PRAISE FOR *INSPIRED BABY NAMES FROM AROUND THE WORLD*

"The sounds in words — a name — are hands that shape us.
The spoken, when from the heart, can bring the sun, moon,
earth, and one's own soul closer when the need is greatest.
A child's name is a prayer all the angels know."

— DANIEL LADINSKY, bestselling Penguin author-poet

"*Inspired Baby Names from Around the World* is a wonderful guide for the joyful and sacred task of discovering your child's 'true name.' Such a unique collection of names with their meanings and spiritual affirmations will be a great addition for your bookshelf for years to come. Light a candle, sip some tea, and enjoy the exploration!"

— DENISE ROY, author of *Momfulness* and *My Monastery Is a Minivan*

"Neala Shane's *Inspired Baby Names from Around the World* is a beautiful and inspiring resource — not only for parents searching for the perfect name, but for all who are interested in one of the roots of who we are in the world. The quotations alone make this a wonderful book. I use Neala's name derivations and meanings in 'Your Soul's Purpose,' a course I teach. Her amazing research provides wonderful clues!"

— JANET CONNER, bestselling journal-writing author of *Writing Down Your Soul*
and *The Lotus and the Lily*

"Impeccably researched, Neala Shane's book is a treasure of wonderfully matched quotes and fascinating information to help you name your child — one of the first and most meaningful gifts we ever bestow."

— BETSY CHASSE, author of *Tipping Sacred Cows*, cocreator of
What the Bleep Do We Know?!, and mom to Elorathea ("goddess of light")
and Maximus Theodore ("greatest divine gift")

"It is said when you say your name, you call in the soul. Choosing your baby's name is a sacred act. Neala Shane has created a timeless gem. What a loving, eloquent gift this is to all mothers- and fathers-to-be."

— RENÉE PETERSON TRUDEAU, author of *Nurturing the Soul of Your Family*

— INSPIRED —
BABY NAMES
from Around the World

— INSPIRED —
BABY NAMES
from Around the World

6,000 International Names
and the Meaning behind Them

NEALA SHANE

New World Library
Novato, California

New World Library
14 Pamaron Way
Novato, California 94949

Text design by Tona Pearce Myers
Permission acknowledgments on page 697 are an extension of the copyright page.

Library of Congress Cataloging-in-Publication Data
Shane, Neala, date.
Inspired baby names from around the world : 6,000 international names and the meaning behind them / Neala Shane.
      pages   cm
Includes indexes.
ISBN 978-1-60868-320-8 (paperback : alkaline paper) — ISBN 978-1-60868-321-5 (ebook)
1. Names, Personal—Dictionaries. I. Title.
CS2377.S435 2015
929.4003—dc23   2014042449

First printing, April 2015
ISBN 978-1-60868-320-8
Printed in Canada on 100% postconsumer-waste recycled paper

New World Library is proud to be a Gold Certified Environmentally Responsible Publisher. Publisher certification awarded by Green Press Initiative.
www.greenpressinitiative.org

10   9   8   7   6   5

To Jake, Adam, and Bethan,

the lights of my love

Thou hast found grace in My sight, and I know thee by name.

— EXODUS 33:17B (KJV)

CONTENTS

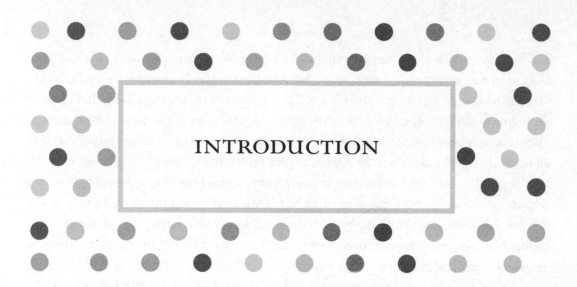

INTRODUCTION

A name pronounced is the recognition of the individual to whom it belongs.
He who can pronounce my name aright, he can call me,
and is entitled to my love and service.

— HENRY DAVID THOREAU,
A Week on the Concord and Merrimack Rivers

Congratulations! If you are reading *Inspired Baby Names from Around the World*, odds are good that you or someone you know is having a baby. What an exciting time in your life! Choosing the perfect name is one of the most important gifts you will give your child. It's a gift that lasts a lifetime.

Your name is a key to who you are. It is the link that connects the inner self with the outer world, the first contact point that ties you to family and the community in which you live. Your name helps to form your character and can affect the outcome of events in your life. To most native cultures, a name reflects the essence of the individual. It is more than a means of identification. It represents the soul and foundation of its bearer.

In many cultures around the world, to name a baby is to bless the baby, to give the child a gift of spiritual meaning. I have always been fascinated by the meaning of names and how parents choose a particular name for a baby. We all know of parents who picked out a baby name that seemed set in stone, but who then suddenly changed their minds after they heard a name that caught their fancy. Their promise to name their baby after beloved Grandma Dorothy melted away, for they simply "knew" the new name was the right one. Many cultures believe that the unborn baby already knows his or her name and gives clues all throughout pregnancy for the parents to pick up on. It's an interesting thought.

Hopefully, the most important consideration when choosing a name will be the welfare of the child, for a name must be borne with pride and pleasure. In fact, many believe that people who are happy with their names are also happy within themselves. In lots of ways, Americans choose names that relate to their cultures and countries of origin. When previous generations immigrated to the United States and landed at Ellis Island, they often changed their names in order to assimilate more easily, but today many people are reidentifying with the names and original spellings of "the old country." People with an Irish or Scottish background are often choosing more authentic Celtic names, and African Americans are using more African names. The significance of baby naming can also bring more stress to parents, who often struggle to find just the right name. Parents want something special for their child, something unique.

Parents facing the often-daunting process of finding the perfect name can consider many factors. Many children are named to honor a relative; in one way or another, incorporating family names is often considered very important. To others, religion is a major factor in choosing a name. Some name their children after historical or popular figures, while others simply want a name that sounds right.

Names also frequently celebrate valued ideals or personal qualities that it is hoped the child will possess. For example, German, Scandinavian, and Scottish names often reflect strength, valor, and other "warrior" traits. American Indian and African names can reflect aspects of nature or other living things. Celtic names usually emphasize physical characteristics, geographic locations, and aspects of gods and goddesses. Though the monikers certainly sound strange to us today, Puritans often named their children after biblical virtues, phrases, or verses, which resulted in such names as Silence, Abstinence, Stedfast, Thankful, Search-the-Scriptures, Sorry-for-Sin, and Zeal-of-the-Land. One of the most unusual Puritan names was Through-Much-Trial-and-Tribulation-We-Enter-the-Kingdom-of-Heaven — or "Tribby" for short (thank goodness!).[1] In colonial times, parents might open the Bible and randomly point to a

---

1.   Elsdon Smith, *Treasury of Name Lore* (New York: Harper & Row, 1967), 191.

word, and so Notwithstanding Griswold and Maybe Barnes were created.[2] That might seem a bit *too* random, but whatever your approach, finding the perfect name for your child can illuminate what your values are. Many parents like traditional names, while others opt for contemporary names. Ask yourself what is more important: tradition or originality, harmony or distinction. Hopefully, *Inspired Baby Names from Around the World* will give you insight and choice in finding that perfect name, a blessing that your child will carry into the future.

Today, several baby name trends are influencing modern prospective parents, particularly names drawn from colors, locations, trees, and flowers. Popular color names include Blue, Hazel, Hunter, Fern, Kelly, Jade, Olive, Ruby, Violet, and Scarlett. A new wave of place-names is often inspired by locations with personal relevance for parents, such as hometowns, memory-filled vacation spots, and even the place of conception. Actress Reese Witherspoon named her son Tennessee in honor of where she was raised. *Girls* star Jemima Kirke named her son Memphis, and Alec Baldwin's daughter is named Ireland. Other city names include Bristol, Brooklyn, Cairo, Dallas, and Paris, and popular country and continent names include Africa, Asia, China, India, and Kenya. Tree names sound strong and stable and include Acacia, Ash, Forest, Juniper, Maple, Olive, and Willow. Poppy and Clover, popular wildflower names, are also on the rise.

Film stars and musicians are adding unusual names to the melting pot by crossing gender boundaries. Actresses Jessica Simpson and Lindsay Sloane each named their daughters Maxwell, and Elizabeth Rohm's daughter is Easton. Actor Jason Lee named his daughter Caspar, while daredevil Johnny Knoxville named his daughter Arlo. Film characters can also inspire baby names; Katniss from *The Hunger Games* and Django from *Django Unchained* are two.

Sometimes, names and naming can be controversial. American singer Beyoncé named her daughter Blue Ivy, and to ward off copycats, she then tried to patent the name, but the US Patent and Trademark Office ruled against her. When a New Zealand couple recently named their baby Messiah, they had to go to court to defend the name …and lost. A New Zealand court ruled that parents cannot legally give their children a name that is excessively lengthy, offensive, or includes an official title "without adequate justification." Since 2001, New Zealand has turned down six Lucifers, two Messiahs, and one Saint, and Justice was turned down sixty-two times. The United States, however, welcomed more than seven hundred new Messiahs in 2012 alone!

---

2. "The Genealogue: What's to Blame for Baby Names," http:/genealogue.com/2007/06.

According to a January 31, 2014, article in *Huff Post Parents*, names that are on the rise include Asa, Azalea, Blaise, Blythe, Celia, Elisa, Freya, Knox, Louis, Persephone, Reed, Ronan, Sasha, and Valentina. More unusual names that are currently in vogue include Beckett, Camber, Costello, Dashiel, Detroit, Kaius, Kipling, Macsen.

Perhaps the largest overall trend in baby naming today is diversity. There is no single dominant trend or source for names. The Internet makes available information on cultures and spiritual traditions worldwide, and parents are choosing names from any source, or they are simply making up wholly original names. And why not?! At some point in history, all names were made up! As a result, the American name base is increasing and diversifying because of all these trends, which also reflects our expanding melting pot. According to the Office of Immigration Statistics, over a million people from over two hundred countries legally immigrated to the United States in 2012. Indeed, such diversity continues to enrich American values and innovation in unparalleled ways.

BLESSING YOUR BABY WITH A SPIRITUAL AFFIRMATION

Inspired Baby Names from Around the World is different from other name books. In addition to providing more than 6,000 multicultural names (all of which are used in the United States today), along with their meanings, origins, and pronunciations, *Inspired Baby Names from Around the World* provides a *spiritual affirmation* for each name. These affirmations are intended as suggested blessings, which can be used to deepen the meaning and intent of the name. In addition, each name is treated as unique and deserving of its own affirmation, even if the name is similar in spelling or derivation with other names. For example, Anita, Ann, Hannah, and Nancy all derive from the Hebrew word *chaanach*, meaning "grace," but each of these names is included and has a different spiritual blessing. Similarly, the spellings Chris, Carl, and Eric are used more often in English-speaking countries, whereas Kris, Karl, and Erik are generally used in German and Scandinavian countries; the French name Félicité is spelled and pronounced differently than the English name Felicity. Yet all these names have their own entry, and each is given an exclusive affirmation.

The spiritual affirmations are carefully matched to each name, so each is specific to the name's meaning and culture of origin. I considered etymology, tribal associations where appropriate, and the most dominant spiritual expression of the culture. For instance, if a name is Irish, I used Irish authors and sources; if it is American Indian, I drew from tribal sources. For many European-based names, I used biblical scriptures, while for many Asian-based names, I used Buddhist quotations. As a result, the affirmations derive from a wide range of sources: in total, they are taken from twenty-two versions of the Bible, two versions of the Hebrew Tanakh, three versions of the Koran, various Hindu Upanishads and Buddhist sutras, and proverbs from Africa, Japan, and Hawaii. They include thousands of inspirational quotes by famous authors and historical figures, such as Shakespeare, Emerson, Thoreau, Gandhi, Mother Teresa, Hafiz, Rumi, Helen Keller, Nietzsche, Muhammad Ali, Alice Walker, Yeats, Black Elk, Bashō, and Nelson Mandela. However, since the affirmations are *suggested blessings only,* feel free to find another one if a certain affirmation does not speak to you or feel appropriate.

As much as possible, *Inspired Baby Names from Around the World* provides the root word etymology for each name, including all European-based names (from which most American first names derive). Most names have more than one traditional meaning, and etymological sources can suggest other or alternate meanings. Knowing all these meanings, definitions, and sources, you can interpret a name's meaning in the way you wish or choose one meaning that fits best. Indeed, your preference may change, and you may feel drawn to different meanings at different times in your life.

Most of the time, a name's affirmation relates directly to the name's meaning, and it uses or repeats the same word or words. Occasionally, however, I matched an affirmation more with the *intent* of the meaning in a less literal way. For example, Jacob literally means "one that takes by the heel, successor, replace with another." The first meaning is a reference to the biblical story of how Jacob was born second after his twin brother, Esau; Jacob held Esau's heel at birth. The second meaning refers to the biblical story of how Jacob took the place of his brother Esau as their father's chosen heir. A third meaning is when God "replaced" Jacob's name with the name Israel. However, for the name Jacob and its derivations, I chose quotes that contained the name "Jacob" or the idea of change and transformation — as the biblical Jacob was made new in name, character, and purpose by God during his lifetime.

Similarly, for names whose meanings relate to animals, I used the qualities associated with those animals. With jewels, I often focused on beauty; for warriors, I stressed strength and courage, and so on. Also, note that spelling and punctuation have varied over the centuries, and in quotes, I have remained true to the spellings in the original text.

Inspired Baby Names from Around the World also includes a range of other helpful resources. In the frontmatter, I include a section describing the baby-naming customs in various countries and religions; a section on guided meditations, which can help you use your intuition to find and confirm the right baby name for your child; a section on the legalities of changing one's name, should any readers be so inspired; and an abbreviation key for scriptural references and a short pronunciation guide. At the end of the book, I include the most popular names by decade over the past one hundred years, names for grandparents, and — just for fun — a list of the most popular names in 2013 given to puppies and kittens. Then I provide two indices — a name meanings index and an index that sorts names by ethnicity — as well as biographies for all quoted authors and texts. The indices will be helpful if you are searching for specific ethnic names — such as all Greek girl names — or a particular meaning or characteristic, such as all names that mean "light" or "courage."

A LINEAGE OF MEANING

A names book is not only useful if you are seeking names for your own children. It can help you discover themes of meaning that run through generations of family names. An interesting exercise I have done is to draw my family tree to look for the connecting links in our first and middle names. Just as your name is a clue to who you are and what you're here to do, family given names often provide similar clues.

For example, my family has very unusual names for women. My great-grandmother's name was Aldora (heavenly gift). My grandmother's name was Stacey Azile (born-again flower), and my mother's name is Trella Fern (star plant). Phillis Jo is my sister's name (God will increase the green plant), and my daughter's name is Bethan Kay (God is purely giving).

My birth name is Sharon Kay (pure fertile field), while my parents' surname is O'Neal (son of the clouds). After I was married (and took my husband's last name, Shane), and upon the death of my father, I decided to move my maiden name forward to become my first name, Neala Kay (pure cloud). Looking at this matrilineal line, I see plants growing out of the earth, initiated by my great-grandmother's gift of life and love, with a bright star looking over it all. These family names have come full circle, as the divine continues to give through my daughter. Plants, with their roots in rich Mother Earth, remind us of how the Divine Hand plants seeds, nurtures their growth, and delights in their blossoming. By moving my maiden name, O'Neal, to become my first name, Neala, the maternal theme of plants, flowers, and a field joins with my father's surname to create the image of rain pouring from the clouds onto earth's greening, helping all to blossom forth to provide beauty to earth's creatures. My family's names connect with God's presence throughout and add a sweet pleasure to my lifelong fascination with names.

You, too, may find turns of interest as you look at your family tree. Write down the names of your family members, along with their meanings. Also include middle names, which often serve as adjectives to describe first names. For example, Nelson Mandela's middle name was Rolihlahla, which means "pulling the branch of a tree" or "troublemaker." Nelson means "cloud," but it also means "champion." This name fits Nelson Mandela extraordinarily well: as everyone knows, he was imprisoned by the South African apartheid government for being a "troublemaker," and yet he became a champion of human rights. His troublemaking cloud had a silver lining, one that inspired millions around the world!

If it helps, download a family tree template from the Internet and explore your family's names. Reflect upon what each name means and look for interesting ties that may connect the meanings. Look again at your own name and at the role you play within your family tree. Who knows what you'll find? Your search might yield surprising, ennobling, or humbling generational ties and attributes, including hidden saints and scoundrels.

Your name — whether given to you by your parents or one you chose on your own — can help you to better understand yourself. Most of all, the name you give your child is a precious gift of a lifetime. Whether you use this book to discover your baby's name or as a pathway to better understanding your own name, it is my hope that you see names as the key to who we are. Blessed be thy name!

NAMING CUSTOMS

The Lord said...you have found favor in my sight,
and I know you by name.

— EXODUS 33:17B (NEB)

Bestowing a name on a child is one of our most important acts as parents, and through a naming ritual we can celebrate and bless our children. A blessing is an acknowledgment of the child's essential nature, the affirmation itself being a gift from the parent to the child. Some rituals are traditional, harkening back thousands of years, while others may be newly created just for this child and this family. Celebrations can take place in the hospital after birth, at home, out of doors, or in a church, mosque, temple, shrine, or any sacred or special setting. They can be done shortly after birth or when the child is old enough to exhibit unique qualities of his or her personality. This section includes but a few examples of such rituals, which serve as a reminder to take every opportunity to celebrate these special milestones.

AMERICAN INDIAN CUSTOMS

According to Wilma Mankiller (1945–2010): "Native Americans regard their names not as mere labels, but as essential parts of their personalities. A native person's name is as vital to his or her identity as the eyes or teeth."[3] American Indian names describe the bearer in some way or tell of an event or action in which she or he took part. Wilma means "determined protector, steadfast guardian." The surname Mankiller refers to a traditional Cherokee military rank. According to Mankiller: "Cherokee women didn't have titled positions. The men had those. But the women had the Women's Council. They had a lot of control.... With the Iroquois the chief was a man, but the women chose the chief, they nurtured him, they installed him. Women could take him out." As the first woman chief of the Cherokee tribe, Mankiller was indeed a warrior woman who protected and guided her people. I find it fascinating that Wilma Mankiller's name was so appropriate to her mission and service in life.

Ella Deloria, a Dakota Sioux anthropologist, has stated: "In Dakota, you do not say... 'What is your name' but, 'In what manner do they say you?' That means 'According to what deed are you known?'"[4] American Indian children often receive a number of names throughout their lifetimes, such as birth names, early childhood names, puberty names, names upon the accomplishment of a major feat, names revealed in a dream, or names that will trick evil spirits if one is critically ill. Ceremonial names are usually kept secret; they are often symbolic, with meanings known only to a chosen few.

Some naming rituals include ear piercing or spirit dancing. In more ancient times, ear piercing was done by the Sioux during the first sun dance held after the child was able to walk. It was done by a man of the tribe through personal invitation of the family, and the man became the child's second father. In his book *The Mystic Warriors of the Plains*, Thomas Mails explains:

> He made a solemn vow taking the child under his protection until one or the other had died. In the mind of the Indian, ear piercing played, in fact, a role very similar to Jewish circumcision and Christian baptism. In all the great ceremonies of the Sioux there was not one which bound two men together so strongly as this. The tie was even stronger than natural brotherhood, because the invited man had assumed a responsibility not placed on him by nature.[5]

---

3. Wilma Mankiller and Michael Wells, *Mankiller: A Chief and Her People* (New York: St. Martin's Press, 1993), 3.
4. Arlene Hirshfielder and Paulette Molin, *Encyclopedia of American Indian Religions* (New York: Facts on File, 2001), 192.
5. Thomas E. Mails, *The Mystic Warriors of the Plains* (Tulsa, OK: Council Oaks Distribution, 1995), 512.

Tom Ration shares the following Navajo blessing:

> Today we are blessed with this beautiful baby. May his feet be to the east; his right hand to the south; his head to the west; his left hand to the north. May he walk and dwell on Mother Earth peacefully.[6]

HAWAIIAN CUSTOMS

Traditional Native Hawaiians carefully craft a new name for each child that contains significant meaning and thought. Names are of great importance to Hawaiians. A child receives his or her name from a parent, grandparent, or other close relative, and the given name is believed to influence the child's spiritual development. Children might be named after relatives, but names are not copied from other families.

A naming ceremony called the *ho`ola`a* is adapted from ancient Hawaiian tradition. The Hawaiian word *ho`ola`a* means "to consecrate, dedicate, or make sacred." In ancient Hawaii, the birth of a child, especially the firstborn male, was celebrated with a consecration ritual that invoked the presence of the family *aumakua*, or primordial guardian spirit, and was then celebrated with a feast. This act of dedication is an important rite because it acknowledges that an *ohana* (family) is willing to commit to the responsibility of rearing the child in love and affirms the child's spiritual connection to *Ke Akua He* (God) and with the spirit of *aina* or the land. This rite helps to "clear the way" for the child to walk the path of life under the care, protection, and guidance of the *ohana*, designated spiritual guides, and godparents.

AFRICAN CUSTOMS

Naming customs vary a great deal among cultures in Africa, although naming is itself taken very seriously. A Yoruban proverb states that a child's name influences his or her behavior, and a proverb from Zaire states that the name is the Spirit. Many Africans see names as carrying a specific function and destiny for a child.

In some tribes, the baby "chooses" his or her own name. While a list of names is recited, adults watch for the infant to respond to one with a smile, cry, sneeze, or other body movement. In other cultures, the baby is offered sticks inscribed with names;

---

6. Tom Ration, "Child Blessing Prayer," cited in *Words of Power: Voices from Indian America*, edited by Norbert S. Hill (Golden, CO: American Indian Science and Engineering Society, 1994), 32.

whichever stick the child grasps is the name she or he "chooses." Some Africans regard a chronically crying child as communicating displeasure with his or her name. A new name is therefore chosen.

In Ethiopia, fathers might fast until the appropriate name for his child comes to him. In West Africa, the Ashanti name their children according to the day of the week on which the child was born. A child born on Monday, for example, would be considered quiet and peaceful, while a Wednesday birth would mean a quick-tempered child.[7]

In the United States, some African families perform the following naming ceremony: around a ritual table laden with foods and objects, a hymn is sung. Then a spiritual leader explains the symbolism of the foods and objects, offering each one to the baby and to the participants to taste or touch. The baby's name is announced, and his or her foot is touched to the ground, symbolizing that the first steps will be guided in the right direction. Prayers, poems, and hymns are then offered to bless and protect the baby and the family's living space.[8]

CHINESE CUSTOMS

A Chinese proverb states that the beginning of wisdom is to call things by their right names. A "milk" name is given in a ceremony a month after the baby is born. The parents usually do not use this name, however; they refer to the child in a way that reflects his or her position in the household (firstborn daughter, and so on). As the child becomes an adult, subsequent other names are given at important times. Traditionally, Chinese surnames are selected from the *Pe-Kia-Sin*, a poem attributed to Chinese Emperor Yao (circa 2300 BCE). The first generation of a family took the first word of the poem, the next generation the second word, and so on, so that each generation's name created a poetic record of the ancestral lineage.[9] In a naming ceremony after birth, Chinese children are given a surname, a generation name, and a first name, the surname being written first.

Chinese tradition also has long used the philosophy of feng shui when naming children. This naming method incorporates the concepts of ying and yang, as well as the five elements of earth, water, fire, metal, and wood. These elements are associated

---

7.   Elsdon Smith, *Treasury of Name Lore* (New York: Harper & Row, 1967), 4.
8.   African Immigrant Folklife Study Project: http://www.folklife.si.edu.
9.   Smith, *Treasury of Name Lore*, 38.

with specific personal characteristics, and they manifest themselves depending on the year, day, and time when a child is born. Choosing an appropriate name is often associated with luck and prosperity, and a Chinese astrologer is frequently consulted when naming a baby.

JAPANESE CUSTOMS

Modern Japanese names usually consist of a surname followed by a given name. Middle names are not generally used. Japanese names are often written in kanji, characters of Chinese origin with Japanese pronunciation. Kanji names and rules of their use in Japan are governed by the Japanese Ministry of Justice. Rules also govern which names are considered inappropriate. In many families, a naming ceremony known as the *Oshichiya Meimeishiki* is done on the seventh night after birth. Once the baby's name is decided, the father has it written in Japanese calligraphy on the *Meimeisho*, or name certificate, which is prominently displayed in the house. Relatives and friends gather around the newborn, who is traditionally dressed in white, and present their monetary gifts, or *shugibukuro*. Two auspicious dishes are usually served: *sekihan* (red rice) and *tai* (sea bream).

KOREAN CUSTOMS

Koreans place the family name first and their given personal names second. Family names are traditional clan names and each has a village from which it comes. Thus, there is a difference between a Kim who comes from Kyong-ju and a Kim who comes from Kimhae. Koreans will generally avoid calling a person by their name when possible. Instead, they will call them by their title, position, trade, profession, scholastic rank, or some other honorific form such as "teacher." Fortune-tellers and baby name specialists are often used for finding an auspicious baby name. Korean babies are usually named by the husband's grandfather, but nowadays that is changing and sometimes they are even given their mother's Korean family name along with their father's.

BUDDHIST CUSTOMS

Unlike in other major world religions, no traditional Buddhist baby-naming ceremonies exist. In more recent times, however, Buddhist rituals have mixed with those of other world cultures. In many countries that practice Theravada Buddhism, outside influences have inspired the development of Buddhist baby-naming rituals. Often these rituals incorporate a visit to the monastery to enlist the naming services of local Buddhist monks. In Sri Lanka, for example, parents will select an auspicious day or full-moon day and take the child to the nearest temple. Babies in Thailand are most often named by either a monk or a grandparent using Thai astrology. In Myanmar, the naming ceremony occurs when the baby is one hundred days old. At this ceremony, monks chant prayers and bless the baby.

CHRISTIAN CUSTOMS

Catholics in various countries often name children after a Catholic saint, a site of a mystery, or a religious feast, such as Santiago, Lourdes, or Pascual. Though there is no special naming ceremony, the Roman Catholic Church takes naming seriously. In Canon 761 of its Code of Canon Law, it states: "Let parish priests take care that a Christian name be given to him who is baptized; if they cannot do this, let them add the name of some saint to the name chosen by the parents and enter both in the register of baptisms."[10] Until recently, priests in Roman Catholic baptisms would ask the baby, *"Quo nomine vocaris?"* (What is your name?) The parents would then answer with the baby's Christian name. In their book *The Language of Names,* authors Justin Kaplan and Anne Bernays continue:

> He then blew gently three times on the infant's face, made the sign of the cross on its forehead, placed consecrated salt in its mouth, with his own saliva touched the ears and nostrils, asked the infant to renounce Satan, and anointed the child with "the oil of salvation," all of this preceding formal baptism at the font, with the water poured three times on the head of the infant.[11]

In Protestant faiths, people frequently celebrate the birth of their child in a church ceremony that welcomes the infant into the congregation. Although not specifically a naming ceremony, this ritual usually confirms a promise made by the parents and the congregation to raise the child in the expression of their faith.

---

10. Smith, *Treasury of Name Lore,* 28.
11. Justin Kaplan and Anne Bernays, *The Language of Names* (New York: Simon & Schuster), 18.

HINDU CUSTOMS

In Hindu practice, names are typically drawn from the names of God, who is both nameless and multinamed. All names are the name of God, as everything in creation is seen as a manifestation of the Divine. The traditional Hindu ceremony of naming the baby is called *namkaran*. Selecting the best name for a child is seen as an important duty of the parents, for the child's name determines the faith of the child, as well as being a social and legal necessity. *Namkaran* is usually performed on the twelfth day after birth, and this naming is considered a highly auspicious occasion that creates a bond between the child and family.

In addition, in Indian astrology, the ecliptic contains twenty-seven *nakshatras*, or clusters, of stars. The birth star of an individual is determined by finding out the position of the moon at the time of birth in relation to these *nakshatras*. For example, if the moon is in the domain of the *nakshatra* Ashvini at birth, then Ashvini would be the person's *nakshatra*. Since Ashvini has four syllables associated with it — Chu, Chay, Cho, and La — parents would choose one of these syllables to begin their child's name, such as Chundadeva, Cholan, or Lalitha, for instance.

JEWISH CUSTOMS

Jewish tradition places a great deal of emphasis on the naming a baby, as a Hebrew name is viewed as the foundation of one's Jewish identity and a link to the countless preceding generations. Jewish ceremonies represent the covenant between God and Israel, called *brit milah* for a boy and *brit bat* for a girl. Adults also have name-changing rituals. The Sephardic Jewish custom is to name a newborn child after a living relative. American Jews, who are predominantly Ashkenazi, tend to give children an English name and a Hebrew name. Often, a child's given name relates to or honors a deceased relative: the first letter of the deceased relative's Hebrew name is used as the first letter of the child's name. For example, a child might be named Adam in memory of a grandfather whose Hebrew name was Avram (Abraham).

The practice of circumcision is known as *brit milah* or the "covenant of our father Abraham." The ceremony takes place on the eighth day after birth, usually in the home. Interestingly, on the eighth day of a baby's life, levels of vitamin K and prothrombin peak in the child. As these are the blood's primary clotting agents, this day is seen as the safest time to perform this operation. A *mohel* performs the circumcision operation, blessings are recited, and a Hebrew name is given to the infant boy.

Traditionally, girls are welcomed into the covenant through a naming ceremony held the first time the father attends a synagogue after the birth. In liberal congregations, a newly invented ceremony for a daughter, called a *brit bat*, usually takes place in the home or in a hall, between seven and thirty days after the birth.

If an adult is critically ill, a life-affirming name is often chosen in order to trick the Angel of Death. The most common names added in these Jewish rituals are Chayim (for a man) or Chayah (for a woman), both meaning "life."

MUSLIM CUSTOMS

Although there are not many specific modern Islamic naming ceremonies, there are naming customs that are considered important. Muslim names usually draw from the Koran and traditional Islamic texts. Customarily, Muslims choose names that refer to the ninety-nine qualities of Allah as described in the Koran or that draw from the more than five hundred names given to the prophet Muhammad and his family. The belief that angels pray in every house where there is a Muhammad (or variation of that name) makes this name the most common in the Muslim world. Muslim names also relate to religious matters, nature, virtues, or occupations.

One interesting naming tradition, known as an *aqeeqah,* is held on the seventh day after the baby's birth. The infant's head is shaved and covered with saffron. The hair is weighed, and the equivalent in money of the hair's weight in gold is given to charity. A goat or lamb is sacrificed on behalf of the child, giving thanks to Allah for the gift of the child. The meat is then distributed to the poor.

These are but a few of the numerous naming rituals used around the world. Create your own naming ritual, perhaps adapting elements of various rituals that appeal to you. Remember, there are as many ways to bless your child's name as there are children in the world. So go ahead — name your child, bless your child, and celebrate!

MEDITATIONS

Good name in man and woman is the immediate jewel
of their souls.

— WILLIAM SHAKESPEARE, *Othello*

I believe, along with most of the world's native cultures, that your name reflects your true essence. A name reveals, clarifies, or indicates one's life purpose and goals. As wonderful as this is, however, naming can feel like a daunting responsibility for prospective parents. No one wants to choose the "wrong" name for their child.

Parents choose names in all sorts of ways, and inspiration can come from many sources, and not just from family or religious traditions. Movie stars, song lyrics, literary characters, and so on may all inspire us with great names. But how do we know whether the name we like is our child's true name or if it is just our own passing fancy? We all know stories of "near misses." My mother wanted to name me Scarlett after the character in *Gone with the Wind*. The movie had taken her, and the nation, by storm, and our last name, O'Neal, sounded close enough to O'Hara to my mom's thinking. Scarlett is more common today, but looking back, I feel luck was with me. I might have felt obligated to maintain an eighteen-inch waist, nor would I have enjoyed repeated taunts of the phrase, "My dear, I don't give a damn!"

One great way to discern and/or confirm your child's true name is to access your intuition through meditation. There are many ways to meditate, and I offer four guided meditations here, along with a basic centering meditation. However, please feel free to adapt these meditations to fit your style. The time to meditate depends upon your schedule and lifestyle. Whenever and wherever you meditate, be sure that you will not be disturbed. Give yourself plenty of time to gear down from the activities and concerns of your day, and proceed when you feel calm and centered. What is important is to set your intention to respect the unique nature of your yet-to-be-born child and to lovingly discern his or her name. Open your heart and your senses, and you may be surprised at the outcome. In addition, meditation can be used to help understand your own name more fully.

CENTERING MEDITATION

I recommend that you do this exercise before each guided meditation. Light a candle in a comfortable, quiet place and think of the Divine's nearness and love surrounding you, flowing through you like light, color, water, or a gentle breeze. In a more personal way, you may want to think of Divine love coming to you through a spiritual master, the Holy Spirit, a saint, an angel, or some person whom you love and trust. Ask that you be protected against confusion, and invite the Divine Presence to anoint your imagination and intuition so that you may trust the images and thoughts that come to mind. Your spiritual guide will always be a totally loving presence. The guide is your friend. Ask your guide to explore the answers with you.

Focus on your breathing. Count slowly to nine as you inhale, hold for a count, then slowly release your breath to a count of nine. If you wish, as you exhale, rest your palms downward in release, and as you inhale, turn your palms upward in reception. You can also vocalize on the breath. One powerful sound is to recite the Hebrew name for God, YHWH (Yahweh). In Hebrew tradition, this tetragrammaton is a manifestation of God's breath.[12] So, as you breathe in, say the syllable "yah," and as you exhale, say the syllable "weh." In so doing, you inhale and exhale the breath of God.

---

12. Rabbi Arthur Waskow describes this in his book *The Breath of Life and Prayer* (Woodstock, VT: Jewish Lights Publishing), 2001.

With each in-breath, imagine the flame of the candle enlarging so as to gently fill and encompass you and your yet-to-be-born child. Draw this light deeply within each cell of your body, from your head down to your toes. With each exhalation, imagine the darkness and fear lodged within being released into this light. Other types of inner visualizations can also be used, such as imagining yourself in a field of flowers and letting your senses evoke the experience: smelling the aromas, feeling the breeze, seeing the colors, and so on. Or, instead of using visualizations, simply listen to music, burn incense, or repeat a name of God or an attribute of the Divine (love, peace, inspiration, and so on) until you feel quiet and at peace. Try different approaches and discover which methods calm and center you best, then continue with one of the more specific guided meditations below.

Finally, when you are finished meditating, ground yourself again by eating, taking a warm bath, or drinking a glass of water or a cup of tea.

MEDITATION 1: PERCEIVING YOUR BABY'S NAME

Once you feel centered, invite your yet-to-be-born child to meet you in a safe place. This may be a favorite spot at the ocean, in a mountain, in a meadow or woods, or in a park. Whatever location comes to mind, notice the details of the setting, such as the brilliant colors, fragrances, the time of day or night, the sound of birds, or the feel of a gentle breeze. Also imagine that you carry a large eraser with you. If there are unwanted thoughts or feelings, use your eraser to literally wipe them out of your mind. Invite your child to be present with you in whatever form she or he feels most comfortable — this might be as a person, but it could be as a butterfly, a puppy, or even a color, a song, or someone you already know and love. Allow your imagination to gently flow.

Be with your child in whatever form best helps you to connect, such as playing with a ball, singing together, or reading a story. Tell her or him your name and who you are, and ask your child to share his or her name with you. Be open to the name appearing in any form in which your child wishes to communicate, such as a whisper in your ear, a picture in your mind, or of someone who bears the same name. In whatever way the name comes to you, express your gratitude and ask the universe to confirm this name in the weeks ahead. If nothing special seems to surface, just enjoy the restfulness of the moment and ask for some indication of the name within the near future. Adopt an attitude of joyful and calm anticipation, saying, "May I patiently anticipate receiving the guidance of this child's true name."

MEDITATION 2: PERCEIVING YOUR BABY'S NAME WITH YOUR GUARDIAN ANGEL

In the calming meditation, you are instructed to invoke the help and protection of a spiritual guide, and you can ask this spiritual guide to help you communicate with your yet-to-be-born child. Many religions believe that God appoints a guardian angel to every person to serve as a loving guide and protector. They serve as emissaries of God, mediating between humankind and the Divine. When you live your life in harmony with the universe, your guardian angel (you may have several) responds gladly to your needs and wants, as long as your requests do not harm yourself or others. They stand on the sidelines waiting for an invitation to act more fully in your life, and one way they help is with realizing the true name of your child.

After becoming centered, invite your spiritual guide to assist you in this sacred name search. Ask your child for permission to allow his or her guardian angels to gather in communion with your own angels. When you feel that communion has been established, ask your child for her or his true name. Your child already knows it, of course, and will willingly tell you. As before, your child may communicate through words, thoughts, or pictures. Trust these images and any names that may come to mind. Then, ask that your guardian angel give you signs and confirmations of this name as the weeks go by, either through family, friends, dreams, or other means.

MEDITATION 3: MAKING A COLLAGE

After doing a calming meditation, sit down with a pile of magazines, catalogs, and travel books you don't mind cutting up, or access the Internet with a device connected to a printer. Gather scissors, glue, and a large sheet of paper. Then, ask your spiritual guide to participate in this process by helping you to relinquish your own projections and fears. Invite your yet-to-be-born child to communicate his or her essence to you through pictures as you leaf through your materials and cut out any pictures and words that attract you. Or search the Internet for appealing images and print them out. Do this over several sittings while relaxing over a cup of tea or by lighting a candle, for example. Sort the pictures into groups, either by color or subject matter, and allow the pictures to speak to you, to tell you a story. If you wish, paste the pictures and words on sheets of paper or poster board to reflect on over time. From these gleanings, you may discover aspects of your child that you never dreamed of.

MEDITATION 4: REPEAT THE NAME

Do this meditation once you have a prospective name for your child, or if you want to focus on exploring your own name. After centering yourself, set your intention to find insight into the essence of your child's possible name. Then, say or write the name repeatedly, as if it were a talisman of sorts. Do this for as long as it feels useful. Once you finish, write down any insights that come to you. Many religions, including Christianity and Hinduism, use the practice of repeating a Divine name in order to attain spiritual awareness. When he couldn't think of something to write, the novelist W. Somerset Maugham wrote his name "over and over and over again," perhaps as a way to refocus on his work.[13] And you, too, may become more conscious of insights as you repeat a prospective name for your baby.

---

13. Kaplan and Bernays, *The Language of Names*, 226.

NAME CHANGE

A good name is rather to be chosen than great riches,
and loving favor rather than silver and gold.

— Proverbs 22:1 (KJV)

In many societies, changing one's name, or acquiring new names, is a natural and expected part of life. For example, some American Indian cultures give a new name when a person enters a new phase of life, such as reaching puberty or accomplishing a notable milestone, like a successful first hunt, a vision quest, or retirement. Kwakiutl Indians have two sets of names: one for use in winter and the other for use in summer.

People give many reasons for changing their names. According to the US Social Security Administration, the most common reasons are that the name is cumbersome and difficult to spell or pronounce, that a new spiritual faith requires legally adopting a religious name, and that the person simply does not like the name. This most often happens with very common names or with very unusual names that cause embarrassment (such as "joke" names like Hazel Nutt, Paige Turner, Stan Still, and so on). At other times, people simply wish to break with the past and start anew, and so they anoint themselves with a new name.

No matter the reason, in the United States, people may change their name freely as long as the request is reasonable and does not impinge on the rights of others. If you wish to change your name, here is the typical process: First, file a petition with the county clerk where you live. They will initiate a state and national FBI search to assure the name change is legally acceptable. Then, you must make a court appearance before a judge or court commissioner, who will either approve or deny your request. If the name change is granted, you must publish the new name in the public notice section of your local newspaper for a designated period of time. Once this process is complete, you will then need to make the change wherever your name is on record, like with your social security number, driver's license, passport, bank accounts, mortgage, credit cards, library, and so on. Some institutions will require a certified copy of the legal name change made in court.

Changing one's name is also an opportunity for celebration. Consider creating a ceremony to affirm your new name and the significance that the name and the change represents. The circle of witnesses can include family members, friends, and religious leaders.

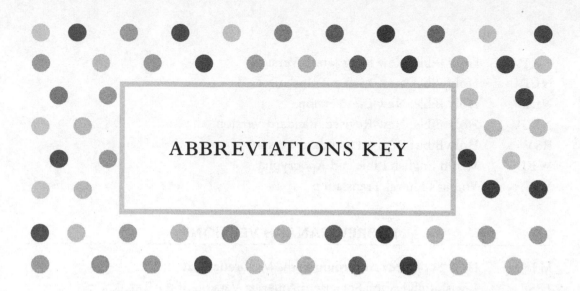

ABBREVIATIONS KEY

BIBLE VERSIONS

ASV	Holy Bible: American Standard Version
CEV	Holy Bible: Contemporary English Version
DR	Douay-Rheims Bible
DT	Darby Translation of the Bible
ESV	Holy Bible: English Standard Version
GNT	Good News Translation and Apocrypha
HCSB	Holman Christian Standard Bible
KJV	Holy Bible: King James Version and The Message: The Bible in Contemporary Apocrypha
KJ21	Holy Bible: 21st Century King James
MSG	The Message: The Bible in Contemporary Language
NASB	Holy Bible: New American Standard Bible
NCV	Holy Bible: New Century Version
NEB	New English Bible
NIV	Holy Bible: New International Version
NIRV	Holy Bible: New International Readers Version

NKJV	Holy Bible: New King James Version
NLT	Holy Bible: New Living Translation
NLV	Holy Bible: New Life Version
NRSV	Holy Bible: New Revised Standard Version
RSV	Holy Bible: Revised Standard Version
WEB	World English Bible and Apocrypha
YLT	Young's Literal Translation

HEBREW TANAKH VERSIONS

| MT | Holy Scriptures According to the Masoretic Text |
| JPS | Jewish Publication Society of America Version of the Tanakh |

KORAN VERSIONS

ALI	The Holy Qur'an, translated by Abdullah Yusuf Ali
PIC	The Meaning of the Glorious Qur'an, translated by Muhammad Marmaduke Pickthall
SKR	Tahrike Tarsile Qur'an, translated by M. H. Shakir

OTHER REFERENCES

cd.	collected by, compiled by
tr.	translated by
Amerind	American Indian

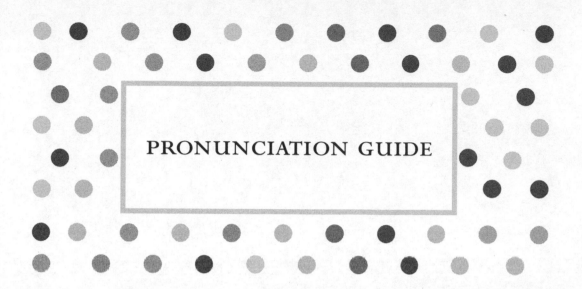

PRONUNCIATION GUIDE

ah	as in *father*
ay	as in *day*
ayr	as in *air* or *care*
ee	as in *beet*
eh	as in *feather*
ehr	as in *air* or *care*
ie	as in *kite*
ih	as in *listen*
kh	as in *loch* (as in German or Scottish, a throat-clearing sound)
oh	as in *boat*
oo	as in *noodle*
uh	as in *utter*

The pronunciation of each name appears in brackets, and the capitalized syllable is the one stressed. If a name does not contain a stressed syllable, it is because the culture stresses each syllable equally or this information was not found in my sources.

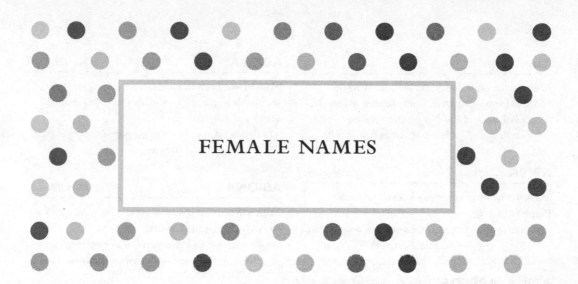

FEMALE NAMES

A

AARONA [ah-ROHN-ah]

MEANING: teaching, singing, shining, mountain, exalted one • USAGE: Spanish feminine form of Aaron, from Hebrew *aharon*
> *She speaks wisely. She teaches faithfully.*
> — Proverbs 31:26 (NIRV)

ABBY, ABBIE [AB-ee]

MEANING: father's joy and delight • USAGE: English form of Abigail, from Hebrew *avigayil*
> *Love is the perfect sum / Of all delight.*
> — Tobias Hume,
> "Fain Would I Change That Note"

ABEBI [ah-BEH-bee]

MEANING: we asked for her and she came, beloved • USAGE: African: Yoruba of Nigeria
> *It is children that make relations.*
> — Nigerian proverb

ABENI [ah-BEH-nee]

MEANING: we asked for her and she came, behold she is ours • USAGE: African: Yoruba of Nigeria
> *It takes a whole village to raise a child.*
> — Yoruban proverb

ABEO [ah-beh-oh]

MEANING: her birth brings happiness • USAGE: African: Yoruba of Nigeria
> *A child is a source of blessings.*
> — Nigerian proverb

ABEY [ah-beh]

MEANING: leaf • USAGE: Amerind: Omaha
> *It may be that some little root of the sacred tree still lives. Nourish it then that it may leaf and bloom and fill with singing birds!*
> — Wallace Black Elk

A

ABI   [AB-ee]

MEANING: father's joy and delight • USAGE:
Scottish form of Abigail, from Hebrew *avigayil*
How beautiful and how pleasant you are, love,
for delights! — Song of Songs 7:6 (WEB)

ABIBA   [ah-bee-bah]

MEANING: beloved, love • USAGE: African:
Bembe of Congo
Mutual love is often better than natural brotherhood.
— Congolese proverb

ABIDA, ABEEDA   [AH-bee-dah, ah-BEE-dah]

MEANING: worshiper (of Allah) • USAGE: Muslim
feminine form of Abid, from Arabic '*aabid*
Who have believed and whose hearts have rest
in the remembrance of Allah. Verily in the
remembrance of Allah do hearts find rest!
— Koran, The Thunder 13.28 (ALI)

ABIELA, ABIELLA   [ah-vee-EH-lah]

MEANING: God is my father • USAGE: Jewish
Honour thy father.
— Deuteronomy 5:16a (MT)

ABIGAIL   [AB-ih-gayl]

MEANING: father's joy and delight • USAGE:
English form of Avigayil, from Hebrew *avigayil*
Abigail...a woman of good understanding, and of a
beautiful countenance. — 1 Samuel 25:3b (KJV)

ABILA   [ah-BEE-lah]

MEANING: beautiful, pretty, lovely • USAGE:
Spanish: from Latin *bella*
How beautiful you are, my darling.
How very beautiful!
*—*Song of Songs 4:1a (HCSB)

ABIOLA   [ah-bee-OH-lah]

MEANING: born in honor, born during the new
yam festival, born into wealth • USAGE: African:
Yoruba of Nigeria
To do one's duty is to eat of the prized fruit of honour.
— Nigerian proverb

ABIONA   [ah-bee-OH-nah]

MEANING: born by the wayside, born on a journey
• USAGE: African: Yoruba of Nigeria
We were not born to experience or go through life
the same way. — Nigerian proverb

ABIRA   [ah-BEE-rah]

MEANING: strength, might • USAGE: Jewish
feminine form of Abir
Strength and dignity are her clothing;
and she laugheth at the time to come.
— Proverbs 31:25 (MT)

ABIRA, ABEERA   [ah-BEE-rah]

MEANING: fragrance, aroma • USAGE: Muslim:
from Arabic '*abir* (fragrance composed of musk,
sandalwood, and rosewater)
Don't plant anything but love..../ A rose opens
because she is the fragrance she loves.
— Jalaluddin Rumi, "Every Tree"
(tr. Coleman Barks, The Glance)

ABRA   [AH-brah]

MEANING: father of a multitude • USAGE: English
feminine form of Abraham, from Hebrew *abh* (father) and *raham* (multitude)
O Lord, you are our Father; we are the clay, and you
are our potter; we are all the work of your hand.
— Isaiah 64:8 (ESV)

ABRIANA, ABRIANNA   *[ah-bree-AH-nah]*

MEANING: father of a multitude, exalted father • USAGE: English feminine form of Abraham (*see* Abra)

To you, O God of my fathers, I give thanks and praise,
for you have given me wisdom and might.
— Daniel 2:23a (ESV)

ABRIL   *[ah-BREEL]*

MEANING: month of April, springtime, opening, goddess Aphrodite • USAGE: Spanish form of April, from Latin *aprilis* (month of Venus, fourth month of the Gregorian calendar) and Latin *aperire* (to open); or from Greek *Aphro*, a form of Aphrodite, the Greek goddess of love and beauty

O thou fair and beauteous garden, / Whose green
republic / Is the chosen clime of April.
— Pedro Calderón de la Barca,
The Secret in Words (tr. Denis MacCarthy)

ACACIA   *[ah-KAH-kee-ah (Greek),*
ah-KAY-shah (English)]

MEANING: acacia tree • USAGE: Greek and English: from Greek *ake* (thorn, point); thorny tree whose wood is light, hard, and durable

I made the ark out of acacia wood and chiseled out
two stone tables...the Lord wrote on these tablets
what he had written before, the ten commandments.
— Deuteronomy 10:3–4 (RSV)

ADA   *[AY-dah (English), AH-dah (German,*
Italian, Scandinavian, Spanish)]

MEANING: noble one, highborn, honorable • USAGE: English, German, Italian, Scandinavian, and Spanish form of Adelaide (*see* Adelaide)

Strength and honor are her clothing;
and she shall rejoice in time to come.
— Proverbs 31:25 (KJV)

ADAH, ADDAH   *[ah-DAH]*

MEANING: adorned, beautiful • USAGE: Jewish

You are beautiful, my darling.
— Song of Songs 6:4a (JPS)

ADALA   *[ah-dah-lah]*

MEANING: act justly, fair, equitable • USAGE: Muslim: from Arabic *'adala*

Be just: that is next to piety.
— Koran, The Table Spread 5.8b (ALI)

ADALINE   *[ad-ah-LIEN]*

MEANING: noble one, highborn, honorable • USAGE: English form of Adelaide or Adele (*see* Adelaide)

You are a noble woman.
— Ruth 3:11b (NIRV)

ADAMA   *[AHD-dah-mah, ah-dah-MAH]*

MEANING: earth, of the red earth, make, create • USAGE: Jewish feminine form of Adam, from Hebrew *adam* (red) or *adamah* (earth); or from Assyrian *adamu* (to make)

My frame was not hidden from Thee,
when I was made in secret, and curiously wrought
in the lowest parts of the earth....Even the days that
were fashioned, when as yet there was none of them.
— Psalm 139:15–16 (MT)

ADAMINA   *[ah-dah-MEEN-ah]*

MEANING: earth, of the red earth, make, create • USAGE: English feminine form of Adam (*see* Adama)

Speak to the earth, and it shall teach thee.
— Job 12:8a (ASV)

ADAMMA   [ah-DAH-mah]

MEANING: beautiful child • USAGE: African: Igbo of Nigeria

> *A child is better than riches.*
> — West African proverb

ADANNA   [ah-DAH-nah]

MEANING: her father's daughter, God's daughter • USAGE: African: Igbo of Nigeria

> *Oneness through blood cannot be severed.*
> — Kenyan proverb

ADARA   [ah-DAH-rah]

MEANING: exalted, praised, worthy • USAGE: Jewish feminine form of Adar

> *Extol her [Wisdom], and she will exalt thee;*
> *She will bring thee to honour, when dost embrace her.*
> — Proverbs 4:8 (MT)

ADDISON   [AD-ih-son]

MEANING: child of Adam, of the red earth, fire, fiery one • USAGE: English surname, a combination of Adam and "son." Adam is from Hebrew *adam* (red) or *adamah* (earth); or from Assyrian *adamu* (to make); or English form of Aidis, from Gaelic *aodh* (fire)

> *Those who contemplate the beauty of the earth find reserves of strength that will endure as long as life lasts.*
> — Rachel Carson, *The Sense of Wonder*

ADEL   [ah-DEL]

MEANING: God is eternal • USAGE: Jewish

> *Eternity is the very essence of God.*
> — Baruch Spinoza, *Ethics* (tr. W. L. White)

ADELA   [ah-DAY-lah (Spanish), ah-DEL-ah (English)]

MEANING: noble one, highborn, honorable • USAGE: Spanish and English form of Adelheid (*see* Adelaide)

> *Honour is a sacred place, which the soul alone inhabits.*
> — Pedro Calderón de la Barca, *The Physician of His Own Honour* (tr. Denis MacCarthy)

ADELAIDE   [AD-eh-layd]

MEANING: noble one, highborn, honorable • USAGE: English form of Adelheid, from German *adal* (noble) and *heid* (sort, type)

> *An honorable person acts honestly and stands firm for what is right.*
> — Isaiah 32:8 (GNT)

ADELE   [ah-DEH-leh (German, Italian), ah-DEL (English)]

MEANING: noble one, highborn, honorable • USAGE: German, Italian, and English form of Adelheid (*see* Adelaide)

> *The being of a noble soul is reliable.*
> — Friedrich Nietzsche

ADELHEID   [AH-dehl-hiet]

MEANING: noble one, highborn, honorable • USAGE: German: from German *adal* (noble) and *heid* (sort, type)

> *Nobility and honor always go together.*
> — Lorenzo da Ponte, *Don Giovanni*

ADELINA   [ah-day-LEE-nah]

MEANING: little noble one, highborn, honorable • USAGE: Italian, Spanish, and Scandinavian form of Adela and diminutive -*ina* (*see* Adelaide)

> *The ones [seeds] that fell on the good ground are those who, having heard the word with a noble and good heart, keep it and bear fruit with patience.*
> — Luke 8:15 (NKJV)

ADELINE   [ah-deh-LEEN (French), ad-eh-LIEN (English)]

MEANING: little noble one, highborn, honorable • USAGE: French and English form of Adelaide or Adele and diminutive —*ine* (*see* Adelaide)

Get wisdom, and with all thy getting get
understanding. Exalt her, and she doth lift thee up.
She honoureth thee, when thou dost embrace her.
— Proverbs 4:7–8 (YLT)

ADELITA   *[ah-day-LEE-tah]*

Meaning: noble one, highborn, honorable •
Usage: Spanish form of Adela (*see* Adelaide)
Whoever pursues righteousness and kindness
will find life, righteousness, and honor.
— Proverbs 21:21 (ESV)

ADELLA   *[ah-DEL-ah]*

Meaning: noble one, highborn, honorable •
Usage: English form of Adelaide (*see* Adelaide)
Many women do noble things, but you excel them all.
— Proverbs 31:29 (WEB)

ADELLE   *[ah-DEL]*

Meaning: noble one, highborn, honorable •
Usage: English form of Adelheid, from German
adal (noble) and *heid* (sort, type)
Do you ask to be the companion of nobles?
Make yourself noble, and you shall be.
— John Ruskin, "Of Kings' Treasuries"

ADI   *[ah-DEE]*

Meaning: jewel, adornment • **Usage:** Jewish
There is gold, and a multitude of rubies,
but the lips of knowledge are a precious jewel.
— Proverbs 20:15 (MT)

ADIA   *[ah-DEE-ah]*

Meaning: gift • **Usage:** African: Swahili
A gift is a fruit from the heart.
— Swahili proverb

ADIBA, ADEEBA   *[ah-DEE-bah]*

Meaning: courteous, considerate • **Usage:**
Muslim feminine form of Adib, from Arabic *'adib*
Consideration is the sign of the wise.
— Hazrat Inayat Khan, *The Gayan*

ADILA, ADEELA   *[ah-DEE-lah]*

Meaning: honest, truthful • **Usage:** Muslim
feminine form of Adil, from Arabic *'adala*
(to act justly)
Truth may walk around unarmed through the world.
— Arabic proverb

ADINA   *[ah-DEE-nah]*

Meaning: tender, gentle, delicate • **Usage:**
Jewish
[God] encompasseth thee with lovingness
and tender mercies. — Psalm 103:4b (MT)

ADINA   *[ah-DEE-nah]*

Meaning: adorned, beautiful • **Usage:** Spanish
form of Hebrew Adah
How beautiful you are, my love; how perfect you are!
— Song of Songs 4:7 (GNT)

ADIRA   *[ah-DEE-rah]*

Meaning: powerful, mighty, noble, glorious •
Usage: Jewish feminine form of Adir
You, O Lord, are a shield about me, my glory,
He who holds my head high.
— Psalm 3:4 (JPS)

ADITI   *[ah-dih-tih]*

Meaning: boundless, unfettered, free •
Usage: Hindu: from Sanskrit *a* (without) and
diti (boundary)
By knowing God one is released from all fetters.
— Shvetashvatara Upanishad

ADIVA   [ah-DEE-vah]

MEANING: gracious, courteous, pleasant • **USAGE:** Jewish feminine form of Adiv

Her ways are ways of pleasantness,
and all her paths are peace.
— Proverbs 3:17 (MT)

ADONA   [ah-DOH-nah]

MEANING: very beautiful • **USAGE:** Greek feminine form of Adonis, associated with being very attractive

How beautiful and pleasant you are.
— Song of Songs 7:6a (ESV)

ADONIA   [ah-DOH-nee-ah]

MEANING: very beautiful • **USAGE:** Greek feminine form of Adonis, associated with being very attractive

I affirm that the good is the beautiful.
— Socrates, *Lysis*

ADORA   [ah-DOR-ah]

MEANING: adore, worship • **USAGE:** Spanish form of Adoracíon (*see* Adoracíon)

Every cell in us worships / God.
— Thomas Aquinas, "Every Foot a Shrine"
(tr. Daniel Ladinsky, *Love Poems from God*)

ADORACÍON   [ah-doh-rah-SEE-ohn]

MEANING: adore, worship • **USAGE:** Spanish: reference to the Adoration of the Magi, from Latin *adorare*

After coming into the house they saw the Child with
Mary His mother; and they fell to the ground and
worshiped Him. Then, opening their treasures,
they presented to Him gifts of gold, frankincense,
and myrrh. — Matthew 2:11 (NASB)

ADRIA   [AY-dree-ah, AH-dree-ah]

MEANING: seaport, sea haven, woman from Hadria • **USAGE:** English and German feminine form of Adrian, from Latin *Hadria* (Italian city on the Adriatic Sea)

The seashore is a sort of neutral ground,
a most advantageous point from which to
contemplate this world.
— Henry David Thoreau, *Cape Cod*

ADRIANA   [ah-dree-AH-nah (Italian, German, Scandinavian, Spanish), ay-dree-AN-eh (English)]

MEANING: seaport, sea haven, woman from Hadria • **USAGE:** Italian, English, German, Scandinavian, and Spanish feminine form of Adrian, from Latin *Hadria* (Italian city on the Adriatic Sea)

Live in the sunshine, swim in the sea, /
Drink the wild air's salubrity.
— Ralph Waldo Emerson,
"Considerations by the Way"

ADRIANNA   [aye-dree-AN-ah]

MEANING: seaport, sea haven, woman from Hadria • **USAGE:** English feminine form of Adrian, from Latin *Hadria* (Italian city on the Adriatic Sea)

Thou shalt hear the music of the sea.
— Thomas Hood, "Hero and Leander"

ADRIANNE   [AY-dree-un]

MEANING: seaport, sea haven, woman from Hadria • **USAGE:** English feminine form of Adrian, from Latin *Hadria* (Italian city on the Adriatic Sea)

The voice of the sea speaks to the soul.
The touch of the sea is sensuous,
enfolding the body in its soft, close embrace.
— Kate Chopin, *The Awakening*

ADRIENNE   *[ah-dree-EN]*

MEANING: seaport, sea haven, woman from Hadria • **USAGE:** French feminine form of Adrian, from Latin *Hadria* (Italian city on the Adriatic Sea)
> *The sea is everything. It covers seven tenths of the terrestrial globe. Its breath is pure and healthy.*
> — Jules Verne, *20,000 Leagues Under the Sea*

ADSILA   *[ahd-see-lah]*

MEANING: blossom, flower • **USAGE:** Amerind: Cherokee
> *Now! I am as beautiful as the very blossoms themselves!* — Cherokee song

AFIFA, AFEEFA   *[ah-FEE-fah]*

MEANING: virtuous, pure • **USAGE:** Muslim feminine form of Afif, from Arabic *'afeef* (virtuous) or *'afifa* (pure, chaste)
> *A woman whom Providence has provided with beauty of spirit and body is a truth, at the same time both open and secret, which we can understand only by love, and touch only by virtue.*
> — Kahlil Gibran, *Broken Wings*

AFIYA   *[ah-FEE-yah]*

MEANING: healthy, vigorous • **USAGE:** African: Swahili of Kenya
> *A good purpose is like a doctor. [It keeps you healthy.]*
> — Swahili proverb

AFRIC   *[AH-frik, AY-frik]*

MEANING: pleasant, noble • **USAGE:** Irish: from Gaelic *aifric* (pleasant) or *fioreach* (noble)
> *The lines have fallen for me in pleasant places; indeed, I have a beautiful inheritance.*
> — Psalm 16:6 (ESV)

AFRICA   *[AF-rih-kah]*

MEANING: land of the African continent • **USAGE:** American: from Latin *africa* (terra, land); originally a Roman reference to the Carthaginian territory of Northern Africa
> *I dream of an Africa which is in peace with itself.*
> — Nelson Mandela

AFROZA   *[ah-FROH-ʒah]*

MEANING: polished, smooth • **USAGE:** Persian
> *The polish for the heart is the remembrance of God.*
> — Hadith of the Prophet Muhammad

AGAFYA   *[ah-GAH-fyah]*

MEANING: good, kind, compassionate • **USAGE:** Russian form of Agatha (*see* Agathe)
> *Compassion is the chief and perhaps the only law of human existence.*
> — Fyodor Dostoevsky, *The Idiot* (tr. Constance Garnett)

AGATA   *[AHG-ah-tah]*

MEANING: good, kind, compassionate • **USAGE:** Italian, Scandinavian, and Spanish form of Agatha (*see* Agathe)
> *I had rather by far that I was adorned with a good disposition than with gold.*
> — Titus Maccius Plautus, *The Young Carthaginian* (tr. Henry Thomas Riley)

AGATHA   *[AG-ah-thah]*

MEANING: good, kind, compassionate • **USAGE:** English form of Agathe (*see* Agathe)
> *Her mouth she hath opened in wisdom, and the law of kindness [is] on her tongue.*
> — Proverbs 31:26 (YLT)

A

AGATHE, AGATHÉ   *[AH-gah-theh (Greek),*
AH-gah-teh (German, French, Scandinavian)]

MEANING: good, kind, compassionate • **USAGE:**
Greek, German, French, and Scandinavian: from
Greek *agathos*

> *Kindness begets kindness evermore.*
> — Sophocles, *Ajax*

AGNA   *[AHG-nah]*

MEANING: pure one, chaste, holy, lamb • **USAGE:**
Scandinavian and German form of Agnes (*see*
Agnes)

> *If your heart be right with God,*
> *then every creature is a book of holy teaching.*
> — Thomas à Kempis, *The Imitation of Christ*
> (tr. Harvey Goodwin)

AGNES   *[AG-nes (English),*
AHG-nes (German, Scandinavian)]

MEANING: pure one, chaste, holy, lamb • **USAGE:**
English, German, and Scandinavian form of *Hagne*,
from Greek *hagnos* (chaste, holy); or from Latin
agnus (lamb)

> *Holiness is the very principle of eternal life, the very*
> *beginning of eternal life in the heart, and that which*
> *will certainly grow up to eternal life.*
> — Jeremiah Burroughs, *The Saints Treasury*

AGNESE   *[ahg-NAY-say]*

MEANING: pure one, chaste, holy, lamb • **USAGE:**
Italian form of Agnes (*see* Agnes)

> *From a pure fountain, pure water flows.*
> — Latin proverb

AGNESSA   *[ahg-NEH-sah]*

MEANING: pure one, chaste, holy, lamb • **USAGE:**
Russian form of Agnes (*see* Agnes)

> *May the God of peace make you holy in every way.*
> — 1 Thessalonians 5:23a (NLT)

AGOSTINA   *[ah-goh-STEE-nah]*

MEANING: great one, revered one, honored •
USAGE: Italian feminine form of Agostino, from
Latin *augustus*

> *You have also given me the shield of Your salvation;*
> *Your gentleness has made me great.*
> — 2 Samuel 22:36 (NKJV)

AGUEDA   *[ah-GAY-dah]*

MEANING: pure, chaste, virtuous • **USAGE:** Portuguese: from Portuguese *agueda*

> *With the pure Thou shewest Thyself pure.*
> — 2 Samuel 22:27a (YLT)

AHARONA   *[ah-hah-ROH-nah]*

MEANING: teaching, singing, shining, mountain,
exalted one • **USAGE:** Jewish feminine form of
Aharon, from Hebrew *aharon*

> *The soul sings all the time; joy and sweetness are her*
> *garments; high-minded tenderness envelops her.*
> — Abraham Isaac Kook

AHAVA, AHAVAH   *[ah-HAH-vah]*

MEANING: beloved, dearly loved • **USAGE:** Jewish

> *Yea, I [God] have loved thee with an everlasting love;*
> *therefore with affection have I drawn thee.*
> — Jeremiah 31:3b (MT)

AHIMSA   *[ah-hihm-sah]*

MEANING: nonviolent, compassionate • **USAGE:**
Hindu: from Sanskrit *a* (without) and *himsa*
(injury)

> *Love in understanding is non-violence and respect*
> *and reverence for all creation.*
> — Sathya Sai Baba

AHONA *[ah-hoh-nah]*

MEANING: red • USAGE: Amerind: Zuni
*Yonder in the south / ... Wherever the ravines open
out, / You hold the world in your keeping; / Ancient
red stone. / You will make your road come hither.*
— Zuni prayer

AHULANI *[ah-hoo-LAH-nee]*

MEANING: heavenly shrine • USAGE: Hawaiian
Strive to reach the highest.
— Queen Kapi'olani (cd. in *'Olelo No'eau*)

AHUVA, AHUVAH *[ah-HOO-vah]*

MEANING: beloved, dearly loved • USAGE: Jewish
The Lord thy God...will love thee and bless thee.
— Deuteronomy 7:12b–13a (MT)

AI *[ah-ee]*

MEANING: love • USAGE: Japanese: from
Japanese *ai*
Ai, the character for "love."
— Morihei Ueshiba, *The Art of Peace*
(tr. John Stevens)

AIKATERINI *[aye-kah-teh-REE-nee]*

MEANING: pure one, unblemished, innocent, virtuous • USAGE: Greek: from Greek *katharos* (pure)
*The forms of Virtue are justice, courage, temperance,
magnificence, magnanimity, liberality,
gentleness, prudence, wisdom.*
— Aristotle, *Rhetoric* (tr. W. Rhys Roberts)

AIKO *[ah-ee-koh]*

MEANING: loving child, child of love • USAGE:
Japanese: from Japanese *ai* (love) and *ko* (child)
*Compassion is a mind that savors only mercy
and love for all sentient beings.*
— Nagarjuna

AILA *[ie-lah]*

MEANING: earth • USAGE: American form of Ila
We have need to be earth-born as well as heaven-born.
— Henry David Thoreau,
A Week on the Concord and Merrimack Rivers

AILANI *[ie-LAH-nee]*

MEANING: one who enjoys the comforts and hon-
ors, and exercises the responsibility of being a chief
• USAGE: Hawaiian
*May the chief remain of highest rank.
[Blessing for a high chief.]*
— Hawaiian proverb
(tr. Mary Pukui in *'Olelo No'eau*)

AILBHE *[AL-bee]*

MEANING: white • USAGE: Irish: from *albho*
(white)
Wash me, and I shall be whiter than snow.
— Psalm 51:7b (DT)

AILEEN, AILENE *[IE-leen]*

MEANING: noble, valorous, light, illumination,
torch • USAGE: Irish, Scottish, and English: from
Gaelic *ail* (noble, valorous); or Irish form of Helen,
from Greek *helene* (torch) or *ele* (light)
*May the blessing of light be on you,
light without and light within.*
— Celtic blessing

AILIS, AILISH *[AYE-lish]*

MEANING: noble one, highborn, nobility •
USAGE: Irish form of Alice, from German *adal*
(noble) and *heid* (sort, type)
*We are all born for love....It is the principle of
existence, and its only end.*
— Benjamin Disraeli, *Sybil*

A

AILSA [AYL-sah]

MEANING: elf island, elf victory • **USAGE:**
Scottish: from Gaelic *Ailse Creag* (elf rock, fairy
rock); or Scottish form of *Alfsigr*, from Norse *alfr*
(elf) and *sigr* (victory, conquest)
> *The Lord be with you that you may be successful.*
> — 1 Chronicles 22:11a (NASB)

AIMÉE [AY-mee]

MEANING: love, beloved, friend • **USAGE:** French:
from French *aimer* (to love) or *ami* (friend)
> *To love another person is to see the face of God.*
> — Victor Hugo, *Les Misérables*

AIMI [ah-EE-mee]

MEANING: beautiful love, beautiful and loving •
USAGE: Japanese: from Japanese *ai* (love) and *mi*
(beautiful)
> *Nurture love, / give joy, / be compassionate, /*
> *create peace.*
> — Shi Wuling, *Path to Peace*

AINSLEE, AINSLEY, AINSLIE [AYNZ-lee]

MEANING: one's own poem, hermitage meadow
• **USAGE:** Scottish and English: from Gaelic *aon*
(one) and *laoi* (poem); or from English *ansetl*
(hermitage) and *leah* (meadow, field)
> *Love makes us poets.*
> — George Santayana, *The Sense of Beauty*

AISHA, AISHAH [ah-EE-shah]

MEANING: life, alive and well • **USAGE:** Muslim:
from Arabic *a'isha* (alive and well) or *a'sha* (to live)
> *Life is the principal thing to consider, and true life is*
> *the inner life, the realization of God.*
> — Hazrat Inayat Khan, *The Gayan*
> (cd. *The Gayani Meditations, Volume 1*,
> tr. Cecil Touchon)

AISLING [AH-shling]

MEANING: dream, vision, visionary • **USAGE:**
Irish: from Gaelic *aisling*
> *Dream lofty dreams, and as you dream,*
> *so you shall become. Your vision is the promise*
> *of what you shall one day be; your ideal is the*
> *prophecy of what you shall at last unveil.*
> — James Allen, *As a Man Thinketh*

AIVEEN [ay-VEEN]

MEANING: beloved, love, sea mistress, bitter
sea, rebellious, well-nourished, healthy, myrrh •
USAGE: Irish form of *Aiobheann*, a form of Mary
(*see* Mary)
> *I pray this: that your love will keep on growing*
> *in knowledge and every kind of discernment.*
> — Philippians 1:9 (HCSB)

AKIFA [ah-KEE-fah]

MEANING: devoted, dedicated, faithful • **USAGE:**
Muslim feminine form of Akif, from Arabic *'aakif*
> *Those who believe and whose hearts are set at rest by*
> *the remembrance of Allah; now surely by*
> *Allah's remembrance are the hearts set at rest.*
> — Koran, The Thunder 15.41 (SKR)

AKIKO [ah-kee-koh]

MEANING: autumn child, bright child • **USAGE:**
Japanese: from Japanese *aki* (autumn, bright) and
ko (child)
> *Autumn drawing near, / My heart of itself / Inclines*
> *to a cosy room / Of four-and-a-half mats.*
> — Matsuo Bashō, *The Narrow Road to the Deep*
> *North* (tr. Nobuyuki Yuasa)

AKILAH, AKEELA [ah-KEE-lah]

MEANING: intelligent, rational, thoughtful •
USAGE: Muslim: from Arabic *aqil* (intelligent) or
akila (one who reasons)

Reason is learned from the ever changing world, but
wisdom comes from the essence of life.
— Hazrat Inayat Khan, *The Gayan* (cd. *The Gayani*
Meditations, Volume 1, tr. Cecil Touchon)

AKILI   *[ah-KEE-lee]*

MEANING: wise, intelligent, clever, insightful •
USAGE: African: Swahili/Kiswahili
Our love opens the doors of our insight.
— Swahili proverb

AKILINA   *[ah-kee-LEE-nah]*

MEANING: little eagle • **USAGE:** Russian: from
Latin *aquila* (eagle) and diminutive *-ina*
They that wait upon the Lord shall renew their
strength; they shall mount up with wings as eagles;
they shall run, and not be weary;
and they shall walk, and not faint.
— Isaiah 40:31 (KJV)

ALAINA   *[ah-LAY-nah]*

MEANING: little rock, beautiful • **USAGE:** French
feminine form of Alain (*see* Alana)
Whatever is very beautiful is,
of necessity, always true.
— Stendhal, *Armance*

ALAIR   *[ah-LAYR]*

MEANING: cheerful, merry, lighthearted, happy •
USAGE: French form of Hilary, from Latin *hilaris*
Joy is the most infallible sign of the presence of God.
— Pierre Teilhard de Chardin

ALAMEDA   *[ah-lah-MAY-dah]*

MEANING: grove of poplar trees • **USAGE:**
Spanish: from Spanish *alameda*
All the trees of the forest will sing for joy.
— Psalm 96:12b (NIV)

ALANA   *[ah-LAH-nah]*

MEANING: awakening, awakened one, an offering
from the soul • **USAGE:** Hawaiian
If a person is awake, aware, mindful, pure,
considerate, self-restrained, and lives according to
duty, that person's glory will increase.
— Buddha, *The Dhammapada* (tr. Sanderson Beck)

ALANA, ALANNA   *[ah-LAH-nah]*

MEANING: little rock, beautiful • **USAGE:** English
and Irish: English feminine form of Alan, from
Breton *alp* (rock) and diminutive *-an*; or from
Scotch Gaelic *alainn* (handsome, fair)
Love is a great beautifier.
— Louisa May Alcott, *Little Women*

ALANDA, ALANDAH   *[ah-LAHN-dah]*

MEANING: little rock, beautiful • **USAGE:** English
form of Alana (*see* Alana)
How beautiful and how pleasing you are.
— Song of Songs 7:6a (NLV)

ALANI   *[ah-LAH-nee]*

MEANING: orange-bearing tree; oahu tree •
USAGE: Hawaiian
A blossom on the topmost branch.
[Praise for an outstanding person.]
— Hawaiian proverb
(tr. Mary Pukui in *'Olelo No'eau*)

ALANI, ALANNI   *[ah-LAH-nee]*

MEANING: little rock, beautiful • **USAGE:**
American form of Alana (*see* Alana)
Behold, you are beautiful, my love.
Behold, you are beautiful.
— Song of Songs 4:1a (ESV)

A

ALANIS, ALANNIS   [ah-LAN-is]

MEANING: little rock, beautiful • **USAGE:** English form of Alana (*see* Alana)

> *God made thee good as thou art beautiful.*
> — Alfred Tennyson, *Idylls of the King*

ALANNAH   [ah-LAH-nah]

MEANING: darling child • **USAGE:** Irish: from Gaelic *a leanbh* (darling)

> *Listen, my child, and be wise,*
> *and guide your heart on the right way.*
> — Proverbs 23:19 (NEB)

ALAYNA   [ah-LAY-nah]

MEANING: little rock, beautiful • **USAGE:** American form of Alana or Alaina (*see* Alana)

> *That pleasure which is at once the most pure,*
> *the most elevating and the most intense, is derived,*
> *I maintain, from the contemplation of the beautiful.*
> — Edgar Allan Poe,
> "The Philosophy of Composition"

ALBA   [AHL-bah]

MEANING: dawn, aurora, sunrise, white • **USAGE:** Italian and Spanish: from Latin *alba* (dawn) or *albus* (white)

> *Dawn is the friend of the Muses.*
> (Aurora musis amica.) — Latin proverb

ALBERTA   [al-BER-tah (English),
ahl-BAYR-tah (German, Italian, Spanish)]

MEANING: noble and brightly shining • **USAGE:** English, German, Italian, and Spanish feminine form of Albert, from German *adal* (noble) and *beraht* (bright, shining)

> *Rely upon your own judgment; be true to your own*
> *conscience; follow the Light that is within you.*
> — James Allen, *From Poverty to Power*

ALBERTINA   [ahl-bayr-TEE-nah]

MEANING: noble and brightly shining • **USAGE:** Portuguese form of Alberta, from German *adal* (noble) and *beraht* (bright, shining)

> *Those who are wise will shine like the brightness*
> *of the sky.* — Daniel 12:3a (NIRV)

ALCINDA   [AL-sin-dah]

MEANING: light, illumination • **USAGE:** American: possibly a form of Lucinda, from Latin *lux*

> *God said, "Let there be light," and there was light.*
> *And God saw that the light was good.*
> — Genesis 1:3–4a (ESV)

ALDORA   [ahl-DOR-ah]

MEANING: winged gift, gift from heaven • **USAGE:** Greek: from Greek *ala* (a wing) and *doron* (gift)

> *Every good gift and perfect present comes from heaven;*
> *it comes down from God, the Creator*
> *of the heavenly lights.* — James 1:17a (GNT)

ALEA, ALEAH   [AH-lee-ah, ah-LEE-ah]

MEANING: ascend, rise upward • **USAGE:** English form of Aliya, from Arabic *ala* (to rise up)

> *You just think lovely wonderful thoughts and they lift*
> *you up in the air.* — James M. Barrie, *Peter Pan*

ALEGRA   [ah-LAY-grah]

MEANING: merry, cheerful, happy • **USAGE:** Spanish: from Latin *allegra*

> *A happy heart is like a continual feast.*
> — Proverbs 15:15b (NCV)

ALEJANDRA   [ah-lay-HAHN-drah]

MEANING: protector and helper of humankind, guardian • **USAGE:** Spanish form of Alexandra (*see* Alexandra)

> *O Lord, you protect me and save me; your help has*
> *made me great.* — 2 Samuel 22:36 (GNT)

A

ALEKA [ah-LEH-kah]

MEANING: protector and helper of humankind, guardian • **USAGE:** Greek feminine form of Alexandros (*see* Alexandra)

Take hold of instruction; do not let go. Guard her, for she is your life. — Proverbs 4:13 (NASB)

ALEKSANDRA [ah-lehk-SAHN-drah]

MEANING: protector and helper of humankind, guardian • **USAGE:** Russian and Polish form of Alexandra (*see* Alexandra)

The Lord will go before you, and...will guard you from behind. — Isaiah 52:12b (NCV)

ALENA [ah-LEH-nah]

MEANING: woman from Magdala, tower • **USAGE:** German form of Magdalene, the Greek form of *Magdala* (a village in Galilee), from Hebrew *migdal* (tower)

The Woman-Soul leadeth us / Upward and on! — Johann Wolfgang von Goethe, *Faust* (tr. Bayard Taylor)

ALESSA [ah-LAY-sah]

MEANING: protector and helper of humankind, guardian • **USAGE:** Italian form of Alessandra (*see* Alexandra)

The Lord is faithful; He will strengthen and guard you. — 2 Thessalonians 3:3a (HCSB)

ALESSANDRA [ah-lay-SAHN-drah]

MEANING: protector and helper of humankind, guardian • **USAGE:** Italian feminine form of Alessandro (*see* Alexandra)

Thou, O Lord art my protector, my glory, and the lifter up of my head. — Psalm 3:3 (DR)

ALESSIA [ah-LAY-see-ah]

MEANING: protector and helper of humankind, guardian • **USAGE:** Italian form of Alessandra (*see* Alexandra)

Lord... Your constant love and truth will always guard me. — Psalm 40:11 (HCSB)

ALETA [ah-LEE-tah (English), ah-LEH-tah (Spanish)]

MEANING: truth • **USAGE:** English and Spanish form of Alethea (*see* Alethea)

Truth is within ourselves. — Robert Browning, *Paracelsus*

ALETHA [ah-LEE-thah]

MEANING: truth • **USAGE:** English form of Alethea (*see* Alethea)

Truth is the one Reality in the universe, the inward Harmony, the perfect Justice, the eternal Love. — James Allen, *From Poverty to Power*

ALETHEA [ah-leh-THEE-ah]

MEANING: truth • **USAGE:** Greek and English: from Greek *aletheia*

Truth is the beginning of every good thing, both in heaven and on earth. — Plato, *Laws*

ALETTE [ah-LET]

MEANING: noble one, highborn, honorable • **USAGE:** French form of Adelaide, from German *adal* (noble) and *heid* (sort, type)

Wisdom is the principal thing, therefore get wisdom; and with all thy getting, get understanding. Exalt her, and she shall promote thee; she shall bring thee honor when thou dost embrace her. — Proverbs 4:7–8 (KJ21)

A

ALEXA　　　　　　　　　*[ah-LEKS-ah]*

MEANING: protector and helper of humankind, guardian • **USAGE:** English form of Alexandra (*see* Alexandra)

The Lord will watch over your coming and going, now and forever. — Psalm 121:8 (NLV)

ALEXANDRA　　*[al-eks-ZAN-drah (English), ah-layks-ZAHN-drah (French), ah-lehk-SAHN-drah (German, Greek, Scandinavian)]*

MEANING: protector and helper of humankind, guardian • **USAGE:** English, French, German, Greek, and Scandinavian feminine form of Alexander, from Greek *alexein* (to defend, to help) and *andros* (man)

The Lord is faithful; he will strengthen you and guard you. — 2 Thessalonians 3:3a (NRSV)

ALEXANDRIA　　　*[al-ek-ZAN-dree-ah]*

MEANING: protector and helper of humankind, guardian • **USAGE:** English feminine form of Alexander (*see* Alexandra)

Discretion shall watch over thee; understanding shall keep thee. — Proverbs 2:11 (ASV)

ALEXIA　　　　　　　*[ah-lehk-SEE-ah]*

MEANING: protector and helper of humankind, guardian • **USAGE:** Greek feminine form of Alexandros (*see* Alexandra)

Keep thy heart with all diligence; for out of it are the issues of life. — Proverbs 4:23 (KJV)

ALEXINA　　　　　　*[al-eks-EE-nah]*

MEANING: protector and helper of humankind, guardian • **USAGE:** Scottish and English form of Alexandra (*see* Alexandra)

Lord, you have examined me and you know me . . . You are all around me on every side; you protect me with your power. — Psalm 139:1, 139:5 (GNT)

ALEXIS　　　*[ah-LEK-sis (English), ah-lek-SEE (French, Scandinavian)]*

MEANING: protector and helper of humankind, guardian • **USAGE:** English, French, and Scandinavian form of Alexandra (*see* Alexandra)

He will put his angels in charge of you, to guard you in all your ways. — Psalm 91:11 (WEB)

ALFREDA　　　　　　*[ahl-FREH-dah]*

MEANING: elf counsel, supernaturally wise • **USAGE:** English, German, and Italian feminine form of Alfred, from English *ælf* (elf) and *raed* (counsel)

Be merry and wise. — English proverb

ALI, ALLIE, ALLY　　　　　*[AL-ee]*

MEANING: noble one, highborn, honorable • **USAGE:** English form of Adelaide, Alice, Alicia (*see* Alice)

Strength and honor are her clothing. — Proverbs 31:25 (HCSB)

ALIANA　　　　　　*[ah-lee-AH-nah]*

MEANING: sun, sunshine • **USAGE:** American: possibly a form of Eliana, a form of Latin family name *Aelianus* (of the sun), from Greek *helios* (sun)

Your light will shine like the dawning sun. — Isaiah 58:8a (CEV)

ALICE　　*[AL-is (English), ah-LEES (French)]*

MEANING: noble one, highborn, nobility • **USAGE:** English and French form of Adelaide, from German *adal* (noble) and *heid* (sort, type)

True love ennobles and dignifies. — Harriet Beecher Stowe, *The Chimney-Corner*

A

ALICIA   *[ah-LEE-see-ah (Spanish),*
ah-LEE-sah (English, Scandinavian),
ah-LEE-shah (English)]

MEANING: noble one, highborn, honorable •
USAGE: Spanish, English, and Scandinavian form
of Alice (*see* Alice)

    There is no noble height thou canst not climb.
    — Ralph Waldo Trine, *In Tune with the Infinite*

ALIFA, ALEEFA   *[ah-LEE-fah]*

MEANING: friendly, sociable, amicable • USAGE:
Muslim feminine form of Alif

    Exchange presents, and grow in friendliness.
    — Hadith of the Prophet Muhammad

ALIMA   *[ah-LEE-mah]*

MEANING: gentle, patient, compassionate •
USAGE: African: Nigerian form of Halima, from
Arabic *halima*

    A patient person has all the wealth in the world.
    — West African proverb

ALIMA   *[ah-LEE-mah, ah-lee-MAH]*

MEANING: strong • USAGE: Jewish

    Be strong and of good courage.
    — 2 Chronicles 32:7a (MT)

ALIMA, ALIMAH   *[ah-LEE-mah]*

MEANING: learned, knowledgeable • USAGE:
Muslim feminine form of Alim, from Arabic *'aleem*

    Those to whom the knowledge has been given see that
    which has been revealed to you from your Lord,
    that is the truth, and it guides into the path of the
    Mighty, the Praised.
    — Koran, Saba 34.6 (SKR)

ALINA   *[ah-LEE-nah]*

MEANING: noble one, highborn, honorable •
USAGE: German, Scandinavian, Italian, Polish,
and Spanish form of Adelina, from German *adal*
(noble) and *heid* (sort, type)

    If you try to be kind and good,
    you will be blessed with life and goodness and honor.
    — Proverbs 21:21 (CEV)

ALISA, ALISSA   *[eh-LEE-sah]*

MEANING: joyful, joyous, happy • USAGE: Jewish
    My heart rejoices, my whole being exults.
    — Psalm 16:9a (JPS)

ALISHA   *[ah-LEE-shah]*

MEANING: noble one, highborn, honorable •
USAGE: English form of Alice (*see* Alice)

    The noblest mind the best contentment has.
    — Edmund Spenser, *The Faerie Queene*

ALISON   *[AL-ih-son (English),*
ah-lee-SAHN (French)]

MEANING: noble one, highborn, honorable •
USAGE: English, Scottish, and French form of
Adelaide or Adele (*see* Alice)

    As one lamp lights another, nor grows less, /
    So nobleness enkindleth nobleness.
    — James Russell Lowell, "Yussouf"

ALISSA, ALYSSA   *[ah-LIS-ah]*

MEANING: noble one, highborn, honorable,
alyssum flower • USAGE: English form of Alicia
(*see* Alice); or from Greek *alyssum* (type of flower)

    As the flower opens its petals to receive the morning
    light, so open your soul more and more
    to the glorious light of Truth.
    — James Allen, *From Poverty to Power*

ALITA
[ah-LEE-tah]

MEANING: noble one, highborn, honorable • **USAGE:** Spanish form of Adelita (*see* Alina)

Whatever is true, whatever is honorable, whatever is just, whatever is pure, whatever is lovely, whatever is commendable, if there is any excellence, if there is anything worthy of praise, think about these things.
— Philippians 4:8 (ESV)

ALITA, ALETA
[ah-LEE-tah]

MEANING: high, excellent • **USAGE:** Jewish

Many women have done well, but you surpass them all.
— Proverbs 31:29 (JPS)

ALIYA, ALIYAH
[ah-LEE-yah]

MEANING: ascend, rise upward • **USAGE:** Jewish: from Arabic *ala* (to rise up)

*Arise, shine, for your light has dawned;
the Presence of the Lord has shone upon you!*
— Isaiah 60:1 (JPS)

ALIYA, ALIYAH
[ah-lee-yah]

MEANING: high, lofty • **USAGE:** Muslim: from Arabic *'ala* (to rise, to ascend) or *'alya* (loftiness, sublimity)

*The higher you rise, the wider becomes
the margin of your view.*
— Hazrat Inayat Khan, *The Bowl of Saki*

ALIZ
[ah-LEEZ]

MEANING: noble one, highborn, honorable • **USAGE:** French and Hungarian form of Alice (*see* Alice)

*Wisdom is the principal thing; therefore get wisdom;
yea, with all thy getting get understanding.
Exalt her, and she will promote thee; she will bring
thee to honor, when thou dost embrace her.*
— Proverbs 4:7–8 (ASV)

ALIZAH, ALEEZA
[ah-LEE-ʒah]

MEANING: joyous, happy • **USAGE:** Jewish

Joy is not incidental to spiritual quest. It is vital.
— Nachman of Breslov

ALLEGRA
[ah-LAY-grah]

MEANING: merry, cheerful, happy • **USAGE:** Italian: from Latin *allegra*

To live happily is an inward power of the soul.
— Marcus Aurelius, *The Meditations*

ALMA
*[AL-mah (English, Irish),
AHL-mah (Spanish)]*

MEANING: good, kind, nourishing, soul • **USAGE:** Irish, English, and Spanish: from Irish Gaelic *almha* (all good); from Spanish *alma* (soul); or from Latin *almus* (nourishing, kind)

Heart on her lip, and soul within her eyes.
— Lord Byron, *Beppo*

ALMAH
[AHL-mah]

MEANING: young woman, maiden • **USAGE:** Jewish

Thou art a virtuous woman.
— Ruth 3:11b (MT)

ALMIRA
[ahl-MEER-ah]

MEANING: noble and famous • **USAGE:** Spanish form of *Adelmira*, from German *adal* (noble) and *meri* (famous)

*The seed on good soil stands for those with a noble and
good heart, who hear the word, retain it,
and by persevering produce a crop.*
— Luke 8:15 (NIV)

ALODIA
[ah-LOH-dee-ah]

MEANING: foreign prosperity, foreign wealth • **USAGE:** German: from German *ali* (foreign, other) and *od* (wealth, prosperity)

*The Lord your God will make you most prosperous
in all the work of your hands.*
— Deuteronomy 30:9a (RSV)

ALOHI   *[ah-LOH-heeh]*

MEANING: bright, shining, brilliant • **USAGE:**
Hawaiian: from Hawaiian *alohi* (to shine, to
sparkle)

*Back [as straight] as a cliff,
face as bright as the moon. [A beautiful woman.]*
— Hawaiian proverb
(tr. Mary Pukui in *'Olelo No'eau*)

ALOMA   *[ah-LOH-mah]*

MEANING: dove, dove-like • **USAGE:** American
form of Paloma, from Spanish *paloma* (dove); a
symbol of peace

*And the dove came in to him in the evening; and, lo, in
her mouth was an olive leaf pluckt off: so Noah knew
that the waters were abated from off the earth.*
— Genesis 8:11 (KJV)

ALONA   *[ah-LOH-nah]*

MEANING: oak tree • **USAGE:** Jewish feminine
form of Alon

Desire fulfilled is a tree of life.
— Proverbs 13:12a (MT)

ALONDA   *[ah-LAHN-dah]*

MEANING: little rock, beautiful • **USAGE:**
English form of Alana, from Breton *alp* (rock)
and diminutive *-an*; or from Scotch Gaelic *alainn*
(handsome, fair)

*Cheerfulness and content are great beautifiers
and famous preserves of good looks.*
— Charles Dickens

ALONDRA   *[ah-LOHN-drah]*

MEANING: lark, protector and helper of
humankind, guardian • **USAGE:** Spanish: from

Spanish *alondra* (lark); or Spanish form of
Alejandra, from Greek *alexein* (to defend, to help)
and *andros* (man)

Sweet is thy voice, and thy countenance is comely.
— Song of Songs 2:14b (ASV)

ALONYA   *[ah-LOHN-yah]*

MEANING: light, illumination, torch • **USAGE:**
Russian form of Yelena, from Greek *helene* (torch)
or *ele* (light)

*God said, Let there be light: and there was light.
And God saw the light, that it was good.*
— Genesis 1:3–4a (ASV)

ALTAGRACIA, ALTAGRAZIA

[ahl-tah-GRAH-see-ah]

MEANING: high grace • **USAGE:** Spanish: from
Spanish *alta* (tall, high) and *gracias* (grace,
favor); commemorates the feast of "Our Lady of
Altagracia"

May God's grace be with you.
— Colossians 4:18b (GNT)

ALTHEA   *[al-THEH-ah, ahl-THEE-ah]*

MEANING: healer • **USAGE:** English form of
Althaia, from Greek *althainein* (to heal)

Health is my expected heaven.
— John Keats (letter of March 1, 1820)

ALVERA   *[ahl-BAYR-ah]*

MEANING: elf army, elfin warrior • **USAGE:**
Spanish feminine form of Álvaro, from English *ælf*
(elf) and *here* (army)

The Lord is with you, mighty warrior!
— Judges 6:12b (NCV)

ALVINA, ALVENA   *[al-VEE-nah]*

MEANING: elf friend, elf ally • **USAGE:** English
feminine form of Alvin, from English *ælf* (elf) and
wine (friend)

Say to wisdom: Thou art my sister:
and call prudence thy friend.
— Proverbs 7:4 (DR)

We must always bear in mind that we are not
going to be free, but are free already.
— Swami Vivekananda, "The Free Soul"

ALYCE, ALYS [AL-is]

MEANING: noble one, highborn, nobility •
USAGE: English form of Alice, from German *adal*
(noble) and *heid* (sort, type)
We are born for a higher destiny than earth.
— Edward Bulwer-Lytton

ALYSON [AL-ih-son]

MEANING: noble one, highborn, honorable •
USAGE: American form of Alison, from German
adal (noble) and *heid* (sort, type)
We are constantly invited to be what we are,
as to something worthy and noble.
— Henry David Thoreau
(journal entry of February 3, 1841)

AMABEL [ah-mah-BEL]

MEANING: lovable, loving • USAGE: English:
from Latin *amabilis*
Be attentive, be intelligent, be reasonable,
be responsible, be in love.
— Bernard Lonergan, *Method in Theology*

AMADA [ah-MAH-dah]

MEANING: beloved • USAGE: Spanish: from Latin
amada
This is my prayer for you: that your love will grow
more and more; that you will have knowledge and
understanding with your love.
— Philippians 1:9 (NCV)

AMALA [ah-mah-lah]

MEANING: immaculate, pure, free from all defects
• USAGE: Hindu: from Sanskrit *a* (without) and
mala (defect, impurity)

AMALIA [ah-MAH-lee-ah (German, Scandinavian), ah-mah-LEE-ah (Spanish)]

MEANING: industrious, hardworking, one
who excels, competitor • USAGE: German,
Scandinavian, and Spanish: from German *amal*
(work, labor); or from Latin *aemulus* (trying to
equal or excel)
Whatsoever you do, do it from the heart.
— Colossians 3:23a (DR)

AMALIE [AH-mah-lee]

MEANING: industrious, hardworking, one who
excels, competitor • USAGE: German form of
Amalia (*see* Amalia)
Surely an earnest word is due to the work which the
earnest hand prepares; when sweet discourse
accompanies it, labour ever prospers there.
— Johann Friedrich von Schiller

AMALYA [ah-MAHL-yah]

MEANING: industrious, hardworking • USAGE:
Jewish feminine form of Amal
Work is the only thing that gives substance to life.
— Albert Einstein

AMANA [ah-MAH-nah]

MEANING: faithful, trustworthy, true • USAGE:
Jewish
Trust draws to heaven, honor to earth.
— Yiddish proverb

AMANDA

*[ah-MAN-dah (English),
ah-MAHN-dah (German, Italian,
Scandinavian, Spanish)]*

MEANING: lovable, beloved • **USAGE:** English,
German, Italian, Scandinavian, and Spanish: from
Latin *amanda*

*Surely goodness and loving kindness
shall follow me all the days of my life.*
— Psalm 23:6a (WEB)

AMANI

[ah-mah-nee]

MEANING: wish, desire • **USAGE:** Muslim: from
Arabic *amani*

*If you wish to draw near to God,
you must seek God in the hearts of others.*
— Abu Sa'id

AMANYA, AMANIA

[ah-MAHN-yah]

MEANING: God's faithful one • **USAGE:** Jewish

*Let me learn of Your faithfulness by daybreak,
for in You I trust; let me know the road I must take,
for on You I have set my hope.*
— Psalm 143:8 (JPS)

AMARA

[ah-MAH-rah]

MEANING: eternal, immortal, infinite • **USAGE:**
Italian form of *Amarantha*, from Latin *amarantus*

*When you grant a blessing, O Lord,
it is an eternal blessing!*
— 1 Chronicles 17:27b (NLT)

AMARETTA

[ah-mah-RET-ah]

MEANING: unfading, immortal, eternal, infinite;
bitter, almond-flavored liquor • **USAGE:** American
form of Amara (*see* Amara); or from Italian *amaro*
(bitter); an Italian almond-flavored liquor

The power of imagination makes us infinite.
— John Muir

AMARYLLIS

[ah-mah-RIL-is]

MEANING: amaryllis flower, shepherdess •
USAGE: English: from Latin *amaryllis* (type of
flower); also from Greek *Amarullis* (a shepherdess
in Greek mythology)

You must perceive with the flower of the mind.
— Henry David Thoreau,
A Week on the Concord and Merrimack Rivers

AMBALA

[ahm-BAH-lah]

MEANING: The Mother • **USAGE:** Hindu: Sanskrit

*The Mother stands above all the worlds and bears in
her eternal consciousness the Supreme Divine.*
— Sri Aurobindo, *The Mother*

AMBER

[AM-ber]

MEANING: amber gemstone, yellow-orange color,
beautiful jewel • **USAGE:** English: from Arabic
anbar (translucent fossil resin, semiprecious gem);
yellow-orange color

How beautiful you are.
— Song of Songs 4:1a (NRSV)

AMBRA

[AHM-brah]

MEANING: amber gemstone, yellow-orange color,
beautiful jewel • **USAGE:** Italian form of Amber
(*see* Amber)

Behold, you are beautiful.
— Song of Songs 1:15b (WEB)

AMBROSIA

*[ahm-BROH-see-ah (Greek),
am-BROH-zhee-ah (English)]*

MEANING: immortal, eternal, food of the gods
• **USAGE:** Greek and English feminine form of
Ambrosius, from Greek *ambrosios*

*The bodily food we take is changed into us, but the
spiritual food we receive changes us into itself.*
— Meister Eckhart, "Deus Charitas Est"
(tr. Franz Pfeiffer in
The Sermons and Collations of Meister Eckhart)

AMELIA
[ah-MEE-lee-ah (English), ah-MEH-lee-ah (German, Italian, Scandinavian, Spanish)]

MEANING: industrious, hardworking, one who excels, competitor • **USAGE:** English, German, Italian, Scandinavian, and Spanish form of Amalia, from German *amal* (work, labor); or from Latin *aemulus* (trying to equal or excel)

If your works are to live, then God must move you from the inside, from the innermost region of the soul — then they will really live.
— Meister Eckhart (tr. Matthew Fox in *Breakthrough: Meister Eckhart's Creation Spirituality*)

AMÉLIE
[AH-meh-lee]

MEANING: industrious, hardworking, one who excels, competitor • **USAGE:** French form of Amalia (*see* Amelia)

Your work will give you what you need. Blessings and good things will come to you.
— Psalm 128:2 (NIRV)

AMELINA
[ah-mah-LEE-nah]

MEANING: industrious, hardworking, one who excels, little competitor • **USAGE:** Spanish form of Amalia and diminutive *-ina* (*see* Amelia)

The Lord thy God will make thee plenteous in every work of thine hand.
— Deuteronomy 30:9a (KJV)

AMERICA
[ah-MER-ih-kah]

MEANING: ruler of the home, universal leader • **USAGE:** American form of Amerigo, from German *heim* (home, house) and *rik* (rule, lead); or from German *ermen* (whole, universal) and *rik* (rule, lead); country named after explorer Amerigo Vespucci

May there be peace inside your walls.... May you enjoy peace.
— Psalm 122:7–8 (NIRV)

AMETHYST
[am-eh-THIST]

MEANING: amethyst, purple gem, precious jewel, sober • **USAGE:** English: from Greek *amethuskein* (not intoxicated, sober), from belief amethyst stone protects from drunkenness

How beautiful and how pleasant you are, love, for delights! — Song of Songs 7:6 (DR)

AMIA
[ah-MEE-ah]

MEANING: love, loved, cherished one, friend • **USAGE:** American form of Amy, from French *aimer* (to love) or *ami* (friend)

Friendship with oneself is all-important, because without it one cannot be friends with anyone else in the world. — Eleanor Roosevelt

AMICE
[ah-MEES]

MEANING: friend, friendship • **USAGE:** English: from Latin *amicitia*

Treat wisdom as a sister, and make understanding your closest friend. — Proverbs 7:4 (NCV)

AMIELA
[ah-mee-EH-lah]

MEANING: God of my people, my nation belongs to God • **USAGE:** Jewish feminine form of Amiel

The Lord will give strength to his people; the Lord will bless His people with peace.
— Psalm 29:11 (MT)

AMINAH, AAMINA, AMEENA
[ah-MEE-nah]

MEANING: trustworthy, faithful, steadfast • **USAGE:** Muslim feminine form of Amin, from Arabic *amuna* (to be trustworthy)

As for those who believe in Allah, and hold fast unto Him, them He will cause to enter into His mercy and grace, and will guide them unto Him by a straight road.
— Koran, The Women 4.175 (PIC)

AMIRA, AMEERA   *[ah-MEE-rah]*

MEANING: speech, utterance, treetop • **USAGE:** Jewish feminine form of Amir

Surely my lips shall not speak unrighteousness,
neither shall my tongue utter deceit.
— Job 27:4 (MT)

AMISHA   *[ah-mih-shah]*

MEANING: honest, forthright, sincere • **USAGE:** Hindu

Always be honest in word and deed,
both in private and in public.
— Taittiriya Upanishad

AMISHA, AMISHIA   *[ah-MEE-shah]*

MEANING: love, beloved, friend • **USAGE:** American: possibly a form of Amy, from French *aimer* (to love) or *ami* (friend)

Beloved, I pray that all may go well with you
and that you may be in good health,
as it goes well with your soul.
— 3 John 1:2 (ESV)

AMITA   *[ah-mee-TAH]*

MEANING: friend, companion • **USAGE:** Jewish
A friend is devoted at all times.
— Proverbs 17:17a (JPS)

AMITI   *[ah-mih-tih]*

MEANING: immeasurable, innumerable, infinite • **USAGE:** Hindu: from Sanskrit *a* (without) and *miti* (measure)

It is the Infinite that is the source of abiding joy
because it is not subject to change.
Therefore seek to know the Infinite.
— Chandogya Upanishad (tr. Eknath Easwaran)

AMITY   *[AM-ih-tee]*

MEANING: friend, friendly, having peaceful relationships • **USAGE:** English: from English *amitie* (friendship, peaceful relations); or from Latin *amicus* (friend)

Say to wisdom, "You are my sister,"
and call understanding your nearest kin.
— Proverbs 7:4 (NKJV)

AMORA   *[ah-MOR-ah]*

MEANING: love, affection • **USAGE:** Spanish: from Latin *amor*

Harmony is pure love, for love is complete agreement.
— Lope de Vega, *Fuenteovejuna*

AMORETTE   *[ah-moh-RET]*

MEANING: little loved one, little beloved • **USAGE:** French: from French *aimer* (to love) and diminutive *-ette*

Mother Agnes asked: "What is the 'little way'
that you would teach?" Therese answered:
"It is the way of spiritual childhood, the way of
trust and absolute surrender."
— Thérèse of Lisieux

AMRITA   *[ahm-REE-tah]*

MEANING: immortal, ambrosia, nectar of immortality • **USAGE:** Hindu: from Sanskrit *a* (without) and *mrita* (death)

Life is immortal youthfulness.
— Rabindranath Tagore, *Sadhana*

AMSHULA   *[ahm-SHOO-lah]*

MEANING: radiant, beaming • **USAGE:** Hindu: Sanskrit

Let your life lightly dance on the edges of Time
like dew on the tip of a leaf.
— Rabindranath Tagore, *The Gardener*

A

AMY, AMI, AMIE   [AY-mee]

MEANING: love, beloved, friend • USAGE: English
form of Aimée, from French *aimer* (to love) or *ami*
(friend)
Love is the greatest of human affections, and friendship
the noblest and most refined improvement of love.
— Robert South, "Sermon XIV"

AN   [ahn]

MEANING: peace, peaceful • USAGE: Chinese
Just as a deep lake is clear and still, even so, on hearing
the teachings and realizing them,
the wise become exceedingly peaceful.
— Buddha, *The Dhammapada* (tr. Irving Babbitt)

ANA   [AH-nah]

MEANING: mother goddess, divine mother •
USAGE: Irish: name of Irish mother goddess (also
known as Dana) of the Tuatha De Danaan, the
ancient folk of Ireland
There is surely a piece of divinity in us, something
that was before the elements, and owes no homage to
the sun. — Thomas Browne, *Religio Medici*

ANA   [AH-nah]

MEANING: grace, gracious • USAGE: Spanish form
of Anna, from Hebrew *chaanach*
Keep thou wisdom and thoughtfulness, and they are life
to thy soul, and grace to thy neck. Then thou goest thy
way confidently, and thy foot doth not stumble.
— Proverbs 3:21–23 (YLT)

ANABEL   [ah-nah-BEHL]

MEANING: gracious and beautiful, lovely and full
of grace • USAGE: Spanish combination of Ana and
Bella (*see* Ana and Bella)
Gracious words are like a honeycomb,
sweetness to the soul and health to the body.
— Proverbs 16:24 (ESV)

ANAÏS   [ah-nah-EES]

MEANING: grace, gracious, merciful • USAGE:
French form of Anne (*see* Ana)
It is good for the heart to be strengthened by grace.
— Hebrews 13:9b (NEB)

ANAMOSA   [ah-nah-MOH-sah]

MEANING: white fawn • USAGE: Amerind: Sauk
My heart is good. — Keokuk

ANANDA   [ah-NAHN-dah]

MEANING: entirely happy, joyful • USAGE: Hindu:
from Sanskrit *a* (entirely) and *nanda* (joyful)
Happiness is when what you think,
what you say, and what you do are in harmony.
— Mahatma Gandhi

ANAROSA   [ah-nah-ROH-sah]

MEANING: graceful rose, rose of grace • USAGE:
Spanish combination of Ana and Rosa (*see* Ana and
Rosa)
Grace to you and peace.
— 2 Corinthians 1:3a (YLT)

ANASTASIA   [ah-nah-STAH-see-yah
(Russian, Greek), an-ah-STAY-zhah (English)]

MEANING: resurrection, reborn, rise up • USAGE:
Russian, Greek, and English form of *Anastasiya*,
from Greek *anastasis* (resurrection), and from
Greek *ana* (up) and *stasis* (standing)
You have been born again, and this new life
did not come from something that dies,
but from something that cannot die.
— 1 Peter 1:23a (NCV)

ANATOLIA   [ahn-nah-TOH-lee-ah]

MEANING: dawn, sunrise, daybreak • USAGE:
Greek feminine form of Anatolius, from Greek
anatole

The path of the righteous is as the dawning light, that
shineth more and more unto the perfect day.
— Proverbs 4:18 (ASV)

ANCI   *[AHN-see]*

MEANING: grace, gracious, merciful • USAGE:
Hungarian form of Ann, from Hebrew *chaanach*
May grace and peace be multiplied to you.
— 1 Peter 1:2b (ESV)

ANDIE, ANDEE   *[AN-dee]*

MEANING: protector and helper of humankind,
courageous, strong • USAGE: English form of
Alexandra, from Greek *alexein* (to defend, to
help) and *andros* (man); or English form of Andra,
Andrea, or Andriana (*see* Andrea)
She puts on strength and honor as if they were her
clothes. She can laugh at the days that are coming.
— Proverbs 31:25a (NIRV)

ANDRA   *[AN-drah, AHN-drah]*

MEANING: man, courageous, strong • USAGE:
English form of Andrea (*see* Andrea)
There is a growing strength in women but it's in the
forehead, not the forearm.
— Beverly Sills

ANDREA   *[AN-dree-ah (English),*
ahn-DRAY-ah (German, Scandinavian)]

MEANING: man, courageous, strong • USAGE:
English, German, and Scandinavian feminine form
of Andrew, from Greek *andros* (man) or *andreios*
(manly)
Real strength never impairs beauty or harmony,
but it often bestows it; and in everything imposingly
beautiful, strength has much to do with the magic.
— Herman Melville, *Moby-Dick*

ANDREANA   *[ahn-dree-AH-nah]*

MEANING: man, courageous, strong • USAGE:
Italian form of Andrea (*see* Andrea)
She is clothed with strength and dignity.
— Proverbs 31:25a (NIV)

ANDRIANA, ANDRIANNA
[ahn-dree-AHN-nah]

MEANING: man, courageous, strong • USAGE:
Greek feminine form of Andreas (*see* Andrea)
Happiness depends on being free,
and freedom depends on being courageous.
— Thucydides,
The History of the Peloponnesian War

ANEEQA, ANIQA   *[ah-NEE-kah]*

MEANING: beautiful, lovely • USAGE: Muslim:
from Arabic *aniq*
Whatever beauty you have known,
you will know a thousand times more.
— Hafiz, "What Madness Is Austerity"
(tr. Daniel Ladinsky in *A Year with Hafiz*)

ANEESA, ANISA   *[ah-NEE-sah]*

MEANING: friendly, sociable • USAGE: Muslim:
from Arabic *anis*
You are with the Friend now. Learn what /
actions of yours delight Him, / what actions of yours
bring freedom and / love.
— Hafiz, "Cast All Your Votes for Dancing"
(tr. Daniel Ladinsky in *A Year with Hafiz*)

ANEMONE   *[ah-NEM-oh-nee]*

MEANING: wind flower • USAGE: English form of
Anemone, from Greek *anemone* (wind flower) and
anemos (wind)
O'er the flower-enamelled glade / More sweetly
breathes wind.
— William Wordsworth, "Lines Composed a Few
Miles above Tintern Abbey"

ANETA   *[ah-NEH-tah]*

MEANING: grace, gracious, merciful • **USAGE:**
Czech form of Anita, from Hebrew *chaanach*
God is able to make all grace abound toward you,
that you, always having all sufficiency in all things,
may have an abundance for every good work.
— 2 Corinthians 9:8 (NKJV)

ANEZKA   *[ah-NEZ-kah]*

MEANING: grace, gracious, merciful • **USAGE:**
Czech form of Anna (*see* Aneta)
Mercy triumphs over judgment.
— James 2:13b (ESV)

ANGEL   *[AYN-jel]*

MEANING: angel, divine messenger • **USAGE:**
English: from Greek *angelos* (messenger); or Latin
angeles (divine messenger, angel)
When angels visit us, we do not hear the rustle of
wings, nor feel the feathery touch of the breast of a
dove; but we know their presence by the love
they create in our hearts.
— Mary Baker Eddy

ANGELA   *[AN-jeh-lah (English), AHN-jeh-lah (German, Scandinavian), ahn-ZEHL-ah (Russian), ahn-JAY-lah (Italian), ahn-HAY-lah (Spanish)]*

MEANING: angel, divine messenger • **USAGE:**
English, Italian, and Spanish form of Angel (*see* Angel)
The angels of divine peace and joy
are always at hand.
— James Allen, *From Poverty to Power*

ANGÈLE   *[ahn-ZHAY-lay]*

MEANING: angel, divine messenger • **USAGE:**
French form of Angela (*see* Angel)
God's angel sets up a circle of protection around us.
— Psalm 34:7a (MSG)

ANGELIA   *[an-JEL-ee-ah]*

MEANING: angel, divine messenger • **USAGE:**
English form of Angela (*see* Angel)
If you woo the company of the angels in your waking
hours, they will be sure to come to you in your sleep.
— George Dennison Prentice

ANGELICA   *[an-JEL-ih-kah (English), ahn-JEH-lee-kah (Italian)]*

MEANING: angel, divine messenger • **USAGE:**
English and Italian form of Angela (*see* Angel)
Thoughts that are calm, pure, and unselfish are so
many angelic messengers sent out into the world with
health, healing, and blessedness upon their wings.
— James Allen, *From Poverty to Power*

ANGELIKA   *[ahn-JEH-lee-kah]*

MEANING: angel, divine messenger • **USAGE:**
German and Hungarian form of Angela (*see* Angel)
We should pray to the angels
who are given to us as guardians.
— St. Ambrose

ANGELIKI   *[ahn-yeh-LEE-kee]*

MEANING: angel, divine messenger • **USAGE:**
Greek form of Angela (*see* Angel)
Behold I will send my angel,
who shall go before thee, and keep thee.
— Exodus 23:20a (DR)

ANGELINA   *[an-jeh-LEE-nah (English, Italian), ahn-zheh-LEE-nah (Russian), ahn-heh-LEE-nah (Spanish)]*

MEANING: angel, divine messenger • **USAGE:**
English, Italian, Russian, and Spanish form of
Angela (*see* Angel)
The glow of the angel in woman.
— Clara Balfour, *Sunbeams for All Seasons*

ANGELINE   *[ahn-ZHAH-leen (French),*
AN-jeh-leen (English)]

MEANING: angel, divine messenger • USAGE:
French and English form of Angela (*see* Angel)
Make friends with the angels, who though invisible
are always with you.... Often invoke them, constantly
praise them, and make good use of their help and
assistance in all your temporal and spiritual affairs.
— Francis de Sales

ANGÉLIQUE   *[ahn-zhay-LEEK]*

MEANING: angel, divine messenger • USAGE:
French form of Angela (*see* Angel)
To love for the sake of being loved is human, but to
love for the sake of loving is angelic.
— Alphonse de Lamartine,
Graziella (tr. James Runnion)

ANGELITA   *[ahn-hay-LEE-tah (Spanish),*
an-jeh-LEE-tah (English)]

MEANING: little angel • USAGE: Spanish and
English form of Angela and diminutive -*ita* (*see*
Angel)
Don't look down on any of these little ones.
For I tell you that in heaven their angels are always
in the presence of my heavenly Father.
— Matthew 18:11 (NLT)

ANGIE   *[AN-jee]*

MEANING: angel, divine messenger • USAGE:
English form of Angela (*see* Angel)
The love and affection of the angels be to you...
The love and affection of heaven be to you,
to guard you and to cherish you.
— Alexander Carmichael, *Carmina Gadelica*

ANIANI   *[ah-nee-AH-nee]*

MEANING: cool, refreshing, to blow softly as a
breeze, a mirror • USAGE: Hawaiian

Love is like the ends of the Ko'olau breeze.
[Love is present even when invisible.]
— Hawaiian proverb
(tr. Mary Pukui in '*Olelo No'eau*)

ANICA   *[ah-NEE-kah]*

MEANING: grace, gracious, merciful • USAGE:
Spanish form of Ana, from Hebrew *chaanach*
May grace and peace be multiplied to you.
— 2 Peter 1:2a (RSV)

ANICE, ANNICE   *[ah-NEES]*

MEANING: pure one, chaste, holy, lamb • USAGE:
English form of Agnes, from Greek *hagnos* (chaste,
holy); or from Latin *agnus* (lamb)
Blessed are the pure in heart, for they shall see God.
— Matthew 5:8 (WEB)

ANIELA   *[ah-nee-EH-lah]*

MEANING: angel, divine messenger • USAGE:
Polish form of Angela (*see* Angel)
He will give his angels charge over thee,
to keep thee in all thy ways.
— Psalm 91:11 (ASV)

ANIKA   *[ah-NEE-kah]*

MEANING: good, goodness • USAGE: African:
Yoruba of Nigeria
Ordinary people are as common as grass,
but good people are dearer than an eye.
— Yoruban proverb

ANIKA   *[ah-NEE-kah, AH-nee-kah]*

MEANING: grace, gracious, merciful • USAGE:
German, Dutch, and Danish form of Anna (*see*
Ann)
Grace is the beauty of form
under the influence of freedom.
— Johann Friedrich von Schiller

ANILA [ah-nih-lah]

MEANING: wind • **USAGE:** Hindu: Sanskrit

Wind and water have patience and tolerance.
— *Sri Guru Granth Sahib*
(Khalsa Consensus Translation)

ANIMA [AH-nee-mah]

MEANING: breath • **USAGE:** English: from Latin *ane* (to breathe)

Deep peace I breathe into you…
Deep peace, deep peace!
— Fiona MacLeod, "Invocation of Peace"

ANINA [ah-nee-nah]

MEANING: wise old woods • **USAGE:** Amerind: Tewa Pueblo

My words are tied in one… / With the great trees, /
In one with my body / And my heart.
— Tewa prayer

ANINA [ah-NEE-nah]

MEANING: grace, gracious, merciful • **USAGE:** German, Danish, and Swedish form of Anna (*see* Ann)

God is able to make all grace abound in you;
that ye always, having all sufficiency in all things,
may abound to every good work.
— 2 Corinthians 9:8 (DR)

ANIQUE [ah-NEEK]

MEANING: grace, gracious, merciful • **USAGE:** American: possibly a form of Ann (*see* Ann)

Everybody can be great…because anybody can
serve.… You only need a heart full of grace.
A soul generated by love.
— Martin Luther King Jr.,
"The Drum Major Instinct"

ANISE [ah-NEES, AN-is]

MEANING: aniseed herb • **USAGE:** English: from English *anis*

Bloom where you're planted.
— Mary Engelbreit, *The Art and the Artist*

ANISHA, ANEESHA [ah-NEE-shah]

MEANING: grace, gracious, merciful • **USAGE:** American: possibly a form of Ann (*see* Ann)

I have found always that mercy bears richer fruits
than strict justice. — Abraham Lincoln

ANITA [ah-NEE-tah]

MEANING: little gracious one • **USAGE:** Spanish, English, German, and Scandinavian form of Anna and diminutive -*ita* (*see* Ann)

She [Wisdom] will give to your head a garland of
grace. She will deliver a crown of splendor to you.
— Proverbs 4:9 (WEB)

ANJA [AHN-yah]

MEANING: grace, gracious, merciful • **USAGE:** Scandinavian and German form of Anna (*see* Ann)

Grace is like a paradise in blessings,
and mercy remaineth for ever.
— Sirach 40:17 (DR Apocrypha)

ANJENI [ahn-jeh-nee]

MEANING: spirit • **USAGE:** Amerind: Algonquin

It's all spirit and it's all connected.
— William Commanda

ANJU [ahn-joo]

MEANING: one who lives in the heart, honor, shine • **USAGE:** Hindu: Sanskrit

What is the soul? The soul is consciousness.
It shines as the light within the heart.
— *Brihadaranyaka Upanishad*

ANKE [AHN-keh]

MEANING: grace, gracious, merciful • **USAGE:** Scandinavian, German, and Dutch form of Annika (*see* Ann)

Grace and peace to you.
— 1 Thessalonians 1:1b (NCV)

ANN [an]

MEANING: grace, gracious, merciful • **USAGE:** English form of Hannah, from Hebrew *chaanach*

Surely goodness and mercy shall follow me all the days of my life.
— Psalm 23:6a (ESV)

ANNA [AH-nah (German, Greek, Italian, Russian, Scandinavian), AN-ah (English)]

MEANING: grace, gracious, merciful • **USAGE:** German, Greek, Italian, Scandinavian, Russian, and English form of Anne (*see* Ann)

It is good that the heart be established by grace.
— Hebrews 13:9b (WEB)

ANNABELLA [ah-nah-BAY-lah]

MEANING: gracious and beautiful, lovely and full of grace • **USAGE:** Italian combination of Anna and Bella (*see* Anna and Bella)

Inasmuch as love grows in you, in so much beauty grows; for love is itself the beauty of the soul.
— Augustine of Hippo

ANNAMARIA [ah-nah-mah-REE-ah (Italian), an-ah-mah-REE-ah (English)]

MEANING: beloved and full of grace • **USAGE:** Italian and English combination of Anna and Maria (*see* Anna and Maria)

Grace be with you.
— 1 Timothy 6:21b (NIV)

ANNE [AH-neh (French, German, Scandinavian), an (English)]

MEANING: grace, gracious, merciful • **USAGE:** French, German, Scandinavian, and English form of Hannah (*see* Ann)

The Lord bless you, and keep you; the Lord make His face shine on you, and be gracious to you; the Lord lift up His countenance on you, and give you peace.
— Numbers 6:24–26 (NASB)

ANNELISE, ANNELIESE [ah-neh-LEES, ah-nah-LEES-ah]

MEANING: graced by God, joined with God, God is my oath, blessed by God • **USAGE:** German and Scandinavian combination of Anne and Liese (*see* Anna and Liese)

With God all things can be done.
— Matthew 19:26b (NLV)

ANNETTE [ah-NET (French, English), ah-NET-eh (German, Scandinavian)]

MEANING: grace, gracious, merciful • **USAGE:** English, French, German, and Scandinavian form of Anne (*see* Ann)

The Lord be with your spirit. God's grace be with you.
— 2 Timothy 4:22 (GNT)

ANNIE [AN-ee]

MEANING: grace, gracious, merciful • **USAGE:** English form of Ann (*see* Ann)

Grace comes into the soul, as the morning sun into the world.
— Thomas Adams, "Heaven Made Sure"

ANNIKA [ah-NEE-kah, AH-nee-kah]

MEANING: grace, gracious, merciful • **USAGE:** Scandinavian, Dutch, and German form of Anna (*see* Ann)

It is good to receive inner strength from God's grace.
— Hebrews 13:9b (GNT)

ANNIS · [AN-is]

Meaning: pure one, chaste, holy, lamb · **Usage:** English form of Agnes, from Greek *hagnos* (chaste, holy); or from Latin *agnus* (lamb)

> *He [God] tends his flock like a shepherd:*
> *He gathers the lambs in his arms*
> *and carries them close to his heart.*
> — Isaiah 40:11a (NIV)

ANNISA · [ah-NIS-ah]

Meaning: grace, gracious, merciful · **Usage:** American: possibly a form of Ann (*see* Ann)

> *Grace to you and peace.*
> — 1 Corinthians 1:3a (ESV)

ANNUNZIATA · [ah-NOON-ʒee-ah-tah]

Meaning: announcement, messenger, herald, Annunciation of the Christ child · **Usage:** Italian: from Italian *annunʒio* (announcement) and Latin *nuntius* (messenger, herald); a reference to the Annunciation of the Christ child to Mary

> *And a little child shall lead them.*
> — Isaiah 11:6b (KJV)

ANNUSHKA · [ah-NOOSH-kah]

Meaning: grace, gracious, merciful · **Usage:** Russian form of Anna (*see* Ann)

> *Grace unto you and peace be multiplied.*
> — 1 Peter 1:2b (KJ21)

ANONNA · [ah-NOH-nah]

Meaning: goddess of harvest, grain goddess · **Usage:** Italian: Roman goddess of grain

> *Plant the seeds of doing what is right. Then you will*
> *harvest the fruit of your faithful love.*
> — Hosea 10:12b (NIRV)

ANOUK · [ah-NOOK]

Meaning: grace, gracious, merciful · **Usage:** French and Dutch form of Anna (*see* Ann)

> *The Lord be with your spirit. Grace be with you.*
> — 2 Timothy 4:22 (NEB)

ANSELMA · [ahn-SEHL-mah]

Meaning: protected by God, divine protection · **Usage:** German and Scandinavian feminine form of Anselm, from German *ans* (God) and *helm* (helmet, protection)

> *The Lord is faithful,*
> *and he will strengthen and protect you.*
> — 2 Thessalonians 3:3a (NASB)

ANTOINETTE · [ahn-twah-NET]

Meaning: invaluable, priceless, excellent · **Usage:** French feminine form of Antoine, from Latin *Antonius,* a Roman family name possibly meaning "invaluable"

> *You are a woman of excellence.*
> — Ruth 3:11b (NASB)

ANTONELLA · [ahn-toh-NAY-lah]

Meaning: invaluable, priceless, excellent · **Usage:** Italian feminine form of Antonio (*see* Antoinette)

> *Think about what is noble, right and pure.*
> *Think about what is lovely and worthy of respect.*
> *If anything is excellent or worthy of praise,*
> *think about those kinds of things.*
> — Philippians 4:8 (NIRV)

ANTONETTE · [AN-toh-NET]

Meaning: invaluable, priceless, excellent · **Usage:** English feminine form of Anthony (*see* Antoinette)

God is able to make every grace overflow to you, so that in every way, always having everything you need, you may excel in every good work.
— 2 Corinthians 9:8 (HCSB)

ANTONIA   *[ahn-TOH-nee-ah]*

MEANING: invaluable, priceless, excellent • **USAGE:** Italian, Spanish, English, German, and Scandinavian feminine form of Antonio (*see* Antoinette)
There are many virtuous and capable women in the world, but you surpass them all!
— Proverbs 31:29 (NLT)

ANURA   *[ah-noo-rah]*

MEANING: knowledge, wisdom, understanding • **USAGE:** Hindu
The true knowledge is the knowledge of our own nature. Know yourself.
— Swami Vivekananda

ANYA   *[AHN-yah]*

MEANING: boundless, infinite • **USAGE:** Hindu: Sanskrit
True love is boundless like the ocean and, swelling within one, spreads itself out and, crossing all boundaries and frontiers, envelops the whole world.
— Mahatma Gandhi

ANYA   *[AHN-yah]*

MEANING: grace, gracious, merciful • **USAGE:** Russian form of Anna, from Hebrew *chaanach*
May grace and peace be yours in abundance.
— 1 Peter 1:2b (NRSV)

AOIFE   *[EE-feh]*

MEANING: cheerful, pleasant, happy, life • **USAGE:** Irish: from Gaelic *aoibh* (face, pleasant); or Irish form of Eve, from Hebrew *hawwah* (life)

Continual cheerfulness is a sign of wisdom.
— Irish proverb

AOLOA   *[ah-oh-LOH-ah]*

MEANING: long cloud, high or distant cloud, distinguished, esteemed • **USAGE:** Hawaiian
My dreams are shaped in the ever-changing clouds.
— Hawaiian proverb

AONANI   *[ah-oh-NAH-nee]*

MEANING: beautiful light • **USAGE:** Hawaiian: from Hawaiian *ao* (light, daylight) and *nani* (beauty, beautiful)
In the first golden light of dawn, nothing is impossible!
— Hawaiian proverb

APHRODITE   *[af-roh-DIE-tee]*

MEANING: sea foam, goddess of love and beauty • **USAGE:** Greek: from Greek *aphros* (sea foam); Greek goddess of love and beauty
The noble; the beautiful.
— Greek proverb

APOLLONIA   *[ah-poh-LOH-nee-ah]*

MEANING: strength, might • **USAGE:** Greek feminine form of Apollo (*see* Apolonia)
In union there is strength.
— Aesop, "The Bundle of Sticks"

APOLONIA   *[ah-poh-LOH-nee-ah]*

MEANING: strength, might • **USAGE:** Spanish feminine form of Apollo, from Greek *apelo*
Like every woman of the people, I have more strength than I appear to have.
— Evita Perón, *La Razón de Mi Vida*

APPLE [AP-el]

MEANING: apple fruit, apple tree • **USAGE:** American: from English *appel*

> Keep me as the apple of the eye;
> hide me under the shadow of Thy wings.
> — Psalm 17:8 (KJ21)

APRIL [AY-pril]

MEANING: month of April, springtime, opening, Aphrodite • **USAGE:** English: from Latin *aprilis* (month of Venus, the fourth month of the Gregorian calendar) and Latin *aperire* (to open); or from Greek *Aphro*, a form of Aphrodite, Greek goddess of love and beauty

> The April's in her eyes. It is love's spring.
> — William Shakespeare, *Antony and Cleopatra*

AQILA, AAQILA, AQEELA [ah-KEE-lah]

MEANING: intelligent, rational, knowledgeable, thoughtful • **USAGE:** Muslim feminine form of Aqil, from Arabic *aqil* (intelligent) or *akila* (one who reasons)

> The intelligent and the brave /
> Open every closet in the future.
> — Hafiz, "The Warrior"
> (tr. Daniel Ladinsky in *The Gift*)

AQUILINA [ah-kee-LEE-nah]

MEANING: little eagle • **USAGE:** Spanish: from Latin *aquila* (eagle) and diminutive *-ina*

> Those who hope in the Lord will renew their strength.
> They will soar on wings like eagles; they will run and
> not grow weary, they will walk and not be faint.
> — Isaiah 40:31 (NIV)

ARABELLA [ah-rah-BAY-lah (Italian), ar-ah-BEL-ah (English)]

MEANING: pray, prayer, answered prayer • **USAGE:** Italian and English: from Latin *orabilis* (yielding to pray)

> More things are wrought by prayer /
> Than this world dreams of.
> — Alfred Tennyson, *Idylls of the King*

ARANRHOD [ah-RAHN-rod]

MEANING: silver wheel, silver circle • **USAGE:** Welsh: from Welsh *ariannaid* (silver) and *rhod* (wheel, circle); Welsh goddess associated with constellation Corona Borealis

> O Being of Brightness, Friend of Light,
> from the Blessed realms of Grace, Gently encircle me,
> sweetly enclosing me, Guarding my soul-shrine
> from harm this day and night.
> — Celtic Blessing of the Guardian Angel

ARDELLA, ARDELA [ar-DEL-ah]

MEANING: hare valley, from the dale of hares • **USAGE:** English feminine form of Ardel, from English *hara* (hare) and *dæl* (dale, valley)

> The valleys…shout for joy, yeah, they sing.
> — Psalm 65:13 (DT)

ARDELLE, ARDELE [ahr-DEL]

MEANING: hare valley, from the dale of hares • **USAGE:** English feminine form of Ardel, from English *hara* (hare) and *dæl* (dale, valley)

> I should be glad if all the meadows on the earth
> were left in a wild state.
> — Henry David Thoreau, *Walden*

ARELA, ARELLA [ah-REH-lah]

MEANING: angel, divine messenger • **USAGE:** Jewish feminine form of Arel

> He will give His angels charge over thee, to keep thee
> in all thy ways. — Psalm 91:11 (MT)

ARETA [ah-REH-tah]

MEANING: charming, pleasant • *Usage:* African: Benin of Nigeria

> A good-humored person has no enemy.
> — Nigerian proverb

ARETHA   *[ah-REE-thah]*

MEANING: virtuous, moral, good • **USAGE:**
English: from Greek *arete*
> *The most natural beauty in the world*
> *is honesty and moral truth.*
> — Earl of Shaftesbury, *Characteristics*

ARIA   *[AH-ree-ah]*

MEANING: song, melody, solo opera piece •
USAGE: English: from Greek *aer* (air, melody, solo
opera piece)
> *Music hath charms to soothe the savage breast, /*
> *To soften rocks, or bend a knotted oak.*
> — William Congreve, *The Mourning Bride*

ARIADNE   *[ah-ree-AHD-neh]*

MEANING: very holy, devout • **USAGE:** Greek:
from Greek *ari* (very) and *adnos* (holy)
> *The root of those who are right with God*
> *will not be moved.* — Proverbs 12:3b (NLV)

ARIANA   *[ah-ree-AH-nah]*

MEANING: silver, silvery • **USAGE:** Welsh and
English: from Welsh *arian*
> *A word aptly spoken is like apples of gold*
> *in settings of silver.* — Proverbs 25:11 (NIV)

ARIANE, ARIANNE   *[ah-ree-AHN*
(French), AYR-ee-an (English)]

MEANING: very holy, utterly pure • **USAGE:**
French and English form of Ariadne (*see* Ariadne)
> *Blessed are the pure in heart: for they shall see God.*
> — Matthew 5:8 (ASV)

ARIANNA   *[ah-ree-AH-nah]*

MEANING: very holy, devout • **USAGE:** Italian
form of Ariadne (*see* Ariadne)
> *The glow of inspiration warms us; it is a holy rapture.*
> — Ovid

ARIELA   *[ah-ree-EL-ah]*

MEANING: lioness of God • **USAGE:** Spanish,
Italian, and English feminine form of Ariel (*see*
Arielle)
> *An honest person is as brave as a lion.*
> — Proverbs 28:1b (GNT)

ARIELLA   *[ah-ree-EL-ah]*

MEANING: lioness of God, lionhearted • **USAGE:**
Jewish feminine form of Ariel (*see* Arielle)
> *The righteous are secure as a young lion.*
> — Proverbs 28:1b (MT)

ARIELLE   *[ah-ree-EL]*

MEANING: lioness of God, lionhearted • **USAGE:**
Jewish, English, and French: from Hebrew *ari 'el*
(lion of God)
> *Beauty rides on her lion.*
> — Ralph Waldo Emerson, *The Conduct of Life*

ARIFA, AARIFA, AREEFA   *[ah-REE-fah]*

MEANING: wise, knowledgeable • **USAGE:** Muslim
feminine form of Arif, from Arabic *arif*
> *Reason is learned from the ever changing world, but*
> *wisdom comes from the essence of life.*
> — Hazrat Inayat Khan, *The Gayan* (cd. *The Gayani*
> *Meditations, Volume 1,* tr. Cecil Touchon)

ARINA   *[ah-REE-nah]*

MEANING: peace, peaceful, calm, serene • **USAGE:**
Russian form of *Irini* from Greek *eirene*
> *We shall find peace. We shall hear angels,*
> *we shall see the sky sparkling with diamonds.*
> — Anton Chekhov, *Uncle Vanya*
> (tr. Ronald Hingley)

ARIZONA   [ayr-ih-ZOH-nah]

MEANING: good oaks, little spring, silver-yielding, barren zone • USAGE: American: from Basque *aritz onak* (good oaks); from American Indian O'odham *ala sonak* (little spring); from Aztec *arizuma* (silver-yielding); or from Spanish *zona árida* (barren zone)

> *Many words rush along like rivers in flood,*
> *but deep wisdom flows up from artesian springs.*
> — Proverbs 18:4 (MSG)

ARLENE   [ahr-LEEN]

MEANING: promise, pledge • USAGE: English: from Welsh *addewid*

> *The Lord your God will bless you just as*
> *he has promised.* — Deuteronomy 15:6a (NEB)

ARLO   [AHR-loh]

MEANING: fortified hill, army hill • USAGE: English form of Harlow, from English *here* (army) and *hlaw* (hill)

> *Let mountains and hills bring peace to the people*
> *through what is right and good.*
> — Psalm 72:3 (NLV)

ARNA   [AHR-nah]

MEANING: eagle power, eagle rule • USAGE: Swedish and Danish feminine form of Arnold, from German *arn* (eagle) and *wald* (rule, power)

> *I carried you on eagles' wings and brought you to Me.*
> — Exodus 19:4b (HCSB)

ARTIA   [AR-tee-ah, AR-shah]

MEANING: bear, strong as a bear, keeper of bears, stone, rock • USAGE: American feminine form of Art, from Welsh *artos* (bear); Greek *arktourous* (keeper of bears); or from Irish Gaelic *art* (stone, rock)

> *I can do all things through Him who strengthens me.*
> — Philippians 4:13 (NASB)

ARUNA   [ah-ROO-nah]

MEANING: red, rosy, color of dawn, sunrise • USAGE: Hindu: from Sanskrit *aruna*

> *Every day / make a fresh beginning.*
> — Shi Wuling, *Path to Peace*

ARYA   [AHR-yah]

MEANING: noble, great • USAGE: Hindu: Sanskrit

> *If you are noble you will find the world noble.*
> — Hindu proverb

ARYN   [AYR-en]

MEANING: peace, peaceful, calm, serene, Ireland • USAGE: American form of Erin, the Irish Gaelic name of Ireland, from Eire (Celtic goddess); or from Greek *eirene* (peace)

> *Peace is at the very center of your own soul,*
> *it is the very Being of your being.*
> — Ernest Holmes, *Your Invisible Power*

ARZU   [ahr-zoo]

MEANING: love, loving • USAGE: Muslim

> *On those who believe and work deeds of righteousness,*
> *will (Allah) Most Gracious bestow love.*
> — Koran, Maryam 19.96 (ALI)

ASAMI   [ah-sah-mee]

MEANING: morning beauty, beautiful morning • USAGE: Japanese: from Japanese *masa* (morning) and *mi* (beautiful)

> *Create each day anew by clothing yourself*
> *with heaven and earth, bathing yourself*
> *with wisdom and love, and placing yourself*
> *in the heart of Mother Nature.*
> — Morihei Ueshiba,
> *The Art of Peace* (tr. John Stevens)

ASHA   [ah-shah]

MEANING: life, alive and well, lively • **USAGE:** Muslim form of Aisha, from Arabic *a'isha* (alive and well) or *a'sha* (to live)

Draw us closer to Thee every moment of our life,
until in us be reflected Thy Grace, Thy Glory,
Thy Wisdom, Thy Joy and Thy Peace.
— Hazrat Inayat Khan, *The Gayan*

ASHANI, ASHANEE   [ah-SHAH-nee]

MEANING: African ethnic group in Ghana • **USAGE:** American: possibly a form of Ashanti, an African ethnic group in Ghana

The lifestyle of good people is like sunlight at dawn
that keeps getting brighter until broad daylight.
— Proverbs 4:18 (CEV)

ASHANTI   [ah-SHAHN-tee]

MEANING: African ethnic group in Ghana • **USAGE:** African: Ghana

You may judge the strength of a nation by the political
consciousness of its women. — Kwame Nkrumah

ASHERA   [ah-SHEH-rah]

MEANING: blessed, happy, fortunate • **USAGE:** Jewish feminine form of Asher

Just to be is a blessing. Just to live is holy.
— Abraham Heschel, "To Grow in Wisdom"

ASHIMA   [ah-shih-mah]

MEANING: free, without limitations • **USAGE:** Hindu

Love does not claim possession, but gives freedom.
— Rabindranath Tagore

ASHIRA   [ah-SHEE-rah]

MEANING: wealthy, prosperous • **USAGE:** Jewish feminine form of Ashir

May the favor of the Lord, our God,
be upon us; let the work of our hands prosper.
— Psalm 90:17a (JPS)

ASHLEIGH   [ASH-lee]

MEANING: ash tree meadow, field of ash trees • **USAGE:** American form of Ashley, from English *aesc* (ash tree) and *leah* (meadow, field)

She [Wisdom] is a tree of life to those who hold her
close. Those who hold on to her will be blessed.
— Proverbs 3:18 (NIRV)

ASHLEY, ASHLIE   [ASH-lee]

MEANING: ash tree meadow, field of ash trees • **USAGE:** English surname: from English *aesc* (ash tree) and *leah* (meadow, field)

A tree provides perhaps our most intimate
contact with nature.
— George Nakashima, *The Soul of a Tree*

ASHLING   [ASH-ling]

MEANING: dream, vision, visionary • **USAGE:** English form of Aisling, from Irish Gaelic *aisling*

Our truest life is when we are in dreams awake.
— Henry David Thoreau,
A Week on the Concord and Merrimack Rivers

ASHLYN, ASHLYNN   [ASH-lin]

MEANING: ash tree lake, ash trees near the lake • **USAGE:** English combination of Ashley and Lynn (*see* Ashley and Lynn)

They are like trees planted by streams of water,
which yield their fruit in its season, and their leaves
do not wither. In all that they do, they prosper.
— Psalm 1:3 (NRSV)

ASHNI   *[ahsh-nih]*

MEANING: flash of lightning • **USAGE:** Hindu

This is the truth of Brahman in relation to nature: whether in the flash of lightning, or in the wink of the eyes, the power that is shown is the power of Brahman.
— *Kena Upanishad* (tr. Swami Prabhavananda)

ASIA   *[AY-zhah]*

MEANING: rising sun, name of largest continent, life, alive and well • **USAGE:** American: from Phoenician *asa* (east) and *ereb(m)* (to enter, of the sun); or form of Aisha, from Arabic *a'isha* (alive and well) and *a'sha* (to live)

Arise, shine, for your light has come.
— Isaiah 60:1a (RSV)

ASILA, ASEELA   *[ah-SEE-lah]*

MEANING: noble, highborn • **USAGE:** Muslim

Surely (as for) the charitable men and the charitable women and (those who) set apart for Allah a goodly portion, it shall be doubled for them and they shall have a noble reward.
— Koran, The Iron 57.18 (SKR)

ASIMA, AASIMA, ASEEMA   *[ah-SEE-mah]*

MEANING: protector, guardian • **USAGE:** Muslim feminine form of Asim, from Arabic *asim*

No human soul but hath a guardian over it.
— Koran, The Night-Comer 86.4 (PIC)

ASIRA, ASIRAH   *[ah-SEE-rah]*

MEANING: chosen • **USAGE:** Muslim feminine form of Asir

He specially chooses for His mercy whom He pleases; and Allah is the Lord of mighty grace.
— Koran, The Family of Imran 3.74 (SKR)

ASIYA   *[ah-sih-yah]*

MEANING: firm, steadfast • **USAGE:** Muslim

O ye who believe! Seek help in steadfastness and prayer. Lo! Allah is with the steadfast.
— Koran, The Cow 2.153 (PIC)

ASMANI   *[ahs-MAH-nee]*

MEANING: heavenly, divine • **USAGE:** Persian

In beauty is the secret of divinity.
— Hazrat Inayat Khan, *The Gayan* (cd. *The Gayani Meditations, Volume 1*, tr. Cecil Touchon)

ASPEN   *[AS-pen]*

MEANING: aspen tree, white poplar • **USAGE:** American: from English *æspe*

Aspens are youth, eternal youth. Endlessly their dancing leaves proclaim youth.
— Enos A. Mills, *Your National Parks*

ASTA   *[AH-stah]*

MEANING: love, beloved, beautiful goddess • **USAGE:** Scandinavian: from Norse *ast* (love); or Scandinavian form of *Astridr*, from Norse *áss* (god) and *fríor* (fair, beautiful)

I pray this, that your love may abound even more and more in knowledge and every kind of insight.
— Philippians 1:9 (NEB)

ASTER   *[AH-ster]*

MEANING: star, starlike, radiant • **USAGE:** African: Ethiopian form of Esther, from Persian *stara*

He telleth the number of the stars; He calleth them all by their names. — Psalm 147:4 (KJ21)

ASTRA   *[AS-trah]*

MEANING: star, starlike, radiant • **USAGE:** English: from Greek *aster*

I think my heart is whiter for its parley with a star.
— Karle Wilson Baker, "Good Company"

ASTRID   *[AH-streed]*

MEANING: beautiful goddess, fair goddess •
USAGE: Scandinavian and German form of *Astrid*
(*see* Asta)

> *How fair and pleasant you are.*
> — Song of Songs 7:6a (NRSV)

ASYA   *[AHS-yah]*

MEANING: resurrection, reborn, rise up • **USAGE:**
Russian form of Anastasia, from Greek *anastasis*
(resurrection); or from Greek *ana* (up) and *stasis*
(standing)

> *You have been given a new birth.*
> *It was from a seed that cannot die.*
> — 1 Peter 1:23a (NLV)

ATARA   *[ah-tah-RAH]*

MEANING: crown, wreath • **USAGE:** Jewish

> *Thou shalt be a crown of beauty in the hand of the*
> *Lord, and a royal diadem in the open hand of thy God.*
> — Isaiah 62:3 (MT)

ATHENA   *[ah-THEE-nah]*

MEANING: goddess, wise, knowledgeable, warrior
• **USAGE:** Greek: from Greek *Athene*, Greek
goddess of wisdom and war, from Greek *a-theo-noa*
(mind of God)

> *Wisdom cometh into thy heart,*
> *and knowledge to thy soul is pleasant.*
> — Proverbs 2:10 (YLT)

ATIANA   *[aht-tee-AH-nah]*

MEANING: father • **USAGE:** American: possibly
a form of Tatiana, from the feminine form of the
Roman family clan name *Tatius*, possibly from
Latin *tata* (father)

> *To You, O God of my fathers, I give thanks and*
> *praise, for You have given me wisdom and power.*
> — Daniel 2:23a (NASB)

ATIFA, ATEEFA   *[ah-TEE-fah]*

MEANING: kind, compassionate • **USAGE:** Muslim
feminine form of Atif, from Arabic *'atif*

> *Nobody appears inferior to us when our heart is*
> *kindled with kindness,*
> *and our eyes are open to the vision of God.*
> — Hazrat Inayat Khan, *The Bowl of Saki*

ATIRA   *[ah-tih-rah]*

MEANING: fragrant, aromatic, perfumed • **USAGE:**
Muslim

> *The God ideal is the flower of creation,*
> *and realization of truth is its fragrance.*
> — Hazrat Inayat Khan, *The Gayan* (cd. *The Gayani*
> *Meditations, Volume 1,* tr. Cecil Touchon)

ATIRA   *[ah-TEE-rah]*

MEANING: crown, wreath • **USAGE:** Jewish
feminine form of Atir

> *Rabbi Shimon said:*
> *"There are three crowns: the crown of Torah,*
> *the crown of priesthood, and the crown of royalty.*
> *However, the crown of a good name is greater*
> *than all of them."*
> — *Pirkei Avot* 4:17

ATIYA, ATIYYAH   *[ah-TEE-yah]*

MEANING: gift, present • **USAGE:** Muslim

> *The best gift comes from the heart.*
> — Arabic proverb

ATSUKO   *[aht-soo-koh]*

MEANING: kind child • **USAGE:** Japanese

> *One kind word can warm three winter months.*
> — Japanese proverb

AUBREY, AUBRIE   [AH-bree]

MEANING: elf queen, elfin power • **USAGE:**
English feminine form of Alberic, from German *alb*
(elf) and *rik* (ruler, leader)
She [Wisdom] shall give to thine head an ornament
of grace; a crown of glory shall she deliver to thee.
— Proverbs 4:9 (KJ21)

AUD   [ahd]

MEANING: rich, prosperous • **USAGE:** Scandina-
vian: from Norse *auðr* (riches, prosperity)
The Lord will make you prosper abundantly.
— Deuteronomy 28:11a (HCSB)

AUDRA   [AH-drah]

MEANING: noble strength, valorous and mighty •
USAGE: English form of Audrey (*see* Audrey)
The better part of valor is discretion.
— William Shakespeare, *Henry IV, Part I*

AUDREY, AUDRIE   [AH-dree]

MEANING: noble strength, valorous and mighty
• **USAGE:** English: from English *æthel* (noble,
valorous) and *thryth* (might, strength)
Strength and dignity are her clothing; and she laugheth
at the time to come. — Proverbs 31:25 (ASV)

AUDRINA   [ah-DREE-nah]

MEANING: noble strength, valorous and mighty •
USAGE: English form of Audrey (*see* Audrey)
Whatever your hand finds to do, do it with your might.
— Ecclesiastes 9:10a (NKJV)

AUGUSTA   [ah-GUS-tah (English),
                    ow-GOOS-tah (German, Scandinavian),
                    eh-GUS-tah (Italian)]

MEANING: great one, revered one, magnificent
• **USAGE:** English, German, Italian, and Scandinavian feminine form of Augustus, from Latin
augustus

Be free all worthy spirits, and stretch yourselves, for
greatness and for height.
— George Chapman, *The Conspiracy and*
Tragedy of Charles, Duke of Byron

AUGUSTINE   [oh-goos-TEEN (French),
                      ow-gus-TEE-neh (German, Scandinavian)]

MEANING: great one, revered one, magnificent
• **USAGE:** French, German, and Scandinavian
feminine form of Augustus (*see* Augusta)
It is passions alone, and strong passions, that can
elevate the soul to great things.
— Denis Diderot, "Philosophic Thoughts"
(tr. Margaret Jourdain)

AURA   [AWR-ah]

MEANING: soft breeze, halo, goddess of breezes
• **USAGE:** English: from Greek *aura* (distinctive
atmosphere, halo); Greek goddess of breezes
What's female beauty but an air divine?
— Edward Young, "Love of Fame"

AURÉLIE   [oh-reh-LEE]

MEANING: gold, golden • **USAGE:** French form of
Aurelius, from Latin *aurum*
Gold like the sun,
which melts wax but hardens clay,
expands souls.
— Antoine de Rivarol

AURORA   [ah-ROR-ah]

MEANING: sunrise, dawn, daybreak • **USAGE:**
English, German, Italian, Scandinavian, and
Spanish: from Latin *aurora* (dawn, daybreak,
sunrise); Roman goddess of the dawn
Your light will shine like the sunrise.
— Isaiah 58:8a (NEB)

AUTUMN   *[AH-tum]*

MEANING: autumn, season of fall, harvesttime • USAGE: English: from Latin *autumnus* (the season from the summer equinox to the winter equinox)

No spring, nor summer beauty hath such grace, /
As I have seen in one autumnal face.
— John Donne, "The Autumnal"

AVA   *[AY-vah]*

MEANING: life, full of life, bird • USAGE: English form of Eve or Eva, from Hebrew *hawwah* (life); or from Latin *avis* (bird)

Surely goodness and mercy
shall follow me all the days of my life.
— Psalm 23:6a (NRSV)

AVALON   *[AV-ah-lahn]*

MEANING: apple, mythological island • USAGE: English: from Welsh *abal* or *afal* (apple); in Arthurian legend, the island paradise where King Arthur goes after death

Keep me as the apple of Your eye;
hide me under the shadow of Your wings.
— Psalm 17:8 (NKJV)

AVANI   *[ah-van-nee]*

MEANING: earth • USAGE: Hindu: from Sanskrit *avana*

Everywhere in this earth the spirit of Paradise
is awake and sending forth its voice.
— Rabindranath Tagore

AVELINA   *[ah-veh-LEE-nah]*

MEANING: little bird • USAGE: English: from Latin *avis* (bird) and suffix *-ina*

He Himself…will cover you with His feathers;
you will take refuge under His wings.
His faithfulness will be a protective shield.
— Psalm 91:3–4 (HCSB)

AVELINE   *[ah-veh-LEEN]*

MEANING: little bird, young bird • USAGE: English: from Latin *avis* (bird) and suffix *-ine*

I'm youth, I'm joy.
I'm a little bird that has broken out of the egg.
— James M. Barrie, *Peter Pan*

AVERY   *[AYE-ver-ee]*

MEANING: elf counsel, supernaturally wise, elf leader • USAGE: English feminine form of Alfred, from English *ælf* (elf) and *raed* (counsel); or English feminine form of Alberic, from German *alb* (elf) and *rik* (ruler, leader)

My mouth shall speak wisdom;
and the meditation of my heart
shall be understanding.
— Psalm 49:3 (ASV)

AVIELA, AVIELLA   *[ah-vee-EH-lah]*

MEANING: my father is God • USAGE: Jewish feminine form of Aviel, from Hebrew *abn 'el*

O Lord, Thou art our Father; we are the clay,
and Thou our potter, and we all are the work
of Thy hand.
— Isaiah 64:7 (MT)

AVIGAYIL   *[ah-vee-GAH-yeel]*

MEANING: father's joy and delight • USAGE: Jewish: from Hebrew *avigayil*

He [God] brought me forth also into a large place;
He delivered me, because He delighted in me.
— Psalm 18:20 (MT)

AVILA   *[ah-VEE-lah]*

MEANING: bird • USAGE: English: from Latin *avis*

A little creature of soft wings.
— Richard Le Gallienne, "To a Bird at Dawn"

A

AVIVA, AVIVAH   [ah-VEE-vah]

MEANING: spring, youthfulness, freshness •
USAGE: Jewish

> Youth is a wreath of roses.
> — Jewish proverb

AVRIELLE   [AYV-ree-el, ahv-ree-EL]

MEANING: elf counsel, supernaturally wise, my
father is God, month of April, springtime, lioness
of God, wild boar warrior • **USAGE:** American:
possibly a form of Avery, Aviela, Avril, Arielle, or
Averil (see those entries)

> She opens her mouth in wisdom,
> and the teaching of kindness is on her tongue.
> — Proverbs 31:26 (NASB)

AVRIL   [ah-VREEL]

MEANING: month of April, springtime, opening,
Aphrodite • **USAGE:** French form of April, from
Latin aprilis (month of Venus, the fourth month of
the Gregorian calendar) and Latin aperire (to open);
or from Greek Aphro, a form of Aphrodite, Greek
goddess of love and beauty

> Love is like…spring.
> — Honoré de Balzac,
> The Wild Ass's Skin (tr. Ellen Marriage)

AYAH   [AH-yah]

MEANING: bright, shining • **USAGE:** African:
Swahili of Kenya and Tanzania

> A good name shines in the dark.
> — Tanzanian proverb

AYDA   [AY-dah]

MEANING: first daughter • **USAGE:** African:
Nigeria

> Early corn is best, so the firstborn
> is the one to delight in.
> — West African proverb

AYDA, AIDA   [ah-EE-dahh]

MEANING: reward, recompense, benefit • **USAGE:**
Muslim: from Arabic a'ida (benefit) or 'ada (to
return)

> Allah is never unjust in the least degree:
> If there is any good (done), He doubleth it,
> and giveth from His own presence a great reward.
> — Koran, The Women 4.40 (ALI)

AYITA   [ah-yeet-tah]

MEANING: first to dance • **USAGE:** Amerind:
Cherokee

> The highest human purpose is always to reinvent
> and celebrate the sacred.
> — N. Scott Momaday

AYLA   [aye-LAH]

MEANING: oak tree, terebinth tree • **USAGE:**
Jewish form of Eilah

> All the trees of the field shall clap their hands.
> — Isaiah 55:12b (JPS)

AYN   [ien]

MEANING: only daughter, only one • **USAGE:**
Russian: from Finnish aino tytti (only daughter,
only one), from Finnish epic Kalevala

> Many daughters have done worthily,
> but thou excellest them all.
> — Proverbs 31:29 (ASV)

AYOKA   [ah-YOH-kah]

MEANING: she brings joy to all • **USAGE:** African:
Yoruba of Nigeria

> If you have friends, you will not be alone.
> — West African proverb

AZALEA, AZALIA   [ah-ZAYL-yah]

MEANING: azalea flower, dry • **USAGE:** English:
from Greek azaleos (dry); type of flower

> Flowers are appearing on the earth.
> The season for singing has come.
> — Song of Songs 2:12 (NIRV)

B

AZALEE, AZALIE [ah-ʒah-LEE]

MEANING: azalea flower, dry • **USAGE:** American form of Azalea (*see* Azalea)
> *Where flowers bloom so does hope.*
> — Lady Bird Johnson

AZAR [ah-ʒahr]

MEANING: fire • **USAGE:** Persian
> *Life itself becomes a scripture to the kindled soul.*
> — Hazrat Inayat Khan, *The Gayan* (cd. *The Gayani Meditations, Volume 1,* tr. Cecil Touchon)

AZILE [aʒ-EEL]

MEANING: azalea flower, dry • **USAGE:** American: possibly a form of Azalea (*see* Azalea)
> *Hiding in every flower, in every leaf,*
> *in every twig and bough are reflections of the God*
> *who once walked with us in Eden.*
> — Tonia Triebwasser, *The Color of Grace*

AZIZAH, AZEEZAH [ah-ZEE-ʒah]

MEANING: beloved, noble, honorable • **USAGE:** Muslim feminine form of Aziz, from Arabic *aʒiʒ*
> *Only the soul knows what love is.*
> — Jalaluddin Rumi
> (tr. Coleman Barks in *Rumi: The Big Red Book*)

AZRIELA [ahʒ-ree-EH-lah]

MEANING: God is my help • **USAGE:** Jewish feminine form of Azriel, from Hebrew *aʒra' el*
> *I strengthen thee, yea, I help thee;*
> *yea, I uphold thee with My victorious right hand.*
> — Isaiah 41:10b (MT)

AZURA [ah-ZHUR-ah]

MEANING: azure, sky blue color, lapis lazuli • **USAGE:** English form of Azure (*see* Azure)
> *The sky is the soul of all scenery.*
> — Thomas Campbell

AZURE [ah-ZHUR]

MEANING: azure, sky blue color, lapis lazuli • **USAGE:** English: from French *aʒur*
> *Come out in the aʒure. Love the day.*
> *Do not leave the sky out of your landscape.*
> — Ralph Waldo Emerson, *The Conduct of Life*

AZZURRA [ah-ZHUH-rah]

MEANING: azure, sky blue color, lapis lazuli • **USAGE:** Italian form of Azure (*see* Azure)
> *If the sight of the blue skies fills you with joy,*
> *if a blade of grass springing up in the fields*
> *has power to move you, if the simple things*
> *of nature have a message that you understand,*
> *rejoice, for your soul is alive.*
> — Eleonora Duse

B

BABETTE [bah-BET]

MEANING: God is my oath, joined with God, blessed by God, foreigner, stranger, visitor • **USAGE:** French form of Elizabeth, from Hebrew *el'ishebha;* or French form of Barbara, from Greek *barbaros* (foreign, other) or *bar-bar* (unintelligible speech)
> *Let us love one another, because love is from God,*
> *and everyone who loves has been born of God*
> *and knows God.*
> — 1 John 4:7 (HCSB)

BABS [babs]

MEANING: foreigner, stranger, visitor • **USAGE:** English form of Barbara (*see* Barbara)
> *Do not forget to show hospitality to strangers,*
> *for by so doing some people have shown hospitality*
> *to angels without knowing it.*
> — Hebrews 13:2 (NIRV)

B

BADRA
[bah-drah]

MEANING: full moon • USAGE: Muslim: from
Arabic *badr*
>There is a moon inside every human being. /
>Learn to be companions with it. /
>Give more of your life to this listening.
>— Jalaluddin Rumi, "Listening"
>(tr. Coleman Barks in *The Glance*)

BAHIRA, BAHIRAH, BAHEERA
[bah-hee-rah]

MEANING: brilliant, bright light • USAGE: Muslim
feminine form of Bahir, Arabic *bahir*
>There are those who are like a lighted candle:
>they can light other candles.
>— Hazrat Inayat Khan, *The Bowl of Saki*

BAHIYA, BAHIYYA
[bah-HEE-yah]

MEANING: dazzling, bright light • USAGE:
Muslim: from Arabic *bahir*
>Beauty is not in the face; beauty is a light in the heart.
>— Kahlil Gibran

BAILEY, BAILEE, BAILIE
[BAY-lee]

MEANING: bailiff, steward, administrator •
USAGE: English surname: from English *bailiff*
>Make fair decisions. Show faithful love
>and compassion to one another.
>— Zechariah 7:9b (HCSB)

BAKHITA
[bahk-hee-tah]

MEANING: blessed, fortunate • USAGE: Muslim
>He it is Who sends His blessings on you, and (so do)
>His angels. — Koran, The Allies 33.43a (SKR)

BALA
[bah-lah]

MEANING: childlike, innocent, youthful • USAGE:
Hindu: from Sanskrit *bala*

>Seen through the eyes of love, all beings are beautiful,
>all deeds are dedicated, all thoughts are innocent.
>— Sathya Sai Baba

BALISSA
[bah-LIS-ah]

MEANING: beautiful, pretty, lovely • USAGE:
American: possibly a form of *Bella*, from Latin
bella
>It was for beauty that the world was made.
>— Ralph Waldo Emerson, *The Conduct of Life*

BAO
[bou]

MEANING: treasure, precious • USAGE: Chinese
>I have just three things to teach: simplicity, patience,
>compassion. These three are your greatest treasures.
>— Lao Tzu, *Tao Te Ching* (tr. Stephen Mitchell)

BARAKA
[bah-rah-kah]

MEANING: blessed, fortunate • USAGE: Muslim
>The grace of Allah and His blessings on you.
>— Koran, Hud 11.73b (ALI)

BARB
[barb]

MEANING: foreigner, stranger, visitor • USAGE:
English form of Barbara (*see* Barbara)
>Remember to welcome strangers,
>because some who have done this
>have welcomed angels without knowing it.
>— Hebrews 13:2 (NCV)

BARBARA
[BAR-bah-rah]

MEANING: foreigner, stranger, visitor • USAGE:
English, Italian, French, German, Scandinavian,
and Spanish: from Greek *barbaros* (foreign, other)
or *bar-bar* (unintelligible speech)
>Beauty is a welcome guest everywhere.
>— Johann Wolfgang von Goethe,
>*Elective Affinities* (tr. Hjalmar Hjorth Boyesen)

B

BARBORA   *[BAR-boh-rah]*

MEANING: foreigner, stranger, visitor • **USAGE:**
Czech form of Barbara (*see* Barbara)
You [God] prepare a banquet for me...you welcome me
as an honored guest and fill my cup to the brim.
— Psalm 23:5 (GNT)

BARBRA   *[BAR-brah]*

MEANING: foreigner, stranger, visitor • **USAGE:**
English form of Barbara (*see* Barbara)
You are no longer foreigners and strangers,
but fellow citizens with God's people
and also members of his household.
— Ephesians 2:19 (NIV)

BARBRO   *[BAR-broh]*

MEANING: foreigner, stranger, visitor • **USAGE:**
Scandinavian form of Barbara (*see* Barbara)
The Lord your God is with you anywhere you go.
— Joshua 1:9b (NLV)

BARI, BARRI, BARRIE   *[BAYR-ee]*

MEANING: spear, spear-like, warrior, fair-haired
• **USAGE:** English feminine form of Barry, from
Irish Gaelic *bearach* (spear, spear-like), or a form of
Fionbharr, from Gaelic *fionn* (white, fair) and *bearr*
(head)
Thou anointest my head with oil.
— Psalm 23:5b (ASV)

BASHA, BASHE   *[bah-shah]*

MEANING: daughter of God • **USAGE:** Yiddish
form of Batya; from Hebrew *bat' yah* (daughter of
Yahweh)
Blessed be thou of the Lord, my daughter.
— Ruth 3:10b (MT)

BASHIRA, BASHIRAH, BASHEERA

[bah-SHEE-rah]

MEANING: bringer of good news • **USAGE:**
Muslim feminine form of Bashir
Convey good news to those who believe and do good
deeds, that they shall have gardens in which rivers flow.
— Koran, The Cow 2.25 (SKR)

BASIMA, BASIMAH   *[bah-see-mah]*

MEANING: smiling, happy, cheerful • **USAGE:**
Muslim: from Arabic *basimah* (to smile)
Cheerfulness is a sign of health.
— Arabic proverb

BASIRA, BASIRAH   *[bah-SEE-rah]*

MEANING: wise, insightful • **USAGE:** Muslim
feminine form of Basir
O my Lord! bestow wisdom on me,
and join me with the righteous.
— Koran, The Poets 26.83 (PIC)

BASMA   *[bahs-mah]*

MEANING: smiling, happy, cheerful • **USAGE:**
Muslim: from Arabic *basimah* (to smile)
One can show generosity by a smile.
— Hazrat Inayat Khan, *The Gayan* (cd. *The Gayani*
Meditations, Volume 1, tr. Cecil Touchon)

BATYA, BATIA   *[BAHT-yah, BAHT-ee-ah]*

MEANING: daughter of God • **USAGE:** Jewish:
from Hebrew *bat' yah* (daughter of Yahweh)
Many daughters have done valiantly,
but thou excellest them all.
— Proverbs 31:29 (MT)

BAYO   *[BAH-yoh]*

MEANING: joy is found, there is joy • **USAGE:**
African: Yoruba of Nigeria

B

Whoever knows how to enjoy life
does not enter into a fight.
— Yoruba of Nigeria proverb

Blessed is the one who finds wisdom.
Blessed is the one who gains understanding.
— Proverbs 3:13 (NIRV)

BEA   *[bee]*

MEANING: blessed, blissful, voyager, traveler •
USAGE: English form of Beatrice (*see* Beatrix)
Send forth loving, stainless, and happy thoughts,
and blessings will fall into your hands, and your
table will be spread with the cloth of peace.
— James Allen, *From Poverty to Power*

BEAH   *[BEH-ah]*

MEANING: blessed, blissful, voyager, traveler •
USAGE: American form of Bea (*see* Beatrix)
The blessing of the Lord be upon you.
— Psalm 129:8b (KJV)

BEATA   *[bay-AH-tah]*

MEANING: blessed, blissful, voyager, traveler,
life, full of life • **USAGE:** Italian, German, and
Scandinavian form of Beatrice (*see* Beatrix); or from
Irish Gaelic *beatha* (life)
May you live a long time! May everything go well
with you and your family! And may things
go well with everything that belongs to you!
— 1 Samuel 25:6 (NIRV)

BEATE   *[bay-AH-tah]*

MEANING: blessed, blissful, voyager, traveler •
USAGE: German form of Beatrix (*see* Beatrix)
The Lord has blessed you and is with you.
— Luke 1:28b (NCV)

BEATRICE, BÉATRICE   *[BEE-ah-tris*
(English), bay-ah-TREE-chay (Italian)
beh-ah-TREES (French)]

MEANING: blessed, blissful, voyager, traveler
• **USAGE:** English, Italian, and French form of
Beatrix (*see* Beatrix)

BEATRIX   *[BEE-ah-triks (English),*
BEH-a-triks (German)]

MEANING: blessed, blissful, voyager, traveler •
USAGE: English and German: from Latin *beátus*
(blessed, blissful); or English form of *Viatrix*, from
Latin *viator* (voyager, traveler)
The Lord your God will bless you
in all your produce and in all the work of your hands,
so that you will be altogether joyful.
— Deuteronomy 16:15b (ESV)

BEATRIZ   *[bay-ah-TREEZ]*

MEANING: blessed, blissful, voyager, traveler •
USAGE: Spanish form of Beatrix (*see* Beatrix)
How blessed you will be.
— Isaiah 32:20a (NIV)

BECCA   *[BEK-ah]*

MEANING: prophet, seer, sage • **USAGE:** African:
Bobangi of Nigeria
Anything that needs [to] be known
can be understood by a wise person.
— Nigerian proverb

BECHIRA   *[beh-KHEER-ah]*

MEANING: chosen, the chosen one, eldest daughter
• **USAGE:** Jewish
The Lord thy God hath chosen thee
to be His own treasure.
— Deuteronomy 7:6b (MT)

BECKA, BECCA, BEKHA   *[BEK-ah]*

MEANING: connection, tie, join, noose, small •
USAGE: English form of Rebecca, from Hebrew
ribhqah (connection), *rivka* (noose), and Hebrew

root *r-b-q* (to tie, to join); or from Scottish *beag* (small)

> *No cord or cable can draw so forcibly,*
> *or bind so fast, as love can do with a single thread.*
> — Robert Burton, *The Anatomy of Melancholy*

BECKY, BECKIE, BECKI *[BEK-ee]*

MEANING: connection, tie, join, noose • **USAGE:** English form of Rebecca, from Hebrew *ribhqah* (connection), *rivka* (noose), and Hebrew root *r-b-q* (to tie, to join)

> *Let not kindness and truth forsake thee, bind them on thy neck, write them on the table of thy heart.*
> — Proverbs 3:3 (YLT)

BEDELIA *[beh-DEEL-yah]*

MEANING: strong, noble, valorous, high, lofty • **USAGE:** Irish form of Bridget, from Gaelic *brígh* (strong, noble, valorous) or *brig* (high, lofty)

> *Be strong and courageous.*
> — Psalm 31:24a (NLT)

BEHIRA *[beh-HEE-rah]*

MEANING: light, clear, brilliant, blinding light of truth • **USAGE:** Jewish

> *God said: "Let there be light"; and there was light. God saw that the light was good.*
> — Genesis 1:3 (JPS)

BELA *[BEH-lah]*

MEANING: flowering vine, time • **USAGE:** Hindu

> *God grows weary of great kingdoms,*
> *but never of little flowers.*
> — Rabindranath Tagore, *Stray Birds*

BELEN *[bay-LEN]*

MEANING: from the house of bread, woman from Bethlehem • **USAGE:** Spanish form of *Bethlehem*, from Hebrew *beit lachem* (house of bread)

> *Give us this day our daily bread.*
> — Matthew 6:11 (KJV)

BELICIA *[bay-LEE-see-ah]*

MEANING: God is my oath, joined with God, blessed by God • **USAGE:** Spanish form of Isabela, from Hebrew *el'ishebha*

> *The Lord your God is the one who goes with you.*
> *He will not fail you or forsake you.*
> — Deuteronomy 31:b (NASB)

BELINDA *[beh-LIN-dah]*

MEANING: tender, gentle, serpent, dragon, beautiful, very pretty • **USAGE:** English and German: from German *linde* (tender, gentle); from German *lind* (serpent, dragon); or from Spanish *linda* (beautiful, pretty)

> *Take the gentle path.*
> — George Herbert, "Discipline"

BELITA *[bay-LEE-tah]*

MEANING: God is my oath, joined with God, blessed by God • **USAGE:** Spanish form of Isabela (*see* Belicia)

> *O Lord, You have searched me and known me.*
> *You know my sitting down and my rising up;*
> *You understand my thoughts afar off.*
> *You comprehend my path and my lying down,*
> *and are acquainted with all my ways.*
> — Psalm 139:1–3 (NKJV)

BELLA *[BAY-lah (Italian and Spanish), BEL-ah (English)]*

MEANING: beautiful, lovely, God is my oath, joined with God, blessed by God • **USAGE:** Italian, English, and Spanish: from Latin *bella* (beautiful, lovely); or Spanish and Italian form of Isabella (*see* Belicia)

> *Your beauty, within and without, is absolute.*
> — Song of Songs 7:6a (MSG)

B

BELLAROSA   *[bay-lah-ROH-sah]*

MEANING: beautiful rose • USAGE: Spanish: from Latin *bella* (beautiful, lovely) and Latin *rosa* (rose)

How beautiful you are and how pleasing.
— Song of Songs 7:6a (NIV)

BELLE   *[bel]*

MEANING: beautiful, lovely, God is my oath, joined with God, blessed by God • USAGE: English: from French *belle* (beautiful, lovely); or English form of Isabelle (*see* Belicia)

Beauty can inspire miracles.
— Benjamin Disraeli, *The Young Duke*

BELLINA   *[bay-LEE-nah]*

MEANING: little beautiful one • USAGE: Italian form of Bella and diminutive *-ina* (*see* Bella)

You shall be a crown of beauty in the hand of the Lord,
and a royal diadem in the hand of your God.
— Isaiah 62:3 (RSV)

BELVA   *[BEL-vah]*

MEANING: beautiful view, married, tied • USAGE: English: from French *belvedere* (beautiful view); or English form of Beulah, from Hebrew *be'ulah* (married woman)

The vista that shines through the eye of the heart.
— Thomas Moore

BENA   *[bee-nah]*

MEANING: partridge • USAGE: Amerind: Chippewa

As my eyes search the prairie /
I feel the summer in the spring.
— Chippewa song

BENEDETTA   *[bay-nay-DAY-tah]*

MEANING: blessed, blessing • USAGE: Italian feminine form of Benedetto, from Latin *benedictus*

The Lord your God will bless you
in all your produce and in all the work of your hands,
and you will have abundant joy.
— Deuteronomy 16:15b (HCSB)

BENEDICTA   *[bay-nay-DEEK-tah]*

MEANING: blessed, blessing • USAGE: Portuguese and Spanish feminine form of Benedicto, from Latin *benedicere* (to bless)

The Lord will bless you.
— Deuteronomy 15:6a (GNT)

BENEDIKTA   *[ben-eh-DEEK-teh]*

MEANING: blessed, blessing • USAGE: Swedish and Finnish feminine form of Benedikt (*see* Benedicta)

May you be blessed by the Lord,
the Maker of heaven and earth.
— Psalm 115:15 (NIV)

BENICIA   *[bay-NEE-chee-ah]*

MEANING: blessed, blessing • USAGE: Italian: from Latin *benedicere* (to bless)

God is able to shower all kinds of blessings on you. In
all things and at all times you will have everything you
need. You will do more and more good works.
— 2 Corinthians 9:8 (NIRV)

BENIGNA   *[bay-NEEN-yah]*

MEANING: good, kind, wellborn • USAGE: Italian: from Latin *benignus*

She openeth her mouth with wisdom;
and in her tongue is the law of kindness.
— Proverbs 31:26 (KJV)

BENISHA   *[beh-NEE-shah]*

MEANING: blessed, blessing • USAGE: American form of Benicia (*see* Benicia)

The Lord thy God shall bless thee in all thy works, and
in all that thou puttest thine hand unto.
— Deuteronomy 15:10b (KJV)

B

BENITA   *[bay-NEE-tah]*

MEANING: blessed, blessing • **USAGE:** Spanish feminine form of Benito (*see* Benicia)
You shall be blessed, and it shall be well with you.
— Psalm 128:2b (ESV)

BENOITE   *[ben-WAH-teh]*

MEANING: blessed, blessing • **USAGE:** French feminine form of Benôit (*see* Benicia)
Blessed be your discretion,
and blessed be you.
— 1 Samuel 25:33a (ESV)

BENTE   *[BEN-teh]*

MEANING: blessed, blessing • **USAGE:** Danish and Norwegian form of Benedikta (*see* Benedicta)
Blessings and prosperity will be yours.
— Psalm 128:2b (NIV)

BEQUITA   *[bay-KEE-tah]*

MEANING: connection, tie, join, noose • **USAGE:** Spanish form of Rebeca, from Hebrew *ribhqah* (connection), *rivka* (noose), and Hebrew root *r-b-q* (to tie, to join)
Never let go of loyalty and faithfulness.
Tie them around your neck; write them on your heart.
— Proverbs 3:3 (GNT)

BERENICE, BÉRÉNICE
[bay-rah-NEE-cheh (Italian),
bay-ray-NEES (French)]

MEANING: bringer of victory, victorious • **USAGE:** Italian and French: from Greek *pherein* (to bring, to bear) and *nike* (victory)
The Lord your God wins victory after victory and is always with you. He celebrates and sings because of you, and he will refresh your life with his love.
— Zephaniah 3:17 (CEV)

BERI, BERRI   *[BAYR-ee]*

MEANING: berry, beryl gemstone, beautiful jewel, bringer of victory • **USAGE:** English: from English *berye* (berry fruit); English form of Beryl, from Greek *beryllos* (sea-green gemstone); or English form of Bernice, from Greek *pherein* (to bring, to bear) and *nike* (victory)
The Spirit produces the fruit of love, joy, peace, patience, kindness, goodness, faithfulness, gentleness, self-control.
— Galatians 5:22–23a (NCV)

BERLIN   *[ber-LIN]*

MEANING: swamp, city in Germany • **USAGE:** American: possibly from German *berl* (swamp)
You will be blessed in the city and blessed in the country.
— Deuteronomy 28:3 (NCV)

BERNADETTA   *[bayr-nah-DET-ah]*

MEANING: strong as a bear, powerful • **USAGE:** Italian feminine form of Bernardo, from German *bern* (bear) and *hart* (hardy, strong, brave)
Be strong and courageous...for it is the Lord your God who goes with you; He will not leave you or forsake you.
— Deuteronomy 31:6 (HCSB)

BERNADETTE
[behr-nah-DET (French),
ber-nah-DET (English)]

MEANING: strong as a bear, powerful • **USAGE:** French and English feminine form of Bernard, from German *bern* (bear) and *hart* (hardy, strong, brave)
Strength bestows Wisdom, then Intelligence; for Strength and Wisdom demand Will.
— Honoré de Balzac, *Seraphita*
(tr. Katharine Wormeley)

B

BERNADINE   *[ber-nah-DEEN]*

MEANING: strong as a bear, powerful • USAGE:
English feminine form of Bernard (*see* Bernadette)
> *Be strong and courageous,*
> *for your work will be rewarded.*
> — 2 Chronicles 15:7 (NLT)

BERNARDA   *[bayr-NAHR-dah]*

MEANING: strong as a bear, powerful • USAGE:
Spanish and Portuguese feminine form of Bernardo
(*see* Bernadette)
> *This is my command — be strong and courageous!*
> *Do not be afraid or discouraged.*
> *For the Lord your God is with you wherever you go.*
> — Joshua 1:9 (NLT)

BERNARDINE   *[bayr-nar-DEEN (French),*
bayr-nahr-DEE-neh (German)]

MEANING: strong as a bear, powerful • USAGE:
French and German feminine form of Bernard (*see*
Bernadette)
> *God did not give us a spirit that makes us afraid but a*
> *spirit of power and love and self-control.*
> — 2 Timothy 1:7 (NCV)

BERNEEN   *[ber-NEEN]*

MEANING: strong as a bear, powerful • USAGE:
Irish feminine form of Bernard (*see* Bernadette)
> *Ye shall be a blessing: fear not,*
> *but let your hands be strong.*
> — Zechariah 8:13b (KJV)

BERNETTA   *[ber-NET-ah]*

MEANING: bringer of victory, victorious • USAGE:
English form of Bernice (*see* Bernice)
> *Peace gives victory on both sides.*
> — Ralph Waldo Emerson
> (journal entry of October 31, 1867)

BERNICE   *[ber-NEES]*

MEANING: bringer of victory, victorious • USAGE:
English form of *Berenike*, from Greek *pherein* (to
bring, to bear) and *nike* (victory)
> *The Lord God is my strength and my song;*
> *he has given me victory.*
> — Isaiah 12:2b (NLT)

BERTA   *[BAYR-tah]*

MEANING: noble and brightly shining • USAGE:
German, Hungarian, Italian, Polish, and Spanish
form of Alberta, from German *adal* (noble) and
beraht (bright, shining)
> *Piety, prudence, wit,*
> *and civility are the elements of true nobility.*
> — German proverb

BERTHA   *[BAYR-tah (German, Spanish),*
BER-thah (English)]

MEANING: brightly shining • USAGE: German,
Spanish, and English: from German *beraht*
> *The wise will shine like the brightness*
> *of the heavenly expanse.*
> — Daniel 12:3a (WEB)

BERTHANA   *[ber-THAH-nah]*

MEANING: brightly shining • USAGE: American
form of Bertha (*see* Bertha)
> *If thy whole body therefore be full of light, having no*
> *part dark, the whole shall be full of light, as when the*
> *bright shining of a candle doth give thee light.*
> — Luke 11:36 (KJV)

BERTHE   *[BAYR-theh]*

MEANING: brightly shining • USAGE: French form
of Bertha (*see* Bertha)
> *Who is this that looks like the dawn,*
> *fair as the moon, bright as the sun?*
> — Song of Songs 6:10 (NRSV)

B

BERTINA   *[bayr-TEE-nah]*

MEANING: noble and brightly shining • **USAGE:** German and Italian form of Alberta (*see* Bertha)

*The path of the righteous is like
the light of dawn, that shines brighter and brighter
until the full day.*
— Proverbs 4:18 (NASB)

BERYL   *[berl]*

MEANING: beryl gemstone, beautiful jewel, seafoam green • **USAGE:** English: from Greek *beryllos* (sea-green gemstone)

This precious stone set in the silver sea.
— William Shakespeare, *Richard II*

BESS   *[bes]*

MEANING: God is my oath, joined with God, blessed by God • **USAGE:** English form of Elizabeth, from Hebrew *el'ishebha*

How blessed you will be.
— Isaiah 32:20a (NASB)

BETANIA   *[bay-TAH-nee-ah]*

MEANING: house of figs • **USAGE:** Spanish form of Bethany, from Hebrew *bet t'eina*

*I will walk within my house
with a right and good heart.*
— Psalm 101:2b (NLV)

BETH   *[beth]*

MEANING: God is my oath, joined with God, blessed by God, house of figs • **USAGE:** English form of Elizabeth (*see* Bess); or English form of Bethany (*see* Bethany)

You are within God. God is within you.
— Peace Pilgrim, *Peace Pilgrim*

BETHAN   *[BETH-an]*

MEANING: God is my oath, joined with God, blessed by God • **USAGE:** Welsh form of Elizabeth (*see* Bess)

*I pray that God will greatly bless you
with kindness, peace and love!*
— Jude 1:2 (CEV)

BETHANY, BETHANIE   *[BETH-ah-nee]*

MEANING: house of figs • **USAGE:** English: from Hebrew *bet t'eina*

*By wisdom a house is built, and through understanding
it is established; through knowledge its rooms are filled
with rare and beautiful treasures.*
— Proverbs 24:3–4 (RSV)

BETSAN   *[BET-san]*

MEANING: God is my oath, joined with God, blessed by God • **USAGE:** Welsh form of Elizabeth (*see* Bess)

*The Lord your God will bless you
in all your work and in everything you do.*
— Deuteronomy 15:10b (HCSB)

BETSY, BETSIE   *[BET-see]*

MEANING: God is my oath, joined with God, blessed by God • **USAGE:** English form of Elizabeth (*see* Bess)

The blessing of the Lord be upon you.
— Psalm 129:8b (NLT)

BETTA   *[BAY-tah]*

MEANING: God is my oath, joined with God, blessed by God • **USAGE:** Italian form of Elisabetta (*see* Bess)

*The Lord is the One who will go before you.
He will be with you.*
— Deuteronomy 31:8a (HCSB)

BETTE
[bet, BET-ee]

MEANING: God is my oath, joined with God, blessed by God • **USAGE:** English form of Elizabeth (see Bess)

There is an agent in my soul which is perfectly sensitive to God. I am as sure of this as I am that I am alive.
— Meister Eckhart

BETTINA
[bay-TEEN-ah]

MEANING: blessed, blessing, God is my oath, joined with God, blessed by God • **USAGE:** Italian, German, and Scandinavian: Italian form of Benedetta, from Latin *benedicere* (to bless); or German and Scandinavian form of Elisabeth, from Hebrew *el'ishebha* (God is my oath)

God bless you.
— Genesis 43:29b (CEV)

BETTY, BETTIE
[BET-ee]

MEANING: God is my oath, joined with God, blessed by God • **USAGE:** English form of Elizabeth (see Bess)

The God that is within you is truth, beauty, harmony and wholeness.
— Ernest Holmes, *Your Invisible Power*

BEULAH
[BYOO-lah]

MEANING: married woman, tied, joined • **USAGE:** Jewish: from Hebrew *be'ulah*

God is a great matchmaker.
— Jewish proverb

BEV
[bev]

MEANING: beaver stream, beaver meadow • **USAGE:** English form of Beverly (see Beverly)

The Lord your God will make you abundantly prosperous in all your undertakings.
— Deuteronomy 30:9a (NRSV)

BEVERLY, BEVERLEY
[BEV-er-lee]

MEANING: beaver stream, beaver meadow • **USAGE:** English: from English *beofor* (beaver) and *leac* (stream) or *leah* (meadow, field)

Happiness consists in activity...
it is a running stream, not a stagnant pool.
— John Mason Good, *The Book of Nature*

BEVIN, BEVAN
[BEV-en]

MEANING: sweet melodious woman, beautiful woman • **USAGE:** Irish form of *Bebhinn*, from Gaelic *be* (woman) and *binn* (sweet, melodious); or from Gaelic *bean* (woman) and *fionn* (fair, white, beautiful)

Let me hear your voice; for your voice is sweet, and your form is lovely.
— Song of Songs 2:14b (NASB)

BHAKTI
[BAHK-tih]

MEANING: devotion, prayer • **USAGE:** Hindu: Sanskrit

Prayer is not asking. It is a longing of the soul.
— Mahatma Gandhi

BHAMINI
[bah-mih-nih]

MEANING: beautiful woman • **USAGE:** Hindu

The real ornament of woman is her character, her purity.
— Mahatma Gandhi

BHUTI
[boo-tih]

MEANING: prosperous, wealthy, rich • **USAGE:** Hindu: Sanskrit

Those who realize the Self within the heart /
Stand firm, grow rich, gather a family / Around them,
and receive the love of all.
— *Taittiriya Upanishad* (tr. Eknath Easwaran)

BIANCA [bee-AHN-kah]

MEANING: white, fair • USAGE: Italian: from Italian *bianca*

Behold, thou art fair, my beloved, yea, pleasant.
— Song of Songs 1:16a (ASV)

BIANKA [bee-AHN-kah]

MEANING: white, fair • USAGE: Hungarian and Polish form of Bianca (*see* Bianca)

Thou art all fair, O my love, and there is not a spot in thee. — Song of Songs 4:7 (DR)

BIBIANA [bee-bee-AH-nah]

MEANING: life, full of life • USAGE: Italian and Spanish form of Viviana, from Latin *vita*

Wisdom will add years to your life.
You are the one who will profit if you have wisdom.
— Proverbs 9:11–12a (GNT)

BIBIANE [bee-bee-AHN]

MEANING: life, full of life • USAGE: French form of Viviana (*see* Bibiana)

Those who become wise are happy;
wisdom will give them life.
— Proverbs 3:18 (GNT)

BIJOU [BEE-joo]

MEANING: jewel, precious gem • USAGE: French: from French *bijou*

You are altogether beautiful, my love;
there is no flaw in you.
— Song of Songs 4:7 (ESV)

BILLIE [BIL-ee]

MEANING: determined protector, steadfast guardian • USAGE: English feminine form of William, from German *wil* (will, resolve) and *helm* (helmet, protection)

Hold on to instruction, do not let it go;
guard it well, for it is your life.
— Proverbs 4:12 (NIV)

BINAH [BEE-nah]

MEANING: dancer • USAGE: African: Bobangi of Nigeria

When the drumbeat changes, the dance changes.
— Nigerian proverb

BINDY, BINDI [BIN-dee]

MEANING: tender, gentle, serpent, dragon, beautiful, very pretty • USAGE: English form of Belinda, from German *linde* (tender, gentle); from German *lind* (serpent, dragon); or from Spanish *linda* (beautiful, pretty)

Patience and Gentleness is Power.
— Leigh Hunt, "The Nile"

BIRGIT, BIRGITTE [BIR-geet]

MEANING: strong, noble, valorous, high, lofty • USAGE: Scandinavian and German form of Brighid, from Irish Gaelic *brígh* (strong, noble, valorous) or *brig* (high, lofty)

Let your love towards life be love towards
your highest hope; and let your highest hope
be the highest idea of life!
— Friedrich Nietzsche,
Thus Spoke Zarathustra (tr. R. J. Hollingdale)

BIRGITTA [beer-GEE-tah]

MEANING: strong, noble, valorous, high, lofty • USAGE: Swedish and Danish form of Brighid (*see* Birgit)

Her clothes are strength and honor.
She is full of joy about the future.
— Proverbs 31:25 (NLV)

B

BLANCA [BLAHN-kah]

MEANING: white, fair • USAGE: Spanish: from Spanish *blanca*

Beloved, you are fair…behold, you are fair!
— Song of Songs 4:1a (NKJV)

BLANCH [blanch]

MEANING: white, fair • USAGE: English form of Blanche (*see* Blanche)

White is a colour. It is not a mere absence of colour;
it is a shining and affirmative thing,
as fierce as red, as definite as black.
— G. K. Chesterton, "A Piece of Chalk"

BLANCHE [blahnch]

MEANING: white, fair • USAGE: French: from French *blanche*

Fair and softly goes far.
— French proverb

BLANKA [BLAHN-kah]

MEANING: white, fair • USAGE: Czech and Polish form of Blanche (*see* Blanche)

Wash me, and I shall be whiter than snow.
— Psalm 51:7b (ASV)

BLEU [bloo]

MEANING: blue color • USAGE: American: from French *bleu*

Colors are the smiles of nature.
— Leigh Hunt, *The Seer*

BLISS [blis]

MEANING: blissful, joyous, extreme happiness • USAGE: English: from English *blisse* (ecstasy, extreme happiness, joyous)

Follow your bliss.
— Joseph Campbell, *The Power of Myth*

BLONDIE, BLONDEE [BLON-dee]

MEANING: blond, fair-haired • USAGE: English: from English *blonde*

Behold, thou art fair, my beloved, yea, pleasant.
— Song of Songs 1:16a (KJV)

BLOSSOM [BLOS-um]

MEANING: bloom, blossom, flower • USAGE: English: from English *blostma*

The nature of this flower is to bloom.
— Alice Walker

BLYTHE [blieth]

MEANING: cheerful, gay, happy, joyous • USAGE: English: from English *blithe*

My heart is glad, and my whole being rejoices.
— Psalm 16:9a (ESV)

BODIL [BOH-deel]

MEANING: remedy for war, warrior who sets things right • USAGE: Scandinavian: from Norse *Bóthildr*, from *bót* (remedy, compensation) and *hildr* (war, battle)

Those who do right for the right reasons…the Lord God, who saves them, will bless and reward them.
— Psalm 24:4–5 (CEV)

BOGDANA [bog-DAH-nah]

MEANING: gift of God • USAGE: Polish feminine form of Bogdan, from Slavic *bog* (God) and *dan* (gift)

Fan into flame the gift of God.
— 2 Timothy 1:6b (ESV)

BOHDANA [boh-DAH-nah]

MEANING: God's gift, gift of God • USAGE: Czech feminine form of Bohdan (*see* Bogdana)

I remind you to help God's gift grow,
just as a small spark grows into a fire.
— 2 Timothy 1:6b (NIRV)

BONA   *[BOH-nah]*

MEANING: good, kind • USAGE: Spanish and
Italian: from Latin *bona*
If you have done something good in little,
do it also in great, as the good will never die.
— Don Juan Manuel, *El Conde Lucanor*

BONITA   *[boh-NEE-tuh]*

MEANING: pretty, beautiful • USAGE: Spanish and
English: from Spanish *bonita*
How pretty you are, how beautiful.
— Song of Songs 7:6a (GNT)

BONNA   *[BON-ah]*

MEANING: good, kind • *Usage:* American: from
Latin *bona*
How goodness heightens beauty.
— Hannah More, *Moses in the Bulrushes*

BONNIE, BONNY   *[BAH-nee, BON-ee]*

MEANING: beautiful, pretty, good-natured •
USAGE: Scottish and English: from Scottish *bonnie*
(beautiful, pretty); or from French *bon* (good)
Beauty lives with kindness.
— William Shakespeare,
The Two Gentlemen of Verona

BRACHA   *[brah-KHAH]*

MEANING: blessing, benediction • USAGE:
Jewish
The Lord your God will bless you.
— Deuteronomy 15:6a (JPS)

BRANDY, BRANDEE, BRANDIE   *[BRAN-dee]*

MEANING: brandy liquor • USAGE: English: from
Dutch *brandewijn* (burnt wine), a liquor
Happiness is a wine of the rarest vintage.
— Logan Pearsall Smith,
"Life and Human Nature"

BRANNA   *[BRAN-ah]*

MEANING: raven • USAGE: Welsh: from Welsh
bran
Consider the ravens, for they neither sow nor reap;
and they have no storeroom nor barn;
and yet God feeds them; how much more valuable
you are than the birds!
— Luke 12:24 (NASB)

BRANWEN   *[BRAN-wen]*

MEANING: holy raven, beautiful raven • USAGE:
Welsh: from Welsh *bran* (raven) and *gwyn* (white,
fair, holy)
Behold, you are beautiful.
— Song of Songs 1:15a (ESV)

BREANA, BREANNA   *[bree-AN-ah, bree-AH-nah]*

MEANING: strong, noble, valorous, high, lofty •
USAGE: American form of Briana (*see* Brighid)
All high beauty has a moral element in it.
— Ralph Waldo Emerson, "Beauty"

BREDA   *[BREE-dah]*

MEANING: strong, noble, valorous, high, lofty •
USAGE: Irish form of Brighid, from Gaelic *brígh*
(strong, noble, valorous) or *brig* (high, lofty)
She is clothed with strength and dignity.
— Proverbs 31:25a (RSV)

B

BREE   [bree]

MEANING: strong, noble, valorous, high, lofty •
USAGE: Irish: from Gaelic *brígh* (strong, noble,
valorous) or *brig* (high, lofty)

> *Be cheerful and strong.*
> — Psalm 31:24 (CEV)

BREENA, BRINA   [BREE-nah]

MEANING: strong, noble, valorous, high, lofty •
USAGE: American form of Brianna (*see* Brianna)

> *Be strong in body, clean in mind, lofty in ideals.*
> — James Naismith

BRENDA   [BREN-dah]

MEANING: sword, lance, little queen, princess,
steep hill • **USAGE:** Scottish and English: from
Norse *brandr* (sword); or Scottish feminine form of
Brendan, from Welsh *brenhin* (king) and diminutive
-an, or from *bryn* (steep hill)

> *Beauty is power; a smile is its sword.*
> — John Ray

BRENNA, BRYNNA   [BREN-ah]

MEANING: little queen, princess, steep hill, sword,
lance • **USAGE:** English feminine form of Brendan,
from Welsh *brenhin* (king) and diminutive *-an,* or
from *bryn* (steep hill); or English form of Brenda
(*see* Brenda)

> *The Lord says… You will be like a royal crown*
> *in my powerful hand.*
> — Isaiah 62:1–3b (NIRV)

BRIA   [BREE-ah]

MEANING: strong, noble, valorous, high, lofty •
USAGE: American form of Bria (*see* Brighid)

> *There are a few noble natures whose very presence*
> *carries sunshine with them wherever they go.*
> — Orison Swett Marden, *Architects of Fate*

BRIANA, BRIANNA   [bree-AN-ah, bree-AH-nah]

MEANING: strong, noble, valorous, high, lofty •
USAGE: Irish and English feminine form of Brian
(*see* Brighid)

> *Strength and honor are her clothing;*
> *she shall rejoice in time to come.*
> — Proverbs 31:25 (NKJV)

BRIANNE, BREANNE   [bree-AN]

MEANING: strong, noble, valorous, high, lofty
• **USAGE:** American feminine form of Brian (*see*
Brighid)

> *Let love be your highest goal!*
> — 1 Corinthians 14:1a (NLT)

BRIDGET   [BRID-jet]

MEANING: strong, noble, valorous, high, lofty
• **USAGE:** English and Irish form of Brighid (*see*
Brighid)

> *She is strong and is respected by the people.*
> *She looks forward to the future with joy.*
> — Proverbs 31:25 (NCV)

BRIGHID, BRIGID   [BRIH-jid]

MEANING: strong, noble, valorous, high, lofty,
goddess • **USAGE:** Irish: from Gaelic *brígh* (strong,
noble, valorous) or *brig* (high, lofty); Celtic goddess
of inspiration, healing, creativity, fire, and poetry;
an Irish saint

> *The Mantle of Brighid about us, the Memory of*
> *Brighid within us, the Protection of Brighid keeping us*
> *from harm, from ignorance, from restlessness, this day*
> *and night, from dawn till dark, from dark till dawn.*
> — Celtic blessing

BRIGIDA   [bree-JEE-dah]

MEANING: strong, noble, valorous, high, lofty •
USAGE: Italian and Spanish form of Brighid (*see*
Brighid)

In valor there is hope.
— Publius Cornelius Tacitus

BRIGITTE [brih-ZHEET]

MEANING: strong, noble, valorous, high, lofty •
USAGE: French and German form of Brighid (*see* Brighid)

Valor is stability, not of legs and arms,
but of courage and the soul.
— Michel de Montaigne, *Essays*

BRISA [BREE-sah]

MEANING: breeze, gentle wind • USAGE: Spanish:
from Spanish *brisa*
The wind blows where it wishes and you hear the sound
of it, but do not know where it comes from and where it
is going: so is everyone who is born of the Spirit.
— John 3:8 (NASB)

BRISEN [BRIE-sen]

MEANING: queen, royal one • USAGE: Welsh:
from Welsh *brenhines*
You will also be a crown of beauty in the hand of the
Lord, and a royal diadem in the hand of your God.
— Isaiah 62:3 (NASB)

BRISTOL [BRIS-tel]

MEANING: site of the bridge • USAGE: English
form of *Bridgestow* (site of the bridge); city in
England
Faith builds a bridge from this world to the next.
— Edward Young, *Night Thoughts*

BRITA, BRITTA [BREE-tah]

MEANING: strong, noble, valorous, high, lofty •
USAGE: Scandinavian form of Brighid (*see*
Brighid)
You can stand strong without fear.
— Job 11:15b (NCV)

BRITES [BREE-tes]

MEANING: strong, noble, valorous, high, lofty •
USAGE: Portuguese form of Bridget (*see* Brighid)
I am your God. I will make you strong and
will help you; I will support you with my right hand
that saves you. — Isaiah 41:10 (NCV)

BRITNEY [BRIT-nee]

MEANING: woman from Bretagne • USAGE:
American form of Brittany (*see* Brittany)
Know that you are a worthy woman.
— Ruth 3:11b (NRSV)

BRITT [brit, breet]

MEANING: strong, noble, valorous, high, lofty •
USAGE: Scandinavian form of Britta (*see* Brighid)
Wise people have great power,
and those with knowledge have great strength.
— Proverbs 24:5 (NCV)

BRITTANY [BRIT-ah-nee]

MEANING: woman from Bretagne • USAGE:
English form of Bretagne, a region in France
The boundary lines have fallen for me
in pleasant places; I have a goodly heritage.
— Psalm 16:6 (NRSV)

BRONWEN, BRONWYN [BRON-wen]

MEANING: white breast, fair breast, holy breast •
USAGE: Welsh: from Welsh *bron* (breast) and *gwyn*
(white, fair, holy)
Modesty seldom resides in a breast
that is not enriched with nobler virtues.
— Oliver Goldsmith, *She Stoops to Conquer*

BROOK, BROOKE [bruk]

MEANING: brook, stream • USAGE: English: from
English *broc*

Wise words are like deep waters;
wisdom flows from the wise like a bubbling brook.
— Proverbs 18:4 (NLT)

BROOKLYN   [BROOK-len]

MEANING: marsh, fen • USAGE: American form of
Breuckelen, from Dutch *broek* (a marsh); borough in
New York City
There's a tree that grows in Brooklyn.
Some people call it the Tree of Heaven.
— Betty Smith, *A Tree Grows in Brooklyn*

BRUNHILDE   [broon-HIL-deh]

MEANING: armed for battle, armor protection,
warrior • USAGE: German: from German *brun*
(armor) and *hild* (battle)
Put on the armour of light.
— Romans 13:12b (DR)

BRYDEN   [BRIE-den]

MEANING: broad forest, broad hill, strong,
valorous, high • USAGE: American feminine form
of Braden, from *brad* (broad) and *dene* (woods,
forest) or *dun* (hill); or possibly a form of Brian,
from Irish Gaelic *brígh* (strong, noble, valorous) or
brig (high, lofty)
The grandeur of the forest tree / Comes not by casting
in a formal mould, / But from its own divine vitality.
— William Wordsworth, "A Poet"

BRYNNA   [BREN-ah]

MEANING: sword, lance, little queen, princess,
steep hill • USAGE: English feminine form of
Brendan, from Welsh *brenhin* (king) and diminutive
-an, or from *bryn* (steep hill); or English form of
Brenda, from Norse *brandr* (sword)
The Lord says... You will be like a royal crown
in my powerful hand.
— Isaiah 62:1–3b (NIRV)

BRYONY, BRIONY   [BRIE-oh-nee]

MEANING: vine, grow, sprout • USAGE: English:
name of flowering vine *bryonia,* from Greek *bryo*
(to grow, to sprout)
Good, the more communicated, more abundant grows.
— John Milton, *Paradise Lost*

BUFFY   [BUF-ee]

MEANING: God is my oath, joined with God,
blessed by God • USAGE: English form of
Elizabeth, from Hebrew *el'ishebha* (God is my oath)
The Lord himself will go ahead of you.
He will be with you.
— Deuteronomy 31:8a (NCV)

BURGUNDY   [BUR-gun-dee]

MEANING: highlander, dark red color, red wine
• USAGE: English: from Latin *burgundiones*
(highlander); red color; red wine
You [God] pour oil of blessing on my head;
you fill my cup to overflowing.
— Psalm 23:5b (NCV)

BUSARA   [buh-sah-rah]

MEANING: wisdom • USAGE: African: Swahili of
Kenya/Tanzania
We must add wisdom to knowledge.
— Kenyan proverb

C

CADENCE   [KAY-dens]

MEANING: flow of rhythm • USAGE: American:
from Latin *cadentia* (a falling, a conclusion of a
movement in music)
When you listen with your soul, you come into rhythm
and unity with the music of the universe.
— John O'Donohue, *Anam Cara*

CADY [KAY-dee]

MEANING: pure one, unblemished, innocent, virtuous • **USAGE:** English form of Katy, from Greek *katharos* (pure)

The means we use must be as pure as the ends we seek.
— Martin Luther King Jr.,
Letter from Birmingham City Jail

CAILIN [KAY-len]

MEANING: girl, girl of marriageable age • **USAGE:** Scottish: from Gaelic *cailín*

A lovely girl is above all rank.
— Charles Robert Buxton

CAIRENN, CAIRAN [KAYR-en]

MEANING: beloved, love • **USAGE:** Irish: from Gaelic *cara*

Beloved, let us love one another, for love is from God; and everyone who loves is born of God and knows God.
— 1 John 4:7 (NASB)

CAIT [kayt]

MEANING: pure one, unblemished, innocent, virtuous • **USAGE:** Scottish and Irish form of Catriona, Caitin, or Caitlin (*see* Caitlin)

Whatsoever things are true, whatsoever things are honest, whatsoever things are just, whatsoever things are pure, whatsoever things are lovely, whatsoever things are of good report; if there be any virtue, and if there be any praise, think on these things.
— Philippians 4:8b (KJV)

CAITANYA [kie-tahn-yah]

MEANING: consciousness • **USAGE:** Hindu: Sanskrit

When we are conscious of our soul, we perceive the inner being that transcends our ego and has its deeper affinity with the All.
— Rabindranath Tagore, *Sadhana*

CAITIN [kah-TEEN]

MEANING: pure one, unblemished, innocent, virtuous • **USAGE:** Irish form of Catriona (*see* Caitlin)

If there's a virtue in the world at which we should always aim, it is cheerfulness.
— Edward Bulwer-Lytton, *My Novel*

CAITLIN [kaht-LEEN (Irish), KAYT-lin (English)]

MEANING: pure one, unblemished, innocent, virtuous • **USAGE:** Irish and English form of Katherine, from Greek *katharos* (pure)

I believe that the highest virtue is to be happy, living in the greatest truth.
— D. H. Lawrence (letter of February 7, 1916)

CALANDRA [kah-LAHN-drah]

MEANING: beautiful woman, skylark • **USAGE:** English form of Kalandra, from Greek *kallos* (beautiful) and *andros* (man); skylark

Your voice is sweet, and your face is lovely.
— Song of Songs 2:14b (ESV)

CALANTHA [kah-LAHN-thah]

MEANING: beautiful flower • **USAGE:** Greek: from Greek *kallos* (beautiful) and *anthos* (flower)

I will sing with the spirit, and I will sing with understanding also.
— 1 Corinthians 14:15b (ASV)

CALDONIA [kal-DOH-nee-ah, kal-DOHN-yah]

MEANING: poetic name of Scotland • **USAGE:** Scottish

The melodies of the poet ascend, and leap, and pierce into the deeps of infinite time.
— Ralph Waldo Emerson, "The Poet"

C

CALEIGH [KAY-lee]

MEANING: pure meadow, slender, narrow •
USAGE: American form of Kayley, from Greek
katharos (pure) and English *leah* (meadow, field); or
from Scotch Gaelic *caol* (slender, narrow)
> *The Lord is my shepherd; I shall not want.*
> *He maketh me to lie down in green pastures;*
> *He leadeth me beside the still waters.*
> — Psalm 23:1–2 (KJ21)

CALIDA [kah-LEE-dah]

MEANING: beautiful, lovely, hot • **USAGE:** Italian
form of Kalidas, from Greek *kallos* (beautiful,
lovely); or from Spanish *calida* (hot)
> *Oh, how beautiful you are!*
> — Song of Songs 1:15b (NEB)

CALÍOPE [kah-LEE-oh-peh]

MEANING: beautiful voice, lyrical, eloquent •
USAGE: Spanish form of Kalliope (*see* Calliope)
> *Music is the divine way to tell beautiful,*
> *poetic things to the heart.*
> — Pablo Casals

CALISSA, CALLISA [kah-LIS-ah]

MEANING: most beautiful, most lovely • **USAGE:**
American form of Calista (*see* Calista)
> *Grace is beauty in motion.*
> — Henry Fuseli

CALISTA [kah-LIS-tah (English), kah-LEE-stah (Italian, Spanish)]

MEANING: most beautiful, most lovely • **USAGE:**
English, Italian, and Spanish form of Kallisto, from
Greek *kalliste*
> *How beautiful you are.*
> — Song of Songs 4:1a (NLV)

CALLIE, CALLI [KAL-ee]

MEANING: most beautiful, most lovely, beautiful
woman, skylark • **USAGE:** English form of Calista
(*see* Calista); or English form of Calandra (*see*
Calandra)
> *Ye shall have a song…and gladness of heart.*
> — Isaiah 30:29a (KJ21)

CALLIOPE [kah-LEE-oh-pay (Italian), kah-LIE-oh-pee (English)]

MEANING: beautiful voice, lyrical, eloquent •
USAGE: Italian form of Kalliope from Greek *kallos*
(beauty, beautiful) and *ops* (voice)
> *Your voice is sweet and your face is lovely.*
> — Song of Songs 2:14b (NCV)

CALLISTO [kah-LEE-stoh]

MEANING: she who is most beautiful • **USAGE:**
Italian form of Kallisto (*see* Calista)
> *Every part of you is so beautiful.*
> — Song of Songs 4:7a (NIRV)

CAMBER [KAM-ber]

MEANING: amber gemstone, beautiful gemstone,
crooked nose • **USAGE:** American: combination of
Cameron and Amber (*see* Cameron and Amber)
> *Beauty connects us to our cosmic connections.*
> — Matthew Fox, *Original Blessing*

CAMELLIA [kah-MEEL-yah]

MEANING: camellia flower • **USAGE:** English:
from Latin *camellia* (type of flower)
> *Flowers are lovely; love is flower-like.*
> — Samuel Taylor Coleridge, "Youth and Age"

CAMERON, CAMRYN [KAM-er-on, KAM-ron]

MEANING: crooked nose • **USAGE:** Scottish and
English: from Gaelic *cam* (crooked, bent) and *shron*
(nose)

Thus saith the Lord...I will go before thee,
and make the crooked places straight.
— Isaiah 45:1–2a (KJV)

CAMILA   [kah-MEE-lah]

MEANING: virgin of pure character, attendant at a religious service • **USAGE:** Spanish form of Camilla (*see* Camilla)

Whatever is true, whatever is worthy of respect,
whatever is just, whatever is pure, whatever is lovely,
whatever is commendable, if something is excellent or
praiseworthy, think about these things.
— Philippians 4:8 (WEB)

CAMILLA   [kah-MEE-lah (Italian, Scandinavian), kah-MIL-ah (English)]

MEANING: virgin of pure character, attendant at a religious service • **USAGE:** Italian, English, and Scandinavian: from Latin *camilla* (virgin of pure character); or from Latin *camillus* (attendant at a religious service)

All our acts have sacramental possibilities.
— Freya Stark, *The Zodiac Arch*

CAMILLE   [kah-MEEL]

MEANING: virgin of pure character, attendant at a religious service • **USAGE:** French and English (*see* Camilla)

To insist on purity is to baptize instinct,
to humanize art, and to deify personality.
— Guillaume Apollinaire

CAMMIE, CAMMY, CAMI   [KAM-ee]

MEANING: virgin of pure character, attendant at a religious service • **USAGE:** English form of Camilla or Camille (*see* Camilla)

As servants of God we commend ourselves in every
way...by purity, knowledge, patience, kindness,
the Holy Spirit, genuine love.
— 2 Corinthians 6:4–6 (ESV)

CANDE   [KAHN-day]

MEANING: candle, candlelight • **USAGE:** Spanish form of Candelaria (*see* Candelaria)

God said, "Let there be light"; and there was light.
And God saw the light, that it was good.
— Genesis 1:3–4a (KJ21)

CANDELARIA   [kahn-deh-LAH-ree-ah]

MEANING: candle, candlelight • **USAGE:** Spanish: from Latin *candela* (candle); in reference to Candlemas, a Christian celebration

For thou wilt light my candle:
the Lord my God will enlighten my darkness.
— Psalm 18:28 (KJV)

CANDICE, CANDACE   [KAN-dis]

MEANING: brilliant white, incandescent, pure, sincere, candid • **USAGE:** English: from Latin *candidus* (brilliant white, shining, pure, sincere)

Deep are the foundations of sincerity.
— Henry David Thoreau,
A Week on the Concord and Merrimack Rivers

CANDIDA   [kan-DEE-dah]

MEANING: brilliant white, incandescent, pure, sincere, candid • **USAGE:** English (*see* Candice)

Behold thou art fair.
— Song of Songs 1:14a (DR)

CANDIDE   [kahn-DEED]

MEANING: brilliant white, incandescent, pure, sincere, candid • **USAGE:** French form of Candida (*see* Candice)

True love is eternal, infinite,
always like unto itself; it is equable, pure.
— Honoré de Balzac, *The Lily of the Valley*

C

CANDRA   *[KAHN-drah]*

MEANING: shining moon • USAGE: Hindu: from Sanskrit *candra*

When I admire the wonder of a sunset or the beauty of the moon, my soul expands in worship of the Creator.
— Mahatma Gandhi, "Indian Problems"

CANDY, CANDI   *[KAN-dee]*

MEANING: brilliant white, incandescent, pure, sincere, candid, candy, sweet • USAGE: English form of Candice (*see* Candice)

All love is sweet.
— Percy Bysshe Shelley, *Prometheus Unbound*

CAPARINA   *[kah-pah-REE-nah]*

MEANING: butterfly • USAGE: Spanish: from Spanish *caparina* (type of butterfly)

Love wishes to soar to the heights.
— Thomas à Kempis, *The Imitation of Christ*
(tr. Joseph Tylenda)

CAPRI   *[kah-PREE]*

MEANING: goat island, island of wild boars • USAGE: Italian: from Latin *capreæ* (goats) or from Greek *kapros* (wild boar)

Let the many isles rejoice.
— Psalm 97:1b (DT)

CAPRINA   *[kah-PREE-nah]*

MEANING: goat island, island of wild boars • USAGE: English form of Capri (*see* Capri)

Hail, happy isle!
— Thomas Augustine Arne, "Britain's Bulwarks"

CARA   *[KAHR-ah]*

MEANING: beloved, love • USAGE: Italian, English, and German: from Latin *carus*

This is my prayer: that your love may abound more and more in knowledge and depth of insight.
— Philippians 1:9 (NIV)

CARAGH   *[KAHR-ah]*

MEANING: friend • USAGE: Irish: from Gaelic *cara*

Help me to find my happiness in my acceptance of what is my purpose: in friendly eyes; in work well done; in quietness born of trust, and most of all, in the awareness of Your presence in my spirit.
— Celtic blessing

CARI   *[KAHR-ee]*

MEANING: beloved, love • USAGE: Welsh: from Welsh *caru*

May the Lord make you increase and abound in love.
— 1 Thessalonians 3:12a (RSV)

CARIDAD   *[kah-ree-DAHD]*

MEANING: generous love • USAGE: Spanish and Portuguese form of Charity, from Latin *caritas*

These three remain: faith, hope, and love; and the greatest of these is love.
— 1 Corinthians 13:13 (NEB)

CARINA   *[kah-REE-nah]*

MEANING: little loved one, beloved • USAGE: Spanish, English, German, Italian, and Scandinavian form of Cara and diminutive *-ina* (*see* Cara)

The love that flows out upon others is a perpetual well-spring from on high.
— Lydia Maria Child, *Letters from New York*

CARINE   *[kah-REEN]*

MEANING: beloved, love • USAGE: French and English form of Cara (*see* Cara)

Love is, above all, the gift of oneself.
— Jean Anouilh, *Ardele* (tr. Lucienne Hill)

CARISA   *[kah-REE-sah]*

MEANING: beloved, love • USAGE: Spanish form of Cara (*see* Cara)

Mercy to you and peace and love be multiplied.
— Jude 1:2 (WEB)

C

CARISSA
[kah-REE-sah (Italian), kah-RIS-ah (English)]

MEANING: beloved, love • **USAGE:** Italian and English form of Cara (*see* Cara)

There is nothing sweeter than love, nothing stronger,
nothing deeper, nothing broader, nothing more
pleasant, nothing better either in heaven or in earth.
— Thomas à Kempis, *The Imitation of Christ*
(tr. Harvey Goodwin)

CARITA
[kah-REE-tah]

MEANING: little beloved one • **USAGE:** Scandinavian form of Charity, from Latin *caritas* and diminutive *-ita*

For love alone is what gives value to all things.
— Teresa of Avila

CARLA
[KAR-lah]

MEANING: one who is free, adult • **USAGE:** English, German, Italian, and Spanish feminine form of Carl, from English *ceorl* (freeman, peasant); or from German *karl* (full-grown man, adult)

If I have freedom in my love, /
And in my soul am free, / Angels alone that soar
above, / Enjoy such liberty.
— Richard Lovelace, "To Althea, from Prison"

CARLANA
[kar-LAH-nah]

MEANING: one who is free, adult • **USAGE:** American form of Carla (*see* Carla)

What is liberty without wisdom and without virtue?
— Edmund Burke,
Reflections on the Revolution in France

CARLEIGH
[KAR-lee]

MEANING: one who is free, adult • **USAGE:** American form of Carla (*see* Carla)

The best road to progress is freedom's road.
— John F. Kennedy
(message to Congress, March 14, 1961)

CARLENE, CARLINE
[kar-LEEN]

MEANING: one who is free, adult • **USAGE:** English feminine form of Carl (*see* Carla)

Now the Lord is a Spirit.
And where the Spirit of the Lord is, there is liberty.
— 2 Corinthians 3:17 (DR)

CARLOTA
[kahr-LOH-tah]

MEANING: one who is free, adult • **USAGE:** Spanish and Portuguese feminine form of Carlos (*see* Carla)

Doing right brings freedom to honest people.
— Proverbs 11:6a (NCV)

CARLOTTA
[kahr-LOH-tah]

MEANING: one who is free, adult • **USAGE:** Italian feminine form of Carlo (*see* Carla)

You will know the truth, and the truth will set you free.
— John 8:32 (ESV)

CARLY, CARLIE
[KAR-lee]

MEANING: one who is free, adult • **USAGE:** English form of Carla (*see* Carla)

Freedom is the open window through which pours the
sunlight of the human spirit and human dignity.
— Herbert Hoover

CARMEL
[kahr-MEL]

MEANING: vineyard, garden, orchard • **USAGE:** Jewish: from Hebrew *karmel*

As the vine I [Wisdom] put forth grace;
and my flowers are the fruit of glory and riches.
— Sirach 24:17 (WEB Apocrypha)

CARMELA
[kahr-MAY-lah]

MEANING: vineyard, garden, orchard • **USAGE:** Spanish and Italian form of Carmel (*see* Carmel)

One is nearer God's heart in a garden /
Than anywhere else on earth.
— Dorothy Gurney, "God's Garden"

C

CARMELITA   [kahr-may-LEE-tah]

MEANING: little vineyard, little garden, little orchard • USAGE: Spanish form of Carmel and diminutive -ita (see Carmel)

I am the Vine and you are the branches.
Get your life from Me. Then I will live in you
and you will give much fruit.
— John 15:5a (NLV)

CARMEN   [KAHR-men]

MEANING: vineyard, garden, orchard • USAGE: Spanish, Italian, and English form of Carmel (see Carmel)

You will be like a garden that has plenty of water,
like a spring of water that never goes dry.
— Isaiah 58:11b (GNT)

CARMENCITA   [kahr-men-SEE-tah]

MEANING: little vineyard, little garden, little orchard • USAGE: Spanish foerm of Carmen and diminutive -ita (see Carmel)

As the vine I [Wisdom] have brought forth a
pleasant odour: and my flowers are the fruit of
honour and riches.
— Sirach 24:23 (DR Apocrypha)

CAROL   [KAYR-ol]

MEANING: celebrate in song, Christmas song, fierce warrior, beloved, one who is free, adult • USAGE: English and Scandinavian: from English *carolen* (celebrate in song), a Christmas song; from Welsh *caru* (to love); from Irish Gaelic *cearbh* (hack with a weapon) or *cearbhall* (fierce warrior); or English feminine form of Carl (see Carla)

Let thy song be love.
— William Shakespeare, *Troilus and Cressida*

CAROLE   [kah-ROH-leh, kah-ROHL]

MEANING: celebrate in song, Christmas song, fierce warrior, beloved, one who is free, adult • USAGE: French form of Carol (see Carol)

With all my heart, I will celebrate.
— Psalm 16:9a (CEV)

CAROLINA   [kahr-oh-LEE-nah (Italian, Spanish), kayr-oh-LIE-nah (English)]

MEANING: one who is free, adult • USAGE: Spanish, Italian, and English feminine form of Carl (see Carla)

Know that you are a woman of worth.
— Ruth 3:11b (RSV)

CAROLINE   [keh-roh-LEEN (French), kayr-oh-LEE-neh (Scandinavian), KAYR-oh-lin, KAYR-oh-lien (English)]

MEANING: one who is free, adult • USAGE: English, French, and Scandinavian feminine form of Carl (see Carla)

You will be strong and free of fear.
— Job 11:15b (NLT)

CAROLYN   [KAYR-oh-len, KAYR-len]

MEANING: one who is free, adult • USAGE: English feminine form of Carl (see Carla)

There are two good things in life —
freedom of thought and freedom of action.
— W. Somerset Maugham, *Of Human Bondage*

CARON   [KAYR-on]

MEANING: loving, kindhearted, compassionate • USAGE: Welsh: from Welsh *caru* (to love)

Be kind and compassionate to one another.
— Ephesians 4:32a (NIV)

CARRIE, CARRY [KAYR-ee]

MEANING: loved, beloved, fortress, castle, dark, black, dark-haired, one who is free, feminine • **USAGE:** English and Irish: from Welsh *caru* (to love) or *caer* (fortress, castle); Irish feminine form of *Ciardha*, from Gaelic *ciar* (dark, black); or English form of Caroline (*see* Carla)

May mercy, peace, and love be lavished on you!
— Jude 1:2 (NEB)

CARSON [KAHR-sen]

MEANING: courteous, polite, courtly, court dweller • **USAGE:** Scottish and English surname: possibly a form of *Curzon,* from French *curteis* (courteous, polite behavior) or *cort* (court)

Life is not so short but that there is always time enough for courtesy.
— Ralph Waldo Emerson, "Social Aims"

CARYL, CARYLL [KAYR-el]

MEANING: celebrate in song, Christmas song, fierce warrior, beloved, one who is free, adult • **USAGE:** Welsh form of Carol (*see* Carol)

Let me see your face, let me hear your voice;
for your voice is sweet, and your face is lovely.
— Song of Songs 2:14b (NRSV)

CARYS [KAYR-is]

MEANING: love, beloved • **USAGE:** Welsh: from Welsh *caru* (to love)

Let all that you do be done in love.
— 1 Corinthians 16:14 (RSV)

CASEY [KAY-see]

MEANING: vigilant, alert, watchful • **USAGE:** English surname: English form of *O'Cathasaigh,* from Irish Gaelic *cathasaigh*

Love is watchful…as a live flame, or a lighted torch, it breaks forth and overcomes all attempts to quench it.
— Thomas à Kempis, *The Imitation of Christ*
(tr. Harvey Goodwin)

CASS [kas]

MEANING: prophetess, seer • **USAGE:** English form of Cassandra (*see* Cassandra)

Wisdom is found in the words of the discerning person.
— Proverbs 10:13 (NEB)

CASSANDRA [kah-SAHN-drah]

MEANING: prophetess, seer • **USAGE:** English form of Kassandra, a Greek prophetess doomed to tell the truth but never to be believed

She speaks with wisdom,
and faithful instruction is on her tongue.
— Proverbs 31:26 (NIV)

CASSIA [KAS-ee-ah, KAH-shah]

MEANING: cinnamon-like, fragrant spice • **USAGE:** English: from Greek *kassia* (cassia tree)

Take the finest spices…
sweet-smelling cinnamon…cassia…
and you shall make of these a sweet anointing oil.
— Exodus 30:23–25 (NRSV)

CASSIDY, CASSIDI [KAS-ih-dee]

MEANING: love, affection, curly-haired • **USAGE:** Irish form of surname *O'Caiside,* from Gaelic *cais* (love, affection) or *cas* (curly-haired)

Love surpasseth all sweetness, strength, height, depth, and breadth; nothing is more pleasing, nothing more full, nothing more excellent in heaven or in earth.
— Thomas à Kempis, *The Imitation of Christ*
(tr. John Payne)

CASSIE [KAS-ee]

MEANING: prophetess, seer • **USAGE:** English form of Cassandra (*see* Cassandra)

Live by intuition and inspiration and let your whole life be a Revelation.
— Eileen Caddy

C

CATALINA   *[kah-tah-LEE-nah]*

MEANING: pure one, unblemished, innocent, virtuous • USAGE: Spanish form of Catherine (*see* Catharine)

> *Keep thy conscious pure,*
> *and God will be thy continual defense.*
> — Thomas à Kempis, *The Imitation of Christ*
> (tr. John Payne)

CATARINA   *[kah-tah-REE-nah]*

MEANING: pure one, unblemished, innocent, virtuous • USAGE: Italian and Spanish form of Catherine (*see* Catharine)

> *Nothing…is more beautiful than virtue;*
> *nothing fairer; nothing more lovely.*
> — Marcus Tullius Cicero

CATE   *[kayt]*

MEANING: pure one, unblemished, innocent, virtuous • USAGE: Welsh form of Catrin (*see* Catharine)

> *You are a virtuous woman.*
> — Ruth 3:11b (NKJV)

CATHARINA, CATHERINA   *[kah-tah-REE-nah]*

MEANING: pure one, unblemished, innocent, virtuous • USAGE: Scandinavian form of Catherine (*see* Catharine)

> *The pure in heart are blessed, for they will see God.*
> — Matthew 5:8 (HCSB)

CATHARINE, CATHRINE, CATHRYN   *[KATH-ah-ren, KATH-ren]*

MEANING: pure one, unblemished, innocent, virtuous • USAGE: English form of Aikaterini, from Greek *katharos* (pure)

> *Love, gentleness, good-will, purity, are cooling airs*
> *which breathe peace upon the soul.*
> — James Allen, *From Poverty to Power*

CATHERINE   *[kah-TREEN (French), KATH-eh-ren, KATH-ren (English)]*

MEANING: pure one, unblemished, innocent, virtuous • USAGE: French and English form of Aikaterini (*see* Catharine)

> *Purity is…supernatural knowledge*
> *of ourselves in the Divine.*
> — Georges Bernanos,
> *The Diary of a Country Priest* (tr. Pamela Morris)

CATHLEEN   *[kath-LEEN]*

MEANING: pure one, unblemished, innocent, virtuous • USAGE: Irish and English form of Kathleen (*see* Catharine)

> *The wisdom that comes from above leads us to be pure,*
> *friendly, gentle, sensible, kind, helpful, genuine,*
> *and sincere.* — James 3:17 (CEV)

CATHY, CATHIE   *[KATH-ee]*

MEANING: pure one, unblemished, innocent, virtuous • USAGE: Irish and English form of Caitlin or Cathleen (*see* Catharine)

> *Better keep yourself clean and bright; you are the*
> *window through which you must see the world.*
> — George Bernard Shaw, *Man and Superman*

CATINA   *[kah-TEE-nah]*

MEANING: pure one, unblemished, innocent, virtuous • USAGE: Spanish form of Catalina or Catarina (*see* Catharine)

> *Thou art a virtuous woman.*
> — Ruth 3:11b (KJV)

CATORI   *[kah-toh-ree]*

MEANING: spirit • USAGE: Amerind: Hopi

> *We do not walk alone. Great Being walks beside us.*
> *Know this and be grateful.*
> — Polingaysi Qöyawayma

CATRICE [kah-TREES]

MEANING: pure one, unblemished, innocent, virtuous • USAGE: American form of Catherine (*see* Catharine)

I believe we are still so innocent.
— Maya Angelou

CATRIN [KAHT-reen]

MEANING: pure one, unblemished, innocent, virtuous • USAGE: Welsh form of Catherine (*see* Catharine)

Keep your heart pure for out of it are the important things of life. — Proverbs 4:23 (NLV)

CATRINA [kah-TREEN-ah]

MEANING: pure one, unblemished, innocent, virtuous • USAGE: Irish and Scottish form of Catriona (*see* Catharine)

Whatever is true, whatever is honorable, whatever is right, whatever is pure, whatever is lovely, whatever is of good repute, if there is any excellence and if anything worthy of praise, let your mind dwell on these things. — Philippians 4:8 (NASB)

CATRIONA [kah-tree-OH-nah, kah-TREE-oh-nah]

MEANING: pure one, unblemished, innocent, virtuous • USAGE: Scottish and Irish form of Catherine (*see* Catharine)

Thou [art] a virtuous woman.
— Ruth 3:11b (YLT)

CAYENNE [kie-AN]

MEANING: hot red pepper, spice, spicy • USAGE: American: from Brazilian *kyynha* (hot red pepper)

Love is of all stimulants the most powerful.
— Amelia B. Edwards

CECILIA [seh-SIL-yah (English, German, Scandinavian), seh-SEE-lee-ah (Italian, Spanish)]

MEANING: blind, dim-sighted • USAGE: English, German, Italian, Scandinavian, and Spanish form of Roman family name *Caecilius*, from Latin *caecus* (blind)

Shut the eyes of your body and open those of your soul.
— Teresa of Avila, *The Way of Perfection*

CECILY, CICELY [SIS-eh-lee]

MEANING: blind, dim-sighted • USAGE: English form of Cecilia (*see* Cecilia)

We live by believing and not by seeing.
— 2 Corinthians 5:7 (NLT)

CELESTE, CÉLESTE [seh-LEST (English), SAY-lest (French)]

MEANING: heavenly, celestial • USAGE: English and French: from Latin *caelestis*

Love is heaven and heaven is love.
— Lord Byron, *Don Juan*

CELESTINA [say-lay-STEE-nah]

MEANING: heavenly, celestial • USAGE: Spanish and Italian form of Celeste (*see* Celeste)

But the wisdom that comes from heaven is pure. That's the most important thing about it. And that's not all. It also loves peace. It thinks about others. It obeys. It is full of mercy and good fruit. It is fair. It doesn't pretend to be what it is not.
— James 3:17 (NIRV)

CÉLESTINE, CELESTINE [seh-leh-STEE-neh (French), sel-es-TEEN (English)]

MEANING: heavenly, celestial • USAGE: French and English form of Céleste (*see* Celeste)

Eyes raised toward heaven are always beautiful.
— Joseph Joubert

C

CELIA   [say-LEE-ah (Spanish, Italian), SIL-yah, SEE-lee-ah (English, Swedish, Danish)]

MEANING: heavenly, celestial • **USAGE:** Spanish, Italian, Swedish, Danish, and English feminine form of Roman family name *Caelia*, from Latin *caelum* (heaven)

> *Love indeed is light from heaven; /*
> *A spark of that immortal fire with angels shared.*
> — Lord Byron, "The Giaour"

CELINA   [cheh-LEE-nah (Italian), seh-LEE-nah (Polish)]

MEANING: heavenly, celestial, moon • **USAGE:** Italian and Polish form of Celia (*see* Celia); or Polish form of Selene, from Greek *selene* (moon)

> *If thou follow thy star,*
> *thou canst not fail of glorious heaven.*
> — Dante Alighieri,
> *The Divine Comedy* (tr. John A. Carlyle)

CELINE, CÉLINE   [seh-LEEN (English), say-LEEN (French)]

MEANING: heavenly, celestial • **USAGE:** English and French: from Latin *caelestis*

> *Of all earthly music that which reaches*
> *the farthest into heaven is the beating of a loving heart.*
> — Henry Ward Beecher

CELYN   [KEH-len]

MEANING: holly bush, holly berry • **USAGE:** Welsh: from Welsh *celyn*

> *Let the gentle bush dig its root deep*
> *and spread upward to split the boulder.*
> — Carl Sandburg

CERI   [KAYR-ee]

MEANING: beautiful poetry • **USAGE:** Welsh form of Ceridwen (*see* Ceridwen)

> *My thoughts will be deep;*
> *I will speak words of wisdom.*
> — Psalm 49:3 (GNT)

CERIDWEN, CERIDWYN   [keh-RID-wen]

MEANING: beautiful poetry, holy poetry • **USAGE:** Welsh: from *cerdd* (poetry) and *gwyn* (white, fair, holy)

> *Let the words of my mouth, and the meditation*
> *of my heart, be acceptable in thy sight,*
> *O Lord, my strength, and my redeemer.*
> — Psalm 19:14 (KJV)

CERISE   [seh-REEZ]

MEANING: cherry fruit, cherry-red color • **USAGE:** French: from French *cerise* (cherry)

> *Color is the fruit of life.*
> — Guillaume Apollinaire

CERULE   [seh-ROOL]

MEANING: cerulean blue, sky blue color • **USAGE:** English: from English *caeruleus*

> *The sky is not blue colour merely; it is blue fire.*
> — John Ruskin, *Art Culture*

CHAGINA   [chah-GEE-nah]

MEANING: courage • **USAGE:** African: Swahili of Kenya/Tanzania

> *Courage is the fruit of the decision in the heart.*
> — Swahili proverb

CHAGIT   [khah-GEET]

MEANING: my feast, holiday, celebration • **USAGE:** Jewish feminine form of Chagai

> *Contentment is a feast without end.*
> — Proverbs 15:15b (JPS)

C

CHAIFA, CHEIFA [KHIE-fah]

MEANING: harbor, safe haven • **USAGE:** Jewish
Truly He is my rock and deliverance, my haven;
I shall never be shaken.
— Psalm 62:3 (JPS)

CHALICE [CHAL-es]

MEANING: cup, chalice • **USAGE:** English: from Latin *calix* (chalice, cup); reference to the Holy Chalice
My cup overflows with blessings.
— Psalm 23:5b (NLT)

CHAMELI [chah-meh-lee]

MEANING: jasmine flower, jasmine fragrance • **USAGE:** Hindu
Enjoy the smell of the flower, but see God in it.
— Paramahansa Yogananda

CHANAH, CHANNAH [khah-NAH]

MEANING: grace, gracious, merciful • **USAGE:** Jewish: from Hebrew *chaanach*
Thou hast found grace in My sight,
and I know thee by name. — Exodus 33:17b (MT)

CHANDA [CHAHN-dah]

MEANING: shining moon • **USAGE:** Hindu: from Sanskrit *candra*
Free woman, be free / As the moon is free /
From the eclipse of the sun.
— "Songs of the Nuns," Buddhist song
(tr. Jack Kornfield)

CHANDA [SHAHN-dah]

MEANING: God is gracious, God is giving, lily, rose • **USAGE:** American: possibly a form of Shawna, from Hebrew *y'hohanan* (Yahweh is gracious); or possibly a form of Shanna, from Hebrew *shoshan* (lily, rose)

May the Lord who created the heavens
and the earth give you his blessing.
— Psalm 115:15 (CEV)

CHANDRA [CHAHN-drah]

MEANING: shining moon • **USAGE:** Hindu (*see* Chanda)
How bright the full moon of wisdom!
— Buddha

CHANELLE [shah-NEL]

MEANING: God is gracious, God is giving, song, singer, lily, rose • **USAGE:** American: possibly a form of Shana, from Hebrew *y'hohanan* (Yahweh is gracious); or possibly a form of Shanna, from Hebrew *shoshan* (lily, rose)
I am . . . a lily of the valleys.
— Song of Songs 2:1 (ASV)

CHANI [KHAH-nee]

MEANING: grace, gracious, merciful • **USAGE:** Jewish form of Chanah (*see* Chanah)
A gracious woman obtaineth honour.
— Proverbs 11:16a (MT)

CHANICE [shah-NEES]

MEANING: lily, rose, God is gracious, God is giving • **USAGE:** American: possibly a form of Shanna, from or possibly a form of Shoshana, from Hebrew *y'hohanan* (Yahweh is gracious)
Music! the greatest good that mortals know, /
And all of heav'n we have below.
— Joseph Addison, *A Song for St. Cecilia's Day*

CHANIYA [CHAH-nee-yah]

MEANING: rich, wealthy • **USAGE:** African: Swahili of Kenya/Tanzania
Wealth is a matter of the heart.
— Swahili proverb

C

CHANNING [CHAN-ing]

MEANING: channel, canal, waterway • USAGE:
English surname: from English *chanel*
> *The water of life is faith.*
> — Anna Jameson

CHANTAL [shahn-TAHL]

MEANING: song, singer, stone, rock, boulder •
USAGE: French and English: from French *cantal*
(stone, boulder) or *chant* (song)
> *I will sing with my spirit, but I will also sing*
> *with my mind.* — 1 Corinthians 14:15b (NIV)

CHANTÉ, CHANTE, CHANTAY
[shahn-TAY]

MEANING: singer, songstress, song • USAGE:
French and American: from French *chanté* (sung) or
chanter (singer)
> *Let me see your lovely face and hear your enchanting*
> *voice.* — Song of Songs 2:14b (GNT)

CHANTELLE, CHANTEL [shahn-TEL]

MEANING: song, singer, stone, rock, boulder •
USAGE: English form of Chantal (*see* Chantal)
> *Life is one grand, sweet song, so start the music.*
> — Ronald Reagan (senior yearbook quotation)

CHANTRA [SHAHN-trah]

MEANING: song, singer, stone, rock, boulder •
USAGE: American form of Chantrelle (*see* Chantal)
> *For sweet is thy voice, and thy countenance is comely.*
> — Song of Songs 2:14b (DT)

CHANTRELLE, CHANTREL [CHAHN-trel,
SHAHN-trel]

MEANING: song, singer, stone, rock, boulder •
USAGE: American form of Chantelle (*see* Chantal)
> *You shall have a song…and gladness of heart.*
> — Isaiah 30:29a (NKJV)

CHANYA [khahn-YAH, KHAHN-yah]

MEANING: grace of God • USAGE: Jewish: from
Hebrew *chaanach* and *yah* (grace of Yahweh)
> *Truly, the Lord is waiting to show you grace.*
> — Isaiah 30:18a (JPS)

CHARA [KAH-rah]

MEANING: joyous, happy • USAGE: Greek: from
Greek *chairein* (to rejoice)
> *Happiness resides not in possessions*
> *and not in gold, the feeling of happiness*
> *dwells in the soul.*
> — Democritus

CHARICE, CHARISE [shah-REES]

MEANING: cherry fruit, cherry-red color, grace,
kindness, joyful, happy • USAGE: American form
of Cerise, from French *cerise* (cherry); or American
form of Charissa (*see* Charis)
> *The fruit of light is found in all that is good*
> *and right and true.*
> — Ephesians 5:9 (RSV)

CHARIS [KAHR-is]

MEANING: grace, kindness, joyful, happy
• USAGE: Greek: from Greek *charis* (grace,
kindness); or from Greek *chairen* (to rejoice)
> *Grant to me that I be made beautiful*
> *in my soul within.*
> — Plato, *Phraedrus* (tr. H. N. Fowler)

CHARISMA [kah-RIZ-mah]

MEANING: personal magnetism, inspiring,
charming • USAGE: English: from Greek *kharisma*
(favor, grace)
> *Charm is a glow from within you*
> *that casts a becoming light on others.*
> — John Mason Brown

CHARISSA   [kah-RIH-sah]

MEANING: grace, kindness, joyful, happy •
USAGE: English form of Charis (*see* Charis)
How deep in us lies this assurance that goodness
and happiness belong together.
— Phillips Brooks,
"The Withheld Completions of Life"

CHARITA   [chah-REE-tah]

MEANING: generous love, little beloved one •
USAGE: English form of Charity and diminutive
-*ita* (*see* Charity)
O spirit of love! How quick and fresh art thou.
— William Shakespeare, *Twelfth Night*

CHARITA   [chah-rih-tah]

MEANING: having a good character, good •
USAGE: Hindu
To be truly united in knowledge, love, and service
with all beings, and thus to realise one's self in the
all-pervading God, is the essence of goodness.
— Rabindranath Tagore, *Sadhana*

CHARITY   [CHAYR-ih-tee]

MEANING: generous love • USAGE: English: from
Latin *caritas*
Charity itself fulfils the law, /
And who can sever love from charity?
— William Shakespeare, *Love's Labour's Lost*

CHARLAINE, CHARLAYNE   [char-LAYN]

MEANING: one who is free, adult • USAGE:
American form of Charlene (*see* Charlene)
You will know the truth,
and the truth will set you free.
— John 8:32 (HCSB)

CHARLENA, SHARLENA   [shahr-LEH-nah]

MEANING: one who is free, adult • USAGE:
American form of Charlene (*see* Charlene)
Almighty God hath created the mind free.
— Thomas Jefferson (inscription on
Jefferson Memorial, Washington, DC)

CHARLENE, CHARLEEN   [SHAHR-leen]

MEANING: one who is free, adult • USAGE:
English feminine form of Charles, from English
ceorl (freeman, peasant); or from German *karl*
(full grown man, adult)
Seek goodness everywhere,
and when it is found,
bring it out of its hiding place
and let it be free.
— William Saroyan, *The Time of Your Life*

CHARLIE, CHARLEY   [CHAR-lee]

MEANING: one who is free, adult • USAGE:
English feminine form of Charles (*see* Charlene)
The Lord is the Spirit,
but where the Spirit of the Lord is, there is liberty.
— 2 Corinthians 3:17 (DT)

CHARLINE   [shahr-LEEN]

MEANING: one who is free, adult • USAGE: French
feminine form of Charles (*see* Charlene)
I know of one freedom
and that is the freedom of the mind.
— Antoine de Saint-Exupéry

CHARLIZE   [shahr-LEEZ]

MEANING: one who is free, adult • USAGE:
African: South African feminine form of Charles
(*see* Charlene)
For to be free is not merely to cast off one's chains,
but to live in a way that respects and enhances
the freedom of others.
— Nelson Mandela, *Long Walk to Freedom*

C

C

CHARLOTTA   [shahr-LOH-tah]

MEANING: one who is free, adult • USAGE:
Scandinavian form of Charlotte (see Charlene)
*You will know the truth, and the truth
will make you free.* — John 8:32 (NCV)

CHARLOTTE   [shahr-LOHT (French),
SHAHR-lot (English), shahr-LOH-teh (German)]

MEANING: one who is free, adult • USAGE:
English, French, and German feminine form of
Charles (see Charlene)
Freedom is a gift from heaven.
— Denis Diderot, "Political Authority"
(tr. Derek Coltman in *Selected Writings*)

CHARMAINE   [shar-MAYN]

MEANING: charming singer • USAGE: English:
from French *charme* (charm) and from the Latin
canere (to sing)
Your charms are more powerful than all the stars above.
— Song of Songs 6:10b (CEV)

CHARMIAN   [SHAR-mee-an]

MEANING: joyous, delighted • USAGE: English:
from Greek *karmia*
Wit to persuade, and beauty to delight.
— John Davies, "Orchestra"

CHARU   [chah-ruh]

MEANING: beautiful, lovely • USAGE: Hindu:
from Sanskrit *charu*
*Love adorns itself;
it seeks to prove inward joy by outward beauty.*
— Rabindranath Tagore

CHASIDA   [khah-see-DAH, kah-SEE-dah]

MEANING: pious, righteous, devout • USAGE:
Jewish feminine form of Chasid

*I believe that I am very important in God's eyes. I
believe that I can return, no matter how far I've strayed.
I believe I have the inner strength to change. I believe
that I can become truly devoted and close to God.*
— Nachman of Breslov

CHASTITY   [CHAS-tih-tee]

MEANING: pure one, chaste, virtuous • USAGE:
English: from Latin *castus*
*Chastity does not mean abstention from sexual wrong;
it means something flaming, like Joan of Arc.*
— G. K. Chesterton, "A Piece of Chalk"

CHAUNCIE   [CHAHN-see]

MEANING: keeper of records, scribe • USAGE:
English feminine form of Chauncey, from French
chancelier
The Lord your God will bless your work.
— Deuteronomy 28:8a (GNT)

CHAVA   [khah-VAH, KAH-vah]

MEANING: life, full of life • USAGE: Jewish: from
Hebrew *hawwah*
*Hold on to resourcefulness and foresight.
They will give life to your spirit and grace to your
throat. Then you will go your way safely.*
— Proverbs 3:21b–23a (JPS)

CHAYA   [KHAH-yah]

MEANING: life, full of life • USAGE: Jewish: from
Hebrew *hawwah*
Only a life lived for others is a life worthwhile.
— Albert Einstein

CHEDVA   [KHED-vah]

MEANING: joyful, happy • USAGE: Jewish
Gladness and joy shall abide.
— Isaiah 51:3b (JPS)

CHELA [CHAY-lah]

MEANING: God is my strength, strong one of God, God is my oath, joined with God, blessed by God • **USAGE:** Spanish form of Gabriela, from Hebrew *gabhri'el* (God is my strength); or Spanish form of Isabela, from Hebrew *el'ishebha*

God is faithful, who will strengthen and keep you.
— 2 Thessalonians 3:3 (DR)

CHELITA [cheh-LEE-tah]

MEANING: grace, graceful, gracious • **USAGE:** Spanish form of Graciela, from Latin *gratia*

Grace and peace be multiplied to you.
— 2 Peter 1:2a (NKJV)

CHELSEA, CHELSIE [CHEL-see]

MEANING: chalk landing place • **USAGE:** English form of *Caelichyth*, from English *cealc* (chalk) and *hyth* (landing place); place where chalk or limestone was unloaded

*Blessed shalt thou be in thy coming in,
and blessed shalt thou be in thy going out.*
— Deuteronomy 28:6 (DT)

CHENG [cheng]

MEANING: successful, sincere • **USAGE:** Chinese

Sincerity is the Way of Heaven.
— Confucius

CHENOA [sheh-noh-ah]

MEANING: white dove • **USAGE:** Amerind: Cherokee

May the Great Spirit's blessings always be with you.
— Cherokee blessing

CHENYA [khen-YAH]

MEANING: grace of God • **USAGE:** Jewish: from Hebrew *chaanach* and *Yah* (Yahweh)

*The Lord make His face to shine upon thee,
and be gracious unto thee.*
— Numbers 6:24 (MT)

CHER [sher]

MEANING: beloved, dear one, one who is free, adult • **USAGE:** American: from French *cherie* (beloved); or American form of Cheryl (*see* Cheryl)

Let me be rapt in love. Let me rise above self in great fervor and wonder. Let me sing the hymn of love.
— Thomas à Kempis, *The Imitation of Christ*
(tr. Aloysius Croft and Harold Bolton)

CHERIE [sheh-REE, SHER-ee]

MEANING: beloved, dear one • **USAGE:** English: from French *cherie*

May mercy, peace, and love be multiplied to you.
— Jude 1:2 (ESV)

CHERISE, CHERICE [sheh-REES]

MEANING: cherry fruit, cherry-red color, grace, kindness, joyful, happy • **USAGE:** English form of Cerise, from French *cerise* (cherry); or English form of Charissa, from Greek *charis* (grace, kindness), or from Greek *chairen* (to rejoice)

My heart rejoices and I am happy.
— Psalm 16:9a (NEB)

CHERISH [CHEHR-ish]

MEANING: adore, cherish, love • **USAGE:** English: from English *cherishen*

*Cherish your visions; cherish your ideals;
cherish the music that stirs in your heart, the beauty
that forms in your mind, the loveliness that drapes
your purest thoughts, for out of them will grow all
delightful conditions, all heavenly environment.*
— James Allen, *As a Man Thinketh*

C

CHERMONA   [kher-MOH-nah]

MEANING: sacred mountain, dedicated • USAGE:
Jewish

> O send out Thy light and Thy truth;
> let them lead me; let them bring me unto
> Thy holy mountain, and to Thy dwelling-places.
> — Psalm 43:3 (MSG)

CHERRY   [CHEHR-ee]

MEANING: cherry tree, cherry fruit, bright red
color, beloved, dear one • USAGE: English: from
Greek kerasos (cherry tree), or from French cherie
(beloved)

> The fruit of the Spirit is love, joy, peace,
> patience, kindness, goodness, faithfulness,
> gentleness, and self-control.
> — Galatians 5:22–23a (NEB)

CHERYL, SHERYL   [SHER-el]

MEANING: beloved, dear one, one who is free,
adult • USAGE: English: from French cherie
(beloved, dear one); or English feminine form of
Charles, from English ceorl (freeman, peasant) or
from German karl (full-grown man, adult)

> Nature has flowers, and night her stars,
> and woman's heart has love.
> — Clara Balfour, Sunbeams for All Seasons

CHEVONNE   [sheh-VON]

MEANING: God is gracious, God is giving •
USAGE: American form of Siobhan, from Hebrew
y'hohanan (Yahweh is gracious)

> The grace of God means something like:
> Here is your life. You might never have been,
> but you are because the party wouldn't
> have been complete without you.
> — Frederick Buechner, Wishful Thinking

CHEYENNE   [shie-AN]

MEANING: foreigner, stranger; name of American
Indian tribe • USAGE: Amerind: Anglicization of
Sioux shaiyena

> Forget not to show love unto strangers:
> for thereby some have entertained angels unawares.
> — Hebrews 13:2 (ASV)

CHIARA   [kee-AHR-ah]

MEANING: clear, transparent • USAGE: Italian
form of Clara, from Latin clarus

> Who is she that looketh forth as the dawn,
> fair as the moon, clear as the sun.
> — Song of Songs 6:10a (DT)

CHIBA   [khee-BAH]

MEANING: love, beloved • USAGE: Jewish

> Hillel said: "Love peace and pursue peace."
> — Pirkei Avot 1:12a

CHINA   [CHIE-nah]

MEANING: country of China, Middle Kingdom,
Central Kingdom • USAGE: American: name of
Qin Dynasty, from Chinese zhóng (middle, central)
and guó (kingdom, state)

> Behold, the kingdom of God is in the midst of you.
> — Luke 17:21b (DT)

CHIYO   [chee-yoh]

MEANING: thousand generations, thousand worlds
• USAGE: Japanese: from chi (thousand) and yo
(generations, world)

> Days and months are travelers of eternity.
> So are the years that pass by.
> — Matsuo Bashō,
> The Narrow Road to the Deep North
> (tr. Nobuyuki Yuasa)

CHLOE [KLOH-ee]

MEANING: green shoot, verdant, new growth • **USAGE:** English: from Greek *khloe* (green shoot) and *khloros* (pale green)

In you God will green.
— Angelus Silesius, *The Cherubinic Wanderer*
(tr. Maria Shrader)

CHO [choh]

MEANING: butterfly • **USAGE:** Japanese

Lift yourself up. Be attentive. Act virtuously.
One who does good deeds lives happily,
both in this life and the life to come.
— Buddha, *The Dhammapada*
(tr. Ananda Maitreya)

CHONDEL, CHANDELLE [shahn-DEL]

MEANING: candle, stone, boulder, song, singer • **USAGE:** American form of Chantelle: from Latin *candela* (candle); or from French *cantal* (stone, boulder) or *chant* (song)

There are two ways of spreading light; to be /
The candle or the mirror that reflects it.
— Edith Wharton, "Vesalius in Zante"

CHONSIE [CHAHN-see]

MEANING: keeper of records, scribe • **USAGE:** American feminine form of Chauncey, from French *chancelier*

The Lord your God will bless you in all your works
and in all to which you put your hand.
— Deuteronomy 15:10b (NKJV)

CHOSOVI [choh-soh-vee]

MEANING: bluebird • **USAGE:** Amerind: Hopi

Great Spirit...Let us be seen in beauty,
the colors of the rainbow.
— Hopi Prayer for Peace

CHRIS [kris]

MEANING: follower of Christ, Christian • **USAGE:** English form of Christina or Christine (*see* Christine)

I am certain that nothing can separate us from his love:
neither death nor life, neither angels nor other heavenly
rulers or powers, neither the present nor the future,
neither the world above nor the world below —
there is nothing in all creation that will ever
be able to separate us from the love of God
which is ours through Christ Jesus.
— Romans 8:38–39 (GNT)

CHRISSIE, CHRISSY [KRIS-ee]

MEANING: follower of Christ, Christian • **USAGE:** English form of Christina or Christine (*see* Christine)

Anyone who belongs to Christ has become a new person.
The old life is gone; a new life has begun!
— 2 Corinthians 5:17 (NLT)

CHRISTA [KRIS-tah]

MEANING: follower of Christ, Christian • **USAGE:** English, German, and Scandinavian form of Christina or Christine (*see* Christine)

Christ will make his home in your hearts
as you trust in him. Your roots will grow down
into God's love and keep you strong.
— Ephesians 3:17 (ESV)

CHRISTELLE [kree-STEHL]

MEANING: follower of Christ, Christian • **USAGE:** French and Scandinavian form of Christiana (*see* Christine)

The peace of God, which passeth all understanding,
shall keep your hearts and minds through Christ Jesus.
— Philippians 4:7 (KJ21)

C

CHRISTIANA [krees-tee-AH-nah (German), kris-tee-AN-ah (English)]

MEANING: follower of Christ, Christian • USAGE: German and English feminine form of Christian (*see* Christine)

The Spirit himself testifies with our spirit that we are children of God; and if children, then heirs; heirs of God, and joint heirs with Christ.
— Romans 8:16–17a (WEB)

CHRISTIANE [kris-tee-AHN]

MEANING: follower of Christ, Christian • USAGE: French form of Christiana (*see* Christine)

I can do all things through Christ who strengthens me.
— Philippians 4:13 (NKJV)

CHRISTIE, CHRISTY, CHRISTI [KRIS-tee]

MEANING: follower of Christ, Christian • USAGE: English form of Christina or Christine (*see* Christine)

For we are God's masterpiece. He has created us anew in Christ Jesus, so we can do the good things he planned for us long ago.
— Ephesians 2:10 (NLT)

CHRISTINA [kris-TEE-nah (English), krees-TEE-nah (Scandinavian)]

MEANING: follower of Christ, Christian • USAGE: English and Scandinavian feminine form of Christian (*see* Christine)

I am persuaded that neither death nor life, nor angels nor principalities nor powers, nor things present nor things to come, nor height nor depth, nor any other created thing, shall be able to separate us from the love of God which is in Christ Jesus.
— Romans 8:38–39 (NKJV)

CHRISTINE [kris-TEEN (English), kris-TEE-neh (Scandinavian)]

MEANING: follower of Christ, Christian • USAGE: English and Scandinavian feminine form of Christian, from Greek *christianos*

You will experience God's peace, which exceeds anything we can understand. His peace will guard your hearts and minds as you live in Christ Jesus.
— Philippians 4:7 (NLT)

CHUN [chwen]

MEANING: spring • USAGE: Chinese

When spring comes every spot is perfumed with flowers.
— Chinese proverb (tr. William Scarborough)

CIANA, CIANNA [kee-AHN-ah]

MEANING: ancient, distant past, enduring • USAGE: Irish: from Gaelic *cian*

The Lord has appeared of old to me, saying: Yes, I have loved you with an everlasting love; therefore with lovingkindness I have drawn you.
— Jeremiah 31:3 (NKJV)

CIARA, CIARRA [kee-AHR-ah]

MEANING: dark, black, dark-haired • USAGE: Irish: from Gaelic *ciar*

Thus saith the Lord...I will give thee the treasures of darkness and hidden riches of secret places.
— Isaiah 45:1–3a (KJ21)

CIEL [seel]

MEANING: sky, heaven • USAGE: French: from French *ciel*

Faith transforms the earth into a paradise. By it our hearts are raised with the joy of our nearness to heaven.
— Jean Pierre de Caussade

CILI [SEE-lee]

MEANING: blind, dim-sighted • USAGE:
Hungarian form of Cecilia, from Latin *caecus*
(blind)

> *The things which are seen are temporal;*
> *but the things which are not seen are eternal.*
> — 2 Corinthians 4:18b (KJV)

CILLA [SEEL-ah]

MEANING: blind, dim-sighted • USAGE:
Scandinavian form of Cecilia, from Latin *caecus*
(blind)

> *We live by what we believe, not by what we see.*
> — 2 Corinthians 5:7 (NCV)

CINDA [SEN-dah]

MEANING: woman of Kynthos, mountain on
Delos, moon • USAGE: American: possibly a form
of Cynthia (*see* Cindy)

> *Happiness is reflective, like the light of heaven.*
> — Washington Irving,
> *The Sketch-Book of Geoffrey Crayon*

CINDY [SEN-dee]

MEANING: woman of Kynthos, mountain on
Delos, moon • USAGE: English form of Cynthia,
from Greek Kynthia, from *Kynthos*, a mountain on
Delos where the Greek goddess Artemis was born
and denotes "moon personified"

> *Like the moon her kindness is.*
> — William Butler Yeats, "Human Dignity"

CINNAMON [SEN-ah-mon]

MEANING: spice, spicy • USAGE: American: from
Latin *Cinnamomum* (tree used to create cinnamon)
and from Latin *canna* (tube)

> *Variety's the very spice of life, /*
> *That gives it all its flavor.*
> — William Cowper, "The Time-Piece"

CINZIA [SEEN-ʒee-ah]

MEANING: woman of Kynthos, mountain on
Delos, moon • USAGE: Italian form of Cynthia (*see*
Cindy)

> *Who is she that cometh forth as the morning rising,*
> *fair as the moon, bright as the sun.*
> — Song of Songs 6:9a (DR)

CLAIRE [klayr]

MEANING: clear, transparent • USAGE: French and
English (*see* Clare)

> *One sees clearly only with the heart.*
> *Anything essential is invisible to the eyes.*
> — Antoine de Saint-Exupéry,
> *The Little Prince* (tr. Richard Howard)

CLARA [KLAYR-ah (English), KLAH-rah (Italian, Spanish)]

MEANING: clear, transparent • USAGE: English,
Italian, and Spanish form of Clare (*see* Clare)

> *We are living in a world that is absolutely transparent*
> *and God is shining through it all the time.*
> — Thomas Merton

CLARE [klayr]

MEANING: clear, transparent • USAGE: Irish and
English: from Latin *clarus*

> *I find that I have four things to learn…to think clearly*
> *without hurry or confusion, to love everybody sincerely,*
> *to act in everything with the highest motives,*
> *to trust God unhesitatingly.*
> — Helen Keller, *The Story of My Life*

CLARETTE [klah-RET]

MEANING: clear, transparent • USAGE: English
form of Clara (*see* Clare)

> *If therefore thy whole body be full of light, having no*
> *part dark, it shall be wholly full of light, as when the*
> *lamp with its bright shining doth give thee light.*
> — Luke 11:36 (ASV)

C

C

CLARICE [klah-REES]

MEANING: clear, transparent • USAGE: English form of Clara (see Clare)

> Eyes so transparent that through them
> one sees the soul.
> — Théophile Gautier

CLARINDA, CLARENDA [klah-RIN-dah]

MEANING: clear, transparent • USAGE: English form of Clara (see Clare)

> Character must be kept bright as well as clean.
> — Lord Chesterfield (letter of January 8, 1750)

CLARISA [klah-REE-sah]

MEANING: clear, transparent • USAGE: Spanish form of Clare (see Clare)

> Those who are wise will shine
> like the bright expanse of the heavens.
> — Daniel 12:3a (HCSB)

CLARISSA [klah-RIS-ah (English), klah-REE-sah (Italian)]

MEANING: clear, transparent • USAGE: English and Italian form of Clare (see Clare)

> The eye is the lamp of your body; when your eye
> is clear, your whole body also is full of light.
> — Luke 11:34 (NASB)

CLARISSE [klah-REES]

MEANING: clear, transparent • USAGE: French form of Claire (see Clare)

> Clarity of mind means clarity of passion, too;
> this is why a great and clear mind loves ardently
> and sees distinctly what it loves.
> — Blaise Pascal

CLARITY [KLAYR-eh-tee]

MEANING: clear, transparent • USAGE: English: from Latin clarus

> The greatest thing a human soul ever does
> in this world is to see something.... To see clearly
> is poetry, prophecy and religion all in one.
> — John Ruskin, Modern Painters

CLARY [KLAYR-ee]

MEANING: clear, transparent • USAGE: English form of Clara, Clarette, or Clarissa (see Clare)

> A clear and innocent conscience fears nothing.
> — Queen Elizabeth I

CLAUDETTE [kloh-DET (French), klah-DET (English)]

MEANING: lame, limping • USAGE: French and English feminine form of Claude (see Claudia)

> Common sense and discernment...keep you safe on
> your way, and your feet will not stumble.
> — Proverbs 3:21–23 (NLT)

CLAUDIA [KLAH-dee-ah (English), KLOW-dee-ah (German, Italian, Scandinavian, Spanish)]

MEANING: lame, limping • USAGE: English, German, Italian, Scandinavian, and Spanish feminine form of Claude, from Latin claudus (lame)

> God, who gives all grace, will make everything right.
> He will make you strong and support you and
> keep you from falling. — 1 Peter 5:10 (NCV)

CLAUDINE [kloh-DEEN]

MEANING: lame, limping • USAGE: French feminine form of Claude (see Claudia)

> The Lord will hold your hand,
> and if you stumble, you still won't fall.
> — Psalm 37:4 (CEV)

CLEMENCIA [klay-MEN-see-ah]

MEANING: clement, mild, gentle, merciful • USAGE: Spanish feminine form of Clemente (see Clementine)

*Clothe yourselves instead with the beauty
that comes from within, the unfading beauty
of a gentle and quiet spirit.*
— 1 Peter 3:4a (NLT)

CLEMENTINE [KLEM-en-tien (English), kleh-mahn-TEEN (French)]

MEANING: clement, mild, gentle, merciful •
USAGE: English and French feminine form of
Clement, from Latin *clemens*
Love makes all hearts gentle.
— George Herbert

CLIO [KLEE-oh]

MEANING: glory, magnificence, splendor •
USAGE: Greek: from Greek *kleos* (glory); the
Greek muse of history
*Arise, shine; for your light has come!
And the glory of the Lord is risen upon you.*
— Isaiah 60:1 (NKJV)

CLIONA, CLEONA [klee-OH-nah]

MEANING: shapely • **USAGE:** Irish meaning
"shapely"; Irish Gaelic goddess
*Thou didst form my inward parts: Thou didst cover me
in my mother's womb. I will give thanks unto thee; for I
am fearfully and wonderfully made: wonderful are thy
works; and that my soul knoweth right well.*
— Psalm 139:13–14 (ASV)

CLODAGH [CLOH-dah]

MEANING: river name, stony beach • **USAGE:**
Irish: possibly from Gaelic *claddagh* (stony beach);
river in Ireland
*For thus says the Lord:
"Behold, I will extend peace to her like a river."*
— Isaiah 66:12a (NKJV)

CLOE [KLOH-ee]

MEANING: green shoot, verdant, new growth •
USAGE: Italian form of Chloe, from Greek *khloe*
(green shoot) and *khloros* (pale green)
The earth is full of the goodness of the Lord.
— Psalm 33:5b (KJV)

CLORIS, CHLORIS [KLOR-es]

MEANING: pale green, new growth, goddess of
flowers, spring, new growth • **USAGE:** English:
from Greek *khloros* (pale green); Greek goddess of
flowers, spring, and new growth
*I adorn all the earth. I am the breeze that nurtures all
things green. I encourage blossoms to flourish with
ripening fruits…I am the yearning for good.*
— St. Hildegard of Bingen

CLOTILDA [kloh-TEEL-dah]

MEANING: famous warrior • **USAGE:** German and
English form of *Hlodhild*, from *hlud* (famous) and
hild (war, battle)
Put on the armor of light.
— Romans 13:12b (WEB)

CLOVER [KLOH-ver]

MEANING: green herb, carefree, comfortable,
prosperous • **USAGE:** English: from English *clafre*
(herb in pea family); reference to living a carefree
life of ease, comfort, or prosperity
*Happiness, health, and prosperity are the result of a
harmonious adjustment of the inner with the outer.*
— James Allen, *As a Man Thinketh*

CODY, CODIE [KOH-dee]

MEANING: helper, aide, helpful • **USAGE:** Irish
and English: from Gaelic *cuidightheach*
*Show love for others by truly helping them,
and not merely by talking about it.*
— 1 John 3:18 (CEV)

C

COLETTE, COLLETTE   [koh-LET]

MEANING: victory of the people, successful, triumphant • USAGE: French feminine form of Nicholas, from Greek *nike* (victory) and *laos* (people)

Success, success to you. Success to those who help you,
because your God helps you.
— 1 Chronicles 12:18b (NCV)

COLLEEN, COLEEN   [koh-LEEN]

MEANING: young girl, maiden • USAGE: Irish and English: from Gaelic *cailín*

Maiden, when such a soul as thine is born, /
The morning stars their ancient music make.
— James Russell Lowell,
"To —, on Her Birthday"

COLOMBE   [koh-LOHM-beh]

MEANING: dove, dove-like • USAGE: Italian: from Latin *columba* (dove); a symbol of peace

Blessed are the peacemakers,
for they shall be called children of God.
— Matthew 5:9 (DR)

COLOMBINA   [koh-lohm-BEE-nah]

MEANING: little dove • USAGE: French: from Latin *columba* (dove) and diminutive *-ina* (see Colombe)

How beautiful art thou, my love,
how beautiful art thou! thy eyes are doves' eyes.
— Song of Songs 4:1a (DR)

CONCEPCIÓN   [kohn-sep-see-OHN]

MEANING: conception, beginning, birth • USAGE: Spanish: from Latin *concipere* (to conceive); reference to the Immaculate Conception

Spirit gives birth to spirit.
— John 3:6b (NIV)

CONCETTA   [kohn-CHEH-tah]

MEANING: conception, beginning, birth • USAGE: Italian form of Concepción (see Concepción)

Everyone born of God overcomes the world.
— 1 John 5:4a (NIV)

CONCHITA   [kohn-CHEE-tah]

MEANING: conception, beginning, birth • USAGE: Spanish form of Concepción (see Concepción)

My bones were not hidden from You when I was
made in secret, when I was formed in the depths
of the earth. Your eyes saw me when I was formless;
all my days were written in Your book and
planned before a single one of them began.
— Psalm 139:15–16 (HCSB)

CONLEE   [KON-lee]

MEANING: hound of valor, courageous hound • USAGE: English feminine form of Conley, an English surname: from Gaelic *con* (hound, dog) and *gal* (valor, courage)

People grow through experience if they meet life honestly and courageously. This is how character is built.
— Eleanor Roosevelt
(journal entry of August 1, 1941)

CONNIE, CONNY   [KON-ee]

MEANING: constant, steadfast, enduring • USAGE: English form of Constance (see Constance)

The secret of success is constancy of purpose.
— Benjamin Disraeli (speech on June 24, 1872)

CONSEJA   [kohn-SAY-hah]

MEANING: counselor, adviser • USAGE: Spanish: from Latin *consilium*

They say that the best counsel is that of a woman.
— Pedro Calderón de la Barca,
The Physician of His Own Honour
(tr. Denis MacCarthy)

C

CONSTANCE [KON-stans (English), kon-STAHNS (French)]

MEANING: constant, steadfast, enduring • **USAGE:** English and French form of *Constantia*, from Latin *constans*

How precious, O God, is your constant love!
— Psalm 36:7a (GNT)

CONSTANCIA [kohn-STAHN-see-ah]

MEANING: constant, steadfast, enduring • **USAGE:** Portuguese form of Constance (*see* Constance)

Those who devise good meet
steadfast love and faithfulness.
— Proverbs 14:22b (ESV)

CONSTANTINA [kohn-stahn-TEE-nah]

MEANING: constant, steadfast, enduring • **USAGE:** Italian feminine form of Constantino, from Latin *constans*

Lord…let your steadfast love
and your faithfulness keep me safe forever.
— Psalm 40:11 (NRSV)

CONSTANZA [kohn-STAHN-ʒah]

MEANING: constant, steadfast, enduring • **USAGE:** Spanish form of Constance, from Latin *constans*
Thou shalt be stedfast, and shalt not fear.
— Job 11:15b (DT)

CONSUELO [kohn-SWEH-loh]

MEANING: consoler, comforter • **USAGE:** Spanish: from Spanish *consuelo*

Do that which makes you complete. Be comforted.
Work to get along with others. Live in peace.
The God of love and peace will be with you.
— 2 Corinthians 13:11b (NLV)

CORA [KOR-ah]

MEANING: maiden, young woman • **USAGE:** English form of Kora, from Greek *kore*

A good woman is hard to find,
and worth far more than diamonds.
— Proverbs 31:10 (MSG)

CORAL [KOR-al]

MEANING: reef, coral, orange-pink color • **USAGE:** English: from Greek *korallion*

Orange is the happiest color.
— Frank Sinatra

CORAZÓN [kohr-ah-ZOHN]

MEANING: heart, a reference to the Sacred Heart of Jesus • **USAGE:** Spanish: from Spanish *corazón*

In Your hand / I place my heart, / Body, life and soul.
— Teresa of Avila, "In the Hands of God"

CORDELIA [kor-DEEL-yah]

MEANING: heart of Delos • **USAGE:** English: from *King Lear* by William Shakespeare, possibly from Latin *cor* (heart) and *Delia* (Greek island of Delos)

Let Love's bright sunshine play upon your heart.
— James Allen, *From Poverty to Power*

CORELLE [kor-EL]

MEANING: reef, coral, orange-pink color • **USAGE:** English form of Coral (*see* Coral)

Colors speak all languages.
— Joseph Addison

CORETTA [kor-REH-tah]

MEANING: little maiden • **USAGE:** English form of Cora and diminutive *-etta* (*see* Cora)

[God] satisfies you with good as long as you live
so that your youth is renewed like the eagle's.
— Psalm 103:5 (NRSV)

C

CORINA [koh-REEN-ah]

Meaning: little maiden, young woman • **Usage:** English, German, and Scandinavian form of Korinna and diminutive -ina (see Corinna)

He [God] wraps you in goodness — beauty eternal.
He renews your faith —
you're always young in his presence.
— Psalm 103:5 (MSG)

CORINNA [koh-RIN-ah]

Meaning: little maiden, young woman • **Usage:** English, German, and Scandinavian form of Korinna, from Greek *kore* (maiden) and diminutive -ina

A Maiden…lovely as Spring's first rose.
— William Wordsworth, *The Borderers*

CORINNE [koh-RIN]

Meaning: maiden, girl, young woman • **Usage:** French and English form of Corinna (see Corinna)

One is not born, but rather becomes, a woman.
— Simone de Beauvoir,
The Second Sex (tr. H. M. Parshley)

CORNELIA [kor-NEEL-yah (English), kor-NEH-lee-ah (German, Italian, Scandinavian)]

Meaning: horn, horn-bearer • **Usage:** English, German, Italian, and Scandinavian feminine form of Cornelius, from Latin *cornu*

My God is my helper, and in him will I put my trust.
My protector and the horn of my salvation,
and my support.
— Psalm 17:3a (DR)

CORONA [koh-ROH-nah]

Meaning: crown, crowned one • **Usage:** German: from Latin *corona*

[God] crowns you with lovingkindness and compassion.
— Psalm 103:4b (NASB)

CORRIE [KOR-ee]

Meaning: maiden, young woman, heart of Delos • **Usage:** English and Dutch form of Cora (see Cora); or English form of Cordelia (see Cordelia)

A worthy woman who can find?
For her price is far above rubies.
— Proverbs 31:10 (ASV)

COSETTE [koh-ZET, koh-SET]

Meaning: little darling • **Usage:** French: from French *cosette*

My darling, you are beautiful! Oh, you are beautiful.
— Song of Songs 1:15a (NCV)

COSIMA [KOH-ʒee-mah]

Meaning: cosmos, order, harmony, the universe • **Usage:** Italian feminine form of Cosimo or Cosmo, from Greek *kosmos* (order, harmony, the universe)

Reverence that which is best in the universe;
and this is that which makes use of all things
and directs all things. And in like manner also
reverence that which is best in thyself.
— Marcus Aurelius, *The Meditations*
(tr. George Long)

COURTLAND, COURTLIN [KORT-land, KORT-lin]

Meaning: courteous, polite, courtly, court dweller • **Usage:** English: from French *curteis* (courteous, polite behavior) or *cort* (court, courtyard)

Manners are of more importance than laws.
Upon them, in a great measure the law depends.
— Edmund Burke, *Letters on a Regicide Peace*

COURTNEY, COURTENAY [KORT-nee]

Meaning: courteous, polite, courtly, court dweller, short nose • **Usage:** English (see Courtland)

*The music that can deepest reach, /
And cure all ill, is cordial speech.*
— Ralph Waldo Emerson,
"Considerations by the Way"

CRESSIDA [KRES-eh-dah]

MEANING: gold, golden • **USAGE:** English form of *Khryseis*, from Greek *khrysos* (golden)
As you proceed, golden opportunities will be strewn across your path, and the power and judgment to properly utilize them will spring up within you.
— James Allen, *From Poverty to Power*

CRISTA [KRIS-tah (English), KREES-tah (Danish, Swedish)]

MEANING: follower of Christ, Christian • **USAGE:** English, Danish, and Swedish form of Christina or Christine, from Greek *christianos*
I can do everything through Christ, who gives me strength.
— Philippians 4:13 (NLT)

CRISTAL [krees-tahl]

MEANING: crystal, transparent quartz, ice • **USAGE:** Spanish form of Crystal (*see* Crystal)
A leaf, a drop, a crystal, a moment of time is related to the whole, and partakes of the perfection of the whole.
— Ralph Waldo Emerson, *Nature*

CRISTIANA [krees-tee-AH-nah]

MEANING: follower of Christ, Christian • **USAGE:** Italian form of Cristina (*see* Crista)
For we are his workmanship, created in Christ Jesus unto good works, which God hath before ordained that we should walk in them.
— Ephesians 2:10 (KJV)

CRISTINA [krees-TEE-nah]

MEANING: follower of Christ, Christian • **USAGE:** Italian and Spanish feminine form of Christian (*see* Crista)
Neither death, nor life, nor angels, nor principalities, nor powers, nor things present, nor things to come, nor height, nor depth, nor any other creature, shall be able to separate us from the love of God, which is in Christ Jesus.
— Romans 8:38–39 (KJV)

CRISTINE [krees-TEEN-ah]

MEANING: follower of Christ, Christian • **USAGE:** Scandinavian feminine form of Christian (*see* Crista)
Let the peace of Christ rejoice in your hearts.
— Colossians 3:15a (DR)

CRYSTAL [KRIS-tal]

MEANING: crystal, transparent quartz, ice • **USAGE:** English: from Greek *krystallos* (ice)
Pure thoughts crystallize into habits of temperance and self-control, which solidify into circumstances of repose and peace.
— James Allen, *As a Man Thinketh*

CYAN [SIE-an]

MEANING: green-blue color • **USAGE:** English: from Greek *kyanos*
Methinks my own soul must be a bright invisible green.
— Henry David Thoreau,
A Week on the Concord and Merrimack Rivers

CYBILL, CYBIL [SIB-el]

MEANING: prophetess, seer • **USAGE:** English form of Sibyl, from Greek *sibylla*
When she speaks, her words are wise and she gives instructions with kindness.
— Proverbs 31:26 (NLT)

CYNTHIA, CINTHIA   [SIN-thee-ah]

MEANING: woman of Kynthos, mountain on Delos, moon • **USAGE:** English form of Kynthia, from Greek *Kynthos*, a mountain on Delos where the Greek goddess Artemis was born and denotes "moon personified"

> *Who is this, arising like the dawn,*
> *as fair as the moon, as bright as the sun?*
> — Song of Songs 6:10a (NLT)

CYRA   [KIE-rah]

MEANING: lady, mistress, like the sun, farsighted • **USAGE:** English feminine form of Cyril or Cyrus, from Greek *kyrios* (lord, master); or possibly from Persian *khur* (sun) or *kûrush* (farsighted)

> *I believe in sunshine, fresh air, friendship,*
> *calm sleep, beautiful thoughts.*
> — Elbert Hubbard

CYRILLA, CIRILLA   [seh-REL-ah, seh-REE-lah]

MEANING: lady, mistress • **USAGE:** English feminine form of Cyril, from Greek *kyrios* (lord, master)

> *You're blessed when you meet Lady Wisdom....*
> *With one hand she gives long life,*
> *with the other she confers recognition.*
> — Proverbs 3:13, 3:16 (MSG)

CYRILLE   [seh-REEL]

MEANING: ruler, mistress • **USAGE:** French feminine form of Cyril (*see* Cyrilla)

> *The hand of the diligent shall bear rule.*
> — Proverbs 12:24a (KJV)

D

DACEY, DACIE, DACY   [DAY-see]

MEANING: south, southern, servant • **USAGE:** Irish: from Gaelic *deas* (south); or from Irish *deise* (servant)

> *Well done, good and faithful servant. You have been faithful over a little; I [God] will set you over much.*
> — Matthew 25:21b (ESV)

DAFINA   [DAH-fee-nah]

MEANING: valuable, precious • **USAGE:** African: Swahili of Kenya/Tanzania

> *Wealth, if you use it, comes to an end; learning,*
> *if you use it, increases.* — Swahili proverb

DAFNA   [dahf-NAH]

MEANING: laurel tree, bay tree, daphne flower • **USAGE:** Jewish

> *She [Wisdom] is a tree of life to those who grasp her,*
> *and whoever holds on to her is happy.*
> — Proverbs 3:18 (JPS)

DAFNE   [DAHF-neh]

MEANING: laurel tree, bay tree, daphne flower • **USAGE:** Italian form of Daphne, from Greek *daphne* (laurel or bay tree); type of flower

> *Happy is the person who finds wisdom,*
> *the one who gets understanding...With her right hand wisdom offers you a long life, and with her left hand she gives you riches and honor.*
> — Proverbs 3:13, 3:16 (NCV)

DAGMAR   [DAHG-mahr]

MEANING: day maiden, glorious day • **USAGE:** Scandinavian and German: from Norse *dagr* (day) and *mar* (splendid, glorious) or *mær* (maiden)

> *Shine! Your new day is dawning.*
> *The glory of the Lord shines brightly on you.*
> — Isaiah 60:1b (CEV)

DAGNA   [DAHG-neh]

MEANING: new day • USAGE: Scandinavian: from Norse *dagr* (day) and *ny* (new)
> *This is the day which the Lord hath made:*
> *let us be glad and rejoice therein.*
> — Psalm 117:24 (DR)

DAHLIA   [DAHL-yah]

MEANING: dahlia flower • USAGE: English: flower named for Swedish botanist Anders Dahl
> *The flowers appear on the earth;*
> *the time of the singing of birds is come.*
> — Song of Songs 2:12a (KJ21)

DAISY   [DAY-ʒee]

MEANING: day's eye, daisy flower • USAGE: English: from English *dæges eage* (day's eye); type of flower; a symbol of dawn
> *Gorgeous flowerets in the sunlight shining /*
> *Blossoms flaunting in the eye of day.*
> — Henry Wadsworth Longfellow, "Flowers"

DAKOTA   [dah-KOH-tah]

MEANING: friend, ally friend, ally, American Indian tribe • USAGE: American: Sioux
> *Friend, whatever hardships threaten, /*
> *If thou call me, / I'll befriend thee; /*
> *All enduring fearlessly, / I'll befriend thee.*
> — Song of the White Horse Society, Lakota Sioux

DALE   [dayl]

MEANING: dale, glen, small valley • USAGE: English: from English *dæl*
> *One sees great things from the valley,*
> *only small things from the peak.*
> — G. K. Chesterton, *The Innocence of Father Brown*

DALLAS   [DAL-es]

MEANING: house in the dale, valley house • USAGE: Scottish and English surname: from Gaelic *dail* (dale, valley) and *fas* (dwelling, house)
> *The peace of God... / Be upon each window,*
> *upon each door / Upon each hole that lets in light. /*
> *Upon the four corners of my house.*
> — Alexander Carmichael, *Carmina Gadelica*

DALYA, DALIA   [DAHL-yah]

MEANING: branch, tree bough • USAGE: Jewish: kibbutz in northern Israel
> *There is hope of a tree...at the scent of water it will*
> *bud and produce branches like a sapling.*
> — Job 14:7–9 (JPS)

DAMARIS   [dah-MAHR-es (Greek),
                  dah-MAYR-es (English)]

MEANING: tame, subdue, discipline • USAGE: Greek and English: from Greek *damao* (to tame)
> *Let us dedicate ourselves to what the Greeks wrote*
> *so many years ago: to tame the savageness of man*
> *and make gentle the life of this world.*
> — Robert F. Kennedy
> (1968 Indiana primary speech)

DAMIANA   [dah-mee-AH-nah]

MEANING: tame, subdue, discipline • USAGE: Italian, Spanish feminine form of Damiano (*see* Damaris)
> *God blessed them; and God said to them, Be fruitful*
> *and multiply, and fill the earth, and subdue it.*
> — Genesis 1:28a (DR)

DAMISI   [dah-mee-see]

MEANING: sociable, cheerful, amiable • USAGE: African: Swahili of Kenya and Tanzania
> *Talking with one another is loving one another.*
> — Kenyan proverb

D

DAN   [dahn]

MEANING: red color • USAGE: Chinese
If you touch red, you become red.
— Chinese proverb

DANA   [DAY-nah]

MEANING: poem, poet, brave, daring, Danish, Irish mother goddess • USAGE: Irish and English: from Irish *dána* (brave, daring) or *dán* (poem); or from Norse *Danr* (a Dane); mother goddess of the mythic early settlers of Ireland, the Tuatha de Danann
Life is either a daring adventure, or nothing. To keep our faces toward change and behave like free spirits in the presence of fate is strength undefeatable.
— Helen Keller

DANA   [DAH-nah]

MEANING: judge, justice, judgment, God is my judge • USAGE: Jewish, feminine form of Dan, from Hebrew *dan* (to judge) or from Hebrew *dani'el* (God is my judge)
Execute true judgment,
and show mercy and compassion.
— Zechariah 7:9b (MT)

DANAE   [dah-NAY]

MEANING: dry, arid • USAGE: Greek: from Greek *danae* (dry, parched); Greek mythological heroine
Be good, keep your feet dry,
your eyes open, your heart at peace.
— Thomas Merton (letter of November 27, 1962)

DANESH   [dah-NESH]

MEANING: wise, knowledgeable • USAGE: Persian
It is the soul's light which is natural intelligence.
— Hazrat Inayat Khan, *The Bowl of Saki*

DANETTE   [dah-NET]

MEANING: God is my judge • USAGE: English feminine form of Daniel (*see* Danielle)
The Lord loves righteousness and justice.
— Psalm 33:5b (NIV)

DANI, DANNI   [DAN-ee]

MEANING: God is my judge • USAGE: English form of Danielle (*see* Danielle)
The Lord…hath led me on the paths of justice,
for his own name's sake.
— Psalm 22:1–3 (DR)

DANIA   [DAHN-ee-ah]

MEANING: God is my judge • USAGE: Scandinavian form of Daniela (*see* Danielle)
The Lord is waiting to show you mercy, and is rising up to show you compassion, for the Lord is a just God.
— Isaiah 30:18a (HCSB)

DANIELA, DANIELLA

[dah-nee-EL-ah (Jewish),
dahn-YEL-ah (German, Italian, Scandinavian,
Spanish), dan-YEL-ah (English)]

MEANING: God is my judge • USAGE: Jewish, English, German, Italian, Scandinavian, and Spanish feminine form of Daniel (*see* Danielle)
When you judge, be fair to everyone; don't act as if one person is more important than another, and don't be afraid of anyone, because your decision comes from God.
— Deuteronomy 1:17a (NCV)

DANIELE, DANIÈLE   [dan-YEL (English),
dahn-YEL (French)]

MEANING: God is my judge • USAGE: English and French feminine form of Daniel (*see* Danielle)
God does not see the same way people see. People look at the outside of a person, but the Lord looks at the heart.
— 1 Samuel 16:7b (NCV)

DANIELLE   *[dah-nee-EHL (Jewish),
dan-YEL (English), dahn-YEHL (Spanish)]*

MEANING: God is my judge • USAGE: Jewish,
English, and Spanish feminine form of Daniel, from
Hebrew *dani'el*
> *There shall be no difference of persons, you shall hear
> the little as well as the great: neither shall you respect
> any man's person, because it is the judgment of God.*
> — Deuteronomy 1:17a (DR)

DANIKA, DANICA   *[DAH-nee-kah]*

MEANING: morning star, God is my judge •
USAGE: Czech: from Slavic *jitjenka* (morning star);
or Czech feminine form of Daniel (*see* Danielle)
> *You still stand watch, O human star, burning without
> a flicker, perfect flame, bright and resourceful spirit.*
> — Karel Capek, *R. U. R.*
> *(Rossum's Universal Robots)*

DANISHA, DANEISHA   *[dah-NEE-shah]*

MEANING: God is my judge • USAGE: American:
possibly a form of Dani (*see* Danielle)
> *Reputation is what men and women think of us;
> character is what God and angels know of us.*
> — Thomas Paine

DANYA   *[DAHN-yah]*

MEANING: God is my judge • USAGE: Jewish
feminine form of Daniel (*see* Danielle)
> *Execute the judgment of truth and peace.*
> — Zechariah 8:16b (MT)

DAPHNE   *[DAHF-nee (Greek),
DAF-nee (English)]*

MEANING: laurel tree, bay tree, daphne flower •
USAGE: Greek and English: from Greek *daphne*
(laurel or bay tree); type of flower
> *The flowers appear on the earth.
> The time of the singing has come.*
> — Song of Songs 2:12a (WEB)

DARA   *[DAH-rah]*

MEANING: good • USAGE: African: Yoruba of
Nigeria
> *Do good and your reward will be with God.*
> — Nigerian proverb

DARA   *[DAH-rah]*

MEANING: oak tree • USAGE: Irish: from Gaelic
dair
> *Beloved, gaze in thine own heart, /
> The holy tree is growing there.*
> — William Butler Yeats, "The Two Trees"

DARCY, DARCIE   *[DAR-see]*

MEANING: dark-haired, woman of Arcy, bear
village • USAGE: Irish and English surname: from
Gaelic *dorchaidhe* (dark-haired); or English form
of French surname *D'Arcy* (Arcy, France), from
French *ars* (bear) and *acum* (village, settlement)
> *You are a worthy woman.*
> — Ruth 3:11b (ESV)

DARIA   *[DAH-ree-ah]*

MEANING: to possess good, possesses a lot,
wealthy • USAGE: Italian feminine form of Dario,
from Persian *daraya* (to possess) and *vahu* (good)
> *Blessed be your good sense, and blessed be you.*
> — 1 Samuel 25:33a (NRSV)

DARICE   *[dah-REES]*

MEANING: to possess good, possesses a lot,
wealthy • USAGE: Greek feminine form of Darius
(*see* Daria)
> *Do good of thine own accord,
> and thou wilt be loved like the Sun.*
> — Epictetus

D

DARLA   [DAR-lah]

MEANING: beloved, dearly loved • USAGE:
English: from English *dereling*
> *Beloved, I pray that you may prosper in all things*
> *and be healthy, even as your soul prospers.*
> — 3 John 1:2 (WEB)

DARLENA   [dar-LAY-nah]

MEANING: little beloved one, little darling •
USAGE: American form of Darlene and diminutive
-*ena* (*see* Darlene)
> *My darling, you are lovely in every way.*
> — Song of Songs 4:7 (CEV)

DARLENE, DARLEEN   [DAR-leen]

MEANING: little beloved one, darling • USAGE:
English: from English *dereling* and diminutive -*een*
> *Beloved, let us love one another,*
> *for love is from God, and whoever loves*
> *has been born of God and knows God.*
> — 1 John 4:7 (ESV)

DARNELLA, DARNELA   [dar-NEL-ah]

MEANING: hidden nook, secret place • USAGE:
American feminine form of Darnell, from English
derne (hidden, secret) and *halh* (nook, alcove)
> *Thou dost desire truth in the innermost being, and in*
> *the hidden part Thou wilt make me know wisdom.*
> — Psalm 51:6 (NASB)

DARRAN   [DAHR-ahn]

MEANING: little oak tree, fruitful, bountiful •
USAGE: Irish: from Gaelic *dair* (oak tree) and
diminutive -*an*; or from Gaelic *dáir* (fruitful,
bountiful)
> *The Lord will open the heavens, the storehouse of his*
> *bounty...to bless all the work of your hands.*
> — Deuteronomy 28:12a (NIV)

DARSHA   [DAR-shah]

MEANING: vision, the vision of God • USAGE:
Hindu: from Sanskrit *darsha* (to see, to perceive)
> *We should develop a habit of visualizing unity in*
> *diversity and not diversity in the unity that is Divine.*
> *God is everywhere and in everyone.*
> *The whole universe is inhabited by Him.*
> *One should find God in every object.*
> — Sathya Sai Baba, *Sathya Sai Baba Speaks*

DARYA   [DAR-yah]

MEANING: to possess good, possesses a lot,
wealthy • USAGE: Russian form of Daria, from
Persian *daraya* (to possess) and *vahu* (good)
> *A good person produces good things*
> *from the treasury of a good heart.*
> — Luke 6:45 (NLT)

DARYL   [DAYR-el]

MEANING: woman of Airelle, open space •
USAGE: English form of French surname *D'Airelle*
(of Airelle, France), from French *arealis* (open
space, threshing floor)
> *You are a good woman.*
> — Ruth 3:11b (NLV)

DASI   [DAH-see]

MEANING: myrtle tree • USAGE: Jewish form of
Hadassah
> *Instead of a nettle, a myrtle shall rise;*
> *these shall stand as a testimony to the Lord,*
> *as an everlasting sign that shall not perish.*
> — Isaiah 55:13b (JPS)

DATYA, DATIA   [DAHT-yah]

MEANING: faith in God, law of God • USAGE:
Jewish
> *The law of the Lord is perfect, restoring the soul; the*
> *testimony of the Lord is sure, making wise the simple.*
> — Psalm 19:8 (MT)

D

DAVETTE [dah-VET]

MEANING: little beloved one • **USAGE:** American feminine form of David and diminutive -ette (*see* Davida)

For certainly there cannot be a higher pleasure
than to think that we love and are beloved
by the most amiable and best Being.
— Mary Astell

DAVIDA [dah-VEE-dah (Jewish, English), dah-BEE-dah (Spanish)]

MEANING: beloved, loved • **USAGE:** Jewish, English, and Spanish feminine form of David, from *dawidh*

Thou has created me not from necessity but from grace. /
And not by compulsion of circumstance /
But by favour and love.
— Solomon ibn Gabirol, "The Royal Crown"

DAVINA [dah-VEE-nah]

MEANING: beloved, loved • **USAGE:** Scottish and English feminine form of David (*see* Davida)

Beloved, if thus did God love us, we also ought one
another to love; God no one hath ever seen;
if we may love one another, God in us doth remain,
and His love is having been perfected in us.
— 1 John 4:11–12 (YLT)

DAVITA [dah-VEE-tah]

MEANING: little beloved one • **USAGE:** American feminine form of David and diminutive -ita (*see* Davida)

It is my prayer that your love abound more and more,
with knowledge and all discernment.
— Philippians 1:9 (ESV)

DAVONA [dah-VOHN-ah]

MEANING: beloved, loved • **USAGE:** American feminine form of David (*see* Davida)

Love can be its own reward.
— Arnold Lobel, "The Ostrich in Love"

DAWN [dahn]

MEANING: sunrise, dawn, daybreak • **USAGE:** English: from English *dauninge*

Who is this that appears like the dawn,
fair as the moon, bright as the sun,
majestic as the stars in procession?
— Song of Songs 6:10 (RSV)

DAYA [dah-yah]

MEANING: mercy, compassion • **USAGE:** Hindu: Sanskrit

Only the intelligence of love and compassion
can solve all problems of life.
— Jiddu Krishnamurti
(journal entry of April 26, 1983)

DAYO [DAH-yoh]

MEANING: joy arrives • **USAGE:** African: Yoruba of Nigeria

A smiling face removes unhappiness.
— Nigerian proverb

DEANA, DEANNA [dee-AN-ah]

MEANING: divine, the shining one, dean, presiding official, valley • **USAGE:** English form of Diana, from Diviana (the shining one) and Latin *dyeu* (to shine); or feminine form of Dean, from English *deen* (dean, presiding official) or *denu* (valley)

Divine love is noble and generous.
— Thomas à Kempis, *The Imitation of Christ*

DEANNE [dee-AN]

MEANING: divine, the shining one, dean, presiding official, valley • **USAGE:** English form of Diana (*see* Deana)

Divine Love always has met
and always will meet every human need.
— Mary Baker Eddy, *Science and Health*

D

DEB   [deb]

MEANING: bee • **USAGE:** English form of
Deborah (*see* Deborah)
Honey be in my mouth, / Affection be in my face.
— Alexander Carmichael, *Carmina Gadelica*

DEBORA, DÉBORA   [DAY-boh-rah]

MEANING: bee • **USAGE:** Italian, German, and
Spanish form of Deborah (*see* Deborah)
The bee is little among such as fly;
but her fruit is the chief of sweet things.
— Ben Sira 11:3 (KJV Apocrypha)

DEBORAH   [DEB-oh-rah]

MEANING: bee • **USAGE:** English form of
Devorah, from Hebrew *devorah*
Hope is the only bee that makes honey without flowers.
— Robert Green Ingersoll

DEBRA   [DEB-rah]

MEANING: bee • **USAGE:** English form of
Deborah (*see* Deborah)
Books are the bees which carry
the quickening pollen from one to another mind.
— James Russell Lowell,
"Nationality in Literature"

DEE   [dee]

MEANING: divine, the shining one, gift of God,
judge, vindicate • **USAGE:** English form of Diana
(*see* Deana); or English form of Deena (*see* Deena)
My appointed work is to awaken
the divine nature that is within.
— Peace Pilgrim, *Peace Pilgrim*

DEENA   [DEE-nah]

MEANING: judge, vindicate • **USAGE:** American
form of Dina, from Hebrew *dinah*

Don't judge each day by the harvest
you reap but by the seeds that you plant.
— Robert Louis Stevenson

DEIDRA   [DEE-drah]

MEANING: end • **USAGE:** English form of Deirdra
(*see* Deirdra)
The end crowneth the work.
— Queen Elizabeth I,
letter to Sir Edward Stafford, 1581

DEIRDRA, DEIRDRE   [DEER-drah]

MEANING: end • **USAGE:** Irish: possibly from
Gaelic *deireadh*
Happiness is not the end of life; character is.
— Henry Ward Beecher

DELANEY   [deh-LAY-nee]

MEANING: dark-haired challenger, trained warrior,
soldier • **USAGE:** Irish and English form of Irish
surname *O'Dubhshlaine*, from Gaelic *dubh* (dark,
black) and *slán* (challenge); or from Gaelic *deagh-
laoch* (trained warrior)
Train me, God, to walk straight.
— Psalm 86:11a (MSG)

DELIA   [DEEL-yah]

MEANING: heart of Delos • **USAGE:** English
form of Cordelia, from *King Lear* by William
Shakespeare, possibly from Latin *cor* (heart) and
Delia (Greek island of Delos)
Of all earthly music, that which reaches the farthest
into heaven is the beating of a loving heart.
— Henry Ward Beecher

DELICE   [deh-LEES]

MEANING: delightful, pleasant • **USAGE:** English
form of *Delicia*, from Latin *deliciae*
How beautiful and how delightful you are.
— Song of Songs 7:6a (NASB)

D

DELILAH, DELILA [deh-LIE-lah]

MEANING: delicate, cord, thread, hair • **USAGE:** Jewish

> *True strength is delicate.*
> — Louise Nevelson

DELLA [DEL-ah]

MEANING: noble one, highborn, honorable, dale, valley • **USAGE:** English form of Adela or Adelaide, from German *adal* (noble) and *heid* (sort, type); or from English *dæl* (dale, valley)

> *The beginning of wisdom is: Get wisdom!*
> *And with all you have gotten, get understanding.*
> *Honor her and she will honor you.*
> *She will honor you if you hold her to your heart.*
> — Proverbs 4:7–8 (NLV)

DELORA [deh-LOR-ah]

MEANING: lady of sorrows, Virgin Mary's sorrows • **USAGE:** English form of Deloros (*see* Delores)

> *Only in the peace and bliss of Truth*
> *is all sorrow vanquished.*
> — James Allen, *From Poverty to Power*

DELORES [deh-LOR-is]

MEANING: lady of sorrows, Virgin Mary's sorrows • **USAGE:** English form of Dolores, from Spanish *dolores* (sorrows), reference to the Virgin Mary's seven sorrows

> *Love comforteth like sunshine after rain.*
> — William Shakespeare, *Venus and Adonis*

DELORIA [deh-LOR-ee-ah]

MEANING: lady of sorrows, Virgin Mary's sorrows • **USAGE:** American form of Delores (*see* Delores)

> *You are with me; Your rod and Your staff,*
> *they comfort me.*
> — Psalm 23:4b (NKJV)

DELPHIA [del-FEE-ah]

MEANING: love for humankind, brotherly love • **USAGE:** English form of Philadelphia, from Greek *phileo* (to love) and *adelphos* (brother)

> *May the Lord make your love grow.*
> — 1 Thessalonians 3:12a (NIRV)

DELPHINA [del-FEE-nah]

MEANING: dolphin, woman from Delphi, delphinium flower • **USAGE:** English: from Greek *delphin* (a dolphin); from Greek *Delphi* (Greek city); also from the delphinium flower

> *Venus among the fishes skips and is a she-dolphin /*
> *she is the gay, delighted porpoise sporting*
> *with love and the sea.*
> — D. H. Lawrence, "Whales Weep Not!"

DELTA [DEL-tah]

MEANING: river mouth, four, door, doorway, triangle • **USAGE:** American: from Greek *delta* (the mouth of a river) or fourth letter in Greek alphabet; also from Hebrew *dalet* (door), the fourth letter of Hebrew alphabet

> *There is no power on earth that*
> *can hold back the river from the ocean.*
> — Henry Ward Beecher, *Life Thoughts*

DELWYN [DEL-wen]

MEANING: beautiful and fair • **USAGE:** Welsh: from Welsh *del* (beautiful) and *gwyn* (white, fair, holy)

> *What's true beauty but fair virtue's face? /*
> *Virtue made visible in outward grace.*
> — Edward Young, "Love of Fame"

DELYTH [DEL-ith]

MEANING: beautiful, pretty, lovely • **USAGE:** Welsh: from Welsh *del*

> *You are lovely, so very lovely.*
> — Song of Songs 4:1a (CEV)

D

DEMETRIA   *[day-MAY-tree-ah]*

MEANING: mother earth, earth lover, earthy •
USAGE: Italian and Spanish form of *Demeter,* from
Greek *Da-mater* (mother earth); Greek goddess of
agriculture and harvest

> *Truth springs up from the earth.*
> — Psalm 85:11a (NLT)

DEMI   *[DEM-ee]*

MEANING: mother earth, earth lover, earthy •
USAGE: English form of *Demeter,* from Greek
Da-mater (mother earth); Greek goddess of
agriculture and harvest

> *Speak to the earth, and it will teach you.*
> — Job 12:8a (NCV)

DENICE   *[deh-NEES]*

MEANING: celebrant, reveler, follower of
Dionysus • **USAGE:** English form of Denise (*see*
Denise)

> *Life is a festival only to the wise.*
> — Ralph Waldo Emerson, "Heroism"

DENISE   *[deh-NEEZ (French),*
deh-NEES (English)]

MEANING: celebrant, reveler, follower of
Dionysus • **USAGE:** French and English feminine
form of Dennis, from *Dionysus,* Greek god of wine
and revelry

> *My heart is glad and my spirit rejoices.*
> — Psalm 16:9a (HCSB)

DERRYTH   *[DEHR-ith]*

MEANING: of the oak tree • **USAGE:** Welsh: from
Gaelic *derw* (oaken)

> *Happy are those who find wisdom, and those who get*
> *understanding.... She is a tree of life to those who lay*
> *hold of her; those who hold her fast are called happy.*
> — Proverbs 3:13, 3:18 (GNT)

DÉSIRÉE, DESIREE   *[deh-ʒih-RAY]*

MEANING: desirable, delightful, loved • **USAGE:**
French and American: from Latin *desiderata*

> *Oh, how beautiful you are!*
> *How pleasing, my love, how full of delights!*
> — Song of Songs 7:6 (YLT)

DESSA   *[DES-ah]*

MEANING: foreigner, traveler, sojourner, explorer
• **USAGE:** American feminine form of *Odysseus,*
from Greek *odysseus* (wandering)

> *The Lord...will send his angel with you.*
> *He will make your journey a success.*
> — Genesis 24:40a (NEB)

DESTINA   *[day-STEE-nah]*

MEANING: destiny, fate • **USAGE:** Spanish: from
Spanish *destino*

> *Love is our true destiny.*
> — Thomas Merton

DESTINY   *[DES-tih-nee]*

MEANING: destiny, fate • **USAGE:** English: from
French *destinée*

> *Destiny is not a matter of chance, it is a matter*
> *of choice; it is not a thing to be waited for,*
> *it is a thing to be achieved.*
> — William Jennings Bryan, *Republic or Empire?*

DEVIKA   *[deh-vee-kah]*

MEANING: divine • **USAGE:** Hindu: from Sanskrit
deva

> *Where love is, there God is also.*
> — Mahatma Gandhi

DEVIN, DEVAN   *[DEV-an]*

MEANING: poet, gift, courageous, fearless •
USAGE: Irish and English: from Gaelic *dámh*
(poet), *dán* (gift), or *dána* (intrepid, courageous)

A poem begins in delight and ends in wisdom.
— Robert Frost

DEVORA, DEVORAH [deh-VOR-ah]

MEANING: bee • USAGE: Jewish: from Hebrew *devorah*

> *Eat thou honey, for it is good,*
> *and the honeycomb is sweet to thy taste;*
> *so know thou wisdom to be unto thy soul;*
> *if thou hast found it, then shall there be a future,*
> *and thy hope shall not be cut off.*
> — Proverbs 24:13–14 (MT)

DHARMINI [dahr-mee-nee]

MEANING: virtuous, pure • USAGE: Hindu: Sanskrit

> *Speak or act with a pure mind / and happiness will*
> *follow you / as your shadow, unshakable.*
> — Buddha, *The Dhammapada* (tr. Thomas Byrom)

DIAMANTE [dee-ah-MAHN-teh]

MEANING: diamond, beautiful gem • USAGE: Italian: from Latin *diamantem* (metal, diamond)

> *You are altogether beautiful, my love;*
> *there is no flaw in you.*
> — Song of Songs 4:7 (NRSV)

DIANA [die-AN-ah (English), dee-AH-nah (Italian, Russian, Spanish)]

MEANING: divine, the shining one, goddess of the moon, goddess of the hunt • USAGE: English, Italian, Russian, and Spanish form of Diviana (the shining one), from Latin *divus* (divine); Roman goddess of the moon and hunting

> *Who is she that looketh forth as the morning,*
> *fair as the moon, clear as the sun?*
> — Song of Songs 6:10a (ASV)

DIANDRE, DIANDRA [die-AN-drah, dee-AN-drah]

MEANING: divine, the shining one • USAGE: American: possibly a form of Diana, from Diviana (the shining one) and Latin *divus* (divine)

> *The spark divine dwells in thee: let it grow.*
> — Ella Wheeler Wilcox, "Resolve!"

DIANE [dee-AHN (French), die-AN (English)]

MEANING: divine, the shining one • USAGE: French and English form of Diana (*see* Diana)

> *Love partakes of the soul, being of the same nature.*
> *Like the soul, it is a divine spark.*
> — Victor Hugo, *Les Misérables*
> (tr. M. Edouard Jolivet)

DIANTHE [dee-AHN-thah]

MEANING: divine flower • USAGE: Greek and English: from Greek *dios* (divine, God) and *anthos* (a flower)

> *Look how the wild flowers grow.*
> *They don't work hard to make their clothes.*
> *But I tell you that Solomon with all his wealth wasn't*
> *as well clothed as one of them.*
> — Matthew 6:28b–29 (CEV)

DIDI, DEE DEE [dee-dee]

MEANING: divine, the shining one, dean, presiding official, valley • USAGE: English form of Diana (*see* Diana); English form of Dorothy, from Greek *doron* (gift) and *theos* (God); or English form of Deena (*see* Dinah)

> *To the divinely wise,*
> *knowledge and Love*
> *are one and inseparable.*
> — James Allen, *From Poverty to Power*

D

D

DIL   [deel]

MEANING: heart • USAGE: Persian
> I looked for Thee in heaven, my Beloved,
> my Pearl, but at last I have found Thee
> hidden in the shell of my heart.
> — Hazrat Inayat Khan, *The Gayan*

DILWYN   [DIL-wen]

MEANING: genuine and holy • USAGE: Welsh:
from Welsh *dilys* and *gwen* (white, fair, holy)
> True holiness consists in doing God's holy will
> with a smile. — Mother Teresa

DILYS   [DIL-es]

MEANING: genuine, true • USAGE: Welsh: from
Welsh *dilys*
> Our love should not be just words and talk;
> it must be true love, which shows itself in action.
> — 1 John 3:18 (GNT)

DIMA   [dee-mah]

MEANING: gentle rain • USAGE: Muslim: from
Arabic *dima* (rain without thunder or lightning)
> A promise is a cloud; fulfillment is rain.
> — Arabic proverb

DIMITRA   [deh-MEE-trah]

MEANING: mother earth, earth lover, earthy •
USAGE: Greek form of *Demeter*, from Greek
Da-mater (mother earth); Greek goddess of
agriculture and harvest
> As for you, be fruitful and multiply;
> bring forth abundantly in the earth.
> — Genesis 9:7a (NKJV)

DINA   [DEE-nah]

MEANING: nice shelter place, haven • USAGE:
African: Mashona of Zimbabwe
> O God, we beseech Thee to bless our native land; /
> The land of our fathers bestowed upon us all; / From
> Zambesi to Limpopo, / May leaders be exemplary; /
> And may the Almighty protect and bless our land.
> — Zimbabwe National Anthem

DINA   [DEE-nah]

MEANING: judge, vindicate • USAGE: English
form of Dinah, from Hebrew *dinah*
> Love justice, you that are the judges of the earth.
> Think of the Lord in goodness,
> and seek him in simplicity of heart.
> — Wisdom of Solomon 1:1 (DR Apocrypha)

DINAH   [DEE-nah (Jewish), DIE-nah (English)]

MEANING: judge, vindicate • USAGE: Jewish and
English: from Hebrew *dinah*
> It shall go well with them who decide justly;
> blessings of good things will light upon them.
> — Proverbs 24:25 (JPS)

DIONE, DIONNE   [dee-OHN]

MEANING: celebrant, reveler, follower of
Dionysus • USAGE: Greek and English feminine
form of Dion (*see* Dionisia)
> I know the best thing we can do is to always enjoy life,
> because God's gift to us is the happiness we get from
> our food and drink and from the work we do.
> — Ecclesiastes 3:12–13 (CEV)

DIONISIA   [dee-oh-NEE-see-ah]

MEANING: celebrant, reveler, follower of
Dionysus • USAGE: Spanish and Italian feminine
form of Dionisio, a form of Dionysus, Greek god of
wine and revelry
> The best thing we can do is to enjoy eating, drinking,
> and working. I believe these are God's gifts to us.
> — Ecclesiastes 2:24 (CEV)

DISA   *[DEE-sah]*

MEANING: goddess, divine • USAGE: Scandinavian: from Norse *dis*

> *All the blessings we enjoy are Divine deposits, committed to our trust on this condition, that they should be dispensed for the benefit of our neighbors.*
> — John Calvin

DIVIANA   *[dee-vee-AH-nah]*

MEANING: the shining one, divine • USAGE: Italian: from Latin *Diviana* (the shining one), from Latin *divus* (divine)

> *You are the light of the world.*
> — Matthew 5:14 (HCSB)

DIVINA   *[dee-VEE-nah]*

MEANING: divine, goddess-like • USAGE: English (*see* Diviana)

> *A good conscience is the best divinity.*
> — Thomas Fuller, *Gnomologia*

DIXIE, DIXEE   *[DIK-see]*

MEANING: ten, tenth, southerner • USAGE: American: from French *dix* (ten); reference to the Confederate states during US Civil War

> *My strength is as the strength of ten, because my heart is pure.*
> — Alfred Tennyson, "Sir Galahad"

DOBRILA   *[doh-BREE-lah]*

MEANING: good, kind, compassionate • USAGE: Czech: from Slavic *dobro*

> *He [God] crowns you with faithful love and compassion.*
> — Psalm 103:4 (HCSB)

DOLI   *[doh-lee]*

MEANING: bluebird • USAGE: Amerind: Navajo
> *Swift and far I journey, / Swift upon the rainbow.*
> — Navajo song

DOLLIE, DOLLY   *[DOL-ee]*

MEANING: lady of sorrows, Virgin Mary's sorrows • USAGE: English form of Dolores (*see* Dolores)

> *There is a comfort in the strength of love.*
> — Henry Wadsworth Longfellow,
> "Michael Angelo"

DOLORES   *[doh-LOH-rehz (Spanish), deh-LOR-is (English)]*

MEANING: lady of sorrows, Virgin Mary's sorrows • USAGE: Spanish and English: from Spanish *dolores* (sorrows), reference to the Virgin Mary's seven sorrows

> *Love thine own soul, and comfort thy heart.*
> — Ben Sira 30:2a (KJV Apocrypha)

DOMENICA   *[doh-MEE-nee-kah]*

MEANING: belonging to God, belonging to the Lord • USAGE: Italian feminine form of Domenico, from Latin *Dominicus*

> *I still belong to You; you hold my right hand.*
> — Psalm 73:23 (NLT)

DOMINGA   *[doh-MEEN-gah]*

MEANING: belonging to God, belonging to the Lord • USAGE: Spanish feminine form of Domingo (*see* Domenica)

> *I have called you by your name; you are Mine.*
> — Isaiah 43:1 (HCSB)

DOMINIKA   *[doh-mee-NEE-kah]*

MEANING: belonging to God, belonging to the Lord • USAGE: Russian feminine form of Dominik (*see* Domenica)

> *God chose you to be his people. You are royal priests. You are a holy nation. You are a people who belong to God.*
> — 1 Peter 2:9a (NIRV)

D

DOMINIQUE   [doh-mih-NEEK]

MEANING: belonging to God, belonging to the Lord • **USAGE:** French form of Domenica (*see* Domenica)

The Lord...keeps safe the way
of those who belong to Him.
— Proverbs 2:6–8a (NLV)

DONALDA   [doh-NAHL-dah]

MEANING: ruler of the world, leader in the world • **USAGE:** Scottish feminine form of Donald, from Gaelic *dumnan* (world) and *val* (rule, ruler)

The wise leaders will shine
with all the brightness of the sky.
— Daniel 12:3a (GNT)

DONANNE   [don-AN]

MEANING: gracious world ruler, grace-filled leader • **USAGE:** English combination of Donna and Anne (*see* Donna and Anne)

Do you wish for kindness? Be kind. / Do you ask for
truth? Be true. / What you give of yourself you find; /
Your world is a reflex of you.
— James Allen, *From Poverty to Power*

DONATA   [doh-NAH-tah]

MEANING: gift • **USAGE:** Italian feminine form of Donato: from Latin *donatio*

Rekindle God's gift that you possess.
— 2 Timothy 1:6b (NEB)

DONATELLA   [doh-nah-TEH-lah]

MEANING: gift • **USAGE:** Italian feminine form of Donatello (*see* Donata)

Every generous act and every perfect gift is from above,
coming down from the Father of lights.
— James 1:17a (HCSB)

DONELLA   [doh-NEL-ah]

MEANING: ruler of the world, leader in the world • **USAGE:** Scottish feminine form of Donald (*see* Donalda)

Leaders will be those who empower others.
— Bill Gates

DONELLE   [don-EL]

MEANING: ruler of the world, leader in the world • **USAGE:** English feminine form of Donald (*see* Donalda)

The hand of the diligent will rule.
— Proverbs 12:24a (ESV)

DONETTE   [DON-et]

MEANING: ruler of the world, leader in the world • **USAGE:** American feminine form of Donald (*see* Donalda)

Leaders must invoke an alchemy of great vision.
— Henry Kissinger

DONIA, DONYA   [DON-yah]

MEANING: lady of nobility, world ruler, leader in the world • **USAGE:** American form of Donna (*see* Donna); or English feminine form of Donald (*see* Donalda)

Thoughtfulness for others, generosity,
modesty, and self-respect, are the qualities
which make a real gentleman, or lady.
— Thomas Henry Huxley
(address of October 9, 1871)

DONNA   [DON-ah]

MEANING: lady of nobility, world ruler, leader in the world • **USAGE:** English: from Latin *donna* (lady of nobility); or English feminine form of Donald (*see* Donalda)

Strength and dignity are her clothing.
— Proverbs 31:25a (NRSV)

DORA   [DOR-ah]

MEANING: gift • **USAGE:** English, Italian, and Spanish form of Dorothy, Theodora, or Isadora: from Greek *doron*

> God said...I will give you wisdom
> and understanding.
> — 1 Kings 3:11–12b (NCV)

DOREEN, DORENE, DORINE
[DOR-een]

MEANING: gift of God • **USAGE:** English form of Dorothy (*see* Dorothy)

> What we are is God's gift to us.
> What we become is our gift to God.
> — Eleanor Powell

DORETTA   [dor-ET-ah]

MEANING: gift of God • **USAGE:** English form of Dorothy (*see* Dorothy)

> Lord...how wonderful are your gifts to me;
> how good they are!
> — Psalm 16:5 (GNT)

DORI, DORIE   [DOR-ee]

MEANING: gift of God • **USAGE:** English form of Dorothy or Theodora (*see* Dorothy and Theodora)

> Great is the power of love; yea, an excellent gift it is.
> — Thomas à Kempis, *The Imitation of Christ*
> (tr. Harvey Goodwin)

DORINDA   [doh-RIN-dah]

MEANING: beautiful gift • **USAGE:** English combination of Dora and Linda (*see* Dora and Linda)

> Keep ablaze the gift of God.
> — 2 Timothy 1:6b (HCSB)

DORIS   [DOR-is]

MEANING: sea goddess, woman of Doria • **USAGE:** English: Greek sea goddess; Greek tribe in Doris region

> Doris, daughter of Ocean...
> passing lovely amongst goddesses.
> — Hesiod, *The Theogony*
> (tr. Hugh G. Evelyn-White)

DORITA   [doh-REE-tah]

MEANING: gift of God • **USAGE:** Spanish form of Dorotea (*see* Dorothy)

> May God give you more and more grace and peace.
> — 1 Peter 1:2b (NLT)

DORKAS, DORCAS   [DOR-kahs]

MEANING: gazelle, antelope, graceful, fleet-footed • **USAGE:** Greek: from Greek *dorkas*

> My beloved is like a gazelle.
> — Song of Songs 2:9a (NASB)

DORONA   [doh-ROH-nah]

MEANING: gift • **USAGE:** English: from Greek *doron*

> The only gift is a portion of thyself.
> — Ralph Waldo Emerson, "Gifts"

DOROTA   [DOH-roh-tah]

MEANING: gift of God • **USAGE:** Polish and Czech form of Dorothy (*see* Dorothy)

> Come, whoever is thirsty; accept the water of life as a gift, whoever wants it.
> — Revelation 22:17b (GNT)

DOROTEA   [dor-oh-TAY-ah]

MEANING: gift of God • **USAGE:** Spanish and Italian form of Dorothea (*see* Dorothy)

> Every good thing bestowed and every perfect gift is from above, coming down from the Father of lights.
> — James 1:17a (NASB)

D

DOROTHEA   *[dor-oh-THEH-ah (Greek, English), dor-oh-THEE-ah (English), dohr-oh-TEH-ah (German)]*

MEANING: gift of God • USAGE: Greek, English, and German (*see* Dorothy)

Virtue comes to the virtuous by the gift of God.
— Plato, *Meno* (tr. Benjamin Jowett)

DOROTHY   *[DOR-oh-thee, DOR-thee]*

MEANING: gift of God • USAGE: English form of Dorothea, from Greek *doron* (gift) and *theos* (God)

God bless you and keep you.
God smile on you and gift you.
God look you full in the face and make you prosper.
— Numbers 6:26 (MSG)

DOVE   *[duv]*

MEANING: dove, dove-like • USAGE: English: from Dutch *duve*

And the dove came in to him in the evening, and behold, in her mouth was a freshly plucked olive leaf. So Noah knew that the waters had subsided from the earth.
— Genesis 8:11 (ESV)

DOVIE, DOVEY   *[DUV-ee]*

MEANING: dove, dove-like • USAGE: English form of Dove (*see* Dove)

The Dove, on silver pinions, winged her peaceful way.
— James Montgomery, "The Pelican Island"

DOVINA   *[doh-VEEN-ah]*

MEANING: little dove, dove-like • USAGE: American form of Dove and diminutive *-ina* (*see* Dove)

You're so beautiful!
And your eyes so beautiful — like doves!
— Song of Songs 1:15a (MSG)

DREA   *[dray]*

MEANING: man, courageous, strong • USAGE: English form of Andrea, from Greek *andros* (man) or *andreios* (manly)

A mode of conduct, a standard of courage, discipline, fortitude and integrity can do a great deal to make a woman beautiful.
— Jacqueline Bisset

DREW   *[droo]*

MEANING: man, courageous, strong • USAGE: courageous, strong English feminine form of Andrew (*see* Drea)

The ideals which have lighted my way and time after time given me new courage to face life cheerfully, have been Truth, Goodness, and Beauty.
— Albert Einstein, "The World as I See It"

DREY, DRAY   *[dray]*

MEANING: noble strength, valorous and mighty • USAGE: American form of Audrey, from English *æthel* (noble, valorous) and *thryth* (might, strength)

In the end, through the long ages of our quest for light, it will be found that truth is still mightier than the sword.
— Douglas MacArthur

DRUSILLA   *[droo-SIL-ah]*

MEANING: strong, mighty, powerful • USAGE: English feminine form of Roman family name *Drusus*, from Celtic for "strong"

Strength and dignity [are] her clothing.
— Proverbs 31:25a (YLT)

DUANA   *[doo-AH-nah]*

MEANING: dark, black, dark-haired • USAGE: Irish and English feminine form of Duane, from Gaelic *dubh*

*Thus says the Lord...I will give you the treasures of
darkness and hidden wealth of secret places.*
— Isaiah 45:1–3a (NASB)

DULCIA [dool-CHEE-ah]

MEANING: sweet one, pleasant • **USAGE:** Italian:
from Latin *dulcis*

Pleasant words — like music — are the food of love.
— Ovid

DULCIE [DUL-see]

MEANING: sweet one, pleasant • **USAGE:** English
form of Dulcia (*see* Dulcia)

All healthy things are sweet-tempered.
— Ralph Waldo Emerson,
"Considerations by the Way"

DULCINEA [dool-say-NAY-ah]

MEANING: sweet one, pleasant • **USAGE:** Spanish
form of Dulcie (*see* Dulcia)

She speaks wise words and teaches others to be kind.
— Proverbs 31:26 (NCV)

DUSANA [doo-SHAH-nah]

MEANING: spirit, soul • **USAGE:** Czech: from
Slavic *dusa*

*It is therefore true, indeed, that the soul unites herself
with God by the affection of love.*
— Catherine of Siena (tr. Algar Thorold)

DUSCHA [DYOO-shah]

MEANING: happy, joyous, cheerful • **USAGE:**
Russian

You will be happy, and it will go well for you.
— Psalm 128:2 (HCSB)

DVORAH, DVORA [DVOR-rah, dvoh-RAH]

MEANING: bee • **USAGE:** Jewish: from Hebrew
devorah

*The bee is small among flying things,
but her fruit hath the chiefest sweetness.*
— Sirach 11:3 Apocrypha (DR Apocrypha)

DYAN [die-AN]

MEANING: divine, the shining one • **USAGE:**
English form of Diane, from *Diviana* (the shining
one) and Latin *divus* (divine)

*Like goodness and beauty,
wisdom is one of the absolute values,
the divine ideas.*
— William Ralph Inge, "The Training of Reason"

DYLAN [DIL-ehn]

MEANING: great ocean, of the sea • **USAGE:** Welsh
and English: from Welsh *dy* (great, large) and *llanw*
(sea, ocean); Welsh god of the sea

*Deep peace of the running wave to you...
Deep peace, deep peace!*
— Fiona MacLeod, "Invocation of Peace"

DZIKO [ZEE-koh]

MEANING: world • **USAGE:** African: Nguni of
South Africa

*Education is the most powerful weapon
which you can use to change the world.*
— Nelson Mandela

D

E

EARLEEN, EARLENE, EARLINE [er-LEEN]

MEANING: noblewoman, warrior • USAGE:
English feminine form of Earl, from English *eorl*
They are never alone that are accompanied
with noble thoughts.
— Philip Sidney,
The Countess of Pembroke's Arcadia

EARTHA [ER-thah]

MEANING: earth, earthy • USAGE: English: from
English *eorthe*
The earth is…mother of all that is natural,
mother of all that is human. She is the mother of all,
for contained in her are the seeds of all.
— Hildegard of Bingen

EASTON [EES-ton]

MEANING: eastern town • USAGE: English
surname: from English *east* (east) and *tun* (town,
settlement)
The Lord God planted a garden in the east.
— Genesis 2:8a (NCV)

EBBA, EBBE [EH-bah]

MEANING: strong as a wild boar, stouthearted •
USAGE: German and Scandinavian feminine form
of *Eberhart*, from German *ebur* (wild boar) and *hart*
(hardy, strong, brave)
Be strong and of good courage…for the Lord thy God,
he it is that doth go with thee; he will not fail thee,
nor forsake thee.
— Deuteronomy 31:6 (KJV)

EBONY, EBONIE [EB-oh-nee]

MEANING: ebony tree, valuable black wood, black
color • USAGE: English: from Greek *ebenos* and
Egyptian *hbny* (ebony tree, valuable black wood,
black color)
I fell in love with black; it contained all color.
— Louise Nevelson

EBUN [eh-BOON]

MEANING: gift • USAGE: African: Yoruba of
Nigeria
What you give you get, ten times over.
— Yoruban proverb

ECHO [EK-oh]

MEANING: echo • USAGE: Greek: from Greek
echo (to echo)
Let me hear your voice; for your voice is sweet.
— Song of Songs 2:14b (RSV)

EDANA [eh-DAH-nah]

MEANING: kernel, fire, little fiery one • USAGE:
Irish: from Gaelic *eithne* (kernel); or Irish feminine
form of Aidan, from *aodh* (fire) and diminutive *-an*
Bless the Lord, O my soul!…He makes
his messengers winds, his ministers a flaming fire.
— Psalm 104:1–4 (ESV)

EDDA [EH-dah]

MEANING: warrior • USAGE: Italian form of
Hedda, from German *hedwig* (battle, war)
Be strong and courageous.
— Joshua 1:6a (NLT)

EDDIE, EDDY [ED-ee]

MEANING: wealthy friend, prosperous friendship,
rich in friendship • USAGE: English form of
Edwina (*see* Edwina)
Treat wisdom as your sister,
and insight as your closest friend.
— Proverbs 7:4 (GNT)

E

EDEN [EH-den, EE-den]

MEANING: delight, delightful, pleasant • **USAGE:** Jewish: from Hebrew *edhen*

The lines are fallen unto me in pleasant places;
yea, I have a goodly heritage.
— Psalm 16:6 (MT)

EDIE [EE-dee]

MEANING: wealthy friend, prosperous friendship, rich in friendship • **USAGE:** English form of Edwina (*see* Edwina)

The Lord will grant you abundant prosperity.
— Deuteronomy 28:11a (NIV)

EDINA [eh-DEE-nah]

MEANING: wealthy friend, prosperous friendship, rich in friendship • **USAGE:** English form of Edwina, from English *ead* (wealth, prosperity) and *wine* (friend)

Be true to your word and your work and your friend.
— John Boyle O'Reilly

EDITH [EE-dith]

MEANING: prosperous in war • **USAGE:** English, German, and Scandinavian: from English *ead* (wealth, prosperity) and *gyth* (war, strife)

Wealth does not bring goodness,
but goodness brings wealth and every other blessing.
— Plato, *The Last Days of Socrates*

EDNA [ED-nah]

MEANING: kernel, fire, fiery • **USAGE:** English and Irish: from Gaelic *eithne* (kernel) or from Gaelic *aodh* (fire)

True love is a durable fire / In the mind ever burning.
— Sir Walter Raleigh,
"As You Came from the Holy Land"

EDNAH [ehd-NAH]

MEANING: delight, delightful • **USAGE:** Jewish: from Hebrew *ednah*

How fair and how pleasant art thou,
O love, for delights!
— Song of Songs 7:7 (MT)

EDUARDA [eh-doo-AHR-dah]

MEANING: wealthy guardian, protector of that which is valuable • **USAGE:** Portuguese feminine form of Eduardo, from English *ead* (wealth, prosperity) and *weard* (guardian, protector)

Discretion shall keep thee, understanding
shall preserve thee. — Proverbs 2:11 (DT)

EDWINA, EDWENA [ed-WEE-nah, ed-WEN-ah]

MEANING: wealthy friend, prosperous friendship, rich in friendship • **USAGE:** English feminine form of Edwin, from English *ead* (wealth, prosperity) and *wine* (friend)

Blessed are they who have the gift of making friends,
for it is one of God's best gifts. It involves many things,
but above all, the power of going out of one's self, and
appreciating whatever is noble and loving in another.
— Thomas Hughes

EFFIE [EF-ee]

MEANING: fair of voice, well-spoken • **USAGE:** English form of Euphemia, from *eu* (good, well) and *pheme* (voice)

How sweetly sounds the voice of a good woman!
— Philip Massinger, *The Old Law*

EFIMIA [eh-fee-MEE-ah]

MEANING: good reputation, good name • **USAGE:** Greek: from Greek *ef* (good) and *fimi* (reputation)

A good name is to be chosen rather than great wealth,
good favor more than silver or gold.
— Proverbs 22:1 (NEB)

E

EFRATA
[eh-FRAH-tah]

MEANING: fruitful, doubly fruitful, abundant, bountiful • **USAGE:** Jewish feminine form of Efrayim, from Hebrew *epharyim*, a derivative of *parah* (was fruitful)

> *The Lord will give you abounding prosperity.*
> — Deuteronomy 28:11a (JPS)

EILA, EILAH
[eh-LAH]

MEANING: oak tree, terebinth tree • **USAGE:** Jewish

> *They might be called terebinths of righteousness,*
> *the planting of the Lord, wherein He might glory.*
> — Isaiah 61:3b (MT)

EILEEN
[IE-leen]

MEANING: light, illumination, torch, radiant face • **USAGE:** English and Irish form of Helen, from Greek *helene* (torch) or *ele* (light); or English form of *Eibhlín*, from Irish Gaelic *aoibhinn* (radiant, cheerful face)

> *Most radiant, exquisite, and unmatchable beauty.*
> — William Shakespeare, *Twelfth Night*

EILIS
[IE-les]

MEANING: God is my oath, joined with God, blessed by God • **USAGE:** Irish form of Elizabeth, from Hebrew *el'ishebha*

> *God can bless you with everything you need,*
> *and you will always have more than enough*
> *to do all kinds of good things for others.*
> — 2 Corinthians 9:8 (CEV)

EILONA
[eh-LOH-nah]

MEANING: oak tree, terebinth tree • **USAGE:** Jewish feminine form of Elon

> *The fruit of the righteous is a tree of life.*
> — Proverbs 11:30a (JPS)

EINYA
[ehn-YAH]

MEANING: eye of God • **USAGE:** Jewish

> *The eyes are the mirror of the soul.*
> — Yiddish proverb

EIRA
[IE-rah]

MEANING: snow, physician, healer • **USAGE:** Welsh: from Welsh *eira* (snow); Norse goddess of medicine

> *There is nothing in the world more beautiful*
> *than the forest clothed to its very hollows in snow.*
> *It is the still ecstasy of nature, wherein every spray,*
> *every blade of grass, every spire of reed,*
> *every intricacy of twig, is clad with radiance.*
> — Fiona MacLeod, "Where the Forest Murmurs"

EIRINI
[ee-REE-nee]

MEANING: peace, peaceful, calm, serene • **USAGE:** Greek: from Greek *eirene*

> *May more and more grace and peace be given to you.*
> — 1 Peter 1:2b (NIRV)

EIRWEN
[EHR-wen]

MEANING: white snow, white as snow • **USAGE:** Welsh: from Welsh *eira* (snow) and *gwyn* (white, fair, holy)

> *Snow is exhilarating.*
> — Sir John Lubbock, *The Use of Life*

EITHNE
[ETH-neh]

MEANING: kernel, fire, fiery • **USAGE:** Irish: from Gaelic *eithne* (kernel) or *aodh* (fire)

> *There is in every true woman's heart*
> *a spark of heavenly fire.*
> — Washington Irving,
> *The Sketch-Book of Geoffrey Crayon*

EKATA   *[eh-kah-tah]*

Meaning: oneness, unity • **Usage:** Hindu: Sanskrit

> *I believe in the absolute oneness of God*
> *and therefore also of humanity. What though we have*
> *many bodies, we have but one soul.*
> — Mahatma Gandhi

EKATERINA   *[yeh-ka-teh-REE-nah]*

Meaning: pure one, unblemished, innocent, virtuous • **Usage:** Russian form of Katherine, from Greek *katharos* (pure)

> *Blessed are the pure in heart,*
> *for they shall see God.*
> — Matthew 5:8 (NASB)

EKENE   *[eh-keh-neh]*

Meaning: praise, thanksgiving • **Usage:** African: Igbo of Nigeria

> *Give thanks for a little and you'll find a lot.*
> — Nigerian proverb

ELAINE, ELAYNE   *[ee-LAYN]*

Meaning: light, illumination, torch • **Usage:** English and French form of Helen, from Greek *helene* (torch) or *ele* (light)

> *Who is this woman?*
> *She is like the sunrise in all of its glory.*
> *She is as beautiful as the moon.*
> *She is as bright as the sun.*
> — Song of Songs 6:10a (NIRV)

ELANDRA   *[eh-LAHN-drah]*

Meaning: little rock, beautiful • **Usage:** American form of Alana, from Breton *alp* (rock) and diminutive *-an*; Irish Gaelic *ailín* (little rock); or from Scotch Gaelic *àlainn* (beautiful, handsome)

> *Oh, how beautiful you are, my darling,*
> *how beautiful you are!*
> — Song of Songs 1:15a (NASB)

ELEANOR, ELEANORE   *[EL-eh-nor]*

Meaning: light, illumination, torch • **Usage:** English form of Helen, from Greek *helene* (torch) or *ele* (light)

> *It is the light that brings a rich harvest of every kind*
> *of goodness, righteousness, and truth.*
> — Ephesians 5:9 (GNT)

ELEANORA   *[eh-leh-NOR-ah]*

Meaning: light, illumination, torch • **Usage:** English form of Eleanor (*see* Eleanor)

> *We must work earnestly in the best light He gives us.*
> — Abraham Lincoln (letter of September 4, 1864)

ELECTRA   *[eh-LEK-trah]*

Meaning: shining one, brilliant, electric • **Usage:** English form of Elektra (*see* Elektra)

> *Love is rapid in its motion as the bolt of heaven;*
> *it acts with ardor, alacrity, and freedom,*
> *and no created power is able to obstruct its course.*
> — Thomas à Kempis, *The Imitation of Christ*

ELEKTRA   *[eh-LEK-trah]*

Meaning: shining one, brilliant, electric • **Usage:** Greek: from Greek *elektor*

> *O Light eternal, transcending all created lights,*
> *cause Thy bright beams to shine into me from above,*
> *and illuminate my inmost heart.*
> — Thomas à Kempis,
> *The Imitation of Christ* (tr. Harvey Goodwin)

ELEN   *[EL-en]*

Meaning: nature spirit, nymph, light, illumination, torch • **Usage:** Welsh: from Welsh *elin* (nymph); or Welsh form of Ellen (*see* Eleni)

E

There is a love of wild nature in everybody,
an ancient mother-love ever showing itself.
— John Muir

ELENA *[eh-LEH-nah (Greek, Italian, Spanish),*
yel-LEH-nah (Russian)]

MEANING: light, illumination, torch • USAGE:
Greek, Italian, Russian, and Spanish form of
Helena (*see* Eleni)
My prayer is that light will flood your hearts
and that you will understand the hope that was given
to you when God chose you. Then you will discover
the glorious blessings that will be yours.
— Ephesians 1:18 (CEV)

ELENI *[eh-LAY-nee]*

MEANING: light, illumination, torch • USAGE:
Greek: from Greek *helene* (torch) or *ele* (light)
Walk in the presence of the light thereof,
that thou mayest be illuminated.
— Baruch 4:2b (KJV Apocrypha)

ELEONOR *[EHL-eh-nor]*

MEANING: light, illumination, torch • USAGE:
English form of Helen, from Greek *helene* (torch)
or *ele* (light)
It is the light that brings a rich harvest of every kind
of goodness, righteousness, and truth.
— Ephesians 5:9 (GNT)

ELEONORA *[el-leh-oh-NOH-rah]*

MEANING: light, illumination, torch • USAGE:
Italian, English, and Scandinavian form of Eleanor
(*see* Eleonor)
Send Your light and Your truth;
let them lead me.
— Psalm 43:3a (HCSB)

ELEONORE *[eh-leh-oh-NOR-ah]*

MEANING: light, illumination, torch • USAGE:
German form of Eleanor (*see* Eleanor)
Laughing cheerfulness throws sunlight
on all the paths of life.
— Jean Paul Richter, *Levana*

ELETTRA *[eh-LEH-trah]*

MEANING: shining one, brilliant, electric • USAGE:
Italian form of Elektra (*see* Elektra)
Arise, shine, for your light has come.
— Isaiah 60:1a (HCSB)

ELIANA *[eh-lee-AH-nah]*

MEANING: sun, sunshine • USAGE: Italian,
Portuguese, and Spanish form of Latin family name
Aelianus (of the sun), from Greek *helios* (sun)
Put your heart into being a bright light.
— Mother Teresa

ELIANA, ELIANNA *[eh-lee-AH-nah]*

MEANING: God has answered me • USAGE: Jewish
Call to Me, and I will answer you;
I will tell you wonderful and marvelous things
that you know nothing about.
— Jeremiah 33:3 (MT)

ÉLIANE *[EH-leh-ahn]*

MEANING: sun, sunshine • USAGE: French (*see*
Eliana)
The Sun, the hearth of affection and life,
pours burning love on the delighted earth.
— Arthur Rimbaud, "Soleil et Chair"

ELIN *[EL-en]*

MEANING: light, illumination, torch • USAGE:
Scandinavian form of Ellen (*see* Eleanor)
Walk as children of light — for the fruit of the light
results in all goodness, righteousness, and truth.
— Ephesians 5:8b–9 (HCSB)

E

ELINOR, ELENOR [EL-eh-nor]

MEANING: light, illumination, torch • USAGE:
English form of Helen (see Eleonor)
God said, "Let there be light"; and there was light.
And God saw the light, that it was good.
— Genesis 1:3–4a (NKJV)

ELIORA [eh-lee-OH-rah]

MEANING: my light is God • USAGE: Jewish
feminine form of Elior
The more I shall recognize my own identity,
and the more I will permit myself to be original,
and to stand on my own feet with an inner conviction
which is based on knowledge, perception, feeling and
song, the more will the light of God shine on me.
— Abraham Isaac Kook

ELISA [eh-LEE-sah]

MEANING: God is my oath, joined with God,
blessed by God • USAGE: German, English, Italian,
and Spanish form of Elizabeth (see Elizabeth)
Live in peace;
and the God of love and peace will be with you.
— 2 Corinthians 13:11b (ESV)

ELISABET [ay-LEES-ah-bet]

MEANING: God is my oath, joined with God,
blessed by God • USAGE: Spanish and Scandinavian
form of Elizabeth (see Elizabeth)
Let no one split apart what God has joined together.
— Matthew 19:6b (NLT)

ELISABETH [eh-LEE-sah-beth]

MEANING: God is my oath, joined with
God, blessed by God • USAGE: German and
Scandinavian form of Elisheva (see Elizabeth)
I am the Lord . . . I am with you,
and will keep you wherever you go.
— Genesis 28:13b, 28:15a (NASB)

ELISABETTA [eh-lee-sah-BAY-tah]

MEANING: God is my oath, joined with God,
blessed by God • USAGE: Italian form of Elizabeth
(see Elizabeth)
We know that God causes everything to work together
for the good of those who love God and are called
according to his purpose for them.
— Romans 8:28 (NLT)

ELISE, ÉLISE [eh-LEES (English), eh-LEE-sah (German, Scandinavian), ay-LEES (French)]

MEANING: God is my oath, joined with God,
blessed by God • USAGE: English, German,
Scandinavian, and French form of Elisabeth (see
Elizabeth)
God hugs you. You are encircled by the arms
of the mystery of God. — Hildegard of Bingen

ELISHA [eh-LEE-shah]

MEANING: God is my oath, joined with God,
blessed by God • USAGE: English form of Elizabeth
(see Elizabeth)
The blessing of the Lord be upon you.
— Psalm 129:8b (ESV)

ELISHEVA [eh-leh-SHEH-vah]

MEANING: God is my oath, joined with God,
blessed by God • USAGE: Jewish: from Hebrew
el'ishebha
I [God] am with you, and I will bless you.
— Genesis 26:24b (JPS)

ELIYA [eh-LEE-yah]

MEANING: the Lord is God • USAGE: Jewish
feminine form of Eliyahu, from Hebrew el'iyahu
(Yahweh is God)
The Lord is with you, while ye are with Him;
and if ye seek Him, He will be found of you.
— 2 Chronicles 15:2b (MT)

E

ELIZA   [eh-LIE-ʒah]

MEANING: God is my oath, joined with God, blessed by God • USAGE: English form of Elizabeth or Isabella (*see* Elizabeth)

> *The kingdom of God is within you.*
> — Luke 17:21b (KJ21)

ELIZABETA   [ay-lee-ʒah-BEH-tah]

MEANING: God is my oath, joined with God, blessed by God • USAGE: Portuguese form of Elizabeth (*see* Elizabeth)

> *Thy God will bless thee in all thy works,*
> *and in all the business of thy hand.*
> — Deuteronomy 28:8b (DT)

ELIZABETH   [eh-LIZ-ah-beth]

MEANING: God is my oath, joined with God, blessed by God • USAGE: English form of Elisheva, from Hebrew *el'ishebha*

> *To be at one with God is to be at peace.*
> — Ralph Waldo Trine, *In Tune with the Infinite*

ELIZAVETA   [yeh-lee-ʒah-VYE-tah]

MEANING: God is my oath, joined with God, blessed by God • USAGE: Russian form of Elizabeth (*see* Elizabeth)

> *I believe in God…whom I understand as Spirit,*
> *as Love, as the Source of all.*
> — Leo Tolstoy,
> "A Reply to the Synod's Edict of Excommunication"
> (tr. Aylmer Maude)

ELKE   [EL-keh]

MEANING: noble one, highborn, honorable • USAGE: German, Dutch, and Scandinavian form of Adelheid, from German *adal* (noble) and *heid* (sort, type)

> *A noble soul alone can noble souls attract.*
> — Johann Wolfgang von Goethe

ELLA   [EL-ah]

MEANING: light, illumination, torch • USAGE: English and Scandinavian form of Ellen (*see* Ellen)

> *You are the light of the world.* — Matthew 5:14 (DR)

ELLEN   [EL-en]

MEANING: light, illumination, torch • USAGE: English form of Helen, from Greek *helene* (torch) or *ele* (light)

> *Look to the light within you.*
> — Susan L. Taylor, *Lessons in Living*

ELLIE, ELLY   [EL-ee]

MEANING: God is my oath, joined with God, blessed by God, light, illumination, torch • USAGE: English form of Elizabeth (*see* Elizabeth); or English form of Ellen or Eleanor (*see* Ellen)

> *The blessing of the Lord be upon you.*
> — Psalm 129:8b (NIV)

ELLINOR   [EH-lee-nor]

MEANING: light, illumination, torch • USAGE: Swedish form of Eleanor (*see* Eleanor)

> *Your eye is a lamp that provides light for your body.*
> *When your eye is good,*
> *your whole body is filled with light.*
> — Luke 11:34a (NLT)

ELMIRA   [ehl-MIE-rah]

MEANING: noble and famous • USAGE: English form of Almira, from German *adal* (noble) and *meri* (famous)

> *God has put something noble and good into every heart*
> *His hand created.* — Mark Twain

ELODIA   [ay-LOH-dee-ah]

MEANING: foreign prosperity, foreign wealth • USAGE: Spanish form of Alodia, from German *ali* (foreign, other) and *od* (wealth, prosperity)

A generous person will prosper;
whoever refreshes others will be refreshed.
— Proverbs 11:25 (NIV)

ÉLODIE   *[EH-loh-dee]*

MEANING: foreign prosperity, foreign wealth •
USAGE: French form of Alodia (*see* Elodia)
Thou shalt make thy way prosperous.
— Joshua 1:8b (KJ21)

ELOISA   *[eh-loh-WEE-sah]*

MEANING: famous warrior, renowned in battle
• **USAGE:** Italian and Spanish form of Louise (*see*
Eloise)
Who shall find a valiant woman?
Far and from the uttermost coasts is the price of her.
— Proverbs 31:10 (DR)

ELOISE, ÉLOISE   *[el-oh-EEZ (English),*
EH-loh-eez (French)]

MEANING: famous warrior, renowned in battle •
USAGE: English form of Louise, from German *hlud*
(famous) and *wig* (war, strife)
Put on the armor of light.
— Romans 13:12b (NRSV)

ELORATHEA   *[eh-lohr-ah-THEE-ah]*

MEANING: goddess of light • **USAGE:** American
form of Eleanor, from Greek *helene* (torch) or *ele*
(light), and Thea, from Greek *theo* (god)
Let your light shine before others.
— Matthew 5:16b (NRSV)

ELSA   *[EL-sah]*

MEANING: God is my oath, joined with God,
blessed by God • **USAGE:** German, Scandinavian,
and English form of Elizabeth (*see* Elizabeth)
The Lord, he it is that doth go before thee;
he will be with thee.
— Deuteronomy 31:8a (KJV)

ELSIE   *[EL-see]*

MEANING: God is my oath, joined with God,
blessed by God • **USAGE:** English form of Elizabeth
(*see* Elizabeth)
Teach me to do your will, for you are my God!
Let your good Spirit lead me on level ground!
— Psalm 143:10 (ESV)

ELSPETH   *[ELS-peth]*

MEANING: God is my oath, joined with God,
blessed by God • **USAGE:** Scottish form of
Elizabeth (*see* Elizabeth)
Teach me your way, O Lord, and I will walk in your
truth; give me an undivided heart.
— Psalm 86:11 (NIV)

ELUNED   *[eh-LOO-ned]*

MEANING: greatly desired • **USAGE:** Welsh: from
Welsh *el* (greatly, much) and *uned* (wish, desire)
Delight yourself also in the Lord,
and He shall give you the desires of your heart.
— Psalm 37:4 (NKJV)

ELVINA   *[el-VEE-nah]*

MEANING: elf friend, elf ally • **USAGE:** English
form of Alvina, from English *ælf* (elf) and *wine*
(friend)
Friendship is the golden thread that ties
the heart of all the world.
— John Evelyn

ELVIRA   *[ayl-BEE-rah (Spanish), el-VIE-rah*
(English), EL-vee-rah (Russian)]

MEANING: all true, truth, noble guardian,
honorable protector • **USAGE:** Spanish, English,
and Russian: from German *al* (all) and *wer* (true);
or from German *adal* (noble) and *ware* (guardian,
protector)
You will know the truth, and the truth will set you free.
— John 8:32 (CEV)

E

ELVIRE   [EL-veer]

MEANING: all true, truth, noble guardian, honorable protector • **USAGE:** French form of Elvira (see Elvira)

Nothing but truth is lovely.
— Nicolas Boileau-Despréaux, "Epistle IX"

ELZA   [EL-ʒah]

MEANING: God is my oath, joined with God, blessed by God • **USAGE:** American form of Elizabeth (see Elizabeth)

The Lord your God is with you wherever you go.
— Joshua 1:9b (HCSB)

ELZA   [el-ZAH]

MEANING: joyous, happy • **USAGE:** Jewish feminine form of Elez

Happy shalt thou be, and it shall be well with thee.
— Psalm 128:2b (MT)

EMA   [AY-mah]

MEANING: whole, universal, strong, powerful • **USAGE:** Spanish form of Emma, from German *ermen* (whole, universal) or *erm* (strength, power)

"For I know the plans I have for you,"
declares the Lord, "plans for wholeness and not for
evil, to give you a future and a hope."
— Jeremiah 29:11 (ESV)

EMANUELA   [ay-mah-noo-EH-lah]

MEANING: God is with us • **USAGE:** Spanish, Italian, and Scandinavian feminine form of Emanuel, from Hebrew *immanu' el*

I am the Lord God…I am with thee,
and will keep thee in all places whither thou goest.
— Genesis 28:13b (KJV)

EMANUELLE   [eh-MAHN-yoo-el]

MEANING: God is with us • **USAGE:** French form of Emanuela (see Emanuela)

May the Lord our God be with us
as he was with our ancestors.
— 1 Kings 8:57a (GNT)

EMELINA   [ay-meh-LEE-nah]

MEANING: industrious, hardworking, one who excels, competitor • **USAGE:** Spanish feminine form of Emilio (see Emily)

She is a hard worker, strong and industrious.
— Proverbs 31:17 (GNT)

EMELINE   [eh-meh-LEEN]

MEANING: industrious, hardworking, one who excels, competitor • **USAGE:** French feminine form of Émile (see Emily)

The Lord your God will bless you in all your work
and in everything you put your hand to.
— Deuteronomy 15:10b (NIV)

EMILIA   [eh-MEE-lee-ah]

MEANING: industrious, hardworking, one who excels, competitor • **USAGE:** Italian and Spanish form of Emily (see Emily)

The Lord your God will make you abound
in all the work of your hand.
— Deuteronomy 30:9a (NKJV)

EMILIANA   [eh-mee-lee-AH-nah]

MEANING: industrious, hardworking, one who excels, competitor • **USAGE:** Italian and Spanish form of Emily (see Emily); or from Latin *aemulus* (trying to equal or excel)

The Lord shall open unto thee his good treasure…
to bless all the work of thine hand.
— Deuteronomy 28:12a (KJV)

E

EMILIE   *[eh-MEEL-yeh]*

MEANING: industrious, hardworking, one who excels, competitor • **USAGE:** Swedish, Norwegian, and Danish form of Emily (*see* Emily)

> *God is able to make all grace abound unto you;*
> *that ye, having always all sufficiency in everything,*
> *may abound unto every good work.*
> — 2 Corinthians 9:8 (ASV)

EMILY   *[EM-eh-lee]*

MEANING: industrious, hardworking, one who excels, competitor • **USAGE:** English form of Amalia, from German *amal* (work, labor); or from Latin *aemulus* (trying to equal or excel)

> *Our work is meant to be a grace. It is a blessing and a*
> *gift, even a surprise and an act of unconditional love.*
> — Matthew Fox, *The Reinvention of Work*

EMMA   *[EM-ah]*

MEANING: whole, universal, strong, powerful • **USAGE:** English, Dutch, French, German, Italian, Russian, and Scandinavian: from German *ermen* (whole, universal) or *erm* (strength, power)

> *What you are, so is your world. Everything in the*
> *universe is resolved into your own inward experience.*
> *It matters little what is without, for it is all a reflection*
> *of your own state of consciousness.*
> — James Allen, *From Poverty to Power*

EMMALINE   *[EM-ah-leen]*

MEANING: industrious, hardworking, one who excels, competitor • **USAGE:** English form of Amelina, from German *amal* (work, labor); or from Latin *aemulus* (trying to equal or excel)

> *When love and skill work together,*
> *expect a masterpiece.*
> — John Ruskin

EMMY, EMMIE   *[EM-ee]*

MEANING: whole, universal, entire, strong, powerful, industrious, hardworking, one who excels, competitor • **USAGE:** English form of Emma (*see* Emma); or English form of Emily (*see* Emily)

> *You are a child of the Universe,*
> *no less than the moon and the stars.*
> — Max Ehrmann, *Desiderata:*
> *A Poem for a Way of Life*

ENA   *[EN-ah]*

MEANING: kernel, fire, fiery • **USAGE:** Irish form of Eithne, from Gaelic *eithne* (kernel) or *aodh* (fire)

> *May the blessed light shine*
> *out of your two eyes like a candle.*
> — Celtic blessing

ENID   *[EE-nid]*

MEANING: soul, spirit • **USAGE:** Welsh and English: from Welsh *enaid*

> *Strong is the Soul, and wise, and beautiful.*
> — Matthew Arnold

ENIDA   *[eh-NEE-dah]*

MEANING: soul, spirit • **USAGE:** Welsh form of Enid (*see* Enid)

> *I know my soul hath power to know all things.*
> — John Davies, *Nosce Teipsum*

ENRICA   *[en-REE-kah]*

MEANING: ruler of the home, house leader • **USAGE:** Italian feminine form of Enrico, from German *heim* (home, house) and *rik* (rule, lead)

> *Look inwards, for you have a lasting fountain*
> *of happiness at home that will always bubble up*
> *if you will but dig for it.*
> — Marcus Aurelius,
> *The Meditations* (tr. Jeremy Collier)

E

ENRIQUA   *[ayn-REE-kah]*

MEANING: ruler of the home, house leader •
USAGE: Spanish feminine form of Enrique (*see* Enrica)

Peace be unto thee, and peace be to thy house, and peace be unto all that thou hast.
— 1 Samuel 25:6b (ASV)

ENYA   *[EN-yah]*

MEANING: kernel, fire, fiery • **USAGE:** Irish form of Eithne, from Gaelic *eithne* (kernel) or *aodh* (fire)

Habitually make many acts of love, for they set the soul on fire and make it gentle.
— Teresa of Avila

EPIFANIA   *[ay-pee-FAH-nee-ah]*

MEANING: manifestation, divine appearance • **USAGE:** Spanish: from Greek *ephiphaneia* (manifestation, appearance); reference to the Christian Epiphany

Your word is the gift that comes directly from God.... What you dream, what you feel, and what you really are, all will be manifested through your word.
— Don Miguel Ruiz, *The Four Agreements*

ERICA   *[AYR-ih-kah]*

MEANING: ruler for eternity, everlasting queen • **USAGE:** English feminine form of Eric, from Norse *ei* (ever, always) and *rikr* (ruler, leader)

You must live in the present, launch yourself on every wave, find your eternity in each moment.
— Henry David Thoreau
(journal entry of April 23, 1859)

ERIKA   *[AYR-ih-kah]*

MEANING: ruler for eternity, everlasting queen • **USAGE:** Scandinavian and German feminine form of Erik (*see* Erica)

Acts of kindness and charity are as lasting as eternity.
— Sirach 40:17 (GNT Apocrypha)

ERIN   *[AYR-in]*

MEANING: peace, peaceful, calm, serene, Ireland • **USAGE:** English form of *Eireann*, the Irish Gaelic name of Ireland, from *Eire* (Celtic goddess); or from Greek *eirene* (peace)

Look at those who are honest and good, for a wonderful future awaits those who love peace.
— Psalm 37:37 (NLT)

ERINA   *[eh-REE-nah]*

MEANING: peace, peaceful, calm, serene, Ireland • **USAGE:** American form of Erin (*see* Erin)

A woman's greatest power lies in serenity.
— Christian Nestell Bovee

ERMA   *[ER-mah]*

MEANING: strong, powerful, whole, universal • **USAGE:** German and English: from German *ermen* (whole, universal) or *erm* (strength, power)

Some thoughts always find us young and keep us so. Such a thought is the love of the universal and eternal beauty.
— Ralph Waldo Emerson, "The Over-Soul"

ERMIN   *[ER-min]*

MEANING: strong, powerful, whole, universal, warrior • **USAGE:** Welsh form of *Erminia*, a feminine form of Herman, from German *hari* (army) and *man* (man); from German *erm* (strength, power); or from German *ermen* (whole, universal)

God did not give us a spirit of fear. He gave us a spirit of power and of love and of a good mind.
— 2 Timothy 1:7 (NLV)

ERNESTA   *[ayr-NAY-stah]*

MEANING: earnest, honest • **USAGE:** Spanish, Italian, and German feminine form of Ernesto (*see* Ernestine)

Joy belongs to those who are honest.
— Psalm 97:11b (NCV)

ERNESTINE   *[ER-nes-teen (English), er-nes-TEE-neh (German)]*

MEANING: earnest, honest • **USAGE:** English and German feminine form of Ernest, from German *ernust*

Nature is in earnest when she makes a woman.
— Oliver Wendell Holmes Sr.,
The Autocrat of the Breakfast Table

ESHANA   *[eh-shah-nah]*

MEANING: wish, desire, search • **USAGE:** Hindu

That which is awake in us even while we sleep, shaping in dream the objects of our desire — that indeed is pure, that is Brahman, and that verily is called the Immortal.
— *Katha Upanishad*

ESHE   *[eh-sheh]*

MEANING: life • **USAGE:** African: Swahili of Kenya/Tanzania

To live long is to see much.
— Swahili proverb

ESMÉE   *[EZ-may]*

MEANING: love, beloved • **USAGE:** French: from French *esmer* (to love)

It is in the heart that God has placed the genius of women, because the works of this genius are all works of love.
— Alphonse de Lamartine

ESMERALDA   *[ays-may-RAHL-dah]*

MEANING: emerald, deep green color, beautiful gemstone • **USAGE:** Spanish: from Spanish *esmeralda*

Green is the prime color of the world, and that from which its loveliness arises.... Green speaks hope, which we always prize as the most precious offering of love.
— Pedro Calderón de la Barca

ESPERANZA   *[ays-PEH-rahn-zah]*

MEANING: hope, faith, trust • **USAGE:** Spanish: from Spanish *esperanza*

May the God of hope fill you with all joy and peace in believing, that you may abound in hope by the power of the Holy Spirit.
— Romans 15:13 (NASB)

ESTÉE   *[EHS-tay]*

MEANING: star, starlike, radiant • **USAGE:** French form of Esther (*see* Estella)

The glory of the stars is the beauty of heaven; the Lord enlighteneth the world on high.
— Sirach 43:10 (DR Apocrypha)

ESTEFANÍA   *[ay-steh-fah-NEE-ah]*

MEANING: crown, crowned one • **USAGE:** Spanish form of Stephanie, from Greek *stephanos*

You will be like a beautiful crown in the Lord's hand.
— Isaiah 62:3a (NCV)

ESTELA   *[ay-STAY-lah]*

MEANING: star, starlike, radiant • **USAGE:** Spanish form of Estella (*see* Estella)

They that are learned shall shine as the brightness of the firmament: and they that instruct many to justice, as stars for all eternity.
— Daniel 12:3 (DR)

ESTELLA   *[ay-STREH-yah]*

MEANING: star, starlike, radiant • **USAGE:** English: from Latin *stella*

O, thou art fairer than the evening air clad in the beauty of a thousand stars.
— Christopher Marlowe,
The Tragical History of Doctor Faustus

E

ESTELLE   [eh-STEL]

MEANING: star, starlike, radiant • USAGE: French and English form of Estella (see Estella)

Women are the poetry of the world in the same sense as the stars are the poetry of heaven. Clear, light-giving, harmonious, they are the terrestrial planets that rule the destinies of mankind.
— Francis Hargrave

ESTER   [ES-ter (Jewish, French), ays-TAHR (Spanish)]

MEANING: star, starlike, radiant • USAGE: Jewish, Scandinavian, and Spanish: from Persian *stara*

The knowledgeable will be radiant like the bright expanse of sky, and those who lead the many to righteousness will be like the stars forever and ever.
— Daniel 12:3a (JPS)

ESTERA   [ehs-TEHR-ah]

MEANING: star, starlike, radiant • USAGE: Polish form of Esther (see Ester)

He counts the number of the stars;
He calls them all by name.
— Psalm 147:4 (NKJV)

ESTHER   [ES-ter]

MEANING: star, starlike, radiant • USAGE: English, French, and German form of Hebrew Ester (see Ester)

Stars arise, and the night is holy.
— Henry Wadsworth Longfellow, *Hyperion*

ESTRELLA   [eh-STREH-yah]

MEANING: star, starlike, radiant • USAGE: Spanish form of Estela (see Estella)

The beauty of heaven, the glory of the stars, an ornament giving light in the highest places of the Lord.
— Ben Sira 43:9 (KJV Apocrypha)

ETANA   [ay-TAH-nah]

MEANING: strong, steadfast, firm • USAGE: Jewish: from Hebrew *ethan*

Create in me a clean heart, O God; and renew a steadfast spirit within me.
— Psalm 51:12 (MT)

ETHEL   [ETH-el]

MEANING: noble, valorous • USAGE: English: from English *æthel*

'Tis only noble to be good.
— Alfred Tennyson, "Lady Clara Vere de Vere"

EUDORA   [yoo-DOR-ah]

MEANING: good gift, gift of wellness • USAGE: Greek: from Greek *eu* (good, well) and *doron* (gift)

When there enters into it a glow from the Divine, the soul gathers strength, spreads true wings...its very nature bears it upwards, lifted by the Giver of that love.
— Plotinus, *The Six Enneads*

EUGENIA   [yoo-HEHN-ee-ah (Greek), yoo-JEH-nee-ah (Italian), yoo-JEE-nee-ah (English), eh-oo-HEH-nee-ah (Spanish)]

MEANING: wellborn, noble • USAGE: Greek, Italian, English, and Spanish feminine form of Eugene, from Greek *eu* (good, well) and *genes* (born)

Harmony and grace and rhythm depend on simplicity...the simplicity of a truly and noble ordered mind.
— Plato, *The Republic* (tr. Benjamin Jowett)

EUGÉNIE   [yoo-ZEH-neh]

MEANING: wellborn, noble • USAGE: French feminine form of Eugene (see Eugenia)

Those who are noble plan noble things, and by noble thing they stand.
— Isaiah 32:8 (NRSV)

EULA [YOO-lah]

MEANING: well-spoken, sweet spoken, eloquent • **USAGE:** English form of Eulalie (*see* Eulalie)

May the words of my mouth and the meditation
of my heart be pleasing in your sight,
O Lord, my Rock and my Redeemer.
— Psalm 19:14 (NIV)

EULALA [yoo-LAH-lah]

MEANING: well-spoken, sweet spoken, eloquent • **USAGE:** American (*see* Eulalie)

Your voice is so sweet. Your face is so lovely.
— Song of Songs 2:14b (NIRV)

EULALIA [yoo-LAH-lee-ah]

MEANING: well-spoken, sweet spoken, eloquent • **USAGE:** Spanish, Italian, and English (*see* Eulalie)

She opens her mouth with wisdom,
and on her tongue is the law of kindness.
— Proverbs 31:26 (NKJV)

EULALIE [yoo-LAH-lee]

MEANING: well-spoken, sweet spoken, eloquent • **USAGE:** French form of Eulalia, from Greek *eu* (good, well) and *lalein* (to talk)

Out of the abundance of the heart
the mouth speaketh.
— Matthew 12:34b (KJV)

EUNICE [YOO-nis]

MEANING: good victory, victorious, triumphant • **USAGE:** English form of *Eunike*, from Greek *eu* (good, well) and *nike* (victory)

You give me your shield of victory;
You stoop down to make me great.
— 2 Samuel 22:36 (NIV)

EUN-SUN [eun-sun]

MEANING: silver goodness • **USAGE:** Korean: from Korean *eun* (silver) and *sun* (goodness)

Do good and be good, and this will take you
to freedom and to whatever truth there is.
— Buddha

EUPHEMIA [yoo-FEE-mee-ah]

MEANING: good voice, sweet voiced • **USAGE:** Greek and English: from Greek *eu* (good, well) and *pheme* (voice)

Thy voice is sweet as if it took
Its music from thy face.
— L. E. Landon, "Poetical Portraits, Number 1"

EVA [EH-vah (Italian, Spanish, Scandinavian), EE-vah (English)]

MEANING: life, full of life • **USAGE:** Italian, English, German, Spanish, and Scandinavian form of Chava, from Hebrew *hawwah*

Surely goodness and mercy shall follow
me all the days of my life.
— Psalm 23:6a (KJV)

EVANGELIA [eh-vahn-yeh-LEE-ah]

MEANING: messenger with good news, angel of good tidings • **USAGE:** Greek and Italian form of Evangeline (*see* Evangeline)

How beautiful on the mountains are the feet of those
who bring good news, who proclaim peace,
who bring good tidings.
— Isaiah 52:7a (NIV)

EVANGELINA [eh-vahn-jeh-LEE-nah (Spanish, Italian), ee-van-jeh-LEE-nah (English)]

MEANING: messenger with good news, angel of good tidings • **USAGE:** Spanish, Italian, and English form of Evangeline (*see* Evangeline)

The work of angels is the will of God,
and the will of God is the work of the angels.
— Meister Eckhart

E

EVANGELINE   *[eh-van-jeh-LEEN]*

MEANING: messenger with good news, angel with good tidings • **USAGE:** English: from Greek *evangelius* (good news) or from Greek *euangelos* (bringing good news)

He shall give His angels charge over thee to keep thee in all thy ways. — Psalm 91:11 (KJ21)

EVE   *[eev]*

MEANING: life, full of life • **USAGE:** English and French form of Chava, from Hebrew *hawwah*

*Realize the inward heaven,
and it will be reflected in all your outward life.*
— James Allen, *From Poverty to Power*

EVELINA   *[eh-veh-LEE-nah (Scandinavian, English), yeh-veh-LEE-nah (Russian)]*

MEANING: life, full of life • **USAGE:** Scandinavian, English, and Russian form of Eve or Eva (*see* Eve)

*Through wisdom your days will be many,
and years will be added to your life.*
— Proverbs 9:11 (NIV)

EVELYN, EVLYN   *[EV-eh-len, EV-len]*

MEANING: light, illumination, torch, life, full of life, little bird • **USAGE:** English form of Helen, from Greek *helene* (torch) or *ele* (light); English form of Eve (*see* Eve); or English form of Aveline, from Latin *avis* (bird) and suffix *-ine*

*This light within you produces
only what is good and right and true.*
— Ephesians 5:9 (NLT)

EVETTE   *[ee-VET]*

MEANING: yew tree, bow maker • **USAGE:** English form of Yvette, from German *iv* (yew tree); yew is used to make bows

*Your roots will grow down into God's love
and keep you strong.*
— Ephesians 3:17b (NLT)

EVITA   *[ay-VEE-tah]*

MEANING: life, full of life • **USAGE:** Spanish form of Eva (*see* Eve)

To life! To love!
— Song of Songs 5:1b (MSG)

F

FABIANA   *[fah-bee-AH-nah]*

MEANING: bean, a sower of beans • **USAGE:** Italian feminine form of Fabian, from Latin *faba* (a broad bean)

Who sows virtue reaps honor.
— Leonardo da Vinci

FABIENNE   *[fah-bee-EN]*

MEANING: bean, a sower of beans • **USAGE:** French feminine form of Fabian (*see* Fabiana)

*Sow righteousness for yourselves,
reap unfailing love.*
— Hosea 10:12a (NEB)

FABIOLA   *[fah-bee-OH-lah]*

MEANING: bean, a sower of beans • **USAGE:** Italian feminine form of Fabian (*see* Fabiana)

*The fruit of righteousness is sown
in peace of them that make peace.*
— James 3:18 (KJV)

FABULA   *[FAB-yoo-lah]*

MEANING: fabulous, incredible, fantastic, wonderful • **USAGE:** English: from Latin *fabula* (fable, mythical)

*You made my whole being;
you formed me in my mother's body.
I praise You because you made me
in an amazing and wonderful way.*
— Psalm 139:13–14 (NCV)

FADILA, FADEELA [fah-DEE-lah]

MEANING: virtuous, generous • **USAGE:** Muslim feminine form of Fadil, from Arabic *fadil* (generous) or *fadala* (to surpass, to be virtuous)

> *The world and all things in it are valuable; but the most valuable thing in the world is a virtuous woman.*
> — Hadith of the Prophet Muhammad

FAHIMA, FAHEEMA [fah-HEE-mah]

MEANING: educated, knowledgeable, rightly guided • **USAGE:** Muslim feminine form of Fahim, from Arabic *fahim*

> *The mind is a gift from God,*
> *knowledge is the gift of the mind.*
> — Arabic proverb

FAINNE [FAH-ih-nie]

MEANING: ring, halo, light • **USAGE:** Irish: from Gaelic *fainne*

> *May the sacredness of your work bring healing, light, and renewal.*
> — Celtic blessing

FAITH [fayth]

MEANING: trust, confident belief, faith • **USAGE:** English: from Latin *fides*

> *Faith makes all things possible,*
> *love makes all them easy.*
> — William H. G. Thomas, *Grace and Power*

FAIZA, FAAZIA, FAYZA [fah-ih-zah]

MEANING: victorious, successful • **USAGE:** Muslim

> *Truth alone is success, and real success is truth.*
> — Hazrat Inayat Khan,
> *The Gayan* (cd. *The Gayani Meditations,*
> *Volume 1*, tr. Cecil Touchon)

FALALA [fah-lah-lah]

MEANING: born into abundance • **USAGE:** African: Fulani of Ghana

> *There is no wealth where there are no children.*
> — West African proverb

FANA [fah-nah]

MEANING: spirited joy • **USAGE:** African: Ethiopia
> *Move your neck according to the music.*
> — Ethiopian proverb

FANCY, FANCIE, FANCEE [FAN-see]

MEANING: imagination, fantasy, whimsical, decorative, elegant • **USAGE:** English: from English *fantasien*

> *Imagination is more important than knowledge.*
> *For knowledge is limited, whereas imagination embraces the entire world, stimulating progress, giving birth to evolution.*
> — Albert Einstein

FANG [fahng]

MEANING: forest, fine jade • **USAGE:** Chinese
> *A great tree affords a pleasant shade.*
> — Chinese proverb

FANNIE, FANNY [FAN-ee]

MEANING: one who is free, native of France, a Franc, spear, spear maiden • **USAGE:** English form of Frances, from Latin *Franciscus* (a Frenchman); from French *franc* (free, freeman); or from *franco* (spear used by the Franks, a Germanic tribe)

> *The Lord and the Spirit are one and the same, and the Lord's Spirit sets us free.*
> — 2 Corinthians 3:17 (CEV)

F

F

FANTASIA   *[fan-TAY-zhah]*

MEANING: fantasy • USAGE: American: from
Latin *phantisa*

Without this playing with fantasy,
no creation work has ever yet come to birth.
— Carl Jung, *Psychological Reflections*

FARAA   *[fah-RAH]*

MEANING: cheerful one • USAGE: African: Hausa
of Nigeria

Spreading of the face is better than the spreading
of the mat. [Cheerfulness is a better welcome
than offering a seat.]
— Hausa proverb

FARAH, FARRAH   *[fah-rah (Muslim),*
                         FAYR-ah (English)]

MEANING: joyous, happy • USAGE: Muslim and
English: from Arabic *farah*

The joy of the heart makes the face fair.
— Persian proverb

FARIDAH, FAREEDA   *[fah-rih-dah]*

MEANING: unique, rare • USAGE: Muslim
feminine form of Farid, from Arabic *farada* (to be
unique)

That which is rare is dear.
— Persian proverb

FARREL, FARROL   *[FAYR-el]*

MEANING: valorous woman, woman of courage •
USAGE: Irish and English surname: feminine form
of *Fearghal*, from Gaelic *fear* (man) and *gal* (valor,
courage)

What is genius or courage without a heart?
— Oliver Goldsmith, *The Vicar of Wakefield*

FATIMA, FATEEMA   *[FAH-tee-mah]*

MEANING: pure, chaste, moderate, one who
abstains from forbidden things, she who weans an
infant • USAGE: Muslim: from Arabic *fatama* (to
wean, to abstain)

God is pure and loveth purity and cleanliness.
— Hadith of the Prophet Muhammad

FAUNA   *[FAH-nah]*

MEANING: animal kingdom • USAGE: American:
from *fauna* (animal life)

Just ask the animals, and they will teach you.
— Job 12:7a (NLT)

FAWN, FAWNE   *[fahn]*

MEANING: fawn, baby deer • USAGE: English:
from English *faon* (young animal, young deer)

The one true God is my mighty refuge; he removes the
obstacles in my way. He gives me the agility of a deer.
— 2 Samuel 22:33–34a (NEB)

FAY, FAYE   *[fay]*

MEANING: fairy, faith, trust • USAGE: English:
from English *faie* (fairy); or English form of Faith,
from Latin *fides* (faith, trust)

The one who has faith can do all things.
— Mark 9:23b (NLT)

FAYOLA   *[fah-YOH-lah]*

MEANING: good fortune walks with honor •
USAGE: African: Yoruba of Nigeria

If a head is blessed with good fortune,
it will affect a hundred others.
— Yoruban proverb

FEBE   *[FEE-bee]*

MEANING: bright, shining, moon goddess •
USAGE: Spanish and Polish form of Phoebe: from

Greek *phoibos* (bright, shining); Greek moon goddess

> *Who is she who looks forth as the morning,*
> *fair as the moon, clear as the sun.*
> — Song of Songs 6:10a (NKJV)

FEDERICA [feh-deh-REE-kah]

MEANING: peaceful ruler, leader of peace • **USAGE:** Italian feminine form of Frederick, from German *frid* (peace, peaceful) and *rik* (rule, lead)

> *May God's peace be with you.*
> — 1 Timothy 6:21b (NLT)

FEIGE [FAY-gee]

MEANING: fig, bird • **USAGE:** Yiddish: from Yiddish *fayg* (fig) or *feigel* (bird)

> *I seek refuge in the shadow of Your wings.*
> — Psalm 57:2b (JPS)

FELICE [fay-LEE-chay (Italian), feh-LEES (English)]

MEANING: happy, lucky, fortunate • **USAGE:** Italian and English feminine form of Felix (*see* Felicia)

> *My heart rejoiceth.*
> — Psalm 16:9a (DT)

FELICIA [fay-LEE-see-ah (Spanish, Italian), feh-LEE-shah (English)]

MEANING: happy, lucky, fortunate • **USAGE:** Spanish, Italian, and English feminine form of Felix, from Latin *felix*

> *A mind always employed is always happy.*
> *This is the true secret, the grand recipe for felicity.*
> — Thomas Jefferson (letter of May 21, 1787)

FELICIDAD [fay-lee-see-DAHD]

MEANING: happy, lucky, fortunate • **USAGE:** Spanish form of Roman *Felicitas* (*see* Felicia)

> *Happy shalt thou be, and it shall be well with thee.*
> — Psalm 128:2b (DT)

FELICIE [feh-LEE-see]

MEANING: happy, lucky, fortunate • **USAGE:** German form of Felix (*see* Felicia)

> *Happy are those who do right,*
> *who do what is fair at all times.*
> — Psalm 106:3 (NCV)

FELICITA [fay-LEE-chee-tah]

MEANING: happy, lucky, fortunate • **USAGE:** Italian feminine form of Felix (*see* Felicia)

> *My heart is glad. My soul is full of joy.*
> — Psalm 16:9a (NLV)

FÉLICITÉ [feh-lee-SEE-teh]

MEANING: happy, lucky, fortunate • **USAGE:** French feminine form of Felix (*see* Felicia)

> *There is only one happiness in this life,*
> *to love and be loved.*
> — George Sand (letter of March 31, 1862)

FELICITY [feh-LIS-eh-tee]

MEANING: happy, lucky, fortunate • **USAGE:** English feminine form of Felix (*see* Felicia)

> *Nothing can sweeten felicity itself but love.*
> — Jeremy Taylor, "The Marriage Ring"

FELINA [feh-LEE-nah]

MEANING: catlike, feline • **USAGE:** English: from Latin *felinus*

> *A cat has absolute emotional honesty.*
> — Ernest Hemingway

FELIPA [fay-LEE-pah]

MEANING: lover of horses • **USAGE:** Spanish feminine form of Felipe, from Greek *philein* (to love) and *hippos* (horse)

> *Love is patient, love is kind.*
> — 1 Corinthians 13:4a (NIV)

F

FELISHA   [feh-LEE-shah]

MEANING: happy, lucky, fortunate • USAGE: American form of Felicia (*see* Felicia)

*I realized that all we can do is be happy
and do the best we can while we are still alive.
All of us should eat and drink and enjoy
what we have worked for. It is God's gift.*
— Ecclesiastes 3:12–13 (GNT)

FEN   [fen]

MEANING: fragrant, aromatic • USAGE: Chinese

*The fragrance of virtue / travels against the wind, /
as far as the ends of the world.*
— Buddha, *The Dhammapada* (tr. Thomas Byrom)

FENELLA   [feh-NEL-ah]

MEANING: white shoulders, beautiful shoulders • USAGE: Scottish form of Fionnuala, from Gaelic *fionn* (fair, white, beautiful) and *guala* (shoulders)

Thou art all fair, my love; there is no spot in thee.
— Song of Songs 4:7 (KJ21)

FERDINANDA   [ferr-deh-NAHN-dah]

MEANING: bold venturer, prepared traveler, courageous journeyer • USAGE: German feminine form of Ferdinand, from German *fardi* (journey, travel) and *nand* (ready, prepared), *nanthi* (venture, adventurous), or *nanths* (courageous)

*Go into yourself and explore the depths
where your life wells forth.*
— Rainer Maria Rilke (letter of February 17, 1903;
tr. Reginald Snell)

FERN, FERNE   [furn]

MEANING: fern • USAGE: English: from English *fearn* (flowerless, seedless plant)

*Rise and put on your foliage, and be seen / To come
forth, like the springtime, fresh and green.*
— Robert Herrick, "Corinna's Going a-Maying"

FERNANDA   [fayr-NAHN-dah]

MEANING: bold venturer, prepared traveler, courageous journeyer • USAGE: Spanish, Portuguese, and Italian feminine form of Fernando (*see* Ferdinanda)

*I am going to send an angel before you
to protect you as you journey.*
— Exodus 23:20a (NEB)

FIALA   [fee-AH-lah]

MEANING: violet flower, purple color • USAGE: Czech: from Slavic *fialka*

*The flowers are in bloom.
This is the time for singing.*
— Song of Songs 2:12a (GNT)

FIDDA   [fee-dah]

MEANING: silver • USAGE: Muslim

*The alchemy is in the stilling of the heart,
when mercy becomes silver.*
— Hazrat Inayat Khan, *The Gayan*

FIDELA   [fee-DAY-lah]

MEANING: faithful, loyal, trustworthy • USAGE: Spanish: from Latin *fidelis*

*Whoever is faithful in very little
is also faithful in much.*
— Luke 16:10a (HCSB)

FIFI   [fee-fee]

MEANING: God will add, God will increase • USAGE: French form of Josephine, from Hebrew *ya'saph* (Yahweh will add)

*May the Lord give you increase,
you and your children.
May you be blessed of the Lord,
Maker of heaven and earth.*
— Psalm 115:14–15 (NASB)

FILIPA [fee-LEE-pah]

MEANING: lover of horses • **USAGE:** Polish feminine form of Philip (*see* Filippa)

Those who show loving-kindness are happy, because
they will have loving-kindness shown to them.
— Matthew 5:7 (NLV)

FILIPPA [fee-LEE-pah]

MEANING: lover of horses • **USAGE:** Italian feminine form of Filippo, from Greek *philein* (to love) and *hippos* (horse)

Kindness to you, and peace,
and love, be multiplied!
— Jude 1:2 (YLT)

FILOMENA [fee-loh-MEE-nah]

MEANING: strong friend • **USAGE:** Italian and Spanish form of Philomena, from Greek *philos* (friend) and *menos* (strength)

Say to wisdom, "You are my sister,"
and call understanding your intimate friend.
— Proverbs 7:4 (NASB)

FINA [FEE-nah]

MEANING: burning one, angel • **USAGE:** Italian form of Serafina, from Hebrew *seraphim* (the burning ones); an order of celestial angels

He [God] maketh winds his messengers;
flames of fire his ministers.
— Psalm 104:4 (ASV)

FINOLA [fih-NOH-lah]

MEANING: white shoulders, beautiful shoulders • **USAGE:** Irish and Scottish form of Fionnuala (*see* Fionnuala)

Behold thou art fair.
— Song of Songs 1:15b (ASV)

FIONA [fee-OH-nah]

MEANING: beautiful, fair, foxglove flower, vine • **USAGE:** Scottish: from Gaelic *fionn* (fair, white, beautiful); from Gaelic *fion* (vine); or from Welsh *ffion* (foxglove)

Beauty is an all-pervading presence.
It unfolds to the numberless flowers of the Spring.
— William Ellery Channing, "Self-Culture"

FIONNUALA [feh-NOO-lah]

MEANING: white shoulders, beautiful shoulders • **USAGE:** Irish form of *Fionnghuala*, from Gaelic *fionn* (fair, white, beautiful) and *guala* (shoulders)

She is fairer than the morning star,
and whiter than the moon.
— Oscar Wilde, *A House of Pomegranates*

FIORELLA [fee-oh-REH-lah]

MEANING: flower • **USAGE:** Italian: from Latin *fiore*

For thee the wonder-working earth
puts forth sweet flowers.
— Lucretius, *De Rerum Natura*

FLAVIA [FLAH-vee-ah]

MEANING: yellow, golden • **USAGE:** Italian and Spanish, from Latin *flavus*

How lovely yellow is!
— Vincent van Gogh

FLEUR [flur]

MEANING: flower, blossom • **USAGE:** French: from Latin *floris*

Blossoms appear through all the land.
The time has come to sing.
— Song of Songs 2:12a (NCV)

F

F

FLORA   *[FLOR-ah]*

MEANING: flower, blossom, goddess of flowers •
USAGE: English, Italian, and Spanish: from Latin
floris (flower, blossom); Roman goddess of flowers
and springtime

Lovely flowers are smiles of God's goodness.
— Samuel Wilberforce

FLORENCE   *[FLOR-ens]*

MEANING: flourishing, prosperous, flower,
blossom • **USAGE:** English: from Latin *florens*
(prospering, flourishing); or from Latin *floris*
(flower, blossom)

*Are not flowers the stars of the earth? /
And are not our stars the flowers of the heaven?*
— Clara Balfour, *Sunbeams for All Seasons*

FLORENS   *[FLOR-ens]*

MEANING: flourishing, prosperous, flower,
blossom • **USAGE:** Polish form of Florence (*see*
Florence)

*May the Lord cause you to flourish,
both you and your children. May you be blessed
by the Lord, the Maker of heaven and earth.*
— Psalm 115:14–15 (NIV)

FLORETTA   *[flor-ET-ah]*

MEANING: little flower • **USAGE:** English form
of Flora, from Latin *floris* (flower, blossom), and
diminutive *-etta* (*see* Flora)

*Little flower — but if I could understand /
What you are, root and all in all, /
I should know what God and man is.*
— Alfred Tennyson,
"Flower in the Crannied Wall"

FLORIANNE   *[flor-ee-AHN]*

MEANING: flower, blossom • **USAGE:** English
form of Flora, from Latin *floris* (flower, blossom)

Life is a flower of which love is the honey.
— Victor Hugo

FLORISSA   *[floh-RIS-ah]*

MEANING: flower, blossom • **USAGE:** English
form of Flora, from Latin *floris* (flower, blossom)

*Spring flowers are in blossom all over. The whole
world's a choir — and singing!*
— Song of Songs 2:11a (MSG)

FOLAMI   *[foh-lah-mee]*

MEANING: respect and honor me • **USAGE:**
African: Yoruba of Nigeria

*A person who is mindful of her image
is not easily disgraced.*
— Yoruban proverb

FOLUKE   *[foh-loo-keh]*

MEANING: placed in God's care • **USAGE:** African:
Yoruba of Nigeria

God does not sleep.
— Nigerian proverb

FONTANA   *[fon-TAN-ah]*

MEANING: fountain, spring • **USAGE:** English:
from French *fontaine*

*You are a garden fountain,
a well of fresh water.*
— Song of Songs 4:15a (NLT)

FORTUNATA   *[for-too-NAH-tah]*

MEANING: fortunate, lucky, goddess of fortune
• **USAGE:** Italian and Spanish, from Latin *fortuna*
(fortune); Roman goddess of fortune

*Whether you speak of nature, fate, fortune,
these are names of the same God....
So likewise justice, honesty, discretion, courage,
frugality, are all the good qualities
of one and the same mind.*
— Seneca, *On Benefits*

FRANCA [*FRAHN-kah*]

MEANING: one who is free, native of France, a Franc, spear, spear maiden • **USAGE:** Italian form of Francesca (*see* Frances)

> *Freedom is a possession of inestimable value.*
> — Marcus Tullius Cicero

FRANCENE [*fran-SEEN*]

MEANING: one who is free, native of France, a Franc, spear, spear maiden • **USAGE:** English form of Frances (*see* Frances)

> *Without Virtue there can be no liberty.*
> — Benjamin Rush

FRANCES [*FRAN-ses*]

MEANING: one who is free, native of France, a Franc, spear, spear maiden • **USAGE:** English feminine form of Francis, from Latin *Franciscus* (a Frenchman); from French *franc* (free, freeman); or from *franco* (spear used by the Franks, a Germanic tribe)

> *You will know the truth,*
> *and the truth will make you free.*
> — John 8:32 (WEB)

FRANCESCA [*frahn-CHEHS-kah*]

MEANING: one who is free, native of France, a Franc, spear, spear maiden • **USAGE:** Italian feminine form of Francesco (*see* Frances)

> *You are free.*
> — 1 Peter 2:16a (NKJV)

FRANCETTE [*frahn-SET*]

MEANING: one who is free, native of France, a Franc, spear, spear maiden • **USAGE:** French form of Frances (*see* Frances)

> *Freedom is nothing else but a chance to be better.*
> — Albert Camus, *Resistance, Rebellion, and Death*
> (tr. Justin O'Brien)

FRANCINE [*frahn-SEEN (French), fran-SEEN (English)*]

MEANING: one who is free, native of France, a Franc, spear, spear maiden • **USAGE:** French and English form of Frances (*see* Frances)

> *Liberty…consists in the ability to choose.*
> — Simone Weil, *The Need for Roots*

FRANCISCA [*frahn-SEES-kah*]

MEANING: one who is free, native of France, a Franc, spear, spear maiden • **USAGE:** Spanish and Portuguese feminine form of Francisco (*see* Frances)

> *Now the Lord is the Spirit:*
> *and where the Spirit of the Lord is, there is liberty.*
> — 2 Corinthians 3:17 (ASV)

FRANÇOISE [*frahn-SWAHZ*]

MEANING: one who is free, native of France, a Franc, spear, spear maiden • **USAGE:** French form of Frances (*see* Frances)

> *For you were called to freedom.*
> — Galatians 5:13 (NASB)

FRANKA [*FRAHN-kah*]

MEANING: one who is free, native of France, a Franc, spear, spear maiden • **USAGE:** German form of Francesca or Frances (*see* Frances)

> *Truth is the free thought, the free idea, the free spirit.*
> — Max Stirner, *The Ego and His Own*
> (tr. Steven T. Byington)

FREDERICA [*fred-eh-REE-kah*]

MEANING: peaceful ruler, leader of peace • **USAGE:** English feminine form of Frederick, from German *frid* (peace, peaceful) and *rik* (rule, lead)

> *Live in peace.*
> *Then the God of love and peace will be with you.*
> — 2 Corinthians 13:11b (NCV)

F

F

FREDONIA   [freh-DOH-nee-ah]

MEANING: peaceful ruler, leader of peace •
USAGE: American: possibly a form of Frederica
(see Frederica)

> There is no way to peace. Peace is the way.
> — A. J. Muste

FREDRIKA   [fred-REE-kah]

MEANING: peaceful ruler, leader of peace •
USAGE: Swedish and Finnish feminine form of
Fredrik (see Frederica)

> May you have peace.
> — Psalm 122:8b (NLT)

FREJA, FREYA   [FRAY-ah]

MEANING: goddess of love and beauty • USAGE:
Norwegian, Danish, and Swedish: Norse goddess
of love, beauty, and fertility

> How beautiful you are, my love!
> How your eyes shine with love.
> — Song of Songs 4:1a (GNT)

FRIDA   [FREE-dah]

MEANING: beautiful, peaceful • USAGE:
Scandinavian and Spanish: from Norse *friða*
(beautiful); or from German *frid* (peace)

> Live in peace and the God of love and peace
> will be with you.
> — 2 Corinthians 13:11b (NIV)

FRIEDA   [FREE-dah]

MEANING: beautiful, peaceful • USAGE: English
form of Frida (see Frida)

> I feel within me a peace above all earthly dignities.
> A still and quiet conscience.
> — William Shakespeare, *Henry VIII*

FRIEDE   [FREE-dah]

MEANING: beautiful, peaceful • USAGE:
Scandinavian and German form of Frida (see Frida)

> God blesses those who work for peace, for they will be
> called the children of God.
> — Matthew 5:9 (NLT)

G

GABRIELA   [gah-bree-AYL-ah]

MEANING: God is my strength, strong woman of
God • USAGE: Spanish feminine form of Gabriel
(see Gabrielle)

> The God of all grace…shall himself perfect,
> establish, strengthen you.
> — 1 Peter 5:10 (ASV)

GABRIELE   [gah-bree-EL]

MEANING: God is my strength, strong woman of
God • USAGE: German feminine form of Gabriel
(see Gabrielle)

> The Lord can be trusted to make
> you strong and protect you from harm.
> — 2 Thessalonians 3:3 (CEV)

GABRIELLA   [gah-bree-AY-lah (Italian),
                         gay-bree-EL-ah (English)]

MEANING: God is my strength, strong woman of
God • USAGE: Italian and English feminine form of
Gabriel (see Gabrielle)

> It is God who covers me
> with strength and makes my way perfect.
> — Psalm 18:32 (NLV)

GABRIELLE   [gah-bree-EL (French),
                          GAY-bree-el (English)]

MEANING: God is my strength, strong woman of
God • USAGE: French and English feminine form
of Gabriel, from Hebrew *gabhri'el*

> God is my strength and power.
> — 2 Samuel 22:33a (KJV)

GAEL   [gayl]

MEANING: Gaelic speaker, one from Ireland or Scotland • USAGE: Irish: from Gaelic *gaedheal*

May the words of my mouth and the meditation
of my heart be pleasing in your sight,
O Lord, my Rock and my Redeemer.
— Psalm 19:14 (NLT)

GAIA, GAEA   [GIE-ah]

MEANING: earth, earth mother • USAGE: Greek: Greek goddess, mother earth, from Greek *ge* (earth)

I will sing of well-founded Earth, mother of all,
eldest of all beings. She feeds all creatures that are
in the world, all that go upon the goodly land,
all that are in the paths of the seas,
and all that fly:
all these are fed of her store.
— Homer, "Hymn XXX"

GAIL, GALE, GAYLE   [gayl]

MEANING: father's joy and delight • USAGE: English form of Abigail, from Hebrew *avigayil*

Make me to hear joy and gladness.
— Psalm 51:8a (ASV)

GALA   [GAH-lah]

MEANING: calm, peaceful • USAGE: Russian form of Galina, from Greek *galene* (calm, peaceful)

Grace unto you, and peace, be multiplied.
— 1 Peter 1:2b (KJV)

GALILA   [gah-LEE-lah]

MEANING: rolling hills • USAGE: Jewish feminine form of Galil

The hills are girded with joy.
— Psalm 65:13b (MT)

GALINA   [gah-LEE-nah]

MEANING: calm, peaceful • USAGE: Russian feminine form of Galen, from Greek *galene* (calm, peaceful)

May there be peace inside your walls…
peace be with you!
— Psalm 122:7–8 (GNT)

GANA   [GAH-nah]

MEANING: garden, orchard • USAGE: Jewish

There are a thousand and one gates leading
into the orchard of mystical truth.
Every human being has his own gate.
We must never make the mistake of wanting
to enter the orchard by any gate but our own.
— Elie Wiesel, *Night*

GANYA, GANIA   [GAHN-yah]

MEANING: garden of God • USAGE: Jewish

Thou shalt be like a watered garden,
and like a spring of water, whose waters fail not.
— Isaiah 58:11b (MT)

GARDENIA   [gar-DEE-nee-ah]

MEANING: gardenia flower, fragrant white flower • USAGE: English: from Latin *gardenia*

Flowers express to us the delicate affections.
— Ralph Waldo Emerson, "Language"

GARNET, GARNETTE   [GAR-net, gar-NET]

MEANING: garnet gemstone, dark-red color, beautiful jewel • USAGE: English from English *grenat* (red like a pomegranate); dark-red gemstone; birthstone of January

How beautiful you are.
— Song of Songs 4:1a (RSV)

G

GAVRIELA, GAVRIELLA   *[gahv-ree-EL-ah]*

MEANING: God is my strength, strong woman of God • **USAGE:** Jewish feminine form of Gavriel (*see* Gavrielle)

Be strong and of good courage, and do it; fear not, nor be dismayed; for the Lord God, even my God, is with thee; He will not fail thee, nor forsake thee.
— 1 Chronicles 28:20a (MT)

GAVRIELLE   *[gahv-ree-EL]*

MEANING: God is my strength, strong woman of God • **USAGE:** Jewish feminine form of Gavriel, from Hebrew *gabhri'el* (man of God) and *gabher* (was strong)

The joy of the Lord is your strength.
— Nehemiah 8:10b (MT)

GAVRILA   *[gahv-REE-lah]*

MEANING: God is my strength, strong woman of God • **USAGE:** Jewish form of Gavriela (*see* Gavrielle)

The Lord is my strength and my shield; my heart trusts in Him.
— Psalm 28:7a (JPS)

GAY, GAYE, GAE   *[gay]*

MEANING: joyful, happy, gay • **USAGE:** English: from French *gale*

Joy, gentle friends! Joy and fresh days of love / Accompany your hearts!
— William Shakespeare, *A Midsummer Night's Dream*

GAYLA, GAILA   *[GAY-lah]*

MEANING: joyful, happy, gay • **USAGE:** English (*see* Gay)

Think joyful thoughts; think loving thoughts; let the elixir of goodwill course through your veins, and you will need no other medicine.
— James Allen, *From Poverty to Power*

GAYLEEN   *[GAY-leen]*

MEANING: joyful, happy, gay • **USAGE:** English (*see* Gay)

Surely joy is the principle of life.
— Henry David Thoreau

GAYORA   *[gay-OR-ah]*

MEANING: valley of light • **USAGE:** Jewish

Light shall shine upon thy ways.
— Job 22:28b (MT)

GEENA   *[JEEN-ah]*

MEANING: queen, royal one • **USAGE:** English form of Gina, from Latin *regina*

I know I have the body of a…woman, but I have the heart and stomach of a king.
— Queen Elizabeth I (speech of August 9, 1588)

GEILES   *[GAY-lesh]*

MEANING: white swan, shining swan • **USAGE:** Irish: from Gaelic *gel* (shining, white) and *geis* (swan)

Wash me, and I shall be whiter than snow.
— Psalm 51:7b (WEB)

GEMMA   *[JEM-ah]*

MEANING: gem, jewel, precious stone • **USAGE:** Italian and English: from Latin *gemma*

Hold on to wisdom and good sense. Don't let them out of your sight. They will give you life and beauty like a necklace around your neck.
— Proverbs 3:21–22 (NCV)

GENESIS   *[JEN-eh-sis]*

MEANING: origin, beginning, birth • **USAGE:** American: from Greek *genus* (race, birth, descent)

In the beginning God created the heaven and the earth.
— Genesis 1:1 (KJV)

GENEVA   *[jeh-NEE-vah]*

MEANING: juniper berry, juniper tree, race of women, matrilineal • **USAGE:** English: from French *genevre* (juniper berry); or English form of Genevieve, from Welsh *genos* (race, lineage) and *wefo* (woman)

> If the first woman God ever made was strong enough to
> turn the world upside down all alone,
> these together ought to be able to turn it back
> and get it right side up again.
> — Sojourner Truth, "Ain't I a Woman"
> (1851 Women's Rights Convention Speech)

GENEVIEVE, GENEVIÈVE   *[JEN-eh-veev (English), zheh-neh-VEEV (French)]*

MEANING: race of women, matrilineal • **USAGE:** English and French: from Welsh *genos* (race, lineage) and *wefo* (woman)

> Women...are the books, the arts, the academies,
> that show, contain and nourish all the world.
> — William Shakespeare, *Love's Labour's Lost*

GENICE, GENISE   *[jeh-NEES]*

MEANING: God is gracious, God is giving • **USAGE:** American: possibly a form of Janice, from Hebrew *y'hohanan* (Yahweh is gracious)

> May your gracious Spirit
> lead me forward on a firm footing.
> — Psalm 143:10b (NLT)

GEONA   *[gee-OH-nah]*

MEANING: glory, exaltation • **USAGE:** Jewish

> The Lord giveth grace and glory.
> — Psalm 84:12b (MT)

GEORGEANNE   *[JOR-jan]*

MEANING: gracious gardener • **USAGE:** American combination of George and Anne (*see* George and Anne)

> Gardening is an instrument of grace.
> — May Sarton, *Journal of a Solitude*

GEORGENE   *[jor-JEEN]*

MEANING: earth worker, farmer, gardener • **USAGE:** English feminine form of George (*see* Georgia)

> By a garden is meant mystically a place of spiritual
> repose, stillness, peace, refreshment, and delight.
> — John Henry Newman, "Rosa Mystica"

GEORGETTE   *[zhor-ZHET (French), jor-JET (English)]*

MEANING: earth worker, farmer, gardener • **USAGE:** French and English feminine form of George (*see* Georgia)

> Gardening is an active participation
> in the deepest mysteries of the universe.
> — Thomas Berry

GEORGIA   *[JOR-jah (English), yeh-oh-REE-ah (Greek)]*

MEANING: earth worker, farmer, gardener • **USAGE:** English and Greek feminine form of George, from Greek *ge* (earth) and *ergein* (to work)

> To cultivate a garden is to walk with God.
> — Christian Nestell Bovee,
> *Intuitions and Summaries of Thought*

GEORGINA   *[jor-JEEN-ah (English, Scottish), zhor-ZHEE-nah (Russian)]*

MEANING: earth worker, farmer, gardener • **USAGE:** Scottish, English, and Russian feminine form of George (*see* Georgia)

> Deep peace of the quiet earth to you...
> Deep peace, deep peace!
> — Fiona MacLeod, "Invocation of Peace"

GEORGINE   *[zhor-ZHEEN]*

MEANING: earth worker, farmer, gardener • **USAGE:** French feminine form of Georges (*see* Georgia)

> Truth will spring up from the earth.
> — Psalm 85:11 (HCSB)

GERALDINE   *[jer-al-DEEN, jerl-DEEN]*

MEANING: rule with a spear, powerful spear •
USAGE: English feminine form of Gerald, from
German *ger* (spear) and *wald* (rule, power)
No matter what you do,
work at it with all your might.
— Ecclesiastes 9:10a (NIRV)

GERDA   *[GAYR-dah]*

MEANING: guarded, protected, stronghold •
USAGE: German, Dutch, and Scandinavian: from
German *gard* (guard, protect); or from Norse *gerðr*
(enclosure, stronghold)
The Lord will protect your coming and going
both now and forever.
— Psalm 121:8 (HCSB)

GERLINDE   *[gayr-LIN-deh]*

MEANING: gentle spear • USAGE: German: from
German *ger* (spear) and *linde* (gentle, tender)
Have faith, love and gentleness.
Hold on to what you believe.
— 1 Timothy 6:11b (NIRV)

GERRIE, GERI   *[JER-ee]*

MEANING: rule with a spear, powerful spear •
USAGE: English form of Geraldine (*see* Geraldine)
I ask God from the wealth of his glory
to give you power through his Spirit
to be strong in your inner selves.
— Ephesians 3:16 (GNT)

GERSHONA   *[gayr-SHOH-nah]*

MEANING: stranger, foreigner • USAGE: Jewish
feminine form of Gershon
Build your home in such a way
that a stranger may feel happy in your midst!
— Theodor Herzl

GERTA   *[GAYR-tah]*

MEANING: spear maiden, strong spear • USAGE:
German form of Gertrud (*see* Gertrude)
Thou [God] didst make me bold
with strength in my soul.
— Psalm 138:3b (NASB)

GERTRUD   *[gayr-TROOD]*

MEANING: spear maiden, strong spear • USAGE:
Spanish form of Gertrude (*see* Gertrude)
She is clothed with strength and dignity,
and she laughs without fear of the future.
— Proverbs 31:25 (NLT)

GERTRUDA   *[gayr-TROO-dah]*

MEANING: spear maiden, strong spear • USAGE:
Polish form of Gertrude (*see* Gertrude)
She girds herself with strength,
and makes her arms strong.
— Proverbs 31:17 (NASB)

GERTRUDE   *[ger-TROOD]*

MEANING: spear maiden, strong spear • USAGE:
English form of Gertrud, from German *ger* (spear)
and *trut* (maiden) or *prup* (strength, power)
God did not give us a spirit of timidity
but a spirit of power and love and self-control.
— 2 Timothy 1:7 (RSV)

GHADA, GHADAH   *[GAH-dah]*

MEANING: graceful, gracious, beautiful • USAGE:
Muslim: from Arabic *ghayada* (to walk gracefully)
Mercy and Grace are just there; they are attributes /
of light, they want nothing but to be.
— Hafiz, "Who Could Read All This?"
(tr. Daniel Ladinsky in *A Year with Hafiz*)

GHADIR   [gah-DEER]

MEANING: stream, brook • **USAGE:** Muslim
> *Love that is progressive is like*
> *the sweet water of the running river.*
> — Hazrat Inayat Khan, *The Gayan*

GHALIYA, GHALIYAH   [gah-lee-ah]

MEANING: beloved, precious • **USAGE:** Muslim
> *Love is inexpressible in its fullness,*
> *but it is a power that speaks louder than words.*
> — Hazrat Inayat Khan, *The Gayan*

GHANIYA, GHANIA   [gah-nee-yah]

MEANING: wealthy, prosperous • **USAGE:** Muslim
feminine form of Ghani
> *Those will prosper who purify themselves,*
> *and glorify the name of their Guardian-Lord,*
> *and (lift their hearts) in prayer.*
> — Koran, The Most High 87.14–15 (ALI)

GHISLAINE   [zhees-LAYN]

MEANING: pledge, promise, vow, oath • **USAGE:**
French form of Giselle: from German *gisil*
> *For the Lord your God blesseth thee,*
> *as He promised thee.*
> — Deuteronomy 15:6a (KJV)

GHITA   [GEET-ah]

MEANING: pearl, beautiful gem • **USAGE:** Italian
form of Margherita, from Greek *margaron*
> *Beauty awakens the soul to act.*
> — Dante Alighieri

GIA   [JEE-ah]

MEANING: God is gracious, God is giving •
USAGE: Italian form of Gianna, from Hebrew
y'hohanan (Yahweh is gracious)
> *For he shall give his angels charge concerning thee,*
> *to keep thee in all thy ways.*
> — Psalm 91:11 (DT)

GIACINTA   [jah-CHEEN-tah]

MEANING: hyacinth flower • **USAGE:** Italian form
of Hyacinth, from Greek *hyakinthos*
> *The blossoms appear in the countryside.*
> *The time of singing has come.*
> — Song of Songs 2:12a (HCSB)

GIADA   [JAH-dah]

MEANING: jade, beautiful gem • **USAGE:** Italian
form of Jade, from Spanish *piedra de ijada* (stone
of the side; the belief that jade cured side pains); a
hard, green jadeite or nephrite stone
> *Everything that is in any way beautiful*
> *is beautiful of itself and complete in itself.*
> — Marcus Aurelius, *The Meditations*
> (tr. George Long)

GIANNA   [jee-AH-nah (Italian),
                    yee-AH-nah (Greek)]

MEANING: God is gracious, God is giving •
USAGE: Italian form of Giovanna, from Hebrew
y'hohanan (Yahweh is gracious)
> *God be gracious to you.*
> — Genesis 43:29b (ESV)

GIBORAH, GIBORA   [gih-BOH-rah]

MEANING: strong, powerful • **USAGE:** Jewish
feminine form of Gibor
> *She is clothed with strength and splendor;*
> *she looks to the future cheerfully.*
> — Proverbs 31:25 (JPS)

GIGI   [zhee-zhee]

MEANING: earth worker, farmer, gardener •
USAGE: French form of Georgette, from Greek *ge*
(earth) and *ergein* (to work)
> *Let us be grateful to people who make us happy;*
> *they are the charming gardeners*
> *who make our souls blossom.*
> — Marcel Proust, *Pleasures and Days*

G

GILAH   [GEE-lah, gee-LAH]

MEANING: joyous, happy • USAGE: Jewish
A joyful heart makes for good health.
— Proverbs 17:22a (JPS)

GILBERTA   [gil-BAYR-tah (German, Dutch), heel-BAYR-tah (Spanish)]

MEANING: shining promise, brilliant pledge, famous oath • USAGE: German, Dutch, and Spanish feminine form of Gilberto, from German *gisil* (pledge, promise) and *beraht* (bright, shining)
For the Lord your God will bless you,
as he promised you.
— Deuteronomy 15:6a (ESV)

GILDA   [GIL-dah]

MEANING: servant of God, gilded, golden one, sacrifice • USAGE: Scottish and English: from Gaelic *giolla* (devotee, servant) and *dia* (God); from English *gyldan* (gild, golden); or from German *gild* (sacrifice)
Live in the right way, serve God,
have faith, love, patience, and gentleness.
— 1 Timothy 6:11b (NCV)

GILL   [jil]

MEANING: young, youthful, of Jupiter • USAGE: English form of Gillian (*see* Gillian)
Youth is to all the glad season of life.
— Thomas Carlyle, "Schiller"

GILLIAN   [JIL-ee-an]

MEANING: young, youthful, of Jupiter • USAGE: English form of Jillian, from Latin *iulus* (downy-chinned, youthful); or form of Jupiter from Latin *dyeus* (Zeus) and *pater* (father)
You're never too old to become younger.
— Mae West

GINA   [JEEN-ah]

MEANING: queen, royal one, earth worker, farmer, gardener • USAGE: Italian and English form of Regina, from Latin *regina* (queen); or Italian form of Georgina, from Greek *ge* (earth) and *ergein* (to work)
A good mind possesses a kingdom.
— Seneca

GINETTE   [zheh-NET]

MEANING: queen, royal one, spring, springlike, flourishing, maiden, virgin • USAGE: French form of Regina, from Latin *regina* (queen); French form of Virginia, from Latin *ver* (spring) or Latin *virgo* (maiden, virgin); or French form of Georgine, from Greek *ge* (earth) and *ergein* (to work)
My kingdom is as wide as the universe.
— Gustave Flaubert, *The Temptation of St. Anthony* (tr. Guy de Maupassant)

GINGER   [JIN-jer]

MEANING: maiden, virgin, spring, springlike, flourishing, spice, spicy • USAGE: English orm of Virginia, from Latin *virgo* (maiden, virgin) or Latin *ver* (spring); or from English *gingifer* (a spice)
There is no time like Spring, /
When life's alive in everything.
— Christina Rossetti, "Spring"

GINNIE, GINNY, GENNY   [JEN-ee]

MEANING: spring, springlike, flourishing, maiden, virgin, race of women, matrilineal • USAGE: English form of Virginia, from Latin *ver* (spring) or Latin *virgo* (maiden, virgin); or English form of Genevieve, from Welsh *genos* (race, lineage) and *wefo* (woman)
Love's gentle spring doth always fresh remain.
— William Shakespeare,
Venus and Adonis

GIOIA [JOY-yah]

MEANING: rejoicing, joyful, glad, delight, delightful • **USAGE:** Italian form of Joy, from French *joie* (to rejoice)

> *I rejoice and am glad.*
> — Psalm 16:9a (NCV)

GIORA [gee-OH-rah]

MEANING: valley of light • **USAGE:** Jewish

> *Glorify ye the Lord in the regions of light.*
> Isaiah 24:15a (MT)

GIOVANNA [jyoh-VAH-na, joh-VAHN-ah]

MEANING: God is gracious, God is giving • **USAGE:** Italian form of Jean, from Hebrew *y'hohanan* (Yahweh is gracious)

> *I pray that the Lord will bless and protect you, and that he will show you mercy and kindness. May the Lord be good to you and give you peace.*
> — Numbers 6:24–26 (CEV)

GISELA [jee-SEH-lah]

MEANING: pledge, promise, vow, oath • **USAGE:** Scandinavian, Dutch, German, and Spanish form of Giselle (*see* Giselle)

> *The rainbow that I have put in the sky will be my sign to you and to every living creature on earth. It will remind you that I will keep this promise forever.*
> — Genesis 9:12–13 (CEV)

GISELLA [jee-ZEH-lah]

MEANING: pledge, promise, vow, oath • **USAGE:** Italian form of Giselle (*see* Giselle)

> *Lord, be good to me as you have promised. Increase my knowledge and give me good sense, because I believe in your commands.*
> — Psalm 119:66 (NIRV)

GISELLE [zhee-ZEL]

MEANING: pledge, promise, vow, oath • **USAGE:** French and English: from German *gisil*

> *For the Lord your God will bless you as He has promised.*
> — Deuteronomy 15:6a (NIV)

GITAH [GEE-tah]

MEANING: wine press • **USAGE:** Jewish

> *My cup runneth over.*
> — Psalm 23:5a (JPS)

GITEL, GITTEL [geh-TEL]

MEANING: good • **USAGE:** Yiddish

> *Among the upright there is good.*
> — Proverbs 14:9b (MT)

GITTA [GEE-tah]

MEANING: strong, noble, valorous, high, lofty • **USAGE:** Danish, Norwegian, and Swedish form of Birgitta, from Irish Gaelic *brígh* (strong, noble, valorous) or *brig* (high, lofty)

> *Be strong, and let your heart take courage.*
> — Psalm 27:14a (ESV)

GITTE [GEE-tah]

MEANING: strong, noble, valorous, high, lofty • **USAGE:** German form of Birgitte (*see* Gitta)

> *She sets about her work vigorously; her arms are strong for her tasks.*
> — Proverbs 31:17 (NIV)

GIULIA [JYOO-lee-ah]

MEANING: young, youthful, of Jupiter • **USAGE:** Italian form of Juliana, from Latin *iulus* (downy-chinned, youthful); or form of Jupiter, from Latin *dyeus* (Zeus) and *pater* (father)

> *There is a fountain of youth: it is your mind, your talents, the creativity you bring to your life and the lives of the people you love. When you learn to tap this source, you will truly have defeated age.*
> — Sophia Loren

G

G

GIZELLA   *[jeh-ZEH-lah]*

MEANING: pledge, promise, vow, oath • USAGE: Hungarian form of Giselle (*see* Giselle)

The Lord has promised
that he will not leave us or desert us.
— Hebrews 13:5b (CEV)

GIZI   *[gee-zee]*

MEANING: pledge, promise, vow, oath • USAGE: Hungarian form of Gizella (*see* Giselle)

God said, "This is the sign of the covenant I am
making between me and you and every living creature
with you, a covenant for all generations to come:
I have set my rainbow in the clouds, and it will be the
sign of the covenant between me and the earth."
— Genesis 9:12–13 (NIV)

GLADYS, GLADDIS   *[GLAD-is]*

MEANING: sword-shaped flower, ruler, leader, country, nation, lame, limping • USAGE: English and Welsh: English form of *gladiolus* (plant with sword-shaped leaves), from Latin *gladius* (sword); from Welsh *gwledig* (ruler) or *gwlad* (country); or Welsh form of Claudia, from Latin *claudus* (lame)

Flowers…are a proud assertion that a ray of beauty
outvalues all the utilities of the world.
— Ralph Waldo Emerson, "Gifts"

GLENDA   *[GLEN-dah]*

MEANING: pure and good, virtuous and holy, valley, secluded wooded valley, glen • USAGE: Welsh and English: from Welsh *glan* (pure, holy) and *da* (good); from Welsh *glyn* (valley, glen); or English feminine form of Glen, from Gaelic *gleann* (secluded wooded valley)

The hand that hath made you fair
hath made you good.
— William Shakespeare, *Measure for Measure*

GLENNA   *[GLEN-ah]*

MEANING: glen, secluded wooded valley • USAGE: Scottish feminine form of Glen, from Gaelic *gleann* (secluded wooded valley); or from Welsh *glyn* (valley, glen)

Going to the woods is going home.
— John Muir, "The Forests of the Yosemite Park"

GLENYS, GLENIS, GLENNIS   *[GLEN-is]*

MEANING: pure and holy valley • USAGE: Welsh: from Welsh *glan* (pure, holy) or *glyn* (valley, glen)

The place you are standing is holy ground.
— Exodus 3:5 (NIV)

GLORIA   *[GLOR-ee-ah]*

MEANING: glory, great praise • USAGE: English: from Latin *gloria*

Look at everything always as though you
were seeing it either for the first time or last time:
Thus is your time on earth filled with glory.
— Betty Smith, *A Tree Grows in Brooklyn*

GLORIANA, GLORIANNA   *[glor-ee-AN-ah]*

MEANING: glory, great praise, exalted • USAGE: English (*see* Gloria)

Your light shall break forth like the morning…
the glory of the Lord shall be your rear guard.
— Isaiah 58:8 (NKJV)

GOLDA   *[GOL-da]*

MEANING: gold, golden one • USAGE: Yiddish and English: from English *gold* (gold metal)

To improve the golden moment of opportunity,
and catch the good that is within our reach,
is the great art of life.
— Samuel Johnson, "The Patriot"

GOLDIE [GOL-dee]

MEANING: gold, golden one • **USAGE:** English: from English *gold* (gold metal)
> *See golden days, fruitful of golden deeds, /*
> *With joy and love triumphing.*
> — John Milton, *Paradise Lost*

GRACA [GRAH-kah]

MEANING: grace, graceful, gracious, blessed • **USAGE:** Portuguese: from Portuguese *graca*
> *Grace…is given not because we have done good works,*
> *but in order that we may have power to do them.*
> — Augustine of Hippo

GRACE [grays]

MEANING: grace, graceful, gracious, blessed • **USAGE:** English: from Latin *gratia*
> *Grace has been defined, the outward expression*
> *of the inward harmony of the soul.*
> — William Hazlitt, "On Manner"

GRACIANA [grah-see-AH-nah]

MEANING: grace, graceful, gracious, blessed • **USAGE:** Spanish form of Grace (*see* Grace)
> *Grace be with you.*
> — 1 Timothy 6:21b (NASB)

GRACIELA [grah-see-AY-lah]

MEANING: grace, graceful, gracious, blessed • **USAGE:** Spanish form of Grace (*see* Grace)
> *Grace is not part of consciousness; it is the amount*
> *of light in our souls, not knowledge nor reason.*
> — Pope Francis

GRANIA, GRAINNE [GRAHN-yah]

MEANING: grain, seedling, loved one, beloved • **USAGE:** Irish: from Gaelic *grainne* (grain, seed) or *graidhte* (loved one); *Grainne* is Irish grain goddess

> *Goodness is the harvest that is produced*
> *from the seeds the peacemakers plant in peace.*
> — James 3:17 (GNT)

GRAZIELLA [graht-ʒee-AY-lah]

MEANING: grace, graceful, gracious, blessed • **USAGE:** Italian (*see* Grace)
> *Thou hast said, I have known thee by name,*
> *and also thou hast found grace in Mine eyes.*
> — Exodus 33:12 (YLT)

GREER [greer]

MEANING: watchful, vigilant, alert • **USAGE:** Scottish and English surname: contraction of Gregor, from Greek *gregorein*
> *Wise choices will watch over you.*
> *Understanding will keep you safe.*
> — Proverbs 2:11 (NLT)

GRETA [GRET-ah]

MEANING: pearl, beautiful gem • **USAGE:** German, English, and Scandinavian form of Margaret, from Greek *margaron*
> *Unity and simplicity are the two true sources of beauty.*
> — Johann Joachim Winckelmann

GRETCHEN [GRET-chen]

MEANING: pearl, beautiful gem • **USAGE:** German and English form of Margaret (*see* Greta)
> *Physical beauty is the sign of an interior beauty,*
> *a spiritual and moral beauty, which is the basis,*
> *the principle, and the unity of the beautiful.*
> — Johann Friedrich von Schiller

GRETEL [GRET-el]

MEANING: pearl, beautiful gem • **USAGE:** German form of Margaret (*see* Greta)
> *O pearl of all things, woman!*
> — Johann Friedrich von Schiller

G

GRIET [greet]

MEANING: pearl, beautiful gem • USAGE: Danish and German form of Margaret (see Greta)

Behold, thou art fair.
— Song of Songs 1:15a (KJV)

GRIGORIA [gree-GOH-ree-ah]

MEANING: watchful, vigilant, alert • USAGE: Greek feminine form of Grigorios, from Greek *gregorein*

With all watchfulness keep thy heart,
because life issueth out from it.
— Proverbs 4:23 (DR)

GRISELDA [grih-SEL-dah]

MEANING: gray battle maid, gray warrior • USAGE: German: from German *gries* (gray) and *hild* (war, strife)

God arms me with strength,
and he makes my way perfect.
— Psalm 18:32 (NLT)

GUADALUPE [gwah-dah-LOO-pay]

MEANING: valley of the wolf • USAGE: Spanish: from Arabic *wadi lupi* (river of the wolves)

Wolves…are gentle-hearted.
— Lois Crisler, *Arctic Wild*

GUDRUN [GOOD-roon]

MEANING: secret lore of the gods, God's secret lore, friend of war, war ally • USAGE: Scandinavian and German: from Norse *guð* (god) and *run* (secret lore); or from Norse *gunnr* (war, strife) and *runa* (friend, ally)

My frame was not hidden from You, when I was made
in secret, and skillfully wrought in the depths of the
earth; Your eyes have seen my unformed substance;
and in Your book were all written the days that were
ordained for me, when as yet there was not one of them.
— Psalm 139:15–16 (NASB)

GUINEVERE [GWEN-eh-veer]

MEANING: white and smooth, fair, holy • USAGE: Welsh: from Welsh *gwyn* (white, fair, holy) and *hwyfar* (smooth, soft)

White as the sun, fair as the lily.
— Henry Constable, "Diaphenia"

GULSHAN [gool-shahn]

MEANING: rose garden • USAGE: Persian

Rosebud, what were you doing at night? /
I was praying to Heaven
with closed hands to open my heart.
— Hazrat Inayat Khan, *The Gayan*

GWEN, GWYN [gwen]

MEANING: white, fair, holy • USAGE: Welsh and English: from Welsh *gwyn*

Behold, you are fair!
— Song of Songs 1:15b (NKJV)

GWENDA [GWEN-dah]

MEANING: holy and good, beautiful and good • USAGE: Welsh: from Welsh *gwyn* (white, fair, holy) and *da* (good)

The good, by affinity, seek the good.
— Ralph Waldo Emerson,
"Divinity School Address"

GWENDOLEN, GWENDOLINE, GWENDOLYN [GWEN-doh-len]

MEANING: holy ring, white bow • USAGE: Welsh: from Welsh *gwyn* (white, fair, holy) and *dolen* (ring, bow)

Keep your minds on whatever is true,
pure, right, holy, friendly, and proper.
Don't ever stop thinking about
what is truly worthwhile and worthy of praise.
— Philippians 4:8 (CEV)

GWENEAL   *[GWEN-ee-el]*

MEANING: fair angel, white angel • **USAGE:**
Welsh: from Welsh *gwen* (white, fair, holy) and
angel (divine messenger, angel)

Behold, I send an Angel before thee,
to keep thee in the way.
— Exodus 23:20a (KJV)

GWYNETH, GWENYTH   *[GWEN-eth]*

MEANING: joyous, happy, fair and holy, white and
smooth • **USAGE:** Welsh and English: from Welsh
gwynaeth (joyous, happy); or from Welsh *gwyn*
(white, fair, holy) and *hwyfar* (smooth, soft)

Happiness is the spiritual experience of living every
minute with love, grace, and gratitude.
— Denis Waitley, *Seeds of Greatness*

GYANDA   *[gie-yahn-dah]*

MEANING: knowledgeable, learned • **USAGE:**
Hindu

Know God, and all fetters will be loosed.
Ignorance will vanish…In him all your desires
will find fulfillment.
— *Svetasvatara Upanishad*
(tr. Swami Prabhavananda)

H

HABIBAH, HABIBA   *[hah-BEE-bah]*

MEANING: beloved, love • **USAGE:** Muslim
feminine form of Habib, from Arabic *habib*

God wants to see /
More love and playfulness in your eyes /
For that is your greatest witness to Him.
— Hafiz, "Your Mother and My Mother"
(tr. Daniel Ladinsky in *The Gift*)

HADARA, HADERA   *[hah-DAH-rah,*
hah-DEH-rah]

MEANING: beautiful, ornamented, honored •
USAGE: Jewish

Ah, you are fair, my darling, ah, you are fair.
— Song of Songs 4:1a (JPS)

HADASSAH   *[hah-DAH-sah]*

MEANING: myrtle tree • **USAGE:** Jewish

Instead of the brier shall come up a myrtle;
and it shall be to the Lord for a memorial,
for an everlasting sign that shall not be cut off.
— Isaiah 55:13b (MT)

HADAYA   *[hah-dah-yah]*

MEANING: gift, present • **USAGE:** Muslim

The giver is greater than the gift.
— Hazrat Inayat Khan, *The Bowl of Saki*

HADIA, HADIYA   *[hah-dee-yah]*

MEANING: religious leader, rightly guided •
USAGE: Muslim feminine form of Hadi, Arabic
hadi (religious leader, one who guides) or *hada* (to
rightly guide)

To treat every human being as a shrine of God
is to fulfill all religion.
— Hazrat Inayat Khan, *The Bowl of Saki*

HADLEY   *[HAD-lee]*

MEANING: heather field, meadow of heather
• **USAGE:** English surname: from English *hæd*
(heathland, heather) and *leah* (meadow, field)

Look how the wild flowers grow!
They don't work hard to make their clothes.
But I tell you that Solomon with all his wealth
wasn't as well clothed as one of these flowers.
— Luke 12:27 (CEV)

H

HAFIZA, HAAFIZA, HAFIZAH
[hah-fee-zah]

MEANING: guardian, protector • **USAGE:** Muslim feminine form of Hafiz, from Arabic *hafiz*
Heaven guards our souls because they are so precious.
— Hafiz, "Ingredients from All Thought"
(tr. Daniel Ladinsky in *A Year with Hafiz*)

HAGAR
[hah-GAHR]

MEANING: emigrant, stranger • **USAGE:** Jewish: from Arabic *hajara* (to forsake, to emigrate)
Love ye therefore the stranger.
— Deuteronomy 10:19a (MT)

HAGIYA
[hah-gee-YAH]

MEANING: my feast, holiday, celebration • **USAGE:** Jewish feminine form of Chagai
Thus saith the Lord God…Gather yourselves on every side to My feast that I do prepare for you.
— Ezekiel 39:17b (JPS)

HAIFA
[HIE-fah]

MEANING: harbor, safe haven • **USAGE:** Jewish
Thou shalt be secure, because there is hope; yea, thou shalt look about thee, and shalt take thy rest in safety.
— Job 11:18 (MT)

HAKIMA, HAKEEMA
[hah-kee-mah]

MEANING: judge, judicious, just • **USAGE:** Muslim feminine form of Hakim, from Arabic *hakama* (to judge) or *hakim* (judicious)
To know the justice of God you must be just yourself.
— Hazrat Inayat Khan, *The Gayan*

HALCYON
[HAL-see-on]

MEANING: kingfisher bird, bright star • **USAGE:** American: from Greek *Halcyon* (kingfisher bird); brightest star of the Pleiades

*In our dreams we are able to fly…
and that is a remembering
of how we were meant to be.*
— Madeleine L'Engle, *Walking on Water*

HALIL
[hah-LEEL]

MEANING: flute • **USAGE:** Jewish feminine form of Chalil
Music…can name the unnameable and communicate the unknowable.
— Leonard Bernstein, "Musical Semantics"

HALIMA, HALIMAH, HALEEMA
[hah-LEE-mah]

MEANING: gentle, patient • **USAGE:** Muslim feminine form of Haleem, from Arabic *halima* (gentle, patient)
God is gentle and loveth gentleness.
— Hadith of the Prophet Muhammad

HALINA
[yah-lee-nah]

MEANING: light, illumination, torch • **USAGE:** Polish form of Helen, from Greek *helene* (torch) or *ele* (light)
Make your light shine, so that others will see the good that you do.
— Matthew 5:16a (CEV)

HALLE
[HAL-ee]

MEANING: ruler of the army, army commander, hay field, hall • **USAGE:** American: from English *here* (army) and *weald* (ruler, leader); from English *heg* (hay) and *leah* (meadow, field); or German surname, from English *heall* (manor, hall)
Beauty and grace command the world.
— Benjamin Park

HALLIE, HALLEY, HALLY
[HAH-lee (German), HAL-ee (English)]

MEANING: ruler of the army, army commander
• USAGE: German and English: German form of
Haralda, from English *here* (army) and *weald* (ruler,
leader)

> *There are many leaders,*
> *but a sensible leader restores law and order.*
> — Proverbs 28:2b (ESV)

HALONA
[hah-loh-nah]

MEANING: of happy fortune • USAGE: Amerind:
Zuni

> *One prays always for "all good fortune,"*
> *never for special and particular benefit.*
> — Ruth Bunzel, *Zuni Ceremonialism*

HAMIDAH, HAAMIDA, HAMIDA
[hah-mee-dah]

MEANING: praised, praiseworthy, exalted, honored
• USAGE: Muslim: from Arabic *hamid*

> *Grant me honourable mention*
> *on the tongue of truth among the latest (generations);*
> *make me one of the inheritors of the Garden of Bliss.*
> — Koran, The Poets 26.84–85 (ALI)

HANA
[hah-nah]

MEANING: flower • USAGE: Japanese: from
Japanese *hana*

> *There is nothing you can see that is not a flower.*
> — Matsuo Bashō

HANANA
[hah-nah-NAH]

MEANING: grace, gracious, merciful • USAGE:
Jewish form of Chanah, from Hebrew *chaanach*

> *A graceful woman obtains honour.*
> — Proverbs 11:16a (JPS)

HANIFA, HANEEFA
[hah-nee-fah]

MEANING: true believer, one of true faith •
USAGE: Muslim feminine form of Hanif, from
Arabic *hanif* (having the right belief)

> *Belief in God is the fuel,*
> *love of God is the glow,*
> *and the realization of God*
> *is the flame of divine light.*
> — Hazrat Inayat Khan, *The Gayan*

HANITA
[hah-nih-tah]

MEANING: divine grace • USAGE: Hindu

> *The Divine Light shines in their hearts,*
> *and like the sun which removes the darkness of night,*
> *it dispels the darkness of ignorance.*
> — Sri Guru Granth Sahib

HANIYYA, HANIYYAH
[hah-nih-yah]

MEANING: happy, joyful • USAGE: Muslim: from
Arabic *hani'a* (to take pleasure in, to be happy)

> *The soul's true happiness lies in*
> *experiencing the inner joy.*
> — Hazrat Inayat Khan, *The Bowl of Saki*

HANNA
[HAHN-ah]

MEANING: happy one • USAGE: African: Hausa of
Nigeria

> *Because you harbor goodwill towards others,*
> *you are happy.*
> — Nigerian proverb

HANNA
[HAH-nah]

MEANING: grace, gracious, merciful, God is
gracious, God is giving • USAGE: Scandinavian,
Dutch, Polish, and German form of Channah (*see*
Hannah)

> *God be gracious to you.*
> — Genesis 43:29b (NIV)

H

HANNAH
[HAN-ah (English),
HAH-nah (French, German, Scandinavian)]

MEANING: grace, gracious, merciful • **USAGE:**
English, French, German, and Scandinavian form
of Channah, from Hebrew *chaanach*
May the Lord bless you and keep you. May the Lord
show you his kindness and have mercy on you.
— Numbers 6:24–25 (NCV)

HARALDA
[hah-RAHL-dah]

MEANING: ruler of the army, army commander •
USAGE: German and Norwegian feminine form of
Harald, from English *here* (army) and *weald* (ruler,
leader)
The diligent person will rule.
— Proverbs 12:24a (NEB)

HAREENA
[hah-REE-nah]

MEANING: goddess of marriage, queen of the
gods, protector, guardian • **USAGE:** English form of
Hera, from Greek *heros* (protector, guardian), the
Greek goddess of marriage and queen of the gods
If you wish to marry suitably, marry your equal.
— Ovid

HARIETTA, HARRIETA, HARRIETTA
[hayr-ee-EH-tah]

MEANING: ruler of the home, ruler of the army,
army commander • **USAGE:** English feminine form
of Harry (*see* Harriet)
Where we love is home, /
Home that our feet may leave, but not our hearts.
— Oliver Wendell Holmes Sr.,
The Poet at the Breakfast Table

HARITA
[hah-rih-tah]

MEANING: yellow, green, brown, a monkey, the
sun, the wind • **USAGE:** Hindu: from Sanskrit *hari*
Joy is everywhere; it is in the earth's green covering of
grass; in the blue serenity of the sky.
—Rabindranath Tagore, *Sadhana*

HARLEY, HARLEIGH
[HAR-lee]

MEANING: hare meadow, from the field of hares •
USAGE: English surname: from English *hara* (hare)
and *leah* (meadow, field)
The Lord is my shepherd; I have everything I need.
He lets me rest in fields of green grass
and leads me to quiet pools of fresh water.
— Psalm 23:1–2 (GNT)

HARLOW
[HAR-loh]

MEANING: rocky hill, army hill • **USAGE:** English
surname: from English *hær* (rock) and *hlaw* (hill) or
from English *here* (army) and *hlaw* (hill)
The Lord said, Behold, there is a place by Me,
and thou shalt stand upon a rock.
— Exodus 33:21 (KJV)

HARMONIA
[har-MOH-nee-ah]

MEANING: harmony, accord • **USAGE:** Greek
form of *Harmonia* (Greek goddess of harmony),
from Greek *harmonia* (harmony, agreement)
Beauty of style and harmony and grace
and good rhythm depend on simplicity.
— Plato, *The Republic* (tr. Benjamin Jowett)

HARMONY, HARMONIE
[HAR-moh-nee]

MEANING: harmony, accord • **USAGE:** English
form of Harmonia (*see* Harmonia)
With an eye made quiet by the power /
Of harmony, and the deep power of joy, /
We see into the life of things.
— William Wordsworth, "Lines Composed
a Few Miles above Tintern Abbey"

HARPER
[HAR-per]

MEANING: harp player • **USAGE:** English
surname: from English *hearpe* (harp, stringed
instrument)
Music is well said to be the speech of angels.
— Thomas Carlyle, "The Opera"

HARRIET, HARRIETTE, HARIETTE

[HAYR-ee-et]

MEANING: ruler of the home, ruler of the army, army commander • **USAGE:** English feminine form of Harry, from German *heim* (home, house) and *rik* (rule, lead), or from English *here* (army) and *weald* (ruler, leader)

> *Home — that blessed word,*
> *which opens to the human heart the most perfect*
> *glimpse of Heaven, and helps to carry it thither,*
> *as on an angel's wings.*
> — Lydia Maria Child, *Letters from New York*

HARSHA

[hahr-shah]

MEANING: joy, happiness • **USAGE:** Hindu: from Sanskrit *harsha*

> *Live in joy, in peace.*
> — Buddha

HASANA, HASSANA

[hah-SAH-nah]

MEANING: beautiful, good • **USAGE:** Muslim feminine form of Hasan, from Arabic *hasan* (handsome) or *hasuna* (to be good)

> *Let the beauty we love be what we do.*
> — Jalaluddin Rumi, "Let the Beauty We Love"
> (tr. Coleman Barks in *The Book of Love*)

HASIBA, HASEEBA

[hah-SEE-bah]

MEANING: noble, honorable • **USAGE:** Muslim feminine form of Hasib, from Arabic *hasib*

> *She who respects others will merit their respect.*
> — Arabic proverb

HASIDA

[hah-SEE-dah]

MEANING: pious, righteous, devout • **USAGE:** Jewish form of Chasida

> *The root of the righteous will not be shaken loose.*
> — Proverbs 12:3b (JPS)

HASIFA, HASEEFA

[hah-SEE-fah]

MEANING: just, judicious • **USAGE:** Muslim feminine form of Hasif

> *If thou judge, judge in equity between them.*
> *For God loveth those who judge in equity.*
> — Koran, The Food 5.42b (ALI)

HASIMA, HASEEMA

[hah-SEE-mah]

MEANING: decisive, firm, resolute • **USAGE:** Muslim feminine form of Hasim, from Arabic *hasama* (to decide) and *hasim* (decisive)

> *Stand through life firm as a rock in the sea,*
> *undisturbed and unmoved by its ever-rising waves.*
> — Hazrat Inayat Khan, *The Gayan*

HASINA, HASEENA

[hah-SEE-nah]

MEANING: strong, secure, protected, guarded • **USAGE:** Muslim

> *Allah is sufficient as a Guardian,*
> *and Allah is sufficient as a Supporter.*
> — Koran, The Women 4.45b (PIC)

HAVA

[HAH-vah]

MEANING: life, full of life • **USAGE:** Jewish form of Chava, from Hebrew *hawwah*

> *Only morality in our actions*
> *can give beauty and dignity for life.*
> — Albert Einstein
> (letter of November 20, 1950)

HAVEN

[HAY-ven]

MEANING: haven, refuge • **USAGE:** English: from English *hæfen*

> *God is my strong place.*
> *He has made my way safe.*
> — 2 Samuel 22:33 (NLV)

H

H

HAYA   [HAH-yah]

MEANING: life, full of life • USAGE: Jewish form
of Chaya, from Hebrew *hawwah*
> *The life of the individual has meaning*
> *only in so far as it aids in making the life*
> *of every living thing nobler and more beautiful.*
> — Albert Einstein,
> *The World as I See It*

HAYDEN   [HAY-den]

MEANING: hay hill, hay valley, fire, fiery one,
heathen, pagan • USAGE: English and Welsh:
English surname, from *heg* (hay) and *dun* (hill)
or *denu* (valley); Welsh feminine form of Aidan,
from Gaelic *aodh* (fire); or from German *heidano*
(heathen)
> *Lord my God…makes winds his messengers,*
> *and flames of fire his servants.*
> — Psalm 104:1–4 (NIRV)

HAYLEY, HAILEY, HALEIGH   [HAY-lee]

MEANING: hay field • USAGE: English surname:
from English *heg* (hay) and *leah* (meadow, field)
> *Who sows a field, or trains a flower, /*
> *Or plants a tree, is more than all.*
> — John Greenleaf Whittier,
> "Lines for an Agricultural Exhibition"

HAZEL   [HAY-zel]

MEANING: hazel tree, hazel nut, brownish-green
color, vision of God, God sees • USAGE: English:
from English *hæsel* (hazel tree, greenish-brown
color); or English form of Hebrew *Haziel* (vision of
God, God sees)
> *The eye of mixed colour*
> *has always a definite character.*
> — Alice Meynell, *The Colour of Life*

HAZIMA   [hah-ʒee-mah]

MEANING: decisive, firm, resolute • USAGE:
Muslim feminine form of Hazim, from Arabic
hasama (to decide) and *hasim* (decisive)
> *Verily whoso is patient and forgiveth — lo! that,*
> *verily, is (of) the steadfast heart of things.*
> — Koran, The Counsel 42.43 (PIC)

HEATHER   [HETH-er]

MEANING: heather flower, heathland • USAGE:
English: from English *hæd*
> *What would the green earth be without its lovely*
> *flowers…. Their beauty fills our hearts with*
> *brightness and their love with tender thoughts.*
> — Louisa May Alcott, "The Frost King"

HEDDA   [HED-ah]

MEANING: warrior • USAGE: Scandinavian form
of Hedvig (*see* Hedwig)
> *Put you on the armour of God.*
> — Ephesians 6:11a (WEB)

HEDVA   [HED-vah]

MEANING: joyful, happy • USAGE: Jewish
> *This is the day which the Lord hath made;*
> *we will rejoice and be glad in it.*
> — Psalm 118:24 (MT)

HEDVIG   [HED-veeg]

MEANING: warrior • USAGE: Scandinavian form
of Hedwig (*see* Hedwig)
> *Be strong and courageous!*
> — Joshua 1:18b (NLT)

HEDWIG   [HED-veeg]

MEANING: warrior • USAGE: German: from
German *adu* (battle, conflict) and *wig* (war)
> *What a vast spirit in a narrow breast!*
> — Johann Wolfgang von Goethe,
> *Torquato Tasso* (tr. Charles des Voeux)

HEIDI, HEIDE [HIE-dee]

MEANING: noble one, highborn, honorable • **USAGE:** German, Scandinavian, and English form of Adelheid, from German *adal* (noble) and *heid* (sort, type)

> *Love and courage are the spirit's wings /*
> *Wafting to noble actions.*
> — Johann Wolfgang von Goethe,
> *Iphigenia in Tauris* (tr. Hjalmar Hjorth Boyesen)

HELEN [HEL-en]

MEANING: light, illumination, torch • **USAGE:** English form of Helene (*see* Helene)

> *Let your light shine for all to see.*
> — Isaiah 60:1b (NLT)

HELENA [heh-LEE-nah (English), heh-LAY-nah (German, Polish, Scandinavian), eh-LAY-nah (Spanish)]

MEANING: light, illumination, torch • **USAGE:** English, German, Polish, Scandinavian, and Spanish form of Helene (*see* Helene)

> *Be a gift and a benediction. Shine with real light.*
> — Ralph Waldo Emerson, "Spiritual Laws"

HELENE, HÉLÈNE [heh-LAY-neh (Greek, German, Scandinavian), HAY-lay-neh (French)]

MEANING: light, illumination, torch • **USAGE:** Greek, German, Scandinavian, and French: from Greek *helene* (torch) or *ele* (light)

> *Give light, and the darkness will disappear of itself.*
> — Erasmus

HELGA [HEL-gah]

MEANING: holy, blessed • **USAGE:** German: from Norse *heilagr*

> *Blessed art thou, and it shall be well with thee.*
> — Psalm 127:2b (DR)

HELGE [HEL-gah]

MEANING: prosperous, successful, blessed • **USAGE:** Scandinavian (*see* Helga)

> *May the Lord be with you and give you success.*
> — 1 Chronicles 22:11a (NLT)

HELMA [HEL-mah]

MEANING: determined protector, steadfast guardian • **USAGE:** German and Dutch form of Wilhelmina, from German *wil* (will, resolve) and *helm* (helmet, protection)

> *Guard, through the Holy Spirit who dwells in us, the treasure which has been entrusted to you.*
> — 2 Timothy 1:14 (NASB)

HÉLOÏSE, HELOISE [EL-oh-eez]

MEANING: warrior • **USAGE:** French form of Eloise, from German *hlud* (famous) and *wig* (war, strife)

> *Who is this who shines like the dawn —*
> *as beautiful as the moon, bright as the sun,*
> *awe-inspiring as an army with banners?*
> — Song of Songs 6:10 (HCSB)

HENRIETTA [hen-ree-ET-ah]

MEANING: ruler of the home, house leader • **USAGE:** English form of Henriette (*see* Henriette)

> *This is the true nature of home —*
> *it is the place of Peace.*
> — John Ruskin, "Of Queens' Gardens"

HENRIETTE [ahn-ree-ET (French), hen-ree-ET-eh (German)]

MEANING: ruler of the home, house leader • **USAGE:** French and German feminine form of Henry, from German *heim* (home, house) and *rik* (rule, lead)

> *By wisdom a house is built,*
> *and through understanding it is established.*
> — Proverbs 24:3 (NIV)

HENRIKA   [HEN-ree-kah]

MEANING: ruler of the home, house leader •
USAGE: Scandinavian feminine form of Hendrik
(*see* Henriette)

> *May there be peace within your walls...*
> *may peace be within you.*
> — Psalm 122:7–8 (NLV)

HENRIQUA   [ahn-REE-kah]

MEANING: ruler of the home, house leader •
USAGE: Spanish and Portuguese feminine form of
Henrique (*see* Henriette)

> *Be pleased to bless the house of your servant,*
> *that it may continue forever in your sight; for you,*
> *O Sovereign Lord, have spoken, and with your blessing*
> *the house of your servant will be blessed forever.*
> — 2 Samuel 7:29 (NIV)

HENYA, HENIA   [hen-YAH]

MEANING: grace of God • **USAGE:** Jewish form of
Chenya, from Hebrew *chaanach* and *Yah* (Yahweh)

> *The Lord your God is gracious and merciful,*
> *and will not turn away His face from you.*
> — 2 Chronicles 30:9b (MT)

HERA   [HEHR-ah]

MEANING: goddess of marriage, queen of the gods,
protector, guardian • **USAGE:** English: from Greek
heros (protector, guardian), the Greek goddess of
marriage and queen of the gods

> *Union gives strength.*
> — Aesop, "The Bundle of Sticks"

HERMIONE   [her-MIE-oh-nee]

MEANING: herald, messenger • **USAGE:** English
feminine form of *Hermes* (Greek god, herald, and
messenger)

> *How beautiful on the mountains are the feet of the*
> *herald, who proclaims peace,*
> *who brings news of good things.*
> — Isaiah 52:7a (HCSB)

HERMOSA   [ayr-MOH-sah]

MEANING: beautiful • **USAGE:** Spanish: from
hermosa

> *How beautiful you are.*
> — Song of Songs 1:15a (NLT)

HERUT   [heh-ROOT]

MEANING: freedom, liberty • **USAGE:** Jewish

> *Nothing is as liberating as joy.*
> *It frees the mind and fills it with tranquility.*
> — Nachman of Breslov

HESPER   [HES-per]

MEANING: evening star • **USAGE:** English: from
Greek *hesperos*

> *The evening star, / Love's harbinger.*
> — John Milton, *Paradise Lost*

HESTER   [HES-ter]

MEANING: star, starlike, radiant • **USAGE:** English
form of Esther, from Persian *stara*

> *The stars are jewels of the night*
> *and perchance surpass anything*
> *which day has to show.*
> — Henry David Thoreau, "Night and Moonlight"

HETTIE   [HET-ee]

MEANING: ruler of the home, ruler of the army,
army commander • **USAGE:** English form of
Harriette, from German *heim* (home, house) and *rik*
(rule, lead) or from English *here* (army) and *weald*
(ruler, leader)

> *Home is a name, a word, it is a strong one;*
> *stronger than magician ever spoke,*
> *or spirit ever answered to,*
> *in the strongest conjuration.*
> — Charles Dickens,
> *The Life and Adventures of Martin Chuzzlewit*

HIALEAH *[hie-ah-leh-ah]*

MEANING: pretty prairie • **USAGE:** Amerind: Seminole-Creek

The Indian talks in poetry…the free and untrammeled poetry of nature, the poetry of the fields, the sky, the river, the sun and the stars.
— Alexander Posey

HIBA *[hee-bah]*

MEANING: gift, present • **USAGE:** Muslim: from Arabic *hiba*

As to those who are made happy, they shall be in the garden, abiding in it as long as the heavens and the earth endure, except as your Lord please; a gift which shall never be cut off.
— Koran, Hud 11.108 (SKR)

HIILANI *[hee-ee-LAH-nee]*

MEANING: held in the arms of heaven • **USAGE:** Hawaiian

Let the selecting be done in heaven.
— Hawaiian proverb
(tr. Mary Pukui in *'Olelo No'eau*)

HIKARI *[hee-kah-ree]*

MEANING: light, radiance • **USAGE:** Japanese: from Japanese *hikari*

Thousands of candles can be lit from a single candle, and the life of the candle will not be shortened. Happiness never decreases by being shared.
— Buddha

HILARIA *[ee-LAHR-yah]*

MEANING: cheerful, joyful, happy • **USAGE:** Spanish form of Hilary (*see* Hilary)

Let me be happy and joyful!
— Psalm 51:8a (CEV)

HILARY, HILLARY *[HIL-ah-ree]*

MEANING: cheerful, joyful, happy • **USAGE:** English: from Latin *hilaris*

She is strong and graceful, as well as cheerful about the future.
— Proverbs 31:25 (CEV)

HILDA *[HIL-dah]*

MEANING: army guard, protecting warrior • **USAGE:** German and Scandinavian form of Hildegard (*see* Hildegard)

I am sending an angel ahead of you to guard you along the way.
— Exodus 23:20a (NIV)

HILDEGARD *[HIL-deh-gahrd]*

MEANING: army guard, protecting warrior • **USAGE:** German and Scandinavian: from German *hild* (war, battle) and *gard* (guard, protect)

The Lord is going before you, and… is your rear guard.
— Isaiah 52:12b (HCSB)

HILLAH *[hee-LAH]*

MEANING: praise, glory • **USAGE:** Jewish feminine form of Hillel

The Lord bestows grace and glory.
— Psalm 84:12b (JPS)

HIRO *[hee-roh]*

MEANING: generous, magnanimous • **USAGE:** Japanese: from Japanese *hiro*

Be charitable to all beings, love is the representative of God.
— Ko-ji-ki

H

H

HIROKO   [hee-roh-koh]

MEANING: generous child, magnanimous child •
USAGE: Japanese: from Japanese *hiro* (generous)
and *ko* (child)

The generous person gives /
not just what they have / but of who they are.
— Shi Wuling, *Path to Peace*

HIROMI   [hee-roh-mee]

MEANING: generous and beautiful, generous
beauty • **USAGE**: Japanese: from Japanese *hiro*
(generous) and *mi* (beautiful)

With generosity comes /
loving-kindness, wisdom, humility, /
thoughts of all others and great joy.
— Shi Wuling, *Path to Peace*

HIYAM   [hee-yahm]

MEANING: love • **USAGE**: Muslim

God is love; when love is awakened in the heart,
God is awakened there.
— Hazrat Inayat Khan, *The Bowl of Saki*

HOKUALA   [hoh-koo-AH-lah]

MEANING: rising star • **USAGE**: Hawaiian

The stars, na hoku, guide me at night —
they show me the way to my destiny.
— Hawaiian proverb

HOLLY, HOLLIE   [HAH-lee]

MEANING: holly bush, holly berry • **USAGE**:
English: from English *holen* (holly, evergreen tree
or shrub)

Earth's crammed with heaven,
and every common bush afire with God.
— Elizabeth Barrett Browning, *Aurora Leigh*

HONI   [HOH-nee]

MEANING: kiss • **USAGE**: Hawaiian

Be one in love.
— Hawaiian proverb
(tr. Mary Pukui in *'Olelo No'eau*)

HONOKA   [hoh-noh-kah]

MEANING: harmony flower • **USAGE**: Japanese:
from Japanese *hono* (harmony) and *ka* (flower)

The blossoms of the heart no wind can touch.
— Kenkō Yoshida, *The Harvest of Leisure*

HONORA   [oh-NOR-ah]

MEANING: honor, honorable • **USAGE**: English
and Irish: from Latin *honor*

Wisdom is more valuable than precious jewels;
nothing you want compares with her.
In her right hand Wisdom holds a long life,
and in her left hand are wealth and honor.
— Proverbs 3:15–16 (CEV)

HONORIA   [oh-noh-REE-ah]

MEANING: honor, honorable • **USAGE**: Spanish:
(*see* Honora)

The Lord bestows favor and honor; he withholds no
good thing from those who have integrity.
— Psalm 84:11b (NEB)

HONORINE   [oh-noh-reen]

MEANING: honor, honorable • **USAGE**: French:
(*see* Honora)

The wise inherit honor.
— Proverbs 3:35a (NIV)

HOPE   [hohp]

MEANING: hope, faith • **USAGE**: English: from
English *hopa*

Whatever enlarges hope will also exalt courage.
— Samuel Johnson,
A Journey to the Western Islands of Scotland

HORTENSE
[or-TAHNS (French),
HOR-tens (English)]

MEANING: garden, gardener • **USAGE:** French and English form of Roman family name *Hortensia*, from Latin *hortus*

A garden is a grand teacher. It teaches patience and careful watchfulness; it teaches industry and thrift; above all it teaches entire trust.
— Gertrude Jekyll, *Wood and Garden*

HORTENSIA
[hor-TEN-see-ah (English),
or TEHN-see-uh (Spanish)]

MEANING: garden, gardener • **USAGE:** English and Spanish feminine form of Hortense (*see* Hortense)

A garden is a lovesome thing.
— Thomas Edward Brown, "My Garden"

HOSHI
[hoh-shee]

MEANING: star, starlike • **USAGE:** Japanese: from Japanese *hoshi*

Always try to be in communion with heaven and earth; then the world will appear in its true light.
— Morihei Ueshiba, *The Art of Peace*
(tr. John Stevens)

HOSHIKO
[hoh-shee-koh]

MEANING: star child • **USAGE:** Japanese: from Japanese *hoshi* (star) and *ko* (child)

Stars on a rainy night. [Something rare.]
— Japanese proverb

HUA
[hwah]

MEANING: flower, blossom • **USAGE:** Chinese

Flowers leave some of their fragrance in the hand that bestows them.
— Chinese proverb

HUAN
[hwahn]

MEANING: happy, joyous • **USAGE:** Chinese

Happiness is Heaven-sent.
— Chinese proverb (tr. William Scarborough)

HUBA
[HOO-bah]

MEANING: love, friendship • **USAGE:** African: Swahili of Kenya/Tanzania

Love is love only when it affects both sides.
— Swahili proverb

HUDA
[HOO-dah]

MEANING: right path, rightly guided • **USAGE:** Muslim: from Arabic *huda* (right guidance) or *hada* (to lead upon the right path)

Love guides its own way.
— Hazrat Inayat Khan, *The Gayan*

HUDSON
[HUD-son]

MEANING: heart, mind, spirit • **USAGE:** English surname: a form of Hugh, from German *hugu* (heart, mind, spirit) and *son*

The best and most beautiful things in this world cannot be seen or even heard, but must be felt with the heart.
— Helen Keller, *The Story of My Life*

HUI
[hwee]

MEANING: benevolent, kind, merciful • **USAGE:** Chinese

Mercy is the root and core.
— Chinese proverb (tr. William Scarborough)

HULDA
[HOOL-dah]

MEANING: lovable, beloved • **USAGE:** Scandinavian and German: from Swedish *huld*

Behold, you are beautiful, my beloved, yes, pleasant.
— Song of Songs 1:16a (WEB)

H

HUMITA   [hoo-mee-tah]

MEANING: shelled corn • USAGE: Amerind: Hopi
> *Corn is the Hopi heart.*
> — Hopi proverb

HYACINTHE, HYACINTH   [hee-ah-SEENT (French), hie-ah-SENTH (English)]

MEANING: hyacinth flower • USAGE: French and English: from Greek *hyakinthos*
> *Flowers always make people better,*
> *happier and more hopeful; they are sunshine,*
> *food and medicine to the soul.*
> — Luther Burbank

HYUN-JA   [hyun-jah]

MEANING: wise woman • USAGE: Korean: from Korean *hyun* (wise) and feminine ending *-ja*
> *Whoever is patient, free from hate and fear,*
> *is said to be wise.*
> — Buddha, *The Dhammapada*
> (tr. Sanderson Beck)

HYUN-JU   [hyun-joo]

MEANING: precious and wise • USAGE: Korean: from Korean *hyun* (wise) and *joo* (precious)
> *Meditation brings wisdom; lack of meditation*
> *leaves ignorance. Know well what leads you*
> *forward and what holds you back,*
> *and choose the path that leads to wisdom.*
> — Buddha

HYUN-YOUNG   [hyun-yung]

MEANING: wise flower, prosperous flower • USAGE: Korean: from Korean *hyun* (wise) and *young* (flower, prosperous)
> *Whoever guides others by a procedure*
> *that is nonviolent and fair*
> *is said to be a guardian of truth, wise and just.*
> — Buddha, *The Dhammapada* (tr. Sanderson Beck)

I

IANTHE   [YAHN-theh]

MEANING: violet flower • USAGE: English: from Greek *ion* (violet) and *anthos* (flower)
> *Look how the wild flowers grow:*
> *they do not work or make clothes for themselves.*
> *But I tell you that not even King Solomon*
> *with all his wealth had clothes as beautiful*
> *as one of these flowers.*
> — Matthew 6:28b–29 (GNT)

IDA   [IE-dah (English), EE-dah (German)]

MEANING: industrious, hard worker • USAGE: English and German: from German *id* (work, labor)
> *Work nourishes the soul…we honor life when we work.*
> — Elisabeth Kübler-Ross

IDE   [EE-dah]

MEANING: thirst for goodness and knowledge • USAGE: Irish: from Gaelic *íde* (thirst, thirst for goodness and knowledge)
> *You will become wise,*
> *and your knowledge will give you pleasure.*
> — Proverbs 2:10 (GNT)

IDETTA   [ie-DET-ah]

MEANING: industrious one, little worker • USAGE: English form of Ida and diminutive *-etta* (see Ida)
> *Perform your work with a whole heart*
> *and you will succeed.*
> — Elbert Hubbard

IDETTE   [ie-DET]

MEANING: industrious one, little worker • USAGE: English form of Ida and diminutive *-ette* (see Ida)
> *She is a hard worker, strong and industrious.*
> — Proverbs 31:17 (NEB)

IGNACIA *[eeg-NAH-see-ah]*

MEANING: fire, fiery • **USAGE:** Spanish feminine form of Ignacio, from Latin *ignis*
> *You [God] make the winds serve as your messengers.*
> *You make flashes of lightning serve you.*
> — Psalm 104:3–4 (NIRV)

IJABA *[ee-jah-bah]*

MEANING: wish fulfilled • **USAGE:** African: Hausa of Nigeria
> *Thatch water can fill the water pot.*
> *[Steadiness and patience can bring success.]*
> — Nigerian proverb

ILA *[ih-lah]*

MEANING: earth • **USAGE:** Hindu: Sanskrit
> *O mother earth, kindly set me down upon a*
> *well-founded place! With (father)*
> *heaven co-operating, O thou wise one,*
> *do thou place me into happiness and prosperity.*
> — *Atharva Veda* (tr. Friedrich Max Müller)

ILANA *[ee-LAH-nah]*

MEANING: tree • **USAGE:** Jewish feminine form of Ilan; symbolic name for girls born on Tu b'Shvat, the New Year of the Trees
> *The root of the righteous shall never be moved.*
> — Proverbs 12:3b (MT)

ILANDRA *[eh-LAHN-drah]*

MEANING: little rock, beautiful • **USAGE:** American: possibly a form of Alana, Breton *alp* (rock) and diminutive *-an*; or from Scotch Gaelic *àlainn* (beautiful, handsome)
> *How beautiful you are, my darling!*
> *Oh, how beautiful!*
> — Song of Songs 4:1a (NIV)

ILANIT *[ee-lah-NEET]*

MEANING: tree • **USAGE:** Jewish feminine form of Ilan
> *The fruit of the righteous is a tree of life.*
> — Proverbs 11:30a (MT)

ILARIA *[ee-LAHR-ee-ah]*

MEANING: cheerful, joyful, happy • **USAGE:** Italian form of Hilary, from Latin *hilaris*
> *The best provision for a happy life is…*
> *to practise honesty in good earnest,*
> *and speak truth from the very soul of you.*
> — Marcus Aurelius, *The Meditations*
> (tr. Jeremy Collier)

ILENE *[IE-leen]*

MEANING: light, illumination, torch • **USAGE:** English form of Eileen, from Greek *helene* (torch) or *ele* (light)
> *God said, "Let there be light."*
> *And there was light!*
> *God saw that the light was good.*
> — Genesis 1:3–4a (NEB)

ILIMA *[ee-LEE-mah]*

MEANING: flower • **USAGE:** Hawaiian
> *The flower is nature's work of art.*
> — Hawaiian proverb

ILONA *[ee-LOH-nah]*

MEANING: light, illumination, torch • **USAGE:** Hungarian and German form of Helen, from Greek *helene* (torch) or *ele* (light)
> *Your light shall break out as the morning.*
> — Isaiah 58:8a (WEB)

ILSA   [EEL-sah]

MEANING: God is my oath, joined with God, blessed by God • USAGE: German form of Elizabeth, from Hebrew *el'ishebha*
> *The Lord your God is with you wherever you go.*
> — Joshua 1:9b (NKJV)

ILSE   [EEL-seh]

MEANING: God is my oath, joined with God, blessed by God • USAGE: Scandinavian form of Elizabeth (*see* Ilsa)
> *God has said,*
> *"Never will I leave you; never will I forsake you."*
> — Hebrews 13:5 (NIV)

ILY   [IE-lee]

MEANING: love, beloved • USAGE: American: acronym for "I Love You"
> *Mercy unto you, and peace and love be multiplied.*
> — Jude 1:2 (KJ21)

IMELDA   [ee-MEL-dah]

MEANING: strong and powerful warrior • USAGE: Italian and Spanish form of *Irmenhild*, from German *erm* (strength, power) and *hild* (war, battle)
> *God did not give us a spirit of cowardice, but rather a*
> *spirit of power and of love and of self-discipline.*
> — 2 Timothy 1:7 (NRSV)

IMINA   [ee-MEE-nah]

MEANING: seeker of truth • USAGE: Hawaiian
> *Those who really seek the path*
> *to Enlightenment dictate terms to their mind.*
> *Then they proceed with strong determination.*
> — Buddha

IMMA   [EM-ah]

MEANING: whole, universal, entire, strong, powerful • USAGE: German form of Irma, from German *ermen* (whole, universal) or *erm* (strength, power)
> *You will be a blessing.*
> *Don't be afraid; let your hands be strong.*
> — Zechariah 8:13b (HCSB)

IMMANUELA   [ee-mah-noo-EH-lah, ee-MAN-yoo-EL-ah]

MEANING: God is with us • USAGE: Jewish feminine form of Immanuel, from Hebrew *immanu' el*
> *I am the Lord...Behold, I am with thee,*
> *and will keep thee whithersoever thou goest.*
> — Genesis 28:13a, 28:15a (MT)

IMOGEN   [EM-oh-jen]

MEANING: maiden, young woman, daughter • USAGE: Irish: possibly from Gaelic *inghean* (maiden) or *inighion* (daughter)
> *Many daughters have done well,*
> *but you excel them all.*
> — Proverbs 31:29 (NKJV)

IMOGENE   [EM-oh-jeen]

MEANING: maiden, young woman, daughter • USAGE: English form of Imogen (*see* Imogen)
> *Who is that young woman*
> *that shines out like the dawn?*
> *She is as pretty as the moon,*
> *as bright as the sun.*
> — Song of Songs 6:10a (NCV)

INA   [EE-nah]

MEANING: follower of Christ, Christian, one who is free, adult • USAGE: Spanish form of Cristina, from Greek *christianos* (follower of Christ); Spanish form of Carolina, from English *ceorl* (freeman, peasant) or German *karl* (full-grown man, adult)
> *Ye shall know the truth,*
> *and the truth shall make you free.*
> — John 8:32 (ASV)

INDA [EN-dah]

MEANING: India, beautiful, very pretty • **USAGE:** English and American: English form of India, from Hindu: Sanskrit *Sindhu* (name of the Indus River); or American, possibly a form of Linda, from Spanish *linda* (beautiful, pretty)

Love is the river of life in this world.
— Henry Ward Beecher, "Of Giving Pleasure"

INDIA [EN-dee-ah]

MEANING: name of country, land of the Indus River • **USAGE:** English: from Hindu Sanskrit *Sindhu* (name of the Indus River)

India chose her places of pilgrimage wherever there was in nature some special grandeur or beauty, so that her mind could come out of its world of narrow necessities and realise its place in the infinite.
— Rabindranath Tagore, *Sadhana*

INDIGO [IN-dih-goh]

MEANING: purplish-blue dye, purple-blue color • **USAGE:** English: from Greek *indikon* (purplish-blue dye from India)

The blue color is everlastingly appointed by the Deity to be a source of delight.
— John Ruskin, *The True and the Beautiful*

INDIRA [in-DEE-rah]

MEANING: beautiful, splendid • **USAGE:** Hindu: from Sanskrit *indira*

She is the most beautiful among women; upon her forehead she wears the Jewel of the Lord's Love.
— Sri Guru Granth Sahib
(Khalsa Consensus Translation)

INÉS, INES [ee-NEHS]

MEANING: pure one, chaste, holy, lamb • **USAGE:** Spanish and Portuguese form of Agnes, from Greek *hagnos* (chaste, holy); or from Latin *agnus* (lamb)

Like a shepherd He will tend His flock, in His arm He will gather the lambs and carry them in His bosom.
— Isaiah 40:11a (NASB)

INESSA [ee-NES-ah]

MEANING: pure one, chaste, holy, lamb • **USAGE:** Russian form of Agnes (*see* Inés)

Blessed are the pure in heart, for they shall see God.
— Matthew 5:8 (NKJV)

INEZ [IE-nez (English), EE-nez (Portuguese)]

MEANING: pure one, chaste, holy, lamb • **USAGE:** English and Portuguese form of Agnes (*see* Inés)

The Lord is my shepherd; I have everything I need.
— Psalm 23:1 (NCV)

INGA [EEN-gah]

MEANING: beautiful Ing, peaceful and fair • **USAGE:** Scandinavian and German feminine form of *Ing* (Norse god of peace and fertility) and *friðr* (fair, beautiful)

Foster the beautiful, and every hour thou callest new flowers to birth.
— Johann Friedrich von Schiller

INGE [EEN-geh]

MEANING: beautiful Ing, peaceful and fair • **USAGE:** Scandinavian form of Inga (*see* Inga)

Behold, thou art fair.
— Song of Songs 1:16a (DT)

INGRID [EEN-grid]

MEANING: beautiful Ing, peaceful and fair • **USAGE:** Scandinavian and German feminine form of *Ing* (*see* Inga)

Peace, peace be to thee!
— 1 Chronicles 12:18b (ASV)

IOANNA   *[ee-oh-AH-nah]*

MEANING: God is gracious, God is giving •
USAGE: Greek feminine form of Ioannis, from
Hebrew *y'hohanan* (Yahweh is gracious)
> *God be gracious unto thee.*
> — Genesis 43:29b (KJV)

IOLA   *[ie-OH-lah]*

MEANING: violet flower, purple color • **USAGE:**
English: from Greek *ion*
> *I smelt the violets in her hand and asked,*
> *half in words, half in signs, a question which meant*
> *"Is love the sweetness of flowers?"*
> — Helen Keller, *The Story of My Life*

IONA   *[ie-OH-nah]*

MEANING: violet flower, purple color, Scottish
island, Greek region • **USAGE:** Scottish and
English: from Greek *ion* (violet flower, purple);
from Norse *ey* (island); island in the Hebrides off
Scotland; or from Ionia, a region in Greece
> *Summer isles of Eden,*
> *lying in dark purple spheres of sea.*
> — Alfred Tennyson, "Locksley Hall"

IRA   *[IH-rah]*

MEANING: earth • **USAGE:** Hindu: Sanskrit
> *The earth has compassion and forgiveness.*
> — *Sri Guru Granth Sahib*
> (Khalsa Consensus Translation)

IRELAND   *[IER-land]*

MEANING: abundant land, name of country •
USAGE: American: from Gaelic *Eiriu* (Gaelic
goddess of the land); or from Sanskrit *pivan*
(suggesting abundant land)
> *Ireland is where strange tales*
> *begin and happy endings are possible.*
> — Charles Haughey

IRENA, IREÑA   *[ee-RAY-nah (Scandinavian,*
Czech, Polish), ee-RAYN-yah (Spanish)]

MEANING: peace, peaceful, calm, serene • **USAGE:**
Scandinavian, Czech, Polish, and Spanish form of
Irene (*see* Irene)
> *May mercy, peace, and love be multiplied to you.*
> — Jude 1:2 (HCSB)

IRENE   *[ie-REEN (English), ee-RAY-neh*
(German, Italian, Scandinavian)]

MEANING: peace, peaceful, calm, serene • **USAGE:**
English, German, Italian, and Scandinavian form of
Eireni, from Greek *eirene*
> *She hath a natural, wise sincerity,*
> *a simple truthfulness, and these have lent her*
> *a dignity as moveless as the centre.*
> — James Russell Lowell, "Irene"

IRENKA   *[ee-RAYN-kah]*

MEANING: peace, peaceful, calm, serene • **USAGE:**
English form of Eirene (*see* Irene)
> *Grace and peace be given to you more and more.*
> — 2 Peter 1:2a (NCV)

IRINA   *[ee-REE-nah]*

MEANING: peace, peaceful, calm, serene • **USAGE:**
Czech form of Irena (*see* Irene)
> *Love truth and peace.*
> — Zechariah 8:19b (NIV)

IRIS   *[EE-rees (Greek, Spanish),*
IE-ris (English)]

MEANING: goddess of the rainbow, iris flower •
USAGE: Greek, English, and Spanish: from Greek
iris (rainbow); Greek goddess of the rainbow; type
of flower
> *When there is love in the heart,*
> *there are rainbows in the eyes.*
> — Henry Ward Beecher,
> *Proverbs from Plymouth Pulpit*

IRMA   *[EER-mah (German, Scandinavian), ER-mah (English)]*

MEANING: strong, powerful, whole, universal, entire • **USAGE:** German, Spanish, and English: from German *ermen* (whole, universal) or *erm* (strength, power)

> *You are the light of the world.*
> — Matthew 5:14 (NKJV)

ISABEL   *[ee-sah-BEL (Spanish), ee-ʒah-BEL (French, German), IZ-ah-bel (English)]*

MEANING: God is my oath, joined with God, blessed by God • **USAGE:** Spanish, English, French and German form of Isabela, from Hebrew *el'ishebha*

> *In all things God works*
> *for good with those who love him,*
> *those whom he has called according to his purpose.*
> — Romans 8:28 (GNT)

ISABELA   *[ee-sah-BAY-lah]*

MEANING: God is my oath, joined with God, blessed by God • **USAGE:** Spanish and Portuguese form of Elizabeth (*see* Isabel)

> *Every one that loveth, is born of God,*
> *and knoweth God.*
> — 1 John 4:7b (DR)

ISABELLA   *[ee-sah-BAY-lah (Italian, German), iʒ-ah-BEL-ah (English)]*

MEANING: God is my oath, joined with God, blessed by God • **USAGE:** Italian, German, and English form of Isabela (*see* Isabel)

> *Thou art the God of my heart,*
> *and the God that is my portion for ever.*
> — Psalm 72:26b (DR)

ISABELLE   *[IZ-ah-bel (English), ee-ʒah-BEL (French)]*

MEANING: God is my oath, joined with God, blessed by God • **USAGE:** English and French form of Isabel (*see* Isabel)

> *I believe that God is in me,*
> *as the sun is in the color and fragrance of a flower,*
> *the Light in my darkness, the Voice in my silence.*
> — Helen Keller, *Midstream*

ISADORA   *[iʒ-ah-DOR-ah]*

MEANING: gift of Isis, fruitful, bounteous • **USAGE:** English form of Isidora (*see* Isidora)

> *You will enjoy the fruit of your labor.*
> *How joyful and prosperous you will be!*
> — Psalm 128:2 (NLT)

ISIDORA   *[ee-seh-DOR-ah]*

MEANING: gift of Isis, fruitful, bounteous • **USAGE:** Greek, Italian, and Spanish: from *Isis* (Egyptian goddess of fertility) and Greek *doron* (gift)

> *As for you, be fruitful.*
> — Genesis 9:7a (NIV)

ISOBEL   *[IS-oh-bel]*

MEANING: God is my oath, joined with God, blessed by God • **USAGE:** Scottish form of Isabela (*see* Isabel)

> *God to enfold me, / God to surround me, /*
> *God in my speaking, / God in my thinking.*
> — Alexander Carmichael, *Carmina Gadelica*

ISOKE   *[ee-soh-keh]*

MEANING: wonderful gift from God, God's gift • **USAGE:** African: Benin of Nigeria

> *No one can uproot the tree which God has planted.*
> — Nigerian proverb

ISOLDE   *[ih-SOLD]*

MEANING: beautiful, fair • USAGE: Welsh: from
Welsh *esyllt*
>   *All beautiful you are, my darling;*
>   *there is no flaw in you.*
>   — Song of Songs 4:7 (RSV)

IVANA   *[ee-VAH-nah]*

MEANING: God is gracious, God is giving •
USAGE: Czech feminine form of Ivan, from
Hebrew *y'hohanan* (Yahweh is gracious)
>   *May grace and peace be yours in full measure.*
>   — 2 Peter 1:2a (GNT)

IVANKA   *[eh-VAHN-kah]*

MEANING: God is gracious, God is giving •
USAGE: Czech form of Ivana (*see* Ivana)
>   *God gives the Spirit without limit.*
>   — John 3:34b (NIV)

IVANNA   *[ee-VAH-nah]*

MEANING: God is gracious, God is giving •
USAGE: Russian feminine form of Ivan (*see* Ivana)
>   *God is gracious and merciful;*
>   *He will not turn His face away from you.*
>   — 2 Chronicles 30:9b (HCSB)

IVONA   *[ee-VOHH-nah]*

MEANING: God is gracious, God is giving •
USAGE: Polish form of Ivana (*see* Ivana)
>   *God saith...I have given to thee a heart,*
>   *wise and understanding.*
>   — 1 Kings 3:11–12b (YLT)

IVONNE   *[ee-VOHN]*

MEANING: yew tree, bow maker • USAGE:
German and Scandinavian form of Yvonne, from
German *iv* (yew tree); yew is used to make bows

>   *Trees are sanctuaries. Whoever knows how*
>   *to listen to them, can learn the truth.*
>   — Hermann Hesse

IVORY   *[IE-vor-ee]*

MEANING: ivory, elephant tusk, shade of white
• USAGE: American: from English *ivorie* (ivory,
elephant tusk); semiprecious substance
>   *Love...will draw an elephant through a key-hole.*
>   — Samuel Richardson, *Clarissa*

IVY   *[IE-vee]*

MEANING: ivy, climbing plant, vine • USAGE:
English: from English *ifig*
>   *That headlong ivy!...bold to leap a height.*
>   — Elizabeth Barrett Browning, *Aurora Leigh*

IZABELLA   *[ee-sah-BAY-lah]*

MEANING: God is my oath, joined with God,
blessed by God • USAGE: Hungarian, Polish, and
Russian form of Isabela (*see* Isabel)
>   *The God of peace shall be with you.*
>   — Philippians 4:9b (DT)

IZZIE, IZZY   *[IZ-ee]*

MEANING: God is my oath, joined with God,
blessed by God, gift of Isis, fruitful, bounteous •
USAGE: English form of Isabelle (*see* Isabel); or
English form of Isidora (*see* Isidora)
>   *The Lord your God will prosper*
>   *you abundantly in all the work of your hand.*
>   — Deuteronomy 30:9a (NASB)

J

JACARANDA   *[hah-kah-RAHN-dah]*

MEANING: tree with lavender flowers • USAGE:
Spanish: *jacaranda* (tree with lavender flowers)

There is hope for a tree...
from the fragrance of water it doth flourish.
— Job 14:7–9a (YLT)

May the God of Jacob protect you....May he give you
what you want and make all your plans succeed.
— Psalm 20:1b, 20:4 (NCV)

JACINTA [hah-SEEN-tah]

MEANING: hyacinth flower • **USAGE:** Spanish
form of Hyacinth (*see* Jacinthe)
Flowers appear on the earth;
the season of singing has come.
— Song of Songs 2:12a (RSV)

JACINTHE [zhah-SEENT]

MEANING: hyacinth flower • **USAGE:** French form
of Hyacinth, from Greek *hyakinthos*
Think how the flowers grow.
They do not work or make cloth.
But I tell you that Solomon in all his greatness
was not dressed as well as one of these flowers.
— Matthew 6:28b–29 (NLV)

JACKIE, JACKY [JAK-ee]

MEANING: replace, change, transform, successor
• **USAGE:** English form of Jacqueline (*see*
Jacqueline)
Love transforms.
— Michael Dorris, "The Power of Love"

JACKLYN [JAK-len]

MEANING: replace, change, transform, successor
• **USAGE:** English feminine form of Jacob (*see*
Jacqueline)
Let God transform you inwardly.
— Romans 12:2b (GNT)

JACOBA [jah-KOH-bah (English), yah-KOH-bah (Dutch)]

MEANING: replace, change, transform, successor •
USAGE: English and Dutch feminine form of Jacob
(*see* Jacqueline)

JACQUELINE [zhahk-LEEN (French), JAK-weh-len (English)]

MEANING: replace, change, transform, successor
• **USAGE:** French and English feminine form of
Jacob, from Hebrew *ya'aqobh* (one that takes by the
heel, replace with another)
To exist is to change, to change is to mature,
to mature is to go on creating oneself endlessly.
— Henri-Louis Bergson

JACQUELYN [JAK-weh-len]

MEANING: replace, change, transform, successor
• **USAGE:** English feminine form of Jacob (*see*
Jacqueline)
Change will not come if we wait
for some other person or some other time.
We are the ones we've been waiting for.
We are the change that we seek.
— Barack Obama (speech of February 5, 2008)

JACQUETTE [zhah-KET]

MEANING: replace, change, transform, successor •
USAGE: French form of Jacqueline (*see* Jacqueline)
Be ye transformed by the renewing of your mind.
— Romans 12:2b (KJ21)

JACQUI, JACQUE [ZHAH-kee (French), JAK-ee (English)]

MEANING: replace, change, transform, successor
• **USAGE:** American form of Jacqueline (*see*
Jacqueline)
Change always comes bearing gifts.
— Price Pritchett,
The Employee Handbook of New Work Habits
for a Radically Changing World

J

JADA   *[JAY-dah]*

MEANING: jade gemstone, beautiful jewel •
USAGE: English form of Jade (*see* Jade)

Whatever the soul desires, that is the jewel of its life.
— Thomas à Kempis,
The Imitation of Christ (tr. John Payne)

JADE   *[jayd (English), ʒhahd (French)]*

MEANING: jade gemstone, jade-green color,
beautiful jewel • **USAGE:** English and French: from
Spanish *piedra de ijada* (stone of the side; the belief
that jade cured side pains); a hard, green jadeite or
nephrite stone

The ideal has many names,
and beauty is but one of them.
— W. Somerset Maugham, *Cakes and Ale*

JADEN, JAIDEN, JADYN   *[JAY-den]*

MEANING: jade gemstone, beautiful jewel •
USAGE: American form of Jade (*see* Jade)

How beautiful you are, my darling.
How beautiful you are!
— Song of Songs 4:1a (NASB)

JAHIDA, JAHEEDA   *[jah-HEE-dah]*

MEANING: diligent, hardworking • **USAGE:**
Muslim feminine form of Jahid, from Arabic *jahada*
(to make an effort)

Lo! those who believe and do good works,
theirs are the Gardens of Paradise for welcome.
— Koran, The Cave 18.107 (PIC)

JAKOVA   *[yah-KOH-vah]*

MEANING: replace, change, transform, successor
• **USAGE:** Hungarian feminine form of Jakov (*see*
Jacqueline)

Come, O house of Jacob,
let us walk in the light of the Lord.
— Isaiah 2:5 (NIV)

JALAINA, JALAYNA   *[jah-LAY-nah]*

MEANING: God will add, God will increase, light,
illumination, torch • **USAGE:** American: possibly
a form of Jolene, from Hebrew *ya'saph* (Yahweh
will add); or possibly a form of Elena, from Greek
helene (torch) or *ele* (light)

May the Lord make your love for each other
and for everyone else grow by leaps and bounds.
— 1 Thessalonians 3:12a (CEV)

JALEH   *[jah-leh]*

MEANING: dew • **USAGE:** Persian

Be aware of your own worth....
Create an ocean from a dewdrop.
— Muhammad Iqbal

JALILA, JALILAH   *[jah-LEE-lah]*

MEANING: great, illustrious, exalted • **USAGE:**
Muslim feminine form of Jalil, from Arabic and
jalla (to be great, to be illustrious)

Do well the little things now; so shall great things come
to thee, by and by, asking to be done.
— Persian proverb

JALINDA   *[jah-LIN-dah]*

MEANING: beautiful, very pretty • **USAGE:**
American: possibly a form of Linda, from Spanish
linda

You are beautiful, my love; ah, you are beautiful.
— Song of Songs 1:15a (NRSV)

JAMEELA, JAMILAH   *[jah-MEE-lah]*

MEANING: beautiful, lovely • **USAGE:** Muslim:
from Arabic *jamula*

Love develops into harmony,
and of harmony is born beauty.
— Hazrat Inayat Khan, *The Gayan*
(cd. *The Gayani Meditations, Volume 1,*
tr. Cecil Touchon)

J

JAMIE   *[JAY-mee]*

Meaning: replace, change, transform, successor • **Usage:** English feminine form of James, from Hebrew *ya'aqobh* (one that takes by the heel, replace with another)

> *Be transformed by the renewing of your mind.*
> — Romans 12:2b (NKJV)

JAN   *[jan]*

Meaning: God is gracious, God is giving • **Usage:** English feminine form of John (*see* Jane)

> *May God be gracious to you.*
> — Genesis 43:29b (NASB)

JANA   *[YAH-nah (Czech, Dutch, German), JAN-ah (English)]*

Meaning: God is gracious, God is giving • **Usage:** Czech, Dutch, German, and English form of Janna (*see* Jane)

> *Thou hast said, "I know thee by name, and thou hast also found grace in My sight."*
> — Exodus 33:12b (KJ21)

JANAE   *[jah-NAY]*

Meaning: God is gracious, God is giving • **Usage:** American: possibly a form of Jane (*see* Jane)

> *God said...wisdom and knowledge have been granted you.*
> — 2 Chronicles 1:11 (NASB)

JANAN   *[jah-nahn]*

Meaning: heart, soul • **Usage:** Muslim: from Arabic *janan*

> *God dwells between a person and their heart.*
> — Arabic proverb

JANE, JAYNE   *[jayn]*

Meaning: God is gracious, God is giving • **Usage:** English feminine form of John, from Hebrew *y'hohanan* (Yahweh is gracious)

> *The Lord be with your spirit. Grace be with you.*
> — 2 Timothy 4:22 (HCSB)

JANELLE   *[jah-NEL]*

Meaning: God is gracious, God is giving • **Usage:** English form of Jane (*see* Jane)

> *God be gracious to you.*
> — Genesis 43:29b (RSV)

JANESSA, JENESSA   *[jah-NES-ah]*

Meaning: God is gracious, God is giving • **Usage:** American: possibly a form of Janice (*see* Jane)

> *"For I know the plans I have for you," declares the Lord, "plans to prosper you and not harm you, plans to give you hope and a future."*
> — Jeremiah 29:11 (NIV)

JANET   *[JAN-et]*

Meaning: God is gracious, God is giving • **Usage:** English form of Jane (*see* Jane)

> *The Lord your God is gracious and merciful, and will not turn away his face from you.*
> — 2 Chronicles 30:9b (KJV)

JANEY, JANIE, JAYNIE   *[JAY-nee]*

Meaning: God is gracious, God is giving • **Usage:** English form of Jane (*see* Jane)

> *Lord, everything you have given me is good. You have made my life secure.*
> — Psalm 16:5 (NIRV)

J

JANICE, JANIS   *[JAN-is]*

MEANING: God is gracious, God is giving •
USAGE: English form of Jane (*see* Jane)

The Lord bless thee and keep thee;
the Lord make His face shine upon thee,
and be gracious unto thee;
the Lord lift up His countenance upon thee,
and give thee peace.
— Numbers 6:24–26 (KJ21)

JANIKA   *[jah-NEE-kah]*

MEANING: God is gracious, God is giving •
USAGE: Hungarian feminine form of John (*see* Jane)

God said…Behold,
I give you a wise and discerning mind.
— 1 Kings 3:11–12b (ESV)

JANINA   *[zhuh-NEE-nah]*

MEANING: garden • **USAGE:** African: Tunisia
To look at green adorns the heart and the eye.
— North African proverb

JANINE   *[jah-NEEN]*

MEANING: God is gracious, God is giving •
USAGE: English form of Jeanine (*see* Jane)
May the Lord be with your spirit.
May God's grace be with you.
— 2 Timothy 4:22 (NIRV)

JANIQUA, JANEKA   *[jah-NEE-kah]*

MEANING: God is gracious, God is giving •
USAGE: American: possibly a form of Jane (*see* Jane)

The God who gives peace will be with you.
— Philippians 4:9b (NLV)

JANIQUE, JENIQUE   *[jah-NEEK]*

MEANING: God is gracious, God is giving •
USAGE: American: possibly a form of Jane (*see* Jane)

May God be gracious to you.
— Genesis 43:29b (NEB)

JANITA   *[yah-NEE-tah (Scandinavian),*
jeh-NEET-ah (English)]

MEANING: God is gracious, God is giving •
USAGE: Scandinavian and American form of Janet (*see* Jane)

May God's grace be with you.
— Colossians 4:18b (NLT)

JANNA   *[YAH-nah (Dutch, Scandinavian),*
JAN-ah (English)]

MEANING: God is gracious, God is giving •
USAGE: Dutch, Scandinavian, and English form of Johanna (*see* Jane)

The gracious, eternal God permits the spirit
to green and bloom and bring forth the
most marvelous fruit, surpassing anything
a tongue can express and a heart conceive.
— Johannes Tauler, "Sermon 24"

JANNA   *[JAH-nah]*

MEANING: garden, paradise • **USAGE:** Muslim:
from Arabic *jinan*

Love reveals the paradise.
— Hafiz, "Selling Your Art"
(tr. Daniel Ladinsky in *A Year with Hafiz*)

JANNE   *[YAH-nah]*

MEANING: God is gracious, God is giving •
USAGE: Scandinavian form of Johanna (*see* Jane)
God is able to give you more than you need,
so that you will always have all you need for yourselves
and more than enough for every good cause.
— 2 Corinthians 9:8 (GNT)

JANNIKE [*YAH-nee-kah*]

MEANING: God is gracious, God is giving •
USAGE: Scandinavian feminine form of Jannik (*see* Jane)

> *Surely goodness and mercy shall follow me*
> *all the days of my life; and I will dwell in the house*
> *of the Lord for ever.*
> — Psalm 23:6 (KJ21)

JASMINE, JASMYN [*JAZ-min*]

MEANING: jasmine flower, jasmine perfume •
USAGE: English: from Persian *yasamin* (shrub with fragrant flowers)

> *Love flowers best in openness and freedom.*
> — Edward Abbey, *Desert Solitaire*

JAVIERA [*hah-bee-AYR-ah*]

MEANING: new house • **USAGE:** Spanish feminine form of Javier, from Basque place-name *Etxabier*

> *Let it please thee to bless the house of thy servant,*
> *that it may continue for ever before thee: for thou,*
> *O Lord God, hast spoken it: and with thy blessing*
> *let the house of thy servant be blessed for ever.*
> — 2 Samuel 7:29 (KJV)

JAYNA [*jay-nah*]

MEANING: victorious, triumphant, successful •
USAGE: Hindu: from Sanskrit *jaya*

> *Purity, patience, and perseverance are the three*
> *essentials to success and, above all, love.*
> — Swami Vivekananda

JAZMIN, JAZMINE [*JAZ-min*]

MEANING: jasmine flower, jasmine perfume •
USAGE: American form of Jasmine (*see* Jasmine)

> *Love is…the perfume of that wondrous flower,*
> *the heart.*
> — Robert Green Ingersoll, "Orthodoxy"

JAZZ [*jaz*]

MEANING: jasmine flower, jasmine perfume, music
• **USAGE:** American form of Jasmine (*see* Jasmine)

> *There is something very wonderful in music…*
> *it speaks straight to our hearts and spirits,*
> *to the very core and root of our souls.*
> — Charles Kingsley, "Sermon XVII"

JEAN [*jeen*]

MEANING: God is gracious, God is giving •
USAGE: English feminine form of John, from Hebrew *y'hohanan* ('Yahweh is gracious')

> *I know you by name,*
> *and you have also found grace in My sight.*
> — Exodus 33:12b (NKJV)

J

JEANA, JEANNA [*JEE-nah*]

MEANING: God is gracious, God is giving •
USAGE: English form of Jean (*see* Jean)

> *May the God of all grace…*
> *establish, strengthen, and settle you.*
> — 1 Peter 5:10 (NKJV)

JEANETTE, JEANNETTE [*jeh-NET (English), zhah-NET (French)*]

MEANING: God is gracious, God is giving •
USAGE: English and French form of Jeanne (*see* Jean)

> *God is able to make all grace abound toward you;*
> *that ye, always having all sufficiency in all things,*
> *may abound to every good work.*
> — 2 Corinthians 9:8 (KJV)

JEANIE, JEANNIE [*JEE-nee*]

MEANING: God is gracious, God is giving •
USAGE: English form of Jean (*see* Jean)

> *May the Lord bring good to you and keep you.*
> *May the Lord make His face shine upon you,*
> *and be kind to you. May the Lord show favor toward*
> *you, and give you peace.*
> — Numbers 6:24–26 (NLV)

JEANINE, JEANNINE   *[ʒhah-NEEN (French), jah-NEEN (English)]*

MEANING: God is gracious, God is giving • **USAGE:** French and English form of Jeanne (*see* Jean)

For it is good that the heart be established by grace.
— Hebrews 13:9b (NKJV)

JEANNE   *[ʒhahn (French), jeen (English)]*

MEANING: God is gracious, God is giving • **USAGE:** French and English feminine form of John (*see* Jean)

God gave us the gift of life;
it is up to us to give ourselves the gift of living well.
— Voltaire

JEANNIQUE   *[ʒhah-NEEK]*

MEANING: God is gracious, God is giving • **USAGE:** French form of Jeanne (*see* Jean)

God be gracious to you.
— Genesis 43:29b (WEB)

JELISSA, JALISSA   *[jeh-LIS-ah]*

MEANING: honeybee, honey • **USAGE:** American: possibly a form of Melissa, from Greek *melissa* (honeybee) or *meli* (honey)

How to extract its honey from the flower
of the world — that is my everyday-business.
I am busy as a bee about it.
— Henry David Thoreau
(journal entry of September 7, 1851)

JEMIMA   *[jeh-MIE-mah]*

MEANING: dove, dove-like • **USAGE:** English form of Yemima, from Hebrew *yemimah;* a symbol of peace

Behold, thou art fair, my love; behold,
thou art fair. Thou hast doves' eyes.
— Song of Songs 4:1a (21KJ)

JEN, JENN   *[jen]*

MEANING: fair and smooth, holy • **USAGE:** English form of Jennifer (*see* Jennifer)

Lo, thou [art] fair, my friend, lo, thou [art] fair.
— Song of Songs 4:1a (YLT)

JENKA   *[YEN-kah]*

MEANING: God is gracious, God is giving • **USAGE:** Czech form of Jane (*see* Jane)

The Lord be with your spirit. Grace be to you.
— 2 Timothy 4:22 (NASB)

JENNA   *[JEN-ah]*

MEANING: fair and smooth, holy • **USAGE:** English form of Jennifer (*see* Jennifer)

For everything that lives is holy, life delights in life.
— William Blake, "America: A Prophecy"

JENNIFER   *[JEN-eh-fer]*

MEANING: fair and smooth, holy • **USAGE:** English form of Guinevere, from Welsh *gwyn* (white, fair, holy) and *hwyfar* (smooth, soft)

How fair and how pleasant art thou,
O love, for delights!
— Song of Songs 7:6 (KJV)

JENNY, JENNIE   *[JEN-ee]*

MEANING: fair and smooth, holy • **USAGE:** English form of Jennifer (*see* Jennifer)

You are all fair, my love, and there is no spot in you.
— Song of Songs 4:7 (NKJV)

JENSEN   *[JEN-sen]*

MEANING: God is gracious, God is giving • **USAGE:** English surname meaning "son of John"; John is from Hebrew *y'hohanan* (Yahweh is gracious)

'Tis grace hath brought me safe thus far
and grace will lead me home.
— John Newton, "Amazing Grace"

JENSINE   *[YEN-see-neh, YEN-seen]*

MEANING: God is gracious, God is giving • **USAGE:** Norwegian feminine form of Jens (*see* Jensen)

May He give you what your heart desires
and fulfill your whole purpose.
— Psalm 20:4 (HCSB)

JERI, JERRI, JERRIE   *[JER-ee]*

MEANING: God will raise up, God will uplift, holy name, sacred name, rules with a spear, spear ruler • **USAGE:** English feminine form of Jerald, from Hebrew *yirmeyahu* (may Yahweh exalt), or from Latin *hieras* (holy) and *onyma* (name); or English form of Geraldine, from German *ger* (spear) and *wald* (rule, power)

You said, "I have known you by name.
You have found favor in My eyes."
— Exodus 33:12b (NLV)

JESENIA, JESSENIA   *[hay-SAY-nee-ah]*

MEANING: palm tree, date palm tree • **USAGE:** Spanish: from *Jessenia*, a South American palm tree

The righteous shall flourish like the palm tree.
— Psalm 92:12a (KJV)

JESSA   *[JES-ah]*

MEANING: God beholds, vision of God, gift • **USAGE:** English form of Jessica (*see* Jessica)

Behold, O Lord, thou hast known all things,
the last and those of old: thou hast formed me,
and hast laid thy hand upon me.
— Psalm 138:5 (DR)

JESSAMINE, JESSAMYN   *[JES-ah-meen,*
JES-ah-men]

MEANING: jasmine flower, jasmine perfume • **USAGE:** English form of Jasmine, from Persian *yasamin* (shrub with fragrant flowers)

Unconscious goodness is the perfume
of the soul in blossom.
— Henry Ward Beecher,
Proverbs from Plymouth Pulpit

JESSICA   *[JES-eh-kah]*

MEANING: God beholds, vision of God, gift • **USAGE:** English feminine form of Jesse, from Hebrew *yishai* (gift); also from *The Merchant of Venice* by William Shakespeare, possibly based on Hebrew *yiskah* (Yahweh beholds)

The eye with which I see God
is the same eye with which God sees me.
— Meister Eckhart,
"True Hearing" (tr. Raymond Blakney)

JESSIE   *[JES-ee]*

MEANING: God beholds, vision of God, gift • **USAGE:** English form of Jessica (*see* Jessica)

The eye repeats every day the first eulogy
on things — "He saw that they were good."
— Ralph Waldo Emerson, *Representative Men*

JESTINA   *[jes-TEE-nah]*

MEANING: just, judicious, fair • **USAGE:** American form of Justine, from Latin *justus*

There is joy for those who deal justly
with others and always do what is right.
— Psalm 106:3 (NLT)

JESÚSA   *[hay-SOO-sah]*

MEANING: God is salvation • **USAGE:** Spanish feminine form of Jesús, from Hebrew *yesha'yah* (Yahweh is salvation)

The Lord makes me very happy;
all that I am rejoices in my God.
He has covered me with clothes of salvation
and wrapped me with a coat of goodness.
— Isaiah 61:10a (NCV)

J

JETTA   [JET-ah]

MEANING: ruler of the home, house leader, coal-black, dark • USAGE: English form of Henriette (see Jette)

Our roots are in the dark....
Not in the light that blinds, but in the dark that
nourishes, where human beings grow human souls.
— Ursula K. Le Guin,
"A Left-Handed Commencement Address"

JETTE   [YET-ah]

MEANING: ruler of the home, house leader, coal-black, dark • USAGE: German, Dutch, and English form of Henriette, from German *heim* (home, house) and *rik* (rule, lead); or from English *jet* (coal-black)

Black is the color of creation.
It is the womb out of which the new is born.
— Ted Andrews, *Animal Speak*

JEWEL, JEWELL   [JOO-el]

MEANING: jewel, gem, precious stone • USAGE: English: from French *jouel*

You shall be a crown of beauty
in the hand of the Lord.
— Isaiah 62:3a (NRSV)

JIA   [jhee-ah]

MEANING: good • USAGE: Chinese

Follow the good, and learn to be so.
— Chinese proverb

JIAN   [jhee-ahn]

MEANING: healthy, strong • USAGE: Chinese

Being deeply loved by someone gives you strength,
while loving someone gives you courage.
— Lao Tzu

JIANG   [jhee-ahng]

MEANING: river • USAGE: Chinese

Human nature is disposed to goodness,
just as water tends to flow downwards.
— Mencius (tr. William Scarborough)

JIAO   [jhee-ow]

MEANING: beautiful, lovely • USAGE: Chinese

Beauty is the wisdom of women.
— Chinese proverb

JIHAN   [jeh-HAHN]

MEANING: world • USAGE: Persian

And do you have worlds within your self? Indeed. /
The night sky a microcosm of you.
— Hafiz, "A Child's Mere Pencil Sketch"
(tr. Daniel Ladinsky in *A Year with Hafiz*)

JILL   [jil]

MEANING: young, youthful, of Jupiter • USAGE: English form of Jillian (see Jillian)

The heart that has once been bathed in love's pure
fountain retains the pulse of youth forever.
— Walter Savage Landor, *Petrarcha*

JILLIAN   [JIL-ee-an]

MEANING: young, youthful, of Jupiter • USAGE: English feminine form of Julian, from Latin *iulus* (downy-chinned, youthful); or form of Jupiter, from Latin *dyeus* (Zeus) and *pater* (father)

Youth...is the freshness of deep springs of life.
— Samuel Ullman, "Youth"

JI-MIN   [jee-min]

MEANING: wise and intelligent • USAGE: Korean: from Korean *ji* (wisdom, heart) and *min* (clever)

A good, all-round education,
appreciation of the arts, a highly trained discipline
and pleasant speech; this is the highest blessing.
— *Sutta Nipata*

JIN [*jhen*]

MEANING: gold, golden • **USAGE:** Chinese
Like a golden beacon signaling on a moonless night,
Tao guides our passage through this transitory realm.
— Loy Ching Yuen

JINAN [*jih-nahn*]

MEANING: garden, paradise • **USAGE:** Muslim:
from Arabic *jinan*
Lo! those who believe and do good works,
theirs will be Gardens underneath which rivers flow.
That is the Great Success.
— Koran, The Constellations 85.11 (PIC)

JIN-SOOK [*jin-sook*]

MEANING: true and pure • **USAGE:** Korean: from
Korean *jin* (truth, honesty) and *sook* (pure)
The teaching is simple. / Do what is right. /
Be pure. / At the end of the way is freedom. /
Till then, patience.
— Buddha, *The Dhammapada* (tr. Thomas Byrom)

JIRANI [*jee-rah-nee*]

MEANING: neighbor • **USAGE:** African: Swahili of
Kenya and Tanzania
God is our neighbor when our brother is absent.
— Swahili proverb

JIRINA [*yee-ree-nah*]

MEANING: earth worker, farmer, gardener •
USAGE: Czech form of George, from Greek *ge*
(earth) and *ergein* (to work)
The earth is full of the lovingkindness of the Lord.
— Psalm 33:5b (NASB)

JIVANI [*jih-vah-nee*]

MEANING: life, enlivening • **USAGE:** Hindu:
Sanskrit

Life is the fire that burns and is the sun that gives light.
Life is the wind and the rain and the thunder in the sky.
Life is matter and is earth, what is and what is not,
and what beyond is in Eternity.
— *Prasna Upanishad* (tr. Juan Mascaró)

JI-WON [*jee-won*]

MEANING: wise and beautiful, beautiful heart •
USAGE: Korean: from Korean *ji* (wisdom, heart)
and *won* (beauty, jewel, garden)
To those who honor the wise and follow them,
four gifts will come in increasing measure:
health, happiness, beauty, and long life.
— Buddha, *The Dhammapada*
(tr. Eknath Easwaran)

JI-YOUNG [*jee-yung*]

MEANING: wise flower bud, heart of the flower
bud • **USAGE:** Korean: from Korean *ji* (wisdom,
heart) and *young* (flower bud)
Compassion, patience, and joy /
are the heart of our true nature: / cherish them.
— Shi Wuling, *Path to Peace*

JO [*joh*]

MEANING: God will add, God will increase, God's
grace, full of grace, gracious, merciful • **USAGE:**
English form of Josephine, Josepha, Joanne, or
Joanna; Josephine and Josepha are from Hebrew
ya'saph (Yahweh will add); Joanna and Joanne are
from Hebrew *y'hohanan* (Yahweh is gracious) and
Hebrew *chaanach* (grace)
May grace and peace be yours in full measure.
— 1 Peter 1:2b (GNT)

JOAN [*jōn*]

MEANING: God is gracious, God is giving •
USAGE: English feminine form of John, from
Hebrew *y'hohanan* (Yahweh is gracious)
Grace and peace to you.
— 1 Thessalonians 1:1b (NIV)

JOANA [ʒhoh-AH-nah]

MEANING: God is gracious, God is giving • **USAGE:** Portuguese form of Johanna (*see* Joan)

> *God is able to make all grace abound to you,*
> *that always having all sufficiency in everything,*
> *you may have an abundance for every good deed.*
> — 2 Corinthians 9:8 (NASB)

JOANIE, JOANI [JOH-nee]

MEANING: God is gracious, God is giving • **USAGE:** English form of Joan (*see* Joan)

> *The Lord be with your spirit. Grace be with you.*
> — 2 Timothy 4:22 (ESV)

JOANNA [joh-AN-ah]

MEANING: grace of God, full of grace • **USAGE:** English combination of Joan and Anna (*see* Joan and Anna)

> *Grace and beauty You have given me.*
> — St. John of the Cross,
> *A Spiritual Canticle of the Soul and the*
> *Bridegroom of Christ* (tr. David Lewis)

JOANNE [joh-AN]

MEANING: grace of God, full of grace • **USAGE:** English combination of Joan and Anne (*see* Joan and Anne)

> *The Lord bless you and keep you; the Lord make his*
> *face shine upon you and be gracious to you; the Lord*
> *turn his face toward you and give you peace.*
> — Numbers 6:24–26 (NIV)

JOAQUINA [hwah-KEE-nah]

MEANING: God will establish • **USAGE:** Spanish feminine form of Joaquín, from Hebrew *yehoyakim* (Yahweh will establish)

> *Commit your works to the Lord,*
> *and your plans will be established.*
> — Proverbs 16:3 (NASB)

JOBETH [joh-BETH]

MEANING: God will increase, God will add, God is my oath, joined with God, blessed by God • **USAGE:** English combination of Jo and Beth (*see* Jo and Beth)

> *The God of love and peace will be with you.*
> — 2 Corinthians 13:11b (HCSB)

JOCELYN, JOCELINE [JAS-eh-lin, JAHS-len (English), ʒhahs-LEEN (French)]

MEANING: Gothic, follower of Odin, warrior, wise • **USAGE:** English and French: from German *Gauts* and Scandinavian *Goth*, both early Germanic tribes; Norse god of war and wisdom

> *The woman warrior who is armed with wit*
> *and courage will be among the first*
> *to celebrate victory.*
> — Maya Angelou,
> *Wouldn't Take Nothing for My Journey Now*

JODINE, JODENE [jod-EEN]

MEANING: praise, thank, glorify, God will add, God will increase • **USAGE:** English form of Jody (*see* Jody)

> *Gratitude is the fairest blossom*
> *which springs from the soul.*
> — Hosea Ballou

JODY, JODIE, JODI [JOH-dee]

MEANING: praise, thank, glorify, God will add, God will increase • **USAGE:** English form of Judith, from Hebrew root *y-d-h* (praised); or English feminine form of Joseph, from Hebrew *ya'saph* (Yahweh will add)

> *Gratitude helps you grow and expand;*
> *gratitude brings joy and laughter into your life*
> *and into the lives of all those around you.*
> — Eileen Caddy

JOELA, JOELLA [joh-EL-ah]

MEANING: the Lord is God, God is willing •
USAGE: English feminine form of Joel, from
Hebrew *yoh'el* (Yahweh is God)

> *Delight thyself also in the Lord;*
> *and he shall give thee the desires of thine heart.*
> — Psalm 37:4 (KJV)

JOELLE, JOËLLE [joh-EL (English), zhoh-EL (French)]

MEANING: the Lord is God, God is willing •
USAGE: English and French feminine form of Joel
(*see* Joela)

> *For God all things are possible.*
> — Matthew 19:26b (NCV)

JOETTE [joh-ET]

MEANING: God will add, God will increase •
USAGE: English feminine form of Joseph, from
Hebrew *ya'saph* (Yahweh will add)

> *May the Lord make you increase and abound in love.*
> — 1 Thessalonians 3:12a (NKJV)

JOHANA [yoh-HAH-nah]

MEANING: God is gracious, God is giving •
USAGE: Norwegian and Czech feminine form
of Johannes, from Hebrew *y'hohanan* (Yahweh is
gracious)

> *The God who gives peace will be with you.*
> — Philippians 4:9b (NCV)

JOHANNA [yoh-HAH-nah]

MEANING: God is gracious, God is giving •
USAGE: German and Scandinavian feminine form
of Johannes (*see* Johana)

> *May the Lord give you success,*
> *and may he give you and your children success.*
> *May you be blessed by the Lord,*
> *who made heaven and earth.*
> — Psalm 115:114–15 (NCV)

JOHNNA, JOHNA [JAHN-ah]

MEANING: God is gracious, God is giving •
USAGE: English feminine form of John (*see* Joan)

> *The Lord your God is gracious and merciful*
> *and will not turn away his face from you.*
> — 2 Chronicles 30:9b (ESV)

JOISSE [jois]

MEANING: rejoicing, joyful, glad, delightful •
USAGE: English form of Joyce, from French *joie* (to
rejoice)

> *Joy is wisdom, /*
> *Time an endless song.*
> — William Butler Yeats,
> "The Land of Heart's Desire"

JOJO [joh-joh]

MEANING: God will add, God will increase •
USAGE: English feminine form of Josephine or
Josepha (*see* Joette)

> *The Lord...will send his angel*
> *with you and prosper your way.*
> — Genesis 24:40a (NKJV)

JOLANA [yoh-LAH-nah]

MEANING: violet flower, purple color • **USAGE:**
Czech form of Yolanda (*see* Jolanda)

> *The flowers appear on the earth;*
> *the time of singing is come.*
> — Song of Songs 2:12a (DT)

JOLANDA [yoh-LAHN-dah]

MEANING: violet flower, purple color • **USAGE:**
Dutch and German form of Yolanda, from
Greek *ion*

> *Colors are the deeds of light.*
> — Johann Wolfgang von Goethe

JOLENE, JOLINE, JOLEEN   *[joh-LEEN]*

MEANING: God will add, God will increase •
USAGE: English form of Josephine (*see* Joette)
The Lord your God will bless you
in all your produce and in all the work of your hands,
so that you surely rejoice.
— Deuteronomy 16:15b (NKJV)

JOLIE   *[ʒhoh-LEE]*

MEANING: beautiful, lovely • USAGE: French:
from French *joli*
Beauty begins with thee.
— Victor Hugo, *Les Misérables*

JONELL, JONELLE   *[joh-NEL]*

MEANING: God is gracious, God is giving •
USAGE: American feminine form of John (*see*
Joan)
[May] God, who gives hope,
bless you with complete happiness and peace.
— Romans 15:13a (CEV)

JONETTA   *[joh-NET-ah]*

MEANING: God is gracious, God is giving •
USAGE: American form of Johnna or Janet (*see*
Joan)
The Lord will give much to you.
— Deuteronomy 28:11a (NLV)

JONI, JONIE   *[JOH-nee]*

MEANING: God is gracious, God is giving •
USAGE: English form of Joan (*see* Joan)
May the Lord…grant your heart's desire;
may he bring all your plans to pass!
— Psalm 20:1a, 20:4 (NEB)

JONINA   *[joh-NEE-nah]*

MEANING: dove, dove-like • USAGE: English
feminine form of Jonah, from Hebrew *yonah*
(dove); a symbol of peace

Behold, thou art fair; thou hast doves' eyes.
— Song of Songs 4:1b (KJV)

JONNA   *[YOH-nah]*

MEANING: God is gracious, God is giving •
USAGE: Scandinavian form of Johana (*see* Johana)
God be gracious to you.
— Genesis 43:29b (NKJV)

JONQUIL   *[JON-kwil]*

MEANING: jonquil flower • USAGE: English: from
Spanish *junquilla*
The Amen! of Nature is always a flower.
— Oliver Wendell Holmes Sr.,
The Autocrat of the Breakfast Table

JOOL   *[jool]*

MEANING: jewel, gem, precious stone • USAGE:
American form of Jewel, from French *jouel*
You shall be a crown of beauty in the hand of the Lord,
and a royal diadem in the hand of your God.
— Isaiah 62:3 (ESV)

JOQUINA   *[ʒhoh-KWEE-nah]*

MEANING: God will establish • USAGE:
Portuguese feminine form of Joachim: from
Hebrew *yehoyakim* (Yahweh will establish)
May the God of all grace…make you perfect,
establish, strengthen, settle you.
— 1 Peter 5:10b (KJ21)

JORDAN, JORDYN   *[JOR-dun]*

MEANING: descend, to flow down, descendant •
USAGE: English feminine form of Jordan, from
Hebrew *yarden* (to descend, to flow down); river in
Israel
Love often knows no limits but overflows all bounds.
— Thomas à Kempis, *The Imitation of Christ*
(tr. Aloysius Croft and Harold Bolton)

JORDANA   *[jor-DAN-ah]*

MEANING: descend, to flow down, descendant
• **USAGE:** English feminine form of Jordan (*see*
Jordan)

Build people up and love them genuinely.
Do them good and their esteem and affection
will flow back toward you.
— Norman Vincent Peale,
The Power of Positive Thinking

JORDANE   *[zhohr-DAYN]*

MEANING: descend, to flow down, descendant
• **USAGE:** French feminine form of Jordan (*see*
Jordan)

May the God of hope fill you with all joy and peace as
you trust in him, so that you may overflow with hope.
— Romans 15:13a (NIV)

JORJA   *[JOR-jah]*

MEANING: earth worker, farmer, gardener •
USAGE: American form of Georgia, from Greek *ge*
(earth) and *ergein* (to work)

Gardening…there the door is always open
into the holy.
— May Sarton, Journal of a Solitude

JOSÉE   *[JOH-see]*

MEANING: God will add, God will increase •
USAGE: French form of Josephine or Josepha (*see*
Josephine)

You shall see and be radiant,
and your heart shall thrill and be enlarged.
— Isaiah 60:5a (WEB)

JOSEFA   *[yoh-SEF-ah (Scandinavian, German), hoh-SEF-ah (Spanish)]*

MEANING: God will add, God will increase •
USAGE: Scandinavian, German, and Spanish
feminine form of Joseph (*see* Josephine)

God doth bless thee in all thine increase,
and in every work of thy hands.
— Deuteronomy 16:15b (YLT)

JOSEFINA   *[yoh-seh-FEE-nah (Scandinavian), hoh-seh-FEE-nah (Spanish)]*

MEANING: God will add, God will increase •
USAGE: Scandinavian and Spanish feminine form
of Josef (*see* Josephine)

The Lord thy God will make thee abound
in all the works of thy hands.
— Deuteronomy 30:9a (DR)

JOSEPHA   *[joh-SEH-fah]*

MEANING: God will add, God will increase •
USAGE: English feminine form of Joseph (*see*
Josephine)

Before me, even as behind, God is, and all is well.
— John Greenleaf Whittier, "My Birthday"

JOSEPHINA   *[joh-seh-FEE-nah]*

MEANING: God will add, God will increase •
USAGE: English feminine form of Joseph (*see*
Josephine)

May the Lord cause you to increase and abound in love.
— 1 Thessalonians 3:12a (NASB)

JOSEPHINE, JOSÉPHINE   *[joh-seh-FEEN (English), zhoh-zeh-FEEN (French)]*

MEANING: God will add, God will increase •
USAGE: English and French feminine form of
Joseph, from Hebrew *ya'saph* (Yahweh will add)

The Lord your God will make you abundantly
prosperous in all the work of your hand.
— Deuteronomy 30:9a (ESV)

JOSETTE   *[zhoh-ZET]*

MEANING: God will add, God will increase •
USAGE: French form of Josephine (*see* Josephine)

May God give you more and more mercy,
peace, and love.
— Jude 1:2 (NLT)

J

JOSIE
[JOH-see]

Meaning: God will add, God will increase • **Usage:** English form of Josephine or Josepha (*see* Josephine)

The Lord thy God shall bless thee in all thine increase
and in all the works of thine hands.
— Deuteronomy 16:15b (KJ21)

JOY, JOYE, JOI
[joi]

Meaning: joyful, happy • **Usage:** English: from French *joie* (to rejoice)

Joy of health, / Joy of friends, /
Joy of peace, / Joy of God!
— Alexander Carmichael, *Carmina Gadelica*

JOYCE
[jois]

Meaning: joyful, happy • **Usage:** English form of Joy (*see* Joy)

Joy delights in joy.
— William Shakespeare, "Sonnet 8"

JOZETTA
[joh-ZEH-tah]

Meaning: God will add, God will increase • **Usage:** English form of Josephine (*see* Josephine)

May the Lord give you increase,
you and your children!
May you be blessed by the Lord,
who made heaven and earth!
— Psalm 115:14–15 (ESV)

JOZETTE
[zhoh-ZET (French), joh-ZET (English)]

Meaning: God will add, God will increase • **Usage:** French and English form of Josephine (*see* Josephine)

May the Lord make you to increase
and abound in love.
— 1 Thessalonians 3:12a (ESV)

JUANA
[HWAH-nah]

Meaning: God is gracious, God is giving • **Usage:** Spanish feminine form of Juan (*see* Juanita)

God be gracious to you.
— Genesis 43:29b (NCV)

JUANITA
[hwah-NEE-tah]

Meaning: God is gracious, God is giving • **Usage:** Spanish feminine form of Juan, from Hebrew *y'hohanan* (Yahweh is gracious)

The Lord will give grace and glory; no good thing will
He withhold from them that walk uprightly.
— Psalm 84:11 (KJ21)

JUBILEE
[joo-bih-LEE]

Meaning: joyous, jubilant, celebrant, joyful celebration • **Usage:** American: from English *jubile* (joyful celebration)

The more you praise and celebrate your life,
the more there is in life to celebrate.
— Oprah Winfrey

JUDIT
[HOO-deet (Spanish),
YOO-deet (Hungarian, Scandinavian)]

Meaning: praise, thank, glorify • **Usage:** Spanish, Hungarian, and Scandinavian form of Judith (*see* Judith)

Whatsoever things are true, whatsoever things are
honorable, whatsoever things are just, whatsoever
things are pure, whatsoever things are lovely,
whatsoever things are of good report; if there be any
virtue, and if there be any praise,
think on these things.
— Philippians 4:8 (ASV)

JUDITA
[yoo-DEE-tah]

Meaning: praise, thank, glorify • **Usage:** Scandinavian form of Judith (*see* Judith)

I thank thee, and praise thee, O thou God of my
fathers, who hast given me wisdom and might.
— Daniel 2:23a (KJV)

JUDITH   *[JOO-dith (English), ʒhoo-DEET*
(French), YOO-dit (German, Scandinavian)]

MEANING: praise, thank, glorify • **USAGE:**
English, French, German, and Scandinavian form
of Yehudit, from Hebrew root *y-d-h* (praised)
If the only prayer you said in your whole life was
"thank you," that would suffice.
— Meister Eckhart

JUDY, JUDIE, JUDI   *[JOO-dee]*

MEANING: praise, thank, glorify • **USAGE:** English
form of Judith (*see* Judith)
Fill me with love, that I may learn the sweetness of
love in my inmost soul. Teach me to sing Thy praises,
and make my heart jubilant with divine love.
— Thomas à Kempis, *The Imitation of Christ*
(tr. Harvey Goodwin)

JULIA   *[JOO-lee-ah (English), YOO-lee-ah*
(German, Scandinavian), HOO-lyah (Spanish)]

MEANING: young, youthful, of Jupiter • **USAGE:**
English, German, Scandinavian, and Spanish
feminine form of Julian, from Latin *iulus* (downy-
chinned, youthful); or form of Jupiter, from Latin
dyeus (Zeus) and *pater* (father)
Youth is not a time of life; it is a state of mind.
— Samuel Ullman, "What Is Youth?"

JULIANA   *[joo-lee-AN-ah (English),*
yoo-lee-AH-nah (Dutch, German, Scandinavian)]

MEANING: young and graceful, gracefully
young • **USAGE:** English, Dutch, German, and
Scandinavian combination of Julia and Anna (*see*
Julia and Anna)
Youth is happy because it has the ability to see beauty.
— Franz Kafka

JULIANE   *[yoo-lee-AH-nah]*

MEANING: young and graceful, gracefully young •
USAGE: German form of Juliana (*see* Julia)
Keep true to the dreams of thy youth.
— Johann Friedrich von Schiller

JULIANNA   *[yoo-lee-AH-nah (Hungarian,*
Polish), joo-lee-AN-ah (English)]

MEANING: young and graceful, gracefully
young • **USAGE:** Hungarian, Polish, and English
combination of Julia and Anna (*see* Julia and
Anna)
Beauty is the mark God sets upon virtue:
every natural action is graceful.
— Ralph Waldo Emerson, *Nature*

JULIE   *[JOO-lee (English), ZHOO-lee (French)]*

MEANING: young, youthful, of Jupiter • **USAGE:**
English and French feminine form of Jules (*see*
Julia)
Beauty is the pilot of the young soul.
— Ralph Waldo Emerson, *The Conduct of Life*

JULIENNE   *[ʒhoo-lee-EN]*

MEANING: young, youthful, of Jupiter • **USAGE:**
French feminine form of Julien (*see* Julia)
Every minute of life carries with it
its miraculous value,
and its face of eternal youth.
— Albert Camus
(tr. Philip Thody in *Notebooks, 1935–1942*)

JULIET   *[joo-lee-ET]*

MEANING: young, youthful, of Jupiter • **USAGE:**
English feminine form of Julian (*see* Julia)
Those who love deeply cannot age.
— Arthur Pinero,
The Princess and the Butterfly

JULIETA   [hoo-lee-ET-ah]

MEANING: young, youthful, of Jupiter • USAGE:
Spanish form of Juliet (see Julia)

> *He [God] fills my life with good things.*
> *My youth is renewed like the eagle's!*
> — Psalm 103:5 (NLT)

JULIETTE   [zhoo-lee-ET]

MEANING: young, youthful, of Jupiter • USAGE:
French feminine form of Julian (see Julia)

> *True love is eternal…*
> *is always young in the heart.*
> — Honoré de Balzac

JULISHA   [joo-LEE-shah]

MEANING: make known • USAGE: African:
Kiswahili of Kenya/Tanzania

> *Love has to be shown by deeds, not words.*
> — Kiswahili proverb

JULITA   [yoo-LEE-tah]

MEANING: young, youthful, of Jupiter • USAGE:
Polish form of Julia (see Julia)

> *Youth is a gift of nature, but age is a work of art.*
> — Stanislaw Lec

JULITTE   [zhoo-LEET]

MEANING: young, youthful, of Jupiter • USAGE:
French feminine form of Julian (see Julia)

> *Wisdom sends us to childhood.*
> — Blaise Pascal, *Pensées* (tr. A.J. Krailsheimer)

JUMANA, JUMANAH   [joo-mah-nah]

MEANING: pearl, precious gem • USAGE: Muslim

> *(There are) fair ones…like unto hidden pearls.*
> — Koran, That Which Is Coming 56.88 (PIC)

JUNE   [joon]

MEANING: month of June • USAGE: English:
month named after Latin *Juno*, the Roman goddess
of marriage and queen of the heavens

> *What is so rare as a day in June?*
> *Then, if ever, come perfect days.*
> — James Russell Lowell,
> "The Vision of Sir Launfal"

JUNG-JA   [jung-jah]

MEANING: chaste woman, pure woman • USAGE:
Korean

> *Truth is said to be the one unequaled means*
> *of purification of the soul.*
> — Narada Dharma Sutra 1:210

JUNIPER   [JOO-nih-per]

MEANING: evergreen shrub, evergreen tree •
USAGE: English: from Latin *junipere* (evergreen
shrub or tree with berrylike fruit)

> *May the God of green hope fill you up with joy.*
> — Romans 15:13a (MSG)

JUNO   [JOO-noh]

MEANING: goddess of marriage, queen of the gods
• USAGE: English: the Roman goddess of marriage
and queen of the heavens

> *Throned in her heart sits love's high majesty.*
> — Giles Fletcher, *The Purple Island*

JUSTINA   [jus-TEE-nah]

MEANING: just, judicious, fair • USAGE: English
feminine form of Justin (see Justine)

> *You will understand what is honest and fair*
> *and what is the good and right thing to do.*
> — Proverbs 2:9 (NCV)

JUSTINE
[zhoo-STEEN (French),
jus-TEEN (English)]

MEANING: just, judicious, fair • **USAGE:** French and English feminine form of Justin, from Latin *justus*

Justice and power must be brought together, so that whatever is just may be powerful, and whatever is powerful may be just.
— Blaise Pascal

JUTTA
[YOO-tah]

MEANING: praise, thank, glorify • **USAGE:** German and Scandinavian form of Judith, from Hebrew root *y-d-h* (praised)

To speak gratitude is courteous and pleasant, to enact gratitude is generous and noble, but to live gratitude is to touch Heaven.
— Johannes Gaertner, *Worldly Virtues*

JYOTI
[jee-OH-teh, JOH-tee]

MEANING: light, the Light • **USAGE:** Hindu: from Sanskrit *jyotis*

Come out into the universe of Light.
Everything in the universe is yours.
Stretch out your arms and embrace it with love.
If you ever felt you wanted to do that,
you have felt God.
— Swami Vivekananda, "Practical Vedanta, Part II" (lecture of November 12, 1896)

K

KABALA
[kah-bah-lah]

MEANING: young, youthful • **USAGE:** African: Rega of Congo

A village never lacks a beautiful young woman.
— Congolese proverb

KABIRA, KABEERA
[kah-BEE-rah]

MEANING: great, magnificent • **USAGE:** Muslim feminine form of Kabir

Experience shows that the spirit is nothing but awareness. Whoever has greater awareness has a greater spirit.
— Jalaluddin Rumi
(tr. William Chitticke in *The Sufi Path of Love*)

KADENCE
[KAY-dens]

MEANING: flow of rhythm • **USAGE:** American form of Cadence, from Latin *cadentia* (a falling, a conclusion of a movement in music)

We're embedded in a rhythm universe....
How we move through that universe
is how we move through life.
— Mickey Hart

KADY, KAYDI, KAYDY
[KAY-dee]

MEANING: first, first in favor • **USAGE:** English: from Gaelic *ceadach* (first)

The wisdom from above is first pure, then peaceable, gentle, accommodating, full of mercy and good fruit, impartial, and not hypocritical.
— James 3:17 (NEB)

KAI
[kie]

MEANING: willow tree • **USAGE:** Amerind: Navajo

Be still and the earth will speak to you.
— Navajo proverb

KAILANI
[kie-LAH-nee]

MEANING: sea and sky • **USAGE:** Hawaiian

The blue of the sky perfectly mirrors the blue of the ocean.
— Hawaiian proverb

KAITI   [KAY-tee]

MEANING: pure one, unblemished, innocent, virtuous • **USAGE:** Greek form of Aikaterini, from Greek *katharos* (pure)

> *Grace and harmony are the twin sisters*
> *of goodness and virtue.*
> — Plato, *The Republic* (tr. Benjamin Jowett)

KAITLIN, KATELIN, KAITLYN

[KAYT-lin]

MEANING: pure one, unblemished, innocent, virtuous • **USAGE:** American form of Caitlin (*see* Kaiti)

> *Bodies are cleansed by water;*
> *the mind is purified by truth.*
> — Horace Mann

KALAMA   [kah-LAH-mah]

MEANING: light, light-bringing, torch-bearer, the one who is light • **USAGE:** Hawaiian: from Hawaiian *ka* (one who is) and *lama* (light, torch, lamp)

> *The standing torch of wisdom. [A wise person.]*
> — Hawaiian proverb
> (tr. Mary Pukui in *'Olelo No'eau*)

KALANDRA   [kah-LAHN-drah]

MEANING: beautiful woman, lovely, skylark • **USAGE:** Greek: from Greek *kallos* (beautiful) and *andros* (man); skylark

> *Your voice is sweet, and your face is lovely.*
> — Song of Songs 2:14b (ESV)

KALEI   [kah-LEH-ee]

MEANING: flower wreath, garland • **USAGE:** Hawaiian: from Hawaiian *lei*

> *Love is worn like a wreath*
> *through the summers and the winters.*
> — Hawaiian proverb
> (tr. Mary Pukui in *'Olelo No'eau*)

KALIA   [kah-LEE-ah]

MEANING: beautiful, lovely • **USAGE:** Hawaiian: from Hawaiian *ka* (one who is) and *lei* (flower wreath, garland)

> *A flower not common.*
> *[Valued like a very rare blossom.]*
> — Hawaiian proverb
> (tr. Mary Pukui in *'Olelo No'eau*)

KALIDAS   [kah-LEE-dahs]

MEANING: beautiful, lovely • **USAGE:** Greek: from Greek *kallos*

> *How beautiful you are!*
> — Song of Songs 7:6a (NEB)

KALISSA   [kah-LIS-ah]

MEANING: true, genuine, sincere • **USAGE:** American form of Khalisa

> *Be true to the highest within your own soul.*
> — Ralph Waldo Trine,
> *In Tune with the Infinite*

KALLI   [KAH-lee]

MEANING: beautiful, lovely, beautiful voice • **USAGE:** Greek form of Kalidas or Kallisto (*see* Kallisto); or Greek form of Kalliope (*see* Kalliope)

> *You are so beautiful, my love! So beautiful!*
> — Song of Songs 1:15a (NIRV)

KALLIOPE   [kah-LEE-oh-pee,
                            kah-LIE-oh-pee]

MEANING: beautiful voice, lyrical, eloquent, muse of poetry and eloquence • **USAGE:** Greek: from Greek *kallos* (beautiful) and *ops* (voice); Greek muse of poetry and eloquence

> *Show me your face, let me hear your voice;*
> *for your voice is sweet, and your face is lovely.*
> — Song of Songs 2:14 (NIV)

KALLISTO [kah-LEES-toh]

MEANING: she who is most beautiful • USAGE: Greek: from Greek *kallos* (most beautiful); nymph in Greek mythology

> *How beautiful you are and how pleasant.*
> — Song of Songs 7:6a (HCSB)

KALYANA [kal-yah-nah]

MEANING: beautiful, auspicious, blessed • USAGE: Hindu: Sanskrit

> *Find your beauty, my heart,*
> *from the world's movement, like the boat*
> *that has the grace of the wind and the water.*
> — Rabindranath Tagore, *Stray Birds*

KAMALIKA [kah-mah-lee-kah]

MEANING: day lotus • USAGE: Hindu: Sanskrit

> *In the lotus / lies knowledge; / here is union. /*
> *Thence bliss / self-experiencing, /*
> *which is* bodhicitta */ and is thought of enlightenment.*
> — *Hevajra Tantra*

KAMALINI [kah-mah-lee-nee]

MEANING: day lotus • USAGE: Hindu: Sanskrit

> *The heart-lotus blossoms forth,*
> *and eternal peace is obtained,*
> *as one's light merges into the Light.*
> — *Sri Guru Granth Sahib*
> (Khalsa Consensus Translation)

KAMEELA, KAMEELAH [kah-MEE-lah]

MEANING: perfected, complete • USAGE: American form of Kamila (*see* Kamila)

> *Where God's love is, there is no fear,*
> *because God's perfect love drives out fear.*
> — 1 John 4:18a (NCV)

KAMILA, KAMILAH [kah-mih-lah]

MEANING: perfected, complete • USAGE: Muslim feminine form of Kamil, from Arabic *kamula* (to become perfect)

> *No one looks for stars when the sun's out. /*
> *A person blended into God does not disappear. He or*
> *she / is just completely soaked in God's qualities.*
> — Jalaluddin Rumi, "Zikr"
> (tr. Coleman Barks in *The Book of Love*)

KAMILLA [kah-MEEL-ah]

MEANING: virgin of pure character, attendant at a religious service • USAGE: German and Scandinavian form of Camilla, from Latin *camilla* (virgin of pure character); or from Latin *camillus* (attendant at a religious service)

> *Purity of heart is the noblest inheritance,*
> *and love the fairest ornament, of woman.*
> — Matthias Claudius

KANANI [kah-NAH-nee]

MEANING: the one who is beautiful • USAGE: Hawaiian: from Hawaiian *ka* (one who is) and *nani* (beauty, beautiful)

> *Bedecked is Halemano with lehua leaves.*
> *[A beautiful person.]*
> — Hawaiian proverb
> (tr. Mary Pukui in *'Olelo No'eau*)

KANEKO [kah-nee-koh]

MEANING: doubly accomplished child, successful child • USAGE: Japanese: Japanese *kane* (successful) and *ko* (child)

> *An accomplishment sticks to a person.*
> — Japanese proverb

KANIT [kah-NEET]

MEANING: songbird • USAGE: Jewish

> *Nature is saturated with melody;*
> *heaven and earth are full of song.*
> — Nachman of Breslov

K

KANTA [kahn-tah]

MEANING: brilliant, radiant, shining light •
USAGE: Hindu: from Sanskrit *kanta*
Like the moon, come out from behind the clouds! Shine.
— Buddha, *The Dhammapada* (tr. Thomas Byrom)

KANTI [kahn-tee]

MEANING: sings • **USAGE:** Amerind: Algonquin
We are the stars which sing, / We sing with our light;
/ We are the birds of fire, / We fly over the sky. /
Our light is a voice: / We make a road for spirits /
For the spirits to pass over.
— "Song of the Stars," Algonquin song

KARA [KAHR-ah]

MEANING: beloved, love • **USAGE:** English form
of Cara, from Latin *carus*
Love springeth upward
and cannot be held down to earth.
— Thomas à Kempis, *The Imitation of Christ*

KAREN [KAYR-en]

MEANING: pure one, unblemished, innocent,
virtuous • **USAGE:** Danish, German, Norwegian,
and English form of Katharine, from Greek *katharos*
(pure)
You are a spring in the garden,
a fountain of pure water.
— Song of Songs 4:15a (CEV)

KARI [KAHR-ee]

MEANING: generous love, pure one, unblemished,
innocent, virtuous • **USAGE:** Scandinavian form of
Karita (*see* Karita); or Norwegian form of Karin (*see*
Karen)
Love is patient and kind....Love never ends.
— 1 Corinthians 13:4, 8a (NCV)

KARIMA, KARIMAH [kah-ree-mah]

MEANING: generous, charitable, noble • **USAGE:**
Muslim feminine form of Karim, from Arabic
karuma (to be noble, to be generous)
Charity is the expansion of the heart.
— Hazrat Inayat Khan, *The Gayan* (cd. *The Gayani*
Meditations, Volume 1, tr. Cecil Touchon)

KARIN [KAHR-en]

MEANING: pure one, unblemished, innocent,
virtuous • **USAGE:** German, Dutch, Polish, and
Swedish form of Karen (*see* Karen)
Love one human being with warmth and purity,
and thou wilt love the world.
— Jean Paul Richter

KARINA [kah-REE-nah]

MEANING: pure one, unblemished, innocent,
virtuous • **USAGE:** Russian, Scandinavian, Polish,
and German form of Karin (*see* Karen)
Know that thou art a virtuous woman.
— Ruth 3:11b (DR)

KARIS [KAR-is]

MEANING: grace, kindness, joyful, happy •
USAGE: American form of Charis, from Greek
charis (grace, kindness); or from Greek *chairen* (to
rejoice)
Kindness can become its own motive.
We are made kind by being kind.
— Eric Hoffer, *The Passionate State of Mind*

KARITA [kah-REE-tah]

MEANING: generous love • **USAGE:** Swedish,
Finnish, and Norwegian form of Charity, from
Latin *charitas*
May mercy, peace, and love be yours in full measure.
— Jude 1:2 (GNT)

KARLA [KAR-lah]

MEANING: adult, one who is free • **USAGE:**
German and Scandinavian feminine form of Karl,

from German *karl* (full-grown man, adult); or from English *ceorl* (freeman, peasant)

> *It is through beauty that we arrive at freedom.*
> — Johann Friedrich von Schiller,
> *Letters on the Aesthetic Education of Man*

KARLEN [*KAR-len*]

MEANING: adult, one who is free • USAGE: English feminine form of Karl (*see* Karla)

> *For you are free.*
> — 1 Peter 2:16a (NLT)

KARLOTTE [*kar-LOH-teh*]

MEANING: adult, one who is free • USAGE: German, Norwegian, and Swedish feminine form of Karl (*see* Karla)

> *Make good use of your freedom.*
> — 1 Corinthians 7:21b (NCV)

KARLY, KARLIE [*KAR-lee*]

MEANING: adult, one who is free • USAGE: Danish, Norwegian, Swedish, and English feminine form of Karl (*see* Karla)

> *Only the person who risks is truly free.*
> — Leo Buscaglia, *Living, Loving, and Learning*

KAROLA [*KAR-oh-lah*]

MEANING: adult, one who is free • USAGE: German and Hungarian feminine form of Karl (*see* Karla)

> *The Lord is the Spirit;*
> *and where the Spirit of the Lord is, there is liberty.*
> — 2 Corinthians 3:17 (NKJV)

KAROLINA, KAROLINE [*kar-oh-LEE-nah*]

MEANING: adult, one who is free • USAGE: German and Scandinavian feminine form of Karl (*see* Karla)

> *Our task is to be free ourselves...by widening our circle*
> *of compassion to embrace all living creatures*
> *and the whole of nature and its beauty.*
> — Albert Einstein

KARUNA [*kah-ROO-nah*]

MEANING: mercy, compassion, kindness • USAGE: Hindu: Sanskrit

> *Whatever is positive, what benefits others,*
> *what conduces to kindness or peace of mind, those states*
> *of mind lead to progress; give them full attention.*
> — Buddha, *The Dhammapada*
> (tr. Eknath Easwaran)

KARUNGA [*kah-ruhn-gah*]

MEANING: beautiful • USAGE: African: Sanskrit

> *Wisdom is the finest beauty of a person.*
> — Yoruban proverb

KARYN [*KAYR-en*]

MEANING: pure one, unblemished, innocent, virtuous • USAGE: English form of Karen (*see* Karen)

> *Let grace and goodness be the principal lodestone*
> *of thy affections. For love which hath ends,*
> *will have an end; whereas that which is founded on*
> *true virtue, will always continue.*
> — Thomas Fuller,
> *The Holy State and the Profane State*

KASEY [*KAY-see*]

MEANING: vigilant, alert, watchful • USAGE: American form of Casey, English form of O'Cathasaigh, from Irish Gaelic *cathasaigh*

> *He has put his angels in charge of you*
> *to watch over you wherever you go.*
> — Psalm 91:11 (NCV)

KASHI [*kah-shee*]

MEANING: shining, luminous • USAGE: Hindu: Sanskrit

> *May the light of wisdom illumine us.*
> — *Taittiriya Upanishad* (tr. Eknath Easwaran)

KASIA, KAZIA   [KAH-zhah, KAH-shah]

MEANING: pure one, unblemished, innocent, virtuous • USAGE: Polish form of Katarzyna (see Katharine)

A pure conscious is the ground of perpetual exultation.
— Thomas à Kempis, *The Imitation of Christ*
(tr. John Payne)

KASSANDRA   [kah-SAHN-drah]

MEANING: prophetess, seer • USAGE: Greek: Greek prophetess doomed to tell the truth but never to be believed

She openeth her mouth with wisdom,
and on her tongue is the law of kindness.
— Proverbs 31:26 (KJ21)

KASSIDY   [KAS-ih-dee]

MEANING: love, affection, curly-haired • USAGE: American form of Cassidy, from Gaelic *cais* (love, affection) or *cas* (curly-haired)

And now abide faith, hope, love, these three;
but the greatest of these is love.
— 1 Corinthians 13:13 (NKJV)

KATANIA, KATANIYA   [kah-TAHN-yah]

MEANING: small, little • USAGE: Jewish
Rabbi [Yehudah HaNasi] said:
What is the right path? One that honors both self
and other. Be as mindful of small acts as great ones,
for you cannot know the consequences of either.
— *Pirkei Avot* 2:1

KATARINA, KATHARINA   [kah-tah-REE-nah]

MEANING: pure one, unblemished, innocent, virtuous • USAGE: German and Scandinavian form of Katharine (see Katharine)

Thou art a virtuous woman.
— Ruth 3:11b (KJ21)

KATARINE   [kah-tah-REE-neh]

MEANING: pure one, unblemished, innocent, virtuous • USAGE: Danish, Finnish, Swedish, and German form of Katharine (see Katharine)

To the pure, all things are pure.
— Titus 1:15a (NASB)

KATARZYNA   [kah-tahr-ZHEH-nah]

MEANING: pure one, unblemished, innocent, virtuous • USAGE: Polish form of Katharine (see Katharine)

The wisdom that is from above is first pure,
then peaceable, gentle, easy to be entreated,
full of mercy and good fruits, without variance,
without hypocrisy.
— James 3:17 (ASV)

KATE   [kayt]

MEANING: pure one, unblemished, innocent, virtuous • USAGE: English and Irish form of Katharine or Kathleen (see Katharine)

An angel is like you, Kate,
and you are like an angel.
— William Shakespeare, *Henry V*

KATERINA   [kah-tah-REE-nah]

MEANING: pure one, unblemished, innocent, virtuous • USAGE: Greek, German, and Russian form of Katharine, from Greek *katharos* (pure)

All virtue is summed up in dealing justly.
— Aristotle, *Nicomachean Ethics*

KATHARINE, KATHERINE, KATHRYN   [KATH-eh-ren, KATH-ren]

MEANING: pure one, unblemished, innocent, virtuous • USAGE: English form of Aikaterini, from Greek *katharos* (pure)

May God himself, the God of peace, make you pure.
— 1 Thessalonians 5:23a (NCV)

KATHLEEN [kath-LEEN]

MEANING: pure one, unblemished, innocent, virtuous • **USAGE:** English and Irish form of Cathleen (*see* Katharine)

That virtue we appreciate is as much ours as another's.
We see so much only as we possess.
— Henry David Thoreau
(journal entry of June 22, 1839)

KATHY, KATHIE [KATH-ee]

MEANING: pure one, unblemished, innocent, virtuous • **USAGE:** English form of Katharine or Kathleen (*see* Katharine)

Who can find a virtuous woman?
For her price is far above rubies.
— Proverbs 31:10 (KJV)

KATIE, KATY [KAY-tee]

MEANING: pure one, unblemished, innocent, virtuous • **USAGE:** English form of Katharine or Kathleen (*see* Katharine)

Live pure, speak true, right wrong.
— Alfred Tennyson, *Idylls of the King*

KATINA [kah-TEE-nah]

MEANING: pure one, unblemished, innocent, virtuous • **USAGE:** Greek form of Katerina (*see* Katharine)

A soul that makes virtue its companion
is like an over-flowing well, for it is clean and pellucid,
sweet and wholesome, open to all, rich,
blameless and indestructible.
— Epictetus

KATINKA [kay-TEEN-kah]

MEANING: pure one, unblemished, innocent, virtuous • **USAGE:** German and Hungarian form of Katarina (*see* Katharine)

Those who are pure in act and in thought...
the Lord will bless them.
— Psalm 24:4–5a (GNT)

KATJA [KAHT-yah]

MEANING: pure one, unblemished, innocent, virtuous • **USAGE:** German, Dutch, and Scandinavian form of Katarina (*see* Katharine)

Cheerfulness is the mother of every virtue.
— Johan Wolfgang von Goethe,
Goetz von Berlichingen

KATJE [KAHT-yah]

MEANING: pure one, unblemished, innocent, virtuous • **USAGE:** Danish form of Katarina (*see* Katharine)

Think about the things that are good
and worthy of praise. Think about the things
that are true and honorable and right and pure
and beautiful and respected.
— Philippians 4:8 (NCV)

KATKA [KAHT-kah]

MEANING: pure one, unblemished, innocent, virtuous • **USAGE:** Czech form of Katharine, from Greek *katharos* (pure)

Now may God himself, the God of peace,
make you pure, belonging only to him.
May your whole self — spirit, soul, and body —
be kept safe and without fault.
— 1 Thessalonians 5:23 (NCV)

KATNISS [KAT-nis]

MEANING: aquatic plant • **USAGE:** American: from Latin *saggitarria*

When peacemakers plant seeds of peace,
they will harvest justice.
— James 3:18 (CEV)

KATRA [KAH-trah]

MEANING: pure one, unblemished, innocent, virtuous • **USAGE:** American: possibly a form of Katharine (*see* Katharine)

Beauty, like truth and justice, lives within us;
like virtue, and like moral law,
it is a companion of the soul.
— George Bancroft, "The People in Art,
Government, and Religion"
(speech of August 1835)

KATRIN [KAHT-reen]

MEANING: pure one, unblemished, innocent, virtuous • **USAGE:** German and Scandinavian form of Katarina (*see* Katharine)

Great thoughts and a pure heart —
that is what we should pray for from God!
— Johann Wolfgang von Goethe,
Wilhelm Meister's Journeyman Years
(tr. Jan van Heurck)

KATRINA [kah-TREEN-ah]

MEANING: pure one, unblemished, innocent, virtuous • **USAGE:** German, Dutch, and Scandinavian form of Katarina (*see* Katharine)

Best of all is it to preserve everything in a pure,
still heart, and let there be for every pulse
a thanksgiving, and for every breath a song.
— Konrad von Gesner

KATRINE [kah-TREE-neh]

MEANING: pure one, unblemished, innocent, virtuous • **USAGE:** Danish and Norwegian form of Katarina (*see* Katharine)

Who can find a virtuous woman?
For her price is far above rubies.
— Proverbs 31:10 (KJ21)

KATRIONA [kat-ree-OH-nah]

MEANING: pure one, unblemished, innocent, virtuous • **USAGE:** English and Scottish form of Catriona (*see* Katharine)

There is no power on earth that can neutralize
the influence of a high, pure, simple and useful life.
— Booker T. Washington,
"The Virtue of Simplicity"

KATYA [KAHT-yah]

MEANING: pure one, unblemished, innocent, virtuous • **USAGE:** Russian form of Ekaterina (*see* Katharine)

Let our lives be pure as snow-fields,
where our footsteps leave a mark, but not a stain.
— Madame Swetchine, "Airelles"

KAUI [KAW-ee]

MEANING: beautiful, lovely • **USAGE:** Hawaiian: Hawaiian goddess of the hula

Surrounded by the reeds that sway in the breeze.
[Beautiful and graceful movements.]
— Hawaiian proverb
(tr. Mary Pukui in *'Olelo No'eau*)

KAVALA [kah-vah-lah]

MEANING: the one, the absolute • **USAGE:** Hindu: Sanskrit

Becoming truthful, we merge with the True One;
remaining blended with Him,
we shall never be separated again.
— *Sri Guru Granth Sahib*
(Khalsa Consensus Translation)

KAY [kay]

MEANING: pure one, unblemished, innocent, virtuous • **USAGE:** English form of Katharine or Kathleen, from Greek *katharos* (pure)

Virtue is bold, and goodness never fearful.
— William Shakespeare, *Measure for Measure*

KAYA [KAH-yah]

MEANING: pure one, unblemished, innocent, virtuous • **USAGE:** American form of Katharine, from Greek *katharos* (pure)

> *The way to true riches is to enrich the soul*
> *by the acquisition of virtue.*
> — James Allen, *From Poverty to Power*

KAYLA [KAY-lah]

MEANING: slender, narrow, pure one, unblemished, innocent, virtuous • **USAGE:** Scottish: from Gaelic *caol* (slender); or English form of Kay, from Greek *katharos* (pure)

> *O Virtue! Peace is all thy own.*
> — Alexander Pope, *Essay on Man*

KAYLEEN [KAY-leen]

MEANING: pure one, unblemished, innocent, virtuous • **USAGE:** American form of Kay, from Greek *katharos* (pure)

> *Blessed are the pure in heart, for they will see God.*
> — Matthew 5:8 (NEB)

KAYLEY, KALEIGH [KAY-lee]

MEANING: pure meadow, slender • **USAGE:** American combination of Kay and Lee (see Kay and Lee)

> *The Lord is my shepherd, I shall not be in want.*
> *He makes me lie down in green pastures,*
> *he leads me beside quiet waters.*
> — Psalm 23:1–2 (RSV)

KAYLIN, KALIN [KAY-lin]

MEANING: pure one, unblemished, innocent, virtuous • **USAGE:** American form of Caitlin, from Greek *katharos* (pure)

> *While our hearts are pure, /*
> *Our lives are happy and our peace is sure.*
> — William Winter, "The Emotion of Sympathy"

KEALA [keh-AH-lah]

MEANING: pathway, the pathway • **USAGE:** Hawaiian

> *A journey of the spirit is never truly finished*
> *— its paths continually unfold before us.*
> — Hawaiian proverb

KEELA [KEE-lah]

MEANING: beautiful, slender • **USAGE:** Irish: from Gaelic *cadhla* (beautiful); or from Gaelic *caol* (slender)

> *There is no cosmetic for beauty like happiness.*
> — Marguerite Gardiner,
> *Desultory Thoughts and Reflections*

KEELIN [KEE-len]

MEANING: slender and beautiful • **USAGE:** Scottish and Irish form of *Caoilfhin*, from Gaelic *caol* (slender) and *fionn* (fair, white, beautiful)

> *Sweetness be in my face, /*
> *Riches be in my countenance.*
> — Alexander Carmichael, *Carmina Gadelica*

KEELY, KEELI [KEE-lee]

MEANING: beautiful, slender • **USAGE:** Irish and English (see Keela)

> *Behold, you are beautiful, my beloved, truly lovely.*
> — Song of Songs 1:16a (RSV)

KEEVA [KEE-vah]

MEANING: beautiful, lovely • **USAGE:** Irish: from Gaelic *caoimhe*

> *Oh, how beautiful you are.*
> — Song of Songs 1:15a (NEB)

KEFIRA [keh-FEE-rah]

MEANING: young lioness • **USAGE:** Jewish feminine form of Kefir

> *I will be…as a young lion.*
> — Hosea 5:14a (JPS)

K

KEHUA   [*KEH-hwah*]

MEANING: dew, mist, dewdrop, gentle land breeze
• **USAGE:** Hawaiian
> *Give me the beauty of nature to restore my spirit,*
> *where the morning dew glistens in the sunlight,*
> *and the wind is the only sound that I hear.*
> — Hawaiian proverb

KEIKI   [*keh-EE-kee*]

MEANING: child of the moon • **USAGE:** Hawaiian
> *I am the moon's child,*
> *born of starlight and dewfall.*
> — Hawaiian proverb

KEIKO   [*keh-EE-koh*]

MEANING: blessed child, lucky child, happy child,
respectful child • **USAGE:** Japanese: from Japanese
kei (lucky, happy, respectful) and *ko* (child)
> *In gain, be honest / in giving, be thoughtful /*
> *in appearance, be warm / in demeanor, be respectful.*
> — Shi Wuling, *Path to Peace*

KEILA   [*KEE-lah*]

MEANING: beautiful, slender, pure one,
unblemished, innocent, virtuous • **USAGE:**
American form of Keela (*see* Keela); or American
form of Kayla (*see* Kayla)
> *You are beautiful, my darling, beautiful beyond words.*
> — Song of Songs 4:1a (NLT)

KEITHA   [*KEE-thah*]

MEANING: forest, woods • **USAGE:** Scottish
and English feminine form of Keith, from Gaelic
ceiteach
> *The wood itself seems to be singing a hopeful song….*
> *In it is the peace, the poetry, the majesty,*
> *and the mystery of the forest.*
> — Enos A. Mills, *Your National Parks*

KELBY   [*KEL-bee*]

MEANING: village by the spring, village well •
USAGE: English surname: from Norse *keld* (spring,
well) and *by* (village, town)
> *Keep your heart with all diligence,*
> *for out of it is the wellspring of life.*
> — Proverbs 4:23 (WEB)

KELDA, KELDAH   [*KEL-dah*]

MEANING: spring, well • **USAGE:** English: from
Norse *keld*
> *You will be like a well-watered garden,*
> *like a spring whose waters never fail.*
> — Isaiah 58:11b (NIV)

KELILA   [*keh-LEE-lah*]

MEANING: crown, wreath, garland • **USAGE:**
Jewish
> *She [Wisdom] will adorn your head with a graceful*
> *wreath; crown you with a glorious diadem.*
> — Proverbs 4:9 (JPS)

KELLEEN   [*keh-LEEN*]

MEANING: young girl, maiden • **USAGE:** Irish
form of Colleen, from Gaelic *cailín*
> *Bless each maiden and youth, /*
> *Each woman and tender youngling, /*
> *Safeguard them beneath Thy shield of strength.*
> — Alexander Carmichael, *Carmina Gadelica*

KELLY, KELLIE, KELLEY, KELI   [*KEL-ee*]

MEANING: warrior, church, forest, holly • **USAGE:**
Irish and English form of surname *O'Ceallagh*,
from Gaelic *ceallagh* (war, warlike), *cill* (church),
or *coille* (woods); or from Welsh *celyn* (holly)
> *Who is she who looks out as the morning,*
> *beautiful as the moon, clear as the sun,*
> *and awesome as an army with banners?*
> — Song of Songs 6:10 (WEB)

KELSEY, KELSIE   *[KEL-see]*

MEANING: victory ship, fierce island • **USAGE:** English surname: a form of *Ceolsige,* from English *ceol* (ship) and *sige* (victory, success); or from English *cenel* (fierce) and *eg* (island)

> *May you have great success.*
> *May those who help you also have success.*
> — 1 Chronicles 12:18b (NIRV)

KENDA   *[KEN-dah]*

MEANING: valley spring, fountain in the valley • **USAGE:** American form of Kendal, from English *dæl* (dale, valley) and Norse *keld* (spring, well)

> *Hope springs eternal in the human breast.*
> — Alexander Pope, *Essay on Man*

KENDA   *[KEN-dah]*

MEANING: magical powers • **USAGE:** Amerind: Sioux

> *Our people possessed remarkable powers of concentration and abstraction, and I sometimes fancy that such nearness to nature as I have described keeps the spirit sensitive to impressions not commonly felt, and in touch with the unseen powers.*
> — Ohiyesa, *The Soul of the Indian*

KENDAL, KENDALL   *[KEN-del]*

MEANING: valley spring, fountain in the valley • **USAGE:** English surname: from English *dæl* (dale, valley) and Norse *keld* (spring, well)

> *You shall be like a watered garden,*
> *and like a spring of water, whose waters do not fail.*
> — Isaiah 58:11b (NKJV)

KENDI   *[KEN-dee]*

MEANING: loved one, beloved • **USAGE:** African: Meru of Kenya

> *Love cannot be divided.*
> — Kenyan proverb

KENDRA   *[KEN-drah]*

MEANING: high hill, mount • **USAGE:** English feminine form of Kendrick, from Welsh *cynwrig*

> *Mountains are the beginning and the end*
> *of all natural scenery.*
> — John Ruskin, *The True and the Beautiful*

KENNA   *[KEN-ah]*

MEANING: born of fire, beautiful • **USAGE:** Scottish feminine form of Kenneth, from Gaelic *cinaed* (born of fire) or *coinneach* (handsome, attractive)

> *'Tis beauty calls, and glory shows the way.*
> — Nathaniel Lee, *Alexander the Great,*
> *Or, The Rival Queens: A Tragedy*

KENNER   *[KEN-er]*

MEANING: born of fire, beautiful • **USAGE:** American surname: possibly a form of Kenna (*see* Kenna)

> *Love is a spirit all compact of fire.*
> — William Shakespeare, *Venus and Adonis*

KENYA   *[KEN-yah]*

MEANING: country in Africa, mountain of the ostrich • **USAGE:** American form of *Kiinyaa,* African Wakamba tribal mountain, meaning "mountain of the ostrich"; an African country

> *We are volcanoes. When we women offer*
> *our experience as our truth, as human truth,*
> *all the maps change. There are new mountains.*
> — Ursula K. Le Guin,
> "Bryn Mawr Commencement Address"

KENZIE   *[KEN-ʒee]*

MEANING: comely child, beautiful child • **USAGE:** English form of MacKenzie, from Gaelic *mac* (son) and *coinneach* (handsome, attractive)

> *Thy voice is sweet, and thy face comely.*
> — Song of Songs 2:14b (DR)

K

KEOLANI   *[keh-oh-LAH-nee]*

MEANING: heaven's continuation, goddess of
healing • USAGE: Hawaiian
>   *Let your love flow outward through the universe,*
>   *to its height, its depth, its broad extent,*
>   *a limitless love, without hatred or enmity.*
>   *Then as you stand or walk, sit or lie down,*
>   *as long as you are awake, strive for this with a*
>   *one-pointed mind; your life will bring heaven to earth.*
>   — Buddha, *Sutta Nipata* (tr. Eknath Easwaran in
>   *God Makes the Rivers to Flow*)

KERANI   *[keh-rah-nee]*

MEANING: sacred bells • USAGE: Hindu
>   *Music is the purest form of art,*
>   *and therefore the most direct expression of beauty.*
>   — Rabindranath Tagore, *Sadhana*

KEREN   *[KER-ehn]*

MEANING: horn, horn of an animal • USAGE:
Jewish
>   *The God who is my rock, in Him I take refuge;*
>   *my shield, and my horn of salvation.*
>   — 2 Samuel 22:3a (MT)

KERRY, KERI, KERRI   *[KER-ee]*

MEANING: dark, black, dark-haired, hollow,
glen, powerful chief • USAGE: Irish and English
surname: form of Irish county name *Ciarraí*,
from Gaelic *ciar* (dark, black); from Gaelic *coire*
(cauldron, a hollow); or English form of surname
Cyneric, from English *cyne* (royal, chief) and *ric*
(power, rule)
>   *The Lord said...I will give you treasures*
>   *hidden in dark and secret places.*
>   — Isaiah 45:1–3a (CEV)

KERSTIN   *[KEHR-stin]*

MEANING: follower of Christ, Christian • USAGE:
German and Scandinavian form of Kristina, from
Greek *christianos*

>   *I pray that the God of our Lord Jesus Christ,*
>   *the glorious Father, would give you a spirit*
>   *of wisdom and revelation in the knowledge of Him.*
>   — Ephesians 1:17b (HCSB)

KESHA, KEESHA, KESHIA   *[KEE-shah]*

MEANING: cinnamon-like, fragrant spice •
USAGE: American form of Kezia (*see* Ketzia)
>   *Take thou also unto thee principal spices,*
>   *of pure myrrh...of sweet cinnamon...of sweet*
>   *calamus...and of cassia...And thou shalt make it*
>   *an oil of holy ointment.*
>   — Exodus 30:23–25a (KJV)

KESHET   *[keh-SHET]*

MEANING: rainbow • USAGE: Jewish
>   *I have set My bow in the cloud,*
>   *and it shall be for a token of a covenant*
>   *between Me and the earth.*
>   — Genesis 9:13 (MT)

KETANA   *[keh-TAH-nah]*

MEANING: small, little • USAGE: Jewish
>   *Small and inauspicious beginnings are often crucial*
>   *for the person to flourish exceedingly in the end.*
>   — Baal Shem Tov aphorism

KETURA   *[keh-TOOR-ah, ktoo-RAH]*

MEANING: perfume, incense • USAGE: Jewish
>   *Ointment and perfume rejoice the heart.*
>   — Proverbs 27:9a (MT)

KETZIA   *[ket-ZIE-ah, ket-ZEE-ah]*

MEANING: cinnamon-like, fragrant spice •
USAGE: Jewish: from Greek *kassia* (cassia tree)
>   *The Lord spoke unto Moses saying: "Take thou also*
>   *unto thee the chief spices, of flowing myrrh...of sweet*
>   *cinnamon...of sweet calamus and of cassia...thou*
>   *shalt make it a holy anointing oil."*
>   — Exodus 30:22–25 (MT)

KEZIA   *[KEE-zhah]*

MEANING: cinnamon-like, fragrant spice •
USAGE: English form of Ketzia (*see* Ketzia)
Taste and see that the Lord is good!
How blessed is the one who takes shelter in him!
— Psalm 34:8 (NEB)

KHABIRA, KHABEERA   *[kah-bee-rah]*

MEANING: learned, knowledgeable • **USAGE:**
Muslim feminine form of Khabir
Let those who have knowledge be honored.
— Hadith of the Prophet Muhammad

KHALIDA, KHALIDAH   *[kah-lee-dah]*

MEANING: eternal, everlasting • **USAGE:** Muslim
feminine form of Khalid, from Arabic *khalada* (to
be eternal)
Indeed God / Has written a thousand promises /
All over your heart / That say, / Life, life, life /
Is far too sacred to / Ever end.
— Hafiz, "God's Bucket"
(tr. Daniel Ladinsky in *The Gift*)

KHALILA, KHALILAH   *[kah-lee-lah]*

MEANING: good friend • **USAGE:** Muslim feminine
form of Khalil, from Arabic *khalil*
Friendship is always a sweet responsibility,
never an opportunity.
— Kahlil Gibran, *Sand and Foam*

KHALISA   *[kah-lees-sah]*

MEANING: true, genuine, sincere • **USAGE:**
Muslim feminine form of Khalis
Sincerity is the jewel that forms in the shell of the heart.
— Hazrat Inayat Khan, *The Bowl of Saki*

KHASHIA   *[kah-shee-ah]*

MEANING: devout, pious • **USAGE:** Muslim

When we devote ourselves to the thought of God,
all illumination and revelation is ours.
— Hazrat Inayat Khan, *The Bowl of Saki*

KHASIBA   *[kah-see-bah]*

MEANING: fruitful, bountiful, prosperous •
USAGE: Muslim feminine form of Khasib
All bounties are in the hand of Allah:
He granteth them to whom He pleaseth:
And Allah careth for all, and He knoweth all things.
— Koran, The Family of Imran 3.7b (ALI)

KHATIRA, KHATIRAH   *[kah-TEE-rah]*

MEANING: wish, desire • **USAGE:** Muslim
Life is opportunity, not only to accomplish what one
desires but even to fulfill what one's soul yearns for.
— Hazrat Inayat Khan, *The Gayan*

KHAYRA, KHAIRA   *[kah-ee-rah]*

MEANING: good, blessed, fortunate • **USAGE:**
Muslim feminine form of Khayr, from Arabic *khair*
Whoso bringeth a good deed will receive tenfold
the like thereof.
— Koran, The Cattle 6.160a (PIC)

KHLOE   *[KLOH-ee]*

MEANING: green shoot, verdant, new growth •
USAGE: American form of Chloe, from Greek
khloe (green shoot) and *khloros* (pale green)
Growth itself contains the germ of happiness.
— Pearl S. Buck, *To My Daughters with Love*

KHRISTINA   *[kree-STEE-nah]*

MEANING: follower of Christ, Christian • **USAGE:**
Russian feminine form of Christian, from Greek
christianos
The Spirit himself testifies with our spirit that we are
God's children. Now if we are children, then we are
heirs — heirs of God and co-heirs with Christ.
— Romans 8:16–17a (NIV)

K

KIA [KEE-ah]

MEANING: follower of Christ, Christian, rising out of the East, rising out of Asia • USAGE: Swedish and Finnish form of Kristina (see Khristina); or from Chinese characters *ki* (rising up) and *a* (Asian)

If I live at the eastern horizon or settle at the western
limits, even there Your hand will lead me;
Your right hand will hold on to me.
— Psalm 139:9–10 (HCSB)

KIANA [kee-AH-nah]

MEANING: divine, the shining one • USAGE: Hawaiian form of Diana, from Latin *divus*

Walk in the paths illuminated by the moon.
— Hawaiian proverb

KIERA, KEIRA [KEER-ah]

MEANING: dark, black, dark-haired • USAGE: English form of Ciara, from Irish Gaelic *ciar*

We are rooted in darkness,
and we grow to the light.
— Joy Widmark, *Simply Rich: The Cosmos Within*

KIERSTEN, KIERSTIN [KEER-sten]

MEANING: follower of Christ, Christian • USAGE: English form of Kristina (see Khristina)

The peace of God is much greater than
the human mind can understand. This peace will keep
your hearts and minds through Christ Jesus.
— Philippians 4:7 (NLV)

KIKU [kee-koo]

MEANING: chrysanthemum flower • USAGE: Japanese

Like a beautiful brightly colored flower
full of fragrance is the well-spoken word
and the deed that matches the word.
— Buddha, *The Dhammapada*
(tr. Ananda Maitreya)

KIM [kim]

MEANING: royal meadow, chief's pasture, diamond-filled rock • USAGE: English form of Kimberly (see Kimberly)

The Lord…hath set me in a place of pasture.
He hath brought me up, on the water of refreshment.
— Psalm 22:1–2 (DR)

KIMBER [KIM-ber]

MEANING: royal meadow, chief's pasture, diamond-filled rock • USAGE: American form of Kimberly (see Kimberly)

The Lord says… Think of the rock from which you
came, the quarry from which you were cut.
— Isaiah 51:1 (GNT)

KIMBERLY [KIM-ber-lee]

MEANING: royal meadow, chief's pasture, diamond-filled rock • USAGE: English: from English *cyne* (royal), *burg* (fortified town), and *leah* (meadow, field); or from English *kimberlite*, a type of peridotite rock containing diamond

In pastures of tender grass He causeth me to lie down,
by quiet waters He doth lead me.
My soul He refresheth.
— Psalm 23:2–3a (YLT)

KIMBRA [KIM-brah]

MEANING: diamond-filled rock, royal meadow, chief's pasture • USAGE: English form of Kimberly (see Kimberly)

The Lord says, "Listen to me, those of you
who try to live right and follow the Lord.
Look at the rock from which you were cut;
look at the stone quarry from which you were dug."
— Isaiah 51:1 (NCV)

KIMIKO [kee-mee-koh]

MEANING: noble child, empress child • USAGE: Japanese: from Japanese *kimi* (noble, empress) and *ko* (child)

Only by exercising harmlessness toward living beings
can one be called noble.
— Buddha, *The Dhammapada*
(tr. Ananda Maitreya)

KIMYA [KEEM-yah]

MEANING: calm, peaceful, quiet • **USAGE:**
African: Swahili of Kenya and Tanzania
For working well, you need a quiet mind.
— Tanzanian proverb

KINDA [KIN-dah]

MEANING: woman of Kynthos, mountain on
Delos, moon • **USAGE:** American: possibly a form
of Kynthia, from Greek *Kynthos*, a mountain on
Delos where the Greek goddess Artemis was born
and denotes "moon personified"
The moon, like a flower /
In heaven's high bower, /
With silent delight /
Sits and smiles on the night.
— William Blake, "Night"

KIONI [kee-OH-nee]

MEANING: she who sees, she sees things • **USAGE:**
African: Kikuyu of Kenya
Seeing is better than hearing.
— East African proverb

KIRA [KEE-rah]

MEANING: lady, mistress, like the sun, far-sighted
• **USAGE:** Russian form of Kyra, from Greek *kyrios*
(lord, master); possibly from Persian *khur* (sun) or
kurush (far-sighted)
Nothing on earth is more beautiful
than the morning sun.
— Ecclesiastes 11:7 (CEV)

KIRSTEN [KEER-sten]

MEANING: follower of Christ, Christian • **USAGE:**
Scandinavian, German, and English form of
Kristina, from Greek *christianos*
Christ lives in you.
— Romans 8:10a (CEV)

KIRSTIE, KIRSTY [KEER-stee]

MEANING: follower of Christ, Christian • **USAGE:**
Scottish form of Kirsten (*see* Kirsten)
Deep peace I breathe into you....Deep peace of the Son
of Peace to you...Deep peace, deep peace!
— Fiona MacLeod, "Invocation of Peace"

KIRSTIN [KEER-sten]

MEANING: follower of Christ, Christian • **USAGE:**
Scottish form of Kristina (*see* Kirsten)
Neither death, nor life, nor angels,
nor principalities, nor things present, nor things to
come, nor powers, nor height, nor depth, nor any other
creature, shall be able to separate us from the love
of God, which is in Christ Jesus our Lord.
— Romans 8:38–39 (ASV)

KISA [KEE-sah]

MEANING: mercy, kind, good • **USAGE:** African:
Uganda
Goodness begets goodness.
— Ugandan proverb

KITRA [keet-RAH, KEH-trah]

MEANING: crown • **USAGE:** Jewish
You shall be a glorious crown in the hand of the Lord,
and a royal diadem in the palm of your God.
— Isaiah 62:3 (JPS)

K

KITTY, KITTIE   [KIT-ee]

MEANING: pure one, unblemished, innocent,
virtuous • **USAGE:** English form of Katharine or
Kathleen, from Greek *katharos* (pure); also from
Latin *cattus* (cat)

With the pure Thou dost show Thyself pure.
— Psalm 18:26a (NASB)

KIYOKO   [kee-yoh-koh]

MEANING: pure child • **USAGE:** Japanese: from
Japanese *kiyo* (pure, clean) and *ko* (child)

*Just as treasures are uncovered from the earth,
so virtue appears from good deeds,
and wisdom appears from a pure and peaceful mind.*
— Buddha

KLARA   [KLAH-rah]

MEANING: clear, transparent • **USAGE:** German,
Polish, Russian, and Scandinavian form of Clara,
from Latin *clarus*

*Your vision will become clear only when you look
into your heart. Who looks outside, dreams.
Who looks inside, awakens.*
— Carl Jung

KLEMENTINA   [klee-men-TEE-nah]

MEANING: clement, mild, gentle, merciful •
USAGE: Russian feminine form of Kliment, from
Latin *clemens*

*The wisdom from above is first pure,
then peaceable, gentle, open to reason,
full of mercy and good fruits, impartial and sincere.*
— James 3:17 (ESV)

KODY   [KOH-dee]

MEANING: helper, aide, helpful • **USAGE:**
American form of Cody, from Gaelic *cuidightheach*

Peace, peace be to thee, and peace to thy helpers.
— 1 Chronicles 12:18b (DR)

KOHANA   [koh-hah-nah]

MEANING: flower child • **USAGE:** Japanese: from
Japanese *ko* (child) and *hana* (flower)

*If we could see the miracle of a single flower clearly,
our whole life would change.*
— Buddha

KOKORO   [koh-koh-roh]

MEANING: heart, spirit, soul • **USAGE:** Japanese:
from Japanese *kokoro*

*All life is a manifestation of the spirit,
the manifestation of love.*
— Morihei Ueshiba, *The Art of Peace*
(tr. John Stevens)

KOLANI   [koh-LAH-nee]

MEANING: heavenly, rising up to heaven • **USAGE:**
Hawaiian: from Hawaiian *ku* (resembling, to stand,
to reach, to rise up) and *lani* (sky, heaven, spiritual)

Heaven above, earth beneath.
— Hawaiian proverb
(tr. Mary Pukui in ʻOlelo Noʻeau)

KOLINA   [koh-LEEN-ah]

MEANING: pure one, unblemished, innocent,
virtuous • **USAGE:** Greek form of Aikaterini, from
Greek *katharos* (pure)

To the pure, all things are pure.
— Titus 1:15a (ESV)

KONANE   [koh-NAH-nee]

MEANING: bright moonlight, to shine as the moon
• **USAGE:** Hawaiian

Face as bright as the moon.
— Hawaiian proverb
(tr. Mary Pukui in ʻOlelo Noʻeau)

KONSTANTINA *[kohn-stahn-TEE-nah]*

MEANING: constant, steadfast • **USAGE:** Greek form of Constantina, from Latin *constans*

> O Lord...let your steadfast love
> and your faithfulness keep me safe forever.
> — Psalm 40:11 (NRSV)

KORA *[KOR-ah]*

MEANING: maiden, young woman • **USAGE:** Greek: from Greek *korë* (maiden); *Kore* is the name for Persephone in Greek mythology

> A heart that loves is always young.
> — Greek proverb

KORINNA *[koh-REEN-ah]*

MEANING: little maiden, young woman • **USAGE:** Greek: from Greek *korë (maiden)* and diminutive *-ina*

> You are a fine woman.
> — Ruth 3:11b (GNT)

KOSHI *[KOH-shee]*

MEANING: full, satisfied • **USAGE:** African: Hausa of West Africa

> Accomplishment of purpose
> is better than making a profit.
> — Hausa proverb

KOTONE *[koh-toh-neh]*

MEANING: sound of the harp, sound of the lute • **USAGE:** Japanese: from Japanese *koto* (harp, lute) and *ne* (sound)

> Just as with a lute / serenity is found
> when one's life is / properly balanced.
> — Shi Wuling, *Path to Peace*

KRIS *[krees (German, Scandinavian), kris (English)]*

MEANING: follower of Christ, Christian • **USAGE:** German, Scandinavian, and English form of Kristina or Kristine (*see* Kristina)

> The peace of God, which surpasses all comprehension,
> will guard your hearts and your minds in Christ Jesus.
> — Philippians 4:7 (NASB)

KRISTA *[KREES-tah (German, Norwegian), KRIS-tah (English)]*

MEANING: follower of Christ, Christian • **USAGE:** German, Norwegian, and English form of Kristina or Kristine (*see* Kristina)

> Christ gives me the strength to face anything.
> — Philippians 4:13 (CEV)

KRISTIE, KRISTY *[KRIS-tee]*

MEANING: follower of Christ, Christian • **USAGE:** English form of Christa (*see* Kristina)

> This Christ within you
> is at the center of every person and every thing.
> — Ernest Holmes, *Your Invisible Power*

KRISTIN, KRISTEN *[KREE-sten (German, Scandinavian), KRIS-ten (English)]*

MEANING: follower of Christ, Christian • **USAGE:** German, Scandinavian, and English form of Kristina (*see* Kristina)

> I pray that you, being rooted and established in love,
> may have power, together with all the saints,
> to grasp how wide and long and high and deep
> is the love of Christ.
> — Ephesians 3:17a–18 (NIV)

KRISTINA *[kree-STEE-nah]*

MEANING: follower of Christ, Christian • **USAGE:** German, Scandinavian, and Russian form of Christina, from Greek *christianos*

> Neither death, nor life, nor angels, nor ruling spirits,
> nothing now, nothing in the future, no powers, nothing
> above us, nothing below us, nor anything else in the
> whole world will ever be able to separate us from the
> love of God that is in Christ Jesus.
> — Romans 8:38–39 (NCV)

K

KRISTINE   *[krees-TEE-neh]*

MEANING: follower of Christ, Christian • **USAGE:** Norwegian, Danish, Swedish, and German feminine form of Christian (*see* Kristina)

The peace of God, which passeth all understanding,
shall keep your hearts and minds
through Christ Jesus.
— Philippians 4:7 (KJV)

KRYSTAL, KRYSTELL   *[KRIS-tal]*

MEANING: crystal, transparent quartz, ice • **USAGE:** American form of Crystal, from Greek *krystallos* (ice)

Our souls should be like a transparent crystal
through which God can be perceived.
— Mother Teresa

KUNDINI   *[kuhn-dih-nee]*

MEANING: jasmine, aromatic flower • **USAGE:** Hindu: Sanskrit

Happiness radiates like the fragrance from a flower,
and draws all good things toward you.
Allow your love to nourish yourself as well as others.
— Maharishi Mahesh Yogi

KUN-SUN   *[kun-sun]*

MEANING: established goodness • **USAGE:** Korean: from Korean *kun* (found, established) and *sun* (goodness)

Set yourself on doing good.
Do it over and over again,
and you will be filled with joy.
— Buddha, *The Dhammapada* (tr. Thomas Byrom)

KUPENDA   *[kuh-pen-dah]*

MEANING: love • **USAGE:** African: Swahili of Kenya/Tanzania

True love is not in the mirror, it is in the heart.
— Swahili proverb

KUPONO   *[koo-poh-noh]*

MEANING: honest, truthful • **USAGE:** Hawaiian

Truth is not changeable.
— Hawaiian proverb
(tr. Mary Pukui in *'Olelo No'eau*)

KWASI   *[KWAH-see]*

MEANING: wealthy • **USAGE:** African: Swahili of Kenya/Tanzania

All wealth is given to us by God.
— Swahili proverb

KYLA   *[KIE-lah]*

MEANING: slender, narrow, church, beautiful • **USAGE:** Scottish and English feminine form of Kyle, from Gaelic *caol* (slender), *cill* (church), or *cadhla* (beautiful)

You can take no credit for beauty at sixteen.
But if you are beautiful at sixty,
it will be your soul's own doing.
— Marie Carmichael Stopes

KYLIE, KILEY   *[KIE-lee]*

MEANING: slender, narrow, church, beautiful • **USAGE:** Scottish and English form of Kyla (*see* Kyla)

Surely your goodness and unfailing love
will pursue me all the days of my life,
and I will live in the house of the Lord forever.
— Psalm 23:6 (NLT)

KYNA   *[KYE-nah]*

MEANING: love, affection • **USAGE:** Irish: from Gaelic *cion*

May mercy, peace,
and love be multiplied to you.
— Jude 1:2 (RSV)

KYNTHIA   [KEEN-thee-ah]

MEANING: woman of Kynthos, mountain on Delos, moon • **USAGE:** Greek: from *Kynthos*, a mountain on Delos where the Greek goddess Artemis was born and denotes "moon personified"

How beautiful on the mountains
are the feet of the messenger who brings good news,
the good news of peace.
— Isaiah 52:7a (NLT)

KYRA   [KIE-rah]

MEANING: lady, mistress, like the sun, far-sighted • **USAGE:** English form of Cyra, from Greek *kyrios* (lord, master); or possibly from Persian *khur* (sun) or *kurush* (far-sighted)

There is a sunshine whose light is golden…
but there is another sunshine, and that the purest,
whose light is white.
— John Ruskin, *Modern Painters*

L

LACY, LACEE   [LAY-see]

MEANING: lace, delicate, net • **USAGE:** English: from English *lace* (ornamental net pattern); or from French *las* (net, noose, string)

You [God] made all the delicate inner parts of my body
and knit me together in my mother's womb.
Thank you for making me so wonderfully complex!
Your workmanship is marvelous — how well I know it.
— Psalm 139:13–14 (NLT)

LA DAWN   [lah-DAHN]

MEANING: sunrise, dawn of day, daybreak • **USAGE:** American: from English *dauninge*
Golden rays will usher in at dawn.
— Sarah Knowles Bolton

LA DONNA, LADONNA   [lah-DON-ah]

MEANING: lady of nobility • **USAGE:** American: from Italian *donna*

It's through me, Lady Wisdom,
that your life deepens, and the years of your life ripen.
— Proverbs 9:11 (MSG)

LAI   [LAH-ee]

MEANING: calm, peaceful, content • **USAGE:** Hawaiian

There is tranquility before the face of the cliff.
[Perfect peace.]
— Hawaiian proverb
(tr. Mary Pukui in *'Olelo No'eau*)

LAILA   [LAY-lah]

MEANING: night, dark beauty • **USAGE:** Jewish, English, and Scandinavian: from Arabic *lei*

I often think that the night is more alive
and more richly coloured than the day.
— Vincent van Gogh (letter of September 8, 1888)

LAILIE, LEILI   [LAY-lee]

MEANING: my night • **USAGE:** Jewish

In the night His song shall be with me,
even a prayer unto the God of my life.
— Psalm 42:9b (MT)

LAKA   [lah-kah]

MEANING: gentle, kind • **USAGE:** Hawaiian

Gentleness is the companion of joy /
tenderness of compassion / serenity of wisdom.
— Shi Wuling, *Path to Peace*

LAKENYA   [lah-KEN-yah]

MEANING: country in Africa, mountain of the ostrich • **USAGE:** American: possibly a form of Kenya, from *Kiinyaa*, the African Wakamba tribal mountain, meaning "mountain of the ostrich"; an African country

Mountains symbolize the indomitable will,
an eternal unbending resolution, a loyalty that is
eternal, and character that is unimpeachable.
— William O. Douglas, *Of Men and Mountains*

LAKISHA, LAKEISHA   *[lah-KEE-shah]*

MEANING: cinnamon-like, fragrant spice •
USAGE: American: possibly from Greek *kassia*
(cassia tree)

Take the finest spices: of liquid myrrh…
of sweet-smelling cinnamon…of cassia…And you
shall make of these a sacred anointing oil blended
as by the perfumer; it shall be a holy anointing oil.
— Exodus 30:23–25 (ESV)

LALASA   *[lah-lah-sah]*

MEANING: love, desire • **USAGE:** Hindu
When our heart is fully awakened in love, or in other
great emotions, our personality is in its flood-tide.
— Rabindranath Tagore, "What Is Art?"

LALIA   *[LAY-lee-ah]*

MEANING: well-spoken, sweet spoken, eloquent
• **USAGE:** English form of Eulalia, from Greek *eu*
(good, well) and *lalein* (to talk)

Let me see your face, let me hear your voice;
for your voice is sweet, and your face is lovely.
— Song of Songs 2:14b (HCSB)

LALITA, LALITHA   *[lah-lih-tah, lah-lee-thah]*

MEANING: lovely, charming, gentle • **USAGE:**
Hindu: from Sanskrit *lalita*

O beauty, find thyself in love,
not in the flattery of thy mirror.
— Rabindranath Tagore, *Stray Birds*

LAN   *[lahn]*

MEANING: orchid flower • **USAGE:** Chinese
The softest things in the world override the hardest.
— Zhuang Zhou

LANA   *[LAH-nah, LAN-ah]*

MEANING: little rock, beautiful • **USAGE:** English
and Irish form of Alana, from Breton *alp* (rock)
and diminutive *-an*; or from Scotch Gaelic *alainn*
(handsome, fair)

My darling, everything about you is beautiful.
— Song of Songs 4:7a (NCV)

LANA   *[LAH-nah]*

MEANING: buoyant, floating, calm as still waters •
USAGE: Hawaiian

As gentle as still water.
— Hawaiian proverb
(tr. Mary Pukui in *'Olelo No'eau*)

LA NEESE, LANICE, LENICE   *[lah-NEES]*

MEANING: celebrant, reveler • **USAGE:** American:
possibly a form of Denise, from *Dionysus*, Greek
god of wine and revelry

The aim of life is to live, and to live means to be
aware, joyously, drunkenly, serenely, divinely aware.
— Henry Miller, *The Wisdom of the Heart*

LANEY, LAINEY   *[LAY-nee]*

MEANING: light, illumination, torch, dark, black,
narrow, country lane • **USAGE:** English form of
Elaine, from Greek *helene* (torch) or *ele* (light);
English form of Melanie, from Greek *melas* (dark,
black); or from English *lane* (narrow road, country
lane)

There is a road from the eye to the heart
that does not go through the intellect.
— G. K. Chesterton

LANI   *[LAH-nee]*

MEANING: sky, heaven, heavenly, spiritual, divine,
highborn, royal one • **USAGE:** Hawaiian: from
Hawaiian *lani*

A heavenly nature; an earthly nature.
— Hawaiian proverb
(tr. Mary Pukui in *'Olelo No'eau*)

LAOLA   *[lah-OH-lah]*

MEANING: day of life • **USAGE:** Hawaiian
Arise with joy to greet the day!
— Hawaiian proverb

LARA   *[LAH-rah]*

MEANING: laurel tree, laurel wreath, cheerful,
joyful, happy • **USAGE:** Russian, English, German,
Italian, Scandinavian, and Spanish form of Laura,
from Latin *laurus* (laurel); or Russian form of
Larisa, from Latin *hilaris* (cheerful, joyful)
Cheerfulness is full of significance:
it suggests good health, a clear conscience,
and a soul at peace with all human nature.
— Charles Kingsley

LARINDA, LARENDA, LAURENDA
[lah-REN-dah]

MEANING: laurel tree, laurel wreath • **USAGE:**
English form of Loren, from Latin *laurus*
To plant trees is to give body and life
to one's dreams of a better world.
— Russell Page, *The Education of a Gardener*

LARISA   *[lah-REE-sah]*

MEANING: cheerful, joyful, happy • **USAGE:**
Russian: probably from Latin *hilaris*
You will be happy and it will be well with you.
— Psalm 128:2b (NASB)

LARISSA   *[lah-RIS-ah]*

MEANING: cheerful, joyful, happy • **USAGE:**
English form of Larisa, probably from Latin *hilaris*
A cheerful countenance
is a token of a heart that is in prosperity.
— Ben Sira 13:26a (KJV Apocrypha)

LARK, LARKE   *[lark]*

MEANING: songbird, lark • **USAGE:** English: from
English *laveroc*
The lark is so brimful of gladness and love.
— Samuel Taylor Coleridge,
"Answer to a Child's Question"

LASAIR   *[lah-SAYR]*

MEANING: flames, fire • **USAGE:** Irish: from
Gaelic *lassa*
Bless the Lord, O my soul…you make the winds
your messengers, and fire and flame your ministers.
— Psalm 104:1–4 (NRSV)

LASHAWNA   *[lah-SHAH-nah]*

MEANING: God is gracious, God is giving •
USAGE: American: possibly a form of Shawna,
from Hebrew *y'hohanan* (Yahweh is gracious)
The Lord your God is kind and loving.
He will not turn His face away from you.
— 2 Chronicles 30:9b (NLV)

LASHONDRA   *[lah-SHAHN-drah]*

MEANING: God is gracious, God is giving •
USAGE: American: possibly a form of Shawna,
from Hebrew *y'hohanan* (Yahweh is gracious)
God is able to give you more than you need,
so that you will always have all you need for yourselves
and more than enough for every good cause.
— 2 Corinthians 9:8 (NEB)

LATANYA, LATAWNYA   *[lah-TAHN-yah]*

MEANING: father • **USAGE:** American: possibly a
form of Tanya or Tatiana, from the feminine form
of the Roman family clan name *Tatius*, possibly
from Latin *tata* (father)
I thank Thee and praise Thee, O Thou God of my
fathers, who hast given me wisdom and might.
— Daniel 2:23a (KJ21)

L

LA TASHA, LATASHA   *[lah-TASH-ah]*

MEANING: born on Christmas Day, Christmas •
USAGE: American: possibly a form of Natasha,
from Latin *natalis dies Domini* (birthday of the
Lord, Christmas)

Christmas is not a time nor a season,
but a state of mind. To cherish peace and goodwill, to
be plenteous in mercy,
is to have the real spirit of Christmas.
— Calvin Coolidge

LATHAM   *[LAY-tham]*

MEANING: barn, animal haven • **USAGE:** English
surname: from Norse *hlatha* (barn)
The animals of the field shall be at peace with you.
— Job 5:23b (WEB)

LATIFAH, LATEEFA   *[lah-TEE-fah]*

MEANING: kind, gentle, gracious, courteous •
USAGE: Muslim feminine form of Latif, from
Arabic *latif*
Verily you have two qualities which God
and His Messenger love — fortitude and gentleness.
— Hadith of the Prophet Muhammad
(tr. Abdullay Al-Mamun Al-Suhrawardy)

LA TISHA, LATISHA   *[lah-TISH-ah]*

MEANING: joyous, happy • **USAGE:** American
form of Leticia, from Latin *laetitia*
You will find happiness and genuine joy.
— Sirach 15:6a (GNT Apocrypha)

LA TOYA, LATOYA   *[lah-TOY-yah]*

MEANING: joyous, happy • **USAGE:** American
form of Victoria, from Latin *vincere* (to conquer)
Ask the Lord to bless your plans,
and you will be successful in carrying them out.
— Proverbs 16:3 (GNT)

LATRICE   *[lah-TREES]*

MEANING: patrician, noble one • **USAGE:**
American: possibly a form of Patrice, from Latin
patricius
O Lord God, we pray that we may be inspired to
nobleness of life in the least things. May we dignify all
our daily life. May we set such a sacredness upon every
part of our life, that nothing shall be trivial, nothing
unimportant, and nothing dull, in the daily round.
— Henry Ward Beecher,
Proverbs from Plymouth Pulpit

LAURA   *[LOR-ah]*

MEANING: laurel tree, laurel wreath • **USAGE:**
English, German, Italian, Spanish feminine form of
Laurence, from Latin *laurus*
There's nothing that keeps its youth,
so far as I know, but a tree and truth.
— Oliver Wendell Holmes Sr.,
The Autocrat of the Breakfast Table

LAURE   *[lohr]*

MEANING: laurel tree, laurel wreath • **USAGE:**
French feminine form of Laurent (*see* Laura)
We have nothing to fear and a great deal
to learn from trees, that vigorous and pacific tribe
which without stint produces strengthening essences for
us, soothing balms, and in whose gracious company we
spend so many cool, silent and intimate hours.
— Marcel Proust, *Pleasures and Regrets*

LAUREL   *[LOR-el]*

MEANING: laurel tree, laurel wreath • **USAGE:**
English feminine form of Laurence (*see* Laura)
We love trees with universal love.
— Henry Ward Beecher

LAUREN   *[LOR-en]*

MEANING: laurel tree, laurel wreath • **USAGE:**
English feminine form of Laurence (*see* Laura)

As a tree produces fruit, wisdom gives life to those who
use it, and everyone who uses it will be happy.
— Proverbs 3:18 (NCV)

LAURIE   *[LOR-ee]*

MEANING: laurel tree, laurel wreath • **USAGE:**
English form of Laura, Laurel, or Lauren (*see*
Laura)

I hear the wind among the trees / Playing the celestial
symphonies; / I see the branches downward bent, /
Like keys of some great instrument.
— Henry Wadsworth Longfellow,
"A Day of Sunshine"

LAVANYA   *[lah-van-yah]*

MEANING: beauty, grace • **USAGE:** Hindu:
Sanskrit

Love gives beauty to everything it touches.
— Rabindranath Tagore

LAVENDER   *[LAV-en-der]*

MEANING: lavender flower, pale purple color •
USAGE: English: from Latin *lividus* (bluish, livid)

The gift of perfume to a flower
is a special grace like genius or like beauty.
— John Burroughs, *Pepaction*

LAVERN, LAVERNE   *[lah-VERN]*

MEANING: spring, springlike, alder tree • **USAGE:**
English: from French *verne* (alder tree); or from
Latin *ver* (spring)

The nobler the tree, the more pliant the twig.
— English proverb

LAVITA   *[lah-VEE-tah]*

MEANING: life, full of life • **USAGE:** American:
from Latin *vita*

Long life to you! Peace be to you, and peace be to your
house, and peace be to all that you have.
— 1 Samuel 25:6b (WEB)

LAVONNE   *[lah-VON]*

MEANING: yew tree, bow maker • **USAGE:** English
form of Yvonne, from German *iv* (yew tree); yew is
used to make bows

She does her work with energy,
and her arms are strong.
— Proverbs 31:17 (NCV)

LAWANDA   *[lah-WAHN-dah]*

MEANING: wand, branch, traveler, wanderer,
sojourner, a Wend • **USAGE:** American form of
Wanda, from German *vond* (wand, branch); or from
German Wend, migrant Slavs of the sixth century

The Lord thy God is with thee
whithersoever thou goest.
— Joshua 1:9b (KJV)

LAYAAN   *[lah-yahn]*

MEANING: gentle, tender • **USAGE:** Muslim

Tenderness and kindness are not symptoms
of weakness and despair but manifestations
of strength and resolution.
— Kahlil Gibran

LAYLA   *[LAY-lah]*

MEANING: night, dark beauty • **USAGE:** English
form of Leila, from Arabic *leila*

Night is the mother of counsels.
— George Herbert

LEA   *[LEE-ah]*

MEANING: meadow, pasture • **USAGE:** English:
from English *leah*

The Lord is my shepherd, I shall not want.
He makes me lie down in green pastures.
— Psalm 23:1–2a (NASB)

LEA   *[LEH-ah]*

MEANING: goddess of canoe makers • **USAGE:**
Hawaiian

One will not be wet on a large canoe.
[Safe in the protection of an important person.]
— Hawaiian proverb
(tr. Mary Pukui in *'Olelo No'eau*)

LEAH   *[LAY-ah (Jewish), LEE-ah (English)]*

MEANING: weary, tired, gazelle • **USAGE:** Jewish
and English: from Hebrew *la'ah* (to be weary) or
le'ah (gazelle, wild cow)
He [God] said: "My presence shall go with thee,
and I will give thee rest."
— Exodus 33:14 (MT)

LEANDRA   *[leh-AHN-drah]*

MEANING: lioness, lionhearted • **USAGE:** Greek,
Spanish, and Italian feminine form of Leander,
from Greek *leon* (lion) and *andros* (man)
I will be to them as a lioness.
— Hosea 13:7a (DR)

LEANN, LEANNE   *[lee-AN]*

MEANING: graceful meadow • **USAGE:** English
combination of Lee and Ann (*see* Lee and Anne)
Grace be with thee.
— 1 Timothy 6:21b (KJV)

LEE   *[lee]*

MEANING: meadow, field, pasture, poem • **USAGE:**
English: from English *leah* (meadow, field); or from
Scotch Gaelic *laoi* (poem)
The Lord is my shepherd, I shall not be in want.
He makes me lie down in green pastures,
he leads me beside quiet waters.
— Psalm 23:1–2 (NIV)

LEEAT, LIAT   *[lee-AHT]*

MEANING: you are mine • **USAGE:** Jewish
I have called you by name, thou art Mine.
— Isaiah 43:1b (MT)

LEENA   *[LEE-nah]*

MEANING: devoted, dedicated, consecrated •
USAGE: Hindu
Now it is time to sit quiet, face to face with Thee,
and to sing dedication of life
in this silent and overflowing leisure.
— Rabindranath Tagore, *Gitanjali*

LEENOY, LINOY   *[lee-NOY]*

MEANING: my beauty, ornament • **USAGE:** Jewish
The noblest of all ornaments is modesty.
— Eleazar Rokeach

LEEONA, LIONA   *[lee-OH-nah]*

MEANING: my strength • **USAGE:** Jewish feminine
form of Leeon
She girds herself with strength,
and performs her tasks with vigor.
— Proverbs 31:17 (JPS)

LEERAZ, LIRAZ   *[lee-RAHZ]*

MEANING: I have a secret • **USAGE:** Jewish
Indeed You desire truth about that which is hidden;
teach me wisdom about secret things.
— Psalm 51:8 (JPS)

LEEYA, LIYA   *[LEE-yah]*

MEANING: I belong to God • **USAGE:** Jewish
I am ever mindful of the Lord's presence;
He is at my right hand;
I shall never be shaken.
— Psalm 16:8 (JPS)

LEHUA   *[leh-HOO-ah]*

MEANING: flower of the island of Hawaii •
USAGE: Hawaiian
A lone tree, a lehua of Ka'ala.
[An outstanding person.]
— Hawaiian proverb
(tr. Mary Pukui in *'Olelo No'eau*)

LEIGH [lee]

MEANING: meadow, field, pasture, poem • **USAGE:** English: from English *leah* (meadow, field); or from Scotch Gaelic *laoi* (poem)

A sweeter meadow ne'er was seen.
— William Wordsworth, "Lines Composed a Few Miles above Tintern Abbey"

LEILA, LAILA [LAY-lah]

MEANING: night, dark beauty • **USAGE:** Muslim: from Arabic *leila*

There is great joy in darkness. Deepen it.
— Hakim Sanai

LEILANI [leh-ee-LAH-nee, lay-LAH-nee]

MEANING: heavenly lei, celestial wreath • **USAGE:** Hawaiian: from Hawaiian *lei* (wreath of flowers) and *lani* (sky, heaven, heavenly, spiritual, divine)

Tiny is the flower, yet it scents the grasses around it.
— Hawaiian proverb
(tr. Mary Pukui in *'Olelo No'eau*)

LEINANI [leh-ee-NAH-nee]

MEANING: beautiful lei, beautiful flowers • **USAGE:** Hawaiian: from Hawaiian *lei* (a wreath of flowers) and *nani* (beauty, beautiful)

A lei of blessings I weave for you.
— Hawaiian proverb

LENA [LAY-nah (German, Greek, Russian, and Scandinavian), LEE-nah (English)]

MEANING: light, illumination, torch, woman from Magdala, tower • **USAGE:** German, English, Greek, Russian, and Scandinavian form of Helena, from Greek *helene* (torch) or *ele* (light); or German and Scandinavian form of Magdalena, from Hebrew *migdal* (tower)

Let your light shine before others.
— Matthew 5:16b (ESV)

LENCI [LEN-see]

MEANING: light, illumination, torch • **USAGE:** Hungarian form of Helen, from Greek *helene* (torch) or *ele* (light)

The fruit of the light consists in all goodness, righteousness and truth.
— Ephesians 5:9 (NIV)

LENE [LEE-neh]

MEANING: light, illumination, torch, woman from Magdala, tower • **USAGE:** Danish and Norwegian form of Helena (*see* Lena)

God said, "Let there be light," and there was light. God saw the light, and saw that it was good.
— Genesis 1:3–4a (KJV)

LENI [LEN-ee]

MEANING: light, illumination, torch • **USAGE:** German form of Helen, from Greek *helene* (torch) or *ele* (light)

When a woman's heart is touched, when it is moved by love, then the electric spark is communicated, and the fire of inspiration kindles.
— Countess Ida von Hahn-Hahn

LENORA [leh-NOR-ah]

MEANING: light, illumination, torch • **USAGE:** English and Russian form of Eleanora, from Greek *helene* (torch) or *ele* (light)

The fruit of the light is all goodness, and justice, and truth.
— Ephesians 5:8b–9 (DR)

LEOLA [lee-OH-lah]

MEANING: lion, lionhearted • **USAGE:** English feminine form of Leo (*see* Leona)

Good people are as brave as a lion.
— Proverbs 28:1b (NCV)

L

LEONA, LIONA [lee-OH-nah]

MEANING: lion, lionhearted • USAGE: English and German feminine form of Leon, from Latin *leo*

Love laughs, and on a lion rides.
— Ralph Waldo Emerson,
"The Dæmonic Love"

LEONIE [lee-OH-nee]

MEANING: lion, lionhearted • USAGE: English feminine form of Leon (*see* Leona)

Rise, like lions after slumber.
— Percy Bysshe Shelley,
"The Masque of Anarchy"

LEONOR [lay-oh-NOR]

MEANING: light, illumination, torch, strong as a lion, lionhearted • USAGE: Spanish and Portuguese form of Eleonor, from Greek *helene* (torch) or *ele* (light); or Spanish feminine form of Leonard, from German *lewo* (lion) and *hart* (hardy, strong, brave)

Truly the light is sweet.
— Ecclesiastes 11:7a (KJV)

LEONORA [leh-oh-NOHR-ah (Italian), lee-oh-NOHR-ah (English)]

MEANING: light, illumination, torch • USAGE: Italian form of Eleonora (*see* Lenora)

Oh, send out Your light and Your truth!
Let them lead me.
— Psalm 43:3a (NKJV)

LEONORE [LEE-oh-nor]

MEANING: light, illumination, torch • USAGE: English form of Eleanor (*see* Lenora)

Let nothing stand between you and the light.
— Henry David Thoreau
(letter of March 7, 1848)

LESLEY, LESLIE [LES-lee, LEZ-lee]

MEANING: lesser meadow, small field, garden of hollies, gray fort • USAGE: Scottish and English surname: from Gaelic *less lea* (lesser field, smaller meadow), *leas chuillin* (garden of hollies), or *liath* (gray, gray fort)

Thou shalt be like a watered garden,
and like a spring of water, whose waters fail not.
— Isaiah 58:11b (KJV)

LETA [LEET-ah]

MEANING: truth, truthful, joyful, happy • USAGE: English form of Aleta, from Greek *aletheia* (truth); or from Latin *laetus* (joyful)

Truth is beautiful within and without, forevermore.
— Ralph Waldo Emerson,
"Divinity School Address"

LETHA [LEE-thah]

MEANING: truth, truthful, healer • USAGE: English form of Alethea, from Greek *aletheia* (truth); or English form of Althea, from Greek *althainein* (to heal)

The knowledge of truth, which is the presence of it,
and the belief of truth, which is the enjoying of it,
is the sovereign good of human nature.
— Francis Bacon, "Of Truth"

LETICIA [lay-TEE-shah]

MEANING: joyous, happy • USAGE: Spanish: from Latin *laetitia*

The spirit of contentment ever wears the hues of joy.
— Pedro Calderón de la Barca,
The Scarf and the Flower (tr. Denis MacCarthy)

LETITIA [leh-TEE-shah]

MEANING: joyous, happy • USAGE: English form of Leticia (*see* Leticia)

You will be happy, and it will be well with you.
— Psalm 128:2b (WEB)

LETIZIA   *[leh-TEE-tsyah]*

MEANING: joyous, happy • **USAGE:** Italian form of Letitia (*see* Leticia)

> *For the happy heart, life is a continual feast.*
> — Proverbs 15:15b (NLT)

LEVANA   *[leh-vah-NAH, leh-VAH-nah]*

MEANING: moon, white • **USAGE:** Jewish

> *Who is she that looketh forth as the dawn,*
> *fair as the moon, clear as the sun?*
> — Song of Songs 6:10a (MT)

LEWA   *[leh-wah]*

MEANING: beautiful • **USAGE:** African: Yoruba of Nigeria

> *Character is beauty.*
> — Yoruba proverb

LEWELLA, LLEWELLA   *[loo-EH-lah]*

MEANING: guiding image, lion, lionhearted • **USAGE:** Welsh form of Llewelyn, from Welsh *llyw* (lead, guide) and *eilun* (image, icon); or from Welsh *llew* (lion)

> *The righteous are bold as a lion.*
> — Proverbs 28:1b (NKJV)

LEXA   *[LEK-sah]*

MEANING: protector and helper of humankind, guardian • **USAGE:** English form of Alexandra or Alexis, from Greek *alexein* (to defend, to help) and *andros* (man)

> *He will command His angels*
> *concerning you to guard you in all your ways.*
> — Psalm 91:11 (NIV)

LEXI, LEXIE, LEXY   *[LEK-see]*

MEANING: protector and helper of humankind, guardian • **USAGE:** English form of Alexandra or Alexis, from Greek *alexein* (to defend, to help) and *andros* (man)

> *Discretion will watch over you.*
> *Understanding will keep you.*
> — Proverbs 2:11 (RSV)

LIA   *[LEE-ah]*

MEANING: messenger with good news, angel of good tidings, weary, tired, gazelle • **USAGE:** Italian form of Evangelia, from Greek *eu* (good, well) and *angelos* (messenger, angel); or Italian form of Leah, from Hebrew *la'ah* (to be weary)

> *Behold, I send an Angel before thee,*
> *to keep thee in the way.*
> — Exodus 23:20a (DT)

LIADAN   *[LEE-den]*

MEANING: gray lady • **USAGE:** Irish: from Gaelic *líadan*

> *A gracious lady is respected.*
> — Proverbs 11:16a (GNT)

LIAN   *[lee-ahn]*

MEANING: lotus flower • **USAGE:** Chinese

> *A flower cannot blossom without sunshine*
> *nor a garden without love.*
> — Chinese proverb

LIANA, LIANNA   *[lee-AH-nah]*

MEANING: graceful meadow, young and graceful, gracefully young • **USAGE:** English combination of Lee and Anna; or English form of Julianna (*see* Lee, Anna, and Julianna)

> *Grace be to you and peace.*
> — 1 Thessalonians 1:2a (DR)

LIANE   *[lee-AH-neh]*

MEANING: young, youthful, of Jupiter • **USAGE:** German form of Juliane, from Latin *iulus* (downy-chinned, youthful); or form of Jupiter, from Latin *dyeus* (Zeus) and *pater* (father)

> *In youth we learn; in age we understand.*
> — Marie von Ebner-Eschenbach

LIANG   [lee-ahng]

Meaning: bright, shining • **Usage:** Chinese
May the star of happiness shine on all your journey.
— Chinese proverb (tr. William Scarborough)

LIANNE   [lee-AN]

Meaning: graceful meadow • **Usage:** English
form of Leann, from English *leah* (meadow, field)
and Hebrew *chaanach* (grace)
Grace to you and peace.
— 1 Corinthians 1:3a (NASB)

LIBBY, LIBBIE   [LIB-ee]

Meaning: God is my oath, joined with God,
blessed by God • **Usage:** English form of
Elizabeth, from Hebrew *el'ishebha*
*Live in peace. And the God who gives
love and peace will be with you.*
— 2 Corinthians 13:11b (NIRV)

LIBENA   [lee-BYEH-nah]

Meaning: loving, affectionate • **Usage:** Czech:
from Slavic *lib* (love)
Love never ends.
— 1 Corinthians 13:8a (NRSV)

LIBERATA   [lee-beh-RAH-tah]

Meaning: freedom, liberty • **Usage:** Italian (*see*
Liberty)
Peace is liberty in tranquility.
— Marcus Tullius Cicero, *Philippics*
(tr. John R. King)

LIBERTY   [LIB-er-tee]

Meaning: freedom, liberty • **Usage:** English:
from Latin *libertas*
Liberty is the soul's right to breathe.
— Henry Ward Beecher,
Proverbs from Plymouth Pulpit

LIBI, LEEBI   [LEE-bee]

Meaning: my heart • **Usage:** Jewish
The Lord…hast put gladness in my heart.
— Psalm 4:3b, 4:8a (MT)

LIBIYA   [lee-bee-YAH]

Meaning: my heart belongs to God • **Usage:**
Jewish
*Let the words of my mouth,
and the meditation of my heart be acceptable before
Thee, O Lord, my Rock, and my Redeemer.*
— Psalm 19:15 (MT)

LIDIA   [LEE-dyah]

Meaning: woman of Lydda, striving • **Usage:**
Spanish, Italian, and Polish form of Lydia, from
Hebrew *lydda* (strife, contention), Greek town in
Israel
*Whatever you find to do with your hands,
do it with all your might.*
— Ecclesiastes 9:10a (NEB)

LIEBA   [LEE-bah]

Meaning: love, beloved • **Usage:** Yiddish and
Russian feminine form of Lieb, from Hebrew *lev*
(love); or from Russian *lieb* (love)
For Your steadfast love toward me is great.
— Psalm 86:13a (JPS)

LIESBETH   [LEES-beth]

Meaning: God is my oath, joined with God,
blessed by God • **Usage:** German form of
Elisabeth (*see* Liese)
With God all things are possible.
— Matthew 19:26b (NASB)

LIESE, LIESA   [LEE-sah]

Meaning: God is my oath, joined with
God, blessed by God • **Usage:** German and

L

Scandinavian form of Elisabeth, from Hebrew *el'ishebha*

> The Lord be with thy spirit. Grace be with you.
> — 2 Timothy 4:22 (ASV)

LIESL [LEE-sel]

MEANING: God is my oath, joined with God, blessed by God • **USAGE:** German and Scandinavian form of Elisabeth (*see* Liese)

> God is an unutterable sigh,
> planted in the depths of the soul.
> — Jean Paul Richter, *Levana*

LIL [lil]

MEANING: lily • **USAGE:** English form of Lilian or Lily (*see* Lily)

> All feelings and affections should open into life like those lilies, and deep amid the blossom petals should be seen the golden crown of love.
> — Henry Ward Beecher, *Life Thoughts*

LILA [LEE-lah]

MEANING: good • **USAGE:** African: Swahili of Kenya/Tanzania

> Where good things go, from there good things return.
> — Swahili proverb

LILA [LEE-lah]

MEANING: playful, divine play • **USAGE:** Hindu: from Sanskrit *lila*

> The Primordial Power is ever at play. She is creating, preserving, and destroying in play, as it were.
> — Sri Aurobindo

LILA [LEE-lah]

MEANING: lilac • **USAGE:** Persian

> What is planted in each person's soul will sprout /
> ...surrender to however that happens.
> — Jalaluddin Rumi, "The Shine in the Fields"
> (tr. Coleman Barks in *The Glance*)

LILIA [lee-LEE-ah, LIL-lee-ah]

MEANING: lily • **USAGE:** Spanish form of Lily or Lilian (*see* Lily)

> Like a lily among thorns is my darling among women.
> — Song of Songs 2:2 (GNT)

LILIAN, LILLIAN [LIL-ee-an]

MEANING: lily • **USAGE:** English (*see* Lily)

> Deep in their roots all flowers keep the light.
> — Theodore Roethke, *Straw for the Fire*

LILIANA [lee-lee-AH-nah]

MEANING: lily • **USAGE:** Polish, Italian, and Spanish form of Lilian (*see* Lily)

> Flowers...are the hieroglyphics of angels.
> — Lydia Maria Child, *Letters from New York*

LILIKE [lee-LEE-keh]

MEANING: lily flower • **USAGE:** Hungarian form of Lilian or Lily (*see* Lily)

> The flowers appear on the earth,
> and the time of singing has come.
> — Song of Songs 2:12a (ESV)

LILITH, LILLITH [LIL-ith]

MEANING: night spirit • **USAGE:** Jewish and English: from Assyrian-Babylonian *lilitu*

> Night unto night revealeth knowledge.
> — Psalm 19:3b (MT)

LILIYA [lee-LEE-yah]

MEANING: lily • **USAGE:** Russian form of Lily or Lilian (*see* Lily)

> I'm like a lily in the valleys.
> — Song of Songs 2:1b (NIRV)

LILY, LILLY, LILLIE [LIL-ee]

MEANING: lily • **USAGE:** English: from Latin *lilium* (lily)

L

Consider the lilies how they grow: they toil not, they
spin not; and yet I say unto you, that Solomon in all
his glory was not arrayed like one of these.
— Luke 12:27 (KJV)

LINA   *[LEE-nah]*

MEANING: one who is free, adult, bringer of good
news, herald • **USAGE:** Spanish and Italian: Spanish
form of Carolina, from English *ceorl* (freeman,
peasant) or from German *karl* (full-grown man,
adult); or Italian form of Evangelina, from Latin
evangelius (bringing good news)
The Lord is the Spirit,
and where the Spirit of the Lord is, there is freedom.
— 2 Corinthians 3:17 (GNT)

LINDA   *[LIN-dah (English),*
LEEN-dah (Dutch, German, Italian)]

MEANING: beautiful, very pretty, tender, gentle •
USAGE: English, Dutch, German, and Italian: from
Spanish *linda* (beautiful, pretty); or from German
linde (tender, gentle)
How beautiful you are, my love!
How your eyes shine with love.
— Song of Songs 1:15 (GNT)

LINDSAY, LINDSEY   *[LIND-see]*

MEANING: lakeside village • **USAGE:** Scottish and
English surname: a form of Lincoln, from Welsh
llyn (lake) and Latin *colonia* (colony, village)
Only in quiet waters do things mirror themselves
undistorted. Only in a quiet mind is adequate
perception of the world.
— Hans Margolius, *Thoughts on Ethics*

LINDY, LINDEY, LINDIE   *[LIN-dee]*

MEANING: lakeside village, beautiful, very pretty,
tender, gentle • **USAGE:** English form of Lindsay
(*see* Lindsay) or Linda (*see* Linda)
What will not woman, gentle woman, dare; /
When strong affection stirs her spirit up?
— Robert Southey, *Madoc in Wales*

LING   *[leeng]*

MEANING: clever, intelligent • **USAGE:** Chinese
Instruction penetrates the hearts of the good.
— Chinese proverb (tr. William Scarborough)

LINNEA   *[leen-NEH-ah]*

MEANING: small blue flower • **USAGE:** Scandina-
vian: Swedish flower *linnaea*, named for Swedish
botanist Carl von Linné
It's not enough merely to live.
One must have freedom, sunshine, and a little flower.
— Hans Christian Andersen, "The Butterfly"

LINNET   *[lih-NET, LIN-et]*

MEANING: songbird, flaxen-haired, blonde •
USAGE: English: from French *linnet* (songbird); or
from French *linette* (flaxen-haired)
Let me see how lovely you are! Let me hear the sound
of your melodious voice.
— Song of Songs 2:14b (CEV)

LINSEY, LINSAY   *[LIN-see]*

MEANING: lakeside village • **USAGE:** English form
of Lindsay (*see* Lindsay)
As water reflects the face,
so the heart reflects the person.
— Proverbs 27:19 (HCSB)

LINZI   *[LIN-ʒee]*

MEANING: lakeside village • **USAGE:** American
form of Lindsay (*see* Lindsay)
My [God's] people will dwell in a peaceful habitation,
in secure dwellings, and in quiet resting places.
— Isaiah 32:18 (NKJV)

LIORA   *[lee-OH-rah]*

MEANING: my light • **USAGE:** Jewish feminine
form of Leor
The Lord lights up my darkness.
— 2 Samuel 22:29b (JPS)

LIRA [LIE-rah]

MEANING: lyre, harp player, star constellation • **USAGE:** English form of Lyra, from Latin *lyra* (lyre, stringed instrument); also constellation shaped like Orpheus's lyre

See deep enough, and you will see music;
the heart of Nature being everywhere music.
— Thomas Carlyle, "The Hero as Poet"

LIRIT [lee-REET]

MEANING: musical, lyrical • **USAGE:** Jewish
Music cleanses the soul from the dust
and dross of every-day life.
— Berthold Auerbach, *On the Heights*
(tr. Simon Adler Stern)

LIRONA [lee-ROH-nah]

MEANING: the song is mine • **USAGE:** Jewish
O sing unto the Lord a new song.
— Psalm 98:1 (MT)

LISA [LEE-sah]

MEANING: God is my oath, joined with God, blessed by God • **USAGE:** English, German, Italian, and Scandinavian form of Elisabeth, from Hebrew *el'ishebha*

God, who gives love and peace,
will be with you.
— 2 Corinthians 13:11b (CEV)

LISBET [LEES-bet]

MEANING: God is my oath, joined with God, blessed by God • **USAGE:** Scandinavian form of Elisabeth (*see* Lisa)

We know that to them that love God
all things work together for good, even to them
that are called according to his purpose.
— Romans 8:28 (ASV)

LISE [LEE-sah]

MEANING: God is my oath, joined with God, blessed by God • **USAGE:** German, French, and Scandinavian form of Elisabeth (*see* Lisa)

Love comes from God. Everyone who loves
has become God's child and knows God.
— 1 John 4:7b (NCV)

LISETTE [lih-ZET]

MEANING: God is my oath, joined with God, blessed by God • **USAGE:** French form of Elisabeth (*see* Lisa)

May you have God's loving-favor.
— Colossians 4:18b (NLV)

LISHA, LICIA, LECIA [LEE-shah]

MEANING: noble one, highborn, honorable, happy, fortunate • **USAGE:** English form of Alisha, from German *adal* (noble) and *heid* (sort, type); or form of Felicia, from Latin *felix* (happy, fortunate)

Happiness is the only good. The place to be happy
is here. The time to be happy is now.
The way to be happy is to make others so.
— Robert Green Ingersoll,
"The Tendency of Modern Thought"

LISSA [LIS-ah]

MEANING: honeybee, sweet • **USAGE:** English form of Melissa, from Greek *melissa* (honeybee) or *meli* (honey)

A bee amongst the flowers in spring, is one of the most
cheerful objects that can be looked upon. Its life appears
to be all enjoyment; so busy, and so pleased.
— William Paley, *Natural Theology*

LIV [leev (Scandinavian), liv (English)]

MEANING: life, full of life, olive, olive tree • **USAGE:** Scandinavian and English: from Norse *lifr* (life); or English form of Olivia, from French *olivia* (olive tree) or Greek *elaia* (olive)

Surely goodness and mercy
shall follow me all the days of my life.
— Psalm 23:6a (NKJV)

LIVIA   [LIV-ee-ah]

MEANING: olive, olive tree • USAGE: English
form of Olivia, from French *olivia* (olive tree) or
Greek *elaia* (olive)
Your branches will spread
with the beauty of an olive tree.
— Hosea 14:6a (CEV)

LIVIE, LIVVIE, LIVVY   [LIV-ee]

MEANING: olive, olive tree • USAGE: English
form of Olivia (*see* Livia)
I am like a green olive tree in the house of God:
I trust in the mercy of God for ever and ever.
— Psalm 52:8 (KJV)

LIVYA   [leev-YAH]

MEANING: crown, wreath • USAGE: Jewish
The fear of the Lord is honour, and glory,
and gladness, and a crown of rejoicing.
— Ben Sira 1:11 (KJV Apocrypha)

LIZ   [liz]

MEANING: God is my oath, joined with God,
blessed by God • USAGE: English form of Elizabeth
(*see* Liza)
God enters by a private door into each individual.
— Ralph Waldo Emerson, "Intellect"

LIZA   [LIE-zah]

MEANING: God is my oath, joined with God,
blessed by God • USAGE: English form of Elizabeth
or Eliza, from Hebrew *el'ishebha*
I, God, am in your midst. Whoever knows me can
never fall, not in the heights, nor in the depths,
nor in the breadths, for I am love.
— Hildegard of Bingen

LIZBET   [LIZ-bet]

MEANING: God is my oath, joined with God,
blessed by God • USAGE: English form of Elizabeth
(*see* Liza)
The Lord be with your spirit. Grace be with you.
— 2 Timothy 4:22 (NCV)

LIZETTE   [lih-ZET]

MEANING: God is my oath, joined with God,
blessed by God • USAGE: English form of Elizabeth
(*see* Liza)
The blessing of the Lord be upon you.
— Psalm 129:8b (KJ21)

LIZZIE, LIZZY   [LIZ-ee]

MEANING: God is my oath, joined with God,
blessed by God • USAGE: English form of Elizabeth
(*see* Liza)
I am the Lord your God,
who teaches you to profit,
who leads you in the way you should go.
— Isaiah 48:17b (NASB)

LODEN   [LOH-den]

MEANING: deep olive green • USAGE: English:
from German *lode*
I am like an olive tree growing in God's house,
and I can count on his love forever and ever.
— Psalm 52:8 (CEV)

LOGAN   [LOH-gan]

MEANING: little hollow • USAGE: Scottish and
English surname: from Gaelic *lag* and diminutive
-an
Little deeds of kindness / Little words of love /
Make our earth an Eden / Like the heaven above.
— Julia Fletcher Carney, "Little Things"

LOIDA   *[loh-EE-dah]*

MEANING: more desirable, better • **USAGE:** Spanish form of Lois (*see* Lois)

A good name is more desirable than great riches,
and loving favor is better than silver and gold.
— Proverbs 22:1 (WEB)

LOIE   *[LOH-ee]*

MEANING: more desirable, better, famous warrior, renown in battle • **USAGE:** English form of Lois, from Greek *loion* (more desirable, better); or English form of Louise, from German *hlud* (famous) and *wig* (war, strife)

She is a theme of honour and renown.
— William Shakespeare, *Troilus and Cressida*

LOIS   *[LOH-es]*

MEANING: more desirable, better • **USAGE:** English: from Greek *loion*

I desire to Radiate Life.
— Elbert Hubbard, "The Radiant Life"

LOLA   *[LOH-lah]*

MEANING: lady of sorrows, Virgin Mary's sorrows • **USAGE:** Spanish and English form of Dolores, from Spanish *dolores* (sorrows); reference Virgin Mary's seven sorrows

Love is a great thing, a good above all others,
which alone maketh every heavy burden light.
— Thomas à Kempis, *The Imitation of Christ*
(tr. William Benham)

LOLIA   *[loh-LEE-ah]*

MEANING: shining star • **USAGE:** African: Nigeria

Guard your light and protect it. Move it forward into the world and be fully confident that if we connect light to light to light, and join the lights together of the one billion young people in our world today, we will be enough to set our whole planet aglow.
— Hafsat Abiola

LOLITA   *[loh-LEE-tah]*

MEANING: lady of sorrows, Virgin Mary's sorrows • **USAGE:** Spanish form of Dolores, from Spanish *dolores* (sorrows), reference to Virgin Mary's seven sorrows

Thou art with me; thy rod and thy staff,
they comfort me.
— Psalm 23:4b (DT)

LOLONYO   *[loh-LOHN-yoh]*

MEANING: love is beautiful • **USAGE:** African: Ewe of Ghana

Love is the greatest of all virtues.
— Ghanian proverb

LONI, LONIE   *[LON-ee]*

MEANING: little rock, beautiful • **USAGE:** English form of Lana, from Breton *alp* (rock) and diminutive *-an*; or from Scotch Gaelic *alainn* (handsome, fair)

You are beautiful and pleasant;
my love, you are full of delights.
— Song of Songs 7:6 (NCV)

LORA   *[LOR-ah]*

MEANING: laurel tree, laurel wreath, light, illumination, torch • **USAGE:** English form of Laura, from Latin *laurus* (laurel); or English form of Eleonora, from Greek *helene* (torch) or *ele* (light)

Only God can make a tree.
— Joyce Kilmer, *Memoirs and Poems*

LORAINA, LORRAINA   *[loh-RAY-nah]*

MEANING: famous warrior, people's army • **USAGE:** English form of Loraine (*see* Loraine)

Put on the armor of light.
— Romans 13:12b (ESV)

L

LORAINE, LORRAINE   *[loh-RAYN]*

MEANING: famous warrior, people's army • USAGE: English: from German *liut* (people) and *hari* (army)

> *She is strong and respected*
> *and not afraid of the future.*
> — Proverbs 31:25 (GNT)

LOREEN   *[loh-REEN]*

MEANING: laurel tree, laurel wreath • USAGE: English form of Laura (*see* Loren)

> *Wherever our race has gone to live,*
> *the trees have given welcome and shelter.*
> — Enos A. Mills, *Your National Parks*

LORELEI   *[LOR-eh-lie]*

MEANING: luring rock • USAGE: German: from German *luren* (to watch) and *lei* (cliff, rock); a siren in German lore who sat in the Rhine River

> *The Lord said, "Behold, there is a place by Me,*
> *and you shall stand there on the rock."*
> — Exodus 33:21 (NASB)

LORELLE   *[loh-REL]*

MEANING: laurel tree, laurel wreath • USAGE: English feminine form of Laurence (*see* Loren)

> *Forests give poetry to the prose of life*
> *and enable us to have and to hold high ideals.*
> — Enos A. Mills, *Your National Parks*

LOREN, LORIN   *[LOR-en]*

MEANING: laurel tree, laurel wreath • USAGE: English feminine form of Laurence, from Latin *laurus*

> *Wisdom is a life-giving tree,*
> *the source of happiness for all who hold on to her.*
> — Proverbs 3:18 (CEV)

LORENA   *[loh-RAY-nah]*

MEANING: laurel tree, laurel wreath, famous warrior, people's army • USAGE: English, Italian, and Spanish (*see* Loren); or Spanish and Italian form of Lorraine (*see* Loraine)

> *Blessed are those who trust in the Lord and have made*
> *the Lord their hope and confidence. They are like trees*
> *planted along a riverbank, with roots that reach deep*
> *into the water. Such trees are not bothered by heat or*
> *worried by long months of drought. Their leaves stay*
> *green, and they never stop producing fruit.*
> — Jeremiah 17:7–8 (NLT)

LORETTA   *[loh-RET-ah]*

MEANING: little laurel tree, little laurel wreath • USAGE: English and Italian form of Laura and diminutive *-etta* (*see* Loren)

> *And the tree was happy.*
> — Shel Silverstein, *The Giving Tree*

LORI, LORIE   *[LOR-ee]*

MEANING: laurel tree, laurel wreath • USAGE: English form of Laura, Laurel, or Lauren (*see* Loren)

> *She [Wisdom] giveth to thy head a wreath of grace,*
> *a crown of beauty she doth give thee freely.*
> — Proverbs 4:9 (YLT)

LORINA, LOREENA   *[loh-REE-nah]*

MEANING: laurel tree, laurel wreath • USAGE: English form of Laura (*see* Loren)

> *A God-shaped life is a flourishing tree.*
> — Proverbs 12:3a (MSG)

LORINDA, LORENDA   *[loh-RIN-dah]*

MEANING: laurel tree, laurel wreath • USAGE: English form of Laura (*see* Loren)

> *Today I have grown taller from walking with the trees.*
> — Karle Wilson Baker, "Good Company"

L

LORIS [LOR-is]

MEANING: lady of sorrows, Virgin Mary's sorrow • **USAGE:** English form of Dolores, from Spanish *dolores* (sorrows), reference to Virgin Mary's seven sorrows

> *Earth has no sorrow that Heaven cannot heal.*
> — Thomas Moore, "Come, Ye Disconsolate"

LORNA [LOR-nah]

MEANING: Scottish place-name, fictional character • **USAGE:** Scottish: title character in R. D. Blackmore's novel *Lorna Doone*, possibly based on Lorne, Scotland

> *God, bless the earth that is beneath my sole; /*
> *Bless, O God, and give to me Thy love.*
> — Alexander Carmichael, *Carmina Gadelica*

LOTEM [LOH-tem]

MEANING: bush with yellow flowers; kibbutz in the Galilee • **USAGE:** Jewish

> *The bush burned with fire,*
> *and the bush was not consumed.*
> — Exodus 3:2 (MT)

LOTTA [LAH-teh]

MEANING: one who is free, adult • **USAGE:** Scandinavian form of Charlotta, from English *ceorl* (freeman, peasant); or from German *karl* (full-grown man, adult)

> *Now the Lord is the Spirit*
> *and where the Spirit of the Lord is, there is liberty.*
> — 2 Corinthians 3:17 (WEB)

LOTTE [LAH-teh]

MEANING: adult, one who is free • **USAGE:** German and Dutch form of Karlotte (*see* Lotta)

> *The truth shall make you free.*
> — John 8:32 (YLT)

LOTUS [LOH-tuhs]

MEANING: lotus flower • **USAGE:** English: from Greek *lotos* (lotus)

> *I'm a wildflower picked from the plains of Sharon,*
> *a lotus blossom from the valley pools.*
> — Song of Songs 2:1 (MSG)

LOU [loo]

MEANING: famous warrior, renowned in battle, pilgrimage site in France • **USAGE:** English form of Louise (*see* Louise); or English form of Lourdes, France, a pilgrimage site related to Virgin Mary

> *Put on the shining armor of right living.*
> — Romans 13:12b (NLT)

LOUELLA, LUELLA [loo-EL-ah]

MEANING: warrior of light, luminous warrior • **USAGE:** English combination of Louisa and Ella (*see* Louisa and Ella)

> *Be strong and courageous…for the Lord your God*
> *is the one who is going with you.*
> *He will not fail you or abandon you!*
> — Deuteronomy 31:6 (NEB)

LOUISA [loo-EE-sah]

MEANING: famous warrior, renowned in battle • **USAGE:** English and German feminine form of Louis (*see* Louise)

> *Lord…you are my shield,*
> *and you give me victory and great honor.*
> — Psalm 3:1–3 (CEV)

LOUISE [loo-EEZ (English), lweez (French)]

MEANING: famous warrior, renowned in battle • **USAGE:** English and French feminine form of Louis, from German *hlud* (famous) and *wig* (war, strife)

> *Who is this who looks down like the dawn,*
> *beautiful as the moon, bright as the sun,*
> *awesome as an army with banners?*
> — Song of Songs 6:10 (ESV)

L

LOURDES   *[luwrd (French), LOOR-des (Spanish), LOR-des (English)]*

MEANING: pilgrimage site in France • USAGE: French, English, and Spanish: French town and pilgrimage site related to Virgin Mary
The road the righteous travel is like the sunrise, getting brighter and brighter until daylight has come.
— Proverbs 4:18 (GNT)

LOVEY, LOVEE   *[LUV-ee]*

MEANING: love, loving, beloved • USAGE: English: from English *lufu*
Now faith, hope, and love abide, these three; and the greatest of these is love.
— 1 Corinthians 13:13 (NRSV)

LOWRI   *[LOW-ree]*

MEANING: laurel tree, laurel wreath • USAGE: Welsh form of Laura, from Latin *laurus*
Wisdom is a tree of life to those who embrace her; happy are those who hold her tightly.
— Proverbs 3:18 (NLT)

LOY, LOI   *[loi]*

MEANING: chosen, elected • USAGE: English surname: from Latin *eligiius* (to choose, to elect)
As God's chosen people, holy and dearly loved, clothe yourselves with compassion, kindness, humility, gentleness and patience.
— Colossians 3:12 (NIV)

LUANA   *[loo-AH-nah]*

MEANING: content, happy • USAGE: Hawaiian
Happiness and fulfillment are found only in our own hearts.
— Hawaiian proverb

LUANA, LUANNA   *[loo-AHN-ah, LWAHN-ah]*

MEANING: graceful warrior, warrior of grace • USAGE: English combination of Lou and Anna (*see* Lou and Anna)
Put on the armour of light.
— Romans 13:12b (KJV)

LUANNE   *[loo-AN]*

MEANING: graceful warrior, warrior of grace • USAGE: English combination of Lou and Anne (*see* Lou and Anne)
Grace is but glory begun, and glory is but grace perfected.
— Jonathan Edwards

LUBA   *[LOO-bah]*

MEANING: love, affection • USAGE: Czech: from Slavic *lub*
There doth remain faith, hope, love — these three; and the greatest of these is love.
— 1 Corinthians 13:13 (YLT)

LUBYA, LYUBA   *[LOOB-yah, LYOOB-yah]*

MEANING: love, affection • USAGE: Russian: from Slavic *lub*
Love is life. All, all I understand, I understand only because I love. Everything is connected with it alone.
— Leo Tolstoy, *War and Peace* (tr. Leo Wiener)

LUCETTA   *[loo-SET-ah]*

MEANING: light, illumination • USAGE: French form of Lucille (*see* Lucille)
Let your light shine.
— Matthew 5:16a (NEB)

LUCETTE   *[loo-SET]*

MEANING: light, illumination • USAGE: English form of Lucille or Lucia (*see* Lucille)

Whoever does what is true comes to the light.
— John 3:21a (ESV)

LUCIA, LUCÍA   *[loo-SEE-ah (Greek, Spanish),*
                   loo-CHEE-ah (Italian)]

MEANING: light, illumination • **USAGE:** Greek, Italian, and Spanish feminine form of Lucius (*see* Lucille)

The soul of each of us is a lamp.
— Symeon the New Theologian, *The Discourses*
(tr. C. J. de Catanzaro)

LUCIANA   *[loo-chee-AH-nah (Italian),*
             loo-see-AH-nah (Spanish)]

MEANING: light, illumination • **USAGE:** Italian and Spanish feminine form of Luciano (*see* Lucille)
The light of the body is the eye: if therefore thine eye be single, thy whole body shall be full of light.
— Matthew 6:22 (KJV)

LUCIENNE   *[looy-SYEN]*

MEANING: light, illumination • **USAGE:** French form of Lucille, Lucia, or Lucinda (*see* Lucille)
You have light from the Lord. So live as people of light! For this light within you produces only what is good and right and true.
— Ephesians 5:8b–9 (NLT)

LUCILA   *[loo-SEE-lah]*

MEANING: light, illumination • **USAGE:** Spanish form of Lucía (*see* Lucille)
Now you are Light in the Lord;
walk as children of Light (for the fruit of the Light consists in all goodness, righteousness and truth).
— Ephesians 5:8b–9 (NASB)

LUCILLE, LUCILE   *[loo-SEEL]*

MEANING: light, illumination • **USAGE:** French and English feminine form of Luc, from Latin *lux*

A light will show you the way
and fill you with happiness.
— Psalm 97:11b (CEV)

LUCINDA   *[loo-SEEN-dah (Spanish),*
             loo-SIN-dah (English)]

MEANING: light, illumination • **USAGE:** Spanish and English feminine form of Lucius, from Latin *lux*
Be a light for other people.
Live so that they will see the good things you do.
— Matthew 5:16b (NCV)

LUCINDE   *[loo-SIND]*

MEANING: light, illumination • **USAGE:** French form of Lucinda (*see* Lucinda)
To love beauty is to see the light.
— Victor Hugo, *Les Misérables*
(tr. Isabel Florence Hapgood)

LUCRETIA   *[loo-KREE-shah]*

MEANING: wealthy, rich, prosperous • **USAGE:** English form of Roman family name *Lucretius*, from Latin *lucrum*
The Lord will make you abound in prosperity.
— Deuteronomy 28:11a (NASB)

LUCY   *[LOO-see]*

MEANING: light, illumination • **USAGE:** English form of Lucille, Lucia, or Lucinda (*see* Lucille)
Your eye is a lamp, lighting up your whole body.
If you live wide-eyed in wonder and belief,
your body fills up with light.
— Luke 11:34 (MSG)

LUDMILA   *[lood-MEE-lah]*

MEANING: beloved people, favored people • **USAGE:** Czech, Polish, and German: from Slavic *lud* (people) and *mil* (love, favor, grace)
I [God] have loved you, my people, with an everlasting love. With unfailing love I have drawn you to myself.
— Jeremiah 31:3 (NLT)

LUISA   *[loo-EE-sah]*

MEANING: famous warrior, renowned in battle •
USAGE: Spanish and Italian form of Louise, from
German *hlud* (famous) and *wig* (war)

> *The woman who is resolved to be respected can make*
> *herself to be so even amidst an army of soldiers.*
> — Miguel de Cervantes

LUISE   *[loo-EE-seh]*

MEANING: famous warrior, renowned in battle •
USAGE: German and Scandinavian form of Louise
(*see* Luisa)

> *Courageous, untroubled, mocking, violent —*
> *thus does Wisdom want us: she is a woman*
> *and always loves only a warrior.*
> — Friedrich Nietzsche,
> *Thus Spoke Zarathustra* (tr. Graham Parkes)

LUIZA   *[loo-EE-ʒah]*

MEANING: famous warrior, renowned in battle
• **USAGE:** Russian and Polish feminine form of
Louisa (*see* Luisa)

> *Put on the armor of light.*
> — Romans 13:12:b (NASB)

LULLA   *[LOO-lah]*

MEANING: prosperous lady, bountiful princess •
USAGE: Irish form of Talulla, from Gaelic *tuile*
(abundance) and *flaith* (princess, lady)

> *Beloved, I desire that in all things thou shouldest*
> *prosper and be in health, even as thy soul prospers.*
> — 3 John 1:2 (DT)

LULU   *[loo-loo]*

MEANING: famous warrior, renowned in battle •
USAGE: German and English form of Luise (*see*
Luisa)

> *Wisdom alone is true ambition's aim, /*
> *Wisdom the source of virtue, and of fame.*
> — William Whitehead, "On Nobility"

LULU   *[loo-loo]*

MEANING: peaceful, calm as the sea • **USAGE:**
Hawaiian

> *Peace within / creates beauty without.*
> — Shi Wuling, *Path to Peace*

LUNA   *[LOO-nah]*

MEANING: moon, moon goddess • **USAGE:**
English, Italian, and Spanish: from Latin *luna*
(moon); Roman goddess of the moon

> *Who is this that grows like the dawn,*
> *as beautiful as the full moon, as pure as the sun.*
> — Song of Songs 6:10a (NASB)

LUNED   *[LOO-ned]*

MEANING: greatly desired • **USAGE:** Welsh form
of Eluned, from Welsh *el* (greatly, much) and *uned*
(wish, desire)

> *Store your treasures in heaven…wherever your treasure*
> *is, there the desires of your heart will also be.*
> — Matthew 6:20–21 (NLT)

LUPE   *[LOO-pay]*

MEANING: valley of the wolf • **USAGE:** Spanish
form of Guadalupe, from Arabic *wadi lupi*

> *A healthy woman is much like a wolf: robust,*
> *chock-full, strong life force, life-giving,*
> *territorially aware, inventive, loyal.*
> — Clarissa Pinkola Estés,
> *Women Who Run with the Wolves*

LURELLA   *[loo-REL-ah]*

MEANING: laurel tree, laurel wreath • **USAGE:**
American: possibly a form of Laura, from Latin
laurus

> *I think that I shall never see /*
> *A poem lovely as a tree.*
> — Joyce Kilmer, "Trees"

LURELLE   [luh-REL]

MEANING: laurel tree, laurel wreath • **USAGE:** American: possibly a form of Laura (*see* Lurella)
Knowing trees, I understand the meaning of patience.
— Hal Borland, *Countryman: A Summary of Belief*

LUZ   [looz]

MEANING: light, illumination, luminous • **USAGE:** Spanish: from Spanish *luz* (light); reference to Virgin Mary
Your Word is a lamp to my feet
and a light to my path.
— Psalm 119:105 (NLV)

LYDA   [LIE-dah]

MEANING: woman of Lydda, striving • **USAGE:** English form of Lydia (*see* Lydia)
Strive to be happy.
— Max Ehrmann, "Desiderata"

LYDIA   [LID-ee-ah (English), LEE-dee-ah (Greek)]

MEANING: woman of Lydda, striving • **USAGE:** English and Greek: from Hebrew *lydda* (strife, contention), Greek town in Israel
The most important human endeavor is the striving for morality in our actions. Our inner balance and even our very existence depend on it. Only morality in our actions can give beauty and dignity for life.
— Albert Einstein

LYDIE   [LID-ee]

MEANING: woman of Lydda, striving • **USAGE:** French form of Lydia (*see* Lydia)
Strive for righteousness, godliness, faith, love, endurance, and gentleness.
— 1 Timothy 6:11b (GNT)

LYLA   [LIE-lah]

MEANING: dark beauty, dark as night, islander, from the island • **USAGE:** English: from Arabic *leila* (night, dark); or from French *de l'isle* (of the island)
Stay near beauty, for she will always / strengthen you.
— Thomas Aquinas, "Capax Universi"
(tr. Daniel Ladinsky in *Love Poems from God*)

LYNDA   [LIND-ah]

MEANING: beautiful, very pretty, tender, gentle • **USAGE:** American form of Linda, from Spanish *linda* (beautiful, pretty); or from German *linde* (tender, gentle)
The Good is always beautiful.
— John Greenleaf Whittier, "Garden"

LYNELLE, LYNNELLE   [leh-NEL]

MEANING: lake, pool, waterfall • **USAGE:** American form of Lynn (*see* Lynn)
Let anyone who is thirsty come. Let anyone who desires drink freely from the water of life.
— Revelations 22:17b (NLT)

LYNETTE, LYNNETTE, LINETTE   [leh-NET]

MEANING: little lake, little pool, little waterfall • **USAGE:** English form of Lynn and diminutive *-ette* (*see* Lynn)
The sounds of falling water and blowing winds make real music that enters the soul and gives it the aural nourishment it needs.
— Thomas Moore,
The Re-Enchantment of Everyday Life

LYNN, LYN   [len]

MEANING: lake, pool, waterfall, cascade • **USAGE:** English: from Welsh *llyn* (lake) or *linn* (pool, waterfall)
Here is a cascade…filled with bounce and dance and joyous hurrah.
— John Muir (letter of October 8, 1872)

LYNNA   [LEN-ah]

MEANING: lake, pool, waterfall, cascade • USAGE:
English form of Lynn (*see* Lynn)
Every desirable and beneficial gift comes out of heaven.
The gifts are rivers of light cascading
down from the Father of Light.
— James 1:17a (MSG)

LYRA, LIRA   [LIE-rah]

MEANING: lyre, harp player, star constellation •
USAGE: English: from Latin *lyra* (lyre, stringed
instrument); also constellation shaped like
Orpheus's lyre
The beauty of a lovely woman is like music.
— George Eliot, *Adam Bede*

LYRICA   [LEER-eh-kah]

MEANING: lyric poem, singing to the lyre •
USAGE: English: from Latin *lyrica* (lyric poem); or
from Greek *lyrikos* (singing to the lyre)
Music soothes us, stirs us up;
it puts noble feelings in us.
— Charles Kingsley, "Sermon XVII"

LYSANDRA   [leh-SAHN-drah]

MEANING: free woman, liberated woman •
USAGE: English feminine form of Lysander, from
Greek *lysis* (release) and *andros* (man)
I believe in freedom — social, economic,
domestic, political, mental, and spiritual.
— Elbert Hubbard

LYSSA   [LIS-ah]

MEANING: noble one, highborn, honorable •
USAGE: English form of Alissa, from German *adal*
(noble) and *heid* (sort, type)
It is noble to seek truth, and it is beautiful to find it.
— Sydney Smith,
"On the Conduct of the Understanding"

M

MABEL   [MAY-bl]

MEANING: lovable, beloved • USAGE: English:
from Latin *amabilis*
May the Lord make you increase and abound in love.
— 1 Thessalonians 3:12a (NRSV)

MACARENA   [mah-kah-RAY-nah]

MEANING: blessed, blessing • USAGE: Spanish
form of Roman family name *Macarius*, from Greek
makaros
May God bless you with his love.
— 2 Corinthians 13:14b (CEV)

MACARIA   [mah-kah-REE-ah]

MEANING: blessed, blessing • USAGE: Spanish
feminine form of Macario, from Greek *makaros*
The blessing of the Lord be upon you.
— Psalm 129:8ba (NASB)

MACKENZIE   [mah-KEN-zee]

MEANING: comely child, beautiful child • USAGE:
Scottish surname: from Gaelic *mac* (son) and
coinneach (handsome, comely)
Behold thou art fair, my beloved, and comely.
— Song of Songs 1:15a (DR)

MACY, MACIE, MACEY   [MAY-see]

MEANING: gift of God • USAGE: English surname:
form of *Massius,* which is a form of Matthew, from
Hebrew *mattah'yah* (gift of Yahweh)
May you have much of God's loving-kindness
and peace and love.
— Jude 1:2 (NLV)

MADA   *[MAH-dah]*

MEANING: woman from Magdala, tower • **USAGE:** Polish, German, and English form of Madeline (*see* Madeline)

> *You are a worthy woman.*
> — Ruth 3:11b (WEB)

MADALENA   *[mah-dah-LAY-nah]*

MEANING: woman from Magdala, tower • **USAGE:** Spanish and Portuguese form of Magdalene (*see* Madeline)

> *Peace be within your walls,*
> *and security within your towers!*
> — Psalm 122:7 (NRSV)

MADDALENA   *[mah-dah-LEH-nah]*

MEANING: woman from Magdala, tower • **USAGE:** Italian form of Magdalene (*see* Madeline)

> *God is my strong fortress,*
> *and he makes my way perfect.*
> — 2 Samuel 22:33 (NLT)

MADDIE, MADDY   *[MAD-ee]*

MEANING: woman from Magdala, tower, warrior's child, powerful child • **USAGE:** English form of Madeline (*see* Madeline) or of Madison (*see* Madison)

> *Let us love one another, because love comes from God.*
> *Whoever loves is a child of God and knows God.*
> — 1 John 4:7 (NEB)

MADELEINE   *[mah-deh-LIEN]*

MEANING: woman from Magdala, tower • **USAGE:** French form of Magdalene (*see* Madeline)

> *Let peace be in thy strength:*
> *and abundance in thy towers.*
> — Psalm 121:7 (DR)

MADELINE, MADELYN   *[MAD-ah-lin]*

MEANING: woman from Magdala, tower • **USAGE:** English form of Magdalene, the Greek form of *Magdala* (a village in Galilee), from Hebrew *migdal* (tower)

> *Who can find a woman of worth?*
> *for her price is far above rubies.*
> — Proverbs 31:10 (DT)

MADGE   *[madj]*

MEANING: pearl, beautiful gem, woman from Magdala, tower • **USAGE:** English form of Margaret, from Greek *margaron* (a pearl); or English form of Magdalene (*see* Madeline)

> *Thou art all fair, my love; and there is no spot in thee.*
> — Song of Songs 4:7 (ASV)

MADINA   *[mah-DEE-nah]*

MEANING: woman from Magdala, tower • **USAGE:** Russian form of Magdalene (*see* Madeline)

> *A woman of worth who doth find?*
> *Yea, far above rubies [is] her price.*
> — Proverbs 31:10 (YLT)

MADISON   *[MAD-ih-son]*

MEANING: powerful warrior's child • **USAGE:** English surname: English combination of Maud and son, from German *maht* (might, power) and *hild* (war, battle)

> *My child, listen and be wise:*
> *keep your heart on the right course.*
> — Proverbs 23:19 (NLT)

MADONNA   *[mah-DON-ah]*

MEANING: my Lady, mother of Jesus • **USAGE:** English: from Latin *donna* (my Lady, lady of nobility), reference to Mary, mother of Jesus

> *The Lord is with you; blessed are you among women!*
> — Luke 1:28b (NKJV)

M

MAEBH   [mayv]

MEANING: child, intoxicating • USAGE: Irish: from Gaelic *meadhbh* (intoxicating); or from Gaelic *mab* (child)

And a little child shall lead them.
— Isaiah 11:6b (NKJV)

MAEVE   [mayv]

MEANING: child, intoxicating • USAGE: English and Irish form of Maebh, from Gaelic *meadhbh* (intoxicating); or from Gaelic *mab* (child)

Give a little love to a child,
and you get a great deal back.
— John Ruskin, "Work"

MAGDA   [MAHG-dah]

MEANING: woman from Magdala, tower • USAGE: German, Scandinavian, Dutch, and Polish form of Magdalene (*see* Magdalene)

Nature meant to make woman as its masterpiece.
— Gotthold Ephraim Lessing, *Emilia Galotti*

MAGDALENA   [mahg-dah-LAY-nah]

MEANING: woman from Magdala, tower • USAGE: German, Scandinavian, and Spanish form of Magdalene (*see* Magdalene)

God is my high tower.
— Psalm 59:9b (ASV)

MAGDALENE   [magh-dah-leh-NEE]

MEANING: woman from Magdala, tower • USAGE: Greek form of *Magdala* (a village in Galilee), from Hebrew *migdal* (tower)

When Jesus was risen early the first day of the week,
he appeared first to Mary Magdalene.
— Mark 16:9 (KJV)

MAGENA   [mah-GEH-nah]

MEANING: protector, guardian • USAGE: Jewish

Above all that thou guardest keep thy heart;
for out of it are the issues of life.
— Proverbs 4:23 (MT)

MAGGIE   [MAG-ee]

MEANING: pearl, beautiful gem • USAGE: English form of Margaret, from Greek *margaron* (a pearl)

Beauty is truth, truth beauty — that is all, /
Ye know on earth, and all ye need to know.
— John Keats, "Ode on a Grecian Urn"

MAGNOLIA   [mag-NOL-yah]

MEANING: magnolia flower • USAGE: English: a flower named after Pierre Magnol, French botanist

God is beauty, and whenever you touch the beauty
of a flower or a sunset you are touching God.
— Peace Pilgrim, *Peace Pilgrim*

MAHDIYA, MAHDIA   [mah-dee-ah]

MEANING: rightly guided • USAGE: Muslim feminine form of Mahdi, from Arabic *mahdi*

Enough is thy Lord to guide and to help.
— Koran, The Criterion 25.31b (ALI)

MAHIMA   [mah-hih-mah]

MEANING: she who is great • USAGE: Hindu: from Sanskrit *maha*

Our roots must go deep down into the universal
if we would attain the greatness of personality.
— Rabindranath Tagore, *Sadhana*

MAHINA   [mah-HEE-nah]

MEANING: moon, moonlight • USAGE: Hawaiian: Hawaiian goddess of the moon

Our seasons are the cycles of the moon,
mahina, and the stars, na hoku.
— Hawaiian proverb

MAHIRA *[mah-HEE-rah]*

MEANING: industrious, energetic • USAGE: Jewish
Extol her for the fruit of her hand,
and let her works praise her.
— Proverbs 31:31a (JPS)

MAHIRAH, MAHEERA *[mah-HEE-rah]*

MEANING: skillful, able, proficient, capable •
USAGE: Muslim: from Arabic *mahara* (to be
skillful)
Ability has no school.
— Turkish proverb

MAI *[mie]*

MEANING: beloved, love, sea mistress, bitter sea,
rebellious, well-nourished, healthy, myrrh, pearl,
beautiful gem • USAGE: Scandinavian form of
Maria (*see* Maria)
Behold, you are beautiful, my beloved,
truly delightful.
— Song of Songs 1:16a (ESV)

MAIA *[MIE-ah]*

MEANING: month of May, goddess of spring, star •
USAGE: English: from Latin *Maius* (month of May,
Roman goddess of spring); Greek name of star in
Taurus constellation
Love is the May-day of the heart.
— Benjamin Disraeli, *Henrietta Temple*

MAIDA *[MAY-dah]*

MEANING: maiden, young woman • USAGE:
English: from English *maide*
Let the maiden with erect soul
walk serenely on her way.
— Ralph Waldo Emerson, "Heroism"

MAIRE *[MAHR-eh]*

MEANING: beloved, love, sea mistress, bitter
sea, rebellious, well-nourished, healthy, myrrh •
USAGE: Irish form of Mary (*see* Mary)
This I pray, that your love may abound still more
and more in real knowledge and all discernment.
— Philippians 1:9 (NASB)

MAIREAD *[MAY-red]*

MEANING: beloved, love, sea mistress, bitter
sea, rebellious, well-nourished, healthy, myrrh •
USAGE: Scottish and Irish form of Mary (*see* Mary)
Love is but the discovery of ourselves in others,
and the delight in the recognition.
— Alexander Smith,
"On the Importance of a Man to Himself"

MAIRONA *[MAY-roh-nah, may-ROH-nah]*

MEANING: beloved, love, sea mistress, bitter
sea, rebellious, well-nourished, healthy, myrrh •
USAGE: Irish form of Maire (*see* Mary)
Now these three remain: faith, hope and love.
But the greatest of these is love.
— 1 Corinthians 13:13 (NIV)

MAISIE *[MAY-ʒee]*

MEANING: pearl, beautiful gem • USAGE: Scottish
form of Margaret (*see* Margaret)
How beautiful you are!
— Song of Songs 1:15b (NLV)

MAITRI *[may-tree]*

MEANING: friendly, benevolent, kind • USAGE:
Hindu: Sanskrit
Friendship and loyalty are an identity of souls seldom
found on earth. The only really lasting and valuable
friendship is between people of a similar nature.
— Mahatma Gandhi

M

MAJA   [MAH-yah]

MEANING: beloved, love, sea mistress, bitter sea, rebellious, well-nourished, healthy, myrrh, pearl, beautiful gem • USAGE: Scandinavian and German form of Maria (see Maria); or Scandinavian and German form of Margaret, from Greek *margaron* (a pearl)

> Peace of mind makes the body healthy.
> — Proverbs 14:30a (GNT)

MAJIDA, MAJEEDA   [mah-JEE-dah]

MEANING: glorious, noble • USAGE: Muslim feminine form of Majid, from Arabic *majada* (to be glorious)

> Celebrate the praises of Allah, and do this often;
> and glorify Him morning and evening.
> He it is Who sends blessings on you.
> — Koran, The Confederates 33.41–43a (ALI)

MAKAELA, MAKAYLA, MIKAYLA   [mah-KAY-lah]

MEANING: Who is like God? • USAGE: American form of Michaela, from Hebrew *mikha'el*

> We are the instruments and expression
> of God Himself.
> — Emmet Fox, *The Sermon on the Mount*

MAKENNA   [mah-keh-nah]

MEANING: happy one, joyous one • USAGE: African: Meru of Kenya

> Happiness is like a field
> you can harvest every season.
> — Kenyan proverb

MALAK   [mah-lahk]

MEANING: angel, divine messenger • USAGE: Muslim: from Arabic *malak*

> He it is Who blesseth you, and His angels (bless you).
> — Koran, The Allies 33.43a (PIC)

MALANA   [mah-LAH-nah]

MEANING: light, buoyant, to move along together • USAGE: Hawaiian

> Let all travel together like water flowing
> in one direction.
> — Hawaiian proverb
> (tr. Mary Pukui in 'Olelo No'eau)

MALATI   [mah-lah-tee]

MEANING: jasmine flower, jasmine fragrance • USAGE: Hindu: from Sanskrit *malati*

> Self-awakening / Means / God-flowering /
> In and through me.
> — Sri Chinmoy Ghose, *The Wings of Joy*

MALENA   [mah-LAY-nah]

MEANING: woman from Magdala, tower • USAGE: Spanish and Scandinavian form of Magdalene, the Greek form of *Magdala* (a village in Galilee), from Hebrew *migdal* (tower)

> The loftiest edifices need the deepest foundations.
> — George Santayana, *The Life of Reason*

MALI   [mah-lee]

MEANING: gardener • USAGE: Hindu Sanskrit

> Love is the seed, courage is the blossom,
> and peace is the fruit that Sages grow
> in the garden of their hearts.
> — Sathya Sai Baba, *Sathya Sai Baba Speaks*

MALIKA   [mah-LEE-kah]

MEANING: jasmine, flower • USAGE: Hindu Sanskrit

> Does a flower, full of beauty, light and loveliness say,
> "I am giving, helping, serving?" It is! And because it
> is not trying to do anything, it covers the earth.
> — Jiddu Krishnamurti,
> *Freedom from the Known*

MALILA   *[mah-lee-lah]*

MEANING: salmon swimming fast • **USAGE:**
Amerind: Salish

*Welcome, O Supernatural One, O Swimmer, who
returns every year in this world that we may live rightly,
that we may be well. I offer you, swimming salmon,
my heart's deep gratitude. I ask that you will come
again, that next year we will meet in this life,
that you will see that nothing evil should befall me.*
— Kwakiutl women's prayer

MALIN   *[MAH-leen, MAY-lin]*

MEANING: woman from Magdala, tower • **USAGE:**
Scandinavian form of Magdalene, the Greek form
of *Magdala* (village in Galilee), from Hebrew
migdal (tower)

You are a good woman.
— Ruth 3:11b (NCV)

MALINA   *[mah-LEE-nah]*

MEANING: calming, soothing, peaceful • **USAGE:**
Hawaiian

*The rippling water where birds gather.
[A quiet, peaceful nature.]*
— Hawaiian proverb
(tr. Mary Pukui in *'Olelo No'eau*)

MALINA   *[mah-LEE-nah]*

MEANING: disciple of St. Columba, follower of
the Dove, God is their king • **USAGE:** Scottish and
English feminine form of Malcolm, from Scotch
Gaelic *mael* (follower, devotee) and *colm* (dove); or
from Hebrew Malkam (God is their king)

*Ye are an elect race, a royal priesthood,
a holy nation, a people for God's own possession,
that ye may show forth the excellencies of him who
called you out of darkness into his marvellous light.*
— 1 Peter 2:9 (ASV)

MALINDA, MELINDA   *[mah-LIN-dah]*

MEANING: dark beauty • **USAGE:** English
combination of Melanie and Linda (*see* Melanie and
Linda)

*She walks in Beauty, like the night / Of cloudless
climes and starry skies; / And all that's best of dark
and bright / Meet in her aspect and her eyes.*
— Lord Byron, "She Walks in Beauty"

MALINI   *[mah-lee-nee]*

MEANING: garland, wreath of flowers • **USAGE:**
Hindu: Sanskrit

Fashion your life as a garland of beautiful deeds.
— Buddha

MALKA, MALKAH   *[MAHL-kah, mahl-KAH]*

MEANING: queen, queenly, regal • **USAGE:** Jewish

A throne shall be established in goodness.
— Isaiah 16:5a (JPS)

MALLORY, MALLERY   *[MAL-oh-ree]*

MEANING: unfortunate, unhappy • **USAGE:**
English surname: from French *malheure*

Love your own soul, and comfort your heart.
— Sirach 30:23a (WEB Apocrypha)

MALOU   *[mah-loo]*

MEANING: famous warrior, beloved warrior, sea
warrior • **USAGE:** Scandinavian combination of
Maria and Lou (*see* Maria and Lou)

*Choose a good reputation over great riches;
being held in high esteem is better than silver or gold.*
— Proverbs 22:1 (NLT)

MALVA   *[MAL-vah]*

MEANING: malva flower, herbal plant • **USAGE:**
English: from Latin *malva* (mallow)

*How could such sweet and wholesome hours
be reckoned, but in herbs and flowers?*
— Andrew Marvell

M

MALVINA   [mahl-VEE-nah]

MEANING: smooth brow • USAGE: Scottish form
of *Malamhin*, from *mala mhin* (smooth brow);
coined by Scottish poet James Macpherson
> *The body says what words cannot.*
> — Martha Graham

MAMIE   [MAY-mee]

MEANING: beloved, love, mistress of the sea, bitter
sea, rebellious, well-nourished, healthy, myrrh,
pearl, beautiful gem • USAGE: English form of
Mary (*see* Mary) or Margaret (*see* Margaret)
> *The Lord your God will...love and bless you.*
> — Deutonomy 7:12a, 23b (NEB)

MANA   [MAH-nah]

MEANING: spiritual or divine power • USAGE:
Hawaiian
> *I am the wild spirit that greets the dawning of this day.*
> — Hawaiian proverb

MANARA   [mah-nah-rah]

MEANING: lighthouse, guiding light • USAGE:
Muslim feminine form of Manar, from Arabic
manar
> *I knew God well when love flashed before me.*
> *It gives me strength by night and day,*
> *and shows what lies ahead.*
> — Sultan Bahu

MANDY, MANDIE   [MAN-dee]

MEANING: lovable, beloved, dear • USAGE:
English form of Amanda, from Latin *amanda*
> *Surely goodness and love will follow me*
> *all the days of my life.*
> — Psalm 23:6a (NIV)

MANJIKA   [mahn-jih-kah]

MEANING: sweet sounding, melodious,
harmonious • USAGE: Hindu

> *In music the heart reveals itself immediately.*
> — Rabindranath Tagore, *Sadhana*

MANON   [mah-NAHN]

MEANING: beloved, love, sea mistress, bitter
sea, rebellious, well-nourished, healthy, myrrh •
USAGE: French form of Marie (*see* Maria)
> *For true love is inexhaustible; the more you give,*
> *the more you have. And if you go to draw*
> *at the true fountainhead, the more water you draw,*
> *the more abundant is its flow.*
> — Antoine de Saint-Exupéry

MANSURA   [mahn-soo-rah]

MEANING: victorious, successful • USAGE:
Muslim feminine form of Mansur, from Arabic
mansur
> *Remember the benefits of Allah,*
> *that you may be successful.*
> — Koran, The Elevated Places 7.69b (SKR)

MANUELA   [mahn-WAY-lah]

MEANING: God is with us • USAGE: Spanish,
Italian, and German feminine form of Manuel, from
Hebrew *immanu'el*
> *The Lord our God be with us, as he was with our*
> *fathers: let him not leave us, nor forsake us.*
> — 1 Kings 8:57 (KJV)

MAPLE   [MAY-pel]

MEANING: maple tree, maple syrup • USAGE:
English: from *mapultreow*
> *The pursuit of perfection is the pursuit*
> *of sweetness and light.*
> — Matthew Arnold, *Sweetness and Light*

MAPUANA   [mah-pwah-nah]

MEANING: sending forth fragrance • USAGE:
Hawaiian
> *A fragrant name. [An esteemed person.]*
> — Hawaiian proverb
> (tr. Mary Pukui in *'Olelo No'eau*)

MARAM   [mah-rahm]

MEANING: wish, desire, aspiration • **USAGE:**
Muslim

> *"God is Love" — three words which open up*
> *an unending realm for the thinker who desires*
> *to probe the depths of the secret of life.*
> — Hazrat Inayat Khan, *The Bowl of Saki*

MARAVILLA   [mar-ah-BEE-yah]

MEANING: marvelous, wonderful, extraordinary •
USAGE: Spanish: from Latin *mirabilis*

> *You formed my inward parts; You wove me in my*
> *mother's womb. I will give thanks to You, for I am*
> *fearfully and wonderfully made; wonderful are Your*
> *works, and my soul knows it very well.*
> — Psalm 139:13–14 (NASB)

MARCELA   [mahr-SAY-lah]

MEANING: warrior • **USAGE:** Spanish form of
Marcelo (*see* Marcia)

> *A warrior treats everything with respect.*
> — Carlos Castañeda, *A Separate Reality*

MARCELINA   [mar-seh-LEE-nah]

MEANING: little warrior • **USAGE:** Spanish and
Polish form of Marcela and diminutive *-ina* (*see*
Marcia)

> *She girds herself with strength.*
> — Proverbs 31:17a (NKJV)

MARCELINE   [mar-seh-LEEN]

MEANING: little warrior • **USAGE:** French form of
Marcela and diminutive *-ine* (*see* Marcia)

> *One who is faithful in very little*
> *is also faithful in much.*
> — Luke 16:10a (ESV)

MARCELLA   [mar-CHEH-lah]

MEANING: warrior • **USAGE:** Italian feminine
form of Marcello (*see* Marcia)

> *You will be confident and fearless.*
> — Job 11:15b (CEV)

MARCIA   [MAR-shah (English, Spanish), MAR-chah (Italian), MAR-see-ah (English)]

MEANING: warrior • **USAGE:** English, Italian,
and Spanish form of Roman family name *Marius*,
reference to Mars (Roman god of war)

> *Put on the armour of light.*
> — Romans 13:12b (DT)

MARCIE, MARCI, MARCY   [MAR-see]

MEANING: warrior • **USAGE:** English form of
Marcia (*see* Marcia)

> *The peaceful warrior's way is not…*
> *about imagined perfection or victory;*
> *it is about love.*
> — Dan Millman,
> *Way of the Peaceful Warrior*

MARCILLE   [mar-SEEL]

MEANING: warrior • **USAGE:** French feminine
form of Marcel (*see* Marcia)

> *The Lord your God is in your midst; he is a warrior*
> *who can deliver. He takes great delight in you; he*
> *renews you by his love; he shouts for joy over you.*
> — Zephaniah 3:17 (NEB)

MAREN   [MAH-ren (Scandinavian), MAYR-en (English)]

MEANING: mariner, sea, ocean, warrior • **USAGE:**
Scandinavian and English form of Marina, from
Latin *marinus* (mariner, seafarer) or *mare* (sea,
ocean); or from Latin *Mars* (Roman god of war)

> *The Ocean is a mighty harmonist.*
> — William Wordsworth,
> "On the Power of Sound"

M

MARETTA   [mah-RET-ah]

MEANING: little Mary, beloved, love • USAGE: American form of Mary and diminutive -etta (see Mary)

Behold, you are beautiful, my beloved, truly lovely.
— Song of Songs 1:16a (NRSV)

MARGALIT   [mar-gah-LEET]

MEANING: pearl, precious gem • USAGE: Jewish (see Margaret)

Dive into the sea of thought,
and find there pearls beyond price.
— Moses ben ibn Ezra

MARGARET   [MAR-gret (English), MAHR-gah-ret (Danish, Norwegian)]

MEANING: pearl, beautiful gem • USAGE: English, Danish, and Norwegian form of *Margarites,* from Greek *margaron* (a pearl)

How fair and how pleasant art thou.
— Song of Songs 7:6a (ASV)

MARGARETE   [mar-gah-REH-teh]

MEANING: pearl, beautiful gem • USAGE: German form of Margaret (see Margaret)

Anyone who keeps the ability to see
beauty never grows old.
— Franz Kafka

MARGARITA   [mar-gah-REE-tah]

MEANING: little pearl, beautiful gem • USAGE: Spanish and Russian form of Margaret and diminutive -ita (see Margaret)

All beautiful you are, my darling;
there is no flaw in you.
— Song of Songs 4:7 (NIV)

MARGE   [marj]

MEANING: pearl, beautiful gem • USAGE: English form of Margaret (see Margaret)

Wisdom is a pearl with most success sought
in still water.
— William Cowper, *The Task*

MARGEA   [mar-GEH-ah]

MEANING: peace • USAGE: Jewish

Peace is a very special gift —
it is our gift to each other.
— Elie Wiesel,
From the Kingdom of Memory: Reminiscences

MARGED   [MAR-ged]

MEANING: pearl, beautiful gem • USAGE: Welsh form of Margaret (see Margaret)

How fair and how pleasant you are.
— Song of Songs 7:6a (NKJV)

MARGERY, MARJERY   [MAR-jer-ee]

MEANING: pearl, beautiful gem • USAGE: English form of Margaret (see Margaret)

Beauty is no beauty without love.
— Thomas Campion, "Thou Art Not Fair,
for All Thy Red and White"

MARGHERITA   [mar-gah-REE-tah]

MEANING: little pearl, beautiful gem • USAGE: Italian form of Margaret and diminutive -ita (see Margaret)

Behold, you are beautiful, my love.
Behold, you are beautiful.
— Song of Songs 4:1a (WEB)

MARGIT   [mar-GEET]

MEANING: pearl, beautiful gem • USAGE: Scandinavian form of Margaret (see Margaret)

You are lovely, so very lovely.
— Song of Songs 1:15b (CEV)

MARGO   [MAR-goh]

MEANING: pearl, beautiful gem • USAGE: English form of Margot (see Margaret)

Beauty itself is not given to us by anyone;
it is…a radiance inside us.
— Marianne Williamson, *A Woman's Worth*

MARGOT, MARGAUX   *[MAR-goh]*

MEANING: pearl, beautiful gem • **USAGE:** French form of Margaret (*see* Margaret)
After the spirit of insight and discernment,
the rarest things in this world are diamonds and pearls.
— Jean de la Bruyère

MARGUERITE   *[mar gyoo-REET]*

MEANING: pearl, beautiful gem • **USAGE:** French form of Margaret (*see* Margaret)
That which is striking and beautiful is not always
good; but that which is good is always beautiful.
— Ninon de L'Enclos

MARI   *[mah-ree]*

MEANING: ball, toy • **USAGE:** Japanese: from Japanese *mari*
Study well, play well.
— Japanese proverb

MARI   *[MAYR-ee]*

MEANING: beloved, love, sea mistress, bitter sea, rebellious, well-nourished, healthy, myrrh • **USAGE:** Welsh form of Mary (*see* Maria)
I am in you and you in me, mutual in divine love.
— William Blake, *Jerusalem*

MARIA, MARÍA   *[mah-REE-ah]*

MEANING: beloved, love, sea mistress, bitter sea, rebellious, well-nourished, healthy, myrrh • **USAGE:** Italian, German, Scandinavian, Greek, English, and Spanish form of Miryam, from Egyptian *mry, mr* (beloved, love); or from Hebrew *mari yam* (sea mistress), *merum yam* (bitter sea), *marah* (rebellious), *mara* (well-nourished, healthy), or *mor* (myrrh)

The Lord is with thee:
blessed art thou among women.
— Luke 1:28b (DR)

MARIAH   *[mah-RIE-ah]*

MEANING: beloved, love, sea mistress, bitter sea, rebellious, well-nourished, healthy, myrrh • **USAGE:** English form of Maria (*see* Maria)
Surely goodness and lovingkindness
shall follow me all the days of my life.
— Psalm 23:6a (ASV)

MARIAM   *[MAYR-ee-um]*

MEANING: beloved, love, sea mistress, bitter sea, rebellious, well-nourished, healthy, myrrh • **USAGE:** English form of Miryam (*see* Maria)
Beloved, I wish above all things that thou mayest
prosper and be in health, even as thy soul prospereth.
— 3 John 1:2 (KJV)

MARIAN   *[MAYR-ee-an]*

MEANING: beloved, love, sea mistress, bitter sea, rebellious, well-nourished, healthy, myrrh • **USAGE:** English form of Miryam (*see* Maria)
The object of love expands and grows
before us to eternity, until it includes
all that is lovely, and we become all that can love.
— Henry David Thoreau
(letter of September 1852)

MARIANA   *[mah-ree-AH-nah]*

MEANING: beloved and full of grace, beloved and gracious • **USAGE:** Spanish combination of Maria and Anna (*see* Maria and Anna)
Beloved, let us love one another;
because love is of God, and every one that loves
has been begotten of God, and knows God.
— 1 John 4:7 (DT)

M

MARIANNA   *[mah-ree-AH-nah, mar-ee-AN-ah (English)]*

MEANING: beloved and full of grace, beloved and gracious • **USAGE:** Italian, Greek, Polish, and Russian combination of Maria and Anna (*see* Maria and Anna)

This I pray, that your love abound yet more and more in knowledge and in all judgment.
— Philippians 1:9 (KJ21)

MARIANNE   *[mayr-ee-AHN (French), mah-ree-AH-neh (German), MAYR-ee-an (English)]*

MEANING: beloved and full of grace, lovely and gracious • **USAGE:** French, German, and English combination of Maria and Anne (*see* Maria and Anne)

God is love, and all who live in love live in God, and God lives in them.
— 1 John 4:16b (NLT)

MARIBEL   *[mah-ree-BAYL]*

MEANING: beloved and joined with God • **USAGE:** Spanish combination of Maria and Isabel (*see* Maria and Isabel)

No one has ever seen God, but if we love each other, God lives in us, and his love is made perfect in us.
— 1 John 4:12 (NCV)

MARICELA   *[mah-ree-SAY-lah]*

MEANING: loved by heaven, celestial love • **USAGE:** Spanish combination of Maria and Celia (*see* Maria and Celia)

The Lord will open up his heavenly storehouse . . . and he will bless everything you do.
— Deuteronomy 28:12a (NCV)

MARIE   *[mah-REE]*

MEANING: beloved, love, sea mistress, bitter sea, rebellious, well-nourished, healthy, myrrh • **USAGE:** French, German, English, and Scandinavian form of Maria (*see* Maria)

Love works miracles every day.
— Marguerite de Valois

MARIEL   *[MAYR-ee-el]*

MEANING: beloved, love, sea mistress, bitter sea, rebellious, well-nourished, healthy, myrrh • **USAGE:** English form of Mary (*see* Mary)

Whoso loves / Believes the impossible.
— Elizabeth Barrett Browning, *Aurora Leigh*

MARIELLA   *[mah-ree-EH-lah]*

MEANING: beloved, love, sea mistress, bitter sea, rebellious, well-nourished, healthy, myrrh • **USAGE:** Italian form of Maria (*see* Maria)

I pray that your love will keep on growing and that you will fully know and understand how to make the right choices.
— Philippians 1:9–10a (CEV)

MARIELLE   *[mah-ree-EL]*

MEANING: beloved, love, sea mistress, bitter sea, rebellious, well-nourished, healthy, myrrh • **USAGE:** French form of Mary (*see* Maria)

The pleasure of love is in loving.
— François de La Rochefoucauld

MARIETA   *[mayr-ee-EH-tah]*

MEANING: little beloved one • **USAGE:** English form of Mary and diminutive *-eta* (*see* Maria)

The God of peace and of love shall be with you.
— Romans 15:13 (DR)

MARIKA   *[mah-REE-kah]*

MEANING: beloved, love, sea mistress, bitter sea, rebellious, well-nourished, healthy, myrrh • **USAGE:** Czech and Hungarian form of Maria (*see* Maria)

Love never ends.
— 1 Corinthians 13:8a (NCV)

MARILEE [mayr-ee-LEE]

MEANING: beloved meadow, lovely meadow •
USAGE: English combination of Mary and Lee (*see*
Mary and Lee)

> *He maketh me to lie down in green pastures;*
> *he leadeth me beside the still waters. He restoreth my*
> *soul; he leadeth me in the paths of righteousness*
> *for his name's sake.*
> — Psalm 23:2–3 (KJV)

MARILLA [mah-RIL-ah]

MEANING: shining sea, blackbird • USAGE:
English form of Muriel, from Irish Gaelic *muir* (sea)
and *geal* (bright, shining); or from French *merle*
(blackbird)

> *Knowledge the wing wherewith we fly to heaven.*
> — William Shakespeare, *Henry VI, Part II*

MARILOU, MARYLOU [MAYR-ee-LOO]

MEANING: famous warrior, beloved warrior, sea
warrior • USAGE: English combination of Mary
and Lou (*see* Mary and Lou)

> *Put on the armor of light.*
> — Romans 13:12b (KJ21)

MARILYN [MAYR-eh-lin, MAYR-lin]

MEANING: beloved lake, beloved pool below a
waterfall • USAGE: English combination of Mary
and Lynn (*see* Mary and Lynn)

> *May the blessing of the great rain be on you; may*
> *they beat upon your spirit and wash it fair and clean,*
> *and leave there many a shining pool where the blue of*
> *heaven shines reflected, and sometimes a star.*
> — Celtic blessing

MARINA [mah-REE-nah]

MEANING: mariner, sea, ocean, warrior • USAGE:
Russian, German, Greek, Italian, Scandinavian, and
Spanish: from Latin *marinus* (mariner, seafarer) or

mare (sea, ocean); or from Latin *Mars* (Roman god
of war)

> *There's nothing stronger than those two warriors,*
> *patience and time.*
> — Leo Tolstoy, *War and Peace*
> (tr. Richard Pevear and Larissa Volokhonsky)

MARINDA [mah-RIN-dah]

MEANING: wonderful, admirable • USAGE:
English: possibly a form of Miranda, from Latin
mirandus

> *For You created my inmost being;*
> *You knit me together in my mother's womb.*
> *I praise you because I am fearfully and wonderfully*
> *made; your works are wonderful,*
> *I know that full well.*
> — Psalm 139:13–14 (NIV)

MARINI [mah-ree-nee]

MEANING: attractive, charming • USAGE: African:
Swahili of Kenya/Tanzania

> *A lovely face does not need adornment.*
> — Swahili proverb

MARIONNE [mah-ree-OHN]

MEANING: beloved, love, sea mistress, bitter
sea, rebellious, well-nourished, healthy, myrrh •
USAGE: French form of Maria (*see* Maria)

> *Love is a flame which burns in heaven,*
> *and whose soft reflections radiate to us.*
> — Aimé Martin

MARIS [MAR-is]

MEANING: of the sea, sea, ocean • USAGE:
English: from Latin *maris* (of the sea)

> *The sea is fresh, the sea is fair.*
> — Mary Howitt, "The White Sea-Gull"

MARISA

[mah-REE-sah (Spanish, Italian), mah-RIS-ah (English)]

MEANING: beloved, love, sea mistress, bitter sea, rebellious, well-nourished, healthy, myrrh, of the sea • USAGE: Spanish, Italian, and English form of Maria (*see* Maria)

This I pray, that your love may abound yet more and more in knowledge and in all judgment.
— Philippians 1:9 (KJV)

MARISE

[mah-REE-seh]

MEANING: beloved, love, sea mistress, bitter sea, rebellious, well-nourished, healthy, myrrh • USAGE: French form of Maria (*see* Maria)

Love alone is capable of uniting living beings in such a way as to complete and fulfill them, for it alone takes them and joins them by what is deepest in themselves.
— Pierre Teilhard de Chardin

MARISOL

[mah-ree-SOHL]

MEANING: beloved sun, sunny sea • USAGE: Spanish combination of Maria (*see* Maria) and Spanish *sol* (sun)

A single sunbeam is enough to drive away any shadows.
— Francis of Assisi

MARISSA

[mah-RIS-ah]

MEANING: beloved, love, sea mistress, bitter sea, rebellious, well-nourished, healthy, myrrh • USAGE: English form of Mary (*see* Mary)

Beauty and health are the chief sources of happiness.
— Benjamin Disraeli, *Lothair*

MARISTELA

[mah-ree-STAY-lah]

MEANING: beloved star • USAGE: Spanish and Italian combination of Maria and Estela (*see* Maria and Estela)

The shining stars make the night sky lovely, brilliant ornaments in the Lord's high heavens.
— Sirach 43:9 (GNT Apocrypha)

MARITA

[mah-REE-tah]

MEANING: beloved, love, sea mistress, bitter sea, rebellious, well-nourished, healthy, myrrh • USAGE: Spanish and German form of Maria (*see* Maria)

A peaceful heart leads to a healthy body.
— Proverbs 14:30a (NLT)

MARIYA

[mah-REE-yah]

MEANING: beloved, love, sea mistress, bitter sea, rebellious, well-nourished, healthy, myrrh • USAGE: Russian form of Maria (*see* Maria)

Seize the moments of happiness, love and be loved! That is the only reality in the world, all else is folly.
— Leo Tolstoy, *War and Peace*
(tr. Louise Maude Shanks and Alymer Maude)

MARJA

[MAHR-yah]

MEANING: beloved, love, sea mistress, bitter sea, rebellious, well-nourished, healthy, myrrh • USAGE: Dutch and Finnish form of Maria (*see* Maria)

Beloved, I pray that all may go well with you and that you may be in health; I know that it is well with your soul.
— 3 John 1:2 (RSV)

MARJAAN

[mar-jahn]

MEANING: pearl, coral • USAGE: Muslim

Human heart is the shell in which sincerity as pearl is formed.
— Hazrat Inayat Khan, *The Gayan*

MARJOLAINE

[marr-zhoh-LAYN]

MEANING: sweet marjoram • USAGE: French: from French *marjolaine* (marjoram)

Love is a springtime plant that perfumes everything with its hope.
— Gustave Flaubert
(letter of October 7, 1846; tr. Francis Steegmuller)

MARJORIE, MARJORY   *[MAR-joh-ree]*

MEANING: pearl, beautiful gem • **USAGE:** English form of Margaret, from Greek *margaron* (a pearl)

In the core of one pearl
all the shade and the shine of the sea.
— Robert Browning, "Summon Bonum"

MARKETA   *[mar-KEH-tah]*

MEANING: pearl, beautiful gem • **USAGE:** Czech form of Margaret (*see* Marjorie)

You are so beautiful!
— Song of Songs 7:6a (NIRV)

MARLA   *[MAR-lah]*

MEANING: beloved woman of Magdala, beloved tower • **USAGE:** English form of Marlene, a contraction of Mary and Magdalene (*see* Marlene)

God…is faithful.
He will keep you safe like a shield or tower.
— Psalm 91:2–4 (NIRV)

MARLENA   *[mar-LAY-nah]*

MEANING: beloved woman of Magdala, beloved tower • **USAGE:** English form of Marlene, a contraction of Maria and Magdalena (*see* Maria and Magdalena)

Thou art a woman of worth.
— Ruth 3:11b (DT)

MARLENE   *[mar-LAY-nah (German),*
mar-LEEN (English)]

MEANING: beloved woman of Magdala, beloved tower • **USAGE:** German and English contraction of Maria and Magdalena (*see* Maria and Magdalena)

Many women are capable, but you surpass them all!
— Proverbs 31:29 (HCSB)

MARLIS   *[MAR-lees]*

MEANING: beloved, love, mistress of the sea, bitter sea, rebellious, well-nourished, healthy, myrrh •

USAGE: German combination of Maria and Liese (*see* Maria and Liese)

Love does not dominate; it cultivates.
— Johann Wolfgang von Goethe

MARLISSA   *[mar-LIS-ah]*

MEANING: beloved, love, mistress of the sea, bitter sea, rebellious, well-nourished, healthy, myrrh • **USAGE:** American form of Mary and diminutive -*issa* (*see* Mary)

The more we nourish our internal world, the more
powerful we grow in the external world.
— Susan L. Taylor, *Lessons in Living*

MARLO   *[MAR-loh]*

MEANING: beloved woman of Magdala, beloved tower • **USAGE:** English form of Marlene, a contraction of Mary and Magdalene (*see* Mary and Magdalene)

Beloved, concerning all things I desire thee to prosper,
and to be in health, even as thy soul doth prosper.
— 3 John 1:2 (YLT)

MARLOW   *[MAR-loh]*

MEANING: lake remnant, bog • **USAGE:** English surname: a form of *Merlave*, from English *mere* (bog, remnants of a lake)

Perhaps the truth depends on a walk around the lake.
— Wallace Stevens,
"Note Toward a Supreme Fiction"

MARLY, MARLEY, MARLIE   *[MAR-lee]*

MEANING: boundary field, pleasant meadow, marten field • **USAGE:** English surname: from English *(ge)mære* (boundary), *myrig* (pleasant), or *mearð* (pine marten) and *leah* (meadow, field)

In the / meadows my spirit becomes so quiet /
that I put my cheek against the earth's body /
I feel the pulse of / God.
— Thomas Aquinas, "The Pulse of God"
(tr. Daniel Ladinsky in *Love Poems from God*)

MARNA   [MAR-nah]

MEANING: mariner, sea, ocean, warrior • USAGE: Scandinavian form of Marina, from Latin *marinus* (mariner, seafarer) or *mare* (sea, ocean); or from Latin *Mars* (Roman god of war)

> *You shall see and become radiant,*
> *and your heart shall swell with joy;*
> *because the abundance of the sea*
> *shall be turned to you.*
> — Isaiah 60:5a (NKJV)

MARNIE   [MAR-nee]

MEANING: mariner, sea, ocean • USAGE: English form of Marna (*see* Marna)

> *The beauteous sea, / Calm as the cloudless heaven.*
> — John Wilson, "It Is the Midnight Ocean"

MARNINA   [mar-nee-NAH]

MEANING: joyful, rejoicing • USAGE: Jewish
> *Joy and gladness shall be found.*
> — Isaiah 51:3b (MT)

MARSHA   [MAR-shah]

MEANING: warrior • USAGE: English feminine form of Marius, in reference to Mars (Roman god of war)

> *Your God is present among you, a strong Warrior*
> *there to save you...he'll calm you with his love*
> *and delight you with his songs.*
> — Zephaniah 3:17 (MSG)

MARTA   [MAR-tah]

MEANING: lady, mistress of the house • USAGE: Spanish, Italian, Portuguese, Scandinavian, Polish, Russian, and English form of Martha (*see* Martha)

> *I will live with a heart of integrity in my house.*
> — Psalm 101:2b (HCSB)

MARTE   [MAR-teh]

MEANING: lady, mistress of the house • USAGE: Norwegian, Danish, and Swedish form of Martha (*see* Martha)

> *Homes are built on the foundation of wisdom and*
> *understanding. Where there is knowledge, the rooms*
> *are furnished with valuable, beautiful things.*
> — Proverbs 24:3–4 (GNT)

MARTHA   [MAR-thah]

MEANING: lady, mistress of the house • USAGE: English, German, Greek, and Scandinavian: from Aramaic *maretha*

> *Peace to thy house, and peace to all that thou hast.*
> — 1 Samuel 25:6b (DR)

MARTHE   [MAR-theh]

MEANING: lady, mistress of the house • USAGE: French, German, and Scandinavian form of Martha (*see* Martha)

> *May it please you to bless the house of your servant,*
> *so that it may continue forever before you. For you*
> *have spoken, and when you grant a blessing to your*
> *servant, O Sovereign Lord, it is an eternal blessing!*
> — 2 Samuel 7:29 (NLT)

MARTINA   [mar-TEE-nah]

MEANING: warrior • USAGE: German, Scandinavian, Italian, Spanish, and English feminine form of Martin, from Latin *Mars* (Roman god of war)

> *Let us conquer the world with our love.*
> — Mother Teresa

MARTINE   [mar-TEEN]

MEANING: warrior • USAGE: French feminine form of Martin, from Latin *Mars* (Roman god of war)

> *Put on the armour of light.*
> — Romans 13:12b (YLT)

MARTITA   *[mar-TEE-tah]*

MEANING: little lady, little mistress of the house •
USAGE: Spanish form of Marta and diminutive *-ita*
(*see* Martha)

> *I will walk with integrity of heart within my house.*
> — Psalm 101:2b (ESV)

MARVA   *[MAR-vah]*

MEANING: sea fortress, prominent sea cliff,
marvelous, wonderful, miraculous • **USAGE:**
English feminine form of Marvin, from Welsh
môr (sea, ocean) and *dunom* (hill, fortress) or *myn*
(eminent, prominent); or English form of Marvela,
from English *marvail* (marvelous)

> *You formed my inward parts;*
> *You covered me in my mother's womb. I will praise*
> *You, for I am fearfully and wonderfully made;*
> *marvelous are Your works,*
> *and that my soul knows very well.*
> — Psalm 139:13–14 (NKJV)

MARVELA   *[mar-VEL-ah]*

MEANING: marvelous, wonderful, miraculous •
USAGE: American: from English *marvail*

> *A gentle word, a kind look, a good-natured smile*
> *can work wonders and accomplish miracles.*
> — William Hazlitt

MARY   *[MAYR-ee]*

MEANING: beloved, love, sea mistress, bitter
sea, rebellious, well-nourished, healthy, myrrh •
USAGE: English form of Miryam, from Egyptian
mry, mr (beloved, love); or from Hebrew *mari
yam* (sea mistress), *merum yam* (bitter sea); *marah*
(rebellious), *mara* (well-nourished, healthy) or *mor*
(myrrh)

> *The Lord is with thee:*
> *blessed art thou among women.*
> — Luke 1:28b (KJV)

MARYA   *[MAR-yah]*

MEANING: beloved, love, sea mistress, bitter
sea, rebellious, well-nourished, healthy, myrrh •
USAGE: Russian form of Maria (*see* Mary)

> *To love deeply in one direction*
> *makes us the more loving in all others.*
> — Madame Swetchine

MARYANNE   *[mayr-ee-AN]*

MEANING: beloved and full of grace, lovely and
gracious • **USAGE:** English combination of Mary
and Anne (*see* Mary and Anne)

> *Grace and peace be multiplied to you.*
> — 2 Peter 1:2a (NASB)

MARYBETH   *[mayr-ee-BETH]*

MEANING: loved by and joined with God •
USAGE: English combination of Mary and Beth (*see*
Mary and Beth)

> *Deep peace from the heart of Mary to you…*
> *Deep peace, deep peace!*
> — Fiona MacLeod, "Invocation of Peace"

MASADA   *[mah-soo-dah]*

MEANING: foundation, basis • **USAGE:** Jewish

> *Our faith has our humanity as its foundation*
> *and our humanity has our faith as its foundation.*
> — Martin Buber, *A Believing Humanism*

MASHA   *[MAH-shah]*

MEANING: beloved, love, sea mistress, bitter
sea, rebellious, well-nourished, healthy, myrrh •
USAGE: Russian form of Maria (*see* Mary)

> *Love all God's creation, the whole and every grain*
> *of sand of it. Love every leaf, every ray of God's light.*
> *Love the animals, love the plants,*
> *love everything. If you love everything,*
> *you will perceive the divine mystery in things.*
> — Fyodor Dostoevsky, *The Brothers Karamazov*
> (tr. Constance Garnett)

M

M

MASHID, MAHSHEED   *[mah-sheed]*

MEANING: moonlight • USAGE: Persian: from
Persian *mah* (moon)

> *Do not beg for light from the moon,*
> *obtain it from the spark within you.*
> — Muhammad

MASIKA   *[mah-sih-kah]*

MEANING: firstborn daughter • USAGE: African:
Xhosa of South Africa

> *You don't choose your family.*
> *They are God's gift to you, as you are to them.*
> — Desmond Tutu, *God Has a Dream*

MASUDA   *[mah-soo-dah]*

MEANING: fortunate, blessed • USAGE: Muslim
feminine form of Masud, from Arabic *mus'ad*

> *O you who believe! remember Allah,*
> *remembering frequently, He it is Who sends*
> *His blessings on you, and (so do) His angels.*
> — Koran, The Allies 33.41–43a (SKR)

MATANA   *[mah-TAHN-ah]*

MEANING: gift • USAGE: Jewish feminine form of
Matan, from Hebrew *mattah*

> *God said…I grant you a wise*
> *and discerning mind.*
> — 1 Kings 3:11–12b (JPS)

MATHILDA, MATILDA   *[mah-TIL-dah*
(English), mah-TEEL-dah (Scandinavian)]

MEANING: mighty warrior, powerful • USAGE:
English and Scandinavian form of Mathilde (*see*
Mathilde)

> *God did not give us a Spirit of fear*
> *but of power and love and self-control.*
> — 2 Timothy 1:7 (NEB)

MATHILDE   *[mah-TEEL-deh]*

MEANING: mighty warrior, powerful • USAGE:
German, Dutch, French, and Scandinavian: from
German *maht* (might, power) and *hild* (war, battle)

> *The eternal God…is your shield and helper*
> *and your glorious sword.*
> — Deuteronomy 33:27, 29b (NIV)

MATILDE   *[mah-TEEL-day]*

MEANING: mighty warrior, powerful • USAGE:
Spanish and Italian form of Mathilda (*see* Mathilde)

> *She dresses herself with strength*
> *and makes her arms strong.*
> — Proverbs 31:17 (ESV)

MATYLDA   *[mah-TEEL-dah]*

MEANING: mighty warrior, powerful • USAGE:
Czech and Polish form of Mathilda (*see* Mathilde)

> *Be strong and courageous…for it is the Lord*
> *your God who goes with you.*
> *He will not leave you or forsake you.*
> — Deuteronomy 31:6 (ESV)

MAUD, MAUDE   *[mahd]*

MEANING: mighty warrior, powerful • USAGE:
English form of Matilda (*see* Mathilde)

> *Mighty hero, the Lord is with you!*
> — Judges 6:12b (NLT)

MAULOA   *[mwah-LOH-ah]*

MEANING: eternal, everlasting • USAGE:
Hawaiian

> *In the tiniest of shells is found the eternal cycle.*
> — Hawaiian proverb

MAUNA   *[MWAH-nah]*

MEANING: mountain • USAGE: Hawaiian

> *I am a part of the land, ka aina.*
> *The soil is my flesh, the mountains my bones.*
> — Hawaiian proverb

MAURA [MOHR-ah]

Meaning: beloved, love, mistress of the sea, bitter sea, rebellious, well-nourished, healthy, myrrh, great, dark-complexioned • **Usage:** Irish, Scottish, and English form of Mary (*see* Mary); from Gaelic *mór* (great one); or from Latin *Maurus* (dark-skinned, a Moor)

Love and affection and friendship for thee.
— Alexander Carmichael, *Carmina Gadelica*

MAUREEN, MAURENE, MOREEN [moh-REEN]

Meaning: little Mary, beloved, love, sea mistress, bitter sea, rebellious, well-nourished, healthy, myrrh • **Usage:** Irish and English form of Mary (*see* Mary)

Let your soul expand, let your heart reach out to others in loving and generous warmth, and great and lasting will be your joy, and all prosperity will come to you.
— James Allen, *From Poverty to Power*

MAVIS [MAY-vis]

Meaning: songbird, my little darling • **Usage:** English: from English *mavys* (songbird, thrush); or from Scotch Gaelic *mo mhuirnin* (my little darling)

The living self has one purpose only: to come into its fullness of being…as a bird into spring beauty.
— D. H. Lawrence

MAXINE, MAXENE [mak-SEEN]

Meaning: greatest, maximum • **Usage:** English feminine form of Maximilian, from Latin *maximus*

What your heart thinks great is great.
The soul's emphasis is always right.
— Ralph Waldo Emerson, "Spiritual Laws"

MAXWELL [MAKS-wel]

Meaning: small child, Maccus's well • **Usage:** Scottish surname: form of *Macsual*, from Gaelic *mac* (son) and *sual* (small, little); or from *Maccus wella* (Maccus's well)

Pretty much all the honest truth-telling there is in the world is done by children.
— Oliver Wendell Holmes,
The Poet at the Breakfast Table

MAY, MAE [may]

Meaning: month of May, mother, pearl, beautiful gem, beloved, love, sea mistress, bitter sea, rebellious, well-nourished, healthy, myrrh • **Usage:** English form of Maia (Latin month of May; Roman goddess of spring), from Latin *maia* (mother); English form of Margaret, from Greek *margaron* (a pearl); or English form of Mary (*see* Mary)

Love, whose month is ever May.
— William Shakespeare, *Love's Labour's Lost*

MAYA [MAH-yah, MIE-ah]

Meaning: water • **Usage:** Jewish: from Hebrew *mayim*

Thou art a fountain of gardens, a well of living waters.
— Song of Songs 4:15a (MT)

MAYA [MAH-yah]

Meaning: of the Mayan civilization, month of May, goddess of springtime • **Usage:** Spanish and English: Spanish reference to ancient Mayan civilization; English form of May (month of May; Roman goddess of spring), from Latin *maia* (mother)

The world's favorite season is the spring.
All things seem possible in May.
— Edwin Way Teale, *North with the Spring*

MAYANA [mah-YAH-nah]

Meaning: spring, fountain • **Usage:** Jewish: from Hebrew *mayim*

[You are] a garden spring, a well of fresh water.
— Song of Songs 4:15 (JPS)

M

MAYIM
[mah-YEEM]

MEANING: water • USAGE: Jewish: from Hebrew *mayim*

You shall be like a watered garden,
like a spring whose waters do not fail.
— Isaiah 58:11b (JPS)

MAYU
[mah-yoo]

MEANING: truly gentle, true and gentle • USAGE: Japanese: from Japanese *ma* (true) and *yu* (gentle)

In the wise and gentle heart /
lies the strength / to change the world.
— Shi Wuling, *Path to Peace*

MAZAL
[mah-ZAHL]

MEANING: good luck, fortune, blessing • USAGE: Jewish

Blessed shall you be in your comings
and blessed shall you be in your goings.
— Deuteronomy 28:6 (JPS)

MCHUMBA
[m-choom-bah]

MEANING: sweetheart • USAGE: African: Swahili

I love to see you my dear, you are the joy of my heart!
— Swahili proverb

MEA, MEAH
[MEE-ah]

MEANING: beloved, love, sea mistress, bitter sea, rebellious, well-nourished, healthy • USAGE: American form of Mia (*see* Maria)

Love is everything. It is the key to life,
and its influences are those that move the world.
— Ralph Waldo Trine,
In Tune with the Universe

MEADOW
[MED-oh]

MEANING: meadow, pasture • USAGE: English: from English *mædwe*

The Lord is my shepherd; I have all that I need.
He lets me rest in green meadows;
he leads me beside peaceful streams.
— Psalm 23:1–2 (NLT)

MEDINA
[meh-dee-NAH, meh-DEE-nah]

MEANING: state, country, symbolic name for girls born on Israeli Independence Day • USAGE: Jewish

The Lord is my allotted share and portion;
You control my fate. Delightful country
has fallen to my lot; indeed is my estate.
— Psalm 16:5–6 (JPS)

MEERA, MIRA
[MEER-ah]

MEANING: wealthy, prosperous • USAGE: Hindu: Sanskrit

True wealth does not burn;
it cannot be stolen by a thief.
— *Sri Guru Granth Sahib*
(Khalsa Consensus Translation)

MEG
[meg]

MEANING: pearl, beautiful gem • USAGE: English form of Margaret (*see* Megan)

Calmness of mind is one of the beautiful jewels
of wisdom.
— James Allen, *As a Man Thinketh*

MEGALYN
[MEG-ah-len]

MEANING: pearl lake, pearl waterfall • USAGE: English combination of Meg and Lynn (*see* Meg and Lynn)

It is a happy world after all. The air, the earth,
the water, teem with delighted existence.
— William Paley, *Natural Theology*

MEGAN, MEGHAN, MEAGAN
[MEG-en, MAY-gen]

MEANING: pearl, beautiful gem • USAGE: Welsh and English form of Margaret, from Greek *margaron* (a pearl)

*There is nothing that makes its way
more directly to the soul than beauty.*
— Joseph Addison

MEHLI [meh-lee]

MEANING: rain • USAGE: Hindu
*Living creatures are nourished by food, and food is
nourished by rain; rain itself is the water of life,
which comes from selfless worship and service.*
— *Bhagavad Gita* (tr. Eknath Easwaran)

MEI [may]

MEANING: beautiful, plum • USAGE: Chinese
*If there is light in the soul,
there will be beauty in the person.*
— Chinese proverb

MEIRA [meh-EE-rah]

MEANING: bright one, shining one • USAGE:
Jewish feminine form of Meir
You will glow.
— Isaiah 60:5a (JPS)

MEISHA [MEE-shah]

MEANING: Who is like God? • USAGE: American
form of Michelle, from Hebrew *mikha'el*
*God is love, and those who live in love live in union
with God and God lives in union with them.*
— 1 John 4:16b (NEB)

MELANIE, MELANY, MELONY [MEL-ah-nee]

MEANING: dark, black • USAGE: English form of
Melaina, from Greek *melas*
*Through the transparent darkness
the stars pour their almost spiritual rays.*
— Ralph Waldo Emerson,
"Divinity School Address"

MELANTHA [meh-LAHN-thah]

MEANING: dark-toned flower, beautiful dark
flower • USAGE: Greek: from Greek *melas* (dark,
black) and *anthos* (flower)
*How beautiful you are, my darling.
How very beautiful!*
— Song of Songs 1:15a (HCSB)

MELBA [MEL-bah]

MEANING: mallow flower • USAGE: English: from
Latin *malva* (mallow)
*Walk into the fields and look at the wildflowers.
They don't fuss with their appearance
— but have you ever seen color and design quite like
it?...If God gives such attention to the wildflowers,
most of them never even seen, don't you think he'll
attend to you, take pride in you, do his best for you?*
— Luke 12:27 (MSG)

MELIA [meh-LEE-ah]

MEANING: plumeria flower • USAGE: Hawaiian
*The birds feed above. [A beautiful person
is like a flower-laden tree that attracts birds.]*
— Hawaiian proverb
(tr. Mary Pukui in *'Olelo No'eau*)

MELIA [MAY-lee-ah]

MEANING: virgin of pure character, attendant at a
religious service • USAGE: Spanish form of Camila,
from Latin *camilla* (virgin of pure character); or
from Latin *camillus* (attendant at a religious service)
Blessed are the pure in heart: for they will see God.
— Matthew 5:8 (NIV)

MELICENT, MELISENT [MEL-eh-sent]

MEANING: strong and industrious, strong worker
• USAGE: English form of Millicent, from German
amal (work, labor) and *swinth* (strength, power)
She is energetic and strong, a hard worker.
— Proverbs 31:17 (NLT)

M

MELIKA   *[meh-LEE-kah]*

MEANING: honeybee, honey • **USAGE:** Hawaiian form of Melissa, from Greek *melissa* (honeybee) or *meli* (honey)

> Look within — the rising and the falling.
> What happiness! How sweet to be free!
> — Buddha, *The Dhammapada* (tr. Thomas Byrom)

MELINA   *[meh-LEE-nah]*

MEANING: quince yellow color, apple, honey, sweet • **USAGE:** Greek: from Greek *melinos* (quince-yellow), *melon* (quince, apple), or *méli* (honey)

> Keep me as the apple of the eye;
> hide me in the shadow of Thy wings.
> — Psalm 17:8 (NASB)

MELISA   *[MAY-LEE-sah]*

MEANING: honeybee, honey • **USAGE:** Spanish form of Melissa (*see* Melissa)

> Compared to most flying things, a bee is very small,
> but the honey it makes is the sweetest of foods.
> — Sirach 11:3 (GNT Apocrypha)

MELISANDE   *[mee-lee-SAHN-deh]*

MEANING: strong and industrious, strong worker • **USAGE:** French form of Millicent, from German *amal* (work, labor) and *swinth* (strength, power)

> A woman's strength is most potent
> when robed in gentleness.
> — Alphonse de Lamartine

MELISSA   *[meh-LIS-ah (English),*
meh-LEE-sah (Greek)]

MEANING: honeybee, honey • **USAGE:** English and Greek: from Greek *melissa* (honeybee) or *meli* (honey)

> Eat honey; it is good. And just as honey
> from the comb is sweet on your tongue,
> you may be sure that wisdom is good for the soul.
> Get wisdom and you have a bright future.
> — Proverbs 24:13–14 (GNT)

MELITA   *[mah-LEE-tah]*

MEANING: little vineyard, little garden, little orchard • **USAGE:** Spanish form of Carmelita, from Hebrew *karmel* (vineyard) and diminutive *-ita*

> The vines are in blossom.
> They give out their fragrance.
> — Song of Songs 2:13b (WEB)

MELODIA   *[may-LOH-dee-ah]*

MEANING: song, melody • **USAGE:** Spanish form of Melodie, from Greek *meoidia* (melody), from Greek *melos* (song) and *aeidein* (to sing)

> Let me see your face, let me hear your voice;
> for your voice is sweet, and your face is lovely.
> — Song of Songs 2:14b (NKJV)

MELODIE, MELODY   *[MEL-oh-dee]*

MEANING: song, melody • **USAGE:** English: from Greek *meoidia* (melody), from Greek *melos* (song) and *aeidein* (to sing)

> We are the music makers, /
> And we are the dreamers of dreams.
> — Arthur O'Shaughnessy, "Ode"

MELVA   *[MEL-vah]*

MEANING: council friend, council protector • **USAGE:** English feminine form of Melvin, from English *mæthel* (council, meeting) and *wine* (friend, protector)

> Get wisdom and insight…do not abandon wisdom,
> and she will protect you; love her,
> and she will keep you safe.
> — Proverbs 4:5–6 (GNT)

MELVINA   *[mel-VEE-nah]*

MEANING: council friend, council protector • **USAGE:** English feminine form of Melvin (*see* Melva)

> She opens her mouth with wisdom,
> and loving instruction is on her tongue.
> — Proverbs 31:26 (NEB)

MEMA [meh-mah]

MEANING: goodness • **USAGE:** African: Swahili of Kenya/Tanzania
We can work together for a better world with men and women of goodwill, those who radiate the intrinsic goodness of humankind.
— Wangari Maathai

MENORA, MENORAH [meh-NOH-rah, men-noh-RAH]

MEANING: candelabrum, candlestick, lamp, symbolic name for girls born on Hanukkah • **USAGE:** Jewish
A lamp for one is a lamp for a hundred.
— Babylonian Talmud: Tractate Sabbath 122a

MEONA [meh-OH-nah]

MEANING: dwelling place, resting place, with special reference to the Temple • **USAGE:** Jewish
God requires no synagogue — except in the heart.
— Baal Shem Tov aphorism

MEORA [meh-OH-rah, meh-oh-RAH]

MEANING: light, luminous, shining • **USAGE:** Jewish
Light shall shine upon your affairs.
— Job 22:28b (JPS)

MERCEDES [mayr-SAY-days]

MEANING: merciful, compassionate, recompense, reward • **USAGE:** Spanish: from Spanish *merced* (mercy, compassion); or from Latin *merces* (reward)
Thy mercy will follow me all the days of my life. And that I may dwell in the house of the Lord unto length of days. — Psalm 22:6 (DR)

MERCY, MERCEE [MER-see]

MEANING: compassionate, merciful, kind • **USAGE:** English: from French *merci* (mercy, compassion) and from Latin *merces* (pay, reward)

Mercy triumphs over judgment.
— James 2:13b (NASB)

MEREDITH [MER-eh-dith]

MEANING: great ruler, guardian of the sea • **USAGE:** Welsh and English: from Welsh *mawr* (great) and *udd* (lord, ruler); or from Welsh *môr* (sea, ocean) and *differaf* (protect, guard)
My bounty is as boundless as the sea, my love as deep.
— William Shakespeare, *Romeo and Juliet*

MERIT [MER-et]

MEANING: reward, merit, worth • **USAGE:** English: from French *merite* (spiritual reward) or Latin *meritus* (to deserve, to earn)
Your kindness will reward you.
— Proverbs 11:17a (NLT)

MERLA [MER-lah]

MEANING: blackbird • **USAGE:** English form of Meryl, from French *merle*
Love hath wings.
— Abraham Cowley, "Constantia and Philetus"

MERRY [MAYR-ee]

MEANING: pleasant, cheerful, happy, merry • **USAGE:** English: from English *mirige*
Heaven give you many, many merry days!
— William Shakespeare,
The Merry Wives of Windsor

MERYL, MERLE [merl]

MEANING: shining sea, blackbird • **USAGE:** English form of Muriel, from Gaelic *muir* (sea) and *geal* (bright, shining); or from French *merle* (blackbird)
You never enjoy the world aright, till the sea itself floweth in your veins, till you are clothed with the heavens and crowned with the stars.
— Thomas Traherne, "First Century"

METTE   [MEH-deh]

Meaning: pearl, beautiful gem • **Usage:** Danish
and Norwegian form of Margaret, from Greek
margaron
> *You are altogether beautiful, my darling,*
> *and there is no blemish in you.*
> — Song of Songs 4:7 (NASB)

MIA   [MEE-ah]

Meaning: beloved, love, sea mistress, bitter
sea, rebellious, well-nourished, healthy, myrrh
• **Usage:** Scandinavian, Dutch, German, and
English form of Maria (*see* Maria)
> *Beloved, I pray that in all things thou mayest prosper*
> *and be in health, even as thy soul prospereth.*
> — 3 John 1:2 (ASV)

MICHAELA   [mee-khah-EL-ah (Jewish),
meh-KAY-lah (English, German, Scandinavian)]

Meaning: Who is like God? • **Usage:** Jewish,
German, English, and Scandinavian feminine form
of Michael, from Hebrew *mikha'el*
> *Beloved, may we love one another,*
> *because the love is of God.*
> — 1 John 4:7a (YLT)

MICHALINA   [mee-chah-LEE-nah]

Meaning: Who is like God? • **Usage:** Polish
feminine form of Michael (*see* Michaela)
> *We are God's coworkers. You are God's field.*
> — 1 Corinthians 3:9a (HCSB)

MICHELA   [mee-KEH-lah]

Meaning: Who is like God? • **Usage:** Italian
form of Michaela (*see* Michaela)
> *For who is God, save the Lord? And who is a rock, save*
> *our God? God is my strength and power;*
> *and he maketh my way perfect.*
> — 2 Samuel 22:32–33 (KJV)

MICHÈLE   [mee-SHEH-leh]

Meaning: Who is like God? • **Usage:** French
feminine form of Michael (*see* Michaela)
> *Only through love can we obtain*
> *communion with God.*
> — Albert Schweitzer

MICHELINE   [meh-sheh-LEEN]

Meaning: Who is like God? • **Usage:** French
feminine form of Michael (*see* Michaela)
> *The essential thing to know about God*
> *is that God is the Good. All the rest is secondary.*
> — Simone Weil, *Gateway to God*

MICHELLE   [mih-SHEL (English),
mih-SHAY-leh (German)]

Meaning: Who is like God? • **Usage:** English
and German (*see* Michaela)
> *God is truth, and whenever you seek truth*
> *you are seeking God.*
> — Peace Pilgrim, *Peace Pilgrim*

MICKI, MIKKI   [MIK-ee]

Meaning: Who is like God? • **Usage:** English
form of Michaela or Michelle (*see* Michaela)
> *God is love. If we keep on loving others,*
> *we will stay one in our hearts with God,*
> *and he will stay one with us.*
> — 1 John 4:16b (CEV)

MIDORI   [mee-dor-ee]

Meaning: green, verdant • **Usage:** Japanese:
from Japanese *midori*
> *Going deeper / And deeper still / green mountains.*
> — Taneda Santōka

MIDRA   [mee-drah]

Meaning: princess • **Usage:** African: Swahili of
Kenya/Tanzania

The princess has all rights in her home.
— Tanzanian proverb

MIGUELA
[mee-GAY-lah (Spanish),
mee-GWEH-lah (Portuguese)]

MEANING: Who is like God? • **USAGE:** Spanish and Portuguese feminine form of Miguel (*see* Michaela)

God is fire and...the soul of each of us is a lamp.
— Symeon the New Theologian,
The Discourses

MIHRI
[mih-ree]

MEANING: sun • **USAGE:** Persian

The sun / Won a beauty contest and became a jewel /
Set upon God's right hand.
— Hafiz, "The Mountain Got Tired of Sitting"
(tr. Daniel Ladinsky in *The Gift*)

MIKA
[MEE-kah]

MEANING: Who is like God? • **USAGE:** Scandinavian form of Mikaela (*see* Michaela)

God is love. Those who live in love live in God,
and God lives in them.
— 1 John 4:16b (NCV)

MIKAELA
[meh-KAY-lah]

MEANING: Who is like God? • **USAGE:** Scandinavian form of Michaela (*see* Michaela)

For who is God, but the Lord? Who is a Rock,
except our God? God is my strong place.
He has made my way safe.
— 2 Samuel 22:32–33 (NLV)

MIKI
[mee-kee]

MEANING: beautiful chronicle, keeper of the family tree • **USAGE:** Japanese: from Japanese *mi* (beautiful) and *ki* (chronicle); or from Japanese *miki* (tree trunk)

A family is a place where minds come in contact
with one another. If these minds love one another
the home will be as beautiful as a flower garden.
— Buddha

MI-KYOUNG
[mee-kyung]

MEANING: beautiful and joyous • **USAGE:** Korean: from Korean *mi* (beauty) and *kyoung* (rejoicing)

We are shaped by our thoughts;
we become what we think. When the mind is pure,
joy follows like a shadow that never leaves.
— Buddha

MILADA
[mee-LAH-dah]

MEANING: love, beloved • **USAGE:** Czech: from Czech *mil*

Love never gives up; and its faith, hope,
and patience never fail.
— 1 Corinthians 13:6 (GNT)

MILAGROS
[mee-LAH-grohs]

MEANING: miracle, wonder • **USAGE:** Spanish: from Spanish *milagro* (miracle, wonder); honors the Virgin Mary

Shalt thou see, and abound,
and thy heart shall wonder and be enlarged.
— Isaiah 60:5a (DR)

MILDRED
[MIL-dred]

MEANING: gentle strength, powerful and kind • **USAGE:** English: from English *milde* (gentle, mild, generous) and *thryth* (strength)

Touched with human gentleness and love.
— William Shakespeare,
The Merchant of Venice

MILI
[MEE-lee]

MEANING: Who is for me? • **USAGE:** Jewish: from Hebrew *mi* (who is) and *li* (for me?)

M

Hillel used to say:
If I am not for myself who will be for me? Yet, if I am
for myself only, what am I? And if not now, when?
— *Pirkei Avot* 1:14

MILIANI   [mee-lee-AH-nee]

MEANING: gentle caress • USAGE: Hawaiian
The birds poise quietly in the gentle breeze.
[At peace with the world.]
— Hawaiian proverb
(tr. Mary Pukui in *'Olelo No'eau*)

MILLA   [MEE-lah]

MEANING: virgin of pure character, attendant at a
religious service • USAGE: German, Scandinavian,
and English form of Camilla, from Latin *camilla*
(virgin of pure character); or from Latin *camillus*
(attendant at a religious service)
Light is spread like seed for those who are right and
good, and joy for the pure in heart.
— Psalm 97:11 (NLV)

MILLICENT   [MIL-ih-sent]

MEANING: strong and industrious, strong worker •
USAGE: German and English form of *Amalswinth*,
from German *amal* (work, labor) and *swinth*
(strength, power)
Work and play are words used to describe
the same thing under differing conditions.
— Mark Twain

MILLIE, MILLY   [MIL-ee]

MEANING: strong and industrious, strong worker,
gentle strength • USAGE: English form of Millicent
(*see* Millicent) or Mildred (*see* Mildred)
Fearless gentleness is the most beautiful of feminine
attractions — born of modesty and love.
— Clara Balfour, *Sunbeams for All Seasons*

MIMI   [mee-mee]

MEANING: beloved, love, sea mistress, bitter
sea, rebellious, well-nourished, healthy, myrrh •
USAGE: French and English form of Maria (*see*
Maria)
This I pray, that your love abound still more
and more in knowledge and all discernment.
— Philippians 1:9 (NKJV)

MINA   [mee-nah]

MEANING: eldest daughter • USAGE: Amerind:
Sioux
The hearts of little children are pure,
and therefore, the Great Spirit may show
to them many things which older people miss.
— Wallace Black Elk

MINA   [MEE-nah]

MEANING: determined protector, steadfast
guardian • USAGE: German and English form of
Wilhelmina (*see* Minna)
Lord…give me health with competence,
a pious heart, and a steadfast mind.
— Ludwig Achim von Arnim

MINDA   [MIN-dah]

MEANING: dark beauty • USAGE: English form
of Malinda, from Greek *melas* (black, dark) and
Spanish *linda* (beautiful, pretty)
You're so beautiful, my darling, so beautiful.
— Song of Songs 4:1a (MSG)

MINDY, MINDIE   [MIN-dee]

MEANING: dark beauty • USAGE: English form of
Malinda (*see* Minda)
Beauty is a name for visible Love.
— Sydney Dobell, "To a Fair Woman"

MING   *[meeng]*

MEANING: light • **USAGE:** Chinese
*To walk safely through the maze of human life, one
needs the light of wisdom and the guidance of virtue.*
— Buddha

MIN-HEE   *[min-hee]*

MEANING: clever and pleasant • **USAGE:** Korean:
from Korean *min* (clever) and *hee* (pleasure)
*Follow one who is wise, intelligent, learned, able to
lead, dutiful and noble; let one follow such a good and
wise one even as the moon follows the path of stars.*
— Buddha, *The Dhammapada* (tr. M. K. Sharan)

MINNA   *[MEEN-ah]*

MEANING: determined protector, steadfast
guardian • **USAGE:** German form of Wilhelmina,
from German *wil* (will, resolve) and *helm* (helmet,
protection)
*Lord, I know you will never stop being merciful to me.
Your love and loyalty will always keep me safe.*
— Psalm 40:11 (GNT)

MINNIE, MINNY   *[MIN-ee]*

MEANING: determined protector, steadfast
guardian • **USAGE:** German and English form of
Wilhelmina (*see* Minna)
Take thought for thy body with steadfast fidelity.
— Johann Wolfgang von Goethe

MIO   *[mee-oh]*

MEANING: beautiful cherry blossom • **USAGE:**
Japanese: from Japanese *mi* (beautiful) and *ou*
(cherry blossom)
*The cherry tree is known among others by its flowers.
[One who stands out.]*
— Japanese proverb

MIRA   *[MEE-rah (Czech, Polish), MIR-ah (English)]*

MEANING: great, famous, renowned • **USAGE:**
Czech, Polish, and English: from Slavic *miri*
Great minds are to make others great.
— William Ellery Channing,
"On the Elevation of the Laboring Classes"

MIRANDA   *[mih-RAN-dah (English), mee-RAHN-dah (Italian, Spanish)]*

MEANING: admirable, wonderful • **USAGE:**
English, Italian, and Spanish: from Latin *mirandus*
*Your eyes are windows into your body.
If you open your eyes wide in wonder and belief,
your body fills up with light.*
— Matthew 6:22 (MSG)

MIRELLA   *[mee-REH-lah]*

MEANING: admirable, wonderful • **USAGE:** Italian:
from Latin *mirari*
You are so beautiful, my love! So beautiful!
— Song of Songs 1:15a (NIRV)

MIRI   *[MEE-ree]*

MEANING: beloved, love, sea mistress, bitter
sea, rebellious, well-nourished, healthy, myrrh •
USAGE: Jewish form of Miryam (*see* Miryam)
Love is the voice of God, Love is the rule of Heaven!
— Grace Aguilar, "The Vale of Cedars"

MIRIAM   *[MIR-ee-am (English), MEER-ee-ahm (Italian)]*

MEANING: beloved, love, sea mistress, bitter
sea, rebellious, well-nourished, healthy, myrrh •
USAGE: English and Italian form of Miryam (*see*
Miryam)
*Beloved, let us love one another: for love is of God;
and every one that loveth is begotten of God,
and knoweth God.*
— 1 John 4:7 (ASV)

M

MIRJAM   [MEER-yahm]

MEANING: beloved, love, sea mistress, bitter sea, rebellious, well-nourished, healthy, myrrh • **USAGE:** German and Dutch form of Miryam (*see* Miryam)

> *To love and to be loved — this /*
> *On earth is the highest bliss.*
> — Heinrich Heine, *Italien*

MIRYAM   [meer-YAHM]

MEANING: beloved, love, sea mistress, bitter sea, rebellious, well-nourished, healthy, myrrh • **USAGE:** Jewish: from Egyptian *mry, mr* (beloved, love); or from Hebrew *mari yam* (sea mistress), *merum yam* (bitter sea), *marah* (rebellious), *mara* (well-nourished, healthy), or *mor* (myrrh)

> *Drink deep of love!*
> — Song of Songs 5:1b (JPS)

MISAKI   [mee-sah-kee]

MEANING: beautiful blossom • **USAGE:** Japanese: from Japanese *mi* (beautiful) and *saki* (blossom)

> *May the perfection of our true selves /*
> *blossom within us.*
> — Shi Wuling, *Path to Peace*

MISHA   [MEE-shah]

MEANING: Who is like God? • **USAGE:** Russian form of Michelle, from Hebrew *mikha'el*

> *God is love.*
> — 1 John 4:8b (ASV)

MISHAILA, MASHAYLA   [mih-SHAY-lah]

MEANING: Who is like God? • **USAGE:** American form of Michelle (*see* Misha)

> *Let us love one another, because love comes from God.*
> *Whoever loves is a child of God and knows God.*
> — 1 John 4:7 (GNT)

MISHALA   [mee-shah-LAH]

MEANING: desire, wish, request • **USAGE:** Jewish

> *Desire realized is a tree of life.*
> — Proverbs 13:12a (JPS)

MISHKA, MISHCHA   [MEESH-kah]

MEANING: Who is like God? • **USAGE:** American form of Michelle (*see* Misha)

> *God is all the goodness in the universe,*
> *available to me here and now.*
> — Wilferd Peterson

MISSIE, MISSY   [MIS-ee]

MEANING: honeybee, honey • **USAGE:** English form of Melissa, from Greek *melissa* (honeybee) or *meli* (honey)

> *The bee is more honored than other animals, not because she labors, but because she labors for others.*
> — John Chrysostom, "Homily XII"

MISTY, MISTIE   [MIS-tee]

MEANING: misty, foggy, clouded • **USAGE:** English: from English *misty*

> *Live free, child of the mist.*
> — Henry David Thoreau, "Walking"

MITZI   [MIT-zee]

MEANING: beloved, love, sea mistress, bitter sea, rebellious, well-nourished, healthy, myrrh • **USAGE:** German and English form of Maria (*see* Maria)

> *We are shaped and fashioned by what we love.*
> — Johann Wolfgang von Goethe

MIYANDA   [mee-YAHN-dah]

MEANING: roots • **USAGE:** African: Zambia

> *A tree is strong because of the roots.*
> — Kaonde of Zambia proverb

MIYU   *[mee-yoo]*

MEANING: beautiful and gentle, gentle beauty •
USAGE: Japanese: from Japanese *mi* (beautiful)
and *yu* (gentleness)

> *Have gentleness in your eyes /*
> *Loving-kindness in your smile.*
> — Shi Wuling, *Path to Peace*

MIZUKI   *[mee-ʒoo-kee]*

MEANING: beautiful moon • **USAGE:** Japanese:
from Japanese *mi* (beautiful) and *ʒuki* (moon)

> *There is nothing you can think that is not the moon.*
> — Matsuo Bashō

MIZUKO   *[mee-ʒoo-koh]*

MEANING: water child • **USAGE:** Japanese: from
Japanese *mizu* (water) and *ko* (child)

> *Study how water flows in a valley stream,*
> *smoothly and freely between the rocks.*
> — Morihei Ueshiba, *The Art of Peace*
> (tr. John Stevens)

MOANA   *[moh-AH-nah, MWAH-nah]*

MEANING: ocean, open sea • **USAGE:** Hawaiian

> *The ocean is the source of all life.*
> — Hawaiian proverb

MOANI   *[moh-AH-nee, MWAH-nee]*

MEANING: gentle breeze, fragrant breeze •
USAGE: Hawaiian

> *There is life in a gentle breath of wind.*
> — Hawaiian proverb
> (tr. Mary Pukui in *'Olelo No'eau*)

MODESTA   *[moh-DAYS-tah]*

MEANING: modest, humble • **USAGE:** Spanish
feminine form of Modesto, from Latin *modestus*

> *The wisdom, that is from above, first indeed is chaste,*
> *then peaceable, modest, easy to be persuaded,*
> *consenting to the good, full of mercy and good fruits,*
> *without judging, without dissimulation.*
> — James 3:17 (DR)

MOIRA, MOYRA, MOIRE   *[MOI-rah]*

MEANING: beloved, love, mistress of the sea, bitter
sea, rebellious, well-nourished, healthy, myrrh •
USAGE: Irish and Scottish form of Maire (*see*
Mary)

> *To love abundantly is to live abundantly,*
> *and to love forever is to live forever.*
> — Henry Drummond,
> *The Greatest Thing in the World*

MOLLY, MOLLIE   *[MAHL-ee]*

MEANING: beloved, love, sea mistress, bitter
sea, rebellious, well-nourished, healthy, myrrh •
USAGE: Irish and English form of Mary (*see* Mary)

> *Dearly beloved, concerning all things I make it my*
> *prayer that thou mayest proceed prosperously,*
> *and fare well as thy soul doth prosperously.*
> — 3 John 1:2 (DR)

MONA   *[MOH-nah]*

MEANING: noble, honorable • **USAGE:** Irish and
English form of *Muadhnait*, from Gaelic *muadh*

> *You are a woman of noble character.*
> — Ruth 3:11b (NIV)

MONEKA   *[moh-neh-kah]*

MEANING: earth • **USAGE:** Amerind: Sioux

> *Grandmother the Earth:*
> *That power is here all the time.*
> *It is continuous, and nobody controls it.*
> — Wallace Black Elk,
> *Black Elk: The Sacred Ways of a Lakota*

M

MONICA   [MAHN-ih-kah]

MEANING: adviser, counselor • USAGE: English and Italian: from Latin *moneo* (to advise)

She opens her mouth with wisdom,
and the teaching of kindness is on her tongue.
— Proverbs 31:26 (RSV)

MONIKA   [MAHN-ih-kah]

MEANING: adviser, counselor • USAGE: German and Scandinavian form of Monica (*see* Monica)

The wise heart will know the proper time and the just way. For there is a time and a way for everything.
— Ecclesiastes 8:5b–6a (ESV)

MONIKA   [moh-nih-kah]

MEANING: little quiet one • USAGE: Hindu: from Sanskrit *mona* (alone, single, quiet) and diminutive *-ka*

With a quiet mind come into that empty house, your heart, and feel the joy of the way beyond the world.
— Buddha, *The Dhammapada* (tr. Thomas Byrom)

MONIQUE   [moh-NEEK]

MEANING: adviser, counselor • USAGE: French form of Monica (*see* Monica)

Blessed be your discernment, and blessed be you.
— 1 Samuel 25:33a (NASB)

MONTANA   [mon-TAN-ah]

MEANING: mountain • USAGE: American: from Latin *montanus*

May your mountains rise into and above the clouds.
— Edward Abbey

MORELA   [moh-RAY-lah]

MEANING: apricot, apricot tree • USAGE: Polish: from Polish *morela*

The fruit of the Spirit is love, joy, peace, patience, kindness, goodness, faithfulness, gentleness and self-control.
— Galatians 5:22–23a (NASB)

MORGAINE   [mohr-GAYN]

MEANING: sea rim, ocean circle, shining sea • USAGE: French form of Morgan (*see* Morgan)

You have encircled me;
You have placed Your hand on me.
— Psalm 139:5 (HCSB)

MORGAN   [MOR-gan]

MEANING: sea rim, ocean circle, shining sea • USAGE: Welsh and English: from Welsh *môr* (sea, ocean) and *cant* (circle, rim) or *can* (bright, gleaming)

Love never contracts its circles;
they widen by as fixed and sure a law
as those around a pebble cast into still water.
— James Russell Lowell

MORGANA   [mor-GAN-ah]

MEANING: sea rim, ocean circle, shining sea • USAGE: Welsh and English form of Morgan (*see* Morgan)

In Life, as in Art, the Beautiful moves in curves.
— Edward Bulwer-Lytton,
What Will He Do with It?

MORIAH, MORIA, MORIYA
[mohr-RIE-ah, moh-ree-YAH]

MEANING: teacher, guide • USAGE: Jewish

Her mouth is full of wisdom,
her tongue with kindly teaching.
— Proverbs 31:26 (JPS)

MORIELA   [moh-ree-EL-ah]

MEANING: God is my teacher, God is my guide • USAGE: Jewish feminine form of Moriel

Thus saith the Lord, thy Redeemer,
the Holy One of Israel, I am the Lord thy God,
who teacheth thee for thy profit, who leadeth thee
by the way that thou shouldest go.
— Isaiah 48:17 (MT)

MORIKO   [moh-ree-koh]

MEANING: child of the forest • **USAGE:** Japanese:
from Japanese *mori* (forest) and *ko* (child)
The forest is a peculiar organism of unlimited kindness
and benevolence…it affords protection to all beings.
— Buddha

MUFIDA, MUFEEDA   [moo-FEE-dah]

MEANING: beneficial, favorable • **USAGE:** Muslim
feminine form of Mufid
Call in remembrance the benefits (ye have received)
from Allah: that so ye shall prosper.
— Koran, The Heights 7:69b (ALI)

MUNA   [MUH-nah]

MEANING: hope • **USAGE:** African: Swahili of
Kenya/Tanzania
Happiness requires something to do,
something to love, and something to hope for.
— Swahili proverb

MUNIFAH   [moo-nee-fah]

MEANING: eminent, exalted, high, lofty • **USAGE:**
Muslim feminine form of Munif, from Arabic *munif*
Such as come to Him as Believers who have worked
righteous deeds, for them are ranks exalted.
— Koran, Ta Ha 20.75 (ALI)

MUNIRAH, MUNEERA   [moo-NEE-rah]

MEANING: luminous, shining, bright • **USAGE:**
Muslim feminine form of Munir, from Arabic
muniir

Our Lord! Perfect our Light for us.
— Koran, Holding (Something) to be Forbidden
66.8b (ALI)

MUNISA   [moo-nee-sah]

MEANING: gentle, kind • **USAGE:** Muslim feminine
form of Munis
There is a smile and a gentleness inside.
— Jalaluddin Rumi, "A Smile and a Gentleness"
(tr. Coleman Barks in *Rumi: The Big Red Book*)

MUNYA, MUNIA   [moon-yah]

MEANING: wish, desire • **USAGE:** Muslim
For those who believe and do righteous deeds,
will be Gardens; beneath which rivers flow:
that is the great Salvation,
(the fulfillment of all desires).
— Koran, The Zodiacal Signs 85.11 (ALI)

MURIEL, MURIAL   [MYOOR-ee-el]

MEANING: shining sea, blackbird • **USAGE:** Irish,
English, and French: Irish form of *Muirgheal*, from
Gaelic *muir* (sea) and *geal* (bright, shining); or from
French *merle* (blackbird)
You will see and be radiant,
and your heart will thrill and rejoice;
because the abundance of the sea
will be turned to you.
— Isaiah 60:5a (NASB)

MURPHY   [MUR-fee]

MEANING: sea warrior, hound of the sea • **USAGE:**
Irish and English surname: from Gaelic *muir* (sea)
and *cath* (battle, war); or from Gaelic *muir* (sea) and
cu (hound, dog)
That the sea is one of the most beautiful
and magnificent sights in Nature, all admit.
— John Joly, *The Birth-Time of the World*

MUSHIRA, MUSHEERA   *[moo-SHEE-rah]*

MEANING: counselor, adviser, guide • USAGE: Muslim feminine form of Mushir

Such as Allah doth guide
there can be none to lead astray.
— Koran, The Crowds 39.37a (ALI)

MYLA   *[MIE-lah]*

MEANING: merciful, compassionate, mild, calm, peaceful, miller, soldier, servant • USAGE: English feminine form of Miles, from Slavic *milu* (merciful, compassionate); from German *mild* (mild, calm) or *milan* (to mill, to rub); from Latin *miles* (soldier, warrior); or from Gaelic *mael* (servant, devotee)

In compassion, justice and peace kiss.
— Meister Eckhart (tr. Matthew Fox in *Meditations with Meister Eckhart*)

MYRA   *[MIE-rah]*

MEANING: beloved, love, sea mistress, bitter sea, rebellious, well-nourished, healthy, myrrh • USAGE: English form of Mary (*see* Mary)

This, then, is the secret of health —
a pure heart and a well-ordered mind.
— James Allen, *From Poverty to Power*

MYRNA   *[MER-nah]*

MEANING: beloved, dear one, darling • USAGE: Irish: from Gaelic *muirne*

You are altogether beautiful, my darling!
There is no blemish in you!
— Song of Songs 4:7 (NEB)

MYRTLE   *[MER-tel]*

MEANING: myrtle tree, evergreen tree • USAGE: English: from Greek *myrtos*

Instead of the brier shall come up the myrtle tree:
and it shall be to the Lord for a name,
for an everlasting sign that shall not be cut off.
— Isaiah 55:13b (KJV)

MYSTIK, MYSTIQUE   *[mih-STEEK]*

MEANING: aura of mystery, mystique, secret • USAGE: American: from Latin *mysticus*

Mystery creates wonder.
— Neil Armstrong

N

NAAMAH, NAMAH   *[nah-ah-MAH, nah-MAH]*

MEANING: pleasant, delightful, kind, graceful • USAGE: Jewish

Deeds of kindness are equal in weight
to all the commandments.
— Babylonian Talmud: Tractate Peah 1:1

NABILA, NABEELA   *[nah-BEE-lah]*

MEANING: noble, honorable • USAGE: Muslim: Arabic *nabil*

Thou endurest with honour whom Thou pleasest.
— Koran, The Women 3.26b (ALI)

NADIA   *[NAHD-yah, NAH-dee-ah]*

MEANING: hope, faith, trust • USAGE: English, French, and Italian form of Nadya, from Russia *nadya*

Faith means being sure of the things we hope for and
knowing that something is real even if we do not see it.
— Hebrews 11:1 (NCV)

NADIE   *[nah-dee]*

MEANING: wise, understanding • USAGE: Amerind: Algonquin

We have to have one mind for the Four Directions.
Until we reach that one mind, we cannot be filled with
understanding.... The Creator will not answer until you
have just one mind, just like if you have one person.
— William Commanda

NADIMA, NADIMAH   *[nah-dee-mah]*

MEANING: friend, companion • **USAGE:** Muslim feminine form of Nadim, Arabic *nadim*

> *You value a friend whom you can trust;*
> *you value a relation in whom you can have confidence.*
> — Hazrat Inayat Khan, *The Gayan*
> (cd. *The Gayani Meditations,*
> *Volume 1,* tr. Cecil Touchon)

NADINE   *[nah-DEEN (French),*
nay-DEEN (English)]

MEANING: hope, faith, trust • **USAGE:** French and English form of Nadia (*see* Nadia)

> *Faith is our light in this life.*
> *By it we possess the truth without seeing it;*
> *we touch what we cannot feel,*
> *and see what is not evident to the senses.*
> — Jean Pierre de Caussade,
> *Abandonment to Divine Providence* (tr. H. Ramiere)

NADIRAH, NADEERA   *[nah-DEE-rah]*

MEANING: rare, precious • **USAGE:** Muslim feminine form of Nadir, from Arabic *nadir*

> *The words that enlighten*
> *are more precious than jewels.*
> — Hazrat Inayat Khan, *The Gayan*

NADJA   *[NAHD-yah]*

MEANING: hope, faith, trust • **USAGE:** German form of Nadya, from Russian *nadya*

> *A strong mind always hopes and has cause to hope.*
> — Karl Ludwig von Knebel

NADYA   *[NAHD-yah]*

MEANING: hope, faith, trust • **USAGE:** Russian: from Russian *nadya*

> *Faith is the force of life.*
> — Leo Tolstoy

NAFISA   *[nah-fee-sah]*

MEANING: precious, gem, treasure • **USAGE:** Muslim

> *If a beautiful woman is a gem,*
> *a good woman is a treasure.*
> — Persian proverb

NAGIDA   *[nah-GEE-dah]*

MEANING: prosperous, wealthy • **USAGE:** Jewish feminine form of Nagid

> *The hand of the diligent shall bear rule.*
> — Proverbs 12:24a (MT)

NAHIDA, NAHIDAH   *[nah-HEE-dah]*

MEANING: Venus, star • **USAGE:** Persian

> *He it is Who has made the stars for you*
> *that you might follow the right way.*
> — Koran, The Cattle 6.97a (SKR)

NAIDA   *[NAY-dah]*

MEANING: water nymph • **USAGE:** English: from Greek *naiad*

> *As water reflects your face,*
> *so your mind shows what kind of person you are.*
> — Proverbs 27:19 (NCV)

NAIMAH, NAIMA   *[nah-EE-mah]*

MEANING: comfortable, contented, at peace • **USAGE:** Muslim feminine form of Naim, from Arabic *na'im* (contented, happy) or *na'ima* (to live in comfort)

> *"Peace!" a word (of salutation)*
> *from a Lord Most Merciful!*
> — Koran, Ya-Sin 36.58 (ALI)

NAJIA, NAJIYA   *[nah-jee-yah]*

MEANING: friend, companion • **USAGE:** Muslim

> *He is our Protecting Friend.*
> *In Allah let believers put their trust!*
> — Koran, Repentance 9.51b (PIC)

NALIN   *[nah-lin]*

MEANING: maiden, young woman • USAGE:
Amerind: Apache
> *May I be well. May I live to old age.*
> *With scattered jewel dust may I live to old age.*
> *May the pollen be on top of my feet.*
> — Jicarilla Apache prayer

NALINI   *[nah-LEE-nee]*

MEANING: gentle, like a lotus • USAGE: Hindu:
Sanskrit
> *With gentleness one defeats the gentle as well as the*
> *hard; there is nothing impossible to the gentle.*
> — *The Mahabharata*

NAMALE   *[nah-mah-leh]*

MEANING: sings well, reed pipe, clouds • USAGE:
African: Ganda of Uganda meaning "that sings
well"; associated with *malenge* (reed pipes)
> *When the heart overflows,*
> *it comes out through the mouth.*
> — East African proverb

NAMI   *[nah-mee]*

MEANING: surf, wave • USAGE: Japanese: from
Japanese *nami* (surf, wave)
> *Consider the ebb and flow of the tide.*
> *When waves come to strike the shore, they crest*
> *and fall, creating a sound. Your breath should follow*
> *the same pattern, absorbing the entire universe*
> *in your belly with each inhalation.*
> — Morihei Ueshiba, *The Art of Peace*
> (tr. John Stevens)

NAMIDA   *[nah-mee-dah]*

MEANING: star dancer • USAGE: Amerind:
Ojibwe-Chippewa
> *The Sun, Moon and Stars are there to guide us.*
> — Dennis Banks

NAN   *[nan]*

MEANING: grace, gracious, merciful, nine • USAGE:
English form of Ann or Nancy, from Hebrew
chaanach; or from Irish Gaelic *naonur* (nine)
> *May grace and peace be yours in fullest measure.*
> — 1 Peter 1:2b (NASB)

NANCY, NANCIE   *[NAN-see]*

MEANING: grace, gracious, merciful • USAGE:
English form of Ann, from Hebrew *chaanach*
> *The light of love, the purity of grace, /*
> *the mind, the music, breathing from her face.*
> — Lord Byron, "The Bride of Abydos"

NANDINI   *[nahn-dih-nee]*

MEANING: joyful, delightful, happy, blissful •
USAGE: Hindu: from Sanskrit *nanda*
> *The mind obtains bliss and eternal peace,*
> *meeting with the Deep and Profound Lord.*
> — *Sri Guru Granth Sahib*
> (Khalsa Consensus Translation)

NANETTE   *[nah-NET]*

MEANING: grace, gracious, merciful • USAGE:
English and French form of Nancy, from Hebrew
chaanach
> *Grace in woman has often more effect than beauty.*
> — William Hazlitt, "On Manners"

NANILOA   *[nah-nee-LOH-ah]*

MEANING: most beautiful • USAGE: Hawaiian
> *Mountain apple in the shade. [A beautiful woman.]*
> — Hawaiian proverb
> (tr. Mary Pukui in *'Olelo No'eau*)

NAOMI   *[nah-oh-MEE (Jewish),*
nay-OH-mee (English)]

MEANING: delightful, pleasant • USAGE: Jewish
and English: from Hebrew *na'omi* (my delight) and
no'am (pleasantness)

Wisdom will enter your heart,
and knowledge will be pleasant to your soul.
— Proverbs 2:10 (RSV)

NAQIYA
[nah-kee-yah]

MEANING: clean, pure, virtuous • **USAGE:** Muslim feminine form of Naqi

What does purity do?…/
It offers what the wise crave:
the priceless treasure of freedom.
— Hafiz, "It Cuts the Plow Reins"
(tr. Daniel Ladinsky in *A Year with Hafiz*)

NASEEM
[nah-seem]

MEANING: morning breeze • **USAGE:** Hindu

God's great power is in the gentle breeze, not in the
storm.
— Rabindranath Tagore, *Stray Birds*

NASHITA
[nah-shee-tah]

MEANING: energetic, dynamic, passionate • **USAGE:** Muslim: from Arabic *nashit*

With / passion pray. / With / passion work.
With passion make love. /
With passion eat and drink and dance and play.
— Jalaluddin Rumi, "With Passion"
(tr. Daniel Ladinsky in *Love Poems from God*)

NASIMA, NASEEMA
[nah-see-mah]

MEANING: breeze, gentle wind • **USAGE:** Muslim feminine form of Nasim

The breeze at dawn has secrets to tell you.
— Jalaluddin Rumi
(tr. Coleman Barks in
Open Secret: Versions of Rumi)

NASIRAH, NASEERA
[nah-SEE-rah]

MEANING: helper, supporter • **USAGE:** Muslim feminine form of Nasir, from Arabic *nasara* (to render victorious, to assist)

Allah is enough for a protector,
and Allah is enough for a Helper.
— Koran, The Women 4.45b (ALI)

NASRIN
[nahs-reen]

MEANING: wild rose • **USAGE:** Persian: from Persian *nasrin*

That which God said to the rose, /
and caused it to laugh in full-blown beauty, /
He said to my heart, / and made it a hundred times
more beautiful. — The rose is…a messenger
from the orchard where the soul lives.
— Jalaluddin Rumi, "A Great Rose Tree"
(tr. Coleman Barks in *The Glance*)

NATALIA
[nah-tah-LEE-ah (Greek),
nah-TAH-lee-ah (Spanish, Italian)]

MEANING: born on Christmas Day, Christmas • **USAGE:** Greek, Spanish, and Italian (*see* Natalie)

It is Christmas every time you let God
love others through you.
— Mother Teresa

N

NATALIE
[NAH-tah-lee (French,
German), NAD-ah-lee (English)]

MEANING: born on Christmas Day, Christmas • **USAGE:** French, German, and English form of Natalia, from Latin *natalis dies Domini* (birthday of the Lord, Christmas)

I will honor Christmas in my heart,
and try to keep it all the year.
— Charles Dickens, *A Christmas Carol*

NATALYA, NATALIYA
[nah-TAHL-yah]

MEANING: born on Christmas Day, Christmas • **USAGE:** Russian form of Natalie (*see* Natalie)

This is the day that the Lord has made;
let us rejoice and be glad in it.
— Psalm 118:24 (ESV)

NATANA [nah-tah-NAH]

MEANING: gift • USAGE: Jewish feminine form of Natan, from Hebrew *nathan*

For I am mindful of the plans I have made concerning you — declares the Lord — plans for your welfare, not for disaster, to give you a hopeful future.
— Jeremiah 29:11 (JPS)

NATANE [nah-TAH-neh]

MEANING: daughter • USAGE: Amerind: Arapaho

My children, my children, /
Here it is, I hand it to you / The earth, the earth.
— Arapaho song

NATANYA [nah-tahn-YAH]

MEANING: gift • USAGE: Jewish feminine form of Natan (*see* Natana)

God said ... Wisdom and knowledge is granted unto thee, and I will give thee riches, and wealth, and honour.
— 2 Chronicles 1:11–12a (MT)

NATASHA [nah-TAH-shah]

MEANING: born on Christmas Day, Christmas • USAGE: Russian and English form of Natalie, from Latin *natalis dies Domini* (birthday of the Lord, Christmas)

Love is born of God, and it cannot find rest in created things, but resteth on him from whom it is derived.
— Thomas à Kempis, *The Imitation of Christ*

NATASHA, NATASIA [nah-TAH-shah]

MEANING: born on Christmas Day, Christmas • USAGE: American form of Natalie (*see* Natasha)

A good conscience is a continual Christmas.
— Benjamin Franklin

NATASSA [nah-TAH-sah]

MEANING: resurrection, reborn, rise up • USAGE: Greek form of Anastasia, from Greek *anastasis*

(resurrection), and from Greek *ana* (up) and *stasis* (standing)

You have been born anew, not of perishable but of imperishable seed, through the living and enduring word of God.
— 1 Peter 1:23a (NIRV)

NAVA [nah-VAH]

MEANING: beautiful, lovely • USAGE: Jewish

Thou art beautiful, O my love.
— Song of Songs 6:4a (MT)

NAVINA [nah-vee-nah]

MEANING: young, youthful • USAGE: Hindu: Sanskrit

In the spiritual life one becomes just like a little child — without resentment, without attachment, full of life and joy.
— Paramahansa Yogananda

NAYANA [nay-yah-nah]

MEANING: lovely eyes, having beautiful eyes • USAGE: Hindu

May we see only what is good for all. /
May we serve you, Lord of Love, all our life. /
May we be used to spread your peace on earth.
— *Mankukya Upanishad* (tr. Eknath Easwaran)

NAYLA [NAY-lah]

MEANING: gain, increase • USAGE: African: Swahili of Kenya/Tanzania

She who does well will be paid likewise.
— Swahili proverb

NAZARA [nah-ʒah-rah]

MEANING: flower, blossom • USAGE: Muslim

What is the soul? Half a leaf. /
What is the heart? A flower opening.
— Jalaluddin Rumi, "Wooden Walking Stick" (tr. Coleman Barks in *The Glance*)

NEA   [NEH-ah]

Meaning: small blue flower • **Usage:**
Scandinavian form of Linnea, from Swedish flower
linnaea, named for Swedish botanist Karl von Linné
Learn how the wildflowers of the field grow: they don't
labor or spin thread. Yet I tell you that not even Solomon
in all his splendor was adorned like one of these!
— Matthew 6:28b–29 (HCSB)

NEALA   [NEE-lah]

Meaning: cloud, champion • **Usage:** Irish and
English feminine form of Neal, from Gaelic *neal*
(cloud) or *niadh* (champion, hero)
I am the daughter of earth and water; /
And the nursling of the sky; / I pass through the pores
of the ocean and shores; / I change, but I cannot die.
— Percy Bysshe Shelley, "The Cloud"

NECHAMA   [neh-KHAH-mah]

Meaning: comforter, consoler • **Usage:** Jewish
Thy rod and Thy staff, they comfort me.
— Psalm 23:4b (MT)

NEDDA   [NED-ah]

Meaning: wealthy guardian, protector of that
which is valuable • **Usage:** English feminine form
of Edward, from English *ead* (prosperity, wealth)
and *weard* (guardian, protector)
I am the Lord your God, Who teaches you to profit,
Who leads you by the way you should go.
— Isaiah 48:17b (NKJV)

NEDIVA   [neh-dee-VAH, neh-DEE-vah]

Meaning: noble, honorable, generous • **Usage:**
Jewish feminine form of Nadav
Keep us under the sway of noble impulses and guide us
ever to perform noble deeds; and bend our nature
so that we may submit wholly to Thy service.
— Jewish prayer

NEDRA, NEDRAH   [NED-drah]

Meaning: wealthy guardian, protector of that
which is valuable • **Usage:** English: feminine form
of Edward, from English *ead* (prosperity, wealth)
and *weard* (guardian, protector)
God said…wisdom and knowledge are granted to you;
and I will give you riches and wealth and honor.
— 2 Chronicles 1:11-12a (NJKV)

NEELA, NILA   [NEE-lah]

Meaning: blue color, sapphire blue • **Usage:**
Hindu
Wherever there is a bit of colour, a note of song,
a grace of form, there comes the call for our love.
— Rabindranath Tagore, *Sadhana*

NEELIE, NEELY   [NEE-lee]

Meaning: cloud, champion • **Usage:** English
feminine form of Neal (*see* Neala)
God said…I set my rainbow in the cloud,
and it will be a sign of a covenant
between me and the earth.
— Genesis 9:12–13 (WEB)

NEEMA   [neh-EH-mah]

Meaning: born during prosperous times •
Usage: African: Swahili of Kenya and Tanzania
God's cup is open.
— Swahili proverb

NEETA, NITA   [nee-tah]

Meaning: gracious, courteous • **Usage:** Hindu
When restraint and courtesy are added to strength,
the latter becomes irresistible.
— Mahatma Gandhi

N

NEGINA [neh-GEE-nah]

MEANING: song, melody • **USAGE:** Jewish
Sing unto the Lord a new song.
— Psalm 98:1 (JPS)

NEHARA [neh-hah-RAH]

MEANING: light, brightness • **USAGE:** Jewish
*Commit thy way unto the Lord; trust also in Him,
and He will bring it to pass. And He will make thy
righteousness to go forth as the light,
and thy right as the noonday.*
— Psalm 37:5–6 (MT)

NELDA [NEL-dah]

MEANING: cloud, champion, light, illumination,
torch • **USAGE:** Irish and English: Irish feminine
form of Neal, from Gaelic *neal* (cloud), or *niadh*
(champion, hero); or English form of Nell, from
Greek *helene* (torch) or *ele* (light)
*Nurture your mind with great thoughts;
to believe in the heroic makes heroes.*
— Benjamin Disraeli, *Coningsby*

NELL [nel]

MEANING: light, illumination, torch • **USAGE:**
English form of Eleanor, from Greek *helene* (torch)
or *ele* (light)
A lovely lady garmented in light.
— Percy Bysshe Shelley, "The Witch of Atlas"

NEORA [neh-oh-RAH]

MEANING: enlightened, cultured, knowledgeable •
USAGE: Jewish feminine form of Naor
*Wisdom shall enter into thy heart,
and knowledge shall be pleasant unto thy soul.*
— Proverbs 2:10 (MT)

NERA [neh-RAH, NEHR-ah]

MEANING: light, candle • **USAGE:** Jewish

*Thy word is a lamp unto my feet,
and a light unto my path.*
— Psalm 119:105 (MT)

NERIAH, NERIYA [neh-ree-YAH]

MEANING: light of God, lamp of God • **USAGE:**
Jewish
We must enhance the light, not fight the darkness.
— Aaron David Gordon

NERIDA [neh-REE-dah]

MEANING: sea nymph • **USAGE:** English form
of *Nereida*, from Greek *neros* (water), reference to
Nereids in Greek myth
The ocean calls.
— Carl Sagan, *Cosmos*

NERINA [neh-REE-nah]

MEANING: sea nymph • **USAGE:** English form of
Nereida (see Nerida)
*Thou shalt see and be radiant,
and thy heart shall thrill and be enlarged;
because the abundance of the sea
shall be turned unto thee.*
— Isaiah 60:5a (ASV)

NERISSA [neh-RIS-ah]

MEANING: sea nymph • **USAGE:** English: from
The Merchant of Venice by William Shakespeare;
possibly a form of *Nereida*, from Greek *neros*
(water), reference to Nereids in Greek myth
The sea, that home of marvels.
— William Ewart Gladstone, *Juventus Mundi*

NESHAMA [neh-shah-MAH]

MEANING: soul, spirit • **USAGE:** Jewish
*My God, the soul that you have
placed within me is pure.*
— Elohai Neshama (Jewish Morning Prayer)

NESSA [NES-ah]

MEANING: pure one, chaste, holy, lamb, strength • **USAGE:** Scottish form of Agnes, from Greek *hagnos* (chaste, holy) or Latin *agnus* (lamb); Irish, from Gaelic *assa* (strength)

> *Truth is not a formal belief;*
> *it is an unselfish, holy, and aspiring heart.*
> — James Allen, *From Poverty to Power*

NETA [NEH-tah]

MEANING: seedling, plant, sapling • **USAGE:** Jewish: symbolic name for girls born on Tu b'Shvat, Arbor Day or New Year of the Trees

> *Rabbi Simon said,*
> *"There is no plant without an angel in Heaven*
> *tending it and telling it, 'Grow!'"*
> — *Midrash*, Rabbah 36:7

NETIVA [nah-TEE-vah]

MEANING: path, way • **USAGE:** Jewish feminine form of Nativ

> *Trust in the Lord with all your heart,*
> *and do not rely on your own understanding.*
> *In all your ways acknowledge Him,*
> *and He will make your paths smooth.*
> — Proverbs 3:5–6 (JPS)

NETTA [NET-ah]

MEANING: cloud, champion • **USAGE:** Scottish feminine form of Niall, from Irish Gaelic *neal* (cloud) or *niadh* (champion, hero)

> *God said... I have placed my rainbow in the clouds.*
> *It is the sign of my covenant with you*
> *and with all the earth.*
> — Genesis 9:12–13 (NLT)

NEVA [NEV-ah]

MEANING: snow, race of women, matrilineal • **USAGE:** English: from Italian *neve* (snow); or English form of Geneva, from Welsh *genos* (race, lineage) and *wefo* (woman)

> *We are, each of us, like beautiful snowflakes*
> *that God has created....Each one of us is born*
> *for a specific reason and purpose.*
> — Elisabeth Kübler-Ross,
> *To Live Until We Say Good-Bye*

NEVAEH [neh-VAY-ah]

MEANING: heaven, heavenly • **USAGE:** American: "heaven" spelled backward; Heaven is from English *heofon* (home of God)

> *Heaven is under our feet as well as over our heads.*
> — Henry David Thoreau, *Walden*

NEVE [neev]

MEANING: brilliant, shining • **USAGE:** English form of Niamh, from Gaelic *niamh*

> *Those who have insight will shine brightly like the*
> *brightness of the expanse of the heaven.*
> — Daniel 12:3a (NASB)

NEVES [NEH-ves]

MEANING: snow • **USAGE:** Portuguese: from Portuguese *neves* (snows); reference to the Virgin Mary, *Nuestra Señora de las Nieves* (Our Lady of the Snows)

> *Trustworthy messengers refresh those who send them,*
> *like the coolness of snow in the summertime.*
> — Proverbs 25:13 (NCV)

NEVONA [neh-voh-NAH]

MEANING: wise, intelligent • **USAGE:** Jewish feminine form of Navon

> *She openeth her mouth with wisdom;*
> *and the law of kindness is on her tongue.*
> — Proverbs 31:26 (MT)

NEZZA [NEZ-ah]

MEANING: pure one, chaste, holy • **USAGE:** American: possibly a form of Agnes or Inez, from Greek *hagnos* (chaste, holy) or from Latin *agnus* (lamb)

N

In that stillness which most becomes a woman,
calm and holy, thou sittest by the fireside
of the heart, feeding its flame.
— Henry Wadsworth Longfellow,
The Spanish Student

NIA   *[nee-ah]*

MEANING: purpose, intention • **USAGE:** African:
Swahili of Kenya and Tanzania
Our task is to make ourselves architects of the future.
— Jomo Kenyatta

NIA   *[NEE-ah]*

MEANING: bright, shining • **USAGE:** Welsh form
of Niamh, from Irish Gaelic *niamh*
If you have good thoughts they will shine out of your
face like sunbeams and you will always look lovely.
— Roald Dahl, *The Twits*

NIAMH   *[neev, nee-iv]*

MEANING: brilliant, shining • **USAGE:** Irish: from
Gaelic *niamh*
Arise, shine; for your light has come.
— Isaiah 60:1a (NASB)

NIARA   *[nee-ah-rah]*

MEANING: of high purpose • **USAGE:** African:
Swahili of Kenya and Tanzania
Every one of us can make a contribution. And quite
often we are looking for the big things and forget that,
wherever we are, we can make a contribution.
— Wangari Maathai

NICCOLA   *[nee-KOH-lah]*

MEANING: victory of the people, successful,
triumphant • **USAGE:** Italian feminine form of
Niccolo (*see* Nicole)
The Lord your God...will make sure you are
successful in everything you do.
— Deuteronomy 28:8a (CEV)

NICOLA   *[NIK-oh-lah (English),*
NEE-koh-lah (German)]

MEANING: victory of the people, successful,
triumphant • **USAGE:** English and German
feminine form of Nicholas (*see* Nicole)
Things won are done; joy's soul lies in the doing.
— William Shakespeare, *Troilus and Cressida*

NICOLE   *[nee-KOHL]*

MEANING: victory of the people, victorious one
• **USAGE:** French, German, and English feminine
form of Nicholas, from Greek *nike* (victory) and
laos (people)
Let love and loyalty always show like a necklace,
and write them in your mind. God and people
will like you and consider you a success.
— Proverbs 3:3–4 (CEV)

NIEVES   *[nee-AY-bays]*

MEANING: snow • **USAGE:** Spanish: from Spanish
nieves (snows); reference to the Virgin Mary,
Nuestra Señora de las Nieves (Our Lady of the
Snows)
Wash me, and I will be whiter than snow.
— Psalm 51:7 (NLV)

NIKA   *[NEE-kah]*

MEANING: wild goose • **USAGE:** Amerind:
Ojibwe-Chippewa
In the center I am standing /
In the form like a bird it appears.
— Chippewa song

NIKA   *[NEE-kah]*

MEANING: true image, bringer of victory •
USAGE: Russian form of Veronika, from Latin *vera*
(true) and *iconicus* (image, icon) or from Greek
pherein (to bring, to bear) and *nike* (victory)
Success to you and those who help you!
— 1 Chronicles 12:18b (GNT)

NIKE [NIE-kee]

MEANING: victorious one, successful, triumphant
• USAGE: Greek: from Greek *nike* (victory), Greek
goddess of victory
> *The true runner comes to the finish*
> *and receives the prize and is crowned.*
> — Plato, *The Republic* (tr. Benjamin Jowett)

NIKKI, NICKI [NIK-ee]

MEANING: victory of the people, victorious one •
USAGE: English form of Nicole (*see* Nicole)
> *You will prosper and be successful.*
> — Joshua 1:8b (NEB)

NIKOLETA [nee-koh-LEH-tah]

MEANING: victory of the people, successful,
triumphant • USAGE: Greek feminine form of
Nikolaos (*see* Nicole)
> *Of all victories,*
> *the first and best is to conquer one's self.*
> — Plato

NILI [NEE-lee]

MEANING: the Everlasting of Israel will not die •
USAGE: Jewish acrostic of the Hebrew words "the
Everlasting of Israel will not die" (cf. 1 Samuel
15:29)
> *In Israel, in order to be a realist*
> *you must believe in miracles.*
> — David Ben-Gurion

NIMAH [nih-mah]

MEANING: content, at peace • USAGE: Muslim:
from Arabic *na'im* (contented, happy) or *na'ima* (to
live in comfort)
> *Verily thy Lord will give unto thee*
> *so that thou wilt be content.*
> — Koran, The Early Hours 93.5 (PIC)

NINA [NEE-nah]

MEANING: mother • USAGE: African: Swahili of
Kenya and Tanzania
> *A mother's tenderness for her children*
> *is as discreet as the dew that kisses the earth.*
> — East African proverb

NINA [NEE-nah]

MEANING: girl, little girl • USAGE: English,
German, and Russian short form of names that end
in *-nina*, such as Anina or Jonina; or from Spanish
niña (little girl)
> *The most potent muse of all is our own inner child.*
> — Stephen Nachmanovitch, *Free Play*

NINA [NEE-nah]

MEANING: having beautiful eyes • USAGE: Hindu
> *Be universal in your love. / You will see the universe /*
> *To be the picture of your own being.*
> — Sri Chinmoy Ghose, *Wings of Joy*

NING [neeng]

MEANING: peaceful, tranquil, calm • USAGE:
Chinese
> *To dwell in peace is great happiness.*
> — Chinese proverb (tr. William Scarborough)

NINON [nee-nohn]

MEANING: grace, gracious, merciful • USAGE:
French form of Anne, from Hebrew *chaanach*
> *Grace and peace to you.*
> — 1 Corinthians 1:3 (NCV)

NISHA [nih-shah]

MEANING: night • USAGE: Hindu
> *Light in my heart the evening star of rest*
> *and then let the night whisper to me of love.*
> — Rabindranath Tagore, *Stray Birds*

NISSANA
[nee-SAH-nah]

MEANING: miracle, wonder • **USAGE:** Jewish feminine form of Nissan

We thank You for the miracles which daily attend us,
for your wonders and favor morning, noon, and night.
— Jewish prayer

NITA
[NEE-tah]

MEANING: grace, gracious, graceful • **USAGE:** Spanish and English form of Anita, from Hebrew *chaanach*

Forgo not a wise and good woman:
for her grace is above gold.
— Ben Sira 7:19 (KJV Apocrypha)

NITYA
[nit-yah]

MEANING: eternal, infinite • **USAGE:** Hindu: Sanskrit

Truth opens up a whole horizon,
it leads us to the infinite.
— Rabindranath Tagore, *Sadhana*

NIYOL
[nee-yohl]

MEANING: wind • **USAGE:** Amerind: Navajo

It was the wind that gave them life. It is the wind that comes out of mouths now that gives us life. When this ceases to blow we die. In the skin at the tips of our fingers we see the trail of the wind; it shows us where the wind blew when our ancestors were created.
— Navajo legend

NOE
[NOH-eh]

MEANING: mist, misty rain • **USAGE:** Hawaiian

A waterfall plummets down the face of the cliffs,
na pali, to be reborn in mist far below.
— Hawaiian proverb

NOELLA
[noh-EL-ah]

MEANING: Christmas, born on Christmas Day • **USAGE:** French feminine form of Noel, from French *nael* (Christmas) and from Latin *natalis dies Domini* (birthday of the Lord)

Beloved, let us love one another:
for love is of God; and everyone that loveth
is born of God, and knoweth God.
— 1 John 4:7 (KJV)

NOELLE, NÖELLE
[noh-EL]

MEANING: Christmas, born on Christmas Day • **USAGE:** English and French feminine form of Noel (*see* Noella)

This is the day the Lord has made;
we will rejoice and be glad in it.
— Psalm 118:24 (NKJV)

NOÉMI, NOEMÍ
[noh-EH-mee (French), noh-eh-MEE (Spanish)]

MEANING: delightful, pleasant • **USAGE:** French and Spanish forms of Naomi, from Hebrew *na'omi* (my delight) and *no'am* (pleasantness)

Wisdom will enter your mind,
and knowledge will delight your heart.
— Proverbs 2:10 (HCSB)

NOLA
[NOH-lah]

MEANING: white shoulders, beautiful shoulders, noble, famous • **USAGE:** Irish form of Finola or Fionnuala, from Gaelic *fionn* (fair, white, beautiful) and *guala* (shoulders); from Gaelic *nola, nuall* (noble, famous)

You are absolutely beautiful, my darling,
with no imperfection in you.
— Song of Songs 4:7 (HCSB)

NOLEEN
[noh-LEEN]

MEANING: white shoulders, beautiful shoulders, noble, famous • **USAGE:** Irish form of Nola (*see* Nola)

The two noblest things…are sweetness and light.
— Jonathan Swift, *Gulliver's Travels*

NONA [NOH-nah]

MEANING: nine, ninth • USAGE: English: from Latin *nonus*

I place the nine pure choice graces / In thy fair fond face, / The grace of form, / The grace of voice, / The grace of fortune, / The grace of goodness, / The grace of wisdom, / The grace of charity, / The grace of choice, / The grace of whole-souled loveliness, / The grace of goodly speech.
— Alexander Carmichael,
"The Invocation of the Graces," *Carmina Gadelica*

NONI [NOH-nee]

MEANING: gift of God • USAGE: African: Swahili of Kenya and Tanzania

All things are done by God. — Swahili proverb

NORA [NOR-ah]

MEANING: honorable, valorous, light, illumination, torch • USAGE: Irish, English, German, Italian, and Scandinavian form of Honora, from Latin *honor* (honor, valor); or from Eleonora, from Greek *helene* (torch) or *ele* (light).

Be Thy light, O Spirit, over me shining... / From the crown of my head to the soles of my feet.
— Alexander Carmichael, *Carmina Gadelica*

NOREEN, NORENE [nor-EEN]

MEANING: honorable, valorous • USAGE: Irish and English form of Honora, from Latin *honor*

Wisdom is the principal thing; therefore get wisdom: and with all thy getting get understanding. Exalt her, and she shall promote thee: she shall bring thee to honour, when thou dost embrace her.
— Proverbs 4:7–8 (KJV)

NORMA [NOR-mah]

MEANING: north, northerner, woman of the north • USAGE: English feminine form of Norman, from German *nord* (north, northern) and *man* (man)

We believe in the dignity of every life, the possibility of every mind, the divinity of every soul. This is our true North.
— Elizabeth Dole (speech of August 31, 2004)

NOSHIN [noh-sheen]

MEANING: sweet, pleasant • USAGE: Persian

Now, / sweet one, be wise.
— Hafiz, "Cast All Your Votes for Dancing" (tr. Daniel Ladinsky in *A Year with Hafiz*)

NOVA [NOH-vah]

MEANING: chases butterflies • USAGE: Amerind: Hopi

Rain all over the cornfields, / Pretty butterfly-maidens / Chasing one another when the rain is done... / How they frolic 'mid the corn, / Laughing, laughing.
— Hopi song

NOVA, NOVAH [NOH-vah]

MEANING: new • USAGE: American: from Latin *novus*

The purpose of life is to live it, to taste experience to the utmost, to reach out eagerly and without fear for newer and richer experience.
— Eleanor Roosevelt

NOYA, NOIA [noy-YAH, NOH-yah]

MEANING: beautiful, lovely, ornamented • USAGE: Jewish

Behold, thou art fair, my love; behold, thou art fair.
— Song of Songs 4:1 (MT)

NUALA [NOO-ah-lah, noo-AH-lah]

MEANING: white shoulders, beautiful shoulders • USAGE: Irish form of Fionnuala, from Gaelic *fionn* (fair, white, beautiful) and *guala* (shoulders)

May the wings of the butterfly kiss the sun / and find your shoulder to light on. / To bring you luck, happiness and riches. / Today, tomorrow and beyond.
— Celtic blessing

N

NUAN   [noo-ahn]

MEANING: warm, friendly, genial • USAGE:
Chinese

> Friendship existence to attain
> must rest on goodness not on gain.
> — Chinese proverb (tr. William Scarborough)

NUNZIA   [NOON-ʒee-ah]

MEANING: announcement, messenger, herald
• USAGE: Italian form of Annunziata, from
Italian annunʒio (announcement) or Latin nuntius
(messenger, herald)

> How wonderful it is to see a messenger coming across
> the mountains, bringing good news, the news of peace!
> — Isaiah 52:7a (GNT)

NUR, NOOR   [noor]

MEANING: light, illumination • USAGE: Muslim:
from Arabic nur

> O Lord! create light within my heart, and in my eyes,
> and in my ears; in right side and my left; light above
> me and under me, before me and behind me.
> — Hadith of the Prophet Muhammad

NURA   [noo-rah]

MEANING: light, illumination • USAGE: Muslim
form of Nur (see Nur)

> Our Lord! Perfect our light for us.
> — Koran, The Prohibition 66.8b (PIC)

NURIA   [noo-rih-yah]

MEANING: statue of Virgin Mary • USAGE:
Spanish: from Spanish Nostra Senyora de Nuria, a
title of the Virgin Mary and of a Spanish sanctuary
with a statue of Mary

> Strength and honor are her clothing;
> and she shall rejoice in time to come.
> — Proverbs 31:25 (KJ21)

NURIT   [noo-REET]

MEANING: buttercup flower • USAGE: Jewish

> The flowers appear on the earth;
> the time of singing is come.
> — Song of Songs 2:12a (MT)

NURIYA, NURIAH   [noo-REE-ah]

MEANING: light, illumination • USAGE: Muslim:
from Arabic nur

> The same light which is fire on earth and the sun
> in the sky, is God in heaven.
> — Hazrat Inayat Khan, The Gayan

NYDIA   [NIH-dee-ah]

MEANING: nest, nestling • USAGE: English:
possibly from Latin nidus (nest); in The Last Days of
Pompeii by Edward Bulwer-Lytton

> Birds and animals have much they could teach you;
> ask the creatures of earth and sea for their wisdom.
> — Job 12:7–8 (GNT)

NYLA, NILA   [NIE-lah]

MEANING: cloud, champion • USAGE: English
feminine form of Niles, from Irish Gaelic neal
(cloud), or niadh (champion, hero)

> The air up there in the clouds is very pure and fine,
> bracing and delicious. And why shouldn't it be?
> It is the same the angels breathe.
> — Mark Twain, Roughing It

O

OBASI   [oh-BAH-see]

MEANING: in honor of the Supreme God •
USAGE: African: Igbo of Nigeria

> You must give honor to whom honor is due.
> — Nigerian proverb

OBIOMA
[oh-bee-OH-mah]

MEANING: kind, compassionate • **USAGE:** African: Igbo of Nigeria

> *A kind word has a good reply.*
> — Igbo proverb

OCEANA
[oh-SHAH-nah]

MEANING: ocean, of the ocean • **USAGE:** English: from Greek *oceanus* (ocean); or from French *ocean* (ocean, sea)

> *For all at last returns to the sea — to Oceanus,*
> *the ocean river, like the everflowing stream of time,*
> *the beginning and the end.*
> — Rachel Carson, *The Sea Around Us*

OCÉANE
[oh-say-AHN]

MEANING: ocean, of the ocean • **USAGE:** French (*see* Oceana)

> *We are like waves that do not move individually but*
> *rise and fall in rhythm. To share, to rise and fall in*
> *rhythm with life around us, is a spiritual necessity.*
> — Albert Schweitzer

OCEANIA
[oh-SHAH-nee-ah]

MEANING: ocean, of the ocean • **USAGE:** English (*see* Oceana)

> *We are tied to the ocean. And when we go back*
> *to the sea, whether it is to sail or to watch —*
> *we are going back from whence we came.*
> — John F. Kennedy (speech of September 14, 1962)

OCTAVIA
[ohk-TAH-bee-ah (Spanish),
ohk-TAH-vee-ah (English)]

MEANING: eight, eighth • **USAGE:** Spanish and English feminine form of Octavio, from Latin *octavus*

> *Teach us to number our days,*
> *that we may get us a heart of wisdom.*
> — Psalm 90:12 (ASV)

ODA
[OH-dah]

MEANING: rich, prosperous • **USAGE:** Scandinavian: from Norse *auðr*

> *Peace and prosperity to you, your family,*
> *and everything you own!*
> — 1 Samuel 25:6 (NLT)

ODELE
[oh-DEH-leh]

MEANING: song, singer • **USAGE:** Greek: from Greek *oide* (song) and *aeidein* (to sing)

> *Ye shall have a song…and gladness of heart.*
> — Isaiah 30:29a (KJV)

ODETTE
[oh-DET]

MEANING: little prosperous one, little wealthy one • **USAGE:** French form of Oda and diminutive -*ette* (*see* Oda)

> *A generous person will be enriched,*
> *and one who gives water will get water.*
> — Proverbs 11:25 (NRSV)

ODILA
[oh-DEE-lah]

MEANING: prosperous, wealthy • **USAGE:** French form of Oda (*see* Oda)

> *I pray that you may prosper in every way and be in*
> *good health physically just as you are spiritually.*
> — 3 John 1:2 (HCSB)

ODILE
[oh-DEEL]

MEANING: prosperous, wealthy • **USAGE:** German form of Oda (*see* Oda)

> *It is the blessing of the Lord that makes rich,*
> *and He adds no sorrow to it.*
> — Proverbs 10:22 (NASB)

ODILIA
[oh-DEE-lee-ah]

MEANING: prosperous, wealthy • **USAGE:** German form of Oda (*see* Odila)

> *The more one is, the richer is all that one experiences.*
> — Rainer Maria Rilke (letter of October 24, 1900;
> tr. Jane Bannard Green and M. D. Norton)

OFELIA   [oh-FAY-lee-ah]

MEANING: helper, helpful • **USAGE:** Spanish and Italian form of Ophelia, from Greek *ophelia*

> *Behold, God is my helper;*
> *the Lord is the upholder of my life.*
> — Psalm 54:4 (ESV)

OFIRA   [oh-FEER-ah]

MEANING: gold, golden, valuable • **USAGE:** Jewish feminine form of Ofir

> *A word fitly spoken is like apples*
> *of gold in settings of silver.*
> — Proverbs 25:11 (MT)

OKSANA   [ohk-SAH-nah]

MEANING: hospitable, giving hospitality • **USAGE:** Russian form of Xenia, from Greek *xenia* (hospitality) and *xenos* (guest, stranger)

> *Do not neglect to show hospitality to strangers,*
> *for thereby some have entertained angels unawares.*
> — Hebrews 13:2 (ESV)

OLA   [OH-lah]

MEANING: ancestor's descendant, heir • **USAGE:** Finnish feminine form of Olaf, from Norse *anu* (ancestor) and *leifr* (descendant, heir)

> *The lines are fallen unto me in pleasant places;*
> *yes, I have a goodly heritage.*
> — Psalm 16:6 (KJV)

OLALLA   [oh-LAH-yah]

MEANING: well-spoken, sweet spoken, eloquent • **USAGE:** Spanish form of Eulalia, from Greek *eu* (good, well) and *lalein* (to talk)

> *Your voice is pleasant, and your face is lovely.*
> — Song of Songs 2:14b (NLT)

OLATHE   [oh-LAH-theh]

MEANING: beautiful • **USAGE:** Amerind: Shawnee

> *Love your life, perfect your life, beautify*
> *all things in your life. Seek to make your life long*
> *and of service to your people.*
> — Tecumseh

OLENKA   [oh-LAYN-kah]

MEANING: holy, blessed • **USAGE:** Polish form of Olga, from Norse *heilagr*

> *God's chosen ones, holy and loved,*
> *put on heartfelt compassion, kindness,*
> *humility, gentleness, and patience.*
> — Colossians 3:12b (HCSB)

OLETA   [oh-LEE-tah]

MEANING: truth • **USAGE:** American form of Oletha (*see* Oletha)

> *Whatever satisfies the soul is truth.*
> — Walt Whitman, "Autumn Rivulets"

OLETHA   [oh-LEE-thah]

MEANING: truth • **USAGE:** American form of Alethea, from Greek *aletheia*

> *There is an inmost centre in us all /*
> *Where Truth abides in fulness.*
> — James Allen, *From Poverty to Power*

OLGA   [OHL-gah]

MEANING: holy, blessed • **USAGE:** Scandinavian, German, and Russian feminine form of Oleg, from Norse *heilagr*

> *You will have God's blessing.*
> — Isaiah 32:20a (CEV)

OLIMPIA   [oh-LEEM-pee-ah]

MEANING: Mt. Olympus, mountain of the gods • **USAGE:** Italian and Spanish form of Olympia, from Greek *Olympos*, Greek home of the gods

Lord...who may live on your holy mountain?
Only those who are innocent and who do what is right.
Such people speak the truth from their hearts.
— Psalm 15:1–2 (NCV)

OLINA   *[oh-LEE-nah]*

MEANING: joyous • **USAGE:** Hawaiian
A joyousness is in the voice of love.
— Hawaiian proverb
(tr. Mary Pukui in *'Olelo No'eau*)

OLIVE   *[AH-lev]*

MEANING: olive, olive tree • **USAGE:** English
form of Olivia (*see* Olivia)
I am like an olive tree growing in the house of God;
I trust in his constant love forever and ever.
— Psalm 52:8 (GNT)

OLIVIA   *[oh-LIV-ee-ah (English), oh-LEE-vee-ah*
(German, Italian, Scandinavian, Spanish)]

MEANING: olive, olive tree • **USAGE:** English,
German, Italian, Scandinavian, and Spanish: from
French *olivier* (olive tree) or from Greek *elaia*
(olive)
Peace puts forth her olive everywhere.
— William Shakespeare, *Henry IV, Part II*

OLWEN, OLWYN   *[OL-wen]*

MEANING: white footprint, holy trace • **USAGE:**
Welsh: from Welsh *ôl* (footprint, trace) and *gwen*
(white, fair, holy)
Trust in the Lord with all thine heart; and lean not
unto thine own understanding. In all thy ways
acknowledge him, and he shall direct thy paths.
— Proverbs 3:5–6 (KJV)

OLYA   *[OL-yah]*

MEANING: holy, blessed • **USAGE:** Russian form
of Olga, from Norse *heilagr*

Blessed are you among women.
— Luke 6:42b (WEB)

OLYMPIA   *[oh-LEEM-pee-ah]*

MEANING: Mt. Olympus, mountain of the gods •
USAGE: English and Greek: from Greek *Olympos*,
Greek home of the gods
In the mountains, there you feel free.
— T. S. Eliot, *The Waste Land*

OMANA   *[oh-mah-nah]*

MEANING: woman • **USAGE:** Hindu
Woman, in your laughter
you have the music of the fountain of life.
— Rabindranath Tagore, *Stray Birds*

OMATRA   *[oh-MAH-trah]*

MEANING: friend, protector • **USAGE:** Hindu:
Sanskrit
May Brahman protect us, may he guide us,
may he give us strength and right understanding.
May love and harmony be with us all.
— *Katha Upanishad* (tr. Prabhavananda)

OMEA   *[oh-MEH-ah]*

MEANING: respected, beloved, esteemed • **USAGE:**
Hawaiian
Braided with the cords of love.
— Hawaiian proverb
(tr. Mary Pukui in *'Olelo No'eau*)

ONATAH   *[oh-nah-tah]*

MEANING: of the earth • **USAGE:** Amerind:
Iroquois
We return thanks to our mother,
the earth, which sustains us.
— Iroquois prayer

ONDINE   [ohn-deen]

MEANING: ocean spirit, mermaid • USAGE:
French: from Latin *unda* (wave)
> *Steep yourself in the sea of the matter,*
> *bathe in its fiery water, for it is the source*
> *of your life and your youthfulness.*
> — Pierre Teilhard de Chardin,
> "The Heart of the Matter" (tr. Rene Hague)

ONDREA   [OHN-dree-ah]

MEANING: man, courageous, strong • USAGE:
Czech form of Andrea, from Greek *andros* (man) or
andreios (manly)
> *Be of good courage,*
> *and He shall strengthen your heart.*
> — Psalm 31:24a (NKJV)

ONELLA   [oh-NEH-lah]

MEANING: light, illumination, torch • USAGE:
Hungarian form of Helen, from Greek *helene*
(torch) or *ele* (light)
> *The light produces what is completely good,*
> *right and true.*
> — Ephesians 5:9 (NIRV)

ONI   [OH-nee]

MEANING: born in a sacred abode • USAGE:
African: Yoruba of Nigeria
> *A person who is born in the house of wisdom*
> *and reared in the house of discernment,*
> *will she lack wisdom or be without discernment?*
> — Yoruban proverb

OONA, OONAGH   [OO-nah]

MEANING: lamb, sheep, one • USAGE: Irish: from
Gaelic *uan* (lamb); or from Latin *una* (one)
> *The Lord is my shepherd; there is nothing I lack.*
> — Psalm 23:1 (HCSB)

OPAL   [OH-pal]

MEANING: opalescent gemstone, beautiful jewel
• USAGE: English: from Sanskrit *upala* (precious
stone, jewel)
> *There is no shade in a rainbow, or in an opal.*
> — John Ruskin, *Giotto and His Works in Padua*

OPHELIA   [oh-FAY-lee-ah (Greek),
                         oh-FEEL-yah (English)]

MEANING: helper, helpful • USAGE: Greek and
English: from Greek *ophelia*
> *God is my helper;*
> *the Lord is the sustainer of my life.*
> — Psalm 54:4 (HCSB)

OPHRAH, OFRA   [oh-FRAH]

MEANING: fawn, young deer, young hind •
USAGE: Jewish
> *Who is God, save the Lord?…*
> *Who maketh my feet like hinds',*
> *and setteth me upon my high places.*
> — Psalm 18:32–34 (MT)

OPRAH   [OH-prah]

MEANING: the back, the neck • USAGE: American
form of Orpah, from Hebrew *orap*
> *You will find as you look back upon your life*
> *that the moments that stand out, the moments*
> *when you have really lived, are the moments*
> *when you have done things in a spirit of love.*
> — Henry Drummond,
> *The Greatest Thing in the World*

ORAH   [OH-rah]

MEANING: light, brightness • USAGE: Jewish
> *The light of the righteous is radiant.*
> — Proverbs 13:9a (JPS)

ORALIE, ORALEE [or-ah-LEE]

MEANING: gold, golden • USAGE: English form of Aurélie, from Latin *aurum*

> *Love is the only gold.*
> — Alfred Tennyson, *Becket*

ORENDA [oh-rehn-dah]

MEANING: magical power, magical strength • USAGE: Amerind: Iroquois

> *I am becoming stronger, stronger. /*
> *Mighty medicine is now within me, /*
> *You cannot now subdue me — /*
> *I am becoming stronger, /*
> *I am stronger, stronger, stronger.*
> — Iroquois chant

ORIANA [oh-ree-AH-nah]

MEANING: gold, golden • USAGE: Italian: from Latin *oroana*

> *A gold key opens every door.*
> — Italian proverb

ORIANE, ORIANNE [oh-ree-AHN]

MEANING: gold, golden one • USAGE: French (*see* Oriana)

> *The right word at the right time*
> *is like precious gold set in silver.*
> — Proverbs 25:11 (CEV)

ORMA [ohr-mah]

MEANING: free people • USAGE: African: Oromo of Kenya

> *Peace is costly, but it is worth the expense.*
> — Kenyan proverb

ORPAH [OHR-pah]

MEANING: the back, the neck • USAGE: Jewish: from Hebrew *orap*

> *Keep sound wisdom and discretion;*
> *so shall they be life unto thy soul,*
> *and grace to thy neck.*
> — Proverbs 3:22 (MT)

OSHRA [ohsh-RAH]

MEANING: happiness, good fortune • USAGE: Jewish

> *I must find my happiness within my inner self.*
> — Abraham Isaac Kook

OTTAVIA [oh-TAH-vee-ah]

MEANING: eight, eighth • USAGE: Italian feminine form of Octavio, from Latin *octavus*

> *Teach us to number our days,*
> *that we may get a heart of wisdom.*
> — Psalm 90:12 (ESV)

OURANIA [yoo-rah-NEE-ah]

MEANING: heavenly, celestial • USAGE: Greek: from Greek *ouranios*, Greek muse of astronomy and astrology

> *Whatsoever that be within us that feels,*
> *thinks, desires, and animates,*
> *is something celestial and divine,*
> *and consequently, it is imperishable.*
> — Aristotle

OWENA [oh-WEN-ah]

MEANING: youthful, young, wellborn, noble • USAGE: English feminine form of Owen, from Welsh *eoghunn* (youth); or from Greek *eu* (good, well) and *genes* (born)

> *The young do not know enough to be prudent,*
> *and therefore they attempt the impossible —*
> *and achieve it, generation after generation.*
> — Pearl S. Buck, *The Goddess Abides*

P

PACÍFICA [pah-SEE-fee-kah]

MEANING: peaceful, serene • USAGE: Spanish:
from Latin *pacificus*
> You cannot perceive beauty but with a serene mind.
> — Henry David Thoreau, *Autumn*

PAGET [PAJ-et]

MEANING: young attendant, young helper •
USAGE: English (*see* Paige)
> Well done, good and faithful servant:
> thou hast been faithful over a few things,
> I will set thee over many things.
> — Matthew 25:21b (ASV)

PAHA [pah-hah]

MEANING: hill, mount • USAGE: Amerind: Sioux
> When we want wisdom
> we go up on the hill to talk to God.
> — Noble Red Man

PAIGE [payj]

MEANING: young attendant, young helper •
USAGE: English surname: from English *page*
> To find joy in work is to discover
> the fountain of youth.
> — Pearl S. Buck

PAISLEY [PAYZ-lee]

MEANING: church, basilica, cathedral, patterned
fabric • USAGE: English: Scottish town name, from
Latin *passeleg* (basilica, church); paisley fabric,
which originated in the town
> For sure, You will give me goodness and
> loving-kindness all the days of my life.
> Then I will live with You in Your house forever.
> — Psalm 23:6 (NLV)

PALOMA [pah-LOH-mah]

MEANING: dove, dove-like • USAGE: Spanish:
from Spanish *paloma*
> How beautiful you are, my darling!
> Oh, how beautiful! Your eyes are doves.
> — Song of Songs 1:15a (RSV)

PAM [pam]

MEANING: all honey, sweet • USAGE: English
form of Pamela (*see* Pamela)
> Kind words are like honey —
> sweet to the taste and good for your health.
> — Proverbs 16:24 (GNT)

PAMELA [PAM-eh-lah]

MEANING: all honey, sweet • USAGE: English:
from Greek *pan* (all) and *meli* (honey); from
Arcadia by Sir Philip Sidney
> The sweet of nature is love.
> — Ralph Waldo Emerson, "Circles"

PANIK [pah-neek]

MEANING: daughter • USAGE: Amerind: Eskimo
(Arctic Nation)
> May you have warmth in your igloo,
> oil in your lamp, and peace in your heart.
> — Eskimo proverb

PANNA [pah-nah]

MEANING: emerald, precious jewel • USAGE:
Amerind: Eskimo (Arctic Nation)
> Keep the perfect jewel of the Lord
> enshrined in your heart.
> — *Sri Guru Granth Sahib*
> (Khalsa Consensus Translation)

PANSY, PANSIE [PAN-see]

MEANING: pansy flower, thoughtful • USAGE:
English: flower name, from French *pensee* (thought)

Thoughtfulness doth watch over thee,
Understanding doth keep thee.
— Proverbs 2:11 (YLT)

PAOLA [POW-lah]

MEANING: small, little • **USAGE:** Italian and
Spanish feminine form of Paolo, from Latin *paulus*
Anyone who can be trusted in little matters
can also be trusted in important matters.
— Luke 16:10a (CEV)

PAOLINA [pow-LEE-nah]

MEANING: small, little • **USAGE:** Italian form of
Paola, from Latin *paulus*
A little spark will kindle a great flame.
— Dante Alighieri, *The Divine Comedy*
(tr. Frederick Pollock)

PAQUITA [pah-KEE-tah]

MEANING: one who is free, native of France, a
Franc, spear, spear maiden • **USAGE:** Spanish form
of Francisca, from Latin *Franciscus* (a Frenchman);
from French *franc* (free, freeman); or from German
franco (spear used by Franks, a Germanic tribe)
You will know the truth,
and the truth will set you free.
— John 8:32 (NLT)

PARIS, PARRIS [PAYR-is]

MEANING: city of Paris, chance, wager • **USAGE:**
American: French city, derived from the *Gallic*
Parissi tribe, from Greek *pari* (wager, chance); in
Greek myth, Paris was abandoned and found by a
shepherd who "took a chance" to save and raise him
You are the light of the world — like a city
on a hilltop that cannot be hidden....
Let your good deeds shine out for all to see.
— Matthew 5:14–16a (NLT)

PARVANI [pahr-vah-nee]

MEANING: full moon, festival, celebration •
USAGE: Hindu
The being who is in the moon and at the same time
in the mind...meditate upon as Brahman.
— *Brihadaranyaka Upanishad*

PASCUALA [pahs-KWAH-lah]

MEANING: Passover, born during Passover •
USAGE: Spanish feminine form of Pascual, from
Hebrew Pesach (Feast of Unleavened Bread)
You shall also observe the Feast of Unleavened Bread,
for on this very day I brought your hosts out of the land
of Egypt; therefore you shall observe this day
throughout your generations as a permanent ordinance.
— Exodus 12:17 (NASB)

PASTORA [pahs-TOR-ah]

MEANING: shepherdess, guide • **USAGE:** Spanish:
from Latin *pastorem*
Your rod and your shepherd's staff comfort me.
— Psalm 23:4b (NCV)

PAT [pat]

MEANING: patrician, noble one • **USAGE:** English
form of Patricia (*see* Patricia)
Many women do noble things,
but you surpass them all.
— Proverbs 31:29 (NIV)

PATIENCE [PAY-shens]

MEANING: patient, enduring, tolerant, forbearing •
USAGE: English: from Latin *pati* (to suffer)
To grow in self-control, in patience,
in equanimity, is to grow in strength and power.
— James Allen, *From Poverty to Power*

PATRICE   *[pah-TREES]*

MEANING: patrician, noble one • USAGE: French
form of Patricia (*see* Patricia)
> *True nobility is invulnerable.*
> — French proverb

PATRICIA   *[pah-TRISH-ah (English),*
pah-TREE-see-ah (German, Scandinavian),
pah-TREE-syah (Spanish)]

MEANING: patrician, noble one • USAGE: English,
German, Scandinavian, and Spanish feminine
form of Patrick, from Latin *patricius* (patrician,
nobleman)
> *You are a woman of noble character.*
> — Ruth 3:11b (HCSB)

PATRINA   *[pah-TREE-nah]*

MEANING: patrician, noble one • USAGE:
American form of Patricia (*see* Patricia)
> *To be good is noble; but to show others*
> *how to be good is nobler and no trouble.*
> — Mark Twain, *Following the Equator*

PATRIZIA   *[pah-TREET-ʒee-ah]*

MEANING: patrician, noble one • USAGE: Italian
form of Patricia (*see* Patricia)
> *Virtue is the only and true nobility.*
> — Juvenal

PATSY, PATSIE   *[PAT-see]*

MEANING: patrician, noble one • USAGE: English
form of Patricia (*see* Patricia)
> *To give happiness is a far nobler goal than to attain it.*
> — Lewis Carroll

PATTY, PATTI, PATTIE   *[PAT-ee]*

MEANING: patrician, noble one • USAGE: English
form of Patricia (*see* Patricia)
> *You are a worthy woman.*
> — Ruth 3:11b (NEB)

PAULA   *[PAHL-ah (English),*
POH-lah (German, Scandinavian)]

MEANING: small, little • USAGE: English,
German, and Scandinavian feminine form of Paul,
from Latin *paulus*
> *To do something, however small, to make others*
> *happier and better, is the highest ambition, the most*
> *elevating hope, which can inspire a human being.*
> — Sir John Lubbock

PAULEEN, PAULENE   *[pah-LEEN]*

MEANING: small, little • USAGE: English feminine
form of Paul (*see* Paula)
> *Lord, make us mindful of the little things*
> *that grow and blossom in these days*
> *to make the world beautiful for us.*
> — W. E. B. DuBois

PAULETTA   *[pah-LET-ah]*

MEANING: small, little • USAGE: English form of
Paula (*see* Paula)
> *Small is the number that see with their own eyes*
> *and feel with their own heart.*
> — Albert Einstein

PAULETTE   *[pah-LET (English),*
poh-LET (French)]

MEANING: small, little • USAGE: French and
English feminine form of Paul (*see* Paula)
> *Remember there's no such thing*
> *as a small act of kindness. Every act creates a ripple.*
> — Scott Adams

PAULINA   *[pah-LEEN-ah (English),*
poh-LEEN (French), poh-LEEN-ah (Spanish)]

MEANING: small, little • USAGE: English, French,
and Spanish form of Paula (*see* Paula)
> *Remember that the smallest seed of faith is of more*
> *worth than the largest fruit of happiness.*
> — Henry David Thoreau
> (letter of January 25, 1843)

PAULINE [pah-LEEN]

MEANING: small, little • **USAGE:** English feminine form of Paul (*see* Paula)

> *The one who is faithful in a very little*
> *is also faithful in much.*
> — Luke 16:10 (NEB)

PAVANA [pah-vah-nah]

MEANING: wind, of the wind • **USAGE:** Hindu

> *The being who is in the wind and who at the same time*
> *is the breath within…meditate upon as Brahman.*
> — *Brihadaranyaka Upanishad*
> (tr. Swami Prabhavananda)

PAVLA [PAHV-lah]

MEANING: small, little • **USAGE:** Czech feminine form of Paul (*see* Paula)

> *Each small task of everyday life*
> *is part of the total harmony of the universe.*
> — Thérèse of Lisieux

PAYTON, PEYTON [PAY-ton]

MEANING: patrician, noble one, from Paega's town • **USAGE:** English and Irish surname: Irish form of Patricia, from Latin *patricius* (patrician, nobleman); or English surname meaning "Pæga's town"

> *Lovely sweetness is the noblest power of woman,*
> *and is far fitter to prevail by parley than by battle.*
> — Philip Sidney

PAZ [pahz]

MEANING: peace, peaceful • **USAGE:** Spanish: from Latin *pax* (peace); Roman Catholic reference to "Our Lady of Peace," the Virgin Mary

> *Blessed are the peacemakers,*
> *for they shall be called children of God.*
> — Matthew 5:9 (KJV)

PEARL [perl]

MEANING: pearl, beautiful gem • **USAGE:** English: from English *perle*

> *The kingdom of heaven is like what happens*
> *when a shop owner is looking for fine pearls.*
> *After finding a very valuable one, the owner goes*
> *and sells everything in order to buy that pearl.*
> — Matthew 13:45–46 (CEV)

PEG, PEGGY, PEGGIE [peg]

MEANING: pearl, beautiful gem • **USAGE:** English form of Margaret (*see* Margaret)

> *Contentment is a pearl of great price.*
> — John Balguy

PEIGI [PEG-ee]

MEANING: pearl, beautiful gem • **USAGE:** Scottish form of Margaret (*see* Peggy)

> *Thou art all fair, my love;*
> *and there is no spot in thee.*
> — Song of Songs 4:7 (DT)

PELE [PEH-leh]

MEANING: goddess of fire and volcanoes • **USAGE:** Hawaiian: Hawaiians did not use this name unless it was revealed in a dream

> *The earth's fire, a wave's caress,*
> *the never-ceasing kiss of the wind —*
> *of these things is my island born.*
> — Hawaiian proverb

PEMA [pem-ah]

MEANING: lotus • **USAGE:** Hindu: Sanskrit

> *The Self is hidden in the lotus of the heart.*
> *Those who see themselves in all creatures go day by day*
> *into the world of the Brahman hidden in the heart.*
> — *Chandogya Upanishad* (tr. Eknath Easwaran)

PENELOPE   [peh-NEL-oh-pee (English), pee-neh-loh-PEE (Greek)]

MEANING: weaver, bobbin, duck • **USAGE:** English and Greek: from Greek *pene* (thread on a bobbin, weaver) or *penelops* (type of duck)

Weave in faith and God will find the thread.
— English proverb

PENNIE, PENNY   [PEN-ee]

MEANING: weaver, bobbin, duck • **USAGE:** English form of Penelope (*see* Penelope)

Strength and dignity are her clothing.
— Proverbs 31:25a (ESV)

PEPITA   [pay-PEE-tah]

MEANING: God will add, God will increase • **USAGE:** Spanish feminine form of Pepito, from Hebrew *ya'saph* (Yahweh will add)

May the Lord cause you to increase and overflow with love for one another and for everyone.
— 1 Thessalonians 3:12a (HCSB)

PEPPER   [PEP-er]

MEANING: spice, spicy, to make lively • **USAGE:** American: from English *peper* (to make lively) and Hindu Sanskirt *pippali* (berry)

Exuberance is beauty.
— William Blake, *The Marriage of Heaven and Hell*

PERLA   [PAYR-lah]

MEANING: pearl, beautiful gem • **USAGE:** Italian and Spanish form of Pearl, from English *perle*

How fair and how pleasant art thou.
— Song of Songs 7:6a (KJ21)

PERPETUA   [per-PAY-twah (Spanish), per-PET-choo-ah (English)]

MEANING: lasting, perpetual, continuous, infinite • **USAGE:** Spanish and English: from Latin *pepetuus*

The windows of the soul are infinite…and it is through the eyes of the soul that paradise is visioned.
— Henry Miller,
Big Sur and the Oranges of Hieronymus Bosch

PERRINE   [peh-REEN]

MEANING: rock, stone • **USAGE:** French feminine form of Pierre, from Greek *petros*

For you shall be in agreement with the stones of the field.
— Job 5:23a (NLV)

PETA   [PET-ah]

MEANING: rock, stone • **USAGE:** English form of Petra, from Greek *petros*

Every charitable act is a stepping stone toward heaven.
— Henry Ward Beecher

PETAH   [peh-tah]

MEANING: golden eagle • **USAGE:** Amerind: Blackfeet

There are many paths to a meaningful sense of the natural world.
— Blackfeet proverb

PETAL   [PET-al]

MEANING: petal, floral leaf • **USAGE:** English: from Greek *petalos* (outspread, broad, flat)

Look at how the wild flowers grow: they don't work or make clothes for themselves. But I tell you that not even King Solomon with all his wealth had clothes as beautiful as one of these flowers.
— Luke 12:27 (GNT)

PETRA   [PET-rah]

MEANING: rock, stone • **USAGE:** Greek, German, Czech, Scandinavian, and English feminine form of Petros, from Greek *petros*; ancient Jordan city

Look to the rock from which you were cut, and to the quarry from which you were dug.
— Isaiah 51:1b (HCSB)

PETRINA [peh-TREE-nah]

MEANING: rock, stone • **USAGE:** Greek feminine form of Petros (*see* Petra)

> *The Lord...set my feet upon a rock,*
> *making my steps secure.*
> — Psalm 40:1–2 (NIRV)

PETRINE [peh-TREE-neh]

MEANING: rock, stone • **USAGE:** Norwegian, Danish, and Swedish feminine form of Peter (*see* Petra)

> *We should build with the stones we have.*
> — Swedish proverb

PETRONA [pay-TROH-nah]

MEANING: rock, stone • **USAGE:** Spanish and Greek feminine form of Peter (*see* Petra)

> *Our Lord and our God, you are my mighty rock, my*
> *fortress, my protector. You are the rock where I am safe.*
> — 2 Samuel 22:2–3a (CEV)

PETULA [peh-TOO-lah]

MEANING: bold, daring, asking, inviting, petunia and tulip • **USAGE:** English: from Latin *petulans* (bold) or *petulare* (to ask); or English combination of *petunia* and *tulip*

> *How does the meadow flower its bloom unfold? /*
> *Because the lovely little flower is free /*
> *Down to its root, and in that freedom, bold.*
> — William Wordsworth, "A Poet"

PHILIPPA [FIL-ih-pah (English), fee-LEE-pah (French, Greek)]

MEANING: lover of horses • **USAGE:** English, French, and Greek feminine form of Philip, from Greek *philein* (to love) and *hippos* (horse)

> *Love is the wind, the tide, the waves, the sunshine.*
> *Its power is incalculable; it is many horse-power.*
> — Henry David Thoreau,
> "A Paradise (To Be) Regained"

PHILLIS [FIL-is]

MEANING: leaf, foliage, green plant • **USAGE:** English and Polish form of Phyllis (*see* Phyllis)

> *Plants are the young of the world,*
> *vessels of health and vigor.*
> — Ralph Waldo Emerson, "Nature"

PHILOMELA [FEE-loh-MEE-lah]

MEANING: lover of song • **USAGE:** Greek: from Greek *philein* (to love) and *melos* (song)

> *Be joyful, you who do what is right!*
> *Sing, all of you whose hearts are honest!*
> — Psalm 32:11b (NIRV)

PHILOMENA [fil-oh-MEE-nah]

MEANING: strong friend • **USAGE:** English and Greek: from Greek *philos* (friend) and *menos* (strength)

> *Let wisdom be your sister*
> *and make common sense your closest friend.*
> — Proverbs 7:4 (CEV)

PHOEBE [FEE-bee]

MEANING: bright, shining, moon goddess • **USAGE:** Greek and English: from Greek *phoibos* (bright, shining); Greek moon goddess

> *She moves a goddess,*
> *and she looks a queen.*
> — Homer, *The Iliad* (tr. Alexander Pope)

PHYLLIS [FEEL-is (Greek), FIL-is (English)]

MEANING: leaf, foliage, green plant • **USAGE:** Greek and English: from Greek *phyllon*

> *A good person will be healthy*
> *like a green leaf.*
> — Proverbs 11:28b (NCV)

P

PIA   *[PEE-ah]*

MEANING: pious, devout, Mt. Olympus, mountain of the gods • USAGE: Greek, Italian, German, and Scandinavian: from Latin *pius* (pious, devout); or Italian form of Olimpia, from Greek *Olympos*, Greek home of the gods

> *You are the light of the world.*
> *You cannot hide a city that is on a mountain.*
> — Matthew 5:14 (NLV)

PIALA   *[pee-AH-lah]*

MEANING: prudent, wise, discreet, good judgment • USAGE: Welsh: from Welsh *pwyll*

> *Sound judgment and good sense*
> *will watch over you.*
> — Proverbs 2:11 (CEV)

PIEDAD   *[pee-ah-DAHD]*

MEANING: merciful, compassionate, kind • USAGE: Spanish: from Spanish *piedad*

> *Clothe yourselves with a heart of mercy,*
> *kindness, humility, gentleness, and patience.*
> — Colossians 3:12b (NEB)

PILAR   *[pee-LAHR]*

MEANING: pillar, column, support • USAGE: Spanish: from Spanish *pilar* (pillar, column); reference to miraculous appearance of Virgin Mary over a pillar in Santiago

> *As golden pillars upon bases of silver,*
> *so are the firm feet upon the soles of a steady woman.*
> — Sirach 26:23 (DR Apocrypha)

PILI   *[PEE-lee]*

MEANING: pillar, column, support • USAGE: Spanish form of Pilar (see Pilar)

> *The God will help; the Lord will support me.*
> — Psalm 54:4 (NCV)

PING   *[peeng]*

MEANING: peaceful, smooth • USAGE: Chinese

> *Peace and joy are more precious than yellow gold.*
> — Chinese proverb (tr. William Scarborough)

PIPER   *[PIE-per]*

MEANING: flute player, pipe player • USAGE: American: from English *pipe* (pipe, flute) or *pipere* (pipe player)

> *There is beauty of a concert, as well as of a flute.*
> — Ralph Waldo Emerson, *Representative Men*

PIPPA   *[PIP-ah]*

MEANING: lover of horses • USAGE: English form of Philippa (see Philippa)

> *Sit loosely in the saddle of life.*
> — Robert Louis Stevenson

PIPPI   *[PIP-ee]*

MEANING: lover of horses • USAGE: English form of Philippa (see Philippa)

> *One's feelings are the source of one's energy;*
> *they provide the horsepower...that makes it possible*
> *for us to accomplish the tasks of living.... Since they*
> *work for us, we should treat them with respect.*
> — M. Scott Peck, *The Road Less Traveled*

PIROSKA   *[pee-ROHSH-kah]*

MEANING: ancient, old, long-lived • USAGE: Hungarian form of Priscilla, from Latin *priscus*

> *With the ancient is wisdom;*
> *and in length of days understanding.*
> — Job 12:12 (KJV)

PLACIDA, PLÁCIDA   *[PLAH-cee-dah]*

MEANING: calm, serene, tranquil, peaceful • USAGE: Italian and Spanish feminine form of Placido, from *placidus*

> *The God of peace will be with you.*
> — Philippians 4:9b (NIV)

POLINA   *[poh-LEE-nah]*

MEANING: small, little • **USAGE:** Russian feminine form of Paul, from Latin *paulus*

If you are faithful in little things,
you will be faithful in large ones.
— Luke 16:10a (NLT)

POLLY, POLLIE   *[PAHL-ee]*

MEANING: beloved, love, sea mistress, bitter sea, rebellious, well-nourished, healthy, myrrh • **USAGE:** Irish and English form of Molly: from Egyptian *mry, mr* (beloved, love); or from Hebrew *mari yam* (sea mistress), *merum yam* (bitter sea), *marah* (rebellious), *mara* (well-nourished, healthy), or *mor* (myrrh)

Beloved, let us love one another,
for love is of God; and everyone who loves
has been born of God, and knows God.
— 1 John 4:7 (WEB)

POLLYANNA   *[pahl-ee-AN-ah]*

MEANING: beloved and gracious • **USAGE:** English combination of Polly and Anna (*see* Polly and Anna)

Grace in women...is an outward and visible sign
of an inward harmony of soul.
— William Hazlitt, "On the Conduct of Life"

PONIA   *[poh-NEE-ah]*

MEANING: consecrated, blessed, anointed • **USAGE:** Hawaiian

We bless the earth...and are blessed by it.
— Hawaiian proverb

POPPY   *[POP-ee]*

MEANING: poppy flower, reddish-orange color • **USAGE:** English: from English *popi*

Earth laughs in flowers.
— Ralph Waldo Emerson, "Hamatreya"

PORTIA   *[POR-shah]*

MEANING: pig, hog • **USAGE:** English form of Roman family name *Porcius*, from Latin *porcus*

Every single creature is full of God
and is a book about God.
Every creature is a word of God.
— Meister Eckhart (tr. Matthew Fox
in *Meditations with Meister Eckhart*)

PRAIRIE   *[PRAYR-ee]*

MEANING: grassland, flat treeless plain • **USAGE:** English: from French *praierie* and Latin *prata* (meadow)

The grass lands are covered with birds....
They call out for joy and sing.
— Psalm 65:13 (NLV)

PRASANNA   *[prah-sah-nah]*

MEANING: pure, serene, gracious • **USAGE:** Hindu: Sanskrit

Control the senses and purify the mind.
In a pure mind there is constant awareness of the Self.
Where there is constant awareness of the Self,
freedom ends bondage and joy ends sorrow.
— *Chandogya Upanishad*

PREMA   *[preh-mah]*

MEANING: love, affection • **USAGE:** Hindu: from Sanskrit *prema*

We find in perfect love the freedom of our self.
— Rabindranath Tagore, *Sadhana*

PRIMAVERA   *[pree-mah-VAYR-ah]*

MEANING: spring, springtime • **USAGE:** Spanish and Italian: from Latin *primavera*

Oh, visit the earth, ask her to join the dance!
Deck her out in spring showers.
— Psalm 65:9 (MSG)

P

PRISCILA   [prih-SEE-lah]

MEANING: ancient, old, enduring • **USAGE:**
Spanish and Portuguese form of Priscilla, from
Latin *priscus*

> *The Lord hath appeared of old unto me, saying,*
> *Yea, I have loved thee with an everlasting love:*
> *therefore with lovingkindness have I drawn thee.*
> — Jeremiah 31:3 (KJV)

PRISCILLA   [prih-SIL-ah]

MEANING: ancient, old, enduring • **USAGE:**
English: from Latin *priscus*

> *I look forward to growing old*
> *and wise and audacious.*
> — Glenda Jackson

PRITA   [PREE-tah]

MEANING: delight, joy • **USAGE:** Hindu: Sanskrit

> *Love is the ultimate meaning of everything around us.*
> *It is not a mere sentiment; it is truth;*
> *it is the joy that is at the root of all creation.*
> — Rabindranath Tagore, *Sadhana*

PRUDENCE   [PROO-dens]

MEANING: prudent, cautious, good judgment
• **USAGE:** English form of Roman family name
Prudentia, from Latin *prudens* (prudence)

> *Truth, frankness, courage, love, humility,*
> *and all the virtues, range themselves*
> *on the side of prudence.*
> — Ralph Waldo Emerson, "Prudence"

PRUNELLA   [proo-NEL-ah]

MEANING: little plum • **USAGE:** English: from
Latin *pruna* (plum) and diminutive *-ella*

> *The fruit of the Spirit is love, joy, peace, patience,*
> *kindness, goodness, faith, gentleness, self-control.*
> — Galatians 5:22–23a (HCSB)

Q

QIAN   [chee-ahn]

MEANING: beautiful, lovely • **USAGE:** Chinese

> *If there is sincerity in the heart,*
> *there will be beauty in the character.*
> — Confucius, *The Analects*

QING   [chee-ing]

MEANING: green-blue color • **USAGE:** Chinese

> *Green comes from blue, but it surpasses blue.*
> — Chinese proverb

QIONG   [chee-ong]

MEANING: red jade • **USAGE:** Chinese

> *One can put a price on gold, but jade is priceless.*
> — Chinese proverb

QIU   [chew]

MEANING: autumn • **USAGE:** Chinese

> *When Autumn comes the hills are covered with beauty.*
> — Chinese proverb (tr. William Scarborough)

QUANDA   [KWAHN-dah]

MEANING: queen, royal one • **USAGE:** English:
from English *cwen* (queen)

> *Love is the magician, the enchanter,*
> *that changes worthless things to joy, and makes right*
> *royals kings and queens of common clay.*
> — Robert Ingersoll, "Orthodoxy"

QUELA   [KAY-lah]

MEANING: ewe, sheep • **USAGE:** Spanish form of
Raquel, from Aramaic *rahla*

> *The Lord God said:*
> *I will look for my sheep and take care of them myself.*
> — Ezekiel 34:11a (CEV)

QUENBY [KWEN-bee]

MEANING: queen's town • **USAGE:** English surname: from English *cwen* (queen) and *by* (town, village)

The kingdom of God is in the midst of you.
— Luke 17:21b (ESV)

QUENNA [KWEN-ah]

MEANING: queen, royal one • **USAGE:** English: from English *cwen* (queen)

I'd like to be a queen of people's hearts.
— Diana Francis, Princess of Wales

QUIANA [kee-AHN-ah]

MEANING: divine, the shining one • **USAGE:** American form of Kiana, from Latin *divus*

It is the divinity within that makes the divinity without.
— Washington Irving (letter of July 21, 1828)

QUILLA [KWIL-ah]

MEANING: quill, feather, pen • **USAGE:** English: from English *quil* (hollow stalk of a feather, writing pen)

The pen is mightier than the sword.
— Edward Bulwer-Lytton, *Richelieu*

QUINCE [kwins]

MEANING: quince fruit, five, fifth • **USAGE:** English: from French *cooin* (quince); or from Latin *quintus* (fifth, five)

The fruit of Spirit is in all goodness and righteousness and truth. — Ephesians 5:9 (KJ21)

QUINN [kwin]

MEANING: wise, intelligent • **USAGE:** Irish and English: form of Irish surname *O'Cuinn*, from Gaelic *conn*

Wisdom will come into your heart, and knowledge will be pleasant to your soul.
— Proverbs 2:10 (NRSV)

R

RABIAH, RAABIA [rah-bee-ah]

MEANING: springtime • **USAGE:** Muslim: from Arabic *rabi'ah*

In the spring God looks happiest it seems, / when it is clear a beautiful force is surely active / on earth.
— Hafiz, "Little Erect Things Feel Proud"
(tr. Daniel Ladinsky in *A Year with Hafiz*)

RACHEL [rah-KHEL (Jewish), RAY-chel (English), rah-SHEL (French)]

MEANING: ewe, sheep • **USAGE:** Jewish, English, and French: from Aramaic *rahla* (ewe)

The Lord is my shepherd; I shall not want.
— Psalm 23:1 (MT)

RACHELA [rah-kheh-LAH]

MEANING: ewe, sheep • **USAGE:** Jewish form of Rachel (*see* Rachel)

For He is our God, and we are the people He tends, the flock in His care.
— Psalm 95:7a (JPS)

RACHELE [rah-KEH-leh]

MEANING: ewe, sheep • **USAGE:** Italian form of Rachel (*see* Rachel)

He will feed His flock like a shepherd. He will gather the lambs in His arms and carry them close to His heart. He will be gentle in leading those that are with young.
— Isaiah 40:11 (NLV)

RACHELLE [rah-SHEL]

MEANING: ewe, sheep • **USAGE:** English form of Rachel (*see* Rachel)

The Lord my pasture shall prepare, / And feed me with a shepherd's care; / His presence shall my wants supply, / And guard me with a watchful eye.
— Joseph Addison, "Trust in God"

R

RAE   *[ray]*

MEANING: wise protector, guards wisely, guiding hand, ewe, sheep, doe • **USAGE:** English feminine form of Ray, from German *ragin* (advice, counsel); English form of Rachel, from Aramaic *rahla* (ewe); or from Scandinavian *rae* (doe, female deer)

Get wisdom; develop good judgment....Don't turn
your back on wisdom, for she will protect you.
Love her, and she will guard you.
— Proverbs 4:5–6 (NLT)

RAELEEN, RAYLENE   *[ray-LEEN]*

MEANING: wise protector, guards wisely, guiding hand, ewe, sheep, doe • **USAGE:** English feminine form of Ray, from German *ragin* (advice, counsel); English form of Rachel, from Aramaic *rahla* (ewe); or from Scandinavian *rae* (doe, female deer)

The Lord will always guide you.
— Isaiah 58:11a (CEV)

RAFAELA   *[rah-fah-AY-lah]*

MEANING: God has healed • **USAGE:** Spanish form of Raphael, from Hebrew *repha'el*

Trust in the Lord with all your heart....Then you will
have healing for your body and strength for your bones.
— Proverbs 3:5–8 (NLT)

RAFIAH, RAFIA   *[rah-fee-ah]*

MEANING: noble, high ranking • **USAGE:** Muslim

Doing good is true nobility.
— Arabic proverb

RAFIDA, RAFEEDA   *[rah-FEE-dah]*

MEANING: helper, assistant, stream • **USAGE:** Muslim feminine form of Rafid, from Arabic *rafid* (one who assists, stream)

The fountain stream of love rises in the love for an
individual, but spreads and falls down
in universal love.
— Hazrat Inayat Khan, *The Gayan* (cd. *The Gayani Meditations, Volume 1,* tr. Cecil Touchon)

RAFIKI   *[rah-FEE-kee]*

MEANING: trusted friend • **USAGE:** African: Swahili of Kenya and Tanzania

A friend is like a source of water
during a long voyage.
— East African proverb

RAGNA   *[RAHN-ah]*

MEANING: adviser, counselor, judge • **USAGE:** Scandinavian: from Norse *ragn*

Life will judge me by the measure of love
I myself am capable of.
— Dag Hammarskjöld

RAHEL   *[rah-HEHL]*

MEANING: ewe, sheep • **USAGE:** Jewish form of Rachel (*see* Rachel)

Like a shepherd He pastures His flock:
He gathers the lambs in His arms and carries them
in His bosom; gently He drives the mother sheep.
— Isaiah 40:11 (JPS)

RAHIMA, RAHIMAH   *[rah-HEE-mah]*

MEANING: compassionate, kind, merciful • **USAGE:** Muslim feminine form of Rahim

He will give you two portions of His mercy,
and make for you a light with which you will walk.
— Koran, The Iron 57.28b (SKR)

RAIDA   *[rah-ee-dah]*

MEANING: pioneer, explorer, guide • **USAGE:** Muslim: Arabic *raid*

If you seek to be a light to guide others, then,
like the sun, you must show the same face to all.
— Abu Sa'id

RAIN, RAINE   *[rayn]*

MEANING: rain, rainfall • **USAGE:** English: from English *regn*

R

Rain is grace; rain is the sky condescending to the
earth; without rain, there would be no life.
— John Updike, *Self-Consciousness*

RAISA   *[ray-EE-sah]*

MEANING: rose • **USAGE:** Yiddish and Russian
I would rather have roses on my table
than diamonds on my neck.
— Emma Goldman

RAIZEL   *[RAY-zǝl]*

MEANING: rose • **USAGE:** Yiddish
I am a rose of Sharon.
— Song of Songs 2:1a (MT)

RAJANI   *[rah-jah-nee]*

MEANING: night, dark • **USAGE:** Hindu: from
Sanskrit *rajani*
Night is like unto the sun,
the (starry) night is similar to day.
— *Atharva Veda*

RAJIA, RAJYA   *[rah-jah]*

MEANING: hope, wish, desire • **USAGE:** Muslim
feminine form of Rajih, from Arabic *raji*
Be a precious donor of peace and hope. /
Give love to all you meet.
— Jalaluddin Rumi, "A Voice that Calms"
(tr. Daniel Ladinsky in *The Purity of Desire*)

RAKEL   *[rah-KEL]*

MEANING: ewe, sheep • **USAGE:** German and
Scandinavian form of Rachel (*see* Rachel)
For this is what the Sovereign Lord says:
I Myself will search for My sheep and look after them.
As a shepherd looks after his scattered flock when he is
with them, so will I look after my sheep.
— Ezekiel 34:11–12a (NIV)

RAKHIMA   *[rahk-hee-mah]*

MEANING: soft, pleasant • **USAGE:** Muslim
The gown of happiness is soft and smooth.
— Arabic proverb

RAKINA, RAKEENA   *[rah-KEE-nah]*

MEANING: reliable, firm, faithful • **USAGE:**
Muslim feminine form of Rakin, Arabic *rakin* (to be
reliable, to be firm)
Allah loveth the steadfast.
— Koran, The Victory 3.146 (PIC)

RALPHINA   *[ral-FEEN-ah]*

MEANING: wise wolf, wolf counsel • **USAGE:**
English form of Ralph, from German *rad* (advice,
counsel) and *wulf* (wolf)
A wise person does the right thing at the right time.
There is a right time and a right way for everything.
— Ecclesiastes 8:5b–6a (NCV)

RAMANI   *[rah-mah-nee]*

MEANING: beautiful girl • **USAGE:** Hindu:
Sanskrit
How beautiful it would be if all of us,
young and old, men and women,
devoted ourselves wholly to truth
in all that we might do.
— Mahatma Gandhi

RAMIRA   *[rah-MEE-rah]*

MEANING: famous counselor, renowned adviser
• **USAGE:** Spanish feminine form of Ramiro, from
German *ragin* (advice) and *mari* (famous)
She openeth her mouth with wisdom;
and upon her tongue is the law of kindness.
— Proverbs 31:26 (DT)

R

RAMONA   [rah-MOH-nah]

MEANING: wise protector, guards wisely, guiding hand • USAGE: Spanish and English feminine form of Ramon, from German *ragin* (advice, counsel) and *mund* (hand, protection)

Her words are sensible,
and her advice is thoughtful.
— Proverbs 31:26 (CEV)

RAMYA   [RAHM-yah]

MEANING: delightful, beautiful • USAGE: Hindu: from Sanskrit *rama*

The moment you have in your heart this
extraordinary thing called love and feel the depth,
the delight, the ecstasy of it, you will discover
that for you the world is transformed.
— Jiddu Krishnamurti

RANDA   [RAHN-dah]

MEANING: admirable, wonderful • USAGE: English form of Miranda, from Latin *mirandus*

All the wonders you seek are within yourself.
— Thomas Browne

RANDA   [RAHN-dah]

MEANING: fragrant desert tree • USAGE: Muslim: from Arabic *randa*

Love is a tree with branches reaching into eternity/
and roots set deep in eternity.
— Jalaluddin Rumi, "One Swaying Being"
(tr. Coleman Barks in *The Book of Love*)

RANDI, RANDIE   [RAN-dee]

MEANING: admirable, wonderful • USAGE: English form of Miranda, from Latin *mirandus*

We live by admiration, hope and love.
— William Wordsworth, "The Excursion"

RANI   [RAH-nee]

MEANING: she is singing • USAGE: Jewish

Ye shall have a song…and gladness of heart.
— Isaiah 30:29a (MT)

RANIA   [RAHN-yah]

MEANING: song of God, psalm • USAGE: Jewish

My glory may sing praise to Thee, and not be silent.
— Psalm 30:13a (MT)

RANIM, RANEEM   [rah-NEEM]

MEANING: song, melody • USAGE: Muslim

When a soul is attuned to God,
its every action becomes music.
— Hazrat Inayat Khan, *The Gayan* (cd. *The Gayani Meditations, Volume 1*, tr. Cecil Touchon)

RANITA   [rah-NEE-tah]

MEANING: she is singing • USAGE: Jewish

For you, there shall be singing.
— Isaiah 30:29a (JPS)

RANIYAH, RANIYA   [RAHN-ee-ah]

MEANING: gazing, seeing • USAGE: Muslim: from Arabic *rana* (to gaze at)

Borrow the Beloved's eyes. Look through them
and you'll see the Beloved's face everywhere.
— Jalaluddin Rumi, "Checkmate"
(tr. Coleman Barks in *The Essential Rumi*)

RAPHAELA   [rah-fah-EH-lah]

MEANING: God has healed • USAGE: German feminine form of Raphael, from Hebrew *repha'el*

Trust in the Lord with all your heart; do not depend
on your own understanding.… This will be healing for
your body and strengthening for your bones.
— Proverbs 3:5–8 (HCSB)

R

RAQUEL [rah-KEL]

Meaning: ewe, sheep • **Usage:** Spanish and English form of Rachel, from Aramaic *rahla* (ewe)

The Lord is my shepherd, I shall not want.
He makes me lie down in green pastures;
he leads me beside still waters.
— Psalm 23:1–2 (NRSV)

RASHIDAH [rah-SHEE-dah]

Meaning: rightly guided • **Usage:** Muslim feminine form of Rashid, from Arabic *rashada* (to follow the right course)

Peace to all who follow guidance!
— Koran, Ta Ha 20:47b (ALI)

RASINA, RASEENA [rah-SEE-nah]

Meaning: calm, peaceful • **Usage:** Muslim feminine form of Rasin

Verily, the heart that receiveth
the divine Peace
is blessed.
— Hazrat Inayat Khan, *The Gayan*

RAUSHANA [rah-SHAH-nah]

Meaning: dawn, sunrise • **Usage:** Muslim

A light came and kindled a flame
in the depth of my soul.
— Jalaluddin Rumi
(tr. Shahram Shiva in *Rumi: Thief of Sleep*)

RAVEN [RAY-ven]

Meaning: raven, crow, shiny black color • **Usage:** English: from English *hræfn*

Look at the ravens, free and unfettered,
not tied down to a job description, carefree
in the care of God. You count far more.
— Luke 12:24 (MT)

RAVENNA [rah-VEN-ah]

Meaning: raven, crow, shiny black color • **Usage:** American: from English *hræfn*

Ask the birds of the sky, and they will tell you.
— Job 12:7b (NLT)

RAYA [rah-yah]

Meaning: beautiful, exuberant • **Usage:** Muslim: from Arabic *rayyan*

It is the exaltation of the spirit
which is productive of all beauty.
— Hazrat Inayat Khan, *The Gayan* (ed. *The Gayani Meditations, Volume 1*, tr. Cecil Touchon)

RAZ [rahz]

Meaning: secret, mystery • **Usage:** Jewish: from Hebrew *raz*

The most beautiful experience we can have
is the mysterious. It is the fundamental emotion
which stands at the cradle of true art and science.
— Albert Einstein, "The World as I See It"

RAZIELA [rah-zee-EL-ah]

Meaning: secret, mystery • **Usage:** Jewish: from Hebrew *raz*

Call to Me, and I will answer you,
and I will tell you wondrous things,
secrets you have not known.
— Jeremiah 33:3 (JPS)

RAZINA, RAZEENA [rah-ZEE-nah]

Meaning: calm, peaceful • **Usage:** Muslim

The peace, it is there; it grows from her soil. /
A few feet beneath her surface, all is always /
perfectly calm.
— Hafiz, "Until They Become a Sky Again"
(tr. Daniel Ladinsky in *A Year with Hafiz*)

R

RAZIYAH, RAAZIA   *[rah-ʒee-ah]*

MEANING: satisfied, content • **USAGE:** Muslim feminine form of Razi, from Arabic *razi*
> *Contentment is an inexhaustible treasure.*
> — Arabic proverb

REAGAN, REGAN   *[RAY-gun]*

MEANING: king's child, little royal one, spontaneous, impulsive • **USAGE:** Irish and English form of Irish surname *O'Riagain,* from Gaelic *ri* (king) and diminutive *-an;* or from Gaelic *riogach* (impulsive, rash)
> *Thou shalt also be a crown of glory*
> *in the hand of the Lord.*
> — Isaiah 62:3a (KJ21)

REBA   *[REE-bah]*

MEANING: connection, tie, join, noose • **USAGE:** English form of Rebecca (*see* Rebekah)
> *For, when with beauty we can virtue join, /*
> *We paint the semblance of a form divine.*
> — Matthew Prior

REBECA   *[reh-BAY-kah]*

MEANING: connection, tie, join, noose • **USAGE:** Spanish form of Rebecca (*see* Rebekah)
> *Everything in the universe is related;*
> *we are all connected.*
> — Rudolfo Anaya, *The Essays*

REBECCA   *[rah-BEK-ah (English), ray-BAY-kah (Italian)]*

MEANING: connection, tie, join, noose • **USAGE:** English and Italian form of Rebekah (*see* Rebekah)
> *Faithful love and truth will join together;*
> *righteousness and peace will embrace.*
> — Psalm 85:10 (HCSB)

REBECKA   *[rah-BEH-kah]*

MEANING: connection, tie, join, noose • **USAGE:** Swedish, Norwegian, and Danish form of Rebecca (*see* Rebekah)
> *What God has joined together,*
> *let no one separate.*
> — Matthew 19:6b (NEB)

REBEKAH   *[reh-BEK-ah]*

MEANING: connection, tie, join, noose • **USAGE:** Jewish: from Hebrew *ribhqah* (connection), *rivka* (noose), and Hebrew root *r-b-q* (to tie, to join)
> *Let not kindness and truth forsake thee;*
> *bind them about thy neck, write them upon the table*
> *of thy heart, so shalt thou find grace*
> *and good favour in the sight of God and man.*
> — Proverbs 3:3–4 (MT)

REBEKKA   *[reh-BEH-kah]*

MEANING: connection, tie, join, noose • **USAGE:** German and Dutch form of Rivka (*see* Rebekah)
> *It is sweet to feel by what fine-spun threads*
> *our affections are drawn together.*
> — Laurence Sterne, *A Sentimental Journey*

REESE   *[rees]*

MEANING: enthusiastic, passionate, ardent • **USAGE:** English surname: from Welsh *rhys*
> *All are speeding on with love's enthusiasm,*
> *singing with the stars the eternal song of creation.*
> — John Muir, "My First Summer in the Sierra"

REFAELA   *[reh-fah-EH-lah]*

MEANING: God has healed • **USAGE:** Jewish feminine form of Refael, from Hebrew *repha'el*
> *Heal me, O Lord, and I shall be healed; save me,*
> *and I shall be saved; for Thou art my praise.*
> — Jeremiah 17:14 (JPS)

R

REGINA [reh-JEE-nah (English, Italian, Russian), reh-GEE-nah (Polish, German)]

MEANING: queen, royal one • **USAGE:** Italian, English, Russian, German, and Polish: from Latin *regina* (queen)

> *Strength and dignity are her clothing,*
> *and she smiles at the future.*
> — Proverbs 31:25 (NASB)

REINA [RAY-nah]

MEANING: queen, royal one • **USAGE:** Spanish: from Spanish *reina*

> *[God] crowneth thee with lovingkindness*
> *and tender mercies.*
> — Psalm 103:4b (KJ21)

REINE [REH-neh]

MEANING: queen, royal one • **USAGE:** French (*see* Reina)

> *I will give you the keys of the kingdom of heaven;*
> *and whatever you shall bind on earth shall be bound*
> *in heaven, and whatever you shall loose*
> *on earth shall be loosed in heaven.*
> — Matthew 16:19 (NASB)

REMBA [rem-bah]

MEANING: beautiful, lovely • **USAGE:** African: Swahili of Kenya/Tanzania

> *A woman's beauty isn't in her face.*
> — Tanzania proverb

RENA [RAY-nah]

MEANING: peace, peaceful, calm, serene • **USAGE:** Greek form of Eirini, from Greek *eirene*

> *Mercy unto you, and peace, and love, be multiplied.*
> — Jude 1:2 (KJV)

RENANA [reh-nah-NAH, reh-NAH-nah]

MEANING: song, joy, exultation, prayer, chant • **USAGE:** Jewish

> *The beating heart of the Universe is holy joy.*
> — Martin Buber

RENATA [reh-NAH-tah]

MEANING: reborn, born again • **USAGE:** Italian, Spanish, German, English, and Russian: from Latin *renascor*

> *For you have been born again,*
> *not of perishable seed, but of imperishable,*
> *through the living and enduring word of God.*
> — 1 Peter 1:23 (DR)

RENATE [reh-NAH-teh]

MEANING: reborn, born again • **USAGE:** German and Scandinavian: from Latin *renascor*

> *You must be born anew. The wind blows*
> *where it wants to, and you hear its sound,*
> *but don't know where it comes from and where it is*
> *going. So is everyone who is born of the Spirit.*
> — John 3:8 (WEB)

RENE, RENEE, RENEÉ [reh-NAY]

MEANING: reborn, born again • **USAGE:** English and French: from Latin *renascor*

> *There is true ascension in our love.*
> — Ralph Waldo Emerson, "Uses of Great Men"

RENITA [reh-NEE-tah]

MEANING: reborn, born again • **USAGE:** English form of Renee: from Latin *renascor*

> *I [God] have given to you a new heart,*
> *and a new spirit I give.*
> — Ezekiel 36:26a (YLT)

REUT [reh-OOT]

MEANING: friend, companion • **USAGE:** Jewish: from Hebrew *re'uth*

> *When two people relate to each other authentically*
> *and humanly, God is the electricity*
> *that surges between them.*
> — Martin Buber

R

REVA   [REE-vah, ree-VAH]

MEANING: connection, tie, join, noose • USAGE:
Jewish form of Rivka, from Hebrew *ribhqah*
(connection), *rivka* (noose), and Hebrew root *r–b–q*
(to tie, to join)

Keep the commandment of thy father,
and forsake not the teaching of thy mother;
bind them continually upon thy heart,
tie them about thy neck.
— Proverbs 6:20–21 (MT)

REXENE   [rek-SEEN]

MEANING: queen, royal one • USAGE: English
feminine form of Rex, from Latin *rex* (king)

Thou shalt also be a...royal diadem
in the hand of thy God.
— Isaiah 62:3 (ASV)

RHEA   [RAY-ah (Greek), REE-ah (English)]

MEANING: flowing stream • USAGE: Greek
and English: from Greek *rheo* (to flow) or *rheos*
(stream); Greek goddess

You will be like a...stream that never runs dry.
— Isaiah 58:11b (CEV)

RHETTA   [RET-ah]

MEANING: adviser, counselor • USAGE: English
feminine form of Rhett, from Dutch *raet*

She opens her mouth with wisdom,
and the teaching of kindness is on her tongue.
— Proverbs 31:26 (ESV)

RHIAN   [HREE-an]

MEANING: great queen, maiden, nymph, sprite,
moon goddess • USAGE: Welsh form of Rhiannon
(*see* Rhiannon)

Regard the moon.
— T. S. Eliot, "Rhapsody on a Windy Night"

RHIANA, RHIANNA, RHEANNA   [ree-AH-nah]

MEANING: great queen, maiden, nymph, sprite,
moon goddess • USAGE: American form of
Rhiannon (*see* Rhiannon)

How bright and goodly shines the moon!
— William Shakespeare, *The Taming of the Shrew*

RHIANNE, RHEANNE   [ree-AN]

MEANING: great queen, maiden, nymph, sprite,
moon goddess • USAGE: American form of
Rhiannon (*see* Rhiannon)

Who is this who appears like the dawn?
Beautiful as the moon, bright as the sun,
awe-inspiring as the stars in procession?
— Song of Songs 6:10 (NEB)

RHIANNON   [hree-AHN-ohn (Welsh), ree-AN-un (English)]

MEANING: great queen, maiden, nymph, sprite,
moon goddess • USAGE: Welsh: from Welsh *rion*
(queen), *rhiain* (maiden), or *rhiannon* (nymph,
sprite); Welsh moon goddess

Deep peace, pure white of the moon to you...
Deep peace, deep peace!
— Fiona MacLeod, "Invocation of Peace"

RHODA   [ROH-dah]

MEANING: rose, fragrant flower • USAGE:
English: from Greek *rhodon*

When we see a soul whose acts are all regal,
graceful, and pleasant as roses, we must thank God
that such things can be and are.
— Ralph Waldo Emerson, "Spiritual Laws"

RHONA   [ROH-nah]

MEANING: rough island, little seal • USAGE:
Scottish and Irish: island in Hebrides, from Norse
hrauen (rough) and *ey* (island); or from Gaelic *rón*
(seal) and diminutive *-an*

R

Deep peace, an ebbing wave to you!...
Deep peace, deep peace!
— Fiona MacLeod, "Invocation of Peace"

RHONDA [RAHN-dah]

MEANING: good lance, good spear, good gift •
USAGE: English: from Welsh *rhon* (spear, lance)
and *da* (good); or from Welsh *rhodd* (gift) and *da*
(good)

Every good gift and every perfect gift
comes down from above, from the Father of lights.
— James 1:17a (DT)

RHONWEN [RAHN-wen]

MEANING: fair-haired, white lance • **USAGE:**
Welsh: from Welsh *rhawn* (hair) and *gwyn* (white,
fair, holy); or from Welsh *rhon* (spear, lance)

Thou art all fair, my love; there is no spot in thee.
— Song of Songs 4:7 (KJV)

RIA [REE-ah]

MEANING: conqueror, victorious, successful,
triumphant, beloved, love, sea mistress, bitter sea,
rebellious, well-nourished, healthy, myrrh, river
• **USAGE:** English form of Victoria, from Latin
vincere (to conquer); English form of Maria (*see*
Maria); or from Spanish *rio* (river)

Time is a flowing river. Happy are those who
allow themselves to be carried, unresisting,
with the current. They float through easy days.
They live, unquestioning, in the moment.
— Christopher Morley, *Where the Blue Begins*

RIANA, RIANNA, REANNA [ree-AH-nah]

MEANING: great queen, maiden, nymph, sprite,
moon goddess • **USAGE:** American form of
Rhiannon (*see* Rhiannon)

Queenly your movement.
— Song of Songs 7:1b (MSG)

RIANNE, REANNE [ree-AN]

MEANING: great queen, maiden, nymph, sprite,
moon goddess • **USAGE:** American form of
Rhiannon (*see* Rhiannon)

The moon is at her full, and riding high.
— William Cullen Bryant, "The Tides"

RICARDA [ree-KAR-dah]

MEANING: powerful ruler, strong leader • **USAGE:**
Spanish feminine form of Ricardo, from German *rik*
(rule, lead) and *hart* (hardy, strong, brave)

The sole advantage of having power
is that you can do greater good.
— Baltasar Gracian, *The Art of Worldly Wisdom*
(tr. Christopher Maurer)

RICHELLE [rih-SHEL]

MEANING: powerful ruler, strong leader • **USAGE:**
English feminine form of Richard, from German *rik*
(rule, lead) and *hart* (hardy, strong, brave)

By the time we have acquired great power, we have
acquired therewith sufficient wisdom to use it well.
— Ralph Waldo Emerson, "Journal XXVIII"

RIHANNA [rih-HAHN-ah]

MEANING: great queen, maiden, nymph, sprite •
USAGE: American: possibly a form of Rianna or
Rhiannon (*see* Rhiannon)

Greatness lives in one who triumphs equally
over defeat and victory.
— John Steinbeck,
The Acts of King Arthur and His Noble Knights

RIJU [rih-juh, ree-joo]

MEANING: pure, clean • **USAGE:** Hindu

The Self, who is to be realized by the purified mind
and the illumined consciousness, whose form is light,
whose thoughts are true...and in whom there is
fullness of joy forever — he is my very Self,
dwelling within the lotus of my heart.
— *Chandogya Upanishad*
(tr. Swami Prabhavananda)

R

RIKKI, RIKI   [RIK-ee]

MEANING: powerful ruler, strong leader, connection, tie, join, noose • USAGE: English feminine form of Richard, from German *rik* (rule, lead) and *hart* (hardy, strong, brave); or English form of Rebecca, from Hebrew *ribhqah* (connection), *rivka* (noose), and Hebrew root *r-b-q* (to tie, to join)

> *Knowledge itself is a power.*
> — Francis Bacon, "Of Heresies"

RILEY   [RIE-lee]

MEANING: courageous, valiant, brave, from the rye meadow • USAGE: Irish and English surname: from Irish Gaelic *raghalach* (courageous, valiant); or from English *ryge* (rye) and *leah* (meadow, field)

> *To have courage for whatever comes in life —*
> *everything lies in that.*
> — Teresa of Avila

RILLA   [RIL-ah]

MEANING: small brook, flowing stream • USAGE: American: possibly from German *rille* (running stream)

> *For this is what the Lord says:*
> *I will make peace flow to her like a river.*
> — Isaiah 66:12a (HCSB)

RIMA   [ree-mah]

MEANING: white gazelle, antelope, graceful, fleet-footed • USAGE: Persian

> *My soul is moved to dance by the charm*
> *of Thy graceful movements.*
> *And my heart beateth*
> *the rhythm of Thy gentle steps.*
> — Hazrat Inayat Khan, *The Gayan*

RIMONA   [ree-MOH-nah]

MEANING: pomegranate • USAGE: Jewish

> *For the Lord your God is bringing you into a good land, a land with streams and springs and fountains issuing from plain and hill; a land of wheat and barley, of vines, figs, and pomegranates, a land of olive trees and honey; a land where…you will lack nothing.*
> — Deuteronomy 8:7 (JPS)

RIONA   [ree-OH-nah]

MEANING: queen, royal one • USAGE: Irish form of *Rioghnach*, from Gaelic *rioghan*

> *You will be like a beautiful crown for the Lord.*
> — Isaiah 62:3 (GNT)

RISHONA   [ree-shoh-NAH, ree-SHOH-nah]

MEANING: first, eldest • USAGE: Jewish

> *Wisdom hath been created before all things, and the understanding of prudence from everlasting.*
> — Ben Sira 1:4 (KJV Apocrypha)

RITA   [rih-tah]

MEANING: true, righteous, proper • USAGE: Hindu: Sanskrit

> *Love in action is morality and right living.*
> — Sathya Sai Baba

RITA   [REE-tah]

MEANING: pearl, beautiful gem • USAGE: Spanish, English, German, Italian, and Scandinavian form of Margarita, from Greek *margaron* (a pearl)

> *How beautiful you are.*
> — Song of Songs 4:1a (NCV)

RIVA   [ree-VAH, REE-vah]

MEANING: young woman, maiden • USAGE: Jewish

> *Thou art a virtuous woman.*
> — Ruth 3:11b (JPS)

RIVKA [REEV-kah, reev-KAH]

MEANING: connection, tie, join, noose • **USAGE:** Jewish: from Hebrew *ribhqah* (connection), *rivka* (noose), and Hebrew root *r-b-q* (to tie, to join)

Let fidelity and steadfastness not leave you;
bind them about your throat,
write them on the tablet of your mind.
— Proverbs 3:3 (JPS)

RIYA [rih-yah]

MEANING: singer, songstress • **USAGE:** Hindu: Sanskrit

Music fills the infinite between two souls.
— Rabindranath Tagore, *The Fugitive*

RIYAZ [ree-ahz]

MEANING: garden • **USAGE:** Muslim

Good News for you this Day! Gardens beneath
which flow rivers! to dwell therein for aye!
This is indeed the highest Achievement!
— Koran, Iron 57.12b (ALI)

ROBERTA [roh-BER-tah (English), roh-BAYR-tah (Italian, Spanish)]

MEANING: brightly famous, shining with fame • **USAGE:** English, Italian, and Spanish feminine form of Robert, from German *hrod* (fame) and *beraht* (bright, shining)

Who is this whose glance is like the dawn!
She is beautiful and bright,
as dazzling as the sun or the moon.
— Song of Songs 6:10 (GNT)

ROBIN, ROBYN [ROB-in]

MEANING: brightly famous, shining with fame, robin, songbird • **USAGE:** English form of Roberta, from German *hrod* (fame) and *beraht* (bright, shining); or from English *robin* (robin)

My heart is like a singing bird.
— Christina Rossetti, "A Birthday"

ROBINA [roh-BEE-nah]

MEANING: brightly famous, shining with fame, robin, songbird • **USAGE:** Scottish form of Robin (*see* Robin)

Arise, shine; for thy light is come.
— Isaiah 60:1a (KJV)

ROCHELLE [roh-SHEL]

MEANING: peace, rest, sheep, ewe • **USAGE:** French form of Roch, from German *hrok* (peace, rest); or English form of Rachel, from Aramaic *rahla* (ewe)

Peace be to you, and peace be to your house,
and peace be to all that you have.
— 1 Samuel 25:6b (NRSV)

ROISIN [RAH-sheen]

MEANING: rose, little rose • **USAGE:** Irish: from Gaelic *róis* and diminutive *-een*

The Rose... so full of virtue, pleasance,
and delight. So full of blissful angelic beauty.
— William Dunbar,
"The Wedding of the Thistle and the Rose"

ROKSANA [rohks-AN-ah]

MEANING: sunrise, dawn, daybreak • **USAGE:** Russian form of Roxanna, from Persian *roschana*

Who is this that looks out like the first light of day?
She is as beautiful as the full moon, as pure as the sun.
— Song of Songs 6:10a (NLV)

ROLANDA [roh-LAHN-dah]

MEANING: fame of the land, famous land, praised estate • **USAGE:** German and English feminine form of Roland, from German *hrod* (fame, praise) and *land* (land, territory)

Goodness is beauty in its best estate.
— Christopher Marlowe

R

ROMANA   [roh-MAH-nah]

MEANING: woman of Rome, Roman • USAGE:
Czech, Polish, and Italian feminine form of Roman,
from Latin *Roma* (Rome, native of Rome)
> *To all that be in Rome, beloved of God,*
> *called to be saints: Grace to you and peace.*
> — Romans 1:7a (NIV)

ROMY   [ROH-mee]

MEANING: rosemary herb, dew of the sea, rose of
Mary, beloved rose • USAGE: German and English
contraction of Rosemary (*see* Rosemary)
> *May God give you of heaven's dew*
> *and of earth's richness.*
> — Genesis 27:28a (NIV)

RONA   [ROH-nah]

MEANING: well-advised ruler, ruler's judgment
• USAGE: English feminine form of Ronald, from
Norse *rögn* (advice, judgment) and *valdr* (to rule)
> *The Lord says, "Do what is right and fair and good."*
> — Jeremiah 22:3a (NLV)

RONA   [ROH-nah]

MEANING: song, joy • USAGE: Jewish feminine
form of Ron
> *Let me hear tidings of joy and gladness.*
> — Psalm 51:10a (JPS)

RONNELL   [ron-EL]

MEANING: well-advised ruler, ruler's judgment •
USAGE: American feminine form of Ronald, from
Norse *rögn* (advice, judgment) and *valdr* (to rule)
> *The hand of the diligent will rule.*
> — Proverbs 12:24a (NRSV)

RONNETTE, RONETTE   [ron-ET]

MEANING: well-advised ruler, ruler's judgment
• USAGE: English feminine form of Ronald, from
Norse *rögn* (advice, judgment) and *valdr* (to rule)
> *She opens her mouth with wisdom.*
> *Faithful instruction is on her tongue.*
> — Proverbs 31:26 (WEB)

RONNIE, RONI   [RON-ee]

MEANING: well-advised ruler, ruler's judgment,
true image, bringer of victory • USAGE: English
feminine form of Ronald (*see* Ronnette); or English
form of Veronica, from Latin *vera* (true) and
iconicus (image, icon) or from Greek *pherein* (to
bring, to bear) and *nike* (victory)
> *A wise person does the right thing at the right time.*
> *There is a right time and a right way for everything.*
> — Ecclesiastes 8:5b–6a (NCV)

ROSA   [ROH-sah]

MEANING: rose, fragrant flower • USAGE: Italian
and Portuguese: from Latin *rosa* (rose)
> *The flowers are springing up,*
> *the season of singing birds has come.*
> — Song of Songs 2:12a (NLT)

ROSABELLA   [roh-sah-BAY-lah]

MEANING: beautiful rose, lovely flower • USAGE:
Italian: from Latin *rosa* (rose) and *bella* (beautiful,
lovely)
> *Treasure wisdom, and it will make you great; hold on*
> *to it, and it will bring you honor. It will be like flowers*
> *in your hair and like a beautiful crown.*
> — Proverbs 4:8–9 (NCV)

ROSALIA   [roh-sah-LEE-ah]

MEANING: rose, fragrant flower • USAGE: Italian
and Spanish (*see* Rosa); Rosalia is the annual
Catholic ceremony of placing rose garlands on
tombs
> *Beauty is an exquisite flower,*
> *and its perfume is virtue.*
> — Giovanni Ruffini

ROSALIE   *[ROH-sah-lee]*

MEANING: rose, fragrant flower • **USAGE:** English form of Rose (*see* Rose)

> *The flowers appear on the earth;*
> *the time of the singing of birds is come.*
> — Song of Songs 2:12a (ASV)

ROSALIND, ROSALYN, ROSLYN
[RAHZ-ah-lind, RAHZ-ah-lin, RAHZ-lin]

MEANING: gentle horse, tender horse • **USAGE:** English: from German *hros* (horse) and *linde* (gentle, tender)

> *From the east to western Ind /*
> *No jewel is like Rosalind.*
> — William Shakespeare, *As You Like It*

ROSALINDA   *[roh-sah-LEEN-dah]*

MEANING: beautiful rose, fair rose • **USAGE:** Spanish combination of Rosa and Linda (*see* Rosa and Linda)

> *You are altogether beautiful, my darling,*
> *beautiful in every way.*
> — Song of Songs 4:7 (NLT)

ROSALINDE   *[roh-sah-LIN-dah]*

MEANING: gentle horse, famous and gentle • **USAGE:** German form of *Roslindis*, from *hros* (horse) or *hrós* (fame) and *lind* (gentle, tender)

> *Follow after righteousness, godliness, faith, love,*
> *patience, and gentleness.*
> — 1 Timothy 6:11b (WEB)

ROSANA   *[roh-SAH-nah]*

MEANING: graceful rose, rose of grace • **USAGE:** Spanish combination of Rosa and Anna (*see* Rosa and Anna)

> *Grace be with you.*
> — Colossians 4:18b (KJV)

ROSANNA   *[roh-SAN-ah]*

MEANING: graceful rose, rose of grace • **USAGE:** English combination of Rose and Anna (*see* Rose and Anna)

> *Flowers are love's truest language.*
> — Park Benjamin,
> "Flowers, Love's Truest Language"

ROSE   *[rohz]*

MEANING: rose flower, reddish-pink color • **USAGE:** English: from Latin *rosa* (rose); reddish-pink color

> *The red rose whispers of passion, / And the white rose*
> *breathes of love; / O, the red rose is a falcon, /*
> *And the white rose is a dove.*
> — John Boyle O'Reilly, "A White Rose"

ROSEANNE   *[roh-ZAN]*

MEANING: graceful rose, rose of grace • **USAGE:** English combination of Rose and Anne (*see* Rose and Anne)

> *It is good for the heart to be strengthened by grace.*
> — Hebrews 13:9b (ESV)

ROSEMARY   *[ROHZ-mah-ree,*
rohs-MAYR-ee]

MEANING: rosemary herb, dew of the sea, rose of Mary, beloved rose • **USAGE:** English: aromatic shrub and herb, from Latin *ros mare* (dew of the sea); also English combination of Rose and Mary (*see* Rose and Mary)

> *Herbs can help the body and give /*
> *the heart more strength / to love.*
> — Catherine of Siena,
> "Give the Heart More Strength"
> (tr. Daniel Ladinsky in *Love Poems from God*)

ROSETTA   *[roh-SET-ah]*

MEANING: little rose • **USAGE:** Italian form of Rosa and diminutive *-etta* (*see* Rosa)

> *I am a rose of Sharon, a lily of the valleys.*
> — Song of Songs 2:1 (RSV)

R

ROSETTE   [roh-ZET]

MEANING: little rose, fragrant flower • USAGE:
French form of Rosa and diminutive *-ette* (*see* Rosa)
The tiniest flower is a thought.
— Honoré de Balzac, *Seraphita*
(tr. Katharine Wormeley)

ROSHANA   [roh-SHAH-nah]

MEANING: shining, splendid • USAGE: Hindu
Follow then the shining ones,
the wise, the awakened, the loving,
for they know how to work and forbear.
— Buddha, *The Dhammapada* (tr. Thomas Byrom)

ROSHANA   [roh-SHAH-nah]

MEANING: dawn, sunrise • USAGE: Persian: from
Persian *roschana*
You are the dawn that arrives in the middle of the
night, dark-haired strands of music filling the reed.
— Jalaluddin Rumi, "Your Morning Shade"
(tr. Coleman Barks in *The Glance*)

ROSHEEN   [roh-SHEEN]

MEANING: rose, fragrant flower • USAGE:
English form of Roisin, from Irish Gaelic *róis* and
diminutive *-een*
Flowers are the brightest things which earth /
On her broad bosom loves to cherish.
— Clara Balfour, *Sunbeams for All Seasons*

ROSIE, ROSY   [ROH-zee]

MEANING: rose, fragrant flower, reddish-pink
color, cheerful, optimistic • USAGE: English form
of Rose (*see* Rose); reddish-pink color
No pessimist ever discovered the secret of the stars,
or sailed to an uncharted land,
or opened a new doorway for the human spirit.
— Helen Keller, "The Practice of Optimism"

ROSINA   [roh-SEE-nah]

MEANING: little rose • USAGE: Italian, Spanish,
German, and English form of Rosa and diminutive
-ina (*see* Rosa)
The flowers appear on the earth;
the time of singing has come.
— Song of Songs 2:12a (NKJV)

ROSITA   [roh-SEE-tah]

MEANING: little rose • USAGE: Spanish and
Portuguese form of Rosa and diminutive *-ita* (*see*
Rosa)
In music, in the sea, in a flower,
in a leaf, in an act of kindness…
I see what people call God in all these things.
— Pablo Casals

ROWENA, ROWINA   [roh-WEE-nah]

MEANING: rowan tree, little redheaded one,
famous friend • USAGE: English feminine form of
Rowan, from Norse *reynir* (rowan tree, mountain
ash); Irish form of *Ruadhan*, from Gaelic *ruadh*
(red) and diminutive *-an*; or from English *hroo*
(fame) and *wine* (friend)
A friend may well be reckoned
the masterpiece of Nature.
— Ralph Waldo Emerson, "Friendship"

ROXANNA, ROXANA   [roks-AN-ah]

MEANING: sunrise, dawn, daybreak • USAGE:
English (*see* Roxanne)
Who is she that looketh forth as the morning,
fair as the moon, clear as the sun.
— Song of Songs 6:10a (KJ21)

ROXANNE   [roks-AN (English),
rahs-AHN [French)]

MEANING: sunrise, dawn, daybreak • USAGE:
English and French: from Persian *roschana* (dawn
of day)

R

All that is good, and living,
and hopeful, rising with the dawn of Day!
— Lewis Carroll, *Sylvie and Bruno*

ROXIE, ROXY [ROKS-ee]

Meaning: sunrise, dawn, daybreak • **Usage:**
English form of Roxanne or Roxanna (*see*
Roxanne)

My soul is heavy with sunshine,
and steeped with strength.
— D. H. Lawrence, *The Plumed Serpent*

ROZ [rahz]

Meaning: gentle horse, tender horse • **Usage:**
English form of Rosalind from German *hros* (horse)
and *linde* (gentle, tender)

There is great force hidden in a gentle command.
— George Herbert

ROZA [ROH-zah]

Meaning: rose, beautiful flower • **Usage:**
Russian form of Rosa, from Latin *rosa* (rose)

The world will be saved by beauty!
— Fyodor Dostoevsky, *The Idiot*

ROZETTA [roh-ZET-ah]

Meaning: little rose • **Usage:** American: from
Latin *rosa* (rose) and diminutive *-etta*

There is simply the rose;
it is perfect in every moment of its existence.
— Ralph Waldo Emerson, "Self-Reliance"

RU [roo]

Meaning: scholar, educated • **Usage:** Chinese

Study thoroughly and think deeply.
— Chinese proverb (tr. William Scarborough)

RUBÍ [roo-BEE]

Meaning: ruby gemstone, red jewel, deep-red
color • **Usage:** Spanish form of Ruby (*see* Ruby)

Oh, you are beautiful.
— Song of Songs 4:1a (NEB)

RUBY [ROO-bee]

Meaning: ruby gemstone, red jewel, deep-red
color • **Usage:** English: from Latin *rubeus* (red);
deep-red jewel

Good name in man and woman...is the immediate
jewel of their souls.
— William Shakespeare, *Othello*

RUE [roo]

Meaning: rue herb, evergreen shrub, friend,
friendship • **Usage:** English: medicinal herb, from
Greek *rhyte* (herb, evergreen shrub); also English
form of Ruth, from Hebrew *re'uth* (friend)

The language of Friendship is not words, but meanings.
It is an intelligence above language.
— Henry David Thoreau,
A Week on the Concord and Merrimack Rivers

RUNA [ROO-nah]

Meaning: secret lore • **Usage:** Scandinavian:
from Norse *run*

This is what the Lord says...call to me
and I will answer you and tell you great and
unsearchable things you do not know.
— Jeremiah 33:1–3 (NIV)

RUT [root]

Meaning: friend, companion • **Usage:** Spanish,
German, and Swedish form of Ruth (*see* Ruth)

Say to wisdom, "You are my sister,"
and call insight your intimate friend.
— Proverbs 7:4 (NRSV)

R

RUTH
[rooth (English), root (German, Scandinavian)]

MEANING: friend, companion • USAGE: English, German, and Scandinavian form of Rut, from Hebrew *re'uth*

A friend is called a guardian of love or, as some would have it, a guardian of the spirit itself.
— Aelred of Rievaulx, *Spiritual Friendship*
(tr. Lawrence Braceland)

RYAN, RYANN, RYANNE
[RIE-an]

MEANING: little queen, little royal one • USAGE: Irish and English surname: from Gaelic *ri* (king) and diminutive *-an*

The beginning of wisdom is this: get wisdom, and whatever you get, get insight. Prize her highly, and she will exalt you; she will honor you if you embrace her. She will place on your head a graceful garland; she will bestow on you a beautiful crown.
— Proverbs 4:7–9 (ESV)

RYANA
[rie-AN-ah]

MEANING: little queen, little royal one • USAGE: English form of Ryan (*see* Ryan)

Strength and dignity are her clothing.
— Proverbs 31:25a (DT)

RYLIE, RYLEE
[RIE-lee]

MEANING: courageous, valiant, brave, from the rye meadow • USAGE: American form of Riley, from Irish Gaelic *raghalach* (courageous, valiant); or from English *ryge* (rye) and *leah* (meadow, field)

The best protection that any woman can have, one that will serve her at all times and in all places, is courage.
— Elizabeth Cady Stanton
(letter of May 16, 1851)

S

SAAFI
[SAH-fee]

MEANING: pure, clean • USAGE: Muslim: from Arabic *safa* (to be pure)

A pure life and a clear conscience are as two eyes for the soul.
— Hazrat Inayat Khan, *The Gayan*

SABAH
[sah-BAH]

MEANING: morning • USAGE: Hindu: from Sanskrit *sabah*

Do not say, "It is morning," and dismiss it with a name of yesterday. See it for the first time as a newborn child that has no name.
— Rabindranath Tagore, *Stray Birds*

SABELA
[sah-BAY-lah]

MEANING: God is my oath, joined with God, blessed by God • USAGE: Spanish form of Isabella, from Hebrew *el'ishebha*

It is God who is working in you, enabling you both to desire and to work out His good purpose.
— Philippians 2:13 (HCSB)

SABELLA
[sah-BAY-lah]

MEANING: God is my oath, joined with God, blessed by God • USAGE: Italian form of Isabella (*see* Sabela)

Have peace; and the God of peace and of love shall be with you.
— 2 Corinthians 13:11b (DR)

SABINA
[sah-BEE-nah]

MEANING: woman from Sabine • USAGE: Italian, Spanish, Polish, and Russian form of Sabine (*see* Sabine)

Who can find a worthy woman? For her price is far above rubies.
— Proverbs 31:10 (WEB)

SABINE
[*sah-BIE-nah (German)*,
sah-BEEN (French)]

Meaning: woman of Sabine • **Usage:** German and French form of *Sabinus* (Sabine), an ancient people of central Italy
> *Thou art a worthy woman.*
> — Ruth 3:11b (ASV)

SABIRA, SABEERA
[*sah-BEE-rah*]

Meaning: patient, tolerant • **Usage:** Muslim feminine form of Sabir, from Arabic *sabara* (to endure)
> *Tolerance is generosity. Tolerance is a sign of faith.*
> — Hadith of the Prophet Muhammad

SABITA, SABEETA
[*sah-BEE-tah*]

Meaning: well-established, certain • **Usage:** Muslim
> *Who establish regular prayers and spend (freely) out of the gifts We have given them for sustenance:*
> *Such in truth are the Believers:*
> *they have grades of dignity with their Lord,*
> *and forgiveness, and generous sustenance.*
> — Koran, The Spoils of War 8.3–4 (ALI)

SABRINA
[*sah-BREE-nah*]

Meaning: river name • **Usage:** English, German, Italian, Spanish, and Welsh: form of *Habren* (original Welsh name of River Severn)
> *For thus says the Lord:*
> *"Behold, I will extend peace to her like a river."*
> — Isaiah 66:12a (ESV)

SACHIKO
[*sah-chee-koh*]

Meaning: happy child, blissful child • **Usage:** Japanese: from Japanese *sachi* (happy, blissful) and *ko* (child)
> *If my heart can become pure and simple like that of a child, I think there probably can be no greater happiness than this.*
> — Kitaro Nishida

SADHANA
[*sahd-hahn-nah*]

Meaning: spiritual practice • **Usage:** Hindu: Sanskrit
> *Best of the paths is the eightfold, best of the truths the four; best of the virtues is freedom from attachment;*
> *best of the people is the one who sees.*
> — Buddha, The Dhammapada (tr. Sanderson Beck)

SADIAH, SADIYAH
[*sah-dee-yah*]

Meaning: happy, joyous • **Usage:** Muslim
> *Happiness lies in thinking or doing that which one considers beautiful.*
> — Hazrat Inayat Khan, The Bowl of Saki

SADIE
[*SAY-dee*]

Meaning: princess, royal one • **Usage:** English form of Sarah, from Hebrew *sarah*
> *You will be a glorious crown…for the Lord your God.*
> — Isaiah 62:3 (CEV)

SAFARA
[*sah-fah-rah*]

Meaning: her place • **Usage:** African: Ethiopia
> *Ethiopia has need of no one;*
> *she stretches out her hands to God.*
> — Menelik II

SAFFRON
[*SAF-ron*]

Meaning: saffron, yellow-orange color • **Usage:** English: from Arabic *za'faran*
> *Although yellow occupies one-twentieth of the spectrum, it is the brightest colour.*
> — Derek Jarman

SAGE
[*sayj*]

Meaning: wise one, sage herb • **Usage:** English: from Latin *sapere* (to be wise); or from English *sauge* (herb)
> *Wisdom will enter your heart,*
> *and knowledge will be pleasant to your soul.*
> — Proverbs 2:10 (NIV)

S

SAGUNA [sah-guh-nah]

MEANING: having good qualities, virtuous • **USAGE:** Hindu: from Sanskrit *sa* (good) and *guna* (quality of nature)

> *Character is based on virtuous action,*
> *and virtuous action is grounded on Truth.*
> — Mahatma Gandhi

SAHAB [sah-hahb]

MEANING: clouds • **USAGE:** Muslim

> *Seest thou not that God makes the clouds move gently?*
> — Koran, Light 24.45a (ALI)

SAHLA [sah-lah]

MEANING: simple, easy • **USAGE:** Muslim

> *Simplicity of nature is the sign of saints.*
> — Hazrat Inayat Khan, *The Gayan* (cd. *The Gayani Meditations, Volume 1*, tr. Cecil Touchon)

SAJIDA, SAJEEDA [sah-JEE-dah]

MEANING: worshiper (of Allah) • **USAGE:** Muslim feminine form of Sajid, from Arabic *sajid*

> *I lift my heart to God / And grace is poured.*
> — Hafiz, "A Crystal Rim"
> (tr. Daniel Ladinsky in *The Gift*)

SAKALAH [sah-kah-lah]

MEANING: complete • **USAGE:** Hindu: from Sanskrit *sa* (with) and *kala* (parts)

> *The wise train the mind to give complete attention*
> *to one thing at a time, here and now.*
> — Buddha, *The Dhammapada*
> (tr. Eknath Easwaran)

SAKI [sah-kee]

MEANING: blossom of hope • **USAGE:** Japanese: from Japanese *sa* (blossom) and *ki* (hope)

> *In joy or sadness, flowers are our constant friends.*
> — Kakuzō Okakura, *The Book of Tea*

SAKURA [sah-koo-rah]

MEANING: cherry blossom • **USAGE:** Japanese: from Japanese *sakura*

> *In the cherry blossom's shade /*
> *there is no such thing / as a stranger.*
> — Issa

SALENA [sah-leh-nah]

MEANING: moon • **USAGE:** Hindu

> *The moon, O disciples,*
> *illumines the world and cannot be hidden.*
> — Buddha

SALIMA, SALIMAH, SALEEMA [sah-LEE-mah]

MEANING: safe, secure, at peace • **USAGE:** Muslim: from *salima*

> *The righteous (will be) amid gardens and fountains*
> *(of clear-flowing water). (Their greeting will be):*
> *"Enter ye here in peace and security."*
> — Koran, The Rocky Tract 15.45–46 (ALI)

SALLY, SALLIE [SAL-ee]

MEANING: princess, royal one • **USAGE:** English form of Sarah, from Hebrew *sarah*

> *She [Wisdom] will put on your head*
> *a crown of loving-favor and beauty.*
> — Proverbs 4:9 (NLV)

SALOME [sah-LOH-meh, SAH-loh-meh]

MEANING: peace, peaceful • **USAGE:** Jewish: from Hebrew *shalom* (peace)

> *I know the thoughts that I think toward you,*
> *saith the Lord, thoughts of peace, and not of evil,*
> *to give you a future and a hope.*
> — Jeremiah 29:11 (MT)

SAMANTA [sah-MAHN-tah]

MEANING: His name is God, name of God • **USAGE:** Italian and Spanish form of Samantha (*see* Samantha)

*I will cause all my goodness to pass in front of you, and
I will announce my name, the Lord, so you can hear it.*
— Exodus 33:19a (NCV)

SAMANTHA   *[sah-MAN-thah]*

MEANING: His name is God, name of God •
USAGE: English feminine form of Samuel, from
Hebrew *shemu 'el*
*You, Lord, are my shepherd....
You are true to your name,
and you lead me along the right paths.*
— Psalm 23:1–3 (CEV)

SAMATA   *[sah-mah-tah]*

MEANING: equal, equanimity of mind • USAGE:
Hindu: Sanskrit
Love and truth are faces of the same coin.
— Mahatma Gandhi

SAMIA, SAAMIA   *[sah-mee-ah]*

MEANING: elevated, eminent, exalted • USAGE:
Muslim: from Arabic *sama* (to be elevated)
*The more elevated the soul,
the broader the outlook.*
— Hazrat Inayat Khan, *The Bowl of Saki*

SAMINA, SAMEENA   *[sah-mee-nah]*

MEANING: happy, joyous • USAGE: Hindu
*May all be happy and safe!
May all beings gain inner joy.*
— Buddha

SAMINA, SAMINAH   *[sah-MEE-nah]*

MEANING: valuable, precious • USAGE: Muslim
All precious things need strong guarding.
— Hazrat Inayat Khan, *The Gayan* (cd. *The Gayani
Meditations, Volume 1*, tr. Cecil Touchon)

SAMUELA   *[sahm-WAY-lah]*

MEANING: His name is God, name of God •
USAGE: Italian feminine form of Samuel (*see*
Samantha)
*O God!...Let all who take refuge in you be glad;
let them ever sing for joy. Spread your protection
over them, that those who love your name
may rejoice in you.*
— Psalm 5:11 (NIV)

SANANDA   *[sah-nahn-dah]*

MEANING: happy, joyous, cheerful • USAGE:
Hindu: from Sanskrit *a* (entirely) and *nanda*
(joyful)
It is the cheerful mind that is persevering.
— Swami Vivekananda, "Bhaki-Yoga"

SANCHIA   *[sahn-CHEE-ah]*

MEANING: sanctified, holy • USAGE: Spanish
feminine form of Sancho, from Latin *sanctus*
May the God of peace sanctify you entirely.
— 1 Thessalonians 5:23 (NRSV)

SANDRA   *[SAN-drah (English),
SAHN-drah (German, Italian, Scandanavian)]*

MEANING: protector and helper of humankind,
prophetess, seer • USAGE: English, German,
Italian, and Scandinavian form of Alexandra, from
Greek *alexein* (to defend, to help) and *andros* (man);
or English form of Cassandra, a Greek prophetess
*For behold God is my helper:
and the Lord is the protector of my soul.*
— Psalm 53:6 (DR)

SANDY, SANDIE, SANDI   *[SAN-dee]*

MEANING: protector and helper of humankind,
prophetess, seer • USAGE: English form of Sandra
or Saundra (*see* Sandra)
*The one who blesses others is abundantly blessed;
those who help others are helped.*
— Proverbs 11:25 (MSG)

S

SANGITA   [san-gee-tah]

MEANING: divine music • **USAGE:** Hindu: Sanskrit
*The divine music
is incessantly going on within ourselves.*
— Mahatma Gandhi

SANG-MI   [sahng-mee]

MEANING: helpful and beautiful • **USAGE:** Korean:
from Korean *sang* (helpful) and *mee* (beautiful)
*Touch the beauty / and truth / within /
to reveal and liberate / our natural joy.*
— Shi Wuling, *Path to Peace*

SANIYYA, SANIA   [sah-nee-yah]

MEANING: shining light, radiance • **USAGE:**
Muslim: from Arabic *sana* (to gleam, to shine)
*Open our hearts towards Thy Beauty,
illuminate our souls with Divine Light.*
— Hazrat Inayat Khan, *The Gayan*

SANJANA   [san-jah-nah]

MEANING: gentle, tolerant, kind • **USAGE:** Hindu
*Right speech, right action, and right occupation follow
from right purpose. They mean living in harmony
with the unity of life: speaking kindly, acting kindly,
living not just for oneself but for the welfare of all.*
— Buddha, *The Dhammapada*
(tr. Eknath Easwaran)

SANNA   [SAHN-ah]

MEANING: lily, rose • **USAGE:** Scandinavian form
of Susan, from Hebrew *shoshan*
*Consider the lilies of the field, how they grow:
they labour not, neither do they spin.
But I say to you, that not even Solomon
in all his glory was arrayed as one of these.*
— Matthew 6:28b–29 (DR)

SANTANA   [sahn-TAH-nah]

MEANING: St. Anne, grace, gracious, merciful,
compassionate • **USAGE:** Spanish: from Spanish *san*
(saint) and Ana, from Hebrew *chaanach*
It is good for our hearts to be strengthened by grace.
— Hebrews 13:9b (NIV)

SAPPHIRA   [sah-FIE-rah (English), sah-FEE-rah (Greek)]

MEANING: sapphire, deep-blue color, beautiful
jewel • **USAGE:** English and Greek: from Greek
sappheiros (sapphire, blue gemstone); or from
Sanskrit *priyah* (precious)
Oh! darkly, deeply, beautifully blue.
— Percy Bysshe Shelley, *Don Juan*

SAPPHIRE   [SAF-ier]

MEANING: sapphire, deep-blue color, beautiful
gemstone • **USAGE:** English: from Greek *sappheiros*
(sapphire, blue gemstone); or from Sanskrit *priyah*
(precious)
Blueness doth express trueness. — Ben Jonson

SARA   [SAYR-ah (English), SAH-rah (German, Italian, Scandinavian, Spanish)]

MEANING: princess, royal, noble • **USAGE:**
English, German, Italian, Scandinavian, and
Spanish: from Hebrew *sarah*
*You shall also be a crown of glory in the hand of the
Lord, and a royal diadem in the hand of your God.*
— Isaiah 62:3 (NKJV)

SARAH   [sah-RAH (Jewish), SAYR-ah (English, French)]

MEANING: princess, royal, noble • **USAGE:** Jewish,
French, and English: from Hebrew *sarah*
*God said unto Abraham: "As for Sarai thy wife,
thou shalt not call her name Sarai, but Sarah shall her
name be....I will bless her, and she shall be a mother
of nations; kings of peoples shall be of her."*
— Genesis 17:15–16 (MT)

SARALA [sah-rah-lah]

Meaning: honest, sincere • **Usage:** Hindu: from Sanskrit *sarala*

> *O how sweet it is to enjoy life, /*
> *living in honesty and strength!*
> — Buddha, *The Dhammapada* (tr. Thomas Byrom)

SARAMA [sah-rah-mah]

Meaning: beautiful, nice • **Usage:** African: Bambara of West Africa

> *All that is in the heart is written in the face.*
> — West African proverb

SARANA, SARANNA [sah-RAH-nah]

Meaning: princess, royal one • **Usage:** American form of Sarah (*see* Sarah)

> *A throne shall be prepared in mercy,*
> *and one shall sit upon it in truth.*
> — Isaiah 16:5a (DR)

SARANI [sah-rah-nih]

Meaning: spiritual path • **Usage:** Hindu: Sanskrit

> *In the attitude of silence, the soul finds the path in a*
> *clearer light, and what is elusive and deceptive resolves*
> *itself into crystal clearness. Our life is a long and*
> *arduous quest after Truth, and the soul requires inward*
> *restfulness to attain its full height.*
> — Mahatma Gandhi

SARINA [sah-REE-nah]

Meaning: princess, royal, noble • **Usage:** Spanish and English form of Sarah (*see* Sarah)

> *If you value Wisdom and hold tightly to her,*
> *great honors will be yours. It will be like wearing*
> *a glorious crown of beautiful flowers.*
> — Proverbs 4:8–9 (CEV)

SARITA [sah-rih-tah]

Meaning: river, to flow, flowing • **Usage:** Hindu

> *A river is flowing in and through you*
> *carrying the message of joy.*
> — Sri Chinmoy Ghose, *Wings of Joy*

SARITA [sah-REE-tah]

Meaning: little princess, little royal one • **Usage:** Spanish form of Sarah: from Hebrew *Sarah* and diminutive *-ita*

> *Praise the Lord, who is good,*
> *who has crowned you with glory!*
> — Sirach 45:26a (GNT Apocrypha)

SARVANI [sahr-vah-nee]

Meaning: the all • **Usage:** Hindu: Sanskrit

> *Always bear this in mind: Everything is in God's*
> *hands, and you are His tool to be used by Him as He*
> *pleases. Try to grasp the significance of "all is His,"*
> *and you will immediately feel free from all burdens.*
> — Sri Anandamayi Ma

SASHA [SAH-shah]

Meaning: protector and helper of humankind, guardian • **Usage:** Russian form of Aleksandra, from Greek *alexein* (to defend, to help) and *andros* (man)

> *He will give His angels charge concerning you,*
> *to guard you in all your ways.*
> — Psalm 91:11 (NASB)

SATI [saht-tee]

Meaning: faithful, truthful • **Usage:** Hindu: Sanskrit

> *On a long journey of human life, faith is the best of*
> *companions; it is the best refreshment on the journey;*
> *and it is the greatest reward at the end.*
> — Buddha

S

SATYA   [saht-yah]

MEANING: true, truth • USAGE: Hindu: Sanskrit
Realize your true nature. That is all there is to do.
Know yourself as you are — infinite spirit.
— Swami Vivekananda

SAUNDRA   [SAHN-drah]

MEANING: protector and helper of humankind, guardian • USAGE: Scottish form of Alexandra (*see* Sandra)
Acquire wisdom, acquire understanding....
Do not forsake wisdom, and she will protect you;
love her, and she will guard you.
— Proverbs 4:5–6 (NEB)

SAUSAN   [sah-sahn]

MEANING: lily flower • USAGE: Persian
Water-lily, what do you represent by your
white garland? The purity of the heart of this lake.
— Hazrat Inayat Khan, *The Gayan*

SAVANNAH, SAVANNA   [sah-VAN-ah]

MEANING: grassland, flat treeless plain • USAGE: English: from Spanish *zabana*
The Lord is my Shepherd. I will have everything
I need. He lets me rest in fields of green grass.
— Psalm 23:1–2a (NLV)

SCARLET, SCARLETT, SCARLETTE   [SKAR-let]

MEANING: vivid red color, dyer • USAGE: English: from English *scarlet* (red color); or from French *escarlate* (scarlet cloth); also an occupational name for a dyer or seller of fabrics
The true colour of life is the colour of the body...
red of the living heart and the pulses.
— Alice Meynell, *The Colour of Life*

SEANA   [SHAH-nah]

MEANING: God is gracious, God is giving • USAGE: Irish and English feminine form of Sean, from Hebrew *y'hohanan* (Yahweh is gracious)
Grant, O God, Thy Protection, and in protection,
strength, and in strength, understanding;
and in understanding, knowledge; and in knowledge,
knowledge of righteousness; and in knowledge of
righteousness, the love it is; and in that love,
the love of everything, and in the love of everything,
the love of God. God and all goodness!
— Celtic prayer

SEFERINA   [say-fay-REE-nah]

MEANING: west wind, mild breeze • USAGE: Spanish: from Greek *zephyros*
The wind bloweth where it will,
and thou hearest the voice thereof, but knowest not
whence it cometh, and whither it goeth:
so is every one that is born of the Spirit.
— John 3:8 (ASV)

SELA   [SEH-lah]

MEANING: rock, cliff, heights, strength • USAGE: Jewish
The Lord said: "Behold, there is a place by Me,
and thou shalt stand upon the rock."
— Exodus 33:21 (MT)

SELBY   [SEL-bee]

MEANING: willow town • USAGE: English surname: from Norse *selja* (willow) and *býr* (town, village)
Love is a young green willow shimmering
at the bare wood's edge.
— William Carlos Williams, "Epitaph"

SELDA   [SEL-dah]

MEANING: friend, companion, gray battle maid, gray warrior, lucky, fortunate • USAGE: German

and English: from English *selda* (companion);
or German form of Griselda, from German *gries*
(gray) and *hild* (war, strife); or English form of
Yiddish *salida* (luck)

> *Say to wisdom, "You are my sister."*
> *Call insight your special friend.*
> — Proverbs 7:4 (NLV)

SELENA [say-LAY-nah (Spanish), seh-LEE-nah (English)]

MEANING: moon, moon goddess • **USAGE:**
Spanish and English form of Selene (*see* Selene)

> *Who is she that looketh forth as the morning,*
> *fair as the moon, clear as the sun.*
> — Song of Songs 6:10a (KJV)

SELENE [seh-LEH-neh (Greek), seh-LEEN (English)]

MEANING: moon, moon goddess • **USAGE:** Greek
and English: from Greek *selene* (moon), Greek
moon goddess

> *Be praised, my Lord, for sister moon and stars,*
> *in the sky you have made them brilliant*
> *and precious and beautiful.*
> — Francis of Assisi, "Canticle of the Sun"

SELINA [seh-LEE-nah]

MEANING: moon, moon goddess • **USAGE:**
Russian, German, and English form of Selene (*see*
Selene)

> *How fair and how pleasant art thou.*
> — Song of Songs 7:6a (KJ21)

SELMA [SEL-mah]

MEANING: protected by God • **USAGE:** German,
Scandinavian, and English form of Anselma, from
German *ans* (God) and *helm* (helmet, protection)

> *God always protects my heart and gives me stability.*
> — Psalm 73:26b (NEB)

SENGA [SEHN-gah]

MEANING: pure one, chaste, holy, lamb • **USAGE:**
Irish form of Agnes (spelled backward), from Greek
hagnos (chaste, holy) or from Latin *agnus* (lamb)

> *May the God of peace himself*
> *make you completely holy.*
> — 1 Thessalonians 5:23a (NEB)

SENNA [SEN-ah]

MEANING: plant with yellow flowers • **USAGE:**
American: from Aramaic *sanya* (thornbush); genus
Cassia plant with yellow flowers and medicinal
properties

> *Plant what is right and good for yourselves.*
> *Gather the fruit of lasting love.*
> — Hosea 10:12a (NLV)

SEONA [SHOH-nah]

MEANING: God is gracious, God is giving •
USAGE: Scottish form of Jane, from Hebrew
y'hohanan (Yahweh is gracious)

> *Bless, O God, my reason and my purpose. /*
> *Bless, O bless Thou them.*
> — Alexander Carmichael, *Carmina Gadelica*

SEPIDEH [seh-PEH-deh]

MEANING: dawn • **USAGE:** Persian

> *The soul comes every day at dawn. / "Good to see you*
> *again, my friend. / The peace of God be with you."*
> — Jalaluddin Rumi, "A World Dense with
> Greeting" (tr. Coleman Barks in *The Glance*)

SERAFINA [sayr-ah-FEE-nah]

MEANING: burning one, angel • **USAGE:** Italian,
Portuguese, and Polish form of Seraphina (*see*
Seraphina)

> *We learn from the testimony of holy scripture,*
> *the orders of angels are nine in number — angels,*
> *archangels, mights, powers, principalities,*
> *dominions, thrones, cherubim, and seraphim.*
> — Gregory the Great

S

SERAPHINA   *[sayr-ah-FEE-nah]*

MEANING: burning one, angel • **USAGE:** Jewish and English: from Hebrew *seraphim* (the burning ones), an order of celestial angels

Bless the Lord, O my soul.... Who makest winds
Thy messengers, the flaming fire Thy ministers.
— Psalm 104:1, 4 (MT)

SÉRAPHINE, SERAPHINE

[SAYR-ah-feen]

MEANING: burning one, angel • **USAGE:** French and English form of Seraphina (*see* Seraphina)

The Lord ... will send his angel
with you and prosper your way.
— Genesis 24:40a (ESV)

SEREN   *[SER-en]*

MEANING: star, starlike • **USAGE:** Welsh: from Welsh *seren*

Deep peace of the Flock of Stars to you...
Deep peace, deep peace!
— Fiona MacLeod, "Invocation of Peace"

SERENA   *[seh-RAY-nah (Italian),*
seh-REE-nah (English)]

MEANING: serene, peaceful, calm • **USAGE:** Italian and English: from Latin *serenus*

To have a quiet mind is to possess one's mind wholly;
to have a calm spirit is to possess one's self.
— Hamilton Mabie, *The Life of the Spirit*

SERENE   *[seh-REEN]*

MEANING: serene, peaceful, calm • **USAGE:** American: from Latin *serenus*

Ultimate peace begins within.
— Peace Pilgrim, *Peace Pilgrim*

SERENITY   *[seh-REN-eh-tee]*

MEANING: serene, peaceful, calm • **USAGE:** American: from Latin *serenus*

God, grant me the serenity to accept the things
I cannot change, the courage to change the things I can,
and the wisdom to know the difference.
— Reinhold Niebuhr

SHACHEE   *[shah-chee]*

MEANING: powerful, helpful • **USAGE:** Hindu: Sanskrit

If by strength is meant moral power, then woman is
immeasurably man's superior. Has she not greater
intuition, is she not more self-sacrificing,
has she not greater powers of endurance, has she not
greater courage? Without her man could not be.
If nonviolence is the law of our being, the future
is with woman. Who can make a more effective
appeal to the heart than woman?
— Mahatma Gandhi

SHADIYA, SHADIA   *[shah-dee-yah]*

MEANING: singer, songstress • **USAGE:** Muslim: from Arabic *shada* (to sing)

The chorus in the heart needs to sing /
Love is sovereign.
— Hafiz, "The Chorus in the Eye"
(tr. Daniel Ladinsky in *The Gift*)

SHAELEIGH, SHAELEE   *[SHAY-lee]*

MEANING: fairy, fairy place • **USAGE:** Irish: from Gaelic

Child of the pure, unclouded brow / And dreaming
eyes of wonder!... / Thy loving smile will surely hail
/ The love-gift of a fairy tale.
— Lewis Carroll, *Through the Looking-Glass*

SHAFIQA, SHAFEEQA   *[shah-FEE-kah]*

MEANING: compassionate, kindhearted, merciful • **USAGE:** Muslim feminine form of Shafiq, from Arabic *shafaqua* (to have compassion)

Lo! Allah loveth the kindly.
— Koran, The Table Spread 5.13 (PIC)

SHAHANA [shah-hah-nah]

MEANING: royal, noble • **USAGE:** Persian
> *If the thought is noble, it will ennoble you.*
> — Jalaluddin Rumi (tr. William Chittick in
> *The Sufi Path of Love*)

SHAIRA [shah-ih-rah]

MEANING: poetess, endowed with insight •
USAGE: Muslim
> *The Holy, like a good poem, may enter you and /*
> *coax your mind . . . to wade out*
> *to more interesting internal space.*
> — Hafiz (tr. Daniel Ladinsky in *A Year with Hafiz*)

SHAKEDA [shah-KEH-dah]

MEANING: almond, almond tree • **USAGE:** Jewish
feminine form of Shaked; symbolic name for
children born on Tu b'Shvat, the New Year of the
Trees
> *The almond trees are white / The sun is shining bright*
> */ Singing birds from every dome /*
> *Tell us Tu b'Shvat has come.*
> — Israeli Tu b'Shvat song

SHAKILAH, SHAKEELA [shah-KEE-lah]

MEANING: beautiful, lovely • **USAGE:** Muslim
feminine form of Shakil, from Arabic *shakil*
> *Beauty is eternity gazing at itself in a mirror.*
> *You are eternity and you are the mirror.*
> — Kahlil Gibran, *The Prophet*

SHAKIRA, SHAKIRAH [shah-KEE-rah]

MEANING: thankful, grateful • **USAGE:** Muslim
feminine form of Shakir, from Arabic *shakara* (to
thank)
> *This being human is a guest house. / Every morning a*
> *new arrival. / . . . Welcome and entertain them all! . . .*
> *Be grateful for whoever comes, / Because each has*
> *been sent / As a guide from Beyond.*
> — Jalaluddin Rumi, "The Guest House"
> (tr. Coleman Barks in *The Essential Rumi*)

SHALVA, SHALVAH [shahl-VAH]

MEANING: peaceful, calm, tranquil • **USAGE:**
Jewish
> *Peace, peace be unto thee.*
> — 1 Chronicles 12:19b (MT)

SHAMEENA [shah-mee-nah]

MEANING: beautiful • **USAGE:** Hindu: Sanskrit
> *Beauty is truth's smile when she beholds*
> *her own face in a perfect mirror.*
> — Rabindranath Tagore, *Fireflies*

SHAMIRA [shah-MEE-rah]

MEANING: guardian, defender, protector •
USAGE: Jewish
> *Discretion shall watch over thee,*
> *discernment shall guard thee.*
> — Proverbs 2:11 (MT)

SHANDA, SHONDA [SHAHN-dah]

MEANING: God is gracious, God is giving •
USAGE: American: possibly a form of Shauna, from
Hebrew *y'hohanan* (Yahweh is gracious)
> *Every best gift, and every perfect gift, is from above,*
> *coming down from the Father of lights, with whom*
> *there is no change, nor shadow of alteration.*
> — James 1:17 (DR)

SHANDELLE [shahn-DEL]

MEANING: song, singer, stone, rock, boulder •
USAGE: American form of Chantelle, from French
cantal (stone, boulder) or *chant* (song)
> *Sing, my tongue; sing, my hand; /*
> *sing, my feet, my knee, / my loins, my /*
> *whole body. / Indeed I am His / choir.*
> — Thomas Aquinas, "His Choir"
> (tr. Daniel Ladinsky in *Love Poems from God*)

S

SHANDRA   [SHAHN-drah]

MEANING: protector and helper of humankind, guardian • USAGE: American: possibly a form of Sandra, from Greek *alexein* (to defend, to help) and *andros* (man)

The more I help others to succeed, the more I succeed.
— Ray Kroc

SHANELLE   [shah-NEL]

MEANING: lily, rose, God is gracious, God is giving • USAGE: American: possibly a form of Shanna, from or possibly a form of Shoshana, from Hebrew *y'hohanan* (Yahweh is gracious)

Help us to be ever faithful gardeners of the spirit, who know that without darkness nothing comes to birth, and without light nothing flowers.
— May Sarton

SHANI   [SHAH-nee]

MEANING: marvel, wondrous • USAGE: African: Swahili of Kenya/Tanzania

The heart's eye sees many things.
— Swahili proverb

SHANI   [SHAH-nee, shah-NEE]

MEANING: crimson thread, scarlet, crimson, red • USAGE: Jewish

Nature uses only the longest threads to weave her patterns, so each small piece of her fabric reveals the organization of the entire tapestry.
— Richard Feynman, *The Character of Physical Law*

SHANIA   [shah-NIE-ah]

MEANING: she is on her way • USAGE: Amerind: Ojibwe

The more you know the more you will trust and the less you will fear.
— Ojibwe saying

SHANICE   [shah-NEES]

MEANING: God is gracious, God is giving, song, singer, stone, boulder, rock, lily, rose • USAGE: American: possibly a form of Shandelle, from Hebrew *y'hohanan* (Yahweh is gracious); possibly a form of Chantelle, from French *chant* (song) or *cantal* (stone, boulder); or possibly a form of Shanna, from Hebrew *shoshan* (lily, rose)

In matters of style, swim with the current; in matters of principle, stand like a rock.
— Thomas Jefferson

SHANKARI   [shahn-kah-ree]

MEANING: bliss-maker, beneficent • USAGE: Hindu: from Sanskrit *sam* (happiness, bliss) and *kara* (maker)

Love in feeling is peace, bliss.
— Sathya Sai Baba

SHANNA, SHANA   [SHAH-noh]

MEANING: lily, rose • USAGE: English form of Shoshanah, from Hebrew *shoshan*

Consider the lilies, how they grow: they neither toil nor spin; and yet I say to you, even Solomon in all his glory was not arrayed like one of these.
— Luke 12:27 (NKJV)

SHANNON, SHANNAN   [SHAN-on]

MEANING: wise, ancient, enduring, river name • USAGE: Irish and English: from Gaelic *sean* (ancient, wise); river in Ireland, known as "the old one"

Wisdom will enter your heart, and knowledge will fill you with joy.
— Proverbs 2:10 (NLT)

SHANTEL, SHANTELLE   [shahn-TEL]

MEANING: song, singer, stone, rock, boulder • USAGE: English form of Chantelle (*see* Shandelle)

Her step is music and her voice is song.
— Philip James Bailey, *Festus*

SHANTI   *[shahn-tee]*

MEANING: peace, peaceful • **USAGE:** Hindu: Sanskrit

> Shanti, shanti, shanti! *Peace, peace, peace!*
> — *Taittiriya Upanishad* (tr. Eknath Easwaran)

SHANTRA   *[SHAHN-trah]*

MEANING: song, singer, stone, rock, boulder • **USAGE:** American form of Shantrel (*see* Shantrel)

> *You will have songs…and gladness of heart.*
> — Isaiah 30:29 (NASB)

SHANTREL, SHANTRELLE   *[SHAHN-trel]*

MEANING: song, singer, stone, rock, boulder • **USAGE:** American form of Chantrelle (*see* Shandelle)

> *I will sing with my spirit,*
> *but I will sing also with my mind.*
> — 1 Corinthians 14:15b (NEB)

SHARI, SHARIE, SHARRIE, SHARRY, SHERRY   *[SHAYR-ee]*

MEANING: plain, fertile plain • **USAGE:** English form of Sharon (*see* Sharon)

> *I am a meadow flower from Sharon,*
> *a lily from the valleys.*
> — Song of Songs 2:1 (NEB)

SHARICE, SHARISE   *[shah-REES]*

MEANING: beloved, dear one, fertile plain, cherry fruit, cherry-red color • **USAGE:** American form of Sherry, from French *cherie* (beloved, dear); American form of Shari, from Hebrew *yesharon* (fertile plain); or American form of Cerise, from French *cerise* (cherry)

> *Love wisdom, and she will make you great.*
> *Embrace her, and she will bring you honor.*
> *She will be your crowning glory.*
> — Proverbs 4:8–9 (GNT)

SHARIFA   *[shah-REE-fah]*

MEANING: noble, distinguished, honorable • **USAGE:** Muslim feminine form of Sharif, from Arabic *sharafa* (to be distinguished)

> *Nobleness of character is an inborn quality as fragrance*
> *in the flower; it cannot be taught or learnt.*
> — Hazrat Inayat Khan, *The Gayan*

SHARITA   *[shah-REE-tah]*

MEANING: little fertile plain • **USAGE:** American form of Sharon, and diminutive *-ita* (*see* Sharon)

> *Let the field be joyful, and all that is in it.*
> — Psalm 96:12a (NKJV)

SHARLA   *[SHAR-lah]*

MEANING: one who is free, adult • **USAGE:** English feminine form of Charles, from English *ceorl* (freeman, peasant); or from German *karl* (full-grown man, adult)

> *Ye shall know the truth,*
> *and the truth shall make you free.*
> — John 8:32 (KJV)

SHARLAINE, SHARLAYNE   *[shar-LAYN]*

MEANING: one who is free, adult • **USAGE:** American feminine form of Charles (*see* Sharla)

> *Freedom is an internal achievement*
> *rather than an external adjustment.*
> — Adam Clayton Powell Jr.,
> *Keep the Faith, Baby!*

SHARLANA, CHARLANA   *[shar-LAH-nah]*

MEANING: one who is free, adult • **USAGE:** American feminine form of Charles (*see* Sharla)

> *In the truest sense,*
> *freedom cannot be bestowed; it must be achieved.*
> — Franklin D. Roosevelt
> (speech of September 22, 1935)

S

SHARLEEN, SHARLENE   *[shar-LEEN]*

MEANING: one who is free, adult • USAGE:
English form of Charlene (*see* Sharla)

> *The Lord is the Spirit,*
> *and where the Spirit of the Lord is, there is freedom.*
> — 2 Corinthians 3:17 (NIV)

SHARMEEN, SHARMIN   *[shahr-meen]*

MEANING: modest, chaste • USAGE: Muslim

> *Without modesty beauty is dead,*
> *for modesty is the spirit of beauty.*
> — Hazrat Inayat Khan, *The Gayan* (cd. *The Gayani*
> *Meditations, Volume 1*, tr. Cecil Touchon)

SHARMINI   *[shahr-mih-nee]*

MEANING: blissful • USAGE: Hindu: Sanskrit

> *Where there is Faith, there is Love; where there is love,*
> *there is peace; where there is peace, there is God, and*
> *where there is God, there is Bliss.*
> — Sathya Sai Baba

SHARON   *[shah-ROHN (Jewish),*
SHAYR-on (English)]

MEANING: plain, fertile plain • USAGE: Jewish and
English: from Hebrew *yesharon* (the Plain, a fertile
coastal plain in Israel)

> *I am a rose in the Plain of Sharon, a lily in the valleys.*
> — Song of Songs 2:1 (NCV)

SHARONA   *[shah-ROH-nah]*

MEANING: plain, fertile plain • USAGE: Jewish (*see*
Sharon)

> *Righteousness shall abide in the fruitful field.*
> — Isaiah 32:16b (MT)

SHASA   *[SHAH-sah]*

MEANING: good water, precious water • USAGE:
African: Bushman of Kalahari (South Africa)

> *Every stream has its source.*
> — South African proverb

SHASHINI   *[shah-shee-nee]*

MEANING: moon • USAGE: Hindu: from Sanskrit
shahsa

> *This moon is honey for all beings,*
> *and all beings are honey for this moon.*
> — *Brihadaranyaka Upanishad*
> (tr. Swami Prabhavananda)

SHASTA   *[SHAH-stah]*

MEANING: white mountain • USAGE: Amerind:
Kuruk (Northern California tribe)

> *The summit of the mountain, the thunder of the sky,*
> *the rhythm of the sea, speaks to me....*
> *And my heart soars.*
> — Dan George, *My Heart Soars*

SHAUNA, SHAWNA   *[SHAH-nah]*

MEANING: God is gracious, God is giving •
USAGE: Irish and English feminine form of Shaun,
from Hebrew *y'hohanan* (Yahweh is gracious)

> *May God be gracious to us and bless us*
> *and make his face shine upon us.*
> — Psalm 67:1 (NIV)

SHAYLA   *[SHAY-lah]*

MEANING: blind, dim-sighted woman • USAGE:
English form of Sheila, from Latin *caecus* (blind,
dim-sighted)

> *Faith makes us sure of what we hope for*
> *and gives us proof of what we cannot see.*
> — Hebrews 11:1 (CEV)

SHEELA   *[shee-lah]*

MEANING: virtuous, dignified • USAGE: Hindu:
from Sanskrit *sila*

> *She is virtuous, and she is very fortunate...*
> *she is beautiful, wise, and clever.*
> — *Sri Guru Granth Sahib*
> (Khalsa Consensus Translation)

SHEENA [*SHEE-nah*]

MEANING: God is gracious, God is giving •
USAGE: English form of Sine, from Hebrew
y'hohanan (Yahweh is gracious)

God is able to make all grace abound toward you,
that ye, always having all sufficiency in all things,
may abound in every good work.
— 2 Corinthians 9:8 (KJ21)

SHEEVA [*SHEE-vah*]

MEANING: good peace • **USAGE:** English form of
Siomha, from Gaelic *sith* (peace) and *maith* (good)

Peace lies not in the external world.
It lies within one's own soul.
— Ralph Waldo Trine, *In Tune with the Infinite*

SHEILA [*SHEE-lah*]

MEANING: blind, dim-sighted • **USAGE:** English
form of Sile, from Latin *caecus* (blind, dim-sighted)

Faith is the substance of things hoped for,
the evidence of things not seen.
— Hebrews 11:1 (KJV)

SHEINA [*SHAY-nah*]

MEANING: beautiful, lovely • **USAGE:** Yiddish:
from German *schoen*

Who is she that shines through like the dawn,
beautiful as the moon, radiant as the sun?
— Song of Songs 6:10 (JPS)

SHELBY, SHELBIE [*SHEL-bee*]

MEANING: willow town, settlement of huts,
settlement near the ledge • **USAGE:** English:
possibly a form of surname Selby, from Norse
selja býr (willow town); or possibly from English
schele (hut) or *scylf* (shelf, ledge) and *by* (farm,
settlement)

May there be peace within your walls...
peace be within you.
— Psalm 122:7–8 (NIV)

SHELLY, SHELLEY, SHELLIE [*SHEL-ee*]

MEANING: clearing on the ledge, Who is like
God?, wealthy, rich • **USAGE:** English surname:
from English *scelf* (shelf, ledge) and *leah* (meadow,
field); English form of Michelle, from Hebrew
mikha'el (Who is like God?); or from Irish Gaelic
selbhach (having many possessions, wealthy)

God is love, and those who abide in love
abide in God, and God abides in them.
— 1 John 4:16b (NRSV)

SHERI, SHERIE, SHERRIE [*SHAYR-ee*]

MEANING: beloved, dear one • **USAGE:** English
form of Cherie: from French *cherie*

Beloved, I pray that all may go well with you
and that you may be in good health,
just as it is well with your soul.
— 3 John 1:2 (NRSV)

SHERIDAN [*SHER-ih-den*]

MEANING: elfin child, eternal treasure, eternal
poem, seeker • **USAGE:** English and Irish surname:
form of Irish *O'Sirideain*, from Gaelic *o* (son of),
siride (elf) and diminutive *-an;* from Gaelic *sior*
(eternal) and *dan* (treasure, poem); or from Gaelic
sirim (to seek)

Lay up for yourselves treasures in heaven...for where
your treasure is, there your heart will be also.
— Matthew 6:20–21 (ESV)

SHIBA, SHEBA [*shee-bah*]

MEANING: beautiful lady, beautiful lady, Ethiopian
queen • **USAGE:** African: Ethiopia

Through wisdom I have dived down in the great sea,
and have seized in the place of her depths a pearl where
I am rich. I went down like the great iron anchor,
whereby men anchor ships for the night on the high
seas, and I received a lamp which lighteth me, and I
came up by the ropes of the boat of understanding.
— Queen of Sheba
(cd. *Kebra Negast*, tr. E. A. Wallis Budge)

S

SHIFRA, SHIFRAH   [shee-FRAH]

MEANING: good, beautiful • USAGE: Jewish
Trust in the Lord and do good.
— Psalm 37:3a (JPS)

SHIKAH   [shih-KAH]

MEANING: peak, mountain peak • USAGE: Hindu:
Sanskrit
For aspirants who wish to climb the mountain of
spiritual awareness, the path is selfless work.
For those who have attained the summit of union with
the Lord, the path is stillness and peace.
— *Bhagavad Gita* (tr. Eknath Easwaran in
The Bhagavad Gita for Daily Living)

SHILOH, SHILO   [SHY-loh]

MEANING: the gift is His, His gift • USAGE:
Jewish: from Hebrew *shai* (gift) and *lo* (his)
The Lord lift up His countenance upon thee,
and give thee peace.
— Numbers 6:26 (MT)

SHIMONA   [shee-MOH-nah]

MEANING: hear, hearken • USAGE: Jewish
feminine form of Shimon, from Hebrew *shim'on*
Make me to hear joy and gladness.
— Psalm 51:10a (MT)

SHIRAH   [shee-RAH]

MEANING: song, melody • USAGE: Jewish
Sweet is thy voice, and thy countenance is comely.
— Song of Songs 2:14b (MT)

SHIRAN   [shee-RAHN]

MEANING: happy song • USAGE: Jewish
Break forth and sing for joy.
— Psalm 98:4b (JPS)

SHIRAZ   [shee-RAHZ]

MEANING: secret song • USAGE: my song, song
is mine
I will sing to the Lord, for He has been good to me.
— Psalm 13:6b (JPS)

SHIREEN   [shih-REEN]

MEANING: sweet, pleasant, fertile plain • USAGE:
American: possibly a form of Shirin, from Persian
shirin (sweet, pleasant); or possibly a form of Shari,
from Hebrew *yesharon* (fertile plain)
Let the fields be jubilant,
and everything in them!
— 1 Chronicles 16:32b (NIV)

SHIREL   [shee-REHL]

MEANING: God's song • USAGE: Jewish
I will sing of the Lord's steadfast love forever.
— Psalm 89:1a (JPS)

SHIRIN   [shee-reen]

MEANING: pleasant, charming, sweet-natured •
USAGE: Persian: from Persian *shirin*
A charming personality is as precious as gold
and as delicious as perfume.
— Hazrat Inayat Khan, *The Gayan* (cd. *The Gayani*
Meditations, Volume 1, tr. Cecil Touchon)

SHIRLENE, SHIRLEEN   [SHER-leen]

MEANING: bright meadow, pasture near the shire •
USAGE: English form of Shirley (*see* Shirley)
He [God] lets me lie down in green pastures;
He leads me beside quiet waters.
— Psalm 23:2 (HCSB)

SHIRLEY   [SHER-lee]

MEANING: bright meadow • USAGE: English:
from English *scir* (bright, shire) and *leah* (meadow,
pasture)

S

The grass grows, the buds burst, the meadow is spotted
with fire and gold in the tint of flowers.
— Ralph Waldo Emerson,
"Divinity School Address"

SHLOMIT [shloh-MEET]

MEANING: peace, peaceful • USAGE: Jewish
feminine form of Shlomo, from Hebrew *shalom*
At peace, at peace with you.
— 1 Chronicles 12:19b (JPS)

SHOBA [SHOH-bah]

MEANING: brilliance, beauty • USAGE: Hindu:
Sanskrit
Look at / beauty's gift to us — her power is so great
she enlivens / the earth, the sky, our / soul.
— Mira, "A Hundred Objects Close By"

SHONA [SHOH-nah]

MEANING: God is gracious, God is giving •
USAGE: Scottish form of Sinead, from Hebrew
y'hohanan (Yahweh is gracious)
The Lord your God is kind and tender.
He won't turn away from you.
— 2 Chronicles 30:9b (NIRV)

SHONA [SHOH-nah]

MEANING: beautiful, lovely • USAGE: Yiddish
form of *Shaina*, from German *schoen*
Thou are all fair, my love; and there is no spot in thee.
— Song of Songs 4:7 (MT)

SHONDEL [shahn-DEL]

MEANING: stone, boulder, song, singer • USAGE:
American form of Shandelle, from French *cantal*
(stone, boulder) or *chant* (song)
I will sing with my spirit,
but I will also sing with my mind.
— 1 Corinthians 14:15b (NCV)

SHOSHANAH, SHOSHANNAH
[shoh-shah-NAH, shoh-SHAH-nah]

MEANING: lily, rose • USAGE: Jewish: from
Hebrew *shoshan*
The flowers of the field,
they are kith and kin to me;
the lily my sister, the rose is my blood and flesh.
— Abraham Moses Klein,
"Out of the Pulver and Polished Lens"

SHREYA [SHRAY-ah]

MEANING: fortunate, auspicious, beautiful •
USAGE: Hindu
Those who find the Lord
are very fortunate and blessed.
— Sri Guru Granth Sahib
(Khalsa Consensus Translation)

SHRILA [SHREE-lah]

MEANING: beautiful, fortunate • USAGE: Hindu:
Sanskrit
Beauty is omnipresent,
therefore everything is capable of giving us joy.
— Rabindranath Tagore, *Sadhana*

SHU [shoo]

MEANING: kind, compassionate, gentle • USAGE:
Chinese
Kindness in giving creates love.
— Lao Tzu

SHUCHEE [shuh-chee]

MEANING: pure • USAGE: Hindu: Sanskrit
The purity of life is the highest
and most authentic art to follow.
— Mahatma Gandhi

S

SHULA [SHOO-lah]

MEANING: peace, peaceful • USAGE: Jewish
> Peace is the beauty of life. It is sunshine.
> It is the smile of a child, the love of a mother,
> the joy of a father, the togetherness of a family....
> Peace is all of these and more and more.
> — Menachem Begin
> (December 10, 1978, Nobel lecture)

SHYLA [SHIE-lah]

MEANING: blind, dim-sighted • USAGE: English
form of Sheila, from Latin *caecus* (blind, dim-
sighted)
> Faith is the confidence that what we hope
> for will actually happen; it gives us assurance
> about things we cannot see.
> — Hebrews 11:1 (NLT)

SIAN [shahn]

MEANING: God is gracious, God is giving •
USAGE: Welsh form of Jane, from Hebrew
y'hohanan (Yahweh is gracious)
> The Lord gives wisdom.
> Knowledge and understanding come from his mouth.
> He stores up success for honest people.
> — Proverbs 2:6–7 (NIRV)

SIBEAL [shih-BAYL, sih-BAYL]

MEANING: God is my oath, joined with God,
blessed by God • USAGE: Irish form of Isabel, from
Hebrew *el'ishebha*
> May God enfold you in the mantle of His love.
> — Celtic blessing

SIBYL [SIB-el]

MEANING: prophetess, seer • USAGE: Greek: from
Greek *sibylla*
> Wisdom is found on the lips of the discerning.
> — Proverbs 10:13a (NIV)

SIBYLLA [sih-BEE-lah]

MEANING: prophetess, seer • USAGE:
Scandinavian, German, and Greek form of Sybil
(*see* Sibyl)
> It is your destiny to see as God sees, /
> to know as God knows, / to feel as God / feels.
> — Meister Eckhart, "To See as God Sees"
> (tr. Daniel Ladinsky in *Love Poems from God*)

SIDNEY, SYDNEY, SYDNIE [SID-nee]

MEANING: broad island, wide island • USAGE:
English surname: from English *sid* (wide, broad)
and *ieg* (island)
> The Lord...brought me forth
> also into a broad place...because He delighted in me.
> — Psalm 18:18a–19 (NASB)

SIEGFRIDA [seeg-FREE-dah]

MEANING: peaceful victory, victorious peace •
USAGE: German feminine form of Sigfried, from
German *sige* (victory, success) and *frid* (peace,
peaceful)
> May grace and peace be yours in full measure.
> — 1 Peter 1:2b (NEB)

SIEGLINDE [SEEG-lin-deh]

MEANING: gentle victory • USAGE: German: from
German *sige* (victory, success) and *linde* (gentle,
soft)
> Blessed are the gentle, for they shall inherit the earth.
> — Matthew 5:5 (NASB)

SIENA, SIENNA [see-EN-ah]

MEANING: earth color, orange-red color, brown-
red color, old, ancient • USAGE: American: from
Latin *sienna* (orange-red, brown-red, earth color)
or *seneo* (old, ancient)
> Some of us come on earth seeing —
> some of us come on earth seeing color.
> — Louise Nevelson

SIERRA   *[see-AYR-ah]*

MEANING: rugged mountains, mountain range • **USAGE:** American: from Latin *serra* (serrated, a saw); a reference to rugged mountains with a serrated profile

> *It seemed to me the Sierra should be called not the Nevada, or Snowy Range, but the Range of Light…the divinely most beautiful of all the mountain-chains I have ever seen.*
> — John Muir, *The Mountains of California*

SIGI   *[SEE-gee]*

MEANING: peaceful victory, victorious peace, gentle victory • **USAGE:** German form of Siegfrida (*see* Siegfrida); or German form of Sieglinde (*see* Sieglinde)

> *May the Lord look on you with favor and give you peace.*
> — Numbers 6:26 (GNT)

SIGNY, SIGNE   *[SEEG-nee]*

MEANING: new victory • **USAGE:** Scandinavian: from Norse *sigr* (victory) and *ny* (new)

> *Win the victory for what is true and right.*
> — Psalm 45:4b (NCV)

SIGRID   *[SEEG-reed]*

MEANING: beautiful victory • **USAGE:** Scandinavian form of *Sigridr*, from Norse *sigr* (victory, conquest) and *friðr* (fair, beautiful)

> *The beautiful word begets the beautiful deed.*
> — Thomas Mann, *The Magic Mountain*

SIGRUN   *[SEEG-run]*

MEANING: secret lore, victory • **USAGE:** Scandinavian: from Norse *sigr* (victory) and *run* (secret lore)

> *O God…you delight in truth in the inward being, and you teach me wisdom in the secret heart.*
> — Psalm 51:1, 51:6 (ESV)

SIHU   *[see-hoo]*

MEANING: flower, blossom • **USAGE:** Amerind: Hopi

> *Sprinkle me, / Cloud, come bathe me!…*
> *Oh, change me now, / Into a cluster of flowers.*
> — Hopi song

SIKIA   *[see-kee-ah]*

MEANING: harmony • **USAGE:** African: Kenya

> *Better to build bridges than to raise walls.*
> — Swahili of Kenya proverb

SILE   *[SHEE-lah]*

MEANING: blind, dim-sighted • **USAGE:** Irish form of Cecilia, from Latin *caecus* (blind, dim-sighted)

> *We walk by faith, not by sight.*
> — 2 Corinthians 5:7 (NKJV)

SILVIA   *[SIL-vee-ah (English), SEEL-vee-ah (German, Italian)]*

MEANING: woods, forest • **USAGE:** English, German, and Italian: from Latin *silva*

> *Now is the time of illuminated woods… every leaf glows like a tiny lamp.*
> — John Burroughs

SIMCHA   *[seem-KHAH]*

MEANING: joy, gladness • **USAGE:** Jewish

> *Thou hast put gladness in my heart.*
> — Psalm 4:8a (MT)

SIMI   *[see-mee]*

MEANING: valley of the wind • **USAGE:** First Nation: Eskimo-Chumash

> *Earth and the great weather / Move me, / Have carried me away / And move my inward parts with joy.*
> — Eskimo song

S

SIMONA   *[see-MOH-nah]*

MEANING: hear, hearken • **USAGE:** Italian form of Simone (*see* Simone)

> *If you love to listen you will gain knowledge,*
> *and if you incline your ear you will become wise.*
> — Ben Sira 6:33 (RSV Apocrypha)

SIMONE   *[see-MOHN]*

MEANING: hear, hearken • **USAGE:** French feminine form of Simon, from Hebrew *shim'on*

> *Let me hear joy and gladness.*
> — Psalm 51:8a (NIV)

SINDRA, CINDRA   *[SEN-drah]*

MEANING: protector and helper of humankind, guardian • **USAGE:** American: possibly a form of Sandra, from Greek *alexein* (to defend, to help) and *andros* (man)

> *For he hath given his angels charge over thee;*
> *to keep thee in all thy ways.*
> — Psalm 90:11 (DR)

SINE   *[SHEE-nah]*

MEANING: God is gracious, God is giving • **USAGE:** Scottish and Irish form of Jean, from Hebrew *y'hohanan* (Yahweh is gracious)

> *The Lord your God is gracious and merciful,*
> *and will not turn His face from you.*
> — 2 Chronicles 30:9b (NKJV)

SINEAD   *[sheh-NAYD]*

MEANING: God is gracious, God is giving • **USAGE:** Irish form of Jane (*see* Sine)

> *The Lord bless you and protect you; the Lord make his*
> *face to shine upon you, and be gracious to you;*
> *the Lord lift up his countenance upon you*
> *and give you peace.*
> — Numbers 6:24–26 (NEB)

SIOBHAN   *[sheh-VAHN]*

MEANING: God is gracious, God is giving • **USAGE:** Irish form of Jean (*see* Sine)

> *God be gracious to you.*
> — Genesis 43:29b (ASV)

SIOMHA   *[SHEE-vah]*

MEANING: good peace • **USAGE:** Irish and English: from Gaelic *sith* (peace) and *maith* (good)

> *Blessed are the peacemakers,*
> *for they shall be called children of God.*
> — Matthew 5:9 (WEB)

SIONA   *[see-OH-nah]*

MEANING: highest point, peak • **USAGE:** Jewish feminine form of Sion

> *God, the Lord, is my strength....*
> *He maketh me to walk upon my high places.*
> — Habakkuk 3:19 (MT)

SIONED   *[SHOH-ned]*

MEANING: God is gracious, God is giving • **USAGE:** Welsh form of Janet (*see* Sine)

> *Your kindness and love will always be*
> *with me each day of my life,*
> *and I will live forever in your house, Lord.*
> — Psalm 23:6 (CEV)

SIRI   *[see-ree]*

MEANING: beautiful victory • **USAGE:** Scandinavian form of Sigrid, from Norse *sigr* (victory, conquest) and *friðr* (fair, beautiful)

> *The boundary lines have fallen for me in pleasant*
> *places; indeed, I have a beautiful inheritance.*
> — Psalm 16:6 (HCSB)

S

SISSY, CISSY   [*SIS-ee*]

MEANING: blind, dim-sighted, sister • **USAGE:**
English form of Cecilia or Cecily: from Latin *caecus*
(blind, dim-sighted); or colloquial name for sister
Say to Wisdom, "You are my sister,"
and call understanding a kinsman.
— Proverbs 7:4 (RSV)

SITARA   [*sih-tahr-ah*]

MEANING: star • **USAGE:** Hindu: from Sanskrit *tara*
Let me think that there is one among those stars
that guides my life through the dark unknown.
— Rabindranath Tagore, *Stray Birds*

SKYE, SKY   [*skie*]

MEANING: cloud, sky, heaven • **USAGE:**
American: from Norse *sky* (cloud)
The sky is the daily bread of the eyes.
— Ralph Waldo Emerson
(journal entry of May 25, 1843)

SKYLA   [*SKIE-lah*]

MEANING: scholar, learned, knowledgeable, cloud,
sky, heaven • **USAGE:** American form of Skylar (*see*
Skylar), or of Skye (*see* Skye)
My soul is the sky.
— William Shakespeare,
A Midsummer Night's Dream

SKYLAR, SKYLER   [*SKIE-ler*]

MEANING: scholar, learned, knowledgeable •
USAGE: American: from Dutch *schuyler* (scholar)
Knowledge is love and light and vision.
— Helen Keller, *The Story of My Life*

SOFIA, SOFÍA   [*soh-FEE-ah*]

MEANING: wise, wisdom, sage • **USAGE:**
Scandinavian, German, Italian, Russian, and
Spanish form of Sophia, from Greek *sophia*
(wisdom) or *sophos* (wise)

Wisdom shall enter into thy heart,
and knowledge shall be pleasant unto thy soul.
— Proverbs 2:10 (ASV)

SOFIE   [*SOH-fee*]

MEANING: wise, wisdom, sage • **USAGE:** German
and Scandinavian form of Sophia (*see* Sofia)
May you be blessed for your wisdom.
— 1 Samuel 25:33a (NCV)

SOFIYA   [*soh-FEE-ah*]

MEANING: wise, wisdom, sage • **USAGE:** Russian
form of Sophia (*see* Sofia)
Wisdom hath been created before all things,
and the understanding of prudence from everlasting.
— Sirach 1:4 (DR Apocrypha)

SOFRONIA   [*soh-FROH-nee-ah*]

MEANING: wise, wisdom, sage • **USAGE:** Greek:
from Greek *sophos* (wise)
Wisdom begins in wonder.
— Socrates

SOJOURNER   [*SOH-jer-ner*]

MEANING: traveler, journeyer • **USAGE:**
American: from English *sojournen* (a temporary
stay)
The soul of a journey is liberty.
— William Hazlitt, "On Going a Journey"

SOLANA   [*soh-LAH-nah*]

MEANING: wind from the east • **USAGE:** Spanish:
from Spanish *solana*
The wind blows wherever it pleases.
You hear its sound, but you cannot tell
where it comes from or where it is going.
So it is with everyone born of the Spirit.
— John 3:8 (NIV)

S

SOLEDAD   [soh-lay-DAHD]

MEANING: solitude, aloneness • USAGE: Spanish: from Spanish *soledad* (solitude); honors the Virgin Mary, "Nuestra Señora de la Soledad" (Our Lady of Solitude)

> *Whoever has God lacks nothing: /*
> *God alone is enough.*
> — Teresa of Avila, "God Alone Is Enough"

SOLINA   [soh-LEE-nah]

MEANING: little sunshine, sunbeam • USAGE: American: possibly from Latin *sol* (the sun) and diminutive *-ina*

> *Those who bring sunshine to the lives*
> *of others cannot keep it from themselves.*
> — James M. Barrie, *A Window in Thrums*

SOLITA   [soh-LEE-tah]

MEANING: little sunshine, sunbeam • USAGE: American: possibly from Latin *sol* (the sun) and diminutive *-ita*

> *The sun does not shine for a few trees and flowers,*
> *but for the wide world's joy.*
> — Henry Ward Beecher

SOMMER   [SUM-er]

MEANING: summertime, fruition, fulfillment • USAGE: American: from English *sumor* (summer)

> *Summer afternoon — summer afternoon;*
> *to me those have always been the two most*
> *beautiful words in the English language.*
> — Henry James

SONDRA   [SON-drah]

MEANING: protector and helper of humankind, defender • USAGE: English form of Sandra, from Greek *alexein* (to defend, to help) and *andros* (man)

> *Discretion shall preserve thee,*
> *and understanding shall keep thee.*
> — Proverbs 2:11 (KJ21)

SONIA   [SOHN-yah]

MEANING: wise, wisdom, sage • USAGE: English, Italian, and Spanish form of Sophia (*see* Sophia)

> *A loving heart is the truest wisdom.*
> — Charles Dickens

SONJA   [SOHN-yah]

MEANING: wise, wisdom, sage • USAGE: Scandinavian form of Sophia (*see* Sophia)

> *The wisdom that is from above is first pure, then*
> *peaceful, gentle, reasonable, full of mercy and good*
> *fruits, without partiality, and without hypocrisy.*
> — James 3:17 (WEB)

SONJE   [SOHN-yah]

MEANING: wise, wisdom, sage • USAGE: German form of Sophia (*see* Sophia)

> *Wisdom…is what Heaven sends, and only to children*
> *of the earth who turn themselves to it.*
> — Paul Fleming

SONNET   [SAHN-et]

MEANING: poem, song • USAGE: English: from French *sonet* (song); a fourteen-line poem

> *You have set yourself to music.*
> *Your days are your sonnets.*
> — Oscar Wilde, *The Picture of Dorian Gray*

SONYA   [SAHN-yah (Russian), SOHN-yah (English)]

MEANING: wise, wisdom, sage • USAGE: Russian and English form of Sophia (*see* Sophia)

> *Wisdom will enter your heart,*
> *and knowledge will be pleasant to your soul.*
> — Proverbs 2:10 (NASB)

SOOK-JA   [sook-jah]

MEANING: virtuous woman • USAGE: Korean: from Korean *sook* (clean, female virtue) and feminine ending *ja*

Virtuous ones are happy in this world and in the next.
They are happy when they think of the good
they have done. They are even happier
when they continue on the good path.
— Buddha, *The Dhammapada*
(tr. Friedrich Max Müller)

SOPHIA   *[soh-FEE-ah]*

MEANING: wise, wisdom, sage • **USAGE:** Greek,
English, German, and Italian: from Greek *sophia*
(wisdom) or *sophos* (wise)
Wisdom and knowledge is granted to you.
— 2 Chronicles 1:12a (WEB)

SOPHIE   *[soh-FEE (French, German),*
SOH-fee (English)]

MEANING: wise, wisdom, sage • **USAGE:** French,
German, and English form of Sophia (*see* Sophia)
Wisdom is best. So get wisdom.
No matter what it costs, get understanding.
Value wisdom, and she will lift you up. Hold her close,
and she will honor you. She will set a beautiful
crown on your head.
She will give you a glorious crown.
— Proverbs 4:7–9 (NIRV)

SORCHA   *[SOR-hah, SOR-kah]*

MEANING: bright, radiant light • **USAGE:** Irish and
Scottish: from Gaelic *sorchae*
The Lord will…fill thy soul with brightness.
— Isaiah 58:11a (DR)

SOTIRIA   *[soh-TEE-ree-ah]*

MEANING: salvation • **USAGE:** Greek feminine
form of Sotirios, from Greek *soteria*
My soul shall be joyful in my God;
for He has clothed me with the garments of salvation,
he has covered me with the robe of righteousness.
— Isaiah 61:10a (NKJV)

SO-YOUNG   *[soh-yung]*

MEANING: smiling flower • **USAGE:** Korean: from
Korean *so* (smile) and *young* (flower)
Butterflies come to pretty flowers.
— Korean proverb

SPARROW   *[SPAYR-oh]*

MEANING: sparrow, small finch • **USAGE:** English:
from English *spearwa*
The first sparrow of spring!
The year beginning with younger hope than ever!
— Henry David Thoreau, *Walden*

SPRING   *[spring]*

MEANING: season of spring, springlike,
flourishing, bountiful, time of sowing • **USAGE:**
English: from Latin *satus* (plant, sow); the season
of spring
Thus came the lovely spring with a rush of blossoms
and music, / Flooding the earth with flowers,
and the air with melodies vernal.
— Henry Wadsworth Longfellow,
Tales of a Wayside Inn

STACY, STACI, STACIE, STACEY
[STAY-see]

MEANING: resurrection, reborn, rise up • **USAGE:**
English form of Anastasia, from Greek *anastasis*
(resurrection), or from Greek *ana* (up) and *stasis*
(standing)
I have been dipped again in God, and new-created.
— D. H. Lawrence, "Shadows"

STAR, STARR   *[star]*

MEANING: star, starlike, radiant • **USAGE:** English:
from English *steorra*
Whatever road I take, the guiding star is within me;
the guiding star and the loadstone which point the way.
— Ayn Rand, *Anthem*

S

STARLA   *[STAR-lah]*

MEANING: star, starlike, radiant • **USAGE:** English: from English *steorra*

> *The glory of the stars is the beauty of heaven,*
> *a glittering array in the heights of the Lord.*
> — Sirach 43:9 (NRSV Apocrypha)

STARLEEN, STARLINE   *[star-LEEN]*

MEANING: star, starlike, radiant • **USAGE:** English: from English *steorra*

> *Ye stars! Which are the poetry of heaven!*
> — Lord Byron, *Childe Harold's Pilgrimage*

STEFANA   *[steh-FAH-nah]*

MEANING: crown, crowned one • **USAGE:** Greek and Dutch feminine form of Stephen (*see* Stephanie)

> *She [Wisdom] will place a garland of grace on your*
> *head; she will give you a crown of beauty.*
> — Proverbs 4:9 (HCSB)

STEFANIA   *[steh-FAH-nee-ah]*

MEANING: crown, crowned one • **USAGE:** Italian and Greek form of Stephanie (*see* Stephanie)

> *Love is the crowning grace of humanity,*
> *the holiest rite of the soul, the golden link*
> *that binds us to duty and truth.*
> — Francesco Petrarch

STELLA   *[STEL-ah (English),*
STAY-lah (Greek)]

MEANING: star, starlike, radiant • **USAGE:** English and Greek: from Latin *stella*

> *Love is more than a candle, love can ignite the stars.*
> — Matthew Stover, *Revenge of the Sith*

STELLINA   *[steh-LEE-nah]*

MEANING: star, starlike, radiant • **USAGE:** Greek form of Stella and diminutive *-ina* (*see* Stella)

> *He counts the number of stars;*
> *He gives names to all of them.*
> — Psalm 147:4 (NASB)

STEPHANIA   *[steh-FAH-nee-ah]*

MEANING: crown, crowned one • **USAGE:** English form of Stephanie (*see* Stephanie)

> *Thou shalt be a crown of glory in the hand of the Lord,*
> *and a royal diadem in the hand of thy God.*
> — Isaiah 62:3 (DR)

STEPHANIE, STEPHANY, STEFANY, STEFANIE   *[STEF-ah-nee]*

MEANING: crown, crowned one • **USAGE:** English feminine form of Stephen, from Greek *stephanos*

> *You will wear Wisdom like a splendid crown.*
> — Sirach 6:31 (GNT Apocrypha)

SUE   *[soo]*

MEANING: lily, rose • **USAGE:** English form of Susan, from Hebrew *shoshan*

> *Lovely as Spring's first rose.*
> — William Wordsworth, "The Borderers"

SUELLEN   *[soo-EL-en]*

MEANING: illumined rose, lily of light, radiant flower • **USAGE:** English combination of Sue and Ellen (*see* Sue and Ellen)

> *In all places, and in all seasons, /*
> *Flowers expand their light and soul-like wings.*
> — Henry Wadsworth Longfellow, "Flowers"

SUELO   *[SWAY-loh]*

MEANING: consoler, comforter • **USAGE:** Spanish form of Consuelo, from Spanish *consuelo*

> *I, even I, am He who comforts you.*
> — Isaiah 51:12a (NKJV)

SUH-HYUN   [suh-hyun]

MEANING: fortunate and kind • **USAGE:** Korean: from Korean *suh* (auspicious, fortunate) and *hyun* (benevolent, kind)

> *Teach this triple truth to all: A generous heart,*
> *kind speech, and a life of service and compassion*
> *are the things which renew humanity.*
> — Buddha

SUKI   [SOO-kee]

MEANING: beloved, dear • **USAGE:** Japanese: from Japanese *suki* (fond of)

> *With love and patience, nothing is impossible.*
> — Daisaku Ikeda, *The Cherry Tree*

SUKIE, SUKI   [SOO-kee]

MEANING: lily, rose • **USAGE:** English form of Susanna, from Hebrew *shoshan*

> *I am a rose of Sharon, the lily of the valleys.*
> — Song of Songs 2:1 (NASB)

SUMA   [soo-mah]

MEANING: flower, blossom • **USAGE:** Hindu: Sanskrit

> *Every morning the day is reborn*
> *among the newly-blossomed flowers.*
> — Rabindranath Tagore, *Sadhana*

SUMITRA   [suh-mih-trah]

MEANING: good friend • **USAGE:** Hindu: from Sanskrit *su* (good, excellent) and *mitra* (friend)

> *There is a magnet in your heart that will attract*
> *true friends. That magnet is unselfishness,*
> *thinking of others first.... When you learn to live*
> *for others, they will live for you.*
> — Paramahansa Yogananda,
> "How to Be More Likeable"

SUMMER   [SUM-er]

MEANING: summertime, fruition, fulfillment • **USAGE:** English: from English *sumor* (summer)

> *Shall I compare thee to a summer's day? /*
> *Thou art more lovely.*
> — William Shakespeare, "Sonnet 18"

SUNITI   [suh-nee-tee]

MEANING: woman with excellent conduct, courteous, gracious, well-mannered • **USAGE:** Hindu: from Sanskrit *su* (good, excellent) and *niti* (conduct, behavior)

> *Be calm and patient,*
> *both in private and in public.*
> — Taittiriya Upanishad

SUNNIVA   [soo-NEE-vah]

MEANING: gift of the sun • **USAGE:** Scandinavian form of *Sunngifu*, from English *sunne* (sun) and *gifu* (gift)

> *The sun shines on me, and the forest kisses.*
> *O, how richly have I been gifted!*
> — Hans Christian Andersen, "The Daisy"

SUNNY, SUNNIE   [SUN-ee]

MEANING: sunny, cheerful, happy • **USAGE:** English: from English *sun*

> *Love...must always create a sunshine,*
> *filling the heart so full of radiance,*
> *that it overflows upon the outward world.*
> — Nathaniel Hawthorne, *The Scarlet Letter*

SURAH, SURA   [SOO-rah]

MEANING: princess, royal one • **USAGE:** Yiddish form of Sarah, from Hebrew *sarah*

> *A throne is established through mercy.*
> — Isaiah 16:5a (MT)

S

SURI   *[SOO-ree]*

Meaning: princess, royal one • **Usage:** English form of Sarah, from Hebrew *sarah*

> *Seek ye first the kingdom of God,*
> *and his righteousness;*
> *and all these things shall be added unto you.*
> — Matthew 6:33 (KJV)

SURINA   *[suh-rih-nah]*

Meaning: goddess, divine • **Usage:** Hindu: from *sura*

> *Will power is what makes you divine.*
> — Paramahansa Yogananda, "Answered Prayers"

SUSAN, SUZAN   *[SOO-ʒan]*

Meaning: lily, rose • **Usage:** English form of Susannah (*see* Susanna)

> *The path of a good woman is indeed strewn with flowers; but they rise behind her steps, not before them.*
> — John Ruskin, "Of Queens' Gardens"

SUSANA   *[soo-SAHN-ah]*

Meaning: lily, rose • **Usage:** Spanish and Italian form of Shoshanah (*see* Susanna)

> *I am the flower of the field, and the lily of the valleys.*
> — Song of Songs 2:1 (DR)

SUSANNA   *[soo-SAH-nah (Scandinavian, Italian, Russian), soo-ZAN-ah (English)]*

Meaning: lily, rose • **Usage:** Scandinavian, English, Italian, and Russian form of Shoshanah, from Hebrew *shoshan*

> *What's in a name? That which we call a rose*
> *by any other name would smell as sweet.*
> — William Shakespeare, *Romeo and Juliet*

SUSANNAH   *[soo-SAN-ah]*

Meaning: lily, rose • **Usage:** English form of Shoshanah (*see* Susanna)

> *I am a rose of Sharon, a lily of the valleys.*
> — Song of Songs 2:1 (ESV)

SUSANNE   *[soo-SAHN-ah (Scandinavian, German), soo-ZAN (English)]*

Meaning: lily, rose • **Usage:** German, English, and Scandinavian form of Shoshanah (*see* Susanna)

> *You are like a flower.*
> — Heinrich Heine, "Du Bist wie eine Blume" (tr. Louis Untermeyer)

SUSHANTI   *[suh-shahn-tih]*

Meaning: calm, peaceful, quiet • **Usage:** Hindu

> *You must learn to be still in the midst of activity*
> *and to be vibrantly alive in repose.*
> — Indira Gandhi

SUSHILA   *[soo-SHEE-lah]*

Meaning: good conduct, greatly virtuous • **Usage:** Hindu: from Sanskrit *su* (good) and *shila* (conduct)

> *Let your conduct be marked by right action…by truthfulness in word, deed, and thought.*
> — *Taittiriya Upanishad* (tr. Swami Prabhavanand)

SUSIE, SUZIE, SUZY   *[SOO-ʒee]*

Meaning: lily, rose • **Usage:** English form of Susan (*see* Susanna)

> *A good woman is the loveliest flower*
> *that blooms under heaven.*
> — William Makepeace Thackeray, *The History of Pendennis*

SUZANNA, SUZANNAH   *[soo-ZAN-ah]*

Meaning: lily, rose • **Usage:** English form of Shoshanah (*see* Susanna)

> *Consider the lilies, how they grow: they neither toil nor spin, yet I tell you, even Solomon in all his glory was not arrayed like one of these.*
> — Luke 12:27 (ESV)

SUZANNE
[soo-ZAHN (French), soo-ZAN (English)]

MEANING: lily, rose • USAGE: French and English form of Susan (*see* Susanna)
> *You become responsible forever for what you have tamed. You're responsible for your rose.*
> — Antoine de Saint-Exupéry, *The Little Prince*
> (tr. Richard Howard)

SUZETTE
[soo-ZET]

MEANING: little lily, little rose • USAGE: French form of Suzanne and diminutive *-ette* (*see* Susanna)
> *Honor women! They strew celestial roses on the pathway of our terrestrial life.*
> — Pierre-Claude-Victor Boiste

SUZUKI
[soo-zoo-kee]

MEANING: bell tree • USAGE: Japanese: from Japanese *suzu* (bell) and *ki* (tree)
> *The temple bell stops but I still hear the sound coming out of the flowers.*
> — Matsuo Bashō

SVENJA
[SVEN-yah]

MEANING: swan, swan-like • USAGE: German: from German *svan*
> *Wash me, and I shall be whiter than snow.*
> — Psalm 51:7b (GNT)

SVETLANA
[svet-LAH-nah]

MEANING: light, illumination, radiance • USAGE: Russian: from Russian *svet* (light)
> *Arise, shine; for thy light is come.*
> — Isaiah 60:1a (ASV)

SYBIL
[SIB-el]

MEANING: prophetess, seer • USAGE: English: from Greek *sibylla*
> *Wisdom is found on the lips of the discerning.*
> — Proverbs 10:13a (NIV)

SYBILLA
[sih-BEE-lah]

MEANING: prophetess, seer • USAGE: German and Dutch form of Sybil (*see* Sybil)
> *She openeth her mouth with wisdom; and the law of kindness is on her tongue.*
> — Proverbs 31:26 (ASV)

SYBILLE
[SEE-beel (French), see-BIL-eh (German)]

MEANING: prophetess, seer • USAGE: French and German (*see* Sybil)
> *Seeing. We might say that the whole of life lies in that verb.*
> — Pierre Teilhard de Chardin, *The Phenomenon of Man*

SYLVA, SILVA
[SIL-vah]

MEANING: woods, forest • USAGE: English: from Latin *silva* (*see* Sylvia)
> *When the Spirit is given to us from heaven, deserts will become orchards thick as fertile forests. Honesty and justice will prosper there, and justice will produce lasting peace and security.*
> — Isaiah 32:15–17 (CEV)

SYLVESTRA
[sil-VES-trah]

MEANING: woods, forest • USAGE: English feminine form of Sylvester, from Latin *silva*
> *Kinship is the spirit of the forest.*
> — Enos A. Mills, *Your National Parks*

SYLVIA
[SEEL-vee-ah (Scandinavian, German), SIL-vee-ah (English)]

MEANING: woods, forest • USAGE: Scandinavian, German, and English: from Latin *silva*
> *The trees of the forest will sing for joy.*
> — 1 Chronicles 16:33a (NIRV)

S

SYLVIE   [SIL-vee (English), SEEL-vee (French, Danish)]

MEANING: woods, forest • USAGE: English, French, and Danish form of Sylvia (see Sylvia)

*If you want to be happy for a year, plant a garden;
if you want to be happy for life, plant a tree.*
— English proverb

T

TAA   [tah-ah]

MEANING: seed, seedling • USAGE: Amerind: Zuni

*With your waters / Your seeds / You will bless
all my children. / All your good fortune /
You will grant to them all.*
— Zuni prayer

TABEA   [tah-BEH-ah]

MEANING: gazelle, antelope, graceful, fleet-footed • USAGE: German form of Tabitha (see Tabitha)

Grace to you and peace be multiplied.
— 1 Peter 1:2b (NKJV)

TABIA   [tah-bee-ah]

MEANING: talent, gift • USAGE: African: Swahili of East Africa

Praise is due to those who have merits.
— Swahili proverb

TABITA   [tah-BEE-tah]

MEANING: gazelle, antelope, graceful, fleet-footed • USAGE: Italian form of Tabitha (see Tabitha)

My beloved is like a gazelle.
— Song of Songs 2:9a (NLV)

TABITHA   [TAH-bee-thah (Greek), TAB-ih-thah (English)]

MEANING: gazelle, antelope, graceful, fleet-footed • USAGE: Greek and English: from Aramaic *tabhyetha*

Love is swift, true, pleasant, and holy.
— Thomas à Kempis, *The Imitation of Christ*
(tr. Harvey Goodwin)

TACEY, TACY   [TAY-see]

MEANING: silent, quiet • USAGE: English: from Latin *tace* (to be silent)

Real action is in silent moments.
— Ralph Waldo Emerson, "Spiritual Laws"

TAHEERA, TAHEERAH   [tah-hee-rah]

MEANING: virtuous, pure, chaste, modest • USAGE: Muslim feminine form of Tahir, from Arabic *tahura* (to be pure, to be clean)

*Allah loves those who turn much (to Him),
and He loves those who purify themselves.*
— Koran, The Cow 2.222b (SKR)

TAINI   [tah-ee-nee]

MEANING: new moon • USAGE: Amerind: Omaha

*My friend, this is a wide world / We're traveling. /
Walking on the moonlight.*
— Omaha song

TAKALA   [tah-kah-lah]

MEANING: corn tassel • USAGE: Amerind: Hopi

*Plant the double ear / Plant the perfect
double corn-ear. / So the fields shall shine /
With tassels white of perfect corn-ears.*
— Wuwuchim Taw, Hopi song

TAKARA   [tah-kah-rah]

MEANING: treasure • USAGE: Japanese: from Japanese *takara*

*More valuable than treasures in a storehouse
are the treasures of the body, and the treasures
of the heart are the most valuable of all . . . strive
to accumulate the treasure of the heart!*
— Nichiren Daishonin

TALIBA, TALEEBA [tah-lee-bah]

MEANING: seeker of knowledge • **USAGE:** Muslim
feminine form of Talib, from Arabic *taliba*
*I searched for God and found only myself.
I searched for myself and found only God.*
— Sufi proverb

TALIMA, TALEEMA [tah-LEE-mah]

MEANING: educated, trained, rightly guided •
USAGE: Muslim feminine form of Talim
*Where the flame of love rises,
the knowledge of God unfolds of itself.*
— Hazrat Inayat Khan, *The Bowl of Saki*

TALISA, TALISSA [tah-LIS-ah]

MEANING: God is my oath, joined with God,
blessed by God, honeybee, honey • **USAGE:**
American: possibly a form of Melissa, from Greek
melissa (honeybee) or *meli* (honey); or possibly a
form of Lisa, from Hebrew *el'ishebha* (God is my
oath)
*Wisdom is like honey for your life —
if you find it, your future is bright.*
— Proverbs 24:13–14 (CEV)

TALISHA, TALISHA [tah-LEE-shah]

MEANING: God is my oath, joined with God,
blessed by God, noble one, highborn, honorable •
USAGE: American: possibly a form of Lisa, from
Hebrew *el'ishebha* (God is my oath); or English
form of Alice, from German *adal* (noble) and *heid*
(sort, type)
*He wants you all to Himself to put His loving,
divine arms around you.*
— Charles Stanley, *How to Listen to God*

TALULLA [tah-LOO-lah]

MEANING: prosperous lady, bountiful princess •
USAGE: Irish form of *Tuilelaith*, from Gaelic *tuile*
(abundance) and *flaith* (princess, lady)
*Peace and prosperity be with you,
and success to all who help you.*
— 1 Chronicles 12:18b (NLT)

TALYA [TAHL-yah]

MEANING: born on Christmas Day, Christmas •
USAGE: Russian form of Natalia, from Latin *natalis
dies Domini* (birthday of the Lord, Christmas)
*This is the day the Lord has made.
We will rejoice and be glad in it.*
— Psalm 118:24 (NLT)

TALYA, TALIA [TAHL-yah]

MEANING: dew • **USAGE:** Jewish
*Blessed of the Lord be his land with the bounty of dew
from heaven, and of the deep that couches below.*
— Deuteronomy 33:13 (JPS)

TAMAH [TAH-mah]

MEANING: wonder, amazement, awe • **USAGE:**
Jewish
*Awe enables us to perceive in the world intimations of
the divine, to sense in small things the beginning of
infinite significance, to sense the ultimate in the common and the simple; to feel in rush of the passing the
stillness of the eternal.*
— Abraham Heschel, *God in Search of Man*

TAMARA [TAM-ah-rah (English), tah-MAH-rah (Italian, Russian, Spanish)]

MEANING: palm tree • **USAGE:** English, Italian,
Russian, and Spanish: from Hebrew *tamar*
*It is the temper of highest hearts,
like the palm-tree, to strive upward.*
— Philip Sidney

TAMIZA, TAMEEZA   *[tah-MEE-ʒah]*

MEANING: judicious, just • USAGE: Muslim feminine form of Tamiz

> *O you who believe! Be upright for Allah,*
> *bearers of witness with justice.*
> — Koran, The Food 5.8a (SKR)

TAMMY, TAMMIE, TAMI   *[TAM-ee]*

MEANING: palm tree • USAGE: English form of Tamara (*see* Tamara)

> *Good people will prosper like palm trees…they will*
> *take root in your house, Lord God, and they will do*
> *well. They will be like trees that stay healthy and*
> *fruitful, even when they are old.*
> — Psalm 92:12–14 (CEV)

TAMSIN, TAMSEN, TAMSYN   *[TAM-sen]*

MEANING: twin, joined, double • USAGE: English feminine form of Thomas, from Aramaic *tau'am* (a twin)

> *Wisdom and goodness are twin-born,*
> *one heart must hold both sisters, never seen apart.*
> — William Cowper, "Expostulation"

TANDRA   *[TAHN-drah, TAN-drah]*

MEANING: protector and helper of humankind, guardian • USAGE: American: possibly a form of Sandra, from Greek *alexein* (to defend, to help) and *andros* (man)

> *Acquire wisdom, acquire understanding….*
> *Do not forsake wisdom, and she will protect you;*
> *love her, and she will guard you.*
> — Proverbs 4:5–6 (NEB)

TANIA, TAWNIA   *[TAHN-yah]*

MEANING: father • USAGE: English form of Tanya (*see* Tanya)

> *The Lord our God be with us,*
> *as he was with our fathers.*
> — 1 Kings 8:57 (ESV)

TANISHA, TANESHA, TANEESHA   *[tah-NEE-shah]*

MEANING: life, alive and well, father • USAGE: American: possibly a form of Aisha, from Arabic *a'isha* (alive and well) and *asha* (to live); or possibly a form of Tania (*see* Tanya)

> *Be glad of life because it gives you the chance to love*
> *and to work and to play and to look up at the stars.*
> — Henry Van Dyke, "The Footpath to Peace"

TANSY   *[tahn-see]*

MEANING: tansy flower • USAGE: Amerind: Hopi

> *My father told me…that Hopi earth does contain my*
> *roots and I am, indeed, from that land. Because my*
> *roots are there, I will find them.*
> — Wendy Rose

TANYA   *[TAHN-yah]*

MEANING: father • USAGE: Russian and English form of Tatiana, from the feminine form of the Roman family clan name *Tatius*, possibly from Latin *tata* (father)

> *O Lord, You are our Father; we are the clay, and You*
> *our potter; and all we are the work of Your hand.*
> — Isaiah 64:8 (NKJV)

TAQIA, TAQIYA   *[tah-kee-ah]*

MEANING: devout, righteous • USAGE: Muslim feminine form of Taqi, from Arabic *taqi*

> *Righteousness comes from the very essence of the soul.*
> — Hazrat Inayat Khan, *The Gayan*

TARA   *[tah-rah]*

MEANING: star • USAGE: Hindu: from Sanskrit *tara*

> *Only in the deepest silence of the night the stars smile*
> *and whisper among themselves.*
> — Rabindranath Tagore, *Gitanjali*

T

TARA   *[TAH-rah, TAYR-ah]*

MEANING: hill, elevated place, mound • **USAGE:** Irish and English: from Gaelic *teamhair* (elevated place); the traditional seat of Irish kingship
May the Irish hills caress you. May her lakes and rivers
bless you. May the luck of the Irish enfold you.
        — Irish blessing

TARANI   *[tah-RAH-nih]*

MEANING: ray of light • **USAGE:** Hindu
We light many candles with the flame
of a single candle. But remember only a
burning candle can light other candles.
— Sathya Sai Baba, *Sathya Sai Baba Speaks*

TARIA   *[tah-RIE-ah, TAR-ee-ah]*

MEANING: to possess good, possesses a lot, wealthy • **USAGE:** American: possibly a form of Daria, from Persian *daraya* (to possess) and *vahu* (good)
Good nature is worth more than knowledge, more than
money, more than honor, to the persons who possess it.
        — Henry Ward Beecher,
          Proverbs from Plymouth Pulpit

TARIKA   *[tah-rih-kah]*

MEANING: savior, star, planet • **USAGE:** Hindu: Sanskrit
Brahman is to be meditated upon as the source of all
thought and life and action. He is the splendor in
wealth; he is the light in the stars. He is all things.
— *Taittiriya Upanishad* (tr. Swami Prabhavananda)

TARINA   *[tah-REE-nah]*

MEANING: little hill • **USAGE:** English form of Tara, from Irish Gaelic *teamhair* (elevated place) and diminutive *-ina*
The hillsides blossom with joy.
        — Psalm 65:12b (NLT)

TARYN, TAREN   *[TER-en, TAH-ren]*

MEANING: hill, elevated place, heights, born on the land of the yew trees • **USAGE:** English form of Tara, from Irish Gaelic *teamhair* (elevated place); or English feminine form of Tyrone, from Irish Gaelic *tir* (land) and *eo gein* (born of the yew tree)
Let us love one another,
for love comes from God.
Everyone who loves has been born
of God and knows God.
        — 1 John 4:7 (NIV)

TASHA   *[TAH-shah]*

MEANING: birthday, born on Christmas Day • **USAGE:** Russian and English form of Natasha, from Latin *natalis dies Domini* (birthday of the Lord, Christmas)
This is the day which the Lord has made;
let us rejoice and be glad in it.
        — Psalm 118:24 (NASB)

TASIA   *[TAH-zhah]*

MEANING: resurrection, reborn, rise up • **USAGE:** Greek form of Anastasia, from Greek *anastasis* (resurrection), or from Greek *ana* (up) and *stasis* (standing)
You have been born again not of seed
which is perishable but imperishable.
        — 1 Peter 1:23a (NASB)

TATE   *[tayt]*

MEANING: cheerful, joyful, happy • **USAGE:** English surname: from Norse *teitr* (cheerful)
Learn the sweet magic of a cheerful face.
        — Oliver Wendell Holmes Sr.,
          "The Morning Visit"

T

TATIANA

[taht-YAH-nah (Russian),
tah-tee-AH-nah (English)]

MEANING: father, queen of fairies • **USAGE:** Russian and English feminine form of the Roman family clan name *Tatius*, possibly from Latin *tata* (father); Tatiana is possibly a form of Titania, the queen of fairies in *A Midsummer Night's Dream* by William Shakespeare

I thank you, and praise you, you God of my fathers,
who have given me wisdom and might.
— Daniel 2:23a (WEB)

TATIENNE

[tah-tee-EHN]

MEANING: father • **USAGE:** French form of Tatiana (*see* Tatiana)

A father is tender and kind to his children.
In the same way, the Lord is tender and kind
to those who have respect for him.
— Psalm 103:13 (NIRV)

TATUM

[TAY-tum]

MEANING: cheerful, joyful, happy • **USAGE:** American form of Tate, from Norse *teitr*

Cheerfulness keeps up a kind of daylight in the mind,
and fills it with a steady and perpetual serenity.
— Joseph Addison

TAYIBA, TAYIBAH

[tah-yee-bah]

MEANING: good, good-natured • **USAGE:** Muslim feminine form of Tayyib

Allah loves those who do good (to others).
— Koran, The Dinner Table 5.13b (SKR)

TAYLOR, TAYLER

[TAY-lor]

MEANING: tailor, garment maker • **USAGE:** English surname: from English *taillour* (cutter of cloth)

Her clothes are well-made and elegant,
and she always faces tomorrow with a smile.
— Proverbs 31:25 (MSG)

TEA

[TAY-ah (Spanish, Scandinavian),
TEE-ah (English)]

MEANING: summer, harvester, reaper • **USAGE:** Spanish, English, and Scandinavian form of Teresa, from Greek *theros* (summer) or *therizo* (to harvest)

Sow with a view to righteousness,
reap in accordance with kindness.
— Hosea 10:12a (NASB)

TEAGAN

[TAY-gen]

MEANING: little poet • **USAGE:** American form of Tegan (*see* Tegan)

Poetry has a natural alliance with our best affections. It
delights in the beauty and sublimity
of the outward creation and of the soul.
— William Ellery Channing,
"On the Character and Writings of Milton"

TEAL, TEALE

[teel]

MEANING: small duck, blue-green color • **USAGE:** English: from English *tele* (small duck, blue-green color)

Blue is the only color
which maintains its own character in all its tones.
— Raoul Dufy

TECLA

[TEH-klah]

MEANING: glory of God, God's glory • **USAGE:** Italian form of *Theokleia*, from Greek *theos* (God) and *kleos* (glory)

The glory of the Lord is shining on you!
— Isaiah 60:1b (GNT)

TEGAN

[TEH-gan]

MEANING: little poet • **USAGE:** Welsh: from Welsh Gaelic *tadhg* (poet) and diminutive *-an*

A good poem helps to change the shape
and significance of the universe.
— Dylan Thomas, *Quite Early One Morning*

TEGWEN   *[TEG-wen]*

MEANING: fair and holy • **USAGE:** Welsh: from Welsh *teg* (fair, lovely) and *gwen* (white, fair, holy)
Behold, thou art fair, my beloved, yea, pleasant.
— Song of Songs 1:16a (KJ21)

TEHILA, TEHILLA   *[teh-hee-LAH]*

MEANING: song of praise, psalm • **USAGE:** Jewish
By day may the Lord vouchsafe His faithful care,
so that at night a song to Him may be with me,
a prayer to the God of my life.
— Psalm 42:9 (JPS)

TEKLA   *[TEH-klah]*

MEANING: glory of God, God's glory • **USAGE:** Russian, Scandinavian, and Polish form of *Theokleia*, from Greek *theos* (God) and *kleos* (glory)
Put your face in the sunlight. God's bright glory
has risen for you.... God rises on you,
his sunrise glory breaks over you.
— Isaiah 60:1, 3 (MSG)

TEMAH   *[tah-MAH]*

MEANING: wonder, wondrous • **USAGE:** Jewish
I will give thanks unto Thee, for I am fearfully
and wonderfully made; wonderful are Thy works;
and that my soul knoweth right well.
— Psalm 139:14 (MT)

TEMIRA, TEMIRAH   *[teh-MEE-rah, teh-mee-RAH]*

MEANING: tall, stately (like a palm tree), upright • **USAGE:** Jewish
Light is sown for the righteous,
and gladness for the upright in heart.
— Psalm 97:11 (MT)

TEMPLE   *[TEM-pel]*

MEANING: place of worship, synagogue • **USAGE:** English: from English *temple*
A temple is a landscape of the soul.
— Joseph Campbell, *The Power of Myth*

TEODORA   *[tay-oh-DOH-rah]*

MEANING: gift of God • **USAGE:** Spanish, Italian, Scandinavian, and Polish feminine form of Teodor or Teodoro, from Greek *theos* (God) and *doron* (gift)
God gives the Spirit without limit.
— John 3:34b (WEB)

TERESA   *[tay-RAY-sah (Spanish, German, Italian, Polish, Scandinavian), teh-REE-sah (English)]*

MEANING: summer, harvester, reaper • **USAGE:** Spanish, Italian, Polish, German, Scandinavian, and English: from Greek *theros* (summer) or *therizo* (to harvest)
The wisdom from above is pure first of all; it is also
peaceful, gentle, and friendly; it is full of compassion
and produces a harvest of good deeds.
— James 3:17 (GNT)

TEREZA   *[teh-RAY-zah]*

MEANING: summer, harvester, reaper • **USAGE:** Czech and Polish form of Theresa (*see* Teresa)
Sow to yourselves in righteousness,
reap according to mercy.
— Hosea 10:12a (DT)

TERIAH   *[teh-REE-ah]*

MEANING: fresh, new • **USAGE:** Jewish
A new heart also will I give you, and a new spirit will I
put within you ... I will put My spirit within you.
— Ezekiel 36:26–27a (MT)

T

TERRA   *[TER-ah]*

MEANING: earth, land • USAGE: English: Latin
terra
> *Those who dwell…among the beauties and mysteries*
> *of the earth are never alone or weary of life.*
> — Rachel Carson, *The Sense of Wonder*

TERRY, TERRI, TERRIE, TERI   *[TER-ee]*

MEANING: summer, harvester, reaper, tender,
polished, smooth • USAGE: English form of
Theresa (*see* Teresa); or English feminine form
of Terence, from Latin *terenus* (soft, tender) or
terentius (polished, smooth)
> *The quality of strength lined with tenderness*
> *is an unbeatable combination.*
> — Maya Angelou,
> *I Know Why the Caged Bird Sings*

TESHI   *[teh-shee]*

MEANING: cheerful, prone to laughter • USAGE:
African: Swahili of Kenya/Tanzania
> *The owner of a cheerful heart*
> *will find joy ever increasing.*
> — Swahili proverb

TESS   *[tes]*

MEANING: summer, harvester, reaper • USAGE:
English form of Theresa (*see* Teresa)
> *We weave with colors all our own, / And in the field of*
> *Destiny, / We reap as we have sown.*
> — John Greenleaf Whittier, "Raphael"

TESSA   *[TES-ah]*

MEANING: summer, harvester, reaper, four, fourth
child • USAGE: English and Greek: English form of
Theresa (*see* Teresa); or from Greek *tessares* (four)
> *From the dew of heaven and the richness of the earth,*
> *may God always give you abundant harvests.*
> — Genesis 27:28a (NLT)

THALIA   *[THAYL-yah]*

MEANING: blossom, Muse of comedy and poetry
• USAGE: Greek: from Greek *thallo* (to blossom);
Greek muse of comedy and pastoral poetry
> *Poetry comes nearer to vital truth than history.*
> — Plato

THANDI   *[tahn-dih]*

MEANING: love, beloved, dear • USAGE: African:
Xhosa of South Africa
> *Love is like a seed:*
> *it does not choose the ground on which it falls.*
> — South African proverb

THEA   *[THAY-ah, THEE-ah]*

MEANING: truth, truthful, true, gift of God
• USAGE: Greek and English: Greek form of
Alethea, from Greek *aletheia* (truth); also English
form of Theodora or Dorothea, from Greek *theo*
(God) and *doron* (gift)
> *To be persuasive we must be believable; to be believable*
> *we must be credible. To be credible we must be truthful.*
> — Edward R. Murrow

THEKLA   *[THEK-lah]*

MEANING: glory of God • USAGE: Greek and
German: from Greek *theos* (God) and *kleos* (glory,
fame)
> *Thy light is come,*
> *and the glory of the Lord is risen upon thee.*
> — Isaiah 60:1b (DR)

THELMA   *[THEL-mah]*

MEANING: will, determination, spirit • USAGE:
English: from Greek *thelema* (will, determination,
spirit); from *Thelma* by Marie Corelli
> *It is the spirit, the will to excel, the will to win;*
> *these are the things that endure.*
> *These are the important things.*
> — Vince Lombardi, *What It Takes to Be #1*

T

THEODORA [theh-oh-DOR-ah (Greek), thee-eh-DOR-ah (English)]

Meaning: gift of God • **Usage:** Greek and English feminine form of Theodore (*see* Theodosia)
The gift of pure love is always attended with bliss.
— James Allen, *From Poverty to Power*

THEODOSIA [theh-oh-DOH-see-ah]

Meaning: gift of God • **Usage:** Greek: from Greek *theos* (God) and *doron* (gift)
Every perfect gift is from above,
coming down from the Father of the lights.
— James 1:17a (YLT)

THERESA [teh-REE-sah (English), teh-RAY-sah (Greek)]

Meaning: summer, harvester, reaper • **Usage:** English and Greek: from Greek *theros* (summer) or *therizo* (to harvest)
Be joyful, because the Lord has blessed
your harvest and your work.
— Deuteronomy 16:15b (GNT)

THERESE, THÉRÈSE [teh-REH-seh]

Meaning: summer, harvester, reaper • **Usage:** German, Scandinavian, and French (*see* Theresa)
Blessed be the Lord for the beauty of summer and
spring, for the air, the water, the verdure,
and the song of birds.
— Carl von Linné, *A Tour in Lapland*

THORA [THOR-ah]

Meaning: of the god of thunder and strength • **Usage:** Norwegian and Swedish feminine form of *Thorvalldr*, from Norse *Þorr* (Thor, god of thunder and strength)
The voice of the Lord is over the waters;
the God of glory thunders,
the Lord thunders over the mighty waters.
— Psalm 29:3 (NIV)

TIANA, TIANNA [tee-AH-nah]

Meaning: follower of Christ, Christian • **Usage:** English form of Christiana, from Greek *christianos*
Let the peace of Christ rule in your hearts.
— Colossians 3:15a (NIV)

TIARA [tee-AHR-ah]

Meaning: crown, diadem, jeweled coronet • **Usage:** American: from Greek *tiara*
She [Wisdom] will place on your head an ornament
of grace; a crown of glory she will deliver to you.
— Proverbs 4:9 (NKJV)

TIERRA [tee-EHR-ah]

Meaning: earth • **Usage:** English and Spanish: from Latin *terra*
Touch the earth, love the earth, honour the earth.
— Henry Beston, *The Outermost House*

TIFARA [tee-fah-RAH, tee-FAH-rah]

Meaning: beautiful, glory, splendor • **Usage:** Jewish
Truth is the vital breath of Beauty;
Beauty the outward form of Truth.
— Grace Aguilar, "Amete and Yafeh"

TIFFANY, TIFFANIE [TIF-ah-nee]

Meaning: epiphany, manifestation of God • **Usage:** English form of French *Tifaine*, from Latin *Theophania* (Epiphany, manifestation of God)
The Lord bless you and keep you; the Lord make His
face shine upon you, and be gracious to you; the Lord
lift up His countenance upon you, and give you peace.
— Numbers 6:24–26 (NKJV)

TIIVA [tee-vah]

Meaning: dances • **Usage:** Amerind: Hopi
To watch us dance is to hear our hearts speak.
— Hopi saying

T

TIKVA, TIKVAH [teek-VAH]

MEANING: hope, hopeful • USAGE: Jewish
You will be secure, for there is hope.
— Job 11:18a (JPS)

TILDA [TEEL-dah]

MEANING: mighty warrior, powerful • USAGE:
German, Scandinavian, and English form of
Mathilda, German *maht* (might, power) and *hild*
(war, battle)
Whatever your hand finds to do,
do it with all your might.
— Ecclesiastes 9:10a (NASB)

TILDE [TIL-deh]

MEANING: mighty warrior, powerful • USAGE:
Scandinavian form of Mathilda (*see* Tilda)
Power over others is weakness disguised as strength.
True power is within, and it is available to you now.
— Eckhart Tolle, *The Power of Now*

TILLIE, TILLY [TIL-ee]

MEANING: mighty warrior, powerful • USAGE:
English form of Mathilda (*see* Tilda)
I thank You and praise You, O God of my fathers;
You have given me wisdom and might.
— Daniel 2:23a (NKJV)

TIMORA [tee-MOH-rah]

MEANING: tall, upright, stately (like a palm tree) •
USAGE: Jewish
Light is sown for the righteous,
radiance for the upright.
— Psalm 97:11 (JPS)

TIMOTHEA [tee-moh-THEH-ah]

MEANING: one who honors God, one who esteems
God • USAGE: Greek feminine form of Timotheos,
from Greek *time* (honor, esteem) and *theos* (God)

Thou shalt love the Lord thy God with all thy heart,
and with all thy soul, and with all thy mind, and with
all thy strength: this is the first commandment.
— Mark 12:30 (KJV)

TINA [TEE-nah]

MEANING: follower of Christ, Christian, warrior
• USAGE: English, German, Italian, Scandinavian,
and Spanish form of names ending in -*tina*, such
as Christina, from Greek *christianos* (Christian), or
Martina, from Latin *Mars* (Roman god of war)
The peace of God, which surpasses all understanding,
will guard your hearts and minds through Christ Jesus.
— Philippians 4:7 (NKJV)

TIPONI [tee-poh-nee]

MEANING: child of importance • USAGE:
Amerind: Hopi
You should water your children like you water a tree.
— Hopi proverb

TIRA [tee-RAH]

MEANING: encampment, small village • USAGE:
Jewish
My people shall abide in a peaceable habitation, and in
secure dwellings, and in quiet resting-places.
— Isaiah 32:18 (MT)

TIRION [TEE-ree-on]

MEANING: gentle, kind • USAGE: Welsh: from
Welsh *tirion*
She speaks with a gentle wisdom.
— Proverbs 31:26 (GNT)

TIRZAH, TIRZA [TEER-zah]

MEANING: cypress tree, desirable, pleasant •
USAGE: Jewish
Instead of the thorn shall come up the cypress...
and it shall be to the Lord for a memorial,
for an everlasting sign that shall not be cut off.
— Isaiah 55:13 (MT)

TISHA   *[TEE-shah]*

MEANING: strong-willed • **USAGE:** African:
Swahili of Kenya/Tanzania

> *Nothing is impossible to a woman of will.*
> — Swahili proverb

TIVA   *[TEE-vah, tee-VAH]*

MEANING: good, goodness • **USAGE:** Jewish: from
Hebrew *tobh*

> *Good will is the best charity.*
> — Yiddish proverb

TIVIAN   *[TIV-ee-an]*

MEANING: life, full of life • **USAGE:** American:
possibly a form of Vivian, from Latin *vita*

> *Life is full of beauty. Notice it....*
> *Smell the rain, and feel the wind.*
> *Live your life to the fullest potential.*
> — Ashley Smith

TOBIE, TOBY   *[TOH-bee]*

MEANING: God is good, goodness of God •
USAGE: English feminine form of Tobias, from
Hebrew *tobhi'yah* (goodness of Yahweh)

> *The Lord will open for you His good storehouse...*
> *to bless all the work of your hand.*
> — Deuteronomy 28:12a (NASB)

TOINETTE   *[twah-NET]*

MEANING: invaluable, priceless, excellent •
USAGE: French form of Antoinette, from Latin
Antonius, a Roman family name possibly meaning
"invaluable"

> *One's life has value so long as one attributes value*
> *to the life of others, by means of love, friendship,*
> *indignation, and compassion.*
> — Simone de Beauvoir, *The Coming of Age*

TOMASA   *[toh-MAH-sah]*

MEANING: twin, joined, double • **USAGE:** Spanish
feminine form of Tomas, from Aramaic *tau'am* (a
twin)

> *No human being must separate,*
> *then, what God has joined together.*
> — Matthew 19:6b (GNT)

TOMASINA   *[toh-mah-SEE-nah]*

MEANING: twin, joined, double • **USAGE:** English
feminine form of Greek Thomas (*see* Tomasa)

> *Heart to heart, one in one, that is what God loves.*
> — Meister Eckhart

TOMOMI   *[toh-moh-mee]*

MEANING: beautiful friend • **USAGE:** Japanese:
from Japanese *tomo* (friend) and *mi* (beautiful)

> *The Art of Peace is based on the Four Great Virtues:*
> *Bravery, Wisdom, Love, and Friendship,*
> *symbolized by Fire, Heaven, Earth, and Water.*
> — Morihei Ueshiba, *The Art of Peace*

TONI, TONIE   *[TOH-nee]*

MEANING: invaluable, priceless, excellent •
USAGE: English form of Antonia, from *Antonius*, a
Roman family name possibly meaning "invaluable"

> *This I believe: That the free, exploring mind*
> *of the individual human is the most valuable*
> *thing in the world.*
> — John Steinbeck, *East of Eden*

TONIA   *[TOHN-yah]*

MEANING: invaluable, priceless, excellent •
USAGE: English form of Antonia (*see* Toni)

> *Excellence is not an act but a habit.*
> *The things you do the most are the things*
> *you will do the best.*
> — Marva Collins

T

TOPAZ   *[TOH-paz]*

MEANING: topaz gemstone, beautiful jewel, smoky-yellow color, heat, fire • **USAGE:** English: from Greek *topazos* (semiprecious gemstone) or possibly from Sanskrit *tapas* (heat, fire)

> *You are all beautiful, my love. You are perfect.*
> — Song of Songs 4:7 (NLV)

TORA   *[TOR-ah]*

MEANING: of the god of thunder and strength • **USAGE:** Scandinavian feminine form of Tor, from Norse *Þorr* (Thor, Norse god of thunder and strength)

> *The voice of the Lord is heard on the seas; the glorious God thunders, and his voice echoes over the ocean.*
> — Psalm 29:3 (GNT)

TORI   *[TOR-ee]*

MEANING: my turtledove • **USAGE:** Jewish

> *Ah, you are fair, my darling, ah, you are fair, with your dove-like eyes!*
> — Song of Songs 1:15 (JPS)

TORI, TORRIE, TORY   *[TOR-ee]*

MEANING: conqueror, victorious, successful, triumphant • **USAGE:** English form of Victoria, from Latin *vincere* (to conquer)

> *The way of peace is the way of love.*
> *Love is the greatest power on earth.*
> *It conquers all things.*
> — Peace Pilgrim, *Peace Pilgrim*

TORIA   *[TOR-ee-ah]*

MEANING: conqueror, victorious, successful, triumphant • **USAGE:** English form of Victoria (*see* Tori)

> *If you think you can win, you can.*
> *Faith is necessary to victory.*
> — William Hazlitt, "On Great and Little Things"

TORIANA   *[tor-ee-AH-nah]*

MEANING: conqueror, victorious, successful, triumphant • **USAGE:** English form of Victoria (*see* Tori)

> *Your success and happiness lie in you.*
> — Helen Keller, *Out of the Dark*

TORRANCE, TORRENCE   *[TOR-ans]*

MEANING: hill, small mount • **USAGE:** English: from Gaelic *torran*

> *The hills are clothed with gladness.*
> — Psalm 65:12b (NIV)

TOVAH   *[toh-VAH, TOH-vah]*

MEANING: good, goodness • **USAGE:** Jewish feminine form of Tov, from Hebrew *tobh*

> *For those who plan good there is joy.*
> — Proverbs 12:20b (JPS)

TRACY, TRACI, TRACIE   *[TRAY-see]*

MEANING: from Tracy-sur-Mer, summer, harvester, reaper • **USAGE:** English surname: English form of *Tracy-sur-Mer* (French town); or form of Theresa, from Greek *theros* (summer) or *therizo* (to harvest)

> *Plant goodness, harvest the fruit of loyalty,*
> *plow the new ground of knowledge.*
> *Look for the Lord until he comes*
> *and pours goodness on you like water.*
> — Hosea 10:12 (NCV)

TREASA   *[TRAY-sah]*

MEANING: summer, harvester, reaper • **USAGE:** Irish form of Theresa, from Greek *theros* (summer) or *therizo* (to harvest)

> *Thy eternal summer shall not fade.*
> — William Shakespeare, "Sonnet 18"

TRELLA [TREL-ah]

Meaning: star, starlike, radiant • **Usage:** English form of Estrella, from Latin *stella*

> *Who is this that appears like the dawn,*
> *fair as the moon, bright as the sun,*
> *majestic as the stars in procession?*
> — Song of Songs 6:10 (NIV)

TRESSA [TRES-ah]

Meaning: strong, powerful, three, third • **Usage:** American: from Welsh *tressa* (third)

> *These three things continue forever: faith, hope,*
> *and love. And the greatest of these is love.*
> — 1 Corinthians 13:13 (NCV)

TRIANA [tree-AH-nah]

Meaning: triply graced, triply blessed • **Usage:** American: possibly a combination of Latin *tri* (three) and Anna, from Hebrew *chaanach*

> *By compassion the soul is made blessed.*
> — Meister Eckhart (tr. Matthew Fox in
> *Meditations with Meister Eckhart*)

TRICIA, TRISHA [TRISH-ah]

Meaning: patrician, noble one • **Usage:** English form of Patricia, from Latin *patricius*

> *Sweet mercy is nobility's true badge.*
> — William Shakespeare, *Titus Andronicus*

TRINA [TREE-nah]

Meaning: pure one, unblemished, innocent, virtuous • **Usage:** Spanish form of Catalina or Catarina, from Greek *katharos* (pure)

> *Create in me a clean heart,*
> *O God, and renew a steadfast spirit within me.*
> — Psalm 51:10 (NKJV)

TRINIDAD [TREE-neh-dahd]

Meaning: trinity, Holy Trinity • **Usage:** Spanish: from Spanish *Trinidad* (reference to the Holy Trinity)

> *God is not solitude, but perfect communion.*
> — Pope Benedict

TRINITY [TRIN-eh-tee]

Meaning: three, triune • **Usage:** English: from English *trinite*

> *Now there remain faith, hope, and charity,*
> *these three: but the greatest of these is charity.*
> — 1 Corinthians 13:13 (DR)

TRIONA [tree-OH-nah]

Meaning: pure one, unblemished, innocent, virtuous • **Usage:** Scottish form of *Caitriona*, from Greek *katharos* (pure)

> *Blessed are the pure in heart; for they shall see God.*
> — Matthew 5:8 (KJV)

TRISH [trish]

Meaning: patrician, noble one • **Usage:** English form of Patricia, from Latin *patricius*

> *Every human person is an aristocrat,*
> *every human person is noble and of royal blood.*
> — Meister Eckhart (tr. Matthew Fox in
> *Meditations with Meister Eckhart*)

TRISTA [TRIS-tah]

Meaning: riotous, chaotic, sad • **Usage:** English feminine form of Tristan, from Welsh *drest* (riotous, tumultuous, chaotic); or from French *triste* (sad, sorrowful)

> *The Lord your God is with you....*
> *The quietness of his love will calm you down.*
> — Zephaniah 3:17b (NIRV)

T

TRIXIE   *[TRIK-see]*

MEANING: blessed, blissful, voyager, traveler • **USAGE:** English form of Beatrix, from Latin *beatus* (blessed, blissful) or *viator* (voyager, traveler)
The blessing of the Lord be upon you.
— Psalm 129:8b (NKJV)

TRUDA   *[TROO-dah]*

MEANING: spear maiden, strong spear • **USAGE:** Polish form of Gertruda, from German *ger* (spear) and *trut* (maiden) or *prup* (strength, power)
*She draws on her strength and reveals
that her arms are strong.*
— Proverbs 31:17 (HCSB)

TRUDY, TRUDIE   *[TROO-dee]*

MEANING: spear maiden, strong spear • **USAGE:** English, Dutch, and German form of Gertrude, from German *ger* (spear) and *trut* (maiden) or *prup* (strength, power)
Strength and dignity are her clothing.
— Proverbs 31:25a (WEB)

TRUTH   *[trooth]*

MEANING: quality of being true and genuine • **USAGE:** American: from English *triewð*
*I believe that unarmed truth and unconditional love
will have the final word in reality.*
— Martin Luther King Jr.
(Nobel Prize acceptance speech, 1964)

TUESDAY   *[TOOS-day]*

MEANING: warrior, protected by Tyr • **USAGE:** American: from English *tuesdai* (day of *Tiu*, Norse god of war), day of the week
*The Lord, your God, is in your midst,
a warrior who gives victory; he will rejoice over you
with gladness, he will renew you in his love.*
— Zephaniah 3:17 (NRSV)

TUWA   *[too-wah]*

MEANING: earth • **USAGE:** Amerind: Hopi
*We pray the Great Spirit that one day our Mother
Earth will be purified into a healthy peaceful one.*
— Hopi prayer

TWYLA, TWILA   *[TWIE-lah]*

MEANING: twilight, dusk, evening • **USAGE:** English: from English *twilighte* (half-light)
*Sunsets are so beautiful that they almost seem
as if we were looking through the gates of Heaven.*
— John Lubbock, *The Use of Life*

TYLER, TYLAR, TYLOR   *[TIE-ler]*

MEANING: tiler, tiler of roofs • **USAGE:** English surname: from Latin *tegere* (to cover)
*By wisdom a house is built,
and by understanding it is established.*
— Proverbs 24:3 (NRSV)

TYRA   *[TIE-rah]*

MEANING: warrior, justice • **USAGE:** Scandinavian feminine form of Tyr, Norse god of war and justice
*Who [is] this that is looking forth as morning,
fair as the moon — clear as the sun,
awe-inspiring as bannered hosts?*
— Song of Songs 6:10 (YLT)

TYRONA   *[tie-ROH-nah]*

MEANING: born on the land of yew trees • **USAGE:** Irish feminine form of Tyrone, from Gaelic *tir* (land) and *eo gein* (born of the yew tree)
The Yew alone burns lamps of peace.
— Walter de la Mare, "Trees"

TZIPORAH   *[tzih-POH-rah]*

MEANING: bird • **USAGE:** Jewish
*He will cover thee with His pinions,
and under His wings shalt thou take refuge.*
— Psalm 91:4a (MT)

U

UILANI [oo-ee-LAH-nee]

MEANING: heavenly beauty • USAGE: Hawaiian
For every loving soul, life brings beauty and joy.
— Hawaiian proverb

ULA [OO-lah, YOO-lah]

MEANING: altar • USAGE: Irish: from Gaelic *ula*
I will go to the altar of God, to God —
the source of all my joy.
— Psalm 43:4a (NLT)

ULANI [oo-LAH-nee]

MEANING: happy nature, optimistic • USAGE:
Hawaiian
Seek love, knowledge, and above all else — happiness.
— Hawaiian proverb

ULLA [oo-lah]

MEANING: will, resolve, she-bear, strong as a bear
• USAGE: Scandinavian: from Norse *ullr* (will,
desire, resolve); or Scandinavian form of Ursula
(*see* Ursula)
Be strong and courageous...for the Lord your God goes
with you; he will never leave you nor forsake you.
— Deuteronomy 31:6 (NIV)

ULYA [ool-yah]

MEANING: higher, highest • USAGE: Muslim
Whoso cometh unto Him a believer, having done good
works, for such are the high stations.
— Koran, Ta Ha 20.75 (PIC)

UMA [oo-mah]

MEANING: serene, tranquil, calm • USAGE: Hindu:
Sanskrit
The highest manifestation of strength is to keep
ourselves calm and on our own feet.
— Swami Vivekananda, *The Vedanta Philosophy*

UMEKO [oo-meh-koh]

MEANING: plum child • USAGE: Japanese: from
Japanese *ume* (plum) and *ko* (child)
The plum blossom is hardy, fragrant, and elegant.
— Morihei Ueshiba, *The Art of Peace*
(tr. John Stevens)

UNA [oo-nah]

MEANING: remember • USAGE: Amerind: Hopi
Know that you yourself are essential to the world.
Believe that! Understand both the blessing
and the burden of that.
You yourself are desperately needed to save
the soul of this World.
Did you think you were put here for something less?
— Arvol Looking Horse

UNITY [YOO-neh-tee]

MEANING: oneness, accordance, harmony, united
• USAGE: American: from Latin *unitas* (oneness,
sameness)
God is One, all our lives have various and unique
places in the harmony of the divine life.
— Josiah Royce, *The Conception of Immortality*

URANIA [yoo-RAY-nee-ah]

MEANING: heavenly, celestial • USAGE: English
form of Ourania, from Greek *ouranios*
The gate of heaven is everywhere.
— Thomas Merton

URIELA, URIELLA [oo-ree-EL-ah]

MEANING: fire of God, God is my flame • USAGE:
Jewish: from Hebrew *uri'el*
Bless the Lord, O my soul...Who makest winds
Thy messengers the flaming fire Thy ministers.
— Psalm 104:1–4 (MT)

U

URIKA   *[oo-REE-kah]*

Meaning: useful to all • **Usage:** Amerind:
Omaha Sioux
Everyone should pray together, cheer along, root along.
That brings the circle together. Everything is together.
— Wallace Black Elk,
Black Elk: The Sacred Ways of a Lakota

URSULA   *[OOR-suh-lah (German,*
Scandinavian), ER-suh-lah (English)]

Meaning: she-bear, strong as a bear • **Usage:**
German, English, and Scandinavian: form of Latin
ursa (she-bear)
She is strong and respected and not afraid of the future.
— Proverbs 31:25 (NEB)

USHARA   *[oo-SHAH-rah]*

Meaning: blessed, fortunate • **Usage:** Jewish
It is the blessing of the Lord that enriches.
— Proverbs 10:22a (JPS)

V

VAL   *[val]*

Meaning: strong, vigorous, healthy • **Usage:**
English form of Valentina or Valerie, from Latin
valens
A strong body makes the mind strong.
— Thomas Jefferson (letter of August 19, 1785)

VALDA   *[VAHL-dah]*

Meaning: truth, true • **Usage:** German: from
Latin *verus* (true)
You shall know the truth,
and the truth shall make you free.
— John 8:32 (NKJV)

VALENCIA   *[bah-LAYN-see-ah]*

Meaning: powerful, strong • **Usage:** Spanish:
from Spanish *valentia*
O God of my fathers, I acknowledge and glorify you,
for you have bestowed wisdom and power on me.
— Daniel 2:23a (NEB)

VALENDA, VALINDA   *[vah-LEN-dah]*

Meaning: strong, vigorous, healthy, beautiful,
pretty • **Usage:** American: possibly a form of
Valerie (*see* Valerie); or possibly a form of Linda,
from Spanish *linda* (beautiful, pretty)
Never forget that the most powerful force
on earth is love.
— Nelson Rockefeller

VALENTINA   *[vah-layn-TEE-nah (Italian,*
Spanish), val-en-TEE-nah (English),
vah-leen-TEE-nah (Russian)]

Meaning: strong, vigorous, healthy • **Usage:**
Italian, English, Russian, and Spanish feminine
form of Valentino, from Latin *valere*
Health and fitness are better than any gold,
and bodily vigour than boundless prosperity.
— Sirach 30:15 (WEB Apocrypha)

VALENTINE   *[vah-len-TEEN (French),*
VAL-en-tien (English)]

Meaning: strong, vigorous, healthy • **Usage:**
English and French form of Valentina, from Latin
valere
Nothing is so strong as gentleness
— nothing is so gentle as real strength.
— Francis de Sales

VALERIA   *[vah-LAY-ree-ah (Italian),*
bah-LAY-ree-ah (Spanish)]

Meaning: strong, vigorous, healthy • **Usage:**
Italian and Spanish feminine form of Valerio, from
Latin *valere*

*I pray that everything may go well with you
and that you may be in good health —
as I know you are well in spirit.*
— 3 John 1:2 (GNT)

VALERIE, VALERY [VAL-er-ee]

MEANING: strong, vigorous, healthy • USAGE:
English feminine form of Roman family name
Valerius, from Latin *valere*
*Strong, pure, and happy thoughts build
up the body in vigour and grace.*
— James Allen, *As a Man Thinketh*

VALERIYA [vah-LYEH-ree-yah]

MEANING: strong, vigorous, healthy • USAGE:
Russian form of Valerie (*see* Valerie)
*Long life to you! Good health to you and your
household! And good health to all that is yours!*
— 1 Samuel 25:6b (NIV)

VANESSA [vah-NES-ah]

MEANING: butterfly, manifester, revealer •
USAGE: English, Italian, and German: possibly
from the name of a butterfly genus, from Greek
Phanes (manifester, revealer); from "Cadenus and
Vanessa" by Jonathan Swift, who rearranged and
combined the initial syllables of his friend's name,
Esther Vanhomrigh
I only ask to be free. The butterflies are free.
— Charles Dickens, *Bleak House*

VANIKA [vah-nih-kah]

MEANING: little forest, little woods • USAGE:
Hindu
*The Self as life /
Supports the tree, which stands firm and enjoys /
The nourishment it receives.*
— *Chandogya Upanishad* (tr. Eknath Easwaran)

VANJA [VAHN-yah]

MEANING: God is gracious, God is giving •
USAGE: Scandinavian form of Vanya (*see* Vanya)
*May God be gracious to us and bless us
and make his face to shine upon us.*
— Psalm 67:1 (ESV)

VANNA [VAH-nah (Italian, Scandinavian), VAN-ah (English)]

MEANING: God is gracious, God is giving •
USAGE: Italian form of Giovanna, or Scandinavian
and English form of Ivana (*see* Vanya)
*Everything comes from love…
God does nothing without this goal in mind.*
— Catherine of Siena

VANYA [VAHN-yah]

MEANING: God is gracious, God is giving •
USAGE: Russian form of Ivana, from Hebrew
y'hohanan (Yahweh is gracious)
*God is gracious and merciful,
and will not turn away his face from you.*
— 2 Chronicles 30:9b (NCV)

VARANA [vah-rah-nah]

MEANING: river, to flow • USAGE: Hindu
*The world is the river of God, /
flowing from him and flowing back to him.*
— Buddha, *Shvetashvatara Upanishad*
(tr. Eknath Easwaran in
God Makes the Rivers to Flow)

VARSHA [vahr-shah]

MEANING: rain shower • USAGE: Hindu
*Please shower me with Your Mercy,
O Lord God, and unite me with Yourself.*
— *Sri Guru Granth Sahib*
(Khalsa Consensus Translation)

VARVARA [vahr-VAHR-vah]

MEANING: foreigner, stranger, visitor • **USAGE:** Russian and Greek form of Barbara, from Greek *barbaros* (foreign, other) or *bar-bar* (foreign unintelligible speech)

Be sure to welcome strangers into your home. By doing this, some people have welcomed angels as guests, without even knowing it.
— Hebrews 13:2 (CEV)

VASHATI [vah-shah-tih]

MEANING: dawn, sunrise • **USAGE:** Hindu: Sanskrit

My thoughts shimmer with these shimmering leaves and my heart sings with the touch of this sunlight; my life is glad to be floating with all things into the blue of space, into the dark of time.
— Rabindranath Tagore, *Stray Birds*

VASHTI [VASH-tee]

MEANING: beautiful, lovely • **USAGE:** Persian

My dear, you are so beautiful.
— Hafiz, "A Man Married to a Blind Woman" (tr. Daniel Ladinsky in *A Year with Hafiz*)

VEERA [VEE-rah]

MEANING: brave, powerful, strong • **USAGE:** Hindu

May my body be strong, my tongue be sweet.
— *Taittiriya Upanishad* (tr. Eknath Easwaran)

VEGA [VEH-gah (Scandinavian), BEH-gah (Spanish)]

MEANING: star, starlight, radiant • **USAGE:** Scandinavian and Spanish: from Latin *vega* (star in Lyra constellation)

The wise people will shine like the brightness of the sky. Those who teach others to live right will shine like stars forever and ever.
— Daniel 12:3a (NCV)

VELMA [VEL-mah]

MEANING: determined protector, steadfast guardian • **USAGE:** English form of Wilma, from German *wil* (will, resolve) and *helm* (helmet, protection)

Doing what is right protects the honest person.
— Proverbs 13:6 (NCV)

VELVET [VEL-vet]

MEANING: velvet cloth • **USAGE:** English: from English *veluet* (shaggy cloth)

Strength and beauty are her clothing.
— Proverbs 31:25a (DR)

VENICIA [veh-nee-CHEE-ah]

MEANING: people of Venice, Venetian • **USAGE:** Italian: from Latin *Veneti* (a northern Italian people)

There is a spirit within people, the breath of the Almighty within them, that makes them intelligent.
— Job 32:8 (NLT)

VENUS [VEE-nus]

MEANING: love, goddess of love and beauty, morning and evening star • **USAGE:** English: from Latin *venus* (love); Roman goddess of beauty and love; planet Venus, known as the morning and evening star

What is love?...It is the morning and it is also the evening star.
— Sinclair Lewis, *Elmer Gantry*

VERA [VER-ah (English), VEER-ah (English, German, Italian, Scandinavian), VYEH-rah (Russian)]

MEANING: true, faith • **USAGE:** English, German, Italian, Russian, and Scandinavian: from Latin *verus* (true); or from Russian *vjera* (faith)

Not only must we speak truth, but we must live it.
— Elbert Hubbard, "The Radiant Life"

VERENA   *[veh-RAY-nah]*

MEANING: true, truth, alder tree, spring, spring-like • **USAGE:** German: from Latin *verus* (true); from Latin *ver* (spring); or from French *verne* (alder tree, alder grove)

> *The love of truth has its reward in heaven,*
> *and already upon earth.*
> — Friedrich Nietzsche, *Beyond Good and Evil*
> (tr. Helen Zimmern)

VERITA   *[veh-REE-tah]*

MEANING: true, truth • **USAGE:** American: from Latin *verus*

> *Truth is the only safe ground to stand upon.*
> — Elizabeth Cady Stanton, *The Woman's Bible*

VERNA   *[VER-nah]*

MEANING: alder tree, spring, springlike • **USAGE:** English feminine form of Vernon, from French *verne* (alder tree); or from Latin *ver* (spring)

> *The trees of the forest will sing for joy.*
> — 1 Chronicles 16:33a (NASB)

VERONA   *[ver-OH-nah]*

MEANING: true image, bringer of victory • **USAGE:** English form of Veronica (*see* Veronica)

> *Everything possible to be believed*
> *is an image of truth.*
> — William Blake, *The Marriage of Heaven and Hell*

VERONDA   *[veh-RON-dah]*

MEANING: true image, bringer of victory • **USAGE:** English form of Veronica (*see* Veronica)

> *As every pool reflects the image of the sun, so every*
> *thought and thing restores us an image and creature of*
> *the supreme Good.*
> — Ralph Waldo Emerson, *Representative Men*

VERONICA   *[veh-ROHN-eh-kah (Italian), veh-RON-eh-kah (English)]*

MEANING: true image, bringer of victory • **USAGE:** English and Italian form of *Veraiconica* (cloth with the image of Christ on it), from Latin *verus* (true) and *iconicus* (image, icon); or English form of *Berenike,* from Greek *pherein* (to bring, to bear) and *nike* (victory)

> *This above all: to thine own self be true.*
> — William Shakespeare, *Hamlet*

VERONIKA   *[veh-ROH-nee-kah (German, Scandinavian), vyeh-rah-NEE-kah (Russian)]*

MEANING: true image, bringer of victory • **USAGE:** German, Russian, and Scandinavian form of Veronica (*see* Veronica)

> *Love is an image of God.*
> — Martin Luther

VÉRONIQUE   *[veh-roh-NEEK]*

MEANING: true image, bringer of victory • **USAGE:** French form of Veronica (*see* Veronica)

> *Whoever brings blessing will be enriched.*
> — Proverbs 11:25a (ESV)

VERUSHA   *[veh-ROO-shah]*

MEANING: true, trustworthy • **USAGE:** Russian: from Latin *verus*

> *Those who plan to do good will be loved and trusted.*
> — Proverbs 14:22 (NCV)

VESTA   *[VES-tah]*

MEANING: goddess of the hearth, sacred fire • **USAGE:** English: Roman goddess of the hearth; "Vestial" virgins tended the sacred fire in the temple of Vesta during Roman times

> *Love must be as much a light, as it is a flame.*
> — Henry David Thoreau
> (letter of September 1852)

V

VIANA, VIANNA   [vee-AH-nah]

MEANING: life, full of life • USAGE: American form of Vivian, from Latin *vita*

> *Believe that life is worth living,*
> *and your belief will help create the fact.*
> — William James, *Is Life Worth Living?*

VICKIE, VICKY, VIKI   [VIK-ee]

MEANING: conqueror, victorious, successful, triumphant • USAGE: English form of Victoria (*see* Victoria)

> *If you wish success in life, make perseverance your*
> *bosom friend, experience your wise counselor, caution*
> *your elder brother, and hope your guardian genius.*
> — Joseph Addison

VICTOIRE   [veek-TWAHR]

MEANING: conqueror, victorious, successful, triumphant • USAGE: French form of Victoria (*see* Victoria)

> *The Lord be with you, so that you may succeed.*
> — 1 Chronicles 22:11a (ESV)

VICTORIA   [vik-TOHR-ee-ah (English), veek-TOHR-ree-ah (Scandinavian), beek-TOHR-ee-ah (Spanish)]

MEANING: conqueror, victorious, successful, triumphant • USAGE: English, Scandinavian, and Spanish feminine form of Victor, from Latin *vincere* (to conquer)

> *If the day and the night are such that you greet them*
> *with joy...that is your success.*
> — Henry David Thoreau, *Walden*

VIDONIA   [bee-DOH-nee-ah]

MEANING: vine, branch • USAGE: Portuguese: from Latin *vinea*

> *The vines are in blossom;*
> *They give forth their fragrance.*
> — Song of Songs 2:13b (ASV)

VIKA   [VEE-kah]

MEANING: conqueror, victorious, successful, triumphant • USAGE: Russian form of Viktoria (*see* Victoria)

> *You will be prosperous and successful.*
> — Joshua 1:8b (NIV)

VIKTORIA   [veek-TOH-ree-ah]

MEANING: conqueror, victorious, successful, triumphant • USAGE: German and Scandinavian feminine form of Victor (*see* Victoria)

> *Minds are conquered, not by arms,*
> *but by Love and Generosity.*
> — Baruch Spinoza, *Ethics*
> (tr. James Allanson Picton)

VIKTORIYA   [veek-TOH-ree-yah]

MEANING: conqueror, victorious, successful, triumphant • USAGE: Russian form of Viktoria (*see* Victoria)

> *Love never fails.*
> — 1 Corinthians 13:8a (NASB)

VIMALA   [vih-mah-lah]

MEANING: pure, clean • USAGE: Hindu: from Sanskrit *vimala*

> *When the senses are purified, the heart is purified;*
> *when the heart is purified, there is constant and*
> *unceasing remembrance of the Self; when there is*
> *constant and unceasing remembrance of the Self,*
> *all bonds are loosed and freedom is attained.*
> — *Chandogya Upanishad* (tr. Swami Prabhavananda)

VINATA   [vih-nah-tah]

MEANING: humble, modest • USAGE: Hindu: Sanskrit

> *Humbleness is the manifestation*
> *of an understanding heart, and sets an example*
> *of greatness for others to follow.*
> — Paramahansa Yogananda

VIOLA
[*vie-OH-lah (English),*
vee-OH-lah (Italian)]

MEANING: violet flower, purple color • USAGE:
English and Italian: from Greek *ion*
Think about how the flowers of the field grow; they do
not work or spin. Yet I tell you that not even Solomon
in all his glory was clothed like one of these!
— Matthew 6:28b–29 (NEB)

VIOLET
[*VIE-oh-let*]

MEANING: violet flower, purple color • USAGE:
English: from Greek *ion*
I do love violets; they tell the history of woman's love.
— L. E. Landon, "Roland's Tower"

VIOLETA
[*vee-oh-LAY-tah*]

MEANING: violet flower, purple color • USAGE:
Spanish form of Violet (*see* Violet)
You're here to be light,
bringing out the God-colors in the world.
— Matthew 5:14b (MSG)

VIOLETTE
[*vee-oh-LET*]

MEANING: violet flower, purple color • USAGE:
French form of Violet (*see* Violet)
Flowers appear on the earth;
the season of singing has come.
— Song of Songs 2:12a (NIV)

VIONA
[*vee-OH-nah*]

MEANING: beautiful, fair, foxglove flower, vine •
USAGE: English and Spanish form of Fiona, from
Gaelic *fionn* (fair, white, beautiful); from Gaelic *fion*
(vine); or from Welsh *ffion* (foxglove)
I am the vine, and you are the branches.
If any remain in me and I remain in them,
they produce much fruit.
— John 15:5a (NCV)

VIRGINIA
[*ver-JEN-yah (English),*
veer-JEE-nyah (Italian), beer-HEE-nyah (Spanish)]

MEANING: spring, springlike, flourishing, maiden,
virgin • USAGE: English, Italian, and Spanish form
of Roman family name *Verginius*, from Latin *ver*
(spring) or Latin *virgo* (maiden, virgin)
Spring…is a natural resurrection,
an experience in immortality.
— Henry David Thoreau
(journal entry of February 24, 1852)

VIRYA
[*VEER-yah*]

MEANING: spiritual strength • USAGE: Hindu:
Sanskrit
Let us have strength enough fully to see and hear thy
universe, and to work with full vigour therein.
— Rabindranath Tagore, *Sadhana*

VITA
[*VEE-tah*]

MEANING: life, full of life • USAGE: Russian and
Scandinavian: from Latin *vita*
The one who pursues righteousness and faithful love
will find life, righteousness, and honor.
— Proverbs 21:21 (HCSB)

VITTORIA
[*vee-TOH-ree-ah*]

MEANING: conqueror, victorious, successful,
triumphant • USAGE: Italian form of Victoria, from
Latin *vincere* (to conquer)
Love conquers all.
— Virgil, *Eclogues* (tr. J. W. Mackail)

VIVI
[*vee-VEE*]

MEANING: life, full of life • USAGE: French and
Scandinavian form of Vivian (*see* Viviana)
Surely your goodness and faithfulness
will pursue me all my days, and I will live in the Lord's
house for the rest of my life.
— Psalm 23:6 (NEB)

V

VIVIAN, VIVIEN   [VIV-ee-an (English), VEE-vee-en (Danish)]

MEANING: life, full of life • **USAGE:** English and Danish (see Viviana)

> *I find ecstasy in living —*
> *the mere sense of living is joy enough.*
> — Emily Dickinson (letter of August 1870)

VIVIANA   [vee-vee-AH-nah (Italian), bee-bee-AH-nah (Spanish)]

MEANING: life, full of life • **USAGE:** Italian and Spanish form of Roman family name *Vivianus*, from Latin *vita*

> *Use common sense and sound judgment!*
> *Always keep them in mind. They will help you*
> *to live a long and beautiful life.*
> *You will walk safely and never stumble;*
> *you will rest without a worry and sleep soundly.*
> — Proverbs 3:21–24 (CEV)

VIVIENNE   [vee-vee-AHN]

MEANING: life, full of life • **USAGE:** French (see Viviana)

> *I pray that the Lord will bless your life*
> *and will be kind to you.*
> — 2 Timothy 4:22 (CEV)

VIVIETTE   [vih-vee-ET]

MEANING: life, full of life • **USAGE:** English form of Vivian (see Viviana)

> *Long life to thee! and peace be to thee,*
> *and peace be to thy house, and peace*
> *be to all that thou hast!*
> — 1 Samuel 25:6b (DT)

VONDA   [VON-dah]

MEANING: wand, branch, traveler, wanderer, sojourner, a Wend • **USAGE:** English and Russian form of Wanda, from German *vond* (wand, branch); or from German *Wend*, migrant Slavs of the sixth century

> *I am sending an angel before you*
> *to protect you on your journey.*
> — Exodus 23:20a (NLT)

VONETTA   [voh-NET-ah]

MEANING: yew tree, bow maker, God is gracious, God is giving • **USAGE:** American: possibly a form of Yvonne, from German *iv* (yew tree; a wood used to make bows); or possibly a form of Vanna, from Hebrew *y'hohanan* (Yahweh is gracious)

> *A single act of kindness throws out roots in all*
> *directions, and the roots spring up and make new trees.*
> — Amelia Earhart

VRENI   [VREH-nee]

MEANING: true, truth, alder tree, spring, spring-like • **USAGE:** German form of Verena, from Latin *verus* (true); from Latin *ver* (spring); or from French *verne* (alder tree, alder grove)

> *Nature smiled again in youthful beauty; the earth*
> *assumed once more its robe of tender green....*
> *Thus the gay morning of the year, delightful spring,*
> *returned to revive and cheer the earth.*
> — Salomon Gessner, *The Death of Abel*

VRINDA   [VREN-dah]

MEANING: cluster of holy basil used in worship • **USAGE:** Hindu: Sanskrit

> *The leaf becomes flower when it loves.*
> *The flower fruit when it worships.*
> — Rabindranath Tagore, *Stray Birds*

W

WAFEEQA, WAFIQA   [wah-FEE-kah]

MEANING: friend, companion • **USAGE:** Muslim feminine form of Wafiq

Your mind and your deep / being walk together as
friends walk along / inside their friendship.
— Jalaluddin Rumi, "Friday"
(tr. Coleman Barks in *The Glance*)

WAFIYA, WAFIYAH   [wah-fee-ah]

MEANING: faithful, loyal, trustworthy, true •
USAGE: Muslim feminine form of Wafi, from
Arabic *wafa*
The Faithful are those who perform their trust and fail
not in their word, and keep their pledge.
— Hadith of the Prophet Muhammad
(tr. Abdullay Al-Mamun Al-Suhrawardy)

WAILANI   [weh-ee-LAH-nee]

MEANING: rain water, heavenly water • USAGE:
Hawaiian
There is life in the water from the clouds.
— Hawaiian proverb
(tr. Mary Pukui in *'Olelo No'eau*)

WAINANI   [weh-ee-NAH-nee]

MEANING: beautiful water • USAGE: Hawaiian
Unfolded by the water are the faces of the flowers.
[The life-giving gift of water.]
— Hawaiian proverb
(tr. Mary Pukui in *'Olelo No'eau*)

WAJIDA, WAJEEDA   [wah-JEE-dah]

MEANING: finder • USAGE: Muslim feminine form
of Wajid
Whichever way you turn, there is the face of God.
That is to say, whichever way you turn your face,
there you will find a road which leads to God.
— Muhyiddin Ibn al-'Arabi

WALLIS   [WAL-is]

MEANING: woman of Wales • USAGE: English
feminine form of Wallace, from French *waleis*
(foreign, Welshman)

Many women have done excellently,
but you surpass them all.
— Proverbs 31:29 (ESV)

WANDA   [WAHN-dah (English), VAHN-dah (German)]

MEANING: wand, branch, traveler, wanderer,
sojourner, explorer, a Wend • USAGE: English
and German: from German *vond* (wand, branch);
or from German *Wend*, migrant Slavs of the sixth
century
Lord, You have searched me and known me.
You know when I sit down and when I stand up;
You understand my thoughts from far away.
You observe my travels and my rest;
You are aware of all my ways.
— Psalm 139:1–3 (HCSB)

WASHTA   [wahsh-tah]

MEANING: good • USAGE: Amerind: Sioux
Put goodness into the world. That's the most important
thing. That's your job as a human being.
— Noble Red Man

WASIMA, WASEEMA   [wah-SEE-mah]

MEANING: beautiful, distinguished • USAGE:
Muslim feminine form of Wasim, from Arabic
wasim (good-looking) or *wasama* (to distinguish)
Your promise is your face,
and performance is its beauty.
— Arabic proverb

WEMA   [weh-mah]

MEANING: good, virtuous • USAGE: African:
Swahili of Kenya/Tanzania
Virtue is better than wealth.
— East African proverb

W

WENDY, WENDI   [WEN-dee]

MEANING: holy ring, white bow, wand, branch, traveler, wanderer, a Wend, character from *Peter Pan* • **USAGE:** English form of Gwendolen, from Welsh *gwyn* (white, fair, holy) and *dolen* (ring, bow); German form of Wanda, German *vand* (wand, branch), or from German *Wend*, migrant Slavs of the sixth century; or from *Peter Pan* by J. M. Barrie (whose nickname *fwendy* means "friend")

> *Though we travel the world over to find the beautiful,*
> *we must carry it with us, or we find it not.*
> — Ralph Waldo Emerson, "Art"

WHITNEY   [WHIT-nee]

MEANING: white island • **USAGE:** English surname: from English *hwit* (white) and *ieg* (island)

> *God paints in many colours; but He never paints so*
> *gorgeously…as when He paints in white.*
> — G. K. Chesterton, "A Piece of Chalk"

WILDA   [WIL-dah]

MEANING: wild, untamed, free-spirited • **USAGE:** English: from German *wilde* (wild)

> *Wilderness is not a luxury*
> *but a necessity of the human spirit.*
> — Edward Abbey, *Desert Solitaire*

WILFREDA   [wil-FRAY-dah]

MEANING: desiring peace, peaceful • **USAGE:** English feminine form of Wilfred, from English *willa* (wish, desire) and *frith* (peace)

> *Peace, peace be to thee!*
> — 1 Chronicles 12:18b (YLT)

WILHELMINA   [veel-hel-MEE-nah]

MEANING: determined protector, steadfast guardian • **USAGE:** German, Swedish, and Danish feminine form of Wilhelm (*see* Willa)

> *Acquire wisdom! Acquire understanding!….*
> *Do not forsake her, and she will guard you;*
> *love her, and she will watch over you.*
> — Proverbs 4:5–6 (NASB)

WILLA   [WIL-ah]

MEANING: determined protector, steadfast guardian • **USAGE:** English feminine form of William, from German *wil* (will, resolve) and *helm* (helmet, protection)

> *Pursue righteousness, godliness, faith,*
> *love, steadfastness, gentleness.*
> — 1 Timothy 6:11b (ESV)

WILLETTA   [wil-ET-ah]

MEANING: determined protector, steadfast guardian • **USAGE:** American feminine form of William (*see* Willa)

> *Lord…let your unfailing love*
> *and faithfulness always protect me.*
> — Psalm 40:11 (NLT)

WILLOW   [WIL-oh]

MEANING: willow tree • **USAGE:** English: from English *wilowe*

> *You will be as secure as a tree with deep roots.*
> — Proverbs 12:3b (CEV)

WILMA   [WIL-mah (English), VIL-mah (German, Dutch)]

MEANING: determined protector, steadfast guardian • **USAGE:** English, German, and Dutch form of Wilhelmina (*see* Willa)

> *Discretion will guard you,*
> *understanding will watch over you.*
> — Proverbs 2:11 (NASB)

WINEMA   [wee-nee-mah]

MEANING: woman chief • **USAGE:** Amerind: Algonquin

I exhort you to peaceable counsels.
— Powhatan

WINIFRED   *[WIN-ih-fred]*

MEANING: holy peace, beautiful and harmonious
• **USAGE:** Welsh and English form of *Gwynfrewi*,
from Welsh *gwyn* (white, fair, holy) and *frewi*
(peace, harmony)
The God of peace shall be with you.
— Philippians 4:9b (KJV)

WINNIE   *[WIN-ee]*

MEANING: holy peace, beautiful and harmonious,
little redheaded one, rowan tree, famous friend •
USAGE: English and Welsh form of Rowena, from
Irish Gaelic *ruadh* (red) and diminutive *-an*; from
Norse *reynir* (rowan tree, mountain ash); or from
English *hroo* (fame) and *wine* (friend); or English
form of Winifred (*see* Winifred)
The present contains all that there is.
It is holy ground; for it is the past, and it is the future.
— Alfred North Whitehead, *The Aims of Education*

WINONA   *[wih-NOH-nah]*

MEANING: firstborn daughter • **USAGE:** Amerind:
Sioux
*Great Spirit, Great Spirit, my Grandfather, all over
the earth the faces of living things are all alike. With
tenderness have these come up out of the ground. Look
upon these faces of children without number and with
children in their arms, that they may face the winds
and walk the good road to the day of quiet.*
— Wallace Black Elk

WINTER, WYNTER   *[WIN-ter]*

MEANING: season of winter • **USAGE:** English:
from English *winter* (winter)
Grace groweth best in winter.
— Samuel Rutherford
(letter of December 30, 1636)

WREN   *[ren]*

MEANING: small songbird • **USAGE:** English: from
English *wrenne*
Let me see your face, let me hear your voice;
for your voice is sweet, and your face is lovely.
— Song of Songs 2:14b (NEB)

WYNNE   *[wen]*

MEANING: white, fair, holy • **USAGE:** Welsh: from
Welsh *gwyn*
For life is holy and every moment is precious.
— Jack Kerouac, *On the Road*

X

XANDRA   *[KSAHN-drah]*

MEANING: protector and helper of humankind,
guardian • **USAGE:** Dutch form of Alexandra,
from Greek *alexein* (to defend, to help) and *andros*
(man)
*The Lord will keep you from all harm — he will watch
over your life; the Lord will watch over your coming
and going both now and forevermore.*
— Psalm 121:7–8 (NIV)

XAVIERA   *[ZAY-vee-ER-ah (English)],*
ʒah-vee-AHR-rah (Spanish)]

MEANING: new house • **USAGE:** English and
Spanish feminine form of Xavier, from Basque
place-name *Etxabier*
Peace be within your walls…peace be within you.
— Psalm 122:7–8 (NKJV)

XENA   *[ZEE-nah]*

MEANING: hospitable, giving hospitality • **USAGE:**
English: from Greek *xenia* (hospitality) and *xenos*
(guest, stranger)

You [God] honor me as your guest,
and you fill my cup until it overflows.
— Psalm 23:1–5b (CEV)

XENIA   *[ZEN-ee-ah]*

MEANING: hospitable, giving hospitality • USAGE:
English and Greek: from Greek *xenia* (hospitality)
and *xenos* (guest, stranger)
> *Don't forget to show hospitality to strangers,*
> *for some who have done this have entertained*
> *angels without realizing it!*
> — Hebrews 13:2 (NLT)

XIAN   *[shee-ahn]*

MEANING: refined and skilled • USAGE: Chinese
This is the work of those who are skilled and peaceful,
who seek the good: May they be able and upright,
straightforward, of gentle speech and not proud. May
they be content and easily supported, unburdened, with
their senses calmed. May they be wise, not arrogant
and without desire for the possessions of others.
> — Buddha, *Metta Sutta*
> (tr. Gil Fronsdal in *Teachings of Buddha*)

XIMENA   *[hee-MAY-nah]*

MEANING: hear, hearken • USAGE: Spanish
feminine form of Ximenes, from Hebrew *shim'on*
If thou love to hear, thou shalt receive understanding:
and if thou bow thine ear, thou shalt be wise.
> — Ben Sira 6:33 (KJV Apocrypha)

Y

YAFA, YAFFAH   *[YAH-fah, yah-FAH]*

MEANING: beautiful, pretty, lovely, worthy •
USAGE: Jewish
> *How fair you are, how beautiful!*
> — Song of Songs 7:7a (JPS)

YAKINI   *[yah-kee-nee]*

MEANING: truth • USAGE: African: Swahili of
Kenya/Tanzania
> *Truth should be in love and love in truth.*
> — Swahili proverb

YAKIRA   *[yah-KEE-rah, yah-kee-RAH]*

MEANING: precious, dear, beloved • USAGE:
Jewish feminine form of Yakir
> *She is more precious than rubies.*
> — Proverbs 3:15a (MT)

YAKOVA   *[yah-KOH-vah, YAH-koh-vah]*

MEANING: replace, change, transform, successor
• USAGE: Jewish feminine form of Yakov, from
Hebrew *ya'aqobh* (one that takes by the heel, replace
with another)
> *O house of Jacob, come ye,*
> *and let us walk in the light of the Lord.*
> — Isaiah 2:5 (MT)

YAMIMA   *[yah-mee-mah]*

MEANING: happy, joyous • USAGE: Muslim: from
Arabic *yamana* (to be happy)
> *Peace be on you, you shall be happy.*
> — Koran, The Companies 39.73b (SKR)

YAMKA   *[yahm-kah]*

MEANING: blossom, flower • USAGE: Amerind:
Hopi
> *Through bright clusters of flowers /*
> *Yellow butterflies / Are chasing at play.*
> — Hopi song

YARA, YAARA   *[YAH-rah, yah-ah-RAH]*

MEANING: honeycomb, honeysuckle • USAGE:
Jewish

Eat honey, for it is good; let its sweet drops be on your
palate. Know: such is wisdom for our soul; if you attain
it, there is a future; your hope will not be cut off.
— Proverbs 24:13–14 (JPS)

YARDENA   *[yahr-deh-NAH]*

Meaning: descend, to flow down, descendant
Usage: Jewish feminine form of Yarden, from
Hebrew *yarden*
God will send down His steadfast love.
— Psalm 57:4b (JPS)

YARONA   *[yah-ROHN-ah]*

Meaning: she will sing, she will be joyous •
Usage: Jewish feminine form of Yaron
I will sing unto the Lord,
because He hath dealt bountifully with me.
— Psalm 13:6b (MT)

YASHARA   *[yah-shah-RAH]*

Meaning: honest, upright, straightforward •
Usage: Jewish feminine form of Yashar
My words bespeak the uprightness of my heart;
my lips utter insight honestly.
— Job 33:3 (JPS)

YASIRA, YASEERA   *[yah-see-rah]*

Meaning: rich, wealthy, prosperous • **Usage:**
Muslim feminine form of Yasir, from Arabic *yasir*
(to be wealthy)
Riches are not from abundance of worldly goods,
but from a contented mind.
— Hadith of the Prophet Muhammad

YASMEEN, YASMIN   *[yahs-meen]*

Meaning: jasmine flower, jasmine fragrance •
Usage: Muslim: from Arabic *yasamin*
You are the origin of all jasmine, narcissi,
and irises to come.
— Jalaluddin Rumi, "One Swaying Being"
(tr. Coleman Barks in *The Book of Love*)

YASU   *[yah-soo]*

Meaning: peaceful, serene, tranquil • **Usage:**
Japanese: from Japanese *yasu* (peace)
Rely on Peace / To activate your /
Manifold powers; / Pacify your environment /
And create a beautiful world.
— Morihei Ueshiba, *The Art of Peace*

YASUKO   *[yah-soo-koh]*

Meaning: peaceful, serene, tranquil • **Usage:**
Japanese: from Japanese *yasu* (peace) and *ko* (child)
From trust / from honesty / come peace.
— Shi Wuling, *Path to Peace*

YEHUDIT   *[yeh-hoo-DEET]*

Meaning: praise, glorify, thank • **Usage:** Jewish
feminine form of Yehudah, from Hebrew root *y-d-h*
(praised)
Let her works praise her in the gates.
— Proverbs 31:31b (MT)

YEIRA   *[yeh-EE-rah, YEE-rah]*

Meaning: light • **Usage:** Jewish
The light is sweet.
— Ecclesiastes 11:7a (MT)

YEKATERINA   *[yeh-kah-teh-REE-nah]*

Meaning: pure one, unblemished, innocent,
virtuous • **Usage:** Russian form of Katherine, from
Greek *katharos* (pure)
To the pure all things are pure.
— Titus 1:15a (ASV)

YELENA   *[yeh-LAY-nah]*

Meaning: light, illumination, torch • **Usage:**
Russian form of Helena, from Greek *helene* (torch)
or *ele* (light)
If you have light, and nothing is dark, then light will
be everywhere, as when a lamp shines brightly on you.
— Luke 11:36 (CEV)

YELIZAVETA   *[yeh-lee-ʒah-VYE-tah]*

MEANING: God is my oath, joined with God, blessed by God • **USAGE:** Russian form of Elizabeth, from Hebrew *el'ishebha*
> *You will become a blessing.*
> — Zechariah 8:13b (NCV)

YEMIMA   *[yeh-MEE-mah]*

MEANING: dove, dove-like • **USAGE:** Jewish: from Hebrew *yemimah*
> *O my dove...let me see your countenance,*
> *let me hear thy voice.*
> — Song of Songs 2:14a (MT)

YERUSHA   *[yeh-roo-SHAH, yeh-ROO-shah]*

MEANING: inheritance, possessions • **USAGE:** Jewish
> *The wise shall inherit honour.*
> — Proverbs 3:35a (MT)

YESENIA   *[yee-SAY-nee-ah]*

MEANING: palm tree, date palm tree • **USAGE:** Spanish: from *Jessenia*, a South American palm tree
> *The tree that is beside the running water*
> *is fresher and gives more fruit.*
> — Teresa of Avila

YEVA   *[YAY-vah]*

MEANING: life, full of life • **USAGE:** Russian form of Eve, from Hebrew *hawwah*
> *Grow a wise heart — you'll do yourself a favor;*
> *keep a clear head — you'll find a good life.*
> — Proverbs 19:8 (MSG)

YI   *[yee]*

MEANING: joyous, happy, harmonious • **USAGE:** Chinese

> *Joy springs spontaneous in harmonious homes.*
> — Chinese proverb (tr. William Scarborough)

YIFAT   *[yee-FAHT]*

MEANING: beauty, brilliance, splendor • **USAGE:** Jewish
> *Behold, thou art fair, my beloved, yea, pleasant.*
> — Song of Songs 1:16a (MT)

YISRAELA   *[yees-rah-EH-lah]*

MEANING: one who wrestles with God • **USAGE:** Jewish feminine form of Yisrael, from Hebrew *yisra'el* (to wrestle with God)
> *For the Lord hath chosen...Israel for His own treasure.*
> — Psalm 135:4 (MT)

YNEZ   *[ee-NAYS]*

MEANING: pure one, chaste, holy, lamb • **USAGE:** Spanish form of Agnes, from Greek *hagnos* (chaste, holy); or from Latin *agnus* (lamb)
> *I pray that God, who gives peace,*
> *will make you completely holy.*
> — 1 Thessalonians 5:23a (CEV)

YOCHANA   *[yoh-KHAH-nah]*

MEANING: God is gracious, God is giving • **USAGE:** Jewish: from Hebrew *y'hohanan* (Yahweh is gracious)
> *The Lord your God is gracious and merciful;*
> *He will not turn away His face from you.*
> — 2 Chronicles 30:9b (JPS)

YOELA   *[yoh-EH-lah]*

MEANING: the Lord is God, God is willing • **USAGE:** Jewish feminine form of Yoel, from Hebrew *yoh'el* (Yahweh is God)
> *The Lord God is a sun and a shield; the Lord giveth grace and glory; no good thing will He withhold from them that walk uprightly.*
> — Psalm 84:12 (MT)

YOKI [yoh-kee]

MEANING: rain • USAGE: Amerind: Hopi

Hither thunder, rain-thunder.... / Moving-rain. /
Everywhere, far and near, /
It will shine — water-shine.
— Hopi song

YOKO [yoh-koh]

MEANING: child of sunlight, sunny child • USAGE: Japanese: from Japanese *you* (sun, sunlight) and *ko* (child)

The sun shines by day; the moon lights up the night;
the warriors shine in their armor;
the holy one shines in meditation;
but the awakened shines radiantly all day and night.
— Buddha, *The Dhammapada* (tr. Sanderson Beck)

YOLANDA [yoh-LAHN-dah]

MEANING: violet flower, purple color • USAGE: Spanish and English: from Greek *ion*

Think how the flowers grow.
They do not work or make cloth. Yet, I tell you,
that King Solomon in all his greatness was
not dressed as well as one of these flowers.
— Luke 12:27 (NLV)

YOLANDE [yoh-LAHND]

MEANING: violet flower, purple color • USAGE: French (*see* Yolanda)

The flowers appear on the earth,
the time of the singing of birds has come.
— Song of Songs 2:12a (KJV)

YONA [yoh-NAH]

MEANING: dove, dove-like • USAGE: Jewish: from Hebrew *yonah* (dove); a symbol of peace

Behold, thou art fair; thine eyes are as doves.
— Song of Songs 1:15b (MT)

YONINA [yoh-NEE-nah]

MEANING: little dove • USAGE: Jewish form of Yona and diminutive -*ina* (*see* Yona)

O my dove...your voice is sweet
and your face is comely.
— Song of Songs 2:14 (JPS)

YOO-JIN [yoo-jeen]

MEANING: plentiful and true, truthful and rich • USAGE: Korean: from Korean *yoo* (plentiful, rich, elm) and *jin* (truth, honesty)

Hold fast to the truth.
Look not for refuge to any one besides yourselves.
— Buddha, *Mahaparinibbana Sutta*

YOSEFA, YOSEPHA [yoh-SEH-fah]

MEANING: God will add, God will increase • USAGE: Jewish feminine form of Yosef, from Hebrew *ya'saph* (Yahweh will add)

The Lord increase you more and more,
you and your children.
— Psalm 115:14 (MT)

YOSHI [yoh-shee]

MEANING: lucky, righteous, good • USAGE: Japanese: from Japanese *yoshi*

We can influence others / for the good /
by the good/ that we are thinking.
— Shi Wuling, *Path to Peace*

YOUNG-HEE [yung-hee]

MEANING: pleasant flower • USAGE: Korean: from Korean *young* (flower) and *hee* (pleasure)

Like garlands woven from a heap of flowers, /
fashion from your life as many good deeds.
— Buddha, *The Dhammapada* (tr. Thomas Byrom)

Y

YRENA   [yeh-RAY-nah]

MEANING: peace, peaceful, calm, serene • **USAGE:** Spanish form of Irene, from Greek *eirene*

Peace be with you! The Lord is with you and has greatly blessed you!
— Luke 1:28b (GNT)

YU   [yoo]

MEANING: jade, peaceful, happy • **USAGE:** Chinese

Happily the peaceful live,
discarding both victory and defeat.
— Buddha, *The Dhammapada*
(tr. Buddharakkhita Thera)

YUKIKO   [yoo-kee-koh]

MEANING: happy child, snow child • **USAGE:** Japanese: from Japanese *yuki* (happiness, snow) and *ko* (child)

The body in motion / the mind at peace. /
These are keys to / contentment and happiness.
— Shi Wuling, *Path to Peace*

YUKO   [yoo-koh]

MEANING: gentle child, kind child • **USAGE:** Japanese: from Japanese *yu* (gentle, kind) and *ko* (child)

Kindness is not for others' sake but for oneself.
— Japanese proverb

YULIYA   [YOO-lee-ah]

MEANING: young, youthful, of Jupiter • **USAGE:** Russian form of Julia, from Latin *iulus* (downy-chinned, youthful); or form of Jupiter, from Latin *dyeus* (Zeus) and *pater* (father)

Youth is, after all, just a moment,
but it is the moment, the spark,
that you always carry in your heart.
— Raisa Gorbachev, *I Hope*

YURI   [yoo-ree]

MEANING: lily flower • **USAGE:** Japanese: from Japanese *yuri*

Your heart is full of fertile seeds, waiting to sprout....
The interaction of the cosmic breath causes the flower of the spirit to bloom and bear fruit in this world.
— Moreihi Ueshiba, *The Art of Peace*

YVETTE   [ee-VET]

MEANING: yew tree, bow maker • **USAGE:** French and English feminine form of Yves, from German *iv* (yew tree); yew is used to make bows

Make love your aim.
— 1 Corinthians 14:1a (RSV)

YVONNE   [ee-VAHN]

MEANING: yew tree, bow maker • **USAGE:** English, French, German, and Scandinavian feminine form of Yves, from German *iv* (yew tree); yew is used to make bows

Blessed is the one who finds wisdom, and the one who obtains understanding. She is like a tree of life to those who obtain her, and everyone who grasps hold of her will be blessed
— Proverbs 3:13, 3:18 (NEB)

Z

ZADA   [ZAY-dah]

MEANING: princess, royal one • **USAGE:** American form of Zadie, from Hebrew *sarah*

Mutual love, the crown of all our bliss.
— John Milton, *Paradise Lost*

ZADIE   [ZAY-dee]

MEANING: princess, royal one • **USAGE:** American form of Sadie, from Hebrew *sarah*

That perfect bliss and sole felicity, /
The sweet fruition of an earthly crown.
— Christopher Marlowe, *Tamburlaine*

Y

ZAFIRA, ZAFIRAH   *[zah-fee-rah]*

MEANING: victorious, successful • **USAGE:**
Muslim feminine form of Zafir, from Arabic *zafira*
(to succeed)

> *Victory cometh only by the help of Allah.*
> *Lo! Allah is Mighty, Wise.*
> — Koran, The Spoils of War 8:10b (PIC)

ZAHARA   *[zah-HAH-rah]*

MEANING: shining, luminous light • **USAGE:**
Jewish

> *How sweet is the light.*
> — Ecclesiastes 11:7a (JPS)

ZAHIDAH, ZAHEEDA   *[zah-HEE-dah]*

MEANING: devout, righteous • **USAGE:** Muslim
feminine form of Zahid

> *When love's fire produces its flame,*
> *it illuminates like a torch the devotee's path in life,*
> *and all darkness vanishes.*
> — Hazrat Inayat Khan, *The Bowl of Saki*

ZAHINA, ZAHEENA   *[zah-HEE-nah]*

MEANING: wise, knowledgeable • **USAGE:** Muslim
feminine form of Zahin

> *My Lord: Grant me wisdom,*
> *and join me with the good.*
> — Koran, The Poets 26.83 (SKR)

ZAHIRAH, ZAHEERA   *[zah-HEE-rah]*

MEANING: helper, supporter • **USAGE:** Muslim
feminine form of Zahir, from Arabic *zahir*

> *Allah sufficeth for a Guide and Helper.*
> — Koran, The Criterion 25.13b (PIC)

ZAHIYA, ZAHIA   *[zah-hee-ah]*

MEANING: beautiful, lovely • **USAGE:** Muslim

> *Beauty / is my teacher /*
> *helping me to know He / cares for / me.*
> — Rabia al-Adawiyya,
> "A Lover Who Wants His Lovers Near"
> (tr. Daniel Ladinsky in *Love Poems from God*)

ZAHRA   *[zah-rah]*

MEANING: flower, blossom • **USAGE:** Muslim:
from Arabic *zahr*

> *Let me grow quietly in Thy garden as a speechless*
> *plant, that some day my flowers and fruits*
> *might sing the legend of my silent past.*
> — Hazrat Inayat Khan, *The Gayan*

ZALENA, ZALINA   *[zah-LEE-nah]*

MEANING: moon, moon goddess • **USAGE:**
American form of Selene, from Greek *selene* (the
moon), Greek moon goddess

> *Under the full moon life is all adventure.*
> — Sigurd Olson, *Wilderness Days*

ZALIRA   *[zah-lee-rah]*

MEANING: flower • **USAGE:** African: Swahili of
Kenya/Tanzania

> *Look after the seedling for it to grow well.*
> — Kenyan proverb

ZAMILA, ZAMEELA   *[zah-MEE-lah]*

MEANING: friend, companion • **USAGE:** Muslim
feminine form of Zamil

> *Make a journey from self to Self, oh friend, for by such*
> *a journey the earth becomes a mine of gold!*
> — Jalaluddin Rumi
> (tr. William Chittick in *The Sufi Path of Love*)

ZAMIRAH, ZAMEERA   *[zah-MEE-rah]*

MEANING: heart • **USAGE:** Muslim feminine form
of Zamir

> *I saw my Lord with the eye of the heart.*
> — Mansur al-Hallaj

Z

ZANDRA   [ZAN-drah]

MEANING: protector and helper of humankind, guardian • USAGE: English form of Alexandra, from Greek *alexein* (to defend, to help) and *andros* (man)

> *Lord, may your love and faithfulness*
> *always protect me.*
> — Psalm 40:11b (NIV)

ZANETA   [zhah-NET-ah]

MEANING: God is gracious, God is giving • USAGE: Russian form of Janet, from Hebrew *y'hohanan* (Yahweh is gracious)

> *God is gracious and merciful*
> *and will not turn away his face from you.*
> — 2 Chronicles 30:9b (ASV)

ZANITA   [zah-NEE-tah]

MEANING: God is gracious, God is giving • USAGE: American: possibly a feminine form of Zane (see Zaneta)

> *I am your God. I will give you strength,*
> *and for sure I will help you. Yes, I will hold you up*
> *with My right hand that is right and good.*
> — Isaiah 41:10b (NLV)

ZANNA   [ZAN-ah]

MEANING: protector and helper of humankind, guardian, lily, rose • USAGE: English form of Alexandra (see Zandra); or English form of Suzanna, from Hebrew *shoshan* (rose, lily)

> *My God is my protection,*
> *and with him I am safe.*
> — 2 Samuel 22:3a (GNT)

ZARA   [ZAH-rah]

MEANING: princess, royal one • USAGE: Jewish form of Sarah, from Hebrew *sarah*

> *She [Wisdom] will give to thy head a chaplet of grace;*
> *a crown of glory will she bestow on thee.*
> — Proverbs 4:7–9 (MT)

ZARIFA, ZAREEFA   [zah-REE-fah]

MEANING: elegant, gracious • USAGE: Muslim feminine form of Zarif

> *Elegant becomes the countenance of one /*
> *who exemplifies patience*
> — Hafiz, "Enduring the Absurb" (tr. Daniel Ladinsky in *A Year with Hafiz*)

ZARITA   [zah-REE-tah]

MEANING: little princess, little royal one • USAGE: Spanish form of Sarah and diminutive *-ita* (see Zara)

> *Seek first His kingdom and His righteousness,*
> *and all these things will be added to you.*
> — Matthew 6:33 (NASB)

ZASHA   [ZAH-shah]

MEANING: protector and helper of humankind, guardian • USAGE: American form of Sasha (see Zandra)

> *He will order his angels to protect you wherever you go.*
> — Psalm 91:11 (NLT)

ZAVANNA, ZAVANNAH   [zah-VAN-ah]

MEANING: grassland, flat treeless plain • USAGE: English form of Savannah, from Spanish *zabana*

> *I believe a leaf of grass is no less*
> *than the journey-work of the stars.*
> — Walt Whitman, "Song of Myself"

ZAYNA   [zay-nah]

MEANING: beautiful, graceful • USAGE: Muslim

> *Great is the Grace of Allah unto thee.*
> — Koran, The Women 4.113b (ALI)

Z

ZEBA [zeh-bah]

MEANING: beautiful, lovely • **USAGE:** Persian
Any beauty the world has, any desire, /
will easily be yours. As you live / deeper in the heart,
the mirror gets / clear and cleaner.
— Jalaluddin Rumi, "Out in Empty Sky"
(tr. Coleman Barks in *The Glance*)

ZEHIRA [zeh-HEER-ah]

MEANING: careful, prudent, guarded, protected •
USAGE: Jewish
Foresight will protect you,
and discernment will guard you.
— Proverbs 2:11 (JPS)

ZELDA, ZELDE [ZEL-dah]

MEANING: happy, joyful, gray warrior • **USAGE:**
Yiddish: from German *salida* (happy); or English
form of Griselda, from German *gries* (gray) and
hild (war, strife)
You shall have nothing but joy.
— Deuteronomy 16:15b (JPS)

ZEMIRA, ZEMIRAH [zeh-MEE-rah]

MEANING: song, melody • **USAGE:** Jewish
Let me hear your voice; for your voice is sweet.
— Song of Songs 2:14b (JPS)

ZENE [ZAY-nay]

MEANING: beautiful • **USAGE:** African: Nigeria
Greatness and beauty do not belong to the gods alone.
— Nigerian proverb

ZENIA [ZEEN-yah, ZEN-ee-ah, ZEN-yah]

MEANING: hospitable, giving hospitality, friendly •
USAGE: English: form of Xenia, from Greek *xenia*
(hospitality) and *xenos* (guest, stranger)

The flowers have appeared in the earth,
the time of the singing hath come.
— Song of Songs 2:12a (YLT)

ZENZI [ZEN-zee]

MEANING: spring up, grow, thrive • **USAGE:**
German form of Latin family name *Crescentius*
(spring up, thriving)
Good is reverence for life...
and all that enhances life, growth, unfolding.
— Erich Fromm, *The Heart of Man*

ZEPHIRA [zeh-FEE-rah]

MEANING: morning, morning light • **USAGE:**
Jewish
Joy cometh in the morning.
— Psalm 30:6b (MT)

ZHANNA [ZHAH-nah]

MEANING: God is gracious, God is giving •
USAGE: Russian form of Jeanne, from Hebrew
y'hohanan (Yahweh is gracious)
He shall give his angels charge over thee,
to keep thee in all thy ways.
— Hebrews 13:2 (CEV)

ZIBA [zee-bah]

MEANING: gazelle, graceful deer • **USAGE:**
Muslim
A dancing soul shows its graceful movements
in all its activities.
— Hazrat Inayat Khan, *The Gayan* (cd. *The Gayani*
Meditations, Volume 1, tr. Cecil Touchon)

ZIHNA [zee-nah]

MEANING: spinning, turning • **USAGE:** Amerind:
Sioux

Z

Our circle is timeless, flowing, it is a new life emerging
from death — life winning out over death.
— John (Fire) Lame Deer,
Lame Deer: Seeker of Visions

ZINA   [ZEE-nah]

Meaning: of Zeus, sky, thunder • **Usage:**
Russian form of *Zinaida,* from Greek *ƺenaide* (of
Zeus, Greek god of sky and thunder)
The voice of the Lord is upon the waters; the God of
glory thundereth; the Lord is upon many waters.
— Psalm 29:3 (KJ21)

ZINNIA   [ZEN-ee-ah]

Meaning: flower • **Usage:** English: from Latin
ƺinnia elegans, named after German botanist Johann
G. Zinn
Flowers are like the pleasures of the world.
— William Shakespeare, *Cymbeline*

ZITA, ZEETA   [ZEE-tah]

Meaning: little girl • **Usage:** Italian
My child, don't lose sight of common sense
and discernment. Hang on to them,
for they will refresh your soul.
— Proverbs 3:21–22 (NLT)

ZIVAH, ZIVA   [ƺih-VAH, ZEE-vah]

Meaning: radiant, light, brilliance, splendor •
Usage: Jewish feminine form of Ziv
They that are wise shall shine
as the brightness of the firmament.
— Daniel 12:3a (MT)

ZIYA   [ƺee-yah]

Meaning: light, radiance • **Usage:** Muslim
Light upon Light!
Allah doth guide whom He will to His Light.
— Koran, Light 24.35b (ALI)

ZLATA   [ZLAH-tah]

Meaning: gold, golden • **Usage:** Czech and
Russian: from Slavic *ƺlato*
A word fitly spoken is like
apples of gold in network of silver.
— Proverbs 25:11 (ASV)

ZOE   [ZOH-ee]

Meaning: life, full of life • **Usage:** Greek,
Italian, and English: from Greek *ƺoe*
Surely, goodness and loving-kindness
shall follow me all the days of my life.
— Psalm 23:6a (DT)

ZOEY   [ZOH-ee]

Meaning: life, full of life • **Usage:** American
form of Zoe (*see* Zoe)
The most important thing in life is to learn
how to give out love, and to let it come in.
— Mitch Albom, *Tuesdays with Morrie*

ZOFIA   [ƺoh-FEE-ah]

Meaning: wise, wisdom, sage • **Usage:** Polish
form of Sophia, from Greek *sophia* (wisdom) or
sophos (wise)
God said…I have given you
a wise and understanding heart.
— 1 Kings 3:11–12b (NLV)

ZOLA   [ZOH-lah]

Meaning: calm, peaceful • **Usage:** African:
Xhosa of South Africa
Together we will work to support courage where there
is fear, foster agreement where there is conflict, and
inspire hope where there is despair.
— Desmond Tutu

Z

ZONTA   *[zohn-tah]*

MEANING: trusted, trustworthy • **USAGE:**
Amerind: Sioux

> *Oh, Great Spirit…Make me always ready to come*
> *to you with clean hands and straight eyes.*
> — Sioux prayer

ZORA, ZORAH   *[ZOHR-ah]*

MEANING: dawn, sunrise • **USAGE:** Czech: from
Slavic *zora*

> *The sun loves to peer into a happy home.*
> — Slovakian proverb

ZORINA   *[zoh-REE-nah]*

MEANING: dawn, sunrise, daybreak • **USAGE:**
Czech: from Slavic *zora*

> *Your light will break forth like the dawn.*
> — Isaiah 58:8a (NIV)

ZOYA   *[ZOY-ah]*

MEANING: life, full of life • **USAGE:** Russian form
of Zoe, from Greek *zoe*

> *Wisdom will multiply your days*
> *and add years to your life.*
> — Proverbs 9:11 (NLT)

ZUHRA   *[zoo-rah]*

MEANING: Venus, star • **USAGE:** Muslim

> *O God, guide me, protect me,*
> *make of me a shining lamp and a brilliant star.*
> — Abdu'l-Bahá

ZUNA   *[ZOO-nah]*

MEANING: abundance, prosperity • **USAGE:**
African: Bobangi of Nigeria

> *Health of the body is prosperity.*
> — Nigerian proverb

ZUSA   *[ZOO-sah]*

MEANING: lily, rose • **USAGE:** Czech, Polish, and
Yiddish form of Suzanna, from Hebrew *shoshan*

> *Time and patience bring roses.*
> — Slovakian proverb

ZUZANNA   *[zoo-ZAH-nah]*

MEANING: lily, rose • **USAGE:** Polish form of
Shoshanah, from Hebrew *shoshan*

> *Consider the lilies how they grow:*
> *they neither toil nor spin; but I say unto you,*
> *not even Solomon in all his glory*
> *was clothed as one of these.*
> — Luke 12:27 (DT)

Z

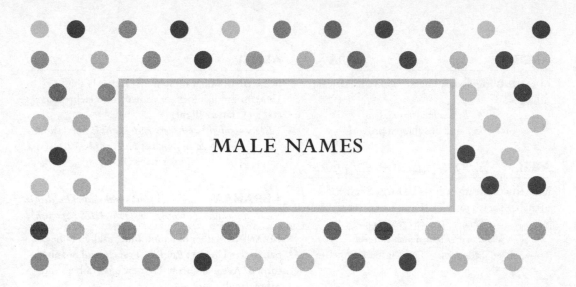

MALE NAMES

A

AARON
[AYR-on]

MEANING: teaching, singing, shining, mountain, exalted one • **USAGE:** English form of Aharon, from Hebrew *aharon*

> *A teacher affects eternity;*
> *he can never tell where his influence stops.*
> — Henry Brooks Adams,
> *The Education of Henry Adams*

ABAN, ABAAN
[ah-bahn]

MEANING: clear, distinct • **USAGE:** Muslim

> *Myself with mine own eyes I saw most clearly, /*
> *But when I looked with God's eyes —*
> *only God I saw.*
> — Baba Kuhi of Shiraz,
> "In the Market, in the Cloister"

ABDALLAH
[ahb-DAH-lah]

MEANING: servant of Allah, devoted to Allah • **USAGE:** Muslim: from Arabic *'abd* (servant) and Allah

> *Love for God is the expansion of the heart.*
> — Hazrat Inayat Khan, *The Bowl of Saki*

ABDUL
[ahb-DOOL]

MEANING: servant, devotee (of Allah) • **USAGE:** Muslim: from Arabic *'abd* (servant)

> *Service of God means we each work for all.*
> — Hazrat Inayat Khan, *The Gayan*

ABE
[ayb]

MEANING: father of a multitude, exalted father, patriarch • **USAGE:** English form of Abraham (*see* Abraham)

> *Out of one man a race / of men innumerable.*
> — John Milton, *Paradise Lost*

363

ABEBE   [ah-BEH-beh]

MEANING: righteous, honest • USAGE: African:
Ethiopia

> *An honest man has no fear.*
> — Kunama of Ethiopia proverb

ABEL   [AY-bel (English), ah-BEL (Spanish)]

MEANING: breath of life • USAGE: English,
French, Spanish form of Hevel, from Hebrew *hebel*

> *Closer is He than breathing, /*
> *and nearer than hands and feet.*
> — Alfred Tennyson, "The Higher Pantheism"

ABHAY   [ahb-hay]

MEANING: brave, courageous • USAGE: Hindu:
Sanskrit

> *If you have confidence in your strength and skill, you*
> *can draw upon the inner springs of courage and raise*
> *yourselves to a higher level of joy and peace.*
> — Sathya Sai Baba, *Sathya Sai Baba Speaks*

ABID, ABEED   [ah-beed]

MEANING: worshiper (of Allah) • USAGE:
Muslim: from Arabic 'aabid

> *To make God a reality is the real object of worship.*
> — Hazrat Inayat Khan, *The Bowl of Saki*

ABIDIN   [ah-bee-deen]

MEANING: worshiper (of Allah) • USAGE:
Muslim: from Arabic 'aabid

> *By respecting every person I meet, I worship God. In*
> *loving every soul on earth, I feel my devotion for Him.*
> — Hazrat Inayat Khan, *The Gayan*

ABIR   [ah-BEER]

MEANING: strength, might • USAGE: Jewish

> *With whom My hand shall be established;*
> *Mine arm also shall strengthen him.*
> — Psalm 89:22 (MT)

ABNER   [AB-ner]

MEANING: father of light, my father is a light •
USAGE: English form of Avner, from Hebrew *abh*
(father) and *ner* (light)

> *Every good gift and every perfect gift is from above,*
> *coming down from the Father of lights.*
> — James 1:17a (ESV)

ABRAHAM   [AY-brah-ham (English),
AH-brah-hahm (French), ah-brah-AHM (Spanish)]

MEANING: father of a multitude, exalted father,
patriarch • USAGE: English, French, and Spanish
form of Avraham, from Hebrew *abh* (father) and
raham (multitude)

> *God said…No longer will you be called Abram;*
> *your name will be Abraham,*
> *for I have made you a father of many nations.*
> — Genesis 17:3b–5 (NIV)

ABRAM   [ah-brahm (Russian, Dutch),
ay-bram (English)]

MEANING: high father, patriarch • USAGE:
Russian, Dutch, and English form of Avram,
Hebrew *abh* (father) and *ram* (high, exalted)

> *The Lord said to Abram…all the peoples on earth*
> *will be blessed through you.*
> — Genesis 12:1–3 (HCSB)

ABRAMO   [ah-BRAH-moh]

MEANING: high father, patriarch • USAGE: Italian
form of Abram (*see* Abram)

> *The word of the Lord came to Abram in a vision:*
> *Do not be afraid, Abram. I am your shield;*
> *your reward will be very great.*
> — Genesis 15:1 (HCSB)

ABRÁN   [ah-BRAHN]

MEANING: father of a multitude, exalted father,
patriarch • USAGE: Spanish form of Abraham (*see*
Abraham)

A

O Lord, thou art our father; we are the clay, and thou
our potter; and we all are the work of thy hand.
— Isaiah 64:8 (KJV)

ABSALOM [AB-sah-lahm]

MEANING: father of a multitude, exalted father,
patriarch • USAGE: Spanish form of Abraham (*see*
Abraham)

O Lord, thou art our father, and we are clay: and thou
art our maker, and we all are the works of thy hands.
— Isaiah 64:8 (DR)

ACE [ays]

MEANING: number one, expert, proficient •
USAGE: English: from Latin *as*

The man who goes farthest is generally
the one who is willing to do and dare.
— Dale Carnegie

ACHIM [ah-KEEM]

MEANING: God will establish • USAGE: German
form of Joachim, from Hebrew *yehoyakim* (Yahweh
will establish)

His heart is fixed, trusting in the Lord.
His heart is established, he shall not be afraid.
— Psalm 112:7b–8a (KJV)

ADAHY [ah-dah-hie]

MEANING: in the woods • USAGE: Amerind:
Cherokee

The native vision, the gift of seeing truly, with wonder
and delight into the natural world, is informed by a
certain attitude of reverence and respect.
— N. Scott Momaday,
"A Vision Beyond Time and Place"

ADAIR [ah-DAYR]

MEANING: prosperous spear, wealthy spearman,
oak grove • USAGE: Scottish and English: from

Gaelic *doire* (oak grove); or English form of Edgar,
from English *ead* (wealth, prosperity) and *gar*
(spear)

Fair be all thy hopes, /
And prosperous be thy life in peace and war!
— William Shakespeare, *King Henry VI, Part I*

ADAM [ah-DAHM (Jewish, French), AD-em (English)]

MEANING: earth, of the red earth, make, create •
USAGE: Jewish, English, and French: from Hebrew
adam (red) or *adamah* (earth); or from Assyrian
adamu (to make)

God said: Let us make man in our image,
after our likeness.... And God created man in
His own image, in the image of God He created him.
— Genesis 1:26–27a (MT)

ADAMO [ah-DAH-moh]

MEANING: earth, of the red earth, make, create •
USAGE: Italian form of Adam (*see* Adam)

Adam, made of earth, came from the earth.
— 1 Corinthians 15:47b (NEB)

ADÁN [ah-DAHN]

MEANING: earth, of the red earth, make, create •
USAGE: Spanish form of Adam (*see* Adam)

God formed man from the dust of the ground,
and breathed into his nostrils the breath of life;
and the man became a living being.
— Genesis 2:7 (NRSV)

ADAR [ah-DAHR]

MEANING: exalted, praised, noble • USAGE:
Jewish

The divine sings in noble deeds.
— Abraham Heschel, *The Earth Is the Lord's*

ADDISON   *[AD-ih-son]*

MEANING: son of Adam, of the red earth, fire, fiery one • **USAGE:** English and Irish: English surname, a combination of Adam and *son*; from Hebrew *adam* (red) or *adamah* (earth), or from Assyrian *adamu* (to make); or English form of Aidis, from Gaelic *aodh* (fire)

> *The divine spark leaps from the finger of God*
> *to the finger of Adam.*
> — Alfred Whitney Griswold,
> *Liberal Education and the Democratic Ideal*

ADEN   *[AY-den]*

MEANING: fire, fiery one • **USAGE:** American form of Aidan, from Irish Gaelic *aodh* (fire)

> *He [God] makes the winds His messengers,*
> *flaming fire His ministers.*
> — Psalm 104:4 (NASB)

ADIB, ADEEB   *[ah-deeb]*

MEANING: courteous, considerate • **USAGE:** Muslim: from Arabic *adib*

> *Humility and courtesy are acts of piety.*
> — Hadith of the Prophet Muhammad

ADIL, ADEEL   *[ah-DEEL]*

MEANING: honest, truthful • **USAGE:** Muslim: from Arabic *'adala* (to act justly)

> *O pray to be honest, / Strong, /*
> *Kind, / And pure.*
> — Hafiz, "Out of This Mess"
> (tr. Daniel Ladinsky in *The Gift*)

ADIO   *[ah-dee-OH]*

MEANING: righteous, moral, guiltless • **USAGE:** African: Yoruba of Nigeria

> *May my outer head not spoil my inner head.*
> — Yoruban proverb

ADIR   *[ah-DEER]*

MEANING: powerful, strong, noble, glorious • **USAGE:** Jewish

> *My hand shall be constantly with him,*
> *and My arm shall strengthen him.*
> — Psalm 89:22 (JPS)

ADISA   *[ah-dee-sah]*

MEANING: one who makes himself clear • **USAGE:** African: Yoruba of Nigeria

> *Intention is the eldest, contemplation is the next,*
> *and plan of action is the third.*
> — Yoruban proverb

ADITYA   *[ah-diht-yah]*

MEANING: the sun • **USAGE:** Hindu: Sanskrit

> *The Self, small as the thumb, dwelling in the heart, /*
> *Is like the sun shining in the sky.*
> — *Shvetashvatara Upanishad* (tr. Eknath Easwaran)

ADIV   *[ah-DEEV]*

MEANING: courteous, gracious, pleasant • **USAGE:** Jewish

> *The words of a wise man's mouth are gracious.*
> — Ecclesiastes 10:12a (MT)

ADLAI   *[AD-lie]*

MEANING: act justly, fair, equitable, judicious • **USAGE:** English: from Arabic *adala* (to act justly)

> *Justice is truth in action.*
> — Benjamin Disraeli (speech of February 11, 1851)

ADOLF   *[AH-dahlf]*

MEANING: noble wolf • **USAGE:** German and Scandinavian: from German *adal* (noble) and *wulf* (wolf)

> *The wolf will dwell with the lamb.*
> — Isaiah 11:6a (NASB)

ADOLFO *[ah-DOHL-foh]*

MEANING: noble wolf • **USAGE:** Spanish and Italian form of Adolf (*see* Adolf)

She [Wisdom] shall give to thy head increase of graces, and protect thee with a noble crown.
— Proverbs 4:9 (DR)

ADOLPH, ADOLPHE *[AY-dolf]*

MEANING: noble wolf • **USAGE:** English form of Adolf (*see* Adolf)

Whatever is true, whatever is noble, whatever is right, whatever is pure, whatever is lovely, whatever is admirable — if anything is excellent or praiseworthy — think about such things.
— Philippians 4:8 (NIV)

ADOM *[ah-DOHM]*

MEANING: God's blessing • **USAGE:** African: Ghana

Oyeʒ! May the Gods pour their blessings upon us!
— Ga of Ghana naming ritual

ADONIS *[ah-DAHN-is]*

MEANING: lord, handsome, exceptionally good-looking • **USAGE:** Greek: from Hebrew *adon* (lord); in Greek mythology, handsome young man loved by Aphrodite

You are the most handsome of all. Gracious words stream from your lips. God himself has blessed you forever.
— Psalm 45:2 (NLT)

ADRIAN *[AY-dree-an (English), ah-dree-AHN (German, Italian, Russian, Scandinavian)]*

MEANING: seaport, sea haven, man from Hadria • **USAGE:** English, German, Italian, Russian, and Scandinavian form of Adriano (*see* Adriano)

The Sea knows all things, for at night when the winds are asleep the stars confide to him their secrets.
— Elbert Hubbard, "The Sea"

ADRIANO *[ah-dree-AHN-oh]*

MEANING: seaport, sea haven, man from Hadria • **USAGE:** Italian: from Latin *Hadria* (Italian city on Adriatic Sea)

I take the wings of morning, I dwell in the uttermost part of the sea, also there Thy hand doth lead me, and Thy right hand doth hold me.
— Psalm 139:9–10 (YLT)

ADRIEL *[ah-dree-EHL]*

MEANING: God is my majesty, of God's flock • **USAGE:** Jewish

For He is our God, and we are the people of His pasture, and the flock of His hand.
— Psalm 95:7a (MT)

ADRIEN *[AH-dree-ehn]*

MEANING: seaport, sea haven, man from Hadria • **USAGE:** French form of Adriano (*see* Adriano)

Man — a free man — always loves the sea.
— Charles Baudelaire, *Les Fleurs du Mal* (tr. Richard Howard)

AEGIS *[AYE-gis]*

MEANING: protection of Zeus • **USAGE:** Greek: from Greek *aigis* (goatskin shield of Zeus)

Let my heart be wise, it is the gods' best gift.
— Euripides, *Medea* (tr. Rex Warner)

AFIF, AFEEF *[ah-feef]*

MEANING: virtuous, chaste • **USAGE:** Muslim: from Arabic ʿafeef (virtuous) or ʿafifa (pure, chaste)

When you speak, speak the truth; perform when you promise; discharge your trust; be chaste in thought and action; and withhold your hand from striking, from taking that which is unlawful, and bad.
— Hadith of the Prophet Muhammad

AGNI [AHG-nee]

MEANING: sacred fire • **USAGE:** Hindu: Sanskrit: Hindu god of fire

The being who is in the fire and at the same time in the heart…meditate upon as Brahman.
— *Brihadaranyaka Upanishad*
(tr. Swami Prabhavananda)

AGOSTINO [ah-goh-STEE-noh]

MEANING: great one, revered one, magnificent • **USAGE:** Italian form of Augustine, from Latin *augustus*

Greatness of spirit adorns greatness of standing.
— Seneca, *De Clementia* (tr. Susanna Braund)

AHARON [ah-hah-ROHN]

MEANING: teaching, singing, shining, mountain, exalted one • **USAGE:** Jewish: from Hebrew *aharon*

Who shall ascend into the mountain of the Lord? And who shall stand in His holy place? He that hath clean hands, and a pure heart; who hath not taken My name in vain, and hath not sworn deceitfully.
— Psalm 24:3–4 (MT)

AHIGA [ah-hee-gah]

MEANING: he fights, warrior • **USAGE:** Amerind: Navajo

A spear is a big responsibility.
— Navajo proverb

AHLF [ahlf]

MEANING: noble wolf • **USAGE:** German form of Adolf (*see* Adolf)

All that is noble is in itself of a quiet nature.
— Johann Wolfgang von Goethe

AHMED, AHMAD [ah-med, ah-mahd]

MEANING: more commendable, more praised • **USAGE:** Muslim: from Arabic *ahmad*

Allah will exalt those of you who believe, and those who are given knowledge, in high degrees; and Allah is Aware of what you do.
— Koran, The Pleading One 58.11b (SKR)

AHULI [ah-hoo-lee]

MEANING: drum • **USAGE:** Amerind: Cherokee

From the beginning there were drums, beating out world rhythm — the booming, never-failing tide on the beach; the four seasons, gliding smoothly, one from the other; when the birds come, when they go, the bear hibernating for his winter sleep. Unfathomable the why, yet all in the perfect. Watch the heartbeat in your wrist — a precise pulsing beat of life's Drum — with loss of timing you are ill.
— Jimalee Burton

AIDAN, AIDEN [AY-den]

MEANING: fire, fiery one • **USAGE:** English form of Aodhan, from Gaelic *aodh* (fire)

Joy is the holy fire that keeps our purpose warm and our intelligence aglow.
— Helen Keller, *Out of the Dark*

AIDIS, ADDIS [AY-dis, AD-es]

MEANING: fire, fiery one • **USAGE:** Irish: from Gaelic *aodh* (fire)

He maketh winds his messengers; flames of fire his ministers.
— Psalm 104:4 (ASV)

AINSLEY [AYNZ-lee]

MEANING: one's own poem, hermitage meadow • **USAGE:** Scottish and English: from Gaelic *aon* (one) and *laoi* (poem); or from English *ansetl* (hermitage) and *leah* (meadow, field)

There is religion in everything around us — a calm and holy religion in the unbreathing things of nature, which man would do well to imitate.…It is the poetry of Nature. It is this which uplifts the spirit within us.
— John Ruskin

AKAMA
[ah-kah-mah]

MEANING: without desire, pure, clean • **USAGE:**
Hindu: from Sanskrit *a* (without) and *kama* (desire)

As pure water poured into pure water becomes the very
same, so does the Self of the illumined man or woman.
— *Taittiriya Upanishad* (tr. Eknath Easwaran)

AKHTAR
[ahk-tahr]

MEANING: star, good fortune, good omen •
USAGE: Persian

Blessed is he who seeth the star of his soul
as the light seen from the sea.
— Hazrat Inayat Khan, *The Gayan*

AKIF
[ah-KEEF]

MEANING: devoted, dedicated, faithful • **USAGE:**
Muslim: from Arabic *'aakif*

The true faithful are those from whose hands
and tongues people remain safe.
— Hadith of the Prophet Muhammad

AKIKI
[ah-kee-kee]

MEANING: friend, friendly • **USAGE:** African:
Egypt

The image of friendship is truth.
— Egyptian proverb

AKIM
[AH-keem, ah-KEEM]

MEANING: God will establish • **USAGE:** Russian
form of Joachim, from Hebrew *yehoyakim* (Yahweh
will establish)

It is good that the heart be established by grace.
— Hebrews 13:9b (ASV)

AKINS
[ah-KEENS]

MEANING: brave, courageous • **USAGE:** African:
Yoruba of Nigeria

There are three friends in life:
courage, sense and insight.
— Nigerian proverb

AKIO
[ah-kee-oh]

MEANING: bright man • **USAGE:** Japanese: from
Japanese *aki* (bright) and *o* (male, man)

One should cultivate (the society of) a good man,
who is intelligent and learned; he who leads
a regular life, having understood what is good
and penetrated the Dharma, will obtain happiness.
— Buddha, *The Dhammapada* (tr. Viggo Fausbøll)

AKIRA
[ah-kee-rah]

MEANING: bright • **USAGE:** Japanese

Always keep your mind as bright and clear as the vast
sky, the great ocean, and the highest peak, and the
deepest ocean, empty of all limiting thoughts.
— Morihei Ueshiba,
The Art of Peace (tr. John Stevens)

AKIVA
[ah-KEE-vah]

MEANING: replace, change, transform, successor
• **USAGE:** Jewish form of Yakov, from Hebrew
ya'aqobh (one that takes by the heel, replace with
another)

The name of Jacob's God keep you safe.... May He
grant you your desire, and fulfill your every plan.
— Psalm 20:2b, 5 (JPS)

AKSEL
[AYK-sel]

MEANING: father of peace, peaceful father,
peaceful ruler • **USAGE:** Danish, Norwegian,
and Swedish form of Absalom, from Hebrew *abh*
(father) and *shalom* (peace)

May God, the source of hope,
fill you with all joy and peace.
— Romans 15:13a (GNT)

AL
[al]

MEANING: little rock, handsome, elf counsel, wise
counselor, elf friend • **USAGE:** English form of Alan,
Albert, Alfred, or Alvin (*see* individual names)

Self-respect — that cornerstone of all virtue.
— John Herschel, *The System Bible Study*

ALAIN [ah-LAYN]

MEANING: little rock, handsome • USAGE: French form of Alan (*see* Alan)

Look unto the rock from whence ye are hewn.
— Isaiah 51:1b (KJ21)

ALAIR [ah-LAYR]

MEANING: cheerful, merry, lighthearted, happy • USAGE: French form of Hilary, from Latin *hilaris*

*The most manifest sign of wisdom
is a continual cheerfulness.*
— Michel de Montaigne,
"Of the Education of Children"

ALAN, ALLAN, ALLEN [AL-an]

MEANING: little rock, handsome • USAGE: English, Irish, and Scottish: from Breton *alp* (rock) and diminutive *-an*; or from Scotch Gaelic *alainn* (handsome, fair)

*He who walks with God, and whose words are good
and honest…he will have a place on high. His safe
place will be a rock that cannot be taken over.*
— Isaiah 33:15–16a (NLV)

ALANDRO [ah-LAHN-droh]

MEANING: protector and helper of humankind, guardian • USAGE: Spanish form of Alejandro, from Greek *alexein* (to defend, to help) and *andros* (man)

You, Lord, are a shield that protects me.
— Psalm 3:3a (NEB)

ALANO [ah-LAH-noh]

MEANING: little rock, handsome • USAGE: Spanish and Italian form of Alan (*see* Alan)

*Thus says the Lord God, "Behold, I am laying…
a stone, a tested stone, a precious cornerstone,
of a sure foundation."*
— Isaiah 28:16 (KJV)

ALASDAIR, ALASTAIR [AL-as-der, AL-as-ter]

MEANING: protector and helper of humankind, guardian • USAGE: Scottish form of Alexander, from Greek *alexein* (to defend, to help) and *andros* (man)

*O Lord, you protect me and save me; your care has
made me great, and your power has kept me safe.*
— Psalm 18:35 (GNT)

ALASTAR, ALASTER [AL-es-ter]

MEANING: protector and helper of humankind, guardian • USAGE: Irish form of Alexander (*see* Alasdair)

*He will command His angels
concerning you to guard you in all your ways.*
— Psalm 91:11 (ESV)

ALBERIC [AHL-beh-rik]

MEANING: elf king, elfin power • USAGE: German: from German *alb* (elf) and *rik* (ruler, leader)

The "kingdom of heaven" is a condition of the heart.
— Friedrich Nietzsche, *Ecce Homo*

ALBERT [AL-bert (English), al-BAYR (French), AHL-bayrt (German, Russian, Scandinavian)]

MEANING: noble and brightly shining • USAGE: English, French, German, Russian, and Scandinavian form of *Adalbrecht*, from German *adal* (noble) and *beraht* (bright, shining)

Noble, courageous, high, unmatchable.
— William Shakespeare, *Antony and Cleopatra*

ALBERTO [ahl-BAYR-toh]

MEANING: noble and brightly shining • USAGE: Spanish, Italian, and Portuguese form of Albert (*see* Albert)

Those who are wise will shine
like the brightness of the heavens.
— Daniel 12:3a (NIV)

ALBRECHT   *[AHL-brekt]*

Meaning: noble and brightly shining • **Usage:**
German and Scandinavian form of *Adalbrecht* (*see*
Albert)

The noble type of man regards himself
as a determiner of values.
— Friedrich Nietzsche, *Beyond Good and Evil*
(tr. Helen Zimmern)

ALDEN   *[AHL-den, AL-den]*

Meaning: old friend • **Usage:** English form of
Ealdwine, from English *eald* (old) and *wine* (friend)
Friendship is a sheltering tree.
— Samuel Taylor Coleridge, "Youth and Age"

ALDO   *[AHL-doh]*

Meaning: noble, highborn, honorable • **Usage:**
Italian and Spanish: from German *adal*
An honorable man makes honorable plans;
his honorable character gives him security.
— Isaiah 32:8 (NEB)

ALEC   *[AL-ek]*

Meaning: protector and helper of humankind,
guardian • **Usage:** English form of Alexander (*see*
Alexander)
May the Lord be with you and help you to do well.
— 1 Chronicles 22:11a (NLV)

ALEEM, ALIM, AALIM   *[ah-leem]*

Meaning: learned, knowledgeable • **Usage:**
Muslim: from Arabic *'aleem*
The knowledge of self is the essential knowledge.
— Hazrat Inayat Khan, *The Bowl of Saki*

ALEJANDRO   *[ah-lay-HAHN-droh]*

Meaning: protector and helper of humankind,
guardian • **Usage:** Spanish form of Alexander (*see*
Alexander)
Lord…let your love and truth always protect me.
— Psalm 40:11 (NCV)

ALEJO   *[ah-LAY-hoh]*

Meaning: protector and helper of humankind,
guardian • **Usage:** Spanish form of Alejandro (*see*
Alexander)
God will put his angels in charge of you
to protect you wherever you go.
— Psalm 91:11 (GNT)

ALEK   *[al-LEEK]*

Meaning: protector and helper of humankind,
guardian • **Usage:** Russian form of Alexander (*see*
Alexander)
Good sense will keep you safe.
Understanding will guard you.
— Proverbs 2:11 (NIRV)

ALEKSY   *[ah-LEHK-see]*

Meaning: protector and helper of humankind,
guardian • **Usage:** Polish form of Alexander (*see*
Alexander)
Lord, you alone are my inheritance,
my cup of blessing. You guard all that is mine.
— Psalm 16:5 (NLT)

ALESSANDRO   *[ah-lay-SAHN-droh]*

Meaning: protector and helper of humankind,
guardian • **Usage:** Italian form of Alexander (*see*
Alexander)
The Lord is faithful,
and he will strengthen
you and protect you.
— 2 Thessalonians 3:3a (NEB)

ALESSIO   *[ah-LAY-see-oh]*

MEANING: protector and helper of humankind, guardian • **USAGE:** Italian form of Alessandro (*see* Alexander)

You [God] are like a wall protecting not only him, but his entire family and all his property. You make him successful in whatever he does.
— Job 1:10a (CEV)

ALEX   *[AL-eks (English), AH-leks (German, Scandinavian)]*

MEANING: protector and helper of humankind, guardian • **USAGE:** English, German, and Scandinavian form of Alexander (*see* Alexander)

Discretion will protect you, understanding will guard you.
— Proverbs 2:11 (NEB)

ALEXANDER   *[al-eks-ZAN-der (English), ah-lek-SAHN-der (German, Russian, Scandinavian)]*

MEANING: protector and helper of humankind, guardian • **USAGE:** English, German, Russian, and Scandinavian form of Alexandros, from Greek *alexein* (to defend, to help) and *andros* (man)

There is a loftier ambition than merely to stand high in the world. It is to stoop down and lift mankind a little higher.
— Henry Van Dyke, *The Open Door*

ALEXANDRE   *[ah-layks-AHN-dray]*

MEANING: protector and helper of humankind, guardian • **USAGE:** French form of Alexander (*see* Alexander)

The Lord is the one who goes ahead of you; He will be with you. He will not fail you or forsake you.
— Deuteronomy 31:8a (NASB)

ALEXANDROS   *[ah-leks-AHN-drohs]*

MEANING: protector and helper of humankind, guardian • **USAGE:** Greek: from Greek *alexein* (to defend, to help) and *andros* (man)

The Lord your God will lead you and protect you on every side.
— Isaiah 52:12b (GNT)

ALEXEI, ALEKSEI   *[ah-LEK-seh]*

MEANING: protector and helper of humankind, guardian • **USAGE:** Russian form of Alexander (*see* Alexander)

Be on guard. Stand firm in the faith. Be courageous. Be strong. And do everything with love.
— 1 Corinthians 16:13–14 (NLT)

ALEXIO   *[an-LESH-ee-oh]*

MEANING: protector and helper of humankind, guardian • **USAGE:** Portuguese form of Alexander (*see* Alexander)

The Lord will protect you in all you do, now and forevermore.
— Psalm 121:8 (NEB)

ALEXIOS   *[ah-LEKS-ee-ohs]*

MEANING: protector and helper of humankind, guardian • **USAGE:** Greek form of Alexandros (*see* Alexandros)

The Lord is faithful, who will establish you and guard you.
— 2 Thessalonians 3:3a (NKJV)

ALEXIS   *[ah-LAYKS-is (German, Scandinavian), ahl-ehk-SEE (French)]*

MEANING: protector and helper of humankind, guardian • **USAGE:** German, English, French, and Scandinavian form of Alexander (*see* Alexander)

Keep thy heart more than anything that is guarded; for out of it are the issues of life.
— Proverbs 4:23 (DT)

ALF   *[alf (English), ahlf (Scandinavian)]*

MEANING: elf counsel, supernaturally wise, elf, elvin • **USAGE:** English form of Alfred,

from English *ælf* (elf) and *raed* (counsel); or
Scandinavian, from Norse *alfr* (elf)

> *Who among you is wise and understands?*
> *Let that one show from a good life by the things*
> *he does that he is wise and gentle.*
> — James 3:13 (NLV)

ALFONS   *[AHL-fohns]*

MEANING: nobly prepared • USAGE: German,
Dutch, Polish, and Scandinavian form of *Adalfuns,*
from German *adal* (noble) and *funs* (ready,
prepared)

> *He is noble / Who both nobly feels and acts.*
> — Heinrich Heine, *Atta Troll*
> (tr. Thomas Selby Egan)

ALFONSO   *[ahl-FOHN-soh]*

MEANING: nobly prepared • USAGE: Spanish,
Italian, and Portuguese form of Alfons (*see* Alfons)

> *The noble man devises noble plans;*
> *and by noble plans he stands.*
> — Isaiah 32:8 (NASB)

ALFRED   *[AL-fred (English), ahl-FRED (French), AHL-fret (German, Scandinavian)]*

MEANING: elf counsel, supernaturally wise
• USAGE: English, French, German, and
Scandinavian: from English *ælf* (elf) and *raed*
(counsel)

> *Wisdom will come into your heart,*
> *and knowledge will be pleasant to your soul.*
> — Proverbs 2:10 (ESV)

ALFREDO   *[ahl-FRAY-doh]*

MEANING: elf counsel, supernaturally wise •
USAGE: Spanish, Italian, and Portuguese form of
Alfred (*see* Alfred)

> *The wise are mightier than the strong, and those with*
> *knowledge grow stronger and stronger.*
> — Proverbs 24:5 (NLT)

ALI   *[ah-lee]*

MEANING: high, lofty, elevated, exalted, honored
• USAGE: Muslim: from Arabic *'ali* (exalted,
elevated) or *'ala* (to ascend, to rise)

> *Whoever comes to Him a believer*
> *(and) he has done good deeds indeed,*
> *these it is who shall have the high ranks.*
> — Koran, Ta Ha 20.75–76 (SKR)

ALIF, ALEEF   *[ah-leef]*

MEANING: friendly, sociable, amicable • USAGE:
Muslim

> *He who maketh room in the heart*
> *will find accommodation everywhere.*
> — Hazrat Inayat Khan, *The Gayan* (cd. *The Gayani*
> *Meditations, Volume 1,* tr. Cecil Touchon)

ALOIS   *[AH-loh-yeez]*

MEANING: famous warrior, renowned in battle •
USAGE: German and Czech form of Louis, from
German *hlud* (famous) and *wig* (war, strife)

> *A good name is to be chosen over great wealth;*
> *favor is better than silver and gold.*
> — Proverbs 22:1 (HCSB)

ALON, ALLON   *[ah-LOHN]*

MEANING: oak tree • USAGE: Jewish

> *He shall be like a tree planted by waters, sending forth*
> *its roots by a stream: it does not sense the coming of*
> *heat, its leaves are ever fresh; it has no care in a year*
> *of drought and never fails to bear fruit.*
> — Jeremiah 17:8 (JPS)

ALONSO   *[ahl-LOHN-soh]*

MEANING: nobly prepared • USAGE: Spanish form
of Alfonso (*see* Alfons)

> *True nobility consists in virtue.*
> — Miguel de Cervantes, *Don Quixote*
> (tr. John Ormsby)

ALONZO [ahl-LOHN-ʒoh]

MEANING: nobly prepared • **USAGE:** Italian form of Alphonso (*see* Alfons)

> *The noble deviseth noble things;*
> *and in noble things shall he continue.*
> — Isaiah 32:8 (ASV)

ALOYSIUS [al-oh-WISH-uhs (English), ah-LOY-ʒee-uhs (German)]

MEANING: famous warrior, renowned in battle • **USAGE:** English and German form of *Aloys*, a form of Louis, from German *hlud* (famous) and *wig* (war, strife)

> *Put on the weapons of light.*
> — Romans 13:12:b (NEB)

ALPHONSE [ahl-FONS]

MEANING: nobly prepared • **USAGE:** French form of Alfons (*see* Alfons)

> *Those who are noble make noble plans,*
> *and stand for what is noble.*
> — Isaiah 32:8 (MSG)

ALPHONSO, ALPHONZO [al-FAHN-soh, al-FAHN-ʒoh]

MEANING: nobly prepared • **USAGE:** English form of Alfons (*see* Alfons)

> *A strong, positive self-image is*
> *the best possible preparation for success in life.*
> — Joyce Brothers

ALTAIR [ahl-TAYR]

MEANING: bright star, the flyer • **USAGE:** English: brightest star in Aquila constellation, from Arabic meaning "the flyer"

> *To you, ye stars, man owes his subtlest raptures,*
> *thoughts unspeakable, yet full of faith.*
> — Herman Melville, *Mardi, and a Voyage Thither*

ALUN [AL-un]

MEANING: little rock, handsome • **USAGE:** Welsh: from Irish Gaelic *ailin* (handsome, fair); or from Scotch Gaelic *alainn* (handsome, fair)

> *You are handsome, truly handsome.*
> — Song of Songs 1:16a (CEV)

ALVAR [AL-vahr]

MEANING: elf army, elfin warrior • **USAGE:** English and Scandinavian: from English *ælf* (elf) and *here* (army); or from Norse *alfr* (elf) and *arr* (warrior)

> *Be strong and courageous.*
> — Joshua 1:18b (ESV)

ÁLVARO, ALVARO [AHL-vah-roh (Spanish), ahl-VAH-roh (Portuguese)]

MEANING: elf army, elfin warrior • **USAGE:** Spanish and Portuguese form of Alvar (*see* Alvar)

> *The Lord is helping you,*
> *and you are a strong warrior.*
> — Judges 6:12b (CEV)

ALVIN [AL-vin]

MEANING: elf friend, elf ally • **USAGE:** English: from English *ælf* (elf) and *wine* (friend, ally)

> *A faithful friend is a strong defence:*
> *and he that hath found him, hath found a treasure.*
> — Sirach 6:14 (DR Apocrypha)

ALWYN [AL-wen]

MEANING: elf friend, elf ally • **USAGE:** Welsh form of Alvin (*see* Alvin)

> *Make new friends, but keep the old; /*
> *Those are silver, these are gold.*
> — Joseph Parry,
> "New Friends and Old Friends"

AMADEUS [ah-mah-DAY-uhs]

MEANING: one who loves God • USAGE: Italian: from Latin *amare* (to love) and *deus* (God)

God is near you, he is with you, he is within you.
— Seneca, "Letter XLI"

AMADO [ah-MAH-doh]

MEANING: beloved • USAGE: Spanish: from Latin *amada*

Surely your goodness and love will be with me all my life, and I will live in the house of the Lord forever.
— Psalm 23:6 (NCV)

AMAL [ah-mahl]

MEANING: work of God, industrious • USAGE: Jewish

Be ye strong, and let not your hands be slack; for your work shall be rewarded.
— 2 Chronicles 15:7 (MT)

AMAL [ah-mahl]

MEANING: hope, wish, desire • USAGE: Muslim: from Arabic *amal* (hope, expectation) or *amala* (to hope)

Whoever desires the reward of this world, I shall give him of it, and whoever desires the reward of the hereafter I shall give him of it; and I will reward the grateful.
— Koran, The Family of Imran 3.145b (SKR)

AMAN [ah-mahn]

MEANING: trustworthy, faithful • USAGE: Muslim: from Arabic *amana* (trustworthy, calm)

Those who are trusted by others / God trusts.
— Rabia al-Adawiyya, "Trying to Work In" (tr. Daniel Ladinsky in *Love Poems from God*)

AMARAN [ah-mah-rahn]

MEANING: infinite, eternal • USAGE: Hindu: from Sanskrit *a* (without) and *mara* (dying)

We do cross the infinite at every step, and meet the eternal in every second.
— Rabindranath Tagore, *Sadhana*

AMBAR [ahm-bahr]

MEANING: fragrant, aromatic • USAGE: Muslim: from Arabic *anbar*

A sincere man has a fragrance about him which is perceived by a sincere heart.
— Hazrat Inayat Khan, *The Gayan* (cd. *The Gayani Meditations, Volume 1*, tr. Cecil Touchon)

AMBROGIO [ahm-BROH-syoh]

MEANING: immortal, eternal, food of the gods • USAGE: Italian form of *Ambrosius*, from Greek *ambrosios*

Taste and see that the Lord is good; blessed is the man who takes refuge in him.
— Psalm 34:8 (NIV)

AMBROS [AHM-brohs]

MEANING: immortal, eternal, food of the gods • USAGE: Spanish form of Ambrogio (*see* Ambrogio)

Love is eternal.
— 1 Corinthians 13:8a (GNT)

AMERIGO [ah-MER-ee-goh]

MEANING: ruler of the home, universal leader • USAGE: Italian form of Emmerich, from German *heim* (home, house) and *rik* (rule, lead); or from German *ermen* (whole, universal) and *rik* (rule, lead)

You have been pleased to bless the house of your servant, that it may continue forever before you, for it is you, O Lord, who have blessed, and it is blessed forever.
— 1 Chronicles 17:27 (ESV)

AMIAD   *[ah-mee-AHD]*

Meaning: my nation is eternal • **Usage:** Jewish
I will also give thee as a light to the nations that My
salvation may be unto the end of the earth.
— Isaiah 49:6a (MT)

AMICHAI   *[ah-mee-KHIE]*

Meaning: my nation lives • **Usage:** Jewish
Surely this great nation is a wise
and understanding people.
— Deuteronomy 4:6b (MT)

AMID, AMEED   *[ah-MEED]*

Meaning: pillar, support • **Usage:** Muslim
Put your trust in God for support, and see
His hidden Hand working through all sources.
— Hazrat Inayat Khan, *The Gayan*

AMIEL   *[ah-mee-EL]*

Meaning: God of my people, my nation belongs
to God • **Usage:** Jewish
When people are loving, brave, truthful,
charitable, God is present.
— Harold Kushner

AMIN, AAMIN, AMEEN   *[ah-MEEN]*

Meaning: trustworthy, faithful, steadfast •
Usage: Muslim: from Arabic *amuna* (to be
trustworthy)
O you who believe! be patient and excel in patience
and remain steadfast, and be careful of your duty
to Allah, that you may be successful.
— Koran, The Family of Imran 3.200 (SKR)

AMIR   *[ah-MEER]*

Meaning: speech, utterance, treetop • **Usage:**
Jewish

The tree grew, and was strong,
and the height thereof reached unto heaven.
— Daniel 4:8 (MT)

AMIR, AAMIR, AMEER   *[ah-MEER]*

Meaning: prince, ruler, commander • **Usage:**
Muslim: from Arabic *amir* (prince, emir) or *amara*
(to command, to rule)
Allah has promised to those of you who believe and do
good that He will most certainly make them rulers.
— Koran, The Light 24.55 (SKR)

AMIRAM   *[ah-mee-RAHM]*

Meaning: my nation is mighty • **Usage:** Jewish
Attend to Me, O My people, and give ear unto Me,
O My nation; for instruction shall go forth from Me,
and My right on a sudden for a light of the people.
— Isaiah 51:4 (MT)

AMIT   *[ah-meet]*

Meaning: friend, companion • **Usage:** Jewish
Friendship is man's greatest gift.
— Moses ben ibn Ezra, *Shirat Yisrael*

AMITAI   *[ah-mee-TIE]*

Meaning: truth, friend • **Usage:** Jewish
The search for truth and knowledge is
one of the finest attributes of man.
— Albert Einstein,
"The Goal of Human Existence"

AMITAN   *[ah-mee-TAHN]*

Meaning: friend, truth • **Usage:** Jewish
A friend loveth at all times.
— Proverbs 17:17a (MT)

AMNON   *[ahm-NOHN]*

Meaning: faithful • **Usage:** Jewish
A faithful man shall abound with blessings.
— Proverbs 28:20a (MT)

AMOS   *[ah-MOHS (Jewish), AY-mos (English)]*

MEANING: burdened, carried, one with many
responsibilities • **USAGE:** Jewish and English
Cast your burden on the Lord, and he will sustain you.
— Psalm 55:23a (JPS)

AN   *[ahn]*

MEANING: peace, peaceful • **USAGE:** Chinese
He who knows patience knows peace.
— Chinese proverb

ANASTASIOS   *[ah-nah-STAH-see-ohs]*

MEANING: resurrection, reborn, rise up • **USAGE:**
Greek: from Greek *anastasis* (resurrection), or from
Greek *ana* (up) and *stasis* (standing)
You have been born again,
not of perishable seed but of imperishable.
— 1 Peter 1:23a (ESV)

ANATOLE   *[ah-nah-TOHL]*

MEANING: dawn, sunrise, daybreak • **USAGE:**
French form of Anatolius (*see* Anatolius)
The morning of life is like the dawn of day,
full of purity, of imagery, and harmony.
— François-René de Chateaubriand

ANATOLIUS   *[ahn-ah-TOH-lee-us]*

MEANING: dawn, sunrise, daybreak • **USAGE:**
Greek form of *Anatolios,* from Greek *anatole*
Put your face in the sunlight. God's bright glory
has risen for you.... God rises on you,
his sunrise glory breaks over you.
— Isaiah 60:1, 3 (MSG)

ANATOLY   *[ahn-nah-TOH-lee]*

MEANING: dawn, sunrise, daybreak • **USAGE:**
Russian form of Anatolius (*see* Anatolius)
Light is sweet; how pleasant to see a new day dawning.
— Ecclesiastes 11:7 (NLT)

ANDEL   *[ahn-del]*

MEANING: angel, divine messenger • **USAGE:**
Czech: from Greek *angelos* (messenger) or Latin
angeles (divine messenger, angel)
The Lord...will send his angel with thee,
and will direct thy way.
— Genesis 24:40a (DR)

ANDERS   *[AHN-ders]*

MEANING: man, manly, masculine • **USAGE:**
Scandinavian form of Andrew (*see* Andrew)
What's a man's first duty?
The answer is brief: to be himself.
— Henrik Ibsen

ANDOR   *[AHN-dor]*

MEANING: thunder eagle, Thor's eagle • **USAGE:**
Norwegian and Swedish: from Norse *arn* (eagle)
and *Thor* (Norse god of thunder)
Those who trust in the Lord will find new strength.
They will soar high on wings like eagles. They will run
and not grow weary. They will walk and not faint.
— Isaiah 40:31 (NLT)

ANDRAS   *[AN-dras]*

MEANING: man, manly, masculine • **USAGE:**
Welsh form of Andrew (*see* Andrew)
The conscience of every man recognizes courage
as the foundation of manliness.
— Thomas Hughes

ANDRÉ, ANDRE   *[ahn-DRAY]*

MEANING: man, manly, masculine • **USAGE:**
French and English form of Andrew (*see* Andrew)
To be a man is, precisely, to be responsible. To feel
shame at the sight of what seems to be unmerited
misery. It is to take pride in a victory won by one's
comrades. It is to feel, when setting one's stone, that one
is contributing to the building of the world.
— Antoine de Saint-Exupéry,
Wind, Sand, and Stars (tr. Lewis Galantier)

ANDREAS [ahn-DREH-ahs]

MEANING: man, manly, masculine • **USAGE:** Greek, German, and Scandinavian form of Andrew (see Andrew)

Man…is merged with the Supreme, sunken into it, one with it: center coincides with center.
— Plotinus, *Enneads*

ANDREI [AHN-dray]

MEANING: man, manly, masculine • **USAGE:** Russian form of Andrew (see Andrew)

A man is good if he makes others better men.
— Russian proverb

ANDRÉS [ahn-DRAYS]

MEANING: man, manly, masculine • **USAGE:** Spanish form of Andrew (see Andrew)

Do manfully and be of good heart… for the Lord thy God he himself is thy leader, and will not leave thee nor forsake thee.
— Deuteronomy 31:6 (DR)

ANDREW [AN-droo]

MEANING: man, manly, masculine • **USAGE:** English form of Andreas, from Greek *andros* (man) or *andreios* (manly)

Man, unlike any other thing organic or inorganic in the universe, grows beyond his work, walks up the stairs of his concepts, emerges ahead of his accomplishments.
— John Steinbeck, *The Grapes of Wrath*

ANDY [AN-dee]

MEANING: man, manly, masculine • **USAGE:** English form of Andrew (see Andrew)

The good man accepts all his being, knowing, loving and working from the innermost heart of goodness.
— Meister Eckhart

ÁNGEL [AHN-hel]

MEANING: angel, divine messenger • **USAGE:** Spanish: from Greek *angelos* (messenger) or Latin *angeles* (divine messenger, angel)

The Lord will command his angels to take good care of you.
— Psalm 91:11 (NIRV)

ANGELO [AHN-jay-loh (Italian, Greek, Portuguese), ahn-HAY-loh (Spanish)]

MEANING: angel, divine messenger • **USAGE:** Italian, Spanish, Greek, and Portuguese (see Ángel)

I [God] am sending an angel before you to keep you safe on the way.
— Exodus 23:20a (NLV)

ANGUS [AYN-gus]

MEANING: vigorous, passionate, strong • **USAGE:** English and Scottish form of Aonghas (see Aonghas)

To him whose elastic and vigorous thought keeps pace with the sun, the day is a perpetual morning.
— Henry David Thoreau, *Walden*

ANJAY [AHN-jay]

MEANING: unconquerable, indomitable • **USAGE:** Hindu

Strength does not come from physical capacity. It comes from an indomitable will.
— Mahatma Gandhi

ANKUR [ahn-koor]

MEANING: sapling, young tree, seedling • **USAGE:** Hindu: Sanskrit

Trees are the earth's endless effort to speak to the listening heaven.
— Rabindranath Tagore, *Fireflies*

ANOLANI [ah-noh-LAH-nee]

MEANING: chief-like nature, of royal character •
USAGE: Hawaiian

> *Peace is a chief, the lord of love.*
> *[Where there is peace, there is love.]*
> — Hawaiian proverb
> (tr. Mary Pukui in 'Olelo No'eau)

ANSEL [AN-sel]

MEANING: protected by God, divine protection •
USAGE: English (*see* Anselm)

> *The Lord is faithful,*
> *and he will strengthen and protect you.*
> — 2 Thessalonians 3:3 (NIV)

ANSELM [AHN-ʒelm (German), AHN-selm (English)]

MEANING: protected by God, divine protection •
USAGE: German form of *Anselme*, from German
ans (God) and *helm* (helmet, protection)

> *The Lord is my rock, my fortress, and my savior;*
> *my God is my rock, in whom I find protection. He is my*
> *shield, the power that saves me, and my place of safety.*
> — 2 Samuel 22:2–3a (NLT)

ANSELMO [ahn-SAYL-moh]

MEANING: protected by God, divine protection •
USAGE: Spanish and Italian form of Anselm (*see*
Anselm)

> *God's way is perfect. All the Lord's promises prove true.*
> *He is a shield for all who look to him for protection.*
> — Psalm 18:30 (NLT)

ANTAL [AHN-tahl]

MEANING: invaluable, priceless, excellent •
USAGE: Hungarian form of Anthony (*see* Anthony)

> *You are the most excellent of the sons of men.*
> *Grace has anointed your lips,*
> *therefore God has blessed you forever.*
> — Psalm 45:2 (WEB)

ANTHONY [AN-thoh-nee]

MEANING: invaluable, priceless, excellent •
USAGE: English form of *Antonius,* a Roman family
name possibly meaning "invaluable"

> *The basis of all excellence is truth:*
> *he that professes love ought to feel its power.*
> — Samuel Johnson

ANTOINE [ahn-TWAHN]

MEANING: invaluable, priceless, excellent •
USAGE: French form of Anthony (*see* Anthony)

> *The excellency of knowledge is*
> *that wisdom preserves the life of him who has it.*
> — Ecclesiastes 7:12b (WEB)

ANTON [AHN-tahn]

MEANING: invaluable, priceless, excellent •
USAGE: German, Russian, and Scandinavian form
of Anthony (*see* Anthony)

> *Try not to become a man of success*
> *but rather to become a man of value.*
> — Albert Einstein

ANTONELLO [ahn-toh-NAY-loh]

MEANING: invaluable, priceless, excellent •
USAGE: Italian form of Antonio (*see* Anthony)

> *The excellency of knowledge is that wisdom*
> *giveth life to them that have it.*
> — Ecclesiastes 7:12b (KJ21)

ANTONIO [ahn-TOH-nee-oh]

MEANING: invaluable, priceless, excellent •
USAGE: Spanish and Italian form of Roman family
name *Antonius* (*see* Anthony)

> *This I pray, that your love may abound yet more*
> *and more in knowledge and all discernment;*
> *so that you may approve the things that are excellent.*
> — Philippians 1:9–10a (WEB)

ANWAR [ahn-wahr]

MEANING: clearer, brighter, full of light, radiant • USAGE: Muslim: from Arabic *anwar* (clearer, brighter)

Gather from the sky's fields and intimate regions /
that rare, unalloyed quality and light. /
Bring it back to your nest. Weave it into your eyes, /
sounds, movements and touch.
— Jalaluddin Rumi, "Fly Heavenward Dear"
(tr. Daniel Ladinsky in *The Purity of Desire*)

ANZELM [AHN-ʒelm]

MEANING: protected by God, divine protection • USAGE: Polish form of Anselm (*see* Anselm)
Discover for yourself that the Lord is kind.
Come to him for protection, and you will be glad.
— Psalm 34:8 (CEV)

AODHAN [AY-den]

MEANING: fire, fiery one, little fire • USAGE: Irish: from Gaelic *aodh* (fire) and diminutive *-an*
God, kindle Thou in my heart within /
A flame of love.
— Alexander Carmichael, *Carmina Gadelica*

AONGHAS [AYN-gus]

MEANING: vigorous, passionate, strong • USAGE: Irish and Scottish: from *oen* (one) and *gus* (strength, vigor); reference to *Aengus Og*, Gaelic god of youth, love, and poetry
We should employ our passions in the service of life,
not spend life in the service of our passions.
— Richard Steele

APOLLO [ah-POH-loh]

MEANING: strong, mighty, Greek god • USAGE: Italian: from Greek *apelo* (strength, might); Greek god of prophecy, healing, light, music, poetry, and reason

A sound mind in a sound body.
— Juvenal

AQIL, AAQIL [ah-KEEL]

MEANING: intelligent, rational, knowledgeable, thoughtful • USAGE: Muslim: from Arabic *aqil* (intelligent) or *akila* (one who reasons)

My thoughtful self! Reproach no one, hold a grudge
against no one, bear malice against no one; be wise,
tolerant, considerate, polite and kind to all.
— Hazrat Inayat Khan, *The Gayan* (cd. *The Gayani Meditations, Volume 1*, tr. Cecil Touchon)

ARA, ARAH [ah-rah]

MEANING: gatherer, reaper, harvester • USAGE: Jewish

Sow righteousness for yourselves;
reap the fruits of goodness.
— Hosea 10:12a (JPS)

ARAFAT [ah-rah-faht]

MEANING: plain • USAGE: Muslim: a plain near Mecca where pilgrims worship Allah during the Hajj

Light / Will someday split you open... / For a divine
seed, the crown, the destiny, / Is hidden and sown on
an ancient, fertile plain / You hold the title to.
— Hafiz, "In a Tree House"
(tr. Daniel Ladinsky in *The Subject Tonight Is Love*)

ARAM [ah-rahm]

MEANING: quiet • USAGE: Persian
Much silence and a good disposition,
there are no two words better than those.
— Hadith of the Prophet Muhammad

ARAVINDA [ahr-ah-vihn-dah]

MEANING: lotus • USAGE: Hindu: Sanskrit
He who knows that Brahman dwells
within the lotus of the heart becomes
one with him and enjoys all blessings.
— *Taittiriya Upanishad* (tr. Swami Prabhavananda)

ARCH [arch]

MEANING: genuinely brave, true and bold, curve, arch • USAGE: English form of Archibald (*see* Archibald)

> *Be brave, be strong.*
> *Let all that you do be done with love.*
> — 1 Corinthians 16:13–14 (NKJV)

ARCHER [AR-cher]

MEANING: archer, one who uses a bow and arrow • USAGE: American surname: from Latin *arcus* (bow)

> *You must not only aim aright,*
> *but draw the bow with all your might.*
> — Henry David Thoreau
> (letter of December 19, 1853)

ARCHIBALD [AR-chee-bahld (English, Scottish), AHR-keh-bahlt (German)]

MEANING: genuinely brave, true and bold • USAGE: English, Scottish, and German: from German *ercan* (genuine, true) and *balt* (bold, brave)

> *Boldness be my friend.*
> — William Shakespeare, *Cymbeline*

ARCHIE [AR-chee]

MEANING: genuinely brave, true and bold • USAGE: English form of Archibald (*see* Archibald)

> *Whatever you can do or dream you can, begin it.*
> *Boldness has genius, magic and power in it.*
> *Begin it now.*
> — William Hutchison Murray, *The Scottish Himalayan Expedition*

ARDEL [ahr-DEL]

MEANING: hare valley, from the dale of hares • USAGE: English: from English *hara* (hare) and *dæl* (dale, valley)

> *In God's wildness lies the hope of the world.*
> — John Muir (journal entry of July 11, 1890)

ARDEN [AR-den]

MEANING: valley of the eagle, high, lofty • USAGE: English surname: from German *earn* (eagle) and English *denu* (valley); or from Irish Celtic *ard* (high)

> *Those who wait for the Lord will gain new strength;*
> *they will mount up with wings like eagles,*
> *they will run and not get tired,*
> *they will walk and not become weary.*
> — Isaiah 40:31 (NASB)

AREL [ahr-EL]

MEANING: angel, messenger, lion of God • USAGE: Jewish

> *I am sending an angel before you*
> *to guard you on the way and to bring you*
> *to the place that I have made ready.*
> — Exodus 23:20a (JPS)

ARGOS [AHR-gohs]

MEANING: bright, shining • USAGE: Greek: from Greek *argos*

> *They that are wise shall shine*
> *as the brightness of the firmament.*
> — Daniel 12:3a (ASV)

ARI [AHR-ee, ah-REE]

MEANING: lion, lionlike • USAGE: Jewish: from Hebrew *ari*

> *The righteous are as confident as a lion.*
> — Proverbs 28:1b (JPS)

ARIB, AREEB [ah-REEB]

MEANING: brilliant, bright light • USAGE: Muslim

> *Thou wilt recognise in their faces*
> *the beaming brightness of Bliss.*
> — Koran, Dealing in Fraud 83.24 (ALI)

A

ARIEL [ah-ree-EHL]

MEANING: lion of God • **USAGE:** Jewish: from Hebrew *ari 'el*

Judah ben Teima used to say: Be strong as the leopard, swift as the eagle, fleet as the gazelle, and brave as the lion to do the will of your Father in Heaven.
— *Pirkei Avot* 5:23

ARIF, AARIF, AREEF [ah-REEF]

MEANING: learned, knowledgeable • **USAGE:** Muslim: from Arabic *arif*

Wisdom is not in words, it is in understanding.
— Hazrat Inayat Khan, *The Bowl of Saki*

ARISTO [ah-REES-toh]

MEANING: best purpose • **USAGE:** Spanish form of Aristotle (*see* Aristotle)

Whatever work you do, do your best.
— Ecclesiastes 9:10a (NCV)

ARISTOTLE [ahr-ee-STAH-tel]

MEANING: best purpose • **USAGE:** Greek form of *Aristotelis*, from Greek *aristos* (best) and *telos* (purpose, aim)

We are what we repeatedly do. Excellence, then, is not an act, but a habit.
— Aristotle

ARIZONA [ayr-ih-ZOH-nah]

MEANING: good oaks, little spring, silver-yielding, barren zone • **USAGE:** American: from Basque *aritz onak* (good oaks); from American Indian O'odham *ala sonak* (little spring); from Aztec *arizuma* (silver-yielding); or from Spanish *zona árida* (barren zone)

Keep your heart with all vigilance, for from it flow the springs of life.
— Proverbs 4:23 (ESV)

ARJUN [ahr-joon]

MEANING: white, the color of milk, clear, pure • **USAGE:** Hindu: Sanskrit

Remember the clear light, the pure bright shining white light of your own nature, it is deathless.
— Buddha (tr. Gil Fronsdal)

ARLEN [AHR-len]

MEANING: promise, pledge, man of Arles • **USAGE:** English: from Welsh *addewid* (promise, pledge); or from French place-name *Arles*

The Lord your God shall bless you as He has promised you.
— Deuteronomy 15:6a (NASB)

ARLO [AHR-loh]

MEANING: fortified hill, army hill • **USAGE:** English form of Harlow, from English *here* (army) and *hlaw* (hill)

Let peace and justice rule every mountain and hill.
— Psalm 72:3 (CEV)

ARMANDO [ahr-MAHN-doh]

MEANING: warrior, soldier, army man • **USAGE:** Spanish, Italian, and Portuguese form of Herman, from German *hari* (army) and *man* (man)

He who is well prepared has won half the battle.
— Portuguese proverb

ARMIN [AHR-men]

MEANING: warrior, soldier, army man • **USAGE:** German form of *Hariman* (*see* Armando)

You can stand firm without being afraid.
— Job 11:15b (NIRV)

ARNALDO [ahr-NAHL-doh]

MEANING: eagle power, eagle rule • **USAGE:** Spanish and Italian form of Arnold (*see* Arnold)

A

*[God] satisfies you with good so that your youth is
renewed like the eagle's.*
— Psalm 103:5 (ESV)

*When thou seest an eagle,
thou seest a portion of genius; lift up thy head!*
— William Blake, *The Marriage of Heaven and Hell*

ARNAUD [ahr-NOH]

MEANING: eagle power, eagle rule • **USAGE:**
French form of Arnold (*see* Arnold)
*Those who wait on the Lord shall renew their strength;
they shall mount up with wings like eagles, they shall
run and not be weary, they shall walk and not faint.*
— Isaiah 40:31 (NKJV)

ARNDT [ahrnd, ahrnt]

MEANING: eagle • **USAGE:** German: from German
arn
*Eagles come in all shapes and sizes,
but you will recognize them chiefly by their attitudes.*
— E. F. Schumacher

ARNE [ahrn]

MEANING: eagle • **USAGE:** Scandinavian and
German: from German *arn*
I bore you on eagles' wings and brought you to Myself.
— Exodus 19:4b (NASB)

ARNO [AHR-noh]

MEANING: eagle power, eagle rule • **USAGE:**
German and Scandinavian form of Arnold (*see*
Arnold)
*Great minds are like eagles,
and build their nest in some lofty solitude.*
— Arthur Schopenhauer, *Counsels and Maxims*
(tr. Thomas Baily Saunders)

ARNOLD [AHR-nold (English),
AHR-nahlt (German)]

MEANING: eagle power, eagle rule • **USAGE:**
English and German form of *Arnwald*, from
German *arn* (eagle) and *wald* (rule, power)

ARNON [AHR-non]

MEANING: roaring stream • **USAGE:** Jewish
*Thus said the Lord…when you pass through the water,
I will be with you; through streams,
they shall not overwhelm you.*
— Isaiah 43:1a, 2a (JPS)

ARON [AHR-on]

MEANING: teaching, singing, shining, mountain,
exalted one • **USAGE:** Scandinavian and Hungarian
form of Aaron, from Hebrew *aharon*
*How beautiful upon the mountains are the feet of him
that bringeth good tidings, that publisheth peace.*
— Isaiah 52:7a (KJV)

ARSENI [ahr-SEH-nee]

MEANING: virile, masculine, manly • **USAGE:**
Russian form of Arsenios (*see* Arsenios)
The true man wants two things: danger and play.
— Friedrich Nietzsche, *Thus Spoke Zarathustra*
(tr. Alexander Tille)

ARSENIO [ahr-SAY-nee-oh]

MEANING: virile, masculine, manly • **USAGE:**
Spanish, Italian, and English form of Arsenios (*see*
Arsenios)
Be strong and be courageous like a man.
— 1 Kings 2:2b (HCSB)

ARSENIOS [ahr-SEH-nee-ohs]

MEANING: virile, masculine, manly • **USAGE:**
Greek: from Greek *arsenios*
*A brave man is clear in his discourse,
and keeps close to truth.*
— Aristotle

ARSHAD [ahr-SHAHD]

MEANING: more rightly guided, more reasonable •
USAGE: Muslim

*Allah desires to explain to you, and to guide you
into the ways of those before you, and to turn to you
(mercifully), and Allah is Knowing, Wise.*
— Koran, The Women 4.26 (SKR)

ART [art]

MEANING: bear, strong as a bear, keeper of bears,
stone, rock • USAGE: English form of Arthur (*see*
Arthur)

Gentleness is to be expected only from the strong.
— Leo Rosten, *Captain Newman, M.D.*

ARTHUR [AHR-thur, (English, Welsh), ahr-TOOR (French, German)]

MEANING: bear, strong as a bear, keeper of bears,
stone, rock • USAGE: Welsh, English, French,
and German: from Welsh *artos* (bear) or Greek
arktourous (keeper of bears); or from Irish Gaelic *art*
(stone, rock)

*With whom My hand is established,
My arm also doth strengthen him.*
— Psalm 89:21 (YLT)

ARTUR [AHR-toor]

MEANING: bear, strong as a bear, keeper of bears,
stone, rock • USAGE: German and Russian form of
Arthur (*see* Arthur)

*Whatever your hand finds to do,
do it with all your strength.*
— Ecclesiastes 9:10a (NLV)

ARTURO [ahr-TOO-roh]

MEANING: bear, strong as a bear, keeper of bears,
stone, rock • USAGE: Spanish and Italian form of
Arthur (*see* Arthur)

*Be strong and have strength of heart....For the Lord
your God is the One Who goes with you. He will be
faithful to you. He will not leave you alone.*
— Deuteronomy 31:6 (NLV)

ARUN [ah-roon]

MEANING: red, rosy, color of dawn, sunrise •
USAGE: Hindu: from Sanskrit *aruna*

*Listen to the Exhortation of the Dawn, /
Look to the Day, for it is Life, the very Life of Life. /
In its brief course lie all the verities /
And realities of your existence, / The bliss of truth, the
glory of action, the splendor of beauty. / For yesterday
is but a dream, / And tomorrow is only a vision. /
But today, well lived, makes every yesterday a dream
of happiness, / And every tomorrow a vision of hope. /
Look well, therefore, to the Day /
Such is the Salutation of the Dawn.*
— Kalidasa, *Salutation to the Dawn*

ARYEH, ARYE [AHR-yeh, ahr-YEH]

MEANING: lion, lionlike • USAGE: Jewish: from
Hebrew *ari*

*The lion is mightiest among the beasts,
and recoils before none.*
— Proverbs 30:30 (JPS)

ASA [AYE-sah]

MEANING: healer, physician • USAGE: American
form of Asah

The best part of health is fine disposition.
— Ralph Waldo Emerson,
"Considerations by the Way"

ASAD [ah-SAHD]

MEANING: lion • USAGE: Muslim

In the heart of every brave man a lion sleeps.
— Arabic proverb

ASAF, ASAPH [ah-SAHF]

MEANING: collector, gatherer, harvester • USAGE: Jewish symbolic name for boys born on Sukkoth or Shavuot

Sow to yourselves according to righteousness,
reap according to mercy.
— Hosea 10:12a (MT)

ASAH [AH-sah]

MEANING: healer, physician • USAGE: Jewish

A calm disposition gives bodily health.
— Proverbs 14:30a (JPS)

ASH [ash]

MEANING: ash tree • USAGE: English: from English *aesc* (ash tree)

He is like a tree growing near a stream and sending
out roots to the water. It is not afraid when hot weather
comes because its leaves stay green; it has no worries
when there is no rain; it keeps on bearing fruit.
— Jeremiah 17:8 (GNT)

ASHER [ah-SHEHR (Jewish), ASH-er (English)]

MEANING: happy, blessed, fortunate • USAGE: Jewish and English

Happy is the man who finds wisdom, the man who
attains understanding....In her right hand is
length of days, in her left, riches and honor.
— Proverbs 3:13, 3:16 (JPS)

ASHFORD [ASH-ford]

MEANING: ash tree ford, from the ford of the ash trees • USAGE: English surname: from English *aesc* (ash tree) and *ford* (ford, shallow river crossing)

He who plants a tree — He plants a hope. /
He who plants a tree — He plants youth. /
He who plants a tree — He plants peace.
— Lucy Larcom, "Plant a Tree"

ASHIR [ah-SHEER]

MEANING: wealthy, prosperous • USAGE: Jewish

You shall enjoy the fruit of your labors;
you shall be happy and you shall prosper.
— Psalm 128:2 (JPS)

ASHLEY [ASH-lee]

MEANING: ash tree meadow, field of ash trees • USAGE: English surname: from English *aesc* (ash tree) and *leah* (meadow, field)

He shall be like a tree planted by the rivers of water,
that brings forth its fruit in its season,
whose leaf also shall not wither;
and whatever he does shall prosper.
— Psalm 1:3 (NKJV)

ASHTON [ASH-ton]

MEANING: ash tree village, from the town of ash trees • USAGE: English surname: from English *aesc* (ash tree) and *tun* (town, village)

Blessed is the man who finds wisdom, the man who
gains understanding....She is a tree of life to those who
embrace her; those who lay hold of her will be blessed.
— Proverbs 3:13, 3:18 (NIV)

ASIM, AASIM, ASEEM [ah-SEEM]

MEANING: protector, guardian • USAGE: Muslim: from Arabic *asim*

For him are angels ranged before him and behind him,
who guard him by Allah's command.
— Koran, The Thunder 3.11a (PIC)

ASIR, ASEER [ah-SEER]

MEANING: chosen • USAGE: Muslim

Allah chooseth for Himself whom He will,
and guideth unto Himself him who turneth
(toward Him).
— Koran, The Counsel 42.13b (PIC)

A

ASIS   [ah-SEES]

MEANING: sun • USAGE: African: Kelenjin of Kenya

May the sun smile upon you.
— Kenyan blessing

ATIF, ATEEF   [ah-TEEF]

MEANING: kind, compassionate • USAGE: Muslim: from Arabic *'atif*

Allah loveth those who are kind.
— Koran, The Table Spread 5.13b (ALI)

ATIR   [ah-TEER]

MEANING: crown, wreath • USAGE: Jewish

What is man, that Thou art mindful of him?
And the son of man, that Thou thinkest of him?
Yet Thou hast made him but little lower than the an-
gels, and hast crowned him with glory and honour.
— Psalm 8:5–6 (MT)

ATTICUS   [AT-ih-kus]

MEANING: man of Athens, of Athena • USAGE: English: from Greek *Attica*, region surrounding Athens, Greece

Ye are the light of the world.
A city that is set on a hill cannot be hid.
— Matthew 5:14 (KJ21)

AUBERON   [AH-ber-on (English),
                       OH-bur-ahn (French)]

MEANING: elf king, elfin ruler • USAGE: English and French form of Oberon, from German *alb* (elf) and *rik* (ruler, leader)

The vision that you glorify in your mind,
the Ideal that you enthrone in your heart —
this you will build your life by, this you will become.
— James Allen, *As a Man Thinketh*

AUBERT   [ah-BAYR]

MEANING: noble and brightly shining • USAGE: French form of Albert, from German *adal* (noble) and *beraht* (bright, shining)

The light of the righteous shines brightly.
— Proverbs 13:9a (NIV)

AUBREY, AUBRIE   [AH-bree]

MEANING: elf king, elfin power • USAGE: English form of Alberic (*see* Auberon)

Power doesn't have to show off. Power is confi-
dent, self-assuring, self-starting and self-stopping,
self-warming and self-justifying.
— Ralph Ellison, *Invisible Man*

AUDEN   [AH-den]

MEANING: enduring friend, lasting friendship • USAGE: English and Norwegian: from Scotch Gaelic *auld* (old, enduring) and English *wine* (friend)

A friend loveth at all times.
— Proverbs 17:17a (KJV)

AUDIE, AUDEY   [AH-dee]

MEANING: enduring friend, lasting friendship • USAGE: English form of Auden (*see* Auden)

The only way to have a friend is to be one.
— Ralph Waldo Emerson, "Friendship"

AUGUST   [AH-goost (German,
                       Scandinavian), AH-gust (English)]

MEANING: great one, revered one, magnificent • USAGE: German, Scandinavian, and English form of Augustine (*see* Augustine)

You have given me the shield of Your salvation;
Your right hand has held me up,
Your gentleness has made me great.
— Psalm 18:35 (NKJV)

AUGUSTINE
[AH-gus-teen]

MEANING: great one, revered one, magnificent • **USAGE:** English form of *Augustinus,* from Latin *augustus*

> *He is greatest whose strength carries up*
> *the most hearts by the attraction of his own.*
> — Henry Ward Beecher, *Life Thoughts*

AUGUSTINO
[ah-goos-TEEN-oh]

MEANING: great one, revered one, magnificent • **USAGE:** Spanish form of Augustine (*see* Augustine)

> *A good name is rather to be chosen than great riches,*
> *and loving favor rather than silver and gold.*
> — Proverbs 22:1 (ASV)

AUGUSTO
[ah-GOOS-toh]

MEANING: great one, revered one, magnificent • **USAGE:** Spanish, Italian, and Portuguese form of Augustine (*see* Augustine)

> *The man of honor makes good plans,*
> *and he stands for what is good.*
> — Isaiah 32:8 (NLV)

AUGUSTUS
[ah-GOOS-tus]

MEANING: great one, revered one, honored • **USAGE:** Italian (*see* Augustine)

> *What is the son of man that you take care of him?*
> *You made him a little lower than the angels.*
> *You placed on him a crown of glory and honor.*
> — Hebrews 2:6b–7 (NIRV)

AUSTIN, AUSTEN
[AH-sten]

MEANING: great one, revered one, magnificent • **USAGE:** English form of Augustine (*see* Augustine)

> *Greatness lies not in being strong,*
> *but in the right using of strength.*
> — Henry Ward Beecher, *Life Thoughts*

AVERIL
[AV-eh-rel, AV-rel]

MEANING: wild boar warrior • **USAGE:** English form of *Eoforhild,* from German *ebur* (wild boar) and *hild* (war, strife)

> *There is in my nature, methinks,*
> *a singular yearning toward all wildness.*
> — Henry David Thoreau,
> *A Week on the Concord and Merrimack Rivers*

AVERY
[AY-ver-ee]

MEANING: elf counsel, supernaturally wise, elf leader • **USAGE:** English form of Alfred, from English *ælf* (elf) and *raed* (counsel); or English form of Alberic, from German *alb* (elf) and *rik* (ruler, leader)

> *We are wiser than we know.*
> — Ralph Waldo Emerson, "The Over-Soul"

AVIEL
[ah-vee-EHL]

MEANING: God is my father • **USAGE:** Jewish: from Hebrew *abn 'el*

> *O Lord, You are our Father; we are the clay, and You are the Potter, we are all the work of Your hands.*
> — Isaiah 64:7 (JPS)

AVIKAR
[ah-vee-kahr]

MEANING: perfect, faultless • **USAGE:** Hindu: Sanskrit

> *The progress of our soul is like a perfect poem.*
> *It has an infinite idea which once realised makes all movements full of meaning and joy.*
> — Rabindranath Tagore, *Sadhana*

AVNER
[ahv-NEHR]

MEANING: father of light, my father is a light • **USAGE:** Jewish: from Hebrew *abh* (father) and *ner* (light)

> *Come hither, and I [God] shall light a candle*
> *of understanding in thine heart.*
> — 2 Esdras 14:25a (KJV Apocrypha)

AVRAHAM   [ahv-rah-HAHM]

MEANING: father of a multitude, exalted father, patriarch • USAGE: Jewish: from Hebrew *abh* (father) and *raham* (multitude)

As for Me, behold, My covenant is with thee, and thou shalt be the father of a multitude of nations.
— Genesis 17:4 (MT)

AVRAM   [ahv-RAHM]

MEANING: high father, patriarch • USAGE: Jewish: from Hebrew *abh* (father) and *ram* (high, exalted)

The Lord said to Abram...
in thee shall all the families of the earth be blessed.
— Genesis 12:1–3 (MT)

AVSHALOM   [ahv-shah-LOHM]

MEANING: father of peace, my father is peaceful • USAGE: Jewish: from Hebrew *abh* (father) and *shalom* (peace)

Love ye truth and peace.
— Zechariah 8:19b (MT)

AXEL   [AYK-sel]

MEANING: father of peace, peaceful father, peaceful ruler • USAGE: Scandinavian and German form of Absalom, from Hebrew *abh* (father) and *shalom* (peace)

Our work for peace must begin within the private world of each one of us. To build for man a world without fear, we must be without fear. To build a world of justice, we must be just.
— Dag Hammarskjöld

AYINDE   [ah-yeen-deh]

MEANING: we gave praises and he came • USAGE: African: Yoruba of Nigeria

When the sharing is hand by hand, the one who is loved will be known.
— Nigerian proverb

AYIZE   [ah-yee-zeh]

MEANING: let it come • USAGE: African: Zulu of South Africa

Let freedom reign. The sun never sets on so glorious a human achievement.
— Nelson Mandela
(inaugural address of May 10, 1994)

AYO   [AH-yoh]

MEANING: happy, joyous • USAGE: African: Yoruba of Nigeria

To be happy in one's home is better than to be a chief.
— Yoruban proverb

AYUSH   [ah-YOOSH]

MEANING: long-lived • USAGE: Hindu: Sanskrit

May the Lord of Love protect us. /
May the Lord of Love nourish us. /
May the Lord of Love strengthen us. /
May we realize the Lord of Love. / May we live with love for all; / May we live in peace with all.
— Katha Upanishad (tr. Eknath Easwaran)

AZ   [ahz]

MEANING: strong, mighty, powerful • USAGE: Jewish

Be strong and of good courage.
— 2 Chronicles 32:7a (JPS)

AZAN   [ah-zahn]

MEANING: strong, mighty, powerful • USAGE: Jewish

A wise man is strength; a knowledgeable man exerts power.
— Proverbs 24:5 (JPS)

AZAR [ah-ʒahr]

MEANING: fire, flame • **USAGE:** Persian
Burning words rise from a glowing heart.
— Hazrat Inayat Khan, *The Gayan*

AZI [ah-ZEE]

MEANING: strong, mighty, powerful • **USAGE:**
Jewish
Have not I commanded thee?
Be strong and of good courage; be not affrighted,
neither be thou dismayed: for the Lord thy God is
with thee whithersoever thou goest.
— Joshua 1:9 (MT)

AZIEL [ah-ʒee-EHL]

MEANING: God is my strength • **USAGE:** Jewish
Riches and honor are Yours to dispense; You have
dominion over all; with You are strength and might,
and it is Your power to make anyone great and strong.
— 1 Chronicles 29:12 (JPS)

AZIZ, AZEEZ [ah-ZEEZ]

MEANING: beloved, noble, honorable • **USAGE:**
Muslim
When love for God has doubled in your heart,
without doubt God has love for you.
— Jalaluddin Rumi
(tr. William Chitticke in *The Sufi Path of Love*)

AZRIEL, AZRAEL [ahʒ-ree-EHL]

MEANING: God is my strength, God is my help •
USAGE: Jewish: from Hebrew *aʒra'el*
I am your God; I strengthen you and I help you.
— Isaiah 41:10a (JPS)

AZUD [ah-ʒood]

MEANING: strong, powerful • **USAGE:** Muslim
It is God alone that gives your arms their power.
— Saadi, "On Gratitude" (tr. Andrew Harvey)

B

BAHIR, BAHEER [bah-hihr, bah-heer]

MEANING: dazzling, bright light • **USAGE:**
Muslim: from Arabic *bahir*
Verily, the heart that reflecteth
the divine Light is illuminated.
— Hazrat Inayat Khan, *The Gayan*

BAI [bie]

MEANING: pure, white • **USAGE:** Chinese
To cease from all evil, to cultivate good,
to purify one's mind — this is the advice
of all the Buddhas.
— Buddha, *The Dhammapada*

BAILEY, BAILY [BAY-lee]

MEANING: bailiff, steward, administrator •
USAGE: English surname: from English *bailiff*
True liberty can exist only when justice
is equally administered to all.
— Lord Mansfield

BAIRD [bayrd]

MEANING: bard, poet, singer, balladeer • **USAGE:**
Scottish surname: from Gaelic *bàrd*
I would rather be remembered by a song
than by a victory.
— Alexander Smith, "Men of Letters"

BAKARI [bah-KAH-ree]

MEANING: one with great promise • **USAGE:**
African: Swahili of Kenya and Tanzania
The wise man's promises
are like dew on the field.
— East African proverb

BALIN

[bah-lihn]

MEANING: powerful warrior, strong warrior • **USAGE:** Hindu

> *The sign of vigour, the sign of life,*
> *the sign of hope, the sign of health,*
> *the sign of everything that is good, is strength.*
> — Swami Vivekananda

BALINT

[BAH-leent]

MEANING: strong, vigorous, healthy • **USAGE:** Hungarian form of Valentine, from Latin *valens*

> *I pray that all may go well with you and that you may*
> *be in good health, just as it is well with your soul.*
> — 3 John 1:2 (NEB)

BALLARD

[BAL-ard]

MEANING: bald-headed, ballad, dancing song • **USAGE:** English surname: from *bal(le)* (hairless patch on the head); or possibly from French *ballade* (ballad) or *balar* (to dance)

> *You shall have a song...and joy of heart.*
> — Isaiah 30:29 (DR)

BANDHU

[bahn-doo]

MEANING: connection, relation • **USAGE:** Hindu: Sanskrit

> *Everything is connected to everything else.*
> *No one part, nothing, is isolated. Everything is linked,*
> *and interdependent. Everywhere everything is*
> *connected to everything else.*
> — Swami Prajnanpad

BAPTISTE

[bah-TEEST]

MEANING: baptizer • **USAGE:** French: from French *baptiste* (a baptist)

> *He will baptize you*
> *with the Holy Spirit and with fire.*
> — Luke 3:16b (NIV)

BAQI, BAKI

[bah-kee]

MEANING: eternal, everlasting • **USAGE:** Muslim

> *The grace of Allah toward thee hath been infinite.*
> — Koran, The Women 4.113b (PIC)

BAQIR

[bah-keer]

MEANING: educated, knowledgeable • **USAGE:** Muslim

> *Those who have been given knowledge see that what is*
> *revealed unto thee from thy Lord is the truth and leadeth*
> *unto the path of the Mighty, the Owner of Praise.*
> — Koran, Sheba 34.6 (PIC)

BARACK

[bah-RAHK]

MEANING: blessed, blessing, lightning • **USAGE:** American form of Hebrew Baruch (blessed, blessing); or Barak (lightning)

> *He who blesses most is blest.*
> — John Greenleaf Whittier, "A Song of Harvest"

BARAK

[bah-RAHK]

MEANING: lightning, flash of light, gleaming, shining • **USAGE:** Jewish

> *As lightning springs out of its concealment in dark*
> *clouds to flash through the world, so the divine light...*
> *emerges through charitable deeds.*
> — Shneur Zalman ben Baruch, "Seder Tefillot"

BARIK, BAREEQ

[bah-reek]

MEANING: brilliant, bright, lightning • **USAGE:** Muslim

> *Most surely the righteous shall be in bliss, on thrones,*
> *they shall gaze. You will recognize in their faces the*
> *brightness of bliss.*
> — Koran, The Defrauders 83.22–24 (SKR)

BARNABAS

[BAR-nah-bus]

MEANING: son of exhortation, son of encouragement, one who encourages • **USAGE:**

English form of Aramaic *Barnebhuah* (son of exhortation)

> *I know of no more encouraging fact*
> *than the unquestionable ability of man to elevate*
> *his life by conscious endeavor.*
> — Henry David Thoreau, *Walden*

BARNABY [*BAR-nah-bee*]

MEANING: son of exhortation, son of encouragement, one who encourages • USAGE: English form of Barnabas (*see* Barnabas)

> *My son, may the Lord be with you.*
> — 1 Chronicles 22:11a (NCV)

BARNY, BARNEY [*BAR-nee*]

MEANING: son of exhortation, son of encouragement, one who encourages • USAGE: English form of Barnabas (*see* Barnabas)

> *Hear thou, my son, and be wise,*
> *and guide thine heart in the way.*
> — Proverbs 23:19 (KJ21)

BARRY, BARRIE [*BAYR-ee*]

MEANING: sharp, pointed, spear-like, fair-haired • USAGE: Irish and English: a form of Bearach, from Irish Gaelic *bearach* (spear, spear-like); or a form of *Fionbharr*, from Gaelic *fionn* (white, fair) and *bearr* (head)

> *You [God] anoint my head with oil.*
> — Psalm 23:5b (WEB)

BART [*bart*]

MEANING: farmer's son, earth worker, gardener • USAGE: English and Dutch form of Bartholomew (*see* Bartholomew)

> *Believe in yourself, your neighbors, your work,*
> *your ultimate attainment of more complete happiness.*
> *It is only the farmer who faithfully plants seeds*
> *in the Spring, who reaps a harvest in Autumn.*
> — B. C. Forbes

BARTHOLOMEW [*bar-THAH-loh-myoo*]

MEANING: farmer's son, earth worker, gardener • USAGE: English form of *Bartholomaios,* from Hebrew *bar* (son) and *talmai* (furrow, plow)

> *Cultivators of the earth are the most valuable citizens.*
> *They are the most vigorous, the most independent,*
> *the most virtuous, and they are tied to their*
> *country and wedded to its liberty and interests*
> *by the most lasting bonds.*
> — Thomas Jefferson (letter of August 23, 1785)

BARTOLI [*bahr-TOH-lee*]

MEANING: farmer's son, earth worker, gardener • USAGE: Spanish form of Bartholomew (*see* Bartholomew)

> *Plow your fields, scatter seeds of justice,*
> *and harvest faithfulness.*
> — Hosea 10:12a (CEV)

BARTOLOMÉ [*bahr-toh-loh-MAY*]

MEANING: farmer's son, earth worker, gardener • USAGE: Spanish form of Bartholomew (*see* Bartholomew)

> *Those who are peacemakers will plant seeds*
> *of peace and reap a harvest of righteousness.*
> — James 3:18 (NLT)

BARTOLOMEO [*bahr-toh-loh-MAY-oh*]

MEANING: farmer's son, earth worker, gardener • USAGE: Italian form of Bartholomew (*see* Bartholomew)

> *My soul can find no stair /*
> *To mount to heaven, save earth's loveliness.*
> — Michelangelo

BARUCH [*bah-ROOK*]

MEANING: blessed, blessing • USAGE: Jewish
> *May you be blessed by the Lord,*
> *Maker of heaven and earth.*
> — Psalm 115:15 (JPS)

B

B

BASHIR, BASHEER   [bah-SHEER]

MEANING: bringer of good news, messenger •
USAGE: Muslim

*Give glad tidings to those who believe
and work righteousness, that their portion is Gardens,
beneath which rivers flow.*
— Koran, The Cow 2.25a (ALI)

BASIL   [BAY-zel]

MEANING: king, royal one • USAGE: English:
from Greek *basileus*

Every inch a king.
— William Shakespeare, *King Lear*

BASILE   [bah-SEE-leh]

MEANING: king, royal one • USAGE: French form
of Basil (*see* Basil)

*You have made him a little lower than the angels,
and You have crowned him with glory and honor.*
— Psalm 8:4–6 (NKJV)

BASILIO   [bah-ZEE-lyo (Italian),
bah-SEE-lee-oh (Spanish)]

MEANING: king, royal one • USAGE: Italian and
Spanish form of Basil (*see* Basil)

*You are a king by your own fireside,
as much as any monarch in his throne.*
— Miguel de Cervantes, *Don Quixote*
(tr. Peter Motteux)

BASIM, BASEEM   [bah-SEEM]

MEANING: smiling, happy, cheerful • USAGE:
Muslim: from Arabic *basama* (to smile)

*Do what most enables you to fly / and brings a feeling
to the heart that makes you / glad to be alive.*
— Hafiz, "Making the Rounds and Causing
Trouble" (tr. Daniel Ladinsky in *A Year with Hafiz*)

BASIR   [bah-SEER]

MEANING: wise, insightful • USAGE: Muslim

*He granteth wisdom to whom He pleaseth;
and he to whom wisdom is granted receiveth
indeed a benefit overflowing.*
— Koran, The Heifer 2.269a (ALI)

BASTIEN   [BAH-stee-en, bahs-TWAHN]

MEANING: man from Sebastia • USAGE: French
form of Sebastien, from Greek *Sebastia*, a town in
Asia Minor

*A good man out of the good treasure
of his heart brings forth good things.*
— Matthew 12:35a (NKJV)

BATTISTA   [bah-TEES-tah]

MEANING: baptist, one who baptizes • USAGE:
Italian: from Latin *baptista* (baptist)

He will baptize you with the Holy Spirit and fire.
— Luke 3:16b (NCV)

BAXTER   [BAK-ster]

MEANING: baker • USAGE: English surname: from
English *baecestre*

The bread of life is love.
— Anna Jameson

BAZ   [bahz]

MEANING: king, royal one • USAGE: English form
of Basil, from Greek *basileus*

*The kingdom of heaven…is not yonder
and of to-morrow, but is now and here.*
— John Burroughs, "Analogy — True and False"

BEARACH, BERACH   [BAHR-ahk]

MEANING: sharp, spear, spear-like, warrior •
USAGE: Irish: from Irish *berach* (spear, spear-like)

Iron sharpens iron, and one man sharpens another.
— Proverbs 27:17 (ESV)

B

BEAU   *[boh]*

MEANING: handsome, good-looking • **USAGE:**
English: from French *beau*

> *You are the most handsome of men;*
> *you are an eloquent speaker.*
> *God has always blessed you.*
> — Psalm 45:2 (GNT)

BEAUMONT   *[BOH-mont]*

MEANING: handsome mountain • **USAGE:** English:
from French *beau* (handsome, good-looking) and
mont (hill)

> *Great things are done when men and mountains meet;*
> */ This is not done by jostling in the street.*
> — William Blake, "Gnomic Verses"

BECK   *[bek]*

MEANING: stream, brook • **USAGE:** English
surname, from Norse *bekkr* (brook); or from
English *bekke* (stream)

> *Words of wisdom are a stream*
> *that flows from a deep fountain.*
> — Proverbs 18:4 (CEV)

BECKETT   *[BEK-et]*

MEANING: shelter, cottage • **USAGE:** English
surname: from English *beo* (shelter) and *cot*
(cottage)

> *May there be peace within your walls.*
> — Psalm 122:7a (HCSB)

BELA   *[BEH-lah]*

MEANING: noble and brightly shining • **USAGE:**
Hungarian: possibly form of Albert, from German
adal (noble) and *beraht* (bright, shining)

> *Arise, shine, for your light has come.*
> — Isaiah 60:1a (ESV)

BEM   *[bem]*

MEANING: he is peaceful • **USAGE:** African: Tiv
of Nigeria

> *Peace is the father of friendship.*
> — Nigerian proverb

BEMIDJI   *[beh-meed-jee]*

MEANING: river crossing a lake • **USAGE:**
Amerind: Chippewa-Ojibwe

> *A part of the Creator's spirit exists in everything*
> *and thus all things are connected.*
> — Larry P. Aitken, *Two Cultures Meet*

BEN   *[ben]*

MEANING: son, son of my right hand, son of
good fortune, blessed, graced • **USAGE:** Jewish
and English: from Hebrew *ben* (son); English form
of Benjamin (*see* Benjamin) or of Benedict (*see*
Benedict)

> *My son, the Lord be with thee; and prosper thou.*
> — 1 Chronicles 22:11a (MT)

BENEDETTO   *[bay-nay-DAY-toh]*

MEANING: blessed, blessing • **USAGE:** Italian form
of Benedict (*see* Benedict)

> *Your discernment is blessed, and you are blessed.*
> — 1 Samuel 25:33a (HCSB)

BENEDICT   *[BEN-eh-dikt]*

MEANING: blessed, blessing, graced • **USAGE:**
English: from Latin *benedicere* (to bless)

> *Honor and majesty You have placed upon him.*
> *For You have made him most blessed forever.*
> — Psalm 21:5b–6a (NKJV)

BENEDICTO   *[bay-nay-DEEK-toh]*

MEANING: blessed, blessing • **USAGE:** Spanish and
Portuguese form of Benedict (*see* Benedict)

> *The blessing of the Lord be upon you.*
> — Psalm 128:8a (DR)

B

BENEDIKT   *[ben-eh-DEEKT]*

MEANING: blessed, blessing • USAGE: Danish,
Swedish, and Russian form of Benedict (*see*
Benedict)

> *A faithful man shall abound with blessings.*
> — Proverbs 28:20a (ASV)

BENIGNO   *[beh-NEEG-noh]*

MEANING: good, kind, wellborn • USAGE: Italian:
from Latin *benignus*

> *Man's true goodness must lie in conformity*
> *with the Deity.*
> — Marcus Aurelius, *The Meditations*
> (tr. Jeremy Collier)

BENITO   *[bay-NEE-toh]*

MEANING: blessed, blessing • USAGE: Spanish and
Italian form of Benedicto (*see* Benedict)

> *The Lord will love you and bless you.*
> — Deuteronomy 7:13a (CEV)

BENJ   *[benj]*

MEANING: son of my right hand, son of good
fortune • USAGE: English form of Benjamin (*see*
Benjamin)

> *Blessed be you of the Lord, my son.*
> — Judges 17:2b (ASV)

BENJAMIN   *[BEN-jah-min (English),*
ben-ʒhah-MIN (French), BEN-yah-meen (German)]

MEANING: son of my right hand, son of good
fortune • USAGE: English, French, and German
form of Binyamin, from Hebrew *ben* (son) and
yamin (right hand)

> *Of Benjamin he said: "This is the tribe the Lord*
> *loves and protects; He guards them all the day long,*
> *and he dwells in their midst."*
> — Deuteronomy 33:12 (GNT)

BEÑO   *[BAYN-yoh]*

MEANING: strong as a bear, powerful • USAGE:
Spanish form of Bernard (*see* Bernard)

> *I pray that you are doing well in every way. I pray*
> *that your body is strong and well even as your soul is.*
> — 3 John 1:2 (NLV)

BENÔIT   *[ben-WAH]*

MEANING: blessed, blessing • USAGE: French
form of Benedict (*see* Benedict)

> *Blessed is your discretion, and blessed are you.*
> — 1 Samuel 25:33a (WEB)

BENTO   *[BAYN-toh]*

MEANING: blessed, blessing • USAGE: Portuguese
form of Benedicto (*see* Benedict)

> *I pray that God will be kind to you*
> *and will bless you with peace!*
> — 1 Thessalonians 1:1b (CEV)

BENVENUTO   *[bayn-veh-NOO-toh]*

MEANING: welcome, good arrival • USAGE:
Italian: from Latin *bene* (well, good, favorable) and
venuto (came, arrived)

> *Anyone working and living*
> *in truth and reality welcomes God-light.*
> — John 3:21a (MSG)

BERK   *[berk]*

MEANING: birch tree meadow, field of birch trees
• USAGE: English surname: from English *beorc*
(birch tree, birch wood) and *leah* (meadow, field)

> *He shall be like a tree planted by the streams of water,*
> *that bringeth forth its fruit in its season,*
> *whose leaf also doth not wither;*
> *and whatsoever he doeth shall prosper.*
> — Psalm 1:3 (ASV)

B

BERNARD [ber-NARD, BER-nerd (English), ber-NAHR (French)]

MEANING: strong as a bear, powerful • **USAGE:** English and French form of Bernhard, from German *bern* (bear) and *hart* (hardy, strong, brave)
Bears are a peaceable people,
and mind their own business.
— John Muir, "The Wild Parks and Forest Reservations of the West"

BERNARDINO [bayr-nahr-DEE-noh]

MEANING: strong as a bear, powerful • **USAGE:** Italian and Spanish form of Bernard (*see* Bernard)
He who has great power should use it lightly.
— Seneca

BERNARDO [bayr-NAHR-doh]

MEANING: strong as a bear, powerful • **USAGE:** Spanish, Italian, and Portuguese form of Bernard (*see* Bernard)
You shall be a blessing:
fear not, let your hands be strengthened.
— Zechariah 8:13b (DR)

BERND [behrnd]

MEANING: bear, strong as a bear • **USAGE:** German: from German *bern* (bear)
So be strong and courageous! . . . for the Lord your God
will personally go ahead of you.
He will neither fail you nor abandon you.
— Deuteronomy 31:6 (NLT)

BERNHARD [BEHR-hahrt]

MEANING: strong as a bear, powerful • **USAGE:** German and Scandinavian form of *Berinhard,* from German *bern* (bear) and *hart* (hardy, strong, brave)
Be strong and have strength of heart.
— Joshua 1:6a (NLV)

BERNT [bernt]

MEANING: strong as a bear, powerful • **USAGE:** Scandinavian and German form of *Berinhard* (*see* Bernhard)
God has not given us a spirit of fear and timidity,
but of power, love, and self-discipline.
— 2 Timothy 1:7 (NLT)

BERT [bert]

MEANING: shining brightly • **USAGE:** English form of names ending with *-bert,* such as Albert, Gilbert, Herbert, Robert, and so on (*see those entries*); from German *beraht* (bright, shining)
As we let our own light shine, we unconsciously give
other people permission to do the same.
— Marianne Williamson, *A Return to Love*

BERTO [BAYR-toh]

MEANING: noble and brightly shining • **USAGE:** Spanish and Italian form of Alberto, from German *adal* (noble) and *beraht* (bright, shining)
He who is noble plans noble things,
and on noble things he stands.
— Isaiah 32:8 (ESV)

BERTRAM [BER-tram]

MEANING: brightly shining raven • **USAGE:** English surname: form of *Berahtram,* from German *beraht* (bright, shining) and *hramn* (raven)
Consider the ravens, that they sow not, neither reap;
which have no store-chamber nor barn; and God feedeth
them: of how much more value are ye than the birds!
— Luke 12:24 (ASV)

BERTRAND [BER-trand]

MEANING: brightly shining raven • **USAGE:** English surname: form of *Berahtram* (*see* Bertram)
Rise up and shine, for your light has come.
— Isaiah 60:1a (NLV)

B

BEVEN, BEVAN   [BEV-an]

MEANING: God is gracious, God is giving, son of Evan • USAGE: Welsh: from Welsh *ap Iefan* (son of Evan), from Hebrew *y'hohanan* (Yahweh is gracious)

> *My son, let not these things depart from thy eyes: keep the law and counsel: and there shall be life to thy soul, and grace to thy mouth.*
> — Proverbs 3:21–22 (DR)

BHANU   [bah-noo]

MEANING: luminous, shining, light, the sun • USAGE: Hindu: Sanskrit

> *The sunshine greets me with a smile.*
> — Rabindranath Tagore, *Stray Birds*

BHARATA   [bah-rah-tah]

MEANING: the supporter, the maintainer • USAGE: Hindu: from Sanskrit *bharata* (being maintained)

> *Seek refuge with the Lord alone, / with your whole being, Bharata. / By His grace, you will reach / supreme peace, and everlasting estate.*
> — *Bhagavad Gita* (tr. Kees Bolle)

BHASU   [bah-soo]

MEANING: shining, like the sun • USAGE: Hindu: Sanskrit

> *As the sun shines and fills all space with light, / Above, below, across, so shines the Lord of Love / and fills the hearts of all created beings.*
> — *Shvetashvatara Upanishad* (tr. Eknath Easwaran)

BILL   [bil]

MEANING: determined protector, steadfast guardian • USAGE: English form of William, from German *wil* (will, resolve) and *helm* (protection, helmet)

> *Thou shalt be stedfast, and shalt not fear.*
> — Job 11:15b (ASV)

BILLY   [BIL-ee]

MEANING: determined protector, steadfast guardian • USAGE: English form of William (*see* Bill)

> *He who guards his way guards his life.*
> — Proverbs 16:17b (NIV)

BINYAMIN   [been-yah-MEEN]

MEANING: son of my right hand, son of good fortune • USAGE: Jewish: from Hebrew *ben* (son) and *yamin* (right hand)

> *The Lord bless you, my son.*
> — Judges 17:2b (MT)

BION   [BEE-ohn]

MEANING: life, full of life • USAGE: Greek: from Greek *bios*

> *Be kind and honest and you will live a long life; others will respect you and treat you fairly.*
> — Proverbs 21:21 (RSV)

BIRGER   [BEER-ger]

MEANING: helper, protector • USAGE: Scandinavian: from Swedish *bjarga* (to help, to save, to protect)

> *Helpful people can always be trusted to make helpful plans.*
> — Isaiah 32:8 (CEV)

BISHOP   [BIH-shop]

MEANING: overseer, watcher, high-ranking Christian cleric • USAGE: English surname: from English *bisceop*

> *Treat everyone fairly. Show faithful love and tender concern to one another.*
> — Zechariah 7:9b (NIRV)

BIZHAN   [bee-jahn]

MEANING: hero, heroic • USAGE: Persian

The lion who breaks the enemy's ranks is a minor hero
compared to the lion who overcomes himself.
— Jalaluddin Rumi

BJORN   *[byorn]*

MEANING: bear • **USAGE:** Swedish and
Norwegian: from Norse *björn* (bear)
Be strong and have strength of heart.
— Deuteronomy 31:7b (NLV)

BLADE   *[blayd]*

MEANING: blade, edge of a sword, knife • **USAGE:**
American: from English *blade*
The everlasting God…is your shield and helper,
your glorious sword.
— Deuteronomy 33:27–29b (NCV)

BLAISE   *[blez]*

MEANING: talks with a lisp • **USAGE:** French form
of Roman family name *Blasius*, from Latin *blaesus*
(talks with a lisp)
My mouth shall speak wisdom; the meditation
of my heart shall be understanding.
— Psalm 49:3 (ESV)

BLAKE   *[blayk]*

MEANING: black, dark, white, fair • **USAGE:**
English surname: from English *blæc* (black, dark)
or from English *blac* (white, fair)
Black is a color of power and strength.
— Hayden Fry

BLAZE   *[blayz]*

MEANING: blaze, flame, fire, torch • **USAGE:**
American: from English *blæse* (torch, flame,
firebrand, lamp)
Life is no brief candle to me. It is a sort of splendid
torch which I have got a hold of for the moment, and
I want to make it burn as brightly as possible before
handing it on to future generations.
— George Bernard Shaw

BO   *[boh]*

MEANING: householder, homeowner • **USAGE:**
Scandinavian: from Norse *bua* (to dwell, to have a
household, to live)
Use wisdom and understanding to establish your home;
let good sense fill the rooms with priceless treasures.
— Proverbs 24:3–4 (CEV)

BOB   *[bob]*

MEANING: brightly famous, shining with fame •
USAGE: English form of Robert, from German *hrod*
(fame) and *beraht* (bright, shining)
Let your good deeds shine out for all to see.
— Matthew 5:16a (NLT)

BOBBY, BOBBIE   *[BOB-ee]*

MEANING: brightly famous, shining with fame •
USAGE: English form of Robert (*see* Bob)
A man's wisdom makes his face shine.
— Ecclesiastes 8:1b (WEB)

BOBEK   *[BOH-bek]*

MEANING: brightly famous, shining with fame •
USAGE: Czech form of Robert (*see* Bob)
Lord… You make my life pleasant,
and my future is bright.
— Psalm 16:5–6 (CEV)

BODEN   *[BOH-den]*

MEANING: bringer of news, herald, bow-shaped
hill, above the hill, bold friend, ground, bottom
• **USAGE:** English surname: from German *bodo*
(herald, bringer of news); English form of *Bowden*,
from English *bufan dune* (above the hill) or *boga*
(bow) and *dun* (hill); English form of *Baldwin*,
from English *beald* (bold) and *wine* (friend); or
from German *goden* (ground, bottom)
How delightful it is to see approaching over the
mountains the feet of a messenger who announces
peace, a messenger who brings good news.
— Isaiah 52:7 (NEB)

B

BODHI [boh-dee]

MEANING: wise, enlightened • USAGE: Hindu: Sanskrit

The Middle Path…gives vision and knowledge, which leads to calm, insight, enlightenment, Nirvana.
— Buddha

BODIE [BOH-dee]

MEANING: bow maker, victorious, successful • USAGE: English surname: from English *boga* (bow) and *bugan* (to bend); or English form of *O'Buadhaigh*, from Irish Gaelic *buadhach* (victorious, successful)

The Lord your God will make you prosper abundantly in all the work of your hands.
— Deuteronomy 30:9a (HCSB)

BOGDAN [BOG-dahn]

MEANING: God's gift, gift of God • USAGE: Russian and Polish: from Slavic *bog* (God) and *dan* (gift)

Every man should eat and drink and enjoy the good of all his labor: it is the gift of God.
— Ecclesiastes 3:13 (KJ21)

BOHDAN [BOH-dahn]

MEANING: God's gift, gift of God • USAGE: Czech (see Bogdan)

Rekindle the gift of God which is in thee.
— 2 Timothy 1:5b (DT)

BOO-CHUN [boo-chun]

MEANING: rich sky • USAGE: Korean: from Korean *boo* (rich) and *chun* (sky)

When you realize how perfect everything is, you will tilt your head back and laugh at the sky.
— Buddha

BOOKER [BOOK-er]

MEANING: bookbinder, scribe • USAGE: English surname: from English *bok* (book)

Books are the quietest and most constant of friends; they are the most accessible and wisest of counselors and the most patient of teachers.
— Charles W. Eliot, *The Happy Life*

BOOTH, BOOTHE [booth]

MEANING: temporary dwelling place, stall • USAGE: American: from English *bothe*

Peace be both to thee, and peace be to thine house, and peace be unto all that thou hast.
— 1 Samuel 25:6b (KJ21)

BORIS [boh-REES (Russian), BOHR-is (English, German)]

MEANING: glorious warrior, famous warrior • USAGE: Russian, English, and German form of *Borislav*, from Slavic *bor* (battle, war) and *slav* (glory, fame)

You, O Lord, are a shield around me; you are my glory, the one who holds my head high.
— Psalm 3:3 (NLT)

BORYS [BOHR-ees]

MEANING: glorious warrior, famous warrior • USAGE: Polish form of Boris (see Boris)

You, O Lord, are always my shield from danger; you give me victory and restore my courage.
— Psalm 3:3 (GNT)

BOWEN [BOH-wen]

MEANING: youthful, young, wellborn, noble • USAGE: Welsh surname: from Welsh *ap* (son) and Owen, from Welsh *eoghunn* (youth), or from Greek *eu* (good, well) and *genes* (born)

The Lord bless you, my son!
— Judges 17:2b (NIV)

B

BRAD   *[brad]*

MEANING: broad ford, wide river crossing, broad meadow, wide field • **USAGE:** English form of Bradford (*see* Bradford) or of Bradley (*see* Bradley)

> *I love a broad margin to my life.*
> — Henry David Thoreau, *Walden*

BRADEN   *[BRAY-den]*

MEANING: broad woods, broad hill, broad-chested, salmon • **USAGE:** English surname: from English *brad* (broad) and *dene* (woods, forest) or *dun* (hill); or from Irish Gaelic *braghadach* (broad-chested) or *bradan* (salmon)

> *The Lord…brought me forth also into a large place…because he delighted in me.*
> — Psalm 18:18a–19 (KJV)

BRADFORD   *[BRAD-ford]*

MEANING: broad ford, broad river crossing • **USAGE:** English surname: from English *brad* (broad) and *ford* (ford, shallow river crossing)

> *This is what the Lord says…when you pass through the waters, I will be with you.*
> — Isaiah 43:1–2a (NIV)

BRADLEY   *[BRAD-lee]*

MEANING: broad meadow • **USAGE:** English surname: from English *brad* (broad) and *leah* (meadow, field)

> *In this broad earth of ours… / Enclosed and safe within its central heart, / Nestles the seed perfection.*
> — Walt Whitman, "Song of the Universal"

BRADY   *[BRAY-dee]*

MEANING: broad island, broad-chested, salmon • **USAGE:** English and Irish surname: from English *brad* (broad, wide) and *ieg* (island); or Irish form of surname *O'Bradaigh*, from Gaelic *braghadach* (broad-chested) or *bradan* (salmon)

> *The larger the island of knowledge, the longer the shoreline of wonder.*
> — Ralph W. Sockman

BRAM   *[bram (English), brahm (Dutch)]*

MEANING: father of a multitude • **USAGE:** English and Dutch form of Abraham, from Hebrew *abh* (father) and *raham* (multitude)

> *I am the God of your father Abraham; do not fear, for I am with you. I will bless you.*
> — Genesis 26:24b (KJV)

BRAN   *[bran]*

MEANING: raven • **USAGE:** Welsh and Irish: from Gaelic *bran*

> *You have a raven's knowledge.*
> — Gaelic proverb

BRANCH   *[branch]*

MEANING: limb of a tree, bough • **USAGE:** English: from English *braunch*

> *The righteous shall flourish as a branch.*
> — Proverbs 11:28b (KJV)

BRANDAN, BRANDON, BRANDEN   *[BRAN-den]*

MEANING: little king, prince, steep hill, gorse-covered hill, little raven • **USAGE:** English form of Breandan, from Welsh *brenhin* (king) and diminutive *-an*; from English *bryn* (steep hill) or *brom* (broom) and *dun* (hill); or from Welsh *bran* (raven, crow) and diminutive *-an*

> *Consider the ravens:*
> *for they neither sow nor reap;*
> *which neither have storehouse nor barn;*
> *and God feedeth them:*
> *how much more are ye better than the fowls?*
> — Luke 12:24 (KJV)

B

BRANT   [brant]

MEANING: blade of a sword • USAGE: English:
from Norse *brandr*
> Each man stands with his face in the light. / Of his
> own drawn sword, / Ready to do what a hero can.
> — Elizabeth Barrett Browning,
> "Napoleon III in Italy"

BREANDAN   [BREN-den]

MEANING: little king, prince • USAGE: Irish: from
Welsh *brenhin* (king) and diminutive *-an*
> The kingdom of God is within you.
> — Luke 17:21b (NIV)

BRECK   [brek]

MEANING: speckled, freckled, dappled • USAGE:
English surname: from Welsh *brych* (speckled)
> Glory be to God for dappled things.
> — Gerard Manley Hopkins, "Pied Beauty"

BRENDAN, BRENDEN, BRENDON   [BREN-den]

MEANING: little king, prince • USAGE: English
form of Breandan (*see* Breandan)
> He is as full of valour as of kindness; /
> Princely in both.
> — William Shakespeare, *Henry V*

BRENT   [brent]

MEANING: fire, flame, burn • USAGE: English
form of Brenton (*see* Brenton)
> Keep up the fires of thought, and all will go well.
> — Henry David Thoreau
> (letter of September 26, 1859)

BRENTON   [BREN-ton]

MEANING: fire, flame, burn • USAGE: English
surname: from English *boernan* (to burn) or *byrne*
(fire, flame)

> You are host to the eternal flame. It glows in the silence
> of your being to illumine your life and light your way.
> — Susan L. Taylor, *Lessons in Living*

BRETT, BRET   [bret]

MEANING: man from Britain, a British man •
USAGE: English surname: from French *Bret* (a
Breton); or from Welsh *Breiz* (Briton, Brittany)
> Think like a man of action
> and act like a man of thought.
> — Henri-Louis Bergson

BRIAN, BRYAN   [BRIE-an]

MEANING: strong, noble, valorous, high, lofty
• USAGE: Irish and English: from Gaelic *brigh*
(strong, noble, valorous) or *brig* (high, lofty)
> He who cherishes a beautiful vision,
> a lofty ideal in his heart, will one day realize it.
> — James Allen, *As a Man Thinketh*

BRISTOL   [BRIS-tel]

MEANING: site of the bridge • USAGE: English
form of *Bridgestow* (site of the bridge); city in
England
> Praise the bridge that carried you over.
> — George Colman, the Younger, *The Heir at Law*

BROCK   [brahk]

MEANING: badger • USAGE: American surname:
from English *brocc*
> The wild animals will be at peace with you.
> — Job 5:23b (NEB)

BRODER   [broh-der]

MEANING: brother • USAGE: Scandinavian: from
Norse *brodir*
> Whoever loves his brother lives in the light,
> and there is nothing in him to make him stumble.
> — 1 John 2:10 (NIV)

B

BRODY, BRODIE [*BROH-dee*]

MEANING: rampart, fortification, muddy place, ditch • **USAGE:** Irish surname: from Gaelic *brothaigh* (rampart) or *brothach* (muddy place)
You are my strength…for you, O God, are my fortress.
— Psalm 59:9 (NLT)

BROOK [*bruk*]

MEANING: brook, stream • **USAGE:** English: from English *broc*
Smooth runs the water where the brook is deep.
— William Shakespeare, *Henry VI, Part I*

BRUCE [*broos*]

MEANING: brushwood hedge, man of Brieuze • **USAGE:** Scottish and English: Scottish surname referring to *Brieuze* (town in France), from French *bruys* (brushwood thicket)
You have hedged me behind and before, and laid Your hand upon me.
— Psalm 139:5 (NKJV)

BRUNO [*BROO-noh*]

MEANING: brown, rich brown color • **USAGE:** German, Italian, and Spanish: from German *bruno*
The whole world, as we experience it visually, comes to us through the mystic realm of color. Our entire being is nourished by it.
— Hans Hofmann, "Search for the Real"

BRYANT [*BRIE-ant*]

MEANING: strong, noble, valorous, high, lofty • **USAGE:** English form of Brian (*see* Brian)
He who lives constantly in the conception of noble and lofty thoughts, who dwells upon all that is pure and unselfish, will, as surely as the sun reaches its zenith and the moon its full, become wise and noble in character, and rise into a position of influence and blessedness.
— James Allen, *As a Man Thinketh*

BRYCE, BRICE [*bries*]

MEANING: son of the ardent one, eager, passionate, speckled, freckled • **USAGE:** Welsh and English: from Welsh *ap* (son) and *rhys* (ardor, passion); or from Welsh *brych* (speckled)
Enthusiasm moves the world.
— Arthur Balfour

BRYN [*bren*]

MEANING: steep hill, mount • **USAGE:** Welsh: from Welsh *bryn*
Lord…who shall dwell on your holy hill? He who walks blamelessly and does what is right and speaks truth in his heart.
— Psalm 15:1–2 (ESV)

BUCK [*buk*]

MEANING: stag, male deer • **USAGE:** English: from English *buc*
This God is my strong refuge; he makes my pathway safe. He makes me sure-footed as a deer.
— 2 Samuel 22:33–34a (GNT)

BURGESS [*BER-jes*]

MEANING: one who is free, freeman of a borough • **USAGE:** English surname: from French *burgeis*
For a man to act himself, he must be perfectly free; otherwise he is in danger of losing all sense of responsibility or of self-respect.
— Henry David Thoreau
(letter of October 27, 1837)

BURK, BURKE [*burk*]

MEANING: strong protection, stronghold, fortress • **USAGE:** English and German form of *Burkhard*, from German *burg* (protection) and *hart* (hardy, strong, brave); or from English *burh* (fortress)
With whom my hand shall be established; Mine arm also shall strengthen him.
— Psalm 89:21 (ASV)

C

BURL, BURLE   *[burl]*

MEANING: cup bearer • USAGE: English: from
English *byrle*

> *My cup runneth over.*
> — Psalm 23:5b (DT)

BURT   *[burt]*

MEANING: fortified town, town near nettles •
USAGE: English form of Burton (*see* Burton)

> *Peace be within thy walls…peace be within thee.*
> — Psalm 122:7–8 (KJV)

BURTON   *[BUR-tun]*

MEANING: fortified town, town near nettles •
USAGE: English surname: from English *burg*
(fortified town) or *burre* (bur, nettle) and *tun* (town,
farm, village)

> *The Lord will protect you from all danger;*
> *he will keep you safe.*
> — Psalm 121:7 (GNT)

BYRON   *[BIE-ron]*

MEANING: barn for cows, shelter for cattle,
cattleman • USAGE: English: from English *byre*
(cattle shed, barn); an occupational name for one
who looked after cattle

> *I trust in Nature for the stable laws*
> *of beauty and utility.*
> — Robert Browning, "A Soul's Tragedy"

C

CABE   *[kayb]*

MEANING: cape, hat, head, rope, lasso • USAGE:
English form of *MacCaba*, from *caba* (cape, hat);
English form of Cabot (*see* Cabot); or American
form of Cable (*see* Cable)

> *He [God] hath clothed me with the garments of salva-*
> *tion: and with the robe of justice he hath covered me.*
> — Isaiah 61:10a (DR)

CABLE   *[KAY-bel]*

MEANING: rope, lasso • USAGE: English: from
Latin *capulum*

> *The threefold cord is not hastily broken.*
> — Ecclesiastes 4:12b (YLT)

CABOT   *[KA-bot]*

MEANING: head • USAGE: English surname: from
French *cabot*

> *You meet him with the blessings of good things;*
> *You set a crown of fine gold on his head.*
> — Psalm 21:3 (NLV)

CADE   *[kayd]*

MEANING: brave in battle, warrior, barrel maker
• USAGE: English and Welsh form of Cadoc, from
Welsh *cathach* (brave in battle); from English *cade*
(cask, barrel), an occupational name for a barrel
maker

> *Masculinity is not something given to you, something*
> *you're born with, but something you gain. And you*
> *gain it by winning small battles with honor.*
> — Norman Mailer

CADEN, CAIDEN   *[KAY-den]*

MEANING: flow of rhythm, warrior • USAGE:
American form of Cadence (*see* Cadence); or form
of Cathan, from Irish Gaelic *cath* (battle)

> *Let him step to the music which he hears,*
> *however measured or far away.*
> — Henry David Thoreau, *Walden*

CADENCE   *[KAY-dens]*

MEANING: flow of rhythm • USAGE: American:
from Latin *cadentia* (a falling, a conclusion of a
movement in music)

Happiness is not a matter of intensity,
but of balance and order and rhythm and harmony.
— Thomas Merton, *No Man Is an Island*

CADHLA   [KAH-lah]

MEANING: handsome, good-looking • **USAGE:** Irish: from Gaelic *cadhla*

How handsome you are, my love. How delightful!
— Song of Songs 1:16a (HCSB)

CADOC   [KAH-dok]

MEANING: brave in battle, warrior • **USAGE:** Welsh: from Welsh *cathach* (brave in battle)

The Lord is with you, courageous warrior!
— Judges 6:12b (NEB)

CAESAR   [SEE-zar]

MEANING: hairy, cut, blue-gray color, emperor, monarch, ruler • **USAGE:** English: from Latin *caesaries* (hairy), *caedo* (to cut), or *caesius* (blue-gray); a title for Roman emperors

Man, who man would be, /
Must rule the empire of himself.
— Percy Bysshe Shelley, "Political Greatness"

CAI   [kay]

MEANING: pathway, warrior • **USAGE:** Welsh: from Welsh *cai* (path, way) or *cad* (battle, war)

May the blessing of the earth be on you,
soft under your feet as you pass along the roads.
— Celtic blessing

CAIGE, CAGE   [kayj]

MEANING: enclosure • **USAGE:** American: from Latin *cavea*

The beloved of the Lord rests in safety —
the High God surrounds him all day long.
— Deuteronomy 33:12b (NRSV)

CAILEAN   [KAY-lan, KAH-lan]

MEANING: pup, cub, whelp • **USAGE:** Irish: from Gaelic *cuilen*

Let your heart cheer you in the days of your youth,
and walk in the ways of your heart.
— Ecclesiastes 11:9b (WEB)

CAIRO   [KIE-roh]

MEANING: the strong, the victorious • **USAGE:** American: from Arabic *al-Kahira*; an Egyptian city

A wise man is strong, yes,
a man of knowledge increases strength.
— Proverbs 24:5 (NKJV)

CAIUS   [KIE-us]

MEANING: joyful, rejoicing • **USAGE:** American: Roman given name, possibly from Latin *gaudere* (to rejoice)

However many years a man may live,
let him enjoy them all.
— Ecclesiastes 11:8a (NIV)

CAL   [kal]

MEANING: bald one, hairless • **USAGE:** English form of Calvin (*see* Calvin)

Thou hast anointed with oil my head.
— Psalm 23:5b (YLT)

CALDER   [KAHL-der]

MEANING: woodland stream • **USAGE:** American: English surname: from English *coille* (wood) and *dur* (stream)

A person's words can be a source of wisdom,
deep as the ocean, fresh as a flowing stream.
— Proverbs 18:4 (GNT)

CALE   [kayl]

MEANING: slender, narrow, dog, heart • **USAGE:** English form of Caley (*see* Caley), or of Caleb (*see* Caleb)

He that walketh uprightly, and worketh righteousness,
and speaketh truth in his heart....
He that doeth these things shall never be moved.
— Psalm 15:2, 15:5b (ASV)

C

CALEB　　　　　　　　　　　　　*[KAY-leb]*

MEANING: dog, heart • **USAGE:** English form of
Kalev, from Hebrew *kalebh*
God give you wisdom in your heart.
— Ben Sira 45:26a (KJV Apocrypha)

CALEY　　　　　　　　　　　　　*[KAY-lee]*

MEANING: slender, narrow • **USAGE:** Scottish:
from Gaelic *caol*
Health lightens the efforts of body and mind. It enables
a man to crowd much work into a narrow compass.
— William Ellery Channing,
"On the Elevation of the Laboring Classes"

CALIX　　　　　　　　　　　　　*[KAL-ex]*

MEANING: most handsome, most attractive •
USAGE: American masculine form of Calista, from
Greek *kalliste* (most beautiful)
You are the most handsome of men; grace flows from
your lips. Therefore God has blessed you forever.
— Psalm 45:2 (HCSB)

CALLUM, CALUM　　　　　　　　*[KAL-um]*

MEANING: dove, dove-like • **USAGE:** Scottish
form of Colm, from Latin *columba* (dove);
reference to St. Columba, who helped convert
Scotland to Christianity
Love truth and peace.
— Zechariah 8:19b (ESV)

CALVIN, KALVIN　　　　　　　　*[KAL-vin]*

MEANING: little bald one, hairless • **USAGE:**
English surname: English form of French *Cauvin*,
from Latin *calvus* (bald) and diminutive *-in*

You [God] honor me by anointing my head with oil.
— Psalm 23:5b (NLT)

CAMDEN　　　　　　　　　　　　*[KAM-den]*

MEANING: crooked valley, winding valley, valley
with camp enclosures • **USAGE:** English surname:
from Gaelic *cam* (crooked) and *denu* (valley); or
from English *camp* (battle, war) and *denu* (valley)
In every walk with Nature one receives
far more than he seeks.
— John Muir, *Steep Trails*

CAMERON　　　　　　　*[KAM-er-un, KAM-run]*

MEANING: crooked nose • **USAGE:** Scottish and
English surname: from Gaelic *cam* (crooked, bent)
and *shron* (nose)
I think your whole life shows in your face
and you should be proud of it.
— Lauren Bacall

CAMPBELL　　　　　　　　　　　*[KAM-bel]*

MEANING: crooked mouth • **USAGE:** Scottish and
English surname: from Gaelic *cam* (crooked, bent)
and *beul* (mouth)
Pursue some path, however narrow and crooked,
in which you can walk with love and reverence.
— Henry David Thoreau
(journal entry of October 18, 1855)

CARL　　　　　　　　　　　　　　*[karl]*

MEANING: one who is free, man, adult • **USAGE:**
English and Scandinavian form of Charles, from
English *ceorl* (freeman, peasant); or from German
karl (full-grown man, adult)
If a man is to live, he must be all alive,
body, soul, mind, heart, spirit.
— Thomas Merton, *Thoughts in Solitude*

C

CARLIN [KAR-len]

MEANING: fierce warrior • **USAGE:** Irish surname: from Gaelic *cearbhall*

> Be strong and brave!
> — Joshua 1:6a (CEV)

CARLITO [kahr-LEE-toh]

MEANING: one who is free, man, adult • **USAGE:** Spanish form of Carlos (*see* Carl)

> *Freedom does not mean that one can do what one wants; freedom implies moral responsibility.*
> — Pope John II

CARLO [KAHR-loh]

MEANING: one who is free, man, adult • **USAGE:** Italian form of Carl (*see* Carl)

> *Who then is free?*
> *The wise man who can command himself.*
> — Horace

CARLOS [KAHR-los]

MEANING: one who is free, man, adult • **USAGE:** Spanish and Portuguese form of Carl (*see* Carl)

> *O God…Grant that I may be strengthened in the inner man, and that my heart may be free.*
> — Thomas à Kempis, *The Imitation of Christ*
> (tr. Harold Bolton)

CARLTON [KARL-tun]

MEANING: town of freeman • **USAGE:** English surname: from English *ceorl* (freeman, peasant) and *tun* (town, village)

> *My [God's] people will live in peaceful dwelling places, in secure homes, in undisturbed places of rest.*
> — Isaiah 32:18 (NIV)

CARMELO [kar-MAY-loh]

MEANING: vineyard, garden, orchard • **USAGE:** Italian masculine form of Carmel, from Hebrew *karmel*

> *I am the Vine, you are the branches. When you're joined with me and I with you, the relation intimate and organic, the harvest is sure to be abundant.*
> — John 15:5a (MSG)

CARMINE [KAHR-mien]

MEANING: vineyard, garden, orchard • **USAGE:** Italian masculine form of Carmel (*see* Carmelo)

> *Righteousness will dwell in the orchard.*
> — Isaiah 32:16b (HCSB)

CAROLOS [KAHR-oh-lohs]

MEANING: one who is free, man, adult • **USAGE:** Greek form of Charles (*see* Carl)

> *Walk upright and free.*
> — Epictetus, *The Discourses* (tr. Elizabeth Carter)

CARRICK [KAYR-ek]

MEANING: rock, rocky place • **USAGE:** Scottish surname: from Gaelic *carrraig*

> *And the Lord said, "Behold, there is a place by me where you shall stand on the rock."*
> — Exodus 33:21 (ESV)

CARROLL [KAYR-ohl]

MEANING: fierce warrior, one who is free, man, adult • **USAGE:** Irish: from Gaelic *cearbhall* (fierce warrior) or *cearbh* (hack with a weapon); or Irish form of Charles (*see* Carl)

> *Liberty means responsibility.*
> — Bernard Shaw, *Man and Superman*

CARSON [KAR-son]

MEANING: courteous, polite, courtly, court dweller • **USAGE:** Scottish and English surname: possibly a form of *Curzon*, from French *curteis* (courteous, polite behavior) or *cort* (court)

> *The small courtesies sweeten life; the greater ennoble it.*
> — Christian Nestell Bovee

C

CARSTEN   [KAHR-sten]

MEANING: follower of Christ, Christian • USAGE:
English form of Christian, from Greek *christianos*

The peace of God, which passeth
all understanding, shall guard your hearts
and your thoughts in Christ Jesus.
— Philippians 4:7 (ASV)

CARTER   [KAHR-ter]

MEANING: cart driver, one who transfers goods •
USAGE: English surname: from English *carte* (cart);
an occupational name for a cart driver

The journey of a thousand leagues begins
with a single step. We must never neglect any work
of peace within our reach, however small.
— Adlai Stevenson (speech of July 21, 1952)

CARY, CAREY   [KAYR-ee]

MEANING: one who is free, man, adult, dark,
black, dark-haired, loved, beloved, fortress, castle •
USAGE: English and Irish: English form of Charles,
from English *ceorl* (freeman, peasant); from
German *karl* (full-grown man, adult); Irish form
of *Ciardha*, from Gaelic *ciar* (dark, black); or from
Welsh *caru* (to love) or *caer* (fortress, castle)

So far as a man thinks, he is free.
— Ralph Waldo Emerson, "Fate"

CASEY   [KAY-see]

MEANING: vigilant, alert, watchful • USAGE:
English surname: English form of *O'Cathasaigh*,
from Irish Gaelic *cathasaigh*

Those who are awake live
in a state of constant amazement.
— Jack Kornfield

CASH   [kash]

MEANING: money box, case maker • USAGE:
English surname: from French *caisse*
For where your treasure is, there will your heart be also.
— Luke 12:34 (ESV)

CASPAR   [KAHS-pahr]

MEANING: treasure master, steward • USAGE:
Scandinavian form of Gaspar, from Persian
genashber

The good man out of the good treasure
of his heart brings forth what is good...for his mouth
speaks from that which fills his heart.
— Luke 6:45 (NASB)

CASPER   [KAS-per]

MEANING: treasure master, steward • USAGE:
English form of Gaspar, from Persian *genashber*
Knowledge is the treasure,
but judgment the treasurer, of a wise man.
— William Penn

CASSIDY   [KAS-ih-dee]

MEANING: love, affection, curly-haired • USAGE:
Irish form of surname *O'Caiside*, from Gaelic *cais*
(love, affection) or *cas* (curly-haired)

Keep love in your heart.... The consciousness of
loving and being loved brings a warmth and richness
to life that nothing else can bring.
— Oscar Wilde

CATHAL   [KAY-hal, KAH-thal]

MEANING: warrior, battle ruler, commander •
USAGE: Irish: from Gaelic *cath* (battle) and *val*
(rule)

God gave us a spirit not of fear
but of power and love and self-control.
— 2 Timothy 1:7 (ESV)

CATHAN   [KAY-than]

MEANING: warrior, warlike, battle • USAGE: Irish:
from Gaelic *cath* (battle)
The Lord is with you, O mighty man of valor.
— Judges 6:12b (ESV)

CAVAN, CAVIN   *[KA-vin]*

MEANING: little calm one, gentle, hollow, glen • **USAGE:** Irish: from Gaelic *caomh* (gentle, calm) and diminutive *-an;* or from Gaelic *cabhan* (hollow)

> *Who among you is wise and understanding?*
> *Let him show by his good behavior*
> *his deeds in the gentleness of wisdom.*
> — James 3:13 (NASB)

CECIL   *[SEE-sil]*

MEANING: blind, dim-sighted • **USAGE:** English form of Roman family name *Caecilius*, from Latin *caecus* (blind)

> *Live by faith, not by sight.*
> — 2 Corinthians 5:7 (NIV)

CECILIO   *[say-SEE-lee-oh]*

MEANING: blind, dim-sighted • **USAGE:** Spanish, Italian, and Portuguese form of Cecil (*see* Cecil)

> *There are moments in life when we need*
> *to trust blindly in intuition.*
> — Paulo Coelho, *The Zahir* (tr. Margaret Costa)

CEDRIC   *[SED-rik]*

MEANING: first choice • **USAGE:** English: possibly from Scotch Gaelic *ceadrith* (first choice); from *Ivanhoe* by Sir Walter Scott

> *Seek ye therefore first the kingdom of God,*
> *and his justice, and all these things*
> *shall be added unto you.*
> — Matthew 6:33 (DR)

CELIO   *[SAY-lee-oh]*

MEANING: heavenly, celestial • **USAGE:** Spanish and Italian form of *Caelius*, from Latin *caelum*

> *Lay up for yourselves treasures in heaven…for where*
> *your treasure is, there your heart will be also.*
> — Matthew 6:20–21 (NKJV)

CÉSAR   *[SAY-sahr]*

MEANING: hairy, cut, blue-gray color, emperor, monarch, ruler • **USAGE:** Spanish form of Caesar, from Latin *caesaries* (hairy), *caedo* (to cut), or *caesius* (blue-gray); a title for Roman emperors

> *You will be a crown of splendor in the Lord's hand,*
> *a royal diadem in the hand of your God.*
> — Isaiah 62:3 (NIV)

CESARE   *[cheh-SAHR-eh]*

MEANING: hairy, cut, blue-gray color, emperor, monarch, ruler • **USAGE:** Italian form of César (*see* César)

> *I am, indeed, a king,*
> *because I know how to rule myself.*
> — Pietro Aretino

CEZAR   *[SEH-zahr]*

MEANING: hairy, cut, blue-gray color, emperor, monarch, ruler • **USAGE:** Polish form of César (*see* César)

> *For thou hast made him but little lower than God,*
> *and crownest him with glory and honor. Thou makest*
> *him to have dominion over the works of thy hands;*
> *Thou hast put all things under his feet.*
> — Psalm 8:5–6 (ASV)

CHAD   *[chad]*

MEANING: warrior • **USAGE:** English form of *Caedda*, from Welsh *cad*

> *A man of courage never wants weapons.*
> — English proverb

CHAGAI   *[khah-GIE]*

MEANING: my feast, holiday, celebration • **USAGE:** Jewish

> *Thus saith the Lord God…*
> *My feast I do prepare for you, even a great feast.*
> — Ezekiel 39:17b (MT)

CHAI   [chie, kie]

MEANING: life, full of life • **USAGE:** Jewish
*Surely goodness and mercy shall follow me
all the days of my life; and I shall dwell
in the house of the Lord for ever.*
— Psalm 23:6 (MT)

CHAIM, CHAYIM   [KHAH-yeem]

MEANING: life, full of life • **USAGE:** Jewish
*I'm passionately involved in life:
I love its change, its color, its movement.
To be alive, to be able to see, to walk,
to have houses, music, paintings
— it's all a miracle.*
— Arthur Rubenstein

CHALIL   [khah-LEEL]

MEANING: flute • **USAGE:** Jewish
*Music is the universal language, the only one that
requires no translation, and in which soul speaks to soul.*
— Berthold Auerbach, *On the Heights*

CHANCE   [chans]

MEANING: chance, random, good fortune •
USAGE: English: from French *cheance* (unexpected
event) and Latin *cadere* (to befall)
*Chance happens to all,
but to turn chance to account is the gift of few.*
— Edward Bulwer-Lytton, *Caxtoniana*

CHANDLER   [CHAND-ler]

MEANING: candle maker • **USAGE:** English
surname: from French *chandelier* (candle) or Latin
candela (candle)
*How far that little candle throws his beams!
So shines a good deed.*
— William Shakespeare, *The Merchant of Venice*

CHANG   [chahng]

MEANING: flourishing, flowing, prosperous,
smooth • **USAGE:** Chinese
*Flow with whatever may happen and let your mind
be free; stay centered by accepting
whatever you are doing. This is the ultimate.*
— Zhuang Zhou

CHANG-HO   [chang-hoh]

MEANING: good and brightly shining • **USAGE:**
Korean: from Korean *chang* (shiny, bright) and *ho*
(goodness or broad)
*The fragrance of the deeds of good men spreads
to the ends of the earth, in all directions,
regardless of the wind.*
— Buddha, *The Dhammapada*
(tr. Ananda Maitreya)

CHANIEL   [khah-nee-EHL]

MEANING: grace of God • **USAGE:** Jewish
Be gracious unto me, O God, be gracious unto me.
— Psalm 57:2a (MT)

CHANNING   [CHAN-ing]

MEANING: channel, canal, waterway • **USAGE:**
English surname: from English *chanel*
*For rightly, every man is a channel
through which heaven floweth.*
— Ralph Waldo Emerson,
"Nominalist and Realist"

CHANOCH   [khah-NOHK]

MEANING: educated, trained, dedicated • **USAGE:**
Jewish: from Hebrew *hanokh*; symbolic name for
those born on Hanukah
*Wisdom will enter your mind and knowledge
will delight you.*
— Proverbs 2:10 (JPS)

CHARLES   *[charlz (English), sharl (French)]*

MEANING: one who is free, man, adult • USAGE:
English and French: from English *ceorl* (freeman,
peasant); or from German *karl* (full-grown man,
adult)

> *Keep your soul free. What matters most in life*
> *is not knowledge, but character.*
> — Antonin G. Sertillanges, *The Intellectual Life*

CHARLIE, CHARLEY   *[CHAR-lee]*

MEANING: one who is free, man, adult • USAGE:
English form of Charles (*see* Charles)

> *Peace and freedom walk together.*
> — John F. Kennedy (address of June 10, 1963)

CHARLTON   *[CHARL-ton]*

MEANING: town of freeman • USAGE: English
surname: from English *ceorl* (freeman, peasant) and
tun (town, village)

> *Live as free men.*
> — 1 Peter 2:16a (NIV)

CHASE   *[chays]*

MEANING: hunter, pursuer, seeker • USAGE:
English: from English *chasen* (to hunt)

> *Pursue a righteous life — a life of wonder,*
> *faith, love, steadiness, courtesy.*
> — 1 Timothy 6:11 (MSG)

CHASID   *[khah-SEED]*

MEANING: pious, righteous, devout • USAGE:
Jewish

> *The work of righteousness shall be peace; and the effect*
> *of righteousness quietness and confidence for ever.*
> — Isaiah 32:17 (MT)

CHATAN   *[chah-tahn]*

MEANING: hawk • USAGE: Amerind: Sioux

> *You have noticed that everything an Indian does is in*
> *a circle, and that is because the Power of the World*
> *always works in circles.... Birds make their nest in*
> *circles, for theirs is the same religion as ours.*
> — Wallace Black Elk

CHAUNCEY   *[CHAHN-see]*

MEANING: keeper of records, scribe • USAGE:
English surname: possibly from French *chancelier*

> *Has he not a calling in his character?*
> *Each man has his own vocation. The talent is the call.*
> — Ralph Waldo Emerson, "Spiritual Laws"

CHAYTON   *[chay-tahn]*

MEANING: falcon • USAGE: Amerind: Sioux

> *For the Lakota...birds, insects, and animals*
> *filled the world with knowledge that defied*
> *the comprehension of man.*
> — Luther Standing Bear, *Land of the Spotted Eagle*

CHAZ   *[chaz]*

MEANING: one who is free, man, adult • USAGE:
English form of Charles (*see* Charles)

> *Resolve, and thou art free.*
> — Henry Wadsworth Longfellow,
> "The Masque of Pandora"

CHE   *[chay]*

MEANING: God will add, God will increase •
USAGE: Spanish form of José, from Hebrew
ya'saph (Yahweh will add); also Argentinian
expression meaning "hey" or "wow"

> *God will...increase the results of your good works.*
> — 2 Corinthians 9:10b (NIRV)

CHENG   *[cheng]*

MEANING: successful, sincere • USAGE: Chinese

> *He who attains to sincerity is he who chooses*
> *the good, and firmly holds it fast.*
> — Confucius, *The Analects* (tr. James Legge)

C

CHEROKEE   [cher-oh-kee]

MEANING: principal people; American Indian tribe
• USAGE: Amerind: Anglicization of Cherokee
Tsalagi (principal people)

I am Cherokee and it's the
proudest little possession I ever hope to have.
— Will Rogers

CHESTER   [CHES-ter]

MEANING: camp, fortification • USAGE: English
surname: from Latin *castra*

The Lord is my rock, my fortress.
— Psalm 18:2a (NLT)

CHET   [chet]

MEANING: camp, fortification • USAGE: English
form of Chester (*see* Chester)

The Lord's angel camps around the Lord's
loyal followers and delivers them.
— Psalm 34:7 (NEB)

CHEVY   [CHEH-vee]

MEANING: knight, horseman • USAGE: English:
from French *chevalier*

Confidence…thrives only on honesty, on honor,
on the sacredness of obligations, on faithful protection,
on unselfish performance; without them it cannot live.
— Franklin D. Roosevelt

CHIBALE   [chee-bah-leh]

MEANING: kinship • USAGE: African: Ngoni of
Malawi

You cannot pick up a pebble with one finger.
— Malawi proverb

CHICO   [CHEE-koh]

MEANING: one who is free, native of France, a
Franc, spearman, small, little • USAGE: Spanish
form of Francisco, from Latin *Franciscus* (a

Frenchman), from French *franc* (free, freeman),
or from German *franco* (spear used by Franks, a
Germanic tribe); or from Spanish *chico* (small, little)

Proclaim liberty throughout all the land
unto all the inhabitants thereof.
— Leviticus 25:10b (KJ21)

CHIMELU   [chee-meh-loo]

MEANING: made by God • USAGE: African:
Igbo of Nigeria; Chi is the Igbo personal god who
remains with a person from conception to death

God! I am in your hands!
— Ibgo of Nigeria proverb

CHINELO   [chee-neh-loh]

MEANING: thought of God • USAGE: African:
Igbo of Nigeria (*see* Chimelu)

Man looks only on the outside of things
while God looks into the very heart.
— Nigerian proverb

CHINUA   [chee-noo-ah]

MEANING: blessings of God • USAGE: African:
Igbo of Nigeria (*see* Chimelu)

When you stand with the blessings of your mother
and God, it matters not who stands against you.
— Nigerian proverb

CHIP   [chip]

MEANING: one who is free, man, adult, chip of
wood • USAGE: English form of Charles (*see*
Charles); or from Dutch *kip* (small strip of wood)

If you want to do right and obey the Lord,
follow Abraham's example.
He was the rock from which you were chipped.
— Isaiah 51:1 (CEV)

CHIRAM   [KHIE-rahm]

MEANING: great, noble, exalted • USAGE: Jewish:
from Hebrew *ahiram*

C

You have granted me the shield of Your protection
and Your providence has made me great.
— 2 Samuel 22:36 (JPS)

CHRIS   *[kris (English), krees (Scandinavian)]*

MEANING: follower of Christ, Christian, bearer of Christ • **USAGE:** English and Scandinavian form of Christian (*see* Christian); or English form of Christopher (*see* Christopher)

No Christian can be a pessimist, for Christianity is
a system of radical optimism.
— William Ralph Inge

CHRISTER   *[KREES-ter]*

MEANING: follower of Christ, Christian, bearer of Christ • **USAGE:** Scandinavian form of Christian (*see* Christian)

If Christ is in you, then the Spirit gives you life.
— Romans 8:10b (NCV)

CHRISTIAN   *[KRIS-chen (English),*
krees-TYAHN (French),
kris-TEE-ahn (German, Scandinavian)]

MEANING: follower of Christ, Christian • **USAGE:** English, French, German, and Scandinavian form of *Christianus,* from Greek *christianos*

To be like Christ is to be a Christian.
— William Penn

CHRISTIANO   *[krees-tee-AH-noh]*

MEANING: follower of Christ, Christian • **USAGE:** Greek (*see* Christian)

We are God's workmanship,
created in Christ Jesus to do good works,
which God prepared in advance for us to do.
— Ephesians 2:10 (NIV)

CHRISTOPHER   *[KRIS-toh-fer]*

MEANING: follower of Christ, Christian, bearer of Christ • **USAGE:** English form of *Christophoros,*

from Greek *Christos* (Christ, the anointed one) and *pherein* (to bear, to bring)

Christ has no body now on earth but yours,
no hands but yours, no feet but yours. Yours are the
eyes through which is to look out Christ's compassion to
the world; Yours are the feet with which he is
to go about doing good; Yours are the hands
with which he is to bless men now.
— Teresa of Avila

CHRISTOPHOROS   *[krees-TOH-foh-rohs]*

MEANING: follower of Christ, Christian, bearer of Christ • **USAGE:** Italian form of Christopher (*see* Christopher)

Neither death, nor life, nor angels, nor principalities,
nor things present, nor things to come, nor powers,
nor height, nor depth, nor any other created things,
shall be able to separate us from the love of God,
which is in Christ Jesus.
— Romans 8:38–39 (NASB)

CHUCK   *[chuk]*

MEANING: one who is free, man, adult • **USAGE:** English form of Charles, from English *ceorl* (freeman, peasant); or from German *karl* (full-grown man, adult)

Circumstance does not make a man,
it reveals him to himself.
— James Allen, *As a Man Thinketh*

CIAN   *[KEE-an]*

MEANING: ancient, distant past, enduring • **USAGE:** Irish: from Gaelic *cian*

For by Wisdom your days will be many,
and years will be added to your life.
— Proverbs 9:11 (HCSB)

CIANAN   *[KEE-nan]*

MEANING: little ancient one, enduring • **USAGE:** Irish: from Gaelic *cian* and diminutive *-an*

Endurance is nobler than strength.
— John Ruskin,
"The Influence of Imagination in Architecture"

CIAR   [keer]

MEANING: dark, black, dark-haired • **USAGE:**
Irish: from Gaelic *ciar*
What visions in the dark of light!
— Samuel Beckett, *Company*

CIARAN, KIERAN   [KEE-ran]

MEANING: dark, black, dark-haired • **USAGE:**
Irish (*see* Ciar)
*The Lord says...I will give you treasures hidden
in the darkness — secret riches.*
— Isaiah 45:1–3a (NLT)

CILLIAN   [KIL-yan]

MEANING: warrior, church, woods, forest, holly •
USAGE: Irish: from Gaelic *ceallach* (war, warlike),
cill (church), or *coill* (woods, forest); or from Welsh
celyn (holly)
The Lord is with you, you mighty man of valor!
— Judges 6:12b (NKJV)

CIRILLO   [see-REE-loh]

MEANING: lord, master • **USAGE:** Italian form of
Cyril, from Greek *kyrios*
The hand of the diligent shall bear rule.
— Proverbs 12:24a (ASV)

CIRINO   [see-REE-noh]

MEANING: lord, master, like the sun, farsighted •
USAGE: Italian and Spanish form of Cyrus, from
Greek *kyrios* (lord, master); possibly from Persian
khur (sun) or *kurush* (farsighted)
*Be praised, my Lord, for all your creatures, and
first for brother sun, who makes the day bright and
luminous. And he is beautiful and radiant with great
splendor, he is the image of you, Most High.*
— Francis of Assisi, "Canticle of the Sun"

CISCO   [SEES-koh]

MEANING: one who is free, native of France,
a Franc, spearman • **USAGE:** Spanish form of
Francisco, from Latin *Franciscus* (a Frenchman);
from French *franc* (free, freeman); or from German
franco (spear used by Franks, a Germanic tribe)
*The Lord is the Spirit; and where the Spirit
of the Lord is, there is liberty.*
— 2 Corinthians 3:17 (NASB)

CLANCY   [KLAN-see]

MEANING: red warrior, redheaded warrior •
USAGE: Irish form of surname *Mac Fhlannchaidh*,
from Gaelic *flann* (red) and *cath* (battle, war)
*Be watchful, stand firm in your faith,
be courageous, be strong.*
— 1 Corinthians 16:13 (RSV)

CLARENCE   [KLAYR-ens]

MEANING: clear, transparent • **USAGE:** English:
from Latin *clarus*
*Simplicity, clarity, singleness: These are the attributes
that give our lives power and vividness and joy.*
— Richard Holloway

CLARK   [klark]

MEANING: clerk, cleric, clergyman, one
committed to spiritual practice • **USAGE:** English
surname: from English *clerc*
To be spiritually minded is life and peace.
— Romans 8:6b (NKJV)

CLAUDE, CLAUD   [klahd]

MEANING: lame, limping • **USAGE:** French and
English form of *Claudius*, from Latin *claudus*
*When you walk, your steps will not be hampered,
and when you run, you will not stumble.
Hold on to instruction, do not let it go;
protect it, because it is your life.*
— Proverbs 4:12–13 (NEB)

CLAUDIO [*KLAH-dee-oh*]

MEANING: lame, limping • **USAGE:** Italian and Spanish form of *Claudius* (*see* Claude)

> *The Lord is your protector,*
> *and he won't go to sleep or let you stumble.*
> — Psalm 121:3 (CEV)

CLAUS [*klows*]

MEANING: victory of the people, successful, triumphant • **USAGE:** German and Scandinavian form of Nikolaus, from Greek *nike* (victory) and *laos* (people)

> *Anyone who gives a lot will succeed.*
> *Anyone who renews others will be renewed.*
> — Proverbs 11:25 (NIRV)

CLAY [*klay*]

MEANING: clay, clay town • **USAGE:** English form of Clayton (*see* Clayton)

> *O Lord, you are our Father. We are the clay, and you*
> *are the potter. We all are formed by your hand.*
> — Isaiah 64:8 (NLT)

CLAYTON [*KLAY-ton*]

MEANING: clay town, clay village • **USAGE:** English surname: from English *clæg* (clay) and *tun* (town, village)

> *Fashioned from the earth, we are souls in clay form.*
> *We need to remain in rhythm*
> *with our inner clay voice and longing.*
> — John O'Donohue, *Anam Cara*

CLEM [*klem*]

MEANING: clement, mild, gentle, merciful • **USAGE:** English form of Clement (*see* Clement)

> *Pursue justice, godliness, faith,*
> *charity, patience, mildness.*
> — 1 Timothy 6:11b (DR)

CLEMENT [*KLEM-ent*]

MEANING: clement, mild, gentle, merciful • **USAGE:** English: from Latin *clemens*

> *Strong men can always afford to be gentle.*
> — Elbert Hubbard, "Courtesy as an Asset"

CLEMENTE [*klay-MEN-tay*]

MEANING: clement, mild, gentle, merciful • **USAGE:** Spanish, Italian, and Portuguese form of Clement (*see* Clement)

> *The merciful man does good to his own soul.*
> — Proverbs 11:17a (WEB)

CLETUS, CLETIS [*KLEE-tus*]

MEANING: invocator, petitioner • **USAGE:** English form of *Anacletus*, from Greek *anakletos* (invoked, called upon)

> *Ask, and it will be given to you;*
> *seek, and you will find; knock,*
> *and it will be opened to you.*
> — Luke 11:9 (NKJV)

CLIFF [*klif*]

MEANING: ford by a cliff, cliff town, riverbank village • **USAGE:** English form of Clifford (*see* Clifford) or of Clifton (*see* Clifton)

> *Those who are honest and fair…*
> *these are the ones who will dwell on high.*
> — Isaiah 33:15 (NLT)

CLIFFORD [*KLIF-ord*]

MEANING: ford by a cliff • **USAGE:** English surname: from English *clif* (cliff, slope, steep embankment) and *ford* (a river crossing)

> *Thus says the Lord…*
> *when you pass through the waters,*
> *I will be with you.*
> — Isaiah 43:1–2a (NASB)

C

CLIFTON   [KLIF-ton]

MEANING: cliff town, riverbank village • **USAGE:** English surname: from English *clif* (cliff, riverbank) and *tun* (town, village)

> *You are the light of the world.*
> *A city located on a hill cannot be hidden.*
> — Matthew 5:14 (NEB)

CLINT   [klint]

MEANING: cliff town, enclosure, fence, town on the River Glyme • **USAGE:** English form of Clinton (*see* Clinton)

> *He who walks righteously and speaks what is right…*
> *this is the man who will dwell on the heights.*
> — Isaiah 33:15–16a (NIV)

CLINTON   [KLIN-ton]

MEANING: cliff town, enclosure, fence, town on the River Glyme • **USAGE:** English: from English *clif* (cliff, riverbank) and *tun* (town, village); from German *glinde* (enclosure, fence) and English *tun* (town, village); or meaning "town on the River Glyme"

> *Our peace shall stand as firm as rocky mountains.*
> — William Shakespeare, *Henry IV, Part II*

CLIVE   [kliev]

MEANING: cliff, rock face, riverbank • **USAGE:** English surname: from English *clif* (cliff, slope, riverbank)

> *God is bedrock under my feet.*
> — Psalm 18:2b (MSG)

CLYDE   [klied]

MEANING: snug, cozy, muddy, Scottish river • **USAGE:** Welsh, Scottish, and English: from Welsh *clyd* (snug); or from Scotch Gaelic *clodach* (muddy); river in Scotland

> *Place yourself in the middle of the stream*
> *of power and wisdom which animates all whom it*
> *floats, and you are without effort impelled to truth,*
> *to right, and a perfect contentment.*
> — Ralph Waldo Emerson, "Spiritual Laws"

COBY   [KOH-bee]

MEANING: replace, change, transform, successor • **USAGE:** English form of Jacob, from Hebrew *ya'aqobh* (one that takes by the heel, replace with another)

> *May the name of the God of Jacob defend you.…*
> *May He grant you according to your heart's desire,*
> *and fulfill all your plans.*
> — Psalm 20:1b–4 (NKJV)

COCHISE   [koh-chees]

MEANING: great chief, hardwood • **USAGE:** Amerind: Apache

> *I was going around the world with the clouds*
> *and the air when God spoke to my thought*
> *and told me to…be at peace with all.*
> — Cochise

CODY   [KOH-dee]

MEANING: helper, aide, helpful • **USAGE:** Irish and English: from Gaelic *cuidightheach*

> *The man who gives much will have much,*
> *and he who helps others will be helped himself.*
> — Proverbs 11:25 (NLV)

COINNEACH   [KIN-uk]

MEANING: handsome, attractive, good • **USAGE:** Irish and Scottish: from Gaelic *caoin*

> *You are so handsome, my love!*
> *So charming!*
> — Song of Songs 1:16a (NIRV)

COLBY   *[KOL-bee]*

MEANING: coal town • **USAGE:** English surname: from Norse *kol* (coal) and *byr* (town)

Your richest veins don't lie nearest the surface.
— Henry David Thoreau (letter of March 17, 1838)

COLE   *[kohl]*

MEANING: victory of the people, victorious, triumphant, coal-black, black-haired • **USAGE:** English form of Nicholas, from Greek *nike* (victory) and *laos* (people); or from English *col* (coal, coal-black)

The making of friends, who are real friends,
is the best token we have of a man's success in life.
— Edward Everett Hale

COLEY   *[KOH-lee]*

MEANING: victory of the people, victorious, triumphant, coal-black, black-haired • **USAGE:** American form of Cole (*see* Cole)

Expect victory and you make victory.
— Preston Bradley

COLIN, COLLIN   *[KAH-len]*

MEANING: pup, cub, young one, victory of the people, successful, triumphant, high, chieftain • **USAGE:** English and Irish: English form of *Cailean*, from Gaelic *cuilen* (pup, cub, whelp); English form of Nicolas, from Greek *nike* (victory) and *laos* (people); or from Irish Gaelic *coll* (high, chieftain)

Youth, full of grace, force, fascination.
— Walt Whitman, "Youth, Maturity, Age"

COLLEN   *[KAH-len]*

MEANING: hazel tree • **USAGE:** Welsh: from Welsh *collen*

He is like a tree planted by streams of water,
that yields its fruit in its season, and its leaf does not
wither. In all that he does, he prospers.
— Psalm 1:3 (RSV)

COLM   *[kolm, KOL-um]*

MEANING: dove, dove-like • **USAGE:** Irish: from Latin *columba* (dove); reference to St. Columba, who helped convert Scotland to Christianity

Deep peace, a soft white dove to you…
Deep peace, deep peace!
— Fiona MacLeod, "Invocation of Peace"

COLT   *[kolt]*

MEANING: colt, young horse • **USAGE:** American: from English *colt*

I'm well and strong and young.
— Clara Barton

CONALL   *[KON-al]*

MEANING: wise, intelligent, hound, dog, high, mighty • **USAGE:** Irish: from Gaelic *conn* (wise, intelligent) or *con, cu* (hound, dog)

He who gets wisdom loves his own soul;
he who cherishes understanding prospers.
— Proverbs 19:8 (NIV)

CONAN   *[KOH-nan]*

MEANING: little wise one, little wolfhound • **USAGE:** Irish: from Gaelic *conn* (wise, intelligent), *con, cu* (hound, dog) and diminutive *-an*; or from Gaelic *coanan* (little wolfhound)

Those who are wise shall shine
like the brightness of the sky above.
— Daniel 12:3a (ESV)

CONG   *[kong]*

MEANING: intelligent • **USAGE:** Chinese

When happiness comes,
the mind grows more intelligent.
— Chinese proverb (tr. William Scarborough)

C

C

CONLEY　　　　　　　　　　[KON-lee]

MEANING: hound of valor, courageous hound
• USAGE: English form of Irish surname
O'Conghaile, from Gaelic *con* (hound, dog) and *gal*
(valor, courage)

> *It often requires more courage to dare*
> *to do right than to fear to do wrong.*
> — Abraham Lincoln

CONN　　　　　　　　　　　[kon]

MEANING: wise, intelligent, hound, dog • USAGE:
Irish: from Gaelic *conn* (wise, intelligent) or *con, cu*
(hound, dog)

> *Wisdom will enter into your heart.*
> *Knowledge will be pleasant to your soul.*
> — Proverbs 2:10 (WEB)

CONOR, CONNOR, CONNER

　　　　　　　　　　　　　　[KON-er]

MEANING: hound lover, hound nobleman, one
who loves dogs • USAGE: Irish surname: form of
Conchobar, from Gaelic *con, cu* (hound, dog) and
cobar (desiring), or *conaire* (hound nobleman)

> *The noble man makes noble plans,*
> *and by noble deeds he stands.*
> — Isaiah 32:8 (NIV)

CONRAD　　　　　　　　　　[KON-rad]

MEANING: bold counsel, wise adviser • USAGE:
English form of *Kuonrat,* from German *kuon* (bold,
courageous) and *rad* (advice, counsel)

> *Speak boldly and speak truly.*
> — John Fletcher, *Wit Without Money*

CONSTANTINE　　　　[kohn-stahn-TEEN]

MEANING: constant, steadfast • USAGE: English
form of *Constantinus,* from Latin *constans*

> *If a man constantly aspires is he not elevated?*
> — Henry David Thoreau

CONSTANTINO　　[kohn-stahn-TEEN-oh]

MEANING: constant, steadfast • USAGE: Italian
form of *Constantinus* (*see* Constantine)

> *His heart is steadfast.*
> — Psalm 112:7b (RSV)

CONWAY　　　　　　　　　　[KON-way]

MEANING: hound of the plains, field dog • USAGE:
Irish form of surname *Cumhaighe,* from Gaelic *con,
cu* (hound, dog) and *mhaigh* (plain, field)

> *Let the fields and everything in them rejoice.*
> — 1 Chronicles 16:32b (NCV)

COOPER　　　　　　　　　　[KOO-per]

MEANING: barrel maker • USAGE: English
surname: from German *kupe* (cask, barrel)

> *Examine everything carefully;*
> *hold fast to that which is good.*
> — 1 Thessalonians 5:21 (NASB)

CORBIN　　　　　　　　　　[KOR-bin]

MEANING: raven • USAGE: English: from French
corbeau

> *Look at the ravens. They don't plant or harvest or store*
> *food in barns, for God feeds them. And you are far*
> *more valuable to him than any birds!*
> — Luke 12:24 (NLT)

CORDELL　　　　　　　　　　[kor-DEL]

MEANING: cord maker, one who makes ropes, one
who tows or pulls with a rope • USAGE: English:
from French *corde* (rope); or from French *cordelle*
(to tow with a rope); occupational name for a rope
maker

> *A three-strand cord is not quickly broken.*
> — Ecclesiastes 4:12b (KJ21)

COREY, CORY   *[KOR-ee]*

MEANING: hollow, cauldron, God's peace •
USAGE: Irish: from Gaelic *coire* (cauldron, a
hollow); or Irish form of Godfrey, from German
gott (God) and *frid* (peace)

> *Peace is the well from which the stream of joy runs.*
> — Irish proverb

CORIN   *[koh-RIN]*

MEANING: spear • **USAGE:** French: from Latin
quiris (spear); mythological god of war later
identified with Romulus

> *As iron sharpens iron, so one man sharpens another.*
> — Proverbs 27:17 (NIV)

CORMAC   *[KOR-mak]*

MEANING: son of the raven • **USAGE:** English:
from French *corbeau*

> *The Lord bless you, my son!*
> — Judges 17:2b (NCV)

CORNEL, CORNELL   *[kor-NEL]*

MEANING: horn, horn-bearer • **USAGE:** English
form of Cornelius (*see* Cornelius)

> *If you don't live it, it won't come out your horn.*
> — Charlie Parker

CORNELIUS   *[kor-NEE-lee-us]*

MEANING: horn, horn-bearer • **USAGE:** English
form of Roman family name, from Latin *cornu*

> *The Lord is my rock and my fortress and my deliverer;*
> *my God, my rock, in whom I take refuge; my shield*
> *and the horn of my salvation, my stronghold.*
> — Psalm 18:2 (ESV)

CORRADO   *[koh-RAH-doh]*

MEANING: bold counsel, wise adviser • **USAGE:**
Italian form of Conrad, from German *kuon* (bold,
courageous) and *rad* (advice, counsel)

> *Dare to be wise.*
> — Horace, "Epistle XVI" (tr. John Benson Rose)

COSIMO   *[KOH-ʒee-moh]*

MEANING: cosmos, order, harmony, the universe •
USAGE: Italian form of Kosmas (*see* Cosmo)

> *Constantly regard the universe as one living being,*
> *having one substance and one soul.*
> — Marcus Aurelius, *The Meditations*
> (tr. George Long)

COSMO   *[KAHZ-moh]*

MEANING: cosmos, order, harmony, the universe
• **USAGE:** English form of Kosmas, from Greek
kosmos (order, harmony, the universe)

> *We and the cosmos are one.*
> — D. H. Lawrence, *Apocalypse*

COSTELLO   *[kos-TEL-oh]*

MEANING: deerlike • **USAGE:** English surname:
from Gaelic *Mac Oisdealbhaigh*, from Gaelic *os*
(deer) and *dealbhach* (resembling)

> *He [God] makes my feet like hinds' feet,*
> *and sets me upon my high places.*
> — Psalm 18:33 (NASB)

COURTLAND   *[KORT-land]*

MEANING: courteous, polite, courtly, court dweller
• **USAGE:** English: from French *curteis* (courteous,
polite behavior) or *cort* (court, courtyard)

> *All doors open to courtesy.*
> — Thomas Fuller, *Gnomologia*

COURTNEY   *[KORT-nee]*

MEANING: courteous, polite, court dweller,
short nose • **USAGE:** English: from French *curteis*
(courteous, polite behavior), *cort* (court, courtyard),
or *court nez* (short nose)

> *The greater man, the greater courtesy.*
> — Alfred Tennyson, *Idylls of the King*

C

C

COYT [koit]

MEANING: pure one, unblemished • **USAGE:** Irish: from Greek *katharos* (pure)

He who has clean hands and a pure heart…
will receive blessing from the Lord.
— Psalm 24:4–5 (ESV)

CRAIG [kryag]

MEANING: rugged rocks, rocky cliff, craggy rock • **USAGE:** Scottish and English: from Gaelic *carraig* (rock) or *creag* (crag, cliff)

He who walks righteously and speaks with sincerity…
will dwell on the heights.
— Isaiah 33:15–16 (NASB)

CRISÓFORO [kree-SOH-foh-roh]

MEANING: follower of Christ, Christian, bearer of Christ • **USAGE:** Spanish form of Christopher (*see* Cristobal)

I can do all things through Christ
which strengtheneth me.
— Philippians 4:13 (KJV)

CRISTIÁN [krees-tee-AHN]

MEANING: follower of Christ, Christian • **USAGE:** Spanish form of Christian (*see* Cristo)

The peace of God, which transcends all understanding,
will guard your hearts and your minds in Christ Jesus.
— Philippians 4:7 (NIV)

CRISTIANO [krees-tee-AH-noh]

MEANING: Christ, the anointed one • **USAGE:** Italian form of Christian (*see* Cristo)

For we are his workmanship, created in Christ Jesus
for good works, which God afore prepared
that we should walk in them.
— Ephesians 2:10 (ASV)

CRISTO [KREES-toh]

MEANING: Christ, the anointed one • **USAGE:** Spanish: from Greek *Christos* (Christ, the anointed) and *chrein* (to anoint)

If any man be in Christ, he is a new creature: old things
are passed away; behold, all things are become new.
— 2 Corinthians 5:17 (KJV)

CRISTOBAL [krees-TOH-bahl]

MEANING: follower of Christ, Christian, bearer of Christ • **USAGE:** Spanish form of Christopher, from Greek *Christos* (Christ, the anointed one) and *pherein* (to bear, to bring)

I pray that… Christ will live in your hearts because of
your faith. Stand firm and be deeply rooted in his love.
— Ephesians 3:16–18 (CEV)

CRISTOFORO [krees-TOH-foh-roh]

MEANING: follower of Christ, Christian, bearer of Christ • **USAGE:** Italian form of Christopher (*see* Cristobal)

I can do all things because Christ gives me strength.
— Philippians 4:13 (NLV)

CROSBY [KROZ-bee]

MEANING: town by the cross • **USAGE:** English surname: from Norse *kross* (cross, crucifix) and *býr* (town, village)

My [God's] people will abide in a peaceful habitation,
in secure dwellings, and in quiet resting places.
— Isaiah 32:18 (ESV)

CUBA [KOO-bah, KWOO-bah]

MEANING: abundant fertile land, country of Cuba • **USAGE:** English and Spanish: from Taino *cubanacan* (where fertile land is abundant); name of country

That country is the fairest
which is inhabited by the noblest minds.
— Ralph Waldo Emerson, "Heroism"

CURT   [kurt]

MEANING: courteous, polite, courtly, court dweller
• **USAGE:** English form of Curtis (*see* Curtis)

> *For manners are not idle, but the fruit /*
> *Of loyal nature and of noble mind.*
> — Alfred Tennyson, *Idylls of the King*

CURTIS   [KUR-tis]

MEANING: courteous, polite, courtly, court dweller
• **USAGE:** English surname: from French *curteis*
(courteous, polite behavior) or *cort* (court)

> *Kind words can be short and easy to speak*
> *but their echoes are truly endless.*
> — Mother Teresa

CY   [sie]

MEANING: lord, master, like the sun, farsighted •
USAGE: English form of Cyrus (*see* Cyrus) or of
Cyril (*see* Cyril)

> *For man is man and master of his fate.*
> — Alfred Tennyson, *Idylls of the King*

CYRIL   [SEER-el]

MEANING: lord, master, ruler • **USAGE:** English,
Czech, and French form of *Kyrillos*, from Greek
kyrios

> *The gentleman is a man of truth, lord of his own*
> *actions, and expressing that lordship in his behavior.*
> — Ralph Waldo Emerson, "Manners"

CYRUS   [SIE-rus]

MEANING: lord, master, like the sun, farsighted •
USAGE: English form of *Kyros*, from Greek *kyrios*
(lord, master); or possibly from Persian *khur* (sun)
or *kûrush* (farsighted)

> *The light of the sun is but the shadow of love…*
> *it can make a paradise within which will dispense*
> *with a paradise without.*
> — Henry David Thoreau,
> "Paradise (to Be) Regained"

D

DABIR, DABEER   [dah-BEER]

MEANING: root, origin • **USAGE:** Muslim

> *Thy Love is rooted in the depth of my heart.*
> — Hazrat Inayat Khan, *The Gayan*

DACK   [dag, dahg]

MEANING: day, badger • **USAGE:** English form of
surname *Dæcca*, from English *dæg* (day) or from
German *dachs* (badger)

> *This is the day which the Lord hath made;*
> *we will rejoice and be glad in it.*
> — Psalm 118:24 (KJV)

DAFYDD   [DAY-vith]

MEANING: beloved, loved • **USAGE:** Welsh form
of David, from Hebrew *dawidh*

> *Beloved, I pray that in all respects you may prosper*
> *and be in good health, just as your soul prospers.*
> — 3 John 1:2 (NASB)

DAG   [dahg]

MEANING: day, daylight • **USAGE:** Scandinavian:
from Norse *dagr*

> *The path of the just, as a shining light,*
> *goeth forwards and increaseth even to perfect day.*
> — Proverbs 4:18 (DR)

DAGAN   [dah-GAHN]

MEANING: grain, corn • **USAGE:** Jewish: symbolic
for those born on Shavuot, known as the Feast of
the Harvest

> *May God give you of the dew of heaven*
> *and the fat of the earth,*
> *abundance of new grain and wine.*
> — Genesis 27:28 (JPS)

D

DAI [day]

MEANING: shining, beloved • **USAGE:** Welsh: from Welsh *dei* (to shine); or form of David, from Hebrew *dawidh* (beloved)

Beloved, let us love one another, for love is of God; and everyone who loves is born of God and knows God.
— 1 John 4:7 (NKJV)

DAIKI [dah-ee-kee]

MEANING: great glory, great noble, great tree • **USAGE:** Japanese: from Japanese *dai* (large, great) and *ki* (glory, noble, tree)

One is called noble,
because one does not injure living beings.
— Buddha, *The Dhammapada*
(tr. Eknath Easwaran)

DAISUKE [dye-soo-kee]

MEANING: great helper • **USAGE:** Japanese: from Japanese *dai* (great, large) and *suke* (help)

Truly help others, / do what is / beneficial, / correct, / honest.
— Shi Wuling, *Path to Peace*

DAKOTA [dah-KOH-tah]

MEANING: friend, ally • **USAGE:** American: from Amerind, Sioux

Friendship is held to be the severest test of character....
To have a friend, and to be true under any and all trials, is the mark of a man!
— Ohiyesa, *The Soul of the Indian*

DAKTARI [DAHK-tah-ree]

MEANING: doctor, healer • **USAGE:** African: Swahili of Kenya/Tanzania

God is the real physician.
— Swahili proverb

DALE [dayl]

MEANING: dale, glen, small valley • **USAGE:** English: from English *dæl*

Take almost any path you please, and ten to one it carries you down in a dale, and leaves you there by a pool in the stream. There is magic in it.
— Herman Melville, *Moby Dick*

DALEN [DAY-len]

MEANING: calm, peaceful, of the sea, oceanic • **USAGE:** American: possibly a form of Galen, from Greek *galene* (calm, peaceful), or possibly a form of Dylan, from Welsh *dy* (great, large) and *llanw* (sea, ocean)

Remain calm. Be kind.
— Colin Powell

DALEY, DALY [DAY-lee]

MEANING: gathering, assembly, attendee of meetings • **USAGE:** Irish and English surname: from Gaelic *dal* (assembly, gathering) or *dalach* (attender of meetings)

Love and faithfulness meet together.
— Psalm 85:10a (NIV)

DALIL [dah-leel]

MEANING: guide, leader • **USAGE:** Muslim

The one who carries the standard must also know the way.
— Arabic proverb

DALLAS [DAL-es]

MEANING: house in the dale, valley house • **USAGE:** Scottish and English surname: from Gaelic *dail* (dale, valley) and *fas* (dwelling, house)

Through wisdom is a house built, and by understanding it is established.
— Proverbs 24:3 (DT)

D

DAMIAN

[DAY-mee-en (English),
dah-mee-AHN (Polish)]

MEANING: tame, subdue, discipline • **USAGE:**
English and Polish form of *Damianos,* from Greek
damao (to tame)

No life ever grows great until it is
focused, dedicated, disciplined.
— Harry Emerson Fosdick

DAMIANO

[dah-mee-AH-noh]

MEANING: tame, subdue, discipline • **USAGE:**
Italian and Spanish form of Damian (*see* Damian)

God said unto them, Be fruitful, and multiply,
and replenish the earth, and subdue it.
— Genesis 1:28a (KJV)

DAMIEN

[DAH-mee-en (French),
DAY-mee-en (English)]

MEANING: tame, subdue, discipline • **USAGE:**
French and English form of Damian (*see* Damian)

What is man, that you think of him?
Or the son of man, that you care for him?
You made him a little lower than the angels.
You crowned him with glory and honor. You have
put all things in subjection under his feet.
— Hebrews 2:6b–7 (WEB)

DAMON, DAMAN

[DAY-mon]

MEANING: tame, subdue, discipline • **USAGE:**
English form of Damian (*see* Damian)

Self-discipline and self-control
are the beginnings of practical wisdom.
— Samuel Smiles, *Self-Help*

DAN

[dahn (Jewish), dan (English)]

MEANING: judge, God is my judge • **USAGE:**
Jewish and English: from Hebrew *dan* (to judge); or
English form of Daniel (*see* Daniel)

Dan shall judge his people,
as one of the tribes of Israel.
— Genesis 49:16 (MT)

DANA

[DAY-nah]

MEANING: brave, daring, poem, poet, God is my
judge, Dane • **USAGE:** English form of Daniel,
from Hebrew *dani'el* (God is my judge); from Irish
dana (brave, daring) or *dan* (poem); or from Norse
Danr (a Dane)

Dare to be true.
— George Herbert, "The Church Porch"

DANAN

[DAY-nan]

MEANING: brave, daring, poem, poet, God is my
judge, Dane • **USAGE:** American form of Dana (*see*
Dana)

The poet sings how the blood flows in his veins.
— Henry David Thoreau,
A Week on the Concord and Merrimack Rivers

DANE

[dayn]

MEANING: presiding official, dean, administrator,
valley, Dane • **USAGE:** English form of Dean,
from English *deen* (dean, presiding official) or *denu*
(valley); or from Norse *Danr* (a Dane)

By a man of understanding and knowledge,
right will be prolonged.
— Proverbs 28:2b (NKJV)

DANIEL

[dah-nee-EHL (Jewish),
DAN-yel (English), dahn-YEHL (French, Spanish),
DAHN-yehl (German, Scandinavian)]

MEANING: God is my judge • **USAGE:** Jewish,
English, French, German, Scandinavian, and
Spanish: from Hebrew *dani'el*

You shall not be partial in judgment: hear out low
and high alike. Fear no man, for judgment is God's.
— Deuteronomy 1:17a (JPS)

DANIIL

[dah-NEEL]

MEANING: God is my judge • **USAGE:** Russian
form of Daniel (*see* Daniel)

The Lord waits to be gracious to you, and therefore he
exalts himself to show mercy to you. For the Lord is a
God of justice; blessed are all those who wait for him.
— Isaiah 30:18 (ESV)

D

DANILO   *[dah-NEE-loh]*

MEANING: God is my judge • USAGE: Spanish and
Italian form of Daniel (*see* Daniel)
He loves righteousness and justice;
the earth is full of the steadfast love of the Lord.
— Psalm 33:5 (ESV)

DANO   *[DAH-noh]*

MEANING: God is my judge • USAGE: Czech form
of Daniel (*see* Daniel)
The Lord seeth not as man seeth;
for man looketh on the outward appearance,
but the Lord looketh on the heart.
— 1 Samuel 16:7b (KJV)

DANTE   *[DAHN-tay]*

MEANING: steadfast, faithful, enduring • USAGE:
Italian form of Durante, from Latin *durare* (to
endure)
Pursue righteousness, godliness, faithfulness, love,
endurance, and gentleness.
— 1 Timothy 6:11b (NEB)

DARAGH, DARRAH   *[DAH-rah]*

MEANING: black oak • USAGE: Irish form of
surname *O'Dubhdarach*, from Gaelic *dubh* (black,
dark) and *dair* (oak)
The lofty oak from a small acorn grows.
— Lewis Duncombe

DARBY   *[DAR-bee]*

MEANING: free from envy, without restriction,
freeman, deer town • USAGE: Irish and English
surname: Irish form of Diarmaid, from Gaelic *di*
(without) and *airmait* (envy, restriction); or English

form of *Derby*, from Norse *diur* (deer) and *býr*
(town, village)
Ah! Freedom is a noble thing!
— John Barbour, *The Brus*

DARCEL   *[dar-SEL]*

MEANING: dark-haired, man of Arcy • USAGE:
American: possibly a form of Darcy (*see* Darcy)
Just be what you are and speak from your guts
and heart — it's all a man has.
— Hubert Humphrey

DARCY   *[DAR-see]*

MEANING: dark-haired, man of Arcy, bear village
• USAGE: Irish and English surname: from Gaelic
dorchaidhe (dark-haired); or English form of French
surname *D'Arcy* (Arcy, France), from French *ars*
(bear) and *acum* (village, settlement)
Thou hast anointed my head with oil;
my cup runneth over.
— Psalm 23:5b (DT)

DARIAN   *[DAYR-ee-an]*

MEANING: to possess good, possesses a lot,
wealthy • USAGE: English form of Darius (*see*
Darius)
Taking the first step with a good thought,
the second with a good word, and the third
with a good deed, I entered Paradise.
— James Allen, *From Poverty to Power*

DARIO   *[DAH-ree-oh]*

MEANING: to possess good, possesses a lot,
wealthy • USAGE: Italian form of Darius (*see*
Darius)
A man of integrity, sincerity, and good-nature can
never be concealed, for his character is
wrought into his countenance.
— Marcus Aurelius,
The Meditations (tr. Jeremy Collier)

DARIUS   *[DAYR-ee-us]*

MEANING: to possess good, possesses a lot, wealthy • **USAGE:** English form of *Darayavahush*, from Persian *daraya* (to possess) and *vahu* (good)
*The inclination to goodness is
imprinted deeply in the nature of man.*
— Francis Bacon, "Of Goodness"

DARNELL   *[dar-NEL]*

MEANING: hidden nook, secret place • **USAGE:** English: from English *derne* (hidden, secret) and *halh* (nook, alcove)
*Behold, You desire truth in the inward parts, and in the
hidden part You will make me to know wisdom.*
— Psalm 51:6 (NKJV)

DAROLD   *[DAYR-old]*

MEANING: man of Airelle, dearly loved • **USAGE:** American: possibly a form of Darryl (*see* Darryl); or from English *dereling* (darling, dearly loved)
*Beloved, if God so loved us, we ought also to love
one another. No one has ever seen God at any time;
if we love one another, God abides in us,
and His love is perfected in us.*
— 1 John 4:11–12 (NASB)

DARREN, DAREN, DARIN, DARON   *[DAYR-un]*

MEANING: little oak tree, fruitful, bountiful • **USAGE:** Irish and English: from Gaelic *dair* (oak tree) and diminutive *-an*; or from Gaelic *dair* (fruitful, bountiful)
*He'll put down deep oak tree roots,
he'll become a forest of oaks!*
— Hosea 14:5 (MSG)

DARRYL, DARREL, DARRELL   *[DAYR-ul]*

MEANING: man of Airelle, open space • **USAGE:** English form of French surname *D'Airelle* (of Airelle, France), from French *arealis* (open space, threshing floor)

*Where there is an open mind,
there will always be a frontier.*
— Charles F. Kettering

DARSHAN   *[dar-SHAHN]*

MEANING: vision, the vision of God • **USAGE:** Hindu: from Sanskrit *darsha* (to see, to perceive)
*He through whom man sees, tastes, smells, hears, feels,
and enjoys, is the omniscient Lord. He, verily, is the
immortal Self. Knowing him, one knows all things.*
— Katha Upanishad

DARSHAN, DARSHAWN, DARSHON   *[dar-SHAHN]*

MEANING: God is gracious, God is giving • **USAGE:** American: possibly a form of Shawn, from Hebrew *y'hohanan* (Yahweh is gracious)
May grace and peace be yours in full measure.
— 2 Peter 1:2a (NEB)

DASHIEL   *[dah-SHEEL]*

MEANING: of heaven, heavenly • **USAGE:** English form of French surname *de Chiel*, of unknown origin; possibly from French *ciel* (sky, heaven)
The heavens are as deep as our aspirations are high.
— Henry David Thoreau (letter of May 2, 1848)

DATAN   *[dah-TAHN]*

MEANING: faith, law • **USAGE:** Jewish
*The law is not thrust upon man; it rests deep within
him, to waken when the call comes.*
— Martin Buber, "Teaching and Deed"

DAUD, DAWUD   *[dah-ood]*

MEANING: beloved, loved • **USAGE:** Muslim form of David (*see* David)
*The creation is as God's family; for its sustenance is
from Him: therefore the most beloved unto God is
the person who doeth good to God's family.*
— Hadith of the Prophet Muhammad

D

DAVE   [dayv]

MEANING: beloved, loved • USAGE: English form
of David (see David)

> May mercy, peace,
> and love be yours in abundance.
> — Jude 1:2 (NRSV)

DAVEN, DAVIN   [DAV-en]

MEANING: dark, black • USAGE: English: from
Irish Gaelic dubh

> When it is dark enough you can see the stars.
> — Charles Beard

DAVID   [dah-VEED (Jewish, French), DAY-vid (English), DAH-vid (German, Scandinavian), dah-VEET (Russian), dah-BEED (Spanish)]

MEANING: beloved, loved • USAGE: Jewish,
English, French, German, Russian, Spanish, and
Scandinavian: from Hebrew dawidh

> Eternal love I conceived for you then;
> therefore I continue My grace to you.
> — Jeremiah 31:3b (JPS)

DAVY, DAVEY   [DAY-vee]

MEANING: beloved, loved • USAGE: English form
of David (see David)

> Beloved, let us love one another,
> for love is of God, and every one that loveth is
> born of God and knoweth God.
> — 1 John 4:7 (KJ21)

DAWID   [dah-VEED]

MEANING: beloved, loved • USAGE: Polish form
of David (see David)

> The Lord said…you have found favor in my sight,
> and I know you by name.
> — Exodus 33:17b (NEB)

DAX   [daks]

MEANING: badger, French place-name • USAGE:
English: from German dachs (badger); or a town in
France

> Ask the animals, and they will teach you.
> — Job 12:7a (NIV)

DEAN   [deen]

MEANING: presiding official, dean, administrator,
valley • USAGE: English surname: from English
deen (dean, presiding official) or denu (valley)

> Administer true justice;
> show mercy and compassion to one another.
> — Zechariah 7:9b (NIV)

DECIMUS   [DES-ih-mus]

MEANING: ten, tenth • USAGE: American: from
Latin deci

> The tenth part…is the Lord's. It is holy to the Lord.
> — Leviticus 27:30 (NLV)

DECLAN   [DEK-lahn]

MEANING: full of goodness, fully good • USAGE:
Irish: from Gaelic deagh (good) and lan (full)

> We are here to add to the sum of human goodness.
> — Josephine Hart, Sin

DEKEL   [deh-KEHL]

MEANING: palm tree • USAGE: Jewish: symbolic
name for boys born on Sukkoth or on Tu b'Shvat

> The righteous bloom like a date-palm…
> planted in the house of the Lord,
> they shall flourish in the courts of our God.
> — Psalm 92:13–14 (JPS)

DEL   [del]

MEANING: of the king, dale, valley, shining valley,
bright dale • USAGE: English form of Delroy (see
Delroy) or of Delbert (see Delbert)

The valleys…shout for joy! They also sing.
— Psalm 65:13b (WEB)

DELANEY, DELANY [deh-LAY-nee]

MEANING: dark-haired challenger, trained warrior, soldier • USAGE: Irish and English form of Irish surname *Dubhshlaine*, from Gaelic *dubh* (dark, black) and *slan* (challenge); or from Gaelic *deagh-laoch* (trained warrior)

God didn't give us a spirit that makes us weak and fearful. He gave us a spirit that gives us power and love. It helps us control ourselves.
— 2 Timothy 1:7 (NIRV)

DELBERT [DEL-bert]

MEANING: shining valley, bright dale • USAGE: English: from English *dæl* (dale, valley) and German *beraht* (bright, shining)

*Come forth into the light of things, /
Let Nature be your teacher.*
— William Wordsworth, "The Tables Turned"

DELMAR [DEL-mahr]

MEANING: of the sea, ocean • USAGE: English: from Spanish *del mar*

*With every drop of water you drink,
every breath you take, you're connected to the sea.
No matter where on Earth you live.*
— Sylvia Earle, *The World Is Blue*

DELROY [DEL-roi]

MEANING: of the king • USAGE: English: from French *de roi*

*Seek first the kingdom of God and His righteousness,
and all these things shall be added to you.*
— Matthew 6:33 (NKJV)

DELWIN [DEL-wen]

MEANING: friend of the valley, valley friend • USAGE: English: from English *dæl* (dale, valley) and *wine* (friend)

*Trust in the Lord, and do good;
dwell in the land and befriend faithfulness.*
— Psalm 37:3 (ESV)

DEMETRIO [day-MAY-tree-oh]

MEANING: mother earth, earth lover, earthy • USAGE: Italian and Spanish masculine form of *Demeter*, from Greek *Da-mater* (mother earth), Greek goddess of agriculture and harvest

My substance was not hid from Thee when I was made in secret, and intricately wrought in the lowest parts of the earth. Thine eyes did see my substance, yet being imperfect; and in Thy book all my members were written, which in continuity were fashioned, when as yet there were none of them.
— Psalm 139:15–16 (KJ21)

DENIS [deh-NEE (French), DEH-nees (Russian)]

MEANING: celebrant, reveler, follower of Dionysus • USAGE: French and Russian form of Dennis (*see* Dennis)

There is nothing better for man than to eat, drink, and enjoy his work. I have seen that even this is from God's hand, because who can eat and who can enjoy life apart from Him?
— Ecclesiastes 2:24 (HCSB)

DENNIS [DEN-is (English), DAY-nis (German)]

MEANING: celebrant, reveler, follower of Dionysus • USAGE: English and German form of *Dionysus*, Greek god of wine and revelry

Celebrate the joy that God hath given us.
— William Shakespeare, *King Henry VI, Part I*

DENZEL [den-ZEL]

MEANING: sunny fort • USAGE: English place-name in Cornwall, England, possibly from English *din* (fort) and *sul* (sun)

*A man has no better thing under the sun,
than to eat, and to drink, and to be joyful.*
— Ecclesiastes 8:15 (WEB)

D

DEON   [DEE-on]

MEANING: celebrant, reveler, follower of
Dionysus • USAGE: English form of Dion (see
Dennis)

Life is meant to be a celebration…Wise is the person
who finds a reason to make every day a special one.
— Leo Buscaglia, *Bus 9 to Paradise*

DEREK, DERICK   [DEHR-ik]

MEANING: leader of the people • USAGE: German
and English form of *Thiudoreiks*, from German
thiuda (people, nation) and *rik* (rule, lead)

Leaders don't create followers,
they create more leaders.
— Tom Peters

DERMOT   [DER-mot]

MEANING: free from envy, without restriction,
freeman • USAGE: Irish form of Diarmaid, from
Gaelic *di* (without) and *airmait* (envy, restriction)

The good-natured and charitable who rejoice at the
good fortune of others, scarcely know what envy means.
— James Allen, *From Poverty to Power*

DERON   [deh-RON]

MEANING: ruling official, ruler of the valley •
USAGE: American combination of Dean and Ron
(see Dean and Ron)

You made him to rule over the works of Your hands;
You have put all things under his feet.
— Psalm 8:6 (NASB)

DERRY   [DER-ee]

MEANING: like an oak • USAGE: Irish: from Gaelic
daraigh

He will be like a tree planted by the streams of water,
that produces its fruit in its season,
whose leaf also does not wither.
Whatever he does shall prosper.
— Psalm 1:3 (WEB)

DES   [dez]

MEANING: man from south Munster in Ireland •
USAGE: English form of Desmond (see Desmond)

A wise man is strong,
and a man of knowledge increases power.
— Proverbs 24:5 (NASB)

DESI, DEZI   [DES-ee, DEZ-ee]

MEANING: desire, wish • USAGE: Spanish and
Italian form of Desiderio (see Desiderio)

Seek your happiness in the Lord,
and he will give you your heart's desire.
— Psalm 37:4 (GNT)

DESIDERIO   [day-say-DAYR-ee-oh]

MEANING: desire, wish • USAGE: Spanish and
Italian: from Latin *desiderium*

Whatever you wish that others would do to you,
do also to them, for this is the Law and the Prophets.
— Matthew 7:12 (ESV)

DESMOND   [DEZ-mond]

MEANING: man of south Munster in Ireland •
USAGE: Irish surname: from Gaelic *Deas-Mumhan*
(Southern Munster, Ireland)

Men of character are the conscience
of the society to which they belong.
— Ralph Waldo Emerson, "Character"

DESTON   [DEST-on]

MEANING: thunder stone, Thor's stone, destiny,
fate • USAGE: American: possibly a form of Dustin,
from *Thor* (Norse god of thunder) and Norse *steinn*
(stone); or possibly from French *destinée* (destiny,
fate)

The Lord said, "There is a place near me
where you may stand on a rock."
— Ezekiel 34:11 (NIV)

DETROIT [dee-TROYT]

MEANING: strait, channel • USAGE: American: from French *le detroit* (strait, refers to a strait of Lake Erie)

> *Man flows at once to God*
> *when the channel of purity is open.*
> — Henry David Thoreau, *Walden*

DEVIN, DEVAN, DEVON [DEV-an]

MEANING: poet, gift, courageous, fearless • USAGE: Irish and English: from Gaelic *damh* (poet), *dan* (gift), or *dana* (intrepid, courageous)

> *Either life entails courage, or it ceases to be life.*
> — E. M. Forster, *Pharos and Pharillon*

DEVIR, DVIR [deh-VEER]

MEANING: innermost room, holy place, sanctuary • USAGE: Jewish

> *A spirit carried me into the inner court, and lo,*
> *the Presence of the Lord filled the Temple.*
> — Ezekiel 43:5 (JPS)

DEX [deks]

MEANING: dyer of cloth • USAGE: English form of Dexter (*see* Dexter)

> *The purest and most thoughtful minds*
> *are those which love color the most.*
> — John Ruskin, *The True and the Beautiful*

DEXTER [DEKS-ter]

MEANING: dyer of cloth • USAGE: English surname: from English *deag* (dye)

> *Whatsoever thy hand is able to do, do it earnestly.*
> — Ecclesiastes 9:10a (DR)

DHIRA [dee-rah]

MEANING: wise, intelligent • USAGE: Hindu: Sanskrit

> *A well-trained mind brings health and happiness.*
> — Buddha, *The Dhammapada*
> (tr. Eknath Easwaran)

DIARMAID [DEER-med]

MEANING: without envy, free from envy, freeman • USAGE: Irish: from Gaelic *di* (without) and *airmait* (envy, rest)

> *To be rich in admiration and free from envy,*
> *to rejoice greatly in the good of others,*
> *to love with such generosity of heart that your love is*
> *still a dear possession in absence or unkindness —*
> *these are the gifts which money cannot buy.*
> — Robert Louis Stevenson, "Lay Morals"

DICK [dik]

MEANING: powerful ruler, strong leader • USAGE: English form of Richard, from German *rik* (rule, lead) and *hart* (hardy, strong, brave)

> *Ultimately, a genuine leader is not*
> *a searcher for consensus, but a molder of consensus.*
> — Martin Luther King Jr.,
> "Domestic Impact of the War"

DIDRIK [DEE-drik]

MEANING: leader of the people • USAGE: Scandinavian form of Dietrich (*see* Dietrich)

> *Order is maintained by a man of understanding*
> *and knowledge.*
> — Proverbs 28:2b (WEB)

DIEGO [dee-EH-goh]

MEANING: replace, change, transform, successor • USAGE: Spanish form of Jaime, from Hebrew *ya'aqobh* (one that takes by the heel, replace with another)

> *Be transformed by the renewing of your mind.*
> — Romans 12:2b (WEB)

D

D

DIETER   *[DEE-ter]*

MEANING: leader of the people • **USAGE:** German form of Dietrich (*see* Dietrich)
Be determined and confident, for you will be the leader.
— Joshua 1:6a (GNT)

DIETRICH   *[DEE-trik]*

MEANING: leader of the people • **USAGE:** German form of *Thiudoreiks*, from German *thiuda* (people, nation) and *rik* (rule, lead)
Be brave and strong as you lead.
— Deuteronomy 31:7b (CEV)

DIJI   *[DEE-jee]*

MEANING: farmer, earth worker • **USAGE:** African: Igbo of Nigeria
The earth provides for those who nourish it.
— Nigerian proverb

DIL   *[deel]*

MEANING: heart, mind • **USAGE:** Persian
As one can see when the eyes are open,
so one can understand when the heart is open.
— Hazrat Inayat Khan, *The Bowl of Saki*

DILBERT   *[DIL-bert]*

MEANING: shining valley, bright dale • **USAGE:** English: from English *dæl* (dale, valley) and German *beraht* (bright, shining)
The valleys…shout for joy and sing.
— Psalm 65:13b (NIV)

DILLON   *[DIL-on]*

MEANING: man from Lyon, great ocean, of the sea, streak of light • **USAGE:** Irish and English: Irish form of surname *O'Duilleain* and *De Leon* (from Lyon, France); Irish form of Dylan, from Welsh *dy* (great, large) and *llanw* (sea, ocean); or from Gaelic *dealan* (streak of light)

The sea! the sea! the open sea! /
The blue, the fresh, the ever free!
— Bryan Waller Procter, "The Sea"

DIMA   *[DEE-mah]*

MEANING: great leader, peaceful ruler, famous ruler, mother earth, earth lover, earthy • **USAGE:** Russian form of Vladimir, from Russian *volod* (rule, lead) and *meri* (great, famous) or *mir* (peace); or Russian form of Dimitri (*see* Dimitri)
Do right as you find and follow the road
that leads to peace.
— 1 Peter 3:11 (CEV)

DIMITRI   *[deh-MEE-tree]*

MEANING: mother earth, earth lover, earthy • **USAGE:** French masculine form of *Demeter*, from Greek *Da-mater* (mother earth), Greek goddess of agriculture and harvest
Speak to the earth, and it shall teach thee.
— Job 12:8a (ESV)

DIMITRIOS   *[dee-MEE-tree-ohs]*

MEANING: mother earth, earth lover, earthy • **USAGE:** Greek masculine form of *Demeter* (*see* Dimitri)
Truth springs out of the earth.
— Psalm 85:11a (WEB)

DIN, DEEN   *[deen]*

MEANING: religion, faith, belief • **USAGE:** Muslim
My religion is to live through Love.
— Jalaluddin Rumi

DINESH   *[dih-nesh]*

MEANING: lord of the day, sun • **USAGE:** Hindu: from Sanskrit *dina* (day) and *isa* (lord, king, ruler)
Lord is the Sun and when His rays fall upon
your heart, not impeded by the clouds of egoism,
the lotus blooms and the petals unfold.
— Sathya Sai Baba, *Sathya Sai Baba Speaks*

DINI [*DEE-nee*]

MEANING: faith, religion • USAGE: African:
Swahili of Kenya/Tanzania

We all depend on God who gives us every breath
and keeps us standing upright.
— Swahili proverb

DINO [*DEE-noh*]

MEANING: strong as a bear, powerful • USAGE:
Italian form of Bernardino, from German *bern*
(bear) and *hart* (hardy, strong, brave)

He is most powerful, who has himself in his power.
— Seneca

DION [*dee-OHN*]

MEANING: celebrant, reveler, follower of
Dionysus • USAGE: French and Greek form of
Dionysus, Greek god of wine and revelry

I have known that there was no better thing
than to rejoice, and to do well in this life.
For every man that eateth and drinketh, and seeth
good of his labour, this is the gift of God.
— Ecclesiastes 3:12–13 (DR)

DIONISIO [*dee-oh-NEE-see-oh*]

MEANING: celebrant, reveler, follower of
Dionysus • USAGE: Spanish and Italian form of
Dionysus (see Dion)

The best that people can do is eat, drink, and enjoy
their work. I saw that even this comes from God,
because no one can eat or enjoy life without him.
— Ecclesiastes 2:24 (NCV)

DIOSDADO [*dee-ohs-DAH-doh*]

MEANING: gift of God, God has given • USAGE:
Spanish: from Spanish *Dios* (God) and *dado* (given)

Go after a life of love as if your life depended
on it — because it does.
Give yourselves to the gifts God gives you.
— 1 Corinthians 14:1 (MSG)

DIPAK, DEEPAK [*dee-pahk*]

MEANING: light, lamp, illumination • USAGE:
Hindu: from Sanskrit *dipa*

Be a lamp unto yourselves.
— Buddha, *The Dhammapada*
(tr. Eknath Easwaran)

DIRK [*dirk*]

MEANING: leader of the people • USAGE: German,
Dutch, and Scandinavian form of Dietrich, from
German *thiuda* (people, nation) and *rik* (rule, lead)

By someone who is discerning
and knowledgeable order is maintained.
— Proverbs 28:2b (NEB)

DITRIK [*DEE-treek*]

MEANING: leader of the people • USAGE:
Hungarian form of Dietrich (see Dirk)

Work hard, and you will be a leader.
— Proverbs 12:24a (CEV)

DJANGO [*JAYN-goh*]

MEANING: building • USAGE: American: possibly
a form of Jengo

We work together with God.
You are God's field. You are God's building also.
— 1 Corinthians 3:9 (NLV)

DMITRI, DMITRY [*deh-MEE-tree*]

MEANING: mother earth, earth lover, earthy •
USAGE: Russian masculine form of *Demeter* (see
Dimitri)

Truth shall spring out of the earth.
— Psalm 85:11 (NKJV)

DOBRY [*DOH-bree*]

MEANING: good, kind, compassionate • USAGE:
Polish and Czech: from Czech *dobro*

Judge ye true judgment,
and shew ye mercy and compassion.
— Zechariah 7:9b (DR)

God shall be my hope, /
My stay, my guide, and lantern to my feet.
— William Shakespeare, *Henry VI, Part II*

DODGE [dodj]

MEANING: famous spear, renowned spearman • USAGE: English surname: from German *hrod* (fame, praise) and *ger* (spear)

A good reputation and respect
are worth much more than silver and gold.
— Proverbs 22:1 (CEV)

DOM [dom]

MEANING: belonging to God, belonging to the Lord • USAGE: English form of Domenico (*see* Domenico)

There is a soul above the soul of each, /
A mightier soul, which yet to each belongs.
— Richard W. Dixon, "Humanity"

DOMENICO [doh-MEE-nee-koh]

MEANING: belonging to God, belonging to the Lord • USAGE: Italian form of *Dominicus*, from Latin *dominus* (lord)

In every good man . . . God dwells.
— Seneca

DOMINGO [doh-MEEN-goh]

MEANING: belonging to God, belonging to the Lord • USAGE: Spanish form of Dominico (*see* Domenico)

God is love; and he that abideth in love abideth
in God, and God abideth in him.
— 1 John 4:16b (ASV)

DOMINIC, DOMINICK [DOM-ih-nik]

MEANING: belonging to God, belonging to the Lord • USAGE: English form of Domenico (*see* Domenico)

DOMINIK [dom-ih-NEEK]

MEANING: belonging to God, belonging to the Lord • USAGE: Russian and Polish form of Domenico (*see* Domenico)

They shall be my people,
and I will be their God in truth and in justice.
— Zechariah 8:8b (KJV)

DOMINIQUE [doh-mih-NEEK]

MEANING: belonging to God, belonging to the Lord • USAGE: French form of Domenico (*see* Domenico)

You are a chosen people, a royal priesthood,
a holy nation, a people belonging to God.
— 1 Peter 2:9a (NIV)

DON [don]

MEANING: ruler of the world, leader in the world • USAGE: Scottish and English form of Donald (*see* Donald)

A man's feet must be planted in his country,
but his eyes should survey the world.
— George Santayana, *The Life of Reason*

DONAL [DOH-nahl]

MEANING: ruler of the world, leader in the world • USAGE: Irish form of Donald (*see* Donald)

Live your beliefs and you can turn the world around.
— Henry David Thoreau

DONALD [DON-ald]

MEANING: ruler of the world, leader in the world • USAGE: Scottish and English: from Gaelic *dumnan* (world) and *val* (rule, ruler)

You made him a little less than the angels
and gave him a crown of greatness and honor.
You made him to rule over the works of Your hands.
You put all things under his feet.
— Psalm 8:5–6 (NLV)

DONALDO   *[doh-NAHL-doh]*

MEANING: ruler of the world, leader in the world •
USAGE: Spanish form of Donald (*see* Donald)
Wise and knowledgeable leaders bring stability.
Proverbs 28:2b (NLT)

DONAT   *[doh-NAHT]*

MEANING: gift • USAGE: French form of Donato
(*see* Donato)
This is how I define talent; it is a gift that God has
given us in secret, which we reveal without knowing it.
— Charles de Montesquieu

DONATELLO   *[doh-nah-TEL-oh]*

MEANING: gift • USAGE: Italian form of Donato
(*see* Donato)
Give to others, and God will give to you. Indeed, you
will receive a full measure, a generous helping, poured
into your hands — all that you can hold. The measure
you use for others is the one that God will use for you.
— Luke 6:38 (GNT)

DONATO   *[doh-NAH-toh]*

MEANING: gift • USAGE: Italian and Spanish: from
Latin *donatio*
There is nothing better for people than to be happy and
to enjoy themselves as long as they live, and also that
everyone should eat and drink, and find enjoyment in
all his toil, for these things are a gift from God.
— Ecclesiastes 3:12–13 (NEB)

DONN   *[don]*

MEANING: brown, brown-haired, chief, leader
• USAGE: Irish and Scottish: from Gaelic *donn*
(brown, chief)

Great leaders are almost always great simplifiers,
who can cut through argument, debate and doubt,
to offer a solution everybody can understand.
— Michael Korda

DONOVAN   *[DON-oh-vun]*

MEANING: brown chief, dark chief, dark-haired
chief • USAGE: Irish and English form of Irish
surname *O'Donnabhain*, from Gaelic *donn* (brown,
chief) and *dubh* (dark, black)
Deep peace, pure brown of the earth to you…
Deep peace, deep peace!
— Fiona MacLeod, "Invocation of Peace"

DOR   *[dor]*

MEANING: generation, era • USAGE: Jewish:
place-name in Israel
Know therefore that the Lord thy God, He is God;
the faithful God, who keepeth covenant and mercy
with them that love Him and keep His
commandments to a thousand generations.
— Deuteronomy 7:9 (MT)

DORIAN   *[DOR-ee-an]*

MEANING: gift, man of Doria • USAGE: English:
from Greek *doron* (gift); or Greek tribe from the
mountainous area of Doria
God said…I will give you a wise
and understanding heart.
— 1 Kings 3:11–12b (NIRV)

DOUG   *[dug]*

MEANING: dark blue, dark green, dark river •
USAGE: Scottish and English form of Douglas (*see*
Douglas)
What makes a river so restful to people is
that it doesn't have any doubt —
it is sure to get where it is going,
and it doesn't want to go anywhere else.
— Hal Boyle

D

DOUGAN [DOO-gan]

MEANING: dark, black, dark-haired • USAGE: Irish form of surname *O'Dubhagain*, from Gaelic *dubh*

> Thus says the Lord...I will give you the treasures of darkness and hidden riches of secret places.
> — Isaiah 45:1–3a (NKJV)

DOUGLAS [DUG-las]

MEANING: dark blue, dark green, dark river • USAGE: Scottish and English: form of Scottish surname *Dubhglas*, from Gaelic *dubh* (dark, black) and *glas* (blue, green); *Dubhglas* is a common Celtic river name

> The words of a man's mouth are deep waters, a flowing river, a fountain of wisdom.
> — Proverbs 18:4 (HCSB)

DOV [duv]

MEANING: bear • USAGE: Jewish

> Be strong, and let your heart take courage.
> — Psalm 31:24a (MT)

DOYLE [doil]

MEANING: dark stranger, dark-haired stranger • USAGE: Irish surname: from *dubh-ghall* (dark stranger)

> Forget not to show love unto strangers: for thereby some have entertained angels unawares.
> — Hebrews 13:2 (ASV)

DRACOS [DRAY-kohs]

MEANING: dragon • USAGE: American: from Latin *draco*

> Every brave youth is in training to ride and rule his dragon.
> — Ralph Waldo Emerson, "Fate"

DRAKE [drayk]

MEANING: dragon, male duck • USAGE: English surname: from Latin *draco* (dragon); or from English *drake* (male duck)

> The wild animals will be at peace with you.
> — Job 5:23b (NIV)

DREW [droo]

MEANING: wise one, druid, man, manly, masculine • USAGE: Irish and English: from Gaelic *druidh* (druid, Celtic priest); or English form of Andrew, from Greek *andros* (man) or *andreios* (manly)

> A Druid in training must be a bard before he is a priest, for music is one of the keys to the laws of the universe.
> — Marion Zimmer Bradley, *The Mists of Avalon*

DROR [dror]

MEANING: freedom, liberty • USAGE: Jewish: symbolic name for boys born on Passover

> You [God] have let me stride on freely, and my feet have not slipped.
> — 2 Samuel 22:37 (JPS)

DRYSTAN [DRIS-ten]

MEANING: riotous, chaotic, sad • USAGE: Welsh form of Tristan, from Welsh *drest* (riotous, tumultuous, chaotic); or from French *triste* (sad, sorrowful)

> One must have a bit of chaos in one's soul if one wishes to give birth to a dancing star.
> — Friedrich Nietzsche

DUANE, DWAYNE [doo-WAYN, d-WAYN]

MEANING: dark, black • USAGE: Irish and English: from Gaelic *dubh*

> We must walk consciously only part way toward our goal, and then leap in the dark to our success.
> — Henry David Thoreau
> (journal entry of March 11, 1859)

D

DUARTE [doo-AHR-teh]

MEANING: wealthy guardian, protector of that which is valuable • **USAGE:** Portuguese form of Edward, from English *ead* (wealth, prosperity) and *weard* (guardian, protector)

> *Store up riches for yourselves in heaven…*
> *for your heart will always be where your riches are.*
> — Matthew 6:20–21 (GNT)

DUDLEY [DUD-lee]

MEANING: covered field, Dudda's field • **USAGE:** English: from English place-name *Dudda's Lea* (Dudda's clearing), from English *dudde* (cloak, mantle) and *leah* (meadow, field)

> *We are God's fellow workers;*
> *you are God's field.*
> — 1 Corinthians 3:9a (NKJV)

DUKA [DOO-kah]

MEANING: all • **USAGE:** African: Hausa of Nigeria

> *Patience is the best of dispositions; one who possesses patience, possesses all things.*
> — Nigerian proverb

DUKE [dook]

MEANING: nobleman, leader, duke • **USAGE:** English: from French *duc* (leader, commander)

> *Yet you have made him a little lower than the heavenly beings and crowned him with glory and honor.*
> *You have given him dominion over the works of your hands; you have put all things under his feet.*
> — Psalm 8:5–6 (ESV)

DUMI [DOO-mee]

MEANING: the northeast wind, considered "the inspirer" • **USAGE:** African: Bavili of West Africa

> *If you want to speak to God, tell the wind.*
> — West African proverb

DUNA [doo-nah]

MEANING: headman, chief, king • **USAGE:** African: Zulu

> *A king is a king because of the people.*
> — Zulu proverb

DUNCAN [DUN-ken]

MEANING: brown warrior, brown-headed warrior • **USAGE:** Scottish and English form of *Donnchadh*, from Gaelic *donn* (brown) and *chadh* (warrior)

> *To the valiant, actions speak alone.*
> — Tobias Smollett, *James I of Scotland*

DURAN [duh-RAN]

MEANING: enduring, long-lasting, durable, firm • **USAGE:** English surname: from Latin *durer* (to endure) or from Latin *durus* (hard, firm)

> *The best food for the soul is a mixture of love, beauty, and excursions out of time where we glimpse the eternal….Eternity is the proper time frame of the soul, whose immortality is ever present and whose endurance knows no limitation.*
> — Thomas Moore, *The Education of the Heart*

DUSAN [doo-shahn]

MEANING: spirit, soul • **USAGE:** Czech: from Slavic *dusa*

> *I saw the soul as large, as if it were an endless world and as if it were a blissful kingdom. And by the details I saw therein, I understood it to be a glorious city.*
> — Julian of Norwich

DUSTIN [DUS-ten]

MEANING: thunder stone, Thor's stone • **USAGE:** English form of *Thorstein*, from *Thor* (Norse god of thunder) and Norse *steinn* (stone)

> *Truth must be the foundation stone, the cement to solidify the entire social edifice.*
> — Pope John II

D

DUSTY   [DUS-tee]

MEANING: thunder stone, Thor's stone, Thor's rock • USAGE: English form of Dustin (*see* Dustin)

> *And the Lord said, "Here is a place by Me,*
> *and you shall stand on the rock."*
> — Exodus 33:21 (NKJV)

DWIGHT   [dwiet]

MEANING: white, fair, blond-haired • USAGE: English: possibly a form of Dutch family name *De Witt* (the white one)

> *Thou art fairer than the children of men:*
> *grace is poured into thy lips: therefore God*
> *hath blessed thee for ever.*
> — Psalm 45:2 (KJV)

DYLAN   [DIL-en]

MEANING: great ocean, of the sea • USAGE: English: from Welsh *dy* (great, large) and *llanw* (sea, ocean); Welsh god of the sea

> *May the fluency of the ocean be yours.*
> — John O'Donohue, *Anam Cara*

E

EAMON   [AY-mon]

MEANING: rich protector, guardian of wealth and prosperity • USAGE: Irish form of Edmund, from English *ead* (wealth, prosperity) and *mund* (hand, protection)

> *Ordinary riches can be stolen from a man.*
> *Real riches cannot. In the treasury-house of your soul,*
> *there are infinitely precious things,*
> *that may not be taken from you.*
> — Oscar Wilde, *The Soul of Man Under Socialism*

EARL   [erl]

MEANING: nobleman, lord, chief, leader, warrior • USAGE: English: from English *eorl*

> *We must have kings, and we must have nobles.*
> *Nature provides such in every society —*
> *only let us have the real instead of the titular.*
> — Ralph Waldo Emerson, "The Young American"

EASTON   [EES-ton]

MEANING: eastern town • USAGE: English surname: from English *east* (east direction) and *tun* (town, settlement)

> *The Lord God planted a garden eastward.*
> — Genesis 2:8a (KJV)

EBAN   [EH-bahn]

MEANING: stone, rock • USAGE: Jewish

> *Hearken to Me, you who pursue justice,*
> *you who seek the Lord: look to the rock you were hewn*
> *from, to the quarry you were dug from.*
> — Isaiah 51:1 (JPS)

EBERHARDT, EBERHARD   [AY-behr-hard]

MEANING: brave boar, strong boar • USAGE: German: from German *ebur* (wild boar) and *hart* (hardy, strong, brave)

> *Confidence…comes from within. It is there all the time.*
> — Anna Freud

ECKART, ECKHART   [EK-harht]

MEANING: hard sword, strong blade • USAGE: German: from German *ecka* (tip, sword blade) and *harti* (hard)

> *The Lord himself is your shield and your sword,*
> *to defend you and give you victory.*
> — Deuteronomy 33:29b (GNT)

ED   [ed]

MEANING: wealthy guardian, protector of that which is valuable, rich and prosperous protector, guardian of wealth, prosperous spear, rich spear, wealthy friend, prosperous friendship, rich in friendship • **Usage:** English form of Edgar, Edmund, Edward, or Edwin (*see those entries*)

> *Riches are for spending,*
> *and spending for honor and good actions.*
> — Francis Bacon, "Of Expense"

EDDIE, EDDY [ED-ee]

Meaning: wealthy guardian, protector of that which is valuable, rich and prosperous protector, guardian of wealth, prosperous spear, rich spear, wealthy friend, prosperous friendship, rich in friendship • **Usage:** English form of Edgar, Edmund, Edward, or Edwin (*see those entries*)

> *If you would have friends, be one.*
> — "Reciprocity," Elbert Hubbard (1856–1915), American author and philosopher

EDEN, EDAN [EH-den, EE-dan]

Meaning: delight, delightful, pleasant • **Usage:** Jewish: from Hebrew *edhen*

> *People's good deeds are used by the Eternal as seeds for planting trees in the Garden of Eden: thus, each of us creates our own Paradise.*
> — Dov Ber of Mezeritch

EDGAR [ED-gar]

Meaning: prosperous spear, wealthy spearman • **Usage:** English: from English *ead* (wealth, prosperity) and *gar* (spear)

> *Thou shalt make thy way prosperous,*
> *and then thou shalt have good success.*
> — Joshua 1:8b (KJV)

EDGARD [ed-GAHR]

Meaning: prosperous spear, wealthy spearman • **Usage:** French form of Edgar (*see* Edgar)

> *Be generous, and you will be prosperous.*
> *Help others, and you will be helped.*
> — Proverbs 11:25 (GNT)

EDMOND [ed-MOHND (French), ED-mund (English)]

Meaning: rich and prosperous protector, guardian of wealth • **Usage:** French and English form of Edmund (*see* Edmund)

> *Good comes from a good man because of the riches he has in his heart.*
> — Luke 6:45a (NLV)

EDMONDO [ayd-MOHN-doh]

Meaning: rich protector, guardian of prosperity • **Usage:** Italian form of Edmund (*see* Edmund)

> *The Lord will make you abound in prosperity.*
> — Deuteronomy 28:11a (ESV)

EDMUND [ED-mund]

Meaning: rich and prosperous protector, guardian of wealth • **Usage:** English: from English *ead* (wealth, prosperity) and *mund* (hand, protection)

> *Your true wealth is your stock of virtue,*
> *and your true power the uses to which you put it.*
> — James Allen, *From Poverty to Power*

EDMUNDO [ehd-MUHN-doh]

Meaning: rich protector, guardian of prosperity • **Usage:** Spanish and Portuguese form of Edmund (*see* Edmund)

> *I pray that you may prosper in all things and be in health, just as your soul prospers.*
> — 3 John 1:2 (NKJV)

EDOARDO [ayd-WAHR-doh]

Meaning: wealthy guardian, protector of that which is valuable • **Usage:** Italian form of Edward (*see* Edward)

> *God said…wisdom and knowledge is granted unto thee; and I will give thee riches, and wealth, and honor.*
> — 2 Chronicles 1:11–12a (ASV)

E

ÉDOUARD · [eh-DWAHR]

MEANING: wealthy guardian, protector of that which is valuable • **USAGE:** French form of Edward (*see* Edward)

It is a good thing to receive wealth from God and the good health to enjoy it. To enjoy your work and accept your lot in life — this is indeed a gift from God.
— Ecclesiastes 5:19 (NLT)

EDUARD · [EH-doo-ahrt (German), ed-DOO-arhd (Russian)]

MEANING: wealthy guardian, protector of that which is valuable • **USAGE:** German and Russian form of Edward (*see* Edward)

Wisdom is protection as money is protection, and the advantage of knowledge is that wisdom preserves the life of its owner.
— Ecclesiastes 7:12 (HCSB)

EDUARDO · [eh-DWAHR-doh (Spanish), eh-doo-AHR-doh (Portuguese)]

MEANING: wealthy guardian, protector of that which is valuable • **USAGE:** Spanish and Portuguese form of Edward (*see* Edward)

Wisdom offers you long life, as well as wealth and honor.
— Proverbs 3:16 (GNT)

EDVARD · [ED-vahr]

MEANING: wealthy guardian, protector of that which is valuable • **USAGE:** Scandinavian form of Edward (*see* Edward)

Every man also to whom God has given riches and wealth, and has given him power to eat of it, and to take his portion, and to rejoice in his labor — this is the gift of God.
— Ecclesiastes 5:19 (WEB)

EDWARD · [ED-ward]

MEANING: wealthy guardian, protector of that which is valuable • **USAGE:** English: from English *ead* (wealth, prosperity) and *weard* (guardian, protector)

How joyful and prosperous you will be!
— Psalm 128:2b (NLT)

EDWIN · [ED-wen]

MEANING: wealthy friend, prosperous friendship, rich in friendship • **USAGE:** English: from English *ead* (wealth, prosperity) and *wine* (friend)

To be capable of steady friendship or lasting love, are the two greatest proofs, not only of goodness of heart, but of strength of mind.
— William Hazlitt, "Characteristics"

EFI, EFFIE · [EH-fee]

MEANING: fruitful, abundant, bountiful • **USAGE:** Jewish and English form of Efrayim (*see* Efrayim)

The Lord will make thee over-abundant for good.
— Deuteronomy 28:11a (MT)

EFRAYIM · [eh-FRAH-yeem]

MEANING: fruitful, abundant, bountiful • **USAGE:** Jewish: from Hebrew *epharyim*

The Lord will open for you His bounteous stores... to bless all your undertakings.
— Deuteronomy 28:12a (JPS)

EFREM · [EF-rem (English), EE-frem (Italian), YEH-frem (Russian)]

MEANING: fruitful, abundant, bountiful • **USAGE:** English, Italian, and Russian form of Efrayim (*see* Efrayim)

The fruit of the Spirit is love, joy, peace, patience, kindness, goodness, faith, gentleness, and self-control.
— Galatians 5:22–23a (WEB)

EGAN   [EE-gan]

MEANING: fire, little fiery one • USAGE: Irish
form of *Aodhgan*, from Gaelic *aodh* (fire) and
diminutive *-an*

> *[God] makest thy angels spirits:*
> *and thy ministers a burning fire.*
> — Psalm 103:4 (DR)

EGBERT   [EG-bert]

MEANING: bright edge • USAGE: English and
Dutch: from English *ecg* (edge of a sword) and
beorht (bright)

> *The light of the righteous shines brightly.*
> — Proverbs 13:9 (NEB)

EGIL   [EG-el]

MEANING: blade, sword point, edge of a sword,
sharp, keen • USAGE: Scandinavian: from Norse *eg*

> *Iron sharpens iron, so one man sharpens another.*
> — Proverbs 27:17 (NASB)

EGON   [EH-gon]

MEANING: edge of a sword • USAGE: German:
from German *eg*

> *The eternal God…is your protecting shield*
> *and your triumphant sword!*
> — Deuteronomy 33:27–29b (NLT)

EHUD   [eh-HOOD]

MEANING: love, union • USAGE: Jewish

> *Rabbi Akiba used to say: "Beloved is man,*
> *for he was created in the image of God;*
> *but it was by a special love that it was made known*
> *to him that he was created in the image of God."*
> — *Pirkei Avot* 3:18

EILAM, ELAM   [eh-LAHM]

MEANING: eternal, everlasting • USAGE: Jewish

> *One cannot help but be in awe when [one] contemplates*
> *the mysteries of eternity, of life, of the marvelous*
> *structure of reality.*
> — Albert Einstein

EILIF   [IE-lif]

MEANING: immortal, eternal • USAGE:
Norwegian and Swedish: from Norse *ei* (always,
ever) and *lifr* (life, alive)

> *He who sows to the Spirit will*
> *from the Spirit reap eternal life.*
> — Galatians 6:8b (WEB)

EINAR   [IE-nahr]

MEANING: lone warrior, one army • USAGE:
Scandinavian: from Norse *einn* (one) and *arr* (army)

> *The strongest man in the world is*
> *he who stands most alone.*
> — Henrik Ibsen, *An Enemy of the People*
> (tr. Eleanor Marx-Aveling)

EITAN, ETAN   [eh-TAHN]

MEANING: strong, firm, steadfast • USAGE:
Jewish: from Hebrew *ethan*

> *He who walketh uprightly, and worketh righteousness,*
> *and speaketh truth in his heart…he that doeth*
> *these things shall never be moved.*
> — Psalm 15:2, 15:5b (MT)

EKON   [eh-kohn]

MEANING: strong, powerful • USAGE: African:
Nigeria

> *The habit of thinking is the habit of gaining strength.*
> — Nigerian proverb

ELAD   [eh-LAHD]

MEANING: God is eternal • USAGE: Jewish

> *Trust ye in the Lord for ever,*
> *for the Lord is God, an everlasting Rock.*
> — Isaiah 26:4 (MT)

E

ELAZAR   *[eh-lah-ZAHR]*

MEANING: God has helped • **USAGE:** Jewish: from Hebrew *el'azar*

Hear, O Lord, and be gracious unto me;
Lord, be Thou my helper.
— Psalm 30:11 (MT)

ELBERT   *[EL-bert]*

MEANING: noble and brightly shining • **USAGE:** Dutch and English form of *Adalbrecht*, from German *adal* (noble) and *beraht* (bright, shining)

Be noble minded! Our own heart, and not other men's
opinions of us, forms our true honor.
— Johann Friedrich von Schiller,
The Death of Wallenstein

ELDAD   *[ehl-DAHD]*

MEANING: beloved of God, friend of God • **USAGE:** Jewish: from Hebrew *el dawidh*

The beloved of the Lord shall dwell in safety by Him.
— Deuteronomy 33:12a (MT)

ELDON   *[EL-don]*

MEANING: old, enduring, long-lived • **USAGE:** English surname: from Scottish Gaelic *auld*

Eternity is the proper time frame of the soul,
whose immortality is ever present and whose
endurance knows no limitation.
— Thomas Moore, *Education of the Heart*

ELEK   *[EHL-ek]*

MEANING: protector and helper of humankind, guardian • **USAGE:** Hungarian form of Alex, from Greek *alexein* (to defend, to help) and *andros* (man)

The Lord is faithful. He will strengthen you.
He will guard you.
— 2 Thessalonians 3:3a (NIRV)

ELEZ   *[EH-lehz]*

MEANING: joyous, happy • **USAGE:** Jewish

There is nothing worthwhile for a man but to eat and
drink and afford himself enjoyment with his means.
And even that…comes from God.
— Ecclesiastes 2:24 (JPS)

ELI   *[EE-lie, eh-LEE]*

MEANING: uplifted, ascended • **USAGE:** Jewish: from Hebrew *eli*

No limits are set to the ascent of man, and to each
and everyone the highest stands open.
Here it is only your personal choice that decides.
— Martin Buber,
Ten Rungs: Collected Hasidic Sayings

ELIAM   *[eh-lee-AHM]*

MEANING: God's people • **USAGE:** Jewish

They shall be My people, and I will be their God,
in truth and in righteousness.
— Zechariah 8:8b (MT)

ELIAS   *[ay-LEE-ahs (Greek, Spanish, German, Scandinavian), eh-LIE-ahs (English)]*

MEANING: the Lord is God • **USAGE:** Greek, English, German, Scandinavian, and Spanish form of Elijah (*see* Elijah)

The Lord your God is gracious and merciful,
and will not turn away his face from you.
— 2 Chronicles 30:9b (RSV)

ELIJAH   *[ee-LIE-zhah]*

MEANING: the Lord is God • **USAGE:** English form of *Eliyahu*, from Hebrew *el'iyahu* (Yahweh is God)

The Lord your God is with you wherever you go.
— Joshua 1:9b (NASB)

ELIOR   *[eh-lee-OHR]*

MEANING: my light is God • USAGE: Jewish
The Lord is God, and hath given us light.
— Psalm 118:27 (MT)

ELISHA   *[ee-LIE-shah, ee-lee-SHAH]*

MEANING: God is my salvation • USAGE: Jewish:
from Hebrew *elishu'a*
He shall receive a blessing from the Lord,
and righteousness from the God of his salvation.
— Psalm 24:5 (MT)

ELLERY   *[EL-er-ee]*

MEANING: cheerful, joyful, happy • USAGE:
English surname: form of Hilary, from Latin *hilaris*
Of cheerfulness, or a good temper,
the more it is spent, the more of it remains.
— Ralph Waldo Emerson,
"Considerations by the Way"

ELLIOT, ELLIOTT, ELIOT   *[EL-ee-ot]*

MEANING: the Lord is my God, noble combat •
USAGE: English surname: English form of Elijah
(*see* Elijah); or English form of *Aliet*, from *aoel*
(noble) and *gyo* (battle)
Teach me to do Your will, for You are my God.
May Your gracious Spirit lead me on level ground.
— Psalm 143:10 (HCSB)

ELLIS   *[EL-es]*

MEANING: God is my salvation, the Lord is God
• USAGE: English surname: English form of Elisha
(*see* Elisha), or of Elijah (*see* Elijah)
You may call God love, you may call God goodness.
But the best name for God is compassion.
— Meister Eckhart

ELMER   *[EL-mer]*

MEANING: noble and famous • USAGE: English:
from English *æthel* (noble, honorable) and *mær*
(famous)
Of all the properties which belong to honorable men,
not one is so highly prized as that of character.
— Henry Clay (speech of June 12, 1827)

ELMO   *[EL-moh]*

MEANING: protector, guardian • USAGE: English
and Italian: form of German *helm* (helmet,
protection)
The Lord is faithful,
who will establish you, and guard you.
— 2 Thessalonians 3:3a (WEB)

ELOF   *[EH-lof]*

MEANING: solo heir, lone descendant • USAGE:
Swedish, Danish, and Finnish: from Norse *einn*
(one) and *leifr* (descendant, heir)
The lines have fallen to me in pleasant places.
Yes, I have a good inheritance.
— Psalm 16:6 (WEB)

ELON, EILON   *[eh-LOHN]*

MEANING: oak tree, terebinth tree • USAGE:
Jewish
He is like a tree planted beside streams of water,
which yields its fruit in season, whose foliage never
fades, and whatever it produces thrives.
— Psalm 1:3 (JPS)

ELROY   *[EL-roi]*

MEANING: the king, the royal one • USAGE:
English form of Leroy, from French *le roi*
[God] crowns you with love and compassion.
— Psalm 103:4b (RSV)

E

ELVIN   *[EL-ven]*

MEANING: elf friend, elf ally • **USAGE:** English form of Alvin, from English *ælf* (elf) and *wine* (friend)

> *A loyal friend is like a safe shelter;*
> *find one, and you have found a treasure.*
> — Sirach 6:14 (GNT Apocrypha)

ELVIS   *[EL-vis]*

MEANING: elf friend, all wise • **USAGE:** English: possibly a form of Alvin, from English *ælf* (elf) and *wine* (friend, ally); or possibly a form of *Alvis*, meaning "all wise"

> *The greatest sweetener of human life is Friendship.*
> *To raise this to the highest pitch of enjoyment,*
> *is a secret which but few discover.*
> — Joseph Addison, "Of Friendship"

EMANUEL   *[eh-mah-noo-EHL (Jewish),*
ee-MAHN-yoo-EHL (Spanish, German,
Scandinavian)]

MEANING: God is with us • **USAGE:** Scandinavian, Jewish, German, and Spanish form of Imanuel, from Hebrew *immanu' el*

> *The Lord our God be with us, as He was with our*
> *fathers; let Him not leave us, nor forsake us.*
> — 1 Kings 8:57 (MT)

EMERY   *[EM-er-ee]*

MEANING: industrious leader, overseer, boss, employer • **USAGE:** English surname: a form of *Amalrich*, from German *amal* (work, labor) and *rik* (rule, lead)

> *You will earn the trust and respect of others*
> *if you work for good.*
> — Proverbs 14:22b (GNT)

EMIL   *[EE-mil (German, Scandinavian),*
ee-MEEL (English)]

MEANING: industrious, hardworking, one who excels, competitor • **USAGE:** German,

Scandinavian, and English: from German *amal* (work, labor); or German form of Roman *Aemilius*, from Latin *aemulus* (trying to equal or excel)

> *Whatever work you do, do it with all your heart.*
> — Colossians 3:23a (NLV)

ÉMILE   *[eh-MEEL]*

MEANING: industrious, hardworking, one who excels, competitor • **USAGE:** French form of Emil (*see* Emil)

> *The Lord your God will bless you*
> *in all your work and in all that you undertake.*
> — Deuteronomy 15:10b (ESV)

EMILIO   *[ay-MEE-lee-oh]*

MEANING: industrious, hardworking, one who excels, competitor • **USAGE:** Spanish and Italian form of Emil (*see* Emil)

> *The Lord thy God shall bless thee in all*
> *thine increase, and in all the works of thine hands,*
> *therefore thou shalt surely rejoice.*
> — Deuteronomy 16:15b (KJV)

EMMERICH   *[EM-er-rik]*

MEANING: ruler of the home, universal leader • **USAGE:** German: from German *heim* (home, house) and *rik* (rule, lead); or from German *ermen* (whole, universal) and *rik* (rule, lead)

> *Peace be within your walls.*
> — Psalm 122:7a (RSV)

EMMET   *[EM-et]*

MEANING: truth, truthful • **USAGE:** Jewish

> *Behold, Thou desirest truth in the inward parts; make*
> *me, therefore, to know wisdom in mine inmost heart.*
> — Psalm 51:9 (MT)

EMMET, EMMETT   *[EM-et]*

MEANING: whole, universal, strong, powerful • **USAGE:** English: from German *ermen* (whole, universal) or *erm* (strength, power)

Within man is the soul of the whole; the wise silence;
the universal beauty, to which every part and particle
is equally related; the eternal ONE.
— Ralph Waldo Emerson, "The Over-Soul"

ENAPAY   *[ehn-ah-pay]*

Meaning: goes forth bravely • **Usage:** Amerind:
Sioux
The true Indian sets no price upon either his property
or his labor. His generosity is limited only by the
strength and ability. He regards it as an honor to be
selected for a difficult or dangerous service.
— Ohiyesa, *The Soul of the Indian*

ENIOLA   *[eh-nee-oh-lah]*

Meaning: wealth, wealthy • **Usage:** African:
Yoruba of Nigeria
A healthy body is the medicine for wealth.
— Yoruban proverb

ENNIS   *[EN-es]*

Meaning: island, river island • **Usage:** Irish form
of Innes, from Gaelic *innis*
An island always pleases my imagination,
even the smallest, as a small continent
and integral portion of the globe.
— Henry David Thoreau,
A Week on the Concord and Merrimack Rivers

ENOCH   *[EE-nok]*

Meaning: educated, trained, dedicated • **Usage:**
English form of Chanoch, from Hebrew *hanokh*
True education combines intellect, beauty, goodness,
and the greatest of these is goodness.
— Helen Keller, *Out of the Dark*

ENOSH   *[eh-NOHSH]*

Meaning: man, human being • **Usage:** Jewish

Man cannot approach the divine by reaching
beyond the human; he can approach Him through
becoming human. To become human is what he,
this individual man, has been created for.
— Martin Buber, "Hasidism and Modern Man"

ENRICO   *[en-REE-koh]*

Meaning: ruler of the home, house leader •
Usage: Italian form of Henry, from German *heim*
(home, house) and *rik* (rule, lead)
Through wisdom a house is built,
and by understanding it is established.
— Proverbs 24:3 (KJ21)

ENRIQUE   *[ehn-REE-kay]*

Meaning: ruler of the home, house leader •
Usage: Spanish form of Henry (*see* Enrico)
Peace be to you, and peace be to your house,
and peace be to all that you have.
— 1 Samuel 25:6b (RSV)

ENZO   *[EHN-zoh]*

Meaning: laurel tree, laurel wreath, conqueror,
victorious, successful, triumphant • **Usage:** Italian
form of Lorenzo, from Latin *laurus* (laurel tree,
laurel wreath); or Italian form of Vincenzo, from
Latin *vincere* (to conquer)
Truth and virtue conquer. [Veritas et virtus viscunt.]
— Latin proverb

EOGHAN   *[OH-wan]*

Meaning: born on the land of the yew trees,
wellborn, noble • **Usage:** Irish: from Gaelic *eo gein*
(born of the yew tree); or Irish form of Eugene,
from Greek *eu* (good, well) and *genes* (born)
He will be like a tree planted by the water, that extends
its roots by a stream and will not fear when the heat
comes; but its leaves will be green, and it will not be
anxious in a year of drought nor cease to yield fruit.
— Jeremiah 17:8 (NASB)

E

E

EOIN [OH-wen]

MEANING: God is gracious, God is giving
• USAGE: Irish form of John, from Hebrew
y'hohanan (Yahweh is gracious)
> *Every man to whom God hath given riches,*
> *and substance, and hath given him power to eat*
> *thereof, and to enjoy his portion, and to rejoice*
> *of his labour: this is the gift of God.*
> — Ecclesiastes 5:18 (DR)

EPHRAIM, EFRAIM [eh-FRIE-em]

MEANING: fruitful, abundant, bountiful • USAGE:
English form of Efrayim, from Hebrew *epharyim*
> *God will bless you in all of your work.*
> *He will bless you in everything you do.*
> — Deuteronomy 15:10b (NIRV)

ERHARD [EHR-hard]

MEANING: honorable and brave • USAGE:
German: from German *era* (honor, respect) and *hart*
(hardy, strong, brave)
> *Be ye strong therefore,*
> *and let not your hands be weak:*
> *for your work shall be rewarded.*
> — 2 Chronicles 15:7 (KJV)

ERIC, ERICK [EHR-ik]

MEANING: ruler for eternity, everlasting king •
USAGE: English form of *Eirikr*, from Norse *ei*
(ever, always) and *rikr* (ruler, leader)
> *I will be honest and fair in my own kingdom.*
> — Psalm 101:2b (CEV)

ERICH [EHR-ik]

MEANING: ruler for eternity, everlasting king •
USAGE: German form of Erik (*see* Eric)
> *For a person will reap what he sows…the one who sows*
> *to the Spirit will reap eternal life from the Spirit.*
> — Galatians 6:7b–8 (NEB)

ERIK [EHR-ik (Scandinavian, English, German), EH-reek (Russian)]

MEANING: ruler for eternity, everlasting king
• USAGE: Scandinavian, English, German, and
Russian form of Eric (*see* Eric)
> *God has made everything beautiful for its own time.*
> *He has planted eternity in the human heart.*
> — Ecclesiastes 3:11a (NLT)

ERNEST [ER-nest]

MEANING: earnest, honest • USAGE: English form
of Ernst, from German *ernust*
> *No legacy is so rich as honesty.*
> — William Shakespeare,
> *All's Well That Ends Well*

ERNESTO [ayr-NAY-stoh]

MEANING: earnest, honest • USAGE: Spanish and
Italian form of Ernst (*see* Ernest)
> *The one who lives honestly, practices righteousness,*
> *and acknowledges the truth in his heart…*
> *will never be moved.*
> — Psalm 15:2, 15:5b (HCSB)

ERNST [ernst]

MEANING: earnest, honest • USAGE: German and
Dutch (*see* Ernest)
> *Walk straight, act right, tell the truth.*
> — Psalm 15:2 (MSG)

ERROL [ER-ol]

MEANING: wanderer, adventurer, earl, count,
nobleman • USAGE: English: from Latin *errare* (to
wander); or from English *earl* (nobleman, count)
> *Life is an adventure, dare it.*
> — Mother Teresa, "Life"

ERWIN   *[ER-veen (German), ER-win (Dutch)]*

MEANING: army friend • USAGE: German and Dutch form of *Hariwini*, from German *hari* (army) and *win* (friend)

My dear friend, I know your soul is doing fine,
and I pray that you are doing well in every way
and that your health is good.
— 3 John 1:2 (NCV)

ERYK   *[EHR-ek]*

MEANING: ruler for eternity, everlasting king • USAGE: Polish form of Eric, from Norse *ei* (ever, always) and *rikr* (ruler, leader)

What is man, that thou art mindful of him?
or the son of man that thou visitest him?
Thou madest him a little lower than the angels;
thou crownedst him with glory and honour,
and didst set him over the works of thy hands.
— Hebrews 2:6b–7 (KJV)

ESTEBAN   *[ay-STAY-bahn]*

MEANING: crown, crowned one • USAGE: Spanish form of Stephen, from Greek *stephanos*

He will find gladness and a crown of rejoicing.
— Ben Sira 15:6a (RSV Apocrypha)

ETHAN   *[EE-than]*

MEANING: strong, firm, steadfast • USAGE: English form of Eitan, from Hebrew *ethan*

His heart is steadfast.
— Psalm 112:7 (ESV)

ÉTIENNE   *[ay-TYEN]*

MEANING: crown, crowned one • USAGE: French form of Stephen, from Greek *stephanos*

What is man, O God, that you should think of him;
mere man, that you should care for him?
You made him for a little while lower than the angels;
you crowned him with glory and honor,
and made him ruler over all things.
— Hebrews 2:6b–7 (GNT)

EUGEN   *[OY-jen]*

MEANING: wellborn, noble • USAGE: German and Scandinavian form of Eugene (*see* Eugene)

Man's main task in life is to give birth to himself.
— Erich Fromm, *Man for Himself*

EUGENE   *[yoo-JEEN]*

MEANING: wellborn, noble • USAGE: English form of *Eugeneios*, from Greek *eu* (good, well) and *genes* (born)

Be NOBLE! and the nobleness that lies /
In other men, sleeping, but never dead /
Will rise in majesty to meet thine own.
— James Russell Lowell, "Sonnet IV"

EUGENIO   *[yoo-JEE-nee-oh (Italian), yoo-HEE-nee-oh (Spanish)]*

MEANING: wellborn, noble • USAGE: Italian and Spanish form of Eugene (*see* Eugene)

It is within the reach of every man to live nobly.
— Seneca, *Ad Lucilium Epistulae Morales*
(tr. Richard Gummere)

EUSTACE   *[YOO-stas]*

MEANING: steadfast, firm • USAGE: English: from Greek *eu* (good, well) and *stenai* (to stand)

And He set my feet upon a rock
making my footsteps firm.
— Psalm 40:2b (NASB)

EVAN   *[EH-van]*

MEANING: God is gracious, God is giving • USAGE: Welsh and English form of John, from Hebrew *y'hohanan* (Yahweh is gracious)

The Lord your God is gracious and compassionate,
and will not turn His face from you.
— 2 Chronicles 30:9b (NASB)

E

E

EVANDER [ee-VAN-der]

MEANING: good man, bowman, archer, warrior
• USAGE: English and Scottish: English form of
Evandrus, from Greek *eu* (good) and *aner* (man); or
Scottish and English form of *Iomhar,* from Norse *yr*
(yew tree) and *arr* (army)

> *A good man out of the good treasure of his heart*
> *brings forth good....For out of the abundance*
> *of the heart his mouth speaks.*
> — Luke 6:45 (NKJV)

EVANGELOS [eh-VAHN-yeh-lohs]

MEANING: angel • USAGE: Greek: from Greek
angelos

> *He will give His angels orders concerning you,*
> *to protect you in all your ways.*
> — Psalm 91:11 (HCSB)

EVERETT [EV-er-et, EV-ret]

MEANING: brave boar, strong boar • USAGE:
English surname: form of Eberhardt, from German
ebur (wild boar) and *hart* (hardy, strong, brave)

> *A wise man is strong: and a knowing man,*
> *stout and valiant.*
> — Proverbs 24:5 (DR)

EVERT [EH-vert]

MEANING: brave boar, strong boar • USAGE:
German form of Eberhardt (*see* Everett)

> *When I called, You answered me;*
> *You made me bold and stouthearted.*
> — Psalm 138:3 (NIV)

EYAL [EH-yahl]

MEANING: powerful, strong, mighty • USAGE:
Jewish

> *Whatsoever thy hand attaineth*
> *to do by thy strength, that do.*
> — Ecclesiastes 9:10a (MT)

EZEKIEL [eh-ZEE-kee-el]

MEANING: God strengthens, God will strengthen
• USAGE: English form of *Yechezkel,* from Hebrew
yechezq' el

> *One in harmony with God's law of love*
> *has more strength than an army.*
> — Peace Pilgrim, *Peace Pilgrim*

EZRA [EZ-rah, ez-RAH]

MEANING: help, aid • USAGE: Jewish: from
Hebrew *ezra*

> *The Lord thy God, He it is that doth go with thee;*
> *He will not fail thee, nor forsake thee.*
> — Deuteronomy 31:6 (MT)

F

FA [fah]

MEANING: beginning, develop, growth • USAGE:
Chinese

> *The beginning and the end reach out*
> *their hands to each other.*
> — Chinese proverb

FABIAN [FAH-bee-ahn (Italian, German), FAY-bee-an (English)]

MEANING: bean, a sower of beans • USAGE:
Italian, English, and German form of Roman family
name *Fabius,* from Latin *faba* (a broad bean)

> *Every thought-seed sown or allowed to fall into*
> *the mind, and to take root there, produces its own,*
> *blossoming sooner or later into act, and bearing its*
> *own fruitage of opportunity and circumstance. Good*
> *thoughts bear good fruit, bad thoughts bad fruit.*
> — James Allen, *As a Man Thinketh*

FABIEN [fah-bee-EN]

MEANING: bean, a sower of beans • USAGE:
French form of Fabian (*see* Fabian)

Whatever a man soweth, that shall he also reap...
he that soweth to the Spirit shall of the Spirit reap
life everlasting.
— Galatians 6:7b–8 (KJV)

FABIO   *[FAH-bee-oh]*

Meaning: bean, a sower of beans • **Usage:**
Italian and Spanish form of Fabian (*see* Fabian)
Sow to yourselves in righteousness,
reap according to kindness.
— Hosea 10.12a (WEB)

FABRICE   *[fah-BREES]*

Meaning: craftsman, skilled workman • **Usage:**
French form of Fabricio (*see* Fabricio)
You shall be a blessing. Do not be afraid,
but let your hands be strong.
— Zechariah 8:13b (NRSV)

FABRICIO, FABRIZIO   *[fah-BREE-see-oh,*
fah-BREET-ʒee-oh]

Meaning: craftsman, skilled workman • **Usage:**
Italian form of Roman family name *Fabricius*, from
Latin *faber*
Whatever your hands find to do,
do with all your strength.
— Ecclesiastes 9:10a (HCSB)

FADIL, FADEEL   *[fah-DEEL]*

Meaning: virtuous, generous • **Usage:** Muslim:
from Arabic *fadil* (generous) or *fadala* (to surpass,
to be virtuous)
Have a good conscience and fear no evil.
— Arabic proverb

FAGAN, FAGEN   *[FAY-gan]*

Meaning: fire, little fiery one • **Usage:** Irish
form of surname O'Faodhagain, from Gaelic *aodh*
(fire) and diminutive *-an*

He...makes His angels spirits
His ministers a flame of fire.
— Psalm 104:3–4 (NKJV)

FAHD   *[fahd]*

Meaning: leopard, panther • **Usage:** Muslim
It is He who is revealed in every face....
Not a single one of His creatures can fail to find
Him in its primordial and original nature.
— Muhyiddin Ibn al-'Arabi

FAHIM, FAHEEM   *[fah-HEEM]*

Meaning: educated, knowledgeable • **Usage:**
Muslim: from Arabic *fahim*
Knowledge is the adornment of the mind.
— Arabic proverb

FALKO, FALCO   *[FAHL-koh]*

Meaning: falcon • **Usage:** German: from
German *falke*
If I ride the wings of the morning, if I dwell by the
farthest oceans, even there your hand will guide me,
and your [God's] strength will support me.
— Psalm 139:9–10 (NLV)

FALLON, FAOLAN   *[FAY-lan]*

Meaning: little wolf • **Usage:** Irish: from Gaelic
faol (wolf) and diminutive *-an*
All things bright and beautiful, / All creatures great
and small, / All things wise and wonderful, /
The Lord God made them all.
— Cecil Frances Alexander,
"All Things Bright and Beautiful"

FANG   *[fahng]*

Meaning: fragrant, virtuous • **Usage:** Chinese
Like a lovely flower, / bright and fragrant,
are the fine and truthful words /
of the man who means what he says.
— Buddha, *The Dhammapada* (tr. Thomas Byrom)

F

FARAJ   [fah-rahj]

MEANING: comfort, restful, ease • USAGE: Muslim
As for him who giveth and is dutiful
(toward Allah) and believeth in goodness;
surely We will ease his way unto the state of ease.
— Koran, The Night 92.5–7 (PIC)

FARID, FAREED   [fah-REED]

MEANING: unique, rare • USAGE: Muslim: from
Arabic *farada* (to be unique)
Your hope in my heart is the rarest treasure /
Your Name on my tongue is the sweetest word /
My choicest hours / Are the hours I spend with You. /
O Allah, I can't live in this world /
Without remembering You.
— Rabia al-Adawiyya,
"My Greatest Need Is You"

FARIH   [fah-rih]

MEANING: happy, joyous • USAGE: Muslim
The key to all happiness is the love of God.
— Hazrat Inayat Khan, *The Gayan*

FARLEY   [FAR-lee]

MEANING: fern meadow, fern clearing • USAGE:
English: from English *fearn* (fern) and *leah*
(meadow, field)
I am in love with this green Earth.
— Charles Lamb, "New Year's Eve"

FARRELL   [FAYR-el]

MEANING: valorous man, man of courage •
USAGE: Irish and English surname: form of
Fearghal, from Gaelic *fear* (man) and *gal* (valor,
courage)
Courage is the ladder
on which all other virtues mount.
— Clare Boothe Luce

FARUQ, FAROUK   [fah-rook]

MEANING: discerner, one who distinguishes
between truth and falsehood • USAGE: Muslim:
from Arabic *faraqa* (to separate, to make a
distinction)
Truth is purifying, truth is most favorable,
truth is peace-giving.
— Hazrat Inayat Khan, *The Gayan*

FAYZ, FAIZ   [fah-eez]

MEANING: abundant, bountiful • USAGE: Muslim:
from Arabic *faid*
He that doeth good
shall have ten times as much to his credit.
— Koran, The Cattle 6.160a (PIC)

FAZL   [fah-zl]

MEANING: kind, merciful • USAGE: Muslim
By the power of prayer man opens the door of the heart,
in which God, the ever-forgiving,
the all-merciful, abides.
— Hazrat Inayat Khan, *The Bowl of Saki*

FEDERICO   [feh-day-REE-koh]

MEANING: peaceful ruler, leader of peace •
USAGE: Spanish and Italian form of Frederick,
from German *frid* (peace, peaceful) and *rik* (rule,
lead)
Love truth and live at peace.
— Zechariah 8:19b (CEV)

FEIVEL, FIVEL   [FIE-vel]

MEANING: bright one, intelligent, shining •
USAGE: Yiddish form of *Phoebus*, from Greek
phoibo
Happy is the man that findeth wisdom,
and the man that obtaineth understanding.
— Proverbs 3:13–14 (MT)

FELIKS

[FEE-leks]

MEANING: happy, lucky, fortunate • **USAGE:** Polish and Russian form of Felix, from Latin *felix*
Keep a good conscience, and you will always be happy.
— Thomas à Kempis, *The Imitation of Christ*
(tr. W. H. Hutchings)

FELIPE

[fay-LEE-pay]

MEANING: lover of horses • **USAGE:** Spanish form of Philip, from Greek *philein* (to love) and *hippos* (horse)
Let all that you do be done in love.
— 1 Corinthians 16:14 (NASB)

FELIPO

[fay-LEE-poh]

MEANING: lover of horses • **USAGE:** Spanish form of Philip (*see* Felipe)
Now these three remain: faith, hope, and love.
But the greatest of these is love.
— 1 Corinthians 13:13 (HCSB)

FELIPPE

[feh-LEE-pay]

MEANING: lover of horses • **USAGE:** Portuguese form of Philip (*see* Felipe)
Follow after love.
— 1 Corinthians 14:1a (DT)

FELIX

[FEE-leks (English),
FEH-leeks (Spanish)]

MEANING: happy, lucky, fortunate • **USAGE:** English and Spanish: from Latin *felix*
The secret of fortune is joy in our hands.
— Ralph Waldo Emerson, "Self-Reliance"

FENG

[fahng]

MEANING: wind, custom • **USAGE:** Chinese
May fair winds attend you!
— Chinese proverb (tr. William Scarborough)

FERDINAND

[FER-dee-nahnt (German),
FER-deh-nand (English)]

MEANING: bold venturer, prepared traveler, courageous journeyer • **USAGE:** German and English: from German *fardi* (journey, travel) and *nand* (ready, prepared), *nanthi* (venture, adventurous), or *nanths* (courageous)
There is only one journey. Going inside yourself.
— Rainer Maria Rilke

FERGAL, FEARGHAL

[FER-gal]

MEANING: brave, courageous, valorous • **USAGE:** Irish: from Gaelic *fearghal*
The best hearts are ever the bravest.
— Laurence Sterne, *The Life and Opinions of Tristram Shandy, Gentleman*

FERGUS, FEARGHAS

[FER-gus]

MEANING: vigorous man, man of strength • **USAGE:** Irish and Scottish: from Gaelic *fear* (man) and *gus* (strength, vigor)
Vigor is contagious, and whatever makes us either think or feel strongly, adds to our power, and enlarges our field of action.
— Ralph Waldo Emerson,
"Considerations by the Way"

FERNAND

[fer-NAHN]

MEANING: bold venturer, prepared traveler, courageous journeyer • **USAGE:** French form of Ferdinand (*see* Ferdinand)
The real voyage of discovery consists of not in seeking new landscapes but in having new eyes.
— Marcel Proust

FERNANDO

[fayr-NAHN-doh]

MEANING: bold venturer, prepared traveler, courageous journeyer • **USAGE:** Spanish, Italian, and Portuguese form of Ferdinand (*see* Ferdinand)

F

To be prepared is half the victory.
— Miguel de Cervantes, *Don Quixote*
(tr. Charles Jarvis)

FERRIS   *[FER-is]*

Meaning: vigorous man, man of strength •
Usage: English surname: English form of Fergus,
from Gaelic *fear* (man) and *gus* (strength, vigor)
*There is no limit to the ingenuity of man
if it is properly and vigorously applied
under conditions of peace and justice.*
— Winston Churchill

FESTER   *[FES-ter]*

Meaning: woods, forest • **Usage:** German and
English form of Silvester, from Latin *silva*
*He is like a tree planted by streams of water,
which yields its fruit in season and whose leaf
does not wither. Whatever he does prospers.*
— Psalm 1:3 (NIV)

FIDEL   *[fee-DEL]*

Meaning: faithful, loyal, trustworthy • **Usage:**
Spanish: from Latin *fidelis*
*Whoever tries to live right and be loyal
finds life, success, and honor.*
— Proverbs 21:21 (NCV)

FILIP   *[fee-leep]*

Meaning: lover of horses • **Usage:** Scandinavian, Hungarian, and Polish form of Philip (*see*
Felipe)
Follow the way of love.
— 1 Corinthians 14:1a (NIV)

FILIPPO   *[fee-LEE-poh]*

Meaning: lover of horses • **Usage:** Italian form
of Philip (*see* Felipe)

*Love consists in sharing what one has and
what one is with those one loves. Love ought
to show itself in deeds more than in words.*
— Ignatius of Loyola

FINBAR   *[FIN-bahr]*

Meaning: blond, fair-headed • **Usage:** Irish
form of *Fionnbharr*, from *fionn* (white, fair) and *barr*
(head)
You [God] anoint my head with oil; my cup overflows.
— Psalm 23:5b (ESV)

FINDLAY, FINDLEY   *[FIND-lee]*

Meaning: white warrior, fair-haired hero •
Usage: Scottish surname: from Gaelic *fionn*
(white, fair) and *laogh* (warrior, hero)
Self-trust is the essence of heroism.
— Ralph Waldo Emerson, "Heroism"

FIONN, FINN   *[fin]*

Meaning: fair, white • **Usage:** Irish: from Gaelic
finn
Wash me, and I shall be whiter than snow.
— Psalm 51:7b (KJV)

FITZ   *[fits]*

Meaning: son • **Usage:** English: from French *fitz*
(son of)
God bless you, my son.
— Genesis 43:29b (GNT)

FLANN   *[flahn]*

Meaning: red, redheaded, ruddy-complexioned •
Usage: Irish: from Gaelic *flann*
*Mere colour, unspoiled by meaning,
and unallied with definite form,
can speak to the soul in a thousand different ways.*
— Oscar Wilde, "The Critic as Artist"

FLAVIO [*FLAH-vee-oh*]

MEANING: yellow, golden • **USAGE:** Italian and Spanish, from Latin *flavus*

Learning is unto a wise man as an ornament of gold,
and like a bracelet upon his right arm.
— Ben Sira 21:21 (KJV Apocrypha)

FLETCH [*fletch*]

MEANING: arrow maker, archer • **USAGE:** English form of Fletcher (*see* Fletcher)

We have not been created to just pass
through this life without aim. And that greater aim
is to love and be loved.
— Mother Teresa

FLETCHER [*FLET-cher*]

MEANING: arrow maker, archer • **USAGE:** English surname: from French *flechier*

The day is always his,
who works in it with serenity and great aims.
— Ralph Waldo Emerson,
"The American Scholar"

FLINT [*flint*]

MEANING: hard rock, strong • **USAGE:** English: from English *flint* (hard quartz rock)

Iron is made sharp with iron,
and one man is made sharp by a friend.
— Proverbs 27:17 (NLV)

FLIP [*flip*]

MEANING: lover of horses • **USAGE:** American form of Philip (*see* Felipe)

Flaming enthusiasm, backed by horse sense
and persistence, is the quality that most
frequently makes for success.
— Dale Carnegie

FLOYD [*floid*]

MEANING: gray, gray-headed • **USAGE:** English form of Lloyd, from Welsh *lwyd*

Thou anointest my head with oil;
my cup runneth over.
— Psalm 23:5b (KJV)

FLYNN [*flin*]

MEANING: red color, redheaded, ruddy-complexioned • **USAGE:** English form of Flann, from Irish Gaelic *flann* (red)

He was ruddy, with bright eyes,
and good-looking.
— 1 Samuel 16:12b (NKJV)

FOLKER [*FOHL-ker*]

MEANING: guardian of the people, people's army, warrior • **USAGE:** German form of *Folkvardr*, from Norse *folk* (people, folk) and *varðr* (guardian, protector) or from German *volk* (people, folk) and *hari* (army)

The Lord will go before you . . .
[and] will be your rear guard.
— Isaiah 52:12b (NIV)

FOLUKE [*foh-loo-keh*]

MEANING: placed in God's care • **USAGE:** African: Yoruba of Nigeria

Planning is man's, doing is God's.
— Yoruban proverb

FONS [*fonz*]

MEANING: nobly prepared • **USAGE:** Dutch and Spanish form of Alfons or Alphonso, from German *adal* (noble) and *funs* (ready, prepared)

Nobility of soul is more honorable
than nobility of birth.
— Dutch proverb

F

F

FORD   [ford]

MEANING: river crossing, river ford • USAGE:
English: from English *ford* (ford, shallow river
crossing)

> *Thus says the Lord…when you pass through*
> *the waters, I will be with you.*
> — Isaiah 43:1–2a (ESV)

FOREST, FORREST   [FOR-est]

MEANING: forest, woods • USAGE: English: from
Latin *forestis*

> *Forests give a universal feeling of good will.*
> — Enos A. Mills, *Your National Parks*

FORTUNATO   [fohr-too-NAH-toh]

MEANING: fortunate, lucky • USAGE: Italian,
Portuguese, and Spanish: from Latin *fortuna*
(fortune)

> *Every man is the architect of his own fortune.*
> — Appius Claudius Caecus

FRANCESCO   [frahn-CHEHS-koh]

MEANING: one who is free, native of France, a
Franc, spearman • USAGE: Italian form of Latin
Franciscus (*see* Francis)

> *He who is brave is fearless; he who is fearless is free*
> *from sadness; he who is free from sadness is happy.*
> — Seneca, *Ad Lucilium Epistolae Morales*

FRANCIS   [FRAN-sis (English),
frahn-SEES (French)]

MEANING: one who is free, native of France, a
Franc, spearman • USAGE: English and French
form of Latin *Franciscus* (a Frenchman); from
French *franc* (free, freeman); or from *franco* (spear
used by the Franks, a Germanic tribe)

> *Only the heart that is free is pure.*
> — Elbert Hubbard, "Consecrated Lives"

FRANCISCO   [frahn-SEES-koh]

MEANING: one who is free, native of France, a
Franc, spearman • USAGE: Spanish and Portuguese
form of Latin *Franciscus* (*see* Francis)

> *God called you to be free.*
> — Galatians 5:13a (NCV)

FRANCO   [FRAHN-koh]

MEANING: one who is free, native of France, a
Franc, spearman • USAGE: Italian form of Francis
(*see* Francis)

> *Always preserve in yourself the virtues of freedom,*
> *of sincerity, sobriety, and good nature.*
> — Marcus Aurelius,
> *The Meditations* (tr. Jeremy Collier)

FRANÇOIS   [frahn-SWAH]

MEANING: one who is free, native of France, a
Franc, spearman • USAGE: French form of Latin
Franciscus (*see* Francis)

> *He who loves, flies, runs, and rejoices;*
> *he is free and nothing holds him back.*
> — Henri Matisse

FRANK   [fraynk (English), frahnk (German)]

MEANING: one who is free, native of France, a
Franc, spearman, straightforward, frank • USAGE:
English and German form of Francis (*see* Francis);
or English *frank* (straightforward, honest)

> *I wish to be simple, honest, natural, frank,*
> *clean in mind and clean in body.*
> — Elbert Hubbard, "The Radiant Life"

FRANKLIN   [FRAYNK-lin]

MEANING: freeman, town of freemen • USAGE:
English surname: from English *frankeleyn* (a
freeman); or from French *franc* (free) and English
tun (town, village)

> *Live as people who are free.*
> — 1 Peter 2:16a (ESV)

FRANS [*frahnz*]

MEANING: one who is free, native of France, a Franc, spearman • **USAGE:** Scandinavian and Dutch form of Latin *Franciscus* (*see* Francis)

The Lord is the Spirit;
and where the Spirit of the Lord is, there is freedom.
— 2 Corinthians 3:17 (NCV)

FRANZ [*frahnts*]

MEANING: one who is free, native of France, a Franc, spearman • **USAGE:** German form of Latin *Franciscus* (*see* Francis)

Man has been created free — is free by birthright.
— Johann Friedrich von Schiller

FRASER [*FRAY-zer*]

MEANING: strawberry • **USAGE:** Scottish form of French surname *de Frisselle*, from French *fraise* (strawberry)

The fruit of the Spirit is love, joy, peace,
patience, kindness, goodness, faithfulness,
gentleness and self-control.
— Galatians 5:22–23a (NIV)

FRED [*fred*]

MEANING: peaceful ruler, leader of peace • **USAGE:** English form of Frederick (*see* Frederick)

Live in peace, and the God of love
and peace will be with you.
— 2 Corinthians 13:11b (WEB)

FREDERICK, FREDRIK [*FRED-eh-rik, FRED-rik*]

MEANING: peaceful ruler, leader of peace • **USAGE:** English form of Friedrich, from German *frid* (peace, peaceful) and *rik* (rule, lead)

Peace hath higher tests of manhood /
Than battle ever knew.
— John Greenleaf Whittier, "The Hero"

FREDERICO [*freh-day-REE-koh*]

MEANING: peaceful ruler, leader of peace • **USAGE:** Portuguese form of Frederick (*see* Frederick)

Mercy unto you, and peace.
— Jude 1:2a (DR)

FREDRIK [*FRED-reek*]

MEANING: peaceful ruler, leader of peace • **USAGE:** Scandinavian form of Frederick (*see* Frederick)

He hath great tranquility and peace of heart…
that hath a good conscience.
— Thomas à Kempis, *The Imitation of Christ*
(tr. Richard Whytford)

FREE [*free*]

MEANING: liberated, unbound, free • **USAGE:** American: English *freo*

All good things are wild and free.
— Henry David Thoreau, "Walking"

FRIEDRICH [*FREE-drik*]

MEANING: peaceful ruler, leader of peace • **USAGE:** German (*see* Frederick)

To life! and thou, peace; and thy house, peace;
and all that thou hast — peace!
— 1 Samuel 25:6b (YLT)

FRITZ [*fritz*]

MEANING: peaceful ruler, leader of peace • **USAGE:** German form of Friedrich (*see* Frederick)

I am a man of peace.
— Psalm 120:7a (NIV)

FRODE [*FROH-dee*]

MEANING: wise, knowing, intelligent • **USAGE:** Norwegian, Danish, and Swedish: from Norse *fróðr* (wise, knowing)

F

Wisdom brings strength, and knowledge gives power.
— Proverbs 24:5 (CEV)

FUAD   *[foo-ahd]*

MEANING: heart • **USAGE:** Muslim: from Arabic *fu'ad*
> *The heart perceives that which the eye cannot see.*
> — Al-Ghazali

FYODOR   *[FYOH-dahr]*

MEANING: gift of God • **USAGE:** Russian form of Theodore, from Greek *theos* (God) and *doron* (gift)
> *When God gives any man wealth and possessions, and enables him to enjoy them, to accept his lot and be happy in his work — this is a gift from God.*
> — Ecclesiastes 5:19 (NIV)

G

GABE   *[gayb]*

MEANING: God is my strength, strong man of God • **USAGE:** English form of Gabriel (*see* Gabriel)
> *It is God who arms me with strength and keeps my way secure.*
> — 2 Samuel 22:33 (NIV)

GABLE   *[GAY-bel]*

MEANING: God is my strength, strong man of God • **USAGE:** English surname: form of Gabriel (*see* Gabriel)
> *God is my strength of my heart and my portion forever.*
> — Psalm 73:26b (NKJV)

GABRIEL   *[GAY-bree-el (English), gah-bree-EL (Spanish, French, German, Scandinavian)]*

MEANING: God is my strength, strong man of God • **USAGE:** English, French, German, Scandinavian, and Spanish form of Gavriel, from Hebrew *gabhri'el*

I am your God. I will make you strong, as I protect you with my arm and give you victories.
— Isaiah 41:10b (CEV)

GABRIELO   *[gah-bree-AY-loh]*

MEANING: God is my strength, strong man of God • **USAGE:** Portuguese form of Gabriel (*see* Gabriel)
> *Your strength comes from God's grace.*
> — Hebrews 13:9b (NLT)

GADIEL   *[gah-dee-EHL]*

MEANING: God is my fortune, God is my blessing • **USAGE:** Jewish
> *He [God] will favor and bless you.*
> — Deuteronomy 7:13a (JPS)

GAGE, GAIGE   *[gayj]*

MEANING: pledge, promise • **USAGE:** American: from French *gage* (pledge, surety against money lent)
> *For the Lord your God will bless you just as He promised you.*
> — Deuteronomy 15:6a (NKJV)

GAI   *[gie]*

MEANING: valley • **USAGE:** Jewish
> *The valleys…shout for joy, yea, they sing.*
> — Psalm 65:14 (MT)

GALE   *[gayl]*

MEANING: joyous, rejoicing, gale, strong wind • **USAGE:** English: from French *gale* (rejoicing); or from English *gaile* (strong wind)
> *The joy of the spirit indicates strength.*
> — Ralph Waldo Emerson, "Considerations by the Way"

GALEN   *[GAY-len]*

MEANING: calm, peaceful, healer • **USAGE:** English: from Greek *galene* (calm, peaceful); reference to Greek physician Claudius Galenus

*The more tranquil a man becomes, the greater
is his success, his influence, his power for good.*
— James Allen, *As a Man Thinketh*

GALENO　　　　　　　　　[gah-LAY-noh]

MEANING: calm, peaceful, healer • **USAGE:**
Spanish and Italian surname (*see* Galen)
May grace and peace be multiplied to you.
— 1 Peter 1:2b (HCSB)

GALIL　　　　　　　　　　[gah-LEEL]

MEANING: rolling hills • **USAGE:** Jewish; region
in Israel
The hills are girded with joy.
— Psalm 65:13b (JPS)

GAMLIEL　　　　　　　　[gahm-lee-EHL]

MEANING: God is my reward • **USAGE:** Jewish;
region in Israel
May the Lord reward your deeds.
May you have a full recompense from the Lord.
— Ruth 2:12a (JPS)

GANDHI　　　　　　　　　[GAHN-dih]

MEANING: fragrant, sweet-smelling • **USAGE:**
Hindu: Sanskrit
Let the wind blow sweetly. Let the rivers run sweetly.
Let the herbs be to us sweet and beneficial.
Let there be sweetness day and night.
Let the particles of the earth be sweetness-bearing.
Let heaven, our father, be sweet to us.
— *Rig Veda*

GANNON　　　　　　　　　[GAN-on]

MEANING: love, affection, beloved • **USAGE:** Irish
surname: from Gaelic *gean*
Affection is a garden, and without it there would not be
a verdant spot on the surface of the globe.
— Henry Ward Beecher

GARED, GARRED　　　　　[GEHR-ed]

MEANING: strong spear, brave with a spear •
USAGE: English surname: form of Gerald, from
German *ger* (spear) and *hart* (hardy, strong, brave)
God will make you complete,
steady, strong, and firm.
— 1 Peter 5:10 (CEV)

GAREN, GARAN, GARREN　　[GEHR-en]

MEANING: guard, guardian, protector • **USAGE:**
English: from German *gard*
The one who guards his way protects his life.
— Proverbs 16:17 (HCSB)

G

GARETH　　　　　　　　　[GEHR-eth]

MEANING: gentle, kind, civilized • **USAGE:** Welsh
and English: from Welsh *gwared* (gentle, kind), or
gwaraidd (civilized)
Be kind and tender-hearted.
— Ephesians 4:32a (GNT)

GARLAND　　　　　　　　[GAR-land]

MEANING: triangular piece of land; moustache •
USAGE: English surname: from English *gara* and
land (triangular piece of land); or from French
gernon (moustache)
Trust in the Lord, and do good; dwell in the land and
cultivate faithfulness. Delight yourself in the Lord;
and He will give you the desires of your heart.
— Psalm 37:3–4 (NASB)

GARNET, GARNETT　　　　[gar-NET]

MEANING: little war, hinge-maker • **USAGE:**
English surname: possibly from French *guarinot*
(little war); or from French *ganetier* (person who
makes hinges)
Be strong and of good courage.
— 2 Chronicles 32:7a (NRSV)

G

GARRET, GARRETT [GAYR-et]

MEANING: rule with a spear, brave with a spear •
USAGE: English surname: form of Gerald, from
German *ger* (spear) and *wald* (rule, power); or
English form of Gerard, from *ger* (spear) and *hart*
(hardy, strong, brave)

Keep on being brave!
It will bring you great rewards.
— Hebrews 10:35 (CEV)

GARRICK [GAHR-ik (German), GAYR-ik (English)]

MEANING: leads with a spear, spear ruler, strong
spear • USAGE: German and English: from German
ger (spear) and *rik* (rule, lead); or English form of
Gerhard, from German *ger* (spear) and *hart* (hardy,
strong, brave)

Whatever your hand finds to do, do it with your might.
— Ecclesiastes 9:10a (RSV)

GARRISON [GAYR-eh-sun]

MEANING: spear son, son of the spear • USAGE:
English surname: from English *gar* (spear) and *son*
(son)

May the Lord bless you, my son!
— Judges 17:2b (CEV)

GARTH [garth]

MEANING: garden, enclosure • USAGE: English
and Scandinavian: from Norse *garðr*

The best place to seek God is in a garden.
You can dig for him there.
— George Bernard Shaw

GARVIN, GARVAN [GAHR-ven]

MEANING: spear friend, little rugged one •
USAGE: Irish: from Gaelic *garbh* (rough, rugged)
and diminutive *-an;* or from English *gar* (spear) and
wine (friend)

As iron sharpens iron, so a friend sharpens a friend.
— Proverbs 27:17 (NLT)

GARY [GAYR-ee]

MEANING: rule with a spear, powerful spear,
brave with a spear, gentle, kind, civilized • USAGE:
English form of Gerald, from German *ger* (spear)
and *wald* (rule, power); form of Gerhard, from
German *ger* (spear) or *hart* (hardy, strong, brave);
or form of Gareth, from Welsh *gwared* (gentle,
kind) or *gwaraidd* (civilized)

For God hath not given us the spirit of fear;
but of power and of love, and of a sound mind.
— 2 Timothy 1:7 (KJV)

GASPAR [gahs-PAHR]

MEANING: treasure master, steward • USAGE:
Spanish: from Persian *genashber*

Where your treasure is, there will your heart be also.
— Luke 12:34 (KJV)

GASPARD [gahs-PAHR]

MEANING: treasure master, steward • USAGE:
French (*see* Gaspar)

A good man out of the good treasure of his
heart bringeth forth that which is good...for out
of the abundance of the heart his mouth speaketh.
— Luke 6:45 (KJV)

GASTON [gahs-TOHN]

MEANING: treasure master, steward • USAGE:
French form of Gaspar (*see* Gaspar)

Our heart is a treasury.
— Honoré de Balzac, *Père Goriot*
(tr. Katharine Wormeley)

GAUTIER [gah-TEER]

MEANING: ruler of the army, army commander •
USAGE: French form of Walter, from German *wald*
(rule, power) and *hari* (army)

To command is to serve, nothing more, nothing less.
— André Malraux, *Man's Hope*

GAVIN   [*GAV-in*]

MEANING: kind, gentle, handsome field hawk, battle hawk, white hawk • **USAGE:** Scottish and English: Scottish form of Gawain (*see* Gawain); or Scottish and English form of Kevin, from Irish Gaelic *caomh* (gentle, kind) or *caem* (handsome, comely)

> *Be kind and honest and you will live a long life; others will respect you and treat you fairly.*
> — Proverbs 21:21 (GNT)

GAVRIEL, GAVRIL   [*gahv-ree-EHL, gahv-REEL*]

MEANING: God is my strength, strong man of God • **USAGE:** Jewish: from Hebrew *gabhri'el*

> *The Lord is my strength and my shield, in Him hath my heart trusted, and I am helped; therefore my heart greatly rejoiceth, and with my song will I praise Him.*
> — Psalm 28:7a (MT)

GAWAIN, GWAYNE   [*gah-WAYN, gwayn*]

MEANING: field hawk, battle hawk, white hawk • **USAGE:** Welsh form of *Gwalchmei*, from Welsh *gwalch* (hawk, falcon) and *gwyn* (white, fair, holy), *maedd* (battle) or *mai* (plain, field); or possibly from Welsh *gwyn* (white, fair, holy) and *mai* (battle)

> *This I declare about the Lord...He will cover you with his feathers. He will shelter you with his wings. His faithful promises are your armor and protection.*
> — Psalm 91:4b (NLT)

GEFEN   [*GEH-fen*]

MEANING: vine • **USAGE:** Jewish: from Hebrew *gefen* (vine); a symbol of peace

> *As my fathers planted for me, so do I plant for my children.*
> — Babylonian Talmud: Tractate Taanit 23a

GENE   [*jeen*]

MEANING: wellborn, noble • **USAGE:** English form of Eugene, from Greek *eu* (good, well) and *genes* (born)

> *Nothing is sweeter than Love; nothing braver, nothing higher, nothing wider, nothing fuller nor better in Heaven and in earth; because Love is born of God, and can only rest in God, above all created things.*
> — Thomas à Kempis, *The Imitation of Christ*

GEOFF   [*jef*]

MEANING: peace of God, God's peace, peaceful territory, peaceful stranger, peaceful traveler, pledge of peace • **USAGE:** English form of Geoffrey (*see* Geoffrey)

> *God, who gives peace, will be with you.*
> — Philippians 4:9b (CEV)

GEOFFREY, GEOFFRY   [*JEF-ree*]

MEANING: peace of God, God's peace, peaceful territory, peaceful stranger, peaceful traveler, pledge of peace • **USAGE:** English: from German *gott* (God) and *frid* (peace); or from German *gawia* (territory), *walah* (stranger), or *gisil* (pledge, promise) and *frid* (peace)

> *He will easily be content and at peace, whose conscience is pure.*
> — Thomas à Kempis,
> *The Imitation of Christ* (tr. W. H. Hutchings)

GEOFFROI   [*JOH-free*]

MEANING: peace of God, God's peace, peaceful territory, peaceful stranger, peaceful traveler, pledge of peace • **USAGE:** French form of Geoffrey (*see* Geoffrey)

> *I am sending an angel ahead of you, who will protect you as you travel.*
> — Exodus 23:20a (NCV)

GEORG   [GAY-ork]

MEANING: earth worker, farmer, gardener •
USAGE: German and Scandinavian form of George
(*see* George)
Earth, isn't this what you want: to arise invisibly in us?
— Rainer Maria Rilke, *Duino Elegies*

GEORGE   [jorj]

MEANING: earth worker, farmer, gardener •
USAGE: English form of Giorgios, from Greek *ge*
(earth) and *ergein* (to work)
The world is upheld by the veracity of good men:
they make the earth wholesome.
— Ralph Waldo Emerson, *Representative Men*

GEORGES   [ʒorʒ]

MEANING: earth worker, farmer, gardener •
USAGE: French form of George (*see* George)
What a person plants, he will harvest....
The one who plants in response to God,
letting God's Spirit do the growth work in him,
harvests a crop of real life, eternal life.
— Galatians 6:7–8 (MSG)

GEORGI, GEORGY   [gee-OHR-gee]

MEANING: earth worker, farmer, gardener •
USAGE: Russian form of George (*see* George)
He loves righteousness and justice;
the earth is full of the goodness of the Lord.
— Psalm 33:5 (NKJV)

GEORGIOS   [yeh-OR-yee-ohs]

MEANING: earth worker, farmer, gardener •
USAGE: Greek (*see* George)
Speak to the earth. It will teach you.
— Job 12:8a (NIRV)

GERAINT   [jeh-RAYNT]

MEANING: old, old man • USAGE: Welsh form of
Gerontios, from Greek *gerontius*

In the evening of life,
we will be judged on love alone.
— St. John of the Cross

GERALD   [JER-ald (English), GEH-rahlt (German)]

MEANING: rule with a spear, powerful spear •
USAGE: English and German form of *Gerwald*,
from German *ger* (spear) and *wald* (rule, power)
In every society some men are born to rule,
and some to advise. Let the powers be well directed,
directed by love, and they would everywhere
be greeted with joy and honor.
— Ralph Waldo Emerson, "The Young American"

GERALDO   [hay-RAHL-doh]

MEANING: rule with a spear, powerful spear •
USAGE: Spanish form of Gerald (*see* Gerald)
We all have gifts. They differ in keeping
with the grace that God has given each of us....
Is it being a leader? Then work hard at it.
— Romans 12:6, 12:8b (NIRV)

GERARD   [jeh-RARD]

MEANING: strong spear, brave with a spear
• USAGE: English and Scandinavian form of
Gerhard, from German *ger* (spear) and *hart* (hardy,
strong, brave)
Life can only be nobly inspired and rightly lived
if you take it bravely and gallantly.
— Annie Besant

GERARDO   [hay-RAHR-doh]

MEANING: strong spear, brave with a spear •
USAGE: Spanish and Italian form of Gerard (*see*
Gerard)
You shall be a blessing. Don't be afraid.
Let your hands be strong.
— Zechariah 8:13b (WEB)

GERAUD [zheh-roh]

MEANING: rule with a spear, powerful spear • **USAGE:** French form of Gerald (*see* Gerald)
> *The most powerful weapon on earth is*
> *the human soul on fire.*
> — Ferdinand Foch

GERHARD, GERHARDT [GEHR-hart]

MEANING: strong spear, brave with a spear • **USAGE:** German and Scandinavian: from German *ger* (spear) and *hart* (hardy, strong, brave)
> *A wise man is strong; yea,*
> *a man of knowledge increaseth might.*
> — Proverbs 24:5 (ASV)

GERMAIN [zher-MAYN]

MEANING: brother, sprout, bud • **USAGE:** French: from *germanus* (brother) or from Latin *germen* (sprout, bud)
> *He who loves his brother abides in the light,*
> *and there is no cause for stumbling in him.*
> — 1 John 2:10 (NKJV)

GERRY [JER-ee]

MEANING: rule with a spear, powerful spear, brave with a spear • **USAGE:** English form of Gerald (*see* Gerald) or of Gerard (*see* Gerard)
> *Whatever your hand finds to do, do it with your might.*
> — Ecclesiastes 9:10a (ESV)

GERSHOM [ger-SHOHM]

MEANING: stranger, foreigner • **USAGE:** Jewish
> *She bore a son whom he named Gershom, for he said,*
> *"I have been a stranger in a foreign land."*
> — Exodus 2:22 (JPS)

GERSHON [gehr-SHOHN]

MEANING: stranger, foreigner • **USAGE:** Jewish
> *The stranger that sojourneth with you shall be unto you*
> *as the home-born among you, and thou shalt love him*
> *as thyself; for ye were strangers in the land of Egypt.*
> — Leviticus 19:34 (MT)

GERVAISE [zher-VEZ]

MEANING: spear-servant, warrior • **USAGE:** French form of *Gervasius*, from German *ger* (spear) and *vass* (servant)
> *It is God who arms me with strength.*
> — Psalm 18:32a (NKJV)

GHALIB [gah-leeb]

MEANING: victorious, successful • **USAGE:** Muslim: from Arabic *ghalaba* (to have victory)
> *Verily he is victorious who has conquered himself.*
> — Hazrat Inayat Khan, *The Gayan*

GHANDI [GAHN-dee]

MEANING: fragrant, sweet-smelling • **USAGE:** Hindu: Sanskrit
> *Let the wind blow sweetly. Let the rivers run sweetly.*
> *Let the herbs be to us sweet and beneficial.*
> *Let there be sweetness day and night. Let the*
> *particles of the earth be sweetness-bearing.*
> *Let heaven, our father, be sweet to us.*
> — *Rig Veda*

GHANI [gah-nee]

MEANING: wealthy, prosperous • **USAGE:** Muslim
> *A man's true wealth hereafter is*
> *the good he does in this world.*
> — Hadith of the Prophet Muhammad

GHAZI [gah-zee]

MEANING: conqueror, victor • **USAGE:** Muslim
> *Victory is only from Allah;*
> *surely Allah is Mighty, Wise.*
> — Koran, The Spoils of War 8.10b (SKR)

G

GIACOBBE   *[jya-KOH-beh]*

MEANING: replace, change, transform, successor
• **USAGE:** Italian form of Jacob, from Hebrew
ya'aqobh (one that takes by the heel, replace with
another)

Put on the new man, which, according to God,
was created in righteousness and kindness of the truth.
        — Ephesians 4:24 (YLT)

GIACOMO   *[jya-KOH-moh,*
        JAHK-ah-moh]

MEANING: replace, change, transform, successor
• **USAGE:** Italian form of James, from Hebrew
ya'aqobh (one that takes by the heel, replace with
another)

Be ye transformed by the renewing of your mind.
        — Romans 12:2b (KJV)

GIANNI   *[JYA-nee]*

MEANING: God is gracious, God is giving •
USAGE: Italian form of Giovanni, from Hebrew
y'hohanan (Yahweh is gracious)

Grace…is given not because we have done good works,
but in order that we may have power to do them.
        — Augustine of Hippo

GIANNIS   *[JYA-nees]*

MEANING: God is gracious, God is giving •
USAGE: Italian form of Ioannis (*see* Gianni)
May God be gracious to you.
        — Genesis 43:29b (NLT)

GIB   *[gib]*

MEANING: shining promise, brilliant pledge,
famous oath • **USAGE:** English form of Gilbert (*see*
Gilbert)

The Lord…gives me new strength. He guides me
in the right paths, as he has promised.
        — Psalm 23:1–3 (GNT)

GIBOR   *[gee-BOHR]*

MEANING: strong, powerful • **USAGE:** Jewish
Be strong and resolute.
        — Joshua 1:6a (JPS)

GIDEON   *[GID-ee-on]*

MEANING: hewer, one who cuts down, mighty
warrior • **USAGE:** English form of Gidon (*see*
Gidon)

When the angel of the Lord appeared to Gideon,
he said, "The Lord is with you, mighty warrior."
        — Judges 6:12 (NIV)

GIDON   *[gee-DOHN]*

MEANING: hewer, one who cuts down, mighty
warrior • **USAGE:** Jewish: from Hebrew *gidh'on*
Your God the Lord is in your midst, a warrior
who brings triumph. He will rejoice over you and be
glad, He will shout over you with jubilation.
He will soothe with His love.
        — Zephaniah 3:17a (JPS)

GIL   *[gil]*

MEANING: shining promise, brilliant pledge,
famous oath, redheaded disciple • **USAGE:** English
form of Gilbert (*see* Gilbert) or of Gilroy (*see*
Gilroy)

His words are bonds, his oaths are oracles…his heart
as far from fraud, as heaven from earth.
        — William Shakespeare,
        The Two Gentlemen of Verona

GIL   *[geel]*

MEANING: joyous, happy • **USAGE:** Jewish
Happy is he who performs a good deed: for he may tip
the scales for himself and the world.
        — *Talmud:* Kiddushin 40a

GILBERT
[GIL-bert (English), ʒhil-BEHR (French), GEEL-bahrt (German)]

MEANING: shining promise, brilliant pledge, famous oath • **USAGE:** English, French, and German form of *Guillebert*, from German *gisil* (pledge, promise) and *beraht* (bright, shining)

God's gift is what you yourself are,
for you are God's gift to yourself; you are God's
promise to yourself, to other people, to God.
— Hans Urs von Balthasar, *Theo-Drama*

GILBERTO
[heel-BAYR-toh (Spanish), jeel-BER-toh (Italian), geel-BAYR-toh (Portuguese)]

MEANING: shining promise, brilliant pledge, famous oath • **USAGE:** Spanish, Italian, and Portuguese form of Gilbert (*see* Gilbert)

An honest man's word is as good as his bond.
— Miguel de Cervantes, *Don Quixote*
(tr. Peter Motteux)

GILEAD
[GIL-ee-ad]

MEANING: hill of testimony, monument • **USAGE:** English form of Gilad

Lord...who may dwell in Your holy hill?
He that walketh uprightly, and worketh righteousness,
and speaketh the truth in his heart.
— Proverbs 15:1–2 (KJV)

GILES
[jiles]

MEANING: shield of Zeus, protecting shield, goatskin • **USAGE:** English: from Greek *aigidion* (young goat, kid) and from Greek *aigis* (shield of Zeus, goatskin); Zeus is Greek father of the gods

Thou, O Lord, art a shield about me, my glory,
and the One who lifts my head.
— Psalm 3:3 (NASB)

GILLEAN
[GIL-yahn]

MEANING: servant of St. John, Christian • **USAGE:** Scottish surname: a form of *Giolla Eoin* (servant of St. John), from Gaelic *giolla* (devotee, servant) and *Eoin* (John)

This embrace of God sets ablaze a fire within
the soul with which the whole soul burns for Christ.
It also produces a light so great that the soul
understands the fullness of God's goodness.
— Angela of Foligno

GILLIS
[GIL-is]

MEANING: servant of Jesus • **USAGE:** Scottish and Dutch surname: a form of *Giolla Iosa*, from Gaelic *giolla* (devotee, servant) and *Iosa* (Jesus)

I can do everything by the power of Christ.
He gives me strength.
— Philippians 4:13 (NIRV)

GILON
[gee-LOHN]

MEANING: joyful, happy • **USAGE:** Jewish

Happy is the man that findeth wisdom,
and the man that obtaineth understanding....
She is a tree of life to them that lay hold upon her,
and happy is every one that holdeth her fast.
— Proverbs 3:13, 3:18 (MT)

GILROY
[GIL-roi]

MEANING: redheaded disciple • **USAGE:** Scottish form of surname *Mac Giolla Ruaidh*, from Gaelic *giolla* (devotee, servant) and *ruadh* (red)

Well done, thou good and faithful servant: thou hast
been faithful over a few things, I will make thee ruler
over many things: enter thou into the joy of thy lord.
— Matthew 25:21 (KJV)

GINO
[JEEN-oh]

MEANING: wellborn, noble • **USAGE:** Italian form of Eugenio, from Greek *eu* (good, well) and *genes* (born)

The noble devises noble things;
and he will continue in noble things.
— Isaiah 32:8 (WEB)

GIOELE   [joh-AY-lay]

MEANING: the Lord is God, God is willing •
USAGE: Italian form of Joel, from Hebrew *yoh' el*
(Yahweh is God)

God will generously provide all you need.
Then you will always have everything you need
and plenty left over to share with others.
— 2 Corinthians 9:8 (NLT)

GIORGIO   [jee-OHR-jee-oh]

MEANING: earth worker, farmer, gardener •
USAGE: Italian form of George, from Greek *ge*
(earth) and *ergein* (to work)

Love alone / is the true seed of every merit in you.
— Dante Alighieri, *The Divine Comedy*
(tr. James I. Minchin)

GIOVANNI   [joh-VAH-nee]

MEANING: God is gracious, God is giving •
USAGE: Italian form of John, from Hebrew
y'hohanan (Yahweh is gracious)

The Lord your God is gracious and compassionate.
He will not turn his face from you.
— 2 Chronicles 30:9b (GNT)

GIRALDO   [jee-RAHL-doh]

MEANING: rule with a spear, powerful spear •
USAGE: Italian form of Gerald, from German *ger*
(spear) and *wald* (rule, power)

All that thy hand findeth to do, with thy power do.
— Ecclesiastes 9:10a (YLT)

GIRI   [gih-rih]

MEANING: he who is like a mountain • **USAGE:**
Hindu: Sanskrit

Like the Himalayas good men shine from afar.
— Buddha, *The Dhammapada* (tr. Thomas Byrom)

GITONGA   [geh-tohn-gah]

MEANING: wealthy one • **USAGE:** African: Kikuyu
of Kenya

Use of brains begets wealth.
— Kenyan proverb

GIULIANO   [jool-YAH-noh]

MEANING: light-bearded, young, youthful, of
Jupiter • **USAGE:** Italian form of Julian, from Latin
iulus (downy-chinned, youthful); or form of *Jupiter*,
from Latin *dyeus* (Zeus) and *pater* (father)

It takes a very long time to become young.
— Pablo Picasso

GIUSEPPE   [joo-SEH-pay]

MEANING: God will add, God will increase •
USAGE: Italian form of Joseph, from Hebrew
ya'saph (Yahweh will add)

The Lord shall increase you more and more,
you and your children. Ye are blessed by the Lord
who made heaven and earth.
— Psalm 115:14–15 (KJ21)

GIVON   [gee-VOHN]

MEANING: hill, mount • **USAGE:** Jewish

Let the mountains produce well-being for the people,
the hills, the reward of justice.
— Psalm 72:3 (JPS)

GLEN, GLENN   [glen]

MEANING: secluded wooded valley, glen • **USAGE:**
Scottish and English: from Gaelic *gleann* (secluded
wooded valley); or from Welsh *glyn* (valley, glen)

Study nature, love nature, stay close to nature.
It will never fail you.
— Frank Lloyd Wright

GLYN   *[glen]*

MEANING: glen, small valley • **USAGE:** Welsh: from Welsh *glyn*

> *How green was my Valley.*
> — Richard Llewellyn, *How Green Was My Valley*

GODFREY   *[GOD-free]*

MEANING: peace of God, God's peace • **USAGE:** English form of Gottfried, from German *gott* (God) and *frid* (peace)

> *The Lord said,*
> *"I will go with you and give you peace."*
> — Exodus 33:14 (CEV)

GODWIN   *[GOD-win]*

MEANING: friend of God • **USAGE:** English: from English *god* (God) and *wine* (friend)

> *We know that all things work together*
> *for good to them that love God, to them who*
> *are called according to his purpose.*
> — Romans 8:28 (KJV)

GOMDA   *[gohm-dah]*

MEANING: wind • **USAGE:** Amerind: Kiowa

> *That wind, that wind / Shakes my tepee,*
> *shakes my tepee, / And sings a song for me /*
> *And sings a song for me.*
> — Kiowa song

GOMER   *[GOH-mehr]*

MEANING: complete, perfected • **USAGE:** Jewish and English

> *The Lord recompense thy work,*
> *and be thy reward complete from the Lord.*
> — Ruth 2:12a (MT)

GORDON, GORDAN   *[GOR-don]*

MEANING: large fort, great fort • **USAGE:** Scottish and English surname: from Gaelic *gor* (large, spacious, great) and *din* (fort)

> *Great men are they who see that spiritual is*
> *stronger than any material force —*
> *that thoughts rule the world.*
> — Ralph Waldo Emerson, "Progress of Culture"

GOTTFRIED   *[GOHT-freed]*

MEANING: God's peace, the peace of God • **USAGE:** German: from German *gott* (God) and *frid*

> *Live in peace: and the God of love*
> *and peace shall be with you.*
> — 2 Corinthians 13:11b (ASV)

GOYO   *[GOY-yoh]*

MEANING: watchful, vigilant, alert • **USAGE:** Spanish form of Gregorio, from Greek *gregorein*

> *Keep alert. Be firm in your faith. Stay brave and*
> *strong. Show love in everything you do.*
> — 1 Corinthians 16:13–14 (CEV)

GRADY   *[GRAY-dee]*

MEANING: noble, honorable • **USAGE:** Irish and English form of surname *O'Gradaigh*, from Irish *grada*

> *In thy face I see the map of honour, truth, and loyalty.*
> — William Shakespeare, *King Henry VI, Part II*

GRAHAM   *[gram]*

MEANING: fierce, gravel home • **USAGE:** Scottish and English surname: from Gaelic *gruaim* (grim, fierce); or from English *grand* (gravel) and *ham* (home)

> *I will walk within my house*
> *in the integrity of my heart.*
> — Psalm 101:2b (NASB)

GRANGER   *[GRAYN-jer]*

MEANING: farmer, gardener, granary barn, seed • **USAGE:** American surname: from Latin *granum* (seed)

The seed whose fruit is righteousness
is sown in peace by those who make peace.
— James 3:18 (NASB)

GRANT   [grant]

MEANING: great, large, tall • **USAGE:** English and
Scottish surname: from French *graunt*
A great soul will be strong to live, as well as to think.
— Ralph Waldo Emerson,
"The American Scholar"

GRAY, GREY   [gray]

MEANING: gray color • **USAGE:** English surname:
from English *græg*
Of all God's gifts to the sighted man, color is holiest,
the most divine, the most solemn.
— John Ruskin

GREER   [greer]

MEANING: watchful, vigilant, alert • **USAGE:**
Scottish and English surname: contraction of
Gregor (*see* Gregory)
The Lord keeps you from all harm and watches
over your life. The Lord keeps watch over you
as you come and go, both now and forever.
— Psalm 121:7–8 (NLT)

GREG   [greg]

MEANING: watchful, vigilant, alert • **USAGE:**
English form of Gregory (*see* Gregory)
Good thinking will keep you safe.
Understanding will watch over you.
— Proverbs 2:11 (NLV)

GREGER   [GREG-ohr, GREE-gohr]

MEANING: watchful, vigilant, alert • **USAGE:**
Scandinavian form of Gregory (*see* Gregory)
The Lord is my shepherd, I lack nothing. He takes me
to lush pastures, he leads me to refreshing water.
— Psalm 23:1–2 (NEB)

GRÉGOIRE   [greh-GWAWR]

MEANING: watchful, vigilant, alert • **USAGE:**
French form of Gregory (*see* Gregory)
Keep alert, stand firm in your faith, be courageous,
be strong. Let all that you do be done in love.
— 1 Corinthians 16:13–14 (NRSV)

GREGOR   [GREG-ohr]

MEANING: watchful, vigilant, alert • **USAGE:**
Scottish and German form of Gregory (*see*
Gregory)
Keep thy heart with all diligence,
for out of it are the outflowings of life.
— Proverbs 4:23 (KJ21)

GREGORIO   [gray-GOH-ree-oh]

MEANING: watchful, vigilant, alert • **USAGE:**
Spanish, Italian, and Portuguese form of Gregory
(*see* Gregory)
Guard your heart above all else,
for it determines the course of your life.
— Proverbs 4:23 (NLT)

GREGORY   [GREG-oh-ree]

MEANING: watchful, vigilant, alert • **USAGE:**
English form of *Gregorios*, from Greek *gregorein*
(watchful, vigilant)
The Lord says, "I will make you wise and show you
where to go. I will guide you and watch over you."
— Psalm 32:8 (NCV)

GRIFFITH   [GRIF-eth]

MEANING: strong lord, strong ruler, red color,
redhaired, ruddy-complexioned • **USAGE:** Welsh
surname: from Welsh *cryf* (strength, power) and
udd (lord, ruler); or from Welsh *gruffydd* (red,
ruddy)
Be strong and do not lose courage,
for there is reward for your work.
— 2 Chronicles 15:7 (NASB)

GRIGOR   [GRIE-gohr]

MEANING: watchful, vigilant, alert • USAGE:
Welsh form of Gregory (*see* Gregory)

I am the Lord God…wherever you go,
I will watch over you.
— Genesis 28:13b, 28:15a (CEV)

GRIGORI, GRIGORY   [gree-GOH-ree]

MEANING: watchful, vigilant, alert • USAGE:
Russian form of Gregory (*see* Gregory)

Discretion will watch over you.
Understanding will keep you.
— Proverbs 2:11 (WEB)

GRIGORIOS   [gree-GOH-ree-ohs]

MEANING: watchful, vigilant, alert • USAGE:
Greek form of *Gregorios* (*see* Gregory)

The Lord will go before you,
and…will keep watch behind you.
— Isaiah 52:12b (NLV)

GROVER   [GROH-ver]

MEANING: grove of trees • USAGE: English: from
English *graf*

The groves were God's first temples.
— William Cullen Bryant, *A Forest Hymn*

GUGLIELMO   [goo-glee-EHL-moh,
                       goo-LYEL-moh]

MEANING: determined protector, steadfast
guardian • USAGE: Italian form of William (*see*
Guillaume)

God will command his angels to protect
you wherever you go.
— Psalm 91:11 (CEV)

GUIDO   [GWEE-doh]

MEANING: guide, leader • USAGE: Italian: from
Italian *guida*

I will instruct you and teach you in the way you should
go; I will guide you with My eye.
— Psalm 32:8 (NKJV)

GUILLAUME   [gee-YOHM]

MEANING: determined protector, steadfast
guardian • USAGE: French form of William, from
German *wil* (will, resolve) and *helm* (protection,
helmet)

Watch over your heart with all diligence,
for from it flow the springs of life.
— Proverbs 4:23 (NASB)

GUILLERMO   [gee-YAYR-moh]

MEANING: determined protector, steadfast
guardian • USAGE: Spanish form of William (*see*
Guillaume)

You shall be steadfast, and shall not fear.
— Job 11:15b (WEB)

GURI   [GOO-ree]

MEANING: my young lion • USAGE: Jewish

The lion which is mightiest
among beasts turneth not away for any.
— Proverbs 30:30 (MT)

GUS   [gus]

MEANING: great one, revered one, magnificent
• USAGE: English form of Augustine, from Latin
augustus

Great hopes make great men.
— Thomas Fuller, *Gnomologia*

GUSTAF, GUSTAV   [GOO-stahf]

MEANING: God's staff, staff of the gods,
meditation staff, staff of the Goths • USAGE:
German and Scandinavian: from German *gott*
(God) and *staf* (staff); German form of *Chustaffus*,
from German *chuton* (meditate) and *staf* (staff); or
from Norse *Gautr* (tribal name of the Goths) and
stafr (staff)

G

You [God] are close beside me.
Your rod and your staff protect and comfort me.
— Psalm 23:4b (NLT)

GUSTAVO   [goo-STAH-voh]

MEANING: God's staff, staff of the gods, meditation staff, staff of the Goths • USAGE: Italian, Portuguese, and Spanish form of Gustaf (*see* Gustaf)

My mouth will speak wisdom;
and the meditation of my heart will be understanding.
— Psalm 49:3 (NASB)

GUTHRIE   [GUTH-ree]

MEANING: breeze, breezy, warrior, warlike • USAGE: Scottish surname: from Gaelic *gaoth* (breeze) or *guth* (warlike, warrior)

The wind bloweth where it listeth,
and thou hearest the sound thereof, but canst
not tell whence it cometh, and whither it goeth;
so is every one that is born of the Spirit.
— John 3:8 (KJV)

GUY   [gee (French), gie (English)]

MEANING: guide, leader • USAGE: French and English: from French *guie*

The Lord will guide you always;
he will satisfy your needs.
— Isaiah 58:11a (NIV)

GYAN   [GYE-ahn]

MEANING: knowledge, wisdom • USAGE: Hindu: from Sanskrit *gyan*

With goodness, / concentration, /
and wisdom, / one will understand.
— Shi Wuling, *Path to Peace*

H

HABIB, HABEEB   [hah-BEEB]

MEANING: beloved, love • USAGE: Muslim: from Arabic *habib*

Lo! those who believe and do good works,
the Beneficent will appoint for them love.
— Koran, Maryam 19.96 (PIC)

HADI   [hah-dee]

MEANING: religious leader, rightly guided • USAGE: Muslim: from Arabic *hadi* (religious leader, one who guides) or *hada* (to rightly guide)

The religion of each one is the attainment
of his soul's desire; when he is on the path
of that attainment he is religious.
— Hazrat Inayat Khan, *The Bowl of Saki*

HADLEY   [HAD-lee]

MEANING: heather meadow, field of heather • USAGE: English: from English *hæd* (heathland, heather) and *leah* (meadow, field)

The Lord is my shepherd; I shall not want.
He makes me to lie down in green pastures.
— Psalm 23:1–2 (NKJV)

HAFI   [hah-fee]

MEANING: greeting, welcome • USAGE: Muslim
Salute one another with a greeting from Allah,
blessed and sweet.
— Koran, The Light 24.61b (PIC)

HAFIZ, HAAFIZ   [hah-feez]

MEANING: guardian, protector • USAGE: Muslim: from Arabic *hafiz* (guardian)

There are (angels) in succession, before and behind
him: They guard him by command of Allah.
— Koran, Thunder 13.11a (ALI)

HAGAI   [hah-GIE]

MEANING: my celebration, my feast, holiday •
USAGE: Jewish form of Chagai
> *He that is of a merry heart hath a continual feast.*
> — Proverbs 15:15 (MT)

HAGAN   [HAY-gan (Irish),
                  HAH-gahn (German)]

MEANING: fire, little fiery one, high son, chosen
descendant • **USAGE:** Irish and German. Irish form
of Egan, from Gaelic *aodh* (fire) and diminutive
-an; or German form of *Hakon*, from Norse *ha*
(high, chosen) and *konr* (son, descendant)
> *The lines are fallen unto me in pleasant places;*
> *yes, I have a goodly heritage.*
> — Psalm 16:6 (ASV)

HAGEN   [HAH-gahn]

MEANING: high son, chosen descendant, enclosure
• **USAGE:** Scandinavian and German form of
Hakon, from Norse *ha* (high, chosen) and *konr* (son,
descendant); or from German *hakan* (enclosure)
> *Blessed be thou of the Lord, my son.*
> — Judges 17:2b (KJ21)

HAIM, HAYYIM   [HIE-yim, hah-YEEM]

MEANING: life, full of life • **USAGE:** Jewish form
of Chaim
> *It is through man's deed that God reveals*
> *himself in life.*
> — Leo Baeck, *Essence of Judaism* (tr. Irving Howe)

HAKIM, HAKEEM   [hah-keem]

MEANING: just, judicious • **USAGE:** Muslim: from
Arabic *hakama* (to judge) or *hakim* (judicious)
> *Lo! Allah enjoineth justice and kindness.*
> — Koran, The Bee 16.90a (PIC)

HAL   [hal]

MEANING: ruler of the home, house leader, ruler
of the army, army commander • **USAGE:** English
form of Henry, from German *heim* (home, house)
and *rik* (rule, lead); also English form of Harold,
from English *here* (army) and *weald* (ruler, leader)
> *For a man's house is his castle.*
> — Edward Coke, *The Third Part of the Institutes*
> *of the Laws of England*

HALE   [hayl]

MEANING: healthy, hardy • **USAGE:** English
surname: from English *hal* (healthy)
> *Your body will glow with health,*
> *your very bones will vibrate with life!*
> — Proverbs 3:8 (MSG)

HALIM, HALEEM   [hah-leem]

MEANING: gentle, patient • **USAGE:** Muslim: from
Arabic *halima* (gentle, patient)
> *Whoever hath been given gentleness hath been given a*
> *good portion, in this world and the next.*
> — Hadith of the Prophet Muhammad

HALLE   [HAHL-eh]

MEANING: rock, stone, ruler of the army, army
commander • **USAGE:** Norwegian and Swedish:
from Norse *hallr* (rock, stone); or Scandinavian
form of Harald, from English *here* (army) and *weald*
(ruler, leader)
> *Look to the rock from which you were hewn,*
> *and to the quarry from which you were dug.*
> — Isaiah 51:1b (ESV)

HALSTEN   [HAHL-sten]

MEANING: rock, stone, hard, solid • **USAGE:**
Swedish: from Norse *hallr* (rock) and *stein* (stone)
> *The Lord said, "Here is a place near me*
> *where you will stand beside the rock."*
> — Exodus 33:21 (CEV)

H

H

HALVARD   [HAHL-vahr]

MEANING: defender of the rock, rock guardian •
USAGE: Scandinavian: from Norse *hallr* (rock) and
varor (guardian, protector)

> *He only is my rock and my salvation;*
> *He is my defense; I shall not be greatly moved.*
> — Psalm 62:2 (NKJV)

HAMISH   [HAY-mish]

MEANING: replace, change, transform, successor
• USAGE: Scottish form of Seamus, from Hebrew
ya'aqobh (one that takes by the heel, replace with
another)

> *I [God] will give you a new heart,*
> *and a new spirit I will put within you.*
> — Ezekiel 36:26a (ESV)

HANEK   [YAH-nek]

MEANING: God is gracious, God is giving •
USAGE: Czech form of Johan, from Hebrew
y'hohanan (Yahweh is gracious)

> *The Lord be with your spirit. Grace be with you.*
> — 2 Timothy 4:22 (NIV)

HANIA   [hah-nee-ah]

MEANING: warrior • USAGE: Amerind: Hopi
> *All I want is right and justice.*
> — Red Cloud

HANIF, HANEEF   [hah-neef]

MEANING: true believer, one of true faith •
USAGE: Muslim: from Arabic *hanif* (having the
right belief)

> *No man is a true believer unless he desireth*
> *for his brother that which he desireth for himself.*
> — Hadith of the Prophet Muhammad

HANK   [hank]

MEANING: ruler of the home, house leader •
USAGE: English form of Henry, from German *heim*
(home, house) and *rik* (rule, lead)

> *Peace be to you, and peace be to your house,*
> *and peace be to all that you have.*
> — 1 Samuel 25:6b (ESV)

HANS   [hahns]

MEANING: God is gracious, God is giving •
USAGE: German, Dutch, and Scandinavian form
of Johannes, from Hebrew *y'hohanan* (Yahweh is
gracious)

> *The joy that the Lord gives will make you strong.*
> — Nehemiah 8:10b (GNT)

HANS   [hahns]

MEANING: swan • USAGE: Hindu: from Sanskrit
hans

> *Swans fly on the path of the sun*
> *by their wonderful power.*
> — Buddha, *The Dhammapada*
> (tr. Eknath Easwaran)

HANUMAN   [HAH-noo-mahn]

MEANING: divine monkey • USAGE: Hindu:
Hanuman, a divine monkey, is from Sanskrit *hanu*
(jaw) and *mant* (disfigured), meaning "one whose
jaw is disfigured"

> *Always do good to others. Be selfless.*
> *Mentally remove everything and be free.*
> *This is divine life.*
> — Saraswati Sivananda

HAO   [how]

MEANING: good, excellent • USAGE: Chinese
> *He [whose goodness] is extensive and solid*
> *is called a beautiful man.*
> — Mencius

HARALD [HAYR-uld]

MEANING: ruler of the army, army commander •
USAGE: German and Scandinavian (*see* Harold)

> *His [God's] faithful promises*
> *are your armor and protection.*
> — Psalm 91:2–4 (NLT)

HAREL [hahr-EL]

MEANING: mountain people, mountaineer, road •
USAGE: Jewish

> *He answers me from His holy mountain.*
> — Psalm 3:5b (JPS)

HARLEY [HAHR-lee]

MEANING: hare meadow, from the field of hares •
USAGE: English surname: from English *hara* (hare)
and *leah* (meadow, field)

> *Life consists of wildness. The most alive is the wildest.*
> *Not yet subdued to man, its presence refreshes him.*
> — Henry David Thoreau, "Walking"

HARLOW [HAR-loh]

MEANING: rocky hill, army hill • **USAGE:** English
surname: from English *hær* (rock) and *hlaw* (hill) or
from English *here* (army) and *hlaw* (hill)

> *The Lord said, "Behold, there is a place*
> *by me where you shall stand upon a rock."*
> — Exodus 33:21 (RSV)

HAROLD [HAYR-uld]

MEANING: ruler of the army, army commander •
USAGE: English form of *Hereweald*, from English
here (army) and *weald* (ruler, leader)

> *We have different gifts, according to the grace given*
> *to each of us…if it is to lead, do it diligently*
> — Romans 12:6, 12:8b (NIV)

HAROUN, HARUN [hah-ROON]

MEANING: teaching, singing, shining, mountain,
exalted one • **USAGE:** Muslim form of Aaron, from
Hebrew *aharon*

> *The Lord dwells in every Being /*
> *None's bereft of Him /*
> *The Being where He manifests /*
> *Shines in His Beam.*
> — Kabir

HARPER [HAR-per]

MEANING: harp player • **USAGE:** English
surname: from English *hearpe* (harp, stringed
instrument)

> *Lord, make me an instrument of thy peace.*
> — Francis of Assisi, "Prayer of St. Francis"

HARRISON [HAYR-eh-son]

MEANING: army commander's son, son of
the house • **USAGE:** English surname: English
combination of Harry and *son* (*see* Harry)

> *When you can do the common things of life*
> *in an uncommon way, you will command*
> *the attention of the world.*
> — George Washington Carver

HARRY [HAYR-ee]

MEANING: ruler of the army, house leader, army
commander, ruler of the home • **USAGE:** English
form of Harold (*see* Harold) or of Henry (*see*
Henry)

> *I will walk within my house*
> *in the integrity of my heart.*
> — Psalm 101:2b (DT)

HARSHAD [hahr-shahd]

MEANING: joy, happiness • **USAGE:** Hindu: from
Sanskrit *harsha*

> *It is our joy of the infinite in us*
> *that gives us our joy in ourselves.*
> — Rabindranath Tagore, *Sadhana*

H

HARV   [harv]

MEANING: battle worthy, warrior • **USAGE:**
English form of Harvey (*see* Harvey)

I praise you, Lord! You are my mighty rock,
and you teach me how to fight my battles.
You are my friend, and you are my fortress
where I am safe. You are my shield.
— Psalm 144:1–2a (CEV)

HARVEY   [HAR-vee]

MEANING: battle worthy, warrior • **USAGE:**
English form of Breton surname *Haerviu*, from
Breton *hær* (battle) and *viu* (worthy)

The battle is not to the strong alone;
it is to the vigilant, the active, the brave.
— Patrick Henry

HASAN, HASSAN   [hah-sahn]

MEANING: good, handsome • **USAGE:** Muslim:
from Arabic *hasuna* (to be good) or from Arabic
hasan (handsome)

Surely Allah enjoins the doing of justice
and the doing of good.
— Koran, The Bee 16.90a (SKR)

HASANAT   [hah-sah-naht]

MEANING: good • **USAGE:** Muslim: from Arabic
hasuna (to be good)

Anticipate good, and you'll find good.
— Arabic proverb

HASIB   [hah-seeb]

MEANING: noble, honorable • **USAGE:** Muslim:
from Arabic *hasib*

The most honoured of you in the sight of God is
(he who is) the most righteous of you.
— Koran, The Chamber 49.13b (ALI)

HASID   [hah-SEED]

MEANING: pious, righteous, devout, stork •
USAGE: Jewish form of Chasid

Instruct a wise man, and he will grow wiser;
teach a righteous man, and he will gain in learning.
— Proverbs 9:9 (JPS)

HASIF   [hah-seef]

MEANING: just, judicious • **USAGE:** Muslim

O ye who believe! stand out firmly for Allah,
as witnesses to fair dealing.
— Koran, The Table Spread 5.8a (ALI)

HASIM, HASEEM   [hah-seem]

MEANING: decisive, firm, resolute • **USAGE:**
Muslim: from Arabic *hasama* (to decide) and *hasim*
(decisive)

If any show patience and forgive,
that would truly be an exercise of courageous will
and resolution in the conduct of affairs.
— Koran, The Counsel 42.43 (ALI)

HASIN, HASEEN   [hah-seen]

MEANING: secure, protected, guarded • **USAGE:**
Muslim

For his sake there are angels following one another,
before him and behind him, who guard him
by Allah's commandment.
— Koran, The Thunder 13:11 (SKR)

HAVEL   [YAH-vel]

MEANING: small, little • **USAGE:** Czech form of
Paul, from Latin *paulus*

Whoever can be trusted with very little
can also be trusted with much.
— Luke 16:10a (NIV)

HAWK, HAWKE   [hauk]

MEANING: hawk, falcon • **USAGE:** American:
from English *hauk*

H

I soar, I am a hawk.
— William Shakespeare, *Henry V*

HAYDEN   *[HAY-den]*

MEANING: hay hill, hay valley, fire, fiery one, heathen, pagan • **USAGE:** English and Welsh: English surname, from *heg* (hay) and *dun* (hill) or *denu* (valley); Welsh form of Aidan, from Gaelic *aodh* (fire); or from German *heidano* (heathen)
What we need / Is the celestial fire to change the flint / Into the transparent crystal, bright and clear. / That fire is genius.
— Henry Wadsworth Longfellow,
The Spanish Student

HAYLEY, HALEY   *[HAY-lee]*

MEANING: hay field • **USAGE:** English surname: from English *heg* (hay) and *leah* (meadow, field)
We are God's fellow workers. You are God's field.
— 1 Corinthians 3:9b (ESV)

HAZIM, HAZEEM   *[hah-ʒeem]*

MEANING: decisive, firm, resolute • **USAGE:** Muslim: from Arabic *hasama* (to decide) and *hasim* (decisive)
Allah Loves those who are firm and steadfast.
— Koran, The Family of Imran 3.146b (ALI)

HEATH   *[heeth]*

MEANING: heathland, moor • **USAGE:** English: from English *hæd*
Speak to the earth, and it will teach you.
— Job 12:8a (NKJV)

HECTOR   *[HEK-tor]*

MEANING: steadfast, constant • **USAGE:** English form of *Hektor*, from Greek *hektor* (hold fast)
His heart is steadfast.
— Psalm 112:7b (NEB)

HEINRICH   *[HIEN-rik]*

MEANING: ruler of the home, house leader • **USAGE:** German: from German *heim* (home, house) and *rik* (rule, lead)
By wisdom a house is built, and by understanding it is established.
— Proverbs 24:3 (NASB)

HELMUT   *[HEL-moot]*

MEANING: spiritual guardian, courageous protector • **USAGE:** German: from German *helm* (helmet, protection) and *muot* (courage, spirit, mind)
Carefully guard your thoughts because they are the source of true life.
— Proverbs 4:23 (CEV)

HEMENE   *[heh-meh-neh]*

MEANING: wolf • **USAGE:** Amerind: Nez Percé
The Wolf-Power I was given made me a great hunter, a sure scout.
— Yellow Wolf
(from *Yellow Wolf: His Own Story* by Lucullus Virgil McWhorter)

HENDRIK   *[HEN-drik]*

MEANING: ruler of the home, house leader • **USAGE:** German (*see* Heinrich)
He is happiest, be he king or peasant, who finds peace in his home.
— Johann Wolfgang von Goethe

HENRI   *[ahn-REE]*

MEANING: ruler of the home, house leader • **USAGE:** French form of Heinrich (*see* Heinrich)
Love begins at home, and it is not how much we do... but how much love we put in that action.
— Mother Teresa (1979 Nobel Peace Prize speech)

H

H

HENRIK   [HEN-rik]

MEANING: ruler of the home, house leader •
USAGE: Scandinavian form of Heinrich (*see*
Heinrich)

> *By wisdom a house is built, and by understanding*
> *it is established; by knowledge the rooms are filled*
> *with all precious and pleasant riches.*
> — Proverbs 24:3–4 (ESV)

HENRIQUE   [ehn-REE-keh]

MEANING: ruler of the home, house leader
• **USAGE:** Portuguese form of Heinrich (*see*
Heinrich)

> *May it please Thee to bless the house of Thy servant,*
> *that it may continue forever before thee. For Thou,*
> *O Lord God, has spoken; and with Thy blessing*
> *may the house of Thy servant be blessed forever.*
> — 2 Samuel 7:29 (NASB)

HENRY   [HEN-ree]

MEANING: ruler of the home, house leader •
USAGE: English form of Heinrich (*see* Heinrich)

> *Peace be both to thee, and peace be to thine house,*
> *and peace be unto all that thou hast.*
> — 1 Samuel 25:6b (KJV)

HERB   [herb]

MEANING: bright army, of the shining army •
USAGE: English form of Herbert (*see* Herbert)

> *Skill and confidence are an unconquered army.*
> — George Herbert, *Jacula Prudentum*

HERBERT   [HER-bert (English),
er-BAYR (French)]

MEANING: bright army, of the shining army •
USAGE: English and French form of *Hereberht*,
from German *hari* (army) and *beraht* (bright,
shining)

> *Put on the armor of light.*
> — Romans 13:12b (NIRV)

HERBERTO   [ayr-BAYR-toh]

MEANING: bright army, of the shining army •
USAGE: Spanish form of Herbert (*see* Herbert)

> *Arise, shine! for thy light is come.*
> — Isaiah 60:1a (DT)

HERMAN, HERMÁN   [HER-man (English),
ehr-MAHN (Spanish)]

MEANING: warrior, soldier, army man • **USAGE:**
English and Spanish form of *Hariman*, from
German *hari* (army) and *man* (man)

> *The Lord is with you, O powerful soldier.*
> — Judges 6:12b (NLV)

HERNANDO   [ayr-NAHN-doh]

MEANING: bold venturer, prepared traveler,
courageous journeyer • **USAGE:** Spanish form of
Fernando, from German *fardi* (journey, travel)
and *nand* (ready, prepared), *nanthi* (venture,
adventurous), or *nanths* (courageous)

> *The brave man carves out his fortune,*
> *and every man is the sum of his own works.*
> — Miguel de Cervantes,
> *Don Quixote* (tr. Peter Motteux)

HERSH, HIRSH   [hersh]

MEANING: deer • **USAGE:** Yiddish form of
Hershel or Hirshel

> *Truly, who is a god except the Lord…who made my*
> *legs like a deer's, and let me stand firm on the heights.*
> — Psalm 18:32–34 (JPS)

HERSHEL, HERSCHEL, HIRSHEL
[HURSH-el]

MEANING: deer • **USAGE:** Yiddish

> *My Lord God is my strength: He makes my feet like*
> *the deer's and lets me stride upon the heights.*
> — Habakkuk 3:19a (JPS)

HEVEL [*HEH-vel*]

MEANING: breath, vapor • **USAGE:** Jewish: from Hebrew *hebel*

> *Truly it is the spirit in men, the breath of Shaddai,*
> *that gives them understanding.*
> — Job 32:8 (JPS)

HIERONYMOUS [*hee-ROHN-ee-mos*]

MEANING: holy name • **USAGE:** Greek: from Greek *hieros* (holy) and *onyma* (name)

> *I have known thee by name,*
> *and also thou hast found grace in Mine eyes.*
> — Exodus 33:12b (YLT)

HILARIO [*ee-LAH-ryoh*]

MEANING: cheerful, joyful, happy • **USAGE:** Spanish form of Hilary (*see* Hilary)

> *A sound, healthy body and a cheerful attitude*
> *are more valuable than gold and jewels.*
> — Sirach 30:15 (GNT Apocrypha)

HILARY [*HIL-ah-ree*]

MEANING: cheerful, joyful, happy • **USAGE:** English: from Latin *hilaris*

> *The gladness of the heart is the life of man,*
> *and the joyfulness of a man prolongeth his days.*
> — Ben Sira 30:22 (KJV Apocrypha)

HILLEL [*hee-LEL*]

MEANING: praise, glory • **USAGE:** Jewish

> *Great is his glory through Your victory;*
> *You have endowed him with splendor and majesty.*
> — Psalm 21:6 (JPS)

HINTO [*heen-toh*]

MEANING: blue • **USAGE:** Amerind: Sioux

> *A very great vision is needed and the man*
> *who has it must follow it as the eagle seeks*
> *the deepest blue of the sky.*
> — Crazy Horse

HIRAM [*HIE-rahm*]

MEANING: freeborn, noble, exalted • **USAGE:** Jewish: from Hebrew *ahiram*

> *He brought me out to freedom…*
> *because He was pleased with me.*
> — Psalm 18:20 (JPS)

HIROSHI [*hee-roh-shee*]

MEANING: generous, magnanimous • **USAGE:** Japanese: from Japanese *hiro*

> *Generosity, morality, patience, diligence,*
> *concentration, wisdom are the means — and the end.*
> — Shi Wuling, *Path to Peace*

HIROTO [*hee-roh-toh*]

MEANING: great, large • **USAGE:** Japanese

> *Health is the greatest gift;*
> *contentment is the greatest wealth; trusting is*
> *the best relationship; nirvana is the highest joy.*
> — Buddha, *The Dhammapada* (tr. Sanderson Beck)

HOB [*hob*]

MEANING: brightly famous, shining with fame • **USAGE:** English form of Robert, from German *hrod* (fame) and *beraht* (bright, shining)

> *A man's wisdom makes his face shine.*
> — Ecclesiastes 8:1b (NKJV)

HODGE [*hodj*]

MEANING: famous spear, renowned spearman • **USAGE:** English surname: from German *hrod* (fame, praise) and *ger* (spear)

> *The Lord will go before you, and…*
> *will be your rear guard.*
> — Isaiah 52:12b (NKJV)

HOGAN [*HOH-gan*]

MEANING: young, youthful • **USAGE:** Scottish: from Gaelic *ogan*

H

My son, from thy youth up receive instruction,
and even to thy grey hairs thou shalt find wisdom.
— Sirach 6:18 (DR Apocrypha)

HOLOKAI   [hoh-loh-KIE]

MEANING: seafarer, mariner • **USAGE:** Hawaiian
We are all voyagers in life's ocean.
— Hawaiian proverb

HOLT   [holt]

MEANING: woods, wooded hill • **USAGE:**
American: from English *holt*
Reading about nature is fine, but if a person walks in
the woods and listens carefully, he can learn more than
what is in books, for they speak with the voice of God.
— George Washington Carver

HOMER   [HOH-mer]

MEANING: pledge, security, promise, hostage •
USAGE: English: from Greek *homeros*
Life is a promise, fulfill it.
— Mother Teresa, "Life"

HONG   [hong]

MEANING: great, vast • **USAGE:** Chinese
He [whose goodness] is abundant and is
brilliantly displayed is called a great man.
— Mencius

HONI   [hoh-nee]

MEANING: wolf • **USAGE:** Amerind: Arapaho
When we show our respect for other living things,
they respond with respect for us.
— Arapaho proverb

HONORÉ   [oh-nohr-REH]

MEANING: honor, honorable • **USAGE:** French:
from Latin *honor*

Happy is the man who finds wisdom, and the man who
gains understanding....Length of days is in her right
hand, in her left hand riches and honor.
— Proverbs 3:13, 3:16 (NKJV)

HORACIO   [oh-RAY-syo]

MEANING: hour, time, season • **USAGE:** Spanish
and Portuguese form of Horatio (*see* Horatio)
A wise man's heart discerneth both time and judgment.
— Ecclesiastes 8:5b (KJV)

HORATIO   [hor-AY-shee-oh]

MEANING: hour, time, season • **USAGE:** English
form of Roman family name *Horatius*, possibly
from Latin *hora*
There are more things in heaven and earth,
Horatio, than are dreamt of in our philosophy.
— William Shakespeare, *Hamlet*

HORST   [horst]

MEANING: wooded hill • **USAGE:** German: from
German *horst*
Who shall dwell in Thy holy hill?
He that walketh uprightly and worketh righteousness,
and speaketh the truth in his heart.
— Psalm 15:1–2 (KJ21)

HOSEA   [hoh-SEH-ah, hoh-SHEH-ah]

MEANING: save, deliver, help • **USAGE:** Jewish
O Lord, be my help!
— Psalm 30:11b (JPS)

HOWARD   [HOW-ard]

MEANING: high guardian, chosen warden,
shepherd • **USAGE:** English form of *Haward*,
from Norse *ha* (high, chosen) and *varor* (guardian,
warden); or English form of *Howeherde*, from *ewe*
(ewe, sheep) and *hierde* (herd)

Discretion will protect you,
and understanding will guard you.
— Proverbs 2:11 (NIV)

HUAN   *[hwahn]*

MEANING: happy, joyous • USAGE: Chinese
The happiness of good men
may be looked on as reward.
— Chinese proverb (tr. William Scarborough)

HUB   *[hub]*

MEANING: round hill • USAGE: English form of
Hubbell (*see* Hubbell)
Groves stand peaceful and prominent on every hill,
in every dale of history that encourages or inspires.
— Enos A. Mills, *Your National Parks*

HUBBELL   *[HUB-el]*

MEANING: round hill • USAGE: English surname:
from *Hubba*, a Danish chief, from Danish *hub*
(heap, lump); may indicate a small, round hill
Let the mountains receive peace for the people:
and the hills justice.
— Psalm 71:3 (DR)

HUBERT   *[HYOO-burt (English),*
HOO-bairt (German), hyoo-BAYR (French)]

MEANING: shining spirit, intelligent • USAGE:
English, French, and German form of *Huguberht*,
from German *hugu* (heart, mind, spirit) and *beraht*
(bright, shining)
Ye stand in your own light.
— John Heywood

HUDD, HUD   *[hud]*

MEANING: heart, mind, spirit • USAGE: English
form of Hudson (*see* Hugh)
Do what you feel in your heart is right.
— Eleanor Roosevelt

HUDSON   *[HUD-sun]*

MEANING: heart, mind, spirit • USAGE: English
surname: a form of Hugh (*see* Hugh)
Let your heart grow large and loving and unselfish,
and great and lasting will be your influence
and success.
— James Allen, *From Poverty to Power*

HUGH   *[hyoo]*

MEANING: heart, mind, spirit • USAGE: English:
from German *hugu* (heart, mind, spirit)
By trusting your own heart, you shall gain
more confidence in other men.
— Ralph Waldo Emerson,
"Divinity School Address"

HUGO   *[HYOO-goh (French, German,*
Scandinavian), OO-goh (Spanish)]

MEANING: shining spirit, bright mind, shining
heart • USAGE: French, German, Scandinavian,
and Spanish form of *Huguberht*, from German *hugu*
(heart, mind, spirit) and *beraht* (bright, shining)
We know the truth, not only by the reason,
but also by the heart.
— Blaise Pascal, *Pensées* (tr. A. J. Krailsheimer)

HULA   *[hoo-lah]*

MEANING: eagle • USAGE: Amerind: Osage
Eagles are symbols of great power.
— Ted Andrews, *Animal Speak*

HUMPHREY, HUMPHRY   *[HUMP-free]*

MEANING: peaceful warrior, peaceful bear cub
• USAGE: English surname: from German *hun*
(warrior) and *frid* (peace, peaceful); or from Norse
hunn (bear cub) and English *frith* (peace, peaceful)
The great mind knows the power of gentleness.
— Robert Browning, *Prince Hohenstiel-Schwangau*

H

HUNTER [HUN-ter]

MEANING: hunter, pursuer, seeker • USAGE:
English surname: from English *hunten* (to hunt)
The woods were made for the hunter of dreams,
the brooks for the fishers of song.
— Sam Walter Foss, *Dreams in Homespun*

HUNTLEY [HUNT-lee]

MEANING: hunting field • USAGE: English
surname: from English *hunten* (hunt) and *leah*
(meadow, field)
Whoever goes hunting for what is right
and kind finds life itself — glorious life!
— Proverbs 21:21 (MSG)

HURITT [hoo-reet]

MEANING: good • USAGE: Amerind: Delaware
Brother, your heart is good,
you speak always sincerely.
— Shingis

HUSAYN, HUSSEIN [hoo-SAYN]

MEANING: good, handsome • USAGE: Muslim:
from Arabic *hasuna* (to be good) or from *hasan*
(beautiful, handsome)
Allah loveth the good.
— Koran, The Cattle 5.93b (PIC)

HUW [hyoo]

MEANING: heart, mind, spirit • USAGE: Welsh
form of Hugh (*see* Hugh)
There is a wisdom of the Head, and...
a wisdom of the Heart.
— Charles Dickens, *Hard Times*

I

IAGO [ee-AH-goh]

MEANING: replace, change, transform, successor
• USAGE: Welsh form of James, from Hebrew
ya'aqobh (one that takes by the heel, replace with
another)
May the name of the God of Jacob keep you safe
from all harm....May he grant your heart's desires
and make all your plans succeed.
— Psalm 20:1b, 20:4 (NLT)

IAN, IAIN [EE-an]

MEANING: God is gracious, God is giving •
USAGE: Scottish form of John, from Hebrew
y'hohanan (Yahweh is gracious)
May the Lord bless you and protect you.
May the Lord smile on you and be gracious to you.
May the Lord show you his favor
and give you his peace.
— Numbers 6:24–26 (NLT)

IBRAHIM [ee-brah-heem]

MEANING: father of a multitude, father of many,
kind father • USAGE: Muslim form of Abraham,
from Hebrew *abh* (father) and *raham* (multitude)
Who is better in religion than he who surrendereth his
purpose to Allah while doing good (to men)
and followeth the tradition of Abraham, the upright?
Allah (Himself) chose Abraham for a friend.
— Koran, The Women 4.125 (PIC)

ICHIRO [ee-chee-roh]

MEANING: first son • USAGE: Japanese: from
Japanese *ichi* (one) and *rou* (son)
Filial piety is the source of many good deeds
and the beginning of all virtue.
— Japanese proverb

IFAN   *[IE-vahn]*

MEANING: God is gracious, God is giving •
USAGE: Welsh form of John, from Hebrew
y'hohanan (Yahweh is gracious)
> *God be gracious to thee.*
> — Genesis 43:29b (DR)

IGNACIO   *[eeg-NAH-see-oh]*

MEANING: fire, fiery • **USAGE:** Spanish form of
Roman family name *Ignatius*, from Latin *ignis*
> *He makes His helpers a burning fire.*
> — Psalm 104:4b (NLV)

IGNAZIO   *[eeg-NAH-zee-oh]*

MEANING: fire, fiery • **USAGE:** Italian: from
Roman family name *Ignatius*, from Latin *ignis*
> *The mind is not a vessel to be filled*
> *but a fire to be ignited.*
> — Plutarch

IGOR   *[ee-gawr]*

MEANING: bowman, archer, warrior • **USAGE:**
Russian and Scandinavian form of Ivar, from Norse
yr (yew tree) and *arr* (army); yew is used to make
bows
> *Ye shall be a blessing: fear ye not,*
> *let your hands be strong.*
> — Zechariah 8:13b (DT)

IHILANI   *[ee-hee-LAH-nee]*

MEANING: heavenly splendor, sacredness of a
chief • **USAGE:** Hawaiian
> *Have the heart of a chief.*
> *[Having kindness and generosity.]*
> — Hawaiian proverb
> (tr. Mary Pukui in *'Olelo No'eau*)

IHSAN   *[ee-sahn]*

MEANING: kind, compassionate, good • **USAGE:**
Muslim
> *For those who do good in this world is good.*
> — Koran, The Companies 39.10b (SKR)

IKE   *[iek]*

MEANING: he will laugh • **USAGE:** English form
of Isaac, from Hebrew *yitshaq*
> *The human race has one really effective weapon,*
> *and that is laughter.*
> — Mark Twain

ILAN   *[ee-LAHN]*

MEANING: tree • **USAGE:** Jewish; symbolic name
for boys born on Tu b'Shvat, the New Year of the
Trees
> *He is like a tree planted beside streams of water,*
> *which yields its fruit in season, whose foliage never*
> *fades, and whatever it produces thrives.*
> — Psalm 1:3 (JPS)

ILAR   *[IE-lar]*

MEANING: cheerful, joyful, happy • **USAGE:**
Welsh form of Hilary, from Latin *hilaris*
> *You will be happy and it will be well with you.*
> — Psalm 128:2b (NLV)

ILARIO   *[ee-LAH-ryoh]*

MEANING: cheerful, joyful, happy • **USAGE:**
Italian: from Latin *hilaris*
> *Living up to your nature, standing boldly*
> *by the truth of your word, and satisfied therewith,*
> *then you will be a happy man.*
> — Marcus Aurelius, *The Meditations*
> (tr. Jeremy Collier)

IMANUEL, IMMANUEL

[ee-mah-noo-EHL]

MEANING: God is with us • USAGE: Jewish: from Hebrew *immanu' el*

> May the Lord our God be with us, as He was with our fathers. May He never abandon or forsake us. May He include our hearts to Him, that we may walk in all His ways and keep the commandments, the laws, and the rules, which He enjoined upon our fathers.
> — 1 Kings 8:57–58 (JPS)

IMRICH

[EEM-rik]

MEANING: ruler of the home, universal leader • USAGE: Czech form of Emmerich, from German *heim* (home, house) and *rik* (rule, lead); or from German *ermen* (whole, universal) and *rik* (rule, lead)

> Have a long life, peace be to you, and peace be to your house, and peace be to all that you have.
> — 1 Samuel 25:6b (NASB)

INDRA

[en-drah]

MEANING: powerful, mighty • USAGE: Hindu: Sanskrit

> The power behind every activity of nature and of man is the power of Brahman. To realize this truth is to be immortal.
> — Kena Upanishad

INGMAR

[EENG-mahr]

MEANING: famous Ing, peaceful, prosperous • USAGE: Scandinavian: from Norse *Ing* (Norse god of peace and fertility) and *mærr* (famous)

> Mercy, peace, and love be multiplied to you.
> — Jude 1:2 (NKJV)

INGVAR

[EENG-vahr]

MEANING: famous Ing, peaceful, prosperous • USAGE: Scandinavian (*see* Ingmar)

> He who pursues righteousness and love finds life, prosperity and honor.
> — Proverbs 21:21 (NIV)

INNES, INNIS

[EN-es]

MEANING: island, river island, vigorous one, robust • USAGE: Scottish surname: from Gaelic *innis* (island, river island); or Scottish form of Aonghus, from Gaelic *oen* (one) and *gus* (strength, vigor)

> Enthusiasm is the genius of sincerity, and truth accomplishes no victories without it.
> — Edward Bulwer-Lytton,
> *The Last Days of Pompeii*

IOANNIS

[ee-oh-AH-nes]

MEANING: God is gracious, God is giving • USAGE: Greek form of John, from Hebrew *y'hohanan* (Yahweh is gracious)

> God be gracious to you.
> — Genesis 43:29b (NRSV)

IOLANI

[ee-oh-LAH-nee]

MEANING: soaring hawk • USAGE: Hawaiian: from Hawaiian *iolana* (to soar through the air as a bird, symbol of royalty), from *'io* (hawk)

> I am a hawk; there is no branch on which I cannot perch. [The highest chief.]
> — Hawaiian proverb
> (tr. Mary Pukui in *'Olelo No'eau*)

IRA

[ee-RAH (Jewish), IE-rah (English)]

MEANING: watchful, awake, alert • USAGE: Jewish and English: from Hebrew *'ur* (to awake, to rouse oneself)

> Awake, awake, put on strength,
> O arm of the Lord.
> — Isaiah 51:9a (MT)

IRAJA   *[eh-rah-jah]*

MEANING: born of the wind • **USAGE:** Hindu: from Sanskrit *ira* (wind) and *ja* (born)

The wind of divine grace is always blowing. You just
need to spread your sail. Whenever you do anything,
do it with your whole heart concentrated on it.
— Swami Vivekananda

IRUNGU   *[ee-roon-guh]*

MEANING: makes right, reformer • **USAGE:** African: Kikuyu of Kenya

The vigor and the quality of a nation depend on its
capacity to renew itself each generation.
— Jomo Kenyatta (address of October 10, 1966)

IRV   *[erv]*

MEANING: wild boar friend, green river, west river • **USAGE:** English form of Irvin (*see* Irvin) or of Irving (*see* Irving)

A river is more than an amenity, it is a treasure.
— Oliver Wendell Holmes Jr.

IRVIN, IRWIN   *[ER-ven, ER-wen]*

MEANING: wild boar friend • **USAGE:** Scottish and English surname: from English *eofor* (wild boar) and *wine* (friend)

There can be no friendship where there is no freedom.
Friendship loves a free air, and will not be
fenced up in straight and narrow enclosures.
— William Penn

IRVING   *[ER-ving]*

MEANING: green river, west river • **USAGE:** Scottish and English surname: from Gaelic *ir* (green) and *afon* (water) or from Gaelic *iar* (west) and *abhuinn* (river)

A river seems a magic thing. A magic, moving,
living part of the very earth itself.
— Laura Gilpin, *The Rio Grande*

ISAAC   *[IE-ʒak]*

MEANING: he will laugh • **USAGE:** English form of Yitzchak, from Hebrew *yitshaq*

God hath made me to laugh,
so that all that hear will laugh with me.
— Genesis 21:6 (KJV)

ISAAK   *[ee-SAHK]*

MEANING: he will laugh • **USAGE:** Russian, German, and Dutch form of Isaac (*see* Isaac)

Nothing shows a man's character
more than what he laughs at.
— Johann Wolfgang von Goethe

ISAD   *[ee-sahd]*

MEANING: blessed, fortunate • **USAGE:** Muslim

The grace of Allah and His blessings on you.
— Koran, Hud 11.73b (PIC)

ISAIAH   *[ie-SAY-ah]*

MEANING: God is salvation • **USAGE:** English form of Yeshaya, from Hebrew *yesha'yah* (Yahweh is salvation)

Thou hast also given me the shield of thy salvation;
and thy right hand hath holden me up,
and thy gentleness hath made me great.
— Psalm 18:35 (ASV)

ISAK   *[EE-sahk]*

MEANING: he will laugh • **USAGE:** Scandinavian form of Isaac (*see* Isaac)

He [God] will make you laugh
and call out with joy.
— Job 8:21 (NLV)

ISAMU   [ee-sah-moo]

MEANING: brave, courageous • **USAGE:** Japanese

A true warrior is always armed with three things:
the radiant sword of pacification,
the mirror of bravery, wisdom, and friendship;
and the precious jewel of enlightenment.
— Morihei Ueshiba,
The Art of Peace (tr. John Stevens)

ISHAH   [eh-shah]

MEANING: ruler, lord, king, one who looks after,
one who protects • **USAGE:** Hindu: from Sanskrit
isa

The Lord dwells in the hearts of all creatures,
and he whirls them round on the wheel of time.
Run to him for refuge with all your strength and peace
profound will be yours through his grace.
— *Bhagavad Gita*

ISHAQ   [ee-shahk]

MEANING: he will laugh • **USAGE:** Muslim form
of Isaac (*see* Isaac)

Laugh / Because that is the purest / Sound.
— Hafiz, "I Got Kin"
(tr. Daniel Ladinsky in *The Gift*)

ISHMAEL   [ish-mah-EL]

MEANING: God hears, God will hear • **USAGE:**
English form of Yishmael, from Hebrew *yishma' el*
(Yahweh hears)

Speak to Him, thou, for He hears, /
and Spirit with Spirit can meet.
— Alfred Tennyson, "The Higher Pantheism"

ISIDORE   [IZ-ah-dohr]

MEANING: gift of Isis, fruitful, bounteous •
USAGE: English form of Isidoros (*see* Isidoros)

The one who pursues righteousness
and love finds life, bounty, and honor.
— Proverbs 21:21 (NEB)

ISIDOROS   [ee-sah-DOR-ohs]

MEANING: gift of Isis, fruitful, bounteous •
USAGE: Greek: from *Isis* (Egyptian goddess of
fertility) and Greek *doron* (gift)

Give, and you will receive. Your gift will return to you
in full — pressed down, shaken together to make room
for more, running over, and poured into your lap.
— Luke 6:38 (NLT)

ISMAIL   [ees-mah-eel]

MEANING: Allah hears, Allah will hear • **USAGE:**
Muslim form of Ishmael (*see* Ishmael)

Your Lord hath said:
Pray unto Me and I will hear your prayer.
— Koran, The Forgiving One 40.60 (PIC)

ITAI   [ee-TIE]

MEANING: friendly, compassionate, God is with
me • **USAGE:** Jewish

Deal loyally and compassionately with one another.
— Zechariah 7:9b (JPS)

ITTAN   [ee-TAHN]

MEANING: strong, firm, steadfast • **USAGE:**
Jewish: from Hebrew *ethan*

His heart is firm, he trusts in the Lord.
His heart is resolute, he is unafraid.
— Psalm 112:7b–8a (JPS)

IVAN   [ee-VAHN (Russian), IE-vun (English)]

MEANING: God is gracious, God is giving •
USAGE: Russian and English form of John, from
Hebrew *y'hohanan* (Yahweh is gracious)

God be gracious unto thee.
— Genesis 43:29b (KJ21)

IVAR [EE-vahr]

MEANING: bowman, archer, warrior • **USAGE:** Scandinavian: from Norse *yr* (yew tree) and *arr* (army); yew is used to make bows

> *Whatsoever thy hand findeth to do,*
> *do it with thy might.*
> — Ecclesiastes 9:10a (KJV)

IVES [ievs]

MEANING: yew tree, bow maker • **USAGE:** English form of Yves, from German *iv* (yew tree); yew is used to make bows

> *He will be like a tree planted by water: it sends its roots*
> *out toward a stream, it doesn't fear when heat comes,*
> *and its foliage remains green. It will not worry in a*
> *year of drought or cease producing fruit.*
> — Jeremiah 17:8 (HCSB)

IVOR [IE-vohr]

MEANING: bowman, archer, warrior • **USAGE:** Scottish, Irish, and Welsh form of Ivar (*see* Ivar)

> *A good archer is not known by his arrows but his aim.*
> — Thomas Fuller, *Gnomologia*

IWAN [EE-vahn]

MEANING: God is gracious, God is giving • **USAGE:** Polish and Welsh form of John, from Hebrew *y'hohanan* (Yahweh is gracious)

> *"For I know the plans I have for you," says the Lord,*
> *"plans for well-being and not for trouble, to give you a*
> *future and a hope."*
> — Jeremiah 29:11 (NLV)

IZZIE, IZZY [IZ-ee]

MEANING: gift of Isis, fruitful, bounteous • **USAGE:** English form of Isidore, from *Isis* (Egyptian goddess of fertility) and Greek *doron* (gift)

> *Mercy, peace and love be yours in abundance.*
> — Jude 1:2 (NIV)

J

JABBAR [jah-bahr]

MEANING: powerful, mighty • **USAGE:** Muslim

> *The more a man explores himself,*
> *the more power he finds within.*
> — Hazrat Inayat Khan, *The Gayan* (cd. *The Gayani Meditations, Volume 1,* tr. Cecil Touchon)

JABIR, JAABIR [jah-BEER]

MEANING: comfort, comforter • **USAGE:** Muslim: from Arabic *jabara* (to restore) or *jabir* (to comfort, to ease)

> *Whatever of comfort ye enjoy, it is from Allah.*
> — Koran, The Spoils of War 8.53b (PIC)

JACE [jays]

MEANING: healer, physician, replace, change, transform, successor • **USAGE:** American: form of Jason, from Greek *iasthai* (to heal); or form of Jacob, from Hebrew *ya'aqobh* (one that takes by the heel, replace with another)

> *I hope all is well with you and that you are*
> *as healthy in body as you are strong in spirit.*
> — 3 John 1:2 (NLT)

JACINTO [hah-SEEN-toh (Spanish), zhah-SEEN-toh (Portuguese)]

MEANING: hyacinth flower • **USAGE:** Spanish and Portuguese masculine form of Hyacinthe, from Greek *hyakinthos*

> *None can have a healthy love for flowers*
> *unless he loves the wild ones.*
> — John Forbes Watson, *Flowers and Gardens*

JACK [jak]

MEANING: God is gracious, God is giving, replace, change, transform, successor • **USAGE:** English: form of John, from Hebrew *y'hohanan* (Yahweh is gracious); or form of Jacob (*see* Jacob)

God hath not given us the spirit of fear,
but of power and of love and of a sound mind.
    — 2 Timothy 1:7 (KJ21)

JACKSON   *[JAK-son]*

MEANING: son of Jack, God is gracious, God is giving, replace, change, transform, successor • **USAGE:** English surname: English combination of Jack and *son* (*see* Jack)
    Blessed be thou of the Lord, my son.
        — Judges 17:2b (KJV)

JACOB   *[JAY-kub]*

MEANING: replace, change, transform, successor • **USAGE:** English form of Yakov, from Hebrew *ya'aqobh* (one that takes by the heel, replace with another)
    May the God of Jacob keep you safe....
    May he give you what your heart longs for.
    May he make all of your plans succeed.
        — Psalm 20:1b, 20:4 (NIRV)

JACOBO   *[hah-koh-voh]*

MEANING: replace, change, transform, successor • **USAGE:** Spanish and Italian form of Jacob (*see* Jacob)
    Now thus says the Lord, he who created you,
    O Jacob...I have called you by name, you are mine.
        — Isaiah 43:1 (ESV)

JACQUES   *[zhahk]*

MEANING: replace, change, transform, successor • **USAGE:** French form of Jacob (*see* Jacob)
    As long as a man is capable of self-renewal,
        he is a living being.
        — Henri Frédéric Amiel
    (journal entry of June 21, 1871)

JAFAR, JAFAAR   *[jah-FAHR]*

MEANING: stream, brook • **USAGE:** Muslim: from Arabic *ja'far*
    When the stream of love flows in its full strength,
        it purifies all that stands in its way.
        — Hazrat Inayat Khan, *The Bowl of Saki*

JAGGER   *[JAG-er]*

MEANING: carter, carrier, packer, peddler • **USAGE:** English surname: from English *jag* (pack, load); occupational name of a peddler
    Hitch your wagon to a star.
        — Ralph Waldo Emerson, "Civilization"

JAHAN   *[jah-hahn]*

MEANING: world • **USAGE:** Persian
    We live in this world when we love it.
        — Rabindranath Tagore, *Stray Birds*

JAHI   *[jah-hee]*

MEANING: dignified, esteemed, honored • **USAGE:** African: Egypt
    Be patient when you speak,
    and you will say distinguished things.
        — Egyptian proverb

JAHID, JAHEED   *[jah-HEED]*

MEANING: diligent, hardworking • **USAGE:** Muslim: from Arabic *jahada* (to make an effort)
    For those who believe and work righteous deeds, there
    will be Gardens of Bliss, to dwell therein. The promise
    of God is true; and He is Exalted in power, Wise.
        — Koran, Luqman 31.8 (ALI)

JAIME   *[HIE-may]*

MEANING: replace, change, transform, successor • **USAGE:** Spanish form of Jacob (*see* Jacob)
    Be changed within by a new way of thinking.
        — Romans 12:2b (NCV)

JAJA   *[jah-jah]*

MEANING: honored one • **USAGE:** African: Igbo of Nigeria

The man who is honoured has first honoured himself.
— Nigerian proverb

JAKE   *[jayk]*

MEANING: replace, change, transform, successor • **USAGE:** English form of Jacob (*see* Jacob)

Always remember, you have within you the strength, the patience, and the passion to reach for the stars to change the world.
— Harriet Tubman

JAKOB   *[YAH-kohb]*

MEANING: replace, change, transform, successor • **USAGE:** German, Dutch, Polish, and Scandinavian form of Jacob (*see* Jacob)

Change alone is eternal, perpetual, immortal.
— Arthur Schopenhauer

JAKOV   *[YAH-kohb]*

MEANING: replace, change, transform, successor • **USAGE:** Hungarian form of Jacob (*see* Jacob)

O Jacob, listen to the Lord who created you...I have called you by name; you are mine.
— Isaiah 43:1 (NLT)

JAKUB   *[YAH-kub]*

MEANING: replace, change, transform, successor • **USAGE:** Polish and Czech form of Jacob (*see* Jacob)

O house of Jacob, come, let us walk in the light of the Lord!
— Isaiah 2:5 (NRSV)

JALAL, JALAAL   *[jah-lahl]*

MEANING: great, illustrious, exalted • **USAGE:** Muslim: from Arabic *jalla* (to be great, to be illustrious)

To those who believe and do deeds of righteousness hath Allah promised forgiveness and a great reward.
— Koran, The Food 5.9 (ALI)

JALEN   *[JAY-len]*

MEANING: calm, peaceful, serene, replace, change, transform, successor • **USAGE:** American: possibly a form of Galen, from Greek *galene* (calm, peaceful); or possibly a form of Jay (*see* Jacob)

Nonviolence is a powerful and just weapon. It is a weapon unique in history, which cuts without wounding and ennobles the man who wields it. It is a sword that heals.
— Martin Luther King Jr., "I Have a Dream" (speech of August 28, 1963)

JALIL, JALEEL   *[jah-leel]*

MEANING: great, illustrious, exalted • **USAGE:** Muslim: from Arabic *jalla* (to be great, to be illustrious)

Thou exaltest whom Thou wilt.
— Koran, The Women 3.26b (PIC)

JAMAL, JAMAAL   *[jah-MAHL]*

MEANING: handsome, attractive • **USAGE:** Muslim: from Arabic *jamula*

He has created the heavens and the earth in just proportions, and has given you shape, and made your shapes beautiful: and to Him is the final Goal.
— Koran, The Mutual Loss 64.3 (ALI)

JAMAR, JAMARR   *[jah-MAHR]*

MEANING: sea, ocean, of the sea • **USAGE:** American: possibly a form of Lamar, from French *le mer* (the sea)

Behold the Sea! / The opaline, the plentiful and strong.
— Ralph Waldo Emerson, "Seashore"

J

JAMES *[jaymz]*

MEANING: replace, change, transform, successor
• **USAGE:** English form of Jacob, from Hebrew *ya'aqobh* (one that takes by the heel, replace with another)

> *Do not be shaped by this world;*
> *instead be changed within by a new way of thinking.*
> — Romans 12:2a (NASB)

JAMIE *[JAY-mee]*

MEANING: replace, change, transform, successor
• **USAGE:** English and Scottish form of James (*see* James)

> *Intelligence is the ability to adapt to change.*
> — Stephen Hawking

JAN *[yahn (Czech, German, Polish, Scandinavian), jan (English)]*

MEANING: God is gracious, God is giving •
USAGE: Scandinavian, Czech, German, Polish, and English form of John, from Hebrew *y'hohanan* (Yahweh is gracious)

> *The Lord bless you and keep you; the Lord make his face shine upon you and be gracious to you; the Lord turn his face toward you and give you peace.*
> — Numbers 6:24–26 (RSV)

JANEK *[YAH-nek]*

MEANING: God is gracious, God is giving •
USAGE: Polish and Czech form of John (*see* Jan)

> *God be gracious to us and bless.*
> *And cause His face to shine upon us.*
> — Psalm 67:1 (NASB)

JANESH *[jah-NEHSH]*

MEANING: lord of the people • **USAGE:** Hindu: from Sanskrit *jan* (life, being) and *isa* (lord)

> *The Lord is hidden in the hearts of all. /*
> *The eternal witness, pure consciousness.*
> — Shvetashvatara Upanishad (tr. Eknath Easwaran)

JANIKA *[YAH-nee-kah]*

MEANING: God is gracious, God is giving •
USAGE: Hungarian form of John (*see* Jan)

> *God said…Behold,*
> *I give you a wise and discerning mind.*
> — 1 Kings 3:11–12b (ESV)

JANNIK *[YAH-neek]*

MEANING: God is gracious, God is giving •
USAGE: Swedish and Danish form of Jan (*see* Jan)

> *I am sure that your goodness and love*
> *will follow me all the days of my life.*
> *And I will live in the house of the Lord forever.*
> — Psalm 23:6a (NIRV)

JANOS *[YAH-nosh]*

MEANING: God is gracious, God is giving •
USAGE: Hungarian form of Jan (*see* Jan)

> *"For surely I know the plans I have for you,"*
> *says the Lord, "plans for your welfare and not for harm, to give you a future with hope."*
> — Jeremiah 29:11 (NRSV)

JARED *[JAYR-ed]*

MEANING: descend, to flow down, descendant, rules with a spear, spear power • **USAGE:** English form of *Yared*, from Hebrew *yared* (to flow down); or Irish form of Gerald, from German *ger* (spear) and *wald* (rule, power)

> *Out of his heart shall flow rivers of living water.*
> — John 7:38 (RSV)

JAREK *[YAH-rek]*

MEANING: spring, fountain • **USAGE:** Czech and Polish: from Czech *jaro*

> *Good sense is a fountain of life to him who has it.*
> — Proverbs 16:22a (ESV)

JAREL   *[jeh-REL]*

MEANING: man of Airelle, open space, rule with a
spear, powerful spear • **USAGE:** American: possibly
a form of Darrell, from French *arealis* (open space,
threshing floor); or possibly a form of Gerald, from
German *ger* (spear) and *wald* (rule, power)

> *The God who has girded me with strength*
> *has opened wide my path.*
> — 2 Samuel 22:33 (NRSV)

JARON, JARAN, JAREN   *[JAYR-on]*

MEANING: guardian, protector, he will sing out •
USAGE: American: possibly a form of Garen, from
German *gard* (guard, protect); or possibly a form of
Yaron (he will sing out)

> *Discretion will watch over you,*
> *and understanding will guard you.*
> — Proverbs 2:11 (HCSB)

JARRET, JARRETT   *[JAYR-et]*

MEANING: rule with a spear, powerful spear, brave
with a spear • **USAGE:** Irish form of Garret, from
German *ger* (spear) and *wald* (rule, power) or *hart*
(hardy, strong, brave)

> *A leader is one who knows the way,*
> *goes the way, and shows the way.*
> — John C. Maxwell

JARVIS   *[JAR-vis]*

MEANING: spear servant, warrior • **USAGE:**
English form of Gervaise, from German *ger* (spear)
and *vass* (servant)

> *The Lord is with thee, thou mighty man of valor.*
> — Judges 6:12b (KJ21)

JASHAWN   *[jah-SHAHN]*

MEANING: God is gracious, God is giving •
USAGE: American: possibly a form of Shawn, from
Hebrew *y'hohanan* (Yahweh is gracious)

> *God can give you all you need. He will give*
> *you more than enough. You will have everything*
> *you need for yourselves. And you will have*
> *enough left over to give when there is a need.*
> — 2 Corinthians 9:8 (NLV)

JASIM, JASEEM   *[jah-SEEM]*

MEANING: great, illustrious, exalted • **USAGE:**
Muslim

> *Know, O beloved, that man was not created*
> *in jest or at random, but marvelously*
> *made and for some great end.*
> — Al-Ghazali

JASIR, JASEER   *[jah-seer]*

MEANING: brave, courageous • **USAGE:** Muslim

> *Whoever is patient and forgiving,*
> *these most surely are actions due to courage.*
> — Koran, The Counsel 42.43 (SKR)

JASON   *[JAY-son]*

MEANING: healer, physician • **USAGE:** English
form of *Iason*, from Greek *iasthai* (to heal)

> *The greatest healing therapy is friendship and love.*
> — Hubert Humphrey

JASPER   *[JAS-per]*

MEANING: treasure master, steward, gemstone •
USAGE: English form of Gaspar, from Persian
genashber (treasure master); a semiprecious
gemstone

> *You have been trusted with a wonderful treasure.*
> *Guard it with the help of the Holy Spirit,*
> *who lives within you.*
> — 2 Timothy 1:14 (CEV)

JATHAN   *[JAY-than]*

MEANING: gift • **USAGE:** American: possibly a
form of Nathan, from Hebrew *nathan*

Life is the first gift, love is the second,
and understanding the third.
— Marge Piercy, *Gone to Soldiers*

JAVED   *[jah-ved]*

MEANING: eternal, everlasting • USAGE: Persian:
from Persian *jaawid*
Constantly serve the truth
and you will become eternal.
— Jalaluddin Rumi
(tr. Shahram Shiva in *Rumi: Thief of Sleep*)

JAVIER   *[hah-bee-AYR]*

MEANING: new house • USAGE: Spanish form
of Xavier, from Basque place-name *Etxabier* (new
house)
I will lead a life of integrity in my own home.
— Psalm 101:2b (NLT)

JAX   *[jaks]*

MEANING: son of Jack, God is gracious, God
is giving, replace, change, transform, successor,
successor • USAGE: American form of Jaxson (*see*
Jaxson)
The Lord gives grace and glory;
no good thing does He withhold from those
who walk uprightly.
— Psalm 84:11b (NASB)

JAXSON   *[JAK-son]*

MEANING: son of Jack, God is gracious, God
is giving, replace, change, transform, successor,
successor • USAGE: American form of Jackson,
from Hebrew *y'hohanan* (Yahweh is gracious)
or Hebrew *ya'aqobh* (one that takes by the heel,
supplanter)
May God be gracious to you, my son.
— Genesis 43:29b (HCSB)

JAY   *[jay]*

MEANING: replace, change, transform, successor
• USAGE: English form of Jacob or James, from
Hebrew *ya'aqobh* (one that takes by the heel, replace
with another)
May the name of the God of Jacob protect you!…
May he grant you your heart's desire
and fulfill all your plans!
— Psalm 20:1a, 20:4 (ESV)

JAYAN   *[jah-yahn]*

MEANING: victorious, triumphant, successful •
USAGE: Hindu: from Sanskrit *jaya*
Endowed with great wisdom, preserve us for fame, for
strength, for victory, for happiness, for prosperity.
— *Rig Veda* (tr. Edward Cowell)

JAYDEN, JADEN   *[JAY-den]*

MEANING: fire, fiery one, broad woods, broad
hill, broad-chested, salmon, hay field • USAGE:
American: possibly from names ending with -*aden*
suffix, such as Aidan, Braden, or Hayden (*see those
entries*)
It is not light that is needed, but fire;
it is not the gentle shower, but thunder.
— Frederick Douglass (speech of July 5, 1852)

JAZON   *[YAH-zohn]*

MEANING: heal, healer • USAGE: Polish form of
Jason (*see* Jason)
The words of the wise bring healing.
— Proverbs 12:18b (NLT)

JEAN   *[zhahn]*

MEANING: God is gracious, God is giving •
USAGE: French form of John, from Hebrew
y'hohanan (Yahweh is gracious)
The Lord your God is gracious and compassionate.
He will not turn His face from you.
— 2 Chronicles 30:9b (NIV)

JEB [jeb]

MEANING: beloved of God, friend of God •
USAGE: English form of Jebediah (*see* Jebediah)
Beloved, let us love one another,
because love is from God; everyone who loves
is born of God and knows God.
— 1 John 4:7 (NRSV)

JEBEDIAH [jeb-eh-DIE-ah]

MEANING: beloved of God, friend of God •
USAGE: English form of Jedidiah, from Hebrew
Yedidya (beloved of Yahweh, friend of Yahweh)
As those who have been chosen of God,
holy and beloved, put on a heart of compassion,
kindness, humility, gentleness and patience.
— Colossians 3:12 (NASB)

JED [jed]

MEANING: beloved of God, friend of God •
USAGE: English form of Jedidiah (*see* Jedidiah)
Let the beloved of the Lord rest secure in him,
for he shields him all day long, and the one the
Lord loves rests between his shoulders.
— Deuteronomy 33:12b (RSV)

JEDIDIAH [jeh-deh-DIE-ah]

MEANING: beloved of God, friend of God •
USAGE: English form of Hebrew *Yedidya* (beloved
of Yahweh, friend of Yahweh)
God is love, and whoever abides in love
abides in God, and God abides in him.
— 1 John 4:16b (ESV)

JEFF [jeff]

MEANING: peace of God, God's peace, peaceful
territory, peaceful stranger, peaceful traveler,
pledge of peace • **USAGE:** English form of Jeffrey
(*see* Jeffrey)

Be at peace with God, whatever you conceive Him to
be, and whatever your labors and aspirations, in the
noisy confusion of life keep peace with your soul.
— Max Ehrmann, "Desiderata"

JEFFERSON [JEF-er-son]

MEANING: peace of God, God's peace, peaceful
territory, peaceful stranger, peaceful traveler,
pledge of peace • **USAGE:** English surname: a form
of Jeffrey and *son* (*see* Jeffrey)
Live in peace.
And the God of love and peace will be with you.
— 2 Corinthians 13:11b (NEB)

JEFFREY, JEFFRY [JEF-ree]

MEANING: peace of God, God's peace, peaceful
territory, peaceful stranger, peaceful traveler, pledge
of peace • **USAGE:** English form of Geoffrey,
from German *gott* (God) and *frid* (peace); or from
German *gawia* (territory), *walah* (stranger), or *gisil*
(pledge, promise), and *frid* (peace)
The Lord bless thee, and keep thee.
The Lord shew his face to thee, and have mercy on thee.
The Lord turn his countenance to thee,
and give thee peace.
— Numbers 6:24–26 (DR)

JENGO [JAYN-goh]

MEANING: building • **USAGE:** African: Swahili
Every door with its own key.
— Swahili proverb

JENO [YEH-noh]

MEANING: wellborn, noble • **USAGE:** Hungarian
form of Eugene, from Greek *eu* (good, well) and
genes (born)
A noble person plans noble things;
he stands up for noble causes.
— Isaiah 32:8 (HCSB)

J

JENS   *[yens]*

MEANING: God is gracious, God is giving •
USAGE: Scandinavian form of John, from Hebrew
y'hohanan (Yahweh is gracious)

> *God is gracious and merciful,*
> *and will not turn away his face from you.*
> — 2 Chronicles 30:9b (WEB)

JENSEN   *[JEN-sen]*

MEANING: God is gracious, God is giving •
USAGE: English surname meaning "son of John"
(*see* John)

> *Grace be with you.*
> — 1 Timothy 6:21b (NKJV)

JERALD   *[JER-ald]*

MEANING: God will raise up, God will uplift, rule
with a spear, powerful spear • **USAGE:** English:
from Hebrew *yirmeyahu* (may Yahweh exalt);
English form of Gerald, from German *ger* (spear)
and *wald* (rule, power)

> *Ye shall be a blessing.*
> *Fear not, but let your hands be strong.*
> — Zechariah 8:13b (ASV)

JEREMIAH   *[jer-eh-MIE-ah]*

MEANING: God will raise up, God will uplift •
USAGE: English: from Hebrew *yirmeyahu* (may
Yahweh exalt)

> *You, O Lord, are a shield for me,*
> *my glory and the One who lifts up my head.*
> — Psalm 3:3 (NKJV)

JEREMY   *[JER-eh-mee]*

MEANING: God will raise up, God will uplift •
USAGE: English form of Jeremiah (*see* Jeremiah)

> *There are two things that raise a man above earthly*
> *things, simplicity and purity.... Simplicity reaches out*
> *after God; purity discovers and enjoys Him.*
> — Thomas à Kempis, *The Imitation of Christ*

JEROME   *[jeh-ROHM]*

MEANING: holy name • **USAGE:** English: from
Latin *hieras* (holy) and *onyma* (name)

> *I have redeemed you;*
> *I have called you by name; you are Mine!*
> — Isaiah 43:1b (NASB)

JERÓNIMO   *[hay-ROH-nee-moh]*

MEANING: holy name • **USAGE:** Spanish form of
Jerome (*see* Jerome)

> *You have found favor in My sight,*
> *and I have known you by name.*
> — Exodus 33:17b (NASB)

JERROD, JERRAD   *[JER-od, jeh-RAUD]*

MEANING: descend, to flow down, descendant,
rules with a spear, spear power • **USAGE:** American:
possibly form of Jared, from Hebrew *yared* (to flow
down); or possibly form of Gerald, from German
ger (spear) and *wald* (ruler, power)

> *Put on the armor of light.*
> — Romans 13:12b (RSV)

JERRY   *[JER-ee]*

MEANING: God will raise up, God will uplift,
holy name, rule with a spear, powerful spear, brave
with a spear • **USAGE:** English: form of Jeremy
(*see* Jeremy); form of Jerome (*see* Jerome); form of
Gerald, from German *ger* (spear) and *wald* (rule,
power); or form of Gerard, from German *ger*
(spear) and *hart* (hardy, strong)

> *My hand will always be with him,*
> *and My arm will strengthen him.*
> — Psalm 89:21 (HCSB)

JESS   *[jes]*

MEANING: gift • **USAGE:** English form of Jesse
(*see* Jesse)

God is able to make every gracious gift abound towards
you, that, having in every way always all-sufficiency,
ye may abound to every good work.
— 2 Corinthians 9:8 (DT)

JESSE, JESSIE   *[JES-ee]*

MEANING: gift • USAGE: English form of Yishai,
from Hebrew *yishai*
Use your gifts faithfully, and they shall be enlarged;
practice what you know, and you shall attain
to higher knowledge.
— Thomas Arnold

JESÚS   *[hay-SOOS]*

MEANING: God is salvation • USAGE: Spanish
form of Yeshua, from Hebrew *yesha'yah* (Yahweh
is salvation)
My salvation and honor depend on God; he is my
strong protector; he is my shelter.
— Psalm 62:7 (GNT)

JETA   *[jeh-tah]*

MEANING: victorious, triumphant, successful •
USAGE: Hindu: Sanskrit
He is the wisest who seeks God. He is the
most successful who has found God.
— Paramahansa Yogananda

JETHRO   *[JETH-roh]*

MEANING: abundant, bountiful, rich • USAGE:
English form of *Yitro*, Hebrew *yether*
God is able to provide you with every blessing in abun-
dance, so that by always having enough of everything,
you may share abundantly in every good work.
— 2 Corinthians 9:8 (NRSV)

JETT   *[jet]*

MEANING: coal-black, dark • USAGE: American:
from English *jet* (coal-black)
Black is the most aristocratic color of all.
— Louise Nevelson

JEVIN   *[JEV-en]*

MEANING: poet, gift, courageous, fearless •
USAGE: American: possibly a form of Devin, from
Gaelic *damh* (poet), *dan* (gift), or *dana* (intrepid,
courageous)
Poetry is the utterance of deep and heart-felt
truth — the true poet is very near the oracle.
— Edwin Hubbell Chapin

JIA   *[jhee-ah]*

MEANING: good • USAGE: Chinese
Keep company with good men,
and good men you'll learn to be.
— Chinese proverb (tr. William Scarborough)

JIAN   *[jhee-ahn]*

MEANING: healthy, strong • USAGE: Chinese
Seeing the small is called clarity;
keeping flexible is called strength.
— Lao Tzu, *Tao Te Ching*
(tr. Thomas Cleary in *The Essential Tao*)

JIE   *[jhee-eh]*

MEANING: heroic, outstanding • USAGE: Chinese
If one man conquer in battle a thousand times
a thousand men, and if another conquers himself,
he is the greatest of conquerors.
— Buddha, *The Dhammapada*

JIM   *[jim]*

MEANING: replace, change, transform, successor
• USAGE: English form of James, from Hebrew
ya'aqobh (one that takes by the heel, replace with
another)
I am the Lord...
A new heart also will I give you,
and a new spirit will I put within you.
— Ezekiel 36:23b, 26a (KJV)

JIN   [jhin]

Meaning: gold, golden • **Usage:** Chinese
True gold fears no fire.
— Chinese proverb (tr. William Scarborough)

JING   [jhing]

Meaning: perfect, clear, crystal • **Usage:**
Chinese
All things are already complete in us. There is no greater delight than to be conscious of right within us. If one strives to treat others as he would be treated by them, he shall not fail to come near the perfect life.
— Mencius

JIRI   [yee-ree]

Meaning: earth worker, farmer, gardener • **Usage:** Czech form of George, from Greek *ge* (earth) and *ergein* (to work)
Truth springs from the earth.
— Psalm 85:11a (NASB)

JIVANA   [jih-vah-nah]

Meaning: life, enlivening • **Usage:** Hindu: Sanskrit
Where there is love there is life.
— Mahatma Gandhi

JOAB   [JOH-ab]

Meaning: God is father, God is willing • **Usage:** English form of Hebrew Yoav
O Lord, you are our Father. We are the clay, you are the potter; we are all the work of your hand.
— Isaiah 64:8 (RSV)

JOACHIM   [JOH-ah-kim (English), ʒhoh-ah-KEEM (French), YOH-ah-keem (German)]

Meaning: God will establish • **Usage:** English, French, and German form of *Yehoyakim*, from Hebrew *yehoyakim* (Yahweh will establish)

The God of grace will Himself perfect, confirm, strengthen and establish you.
— 1 Peter 5:10b (NASB)

JOAKIM   [yoh-AH-keem]

Meaning: God will establish • **Usage:** Scandinavian form of Joachim (*see* Joachim)
You will be firmly established and unafraid.
— Job 11:15b (HCSB)

JOAQUÍN, JOACHIN   [hwah-KEEN]

Meaning: God will establish • **Usage:** Spanish and English form of Joachim (*see* Joachim)
The Lord is faithful, who shall establish you, and guard you.
— 2 Thessalonians 3:3a (ASV)

JOCK   [jawk]

Meaning: God is gracious, God is giving, replace, change, transform, successor • **Usage:** Scottish form of Jack, from Hebrew *y'hohanan* (Yahweh is gracious), or from Hebrew *ya'aqobh* (one that takes by the heel, replace with another)
The God of all grace…will himself perfect you and give you firmness, strength, and a sure foundation.
— 1 Peter 5:10 (NEB)

JODY   [JOH-dee]

Meaning: God will add, God will increase • **Usage:** English form of Joseph (*see* Joe)
May He give you the desire of your heart, and make all your plans go well.
— Psalm 20:4 (NLV)

JOE   [joh]

Meaning: God will add, God will increase • **Usage:** English form of Joseph, from Hebrew *ya'saph* (Yahweh will add)
May the Lord make your love increase and overflow.
— 1 Thessalonians 3:12a (NIV)

JOEL [*JOH-el, joh-l*]

Meaning: the Lord is God, God is willing •
Usage: English form of Yoel, from Hebrew *yoh'el*
(Yahweh is God)

The Lord will be happy to do good things for you.
— Deuteronomy 30:9a (CEV)

JOEY [*JOH-ee*]

Meaning: God will add, God will increase •
Usage: English form of Joseph (*see* Joe)

May the Lord give you increase more and more,
you and your children. May you be blessed
by the Lord, who made heaven and earth.
— Psalm 115:14–15 (NKJV)

JOHAN, JOHANN [*YOH-hahn*]

Meaning: God is gracious, God is giving •
Usage: German, Czech, and Scandinavian form of
John (*see* John)

God is able to make all grace abound to you,
so that in all things at all times, having all that you
need, you will abound in every good work.
— 2 Corinthians 9:8 (NIV)

JOHANNES [*yoh-HAH-nes*]

Meaning: God is gracious, God is giving •
Usage: Scandinavian and German form of John
(*see* John)

The Lord gives grace and glory; He does not withhold
the good from those who live with integrity.
— Psalm 84:11b (HCSB)

JOHN [*jon*]

Meaning: God is gracious, God is giving •
Usage: English: from Hebrew *y'hohanan* (Yahweh
is gracious)

The Lord bless thee, and keep thee:
the Lord make his face shine upon thee,
and be gracious unto thee: the Lord lift up his
countenance upon thee, and give thee peace.
— Numbers 6:24–26 (KJV)

JOHNNY, JOHNNIE [*JON-ee*]

Meaning: God is gracious, God is giving •
Usage: English form of John (*see* John)

God be gracious to thee.
— Genesis 43:29b (DT)

JOJO [*joh-joh*]

Meaning: God will add, God will increase •
Usage: English form of Joseph (*see* Joseph)

On the day I called, You answered me;
You increased strength within me.
— Psalm 138:3b (HCSB)

JOMO [*joh-moh*]

Meaning: burning spear • **Usage:** African:
Kikuyu of Kenya

Do not wait until tomorrow to hunt.
— East African proverb

JON [*jon*]

Meaning: God has given • **Usage:** English form
of Jonathan (*see* Jonathan)

As for every man to whom God has given riches
and wealth, and given him power to eat of it,
to receive his heritage and rejoice in his labor —
this is the gift of God.
— Ecclesiastes 5:19 (NKJV)

JONAH [*JOH-nah*]

Meaning: dove, dove-like • **Usage:** English form
of Yonah, from Hebrew *yonah* (dove); a symbol of
peace

This is the way of peace: overcome evil with good,
falsehood with truth, and hatred with love.
— Peace Pilgrim, *Peace Pilgrim*

JONAS [*JOH-nas*]

Meaning: dove, dove-like • **Usage:** English form
of Jonah (*see* Jonah)

Blessed are the peacemakers:
for they shall be called sons of God.
— Matthew 5:9 (ASV)

JONATHAN   *[JON-ah-than]*

MEANING: God has given • **USAGE:** English form
of Yehonatan, from Hebrew *yehonathan* (Yahweh
has given)

God said...I have given thee
a wise and an understanding heart.
— 1 Kings 3:11–12b (KJV)

JONG-SOO   *[jong-soo]*

MEANING: excellent leader • **USAGE:** Korean:
from Korean *jong* (leader) and *soo* (excellent)

A man should first direct himself in the way
he should go. Only then should he instruct others.
— Buddha

JONNY   *[JON-ee]*

MEANING: God has given • **USAGE:** English form
of Jonathan (*see* Jonathan)

Grace and peace be given to you more and more.
— 2 Peter 1:2a (NCV)

JOOLS   *[joolz]*

MEANING: light-bearded, young, youthful, of
Jupiter • **USAGE:** English form of Julius, from Latin
iulus (downy-chinned, youthful); or form of *Jupiter*,
from Latin *dyeus* (Zeus) and *pater* (father)

It is not possible for civilization to flow backwards
while there is youth in the world.
— Helen Keller, *Midstream*

JOON-HO   *[joon-hoh]*

MEANING: excellent and good • **USAGE:** Korean:
from Korean *joon* (excellent, outstanding) and *ho*
(goodness, broad)

Whatsoever, after due examination and analysis,
you find to be conducive to the good, the benefit,
the welfare of all beings — that doctrine believe
and cling to, and take it as your guide.
— Buddha

JORDAN, JORDON   *[JOR-dan]*

MEANING: descend, to flow down, descendant •
USAGE: English form of Yarden, from Hebrew
yarden (to descend, to flow down); river in Israel

Out of his heart will flow rivers of living water.
— John 7:38b (ESV)

JORG   *[yoork]*

MEANING: earth worker, farmer, gardener •
USAGE: German and Scandinavian form of George
(*see* Jorge)

The earth is the very quintessence
of the human condition.
— Hannah Arendt, *The Human Condition*

JORGE   *[HOHR-hay (Spanish),*
                  ZHOR-zhee (Portuguese)]

MEANING: earth worker, farmer, gardener •
USAGE: Spanish and Portuguese form of George,
from Greek *ge* (earth) and *ergein* (to work)

Sow righteousness for yourselves and reap faithful love.
— Hosea 10:12a (HCSB)

JORGEN   *[YOHR-gen]*

MEANING: earth worker, farmer, gardener •
USAGE: Swedish and Norwegian form of George
(*see* Jorge)

Speak to the earth, and it will teach you.
— Job 12:8a (NIV)

JOSÉ   *[hoh-SAY]*

MEANING: God will add, God will increase •
USAGE: Spanish form of Joseph (*see* Joseph)

The Lord thy God will bless thee in all thy fruits, and in every work of thy hands, and thou shalt be in joy.
— Deuteronomy 16:15b (DR)

JOSEF   *[YOH-sef (German, Scandinavian), hoh-sef (Spanish)]*

MEANING: God will add, God will increase • **USAGE:** German, Scandinavian, and Spanish form of Joseph (*see* Joseph)

God is able to provide you with every blessing in abundance, so that you may always have enough of everything and may provide in abundance for every good work.
— 2 Corinthians 9:8 (RSV)

JOSEPH   *[JOH-sef (English), zhoh-ZEF (French), YOH-zef (German)]*

MEANING: God will add, God will increase • **USAGE:** English and French form of Yosef, from Hebrew *ya'saph* (Yahweh will add)

The Lord will make you prosperous in all that you do.
— Deuteronomy 30:9a (GNT)

JOSH   *[josh]*

MEANING: God is salvation • **USAGE:** English form of Joshua (*see* Joshua)

I am your God. I will strengthen you; I will help you.
— Isaiah 41:10b (HCSB)

JOSHUA   *[JOSH-yoo-ah]*

MEANING: God is salvation • **USAGE:** English form of Yehoshua, from Hebrew *yesha'yah* (Yahweh is salvation)

Be confident, and never be afraid of anything or get discouraged. The Lord my God will help you do everything needed.
— 1 Chronicles 28:20b (CEV)

JOSIAH   *[joh-SIE-ah]*

MEANING: God is salvation • **USAGE:** English form of Hebrew *Yoshiyah*, from Hebrew *yesha'yah* (Yahweh is salvation)

The Lord your God in your midst, the Mighty One, will save; He will rejoice over you with gladness, He will quiet you with His love, He will rejoice over you with singing.
— Zephaniah 3:17 (NKJV)

JOURDAIN   *[zhohr-DAYN]*

MEANING: descend, to flow down, descendant • **USAGE:** French form of Jordan (*see* Jordan)

From his innermost being shall flow rivers of living water.
— John 7:38b (NASB)

JOZEF   *[YOH-zehf]*

MEANING: God will add, God will increase • **USAGE:** Dutch and Polish form of Joseph (*see* Joseph)

The Lord shall increase you more and more, you and your children.
— Psalm 115:14 (KJV)

JUAN   *[hwahn]*

MEANING: God is gracious, God is giving • **USAGE:** Spanish form of John, from Hebrew *y'hohanan* (Yahweh is gracious)

The Lord bless you and keep you; the Lord make his face to shine upon you, and be gracious to you; the Lord lift up his countenance upon you, and give you peace.
— Numbers 6:24–26 (NRSV)

JUBAL   *[JOO-bal]*

MEANING: stream, river • **USAGE:** English form of Yuval

To put your hands in a river is to feel the chords that bind the earth together.
— Barry Lopez, *River Notes*

J

JUDAH   *[JOO-dah]*

Meaning: praise, glorify, thank • **Usage:**
English form of Yehudah, from Hebrew root *y-d-h*
(praised)

Praise God, from whom all blessings flow!
— Thomas Ken, "Morning and Evening Hymn"

JUDD   *[jud]*

Meaning: descend, to flow down, descendant,
praise, glorify, thank • **Usage:** English form of
Jordan (*see* Jordan) or of Judah (*see* Judah)

Out of his heart shall flow rivers of living water.
— John 7:38 (NKJV)

JUDE   *[jood]*

Meaning: praise, thank, glorify • **Usage:** English
form of Judah (*see* Judah)

As we express our gratitude,
we must never forget that the highest appreciation
is not to utter words, but to live by them.
— John F. Kennedy
(Thanksgiving Day Proclamation, 1963)

JULES   *[ʒhoolʒ (French), joolʒ (English)]*

Meaning: light-bearded, young, youthful, of
Jupiter • **Usage:** French and English form of Julius
(*see* Julius)

Those whom the gods love grow young.
— Oscar Wilde, "A Few Maxims for the
Instruction of the Over-Educated"

JULIAN   *[JOO-lee-an, JOOL-yan (English), YOO-lee-ahn (German)]*

Meaning: light-bearded, young, youthful, of
Jupiter • **Usage:** English and German form of
Julius (*see* Julius)

Dream, O youth! dream manfully and nobly,
and thy dreams shall be prophets.
— Edward Bulwer-Lytton, *The Caxtons*

JULIEN   *[ZHOOL-yen]*

Meaning: light-bearded, young, youthful, of
Jupiter • **Usage:** French form of Julius (*see* Julius)

The glory of young men is their strength.
— Proverbs 20:29a (KJV)

JULIO   *[HOO-lee-oh (Spanish), ZHOO-lee-oh (Portuguese)]*

Meaning: light-bearded, young, youthful, of
Jupiter • **Usage:** Spanish and Portuguese form of
Julian (*see* Julius)

Youth has no age.
— Pablo Picasso

JULIUS   *[JOO-lee-us]*

Meaning: light-bearded, young, youthful, of
Jupiter • **Usage:** English form of Italian Roman
family name Julius, possibly from Latin *iulus*
(downy-chinned, youthful); or form of *Jupiter*,
from Latin *dyeus* (Zeus) and *pater* (father), Roman
father of the gods

Youth has a kingdom waiting for it.
Every one is born a king.
— Oscar Wilde, *A Woman of No Importance*

JUMBE   *[jum-beh]*

Meaning: important person • **Usage:** African:
Swahili of Kenya/Tanzania

A man's deeds are of greater importance
than the facts of his birth.
— East African proverb

JUN   *[jhun]*

Meaning: ruler, talented, handsome • **Usage:**
Chinese

Avoid putting yourself before others
and you can become a leader.
— Lao Tzu, *Tao Te Ching* (tr. Lionel Giles)

JUNG-HO [*jung-hoh*]

MEANING: just and good, righteous and good • **USAGE:** Korean: from Korean *jung* (righteous, justice) and *ho* (goodness, broad)

> *Act righteously. Refuse to do otherwise.*
> *One who follows this path lives happily,*
> *both in this life and the life to come.*
> — Buddha, *The Dhammapada*
> (tr. Ananda Maitreya)

JUNG-SOO [*jung-soo*]

MEANING: righteous and excellent, just and excellent • **USAGE:** Korean: from Korean *jung* (righteous, justice) and *soo* (excellent, long life)

> *People cherish the person committed to right action*
> *and rich in understanding. That person,*
> *knowing the truth, walks steadfastly on the path.*
> — Buddha, *The Dhammapada*
> (tr. Ananda Maitreya)

JUNIOR [*JOON-yur*]

MEANING: young, young man, son of • **USAGE:** English: from Latin *juvenis* (young man)

> *The Youth of a Nation are the trustees of Posterity.*
> — Benjamin Disraeli, *Sybil*

JUR [*yur*]

MEANING: earth worker, farmer, gardener • **USAGE:** Czech form of George, from Greek *ge* (earth) and *ergein* (to work)

> *Plant the good seeds of righteousness,*
> *and you will harvest a crop of love.*
> — Hosea 10:12a (NLT)

JUREK [*YUHR-ek*]

MEANING: earth worker, farmer, gardener • **USAGE:** Polish form of George (*see* Jur)

> *Speak to the earth, and it shall answer thee.*
> — Job 12:8a (DR)

JUSTICE [*JUS-tis*]

MEANING: just, judicious, fair • **USAGE:** English (*see* Justin)

> *The fruit of justice is sown in peace,*
> *to them that make peace.*
> — James 3:18 (DR)

JUSTIN [*JUS-ten (English), zhoo-STIN (French)*]

MEANING: just, judicious, fair • **USAGE:** English and French: from Latin *justus*

> *Yet I shall temper so / Justice with mercy.*
> — John Milton, *Paradise Lost*

JUSTINO [*hoos-TEE-noh*]

MEANING: just, judicious, fair • **USAGE:** Spanish form of Justin (*see* Justin)

> *You will know what is right, just, and fair.*
> *You will know what you should do.*
> — Proverbs 2:9 (GNT)

JUSTUS [*YOO-stus*]

MEANING: just, fair, lawful • **USAGE:** German and Dutch: from Latin *justus* (just)

> *Two things fill the mind with ever new*
> *and increasing admiration and reverence,*
> *the oftener and more steadily we reflect on them: the*
> *starry heavens above and the moral law within.*
> — Immanuel Kant, *The Critique of Practical Reason*
> (tr. Thomas Kingsmill Abbott)

K

KABIR, KABEER [*kah-BEER*]

MEANING: great, magnificent • **USAGE:** Muslim

> *Most Merciful and Compassionate God,*
> *give us Thy Great Goodness.*
> — Hazrat Inayat Khan, *The Gayan*

K

KADE [kayd]

MEANING: brave in battle, warrior, barrel maker • USAGE: American form of Cade, from Welsh *cathach* (brave in battle); from English *cade* (cask, barrel), occupational name for a barrel maker

Be brave, be strong. Do all your work in love.
— 1 Corinthians 16:13a–14 (GNT)

KADEN [KAY-den]

MEANING: flow of rhythm, warrior • USAGE: American form of Kadence (*see* Kadence); or form of Cathán, from Irish Gaelic *cath* (battle)

The Lord, your God, is in your midst, a warrior who gives victory; he will rejoice over you with gladness, he will renew you in his love.
— Zephaniah 3:17 (RSV)

KADENCE [KAY-dens]

MEANING: flow of rhythm • USAGE: American form of Cadence, from Latin *cadentia* (a falling, a conclusion of a movement in music)

Life is about rhythm. We vibrate, our hearts are pumping blood, we are a rhythm machine.
— Mickey Hart

KADHI [kah-dih]

MEANING: ocean, sea, water receptacle • USAGE: Hindu: from Sanskrit *kam* (water) and *dhi* (receptacle)

You have come from God, you are a spark of His Glory; you are a wave of that Ocean of Bliss; you will get peace only when you again merge in Him.
— Sathya Sai Baba, *Sathya Sai Baba Speaks*

KAHANU [kah-HAH-noo]

MEANING: breath from heaven • USAGE: Hawaiian

Continue to do good until the heavens come down to you.
— Hawaiian proverb
(tr. Mary Pukui in *'Olelo No'eau*)

KAHILI [kah-HEE-lee]

MEANING: segment of a rainbow, a feather standard symbolic of royalty • USAGE: Hawaiian; ancient chiefs wore feather capes and helmets that looked like rainbows, which were considered a sign of royalty

Heated rain. [A rainbow.]
— Hawaiian proverb
(tr. Mary Pukui in *'Olelo No'eau*)

KAI [kie]

MEANING: ocean, water from the sea • USAGE: Hawaiian

In my mind is the fire of knowledge; in my blood run the currents of the ocean; in the wind do I hear the song of my spirit.
— Hawaiian proverb

KAI [kay]

MEANING: pathway, warrior • USAGE: Welsh: from Welsh *cai* (path, way) or *cad* (battle, war)

You will understand righteousness, justice, and integrity — every good path.
— Proverbs 2:9 (HCSB)

KAINUI [kie-NOO-ee]

MEANING: high tide, big sea • USAGE: Hawaiian

The song of the sea is never ending.
— Hawaiian proverb

KAIUS [KIE-us]

MEANING: joyful, rejoicing • USAGE: American: Roman given name, possibly from Latin *gaudere* (to rejoice)

You will be filled with joy.
— Isaiah 30:29b (NLT)

KAL [kal]

MEANING: bald one, hairless • USAGE: English form of Calvin (*see* Kalvin)

[Wisdom] will give you a garland to grace your head
and present you with a glorious crown.
— Proverbs 4:9 (NIV)

KALEA [kah-LEH-ah]

MEANING: joyous, happy, the one who is joyful • USAGE: Hawaiian

Dance the joy your heart feels.
— Hawaiian proverb

KALEI [kah-LEH-ee]

MEANING: one who works for the king • USAGE: African: Angola

When a king has good counselors, his reign is peaceful.
— West African proverb

KALEO [kah-LEH-oh]

MEANING: singer, the one who sings • USAGE: Hawaiian: from Hawaiian *ka* (the one who is) and *leo* (voice, sound, tune)

Music is the key to the inner spirit.
— Hawaiian proverb

KALEV, KALEB [kah-LEHV, KAH-lehv]

MEANING: dog, heart • USAGE: Jewish: from Hebrew *kalebh*

The teaching of his God is in his heart;
his feet do not slip.
— Psalm 37:31 (JPS)

KALIL [kah-LEEL]

MEANING: crown, wreath, garland • USAGE: Jewish

You [God] have proffered him blessings of good things,
have set upon his head a crown of fine gold.
— Psalm 21:4 (JPS)

KALVIN [KAL-vin]

MEANING: bald one, hairless • USAGE: English form of Calvin, from Latin *calvus*

You [God] meet him with the blessings of good things;
You set a crown of fine gold on his head.
— Psalm 21:3 (NASB)

KAMA [KAH-mah]

MEANING: love, desire • USAGE: Hindu: Sanskrit

The more we grow in love and virtue and holiness,
the more we see love and virtue and holiness outside.
— Swami Vivekananda

KAMAL, KAMAAL [kah-MAHL]

MEANING: perfected, complete • USAGE: Muslim: from Arabic *kamula* (to become perfect)

In the complete unfoldment of human nature
is the fulfillment of life's purpose.
— Hazrat Inayat Khan, *The Gayan* (cd. *The Gayani Meditations, Volume 1*, tr. Cecil Touchon)

KAMIL, KAMEEL [kah-MEEL]

MEANING: perfected, complete • USAGE: Muslim (*see* Kamal)

As the light of the sun helps the plant to grow, so the
divine Spirit helps the soul towards its perfection.
— Hazrat Inayat Khan, *The Bowl of Saki*

KANE [KAH-neh]

MEANING: man, eastern sky • USAGE: Hawaiian

The joyous heart has as many blessings
as the stars in the sky.
— Hawaiian proverb

KANE [kayn]

MEANING: battle, warrior • USAGE: Irish form of Cathan, from Gaelic *cath* (battle)

K

In everyday affairs, as in battle, we are given
one life to live, and the decision is ours,
whether to wait for circumstances to
make up our mind — or to act, and in acting, to live.
— Omar Bradley

KANG   *[kahng]*

MEANING: healthy, happy • **USAGE:** Chinese
The secret health for both mind and body is
not to mourn for the past, not to worry about the future,
or not to anticipate troubles, but to live in the present
moment wisely and earnestly.
— Buddha

KANGEE, KANGI   *[kahn-gee]*

MEANING: raven • **USAGE:** Amerind: Sioux
In the animal and bird world there existed a
brotherly feeling that kept the Lakota safe among them.
And so close did some of the Lakotas come
to their feathered and furred friends that in true
brotherhood they spoke a common tongue.
— Luther Standing Bear, *Land of the Spotted Eagle*

KANIEL   *[kah-nee-EHL]*

MEANING: God is my reed, God is my support •
USAGE: Jewish
The steps of a man are made firm by the Lord,
when He delights in his way. Though he stumbles,
he does not fall down, for the Lord gives him support.
— Psalm 37:23–24 (JPS)

KANOA   *[kah-NOH-ah]*

MEANING: free one • **USAGE:** Hawaiian
Peace — the foremost joy. / Oneness — the foremost
reality. / Enlightenment — the foremost freedom.
— Shi Wuling, *Path to Peace*

KAPONO   *[kah-POH-noh]*

MEANING: righteous, just • **USAGE:** Hawaiian

Whoever leads others evenhandedly, but not by force, is
a guardian of justice and is called righteous.
— Buddha, *The Dhammapada*
(tr. Ananda Maitreya)

KAPUNI   *[kah-POO-nee]*

MEANING: chosen • **USAGE:** Hawaiian
The spirit of the land guides me
in every choice that I must make.
— Hawaiian proverb

KARIM, KAREEM   *[kah-reem]*

MEANING: generous, charitable, noble • **USAGE:**
Muslim: from Arabic *karuma* (to be noble, to be
generous)
In thought, word, and deed, in every manner
and form one can show that generous spirit
which is the sign of the godly.
— Hazrat Inayat Khan, *The Gayan* (cd. *The Gayani*
Meditations, Volume 1, tr. Cecil Touchon)

KARL   *[karl]*

MEANING: man, adult, one who is free • **USAGE:**
German, Russian, and Scandinavian: from German
karl (full-grown man, adult) or German form of
Charles, from English *ceorl* (freeman, peasant)
What is the freedom of the most free? To do right!
— Johann Wolfgang von Goethe, *Egmont*
(tr. Theodore Martin)

KAROL   *[KAHR-ol]*

MEANING: man, adult, one who is free • **USAGE:**
Polish and Czech form of Karl (*see* Karl)
He hath shewed, O man, what is good; and what doth
the Lord require of thee, but to do justly, and to love
mercy, and to walk humbly with thy God.
— Micah 6:8 (KJV)

KARSTEN [KAHR-sten]

MEANING: follower of Christ, Christian • **USAGE:**
German form of Christian, from Greek *christianos*

For we are His workmanship,
created in Christ Jesus for good works,
which God prepared beforehand
that we should walk in them.
— Ephesians 2:10 (NKJV)

KARU [kah-ruh]

MEANING: singer, poet • **USAGE:** Hindu: Sanskrit
The singer has everything within him.
The notes come out from his very life.
— Rabindranath Tagore, *Sadhana*

KASEY [KAY-see]

MEANING: vigilant, alert, watchful • **USAGE:**
American form of Casey, English form of
O'Cathasaigh, from Irish Gaelic *cathasaigh*
You can observe a lot by watchin'.
— Yogi Berra

KASPAR [KAHS-pahr]

MEANING: treasure master, steward • **USAGE:**
German and Scandinavian form of Gaspar, from
Persian *genashber*
A good man out of the good treasure
of the heart bringeth forth good things.
— Matthew 12:35a (KJ21)

KASSIDY [KAS-ih-dee]

MEANING: love, affection, curly-haired • **USAGE:**
American form of Cassidy, from Gaelic *cais* (love,
affection) or *cas* (curly-haired)
Do everything in love.
— 1 Corinthians 16:14 (NCV)

KATASHI [kah-tah-shee]

MEANING: firm, steadfast • **USAGE:** Japanese:
from Japanese *kata*
The one who lives mindfully, senses under control,
moderate in eating, devout, energetic,
cannot be overthrown by Mara,
just as the wind cannot shake a rocky mountain.
— Buddha, *The Dhammapada*
(tr. Ananda Maitreya)

KATSURO [kaht-soo-roh]

MEANING: victorious son • **USAGE:** Japanese:
from Japanese *katsu* (victory) and *rou* (son)
A person of faith, who is virtuous, well-known and
successful, and is respected wherever one may be.
— Buddha, *The Dhammapada* (tr. Sanderson Beck)

KAULANA [kwah-LAH-nah]

MEANING: famous, celebrated • **USAGE:** Hawaiian
A man from the top of the cliff. [Praising someone.]
— Hawaiian proverb
(tr. Mary Pukui in *'Olelo No'eau*)

K

KAVALA [kah-vah-lah]

MEANING: the one, the absolute • **USAGE:** Hindu:
Sanskrit
Becoming truthful, we merge with the True One;
remaining blended with Him,
we shall never be separated again.
— *Sri Guru Granth Sahib*
(Khalsa Consensus Translation)

KAVAN [kah-vahn]

MEANING: handsome • **USAGE:** Amerind: Sylvan
Tribes
The Old Man said, "you are both ugly and handsome
and you must accept your ugliness as well as your
handsomeness in order to really accept yourself."
— Larry P. Aitken, *Two Cultures Meet*

KAVI   [kah-vih]

MEANING: poet, sage, seer • USAGE: Hindu:
Sanskrit

> All our poetry, philosophy, science, art,
> and religion are serving to extend the scope of our
> consciousness towards higher and larger spheres.
> — Rabindranath Tagore

KAWA   [kah-wah]

MEANING: great, powerful • USAGE: Amerind:
Apache

*Just what Power is I cannot explain, for it is beyond my
comprehension. Those who seek it go alone that they
may be tested for worthiness. It is a gift to be bestowed
not only for virtue but for prayer and courage.*
> — Victorio

KAZI   [KAH-ʒee]

MEANING: industrious, hardworking man •
USAGE: African: Swahili of Kenya/Tanzania

> Work the clay while it is still wet.
> — Swahili proverb

KEAHI   [keh-AH-hee]

MEANING: fire • USAGE: Hawaiian

> Fire is the garment for warmth.
> — Hawaiian proverb
> (tr. Mary Pukui in 'Olelo No'eau)

KEAN, KEANE   [kayn]

MEANING: ancient, long-lasting • USAGE: Irish:
from Gaelic cian

> In the ancient is wisdom,
> and in length of days prudence.
> — Job 12:12 (DR)

KEANU   [kee-AH-noo]

MEANING: cool breeze, cool breeze over the
mountain • USAGE: Hawaiian

> Took off into the breeze.
> [Someone who rises successfully.]
> — Hawaiian proverb
> (tr. Mary Pukui in 'Olelo No'eau)

KEATON   [KEE-ton]

MEANING: village on the bank, town near the
hedges • USAGE: American surname: from English
kee (bank, hedge) and tun (town, village)

> Hast Thou not made a hedge about him
> and his house and all that he has, on every side?
> Thou hast blessed the work of his hands,
> and his possessions have increased in the land.
> — Job 1:10 (NASB)

KEAWE   [kee-AH-weh]

MEANING: name of southern star • USAGE:
Hawaiian

Follow the paths of the stars, and you will never be lost.
> — Hawaiian proverb

KEB, QEB   [keb]

MEANING: Egyptian god of the earth • USAGE:
African: Egypt

> Plant shade trees around the edge of your pond,
> and let your spirit rest under them.
> — Neferhotep

KEEFE   [keef]

MEANING: gentle, noble, lovable • USAGE: Irish
surname: from Gaelic caomh

*God's Spirit makes us loving, happy, peaceful, patient,
kind, good, faithful, gentle, and self-controlled.*
> — Galatians 5:22–23a (CEV)

KEEGAN   [KEE-gan]

MEANING: fire, little fiery one • USAGE: Irish and
English surname: form of Aodhan, from Gaelic
aodh and diminutive -an

*Love is ever the beginning of Knowledge
as fire is of light.*
— Thomas Carlyle, "Death of Goethe"

KEELAN, KEALAN [KEE-lan]

MEANING: slender and handsome • **USAGE:** Irish form of *Caoilfhin*, from Gaelic *caol* (slender) and *fionn* (fair, white, beautiful)
*Beauty, like a lantern's light,
will shine outward from within him.*
— George Garrett, *The Succession*

KEENAN [KEE-nan]

MEANING: little ancient one, enduring • **USAGE:** Irish surname: from Gaelic *cian* and diminutive -*an*
*Gladness of heart is the life of a man;
and the joyfulness of a man is length of days.*
— Sirach 30:22 (WEB Apocrypha)

KEFIR [keh-FEER]

MEANING: young lion • **USAGE:** Jewish: from Hebrew *kefir*
For I will be…as a young lion.
— Hosea 5:14a (MT)

KEIR [keer]

MEANING: dark, black, dark-haired • **USAGE:** Scottish surname: from Gaelic *ciar*
*The Lord says…I will give you the treasures
of darkness and riches from secret places.*
— Isaiah 45:1–3a (HCSB)

KEITH [keeth]

MEANING: forest, woods • **USAGE:** Scottish and English surname: from Gaelic *ceiteach*
In the woods we return to reason and faith.
— Ralph Waldo Emerson, "Nature"

KEKOA [keh-KOH-ah]

MEANING: warrior, courageous one • **USAGE:** Hawaiian
*One who has the face of a warrior in his birthplace.
[One who is loyal and honored.]*
— Hawaiian proverb
(tr. Mary Pukui in *'Olelo No'eau*)

KELBY [KEL-bee]

MEANING: village by the spring, village well • **USAGE:** English surname: from Norse *keld* (spring, well) and *by* (village, town)
*The words of a man's mouth are deep waters;
the wellspring of wisdom is a flowing brook.*
— Proverbs 18:4 (NKJV)

KELE [keh-lee]

MEANING: sparrow, hawk • **USAGE:** Amerind: Hopi
*The bird song, and the people's song
and the song of life will become one.*
— Frank Waters, *Book of the Hopi*

KELLY, KELLEY [KEL-ee]

MEANING: warrior, church, forest, holly • **USAGE:** Irish and English form of surname *O'Ceallagh*, from Gaelic *ceallagh* (war, warlike), *cill* (church), or *coille* (woods); or from Welsh *celyn* (holly)
Wise warriors are better than strong ones, and those who have knowledge than those who have strength.
— Proverbs 24:5 (NRSV)

KELSEY, KELCEY [KEL-see]

MEANING: victory ship, fierce island • **USAGE:** English surname: a form of *Ceolsige*, from English *ceol* (ship) and *sige* (victory, success); or from English *cenel* (fierce) and *eg* (island)
'Tis skill, not strength, that governs a ship.
— Thomas Fuller, *Gnomologia*

K

KELVIN   [KEL-ven]

MEANING: slender, narrow • **USAGE:** Scottish and English: from Gaelic *caol* (slender, narrow); a Scottish river

> *Honour travels in a strait so narrow where one but goes abreast: keep then the path.*
> — William Shakespeare, *Troilus and Cressida*

KEMP   [kemp]

MEANING: champion, battlefield • **USAGE:** English surname (*see* Kemper)

> *The hero is he who is immovably centered.*
> — Ralph Waldo Emerson, "Considerations by the Way"

KEMPER   [KEM-per]

MEANING: champion, battlefield • **USAGE:** English surname: from English *kempa* (champion, as of jousting or wrestling) or from English *campus* (battlefield)

> *You shall be a blessing. Do not fear. Let your hands be strong.*
> — Zechariah 8:13b (NKJV)

KEN   [ken]

MEANING: healthy, strong • **USAGE:** Japanese: from Japanese *ken*

> *In compassion lies the world's true strength.*
> — Buddha

KEN   [ken]

MEANING: born of fire, handsome • **USAGE:** Scottish and English form of Kenneth (*see* Kenneth)

> *He makes His helpers a burning fire.*
> — Psalm 104:4b (NLV)

KENDAL, KENDALL   [KEN-dal]

MEANING: valley spring, well in the valley • **USAGE:** English surname: from English *dæl* (dale, valley) and Norse *keld* (spring, well)

> *Knowing what is right is like deep water in the heart; a wise person draws from the well within.*
> — Proverbs 20:5 (MSG)

KENDRICK   [KEN-drik]

MEANING: high hill, mount • **USAGE:** Scottish surname: from Welsh *cynwrig*

> *The mountains are fountains not only of rivers and fertile soil, but of men.*
> — John Muir, *Steep Trails*

KENNARD   [KEN-ard]

MEANING: royal guardsman, royal and brave • **USAGE:** English surname: a form of *Cyneweard*, from English *cyne* (royal) and *weard* (guardian, protector); or a form of *Cyneheard*, from *cyne* (royal) and *heard* (brave, hardy)

> *The Lord will protect you from all dangers; he will guard your life.*
> — Psalm 121:7 (NCV)

KENNER   [KEN-er]

MEANING: born of fire, handsome • **USAGE:** American surname: possibly a form of Kenneth (*see* Kenneth)

> *He will baptize you in the Holy Spirit and fire.*
> — Luke 3:16b (WEB)

KENNET   [KEN-et]

MEANING: born of fire, handsome • **USAGE:** Scandinavian form of Kenneth (*see* Kenneth)

> *Fan into flames the spiritual gift God gave you.*
> — 2 Timothy 1:6 (NLT)

KENNETH   [KEN-eth]

MEANING: born of fire, handsome • **USAGE:** Scottish and English: from Gaelic *cinaed* (born of fire) or *coinneach* (handsome, attractive)

> *Be praised, my Lord, for brother fire, through whom you illuminate the night.*
> *And he is beautiful and joyous and robust and strong.*
> — Francis of Assisi, "Canticle of the Sun"

KENNY   *[KEN-ee]*

MEANING: born of fire, handsome • **USAGE:**
English form of Kenneth (*see* Kenneth)

> *God is fire and…the soul of each of us is a lamp.*
> — Symeon the New Theologian, *The Discourses*

KENT   *[kent]*

MEANING: borderland, white, bright • **USAGE:**
English surname: from Welsh *cant* (rim, border) or
cant (white, bright)

> *Arise, be bright, for come hath thy light.*
> — Isaiah 60:1a (YLT)

KENTA   *[KEN-tah]*

MEANING: healthy, strong, big • **USAGE:**
Japanese: from *ken* (healthy, strong) and *ta* (big)

> *To keep the body in good health is a duty…*
> *otherwise we shall not be able to keep our mind*
> *strong and clear.*
> — Buddha

KENTON   *[KENT-on]*

MEANING: royal settlement, from the king's town •
USAGE: English surname: from English *cyne* (king,
royal) and *tun* (town, village)

> *The kingdom of God is within you.*
> — Luke 17:21b (ASV)

KENZIE   *[KEN-ʒee]*

MEANING: handsome son • **USAGE:** English form
of MacKenzie, from Gaelic *mac* (son) and *coinneach*
(handsome, attractive)

> *May the Lord bless you, my son!*
> — Judges 17:2b (GNT)

KEOKUK   *[keh-oh-kuk]*

MEANING: one who is alert • **USAGE:** Amerind:
Sauk

> *It is my duty as your chief to be your father*
> *while in the paths of peace, and your leader*
> *and champion while on the war path.*
> — Keokuk

KEOLA   *[keh-OH-lah]*

MEANING: life, the one who is life, the one who is
healthy • **USAGE:** Hawaiian: from Hawaiian *ka* (the
one who is) and *ola* (life, health)

> *Love gives life within.*
> — Hawaiian proverb
> (tr. Mary Pukui in *'Olelo No'eau*)

KERMIT   *[KER-met]*

MEANING: free from envy, one without envy •
USAGE: Irish and English form of surname *Mac
Dhiarmaid*, from Gaelic *di* (without) and *airmait*
(envy)

> *Endeavour with diligence that…thou mayest be*
> *inwardly free and master of thyself.*
> — Thomas à Kempis, *The Imitation of Christ*
> (tr. Charles Bigg)

KERRY, KEARY   *[KEHR-ee]*

MEANING: dark, black, dark-haired, hollow, glen,
powerful chief • **USAGE:** Irish, Welsh, and English
surname: form of Irish county name *Ciarrai*,
from Gaelic *ciar* (dark, black); from Gaelic *coire*
(cauldron, a hollow); or English form of surname
Cyneric, from English *cyne* (royal, chief) and *ric*
(power, rule)

> *All growth is a leap in the dark.*
> — Henry Miller, *The Wisdom of the Heart*

KESI   *[KEH-see]*

MEANING: judging, rational • **USAGE:** African:
Kiswahili of Kenya/Tanzania

> *Discern with attention and it will be right.*
> — Kiswahili proverb

KESTER   *[KES-ter]*

MEANING: follower of Christ, Christian, bearer
of Christ • **USAGE:** Scottish form of Christopher,
from Greek *Christos* (Christ, the anointed one) and
pherein (to bear, to bring)

K

God's Spirit makes us sure that we are his children. His
Spirit lets us know that together with Christ we will be
given what God has promised.
— Romans 8:16–17a (CEV)

KEVIN   *[KEV-en]*

MEANING: little gentle one, kind, handsome •
USAGE: Irish and English form of *Caoimhin*, from
Gaelic *caomh* (gentle, kind) or *caem* (handsome,
comely) and diminutive *-an*

> *Let no one ever come to you without leaving better*
> *and happier. Be the living expression of God's*
> *kindness: kindness in your face,*
> *kindness in your eyes, kindness in your smile.*
> — Mother Teresa, *Love: A Fruit Always in Season*

KHABIR, KHABEER   *[kah-BEER]*

MEANING: learned, knowledgeable • **USAGE:**
Muslim

> *Disclose to us Thy Divine Light, which is hidden in*
> *our souls, that we may know and understand life better.*
> — Hazrat Inayat Khan, *The Gayan*

KHALID, KHALEED   *[kah-LEED]*

MEANING: eternal, everlasting, infinite • **USAGE:**
Muslim: from Arabic *khalada* (to be eternal)

> *Love has the power to open the door of eternal life.*
> — Hazrat Inayat Khan, *The Bowl of Saki*

KHALIL, KHALEEL   *[kah-LEEL]*

MEANING: friend, companion • **USAGE:** Muslim:
from Arabic *khalil*

> *Hold fast to Allah; He is your Protecting friend.*
> *A blessed Patron and a blessed Helper!*
> — Koran, The Pilgrimage 22.78b (PIC)

KHALIS   *[kah-lees]*

MEANING: true, genuine, sincere • **USAGE:**
Muslim

Man proves to be genuine by his sincerity.
— Hazrat Inayat Khan, *The Gayan*

KHASIB   *[kah-seeb]*

MEANING: fruitful, bountiful • **USAGE:** Muslim
> *Whoever brings a good deed, he shall have ten like it.*
> — Koran, The Cattle 6.160a (SKR)

KHAYR, KHAIR   *[kah-eer]*

MEANING: good, blessed, fortunate • **USAGE:**
Muslim: from Arabic *khair*
> *Allah loveth those who do good.*
> — Koran, The Table Spread 5.93a (ALI)

KHAYYAM   *[kah-yahm]*

MEANING: tent maker • **USAGE:** Muslim
> *Only the tent pitched by your own hands*
> *will keep standing.*
> — Arabic proverb

KIAN   *[KEE-an]*

MEANING: ancient, distant past, enduring •
USAGE: Welsh form of Cian, from Irish Gaelic *cian*
> *I believe that man will not merely endure:*
> *he will prevail. He is immortal,*
> *not because he alone among creatures has*
> *an inexhaustible voice, but because he has a soul,*
> *a spirit capable of compassion and sacrifice*
> *and endurance.*
> — William Faulkner
> (1950 Nobel Prize acceptance speech)

KICHIRO   *[kee-chee-roh]*

MEANING: fortunate son, lucky son • **USAGE:**
Japanese: from Japanese *kichi* (good luck) and *rou*
(son)
> *Being generous, just, helping one's relatives and being*
> *blameless in one's actions; this is the best good luck.*
> — Buddha

KIEFER, KEIFER [KEE-fer]

Meaning: young lion • **Usage:** English form of Kefir, from Hebrew *kefir*

> *You are a lion's cub…Like a lion he crouches*
> *and lies down…who dares to rouse him?*
> — Genesis 49:9 (NIV)

KILLIAN [KIL-yan]

Meaning: warrior, church, woods, forest, holly • **Usage:** American form of Cillian, from Gaelic *ceallach* (war, warlike), *cill* (church), or *coill* (woods, forest); or from Welsh *celyn* (holly)

> *After a whole day in the woods,*
> *we are already immortal.*
> — John Muir

KILO [KEE-loh]

Meaning: stargazer, reader of omens • **Usage:** Hawaiian

> *Wishes made by starlight are wishes born of the heart.*
> — Hawaiian proverb

KIM [kim (English), keem (Scandinavian)]

Meaning: war chief, God will establish • **Usage:** English and Scandinavian: English form of *Cynbel*, from Welsh *cyne* (royal) and *bel* (war); or Scandinavian form of Joakim, from Hebrew *yehoyakim* (Yahweh will establish)

> *With whom My hand will be established;*
> *My arm also will strengthen him.*
> — Psalm 89:21 (NASB)

KIMBEL [KIM-bel]

Meaning: royal and brave, bold chieftain • **Usage:** English surname: English form of *Cynebeal*, from English *cyne* (royal, chief) and *beald* (bold, brave)

> *Cast not away therefore your boldness, which hath*
> *great recompense of reward.*
> — Hebrews 10:35 (ASV)

KINGSTON [KING-ston]

Meaning: king's stone • **Usage:** English surname: from English *cyne* (king, royal) and *stan* (stone)

> *For you shall be allied with the stones of the field.*
> — Job 5:23a (WEB)

KIPLING [KIP-ling]

Meaning: people of Cyppel • **Usage:** English surname: from English *Cybbelingcot* (people of Cyppel, in England)

> *They shall be my people,*
> *and I will be their God in truth and in justice.*
> — Zechariah 8:8b (DR)

KIPP [kip]

Meaning: edge, cliff • **Usage:** German and Dutch surname, from German *kippe* (cliff, edge of a hill or mountain)

> *On the mountains is freedom.*
> — Johann Friedrich von Schiller,
> *The Bride of Messina*

KIRBY [KER-bee]

Meaning: church village • **Usage:** English: from Norse *kirkja* (church) and *býr* (town, village)

> *You are part of that building Christ has built*
> *as a place for God's own Spirit to live.*
> — Ephesians 2:22 (CEV)

KIRIL, KIRILL [KEE-rel]

Meaning: lord, master, ruler • **Usage:** Russian form of *Kyrillos*, from Greek *kyrios*

> *Work hard and become a leader.*
> — Proverbs 12:24a (NLT)

KIRK [kirk]

Meaning: church, basilica, cathedral • **Usage:** English: from Norse *kirkja*

K

*Surely goodness and mercy shall follow me
all the days of my life; and I shall dwell
in the house of the Lord for ever.*
— Psalm 23:6 (RSV)

KIRWIN   [KER-wen]

MEANING: dark, black, dark-haired • **USAGE:**
Irish surname: from Gaelic *ciar*
*Thus saith the Lord . . . I will give thee the treasures
of darkness, and hidden riches of secret places.*
— Isaiah 45:1–3a (KJV)

KLAUS   [klows]

MEANING: victory of the people, successful,
triumphant • **USAGE:** German and Scandinavian
form of Nikolaus, from Greek *nike* (victory) and
laos (people)
*The Lord said, "I will go with you,
and I will give you victory."*
— Exodus 33:14 (GNT)

KLIMENT   [klee-MENT]

MEANING: clement, mild, gentle, merciful •
USAGE: Russian form of Clement, from Latin
clemens
A merciful man doeth good to his own soul.
— Proverbs 11:17a (KJV)

KNIGHT   [niet]

MEANING: knight, champion • **USAGE:** English
surname: from English *criht* (servant, attendant),
such as a military follower of a king
*He that respects himself is safe from others.
He wears a coat of mail that none can pierce.*
— Henry Wadsworth Longfellow,
"Michael Angelo"

KNOX   [nahks]

MEANING: hillock, rounded-top hill • **USAGE:**
Scottish surname: from Gaelic *cnoc* (rounded-top
hill)

He that comes first to the hill, may sit where he will.
— Scottish proverb

KNUT   [k-NOOT, noot]

MEANING: knot, tie, binding • **USAGE:**
Scandinavian: from Norse *knutr*
*Verily I say unto you, whatsoever ye shall bind
on earth shall be bound in heaven: and whatsoever
ye shall loose on earth shall be loosed in heaven.*
— Matthew 18:18 (KJV)

KOA   [KOH-ah]

MEANING: brave, bold, fearless, soldier, warrior,
hero • **USAGE:** Hawaiian
Heart of steel. [Fearless and brave.]
— Hawaiian proverb
(tr. Mary Pukui in *'Olelo No'eau*)

KOBE   [koh-beh]

MEANING: tortoise • **USAGE:** African: Swahili
Patience is the key to tranquility.
— Swahili proverb

KOBY   [KOH-bee]

MEANING: replace, change, transform, successor
• **USAGE:** American form of Coby, from Hebrew
ya'aqobh (one that takes by the heel, replace with
another)
*I [God] will give you a new heart,
and I will put a new spirit within you.*
— Ezekiel 36:26a (NEB)

KODY   [KOH-dee]

MEANING: helper, aide, helpful • **USAGE:**
American form of Cody, from Gaelic *cuidightheach*
*Peace, peace be to thee!
And peace be to thy helpers!
For thy God helps thee.*
— 1 Chronicles 12:18b (DT)

KONA   [*KOH-nah*]

MEANING: ruler of the world, leader in the world • **USAGE:** Hawaiian form of Donald, from Gaelic *dumnan* (world) and *val* (rule, ruler)

> *The imu is not heated by mamane*
> *and 'ulei wood alone, but also by the kindling.*
> *[A ruler needs the loyalty of the people*
> *as well as the chiefs.]*
> — Hawaiian proverb
> (tr. Mary Pukui in *'Olelo No'eau*)

KONANI   [*koh-NAH-nee*]

MEANING: bright, shining • **USAGE:** Hawaiian

> *The seeker who sets out upon the way shines*
> *bright over the world.*
> — Buddha, *The Dhammapada*
> (tr. Thomas Byrom)

KONDO   [*KON-doh*]

MEANING: war, warrior • **USAGE:** African: Swahili of Kenya / Tanzania

> *A hunter is not afraid of thorns.*
> — Swahili proverb

KONRAD   [*KAHN-rad*]

MEANING: bold counsel, wise adviser • **USAGE:** German and Scandinavian form of *Kuonrat*, from German *kuon* (bold, courageous) and *rad* (advice, counsel)

> *God said ... I will give you a wise*
> *and understanding heart.*
> — 1 Kings 3:11–12b (HCSB)

KONSTANTIN   [*kahn-stahn-TEEN*]

MEANING: constant, steadfast • **USAGE:** Russian form of *Constantinus*, from Latin *constans*

> *His heart is steadfast.*
> — Psalm 112:7b (NKJV)

KONSTANTINOS   [*kohn-stahn-TEE-nohs*]

MEANING: constant, steadfast • **USAGE:** Greek form of Constantine (*see* Konstantin)

> *Aim at righteousness, godliness, faith,*
> *love, steadfastness, gentleness.*
> — 1 Timothy 6:11b (RSV)

KOOL   [*kool*]

MEANING: calm and self-controlled • **USAGE:** American: from English *cool* (moderately cold, calm)

> *True courage is cool and calm.*
> — Earl of Shaftesbury, "Social Affections"

KORESH   [*kohr-ESH*]

MEANING: sun, farsighted • **USAGE:** Jewish: possibly from Persian *khur* (sun) or *kurush* (farsighted)

> *The path of the righteous is like radiant sunlight,*
> *ever brightening until noon.*
> — Proverbs 4:18 (JPS)

KOREY, KORY   [*KOR-ee*]

MEANING: hollow, cauldron, God's peace • **USAGE:** English form of Corey, from Irish Gaelic *coire* (cauldron, a hollow); or from German *gott* (God) and *frid* (peace)

> *He who knows about depth knows about God.*
> — Paul Tillich, *The Shaking of the Foundations*

KORT   [*kort*]

MEANING: bold counsel, wise adviser • **USAGE:** Danish and Swedish form of Konrad, from German *kuon* (bold, courageous) and *rad* (advice, counsel)

> *Act honestly and answer boldly.*
> — Danish proverb

KOSMAS   [*KOHS-mahs*]

MEANING: cosmos, order, harmony, the universe • **USAGE:** Greek: from Greek *kosmos*

K

The universe is wider than our views of it.
— Henry David Thoreau, *Walden*

KOSTAS   [KOHS-tahs]

MEANING: constant, steadfast • USAGE: Greek
form of Konstantinos, from Latin *constans*
Thou shalt be steadfast and shalt not fear.
— Job 11:15b (KJ21)

KRIS   [kris]

MEANING: follower of Christ, Christian, bearer
of Christ • USAGE: Scandinavian, English,
and German form of Kristian (*see* Kristian); or
Scandinavian form of Kristofer (*see* Kristofer)
God's peace, which is so great we cannot understand it,
will keep your hearts and minds in Christ Jesus.
— Philippians 4:7 (NCV)

KRISTER   [KREES-ter]

MEANING: follower of Christ, Christian, bearer of
Christ • USAGE: Scandinavian form of Kristian (*see*
Kristian)
Now these two things, to believe and to love,
make up the whole sum of Christianity.
— Martin Luther,
"Concerning the Ten Lepers" (tr. Henry Cole)

KRISTIAN   [krees-tee-AHN]

MEANING: follower of Christ, Christian • USAGE:
Scandinavian and German form of Christian, from
Greek *christianos*
Above all the grace and gifts that Christ gives
to his beloved is that of overcoming self.
— Francis of Assisi

KRISTOFER, KRISTOFFER, KRISTOPHER   [KREES-toh-fer]

MEANING: follower of Christ, Christian, bearer of
Christ • USAGE: Scandinavian form of Christopher,
from Greek *Christos* (Christ, the anointed one) and
pherein (to bear, to bring)

For we are His workmanship,
created in Christ Jesus for good works,
which God prepared beforehand,
that we should walk in them.
— Ephesians 2:10 (NASB)

KUBA   [KOO-bah]

MEANING: replace, change, transform, successor
• USAGE: Czech and Polish form of Jakub, from
Hebrew *ya'aqobh* (one that takes by the heel, replace
with another)
Put on the new man,
who according to God is created
in justice and holiness of truth.
— Ephesians 4:24 (DR)

KUNO   [KOO-noh]

MEANING: brave, courageous • USAGE: German:
from German *kuoni*
The courage to be
is the courage to accept oneself.
— Paul Tillich, *The Courage to Be*

KUNTO   [koon-toh]

MEANING: third-born child • USAGE: African:
Akan of Ghana
If you patiently endure, you come out victorious.
— Ghanaian proverb

KURT   [kurt]

MEANING: bold counsel, wise adviser, courteous,
polite, courtly, court dweller • USAGE: German
form of Konrad, from German *kuon* (bold,
courageous) and *rad* (advice, counsel); or English
form of Curt, from French *curteis* (courteous, polite
behavior) or *cort* (court)
A wise man, a strong man.
— German proverb

K

KURUK [koo-rook]

Meaning: bear • **Usage:** Amerind: Pawnee

In the beginning of all things, wisdom and knowledge
were with the animals, for Tirawa, the One Above,
did not speak directly to man. He sent certain
animals to tell men that he showed himself through
the beasts, and that from them, and from the stars
and the sun and the moon should man learn.
— Letakots-Lesa

KWANG-HO [kwahng-hoh]

Meaning: bright and good, shining and good •
Usage: Korean: from Korean *kwang* (bright, shiny,
broad) and *ho* (goodness, broad)

Good people shine from far away,
like the Himalaya mountains.
— Buddha, *The Dhammapada* (tr. Sanderson Beck)

KWANZA [KWAN-ʒah]

Meaning: beginning, start • **Usage:** African:
Swahili of Kenya/Tanzania

The beginning is a bud, the end is a coconut.
— Swahili proverb

KYLE [kiel]

Meaning: slender, narrow, church • **Usage:**
Scottish and English surname: from Gaelic *caol*
(slender, narrow); or from Irish Gaelic *cill* (church)

Surely goodness and lovingkindness will follow me
all the days of my life, and I will dwell in the house
of the Lord forever.
— Psalm 23:6 (NASB)

KYLER [KIE-ler]

Meaning: slender, tiler, tiler of roofs • **Usage:**
American contraction of Kyle and Tyler (*see* Kyle
and Tyler)

All work feeds the soul if it is honest and done to the
best of our abilities and if it brings joy to others.
— Elisabeth Kübler-Ross

L

LAHAR [lah-hahr]

Meaning: small wave • **Usage:** Hindu

The universe is not ruled by arbitrary,
temporary martial law....
We can thus understand the vast serenity of the sea,
to which all the waves are connected,
and to which they must all subside
in the rhythm of marvelous beauty.
— Rabindranath Tagore

LAHIKI [lah-HEE-kee]

Meaning: rising sun, eastern sun • **Usage:**
Hawaiian

Arise, Oh Sun, and warm the land with your passage!
— Hawaiian proverb

LAIRD [layrd]

Meaning: lord, master, ruler • **Usage:** Scottish:
from Gaelic *laird* (lord)

He who is slow to anger is better
than the mighty,
and he who rules his spirit,
than he who captures a city.
— Proverbs 16:32 (NASB)

LALAMA [lah-LAH-mah]

Meaning: daring, fearless, clever • **Usage:**
Hawaiian

A canoe steersman for a stormy day. [A brave person.]
— Hawaiian proverb
(tr. Mary Pukui in *'Olelo No'eau*)

LALI [lah-lee]

Meaning: flexible • **Usage:** African: Swahili of
Kenya/Tanzania

Where there is bending there will be rising up.
— Swahili proverb

L

LALO [LAH-loh]

MEANING: wealthy guardian, protector of that which is valuable • USAGE: Spanish form of Eduardo, from English *ead* (wealth, prosperity) and *weard* (guardian, protector)

Wisdom provides safety, just as money provides
safety. But here's the advantage of wisdom.
It guards the lives of those who have it.
— Ecclesiastes 7:12 (NIRV)

LAMAR [lah-MAR]

MEANING: the sea, ocean, of the sea • USAGE: English: from French *le mer*

Why do we love the sea? It is because it has some
potent power to make us think things we like to think.
— Robert Henri, *The Art Spirit*

LAMONT [lah-MONT]

MEANING: lawman, lawgiver • USAGE: Scottish and English surname: form of *Logmadr*, from Norse *log* (law) and *madr* (man)

Thy Law is within my heart.
— Psalm 40:8b (NIV)

LANCE [lans]

MEANING: lance, spear, church, land • USAGE: Welsh and English: from French *lance* (lance, spear); from Celtic *llan* (church); or from German *land* (land, territory)

The Lord is with you, mighty warrior.
— Judges 6:12b (HCSB)

LANDO [LAHN-doh]

MEANING: fame of the land, famous land, praised estate • USAGE: Spanish form of Rolando, from German *hrod* (fame, praise) and *land* (land, territory)

A good name is to be chosen rather than great riches,
loving favor rather than silver and gold.
— Psalm 31:24a (NKJV)

LANDON, LANDAN [LAN-dan]

MEANING: long hill, ridge, slope • USAGE: English surname: from English *lang* (long) and *dun* (hill)

A people who climb the ridges and sleep
under the stars in high mountain meadows…
these people will give the country some
of the indomitable spirit of the mountains.
— William O. Douglas, *Of Men and Mountains*

LANE, LAINE [layn]

MEANING: country road, narrow passage • USAGE: English surname: from English *lane*

Where his clear spirit leads him, there's his road.
— Ralph Waldo Emerson, "Wood Notes"

LANGDON [LAYNG-dun]

MEANING: long hill, ridge, slope • USAGE: English surname: from English *lang* (long) and *dun* (hill)

The Lord is my high ridge, my stronghold,
my deliverer.
— Psalm 18:2a (NEB)

LANILOA [lah-nee-LOH-ah]

MEANING: vast sky, tall majesty • USAGE: Hawaiian

A tall tree stands above the others.
[A person of outstanding achievements.]
— Hawaiian proverb
(tr. Mary Pukui in 'Olelo No'eau)

LANN [lan]

MEANING: sword • USAGE: Irish: from Gaelic *lann*

Let your courage be as keen,
but at the same time as polished as your sword.
— Richard Brinsley Sheridan, *The Rivals*

LANSA
[lahn-sah]

Meaning: lance, spear • **Usage:** Amerind: Hopi

All things have inner meaning and form and power.
— Hopi proverb

LANZO
[LAHN-ƺoh]

Meaning: land, earth • **Usage:** German: from German *land*

Remain true to the earth.
— Friedrich Nietzsche, *Thus Spoke Zarathustra*
(tr. Thomas Common)

LARKIN
[LAR-ken]

Meaning: laurel tree, laurel wreath • **Usage:** English surname: a form of Laurence (*see* Laurence)

I willingly confess to so great a partiality for trees as tempts me to respect a man in exact proportion in his respect for them.
— James Russell Lowell

LARRY
[LAYR-ee]

Meaning: laurel tree, laurel wreath • **Usage:** English form of Laurence (*see* Laurence)

He will be strong, like a tree planted near water that sends its roots by a stream. It is not afraid when the days are hot; its leaves are always green. It does not worry in a year when no rain comes; it always produces fruit.
— Jeremiah 17:8 (NCV)

LARS
[lahrs]

Meaning: laurel tree, laurel wreath • **Usage:** Scandinavian form of Laurence (*see* Laurence)

Happy is the man who finds wisdom, and the man who gains understanding.... She is a tree of life to those who take hold of her, and happy are all who retain her.
— Proverbs 3:13, 3:18 (NKJV)

LASHON, LASHAWN
[lah-SHAHN]

Meaning: God is gracious, God is giving • **Usage:** American: possibly a form of Shawn, from Hebrew *y'hohanan* (Yahweh is gracious)

I know that here is nothing better for them than to rejoice and to do good in one's lifetime; moreover, that every man who eats and drinks sees good in all his labor — it is the gift of God.
— Ecclesiastes 3:12b–13 (NASB)

LATIF, LATEEF
[lah-TEEF]

Meaning: kind, gentle, gracious, courteous • **Usage:** Muslim: from Arabic *latif*

Truth is a deep kindness that teaches us to be content in our everyday life and share with the people the same happiness.
— Kahlil Gibran

LAURENCE, LAWRENCE
[LOR-ens]

Meaning: laurel tree, laurel wreath • **Usage:** English form of *Laurentius*, from Latin *laurus* (laurel tree, laurel wreath)

If you would know strength and majesty and patience, welcome the company of trees.
— Hal Borland, *Beyond Your Doorstep*

LAURENT
[loh-RAHN]

Meaning: laurel tree, laurel wreath • **Usage:** French form of Laurence (*see* Laurence)

He is like a tree planted by streams of water that yield its fruit in season, and its leaf does not wither. In all that he does, he prospers.
— Psalm 1:3 (ESV)

LAZ
[laƺ]

Meaning: laurel tree, laurel wreath, God has helped • **Usage:** English form of Laurence (*see* Laurence); or English form of Lazarus (*see* Lazarus)

The Lord will lead you....
He will always be with you and help you.
— Deuteronomy 31:8a (CEV)

LAZAR, LAZER   *[lah-ZAHR (Yiddish),*
LAY-zer (English)]

MEANING: God has helped • **USAGE:** Yiddish and English form of Elazar or Lazarus (*see* Lazarus)
Thus saith the Lord: In an acceptable time have
I answered thee, and in a day of salvation
have I helped thee; and I will preserve thee.
— Isaiah 49:8a (MT)

LAZARUS   *[LAZ-ahr-us]*

MEANING: God has helped • **USAGE:** English form of Elazar, from Hebrew *el'azar*
I am the Lord your God,
and I will be there to help you wherever you go.
— Joshua 1:9b (CEV)

LAZLO   *[LAHZ-loh]*

MEANING: glorious ruler, famous leader • **USAGE:** Hungarian form of *Vladislav,* from Slavic *volod* (rule, lead) and *slav* (glory, fame)
My heart is glad, and my glory rejoiceth.
— Psalm 16:9a (KJV)

LAZZARO   *[lah-ZAHR-oh]*

MEANING: God has helped • **USAGE:** Italian form of Lazarus (*see* Lazarus)
Peace, peace to you, and peace to him who helps you;
Indeed, your God helps you!
— 1 Chronicles 12:18b (KJ21)

LEANDER   *[lee-AHN-der]*

MEANING: lion-man, lionhearted • **USAGE:** Greek: from Greek *leon* (lion) and *andros* (man)
That man is bravest who is timid
in counsel and bold in action.
— Herodotus

LEANDRO   *[lay-AHN-droh]*

MEANING: lion-man, lionhearted • **USAGE:** Spanish and Italian form of Leander (*see* Leander)
I am like a lion.
— Hosea 13:7a (WEB)

LECH   *[lek]*

MEANING: uncultivated field, name of river • **USAGE:** Polish reference to the tribe of *Ledzianie,* from Slavic *leda* (uncultivated field); also river in Austria and Germany
Rivers of living water will flow from his heart.
— John 7:38b (NLT)

LEE   *[lee]*

MEANING: strong as a lion, lionhearted, meadow, field, poem • **USAGE:** English form of Leo, Leon, or Leonard, from Latin *leo* (lion) or German *lewo* (lion) and *hart* (hardy, strong, brave); from English *leah* (meadow, field); or from Irish Gaelic *laoi* (poem)
Courage is rightly esteemed
the first of human qualities because...
it is the quality which guarantees all others.
— Winston Churchill, "Alfonso XIII"

LEEON   *[lee-OHN]*

MEANING: my strength • **USAGE:** Jewish
In quietness and in confidence shall be your strength.
— Isaiah 30:15b (MT)

LEE RON, LERON   *[LEE-ron]*

MEANING: lionhearted ruler, lionhearted adviser • **USAGE:** American combination of Lee and Ron (*see* Lee and Ron)
The real leader has no need to lead —
he is content to point the way.
— Henry Miller, *The Wisdom of the Heart*

LEERON, LERON, LIRON [leh-ROHN, lee-ROHN]

MEANING: song of my soul • **USAGE:** Jewish

Surely, the Soul sings continuously.
It is robed in Might and Joy. A Sublime Delight
surrounds it. And a person needs to elevate himself
to the lofty heights of meeting his Soul.
— Abraham Isaac Kook

LEFA [leh fah]

MEANING: inheritance • **USAGE:** African: Lesotho

Search in your past for what is good and beautiful.
Build your future from there.
— Paul Kruger

LEIB [leeb]

MEANING: lion, lionlike • **USAGE:** Yiddish: from Hebrew *labi*

He couched, he lay down as a lion...
who shall rouse him up?
— Numbers 24:8a (JPS)

LEIF [layf]

MEANING: descendant, heir • **USAGE:** Scandinavian: from Norse *leifr*

The lines have fallen to me in pleasant places;
yes, I have a good inheritance.
— Psalm 16:6 (NKJV)

LEITH [leeth]

MEANING: wet, moist, Scottish river • **USAGE:** Scottish surname: from Gaelic *lite* (wet) or *llaith* (damp, moist); Scottish river

There's no music like a little river's....
It quiets a man down.
— Robert Louis Stevenson, *Prince Otto*

LELAND [LEE-land]

MEANING: one who lives near fallow field • **USAGE:** English surname: from English *laege* (fallow) or *leah* (meadow, field) and *land* (land, territory)

Sow for yourselves righteousness; reap in mercy.
Break up your fallow ground,
for it is time to seek the Lord,
till He comes and rains righteousness on you.
— Hosea 10:12 (NKJV)

LEN, LENNY [len]

MEANING: strong as a lion, lionhearted • **USAGE:** English form of Leonard, from German *lewo* (lion) and *hart* (hardy, strong, brave)

The just, bold as a lion, shall be without dread.
— Proverbs 28:1b (DR)

LENCHO [LEN-choh]

MEANING: lion • **USAGE:** African: Oromo of Ethiopia and Kenya

When the lion roars all the animals are quiet.
— East African proverb

LENNART [LEN-ert]

MEANING: strong as a lion, lionhearted • **USAGE:** German and Scandinavian form of Leonard, from German *lewo* (lion) and *hart* (hardy, strong, brave)

Those who do what is right are as bold as lions.
— Proverbs 28:1b (NIRV)

LENNOX [LEN-nuks]

MEANING: elm tree • **USAGE:** Scottish surname: from Gaelic *leamhan*

He that plants trees loves others beside himself.
— Thomas Fuller, *Gnomologia*

L

LENZ [lehnz]

MEANING: laurel tree, laurel wreath • **USAGE:**
German form of Lorenz, from Latin *laurus*

> *God writes the gospel not in the Bible alone,*
> *but on trees and flowers and clouds and stars.*
> — Martin Luther

LEO [LEE-oh (English), LEH-oh (German, Italian, Russian, Scandinavian, Spanish)]

MEANING: lion, lionhearted • **USAGE:** English,
German, Italian, Russian, Scandinavian, and
Spanish: from Latin *leo*

> *Let not thy will roar,*
> *when thy power can but whisper.*
> — Thomas Fuller, *Introductio ad Prudentiam*

LEOLANI [leh-oh-LAH-nee]

MEANING: lofty, tall, chiefly height, rank •
USAGE: Hawaiian

> *Majestic are the tall cliffs of Wailau. [A regal person.]*
> — Hawaiian proverb
> (tr. Mary Pukui in *'Olelo No'eau*)

LEON [LEE-on (English), LEH-ohn (German)]

MEANING: lion, lionhearted • **USAGE:** English and
German form of Leo (*see* Leo)

> *Honest people are relaxed and confident, bold as lions.*
> — Proverbs 28:1b (MSG)

LEONARD, LENNARD [LEN-ard]

MEANING: strong as a lion, lionhearted • **USAGE:**
English form of *Lewenhart*, from German *lewo*
(lion) and *hart* (hardy, strong, brave)

> *God has not given us a spirit of fearfulness,*
> *but one of power, love, and sound judgment.*
> — 2 Timothy 1:7 (HCSB)

LEONARDO [lay-oh-NAHR-doh (Italian, Portuguese, Spanish), lee-oh-NAHR-doh (English)]

MEANING: strong as a lion, lionhearted • **USAGE:**
Italian, Spanish, Portuguese, and English form of
Leonard (*see* Leonard)

> *Those who are right with God*
> *have as much strength of heart as a lion.*
> — Proverbs 28:1b (NLV)

LEONID [lee-ah-NEET]

MEANING: lion, lionhearted • **USAGE:** Russian
form of *Leonidas*, from Greek *leon* (lion)

> *The lion, king of animals…*
> *won't turn aside for anything.*
> — Proverbs 30:30 (NLT)

LEOPOLD [LEH-oh-pohlt]

MEANING: bold people, brave race • **USAGE:**
German and Dutch form of *Liutbalt*, from German
liut (people, race) and *balt* (bold, brave)

> *Walk a bold step, take a brave step, /*
> *The world is great and yours.*
> — Albrecht Goes, "The Steps"

LEOR, LEEOR [lee-OHR]

MEANING: my light • **USAGE:** Jewish

> *A man's wisdom lights up his face.*
> — Ecclesiastes 8:1b (JPS)

LEROY [LEE-roi]

MEANING: king, royal one • **USAGE:** English:
from French *le roi* (the king)

> *What is man, that Thou art mindful of him?*
> *Or the son of man, that Thou visitest him?*
> *Thou madest him a little lower than the angels;*
> *Thou crowned him with glory and honor*
> *and set him over the works of Thy hands.*
> — Hebrews 2:6b–7 (KJ21)

L

LES [les]

Meaning: lesser meadow, small pasture, garden of hollies, gray fort, dyer of cloth, man from Leicester, of the Roman legion • **Usage:** English form of Leslie (*see* Leslie) or of Lester (*see* Lester)

> *You will be like a well-watered garden,*
> *like an ever-flowing spring.*
> — Isaiah 58:11 (NLT)

LESLIE, LESLEY [LES-lee, LEZ-lee]

Meaning: lesser meadow, small field, garden of hollies, gray fort • **Usage:** Scottish and English surname: from Gaelic *less lea* (lesser field, smaller meadow), *leas chuillin* (garden of hollies), or *liath* (gray, gray fort)

> *God Almighty planted a garden.*
> *And indeed it is the purest of human pleasures.*
> *It is the greatest refreshment to the spirits of man.*
> — Francis Bacon, "Of Gardens"

LESTER [LES-ter]

Meaning: dyer of cloth, man from Leicester, of the Roman legion • **Usage:** English: from English *lite*, *litte* (to dye); or from *Leicester* (English city), from Latin *Ligora castra* (Ligora's camp, Roman legion camp)

> *Clothe yourselves with the full armor of God.*
> — Ephesians 6:11a (NEB)

LEV [lehv]

Meaning: heart • **Usage:** Jewish: from Hebrew *lev* (heart)

> *Words that come from the heart enter the heart.*
> — Jewish proverb

LEVI [leh-VEE (Jewish), LEE-vie (English)]

Meaning: joined, united • **Usage:** Jewish and English: from Hebrew *lewi* (joining) and *lewah* (he joined)

> *This is the secret of the unity of God: no matter*
> *where I take hold of a shred of it, I hold the whole*
> *of it. And since the teachings and all the*
> *commandments are radiations of his being,*
> *he who lovingly does one commandment utterly*
> *and to the core, and in this one commandment takes*
> *hold of a shred of the unity of God, holds the whole*
> *of it in his hand, and has fulfilled all.*
> — Martin Buber,
> *Ten Rungs: Collected Hasidic Sayings*

LEWIS [LOO-es]

Meaning: famous warrior, renowned in battle • **Usage:** English form of Louis, from German *hlud* (famous) and *wig* (war, strife)

> *God gave us not a spirit of fearfulness;*
> *but of power and love and discipline.*
> — 2 Timothy 1:7 (ASV)

LEX [leks]

Meaning: protector and helper of humankind, guardian • **Usage:** English and Dutch form of Alexander, from Greek *alexein* (to defend, to help) and *andros* (man)

> *An effort made for the happiness of others*
> *lifts us above ourselves.*
> — Lydia Maria Child, *Looking Toward Sunset*

LI [lee]

Meaning: strength, might • **Usage:** Chinese

> *The mightiest manifestations of active force*
> *flow solely from Tao.*
> — Lao Tzu

LIAM [LEE-am]

Meaning: determined protector, steadfast guardian • **Usage:** Irish form of William, from German *wil* (will, resolve) and *helm* (protection, helmet)

> *Thou shalt be steadfast, and shalt not fear.*
> — Job 11:15b (DR)

LIANG   *[LEE-ahng]*

Meaning: good, excellent • **Usage:** Chinese
Heaven stands by a good man.
— Chinese proverb (tr. William Scarborough)

LIBERATO   *[lee-beh-RAH-toh]*

Meaning: freedom, liberty • **Usage:** Italian (*see* Liberty)
Where the Spirit of the Lord is, there is liberty.
— 2 Corinthians 3:17b (KJV)

LIBERTY   *[LIB-er-tee]*

Meaning: freedom, liberty • **Usage:** English: from Latin *libertas*
Liberty is the soul's right to breathe.
— Henry Ward Beecher,
Proverbs from Plymouth Pulpit

LIBOR   *[lee-bor]*

Meaning: freedom, liberty • **Usage:** Czech (*see* Liberty)
Proclaim freedom in the land for all its inhabitants.
— Leviticus 25:10b (HCSB)

LIEB, LIEV   *[leeb, leev]*

Meaning: love, beloved • **Usage:** Yiddish and Russian: from Hebrew *lev* (love); or from Russian *lieb* (love)
Minds are not conquered by force,
but by love and high-mindedness.
— Baruch Spinoza, *Ethics* (tr. R. H. M. Elwes)

LIF   *[leef]*

Meaning: life, full of life • **Usage:** Norwegian and Danish: from Norse *lifr*
I commend the enjoyment of life, because nothing is better for a man under the sun than to eat and drink and be glad. Then joy will accompany him in his work all the days of the life God has given him under the sun.
— Ecclesiastes 8:15 (NIV)

LIN   *[leen]*

Meaning: voice • **Usage:** African: Ngoni of Malawi
If you can walk you can dance.
If you can talk you can sing.
— Southern Africa proverb

LIN   *[leen]*

Meaning: forest, fine jade • **Usage:** Chinese
My mind is like the autumn moon /
clear and bright in a pool of jade.
— Han Shan

LINCOLN   *[LEEN-kon]*

Meaning: lake colony • **Usage:** English: from Welsh *llyn* (lake) and Latin *colonia* (colony, village)
A lake is the landscape's most beautiful and expressive feature. It is earth's eye; looking into which the beholder measures the depth of his own nature.
— Henry David Thoreau, *Walden*

LINDEN   *[LIN-den]*

Meaning: hill of linden trees, lime-tree hill • **Usage:** English surname: from English *lind* (linden tree, lime tree) and *dun* (hill)
He shall be like a tree planted by the waters,
and that spreadeth out its roots by the stream,
and he shall not see when heat cometh,
but his leaf shall be green;
and in the year of drought he shall not be careful,
neither shall he cease to yield fruit.
— Jeremiah 17:8 (DT)

LINUS   *[LIE-nus]*

Meaning: flaxen-haired, fair-headed, blond • **Usage:** English form of *Linos,* from Greek *flax*
You [God] anoint my head with oil;
my cup overflows.
— Psalm 23:5b (NIV)

LIONEL   *[lee-oh-NEL (French), LIE-oh-nel (English)]*

MEANING: lion, lionhearted • **USAGE:** French and English form of Leon, from Latin leo

I am like a lion.
— Hosea 13:7a (NASB)

LLEW   *[hloo]*

MEANING: lion, lionhearted • **USAGE:** Welsh, from Welsh *llew*

The lion, mighty among beasts…
turneth not away for any.
— Proverbs 30:30 (DT)

LLEWELYN   *[hleh-WEL-en]*

MEANING: guiding image, lion, lionhearted • **USAGE:** Welsh: from Welsh *llyw* (lead, guide) and *eilun* (image, icon); or from Welsh *llew* (lion)

The righteous are bold as a lion.
— Proverbs 28:1b (KJV)

LLOYD   *[loid]*

MEANING: gray, gray-headed • **USAGE:** English form of *Llwyd*, from Welsh *llwyd*

Grey is a colour, and can be a very powerful
and pleasing colour.
— G. K. Chesterton, "The Glory of Grey"

LOBO   *[LOH-boh]*

MEANING: wolf • **USAGE:** Spanish: from Spanish *lobo*

He who accompanies wolves will learn to howl.
— Spanish proverb

LODEN   *[LOH-den]*

MEANING: deep olive green • **USAGE:** English: from German *lode*

I am like an olive tree, thriving in the house of God.
— Psalm 52:8a (NLT)

LOGAN   *[LOH-gun]*

MEANING: little hollow • **USAGE:** Scottish and English surname: from Gaelic *lag* and diminutive *-an*

May Spirit bathe you on the slopes. /
In hollow, on hill, on plain. /
Mountain, valley and plain.
— Alexander Carmichael,
Carmina Gadelica

LON, LONNIE, LONNY   *[lon, LON-ee]*

MEANING: nobly prepared • **USAGE:** English form of Alphonso, from German *adal* (noble) and *funs* (ready, prepared)

I long to accomplish a great and noble task,
but it is my chief duty to accomplish small tasks
as if they were great and noble.
— Helen Keller

LONG   *[long]*

MEANING: dragon • **USAGE:** Chinese

Any man who shows ability may leap the dragon gate.
— Chinese proverb (tr. William Scarborough)

LOPE   *[LOH-pay]*

MEANING: wolf • **USAGE:** Spanish: from Latin *lupus*

If you want to learn,
then go and ask the wild animals.
— Job 12:7 (CEV)

LORCAN   *[LOR-kan]*

MEANING: little fierce one • **USAGE:** Irish: from Gaelic *lorcc* (fierce) and diminutive *-an*

There is always room for a man of force,
and he makes room for many.
— Ralph Waldo Emerson,
The Conduct of Life

L

LOREN   *[LOR-en]*

MEANING: laurel tree, laurel wreath • **USAGE:**
English form of Laurence, from Latin *laurus*

He is like a tree planted by flowing streams;
it yields its fruit at the proper time, and its leaves
never fall off. He succeeds in everything he attempts.
— Psalm 1:3 (NEB)

LORENCIO   *[loh-RAYN-see-oh]*

MEANING: laurel tree, laurel wreath • **USAGE:**
Spanish form of Laurence (*see* Loren)

Happy is the man that findeth wisdom....
She is a tree of life to them that lay hold upon her,
and happy is everyone that retaineth her.
— Proverbs 3:13, 3:18 (KJ21)

LORENS   *[LOHR-enz]*

MEANING: laurel tree, laurel wreath • **USAGE:**
Swedish and Danish form of Laurence (*see* Loren)

You will find something far greater
in the woods than you will find in books.
Stones and trees will teach you
that which you will never learn from masters.
— Bernard of Clairvaux

LORENZ   *[LOHR-aynz]*

MEANING: laurel tree, laurel wreath • **USAGE:**
German and Scandinavian form of Laurence (*see*
Loren)

For in the true nature of things,
if we rightly consider, every green tree is far more
glorious than if it were made of gold or silver.
— Martin Luther, *Watchwords for the Warfare of Life*

LORENZO   *[loh-RAYN-zoh]*

MEANING: laurel tree, laurel wreath • **USAGE:**
Italian form of Laurence (*see* Loren)

He shall be like a tree planted by the rivers of water
that bringeth forth his fruit in his season; his leaf also
shall not wither, and whatsoever he doeth shall prosper.
— Psalm 1:3 (KJ21)

LORIS   *[LOR-ees]*

MEANING: laurel tree, laurel wreath • **USAGE:**
Italian form of Lorenzo, from Latin *laurus*

A tree is known by its fruit; a man by his deeds.
— Basil of Caesarea

LORNE   *[lorn]*

MEANING: Scottish place-name • **USAGE:** Scottish
and English: from Lorne, Scotland

My [God's] people shall dwell
in a peaceable habitation, and in sure dwellings,
and in quiet resting places.
— Isaiah 32:18 (KJV)

LOTHAR   *[LOH-thar]*

MEANING: famous army • **USAGE:** German: from
German *hlud* (famous) and *hari* (army)

The Lord will go before you, and...
will be your rear guard.
— Isaiah 52:12b (RSV)

LOU, LEW   *[loo]*

MEANING: famous warrior, renowned in battle •
USAGE: English form of Louis (*see* Louis)

The legacy of heroes — the memory of a great name
and the inheritance of a great example.
— Benjamin Disraeli (speech of February 1, 1849)

LOUIS   *[lwee (French), LOO-es (English,*
German, Scandinavian)]

MEANING: famous warrior, renowned in
battle • **USAGE:** French, English, German, and
Scandinavian form of Ludwig, from German *hlud*
(famous) and *wig* (war, strife)

Every brave man is a man of his word.
— Pierre Corneille

LOVELL [LUV-el]

MEANING: wolf cub, young wolf • **USAGE:**
English surname: from French *lou* (wolf) and
diminutive *-el*

> The wolf shall dwell with the lamb.
> — Isaiah 11:6a (KJV)

LUAM [loo-AHM]

MEANING: peaceful, calm • **USAGE:** African:
Tigrinya of Ethiopia/Eritrea

> We are at peace as long as our children are with us
> and our land is under our control.
> — Ethiopian proverb

LUC [luke]

MEANING: light, illumination • **USAGE:** French
form of Luke (*see* Lucas)

> God said, "Let there be light," and there was light.
> And God saw that the light was good.
> — Genesis 1:3–4a (NIV)

LUCA [LOO-kah]

MEANING: light, illumination • **USAGE:** Italian
form of Luke (*see* Lucas)

> Whoever loves his brother abides in the light,
> and in him there is no cause for stumbling.
> — 1 John 2:10 (ESV)

LUCAS [LOO-kas]

MEANING: light, illumination • **USAGE:** English
and Spanish form of Lucius, from Latin *lux*

> Hail, holy light! Offspring of heaven first-born.
> — John Milton, *Paradise Lost*

LUCIAN [LOO-shan]

MEANING: light, illumination • **USAGE:** English
form of Lucius, from Latin *lux*

> Light imparts strength to all.
> — Angelus Silesius, *The Cherubinic Wanderer*

LUCIANO [loo-chee-AH-noh]

MEANING: light, illumination • **USAGE:** Italian
form of Lucius, from Latin *lux*

> O send Thy light and Thy truth, let them lead me.
> — Psalm 43:3a (NASB)

LUCIEN [LOO-see-en]

MEANING: light, illumination • **USAGE:** French
form of Lucius, from Latin *lux*

> Your light will shine like the dawn.
> — Isaiah 58:8a (NCV)

LUCIO [loo-CHEE-oh, loo-SEE-oh]

MEANING: light, illumination • **USAGE:** Italian
form of Lucius (*see* Lucius)

> Arise, shine, for thy light is come,
> and the glory of the Lord is risen upon thee.
> — Isaiah 60:1 (KJ21)

LUCIUS [LOO-shuhs]

MEANING: light, illumination • **USAGE:** English:
from Latin *lux*

> There is only one Divine Light,
> and every man in his own measure is enlightened by it.
> — William Temple, *Readings in St. John's Gospel*

LUDWIG [LOOD-veeg]

MEANING: famous warrior, renowned in battle •
USAGE: German form of *Hludowig*, from German
hlud (famous) and *wig* (war, strife)

> Be strong and courageous!
> — 2 Chronicles 32:7a (NLT)

LUFTI [loof-tee]

MEANING: kind, friendly, courteous • **USAGE:**
Muslim

> Be civil in public and gentle in private.
> — Arabic proverb

L

LUGANDA [luh-gahn-dah]

MEANING: brotherhood, kinship • **USAGE:** African: Ganda of Uganda

> *A united family eats from the same plate.*
> — Ugandan proverb

LUGH [loo]

MEANING: light, like the sun, shining • **USAGE:** Irish: from Gaelic *lugu* (light); Celtic sun god

> *May the blessed sunshine shine on you*
> *and warm your heart till it glows.*
> — Celtic blessing

LUIGI [loo-EE-jee]

MEANING: famous warrior, renowned in battle • **USAGE:** Italian form of Louis (*see* Luis)

> *The desire for honour, command, power and glory*
> *usually exist in men of the greatest spirit.*
> — Marcus Tullius Cicero,
> *On Duties* (tr. Margaret Atkins)

LUIS [loo-EES]

MEANING: famous warrior, renowned in battle • **USAGE:** Spanish form of Louis, from German *hlud* (famous) and *wig* (war, strife)

> *A warrior of light makes decisions.*
> *His soul is as free as the clouds in the sky,*
> *but he is committed to his dream.*
> — Paulo Coelho, *Manual of the Warrior of Light*
> (tr. Margaret Costa)

LUKA [LOO-kah]

MEANING: light, illumination • **USAGE:** Russian form of Luke (*see* Luke)

> *He who practices the truth comes to the light.*
> — John 3:21a (NASB)

LUKAS [LOO-kahs]

MEANING: light, illumination • **USAGE:** German, Greek, and Scandinavian form of Lucius (*see* Luke)

> *The sole purpose of human existence is to kindle*
> *a light in the darkness of mere being.*
> — Carl Jung, *Memories, Dreams, Reflections*

LUKE [luke]

MEANING: light, illumination • **USAGE:** English form of Lucius, from Latin *lux*

> *Man is his own star; and the soul that can /*
> *Render an honest and a perfect man /*
> *Commands all light, all influence, all fate.*
> — John Fletcher, "An Honest Man's Fortune"

LUTHER [LOO-thur]

MEANING: famous warrior, people's army • **USAGE:** German and English form of Lothar, from German *liut* (people) and *hari* (army); or from German *hlud* (famous) and *hari* (army)

> *Do right and fear no man.*
> — English proverb

LUX [luks]

MEANING: light, illumination • **USAGE:** English: from Latin *lux*

> *Ye are the light of the world.*
> — Matthew 5:14a (ASV)

LYLE [liel]

MEANING: islander, from the island • **USAGE:** English surname: from French *de l'isle*

> *In the ocean of life the isles of Blessedness*
> *are smiling, and sunny shore of your ideal*
> *awaits your coming.*
> — James Allen, *As a Man Thinketh*

LYNARD *[LEN-ard]*

MEANING: strong as a lion, lionhearted • **USAGE:** American form of Leonard, from German *lewo* (lion) and *hart* (hardy, strong, brave)

The lion…is mighty among beasts
and does not retreat before any.
— Proverbs 30:30 (NASB)

LYNDON *[LEN-don]*

MEANING: hill of linden trees, lime-tree hill • **USAGE:** English: from English *lind* (linden tree, lime tree) and *dun* (hill)

A nation's growth from sea to sea /
Stirs in his heart who plants a tree.
— Henry Cuyler Bunner, "The Heart of the Tree"

LYRONT *[LEE-rahnt]*

MEANING: laurel tree, laurel wreath • **USAGE:** Hungarian form of Laurence, from Latin *laurus*

He is like a tree planted beside streams of water
that bears its fruit in season and whose leaf does not
wither. Whatever he does prospers.
— Psalm 1:3 (HCSB)

LYSANDER *[leh-SAHN-der]*

MEANING: free man, liberated man • **USAGE:** English: from Greek *lysis* (release) and *andros* (man)

Only the free man is truthful.
— Elbert Hubbard, "Consecrated Lives"

M

MAC, MACK *[mak]*

MEANING: son, son of • **USAGE:** Scottish and English: from Gaelic *mac*

My son, keep sound wisdom and discretion;
let them not escape from your sight,
and they will be life for your soul and adornment
for your neck. Then you will walk on your way
securely and your foot will not stumble.
— Proverbs 3:21–23 (RSV)

MACARIO *[mah-kah-REE-ah]*

MEANING: blessed, blessing • **USAGE:** Spanish and Italian form of Roman family name *Macarius*, from Greek *makaros*

God can give you more blessings than you need.
Then you will always have plenty of everything —
enough to give to every good work.
— 2 Corinthians 9:8 (NCV)

MACEY, MACY *[MAY-see]*

MEANING: gift of God • **USAGE:** English surname: form of *Massius*, a form of Matthew, from Hebrew *mattah'yah* (gift of Yahweh)

If God gives us wealth and property and lets us enjoy
them, we should be grateful and enjoy what we have
worked for. It is a gift from God.
— Ecclesiastes 5:19 (GNT)

MACKENZIE *[mah-KEN-zee]*

MEANING: handsome son • **USAGE:** Scottish surname: from Gaelic *mac* (son) and *coinneach* (handsome, attractive)

May God show you loving-favor, my son.
— Genesis 43:29b (NLV)

MACON *[MAY-kun]*

MEANING: stone cutter, stone carver, sculptor, stone mason • **USAGE:** English surname: from French *masson*

God will make you plenteous in all the work
of your hand.
— Deuteronomy 30:9a (WEB)

MACSEN, MACSON [MACKS-sen]

MEANING: greatest, maximum • USAGE: Welsh
form of Maximus, from Latin *maximus*

All the great things are simple,
and many can be expressed in a single word:
freedom, justice, honor, duty, mercy, hope.
— Winston Churchill, "United Europe"
(speech of May 14, 1947)

MADDOX [MAD-oks]

MEANING: good, fortunate • USAGE: Welsh form
of surname Madoc, from Welsh *mad*

The measure of mental health is
the disposition to find good everywhere.
— Ralph Waldo Emerson,
"Natural History of Intellect"

MADISON [MAD-ih-son]

MEANING: son of Maud, warrior's son • USAGE:
English surname: English combination of feminine
Maud and *son*, from German *maht* (might, power)
and *hild* (war, battle)

Listen, my son, and be wise,
and keep your heart on the right path!
— Proverbs 23:19 (WEB)

MADOC [MAD-ok]

MEANING: good, fortunate • USAGE: Welsh
surname: from Welsh *mad*

Every man is the architect of his own fortune.
But chiefly, the mould of a man's fortune is
in his own hands.
— Francis Bacon, "Of Fortune"

MAGEN [mah-GEHN]

MEANING: protector, guardian • USAGE: Jewish

The Lord is your guardian, the Lord is your protection
at your right hand.
— Psalm 121:5 (JPS)

MAGNUS [MAHG-nus]

MEANING: great, magnificent • USAGE:
Scandinavian and German: from Norse *magnus*

Do not throw away your confidence,
which has a great reward.
— Hebrews 10:35 (ESV)

MAHARI [mah-HAH-ree]

MEANING: forgiver, one who gives mercy,
compassionate • USAGE: African: Tigrinya of
Ethiopia/Eritrea

If you offend, ask for pardon; if offended, forgive.
— Ethiopian proverb

MAHDI [mah-dih]

MEANING: rightly guided • USAGE: Muslim: from
Arabic *mahdi*

Follow the best that has been revealed
to you from your Lord.
— Koran, The Companies 39.55a (SKR)

MAHIB [mah-heeb]

MEANING: majestic, magnificent, exalted •
USAGE: Muslim

Whoever is humble to men for God's sake,
may God exalt his eminence.
— Hadith of the Prophet Muhammad

MAHIR, MAHEER [mah-HEER]

MEANING: skillful, able, capable • USAGE:
Muslim: from Arabic *mahara* (to be skillful)

If you are able, that is what God wills for you;
if you are able and good, that is what makes
Him glad about you.
— Hadith of the Prophet Muhammad

MAHKAH [mah-kah]

MEANING: earth • USAGE: Amerind: Sioux

Grandfather Great Spirit, fill us with the Light. Give us the strength to understand, and the eyes to see. Teach us to walk the soft Earth as relatives to all that live.
— Sioux prayer

MAHMUD, MAHMOUD [mah-mood]

MEANING: praiseworthy, esteemed, honorable • **USAGE:** Muslim: from Arabic *hamida* (to praise) or *mahmud* (praiseworthy)

The good reputation is a trust given to man from people, and it is the sacred duty of man to prove worthy of this trust.
— Hazrat Inayat Khan, *The Gayan*

MAJID, MAJEED [mah-JEED]

MEANING: glorious, noble, praiseworthy • **USAGE:** Muslim: from Arabic *majada* (to be glorious)

The shadow of a noble man is large. [A generous, brave, and wise ruler.]
— Arabic proverb

MAKAHA [mah-KAH-hah]

MEANING: fierce, ferocious, patron star of warriors • **USAGE:** Hawaiian

An eel with pointed teeth. [A fearless warrior.]
— Hawaiian proverb
(tr. Mary Pukui in *'Olelo No'eau*)

MAKANI [mah-KAH-nee]

MEANING: wind • **USAGE:** Hawaiian
Though I have no wings, my spirit flies upon the wind!
— Hawaiian proverb

MAKAR [mah-KAHR]

MEANING: blessed, blessing • **USAGE:** Russian form of Makarios, from Greek *makaros*
The Lord your God will bless you in all your work and in all your undertakings.
— Deuteronomy 15:10b (NASB)

MAKARIOS [mah-KAH-ree-ohs]

MEANING: blessed, blessing • **USAGE:** Greek: from Greek *makaros*
Wherever you go and whatever you do, you will be blessed.
— Deuteronomy 28:6 (NLT)

MAKOA [mah-KOH-ah]

MEANING: fearless, courageous, brave • **USAGE:** Hawaiian
It takes more courage / to create peace, / than it takes / to create war.
— Shi Wuling, *Path to Peace*

MAKOTO [mah-koh-toh]

MEANING: sincere, genuine, true • **USAGE:** Japanese
Sincerity the single virtue is / That binds Divinity and man in one.
— Senge Takatomi

MAKS [mahks]

MEANING: greatest, maximum, Maccus's well • **USAGE:** Hungarian form of Maximilian, from Latin *maximus* (greatest); or Czech form of Maxwell, from *Maccus wella* (Maccus's well)
Your right hand holds me up. And Your care has made me great.
— Psalm 18:35 (NLV)

MAKYA [mahk-yah]

MEANING: eagle hunter • **USAGE:** Amerind: Hopi
Search for the truth.
— Al Qöyawayma

MALACHI [mah-lah-CHEE, MAHL-ah-kie]

MEANING: my messenger, my angel • **USAGE:** Jewish: from Hebrew *mal'akhi*

M

Behold, I send an angel before thee,
to keep thee by the way.
— Exodus 23:20a (MT)

MALCOLM   *[MAL-kom]*

Meaning: disciple of St. Columba, follower of
the Dove, God is their king • **Usage:** Scottish
and English form of *Mael Colum* (Dove of the
Church), from Gaelic *mael* (follower, devotee) and
colm (dove); reference to St. Columba, who helped
convert Scotland to Christianity; also from Hebrew
Malkam (God is their king)
  Seek first God's kingdom and what God wants.
  Then all your other needs will be met as well.
      — Matthew 6:33 (NCV)

MALEK   *[mah-LEK]*

Meaning: name of river spirit • **Usage:** African:
Sudan
    Where a river flows, there is abundance.
          — Nilot of Sudan proverb

MALI   *[mah-lih]*

Meaning: let there be peace • **Usage:** African:
Xhosa of South Africa
        Peace, rain, prosperity.
    [With peace and rain, people prosper.]
          — South African proverb

MALINO   *[mah-LEE-noh]*

Meaning: calm, quiet as the sea, peaceful •
Usage: Hawaiian
    The sea is very calm. [A peaceful person.]
          — Hawaiian proverb
      (tr. Mary Pukui in *'Olelo No'eau*)

MALKAM   *[mahl-KAHM]*

Meaning: God is their king • **Usage:** Jewish
    Your kingship is an eternal kingship;
    Your dominion is for all generations.
          — Psalm 145:13 (JPS)

MALU   *[MAH-loo]*

Meaning: shade, shelter, protection, peace •
Usage: Hawaiian
  Make your mind a quiet place of peace and solitude.
          — Hawaiian proverb

MANAR   *[mah-nahr]*

Meaning: guiding light, lighthouse • **Usage:**
Muslim: from Arabic *manar*
          Light upon light.
  Allah guideth unto His light whom He will.
      — Koran, The Light 24.35b (PIC)

MANDAR   *[mahn-dahr]*

Meaning: coral tree • **Usage:** Hindu: Sanskrit
  Be still, my heart, these great trees are prayers.
      — Rabindranath Tagore, *Stray Birds*

MANDARA   *[mahn-dah-rah]*

Meaning: leader, headman • **Usage:** African:
Swahili of Kenya and Tanzania
      All authority is borrowed from God.
          — Swahili proverb

MANDEEP   *[man-deep]*

Meaning: mind full of light, light of the mind •
Usage: Hindu
    Deep within the self is the Light of God.
          — *Sri Guru Granth Sahib*
        (Khalsa Consensus Translation)

MANDO   *[MAHN-doh]*

Meaning: warrior, soldier, army man • **Usage:**
Spanish form of Armando, from German *hari*
(army) and *man* (man)
    God's Spirit doesn't make cowards out of us.
  The Spirit gives us power, love, and self-control.
          — 2 Timothy 1:7 (CEV)

MANDU [mahn-duh]

MEANING: joyous, happy • **USAGE:** Hindu: Sanskrit

Health, contentment and trust are your greatest possessions, and freedom your greatest joy.
— Buddha, *The Dhammapada* (tr. Thomas Byrom)

MANFRED [MAHN-fred, MAN-fred]

MEANING: powerful peace, peaceful and mighty • **USAGE:** German, Dutch, English, and Scandinavian form of *Maginfred*, from German *magin* (power, might) and *frid* (peace, peaceful)
Love truth and peace.
— Zechariah 8:19b (NASB)

MANO [MAH-noh]

MEANING: shark, passionate lover • **USAGE:** Hawaiian

Mano', the shark god, guides me to a safe harbor.
— Hawaiian proverb

MANOLO [mah-NOH-loh]

MEANING: God is with us • **USAGE:** Spanish form of Manuel (*see* Manuel)

The Lord Himself goes before you and will be with you; he will never leave you nor forsake you.
— Deuteronomy 31:8a (NIV)

MANSUR [mahn-SOOR]

MEANING: victorious, successful • **USAGE:** Muslim: from Arabic *mansur*

Remember (all) the bounties of your Lord, that haply ye may be successful.
— Koran, The Places Elevated 7:69 (PIC)

MANUEL [mahn-WEL]

MEANING: God is with us • **USAGE:** Spanish and Italian form of Emanuel, from Hebrew *immanu' el*

The Lord will protect you and keep you safe from all dangers. The Lord will protect you now and always wherever you go.
— Psalm 121:7–8 (CEV)

MANUS [MAH-nus]

MEANING: great, magnificent • **USAGE:** Irish form of Magnus, from Latin *magnus*

Be not afraid of greatness. Some are born great, some achieve greatness, and some have greatness thrust upon 'em.
— William Shakespeare, *Twelfth Night*

MARC [mark]

MEANING: warrior • **USAGE:** French form of Marcus (*see* Marcus)

Be strong, and let your heart take courage.
— Psalm 31:24a (ESV)

MARCEL [mahr-SEL]

MEANING: warrior • **USAGE:** French form of Marcus (*see* Marcus)

The Lord will go before you, and… will be your rear guard.
— Isaiah 52:12b (NASB)

MARCELLO [mahr-CHEH-loh]

MEANING: warrior • **USAGE:** Italian form of Marcus (*see* Marcus)

A man of courage is also full of faith.
— Cicero, *Tusculan Disputations*

MARCELO [mahr-SAY-loh]

MEANING: warrior • **USAGE:** Spanish and Portuguese form of Marcus (*see* Marcus)

Warriors jump over walls; they don't demolish them.
— Carlos Castañeda, *Tales of Power*

M

M

MARCO   *[MAHR-koh]*

MEANING: warrior • **USAGE:** Italian form of Marcus (*see* Marcus)

> *Thou shalt be stedfast, and shalt not fear.*
> — Job 11:15b (KJV)

MARCOS   *[MAHR-kohs]*

MEANING: warrior • **USAGE:** Spanish form of Marcus (*see* Marcus)

> *There's no emptiness in the life of a warrior. Everything is filled to the brim.*
> — Carlos Castañeda, *A Separate Reality*

MARCUS   *[MAR-kus]*

MEANING: warrior • **USAGE:** English and Italian: from Latin *Mars* (Roman god of war)

> *Conscience in the soul is the root of all true courage. If a man would be brave, let him learn to obey his conscience.*
> — James Freeman Clarke, *Self-Culture*

MAREK   *[MAHR-ek]*

MEANING: warrior • **USAGE:** Polish form of Marcus (*see* Marcus)

> *The Lord is with you, you mighty man of valor.*
> — Judges 6:12b (RSV)

MARICI   *[mah-ree-cee]*

MEANING: light, ray of light • **USAGE:** Hindu: Sanskrit

> *The world has opened its heart of light in the morning. Come out, my heart, with thy love to meet it.*
> — Rabindranath Tagore, *Stray Birds*

MARIN   *[mah-RIN]*

MEANING: mariner, seafarer, ocean, sea • **USAGE:** French (*see* Marino)

> *The sea, once it casts its spell, holds one in its net of wonder forever.*
> — Jacques-Yves Cousteau,
> *Life and Death in a Coral Sea*

MARINO   *[mah-REE-noh]*

MEANING: mariner, seafarer, ocean, sea • **USAGE:** Italian form of Roman family name Marinus, from Latin *marinus* (mariner, seafarer) or *mare* (sea, ocean)

> *All the rivers run into the sea, yet the sea doth not overflow: unto the place from whence the rivers come, they return, to flow again.*
> — Ecclesiastes 1:7 (DR)

MARIO   *[MAH-ree-oh]*

MEANING: warrior • **USAGE:** Italian and Portuguese form of Roman family name Marius, from Latin *Mars* (Roman god of war)

> *Put on the armor of light.*
> — Romans 13:12b (ASV)

MARION   *[MAYR-ee-un]*

MEANING: beloved, love, bitter sea, rebellious, well-nourished, healthy, myrrh • **USAGE:** English masculine form of Marian, from Egyptian *mry, mr* (beloved, love); or from Hebrew *mari yam* (sea mistress), *merum yam* (bitter sea), *marah* (rebellious), *mara* (well-nourished, healthy), or *mor* (myrrh)

> *A healthy man, indeed, is the complement of the seasons, and in winter, summer is in his heart.*
> — Henry David Thoreau, "A Winter Walk"

MARIUS   *[MAH-ree-uhs (German, Dutch, Scandinavian), MAHR-yoos (French)]*

MEANING: warrior • **USAGE:** German, Dutch, French, and Scandinavian: from Roman family name Marius, from Latin *Mars* (Roman god of war)

> *A wise warrior is strong, and a man of knowledge makes his strength stronger.*
> — Proverbs 24:5 (NEB)

MARK   *[mark]*

MEANING: warrior • **USAGE:** English, Russian, and Scandinavian form of Marcus (*see* Marcus)

The Spirit that God has given us does not make us
timid; instead, his Spirit fills us with power, love,
and self-control.
— 2 Timothy 1:7 (GNT)

MARKOS [MAHR-kohs]

MEANING: warrior • USAGE: Greek form of
Marcus (*see* Marcus)
Whatever your hand finds to do, do it with your might.
— Ecclesiastes 9:10a (WEB)

MARKUS [MAR-koos]

MEANING: warrior • USAGE: German and
Scandinavian form of Marcus (*see* Marcus)
A wise warrior is better than a strong one,
and a man of knowledge than one of strength.
— Proverbs 24:5 (HCSB)

MARLEY [MAR-lee]

MEANING: boundary field, pleasant meadow,
marten field • USAGE: English surname: from
English *(ge)mære* (boundary), *myrig* (pleasant), or
mearð (pine marten) and *leah* (meadow, field)
The Lord is my shepherd. There is nothing I lack.
He lets me lie down in green pastures;
He leads me beside quiet waters.
— Psalm 23:1–2 (HCSB)

MARLON [MAR-lon]

MEANING: from the moorland • USAGE: English
surname: from *mor* (moor, grassland, marsh) and
land (land, territory)
You, Lord, are my shepherd.
You let me rest in fields of green grass.
— Psalm 23:1–2a (CEV)

MARLOW [MAR-loh]

MEANING: lake remnant, bog • USAGE: English
surname: a form of *Merlave*, from English *mere*
(bog, remnants of a lake)

This is what the Lord says…
when you pass through the waters, I am with you.
— Isaiah 43:1–2a (NEB)

MARSHALL, MARSHAL [MAR-shal]

MEANING: horse groomer, caretaker of horses •
USAGE: English form of French *Mareschal*, from
German *morah* (horse) and *scalc* (servant)
What happens when we live God's way?…
We find ourselves involved in loyal commitments,
not needing to force our way in life,
able to marshal and direct our energies wisely.
— Galatians 5:22–23 (MSG)

MARTIN, MARTÍN [MAR-tin (English, French), mar-TEEN (German, Russian, Scandinavian, Spanish)]

MEANING: warrior • USAGE: English, French,
German, Russian, Scandinavian, and Spanish form
of *Martinus*, from Latin *Mars* (Roman god of war)
The man of character in peace is
a man of courage in war.
— Lord Moran, *The Anatomy of Courage*

MARTINO [mar-TEE-noh]

MEANING: warrior • USAGE: Spanish and Italian
form of Martin (*see* Martin)
The humbleness of a warrior is not
the humbleness of the beggar.
The warrior lowers his head to no one,
but at the same time, he doesn't permit anyone
to lower his head to him.
— Carlos Castañeda, *Tales of Power*

MARTY [MAR-tee]

MEANING: warrior • USAGE: English form of
Martin (*see* Martin)
To be a warrior one needs to be light and fluid.
— Carlos Castañeda

M

MARV   *[marv]*

MEANING: sea fortress, prominent sea cliff, thriving essence, marrow • **USAGE:** English form of Marvin (*see* Marvin)

> *We are as near to heaven by sea as by land.*
> — Humphrey Gilbert

MARVEL, MARVELL   *[mar-VEL]*

MEANING: marvelous, wonderful, miraculous • **USAGE:** American: from English *marvail*

> *Where there is great love, there are always miracles.*
> — Willa Cather, *Death Comes for the Archbishop*

MARVIN   *[MAR-vin]*

MEANING: sea fortress, prominent sea cliff, thriving essence, marrow • **USAGE:** English and Welsh: from Welsh *môr* (sea, ocean) and *dunom* (hill, fortress) or *myn* (eminent, prominent); or English form of Merfyn, from Welsh *mer* (marrow, essence) and *ffynu* (thriving)

> *It is with the soul that we grasp the essence of another human being, not with the mind, not even with the heart.*
> — Henry Miller, *The Books in My Life*

MARZUK   *[mar-ʒook]*

MEANING: blessed, fortunate • **USAGE:** Muslim

> *He it is Who sends blessings on you, as do His angels.*
> — Koran, The Allies 33.43a (ALI)

MASIR, MASEER   *[mah-SEER]*

MEANING: destiny, fate • **USAGE:** Muslim

> *Your destiny is winding toward the Perfect.*
> — Hafiz, "Why Saadi Sits Alone"
> (tr. Daniel Ladinsky in *A Year with Hafiz*)

MASON   *[MAY-son]*

MEANING: stone cutter, stone carver, sculptor, stone mason • **USAGE:** English surname: from French *masson*

> *I saw the angel in the marble and carved until I set him free.*
> — Michelangelo

MASSIMO   *[mah-SEE-moh]*

MEANING: greatest, maximum • **USAGE:** Italian form of Maximus, from Latin *maximus*

> *Thou hast also given me the shield of Thy salvation, and Thy right hand upholds me; and Thy gentleness makes me great.*
> — Psalm 18:35 (NASB)

MASUD   *[mah-sood]*

MEANING: fortunate, blessed • **USAGE:** Muslim: from Arabic *mus'ad*

> *Blessed is he who has found in life his life's purpose. Blessed is he who resteth in the abode of his soul.*
> — Hazrat Inayat Khan, *The Gayan*

MATAN   *[mah-TAHN]*

MEANING: gift • **USAGE:** Jewish: from Hebrew *mattah*

> *Whenever a man does eat and drink and get enjoyment out of all his wealth, it is a gift of God.*
> — Ecclesiastes 3:13 (JPS)

MATAR   *[mah-TAR]*

MEANING: rain • **USAGE:** Jewish

> *The Lord will open unto thee His good treasure, the heaven to give the rain of thy land in its season, and to bless all the work of thy hand.*
> — Deuteronomy 28:12 (MT)

MATEO   *[mah-TAY-oh]*

MEANING: gift of God • **USAGE:** Spanish form of Matthew (*see* Matthew)

> *For God didn't give us a spirit of fear, but of power, love, and self-control.*
> — 2 Timothy 1:7 (WEB)

MATHIAS [*mah-TEE-as*]

MEANING: gift of God • **USAGE:** German and Scandinavian form of Matthew (*see* Matthew)

God's love gives in such a way that it flows from a Father's heart, the well-spring of all good.
— Martin Luther

MATHIEU, MATTHIEU [*MA-tyoo*]

MEANING: gift of God • **USAGE:** French form of Matthew (*see* Matthew)

God has also given riches and wealth to every man, and He has allowed him to enjoy them, take his reward, and rejoice in his labor. This is a gift of God.
— Ecclesiastes 5:19 (HCSB)

MATHIS [*MAH-tees*]

MEANING: gift of God • **USAGE:** German form of Matthew (*see* Matthew)

Every man also to whom God hath given riches and wealth, and hath given him power to eat thereof, and to take his portion, and to rejoice in his labour; this is the gift of God.
— Ecclesiastes 5:19 (KJV)

MATO [*mah-toh*]

MEANING: bear • **USAGE:** Amerind: Sioux

We will be known by the tracks we leave behind.
— Sioux proverb

MATT [*mat*]

MEANING: gift of God • **USAGE:** English form of Matthew (*see* Matthew)

Your talent is God's gift to you. What you do with it is your gift back to God.
— Leo Buscaglia

MATTEUS [*mah-TAY-oos*]

MEANING: gift of God • **USAGE:** Portuguese form of Matthew (*see* Matthew)

Kindle afresh the gift of God which is in you.
— 2 Timothy 1:6b (NASB)

MATTHEW [*MATH-yoo*]

MEANING: gift of God • **USAGE:** English form of *Mattathias*, from Hebrew *mattah'yah* (gift of Yahweh)

Trust in the Lord and do good....
Delight thyself also in the Lord, and He shall give thee the desires of thine heart.
— Psalm 37:3–4 (KJ21)

MATTHIAS [*mah-THEE-ahs*]

MEANING: gift of God • **USAGE:** Greek form of Matthew (*see* Matthew)

God said...I have given you a wise and discerning heart.
— 1 Kings 3:11–12b (WEB)

MATUS [*MAH-tus*]

MEANING: gift of God • **USAGE:** Czech form of Matthew (*see* Matthew)

I commend everyone to enjoy life. A man on this earth can't do anything better than eat and drink and be glad. Then he will enjoy his work. He'll be happy all the days of the life God has given him on earth.
— Ecclesiastes 8:15 (NIRV)

MAURICE [*moh-REES*]

MEANING: Moor, dark-skinned • **USAGE:** French and English: from Latin *Maurus*

The Lord says...
I will give you riches hidden in the darkness and things of great worth that are hidden in secret places.
— Isaiah 45:1–3a (NLV)

M

MAVERICK [MAV-er-ik]

MEANING: independent • **USAGE:** American: reference to Samuel A. Maverick, a Texas cattle owner famous for not branding his calves; originally, a "calf without a brand," and today an unconventional or independent person
Whoso would be a man must be a nonconformist.
— Ralph Waldo Emerson, "Self-Reliance"

MAX [maks (English), mahks (German)]

MEANING: greatest, maximum, Maccus's well • **USAGE:** English and German form of Maximilian (*see* Maximilian); or English form of Maxwell (*see* Maxwell)
Understanding is a wellspring of life to him who has it.
— Proverbs 16:22a (NKJV)

MAXIM [mahk-SEEM]

MEANING: greatest, maximum • **USAGE:** Russian form of Maximus (*see* Maximilian)
There is no greatness where simplicity, goodness, and truth are absent.
— Leo Tolstoy, *War and Peace*
(tr. Louise Maude Shanks and Alker Maude)

MAXIMILIAN [mahk-sih-MIH-lee-ahn (German, Scandinavian), maks-eh-MIL-yan (English)]

MEANING: greatest, maximum • **USAGE:** German, English, and Scandinavian form of Maximus, from Latin *maximus*
He who prizes little things is worthy of great ones.
— German proverb

MAXIMILIEN [mahk-sih-MIL-yen]

MEANING: greatest, maximum • **USAGE:** French form of Maximilian (*see* Maximilian)
The greatest thing in the world is to know how to belong to oneself.
— Michel de Montaigne, "On Solitude"
(tr. Donald Frame)

MÁXIMO [MAHK-see-moh]

MEANING: greatest, maximum • **USAGE:** Spanish form of Maximilian (*see* Maximilian)
Thou hast also given me the shield of Thy salvation, and Thy gentleness hath made me great.
— 2 Samuel 22:36 (KJ21)

MAXIMUS [MAHKS-ih-mus]

MEANING: greatest, maximum • **USAGE:** Italian (*see* Maximilian)
Both riches and honor come from You, and You reign over all. In Your hand is power and might; in Your hand it is to make great and to give strength to all.
— 1 Chronicles 29:12 (NKJV)

MAXWELL [MAKS-wel]

MEANING: little son, Maccus's well • **USAGE:** Scottish surname: form of *Macsual*, from Gaelic *mac* (son) and *sual* (small, little); or from *Maccus wella* (Maccus's well)
The words of a man's mouth are as deep waters, and the wellspring of wisdom as a flowing brook.
— Proverbs 18:4 (KJV)

MAYNARD [MAY-nard]

MEANING: powerful and strong, mighty • **USAGE:** English form of *Maganhard*, from German *magin* (power, might) and *hart* (hardy, strong, brave)
The strong, calm man is always loved and revered.
— James Allen, *As a Man Thinketh*

MAZID [mah-zeed]

MEANING: increase, abundance • **USAGE:** Muslim
Allah increases in guidance those who go aright.
— Koran, Maryam 19.76a (SKR)

MEADE, MEAD [meed]

MEANING: honey wine, meadow • **USAGE:** English surname: from English *meodu* (mead, fermented honey beverage); or from English *medoue* (meadow)

My cup overflows.
— Psalm 23:5b (RSV)

MEGED [MEH-gehd]

MEANING: goodness, excellence, sweetness •
USAGE: Jewish

A man gets his fill of good from the fruit of his speech;
one is repaid in kind for one's deeds.
— Proverbs 12:14 (JPS)

MEINARD, MEINHARD [MIE-nahrt]

MEANING: powerful and strong, mighty • USAGE:
German: from German *magin* (power, might) and
hart (hardy, strong, brave)

Whatever thy hand findeth to do, do with thy might.
— Ecclesiastes 9:10a (DT)

MEIR [meh-EER]

MEANING: bright one, shining one • USAGE:
Jewish

The path of the righteous is as the light of dawn,
that shineth more and more unto the perfect day.
— Proverbs 4:18 (MT)

MEL [mel]

MEANING: council friend, council protector •
USAGE: English form of Melvin (*see* Melvin)

Let the counsel of thine own heart stand;
for there is no man more faithful unto thee than it.
— Ben Sira 37:13 (KJV Apocrypha)

MELVIN [MEL-vin]

MEANING: council friend, council protector
• USAGE: English form of *Mæthelwine*, from
English *mæthel* (council, meeting) and *wine* (friend,
protector)

The greatest trust between man and man
is the trust of giving counsel.
— Francis Bacon, "Of Counsel"

MENACHEM [meh-NAH-kem]

MEANING: comforter, consoler, comforting •
USAGE: Jewish

I, even I, am He that comforteth you.
— Isaiah 51:12a (MT)

MENEWA [men-eh-wah]

MEANING: fierce warrior • USAGE: Amerind:
Creek

Your feet shall be as swift as the forked lightning; your
arm shall be as the thunderbolt, and your soul fearless
as the cataract that dashes from the mountain precipice.
— Methoataske

MENG [mehng]

MEANING: fierce, vigorous • USAGE: Chinese

The superior man in everything
puts forth his utmost endeavors.
— Confucius, *The Analects* (tr. K'ung-fu Tzu)

MEREDITH [MEHR-eh-dith]

MEANING: great ruler, great lord, guardian of the
sea • USAGE: Welsh and English: from Welsh *mawr*
(great) and *udd* (lord, ruler); or from Welsh *môr*
(sea, ocean) and *differaf* (protect, guard)

He who is lord of himself, and exists upon
his own resources, is a noble but a rare being.
— Samuel Egerton Brydges,
The Autobiography, Times, Opinions and
Contemporaries of Sir Egerton Brydges

MERIT [MEHR-et]

MEANING: reward, merit, worth • USAGE:
English: from French *merite* (spiritual reward) or
Latin *meritus* (to deserve, to earn)

You alone are the judge of your worth,
and your goal is to discover infinite worth in yourself,
no matter what anyone else thinks.
— Deepak Chopra, *Ageless Body, Timeless Mind*

M

MERLE [merl]

MEANING: blackbird, shining sea • **USAGE:**
English form of Merrill, from French *merle*
(blackbird); or English masculine form of Muriel,
from Irish Gaelic *muir* (sea) and *geal* (bright,
shining)

> *If I take the wings of the dawn,*
> *if I dwell in the remotest part of the sea,*
> *even there Thy hand will lead me,*
> *and Thy right hand will lay hold of me.*
> — Psalm 139:9–10 (NASB)

MERLIN [MER-lin]

MEANING: thriving essence, marrow, sea fortress,
prominent sea cliff • **USAGE:** Welsh: from Welsh
mer (marrow, essence) and *ffynu* (thriving); or a
form of *Myrddyn*, from Welsh *môr* (sea, ocean) and
dunom (hill, fortress) or *myn* (eminent, prominent)

> *God is the essence of all —*
> *so you are within God and God is within you —*
> *you could not be where God is not.*
> — Peace Pilgrim, *Peace Pilgrim*

MERRILL [MER-il]

MEANING: shining sea, blackbird • **USAGE:**
English surname: English masculine form of
Muriel, from Irish Gaelic *muir* (sea) and *geal*
(bright, shining); or from French *merle* (blackbird)

> *The seas are the heart's blood of the earth.*
> — Henry Beston, *The Outermost House*

MERV [merv]

MEANING: sea fortress, prominent sea cliff,
thriving essence, marrow • **USAGE:** English form
of Mervin (*see* Mervin)

> *The Lord is my rock, and my fortress...*
> *and my high tower.*
> — Psalm 18:2 (KJV)

MERVIN, MERVYN [MER-ven]

MEANING: thriving essence, marrow, sea fortress,
prominent sea cliff • **USAGE:** Welsh and English
form of *Merfyn*, from Welsh *mer* (marrow, essence)
and *ffynu* (thriving); or form of Welsh *Myrddyn*,
from Welsh *môr* (sea, ocean) and *dunom* (hill,
fortress) or *myn* (eminent, prominent)

> *He that walketh righteously and speaketh uprightly...*
> *he shall dwell on high.*
> — Isaiah 33:15–16a (ASV)

METAV [meh-TAHV]

MEANING: best, choicest • **USAGE:** Jewish
> *Man's destiny: To seek truth, love beauty,*
> *will the good, and do the best.*
> — Moses Mendelssohn

MICAH [MIE-kah]

MEANING: Who is like God? • **USAGE:** English
form of Micha (*see* Michael)

> *The first step toward finding God, Who is Truth,*
> *is to discover the truth about myself.*
> — Thomas Merton, *No Man Is an Island*

MICHA [mee-KHAH]

MEANING: Who is like God? • **USAGE:** Jewish (*see*
Michael)

> *Who is God, save the Lord? And who is the Rock,*
> *except our God? The God that girdeth me with*
> *strength, and maketh my way straight.*
> — 2 Samuel 22:32–33 (MT)

MICHAEL [mee-kah-EHL (Jewish, German), MIE-kel (English, Scandinavian)]

MEANING: Who is like God? • **USAGE:** Jewish,
English, German, and Scandinavian: from Hebrew
mikha'el

> *Through the Thou a man becomes I.*
> — Martin Buber, *I and Thou*

MICHAIL [mee-kah-EEL]

MEANING: Who is like God? • **USAGE:** Greek form of Michael (*see* Michael)

> *We ought to fly away from earth to heaven*
> *as quickly as we can; and to fly away*
> *is to become like God, as far as this is possible;*
> *and to become like him is to become*
> *holy, just, and wise.*
> — Plato, *Theaetetus* (tr. Benjamin Jowett)

MICHEL [mee-SHEL]

MEANING: Who is like God? • **USAGE:** French form of Michael (*see* Michael)

> *To get into the core of God at his greatest,*
> *one must first get into the core of himself.*
> — Meister Eckhart

MICHELANGELO [mee-keh-LAHN-jeh-loh]

MEANING: angel who is like God • **USAGE:** Italian combination of Michael and Angelo (*see* Michael and Angelo)

> *Behold, I send an angel before thee*
> *to keep thee in the way.*
> — Exodus 23:20a (ASV)

MICHI [mee-chee]

MEANING: path, pathway • **USAGE:** Japanese: from Japanese *michi*

> *I am open to the guidance of synchronicity,*
> *and I do not let expectations hinder my path.*
> — The Dalai Lama

MICK [mik]

MEANING: Who is like God? • **USAGE:** English form of Michael (*see* Michael)

> *God is love, and the one who remains in love*
> *remains in God, and God remains in him.*
> — 1 John 4:16b (HCSB)

MICKIE, MICKY, MICKEY [MIK-ee]

MEANING: Who is like God? • **USAGE:** English form of Michael (*see* Michael)

> *God is what man finds that is divine in himself.*
> — Max Lerner, *The Unfinished Country*

MICO [MEE-koh]

MEANING: Who is like God? • **USAGE:** Spanish form of Miguel (*see* Michael)

> *God is love, and he who abides in love*
> *abides in God, and God in him.*
> — 1 John 4:16b (NKJV)

MIGUEL [mee-GAYL (Spanish), mee-GWEL (Portuguese)]

MEANING: Who is like God? • **USAGE:** Spanish and Portuguese form of Michael (*see* Michael)

> *Beloved, if God so loved us, we ought also to love*
> *one another. No man hath seen God at any time.*
> *If we love one another, God dwelleth in us,*
> *and His love is perfected in us.*
> — 1 John 4:11–12 (KJ21)

MIKE [miek]

MEANING: Who is like God? • **USAGE:** English form of Michael (*see* Michael)

> *God is love, and whenever you reach out in loving*
> *kindness you are expressing God.*
> — Peace Pilgrim, *Peace Pilgrim*

MIKHAIL [mee-kah-EEL]

MEANING: Who is like God? • **USAGE:** Russian form of Michael (*see* Michael)

> *For who is God besides the Lord?*
> *And who is the Rock except our God? It is God who*
> *arms me with strength and keeps my way secure.*
> — 2 Samuel 22:32–33 (NIV)

M

MIKKEL   [MIE-kel, MEE-kel]

MEANING: Who is like God? • USAGE: Scandinavian form of Michael (see Michael)

We are partners working together for God,
and you are God's field. You are also God's building.
— 1 Corinthians 3:9 (GNT)

MIKLOS   [MEE-lohsh]

MEANING: victory of the people, successful, triumphant • USAGE: Hungarian form of Nicholas, from Greek *nike* (victory) and *laos* (people)

There are victories of the soul and spirit.
Sometimes, even if you lose, you win.
— Elie Wiesel

MILAN   [mih-LAHN]

MEANING: union • USAGE: Hindu

The meaning of our self is not to be found
in its separateness from God and others,
but in the ceaseless realisation of yoga, of union.
— Rabindranath Tagore, *Sadhana*

MILES, MYLES   [mielz]

MEANING: merciful, compassionate, mild, calm, peaceful, miller, soldier, servant • USAGE: English: from Slavic *milu* (merciful, compassionate); from German *mild* (mild, calm) or *milan* (to mill, to rub); from Latin *miles* (soldier, warrior); or from Irish Gaelic *mael* (servant, devotee)

Peace demands the most heroic labor and the most
difficult sacrifice. It demands greater heroism than war.
It demands greater fidelity to the truth
and a much more perfect purity of conscience.
— Thomas Merton, *Seeds of Destruction*

MILO   [MEE-loh (Spanish, Italian), MIE-loh (English)]

MEANING: merciful, compassionate, mild, calm, peaceful, miller, soldier, servant, industrious, hardworking • USAGE: Spanish, Italian, and English form of Miles (see Miles); or Spanish form of Emilio, from Latin *aemulus* (trying to equal or excel) or German *amal* (work, labor)

A mind at peace, a mind centered
and not focused on harming others,
is stronger than any physical force in the universe.
— Wayne Dyer, *Real Magic*

MILOS   [mee-LOHSH]

MEANING: lover of glory • USAGE: Czech form of Miloslav (see Miloslav)

The Lord will give grace and glory; no good thing
will He withhold from those who walk uprightly.
— Psalm 84:11b (NKJV)

MILOSLAV   [mee-loh-slahv]

MEANING: lover of glory • USAGE: Czech: from Slavic *mil* (love, favor, grace) and *slav* (glory)

The wise shall inherit glory.
— Proverbs 3:35a (KJV)

MILT   [milt]

MEANING: milltown, middle village, central town • USAGE: English form of Milton (see Milton)

Every man sees that he is that middle point,
whereof every thing may be affirmed
and denied with equal reason.
— Ralph Waldo Emerson, "Spiritual Laws"

MILTON   [MIL-ton]

MEANING: milltown, middle village, central town • USAGE: English surname: from English *mylen* (mill) and *tun* (town, village); or from English *middel* (middle) and *tun* (town, village)

Character is centrality,
the impossibility of being displaced or overset.
— Ralph Waldo Emerson, "Character"

MIN   [meen]

MEANING: clever, intelligent, sharp, sensitive • USAGE: Chinese

A mind enlightened is like heaven.
— Chinese proverb (tr. William Scarborough)

MINCO [*meen-koh*]

MEANING: chief • **USAGE:** Amerind: Choctaw
I shall exercise my calm,
deliberate judgment in behalf of those most dear to me.
— Pushmataha

MING [*moong*]

MEANING: shining, bright, brilliant • **USAGE:** Chinese
He whose completed goodness is brightly displayed,
is what is called a great man.
— Mencius (tr. James Legge)

MIREK [*MEE-rehk*]

MEANING: glorious peace, glory of peace • **USAGE:** Czech form of Miroslav (*see* Miroslav)
Grace to you and peace be multiplied!
— 1 Peter 1:2b (YLT)

MIRON [*MEE-ron*]

MEANING: myrrh, fragrant resin, incense • **USAGE:** Polish and Russian form of Myron, from Greek *myron* (myrrh)
Ointment and perfume rejoice the heart, and the
sweetness of one's friend — from counsel of the soul.
— Proverbs 27:9 (YLT)

MIROSLAV [*MEE-roh-slahv*]

MEANING: glorious peace, glory of peace • **USAGE:** Czech: from Czech *mir* (peace) and *slav* (glory)
First keep thyself in peace, and then shalt thy
be able to be peacemaker toward others.
— Thomas à Kempis, *The Imitation of Christ*
(tr. William Benham)

MISHA [*MEE-shah*]

MEANING: Who is like God? • **USAGE:** Russian form of Mikhail (*see* Mitchell)
God is love, and he who abides in love abides in God,
and God abides in him.
— 1 John 4:16b (RSV)

MITCH [*mitch*]

MEANING: Who is like God? • **USAGE:** English form of Mitchell (*see* Mitchell)
The glory of God is the human person fully alive.
— Irenaeus

MITCHELL, MITCHEL [*MITCH-el*]

MEANING: Who is like God? • **USAGE:** English surname: form of Michael, from Hebrew *mikha'el*
For who is God, but the Lord? And who is a rock,
except our God? This God is my strong refuge,
and has made my way safe.
— 2 Samuel 22:32–33 (RSV)

MITI [*mee-tee*]

MEANING: trees • **USAGE:** African: Ganda of Uganda
Even the mightiest eagle comes down
to the treetops to rest.
— Ugandan proverb

MO [*moh*]

MEANING: the substance of life • **USAGE:** African: Lingala of Congo
A tree cannot stand without its roots.
— Congolese proverb

MO, MOE [*moh*]

MEANING: drawn out of the water, Moor, dark-skinned • **USAGE:** English form of Moses, from Hebrew *mosheh* (drawn out of the water); or English form of Maurice or Morris, from Latin *Maurus* (Moor)

M

Thus saith the Lord...when thou passeth through the
waters, I will be with you.
— Isaiah 43:1–2a (KJV)

MODESTO   [moh-DAYS-toh]

MEANING: modest, humble • **USAGE:** Spanish,
Portuguese, and Italian: from Latin *modestus*
Speak always according to your conscience,
but let it be done in the terms of good nature
and modesty and sincerity.
— Marcus Aurelius, *The Meditations*
(tr. Jeremy Collier)

MOI   [MOH-ee]

MEANING: king, chief, royal one • **USAGE:**
Hawaiian
Love is like a chief: the best prize to hold fast to.
— Hawaiian proverb
(tr. Mary Pukui in *'Olelo No'eau*)

MOISE   [moy-SAY (Russian),
                      moy-SAYS (Spanish)]

MEANING: drawn out of the water • **USAGE:**
Russian form of Moses, from Hebrew *mosheh*
Counsel in a person's heart is like deep water,
but an understanding person draws it out.
— Proverbs 20:5 (NEB)

MONDE   [mohn-deh]

MEANING: patience, perseverance • **USAGE:**
African: Xhosa of South Africa
The quick one may not win, the enduring one will.
— South African proverb

MONGO   [MOHN-goh]

MEANING: famous • **USAGE:** African: Yoruba of
Nigeria
Wherever a man goes to dwell,
his character goes with him.
— Yoruban proverb

MONROE, MUNROE, MUNRO
                              [mun-ROH]

MEANING: redheaded tonsured one, red-haired
priest, from the mossy place on the River Roe •
USAGE: Scottish form of surname *Maolruadh*, from
Scottish *maol* (bald, or tonsured) and *ruadh* (red); or
from Irish *moine roe* (mossy place on the River Roe)
But ye are a chosen generation, a royal priesthood.
— 1 Peter 2:9a (KJV)

MONTANA   [mon-TAN-ah]

MEANING: mountain • **USAGE:** American: from
Latin *montanus*
Climb the mountains and get their good tidings.
Nature's peace will flow into you as sunshine flows
into trees. The winds will blow their own freshness
into you, and the storms their energy,
while cares will drop off like autumn leaves.
— John Muir, "The Yellowstone National Park"

MONTGOMERY   [mont-GUM-er-ee]

MEANING: hill, Gomer's hill • **USAGE:** English
surname: a form of *Mont Goumeril* (Gomer's
mount), from French *mont* (hill)
May the mountains bring prosperity to the people,
the hills the fruit of righteousness.
— Psalm 72:3 (NIV)

MONTY, MONTE   [MON-tee]

MEANING: hill, Gomer's hill • **USAGE:** English
form of Montgomery (*see* Montgomery)
He that walketh righteously and speaketh uprightly...
he shall dwell on high.
— Isaiah 33:15–16a (DT)

MORDECHAI   [mor-deh-KIE]

MEANING: warrior • **USAGE:** Jewish: reference to
the Marduk, the Babylonian god of war
The Lord will go before you;
and the God of Israel will be your rear guard.
— Isaiah 52:12b (MT)

MORGAN [MOR-gan]

MEANING: sea rim, ocean circle, shining sea
• **USAGE:** Welsh and English: from Welsh *môr* (sea, ocean) and *cant* (circle, rim) or *can* (bright, gleaming)

All the streams flow into the sea,
but the sea is not full, and to the place where the
streams flow, there they will flow again.
— Ecclesiastes 1:7 (NEB)

MORIEL [moh-ree-EHL]

MEANING: God is my teacher, God is my guide •
USAGE: Jewish

Hearken to Me, My people, and give ear to Me,
O My nation, for teaching shall go forth from Me,
My way for the light of peoples.
— Isaiah 51:4 (JPS)

MORRIE, MORRY, MAURY [MOR-ee]

MEANING: Moor, dark-skinned • **USAGE:** English form of Maurice (*see* Morris)

Creativity — like human life itself —
begins in darkness.
— Julia Cameron, *The Artist's Way*

MORRIS [MOR-es]

MEANING: Moor, dark-skinned • **USAGE:** English form of Maurice, from Latin *Maurus* (Moor)

A walk in the dark can lead to wisdom, deliver us from
fear, and bring us closer to God.
— Barbara Brown Taylor,
Learning to Walk in the Dark

MORT [mohrt]

MEANING: village on the moor, town on the grassland, calm sea, still water • **USAGE:** English form of Morton (*see* Morton), or of Mortimer (*see* Mortimer)

Each blade of grass has its spot on earth
whence it draws its life, its strength;
and so is man rooted to the land from which
he draws his faith together with his life.
— Joseph Conrad, *Lord Jim*

MORTIMER [MOR-tih-mer]

MEANING: calm sea, still water • **USAGE:** English: from French *mort* (dead, still) and *mer* (sea, ocean)

It is not the billows, but the calm level of the sea
from which all heights and depths are measured.
— James A. Garfield (speech of June 2, 1880)

MORTON [MOR-ton]

MEANING: village on the moor, town on the grassland • **USAGE:** English: from English *mor* (moor, grassland, marsh) and *tun* (town, village)

Knowing grass, I can appreciate persistence.
— Hal Borland, *Countryman: A Summary of Belief*

MORTY [MOR-tee]

MEANING: village on the moor, town on the grassland, calm sea, still water • **USAGE:** English form of Morton (*see* Morton) or of Mortimer (*see* Mortimer)

He maketh me to lie down in green pastures;
He leadeth me beside still waters.
— Psalm 23:1–2 (ASV)

MOSES [MOH-ses]

MEANING: drawn out of the water • **USAGE:** English form of Moshe (*see* Moshe)

The knowledge of man is as the waters,
some descending from above, and some springing
from beneath; the one informed by the light of nature,
the other inspired by divine revelation.
— Francis Bacon,
Of the Proficiency and Advancement of Learning

M

MOSHE   *[MOH-sheh, moh-SHEH]*

MEANING: drawn out of the water • USAGE:
Jewish: from Hebrew *mosheh*

> *Thus saith the Lord...*
> *when thou passest through the waters,*
> *I will be with thee, and through the rivers,*
> *they shall not overflow thee.*
> — Isaiah 43:2 (MT)

MTIMA   *[m-TEE-mah]*

MEANING: heart • USAGE: African: Malawi

> *It is the heart that knows.*
> — Lamba of Malawi proverb

MUAMAR, MUAMMAR   *[moo-ah-mahr]*

MEANING: long-lived • USAGE: Muslim

> *Nor is a man long-lived granted length of days,*
> *nor is a part cut off from his life,*
> *but is in a Decree (ordained).*
> *All this is easy to Allah.*
> — Koran, The Originator of Creation 35.11b (ALI)

MUBARAK   *[moo-bah-rahk]*

MEANING: blessed, fortunate • USAGE: Muslim:
from Arabic *mubarak*

> *The mercy of Allah and His blessings are on you.*
> — Koran, Hud 11.73b (SKR)

MUFID, MUFEED   *[moo-FEED]*

MEANING: beneficial, favorable • USAGE: Muslim

> *Whatever benefit comes to you (O man!),*
> *it is from Allah.*
> — Koran, The Women 4.79a (SKR)

MUFIZ   *[moo-feez]*

MEANING: charitable, magnanimous • USAGE:
Muslim

> *Your smiling in your brother's face is charity, and acts*
> *which your exhorting mankind to virtuous deeds is*
> *alms; and your prohibiting the forbidden is alms; and*
> *your showing men the road, in the land in which they*
> *lose it, is charity for you.*
> — Hadith of the Prophet Muhammad
> (tr. A. N. Matthews)

MUGABI   *[muh-gah-bee]*

MEANING: generous, liberal • USAGE: African:
Ganda of Uganda

> *If you have a lot, give some of your possessions;*
> *if you have little, give some of your heart.*
> — East African proverb

MUHAMMAD, MOHAMMED   *[mooh-HAH-mad, moh-HAH-med]*

MEANING: praiseworthy, esteemed, honored
• USAGE: Muslim: from Arabic *muhammad*
(praiseworthy) or *hamida* (to praise) or *mahmud*
(praiseworthy)

> *Give glad tidings (O Muhammad) unto those who*
> *believe and work righteousness, that their portion is*
> *Gardens, beneath which rivers flow.*
> — Koran, The Cow 2.25a (PIC)

MUHIB, MUHEEB   *[moo-HEEB]*

MEANING: loving, affectionate • USAGE: Muslim

> *It is love that brings happiness to people. /*
> *It is love that gives joy to happiness.*
> — Jalaluddin Rumi
> (tr. Shahram Shiva in *Rumi: Thief of Sleep*)

MUNDO   *[MOON-doh]*

MEANING: counselor's protection, rich protector,
guardian of prosperity • USAGE: Spanish form of
Raimundo, from German *ragin* (advice, counsel)
and *mund* (hand, protection); or Spanish form of
Edmundo, from English *ead* (wealth, prosperity)
and *mund* (hand, protection)

Good sense will protect you;
understanding will guard you.
— Proverbs 2:11 (NCV)

MUNI [muh-nih]

MEANING: truth seeker • USAGE: Hindu: Sanskrit
Truth is within ourselves.
There is an inmost center in us all,
where truth abides in fullness.
— Mahatma Gandhi

MUNIF [moo-neef]

MEANING: eminent, exalted • USAGE: Muslim:
from Arabic *munif*
Those who keep up prayer and spend
(benevolently) out of what We have given them.
These are the believers in truth;
they shall have from their Lord exalted grades
and forgiveness and an honorable sustenance.
— Koran, The Spoils of War 8.3–4 (SKR)

MUNIR, MUNEER [moo-NEER]

MEANING: luminous, shining, bright • USAGE:
Muslim: from Arabic *muniir*
He will give you twofold of His mercy and
will appoint for you a light wherein ye shall walk.
— Koran, The Iron 57.28b (PIC)

MUNIS [moo-nees]

MEANING: gentle, kind • USAGE: Muslim
A tongue of flame arose out of the twinkling spark
of my heart by Thy gentle blowing.
— Hazrat Inayat Khan, *The Gayan*

MURPHY [MUR-fee]

MEANING: sea warrior, hound of the sea • USAGE:
Irish and English surname: from Gaelic *muir* (sea)
and *cath* (battle, war); or from Gaelic *muir* (sea) and
cu (hound, dog)

There is a tide in the affairs of men, which taken
at the flood, leads on to fortune.... On such a full sea
are we now afloat. And we must take the current
when it serves, or lose our ventures.
— William Shakespeare, *Julius Caesar*

MUSA [moo-sah]

MEANING: drawn out of the water • USAGE:
Muslim form of Moses, from Hebrew *mosheh*
We made from water every living thing.
— Koran, The Prophets 21.30b (ALI)

MUSHIR, MUSHEER [moo-SHEER]

MEANING: counselor, adviser, guide • USAGE:
Muslim
He, then, that receives guidance benefits his own soul.
— Koran, The Crowds 39.41b (ALI)

MUSTAFA [moo-stah-fah]

MEANING: chosen, selected • USAGE: Muslim
For His Mercy He specially chooseth whom He
pleaseth; for Allah is the Lord of bounties unbounded.
— Koran, The Family of Imran 3.74 (ALI)

MWARA [MWAH-rah]

MEANING: intelligent • USAGE: African: Kenya
Wisdom outweighs strength.
— Kikuyu of Kenya proverb

MYRON [MEE-ron (Greek), MIE-ron (English)]

MEANING: myrrh, fragrant resin, incense •
USAGE: Greek and English: from Greek *myron*
(myrrh)
Oil and perfume make the heart glad,
so are a man's words sweet to his friend.
— Proverbs 27:9 (NLV)

M

N

NABHA [nah-bah]

MEANING: heart, the heart center • USAGE:
Hindu: Sanskrit

> Forget not the central truth,
> that God is seated in your own heart.
> — Swami Ramdas, *In the Vision of God*

NABIL, NABEEL [nah-beel]

MEANING: noble, honorable • USAGE: Muslim

> No rank, position, or power can prove one noble; truly
> noble is he who is generous of heart.
> — Hazrat Inayat Khan, *The Gayan* (cd. *The Gayani
> Meditations, Volume 1*, tr. Cecil Touchon)

NADAV [nah-DAHV]

MEANING: donor, generous, beneficent • USAGE:
Jewish

> We must observe the commandment to give charity
> with greater care than any other positive precept....
> For charity is the sign of the righteous man.
> — Maimonides

NADIM [nah-deem]

MEANING: friend, companion • USAGE: Muslim

> A friend is a mirror of his friend.
> — Arabic proverb

NADIR, NADEER [nah-DEER]

MEANING: rare, precious • USAGE: Muslim: from
Arabic *nadir*

> No one anywhere can keep us /
> From carrying the Beloved wherever we go. /
> No one can rob His precious Name /
> From the rhythm of my heart.
> — Hafiz, "Carrying God"
> (tr. Daniel Ladinsky in
> *The Subject Tonight Is Love*)

NADISH [nah-dish]

MEANING: river, stream • USAGE: Hindu: Sanskrit

> In the music of the rushing stream sounds the joyful
> assurance, "I shall become the sea." It is not a vain
> assumption; it is true humility, for it is the truth.
> — Rabindranath Tagore, *Sadhana*

NAFTALI, NAPHTALI [nahf-tah-LEE]

MEANING: wrestle, struggle • USAGE: Jewish

> Of Naphtali he said: O Naphtali, satisfied with
> favour, and full with the blessing of the Lord:
> possess thou the sea and the south.
> — Deuteronomy 34:23 (MT)

NAGID [nah-GEED]

MEANING: ruler, leader • USAGE: Jewish

> He that is slow to anger is better than the mighty;
> and he that ruleth his spirit than he that taketh a city.
> — Proverbs 16:32 (MT)

NAHELE [nah-HEH-leh]

MEANING: forest, forester, woodsman • USAGE:
Hawaiian

> Deep forest of the ancient days — sustain my spirit.
> — Hawaiian proverb

NAHOA [nah-HOH-ah]

MEANING: bold, daring • USAGE: Hawaiian

> One who faced the mountain showers.
> [A courageous person.]
> — Hawaiian proverb
> (tr. Mary Pukui in *'Olelo No'eau*)

NAIM [nah-eem]

MEANING: comfortable, contented, at peace •
USAGE: Muslim: from Arabic *na'im* (contented,
happy) or *na'ima* (to live in comfort)

> Peace be upon you!
> — Koran, The Companies 39.73b (ALI)

NAJIB, NAJEEB   *[nah-JEEB]*

MEANING: noble, honorable • **USAGE:** Muslim: from Arabic *najuba* (of noble birth)

> *Lo! the noblest of you, in the sight of Allah,*
> *is the best in conduct. Lo! Allah is Knower, Aware.*
> — Koran, The Chamber 49.13b (PIC)

NAJIH   *[nah-jih]*

MEANING: steadfast, constant, sound • **USAGE:** Muslim

> *O ye who believe!*
> *Be steadfast witnesses for Allah in equity.*
> — Koran, The Table Spread 5.8a (PIC)

NAKIN   *[nah-kin]*

MEANING: one who dwells in heaven, heavenly • **USAGE:** Hindu: Sanskrit

> *This is the ultimate end of man, to find the One*
> *which is in him; which is his truth, which is his soul;*
> *the key with which he opens the gate of the spiritual*
> *life, the heavenly kingdom.*
> — Rabindranath Tagore, *Sadhana*

NAKOS   *[nah-kohs]*

MEANING: sagebrush • **USAGE:** Amerind: Arapaho

> *All plants are our brothers and sisters.*
> *They talk to us and if we listen, we can hear them.*
> — Arapaho proverb

NALU   *[NAH-loo]*

MEANING: wave, surf • **USAGE:** Hawaiian

> *A wave upon the sand takes only a little of the land*
> *and gives the blessings of the sea in return.*
> — Hawaiian proverb

NAMDI   *[nahm-dee]*

MEANING: father's name lives on • **USAGE:** African: Igbo of Nigeria

> *A wise child gladdens the heart of his father.*
> — Nigerian proverb

NANDAN   *[nahn-dahn]*

MEANING: joyful, happy • **USAGE:** Hindu: from Sanskrit *nanda*

> *In the world of Brahman there is a lake*
> *whose waters are like nectar, and whosoever tastes*
> *thereof is straightway drunk with joy.*
> — *Chandogya Upanishad*
> (tr. Swami Prabhavananda)

NANDI   *[nahn-dih]*

MEANING: joyful, delightful, happy • **USAGE:** Hindu: from Sanskrit *nanda*

> *Joy is your birthright; peace is your inmost nature.*
> — Sathya Sai Baba, *Sathya Sai Baba Speaks*

NANDO   *[NAHN-doh]*

MEANING: bold venturer, prepared traveler, courageous journeyer • **USAGE:** Spanish form of Fernando, from German *fardi* (journey, travel) and *nand* (ready, prepared), *nanthi* (venture, adventurous), or *nanths* (courageous)

> *Adventure is not outside a man; it is within.*
> — David Grayson, *Adventures in Solitude*

NANTAN   *[nahn-tahn]*

MEANING: spokesperson • **USAGE:** Amerind: Apache

> *You must speak straight so that your words*
> *may go as sunlight into our hearts.*
> — Geronimo

NAOR   *[nah-OHR]*

MEANING: enlightened, cultured, knowledgeable • **USAGE:** Jewish

> *With a man who has understanding and knowledge,*
> *stability will last.*
> — Proverbs 28:2b (JPS)

NAQI   [nah-kee]

MEANING: clean, pure, virtuous • USAGE: Muslim
Truly Allah loveth those who turn unto Him,
and loveth those who have a care for cleanness.
— Koran, The Cow 2.222b (PIC)

NARA   [nah-rah]

MEANING: man, masculine • USAGE: Hindu: from
Sanskrit *nara*
The fish in the water is silent, the animal
on the earth is noisy, the bird in the air is singing.
But man has in him the silence of the sea,
the noise of the earth and the music of the air.
— Rabindranath Tagore, *Stray Birds*

NAREN   [nah-rehn]

MEANING: the best among men, king of men •
USAGE: Hindu: from Sanskrit *nara* (male, man)
One may conquer a million men in a single battle;
however, the greatest and best warrior conquers himself.
— Buddha, *The Dhammapada* (tr. Ananda Maitre)

NARYA   [nahr-yah]

MEANING: powerful, heroic, manly • USAGE:
Hindu
Power is of two kinds. One is obtained by the fear
of punishment and the other by acts of love.
Power based on love is a thousand times
more effective and permanent than the one derived
from fear of punishment.
— Mahatma Gandhi

NASH   [nash]

MEANING: ash tree, at the ash tree • USAGE:
English: from English *atten ash*
He will be like a tree firmly planted by streams of
water, which yields its fruit in its season, and its leaf
does not wither; and in whatever he does, he prospers.
— Psalm 1:3 (NASB)

NASIM, NASEEM   [NAH-seem]

MEANING: breeze, gentle wind • USAGE: Muslim
Lord, the air smells good today, straight from the
mysteries within the inner courts of God.
— Jalaluddin Rumi,
"Walking Out of the Treasury Building"
(tr. Coleman Barks in
Open Secret: Versions of Rumi)

NASIR, NAASIR   [nah-seer]

MEANING: helper, supporter • USAGE: Muslim:
from Arabic *nasara* (to render victorious, to assist)
Put your trust in God for support,
and see His hidden Hand working through all sources.
— Hazrat Inayat Khan, *The Gayan*

NAT   [nat]

MEANING: gift of God, gift • USAGE: English
form of Nathan (*see* Nathan) or Nathaniel (*see*
Nathaniel)
Delight yourself in the Lord,
and he will give you the desires of your heart.
— Psalm 37:4 (ESV)

NATAN   [nah-TAHN]

MEANING: gift • USAGE: Jewish: from Hebrew
nathan
Whenever a man is given riches and property by God,
and is also permitted by Him to enjoy them
and to take his portion and get pleasure for his gains
— that is a gift of God. For [such a man] will not
brood much over the days of his life, because
God keeps him busy enjoying himself.
— Ecclesiastes 5:18–19 (JPS)

NATE   [nayt]

MEANING: gift of God, gift • USAGE: English
form of Nathan (*see* Nathan) or Nathaniel (*see*
Nathaniel)

N

*As for every man to whom God has given riches
and wealth, He has also empowered him to eat
from them and to receive his reward and rejoice
in his labor; this is the gift of God.*
— Ecclesiastes 5:19 (NASB)

NATHAN [NAY-than]

MEANING: gift • **USAGE:** English form of Natan,
from Hebrew *nathan*
God said…I give you a wise and discerning mind.
— 1 Kings 3:11–12b (DR)

NATHANIEL [nah-THAN-yel]

MEANING: gift of God, God's gift • **USAGE:**
English form of Netanel, from Hebrew *nathan 'el*
Every good action and every perfect gift is from God.
— James 1:17a (NCV)

NATIV [nah-TEEV]

MEANING: path, road • **USAGE:** Jewish
*Make plain the path of thy feet,
and let all thy ways be established.*
— Proverbs 4:26 (MT)

NAVID, NAVEED [nah-VEED]

MEANING: glad tidings, good news • **USAGE:**
Muslim
*Anything good in your past is a harbinger
of what is to come / in greater quantities.*
— Hafiz, "What Madness Is Austerity"
(tr. Daniel Ladinsky in *A Year with Hafiz*)

NAVON [nah-VOHN]

MEANING: wise, intelligent, knowledgeable •
USAGE: Jewish
*Get Wisdom, get understanding…and she will
preserve thee; love her, and she will keep thee.*
— Proverbs 4:5–6 (MT)

NAZEEM, NAAZIM [nah-ZEEM]

MEANING: leader, organizer • **USAGE:** Muslim
The first step to lead is to consult.
— Arabic proverb

NAZIF [nah-zeef]

MEANING: pure, clean • **USAGE:** Muslim
Purity of the soul is reflected in the cleanliness of body.
— Hazrat Inayat Khan, *The Gayan*

NDIDI [n-dee-dee]

MEANING: patient • **USAGE:** African: Igbo of
Nigeria
*Let us not run the world hastily,
let us not grasp at the rope of wealth impatiently,
what should be treated with mature judgment.*
— Nigerian proverb

NECHEMYA [neh-khem-YAH]

MEANING: God comforts, comforted by God •
USAGE: Jewish: from Hebrew *nechemyah* (Yahweh
comforts)
I, even I, am He that comforteth you.
— Isaiah 51:12a (JPS)

NED [ned]

MEANING: wealthy guardian, protector of that
which is valuable, prosperous • **USAGE:** English
form of Edward, from English *ead* (wealth,
prosperity) and *weard* (guardian, protector)
*God said…wisdom and knowledge will be given you.
And I will also give you wealth, possessions and honor.*
— 2 Chronicles 1:12a (NIV)

NEEL [neel]

MEANING: blue color, sapphire blue • **USAGE:**
Hindu

N

Your simplicity, like the blueness of the lake,
reveals your depth of truth.
— Rabindranath Tagore, *Stray Birds*

NEGASI   [neh-GAH-see]

MEANING: he will be crowned, he will become
royalty • USAGE: African: Ethiopia
A great one must have a long heart.
[Said of leadership.]
— Ethiopian proverb

NEHEMIAH   [nee-ah-MIE-ah]

MEANING: God comforts, comforted by God •
USAGE: English form of Nechemya, from Hebrew
nechemyah (Yahweh comforts)
Thy art with me; thy rod and thy staff they comfort me.
— Psalm 23:4b (KJV)

NEHRU   [NEH-roo]

MEANING: canal, water channel • USAGE: Hindu
As irrigators guide water to their fields,
as archers make their arrows, as carpenters carve wood,
the wise shape their lives.
— Buddha, *The Dhammapada*
(tr. Eknath Easwaran)

NEIL, NEAL   [neel]

MEANING: cloud, champion • USAGE: Irish,
English, and Scottish (*see* Niall)
Champions are made from something they have
deep inside them — a desire, a dream, a vision.
They have to have the skill, and the will.
But the will must be stronger than the skill.
— Muhammad Ali, *The Greatest: My Own Story*

NELSON, NELSEN   [NEL-son]

MEANING: son of Neal, champion's son • USAGE:
English surname: English combination of Neal
and *son*, from Irish Gaelic *neal* (cloud) or *niadh*
(champion, hero)

My son, let them not depart from thine eyes; keep
sound wisdom and discretion.... Then shalt thou walk
in thy way securely, and thy foot shall not stumble.
— Proverbs 3:21–23 (ASV)

NEO   [NEE-oh]

MEANING: new, one • USAGE: American: from
Greek *neos* (new); also homophone of "one"
To become completely transparent and allow Love
to shine by itself is the maturity of the "New Man."
— Thomas Merton, *Love and Living*

NETANEL   [neh-tahn-EHL]

MEANING: gift of God, God's gift • USAGE:
Jewish: from Hebrew *nathan 'el*
I will instruct thee and teach thee in the way which thou
shalt go; I will give counsel, Mine eye being upon thee.
— Psalm 32:8 (MT)

NETRA   [neh-trah]

MEANING: leader, guide • USAGE: Hindu:
Sanskrit
Be the change you want to see in the world.
— Mahatma Gandhi

NEVADA   [neh-VAD-ah]

MEANING: snow, snow-clad, snowcapped •
USAGE: American: from Spanish *neve*
Nature is full of genius, full of the divinity;
so that not a snowflake escapes its fashioning hand.
— Henry David Thoreau
(journal entry of January 5, 1856)

NEVILLE   [NEV-il]

MEANING: new town • USAGE: English form of
Neuville, from French *neuve* (new) and *ville* (town)
Walk in newness of life.
— Romans 6:4b (KJ21)

NEVIN, NEVAN [NEV-en]

MEANING: saint, holy one • USAGE: Scottish and Irish surname *Naomhan*, from Gaelic *naomh*

I pray that you, being rooted and firmly established in love, may be able to comprehend with all the saints what is the length and width, height and depth of God's love.
— Ephesians 3:17b–18 (HCSB)

NGARE [n-gahr oh]

MEANING: leopard • USAGE: African: Kikuyu of Kenya

Even a small leopard is called leopard.
— Kenyan proverb

NGOZI [n-GOH-zee]

MEANING: blessing • USAGE: African: Igbo of Nigeria

The gods may send a gentle breeze when they want to bless us.
— Nigerian proverb

NIALL [NEE-ahl]

MEANING: cloud, champion • USAGE: Irish: from Gaelic *neal* (cloud), or *niadh* (champion, hero); reference to Niall of the Nine Hostages, a fourth-century Irish king

The hero is a mind of such balance that no disturbances can shake his will, but pleasantly, and, as it were, merrily, he advances to his own music.
— Ralph Waldo Emerson, "Heroism"

NIC [nik]

MEANING: belonging to God, belonging to the Lord, victory of the people, successful, triumphant • USAGE: English form of Dominic, from Latin *Dominicus* (belonging to God); or English form of Nicholas (*see* Nicholas)

Joy is of the will which labours, which overcomes obstacles, which knows triumph.
— William Butler Yeats

NICCOLO [NEE-koh-loh]

MEANING: victory of the people, successful, triumphant • USAGE: Italian form of Nicholas (*see* Nicholas)

May the Lord protect you.…May he give you the desire of your heart and make all your plans succeed.
— Psalm 20:1a, 20:4 (NIV)

NICHOLAS [NIK-oh-las (English), nee-koh-LAH (French)]

MEANING: victory of the people, successful, triumphant • USAGE: English and French form of Nikolaos, from Greek *nike* (victory) and *laos* (people)

The ultimate victory…is derived from the inner satisfaction of knowing that you have done your best and that you have gotten the most out of what you had to give.
— Howard Cosell

NICK [nik]

MEANING: victory of the people, victorious one • USAGE: English form of Nicholas (*see* Nicholas)

The one who acquires good sense loves himself; one who safeguards understanding finds success.
— Proverbs 19:8 (HCSB)

NICKY [NIK-ee]

MEANING: victory of the people, successful, triumphant • USAGE: English form of Nicholas (*see* Nicholas)

Men were born to succeed, not to fail.
— Henry David Thoreau
(journal entry of March 21, 1854)

NICO [NEE-koh]

MEANING: victory of the people, victorious one • USAGE: Italian form of Niccolo (*see* Nicholas)

The Lord your God is with you; his power gives you victory.
— Zephaniah 3:17a (GNT)

N

NICOLA   [nee-KOH-lah]

MEANING: victory of the people, successful, triumphant • **USAGE:** Italian form of Nicholas (*see* Nicholas)

> *The Lord...will make you successful*
> *in everything you do.*
> — Deuteronomy 28:12a (CEV)

NICOLAS   [nee-koh-LAH]

MEANING: victory of the people, successful, triumphant • **USAGE:** French form of Nicholas (*see* Nicholas)

> *It is in the compelling zest of high adventure*
> *and of victory, and in creative action,*
> *that man finds his supreme joys.*
> — Antoine de Saint-Exupéry,
> *The Wisdom of the Sands*

NIGEL   [NIE-jil]

MEANING: cloud, champion, black • **USAGE:** English form of Niall (*see* Niall) or from Latin *niger* (black)

> *God said, "This is the sign of the agreement between*
> *me and you and every living creature that is with you.*
> *I am putting my rainbow in the clouds as the sign*
> *of the agreement between me and the earth."*
> — Genesis 9:12–13 (NCV)

NIKAN   [nih-kahn]

MEANING: friend • **USAGE:** Amerind: Potawatomi

> *The red man is your brother,*
> *and God is the father of all.*
> — Simon Pokagon, *Queen of the Woods*

NIKITA   [nee-KEE-tah]

MEANING: victory of the people, successful, triumphant • **USAGE:** Russian form of Nikolai (*see* Nikolaos)

> *Win victories for truth and mercy and justice.*
> — Psalm 45:4b (CEV)

NIKLAS   [NEEK-lahs]

MEANING: victory of the people, successful, triumphant • **USAGE:** Scandinavian form of Nicholas (*see* Nikolaos)

> *Life yields only to the conqueror.*
> *Never accept what can be gained by giving in.*
> — Dag Hammarskjöld

NIKO   [NEE-koh]

MEANING: I am here, I am present • **USAGE:** African: Kiswahili of Kenya/Tanzania

> *Every man leaves his footprints.*
> — East African proverb

NIKOLAI   [nee-koh-LIE]

MEANING: victory of the people, victorious one • **USAGE:** Russian form of Nicholas (*see* Nikolaos)

> *Anyone who gets wisdom loves himself.*
> *Anyone who values understanding succeeds.*
> — Proverbs 19:8 (NIRV)

NIKOLAOS   [nee-KOH-lah-ohs]

MEANING: victory of the people, victorious one • **USAGE:** Greek: from Greek *nike* (victory) and *laos* (people)

> *You will make your way prosperous,*
> *and then you will have good success.*
> — Joshua 1:8b (NKJV)

NIKOLAUS   [NEEK-oh-lahs]

MEANING: victory of the people, successful, triumphant • **USAGE:** German and Scandinavian form of Nikolaos (*see* Nikolaos)

> *Success, success to you,*
> *and success to those who help you.*
> — 1 Chronicles 12:18b (NIV)

NIKOS   *[NEE-kohs]*

MEANING: victory of the people, successful, triumphant • USAGE: Greek form of Nikolaos (*see* Nikolaos)

> *Pay attention to what you are taught,*
> *and you will be successful.*
> — Proverbs 16:20b (GNT)

NILES   *[niels]*

MEANING: cloud, champion • USAGE: English form of Neil (*see* Niall)

> *I have placed My bow in the clouds, and it will be a*
> *sign of the covenant between Me and the earth.*
> — Genesis 9:13 (HCSB)

NILS, NIELS   *[neelʒ]*

MEANING: victory of the people, successful, triumphant • USAGE: Scandinavian form of Nicholas (*see* Nikolaos)

> *You will accomplish your objectives*
> *and you will succeed.*
> — Joshua 1:8b (CEV)

NING   *[neeng]*

MEANING: peaceful, tranquil • USAGE: Chinese

> *Peace leads to calmness and calmness leads*
> *to enlightenment.*
> — Ch'eng Hao

NIRVAN   *[nihr-VAHN]*

MEANING: state of extreme bliss and peace • USAGE: Hindu: from Sanskrit *nirvana* (a blowing out); reference to the blissful absorption of the soul into the supreme spirit

> *Nirvana is not the blowing out of a candle.*
> *It is the extinguishing of the flame because day is come.*
> — Rabindranath Tagore

NISSAN, NISAN   *[nee-SAHN]*

MEANING: miracle, wonder • USAGE: Jewish: from Hebrew *nisan;* Jewish month containing Pesach

> *It was You who created my conscience;*
> *You fashioned me in my mother's womb.*
> *I praise You, for I am awesomely, wondrously made;*
> *Your work is wonderful, I know it very well.*
> — Psalm 139:13–14

NITIS   *[nit-is]*

MEANING: friend • USAGE: Amerind: Delaware

> *We shall live as brothers as long as sun and moon shine*
> *in the sky. We have a broad path to walk.*
> — Tammany

NITYAN   *[niht-yan]*

MEANING: eternal, infinite • USAGE: Hindu: Sanskrit

> *To him who sees the Self revealed in his own heart*
> *belongs eternal peace — to none else, to none else!*
> — *Katha Upanishad* (tr. Swami Prabhavananda)

NKOSI   *[n-KOH-see]*

MEANING: ruler, leader • USAGE: African: Zulu of South Africa

> *The leader is the servant. So leadership is not having*
> *your own way. It's not for self-aggrandizement.*
> *But oddly, it is for service. It is for the sake of the led.*
> *It is a proper altruism.*
> — Desmond Tutu, "Forging Equality in South
> Africa" (interview of June 12, 2004)

NOACH   *[noh-AHKH]*

MEANING: rest, comfort, peace • USAGE: Jewish: from Hebrew *noach*

> *The Lord bless you and protect you! The Lord deal*
> *kindly and graciously with you. The Lord bestow His*
> *favor upon you and grant you peace.*
> — Numbers 6:24–26 (JPS)

NOAH [NOH-ah]

MEANING: rest, comfort, peace • **USAGE:** English form of Noach (*see* Noach)

> The Lord said, "My presence will go with you,
> and I will give you rest."
> — Exodus 33:14 (NEB)

NOAM [NOH-ahm, nohm]

MEANING: kind, pleasant • **USAGE:** Jewish: from Hebrew *no'am*

> The highest wisdom is kindness.
> — Babylonian Talmud: Berakot 17a

NOCONA [noh-koh-nah]

MEANING: wanderer, camper • **USAGE:** Amerind: Comanche

> I was born upon the prairie, where the wind blew free,
> and there was nothing to break the light of the sun.
> I was born where there were no enclosures,
> and where everything drew a free breath....I lived like
> my fathers before me, and like them, I lived happily.
> — Ten Bears

NODIN [noh-din]

MEANING: wind • **USAGE:** Amerind: Chippewa-Ojibwe

> Sometimes / I go about pitying myself /
> While I am carried by the wind / Across the sky.
> — Chippewa song

NOEL, NOËL [NOH-l (English), noh-EL (French)]

MEANING: Christmas, born on Christmas Day, Christmas carol • **USAGE:** English and French: from French *nael* (Christmas), from Latin *natalis dies Domini* (birthday of the Lord); also a Christmas carol

> This is the day the Lord has made;
> let us rejoice and be glad in it.
> — Psalm 118:24 (HCSB)

NOHEA [noh-HEH-ah]

MEANING: handsome, of fine appearance • **USAGE:** Hawaiian

> Unfolded well are the fronds of the ferns.
> [A handsome person.]
> — Hawaiian proverb
> (tr. Mary Pukui in 'Olelo No'eau)

NOLAN [NOH-lan]

MEANING: little famous one, little champion, little proud one • **USAGE:** English surname: form of *Nuallan*, from Gaelic *nuall* (noble, famous), *niul* (champion), or *uallach* (proud) and diminutive *-an*

> He that is faithful in a very little
> is faithful also in much.
> — Luke 16:10a (ASV)

NOMA [NOH-mah]

MEANING: farmer, earth keeper • **USAGE:** African: Hausa of West Africa

> Knowledge is like a garden; if it is not cultivated,
> it cannot be harvested.
> — West African proverb

NORBERT [NOR-bert]

MEANING: northern brightness, shining one from the north • **USAGE:** German and English: from German *nord* (north, northern) and *beraht* (bright, shining)

> They that are wise shall shine
> as the brightness of the expanse.
> — Daniel 12:3a (DT)

NORM [norm]

MEANING: north, northerner, man of the north • **USAGE:** English form of Norman (*see* Norman)

> Will is the north, action the south pole....Character
> may be ranked as having its natural place in the north.
> — Ralph Waldo Emerson, "Character"

NORMAN　　　　　　　*[NOR-man]*

MEANING: north, northerner, man of the north
• **USAGE:** English form of French *Normant*, from
German *nord* (north, northern) and *man* (man)
I find the great thing in this world is, not so much where
we stand, as in what direction we are moving.
— Oliver Wendell Holmes Sr.,
The Autocrat of the Breakfast Table

NORRIS　　　　　　　*[NOR-is]*

MEANING: north, northerner, novice, priest in
training • **USAGE:** English surname: from French
norreis (north); or from Latin *novitas* (novice, a
monk in training)
I am the Lord your God, who teaches you
what is good for you and leads you along the paths
you should follow.
— Isaiah 48:17b (NLT)

NOVIS　　　　　　　*[NAH-vis]*

MEANING: north, northerner, novice, priest in
training • **USAGE:** English surname (*see* Norris)
You are a chosen race, a royal priesthood.
— 1 Peter 2:9a (NASB)

NUNCIO　　　　　　　*[NOON-see-oh]*

MEANING: announcement, messenger, herald •
USAGE: Spanish (*see* Nunzio)
I am sending a messenger before thee
to keep thee in the way.
— Exodus 23:20a (YLT)

NUNZIO　　　　　　　*[NOON-zee-oh]*

MEANING: announcement, messenger, herald •
USAGE: Italian masculine form of Annunziata,
from Italian *annunzio* (announcement) or Latin
nuntius (messenger, herald)
How beautiful on the mountains are the feet of him
who brings good news, who tells of peace
and brings good news of happiness.
— Isaiah 52:7a (NLV)

NUR, NOOR　　　　　　*[noor]*

MEANING: light, illumination • **USAGE:** Muslim:
from Arabic *nur*
See how your soul is a sire of light.
— Hafiz, "Brings Life to a Field"
(tr. Daniel Ladinsky in *A Year with Hafiz*)

O

OBA　　　　　　　*[OH-bah]*

MEANING: king • **USAGE:** African: Yoruba of
Nigeria
It is in a king that regality resides.
— Yoruban proverb

OBADIAH　　　　　　*[oh-bah-DIE-yah]*

MEANING: servant of God, he who serves God
fully • **USAGE:** English form of Hebrew *Ovadya*
Well done, good and faithful servant!
You have been faithful with a few things;
I will put you in charge of many things.
— Matthew 25:21b (NIV)

OBAMA　　　　　　*[oh-BAH-mah]*

MEANING: bending, leaning, flexible • **USAGE:**
African: Luo of Kenya
The wind does not break a tree that bends.
— East African proverb

OBERON　　　　　　*[OH-ber-ahn]*

MEANING: elf king, elfin ruler • **USAGE:** English
form of Alberic, from German *alb* (elf) and *rik*
(ruler, leader)
The kingdom of heaven is in the condition of the heart.
— John Burroughs,
"Natural Versus Supernatural"

O

OCEAN   [oh-SHEN]

MEANING: ocean, of the ocean • USAGE: English:
from Greek *oceanus* (ocean) or French *ocean* (ocean,
sea)

All the rivers run into the sea; yet the sea is not full;
unto the place from whence the rivers come,
thither they return again.
— Ecclesiastes 1:7 (KJV)

OCTAVIO   [ohk-TAH-bee-oh (Spanish),
ohk-TAH-vee-oh (English)]

MEANING: eight, eighth • USAGE: Spanish and
English form of Roman family name *Octavius*, from
Latin *octavus*

Man is not an end but a beginning.
We are at the beginning of the second week.
We are children of the eighth day.
— Thornton Wilder, *The Eighth Day*

ODRAN, ODHRAN   [OHD-ran]

MEANING: pale green, otter, dark-haired • USAGE:
Irish: from Gaelic *odhran* (pale green), *odran*
(otter), or *odhra* (dark-haired)

Deep peace, pure green of the grass to you...
Deep peace, deep peace!
— Fiona MacLeod, "Invocation of Peace"

OFER   [OH-fehr]

MEANING: young deer • USAGE: Jewish

Who is a god except the Lord...Who kept
my path secure. Who made my legs like a deer's,
and set me firm on the heights.
— 2 Samuel 22:32–33 (JPS)

OFIR   [oh-FEER]

MEANING: gold, golden, valuable • USAGE:
Jewish

For Thou meetest him with choicest blessings;
Thou settest a crown of fine gold on his head.
— Psalm 21:4 (MT)

OGEN   [OH-gen]

MEANING: anchor, secure • USAGE: Jewish

He that walketh uprightly walketh securely.
— Proverbs 10:9a (MT)

OHANZEE   [oh-hahn-ʒee]

MEANING: shadow • USAGE: Amerind: Sioux

What you see with your eyes shut is what counts.
— John (Fire) Lame Deer,
Lame Deer: Seeker of Visions

OISIN   [OH-sheen]

MEANING: little deer • USAGE: Irish: from Gaelic
os (deer) and diminutive *-an*

Ask the animals and they will teach you.
— Job 12:7 (NEB)

OKAL   [oh-kahl]

MEANING: to go beyond, to cross • USAGE:
African: Luo of Kenya

The wind and the imagination can travel
far and wide at no cost.
— East African proverb

OLA   [OH-lah]

MEANING: wealthy, rich • USAGE: African:
Yoruba of Nigeria

Generosity is wealth.
— Nigerian proverb

OLAF, OLAV   [OH-lahf, OH-lahv]

MEANING: ancestor's descendant, heir • USAGE:
Scandinavian: from Norse *anu* (ancestor) and *leifr*
(descendant, heir)

The lines are fallen unto me in goodly places:
for my inheritance is goodly to me.
— Psalm 15:6 (DR)

OLEG [ah-LEK]

MEANING: holy, blessed • USAGE: Russian: from Norse *heilagr*

> *Put on then, as God's chosen ones,*
> *holy and beloved, compassion, kindness, humility,*
> *meekness, and patience.*
> — Colossians 3:12 (ESV)

OLIVER [OL-ih-ver (English), OH-lee-vahr (German, Scandinavian)]

MEANING: olive, olive tree, elf army • USAGE: English, German, and Scandinavian: from Latin *oliva* (olive tree), or from Greek *elaia* (olive); or English form of *Alfihar*, from Norse *alfr* (elf) and *arr* (army)

> *I am like an olive tree flourishing in the house of God;*
> *I trust in God's unfailing love for ever and ever.*
> — Psalm 52:8 (NIV)

OLIVIER [oh-lee-VYAY]

MEANING: olive, olive tree, elf army • USAGE: French form of Oliver (*see* Oliver)

> *His splendor will be like an olive tree.*
> — Hosea 14:6 (NIV)

OLU [OH-loo]

MEANING: preeminent, first, chief • USAGE: African: Yoruba of Nigeria

> *Truthfulness is the chief of attributes.*
> — Yoruban proverb

OMAN [oh-mahn]

MEANING: friend, protector • USAGE: Hindu: Sanskrit

> *May all beings look on me with the eye of a friend!*
> *May I look on all beings with the eye of a friend! May*
> *we look on one another with the eye of a friend!*
> — *Yajur Veda*

OMAR [oh-mahr]

MEANING: prosperous, thriving, full of life • USAGE: Muslim: from Arabic *amara* (to live long, to prosper) or *amir* (flourishing, thriving)

> *He who can quicken the feeling of another to joy*
> *or to gratitude, by that much he adds to his own life.*
> — Hazrat Inayat Khan, *The Bowl of Saki*

OMETZ [oh-MEHTZ]

MEANING: courageous, brave • USAGE: Jewish

> *Wait and hope for and expect the Lord; be brave and of*
> *good courage and let your heart be stout and enduring.*
> — Psalm 27:14 (JPS)

OMID [oh-meed]

MEANING: hope, wish, desire • USAGE: Persian

> *When all your desires are distilled / You will cast just*
> *two votes: / To love more, / And be happy.*
> — Hafiz, "Your Seed Pouch"
> (tr. Daniel Ladinsky in *The Gift*)

ONAM [oh-NAHM]

MEANING: strong, powerful, mighty • USAGE: Jewish

> *Whatever it is in your power to do,*
> *do with all your might.*
> — Ecclesiastes 9:10a (JPS)

ONDRO [OHN-droh]

MEANING: man, manly, masculine • USAGE: Czech form of Andrew, from Greek *andros* (man) or *andreios* (manly)

> *Take courage and be a man. Observe the*
> *requirements of the Lord your God, and follow*
> *all his ways…so that you will be successful*
> *in all you do and wherever you go.*
> — 1 Kings 2:2b–3 (NLT)

ORAN [oh-RAHN]

MEANING: light, bright • **USAGE:** Jewish
Arise, shine, for thy light is come,
and the glory of the Lord is risen upon thee.
— Isaiah 60:1 (MT)

ORAN, OREN, ORIN [OR-an]

MEANING: pale green, otter, dark-haired • **USAGE:**
Irish form of Odran, from Gaelic *odhran* (pale
green), *odran* (otter), or *odhra* (dark-haired)
You'll be on good terms with rocks and mountains;
wild animals will become your good friends.
You'll know that your place on earth is safe.
— Job 5:23–24a (MSG)

ORION [oh-RIE-un]

MEANING: star constellation, boundary • **USAGE:**
Greek: from Greek *horion* (boundary, limit); great
hunter constellation
From the stars, Knowledge. [Ex astris, Scientia.]
— Latin proverb

ORLANDO [ohr-LAHN-doh (Italian, Spanish), ohr-LAN-doh (English)]

MEANING: fame of the land, famous land, praised
estate • **USAGE:** Italian, English, and Spanish form
of Roland, from German *hrod* (fame, praise) and
land (land, territory)
A man's true estate of power and riches is to be himself;
not in his dwelling, or position; not in his external
relations; but in his own essential character.
— Henry Ward Beecher

ORSON [OR-son]

MEANING: bear cub, young bear • **USAGE:**
English: from French *ors* (bear) and diminutive *-on*
Bears…know no beginning, no ending, to him life
unstinted, unplanned, is above the accident of time,
and his years, markless, boundless, equal eternity.
— John Muir

ORVILLE, ORVIL [OR-vil]

MEANING: golden city • **USAGE:** English: from
French *or* (gold) and *ville* (village, town)
A good heart's worth gold.
— William Shakespeare, *King Henry IV, Part II*

OSAMU [oh-SAHM-oo]

MEANING: disciplined, studious • **USAGE:**
Japanese
The Art of Peace is the art of learning deeply,
the art of knowing oneself.
— Morihei Ueshiba, *The Art of Peace*
(tr. John Stevens)

OSCAR, ÓSCAR [OS-ker (English, Irish), OHS-kahr (Spanish)]

MEANING: champion, warrior, friend of deer, one
who loves deer, spear of the gods • **USAGE:** Irish,
English, and Spanish: from Gaelic *oscar* (champion,
warrior) or Gaelic *os* (deer) and *cara* (friend); or
from English *os* (God) and *gar* (spear)
The characteristic of heroism is its persistency.
— Ralph Waldo Emerson, "Heroism"

OSEI [oh-SEH-ee]

MEANING: noble, honorable • **USAGE:** African:
Fante of Ghana
If you are honored, honor yourself.
— Ghanaian proverb

OSHER [OH-sher]

MEANING: wealthy, prosperous • **USAGE:** Jewish
[Ben Zoma said]: Who is rich?
One who rejoices in his portion. As it is said:
"When you eat the labor of your hands, you are happy,
and it will be well with you (Psalm 128:2)."
— *Pirkei Avot* 4:1

OSKAR [*AHS-kur*]

MEANING: champion, warrior, friend of deer, one who loves deer, spear of the gods • **USAGE:** German and Scandinavian form of Oscar (*see* Oscar)

> *There is nothing on this earth*
> *more to be prized than true friendship.*
> — Thomas Aquinas

OSWALD [*OZ-wahld*]

MEANING: divine power • **USAGE:** English and Scottish surname: from English *os* (god) and *weald* (rule)

> *There is nothing on this earth*
> *more to be prized than true friendship.*
> — Percy Bysshe Shelley, "Love's Philosophy"

OTIS [*OH-tis*]

MEANING: prosperous, wealthy • **USAGE:** English surname: from German *od*

> *Lord, you give me stability and prosperity;*
> *you make my future secure.*
> — Psalm 16:5 (NEB)

OTTAVIO [*oh-TAH-vee-oh*]

MEANING: eight, eighth • **USAGE:** Italian form of *Octavious,* from Latin *octavus*

> *Teach us to number our days,*
> *that we may gain a heart of wisdom.*
> — Psalm 90:12 (NKJV)

OTTO [*OH-toh, AU-toh*]

MEANING: prosperous, wealthy • **USAGE:** German and Scandinavian form of *Otho,* from German *od*

> *Not he who has much is rich,*
> *but he who gives much.*
> — Erich Fromm, *The Art of Loving*

OWAIN [*OH-wen*]

MEANING: youthful, young, wellborn, noble • **USAGE:** Welsh: from Welsh *eoghunn* (youth); or Welsh form of Eugene, from Greek *eu* (good, well) and *genes* (born)

> *Become aware of what is in you.*
> *Announce it, pronounce it, produce it,*
> *and give birth to it.*
> Meister Eckhart
> (tr. Matthew Fox in *Creation Spirituality*)

OWEN [*OH-wen*]

MEANING: youthful, young, wellborn, noble • **USAGE:** English form of Owain, from Welsh *eoghunn* (youth), or from Greek *eu* (good, well) and *genes* (born)

> *Youth is a quality,*
> *not a matter of circumstances.*
> — Frank Lloyd Wright

OZ [*oz*]

MEANING: strong, powerful, mighty • **USAGE:** English form of Hebrew Az

> *The Lord is with you, brave and mighty man!*
> — Judges 6:12b (GNT)

OZZIE [*OZ-ee*]

MEANING: strong, powerful, mighty, divine power • **USAGE:** English form of Oz (*see* Oz) or of Oswald (*see* Oswald)

> *Whatever your hand finds to do,*
> *do it with all your might.*
> — Ecclesiastes 9:10a (NIV)

P

PABLO   [PAH-bloh]

MEANING: small, little • USAGE: Spanish form of
Paul, from Latin *paulus*

He that is faithful
in that which is least is faithful also in much.
— Luke 16:10a (KJV)

PACÍFICO   [pah-SEE-fee-koh]

MEANING: peaceful, serene • USAGE: Spanish:
from Latin *pacificus*

Peace begins with a smile.
— Mother Teresa, *Love: A Fruit Always in Season*

PACO   [PAH-koh]

MEANING: one who is free, native of France,
a Franc, spearman • USAGE: Spanish form of
Francisco, from Latin *Franciscus* (a Frenchman);
from French *franc* (free, freeman); or from German
franco (spear used by the Franks, a Germanic tribe)

Ye shall know the truth, and the truth shall set you free.
— John 8:32 (DT)

PADDY   [PAD-ee]

MEANING: patrician, noble one • USAGE: Irish
form of Patrick (*see* Padraic)

Life at its noblest leaves mere happiness far behind…
Happiness is not the object of life: life has no object:
it is an end in itself.
— George Bernard Shaw

PADRAIC, PADRAIG   [PAH-drik, PAH-drig]

MEANING: patrician, noble one • USAGE: Irish
and Scottish form of Patrick, from Latin *patricius*
(patrician, nobleman)

The man who is noble makes noble plans.
And by doing noble things he succeeds.
— Isaiah 32:8 (NIRV)

PAGE   [payj]

MEANING: young attendant, young helper •
USAGE: English surname: from English *page*

When Duty whispers low, Thou must, /
The youth replies, I can.
— Ralph Waldo Emerson, "Voluntaries"

PAGET   [PAJ-et]

MEANING: young attendant, young helper •
USAGE: English (*see* Page)

Youth has a kingdom waiting for it.
— Oscar Wilde, *A Woman of No Importance*

PAISLEY   [PAYZ-lee]

MEANING: church, basilica, cathedral, patterned
fabric • USAGE: English: Scottish town, from Latin
passeleg (basilica, church); paisley fabric, which
originated in town

Thy mercy will follow me all the days of my life.
And that I may dwell in the house of the Lord
unto length of days.
— Psalm 22:6 (DR)

PAKALA   [pah-KAH-lah]

MEANING: shining sun • USAGE: Hawaiian

The sun bathes me in its perfect warmth.
— Hawaiian proverb

PAKI   [pah-kee]

MEANING: witness • USAGE: African: Xhosa of
South Africa

You have to be someone who affirms others,
someone who is ready to see the good that is in others,
and perhaps help to coax it from them.
— Desmond Tutu,
"Forging Equality in South Africa"
(interview of June 12, 2004)

PALA [pah-lah]

MEANING: guardian, protector • USAGE: Hindu: Sanskrit

Let the wise man guard his thoughts,
which are difficult to perceive, extremely subtle,
which wanders at will. Thought which is well guarded
is the bearer of happiness.
— Buddha

PANCHO [PAHN-choh]

MEANING: one who is free, native of France, a Franc, spearman • USAGE: Spanish form of Francisco (*see* Paco)

The Lord is the Spirit,
and where the Spirit of the Lord is, there is freedom.
— 2 Corinthians 3:17 (ESV)

PANDITA [pan-dee-tah]

MEANING: scholarly, intelligent • USAGE: Hindu: Sanskrit

Discipline is the mark of intelligent living.
— Sathya Sai Baba, *Sathya Sai Baba Speaks*

PANOS [PAH-nohs]

MEANING: all holy • USAGE: Greek form of *Panagiotis*, from Greek *pan* (all) and *hagios* (holy)

May the God of peace make you holy in every way.
— 1 Thessalonians 5:23 (GNT)

PAOLO [POW-loh]

MEANING: small, little • USAGE: Italian form of Paul, from Latin *paulus*

He who is faithful in a very little
is faithful also in much.
— Luke 16:10 (WEB)

PARAMA [pah-rah-mah]

MEANING: supreme, highest • USAGE: Hindu: Sanskrit

Your heart's cry is a real treasure. /
Your heart's cry flies like an eagle /
To reach the highest goal of your purest soul.
— Sri Chinmoy Ghose, *The Wings of Joy*

PARKE, PARK [park]

MEANING: keeper of the park grounds, forest ranger • USAGE: American (*see* Parker)

If a person walks in the woods and listens carefully,
he can learn more than what is in books,
for they speak with the voice of God.
— George Washington Carver

PARKER [PAHR-ker]

MEANING: keeper of the park, forest ranger, park grounds • USAGE: English: from French *parc* (enclosure) or Latin *parricus* (park, grounds)

Nature never did betray the heart that loved her.
— William Wordsworth, "Lines Composed a Few Miles above Tintern Abbey"

PARNEL, PARNELL [par-NEL]

MEANING: rock, stone • USAGE: English form of *Petronel*, from Latin *petro*

Lord… You let me stand on a rock, with my feet firm.
— Psalm 40:1–2 (CEV)

PASCAL [pahs-KAHL]

MEANING: Passover, born during Passover • USAGE: French and German form of Hebrew *Pesach* (the Feast of Unleavened Bread)

Celebrate this Festival of Unleavened Bread,
for it will remind you that I brought your forces out
of the land of Egypt on this very day. This festival
will be a permanent law for you; celebrate this day
from generation to generation.
— Exodus 12:17 (NLT)

P

PASCUAL   [pahs-KWAHL]

MEANING: Passover, born during Passover • USAGE: Spanish form of Pascal (see Pascal)

A cheerful heart has a continual feast.
— Proverbs 15:15b (HCSB)

PASHA   [PAH-shah]

MEANING: small, little • USAGE: Russian form of Pavel (see Paul)

If you're honest in small things,
you'll be honest in big things.
— Luke 16:10a (MSG)

PAT   [pat]

MEANING: patrician, noble one • USAGE: English form of Patrick (see Patrick)

He who does a good deed, is instantly ennobled.
— Ralph Waldo Emerson,
"Divinity School Address"

PATRICIO   [pah-TREE-see-oh]

MEANING: patrician, noble one • USAGE: Spanish form of Patrick (see Patrick)

The noble deviseth noble things;
and to do noble things doth he stand.
— Isaiah 32:8 (DT)

PATRICK   [PAT-rik (Irish, English), pat-REEK (French), PAHT-rik (German)]

MEANING: patrician, noble one • USAGE: Irish, English, French, and German form of Roman family name *Patricius*, from Latin *patricius* (patrician, nobleman)

I arise today, through the strength of Heaven: /
light of Sun, brilliance of Moon, splendour of Fire, /
speed of Lightning, swiftness of Wind, depth of Sea, /
stability of Earth, firmness of Rock.
— "The Breastplate of Saint Patrick"

PATRIZIO   [pah-TREET-zee-oh]

MEANING: patrician, noble one • USAGE: Italian form of Patrick (see Patrick)

Nothing is more noble, nothing more venerable than fidelity. Faithfulness and truth are the most sacred excellences and endowments of the human mind.
— Marcus Tullius Cicero

PAUL   [pahl]

MEANING: small, little • USAGE: English, French, and German form of Roman family name *Paulinus*, from Latin *paulus*

Character may be manifested in the great moments,
but it is made in the small ones.
— Phillips Brooks

PAVEL   [PAH-vel]

MEANING: small, little • USAGE: Russian form of Paul (see Paul)

Be faithful in small things
because it is in them that your strength lies.
— Mother Teresa

PAVLOS   [PAHV-lohs]

MEANING: small, little • USAGE: Greek form of Paul (see Paul)

No act of kindness,
no matter how small, is ever wasted.
— Aesop, "The Lion and the Mouse"

PAX   [paks]

MEANING: peace • USAGE: English form of Paxton, from Latin *pax*

The Lord bless you and keep you;
the Lord make his face to shine upon you,
and be gracious to you; the Lord turn his
countenance upon you and give you peace.
— Numbers 6:24–26 (NIRV)

PAXTON [PAKS-ton]

MEANING: peace, peaceful village • **USAGE:**
English: from Latin *pax* (peace) and English *tun*
(town, village)

Live in harmony and peace.
Then the God of love and peace will be with you.
— 2 Corinthians 13:11b (NLT)

PAYTON, PEYTON [PAY-ton]

MEANING: patrician, noble one, from Paega's town
• **USAGE:** English and Irish surname: Irish form of
Patrick (*see* Patrick); or English surname meaning
Pæga's town
Instead of noblemen, let us have noble villages of men.
— Henry David Thoreau, *Walden*

PEADAR [PAH-der]

MEANING: rock, stone • **USAGE:** Irish and Scottish
form of Peter (*see* Peter)
Deep peace I breathe into you....Deep peace of the
sleeping stones to you!...Deep peace, deep peace!
— Fiona MacLeod, "Invocation of Peace"

PEDER [PEH-der]

MEANING: rock, stone • **USAGE:** Scandinavian
form of Peter (*see* Peter)
The Lord said, "Here is a place near Me.
You are to stand on the rock."
— Exodus 33:21 (HCSB)

PEDR [PEE-dr]

MEANING: rock, stone • **USAGE:** Welsh form of
Peter (*see* Peter)
This stone, which I have set up for a title,
shall be called the house of God.
— Genesis 28:22a (NCV)

PEDRO [PAY-droh]

MEANING: rock, stone • **USAGE:** Spanish form of
Peter (*see* Peter)
Whoso is walking righteously, and is speaking
uprightly...he high places doth inhabit,
strongholds of rock [are] his high tower.
— Isaiah 33:15–16a

PELE, PELEH [PEH-leh]

MEANING: miracle, wonder • **USAGE:** Jewish
There are only two ways to live your life.
One is as though nothing is a miracle.
The other is as though everything is a miracle.
— Albert Einstein

PEPE [PAY-pay]

MEANING: God will add, God will increase •
USAGE: Spanish form of José, from Hebrew
ya'saph (Yahweh will add)
The Lord is faithful and will give you strength.
— 2 Thessalonians 3:3a (NCV)

PEPITO [pay-PEE-toh]

MEANING: God will add, God will increase •
USAGE: Spanish form of José (*see* Pepe)
The Lord make you to increase and abound
in love one toward another.
— 1 Thessalonians 3:12a (WEB)

PERCE [pers]

MEANING: pierce the veil, pierce the valley •
USAGE: English form of Percival (*see* Percival)
Of what significance the light of day, if it is not
the reflection of an inward dawn?—
to what purpose is the veil of night withdrawn,
if the morning reveals nothing to the soul?
— Henry David Thoreau, "Night and Moonlight"

PERCIVAL   [PER-sih-val]

MEANING: pierce the veil, pierce the valley •
USAGE: English: from French *percer voile* (pierce
the veil) or *percer val* (pierce the valley); an
Arthurian knight in writings of Chrétien de Troyes
This hope we have as an anchor of the soul, a hope both
sure and steadfast and one which enters within the veil.
— Hebrews 6:19 (NASB)

PERCY   [PER-see]

MEANING: pierce the veil, pierce the valley •
USAGE: English form of Percival (*see* Percival)
All that is sweet, delightful, and amiable in this world,
in the serenity of the air, the fineness of seasons, the joy
of light, the melody of sounds, the beauty of colours,
the fragrancy of smells, the splendour of precious
stones, is nothing else but Heaven breaking through
the veil of this world, manifesting itself in such
a degree, and darting forth in such variety
so much of its own nature.
— William Law,
An Appeal to All Who Doubt the Truths of the Gospel

PERRY   [PER-ee]

MEANING: pear tree • **USAGE:** English surname:
English *pirige*
For he shall be as a tree planted by the waters,
and that spreadeth out her roots by the river, and shall
not see when heat cometh, but her leaf shall be green;
and shall not be disquieted in the year of drought,
neither shall cease from yielding fruit.
— Jeremiah 17:8 (KJ21)

PETE   [peet]

MEANING: rock, stone • **USAGE:** English form of
Peter (*see* Peter)
Love is the wise man's stone: It divides gold from mud.
— Angelus Silesius, *The Cherubinic Wanderer*
(tr. Maria Shrader)

PETER   [PEE-ter (English), PEH-ter (German)]

MEANING: rock, stone • **USAGE:** English and
German form of Petros, from Greek *petros*
The Lord says, "I'm laying a firm foundation...
a valuable cornerstone proven to be trustworthy."
— Isaiah 28:16 (CEV)

PETROS   [PEH-trohs]

MEANING: rock, stone • **USAGE:** Greek: from
Greek *petros*
You, Lord God, are my fortress,
that mighty rock where I am safe.
— Psalm 94:22 (CEV)

PEZI   [peh-ʒee]

MEANING: grass • **USAGE:** Amerind: Sioux
The Six Grandfathers have placed in this world many
things, all of which should be happy....Like the grasses
showing tender faces to each other, thus we should do,
for this was the wish of the Grandfathers of the World.
— Wallace Black Elk

PHIL   [fil]

MEANING: lover of horses, love • **USAGE:** English
form of Philip (*see* Philip)
Love give me strength!
— William Shakespeare, *Romeo and Juliet*

PHILIP, PHILLIP   [FIL-ip]

MEANING: lover of horses • **USAGE:** English form
of *Philippos*, from Greek *philein* (to love) and *hippos*
(horse)
The horse, the horse! The symbol of surging potency
and power of movement, of action, in man.
— D. H. Lawrence, *Apocalypse*

PHILIPPE   [fee-LEEP]

MEANING: lover of horses • **USAGE:** French form
of Philip (*see* Philip)

Love is always supportive, loyal, hopeful,
and trusting. Love never fails!
— 1 Corinthians 13:7–8a (CEV)

PHOENIX   *[FEE-niks]*

MEANING: dark red, immortal, resurrected, phoenix bird • **USAGE:** English: from Greek *phoinix* (dark red); Greek symbol of immortality and resurrection

Love is life. And life hath immortality.
— Emily Dickinson, "Proof"

PIERCE   *[peers]*

MEANING: rock, stone • **USAGE:** English and Irish form of Peter (*see* Peter)

Look to the rock from which you were cut
and to the quarry from which you were hewn.
— Isaiah 51:1b (NIV)

PIERO   *[pee-AYR-oh]*

MEANING: rock, stone • **USAGE:** Italian form of Peter (*see* Peter)

He like a rock in the sea unshaken stands his ground.
— Virgil

PIERRE   *[pee-AYR]*

MEANING: rock, stone • **USAGE:** French form of Peter (*see* Peter)

A rock pile ceases to be a rock pile
the moment a single man contemplates it,
bearing within him the image of a cathedral.
— Antoine de Saint-Exupéry, *Flight to Arras*
(tr. Lewis Galantière)

PIERS   *[peers]*

MEANING: rock, stone • **USAGE:** English and Irish form of Peter (*see* Peter)

The Lord God says: I will put a stone in the
ground…a tested stone. Everything will be built
on this important and precious rock.
— Isaiah 28:16a (NCV)

PIETRO   *[pee-EH-troh]*

MEANING: rock, stone • **USAGE:** Italian form of Peter, from Greek *petros*

The Lord is my rock, my protection.
— Psalm 18:2a (NCV)

PING   *[peeng]*

MEANING: peaceful, smooth • **USAGE:** Chinese

Whoever has reached a state of freedom through perfect
wisdom, peaceful and unshakable, is nonviolent in his
mind, his speech, his action.
— Buddha, *The Dhammapada*
(tr. Ananda Maitreya)

PIP   *[pip]*

MEANING: lover of horses • **USAGE:** English form of Philip (*see* Philip)

Love is kind and patient.
— 1 Corinthians 13:4a (CEV)

PIPER   *[PIE-per]*

MEANING: flute player, pipe player • **USAGE:** American: from English *pipe* (pipe, flute) or *pipere* (pipe player)

Make me an instrument which only truth can speak.
— Peace Pilgrim, *Peace Pilgrim*

PIR   *[peer]*

MEANING: spiritual guide • **USAGE:** Persian

The spiritual guide performs the role of Cupid in
bringing the seeking souls closer to God.
— Hazrat Inayat Khan, *The Gayan* (cd. *The Gayani*
Meditations, Volume 1, tr. Cecil Touchon)

PLACIDO, PLÁCIDO   *[plah-SEE-doh*
(Italian), PLAH-cee-doh (Spanish)]

MEANING: calm, serene, tranquil, peaceful • **USAGE:** Italian and Spanish: from Latin *placidus* (placid, calm)

Peace be within thy walls…peace be within thee.
— Psalm 122:7–8 (ASV)

PLATO   [PLAY-toh]

MEANING: broad-shouldered, strong-shouldered •
USAGE: Greek: from Greek *platys*
Let the beloved of the Lord rest secure in Him,
for he shields him all day long, and the one the Lord
loves rests between his shoulders.
— Deuteronomy 33:12 (NIV)

POLANI   [poh-LAH-nee]

MEANING: handsome, clean, pure • **USAGE:**
Hawaiian
Handsome is the man; good are his words.
— Hawaiian proverb
(tr. Mary Pukui in *'Olelo No'eau*)

PORTER   [POR-ter]

MEANING: gate, gatekeeper, one who carries •
USAGE: English: from Latin *porte* (gate, door); or
from English *portour* (to carry)
Enter by this gateway and seek the way of honor,
the light of truth, the will to work for men.
— Edwin A. Alderman (inscription on the
University of Virginia Medical College archway)

PRADEEP, PRADIP   [prah-deep]

MEANING: light, luminous, radiant • **USAGE:**
Hindu: from Sanskrit *pradipa*
By the day and night the man who is awake
shines in the radiance of the spirit.
— Buddha, *The Dhammapada* (tr. Thomas Byrom)

PRADOSH   [prah-dohsh]

MEANING: twilight, sunset • **USAGE:** Hindu:
Sanskrit
The prelude of the night is commenced in the music of
the sunset, in its solemn hymn to the ineffable dark
— Rabindranath Tagore, *Stray Birds*

PRAJNA   [prahj-nah]

MEANING: wise, supremely wise • **USAGE:** Hindu:
Sanskrit
Just as an arrowsmith shapes an arrow to perfection
with fire, so does the wise man shape his mind.
— Buddha, *The Dhammapada*
(tr. Ananda Maitreya)

PRANA   [PRAH-nah]

MEANING: life-breath, life-force • **USAGE:** Hindu:
from Sanskrit *pra* (forth) and *ana* (breathing)
The same stream of life that runs through
my veins night and day runs through the world
and dances in rhythmic measure.
— Rabindranath Tagore, "The Stream of Life"

PREM   [prem]

MEANING: love, affection • **USAGE:** Hindu: from
Sanskrit *prema*
Love is the song of the soul, singing to God.
— Paramahansa Yogananda, *Songs of the Soul*

PRESCOT, PRESCOTT   [PRES-kot]

MEANING: priest's cottage • **USAGE:** English
surname: from English *preost* (priest) and *cote*
(cottage, hut)
You are living stones that God is building
into his spiritual temple.
What's more, you are his holy priests.
— 1 Peter 2:5a (NLT)

PRESLEY   [PRES-lee]

MEANING: priest's field • **USAGE:** English
surname: from English *preost* (priest) and *leah*
(meadow, field)
I shall always be a priest of love.
— D. H. Lawrence (letter of December 25, 1912)

PRIMO [PREE-moh]

MEANING: first • USAGE: Italian, Portuguese, and Spanish: from *primus*

> *Seek ye first the Kingdom of God and His*
> *righteousness, and all these things*
> *shall be added unto you.*
> — Matthew 6:33 (KJ21)

PRINCE [prins]

MEANING: chief, first, royal title, son of the king • USAGE: English: from Latin *princeps*

> *Thou shalt be a...*
> *royal diadem in the hand of thy God.*
> — Isaiah 62:3 (DT)

PRYCE [pries]

MEANING: son of Rhys, enthusiastic, passionate, ardent • USAGE: Welsh: from *ap* (son) and Rhys (from Welsh *rhys*)

> *Nothing great was ever achieved without enthusiasm.*
> — Ralph Waldo Emerson, "Circles"

PUNEET [poo-neet]

MEANING: pure • USAGE: Hindu

> *True knowledge is the greatest purifier of the soul.*
> — *Bhagavad Gita* (tr. Eknath Easwaran)

PYOTR [pee-OH-ter]

MEANING: rock, stone • USAGE: Russian form of Peter, from Greek *petros*

> *He alone is my rock and the One Who saves me.*
> *He is my strong place. I will not be shaken.*
> — Psalm 62:2 (NLV)

Q

QAIM [kah-eem]

MEANING: one who performs (a duty), upright • USAGE: Muslim

> *Surely the most honorable of you with Allah*
> *is the one among you most careful (of his duty)*
> — Koran, The Star 50.16b (SKR)

QIANG [chee-ahng]

MEANING: strong, powerful • USAGE: Chinese

> *He who knows men is clever; / He who knows himself*
> *has insight. / He who conquers men has force; /*
> *He who conquers himself is truly strong.*
> — Lao Tzu, *Tao Te Ching* (tr. Lionel Giles)

QUANAH [kwah-nah]

MEANING: fragrant, sweet aroma • USAGE: Amerind: Comanche

> *May the rain always fall in due season; and in the*
> *warmth of the sunshine after the rain, may the earth*
> *yield bountifully. May peace and contentment dwell*
> *with you and your children forever.*
> — Quanah Parker

QUENTIN, QUINTEN, QUINTON [KWIN-tin]

MEANING: queen's town, fifth, five • USAGE: English: from English *cwen* (queen) and *tun* (town, village); or from Latin *quintus* (fifth, five); a fifth-born child

> *Lo, the kingdom of God is within you.*
> — Luke 17:21b (DR)

QUINCY [KWIN-see]

MEANING: five, fifth • USAGE: English form of *Quintus*, from Latin *quintus* (fifth, five)

> *Man has no Body distinct from his Soul; for that called*
> *Body is a portion of Soul discerned by the five Senses,*
> *the chief inlets of Soul in this age.*
> — William Blake, *The Marriage of Heaven and Hell*

QUINLAN [KWIN-len]

MEANING: handsome, slender • USAGE: Irish surname: from Gaelic *caoin* (fair, handsome) and *dealbh* (form); or from Gaelic *caoinlean* (slender)

Q

You are the most handsome of all men!
You speak in an impressive and fitting manner!
— Psalm 45:2 (NEB)

QUINN   *[kwin]*

MEANING: wise, intelligent • **USAGE:** Irish and
English: form of Irish surname *O'Cuinn*, from
Gaelic *conn*

A wise man shall be filled with blessing;
and all they that see him shall count him happy.
— Ben Sira 37:24 (KJV Apocrypha)

QUINO   *[KEE-noh]*

MEANING: God will establish • **USAGE:** Spanish
form of Joaquín, from Hebrew *yehoyakim* (Yahweh
will establish)

Commit your work to the Lord,
and your plans will be established.
— Proverbs 16:3 (ESV)

QUIQUE   *[KEE-kay]*

MEANING: ruler of the home, house leader •
USAGE: Spanish form of Enrique, from German
heim (home, house) and *rik* (rule, lead)

May it please thee to bless the house of thy servant,
that it may continue for ever before thee; for what thou,
O Lord, hast blessed is blessed for ever.
— 1 Chronicles 17:27 (RSV)

QUITO   *[KEE-toh]*

MEANING: one who is free, native of France,
a Franc, spearman • **USAGE:** Spanish form of
Francisco, from Latin *Franciscus* (a Frenchman);
from French *franc* (free, freeman); or from German
franco (spear used by the Franks, a Germanic tribe)

A man is morally free when, in full possession of his
living humanity, he judges the world, and judges other
men, with uncompromising sincerity.
— George Santayana (letter of December 11, 1934)

R

RAAID   *[rah-eed]*

MEANING: pioneer, explorer, guide • **USAGE:**
Muslim: from Arabic *raid*

A traveler am I and a navigator, and every day
I discover a new region within my soul.
— Kahlil Gibran, *Sand and Foam*

RADEK   *[rah-dek]*

MEANING: famous ruler, renowned leader •
USAGE: Czech and Polish form of Roderick, from
German *hrod* (fame, praise) and *rik* (rule, lead)

A good name is to be chosen rather than great riches,
and favor is better than silver or gold.
— Proverbs 22:1 (ESV)

RADIMIR   *[rah-dee-meer]*

MEANING: great joy, happy and peaceful • **USAGE:**
Russian and Czech: from Slavic *rad* (happy, joyful)
and *meri* (great, famous) or *mir* (peace)

Happy shalt thou be, and it shall be well with thee.
— Psalm 128:2b (KJ21)

RADLEY   *[RAD-lee]*

MEANING: red meadow, red field • **USAGE:**
English surname: from English *read* (red) and *leah*
(meadow, field)

For we are God's fellow workers; you are God's field.
— 1 Corinthians 3:9b (NASB)

RADULF   *[RAHD-ulf]*

MEANING: wolf counsel, wolf adviser • **USAGE:**
German: from German *rad* (counsel, advice) and
wulf (wolf)

Counsel shall keep thee,
and prudence shall preserve thee.
— Proverbs 2:11 (DR)

RAFAEL [rah-fah-AYL]

MEANING: God has healed • USAGE: Spanish and German form of Raphael, from Hebrew *repha'el*
There is a light in this world, a healing spirit more powerful than any darkness we may encounter.
— Mother Teresa

RAFE [rayf]

MEANING: wise wolf, wolf counsel • USAGE: English form of Ralph, from German *rad* (advice, judgment) and *wulf* (wolf)
May He grant thee according to thine own heart, and fulfill all thy counsel.
— Psalm 20:4 (KJ21)

RAFER [RAY-fer]

MEANING: wolf adviser, wolf counsel, God has healed • USAGE: American form of Ralph (see Rafe) or of Rafael (see Rafael)
One cool judgment is worth a thousand hasty counsels. The thing to be supplied is light, not heat.
— Woodrow Wilson (speech of January 29, 1916)

RAFFERTY [RAF-er-tee]

MEANING: prosperous, wealthy • USAGE: Irish surname: from Gaelic *rafaireacht*
The blessing of the Lord brings wealth, and he adds no trouble to it.
— Proverbs 10:22 (NIV)

RAFI [RAH-fee]

MEANING: God has healed • USAGE: Jewish form of Refael (see Rafael)
I am the Lord that healeth thee.
— Exodus 15:26 (MT)

RAFI [rah-fee]

MEANING: friend, companion • USAGE: Muslim form of Rafiq (see Rafiq)

To love is one thing, to understand is another; he who loves is a devotee, but he who understands is a friend.
— Hazrat Inayat Khan, *The Bowl of Saki*

RAFID, RAFEED [rah-feed]

MEANING: helper, assistant, stream • USAGE: Muslim: from Arabic *rafid* (one who assists, stream)
If Allah is your helper none can overcome you.
— Koran, The Family of Imran 3.160a (PIC)

RAFIQ, RAFEEQ [rah-FEEK]

MEANING: friend, companion • USAGE: Muslim: from Arabic *rafaqa* (be a friend)
Harmony is the soul of companionship.
— Arabic proverb

RAGNAR [RAHN-ahr]

MEANING: army counselor • USAGE: Scandinavian: from Norse *ragn* (advice, judgment) and *arr* (army)
A good man's words are wise, and he is always fair.
— Psalm 37:30 (GNT)

RAGNVALD [RAHN-vahlt]

MEANING: adviser to the ruler • USAGE: Scandinavian: from Norse *ragn* (adviser) and *valdr* (to rule)
A wise man will hear and increase in learning, and a man of understanding will acquire wise counsel.
— Proverbs 1:5 (NASB)

RAHIM, RAHEEM [rah-HEEM]

MEANING: compassionate, kind, merciful • USAGE: Muslim
The wise man learns what draws God / Near. / It is the beauty of compassion / In your heart.
— Hafiz, "It Is Unanimous"
(tr. Daniel Ladinsky in *The Gift*)

R

RAIMUND [RIE-moont]

MEANING: counselor's protection • **USAGE:** German form of Raymond, from German *ragin* (advice, counsel) and *mund* (hand, protection)

Counsel in the heart of man is like deep water.
— Proverbs 20:5a (NKJV)

RAIMUNDO [rie-MOON-doh]

MEANING: counselor's protection • **USAGE:** Spanish form of Raymond (*see* Raimund)

Make the counsel of your heart to stand;
for there is none more faithful to you than it.
— Sirach 37:13 (WEB Apocrypha)

RAIN, RAINE [rayn]

MEANING: rain, rainfall • **USAGE:** English: from English *regn*

A single gentle rain makes the grass
many shades greener. So our prospects brighten
on the influx of better thoughts.
— Henry David Thoreau, *Walden*

RAINER, REINER [RIE-ner]

MEANING: army adviser • **USAGE:** German form of *Raganhar*, from German *ragin* (advice, counsel) and *hari* (army)

A wise man has great power, and a man who has
knowledge increases his strength.
— Proverbs 24:5 (NIRV)

RAJIH, RAAJI [rah-jee]

MEANING: hope, wish, desire • **USAGE:** Muslim: from Arabic *raji*

Whoso desireth the reward of the world,
We bestow on him thereof; and whoso desireth the
reward of the Hereafter, We bestow on him thereof.
We shall reward the thankful.
— Koran, The Family of Imran 3.145b (PIC)

RAKIN, RAKEEN [rah-keen]

MEANING: reliable, firm, steadfast • **USAGE:** Muslim: from Arabic *rakin* (to be reliable, to be firm)

Be steadfast! Lo! Allah is with the steadfast.
— Koran, The Spoils of War 8.46b (PIC)

RALPH [ralf, rayf (English), rahlf (German, Scandinavian)]

MEANING: wise wolf, wolf counsel • **USAGE:** English, German, and Scandinavian form of *Radulf*, from German *rad* (advice, counsel) and *wulf* (wolf)

For the strength of the Pack is the Wolf,
and the strength of the Wolf is the Pack.
— Rudyard Kipling, *The Jungle Book*

RAM [rahm]

MEANING: high, lofty, exalted • **USAGE:** Jewish

He that walketh righteously,
and speaketh uprightly…
He shall dwell on high.
— Isaiah 33:15–16a (MT)

RAMA [rah-mah]

MEANING: pleasing, delightful • **USAGE:** Hindu: from Sanskrit *rama*

The wise person delights in the truth
and follows the law of the awakened.
— Buddha, *The Dhammapada* (tr. Thomas Byrom)

RAMIRO [rah-MEE-roh]

MEANING: famous counselor, renowned adviser • **USAGE:** Spanish form of *Ramirus*, from German *ragin* (advice) and *mari* (famous)

Blessed be thy advice, and blessed be thou.
— 1 Samuel 25:33a (KJV)

RAMON [rah-MOHN]

MEANING: counselor's protection • **USAGE:**
Spanish form of Raymond (*see* Raimund)
Counsel in the heart of man is like deep water.
— Proverbs 20:5a (ASV)

RAMSEY, RAMSAY [RAM-see]

MEANING: raven island, ram island, wild garlic
island • **USAGE:** Scottish surname: from English
hræfn (raven) and *eg* (island), *ramm* (ram) and *eg*
(island), or *hramsa* (wild garlic) and *eg* (island)
*If I take the wings of the morning, and dwell in the
uttermost parts of the sea, even there Your hand shall
lead me, and Your right hand shall hold me.*
— Psalm 139:9–10 (NKJV)

RAN [rahn]

MEANING: he is singing • **USAGE:** Jewish
*The psalm reads: "For singing to our God is good."
It is good if man can so bring it about
that God sings within him.*
— Martin Buber,
Ten Rungs: Collected Hasidic Sayings

RANDALL, RANDAL [RAN-del]

MEANING: wolf shield, shield wolf • **USAGE:**
English surname: from German *rand* (edge of a
shield) and *wolf* (wolf)
The gaze of the wolf reaches into our soul.
— Barry Lopez

RANDOLF, RANDOLPH [RAN-dolf (English), RAHN-dolf (German)]

MEANING: wolf shield, shield wolf • **USAGE:**
English and German form of *Randulfr*, from
German *rand* (edge of a shield) and *wulf* (wolf)
*My God is my protection, and with him I am safe.
He protects me like a shield;
he defends me and keeps me safe.*
— 2 Samuel 22:3–4 (NEB)

RANDY [RAN-dee]

MEANING: wolf shield, shield wolf • **USAGE:**
English form of Randall or Randolf (*see* Randolf)
*Lord, you bless those who live right,
and you shield them with your kindness.*
— Psalm 5:12 (CEV)

RANGER [RAN-ger]

MEANING: forest ranger • **USAGE:** American:
from English *ranger*
*It is not so much for its beauty that the forest makes a
claim upon men's hearts, as for that subtle something,
that quality of air that emanates from old trees, that so
wonderfully changes and renews a weary spirit.*
— Robert Louis Stevenson, "Forest Notes"

RANJAN [rahn-jahn]

MEANING: delighted, happy, joyous • **USAGE:**
Hindu
*Your soul, being the reflection of
the ever-joyous Spirit, is happiness itself.*
— Paramahansa Yogananda

RAOUL [rah-OOL]

MEANING: wise wolf, wolf counsel • **USAGE:**
French form of Ralph, from German *rad* (advice,
counsel) and *wulf* (wolf)
Blessed be thy discretion, and blessed be thou.
— 1 Samuel 25:33a (ASV)

RAPHAEL [rah-feh-EL]

MEANING: God has healed • **USAGE:** French and
English form of Refael, from Hebrew *repha'el*
*A deep man believes in miracles,
waits for them, believes…that the heart's blessing
can heal; that love can exalt talent;
can overcome all odds.*
— Ralph Waldo Emerson, *The Conduct of Life*

R

RASA   [rah-sah]

MEANING: taste, essence, nectar • USAGE: Hindu: Sanskrit

That which is the Self-Creator is verily Nectar; for having gained that very Nectar, one becomes blissful.
— *Taittiriya Upanishad*

RASHAD, RAASHAD   [rah-shahd]

MEANING: rightly guided • USAGE: Muslim: from Arabic *rashada* (to follow the right course)

Wherewith Allah guideth all who seek His good pleasure to ways of peace and safety, and leadeth them out of darkness, by His will, unto the light, guideth them to a path that is straight.
— Koran, The Table Spread 5.16 (ALI)

RASHID, RAASHID   [rah-sheed]

MEANING: rightly guided • USAGE: Muslim: from Arabic *rashada* (to follow the right course)

*Whom Allah guides,
there is none that can lead him astray.*
— Koran, The Companies 39.37a (SKR)

RASIN, RASEEN   [RAH-seen]

MEANING: calm, peaceful • USAGE: Muslim

Peace be on you.
— Koran, The Bee 16.32b (SKR)

RASMUS   [RAHS-mus]

MEANING: love • USAGE: Scandinavian form of *Erasmus,* from Greek *erasmios* (to love)

This I pray, that your love may abound yet more and more in full knowledge and all intelligence.
— Philippians 1:9 (DT)

RAUL, RAÚL   [rah-OOL]

MEANING: wolf counsel, wolf adviser • USAGE: German, Italian, and Spanish form of Ralph, from German *rad* (advice, counsel) and *wulf* (wolf)

*May He grant you your heart's desire,
and fulfill all your counsel.*
— Psalm 20:4 (WEB)

RAVI   [rah-VEE, RAH-vee]

MEANING: teacher • USAGE: Jewish
It is the supreme art of the teacher to awaken joy in creative expression and knowledge.
— Albert Einstein (motto for the Astronomy Building, Pasadena Junior College)

RAY   [ray]

MEANING: counselor's protection • USAGE: English form of Raymond (*see* Raymond)
Your insight and understanding will protect you.
— Proverbs 2:11 (GNT)

RAYMOND   [RAY-mond (English), ray-MOHN (French)]

MEANING: counselor's protection • USAGE: English and French form of *Raginmund,* from German *ragin* (advice, counsel) and *mund* (hand, protection)

*Heed the counsel of your own heart,
for no one is more faithful to you than it is.*
— Sirach 37:13 (NIRV Apocrypha)

RAYNER, RAYNOR   [RAY-ner]

MEANING: army adviser • USAGE: English surname: form of *Raganhar,* from German *ragin* (advice, counsel) and *hari* (army)

He who has put forth his total strength in fit actions, has the richest return of wisdom.
— Ralph Waldo Emerson, "The American Scholar"

RAZI   [rah-ʒee]

MEANING: satisfied, content • USAGE: Muslim: from Arabic *razi*

Peace be on you.
— Koran, The Bee 16:32b (ALI)

R

REAGAN [*RAY-gan*]

MEANING: little king, little royal one, spontaneous, impulsive • USAGE: Irish and English form of Irish surname *O'Riagain*, from Gaelic *ri* (king) and diminutive *-an;* or from Gaelic *riogach* (impulsive, rash)

> *The only rule is, do what you really,*
> *impulsively, wish to do. But always act*
> *on your own responsibility, sincerely.*
> *And have the courage of your own strong emotion.*
> — D. H. Lawrence, *Fantasia of the Unconscious*

RED, REDD [*red*]

MEANING: red, redheaded, ruddy • USAGE: English: from English *read* (red)

> *He was ruddy,*
> *with beautiful eyes and a handsome appearance.*
> — 1 Samuel 16:12b (NASB)

REESE [*rees*]

MEANING: enthusiastic, passionate, ardent • USAGE: English form of Rhys, from Welsh *rhys*

> *The world belongs to the energetic man.*
> — Ralph Waldo Emerson, "Resources"

REEVE [*reev*]

MEANING: steward, bailiff • USAGE: English surname: from English *reeve*

> *Dispense true justice,*
> *and practice kindness and compassion.*
> — Zechariah 7:9b (NASB)

REFAEL, REPHAEL [*reh-fah-EHL*]

MEANING: God has healed • USAGE: Jewish: from Hebrew *repha'el*

> *I am the Lord your healer.*
> — Exodus 15:26b (JPS)

REGIN [*REE-gin*]

MEANING: adviser, counselor, judge • USAGE: Scandinavian: from Norse *ragn*

> *Thou [shalt] understand justice, and judgment,*
> *and equity, and every good path.*
> — Proverbs 2:10 (DR)

REGINALD, REGINOLD [*REJ-eh-nahld*]

MEANING: ruling with power, powerful adviser • USAGE: English form of *Raganald*, from German *ragin* (advice, counsel) and *wald* (rule, power)

> *Praised be your good judgment!*
> — 1 Samuel 25:33a (NEB)

RÉGIS, REGIS [*REH-zhee (French), REE-jis (English)*]

MEANING: ruler, manager, leader • USAGE: French and English: from French *régir*

> *A leader must aim high,*
> *see big, judge widely.*
> — Charles de Gaulle

REID, REED [*reed*]

MEANING: red, redheaded, ruddy-complexioned • USAGE: Scottish and English surname: from English *read* (red)

> *Red is the secret of life.*
> — Alice Meynell, *The Colour of Life*

REINALDO [*rie-NAHL-doh*]

MEANING: ruling with power, powerful adviser • USAGE: Spanish form of Reginald (*see* Reginald)

> *Blessed is your advice and blessed are you.*
> — 1 Samuel 25:33a (NKJV)

REINE [*RIE-neh*]

MEANING: adviser, counselor • USAGE: Swedish, Finnish, and Norwegian: from Norse *ragn*

R

A wise man will hear, and will increase learning; and a man of understanding shall attain unto wise counsels.
— Proverbs 1:5 (KJV)

RÉMY   *[REH-mee]*

MEANING: oarsman, rower • **USAGE:** French: from Latin *remigis*
The Lord will send a blessing…
on everything you put your hand to.
— Deuteronomy 28:8 (NIV)

RENARD   *[reh-NAHR]*

MEANING: brave counselor, strong adviser • **USAGE:** French: from German *ragin* (advice, counsel) and *hart* (hardy, strong, brave)
A wise person knows the proper time and procedure. For there is a proper time and procedure for every matter.
— Ecclesiastes 8:5b–6a (NEB)

RENATO   *[ray-NAH-toh]*

MEANING: reborn, born again • **USAGE:** Spanish, Italian, and Portuguese: from Latin *renascor*
You have been born again — not of perishable seed but of imperishable.
— 1 Peter 1:23a (HCSB)

RENAUD   *[reh-NOH]*

MEANING: ruling with power, powerful adviser • **USAGE:** French form of Reginald (*see* Reginald)
Thou shalt understand righteousness, and judgment, and equity; yea, every good path.
— Proverbs 2:9 (KJV)

RENÉ   *[reh-NAY]*

MEANING: reborn, born again • **USAGE:** French: from Latin *renascor*
We are born, so to speak, twice over;
born into existence, and born into life;
born a human being, and born a man.
— Jean-Jacques Rousseau, *Emile*

RENNY   *[REN-ee]*

MEANING: ruling with power, powerful adviser • **USAGE:** English form of Reginald (*see* Reginald)
A wise man's heart discerns
both time and judgment, because for every matter
there is a time and judgment.
— Ecclesiastes 8:5b–6a (NKJV)

RENO   *[REE-noh]*

MEANING: flowing, to flow • **USAGE:** Irish: from Gaelic *reie* (to flow); rivers in Italy and Nevada
The good man brings good things
out of the good stored up in his heart….
For out of the overflow of his heart his mouth speaks.
— Luke 6:45 (NIV)

RENZO   *[RAYN-ʒoh]*

MEANING: laurel tree, laurel wreath • **USAGE:** Italian form of Lorenzo, from Latin *laurus*
Blessed is the man who trusts in the Lord,
and whose hope is the Lord. For he shall be like a tree planted by the waters, which spreads out its roots by the river, and will not fear when heat comes; but its leaf will be green, and will not be anxious in the year of drought, nor will cease from yielding fruit.
— Jeremiah 17:8 (NKJV)

REUBEN   *[ROO-ben]*

MEANING: Behold, a son! • **USAGE:** English form of Reuven (*see* Reuven)
Now, my son, the Lord be with thee; and prosper thou.
— 1 Chronicles 22:11a (KJ21)

REUVEN   *[reh-oo-VEHN, ROO-ven]*

MEANING: Behold, a son! • **USAGE:** Jewish: from Hebrew *ra'ah* (he saw) and *ben* (son)
Blessed of the Lord be my son.
— Judges 17:2b (JPS)

REX [reks]

MEANING: king, royal one • **USAGE:** English: from Latin *rex* (king)

> *What is man that You remember him,*
> *or the son of man that You care for him?*
> *You made him lower than the angels for a short time;*
> *You crowned him with glory and honor.*
> — Hebrews 2:6b–7 (HCSB)

RHETT [ret]

MEANING: adviser, counselor • **USAGE:** English and Welsh: from Dutch *raet*

> *May He grant you your heart's desire*
> *and fulfill all your counsel!*
> — Psalm 20:4 (NASB)

RHYS [hrees (Welsh), rees (English)]

MEANING: enthusiastic, passionate, ardent • **USAGE:** Welsh and English: from Welsh *rhys*

> *Enthusiasm is the height of man;*
> *it is the passing from the human to the divine.*
> — Ralph Waldo Emerson, "The Superlative"

RICARDO [ree-KAHR-doh]

MEANING: powerful ruler, strong leader • **USAGE:** Spanish and Portuguese form of Richard (*see* Richard)

> *A wise man is strong,*
> *and a man of knowledge increaseth strength.*
> — Proverbs 24:5 (DT)

RICCARDO [ree-KAHR-doh]

MEANING: powerful ruler, strong leader • **USAGE:** Italian form of Richard (*see* Richard)

> *Reason and calm judgment:*
> *the qualities especially belonging to a leader.*
> — Publius Cornelius Tacitus

RICH [rich]

MEANING: powerful ruler, strong leader • **USAGE:** English form of Richard (*see* Richard)

> *Be a good and strong leader.*
> — 1 Kings 2:2b (NCV)

RICHARD [RICH-ard (English), ree-SHAHR (French), RIHK-art (German)]

MEANING: powerful ruler, strong leader • **USAGE:** English, French, and German form of *Richart*, from German *rik* (rule, lead) and *hart* (hardy, strong, brave)

> *He who reigns within himself and rules passions,*
> *desires, and fears is more than a king.*
> — John Milton, *Paradise Regained*

RICK [rik]

MEANING: powerful ruler, strong leader • **USAGE:** English form of Richard (*see* Richard)

> *Self-control is strength; Right Thought is mastery;*
> *Calmness is power.*
> — James Allen, *As a Man Thinketh*

RICO [REE-koh]

MEANING: powerful ruler, strong leader, peaceful ruler, leader of peace, ruler of the home • **USAGE:** Spanish: form of Ricardo (*see* Richard); form of Federico, from German *frid* (peace) and *rik* (rule, lead); or form of Enrico, from German *heim* (home, house) and *rik* (rule, lead)

> *Peace be within your walls…peace be within you.*
> — Psalm 122:7–8 (ESV)

RIKARD [rih-KAHR, REE-kahr]

MEANING: powerful ruler, strong leader • **USAGE:** Scandinavian form of Richard (*see* Richard)

> *God has not given us a spirit of fear,*
> *but of power and of love and of a sound mind.*
> — 2 Timothy 1:7 (NKJV)

R

RILEY [RIE-lee]

MEANING: courageous, valiant, brave, from the rye meadow • USAGE: Irish and English surname: from Gaelic *raghalach* (courageous, valiant); or from English *ryge* (rye) and *leah* (meadow, field)

The Lord is with thee, O most valiant of men.
— Judges 6:12b (DR)

RINALDO [ree-NAHL-doh]

MEANING: ruling with power, powerful adviser • USAGE: Italian form of Reginald, from German *ragin* (advice, counsel) and *wald* (rule, power)

Judge fairly between each person
and his fellow or foreigner. Don't play favorites;
treat the little and the big alike;
listen carefully to each.
— Deuteronomy 1:17a (MSG)

RIORDAN [REE-or-den]

MEANING: little poet-king • USAGE: Irish form of *Rioghbhardan*, from Gaelic *riogh* (king), *bard* (poet), and diminutive *-an*

For You meet him with the blessings of goodness;
You set a crown of pure gold upon his head.
— Psalm 21:3 (NKJV)

RISHI [rih-shih]

MEANING: sage, wise • USAGE: Hindu: Sanskrit

The flowing river has become the sea; /
The illumined sage has become the Self.
— *Mundaka Upanishad* (tr. Eknath Easwaran)

RIVER [RIV-er]

MEANING: river, abundant flow of water • USAGE: American: from English *rivere*

Eventually, all things merge into one,
and a river runs through it.
— Norman Maclean, *A River Runs Through It*

ROALD [ROH-ahl]

MEANING: famous ruler • USAGE: Norwegian: from Norse *hroðr* (famous) and *valdr* (to rule)

O Lord…you meet him with rich blessings;
you set a crown of fine gold upon his head.
— Psalm 21:1–3 (ESV)

ROB [rob]

MEANING: brightly famous, shining with fame • USAGE: English form of Robert (*see* Robert)

Knowledge is power as well as fame.
— Rufus Choate, "The Power of a State Developed by Mental Culture"

ROBERT [ROB-ert (English), roh-BAYR (French), ROH-barht (German, Scandinavian), ROH-bert (Russian)]

MEANING: brightly famous, shining with fame • USAGE: English, French, German, Russian, and Scandinavian form of *Hrodberht*, from German *hrod* (fame) and *beraht* (bright, shining)

A reputation, then, for good judgment, for fair dealing,
for truth, and for rectitude, is itself a fortune.
— Henry Ward Beecher,
"Morality the Basis of Piety"

ROBERTO [roh-BAYR-toh]

MEANING: brightly famous, shining with fame • USAGE: Spanish and Italian form of Robert (*see* Robert)

Make your light shine.
Be good and honest and truthful.
— Ephesians 5:9 (CEV)

ROBIN [ROB-in]

MEANING: brightly famous, shining with fame, robin, songbird • USAGE: English form of Robert (*see* Robert); or from English *robin* (robin, songbird)

No bird soars too high if he soars with his own wings.
— William Blake, *The Marriage of Heaven and Hell*

ROC [rok]

MEANING: curly-haired • USAGE: Irish: from Gaelic *rocai*
You [God] anoint my head with oil; my cup runs over.
— Psalm 23:5b (NKJV)

ROCCO [ROK-oh]

MEANING: rest, peace • USAGE: Italian form of Roch (*see* Roch)
The God of peace will be with you.
— Philippians 4:9b (NLT)

ROCH [rosh]

MEANING: rest, peace • USAGE: French form of Rocco, from German *hrok*
You will rest safe and secure,
filled with hope and emptied of worry.
— Job 11:18 (CEV)

ROCKY [ROK-ee]

MEANING: rock, stone, rest • USAGE: English: from English *rocc* (stone, rock); or form of Rocco (*see* Roch)
He raiseth up on a rock my feet,
He is establishing my steps.
— Psalm 40:2b (YLT)

ROD [rod]

MEANING: famous ruler, renowned leader, famous island • USAGE: English: form of Roderick (*see* Roderick) or of Rodney (*see* Rodney)
A leader has the vision and conviction
that a dream can be achieved. He inspires
the power and energy to get it done.
— Ralph Nader

RODERICK [ROD-eh-rik (Scottish, English), ROH-deh-rik (German)]

MEANING: famous ruler, renowned leader • USAGE: Scottish, English, and German form of *Hrodrik*, from German *hrod* (fame, praise) and *rik* (rule, lead)
Conscience and love, when they govern the character,
are accepted as its rulers.
— James Freeman Clarke, *Self-Culture*

RODGE [rodj]

MEANING: famous spear, renowned spearman • USAGE: English form of Roger (*see* Roger)
It is God who arms me with strength
and keeps my way secure.
— Psalm 18:32 (NIV)

RODNEY [ROD-nee]

MEANING: famous island • USAGE: English: from German *hrod* (fame, praise) and Norse *ey* (island)
No man is an island entire of itself; every man is a part
of the continent, a piece of the main.
— John Donne, "Devotion XVII"

RODOLFO [roh-DAHL-foh]

MEANING: famous wolf, wolf fame • USAGE: Italian and Spanish form of Rudolph, from German *hrod* (fame, praise) and *wulf* (wolf)
A good name is more desirable than great riches;
to be esteemed is better than silver or gold.
— Proverbs 22:1 (NIV)

RODRIGO [rohd-REE-goh]

MEANING: famous ruler, renowned leader • USAGE: Spanish and Italian form of Roderick (*see* Roderick)
A good leader plans to do good,
and those good things make him a good leader.
— Isaiah 32:8 (NCV)

R

RODRIGUE [roh-DREEG]

MEANING: famous ruler, renowned leader •
USAGE: French form of Roderick (see Roderick)
Example is not the main thing in influencing others.
It is the only thing.
— Albert Schweitzer

ROGAN [ROH-gan]

MEANING: red, redheaded, ruddy-complexioned •
USAGE: Irish: from Gaelic *ruadh*
He was ruddy, and withal of a beautiful countenance,
and goodly to look to.
— 1 Samuel 16:12b (KJV)

ROGELIO [roh-HEE-lee-oh]

MEANING: requested, prayed for, wished for •
USAGE: Spanish form of *Rogelius*, from Latin
rogatus (request)
I pray that you may enjoy good health
and that all may go well with you,
even as your soul is getting along well.
— 3 John 1:2 (NIV)

ROGER [RAH-jer (English), roh-ZHEH (French), ROH-jehr (German)]

MEANING: famous spear, renowned spearman
• USAGE: English, French, and German form of
Hrodger, from German *hrod* (fame, praise) and *ger*
(spear)
The winning of honour is but the revealing
of a man's virtue and worth.
— Francis Bacon, "Of Honour and Reputation"

ROGÉRIO [roh-HAY-ree-oh]

MEANING: famous spear, renowned spearman •
USAGE: Spanish form of Roger (see Roger)
Ye shall be a blessing. Fear not,
but let your hands be strong.
— Zechariah 8:13b (KJ21)

ROHAN [roh-hahn]

MEANING: ascending, rising • USAGE: Hindu:
from Sanskrit *rohana*
We are what we think. All that we are arises
with our thoughts. With our thoughts we make the
world. Speak or act with a pure mind and happiness
will follow you as your shadow, unshakable.
— Buddha

ROLAN [roh-lahn]

MEANING: fame of the land, famous land, praised
estate • USAGE: Russian form of Roland (see
Roland)
A good name is rather to be chosen than great riches,
and loving favor rather than silver and gold.
— Proverbs 22:1 (KJV)

ROLAND [ROH-land (English), roh-LAHN (German, French, Scandinavian)]

MEANING: fame of the land, famous land, praised
estate • USAGE: German, English, French, and
Scandinavian form of *Hrodland*, from German *hrod*
(fame, praise) and *land* (land, territory)
A good reputation is a fair estate.
— English proverb

ROLANDO [roh-LAHN-doh]

MEANING: fame of the land, famous land, praised
estate • USAGE: Spanish and Italian form of Roland
(see Roland)
Trust in the Lord and live right!
The land will be yours, and you will be safe.
— Psalm 37:3 (CEV)

ROLF [rahlf]

MEANING: famous wolf, wolf fame, wolf counsel,
wolf adviser • USAGE: German and Scandinavian
form of Rudolf, from German *hrod* (fame, praise)
and *wulf* (wolf); or German form of Ralph, from
German *rad* (counsel, advise) and *wulf* (wolf)

Establish within thyself a heart of good counsel: for there is no other thing of more worth to thee than it.
— Sirach 37:17 (DR Apocrypha)

ROLLO   *[ROH-loh]*

MEANING: fame of the land, famous land, praised estate • **USAGE:** English form of Roland (*see* Roland)

Being respected is more important than having great riches. To be well thought of is better than silver or gold.
— Proverbs 22:1 (NCV)

ROM   *[rohm]*

MEANING: height, altitude, eminence • **USAGE:** Jewish

He who walks in righteousness, speaks uprightly…such a one shall dwell in lofty security.
— Isaiah 33:15–16a (JPS)

ROMAN   *[rah-MAHN (Czech, Polish, Russian), ROH-man (English)]*

MEANING: man from Rome, Roman • **USAGE:** Czech, English, Polish, and Russian: from Latin *Roma* (Rome, native of Rome)

To all that be in Rome, beloved of God, called to be saints: Grace to you and peace.
— Romans 1:7 (NASB)

ROMANO   *[roh-MAH-noh]*

MEANING: man from Rome, Roman • **USAGE:** Italian (*see* Roman)

We are pilgrims together, wending through unknown country, home.
— Fra Giovanni Giocondo
(Christmas Eve letter, 1513)

ROMEO   *[ROH-may-oh (Italian), ROH-mee-oh (English)]*

MEANING: man from Rome, Roman • **USAGE:** Italian and English (*see* Roman)

To all those in Rome who are loved by God and called to be saints: Grace to you and peace.
— Romans 1:7a (ESV)

RON   *[ron]*

MEANING: well-advised ruler, ruler's judgment • **USAGE:** English form of Ronald (*see* Ronald)

Leadership is practiced not so much in words as in attitude and in actions.
— Harold Geneen

RON   *[ron]*

MEANING: song, joy • **USAGE:** Jewish

Break forth and sing for joy.
— Psalm 98:4b (MT)

RONALD   *[RON-ald]*

MEANING: well-advised ruler, ruler's judgment • **USAGE:** Scottish and English: from Norse *rögn* (advice, judgment) and *valdr* (to rule)

You must see that justice is done, and must show kindness and mercy to one another.
— Zechariah 7:9b (GNT)

RONALDO   *[roh-NAHL-doh]*

MEANING: well-advised ruler, ruler's judgment • **USAGE:** Spanish form of Ronald (*see* Ronald)

Do not show partiality when deciding a case; listen to small and great alike. Do not be intimidated by anyone, for judgment belongs to God.
— Deuteronomy 1:17a (HCSB)

RONAN   *[ROH-nan]*

MEANING: little seal • **USAGE:** Irish: from Gaelic *ron* (seal) and diminutive *-an*

There is hope from the sea.
— Irish proverb

R

RONSON   [RON-son]

MEANING: son of Ronald, son of the well-advised ruler • **USAGE:** English surname: from Norse *rögn* (advice, judgment) and *valdr* (to rule) and *son*

> *Trust your own judgment;*
> *no one's advice is more reliable.*
> — Sirach 37:13 (GNT Apocrypha)

ROOK   [rook]

MEANING: crow, raven • **USAGE:** American: from English *hroc* (European crow)

> *Consider the ravens: They do not sow or reap,*
> *they have no storeroom or barn; yet God feeds them.*
> *And how much more valuable you are than birds!*
> — Luke 12:24 (NIV)

ROQUE   [ROH-kay]

MEANING: rest, peace • **USAGE:** Spanish form of Rocco, from German *hrok*

> *Peace be within thy walls…peace be within thee.*
> — Psalm 122:7–8 (KJ21)

RORY, RUAIRI   [ROHR-ee]

MEANING: redheaded king • **USAGE:** Irish and Scottish: from Gaelic *ruad* (red) and *ri* (king)

> *The Lord will hold you in his hand for all to see —*
> *a splendid crown in the hand of God.*
> — Isaiah 62:3 (NLT)

ROSCOE   [RAHS-koh]

MEANING: roe-deer forest, from the deer woods • **USAGE:** English: from Norse *ra* (roe-deer) and *skogr* (copse, wood)

> *He [God] makes my feet like the feet of a deer; he*
> *enables me to stand on the heights.*
> — Psalm 18:33 (NIV)

ROSH   [rohsh]

MEANING: leader, head, chief • **USAGE:** Jewish

> *For an intelligent man the path of life*
> *leads upward.*
> — Proverbs 15:24a (JPS)

ROSS   [ros]

MEANING: promontory, sea cliff, headland • **USAGE:** Scottish and English surname: from Gaelic *ros*

> *He who walks righteously and speaks uprightly…*
> *will dwell on heights.*
> — Isaiah 33:15–16a (ESV)

ROWAN   [ROH-wan]

MEANING: rowan tree, little redheaded one, famous friend • **USAGE:** English and Irish: from Norse *reynir* (rowan tree, mountain ash); from Irish form of *Ruadhan*, from Irish Gaelic *ruadh* (red) and diminutive *-an*; or from English *hroo* (fame) and *wine* (friend)

> *In the degree that we become friends to the highest*
> *and best within us, do we become friends to all.*
> — Ralph Waldo Trine, *In Tune with the Infinite*

ROY   [roi]

MEANING: king, royal one • **USAGE:** Scottish and English: from French *roi*

> *O God of light, crown Thou to me Thy gladness.*
> — Alexander Carmichael, "Repose of Sleep,"
> *Carmina Gadelica*

ROYCE   [rois]

MEANING: rose, dweller in a house bearing the sign of the rose • **USAGE:** English surname: from Latin *rosa*

> *Peace be within your walls.*
> — Psalm 122:7a (WEB)

ROYLE   [royl]

MEANING: rye hill • **USAGE:** English surname: from English *ryge* (rye) and *hyll* (hill)

May the mountains bring prosperity to the people,
and the hills, righteousness.
— Psalm 72:3 (HCSB)

RU [roo]

MEANING: scholar, educated • USAGE: Chinese
Knowing others is intelligence;
knowing yourself is true wisdom. Mastering others is
strength; mastering yourself is true power.
— Lao Tzu, *Tao Te Ching* (tr. Stephen Mitchell)

RUBEN [ROO-ben]

MEANING: Behold, a son! • USAGE: Scandinavian
and Dutch form of Reuven, from Hebrew *ra'ah* (he
saw) and *ben* (son)
My son, let them not depart from thine eyes;
keep sound wisdom and discretion, so shall they be life
unto thy soul, and grace unto thy neck.
Then shalt thou walk in thy way securely,
and thy foot shall not stumble.
— Proverbs 3:21–23 (DT)

RUBERT [ROO-bert]

MEANING: brightly famous, shining with fame •
USAGE: Czech form of Robert, from German *hrod*
(fame) and *beraht* (bright, shining)
The path of the righteous is like the first gleam of
dawn, shining ever brighter till the full light of day.
— Proverbs 4:18 (NIV)

RUDOLF [ROO-dahlf]

MEANING: famous wolf, wolf fame • USAGE:
German and Scandinavian form of *Hrodwulf*, from
German *hrod* (fame, praise) and *wulf* (wolf)
Man is the noblest of animals,
therefore the virtue of prudence.
— Aristotle

RUDOLPH [ROO-dahlf]

MEANING: famous wolf, wolf fame • USAGE:
English form of Rudolf (*see* Rudolf)
The best wolf habitat resides in the human heart.
— Ed Bangs

RUDY [ROO-dee]

MEANING: famous wolf, wolf fame • USAGE:
German, Scandinavian, and English form of Rudolf
(*see* Rudolf)
A good name is to be more desired
than great riches, favor is better
than silver and gold.
— Proverbs 22:1 (NASB)

RUFUS [ROO-fus]

MEANING: red color, redheaded, ruddy-
complexioned • USAGE: English: from Latin *rous*
(red)
He [is] ruddy, with beauty of eyes,
and of good appearance.
— 1 Samuel 16:12b (YLT)

RUHI [roo-hee]

MEANING: spirit, spiritual • USAGE: Muslim: from
Arabic *ruh*
Spiritual awakening is the most essential thing in
man's life, and it is the sole purpose of being.
— Kahlil Gibran, "The Tempest"

RUPERT [ROO-pert]

MEANING: brightly famous, shining with fame
• USAGE: German, Dutch, and Polish form of
Robert, from German *hrod* (fame) and *beraht*
(bright, shining)
The wisdom of a man shineth in his countenance.
— Ecclesiastes 8:1b (DR)

R

RUSH [rush]

MEANING: red, redheaded, ruddy-complexioned • **USAGE:** American: from Latin *rous*
Of all the hues, reds have the most potency.
— Jack Lenor Larsen

RUSHDI [RUSH-dee]

MEANING: wise, prudent, judicious, rightly guided • **USAGE:** Muslim: from Arabic *rashada* (to follow the right course)
Wisdom surpasses power.
— Arabic proverb

RUSS [rus]

MEANING: red, redheaded, ruddy-complexioned • **USAGE:** English form of Russell (*see* Russell)
Red is the ultimate cure for sadness.
— Bill Blass

RUSSELL [RUS-el]

MEANING: red, redheaded, ruddy-complexioned • **USAGE:** English: from French *roussell*
Red has been praised for its nobility
as the colour of life.
— Alice Meynell, *The Colour of Life*

RUSTY [RUS-tee]

MEANING: red, redheaded, ruddy-complexioned • **USAGE:** English: from English *rust*
You [God] have anointed my head with oil;
my cup overflows.
— Psalm 23:5b (NASB)

RYAN [RIE-en]

MEANING: little king, little royal one • **USAGE:** Irish and English surname: from Gaelic *ri* (king) and diminutive *-an*
Thou shalt also be a crown of glory in the hand of the
Lord, and a royal diadem in the hand of thy God.
— Isaiah 62:3 (KJV)

RYDER [RIE-der]

MEANING: rider, rider of horses, traveler • **USAGE:** American: from English *riden* (rider, especially of horses)
The great affair, the love affair with life,
is to live as variously as possible, to groom one's
curiosity like a high-spirited thoroughbred,
climb aboard, and gallop over the thick,
sunstruck hills every day.
— Diane Ackerman, *A Natural History of the Senses*

RYE [rie]

MEANING: rye grain • **USAGE:** English: from English *ryge*
God will bless you, my son, with dew from heaven
and with fertile fields, rich with grain and grapes.
— Genesis 27:28 (CEV)

RYKER [RIE-ker]

MEANING: ruler, leader • **USAGE:** English surname: from German *rik*
The function of leadership is to produce more leaders,
not more followers.
— Ralph Nader

RYLAN [RIE-lan]

MEANING: rye land • **USAGE:** English: from English *ryge* (rye) and *land* (land, territory)
Thou has blessed the work of his hands,
and his substance is increased in the land.
— Job 1:10b (KJV)

RYUU [ree-oo]

MEANING: dragon spirit • **USAGE:** Japanese
Unify the material and spiritual realms,
and that will enable you to become truly brave,
wise, loving and empathetic.
— Morihei Ueshiba, *The Art of Peace*

S

SABALA [sah-bah-lah]

MEANING: powerful, mighty, strong • USAGE:
Hindu: from Sanskrit *sa* (with) and *bala* (strength)
There is no weapon more powerful in achieving
the truth than acceptance of oneself.
— Swami Prajnanpad

SABIR, SABEER [sah-BEER]

MEANING: patient, tolerant, enduring • USAGE:
Muslim: from Arabic *sabara* (to endure)
The first sign of the realization of truth is tolerance.
— Hazrat Inayat Khan, *The Bowl of Saki*

SACHI [sah-chee]

MEANING: blissful, happy • USAGE: Japanese:
from Japanese *sachi*
The virtuous are happy in this world, and they are
happy in the next; they are happy in both. They are
happy when they think of the good they have done.
They are even happier when going on the good path.
— Buddha, *The Dhammapada*
(tr. Friedrich Max Müller)

SADID, SADEED [sah-DEED]

MEANING: righteous, true • USAGE: Muslim
No man is true in the truest sense of the word but he
who is true in word, in deed, and in thought.
— Hadith of the Prophet Muhammad
(tr. Abdullay Al-Mamun Al-Suhrawardy)

SAFIR, SAFEER [sah-FEER]

MEANING: mediator, intercessor • USAGE: Muslim
If you judge, judge between them with equity;
surely Allah loves those who judge equitably.
— Koran, The Food 5.42b (SKR)

SAGE [sayj]

MEANING: wise one, sage herb • USAGE: English:
from Latin *sapere* (to be wise); or from English
sauge (herb plant)
God said...I have given thee a wise
and an understanding heart.
— 1 Kings 3:11–12b (ASV)

SAJAN [sah-jahn]

MEANING: beloved, love • USAGE: Hindu
He who wants to do good knocks at the gate:
he who loves finds the door open.
— Rabindranath Tagore, *Stray Birds*

SAJID, SAJEED [sah-JEED]

MEANING: worshiper (of Allah) • USAGE:
Muslim: from Arabic *sajid*
Allah must thou serve, and be among the thankful!
— Koran, The Companies 39.66 (PIC)

SAL [sahl]

MEANING: peace, peaceful, savior, salvation •
USAGE: Spanish: form of Salomon (*see* Salomon)
or of Salvador (*see* Salvador)
I pray that God will be kind to you
and will keep on giving you peace!
— 1 Peter 1:2b (CEV)

SALAAM, SALAM [sah-lahmn]

MEANING: safe, secure, at peace • USAGE: Muslim
Peace be unto you!
— Koran, The Bee 16.32b (PIC)

SALADIN, SALADEEN [sah-lah-deen]

MEANING: righteous faith • USAGE: Muslim:
from Arabic *salah* (righteousness) and *din* (faith,
religion)

S

Prayers lighten the heart,
and charity is proof of imam (faith).
— Hadith of the Prophet Muhammad

Be kind to all, tolerant to all, considerate to all, polite
to all, O my thoughtful self.
— Hazrat Inayat Khan, *The Gayan*

SALOMON, SALOMÓN   *[SAHL-oh-mahn]*

MEANING: peace, peaceful • USAGE: French,
Scandinavian, and Spanish form of Solomon, from
Hebrew *shalom*
Have a long life. Peace be to you. Peace be to your
family. And peace be to all that you have.
— 1 Samuel 25:6 (NKJV)

SALVADOR   *[SAHL-vah-dor]*

MEANING: savior, salvation • USAGE: Spanish:
from Latin *salvator* (savior) or Latin *salvation*
(salvation)
Upon God alone doth my soul rest peacefully; from
him is my salvation.
— Psalm 62:1 (DT)

SALVATORE   *[sahl-vah-TOH-reh]*

MEANING: savior, salvation • USAGE: Italian (*see*
Salvador)
Surely God is my salvation; I will trust and not be
afraid. The Lord, the Lord, is my strength and my
song; he has become my salvation.
— Isaiah 12:2 (NIV)

SAM   *[sam]*

MEANING: His name is God, name of God •
USAGE: English form of Samuel (*see* Samuel)
Let all those that put their trust in thee [God]
rejoice.... Let them also that love thy name
be joyful in thee.
— Psalm 5:11 (KJV)

SAMIH   *[sah-mih]*

MEANING: tolerant, forgiving • USAGE: Muslim:
from Arabic *samuha* (to be tolerant, to forgive)

SAMMY   *[SAM-ee]*

MEANING: His name is God, name of God •
USAGE: English form of Samuel (*see* Samuel)
Bless the Lord, O my soul:
and let all that is within me bless his holy name.
— Psalm 102:1 (DR)

SAMSON   *[SAM-son]*

MEANING: sun, like the sun • USAGE: English
form of *Shimson*, possibly from Hebrew *shimson*
(the sun)
One can make a day of any size,
and regulate the rising and setting of his own
sun and the brightness of its shining.
— John Muir

SAMUEL   *[SAM-yoo-el, SAM-yool]*

MEANING: His name is God, name of God •
USAGE: English form of Shmuel, from Hebrew
shemu 'el
He restoreth my soul: He guideth me in the paths
of righteousness for his name's sake.
— Psalm 23:3 (ASV)

SAMUELO   *[sahm-WAY-loh]*

MEANING: His name is God, name of God •
USAGE: Spanish form of Samuel (*see* Samuel)
I will make all my goodness pass before thee,
and I will proclaim the name of the Lord before thee;
and will be gracious to whom I will be gracious,
and will shew mercy on whom I will shew mercy.
— Exodus 33:19 (KJV)

SANCHO   *[SAHN-choh]*

MEANING: sanctified, holy • **USAGE:** Spanish form
of *Sanctius*, from Latin *sanctus*
May the God of peace Himself sanctify you entirely.
— 1 Thessalonians 5:23a (NASB)

SANDEEP, SANDIP   *[sahn-DEEP]*

MEANING: enlightened, blazing • **USAGE:** Hindu
*To be able to enjoy good health, to bring true
happiness to one's family, to bring a sense of
peacefulness to everybody, one must first discipline
and control his mind. If he can control his mind he can
find the way of enlightenment and all wisdom
and virtue will naturally come to him.*
— Buddha

SANDER   *[SAHN-der]*

MEANING: protector and helper of humankind,
guardian • **USAGE:** Scandinavian, Dutch, and
German form of Alexander, from Greek *alexein*
(to defend, to help) and *andros* (man)
*The Lord is faithful; he will strengthen you
and guard you from evil.*
— 2 Thessalonians 3:3 (RSV)

SANDROS   *[SAHN-drohs]*

MEANING: protector and helper of humankind,
guardian • **USAGE:** Greek form of Alexandros (*see*
Sander)
*Give me a place to stand upon,
and I will move the world!*
— Archimedes

SANDY   *[SAN-dee]*

MEANING: protector and helper of humankind,
guardian • **USAGE:** English form of Alexander (*see*
Sander)
*Having hope will give you courage.
You will be protected and will rest in safety.*
— Job 11:18 (NLT)

SANG-HO   *[sahng-hoh]*

MEANING: helpful and good • **USAGE:** Korean:
from Korean *sang* (helpful) and *ho* (goodness or
broad)
*O good man! One who acts good is the "true thinking."
The true thinking is compassion.*
— Mahaparinibbana Sutra

SANG-MIN   *[sahng-min]*

MEANING: helpful and clever • **USAGE:** Korean:
from Korean *sang* (helpful) and *min* (clever)
*Whoever has virtue and insight, who is just, truthful,
and does one's own work, the world will love.*
— Buddha, *The Dhammapada* (tr. Sanderson Beck)

SANJAY   *[sahn-jay]*

MEANING: triumphant, victorious • **USAGE:**
Hindu: from Sanskrit *samjaya*
*Truth obtains victory, not untruth. /
Truth is the way; truth is the goal of life.*
— *Mundaka Upanishad* (tr. Eknath Easwaran)

SANTIAGO   *[sahn-tee-AH-goh]*

MEANING: follower of St. James, replace, change,
transform, successor • **USAGE:** Spanish and
Portuguese: from Spanish *san* (saint) and Iago
(James), from Hebrew *ya'aqobh* (one that takes by
the heel, replace with another)
*He who follows after righteousness and kindness
finds life, righteousness, and honor.*
— Proverbs 21:21 (WEB)

SAPA   *[sah-pah]*

MEANING: black, dark • **USAGE:** Amerind: Sioux
*Bright days and dark days were both expressions
of the Great Mystery, and the Indian reveled
in being close to the Big Holy.*
— Luther Standing Bear,
Land of the Spotted Eagle

S

SASHA   [SAH-shah]

MEANING: protector and helper of humankind, guardian • **USAGE:** Russian form of Alexander, from Greek *alexein* (to defend, to help) and *andros* (man)

> *The Lord will protect you now*
> *and always wherever you go.*
> — Psalm 121:8 (CEV)

SATANTA   [sah-tahn-tah]

MEANING: white bear • **USAGE:** Amerind: Kiowa

> *I have nothing bad hidden in my breast at all;*
> *everything is all right there.*
> — Satanta

SATYAKI   [SAHT-yah-kee]

MEANING: truthful • **USAGE:** Hindu: from Sanskrit *satya*

> *Realization of Truth is higher than all else; /*
> *Higher still is truthful living.*
> — Sri Guru Granth Sahib

SAUL   [sahl]

MEANING: asked for, prayed for • **USAGE:** English form of Shaul, from Hebrew *sha'ul*

> *Ask and you will receive, and your joy will be complete.*
> — John 16:24b (NIV)

SAWYER   [SAH-yer]

MEANING: woodworker, carpenter • **USAGE:** English surname: from English *saphier* (to saw)

> *The house praises the carpenter.*
> — Ralph Waldo Emerson

SAYYID, SAYYED   [sah-yeed]

MEANING: master, lord • **USAGE:** Muslim: from Arabic *sayyid*

> *Master is he who masters self. Teacher is he who*
> *teaches self. Governor is he who governs self,*
> *and ruler is he who rules self.*
> — Hazrat Inayat Khan, *The Gayan*

SCOTT   [skot]

MEANING: man from Scotland, Scottish • **USAGE:** English surname: from English *Scottas* (a Scotchman)

> *The man who is aware of himself is*
> *henceforward independent; and he is never bored.*
> — Virginia Woolf, *The Common Reader*

SCOUT   [skowt]

MEANING: explorer, observer, guide, scout • **USAGE:** English: from English *scoute*

> *Good Sense will scout ahead for danger,*
> *insight will keep an eye out for you.*
> — Proverbs 2:11 (MSG)

SEAMUS   [SHAY-mus]

MEANING: replace, change, transform, successor • **USAGE:** Irish form of James, from Hebrew *ya'aqobh* (one that takes by the heel, replace with another)

> *He who has realized the Love that is divine has*
> *become a new man, and has ceased to be swayed and*
> *dominated by the old elements of self. He is known*
> *for his patience, his purity, his self-control, his deep*
> *charity of heart, and his unalterable sweetness.*
> — James Allen, *From Poverty to Power*

SEAN   [shahn]

MEANING: God is gracious, God is giving • **USAGE:** Irish and English: Irish form of John, from Hebrew *y'hohanan* (Yahweh is gracious)

> *May the road rise to meet you. May the wind always be*
> *at your back. May the sun shine warm upon your face.*
> *The rains fall soft upon your fields; and, until we meet*
> *again, may God hold you in the palm of his hand.*
> — Celtic blessing

SEANAN, SIONAN   [sheh-NAHN]

MEANING: little wise one, little ancient one • **USAGE:** Irish: from Gaelic *sean* (ancient, wise) and diminutive *-an*

*With wisdom you will learn what is right
and honest and fair.*
— Proverbs 2:9 (CEV)

SEBASTIAN [seh-BAS-chin, zeh-BAHS-tee-ahn (German)]

MEANING: man from Sebastia • **USAGE:** English
form of Roman family name *Sebastianus* (from
town of Sebastia)
*A man can do nothing better than to eat and drink
and find satisfaction in his work. This too, I see,
is from the hand of God.*
— Ecclesiastes 2:24 (NIV)

SEBASTIANO [say-bahs-tee-AHN-oh]

MEANING: man from Sebastia • **USAGE:** Italian
form of Sebastian (*see* Sebastian)
The virtues of a man are seen in his actions.
— Marcus Tullius Cicero

SEBASTIEN, SÉBASTIEN [seh-BAH-stee-en]

MEANING: man from Sebastia • **USAGE:** German
and French form of Sebastian (*see* Sebastian)
*Each man must look to himself to teach him the
meaning of life. It is not something discovered:
it is something moulded.*
— Antoine de Saint-Exupéry,
Wind, Sand, and Stars (tr. Lewis Galantier)

SEFERINO [say-fay-REE-noh]

MEANING: west wind, mild breeze • **USAGE:**
Spanish: from Greek *zephyros*
*The wind blows where it wishes, and you hear the
sound of it, but cannot tell where it comes from and
where it goes. So is everyone who is born of the Spirit.*
— John 3:8 (NKJV)

SEFF [sef]

MEANING: wolf • **USAGE:** Yiddish
The wolf shall dwell with the lamb.
— Isaiah 11:6a (MT)

SEFI [SEH-fee]

MEANING: God will add, God will increase •
USAGE: Jewish form of Yosef, from Hebrew
ya'saph (Yahweh will add)
*Thou hast enlarged my steps under me,
and my feet have not slipped.*
— Psalm 18:37 (MT)

SEKOU [seh-kow]

MEANING: learned, knowledgeable • **USAGE:**
African: Guinea
*We should go down to the grassroots of our culture,
not to remain there, not to be isolated there,
but to draw strength and substance therefrom, and with
whatever additional resources of strength and material
we acquire, proceed to set up a new form of society
raised to the level of human progress.*
— Ahmed Sékou Touré

SEM [sem]

MEANING: name, renown, reputation • **USAGE:**
Dutch form of Shem, from Hebrew *shem*
*A good name is better than great riches:
and good favour is above silver and gold.*
— Proverbs 22:1 (DR)

SEPP [sep]

MEANING: God will add, God will increase •
USAGE: German form of Yosef, from Hebrew
ya'saph (Yahweh will add)
*May the Lord cause you to increase and abound
in love for one another.*
— 1 Thessalonians 3:12a (NEB)

SERAFIM [SAYR-ah-feem]

MEANING: burning one, angel • **USAGE:**
Portuguese and Russian: from Hebrew *seraphim*
(the burning ones), an order of celestial angels
*For His messengers He chargeth for thee,
to keep thee in all thy says.*
— Psalm 91:11 (YLT)

S

SERGEI   [SEHR-gay]

MEANING: servant, attendant, helper • **USAGE:**
Russian form of Sergio (see Sergio)

> *Well done, good and faithful servant;*
> *you were faithful over a few things,*
> *I will make you ruler over many things.*
> — Matthew 25:21b (NKJV)

SERGIO   [SAYR-jee-oh]

MEANING: servant, attendant, helper • **USAGE:**
Spanish and Italian form of Roman family name
Sergius, possibly meaning "servant"

> *Thou hast begun to bless the house of thy servant,*
> *that it may be always before thee: for seeing thou*
> *blessest it, O Lord, it shall be blessed for ever.*
> — 1 Chronicles 17:27 (DR)

SERGIOS   [SEHR-jee-ohs]

MEANING: servant, attendant, helper • **USAGE:**
Greek form of Sergio (see Sergio)

> *Peace, peace be unto thee, and peace be to thine helps;*
> *for thy God helpeth thee.*
> — 1 Chronicles 12:18b (KJV)

SETH   [seth]

MEANING: appointed, chosen • **USAGE:** English:
from Hebrew *shith* (to put, to set)

> *The Lord your God has set you apart for himself.*
> *He has chosen you to be his special treasure.*
> — Deuteronomy 7:6b (NIRV)

SEYMOUR   [SEE-mor]

MEANING: lake by the sea, pond by the sea •
USAGE: English surname: from English *sae* (sea)
and *mere* (lake, pond)

> *Still waters run deep.*
> — English proverb

SHAD   [shad]

MEANING: one who is free, man, adult • **USAGE:**
American: possibly a form of Chad, from English
ceorl (freeman, peasant); or from German *karl* (full-
grown man, adult)

> *A man is not a farmer, or a professor, or an engineer,*
> *but he is all. Man is priest, and scholar,*
> *and statesman, and producer, and soldier.*
> — Ralph Waldo Emerson,
> "The American Scholar"

SHAFAT   [shah-FAHT]

MEANING: God is my judge • **USAGE:** Jewish

> *Truth springs up from the earth;*
> *justice looks down from heaven.*
> — Psalm 85:12 (JPS)

SHAFIQ, SHAFEEQ   [shah-feek]

MEANING: compassionate, kindhearted, merciful
• **USAGE:** Muslim: from Arabic *shafaqua* (to have
compassion)

> *Allah is kind, and he likes those who are kind too.*
> — Arabic proverb

SHAI   [shay]

MEANING: gift, present • **USAGE:** Jewish form of
Yishai, from Hebrew *yishai*

> *God said … Wisdom and knowledge is granted*
> *unto thee, and I will give thee riches,*
> *and wealth, and honour.*
> — 2 Chronicles 1:11–12a (JPS)

SHAKED   [shah-KED]

MEANING: almond, almond tree • **USAGE:** Jewish:
symbolic name for children born on Tu b'Shvat, the
New Year of the Trees

> *The tree grew and became mighty;*
> *its top reached heaven.*
> — Daniel 4:8 (JPS)

SHAKIL, SHAKEEL   *[shah-keel]*

MEANING: handsome, well-formed • **USAGE:** Muslim: from Arabic *shakil*

Allah it is Who…fashioned you and perfected your shapes, and hath provided you with good things.
— Koran, The Forgiving One 40.64b (PIC)

SHAKIR, SHAKEER   *[shah-keer]*

MEANING: thankful, grateful • **USAGE:** Muslim: from Arabic *shakara* (to thank)

Remember Me, I will remember you, and be thankful to Me.
— Koran, The Cow 2.152 (SKR)

SHAKRA   *[shah-krah]*

MEANING: strong, powerful • **USAGE:** Hindu: Sanskrit

Patience is all the strength that man needs.
— Sathya Sai Baba

SHAMA   *[shah-mah]*

MEANING: quiet, tranquil, calm • **USAGE:** Hindu: Sanskrit

Now it is time to sit quiet, face to face with Thee, and to sing dedication of life in this silent and overflowing leisure.
— Rabindranath Tagore, *Gitanjali*

SHAMA, SHAMAH   *[shah-MAH]*

MEANING: hear, understand, listen • **USAGE:** Jewish: from Hebrew *shamah*

Hear, O Israel! The Lord is our God, the Lord alone. You shall love the Lord your God with all your heart and with all your soul and with all your might.
— Deuteronomy 6:4–5 (JPS)

SHAMBE   *[SHAHM-beh]*

MEANING: leader • **USAGE:** African: Swahili of Kenya/Tanzania

When the leaders are wise, so are the people.
— East African proverb

SHAMIR   *[shah-MEER]*

MEANING: strong, flint, rocklike • **USAGE:** Jewish

Be strong and of good courage.
— Joshua 1:6a (MT)

SHANE   *[shayn]*

MEANING: God is gracious, God is giving • **USAGE:** Irish and English form of Sean, from Hebrew *y'hohanan* (Yahweh is gracious)

The Lord bless you and keep you; the Lord make his face shine upon you and be gracious to you; the Lord lift up his countenance upon you and give you peace.
— Numbers 6:24–26 (ESV)

SHANGE   *[SHAHN-gay]*

MEANING: who walks like a lion, courageous • **USAGE:** African: Zulu of South Africa

I learned that courage was not the absence of fear, but the triumph over it.… The brave man is not he who does not feel afraid, but he who conquers that fear.
— Nelson Mandela

SHANKAR   *[SHAHN-kahr]*

MEANING: bliss-maker, auspicious • **USAGE:** Hindu: from Sanskrit *sam* (auspicious, lucky) and *kara* (making)

Love is the highest bliss that man can attain to, for through it alone he truly knows that he is more than himself, and that he is at one with the All.
— Rabindranath Tagore, *Sadhana*

SHANLEY   *[SHAN-lee]*

MEANING: venerable warrior, esteemed warrior • **USAGE:** Irish surname: from Gaelic *sean laoch*

You shall be a blessing. Fear not, but let your hands be strong.
— Zechariah 8:13b (RSV)

S

SHANNON, SHANNAN   [SHAN-on]

MEANING: wise, ancient, enduring, river name
• USAGE: Irish and English: from Gaelic *sean*
(ancient, wise); river in Ireland, known as "the old
one"

*I've known rivers ancient as the world and older
than the flow of human blood in human veins.
My soul has grown deep like the rivers.*
— Langston Hughes

SHAPPA   [shah-pah]

MEANING: red thunder • USAGE: Amerind: Sioux
*Behold! A sacred voice is calling you!
All over the sky a sacred voice is calling!*
— Wallace Black Elk

SHARIF   [shah-REEF]

MEANING: noble, distinguished, honorable •
USAGE: Muslim: from Arabic *sharafa* (to be
distinguished)

Man proves to be noble by his charity of heart.
— Hazrat Inayat Khan, *The Gayan*

SHASTA   [shah-stah]

MEANING: teacher • USAGE: Hindu: Sanskrit
*What is education? It is the teacher above and the
disciple below — and the wisdom that connects them.*
— *Taittiriya Upanishad*

SHAUL   [shah-OOL]

MEANING: asked for, prayed for • USAGE: Jewish:
from Hebrew *sha'ul*

*I call upon Thee, for Thou wilt answer me, O God;
incline Thine ear unto me, hear my speech.*
— Psalm 17:6 (JPS)

SHAUN, SHAWN   [shahn]

MEANING: God is gracious, God is giving •
USAGE: English form of Sean, from Hebrew
y'hohanan (Yahweh is gracious)

*God did not give us a spirit of fear, but of power,
and of love, and of a sound mind.*
— 2 Timothy 1:7 (YLT)

SHAVIT   [shah-VEET]

MEANING: star, comet • USAGE: Jewish
*He countest the number of the stars;
He giveth them all their names.*
— Psalm 147:4 (MT)

SHAVIV   [shah-VEEV]

MEANING: spark, ray of light • USAGE: Jewish
*All souls are one. Each is a spark from the original
soul, and this soul is inherent in all souls, just as your
soul is inherent in all the members of your body.*
— Martin Buber,
Ten Rungs: Collected Hasidic Sayings

SHAW   [shah]

MEANING: woods, forest, grove • USAGE: Scottish
form of Gaelic surname *Seaghdh*, from English
schagh, shawe

*The clearest way into the Universe
is through a forest wilderness.*
— John Muir (journal entry of July 1890)

SHAWNEL   [shaw-NEL]

MEANING: God is gracious, God is giving •
USAGE: American: possibly a form of Shawn (see
Shaun)

*The Lord your God is merciful,
and will not turn away his face from you.*
— 2 Chronicles 30:9b (DR)

SHAY   [shay]

MEANING: replace, change, transform, successor
• USAGE: Irish form of Seamus, from Hebrew
ya'aqobh (one that takes by the heel, replace with
another)

Be transformed by the renewing of your mind.
— Romans 12:2b (YLT)

S

SHAY   [shay]

MEANING: God is salvation • **USAGE:** Jewish form of Yeshaya, from Hebrew *yesha'yah* (Yahweh is salvation)

Thus said the Lord, in an hour of favor I answer you,
and on a day of salvation I help you.
— Isaiah 49:8a (JPS)

SHAYA   [SHAH-yah]

MEANING: God is salvation • **USAGE:** Jewish form of Yeshaya (*see* Shay)

His glory is great through Thy salvation;
honour and majesty dost Thou lay upon him.
For Thou makest him most blessed for ever;
Thou makes him glad with joy in Thy presence.
— Psalm 21:5–6 (MT)

SHEA   [shay]

MEANING: hawk, hawk-like • **USAGE:** Irish, from Gaelic *se* (like a hawk)

If I take the wings of the morning
and dwell in the uttermost parts of the sea,
even there shall Thy hand lead me,
and Thy right hand shall hold me.
— Psalm 139:9–10 (KJ21)

SHEFI   [SHEH-fee]

MEANING: comfort, peace • **USAGE:** Jewish
Your rod and Your staff— they comfort me.
— Psalm 23:4b (JPS)

SHELBY   [SHEL-bee]

MEANING: willow town, settlement of huts, settlement near the ledge • **USAGE:** English surname: from Norse *selja býr* (willow town); or possibly from English *schele* (hut) or *scelf* (shelf, ledge) and *by* (farm, settlement)

Peace be to you, peace to your house,
and peace to all that you have!
— 1 Samuel 25:6b (NKJV)

SHELDON, SHELTON   [SHEL-don, SHEL-ton]

MEANING: ledge on a steep-sided valley • **USAGE:** English surname: from English *scylf* (shelf, slope) and *denu* (steep-sided valley)

The valleys…they shout for joy, they also sing.
— Psalm 65:13b (KJV)

SHELLY, SHELLEY   [SHEL-ee]

MEANING: clearing on a ledge, shelf on a hill, wealthy, rich • **USAGE:** English surname: from English *scelf* (shelf, ledge) and *leah* (meadow, field); English form of Sheldon (*see* Sheldon); or from Irish Gaelic *selbhach* (having many possessions, wealthy)

Wealth is not his that has it,
but his that enjoys it.
— Benjamin Franklin,
Poor Richard's Almanack

SHEM   [shem]

MEANING: name, renown, reputation • **USAGE:** Jewish: from Hebrew *shem*

A good name is rather to be chosen than great riches,
and loving favour rather than silver and gold.
— Proverbs 22:1 (MT)

SHEN   [shehn]

MEANING: deep thought, spirit • **USAGE:** Chinese
The superior man must make his thoughts sincere.
— Confucius, *The Analects* (tr. James Legge)

SHENG   [sheh-ENG]

MEANING: victorious, successful • **USAGE:** Chinese

S

*Man has received from heaven a nature innately good,
to guide him in all his movements. By devotion to this
divine spirit within himself, he attains an unsullied
innocence that leads him to do right with instinctive
sureness and without any ulterior thought of reward
and personal advantage. This instinctive certainty
brings about supreme success.*
— The I Ching: The Book of Changes,
Hexagrams 25, 43

SHEPPARD   *[SHEP-ard]*

MEANING: shepherd, spiritual guide • **USAGE:**
English surname: from English *sceap* (sheep) and
hierde (herder)
The Lord is my shepherd; I shall not want.
— Psalm 23:1 (KJV)

SHERIDAN   *[SHER-ih-dan]*

MEANING: elfin child, eternal treasure, eternal
poem, seeker • **USAGE:** English and Irish surname:
form of Irish *O'Sirideain*, from Gaelic *o* (son of),
siride (elf) and diminutive *-an;* from Gaelic *sior*
(eternal) and *dan* (treasure, poem); or from Gaelic
sirim (to seek)
*Lay up for yourselves treasures in heaven...
for where thy treasure is, there will thy heart be also.*
— Matthew 6:20–21 (ASV)

SHERLOCK   *[SHER-lok]*

MEANING: fair-haired, blond, bright locks •
USAGE: English surname: from English *schirloc*
(bright locks)
Thou anointest my head with oil; my cup runneth over.
— Psalm 23:5b (KJ21)

SHERMAN   *[SHER-mun]*

MEANING: shireman, sheepshearer • **USAGE:**
English surname: from English *scearra* (shears) and
mann (man)
He [God] will tend his flock like a shepherd.
— Isaiah 40:11a (ESV)

SHEVA   *[SHEH-vah]*

MEANING: oath, promise • **USAGE:** Jewish: from
Hebrew *shebha*
*The Lord thy God will bless thee,
as He promised thee.*
— Deuteronomy 15:6 (MT)

SHILOH, SHILO   *[shee-LOH, SHY-loh]*

MEANING: the gift is His, His gift • **USAGE:**
Jewish: from Hebrew *shai* (gift) and *lo* (his)
*God said...I have given thee a wise
and an understanding heart.*
— 1 Kings 3:11–12b (MT)

SHIM   *[shim]*

MEANING: hear, hearken • **USAGE:** American
form of Simon (*see* Shimon)
*A wise man will hear and increase learning,
and a man of understanding will attain wise counsel.*
— Proverbs 1:5 (NKJV)

SHIMON   *[shee-MOHN]*

MEANING: hear, hearken • **USAGE:** Jewish: from
Hebrew *shim'on*
*Ye shall not respect persons in judgment; ye shall hear
the small and the great alike; ye shall not be afraid of
the face of any man; for judgment is God's.*
— Deuteronomy 1:17a (MT)

SHIMSHON   *[sheem-SHOHN]*

MEANING: sun, like the sun • **USAGE:** Jewish:
from Hebrew *shemesh*
A sunbeam took human shape when he was born.
— Israel Zangwell, *The Melting-Pot*

SHIN   *[sheen]*

MEANING: truth, true • **USAGE:** Japanese: from
Japanese *shin*

The gift of truth surpasses all gifts;
the sweetness of truth surpasses all sweetness;
joy in the truth surpasses all pleasures.
— Buddha, *The Dhammapada* (tr. Sanderson Beck)

SHINDA   [SHEEN-dah]

MEANING: successful, victorious • **USAGE:**
African: Swahili of Kenya/Tanzania
Where there is purpose, there is no failure.
— Swahili proverb

SHLOMI   [SHLOH-mee]

MEANING: peace, peaceful • **USAGE:** Jewish form
of Shlomo (*see* Shlomo)
Rabban Shimon ben Gamaliel said: On three things
the world is sustained: on truth, on judgment, and on
peace, as it is said (Zechariah 8:16): "Speak the truth
to one another, render in your gates judgments that are
true and make for peace."
— *Pirkei Avot* 1.18

SHLOMO   [shloh-MOH, SHLOH-moh]

MEANING: peace, peaceful • **USAGE:** Jewish: from
Hebrew *shalom*
Mark the man of integrity, and behold the upright;
for there is a future for the man of peace.
— Psalm 37:37 (MT)

SHMUEL   [shmoo-EHL, shmool]

MEANING: His name is God, name of God •
USAGE: Jewish: from Hebrew *shem' el* (His name is
God) or *yishma'el* (Yahweh hears)
All God's names are hallowed, for in them He is not
merely spoken about, but also spoken to.
— Martin Buber, *I and Thou*

SHO   [shoh]

MEANING: to fly, to soar • **USAGE:** Japanese: from
Japanese *sho*

Higher than the lark / I climbed into the air, /
Taking breath / At the summit of a pass.
— Matsuo Bashō, *The Narrow Road to the Deep*
North (tr. Nobuyuki Yuasa)

SHOFAR   [shoh-FAHR]

MEANING: horn, ram's horn • **USAGE:** Jewish
The Lord is my rock, and my fortress, and my
deliverer; my God, my rock, in Him I take refuge;
my shield, and my horn of salvation, my high tower.
— Psalm 18:3 (MT)

SHOMER   [shoh-MER]

MEANING: watchman, guardian • **USAGE:** Jewish
I have appointed thee a watchman
unto the house of Israel.
— Ezekiel 3:17a (MT)

SHRINI   [SHREE-nee]

MEANING: divine beauty, fortunate, blessed •
USAGE: Hindu: Sanskrit
Bring us, Powerful One, all blessings, all facility…the
best of treasures: the efficient mind and spiritual luster.
— *Rig Veda*

SHU   [shoo]

MEANING: kind, compassionate, gentle • **USAGE:**
Chinese
Wisdom, compassion, and courage are the three
universally recognized moral qualities of men.
— Confucius, *The Analects*

SHUA   [SHOO-ah]

MEANING: God is salvation • **USAGE:** Jewish form
of Yehoshua, from Hebrew *yesha'yah* (Yahweh is
salvation)
The Lord is my strength and song;
and He is become my salvation.
— Psalm 118:14 (MT)

S

SHUI   *[shoo-wee]*

MEANING: water • **USAGE:** Chinese
*The tendency of man's nature to good
is like the tendency of water to flow downward.
As there is no water but tends to that direction,
so there is no man but tends to good.*
— Mencius

SHUN   *[shu-en]*

MEANING: smooth, agreeable • **USAGE:** Chinese
*Wise people, after they have listened to the laws,
become serene like a deep, smooth, and still lake.*
— Buddha, *The Dhammapada*
(tr. Friedrich Max Müller)

SID, CID   *[sid]*

MEANING: broad island, wide island • **USAGE:**
English form of Sidney, from English *sid* (wide,
broad) and *ieg* (island)
*The God who has girded me with strength
has opened wide my path.*
— 2 Samuel 22:33 (GNT)

SIDDHA   *[sid-hah]*

MEANING: perfected, accomplished • **USAGE:**
Hindu: Sanskrit
*The connection of love is total. In love,
differences disappear and the human soul accomplishes
its object in perfection, exceeding its own boundaries
and traversing the threshold of infinity.*
— Rabindranath Tagore

SIDNEY, SYDNEY   *[SID-nee]*

MEANING: broad island, wide island • **USAGE:**
English surname: from English *sid* (wide, broad)
and *ieg* (island)
*The Lord helped me.
He brought me out into a wide open place.*
— Psalm 18:18a–19a (NEB)

SIGFRIED, SIEGFRIED   *[SIG-freed,
SEEG-freed]*

MEANING: peaceful victory, victorious peace
• **USAGE:** German: from German *sige* (victory,
success) and *frid* (peace, peaceful)
*Blessed are the peacemakers,
for they shall be called sons of God.*
— Matthew 5:9 (ESV)

SIGI   *[SEE-gee]*

MEANING: peaceful victory, victorious peace,
guardian of peace, victorious protector • **USAGE:**
German form of Sigfried (*see* Sigfried) or of
Sigmund (*see* Sigmund)
*Live in peace and the God of love and peace
shall be with you.*
— 2 Corinthians 13:11b (KJV)

SIGMUND, SIEGMUND   *[SEEG-mund,
SIG-mund]*

MEANING: guardian of victory, victorious
protector • **USAGE:** German: from German *sige*
(victory, success) and *mund* (hand, protection)
*Discretion will watch over you,
understanding will guard you.*
— Proverbs 2:11 (ESV)

SIGURD   *[SEE-gur]*

MEANING: guardian of victory, victorious
protector • **USAGE:** Scandinavian: from Norse *sigr*
(victory, conquest) and *varor* (guardian, protector)
*You, Lord, are a shield around me, my glory,
and the One who lifts up my head.*
— Psalm 3:3 (HCSB)

SILAS   *[SIE-las]*

MEANING: woods, forest • **USAGE:** English: Latin
form of *Silvanus* (Roman god of forests), from
Latin *silva*

S

*Of the infinite variety of fruits which spring
from the bosom of the earth, the trees of the wood are
the greatest in dignity.*
— Susan Fenimore Cooper, *Rural Hours*

SILVANO   [seel-VAH-noh]

MEANING: woods, forest • USAGE: Italian and
Spanish: from Latin *silva*
All the trees of the wood rejoice.
— Psalm 96:12b (KJ21)

SILVESTER   [seel-VES-ter]

MEANING: woods, forest • USAGE: German form
of Sylvester, from Latin *silva* (woods, forest);
Silvanus is the Roman god of forests
*In the country it is as if every tree said to me, "Holy!
Holy!" Who can ever express the ecstasy of the woods?*
— Ludwig van Beethoven

SILVINO   [seel-VEE-noh]

MEANING: woods, forest • USAGE: Portuguese:
from Latin *silva*
*They will be like trees growing beside a stream
— trees with roots that reach down to the water, and
with leaves that are always green. They bear fruit every
year and are never worried by a lack of rain.*
— Jeremiah 17:8 (CEV)

SILVIO   [SEEL-vee-oh (Italian),
                   SEEL-bee-oh (Spanish)]

MEANING: woods, forest • USAGE: Italian and
Spanish: from Latin *silva*
The trees of the forest will sing for joy.
— 1 Chronicles 16:33a (WEB)

SIMBA   [SEEM-bah]

MEANING: lion • USAGE: African: Swahili of
Kenya/Tanzania
A lion is a lion even if it eats grass.
— Swahili proverb

SIMON   [SIE-mon (English), see-MAHN
                   (French), ZEE-mahn (German)]

MEANING: hear, hearken • USAGE: English,
French, and German form of Shimon, from Hebrew
shim'on
Let me hear the sounds of joy and gladness.
— Psalm 51:8a (GNT)

SINCLAIR, SINCLARE   [sin-KLAYR]

MEANING: sanctified and clear, holy and
transparent • USAGE: English and Scottish
surname: English form of *Saint Claire*, from
Latin *sanctus* (sanctified, holy) and *clarus* (clear,
transparent)
May the God of peace himself sanctify you completely.
— 1 Thessalonians 5:23a (WEB)

SION   [see-OHN]

MEANING: highest point, peak • USAGE: Jewish
*The mountain of the Lord's house
shall be established as the top of the mountains,
and shall be exalted above the hills.*
— Isaiah 2:2b (MT)

SION   [shahn]

MEANING: God is gracious, God is giving •
USAGE: Welsh form of John, from Hebrew
y'hohanan (Yahweh is gracious)
*Only goodness and faithful love will pursue me
all the days of my life, and I will dwell in the house
of the Lord as long as I live.*
— Psalm 23:6a (HCSB)

SKIP   [skip]

MEANING: skipper, captain of a ship, seafarer,
skip, leap • USAGE: English: from Dutch *scipper*
(captain, master of a ship); or from Norse *skopa* (to
skip, to leap)
*I am the master of my fate;
I am the captain of my soul.*
— William Ernest Henley, "Invictus"

S

SKY   [skie]

MEANING: cloud, sky, heaven • USAGE:
American: from Norse *sky* (cloud)

> *Heaven is large, and affords space*
> *for all modes of love and fortitude.*
> — Ralph Waldo Emerson, "Spiritual Laws"

SKYLAR, SKYLER   [SKIE-ler]

MEANING: scholar, learned, knowledgeable •
USAGE: American: from Dutch s*chuyler*

> *The soul of man is larger than the sky.*
> — Hartley Coleridge, "To Shakespeare"

SLADE   [slayd]

MEANING: small valley, flat valley, level ground
between hills • USAGE: American surname: from
English *slade* (small valley); a slip or flat ground
between hills

> *Let your good Spirit lead me on level ground.*
> — Psalm 143:10b (NCV)

SLATE   [slayt]

MEANING: rock with smooth-surfaced layers, gray
color • USAGE: American surname: from English
sclate (splinter, layer)

> *Go deep enough and there is the bedrock of truth.*
> — May Sarton, *Journal of a Solitude*

SLOAN   [slohn]

MEANING: raider • USAGE: English surname:
from Irish Gaelic *sluaghadh* (military expedition,
raid)

> *Put on the full armor of God.*
> — Ephesians 6:11a (NIV)

SLY   [slie]

MEANING: woods, forest • USAGE: English form
of Sylvester, from Latin *silva*

> *One impulse from a vernal wood may teach you more of*
> *a man, of moral evil and of good, than all the ages can.*
> — William Wordsworth, "The Tables Turned"

SOCRATES   [SOH-krah-tees]

MEANING: whole power, safe power • USAGE:
Greek: possibly from Greek *sos* (whole,
unwounded, safe) and *kratos* (power)

> *The true lover of knowledge is always striving after*
> *being — that is his nature; he will not rest…until he*
> *has attained the knowledge of the true nature of all*
> *essence by a sympathetic and kindred power in the soul.*
> — Plato, *The Republic* (tr. Benjamin Jowett)

SOHRAB   [sohr-ahb]

MEANING: bright light, radiance • USAGE: Persian

> *Our Lord! make perfect for us our light.*
> — Koran, The Prohibition 66.8b (SKR)

SOL   [sahl]

MEANING: peace, peaceful • USAGE: English form
of Solomon (*see* Solomon)

> *Solomon, my son, the Lord be with you!*
> — 1 Chronicles 22:11a (NEB)

SOLOMON   [SAHL-oh-man]

MEANING: peace, peaceful • USAGE: English form
of Shlomo, from Hebrew *shalom*

> *God gave Solomon wisdom and understanding*
> *exceeding much, and largeness of heart.*
> — 1 Kings 3:9a (KJV)

SOMA   [soh-mah]

MEANING: nectar of immortality • USAGE: Hindu:
Sanskrit

> *The secret of immortality is to be found in purification*
> *of the heart, in meditation, in realization of the identity*
> *of the Self within and Brahman without.*
> *For immortality is simply union with God.*
> — *Katha Upanishad* (tr. Swami Prabhavananda)

S

SONG [sahng]

MEANING: pine tree • USAGE: Chinese
> *Of those that receive life from the earth,*
> *the pine and cypress alone are the best —*
> *they stay as green as ever in winter or summer.*
> — Zhuang Zhou

SONNY [SON-ee]

MEANING: son • USAGE: English: from English *sunu*
> *My son, do not lose sight of these — keep sound*
> *wisdom and discretion, and they will be life for your*
> *soul.... Then you will walk on your way securely,*
> *and your foot will not stumble.*
> — Proverbs 3:21–23 (ESV)

SORA [soh-rah]

MEANING: sky • USAGE: Japanese: from Japanese *sora*
> *How boundless and free is the sky of Awareness!*
> — Buddha

SOREN [SOHR-en]

MEANING: stern, firm • USAGE: Scandinavian form of Roman family name *Severinus*, from Latin *severus*
> *Those who lead blameless lives and do what is right,*
> *speaking the truth from sincere hearts...*
> *such people will stand firm forever.*
> — Psalm 15:2, 15:5b (NLT)

SOTIRIOS [soh-TEE-ree-ohs]

MEANING: salvation • USAGE: Greek: from Greek *soterios*
> *With joy you will draw water*
> *from the wells of salvation.*
> — Isaiah 12:3 (NIV)

SPENCE [spens]

MEANING: steward, dispenser, administrator • USAGE: English form of Spencer (*see* Spencer)
> *You will discern righteousness and justice*
> *and equity and every good course.*
> — Proverbs 2:9 (NASB)

SPENCER [SPEN-ser]

MEANING: steward, dispenser, administrator • USAGE: English surname: from English *dispensen* (to dispense, to distribute)
> *Render true judgments,*
> *show kindness and mercy to one another.*
> — Zechariah 7:9b (NRSV)

SPIKE [spiek]

MEANING: thorn, spine, sharp, heavy nail, ear of grain • USAGE: English: from Norse *spik* (heavy nail), from Latin *spina* (thorn, spine), or from Latin *spica* (ear of grain)
> *Just as iron sharpens iron,*
> *friends sharpen the minds of each other.*
> — Proverbs 27:17 (CEV)

SPIRO, SPYRO [SPEE-roh]

MEANING: spirit • USAGE: Greek form of *Spyridon*, from Greek *spiritus*
> *It is the spirit in man, the breath of the Almighty,*
> *that makes him understand.*
> — Job 32:8 (ESV)

STACEY, STACY [STAY-see]

MEANING: resurrection, reborn, standing up • USAGE: English form of Anastasios, from Greek *anastasis* (resurrection), or from Greek *ana* (up) and *stasis* (standing)
> *Each day the world is born anew /*
> *For him who takes it rightly.*
> — James Russell Lowell,
> "Gold Egg: A Dream-Fantasy"

S

STAN [stan]

MEANING: stony meadow, stony field • USAGE:
English form of Stanley (see Stanley)

The whole wilderness seems to be alive and familiar,
full of humanity. The very stones seem talkative,
sympathetic, brotherly.
— John Muir, "My First Summer in the Sierra"

STANLEY [STAN-lee]

MEANING: stony meadow, stony field • USAGE:
English: from English *stan* (stone) and *leah*
(meadow, field)

You will be at peace with the stones of the field,
and its wild animals will be at peace with you.
— Job 5:23 (NLT)

STEFAN [STEH-fen]

MEANING: crown, crowned one • USAGE:
German, Russian, and Scandinavian form of
Stephen (see Stephen)

He shall find joy and a crown of gladness.
— Sirach 15:6a (KJV Apocrypha)

STEFANO [STEH-fahh-noh]

MEANING: crown, crowned one • USAGE: Italian
form of Stephen (see Stephen)

[God] crowneth thee with lovingkindness
and tender mercies.
— Psalm 103:4 (KJV)

STEINAR [STIE-nahr]

MEANING: stone warrior • USAGE: Scandinavian:
from Norse *steinn* (stone) and *hari* (warrior)

And the Lord said, "Behold, there is a place by Me,
and thou shalt stand upon a rock."
— Exodus 33:21 (KJ21)

STEN [sten]

MEANING: stone, rock • USAGE: Scandinavian:
from Norse *steinn*

Look at the rock from which you were chiseled,
at the quarry from which you were dug!
— Isaiah 51:1b (NEB)

STEPAN [steh-pahn]

MEANING: crown, crowned one • USAGE: Russian
form of Stephen (see Stephen)

What is man that You are mindful of him,
or the son of man that You take care of him?
You have made him a little lower than the angels;
You have crowned him with glory and honor,
and set him over the works of Your hands.
— Hebrews 2:6b–7 (NKJV)

STEPHAN [STEH-fen]

MEANING: crown, crowned one • USAGE:
Scandinavian and German form of Stephen (see
Stephen)

[God] crowns you with steadfast love and mercy.
— Psalm 103:4 (ESV)

STEPHANOS, STEFANOS [steh-FAH-nohs]

MEANING: crown, crowned one • USAGE: Greek
(see Stephen)

You will be a majestic crown in the hand of the Lord.
— Isaiah 62:3a (NEB)

STEPHEN [STEE-ven]

MEANING: crown, crowned one • USAGE: English
form of Stephanos, from Greek *stephanos*

My crown is in my heart, not on my head.
— William Shakespeare, *King Henry VI, Part II*

S

STERLING [STER-ling]

MEANING: sterling silver, star, stellar • **USAGE:** English: from English *sterlinc* (name of silver coin) or *sterre* (star, starlike, stellar)

A sterling reputation is better than striking it rich;
a gracious spirit is better than money in the bank.
— Proverbs 22:1 (MSG)

STEVE [steev]

MEANING: crown, crowned one • **USAGE:** English form of Stephen (*see* Stephen)

Thou goest before him with the blessings of goodness;
Thou settest a crown of pure gold on his head.
— Psalm 21:3 (KJ21)

STEVEN [STEEV-en]

MEANING: crown, crowned one • **USAGE:** English form of Stephen (*see* Stephen)

The spirit of Love, when manifested as a perfect
and rounded life, is the crown of being
and the supreme end of knowledge upon this earth.
— James Allen, *From Poverty to Power*

STEWART [STOO-wart]

MEANING: steward, administrator, treasurer • **USAGE:** English surname: from English *stig* (house) and *weard* (guard)

Enter eagerly into the treasure house that is within you,
and you will see the things that are in heaven.
— Isaac of Nineveh

STIAN [STEE-an]

MEANING: wanderer, journeyer, sojourner • **USAGE:** Norwegian and Danish form of *Stigandr* (wanderer), from Norse *stig* (step, mounting upward)

You shall be blessed when you come in,
and you shall be blessed when you go out.
— Deuteronomy 28:6 (WEB)

STIG [steeg]

MEANING: wanderer, traveler, sojourner • **USAGE:** Scandinavian form of *Stigandr* (wanderer), from Norse *stig* (step, mounting upward)

The Lord...will send His angel with you
and make your journey a success.
— Genesis 24:40a (NIV)

STONEWALL [STOHN-wahl]

MEANING: wall of stone, rock wall • **USAGE:** American: from English *stan* (stone) and *weall* (wall)

He will cover you with His wings.
And under His wings you will be safe. He is faithful
like a safe-covering and a strong wall.
— Psalm 91:4a (NLV)

STROM [strahm]

MEANING: storm • **USAGE:** English form of Swedish surname, from Swedish *strom*

There are some things you learn best in calm,
and some in storm.
— Willa Cather, *The Song of the Lark*

STU, STEW [stoo]

MEANING: steward, administrator, treasurer • **USAGE:** English form of Stuart or Stewart (*see* Stuart)

Lay up for yourselves treasures in heaven...
for where your treasure is, there will your heart be also.
— Matthew 6:20–21

STUART [STOO-wart]

MEANING: steward, administrator, treasurer • **USAGE:** Scottish and English surname: from English *stig* (house) and *weard* (guard)

A good man of the good treasure of his heart
bringeth forth good things.
— Matthew 12:35a (KJV)

S

SUDAMA   [suh-dah-mah]

MEANING: generous, magnanimous • USAGE: Hindu: from Sanskrit *su* (greatly) and *dama* (giving)

> *Give with faith. Give with love. Give with joy.*
> — *Taittiriya Upanishad* (tr. Eknath Easwaran)

SUJAY   [suh-jay]

MEANING: great victory • USAGE: Hindu: from Sanskrit *su* (great) and *jaya* (victory)

> *Satisfaction lies in the effort,*
> *not in the attainment. Full effort is full victory.*
> — Mahatma Gandhi, "The Practice of Satyagraha"

SULLIVAN   [SUL-ih-van]

MEANING: dark-eyed, keen-eyed • USAGE: Irish and English surname: English form of *O'Suileabhain,* from Gaelic *suil* (eye) and *dubh* (black, dark); or from Gaelic *suilaibi* (keen-eyed)

> *The eyes indicate the antiquity of the soul.*
> — Ralph Waldo Emerson, "Behaviour"

SULLY   [SUL-ee]

MEANING: dark-eyed • USAGE: English form of Sullivan (*see* Sullivan)

> *Nobody sees with his eyes alone;*
> *we see with our souls.*
> — Henry Miller, *The Cosmological Eye*

SUMAN   [suh-mahn]

MEANING: good-natured, good minded • USAGE: Hindu: from Sanskrit *su* (good) and *manas* (mind)

> *The emancipation of our physical nature is*
> *in attaining health, of our social being in attaining*
> *goodness, and of our self in attaining love.*
> — Rabindranath Tagore, *Sadhana*

SUNARA   [soo-nah-rah]

MEANING: joyful, glad, happy • USAGE: Hindu: Sanskrit

> *The laughter of the infinite God must vibrate*
> *through your smile.*
> — Paramahansa Yogananda

SUNG-HO   [sung-hoh]

MEANING: prosperous and good • USAGE: Korean: from Korean *sung* (achievement, prosperous) and *ho* (goodness, broad)

> *For the doer of good deeds there is rejoicing,*
> *here as well as hereafter. Joy and more joy are his,*
> *as he sees his own right action.*
> — Buddha, *The Dhammapada*
> (tr. Ananda Maitreya)

SUNG-WOOK   [sung wook]

MEANING: prosperous and bright, prosperous and shining • USAGE: Korean: from Korean *sung* (prosperous) and *wook* (shiny, bright)

> *The wise keep awareness as their best treasure*
> — Buddha, *The Dhammapada* (tr. Sanderson Beck)

SVEN   [sven]

MEANING: boy, page, youth attending a knight or at court, strong, capable, wise, swan • USAGE: Scandinavian: from Norse *sven* (boy, page) or *svinn* (strong, able, wise); or from German *svan* (swan)

> *Capax universi, capable of the universe*
> *are your arms / when they move with love.*
> — Thomas Aquinas, "Capax Universi"
> (tr. Daniel Ladinsky in *Love Poems from God*)

SWEENEY   [SWEE-nee]

MEANING: pleasant, well-going • USAGE: Irish surname: from Gaelic *subhuigh*

> *The lines have fallen for me in pleasant places;*
> *yea, I have a goodly inheritance.*
> — Psalm 16:6 (KJ21)

S

SYLVESTER [sil-VES-ter]

MEANING: woods, forest • **USAGE:** English: from Latin *silva* (woods, forest); *Silvanus* is the Roman god of forests

> *The trees are friends of mankind.*
> — Enos A. Mills, *Your National Parks*

T

TAD [tad]

MEANING: gift of God, poet, philosopher • **USAGE:** English form of Theodore, from Greek *theos* (God) and *doron* (gift); or English of Tadhg, from Irish Gaelic *tadhg*

> *Every good gift and every perfect gift is from above,*
> *and cometh down from the Father of lights.*
> — James 1:17a (KJV)

TADDEO [tah-DAY-oh]

MEANING: given of God, gift of God • **USAGE:** Italian form of Thaddeus, from Greek *theo* (God) and *dotos* (given)

> *Take delight in the Lord,*
> *and he will give you your heart's desires.*
> — Psalm 37:4 (NLT)

TADEN, TAYDEN [TAY-den]

MEANING: fire, fiery one, broad woods, broad hill, broad-chested, salmon, hay field • **USAGE:** American: possibly a form of names rhyming with suffix *-aden*, such as Aidan, Braden, or Hayden (*see those entries*)

> *The woods are made for the wise and strong.*
> *In their very essence they are the counterparts of man.*
> — John Muir

TADEO [tah-DAY-oh]

MEANING: given of God, gift of God • **USAGE:** Spanish form of Thaddeus, from Greek *theo* (God) and *dotos* (given)

> *The Lord is my shepherd.*
> *He gives me everything I need.*
> — Psalm 23:1 (NIRV)

TADHG [tayg]

MEANING: poet, philosopher • **USAGE:** Irish: from Gaelie *tadhg*

> *The poet is the supreme artist,*
> *for he is the master of colour and of form.*
> — Oscar Wilde, "Mr. Whistler's Ten O'Clock"

TAHIR, TAHEER [tah-HEER]

MEANING: virtuous, pure, chaste, modest • **USAGE:** Muslim: from Arabic *tahura* (to be pure, to be clean)

> *The purest people are the ones with good manners.*
> — Arabic proverb

TAI [tie]

MEANING: great • **USAGE:** Chinese

> *The great man is he who does not lose his child's heart.*
> — Mencius (tr. James Legge)

TAIT [tayt]

MEANING: cheerful, joyful, happy • **USAGE:** Scandinavian: from Norse *teitr*

> *Happy shalt thou be, and it shall be well with thee.*
> — Psalm 128:2b (ASV)

TAJ [tahj]

MEANING: crown, crowned one • **USAGE:** Hindu

> *Blessed is he whose fame does not outshine his truth.*
> — Rabindranath Tagore, *Stray Birds*

T

TAKASHI   *[tah-kah-shee]*

MEANING: elevated, praiseworthy • **USAGE:**
Japanese
> *Whom the discriminating praise as behaving*
> *impeccably in life, displaying wisdom, insight, and*
> *virtue, who is like a coin of pure gold. He is praised.*
> — Buddha, *The Dhammapada*
> (tr. Ananda Maitreya)

TAKUMI   *[tah-koo-mee]*

MEANING: artisan, skilled • **USAGE:** Japanese:
from Japanese *takumi*
> *Being deeply learned and skilled;*
> *being well-trained and using well-spoken words —*
> *this is the best good luck.*
> — Buddha

TALIB, TALEEB   *[tah-leeb]*

MEANING: seeker of knowledge • **USAGE:** Muslim:
from Arabic *taliba*
> *All things which one seeks in God, such as light,*
> *life, strength, joy and peace,*
> *these all can be found in Truth.*
> — Hazrat Inayat Khan, *The Gayan*

TALIM, TALEEM   *[tah-leem]*

MEANING: educated, trained, rightly guided •
USAGE: Muslim
> *Allah will exalt those who believe among you,*
> *and those who have knowledge, to high ranks.*
> — Koran, She Who Pleaded 58.11b (PIC)

TAMBE   *[tahm-bee]*

MEANING: drum • **USAGE:** Amerind: Tewa
Pueblo
> *The drum dance offers an opportunity for those*
> *people who want to participate in the consciousness of*
> *the planet. In addition to what happens on the*
> *collective level, each dancer is uplifted mentally,*
> *emotionally, physically, and spiritually.*
> — Joseph Rael, *Being and Vibration*

TAMIZ, TAMEEZ   *[tah-meez]*

MEANING: judicious, just • **USAGE:** Muslim
> *Allah commands justice, the doing of good.*
> — Koran, The Bee 16.90a (ALI)

TANNER   *[TAN-er]*

MEANING: leather worker, tanner • **USAGE:**
English surname: from English *tannian* (to convert
hide into leather)
> *Your work will provide for your needs;*
> *you will be happy and prosperous.*
> — Psalm 128:2 (GNT)

TANNIS   *[TAN-es]*

MEANING: leather worker, tanner • **USAGE:**
American form of Tanner (*see* Tanner)
> *Along with love and friendship,*
> *one of the most durable satisfactions in life*
> *is to lose oneself in one's work.*
> *Every wise man seeks a task to dignify his days.*
> — Harry Emerson Fosdick,
> *On Being a Real Person*

TANNON   *[TAN-on]*

MEANING: leather worker, tanner • **USAGE:**
American form of Tanner (*see* Tanner)
> *The Lord your God will make you*
> *most prosperous in all the work of your hands.*
> — Deuteronomy 30:9a (NIV)

TAPCO   *[tahp-koh]*

MEANING: antelope • **USAGE:** Amerind: Kiowa
> *I love to roam over the prairies.*
> *There I feel free and happy.*
> — Satanta

TAQI   *[tah-kee]*

MEANING: devout, pious • **USAGE:** Muslim: from
Arabic *taqi*

It is not a sixth or a tenth of a man's devotion
which is acceptable to God, but only such portions
thereof as he offereth with understanding
and true devotional spirit.
— Hadith of the Prophet Muhammad
(tr. Abdullay Al-Mamun Al-Suhrawardy)

TARAN   *[TAH-ran]*

MEANING: thunder, god of thunder • **USAGE:** Irish
form of *Taranis* (Celtic god of thunder)
The voice of the Lord is over the waters;
the God of glory thunders, the Lord,
over many waters.
— Psalm 29:3 (ESV)

TARIK, TAREEK, TARIQ   *[tah-reek]*

MEANING: one who knocks at the door, seeker,
morning star • **USAGE:** Muslim: from Arabic *taraqa*
(to knock); the morning star
The first lesson that the seeker
after truth must learn is to be true to himself.
— Hazrat Inayat Khan, *The Gayan* (cd. *The Gayani*
Meditations, Volume 1, tr. Cecil Touchon)

TARUN   *[tah-roon]*

MEANING: young, youthful • **USAGE:** Hindu:
from Sanskrit *taruna*
Now is the time to wake up,
when you are young and strong.
— Buddha, *The Dhammapada*
(tr. Eknath Easwaran)

TASHUNKA   *[tah-shoon-kah]*

MEANING: horse • **USAGE:** Amerind: Sioux
Out of the earth, I sing for them. / A horse nation,
I sing for them. / Out of the earth, / I sing for them. /
The animals, I sing for them.
— "I Sing for the Animals," Teton Sioux song

TASLIM   *[tahs-leem]*

MEANING: greeting, welcome • **USAGE:** Muslim
If ye enter houses, salute each other —
a greeting of blessing and purity as from Allah.
— Koran, Light 24.61b (ALI)

TASOS, TASSOS   *[TAH-sohs]*

MEANING: resurrection, reborn, rise up • **USAGE:**
Greek form of Anastasios, from Greek *anastasis*
(resurrection), or from Greek *ana* (up) and *stasis*
(standing)
Arise, shine; for your light has come.
— Isaiah 60:1a (NRSV)

TATE   *[tayt]*

MEANING: cheerful, joyful, happy • **USAGE:**
English surname: from Norse *teitr*
Cheerfulness is, in the first place,
the best promoter of health...it bears
the same friendly regard to the mind as to the body.
— Joseph Addison

TATUM   *[TAY-tum]*

MEANING: cheerful, joyful, happy • **USAGE:**
American form of Tate (*see* Tate)
He that is of a merry heart hath a continual feast.
— Proverbs 15:15b (KJV)

TAVI   *[TAH-vee, tah-VEE]*

MEANING: beloved, loved • **USAGE:** Jewish form
of David, from Hebrew *dawidh*
Only goodness and steadfast love shall pursue
me all the days of my life, and I shall dwell
in the house of the Lord for many long years.
— Psalm 23:6 (JPS)

T

TAVIN, TAVEN [TAV-en]

MEANING: white hawk, plains falcon, kind, gentle, handsome, dark, black • **USAGE:** American: possibly a form of Gavin, from Welsh *gwalch* (hawk, falcon) and *gwyn* (white, fair, holy), *maedd* (battle) or *mai* (plain, field), or from Irish Gaelic *caomh* (gentle, kind) or *caem* (handsome); or possibly a form of Daven, from Irish Gaelic *dubh* (dark, black)

How truly is a kind heart a fountain of gladness, making everything in its vicinity freshen into smiles!
— Washington Irving, "The Christmas Dinner"

TAVIS [TAV-is]

MEANING: twin, joined, toll keeper, crossover • **USAGE:** Scottish form of Thomas, from Aramaic *tau'am* (a twin); or American form of Travis, from French *traverse* (to cross a river or bridge); occupational name for a toll collector

Blessed shall you be when you come in, and blessed shall you be when you go out.
— Deuteronomy 28:6 (NKJV)

TAVISH [TAV-ish]

MEANING: twin, joined • **USAGE:** Scottish form of Thomas, from Aramaic *tau'am* (a twin)

What God has joined together, let not man separate.
— Matthew 19:6 (NIV)

TAWA [tah-wah]

MEANING: sun • **USAGE:** Amerind: Hopi

Your beautiful rays, may they color our faces.
— Hopi prayer

TAWHID, TAWHEED [tah-heed]

MEANING: belief in the unity of Allah • **USAGE:** Muslim

God is a unit, and liketh unity.
— Hadith of the Prophet Muhammad
(tr. Abdullay Al-Mamun Al-Suhrawardy)

TAYE [tay]

MEANING: tailor, garment maker • **USAGE:** English form of Taylor (*see* Taylor)

God — He clothes me with strength and makes my way perfect.
— Psalm 18:32 (HCSB)

TAYLOR, TAYLER [TAY-lor]

MEANING: tailor, garment maker • **USAGE:** English surname: from English *taillour* (cutter of cloth)

Clothe yourselves with compassion, kindness, humility, gentleness, and patience.
— Colossians 3:12b (GNT)

TAYYIB [tah-yeeb]

MEANING: good, good-natured, generous • **USAGE:** Muslim

He that doeth good shall have ten times as much to his credit.
— Koran, Cattle 6.160a (ALI)

TEAGUE [teeg]

MEANING: poet, philosopher • **USAGE:** Irish form of Tadhg, from Gaelic *tadhg*

Poetry is the mysticism of mankind.
— Henry David Thoreau,
A Week on the Concord and Merrimack Rivers

TED [ted]

MEANING: gift of God • **USAGE:** English form of Theodore (*see* Teodor)

Every man also to whom God hath given riches and wealth, and hath given him power to eat thereof, and to take his portion, and to rejoice in his labor — this is the gift of God.
— Ecclesiastes 5:19 (ASV)

TEIGE   *[teeg]*

Meaning: poet, philosopher • **Usage:** Irish form of Tadhg, from Gaelic *tadhg*

> *Let the words of my mouth and the meditation*
> *of my heart be acceptable in your sight,*
> *O Lord, my rock and my redeemer.*
> — Psalm 19:14 (ESV)

TELLY   *[TEL-ee]*

Meaning: best purpose • **Usage:** English form of *Aristotelis*, from Greek *aristos* (best) and *telos* (purpose, aim)

> *When we do the best that we can, we never know what*
> *miracle is wrought in our life, or in the life of another.*
> — Helen Keller, *Out of the Dark*

TEMPLE   *[TEM-pel]*

Meaning: place of worship, synagogue • **Usage:** English: from English *temple*

> *You yourselves are being built like*
> *living stones into a spiritual temple.*
> — 1 Peter 2:6 (CEV)

TENNESSEE   *[ten-eh-SEE]*

Meaning: winding river, name of U.S. state • **Usage:** American: from Cherokee *tanisi*

> *We ought to begin life as at the source of a river,*
> *growing deeper every league to the sea.*
> — Henry Ward Beecher, *Life Thoughts*

TEO   *[TAY-oh]*

Meaning: gift of God • **Usage:** Spanish and Italian form of Mateo, from Hebrew *mattah'yah* (gift of Yahweh)

> *So with any gift of God: these are meted out*
> *according to the taker, not according to the giver.*
> — Meister Eckhart

TEODOR   *[TEH-oh-dohr]*

Meaning: gift of God • **Usage:** Polish, Czech, Hungarian, and Scandinavian form of Theodore, from Greek *theos* (God) and *doron* (gift)

> *Every good and perfect gift comes down from the*
> *Father who created all the lights in the heavens.*
> — James 1:17a (CEV)

TEODORO   *[tay-oh-DOR-oh]*

Meaning: gift of God • **Usage:** Spanish and Italian form of Theodore (*see* Teodor)

> *God said...wisdom and knowledge are granted to you.*
> — 2 Chronicles 1:12a (NRSV)

TERENCE, TERRENCE   *[TER-ens]*

Meaning: tender, polished, smooth • **Usage:** English: possibly form of Roman family name *Terentius*, from Latin *terenus* (soft, tender) or *terentius* (polished, smooth)

> *The bravest are the tenderest. /*
> *The loving are the daring.*
> — Bayard Taylor, "The Song of the Camp"

TERRAN   *[TER-an]*

Meaning: of the earth, earthy • **Usage:** English masculine form of Terra, from Latin *terra*

> *It is a wholesome and necessary thing for us to turn*
> *again to the earth and in the contemplation of her*
> *beauties to know of wonder and humility.*
> — Rachel Carson

TERRELL, TERREL   *[TER-el]*

Meaning: stubborn, warrior, justice • **Usage:** English surname: possibly from French *tirel* (to pull, stubborn); or possibly a form of Tyr, Norse god of war and justice

> *Prove all things; hold fast that which is good.*
> — 1 Thessalonians 5:21 (DR)

TERRONE   [teh-ROHN]

MEANING: born on the land of yew trees • **USAGE:** American form of Tyrone, from Irish Gaelic *tir* (land) and *eo gein* (born of the yew tree)

When a man plants a tree he plants himself.... The seeds he plants are his prayers, and, by God he works grander miracles every day than ever were written.
— John Muir, *Steep Trails*

TERRY   [TER-ee]

MEANING: tender, polished, smooth • **USAGE:** English form of Terence (*see* Terence)

Tenderness is a virtue.
— Oliver Goldsmith, *The Good-Natured Man*

TEX   [teks]

MEANING: friend, man from Texas • **USAGE:** American: from Caddo Indian *Tejas* (those who are friends)

The better part of one's life consists of his friendships.
— Abraham Lincoln (letter of July 13, 1849)

THABO   [tah-boh]

MEANING: joyful, lighthearted, happy • **USAGE:** African: Sotho of South Africa

Man must always be happy in order to perform well.
— Sotho proverb

THAD   [thad]

MEANING: given of God, gift of God • **USAGE:** English form of Thaddeus (*see* Thaddeus)

I thank thee, and praise thee, O thou God of my fathers, who hast given me wisdom and might.
— Daniel 2:23a (ASV)

THADDEUS   [THAD-ee-uhs]

MEANING: given of God, gift of God • **USAGE:** English form of *Theodotos*, from Greek *theo* (God) and *dotos* (given)

Take delight in the Lord, and he will give you your heart's desires.
— Psalm 37:4 (NLT)

THANOS   [THAH-nohs]

MEANING: immortal, eternal • **USAGE:** Greek form of *Athanasios*, from Greek *athanatos*

For whatever a man sows he will also reap... the one who sows to the Spirit will reap eternal life from the Spirit.
— Galatians 6:7b–8 (HCSB)

THATCHER   [THAT-cher]

MEANING: one who thatches a roof • **USAGE:** English surname: from English *þæc* (a roof of thatch), occupational name

Through wisdom a house is built, and by understanding it is established.
— Proverbs 24:3 (NKJV)

THEMBA   [tem-bah]

MEANING: hope, expectation • **USAGE:** African: Xhosa and Zulu of South Africa

Hope does not disappoint.
— Xhosa proverb

THEO   [THEE-oh]

MEANING: gift of God • **USAGE:** English and Greek form of Theodore (*see* Theodore)

Every good gift and every perfect gift is from above, coming down from the Father of lights.
— James 1:17a (ASV)

THEODOR   [THEH-oh-dor]

MEANING: gift of God • **USAGE:** German and Scandinavian form of Theodoros (*see* Theodore)

There are souls in the world who have the gift of finding joy everywhere, and of leaving it behind them when they go.
— Jean Paul Richter

THEODORE   *[THEE-oh-dohr]*

MEANING: gift of God • **USAGE:** English form of Theodoros, from Greek *theos* (God) and *doron* (gift)

No eye has seen, no ear has heard,
and no mind has imagined what God has prepared
for those who love him.
— 1 Corinthians 2:9b (NLT)

THEODORO   *[thay oh-DOH-roh]*

MEANING: gift of God • **USAGE:** Portuguese form of Theodore (*see* Theodore)

Thou [God] hast given me wisdom and power.
— Daniel 2:23b (NASB)

THEODOROS   *[theh-oh-DOR-os]*

MEANING: gift of God • **USAGE:** Greek (*see* Theodore)

There is nothing better than to enjoy food and drink
and to find satisfaction in work…these pleasures
are from the hand of God.
— Ecclesiastes 2:24 (NLT)

THEON   *[THEE-on]*

MEANING: gift of God • **USAGE:** American form of Theo or Theodore (*see* Theodore)

The Power within you is a Divine Authority. It is a
dispenser of the Divine Gifts. It is a giver of life, of joy.
— Ernest Holmes

THIBAULT   *[TEE-boh]*

MEANING: brave people • **USAGE:** French form of *Theobald*, from German *theuda* (people, nation) and *bald* (bold, brave)

The Lord gives his people strength.
The Lord blesses them with peace.
— Psalm 29:11 (NLT)

THOM   *[tom]*

MEANING: twin, joined, double • **USAGE:** English form of Thomas (*see* Thomas)

What therefore God hath joined together,
let not man put asunder.
— Matthew 19:6 (KJV)

THOMAS   *[TOM-as (English),*
toh-MAH (French), toh-MAHS (German,
Scandinavian), thoh-MAHS (Greek)]

MEANING: twin, joined, double • **USAGE:** English, French, German, Greek, and Scandinavian: from Aramaic *tau'am* (a twin)

Happiness was born a twin.
— Lord Byron, *Don Juan*

THONAH   *[thoh-nah]*

MEANING: thunder • **USAGE:** Amerind: Navajo

Thonah! Thonah! / There is a voice above, /
The voice of the thunder. / Within the dark cloud, /
Again and again it sounds.
— Navajo song

THORIN   *[THOR-in]*

MEANING: of Thor, the god of thunder and strength • **USAGE:** American form of *Thor*, Norse god of thunder and strength

The Lord's voice is heard over the sea. The glorious
God thunders; the Lord thunders over the ocean.
— Psalm 29:3 (GNT)

TIAGO   *[tee-AH-goh]*

MEANING: follower of St. James, replace, change, transform, successor • **USAGE:** Spanish form of Santiago, from Spanish *san* (saint) and Iago (James), from Hebrew *ya'aqobh* (one that takes by the heel, replace with another)

He that followeth justice and mercy,
shall find life, justice, and glory.
— Proverbs 21:21 (DR)

T

TIERNAN   *[TEER-nan]*

MEANING: little chief, little lord, leader • **USAGE:** Irish form of *Tighearnan* and diminutive *-an* (*see* Tierney)

> *Always be faithful in little things,*
> *for in them our strength lies.*
> — Mother Teresa

TIERNEY   *[TEER-nee]*

MEANING: chief, lord, leader • **USAGE:** Irish surname: form of *Tighearnan*, from Gaelic *tighern* (lord)

> *We all have different gifts, each of which came because of the grace God gave us....Anyone who has the gift of being a leader should try hard when he leads.*
> — Romans 12:6, 12:8b (NCV)

TIM   *[tim]*

MEANING: one who honors God, one who esteems God • **USAGE:** English form of Timothy (*see* Timothy)

> *He leads me in the way of living right with Himself which brings honor to His name.*
> — Psalm 23:3 (NLV)

TIMON   *[tee-MOHN]*

MEANING: honor, esteem • **USAGE:** Greek: from Greek *time*

> *Above all things, reverence yourself.*
> — Pythagoras

TIMOTEO   *[tee-moh-TAY-oh]*

MEANING: one who honors God, one who esteems God • **USAGE:** Spanish and Italian form of Timothy (*see* Timothy)

> *I delight to do thy will,*
> *O my God: yea, thy law is within my heart.*
> — Psalm 40:8 (KJV)

TIMOTHEE   *[tee-moh-TEH]*

MEANING: one who honors God, one who esteems God • **USAGE:** French form of Timothy (*see* Timothy)

> *We know that to them that love God,*
> *all things work together unto good.*
> — Romans 8:28 (DR)

TIMOTHEOS   *[tee-moh-THEH-ohs]*

MEANING: one who honors God • **USAGE:** Greek: from Greek *time* (honor, esteem) and *theos* (God)

> *Only love honors God.*
> — Francis of Assisi, "Only Love Honors God" (tr. Daniel Ladinsky in *Love Poems from God*)

TIMOTHY   *[TIM-oh-thee]*

MEANING: one who honors God, one who esteems God • **USAGE:** English form of Timotheos, from Greek *time* (honor, esteem) and *theos* (God)

> *Teach me your way, O Lord, that I may walk in your truth; give me an undivided heart to revere your name.*
> — Psalm 86:11 (NRSV)

TINO   *[TEE-noh]*

MEANING: great one, revered one, honored • **USAGE:** Spanish form of Augustino, from Latin *augustus* (great, revered); or Spanish form of Martino, from Latin *Mars* (Roman god of war)

> *His honor is great because of Your help.*
> *You have given him greatness and power.*
> — Psalm 21:5 (NLV)

TIP, TIPP   *[tip]*

MEANING: twin, joined, double • **USAGE:** English form of Thomas (*see* Thomas)

> *They are no longer two but one.*
> *Let no man divide what God has put together.*
> — Matthew 19:6 (NLV)

T

TITO [*TEE-toh*]

MEANING: title of honor, esteemed, white clay, great one, revered one, valorous • **USAGE:** Italian and Spanish form of Titus, from Greek *titulus* (title of honor) or *titauos* (white clay, white earth); Spanish form of Augusto, from Latin *augustus* (great, magnificent); or from Greek *tio* (honor, valor)

> *What is becoming in behavior is honorable,*
> *and what is honorable is becoming.*
> — Marcus Tullius Cicero

TITUS, TITOS [*TEE-tus, TEE-tohs*]

MEANING: honorable, valorous, white clay, white earth • **USAGE:** Greek: from Greek *titulus* (title of honor) or *titauos* (white clay, white earth)

> *O Lord, you are our Father; we are the clay, and you*
> *are our potter; we are all the work of your hand.*
> — Isaiah 64:8 (NRSV)

TIV [*teev, tiv*]

MEANING: good, goodness • **USAGE:** Jewish

> *You will then understand what is right, just,*
> *and equitable — every good course.*
> — Proverbs 2:9 (JPS)

TIVON [*tee-VOHN*]

MEANING: naturalist, lover of nature • **USAGE:** Jewish

> *Look deep into nature,*
> *and then you will understand everything better.*
> — Albert Einstein

TOBIAH [*toh-BIE-ah*]

MEANING: God is good, goodness of God • **USAGE:** English form of Tuvya (*see* Tobias)

> *You will be full of joy because the Lord your God*
> *will bring good to you.*
> — Deuteronomy 16:15b (NLV)

TOBIAS [*toh-BIE-ahs (English),*
toh-BEE-ahs (German, Scandinavian)]

MEANING: God is good, goodness of God • **USAGE:** English, German, and Scandinavian form of Tuvya, from Hebrew *tobhi'yah* (goodness of Yahweh)

> *God plays and laughs in good deeds.*
> — Meister Eckhart (tr. Raymond Blakney)

TOBIN [*TOH-ben*]

MEANING: God is good, goodness of God • **USAGE:** English form of Tobias (*see* Tobias)

> *Goodness…of all virtues and dignities of the mind is*
> *the greatest, being the character of the Deity.*
> — Francis Bacon, "Of Goodness"

TOBY, TOBIE [*TOH-bee*]

MEANING: my good, my goodness • **USAGE:** English form of Tobias (*see* Tobias)

> *Oh, taste and see that the Lord is good;*
> *blessed is the man who trusts in Him!*
> — Psalm 34:8 (NKJV)

TODD, TOD [*tod*]

MEANING: fox • **USAGE:** English: from English *tod*

> *What the lion cannot manage to do, the fox can.*
> — German proverb

TOKOTA [*toh-koh-tah*]

MEANING: friends to all • **USAGE:** Amerind: Sioux

> *With all things and in all things, we are relatives.*
> — Sioux proverb

TOM [*tom*]

MEANING: twin, joined, double • **USAGE:** English form of Thomas, from Aramaic *tau'am* (a twin)

> *A joy that is shared is a joy made double.*
> — English proverb

TOMAS, TOMÁS   *[TOM-as (Irish, Welsh), toh-MAHS (Spanish)]*

MEANING: twin, joined, double • **USAGE:** Irish, Welsh, and Spanish: form of Thomas (*see* Tom)

May you have the love of God.
May you be joined together by the Holy Spirit.
— 2 Corinthians 13:14b (NLV)

TOMER   *[TOH-mer]*

MEANING: palm tree, date tree • **USAGE:** Jewish: a place in Israel's Jordan Valley

He shall be as a tree planted by the waters, and that
spreadeth out its roots by the river, and shall not see
when heat cometh, but its foliage shall be luxuriant;
and shall not be anxious in the year of drought,
neither shall cease from yielding fruit.
— Jeremiah 17:8 (MT)

TOMMASO   *[toh-MAH-soh]*

MEANING: twin, joined, double • **USAGE:** Italian form of Thomas (*see* Tom)

For his Spirit joins with our spirit to affirm
that we are God's children.
— Romans 8:16 (NLT)

TONIO   *[TOH-nee-oh]*

MEANING: invaluable, priceless, excellent • **USAGE:** Italian form of Antonio (*see* Tony)

The excellency of knowledge is,
that wisdom preserveth the life of him that hath it.
— Ecclesiastes 7:12b (ASV)

TOÑO   *[TOHN-yoh]*

MEANING: invaluable, priceless, excellent • **USAGE:** Spanish form of Antonio (*see* Tony)

You are the most excellent of men,
and your lips have been anointed with grace,
since God has blessed you forever.
— Psalm 45:2 (RSV)

TONY   *[TOH-nee]*

MEANING: invaluable, priceless, excellent • **USAGE:** English form of Anthony, from Latin *Antonius*, a Roman family name possibly meaning "invaluable"

The one thing in the world, of value,
is the active soul. This every man is entitled to;
this every man contains within him.
— Ralph Waldo Emerson,
"The American Scholar"

TOPHER   *[TOH-fer]*

MEANING: follower of Christ, Christian, bearer of Christ • **USAGE:** English form of Christopher, from Greek *Christos* (Christ, the anointed one) and *pherein* (to bear, to bring)

All that is necessary to make this world
a better place to live in is to love — to love as
Christ loved, as Buddha loved.
— Isadora Duncan (memoir of December 20, 1924)

TOR   *[tor]*

MEANING: king • **USAGE:** African: Tiv of Nigeria

Whoever has riches should act like a king.
— Nigerian proverb

TOR   *[tor]*

MEANING: turn, appointed time • **USAGE:** Jewish

To every thing there is a season and a time to every
purpose under the heaven.
— Ecclesiastes 3:1 (MT)

TOR   *[tor]*

MEANING: of Thor, of the god of thunder and strength • **USAGE:** Scandinavian form of *Thorvalldr*, from Norse *Þorr* (Thor, Norse god of thunder and strength)

The voice of the Lord echoes above the sea. The God of
glory thunders. The Lord thunders over the mighty sea.
— Psalm 29:3 (NLT)

TORIN   [TOR-en]

MEANING: chief, ruler, leader • **USAGE:** Irish: from Gaelic *tighern*
> *I'll walk where my own nature would be leading.*
> — Emily Brontë, *The Professor*

TORRANCE, TORRENCE   [TOR-ens]

MEANING: hillock, mound • **USAGE:** Scottish surname: from Gaelic *torran*
> *You are the light of the world.*
> *A city on a hill can't be hidden.*
> — Matthew 5:14 (NIRV)

TORSTEN   [TOR-sten]

MEANING: thunder stone, Thor's stone, Thor's rock • **USAGE:** Scandinavian and German: from *Thor* (Norse god of thunder) and *steinn* (stone, rock)
> *God alone is the mighty rock that keeps me safe,*
> *and he is the fortress where I feel secure.*
> — Psalm 62:6 (CEV)

TORY, TORRIE   [TOR-ee]

MEANING: tender, polished, smooth, hillock, mound • **USAGE:** English form of Terence, from Latin *terenus* (soft, tender) or *terentius* (polished, smooth); or English form of Torrance (*see* Torrance)
> *Open your hearts to the love of God which he will give*
> *you. He loves you with tenderness.*
> — Mother Teresa

TOSHIO   [toh-shee-oh]

MEANING: wise man, brilliant man • **USAGE:** Japanese: from Japanese *toshi* (wise) and *o* (man)
> *A wise man should pay attention to his mind....*
> *The mind, well-guarded and controlled,*
> *will bring him happiness.*
> — Buddha, *The Dhammapada*
> (tr. Ananda Maitreya)

TOV   [tohv]

MEANING: good, goodness • **USAGE:** Jewish: from Hebrew *tobh*
> *He who strives to do good and kind deeds*
> *attains life, success, and honor.*
> — Proverbs 21:21 (JPS)

TOVE   [TOH-veh]

MEANING: Thor's rule, ruler of thunder • **USAGE:** Swedish form of *Thorvaldr*, from *Thor* (Norse god of thunder) and *valdr* (to rule)
> *The voice of the Lord is over the waters; the God of*
> *glory thunders; the Lord is over many waters.*
> — Psalm 29:3 (NKJV)

TOVI   [TOH-vee]

MEANING: my good, my goodness • **USAGE:** Jewish: from Hebrew *tobh*
> *The merciful man doeth good to his own soul.*
> — Proverbs 11:17a (MT)

TRACE   [trays]

MEANING: from Tracy-sur-Mer, visible mark • **USAGE:** English form of Tracy (*see* Tracy)
> *The invariable mark of wisdom is to see*
> *the miraculous in the common.*
> — Ralph Waldo Emerson, "Prospects"

TRACY, TRACEY   [TRAY-see]

MEANING: from Tracy-sur-Mer • **USAGE:** English surname: English form of *Tracy-sur-Mer* (French town)
> *The lines are fallen unto me in pleasant places;*
> *yea, I have a goodly heritage.*
> — Psalm 16:6 (DT)

TRAVERS   [TRAV-ers]

MEANING: traverser, toll keeper, crossover • **USAGE:** English surname (*see* Travis)

T

*Guard Clear Thinking and Common Sense
with your life.... They'll keep your soul alive and well,
and they'll keep you fit and attractive.
You'll travel safely, you'll neither tire nor trip.*
— Proverbs 3:21, 3:23 (MSG)

TRAVIS   [TRAV-es]

MEANING: traverser, crossover, toll keeper •
USAGE: English surname: from French *traverse* (to
cross a river or bridge); occupational name for a toll
collector
*You will understand what is right, just,
and fair, and you will find the right way to go.*
— Proverbs 2:9 (NLT)

TREFOR, TREVOR   [TREH-for, TREH-vor]

MEANING: from the big city • USAGE: Welsh:
from Welsh *tref* (town, village) and *for* (large, big)
*A city is not gauged by its length and width, but by the
broadness of its vision and the height of its dreams.*
— Herb Caen, *San Francisco: City on Golden Hills*

TRENT   [trent]

MEANING: flooding over, river name • USAGE:
English surname: possibly from Welsh *tros* (over)
and *hynt* (way), indicating "strongly flooding"; an
English river
*The Lord who created you says...when you pass
through deep waters, I will be with you.*
— Isaiah 43:1–2a (GNT)

TREV   [trev]

MEANING: from the big city • USAGE: Welsh form
of Trevor (*see* Trefor)
Good will come to you in the city.
— Deuteronomy 28:3a (NLV)

TREVIS   [TREV-es]

MEANING: traverser, crossover, toll keeper •
USAGE: American form of Travis (*see* Travis)

*Make the path of your feet level.
Let all of your ways be established.*
— Proverbs 4:26 (WEB)

TREY   [tray]

MEANING: three • USAGE: English: from Latin *tres*
A rope that is woven of three strings is hard to break.
— Ecclesiastes 4:12b (NCV)

TRINI   [TREE-nee]

MEANING: trinity, Holy Trinity • USAGE: Spanish
form of Trinidad (*see* Trinidad)
*Now abide faith, hope, love, these three;
but the greatest of these is love.*
— 1 Corinthians 13:13 (NASB)

TRINIDAD   [TREE-neh-dahd]

MEANING: trinity, Holy Trinity • USAGE: Spanish:
from Spanish *trinidad* (the Holy Trinity)
*I arise today through a mighty strength, the invocation
of the Trinity, through belief in the Threeness, through
confession of the Oneness of the Creator of creation.*
— Saint Patrick, "The Deer's Cry"

TRISTAN   [TRIS-ten]

MEANING: riotous, chaotic, sad • USAGE:
Welsh and English: from Welsh *drest* (riotous,
tumultuous, chaotic) or from French *triste* (sad,
sorrowful)
*In all chaos there is a cosmos,
in all disorder a secret order.*
— Carl Jung, *The Archetypes and the Collective
Unconscious* (tr. R. F. C. Hull)

TRISTIAN   [TRIS-chan]

MEANING: riotous, chaotic, sad, follower of
Christ, Christian • USAGE: American: possibly a
form of Tristan (*see* Tristan); or possibly a form of
Christian, from Greek *christianos*

Neither death nor life, nor angels nor rulers, nor things present nor things to come, nor powers, nor height nor depth, nor anything else in all creation, will be able to separate us from the love of God in Christ Jesus.
— Romans 8:38–39 (ESV)

TROY [troi]

MEANING: Trojan warrior, man of Troyes •
USAGE: English form of Troyes (city in France); or ancient Phrygian city
*Your light will break out like the dawn…
and your righteousness will go before you;
the glory of the Lord will be your rear guard.*
— Isaiah 58:8 (NASB)

TRUMAN [TROO-man]

MEANING: true man, trustworthy, faithful, loyal
• **USAGE:** English surname: from English *treowe* (true, trustworthy) and *mann* (man)
Trust men and they will be true to you; treat them greatly, and they will show themselves great.
— Ralph Waldo Emerson, "Prudence"

TUCSON [TOO-sahn]

MEANING: spring at the foot of a black mountain
• **USAGE:** American: from American Indian Pima *Chuk-son* (spring at the foot of a black mountain)
*You will be like a watered garden and like
a spring whose waters never run dry.*
— Isaiah 58:11b (HCSB)

TULLY, TULLIE [TUL-ee]

MEANING: leader of the people • **USAGE:** Irish surname: from Gaelic *tuathal*
*If you would be a leader of men you must lead
your own generation, not the next.*
— Woodrow Wilson,
"The Individual and Society"

TUVIAH, TUVIA, TUVIYA, TUVYA
[too-vee-YAH, TOO-vee-ah, TOOV-yah]

MEANING: goodness of God, God is good •
USAGE: Jewish: from Hebrew *tobhi'yah* (goodness of Yahweh)
*God is perfect goodness,
and all that comes from Him is absolutely good.*
— Maimonides, *Guide for the Perplexed*
(tr. M. Friedländer)

TY, TYE [tie]

MEANING: born on the land of the yew trees, tiler, firebrand, torch • **USAGE:** English form of Tyler, Tyson, or Tyrone (*see those entries*)
*He is like a tree planted by water, that sends out its
roots by the stream, and does not fear when heat comes,
for its leaves remain green, and is not anxious in the
year of drought, for it does not cease to bear fruit.*
— Jeremiah 17:8 (ESV)

TYCE [ties]

MEANING: firebrand, torch • **USAGE:** English form of Tyson, from French *tison*
*Bless the Lord, O my soul!…He makes his messengers
winds, his ministers a flaming fire.*
— Psalm 104:1–4 (ESV)

TYLER, TYLAR, TYLOR [TIE-ler]

MEANING: tiler, tiler of roofs • **USAGE:** English surname: from Latin *tegere* (to cover); occupational name
*May not but honest and wise men
ever rule under this roof.*
— John Adams (letter of November 2, 1800)

TYR [tier]

MEANING: warrior, justice • **USAGE:** Swedish: Norse god of war and justice
To build a world of justice, we must be just.
— Dag Hammarskjöld

T

TYREL, TYRELL, TYRRELL　　　[tie-REL]

MEANING: stubborn, warrior, justice • **USAGE:** American form of Terrel, possibly from French *tirel* (to pull, stubborn); or possibly a form of Tyr (*see* Tyr)

> *Yet I shall temper so / Justice with mercy.*
> — John Milton, *Paradise Lost*

TYRONE　　　[tie-ROHN]

MEANING: born of the yew trees • **USAGE:** Irish form of *Tir Eoghan* (Eoghan's land), from Gaelic *tir* (land) and *eo gein* (born of the yew tree); a county in Northern Ireland

> *They will be called "Trees of Justice,"*
> *planted by the Lord to honor his name.*
> — Isaiah 61:3b (CEV)

TYRUS　　　[TIE-rus]

MEANING: ruler, tyrant, coastal city, torch • **USAGE:** English form of *Tyrannus*, from Greek meaning "tyrant, ruler"; English form of Tyre, an ancient Mediterranean coastal city; or English form of Tyson, from French *tison* (firebrand, torch)

> *He will baptize you with the Holy Spirit and with fire.*
> — Luke 3:16b (KJV)

TYSON　　　[TIE-son]

MEANING: firebrand, torch • **USAGE:** English: from French *tison*

> *Enthusiasm is a kind of faith that has been set afire.*
> — George Matthew Adams

TZION　　　[tzee-YOHN]

MEANING: excellent • **USAGE:** Jewish: Zion, which can refer to Jewish people and to Israel

> *May the Lord, maker of heaven and earth,*
> *bless you from Zion.*
> — Psalm 134:3 (JPS)

U

UBERTO　　　[oo-BAYR-toh]

MEANING: shining spirit, intelligent • **USAGE:** Italian form of Hubert, from German *hugu* (heart, mind, spirit) and *beraht* (bright, shining)

> *There resides within us a divine spirit,*
> *which guards us and watches us.... He it is that*
> *prompts us to noble and exalted endeavours.*
> — Seneca

UDARA　　　[oo-dahr-ah]

MEANING: great, exalted • **USAGE:** Hindu: Sanskrit

> *As human beings, our greatness lies*
> *not so much in being able to remake the world...*
> *as in being able to remake ourselves.*
> — Mahatma Gandhi

UILLIAM　　　[OOL-yam]

MEANING: determined protector, steadfast guardian • **USAGE:** Irish form of William, from German *wil* (will, resolve) and *helm* (helmet, protection)

> *The Lord will guard you as you come and go,*
> *both now and forever.*
> — Psalm 121:8 (NCV)

ULF　　　[oolf]

MEANING: wolf • **USAGE:** Scandinavian and German: from Norse *ulfr*

> *The wolf shall dwell with the lamb.*
> — Isaiah 11:6a (ESV)

UMAR　　　[oo-mahr]

MEANING: long-lived, prosperous • **USAGE:** Muslim: from Arabic *amara* (to live long, to prosper)

T

O ye who believe! Persevere in patience and constancy;
vie in such perseverance; strengthen each other;
and fear Allah; that ye may prosper.
— Koran, The Family of Imran 3.200 (ALI)

UNIKA [oo-nee-kah]

MEANING: light up, shine • **USAGE:** African:
Lomwe of Malawi
While it shines, bask!
— Malawian proverb

URAM [oo-RAHM]

MEANING: light of the nation • **USAGE:** Jewish
I the Lord have called thee in righteousness, and have
taken hold of thy hand, and kept thee, and set thee for
a covenant of the people, for a light of the nations.
— Isaiah 42:6 (MT)

URBAN [oor-bahn]

MEANING: city dweller • **USAGE:** Scandinavian
and Polish: from Latin *urbanus* (from the city)
You are the light of the world.
A city on a hill cannot be hidden.
— Matthew 5:14 (NIV)

URBANO [oor-BAHN-oh]

MEANING: city dweller • **USAGE:** Italian: from
Latin *urbanus* (from the city)
You will be blessed in the city
and blessed in the country.
— Deuteronomy 28:3 (NIV)

URI [YOOR-ee, OO-ree]

MEANING: my flame, my light • **USAGE:** Jewish
Hitlahavut is "the burning," the ardor of ecstasy....
Hitlahavut unlocks the meaning of life.
— Martin Buber, *The Legend of the Baal-Shem*
(tr. Maurice Friedman)

URIAH [oo-ree-YAH, oo-RIE-ah, yoo-RIE-ah]

MEANING: God is my flame, God is my light •
USAGE: Jewish: from Hebrew *uriyyah* (flame of
Yahweh)
Send forth Your light and Your truth;
they will lead me.
— Psalm 43:3a (JPS)

URIEL [YOO-ree-el, oo-ree-EL]

MEANING: fire of God, God is my flame • **USAGE:**
Jewish: from Hebrew *uri'el*
Blessed is the flame that burns
in the secret fastness of the heart.
— Hannah Senesh, "Blessed Is the Match"

URVIL [uhr-vil]

MEANING: ocean, sea • **USAGE:** Hindu
The Spirit, without moving, is swifter than the mind;
the senses cannot reach him; He is ever beyond them....
To the ocean of his being, the spirit of life
leads the streams of action.
— Isa Upanishad (tr. Juan Mascaro)

USAMAH [oo-sah-mah]

MEANING: lion • **USAGE:** Muslim: from Arabic
usama
A pure conscience gives one the strength of a lion.
— Hazrat Inayat Khan, *The Gayan* (cd. *The Gayani*
Meditations, Volume 1, tr. Cecil Touchon)

UTAH [YOO-tah]

MEANING: one that is higher up, people of the
mountain • **USAGE:** American: from Apache
yuttahih (one that is higher up, reference to living
on a mountain)
I came to life in the cool winds
and crystal waters of the mountains.
— John Muir (letter of July 26, 1868)

U

UZI   *[OO-ʒee]*

MEANING: courageous, brave • **USAGE:** Jewish
Courage is a special kind of knowledge:
the knowledge of how to fear what ought to be feared
and how not to fear what ought not to be feared.
— David Ben-Gurion

UZIAH, UZIYA   *[yoo-ZIE-ah, oo-ZIE-ah]*

MEANING: God is my strength • **USAGE:** Jewish
I am ever mindful of the Lord's presence;
He is at my right hand; I shall never be shaken.
— Psalm 16:8 (JPS)

V

VADIM   *[vah-DEEM]*

MEANING: ruler, leader • **USAGE:** Russian:
possibly from Slavic *volod* (rule, lead)
A gifted leader is one who is capable
of touching your heart.
— Jacob Potofsky

VAL   *[vahl (Italian), val (English)]*

MEANING: strong, vigorous, healthy • **USAGE:**
English form of Valentine (*see* Valentin)
A strong body makes the mind strong.
— Thomas Jefferson (letter of August 19, 1785)

VALENTIN   *[vah-len-TEEN]*

MEANING: strong, vigorous, healthy • **USAGE:**
French, German, Russian, and Scandinavian form
of Roman family name *Valentinus*, from Latin
valens
Health of the soul in holiness of justice,
is better than all gold and silver: and a sound body,
than immense revenues.
— Sirach 30:15 (DR Apocrypha)

VALENTINE   *[VAL-en-tien]*

MEANING: strong, vigorous, healthy • **USAGE:**
English form of Valentino (*see* Valentin)
Reason's whole pleasure, all the joys of sense, /
Lie in three words: health, peace, and competence.
— Alexander Pope, *An Essay on Man*

VALENTINO   *[vah-len-TEE-noh]*

MEANING: strong, vigorous, healthy • **USAGE:**
Italian form of Roman family name *Valentinus* (*see*
Valentin)
Health is the soul that animates
all the enjoyments of life.
— Seneca

VALERIO   *[vah-LAY-ree-roh (Italian),*
bah-LAY-ree-yoh (Spanish)]

MEANING: strong, vigorous, healthy • **USAGE:**
Italian and Spanish form of Roman family name
Valerius, from Latin *valere*
Health and a good estate of body are above all gold,
and a strong body above infinite wealth.
— Ben Sira 30:15 (KJV Apocrypha)

VAN   *[van]*

MEANING: fen, marsh, small, little, God is
gracious, God is giving • **USAGE:** English: form of
Vance, from English *fenn* (marsh); form of Vaughn,
from *bychan* (small); or form of Ivan, from Hebrew
y'hohanan (Yahweh is gracious)
That best portion of a good man's life; /
His little, nameless, unremembered acts /
Of kindness and of love.
— William Wordsworth, "Lines Composed a Few
Miles above Tintern Abbey"

VANCE   *[vans]*

MEANING: marsh, fen • **USAGE:** English: from
English *fenn*

I enter a swamp as a sacred place, a sanctum sancto-
rum. There is the strength, the marrow, of Nature.
— Henry David Thoreau, "Walking"

VANYA   *[VAHN-yah]*

MEANING: God is gracious, God is giving •
USAGE: Russian form of Ivan, from Hebrew
y'hohanan (Yahweh is gracious)
The God who gives us peace will be with you.
— Philippians 4:9b (GNT)

VARADA   *[vah-rah-dah]*

MEANING: giver of blessings, beneficent • USAGE:
Hindu
God the Rescuer, / God the Savior, / Almighty, whom
we joyfully adore, / Powerful God, / Invoked by all
men, / May he, the bounteous, grant us his blessings!
— *Rig Veda*

VAREN   *[vah-ren]*

MEANING: best, superior • USAGE: Hindu
I cannot choose the best. The best chooses me.
— Rabindranath Tagore, *Stray Birds*

VARESH   *[vahr-esh]*

MEANING: superior ruler, honorable king •
USAGE: Hindu: from Sanskrit *vara* (best, superior)
and *isa* (lord, king, ruler)
There is nothing noble in being superior to some
other person. True nobility comes from being superior
to your previous self.
— Hindu proverb

VARIL   *[vah-ril]*

MEANING: water • USAGE: Hindu
Only he who is ready to question, to think for himself,
will find the truth! To understand the currents
of a river, he who wishes to know
the truth must enter the water.
— Nisargadatta Maharaj

VASILY   *[vah-SEE-lee]*

MEANING: king, royal one • USAGE: Russian form
of Basil, from Greek *basileus*
You meet him with rich blessings;
You place a crown of fine gold on his head.
— Psalm 21:3 (HCSB)

VASU   *[vah-suh]*

MEANING: wealthy, prosperous • USAGE: Hindu:
from Sanskrit *vasu*
Life finds its wealth by the claims of the world,
and its worth by the claims of love.
— Rabindranath Tagore, *Stray Birds*

VAUGHN, VAUGHAN   *[vahn]*

MEANING: small, little • USAGE: Welsh and
English: from Welsh *bychan*
Make small commitments and keep them.
Be a light, not a judge. Be a model, not a critic.
Be a part of the solution, not the problem.
— Stephen Covey,
Daily Reflections for Highly Effective People

VENTURO   *[been-TOOR-oh]*

MEANING: good fortune, lucky • USAGE: Spanish
form of *Bonaventura*, from Latin *bona* (good) and
ventura (luck, fortune)
Good will come to you when you come in,
and when you go out.
— Deuteronomy 28:6 (NLV)

VERN, VERNE   *[vern]*

MEANING: alder tree • USAGE: English form of
Vernon (*see* Vernon)
The grandeur of the forest tree / Comes not by casting
in a formal mould, / But from its own divine vitality.
— William Wordsworth, "A Poet"

V

VERNON   *[VER-non]*

MEANING: alder tree • **USAGE:** English: from French *verne*

He shall be like a tree which is planted near the running
waters, which shall bring forth its fruit,
in due season. And his leaf shall not fall off:
and all whosoever he shall do shall prosper.
— Psalm 1:3 (DR)

VIAN   *[VEE-an]*

MEANING: life, full of life • **USAGE:** English masculine form of Vivian, from Latin *vita*

It is not length of life, but depth of life.
— Ralph Waldo Emerson, "Immortality"

VIC, VICK, VIK   *[vik]*

MEANING: conqueror, victorious, successful, triumphant • **USAGE:** English form of Victor (*see* Victor)

He who has conquered self has conquered the universe.
— James Allen, *From Poverty to Power*

VICENTE   *[vee-SAYN-tay]*

MEANING: conqueror, victorious, successful, triumphant • **USAGE:** Italian form of Vincenzo (*see* Victor)

He nevertheless got the better of himself,
and that is the best kind of victory one can wish for.
— Miguel de Cervantes, *Don Quixote*

VICO   *[VEE-koh]*

MEANING: conqueror, victorious, successful, triumphant • **USAGE:** Italian form of Vincenzo (*see* Victor)

The Lord be with you,
and may you have success.
— 1 Chronicles 22:11a (NIV)

VICTOR, VÍCTOR   *[VIK-tor (English),*
VEEK-tor (French, Scandinavian),
BEEK-tor (Spanish)]

MEANING: conqueror, victorious, successful, triumphant • **USAGE:** English, French, Scandinavian, and Spanish: from Latin *vincere* (to conquer)

This is the art of courage: to see things as they are
and still believe that the victory lies not
with those who avoid the bad, but those who taste,
in living awareness, every drop of the good.
— Victoria Lincoln, "The Art of Courage"

VIDAL   *[bee-DAHL]*

MEANING: life, full of life, vital • **USAGE:** Spanish form of Roman family name *Vitalis*, from Latin *vitalis* (vital, of life)

The excellency of knowledge is,
that wisdom giveth life to them that have it.
— Ecclesiastes 7:12 (KJV)

VIDURA   *[vih-doo-rah]*

MEANING: wise • **USAGE:** Hindu: Sanskrit

In this world the wise man /
becomes himself a light, / pure, shining, free.
— Buddha, *The Dhammapada* (tr. Thomas Byrom)

VIGGO   *[VEE-goh]*

MEANING: warrior • **USAGE:** Scandinavian: from Norse *vig* (war)

You will stand firm and without fear.
— Job 11:15b (NIV)

VIJAY   *[vih-jay]*

MEANING: victorious, triumphant, all-conquering • **USAGE:** Hindu: from Sanskrit *vijaya*

When soul force awakens, it becomes irresistible
and conquers the world. This power is inherent
in every human being.
— Mahatma Gandhi

VIKTOR [VEEK-tor]

MEANING: conqueror, victorious, successful, triumphant • **USAGE:** German, Scandinavian, and Russian form of Victor (*see* Victor)
> *You will be prosperous and successful.*
> — Joshua 1:8b (GNT)

VILHELM [VEEL-helm]

MEANING: determined protector, steadfast guardian • **USAGE:** Scandinavian and Hungarian form of William, from German *wil* (will, resolve) and *helm* (protection, helmet)
> *The Lord will guard your going out and your coming*
> *in from this time forth and forever.*
> — Psalm 121:8 (NASB)

VILI [VEE-lee]

MEANING: determined protector, steadfast guardian • **USAGE:** Hungarian form of Vilhelm (*see* Vilhelm)
> *Guard your heart with all vigilance,*
> *for from it are the sources of life.*
> — Proverbs 4:23 (NIRV)

VIMAL [vih-mahl]

MEANING: pure, clean • **USAGE:** Hindu: from Sanskrit *vimala*
> *As a man acts, so does he become....*
> *A man becomes pure through pure deeds.*
> — Brihadaranyaka Upanishad
> (tr. Swami Prabhavananda)

VINCE [vins]

MEANING: conqueror, victorious, successful, triumphant • **USAGE:** English form of Vincent (*see* Vincent)
> *A man can only rise, conquer,*
> *and achieve by lifting up his thoughts.*
> — James Allen, *As a Man Thinketh*

VINCENS, VINZENZ [veen-SENZ]

MEANING: conqueror, victorious, successful, triumphant • **USAGE:** German form of Vincent (*see* Vincent)
> *The one who understands a matter finds success.*
> — Proverbs 16:20a (HCSB)

VINCENT [VIN-sent (English), ven-SAHN (French), VEEN-sent (Dutch)]

MEANING: conqueror, victorious, successful, triumphant • **USAGE:** English, French, and Dutch form of Roman family name *Vincentius*, from Latin *vincere* (to conquer)
> *The sword conquered for a while,*
> *but the spirit conquers for ever!*
> — Sholem Asch, *The Apostle*

VINCENTE [veen-CHEHN-tay]

MEANING: conqueror, victorious, successful, triumphant • **USAGE:** Spanish and Portuguese form of Vincent (*see* Vincent)
> *Victory increases with harmony.*
> [Victoria concordia crescit.]
> — Latin proverb

VINCENZO [ven-CHEN-zoh]

MEANING: conqueror, victorious, successful, triumphant • **USAGE:** Italian form of Vincent (*see* Vincent)
> *Courage conquers all things:*
> *it even gives strength to the body.* — Ovid

VINSON [VIN-son]

MEANING: son of Vince, son of the conqueror, successful, victorious • **USAGE:** English surname: from Latin *vincere* (to conquer) and *son*
> *If one advances confidently in the direction*
> *of his dreams, and endeavors to live the life*
> *which he has imagined, he will meet with success*
> *unexpected in common hours.*
> — Henry David Thoreau, *Walden*

V

VIRGIL   [VIR-jil]

MEANING: staff-bearer, rod • **USAGE:** English: possibly form of Roman family name *Vergilius*, from Latin *virga* (rod, staff)

> *Thou art with me; Thy rod and thy staff,*
> *they comfort me.*
> — Psalm 23:4b (ASV)

VIT   [veet]

MEANING: life, full of life • **USAGE:** Czech form of Roman family name *Vitus* (*see* Vital)

> *Let them not depart from your eyes — keep sound*
> *wisdom and discretion; so they will be life to your soul.*
> — Proverbs 3:21–22b (NKJV)

VITAL   [vee-TAHL]

MEANING: life, full of life • **USAGE:** German form of Roman family name *Vitus*, from Latin *vita*

> *Talent develops in solitude,*
> *character in the stream of life.*
> — Johann Wolfgang von Goethe

VITALE   [veh-TAH-leh]

MEANING: life, full of life • **USAGE:** Italian form of Roman family name *Vitalis*, from Latin *vita*

> *Life is so full of meaning and of purpose,*
> *so full of beauty.*
> — Fra Giovanni Giocondo
> (Christmas Eve letter, 1513)

VITALY, VITALI   [veh-TAH-leh]

MEANING: life, full of life • **USAGE:** Russian form of Vitale (*see* Vitale)

> *There's nothing better to do than go ahead*
> *and have a good time and get the most*
> *we can out of life. That's it — eat, drink,*
> *and make the most of your job. It's God's gift.*
> — Ecclesiastes 3:13 (MSG)

VITO   [VEE-toh]

MEANING: life, full of life • **USAGE:** Italian and Spanish form of Roman family name *Vitus* (*see* Vital)

> *If a man should live many years,*
> *let him have joy in them all.*
> — Ecclesiastes 11:8a (NLV)

VITTORIO   [vee-TOH-ree-oh]

MEANING: conqueror, victorious, successful, triumphant • **USAGE:** Italian form of Victor, from Latin *vincere* (to conquer)

> *You will make your way prosperous,*
> *and then you will have success.*
> — Joshua 1:8b (NASB)

VLAD   [vlahd]

MEANING: great leader, peaceful ruler • **USAGE:** Russian form of Vladimir (*see* Vladimir)

> *Be at peace, and the God of the love*
> *and peace shall be with you.*
> — 2 Corinthians 13:11b (YLT)

VLADIMIR   [vlah-DEE-meer]

MEANING: great leader, peaceful ruler • **USAGE:** Russian: from Russian *volod* (rule, lead) and *meri* (great, famous) or *mir* (peace)

> *First put yourself at peace, and then you may*
> *the better make others be at peace.*
> — Thomas à Kempis, *The Imitation of Christ*
> (tr. Harvey Goodwin)

VOLKER   [VOHL-ker]

MEANING: guardian of the people, people's army, warrior • **USAGE:** German form of *Folkvardr*, from Norse *folk* (people, folk) and *varðr* (guardian, protector), or from German *volk* (people, folk) and *hari* (army)

> *Get wisdom, get understanding....*
> *Do not forsake her and she will guard you;*
> *love her, and she will watch over you.*
> — Proverbs 4:5–6 (NIV)

V

W

WADE   [wayd]

MEANING: wade, ford • USAGE: English surname: from English *waden* (to wade)

> *Thus says the Lord...when you pass through*
> *the waters, I will be with you.*
> — Isaiah 43:1–2a (NKJV)

WAFI   [wah-fee]

MEANING: faithful, trustworthy, true • USAGE: Muslim: from Arabic *wafa*

> *Beyond goodness is trueness, which is a divine quality.*
> — Hazrat Inayat Khan, *The Gayan*

WAFIQ, WAFEEQ   [wah-FEEK]

MEANING: friend, companion • USAGE: Muslim

> *The more people you can get on with,*
> *the wiser man you are.*
> — Hazrat Inayat Khan, *The Gayan*

WAHIB, WAHEEB   [wah-HEEB]

MEANING: generous, charitable • USAGE: Muslim: from Arabic *wahaba* (to give)

> *He who has given has saved his treasure forever.*
> — Hazrat Inayat Khan, *The Gayan* (cd. *The Gayani Meditations, Volume 1*, tr. Cecil Touchon)

WAJID, WAJEED   [wah-JEED]

MEANING: finder • USAGE: Muslim

> *If you search for God, you will find Him.*
> — Arabic proverb

WALDO   [WAL-doh (English), VAHL-doh (German)]

MEANING: ruler, leader • USAGE: English and German: from German *wald*

> *If we are leaders, we should do our best.*
> — Romans 12:6 (CEV)

WALKER   [WAL-ker]

MEANING: one who thickens cloth, cloth maker • USAGE: English surname: from English *wealcere* (to walk, tread); occupational name, refers to medieval practice of "walking" on wool cloth to ready it for use

> *Compassion clothes the soul with the robe of God*
> *and divinely adorns it.*
> — Meister Eckhart
> (*Meditations with Meister Eckhart*, tr. Matthew Fox)

WALLACE   [WAL-us]

MEANING: man from Wales, Welshman • USAGE: Scottish and English surname: from French *waleis* (foreign, Welshman)

> *A faithful man will abound with blessings.*
> — Proverbs 28:20a (NASB)

WALLY   [WAL-ee]

MEANING: man from Wales, Welshman • USAGE: English form of Wallace (*see* Wallace)

> *Nothing is better for a man than that he should eat and*
> *drink, and that his soul should enjoy good in his labor.*
> *This also, I saw, was from the hand of God.*
> — Ecclesiastes 2:24 (NKJV)

WALT   [walt]

MEANING: ruler of the army, army commander • USAGE: English form of Walter (*see* Walter)

> *We all have different gifts that God has given*
> *to us by His loving-favor. We are to use them....*
> *If someone has the gift of leading other people,*
> *he should lead them.*
> — Romans 12:6, 12:8 (NLV)

WALTER   [WAL-ter (English), VAHL-tehr (Polish, German, Scandinavian)]

MEANING: ruler of the army, army commander • USAGE: English, German, Polish, and

W

Scandinavian form of *Waldhere*, from German *wald* (rule, power) and *hari* (army)

God did not give us a spirit of timidity,
but a spirit of power, of love and of self-discipline.
— 2 Timothy 1:7 (NIV)

WALTHER   *[VAHL-ter]*

MEANING: ruler of the army, army commander • USAGE: German and Scandinavian form of Walter (*see* Walter)

Principles and rules are intended to provide
a thinking man with a frame of reference.
— Carl von Clausewitz, *On War* (tr. J. J. Graham)

WAMBLEE   *[wahm-blee]*

MEANING: eagle • USAGE: Amerind: Sioux

The eagle is the witness of the Great Spirit,
the eyes of God.
— Noble Red Man

WANETA   *[wah-neh-tah]*

MEANING: he who charges • USAGE: Amerind: Sioux

Try to do something that is brave.
That man is most successful who is foremost.
— Jumping Bull

WARD   *[ward]*

MEANING: guard, watchman, sentinel • USAGE: English surname: from English *weard*

Keep your heart with all vigilance,
for out of it spring the issues of life.
— Proverbs 4:23 (NKJV)

WARREN   *[WAR-en]*

MEANING: game preserve, protection, shelter • USAGE: English surname: from French *warenne* (warren, game preserve); or from German *warin* (protection, shelter)

The beloved of the Lord shall dwell in safety by Him,
Who shelters him all the day long.
— Deuteronomy 33:12 (NKJV)

WASI   *[wah-see]*

MEANING: broad-minded, liberal • USAGE: Muslim

For those who give in Charity, men and women,
and loan to Allah a Beautiful Loan,
it shall be increased manifold (to their credit),
and they shall have (besides) a liberal reward.
— Koran, Iron 57.18 (ALI)

WASIM, WASEEM   *[wah-SEEM]*

MEANING: handsome, distinguished • USAGE: Muslim: from Arabic *wasim* (good-looking) or *wasama* (to distinguish)

He created the heavens and the earth with truth,
and He formed you, then made goodly your forms,
and to Him is the ultimate resort.
— Koran, Loss and Gain 64.3 (SKR)

WAYLAND   *[WAY-land]*

MEANING: battlefield • USAGE: English form of *Weiland* (Scandinavian blacksmith), from German *wig* (war, strife) and *land* (land, territory)

Real courage is not limited to the battlefield.
— Charles Swindoll,
Growing Strong in the Seasons of Life

WAYNE   *[wayn]*

MEANING: wagon maker, wagoner • USAGE: English surname: from English *waen* (wagon, cart); occupational name of a wagoner

Listen for God's voice in everything you do,
everywhere you go;
he's the one who will keep you on track.
— Proverbs 3:5–6 (MSG)

WEI   *[way]*

MEANING: great, big, mighty, powerful, strong •
USAGE: Chinese

*The man of perfect virtue, wishing to be established
himself, seeks also to establish others; wishing to be
enlarged himself, he seeks also to enlarge others.*
— Confucius, *The Analects* (tr. James Legge)

WEN   *[wen]*

MEANING: culture, literacy, refined, gentle •
USAGE: Chinese

*The gentleman by his culture collects friends about
him, and through these friends promotes goodness.*
— Confucius, *The Analects* (tr. Arthur Waley)

WENDEL, WENDELL   *[WEN-del (English),*
                       VEN-del (German, Dutch)]

MEANING: traveler, sojourner, wanderer, a Wend
• **USAGE:** English, Dutch, and German: from
German *Wend*, migrant Slavs of the sixth century
*A man that hath travelled knoweth many things; and
he that hath much experience will declare wisdom.*
— Ben Sira 34:9 (KJV Apocrypha)

WERNER   *[VER-ner (German,*
                    Scandinavian), WER-ner (English)]

MEANING: army guard, defending warrior •
USAGE: German and Scandinavian: from German
ware (guardian, protector) and *hari* (army)
*Courage, above all things,
is the first quality of a warrior.*
— Carl von Clausewitz, *On War*
(tr. Colonel J. J. Graham)

WES   *[wes]*

MEANING: west meadow, western field, western
town • **USAGE:** English form of Wesley (*see*
Wesley) or of Weston (*see* Weston)

*Out where the handclasp's a little stronger, /
Out where the smile dwells a little longer, /
That's where the West begins.*
— Arthur Chapman,
"Out Where the West Begins"

WESLEY   *[WES-lee, WEZ-lee]*

MEANING: west meadow, western pasture •
USAGE: English: from English *west* (west) and *leah*
(meadow, pasture)
*The west is color…
the colors of earth and sunlight and ripeness.*
— Jessamyn West

WESTON   *[WES-ton]*

MEANING: western town • **USAGE:** English
surname: from English *west* (west) and *tun* (town)
Westward the course of empire takes its way.
— George Berkeley

WHAKAN   *[whah-kahn]*

MEANING: sacred • **USAGE:** Amerind: Sioux
*I saw the sacred hoop of my people was one of the many
hoops that made one circle, wide as daylight and as
starlight, and in the center grew one mighty flowering
tree to shelter all the children of one mother and one
father. And I saw that it was holy.*
— Wallace Black Elk

WHITLEY   *[WHIT-lee]*

MEANING: white meadow • **USAGE:** English
surname: from English *hwit* (white) and *leah*
(meadow, field)
*When you gaze on a bright white ground,
it is like looking through colour rather than at it —
like looking through stained glass.*
— Fred Machetanz

W

WHITNEY   *[WHIT-nee]*

MEANING: white island • **USAGE:** English surname: from English *hwit* (white) and *ieg* (island)

Nature always wears the colours of the spirit.
— Ralph Waldo Emerson, *Nature*

WICASA   *[wee-kah-sah]*

MEANING: sage, wise • **USAGE:** Amerind: Sioux

The man who preserves his selfhood ever calm and unshaken by the storms of existence — not a leaf, as it were, astir on the tree, not a ripple upon the surface of the shining pool — his, in the mind of the unlettered sage, is the ideal attitude and conduct of life.
— Ohiyesa, *The Soul of the Indian*

WILBERT   *[WIL-bert (English), VEEL-bert (Dutch, Scandinavian)]*

MEANING: bright resolve, shining desire • **USAGE:** English, Dutch, and Scandinavian: from German *wil* (will, desire, resolve) and *beraht* (bright, shining)

Nothing is impossible to a willing heart.
— John Heywood

WILBUR, WILBER   *[WIL-ber]*

MEANING: shining desire, bright resolve • **USAGE:** English: from German *wil* (will, desire, resolve) and *beraht* (bright, shining)

Have the courage of your desire.
— George Gissing,
The Private Papers of Henry Ryecroft

WILFRED, WILFRID   *[WIL-fred]*

MEANING: desiring peace, peaceful • **USAGE:** English: from English *willa* (wish, desire) and *frith* (peace)

*Blessed are the peacemakers,
for they shall be called sons of God.*
— Matthew 5:9 (NASB)

WILHELM   *[VEEL-helm]*

MEANING: determined protector, steadfast guardian • **USAGE:** German and Scandinavian: from German *wil* (will, resolve) and *helm* (helmet, protection)

Be strong, be resolute; do not be fearful or dismayed, for the Lord your God is with you wherever you go.
— Joshua 1:9 (NEB)

WILL   *[wil]*

MEANING: determined protector, steadfast guardian • **USAGE:** English form of William, Wilhelm, or Willard (*see those entries*)

Courage and resolution are the spirit and soul of virtue.
— Thomas Fuller, *Gnomologia*

WILLARD   *[WIL-ard]*

MEANING: strong-willed, determined, resolute, steadfast • **USAGE:** English surname: form of *Wilheard*, from English *wolde* (will, determination) and *heard* (brave, hardy, strong)

We must remember that one determined person can make a significant difference, and that a small group of determined people can change the course of history.
— Sonia Johnson

WILLEM   *[VEE-lem]*

MEANING: determined protector, steadfast guardian • **USAGE:** Dutch and Scandinavian form of William (*see* William)

*Keep thy heart with all diligence;
for out of it are the issues of life.*
— Proverbs 4:23 (ASV)

WILLI   *[VEEL-ee]*

MEANING: determined protector, steadfast guardian • **USAGE:** German form of William (*see* William)

W

You will live secure and full of hope;
God will protect you and give you rest.
— Job 11:18 (GNT)

WILLIAM   *[WIL-yam]*

MEANING: determined protector, steadfast
guardian • **USAGE:** English form of Wilhelm,
from German *wil* (will, resolve) and *helm* (helmet,
protection)

An able man shows his spirit
by gentle words and resolute actions.
— Lord Chesterfield (letter of January 15, 1753)

WILMER   *[WIL-mer]*

MEANING: famous resolve • **USAGE:** English form
of *Willamar,* from German *wil* (will, resolve) and
meri (famous)

He who walks with integrity, and works righteousness,
and speaks truth in his heart....He who does these
things will never be shaken.
— Psalm 15:2, 15:5b (NASB)

WINFRED   *[WEN-fred]*

MEANING: friend of peace, peaceful friend •
USAGE: English: from English *wine* (friend) and
frid (peace)

To think well of all, to be cheerful with all, to patiently
learn to find the good in all — such unselfish thoughts
are the very portals of heaven; and to dwell day by day
in thoughts of peace toward every creature will bring
abounding peace to their possessor.
— James Allen, *As a Man Thinketh*

WINFRIED   *[WEN-freed]*

MEANING: friend of peace, peaceful friend •
USAGE: German form of Winfred, from English
wine (friend) and *frid* (peace)

Peace is not mere absence of war,
but is a virtue that springs from force of character.
— Baruch Spinoza, "Tractatus Politicus"
(tr. R. H. M. Elwes)

WINSTON   *[WIN-ston]*

MEANING: friendly town, joy stone, good place
• **USAGE:** English surname: from English *wine*
(friend) and *tun* (town, village); from English *wynn*
(joy) and *stan* (stone); or from Norse *wynn* (good,
beautiful) and *stonn* (town, place)

A people free to choose will always choose peace.
— Ronald Reagan
(speech at Moscow State University, 1988)

WOLF, WOLFE   *[wulf]*

MEANING: wolf • **USAGE:** English: from German
wulf

The wolf will live with the lamb.
— Isaiah 11:6a (NIV)

WOLFGANG   *[VOLF-gahng]*

MEANING: pathway of the wolf • **USAGE:**
German: from German *wulf* (wolf) and *gang*
(pathway, path)

The path of life leads upward for the wise.
— Proverbs 15:24a (NASB)

WOODROW   *[WUD-roh]*

MEANING: woods, forest • **USAGE:** English: from
English *wudu*

All the trees of the wood sing for joy.
— Psalm 96:12 (ASV)

WOODY   *[WUD-ee]*

MEANING: woods, forest • **USAGE:** English form
of Woodrow (*see* Woodrow)

Keep close to Nature's heart...spend a week
in the woods. Wash your spirit clean.
— John Muir

WYATT   *[WIE-et]*

MEANING: brave in battle, strong warrior •
USAGE: English form of *Wigheard,* from English
wig (war, strife) and *heard* (brave, hardy, strong)

W

The God Who lives forever...is the battle-covering
Who helps you. He is the sword of your great power.
— Deuteronomy 33:27–29b (NLV)

WYNN, WYN   *[wen]*

MEANING: handsome, white, holy • **USAGE:**
Welsh: from Welsh *gwyn*
   Thou art fairer than the children of men;
grace is poured into thy lips: Therefore God hath
blessed thee for ever.
— Psalm 45:2 (ASV)

X

XANDER   *[KSAHN-der]*

MEANING: protector and helper of humankind,
guardian • **USAGE:** Dutch and English form of
Alexander, from Greek *alexein* (to defend, to help)
and *andros* (man)
   I am going to send an angel before you
to protect you on the way.
— Exodus 23:20a (HCSB)

XAVIER   *[ZAY-vyer (English),*
ʒah-vee-AHR-ah (Portuguese, Spanish),
ʒah-VYAY (French)]

MEANING: new house • **USAGE:** English, French,
Portuguese, and Spanish: from Basque place-name
Etxabier (new house)
Peace to you and your house! Peace to all that is yours!
— 1 Samuel 25:6b (NEB)

XIMENES   *[hee-MAY-nes]*

MEANING: hear, hearken • **USAGE:** Spanish form
of Simon, from Hebrew *shim'on*
   If you are willing to listen,
you will learn and become wise.
— Sirach 6:33 (GNT Apocrypha)

XIONG   *[shee-ohng]*

MEANING: male, masculine, powerful, mighty •
USAGE: Chinese
A real man is one whose goodness is a part of himself.
— Mencius

XUE   *[shu-eh]*

MEANING: study, learning • **USAGE:** Chinese
Only he who has studied his mental constitution knows
his nature; knowing his nature, he knows Heaven.
— Mencius

Y

YADID   *[yah-DEED]*

MEANING: friend, beloved • **USAGE:** Jewish
   He who acquires wisdom is his own best friend;
he preserves understanding and attains happiness.
— Proverbs 19:8 (JPS)

YAKIM   *[yah-KEEM]*

MEANING: he will establish, God will establish •
USAGE: Jewish
   Thou shouldest enter into the covenant
of the Lord thy God...that He may establish
thee this day unto Himself for a people.
— Deuteronomy 29:11–12a (MT)

YAKIR   *[yah-KEER]*

MEANING: precious, dear, beloved • **USAGE:**
Jewish

   Beloved of the Lord,
he rests securely beside Him;
ever does He protect him,
as he rests between His shoulders.
— Deuteronomy 33:12b (JPS)

X

YAKOV [yah-KOHV, YAHK-ohv]

MEANING: replace, change, transform, successor • **USAGE:** Jewish and Russian: from Hebrew *ya'aqobh* (one that takes by the heel, replace with another)

Now thus said the Lord — Who created you, O Jacob, Who formed you, O Israel: fear not, for I will redeem you; I have singled you out by name, You are Mine.
— Isaiah 2:5b (JPS)

YAMATO [yah-muh-toh]

MEANING: great harmony • **USAGE:** Japanese

Concord gladdens one, one delights and rejoices in concord; and it is concord that one spreads by one's words.
— Buddha

YANCY, YANCEY [YAN-cee]

MEANING: God is gracious, God is giving, Yankee • **USAGE:** American form of Dutch surname *Jansen*, meaning "son of Jan," from Hebrew *y'hohanan* (Yahweh is gracious); or possibly an American Indian mispronunciation of "English"

The God of grace…will perfect you and give you firmness, strength, a sure foundation.
— 1 Peter 5:10 (GNT)

YANKEL [YAHN-kel]

MEANING: replace, change, transform, successor • **USAGE:** Yiddish form of Yakov (*see* Yakov)

Whoever reaches his ideal transcends it.
— Friedrich Nietzsche, *Beyond Good and Evil* (tr. Walter Kaufmann)

YANN [yahn]

MEANING: God is gracious, God is giving • **USAGE:** French form of John, from Hebrew *y'hohanan* (Yahweh is gracious)

May God be gracious to you.
— Genesis 43:29b (NIRV)

YANNI, YIANNI [YAH-nee]

MEANING: God is gracious, God is giving • **USAGE:** Greek form of John (*see* Yann)

There is nothing better for man under the sun than to eat, drink, and enjoy himself, for this will accompany him in his labor during the days of his life that God gives him under the sun.
— Ecclesiastes 8:15 (HCSB)

YANNIS, YIANNIS [YAH-nes]

MEANING: God is gracious, God is giving • **USAGE:** Greek form of John (*see* Yann)

God said…I have given thee a wise and an understanding heart.
— 1 Kings 3:11–12b (KJ21)

YAQUB [yah-koob]

MEANING: replace, change, transform, successor • **USAGE:** Muslim form of Jacob (*see* Yakov)

Say ye: "We believe in Allah, and the revelation given to us, and to Abraham, Isma'il, Isaac, Jacob."
— Koran, The Cow 2.136a (ALI)

YAQUT [yah-koot]

MEANING: ruby, precious gem • **USAGE:** Muslim

The jewels you get when you meet the Beloved / Go on multiplying themselves; / They take root / everywhere.
— Hafiz, "Burglars Hear Watchdogs" (tr. Daniel Ladinsky in *The Gift*)

YARDEN [yahr-DEN, YAHR-den]

MEANING: descend, to flow down, descendant • **USAGE:** Jewish: from Hebrew *yarden* (to descend, to flow down)

The words a man speaks are deep waters, a flowing stream, a fountain of wisdom.
— Proverbs 18:4 (JPS)

YARON [yah-ROHN]

MEANING: he will sing out, he will be joyous • **USAGE:** Jewish

Satisfy us at daybreak with Your steadfast love
that we may sing for joy all our days.
— Psalm 90:14 (JPS)

YASH [yahsh]

MEANING: glory, fame • **USAGE:** Hindu: from Sanskrit *yasah*

For from joy all beings are born, by joy they are
sustained, being born, and into joy they enter
after death....He who attains this wisdom wins glory,
grows rich, enjoys health and fame.
— *Taittiriya Upanishad* (tr. Swami Prabhavananda)

YASHAR [yah-SHAHR]

MEANING: honest, upright, straightforward • **USAGE:** Jewish

My words shall utter the uprightness of my heart;
and that which my lips know they shall speak sincerely.
— Job 33:3 (MT)

YASIR, YASSIR [yah-SEER]

MEANING: rich, wealthy, prosperous • **USAGE:** Muslim: from Arabic *yasir* (to be wealthy)

A man's true wealth hereafter
is the good he does in this world.
— Hadith of the Prophet Muhammad

YASU [yah-soo]

MEANING: peaceful, serene, tranquil • **USAGE:** Japanese: from Japanese *yasu*

As a deep lake is clear and calm, so the wise become
tranquil after they listened to the truth.
— Buddha, *The Dhammapada*
(tr. Sanderson Beck)

YASUO [yah-soo-oh]

MEANING: peaceful man, tranquil man • **USAGE:** Japanese: from Japanese *yasu* (peaceful, tranquil) and *o* (man)

Peace originates with the flow of things —
its heart is like the movement of the wind and waves.
— Morihei Ueshiba, *The Art of Peace*
(tr. John Stevens)

YEHONATAN [yeh-HOH-nah-tahn]

MEANING: God has given • **USAGE:** Jewish: from Hebrew *yehonathan* (Yahweh has given)

O God of my fathers,
You who have given me wisdom and power.
— Daniel 2:23b (JPS)

YEHOSHUA [ye-hoh-SHOO-ah]

MEANING: God is salvation • **USAGE:** Jewish form of *Yeshayahu*: from Hebrew *yesha'yah* (Yahweh is salvation)

The Lord is my strength and might;
He has become my deliverance.
— Psalm 118:14 (JPS)

YEHUDAH [yeh-hoo-DAH, yah-HOO-dah]

MEANING: praise, glorify, thank • **USAGE:** Jewish: from Hebrew root *y-d-h* (praised)

Praise the Lord, O my soul...who encompasseth
thee with lovingkindness and tender mercies.
— Psalm 103:1a, 103:4a (JPS)

YESHAYA [yeh-SHAH-yah, yeh-shah-YAH]

MEANING: God is salvation • **USAGE:** Jewish (see Yehoshua)

Behold, God is my salvation; I will trust,
and will not be afraid; for God the Lord is my strength
and song; and He is become my salvation.
— Isaiah 12:2 (MT)

Y

YESHUA   *[yeh-shoo-AH, yeh-SHOO-ah]*

MEANING: God is salvation • **USAGE:** Jewish form of Yehoshua (*see* Yehoshua)

I will greatly rejoice in the Lord,
my soul shall be joyful in my God;
for He hath clothed me with the garments of salvation,
He hath covered me with a robe of victory.
— Isaiah 61:10a (MT)

YETZER   *[YET-zehr]*

MEANING: nature, inclination, instinct, desire • **USAGE:** Jewish

Desire realized is a tree of life.
— Proverbs 13:12a (JPS)

YILMA   *[yihl-mah]*

MEANING: may he prosper • **USAGE:** African: Ethiopia

Anticipate the good so that you may enjoy it.
— Ethiopian proverb

YIRMEYAHU   *[yeerr-mee-YAH-hoo]*

MEANING: God will raise up, God will uplift • **USAGE:** Jewish: from Hebrew *yirmeyahu* (may Yahweh exalt)

Behold, My servant shall prosper,
He shall be exalted and lifted up,
and shall be very high.
— Isaiah 52:13 (MT)

YISHAI   *[yee-SHAY]*

MEANING: gift • **USAGE:** Jewish: from Hebrew *yishai*

Every man also to whom God hath given riches
and wealth, and hath given him power to eat thereof,
and to take his portion, and to rejoice in his labour —
this is the gift of God.
— Ecclesiastes 5:18 (MT)

YISHMAEL   *[yeesh-mah-EHL]*

MEANING: God hears, God will hear • **USAGE:** Jewish: from Hebrew *yishma'el* (Yahweh hears)

I will call upon Thee, for Thou wilt answer me,
O God; incline Thine ear unto me, hear my speech.
— Psalm 17:6 (MT)

YISKA   *[yees-kah]*

MEANING: night has passed • **USAGE:** Amerind: Navajo

And the night of darkness /
And the dawn of light, /
Meeting, joining one another, /
Helpmates ever, they.
— Navajo song

YISRAEL   *[yees-rah-EL]*

MEANING: one who wrestles with God • **USAGE:** Jewish: from *yisra'el* (to wrestle with God); reference to God changing Jacob's name after he wrestled with an angel

Hear, O Israel: the Lord our God, the Lord is one.
And thou shalt love the Lord thy God with all thy
heart, and with all thy soul, and with all thy might.
— Deuteronomy 6:4–5 (MT)

YITZCHAK   *[yeetz-KHAHK]*

MEANING: he will laugh • **USAGE:** Jewish: from Hebrew *yitshaq*

He [God] will yet fill your mouth with laughter,
and your lips with shouts of joy.
— Job 8:21 (JPS)

YITZHAR   *[yeetz-HAHR]*

MEANING: pure oil, poetic name for a scholar • **USAGE:** Jewish

Thou hast anointed my head with oil;
my cup runneth over.
— Psalm 23:5 (MT)

YIZHAR   [yeez-HAHR]

MEANING: he will shine, he will brighten •
USAGE: Jewish

> *With Thee is the fountain of life;*
> *in Thy light do we see light.*
> — Psalm 36:10 (MT)

YOAV   [YOH-ahv]

MEANING: God is my father, God is willing •
USAGE: Jewish

> *Honor your father.*
> — Deuteronomy 5:16a (JPS)

YOCHAI   [yoh-KHIE]

MEANING: God lives • **USAGE:** Jewish

> *The foundation of faith and the pillar of divine service*
> *is to believe that the Creator, blessed be He,*
> *is one, single, and unique, that He watches over*
> *and directs all the worlds and all the nations of men....*
> *He fills all worlds and surrounds all worlds,*
> *and there is no place where He is not present.*
> — Baal Shem Tov aphorism

YOEL   [yoh-EHL]

MEANING: the Lord is God, God is willing •
USAGE: Jewish: from Hebrew *yoh'el* (Yahweh is
God)

> *The Lord Himself will go before you.*
> *He will be with you;*
> *He will not fail you or forsake you.*
> — Deuteronomy 31:8 (JPS)

YONAH   [yoh-NAH]

MEANING: dove, dove-like • **USAGE:** Jewish: from
Hebrew *yonah* (dove); a symbol of peace

> *May the Lord grant peace to His people;*
> *may the Lord bestow on His people well being.*
> — Psalm 29:11 (JPS)

YONATAN   [yoh-nah-TAHN]

MEANING: gift of God • **USAGE:** Jewish form of
Yehonatan, from Hebrew *yehonathan* (Yahweh has
given)

> *The world is new to us every morning —*
> *this is God's gift; and every man should believe*
> *he is reborn each day.*
> — Baal Shem Tov aphorism

YONG   [yohng]

MEANING: brave, courageous • **USAGE:** Chinese

> *Let every man have the courage to think for himself.*
> *In this capacity of man to think for himself...*
> *lies the true motive force of all human progress.*
> — Lin Yutang, *The Pleasures of a Nonconformist*

YOSEF   [yoh-SEF]

MEANING: God will add, God will increase •
USAGE: Jewish: from Hebrew *ya'saph* (Yahweh
will add)

> *The Lord thy God shall bless thee in all thine increase,*
> *and in all the work of thy hands,*
> *and thou shalt be altogether joyful.*
> — Deuteronomy 15:16 (MT)

YOSHER   [yoh-SHEHR]

MEANING: honest, upright, straightforward •
USAGE: Jewish

> *You must love honesty and integrity.*
> — Zechariah 8:19b (JPS)

YOSHIRO   [yoh-shee-roh]

MEANING: lucky son, righteous son • **USAGE:**
Japanese: from Japanese *yoshi* (lucky, righteous)
and *rou* (son)

> *A wise man calmly considers what is right and what*
> *is wrong, and faces different opinions with truth,*
> *non-violence and peace. This man is guarded*
> *by truth and is a guardian of truth.*
> *He is righteous and he is wise.*
> — Buddha, *The Dhammapada* (tr. Juan Mascaro)

Y

YOSSI [YOH-see]

MEANING: God will add, God will increase • USAGE: Jewish form of Yosef (*see* Yosef)

God will…increase the results of your good works.
— Deuteronomy 16:15 (MT)

YU [yoo]

MEANING: jade, peaceful, happy • USAGE: Chinese

There is happiness in doing good,
and secret merit in virtuous deeds.
— Chinese proverb (tr. William Scarborough)

YUL [yool]

MEANING: light-bearded, young, youthful, of Jupiter • USAGE: Russian form of Julian (*see* Yulian)

[God] satisfies your desires with good things
so that your youth is renewed like the eagle's.
— Psalm 103:5 (RSV)

YULIAN [YOO-lee-ahn]

MEANING: light-bearded, young, youthful, of Jupiter • USAGE: Russian form of Julian, from Latin *iulus* (downy-chinned, youthful); or form of *Jupiter*, from Latin *dyeus* (Zeus) and *pater* (father), Roman father of the gods

Rejoice, young man, while you are young, and let your heart be glad in the days of your youth. And walk in the ways of your heart and in the sight of your eyes.
— Ecclesiastes 11:9a (HCSB)

YURI [YOO-ree]

MEANING: earth worker, farmer, gardener • USAGE: Russian form of Georgi, from Greek *ge* (earth) and *ergein* (to work)

A good deed is never lost; he who sows courtesy reaps friendship, and he who plants kindness gathers love.
— Basil of Caesarea

YUVAL [YOO-vahl, yoo-VAHL]

MEANING: stream, river • USAGE: Jewish

Let justice well up as waters,
and righteousness as a mighty stream.
— Amos 5:24 (JPS)

YVES [eev]

MEANING: yew tree, bow maker • USAGE: French: from German *iv* (yew tree); yew is used to make bows

He shall be as a tree planted by the waters,
who spreads out its roots by the river,
and shall not fear when heat comes, but its leaf shall be green; and shall not be careful in the year of drought, neither shall cease from yielding fruit.
— Jeremiah 17:8 (WEB)

Z

ZACARÍAS [zah-kah-REE-ahs]

MEANING: remembrance of the Lord, God remembers • USAGE: Spanish form of Zacharias (*see* Zacharias)

Remember, O Lord, Thy tender mercies and Thy lovingkindnesses; for they have been ever of old.
— Psalm 25:6 (KJV)

ZACHARIAH [zak-ah-RIE-ah]

MEANING: remembrance of the Lord, God remembers • USAGE: English form of Zecharias (*see* Zacharias)

Keep your eyes on the stars,
but remember to keep your feet on the ground.
— Theodore Roosevelt (address of May 24, 1904)

ZACHARIAS [zah-kah-REE-ahs]

MEANING: remembrance of the Lord, God remembers • USAGE: Greek form of Zecharya: from Hebrew *zekharyal* (Yahweh remembers)

Z

*Trust the Lord with all your heart, and don't depend
on your own understanding. Remember the Lord
in all you do, and he will give you success.*
— Proverbs 3:5–6 (NCV)

ZACHARY   [ZAK-ar-ee]

MEANING: remembrance of the Lord, God
remembers • USAGE: English form of Zacharias
(*see* Zacharias)
The true art of memory is the art of attention.
— Samuel Johnson, "The Idler"

ZACK, ZACH, ZAC, ZAK   [zak]

MEANING: remembrance of the Lord, God
remembers, he will laugh • USAGE: English form
of Zachariah or Zachary (*see* Zacharias); or English
form of Isaac, from Hebrew *yitshaq* (he will laugh)
*I am the Lord…Remember,
I will be with you and protect you wherever you go.*
— Genesis 28:13b, 28:15a (GNT)

ZAFIR   [zah-feer]

MEANING: victorious, successful • USAGE:
Muslim, from Arabic *zafira* (to succeed)
*As for him whose good deeds are preponderant,
these are the successful.*
— Koran, The Believers 23.102 (SKR)

ZAHID, ZAHEED   [zah-HEED]

MEANING: devout, pious • USAGE: Muslim
*It is the lover of God whose heart is filled with devotion
who can commune with God, not he who makes an
effort with his intellect to analyze God.*
— Hazrat Inayat Khan, *The Bowl of Saki*

ZAHIN, ZAHEEN   [zah-HEEN]

MEANING: wise, knowledgeable • USAGE: Muslim
*He giveth wisdom unto whom He will,
and he unto whom wisdom is given,
he truly hath received abundant good.*
— Koran, The Cow 2.269a (PIC)

ZAHIR, ZAHEER   [zah-HEER]

MEANING: helper, supporter • USAGE: Muslim:
from Arabic *zahir*
*If Allah helps you, none can overcome you…
in Allah, then, let believers put their trust.*
— Koran, The Family of Imran 3.160a (ALI)

ZAKAI   [zah-KIE]

MEANING: pure, clean, innocent • USAGE: Jewish
*He that hath clean hands and a pure heart…
He shall receive a blessing from the Lord.*
— Psalm 24:4–5a (MT)

ZAKI   [zah-kee]

MEANING: lion, prowess • USAGE: African: Hausa
of Nigeria
Strategy is better than strength.
— Hausa proverb

ZALMAN, ZALMEN, ZALMON   [ZAHL-mahn]

MEANING: peace, peaceful • USAGE: Yiddish form
of Shlomo, from Hebrew *shalom*
Where there is peace, there is blessing.
— Yiddish proverb

ZAMIL, ZAMEEL   [zah-MEEL]

MEANING: friend, companion • USAGE: Muslim
*Our friendship can be like this: a needed lift, a sail, /
a pillar, a springboard to taste the unfathomable.*
— Jalaluddin Rumi, "Together Through the Years"
(tr. Daniel Ladinsky)

ZAMIR, ZAMEER   [zah-MEER]

MEANING: heart • USAGE: Muslim
*The heart is deeper than rivers and seas — /
Who has fathomed the heart!…He who learns
the secret of the heart / Comes to know God.*
— Sultan Bahu

Z

ZAN [jhahn]

MEANING: support, favor • USAGE: Chinese
> *If a man's in luck he always finds,*
> *wherever he goes to, favoring winds.*
> — Chinese proverb (tr. William Scarborough)

ZANDER [ZAN-der]

MEANING: protector and helper of humankind,
guardian • USAGE: English form of Alexander,
from Greek *alexein* (to defend, to help) and *andros*
(man)
> *The Lord is faithful.*
> *He will establish you and guard you.*
> — 2 Thessalonians 3:3a (ESV)

ZANE [ʒayn]

MEANING: God is gracious, God is giving •
USAGE: English form of John, from Hebrew
y'hohanan (Yahweh is gracious)
> *God is able to make all grace abound to you,*
> *that you, always having all sufficiency in everything,*
> *may abound to every good work.*
> — 2 Corinthians 9:8 (WEB)

ZARIF, ZAREEF [ʒah-REEF]

MEANING: elegant, gracious • USAGE: Muslim
> *Allah's grace on you is very great.*
> — Koran, The Women 4.113b (SKR)

ZAVAD [ʒah-VAHD]

MEANING: gift, bounty • USAGE: Jewish
> *Each day has its own bountifulness, and certainly,*
> *there has been set aside for you in this day much good.*
> — Nachman of Breslov

ZAYD [ʒah-eed]

MEANING: increase, abundance • USAGE: Muslim:
from Arabic *ʒada* (to increase)

> *Allah increaseth in right guidance*
> *those who walk aright.*
> — Koran, Maryam 19.76a (PIC)

ZEB [ʒeb]

MEANING: gift of God • USAGE: English form of
Zebedee (*see* Zebedee)
> *Every man also to whom God hath given*
> *riches and wealth, and hath given power*
> *to eat thereof and to take his portion and to rejoice*
> *in his labor, this is the gift of God.*
> — Ecclesiastes 5:19 (KJ21)

ZEBEDEE [ZEB-eh-dee]

MEANING: gift of God • USAGE: Jewish: from
Hebrew *ʒebhad* (gift) and *Yah* (Yahweh)
> *Every man should eat and drink, and enjoy pleasure*
> *for all his labour, is the gift of God.*
> — Ecclesiastes 3:13 (MT)

ZECHARYA [ʒeh-KAHR-yah, ʒchahr-YAH]

MEANING: remembrance of the Lord, God
remembers • USAGE: Jewish: from Hebrew
ʒekharyal (Yahweh remembers)
> *Remember, I [God] am with you:*
> *I will protect you wherever you go.*
> — Genesis 28:15a (JPS)

ZED [ʒed]

MEANING: God is righteousness, justice of the
Lord • USAGE: English form of Zedekiah (*see*
Zedekiah)
> *God does not view things the way men do.*
> *People look on the outward appearance,*
> *but the Lord looks at the heart.*
> — 1 Samuel 16:7b (NEB)

ZEDEKIAH [ʒeh-deh-KIE-ah]

MEANING: God is righteousness, justice of the
Lord • USAGE: English form of Hebrew *Tʒidkiya*

Z

He loves whatever is just and good;
the unfailing love of the Lord fills the earth.
— Psalm 33:5 (NLT)

ZEKE   *[zeek]*

MEANING: God strengthens, God will build,
remembrance of the Lord, God remembers •
USAGE: English form of Ezekiel, from Hebrew
yechezq' el (God strengthens); or English form of
Zachariah (*see* Zecharya)
The Lord is faithful, and he will strengthen you.
— 2 Thessalonians 3:3a (GNT)

ZENDE   *[zen-deh]*

MEANING: strong, firm • USAGE: African: Swahili
of Kenya/Tanzania
Perseverance wins the battle.
— Kenyan proverb

ZENO   *[ZEE-noh]*

MEANING: stoic, disciplined, of Zeus • USAGE:
Greek: from Greek *Zeus* (Greek father of the gods);
Greek philosopher and founder of Stoicism
Blessed is the man you discipline,
O Lord, the man you teach from your law.
— Psalm 94:12 (NIV)

ZEPHYR   *[ZEF-er]*

MEANING: west wind, mild breeze • USAGE:
English: from Greek *zephyros*
Softly blow, thou western breeze.
— John Leyden, "The Mermaid"

ZEPHYRN   *[ZEF-ren]*

MEANING: west wind, mild breeze • USAGE:
American form of Zephyr (*see* Zephyr)
Low, low, breathe and blow /
Wind of the western sea.
— Alfred Tennyson, "Sweet and Low"

ZERACH   *[zeh-RAHCH]*

MEANING: shine, glow, light, lamp • USAGE:
Jewish
For Thy art my lamp, O Lord;
and the Lord doth lighten my darkness.
— 2 Samuel 22:29 (MT)

ZETHUS   *[ZEE-thus]*

MEANING: Zeus-like, leader, ruler • USAGE:
American: possibly a form of Greek *Zeus*, Greek
father of the gods and ruler of Olympus
I don't know any other way to lead but by example.
— Don Shula

ZEVULON   *[zeh-voo-LON]*

MEANING: lofty house, heavenly mansion, exalt,
honor • USAGE: Jewish: from Hebrew *zebhul* (a
dwelling)
It hath pleased Thee to bless the house
of Thy servant, that it may continue for ever before
Thee; for Thou, O Lord, hast blessed,
and so let [Thy servant] be blessed for ever.
— 1 Chronicles 17:27 (MT)

ZHI   *[jheh]*

MEANING: will, purpose, wisdom, knowledge •
USAGE: Chinese
He who acts with energy
has strength of purpose.
— Lao Tzu, *Tao Te Ching* (tr. Lionel Giles)

ZHONG   *[zohng]*

MEANING: loyal, true, middle • USAGE: Chinese
One who is sincere with himself
is called a true man.
— Mencius

Z

ZHUANG [jhoo-ahng]

MEANING: robust, strong, hale • USAGE: Chinese
The older you grow, the more hale may you be!
— Chinese proverb (tr. William Scarborough)

ZIF, ZIFF [zif]

MEANING: wolf • USAGE: Yiddish
Thou [God] hast enlarged my steps under me,
and my feet have not slipped.
— 2 Samuel 22:37 (MT)

ZION [ZIE-on]

MEANING: excellent, sign, reference to Jewish people, Israel • USAGE: Jewish
They shall call thee the city of the Lord,
the Zion of the Holy One of Israel.
— Isaiah 60:15b (MT)

ZISSIS [ZEE-sees]

MEANING: lifetime • USAGE: Greek: from Greek *zissis*
Have a long life. Peace be to you. Peace be to your
family. And peace be to all that you have.
— 1 Samuel 25:6 (NLV)

ZIV [ziv, zeev]

MEANING: shining, brilliant, light, illuminated, glory, second month in Jewish calendar • USAGE: Jewish
God said: "Let there be light." And there was light.
And God saw the light, that it was good.
— Genesis 1:3–4 (MT)

ZIVEN [ZEE-ven]

MEANING: life, full of life • USAGE: Polish: from Slavic *zhiv*
Guard your heart above all else,
for it is the source of life.
— Proverbs 4:23 (HCSB)

ZOHAR [ZOH-hahr]

MEANING: light, brilliance • USAGE: Jewish
With You is the fountain of life;
by Your light do we see light.
— Psalm 36:10 (JPS)

ZOLTAN [zohl-TAHN]

MEANING: life, full of life • USAGE: Hungarian: from Greek *zoe*
I am sure that your goodness and love
will follow me all the days of my life.
And I will live in the house of the Lord forever.
— Psalm 23:6a (NIRV)

ZURI [ZUH-ree]

MEANING: good-looking, handsome • USAGE: African: Swahili of Kenya/Tanzania
A man's face shows what is in his heart.
— Swahili proverb

Z

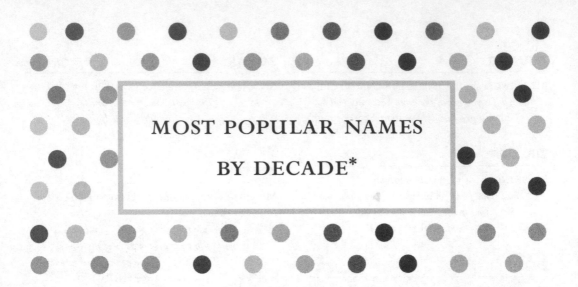

MOST POPULAR NAMES

BY DECADE*

2013

Noah	Sophia
Liam	Emma
Jacob	Olivia
Mason	Isabella
William	Ava
Ethan	Mia
Michael	Emily
Alexander	Abigail
Jayden	Madison
Daniel	Elizabeth

2010

Jacob	Isabella
Ethan	Sophia
Michael	Emma
Jayden	Olivia
William	Ava
Alexander	Emily
Noah	Abigail
Daniel	Madison
Aiden	Chloe
Anthony	Mia

2000

Jacob	Emily
Michael	Hannah
Matthew	Madison
Joshua	Ashley
Christopher	Sarah
Nicholas	Alexis
Andrew	Samantha
Joseph	Jessica
Daniel	Elizabeth
Tyler	Taylor

1990

Michael	Jessica
Christopher	Ashley
Matthew	Brittany
Joshua	Amanda
Daniel	Samantha
David	Sarah
Andrew	Stephanie
James	Jennifer
Justin	Elizabeth
Joseph	Lauren

1980

Michael	Jennifer
Christopher	Amanda
Jason	Jessica
David	Melissa
James	Sarah
Matthew	Heather
Joshua	Nicole
John	Amy
Robert	Elizabeth
Joseph	Michelle

1970

Michael	Jennifer
James	Lisa
David	Kimberly
John	Michelle
Robert	Amy
Christopher	Angela
William	Melissa
Brian	Tammy
Mark	Mary
Richard	Tracy

1960	
David	Mary
Michael	Susan
James	Linda
John	Karen
Robert	Donna
Mark	Lisa
William	Patricia
Richard	Cynthia
Thomas	Deborah
Steven	Sandra

1950	
James	Linda
Robert	Mary
John	Patricia
Michael	Barbara
David	Susan
William	Nancy
Richard	Deborah
Thomas	Sandra
Charles	Carol
Gary	Kathleen

1940	
James	Mary
Robert	Barbara
John	Patricia
William	Judith
Richard	Betty
Charles	Carol
David	Nancy
Thomas	Linda
Donald	Shirley
Ronald	Sandra

1930	
Robert	Mary
James	Betty
John	Dorothy
William	Helen
Richard	Margaret
Charles	Barbara
Donald	Patricia
George	Joan
Joseph	Doris
Edward	Ruth

1920	
John	Mary
William	Dorothy
Robert	Helen
James	Margaret
Charles	Ruth
George	Mildred
Joseph	Virginia
Edward	Elizabeth
Frank	Frances
Richard	Anna

1910	
John	Mary
James	Helen
William	Margaret
Robert	Dorothy
George	Ruth
Joseph	Anna
Charles	Elizabeth
Frank	Mildred
Edward	Marie
Henry	Alice

* According to the Social Security Administration. Names are listed in order of popularity, with the most popular names first.

GRANDPARENT NAMES

GRANDMOTHER NAMES

AMERICAN

Ganny
Gigi
G-Ma
Gram
Grammy
Grams
Gran
Grandma
Grandmama
Grandmother
Granny
Jamma
Mamaw
Mamie
Mams
Meema
Memaw
Mimi
Nan
Nana

Nokomis (Chippewa)
Nonna
Puna (Hawaiian)
Tutu (Hawaiian)

INTERNATIONAL

Abuela (Spanish)
Ajji (Indian)
Amma (Swedish)
Anya (Hungarian)
Avo (Portuguese)
Baba (Serbian)
Babushka (Russian)
Bibi (Swahili)
Bomma (Flemish)
Bubbe (Yiddish)
Gogo (Creole/Haitian)
Gotmor (Norwegian)
Grand-mère (French)
Grootmoeder (Dutch)
Grossmutter (German)

Halmoni (Korean)
Jaddah (Arabic)
Lita (Spanish, informal)
Lola (Filipino)
Meme (French)
Mémère (French)
Mica (Serbian)
Mor Mor (Danish)
Nana (Jewish)
Nanu (Indian)
Nonna (Italian)
Obaasan (Japanese)
Oma (German)
Popo (Mandarin)
Teta (Arabic)
Tita (Spanish, informal)
Yaya (Greek)

GRANDFATHER NAMES

AMERICAN

Bobo
Da
G-Pa
Gampa
Gamps
Gramps
Grampy
Gran
Grandda
Granddad
Grandfather
Grandpa
Granpoppa
Gumpa
Papa
Papaw
Papps
Pappy
Pop
Poppa
Poppy
Pops
Tatu-kane (Hawaiian)

INTERNATIONAL

Abuelo (Spanish)
Ajja (Indian)
Ayo (Portuguese)
Babu (Georgian)
Dadju (Ukrainian, formal)
Dadu (Indian)
Deda (Serbian)
Dedushka (Russian)
Didi (Serbian)
Farfar (Scandinavian, paternal)
Farmor (Danish)
Gigi (Ukrainian, informal)
Gong Gong (Chinese, paternal)
Grand-père (French)
Grootvader (Dutch)
Grossvader (German)
Halabeoji (Korean)
Jaad (Arabic)
Lolo (Filipino)
Morfar (Scandinavian, paternal)
Nonno (Italian)
Ojiisan (Japanese)
Opa (German)

Papau, Pappou (Greek)
Pepe (French)
Seedo (Arabic, informal)
Taidie (Welsh)
Tata (Hungarian)
Tito (Spanish, informal)
Ukki (Finnish)
Yeh Yeh (Chinese, paternal)
Zaide, Zeide (Yiddish)

MOST POPULAR
PET NAMES*

PUPPY NAMES

FEMALE

1. Bella
2. Daisy
3. Molly
4. Lucy
5. Sadie
6. Maggie
7. Bailey
8. Chloe
9. Sophie
10. Lola
11. Lily, Lilly
12. Roxy
13. Zoe, Zoey
14. Ginger
15. Ruby
16. Abby
17. Princess
18. Gracie
19. Emma
20. Angel
21. Sasha
22. Belle
23. Penny
24. Lady
25. Coco

MALE

1. Max
2. Charlie
3. Jack
4. Buddy
5. Jake
6. Tucker
7. Duke
8. Toby
9. Bear
10. Oscar
11. Cooper
12. Shadow
13. Rocky
14. Oliver
15. Riley
16. Bailey
17. Jasper
18. Lucky
19. Bentley
20. Buster
21. Harley
22. Gizmo
23. Bandit
24. Murphy
25. Baxter

KITTEN NAMES

FEMALE

1. Bella
2. Lucy
3. Chloe
4. Lily, Lilly
5. Molly
6. Kitty
7. Luna
8. Sophie
9. Lola
10. Misty
11. Abby
12. Daisy
13. Sasha
14. Nala
15. Jasmine
16. Princess
17. Gracie
18. Kiki
19. Sadie
20. Cleo
21. Callie
22. Belle
23. Maggie
24. Stella
25. Rosie

MALE

1. Max
2. Tigger
3. Oliver
4. Jack
5. Tiger
6. Jasper
7. Oscar
8. Charlie
9. Leo
10. Toby
11. Oreo
12. Buddy
13. Simon
14. Smokey
15. Milo
16. Simba
17. Dexter
18. Shadow
19. Sammy
20. Pumpkin
21. Casper
22. Lucky
23. Chester
24. Harley
25. Boots

*   According to www.petbabynames.com, copyright 2015. Names are listed in order of popularity.

NAMES BY MEANING

INDEX

AIR-RELATED — FEMALE

Anemone, Aniani, Anila, Anima, Aoloa, Brisa, Ciel, Electra, Elektra, Elettra, Kailani, Laniloa, Naseem, Naseema, Nasima, Neala, Neelie, Neely, Nelda, Netta, Nila, Niyol, Nyla, Pavana, Sahab, Seferina, Simi, Sky, Skye, Skyla, Solana, Thora, Tora

AIR-RELATED — MALE

Abel, Andor, Dumi, Dustin, Dusty, Feng, Gale, Gomda, Guthrie, Hevel, Iraja, Kahuna, Keanu, Makani, Naseem, Nasim, Neal, Neil, Niall, Nigel, Niles, Nodin, Seferino, Shappa, Sky, Sora, Strom, Taran, Thonah, Thorin, Tor, Torsten, Tove, Zephyr, Zephyrn

ANGEL, HEAVEN — FEMALE

Ahulani, Aldora, Angel, Angela, Angèle, Angelia, Angelica, Angelika, Angeliki, Angelina, Angeline, Angélique, Angelita, Angie, Aniela, Arela, Arella, Asmani, Celeste, Céleste, Celestina, Celestine, Celia, Celina, Celine, Ciel, Evangelia, Evangelina, Evangeline, Fina, Gweneal, Hiilani, Keolani, Kolani, Lani, Leilani, Lia, Malak, Maricela, Nevaeh, Ourania, Serafina, Seraphina, Seraphine, Séraphine, Sky, Uilani, Urania, Wailani

ANIMAL — FEMALE

Agna, Agnes, Agnese, Agnessa, Amaryllis, Anamosa, Anice, Annice, Annis, Ardela, Ardele, Ardella, Ardelle, Ariela, Ariella, Arielle, Artia, Avrielle, Belinda, Bernadetta, Bernadette, Bernadine, Bernarda, Bernardine, Berneen, Beverley, Beverly, Bindi, Bindy, Caparina, Capri, Caprina, Cho, Conlee, Darcie, Darcy, Deb, Debbie, Debby, Debora, Deborah, Debra, Delphina, Devora, Devorah, Dorcas, Dorkas, Dvora, Dvorah, Ebba, Ebbe, Fauna, Fawn, Fawne, Felina, Felipa, Filipa, Filippa, Guadalupe, Harleigh, Harley, Ines, Inessa, Inez, Ivory, Jalissa, Jelissa, Kefira, Keren, Leandra, Leola, Leona, Leonie,

Leonor, Lewella, Liona, Lissa, Llewella, Lupe, Malila, Melika, Melisa, Melissa, Missie, Missy, Nessa, Nova, Ofra, Oona, Oonagh, Ophrah, Philippa, Pippa, Pippi, Portia, Quela, Rachel, Rachela, Rachele, Rachelle, Rae, Raeleen, Rahel, Rakel, Ralphina, Raquel, Raylene, Rhona, Rima, Rochelle, Rona, Rosalind, Rosalinde, Rosalyn, Roslyn, Roz, Senga, Shofar, Tabea, Tabita, Tabitha, Talisa, Talissa, Ulla, Ursula, Vanessa, Ynez

ANIMAL — MALE

Adolf, Adolfo, Adolph, Adolphe, Adriel, Ahlf, Ardel, Arel, Ari, Ariel, Art, Arthur, Artur, Arturo, Arye, Aryeh, Asad, Averil, Beño, Bernard, Bernardino, Bernardo, Bernd, Bernhard, Bernt, Bjorn, Braden, Brady, Brock, Buck, Byron, Cale, Caleb, Chevy, Colt, Conall, Conan, Conley, Conn, Conner, Connor, Conor, Conway, Costello, Darby, Darcy, Dax, Dino, Dov, Dracos, Drake, Eberhard, Eberhardt, Everet, Everett, Fahd, Fallon, Faolan, Felipe, Felipo, Felippe, Filip, Filippo, Flip, Guri, Hanuman, Harley, Hemene, Hersh, Hershel, Hirsh, Hirshel, Honi, Humphrey, Humphry, Irv, Irvin, Irwin, Jaden, Jayden, Kaleb, Kalev, Kefir, Keifer, Kiefer, Kobe, Kuruk, Leander, Leandro, Lee, LeeRon, Leib, Len, Lencho, Lenny, Leo, Leon, Leonard, Leonardo, Leonid, Leron, Lionel, Llew, Llewelyn, Lobo, Long, Lope, Lovell, Lynard, Mano, Marshal, Marshall, Mato, Ngare, Odhran, Odran, Ofer, Oisin, Oran, Oren, Orin, Orson, Oscar, Oskar, Phil, Philip, Philippe, Phillip, Pip, Rafe, Rafer, Ralph, Ramsay, Ramsey, Randal, Randall, Randolf, Randolph, Randy, Raoul, Raul, Rodolfo, Ronan, Roscoe, Rudolf, Rudolph, Rudy, Ryder, Ryuu, Satanta, Seff, Shange, Shofar, Simba, Taden, Tapco, Tashunka, Tashunke, Tayden, Tod, Todd, Ulf, Usamah, Wolf, Wolfe, Wolfgang, Zaki, Zif, Ziff

BEAUTIFUL — FEMALE

Abila, Adah, Adamma, Addah, Adina, Adona, Adonia, Aimi, Alaina, Alana, Alanda, Alandah,

Alanis, Alanna, Alannis, Alayna, Alonda, Anabel, Aneeqa, Aniqa, Annabella, Aonani, Aphrodite, Asami, Asta, Astrid, Balissa, Belinda, Bella, Bellarosa, Belle, Belva, Bevan, Bevin, Bhamini, Bindi, Bindy, Bonita, Bonnie, Bonny, Branwen, Calandra, Calantha, Calida, Calíope, Calli, Callie, Calliope, Callisto, Ceri, Ceridwen, Ceridwyn, Charu, Delwyn, Delyth, Dorinda, Elandra, Fenella, Finola, Fiona, Fionnuala, Freja, Freya, Frida, Frieda, Friede, Ghada, Ghadah, Gwenda, Hadara, Hasana, Hassana, Hermosa, Hiromi, Ilandra, Inda, Indira, Inga, Inge, Ingrid, Isolde, Jalinda, Jameela, Jamilah, Jiao, Ji-Won, Jolie, Kalandra, Kalidas, Kalli, Kalliopi, Kallisto, Kalyana, Karungi, Kaui, Keela, Keeli, Keelin, Keely, Keeva, Keila, Kenna, Kenner, Kenzie, Kiley, Kyla, Kylie, Laila, Lalita, Lalitha, Lana, Lavanya, Layla, Leenoy, Leila, Leinani, Lewa, Linda, Lindie, Lindy, Linoy, Lolonyo, Loni, Lonie, Lyla, Lynda, MacKenzie, Malinda, Mei, Melinda, Miki, Mi-Kyoung, Minda, Mindie, Mindy, Mio, Misaki, Miyu, Mizuki, Naniloa, Nava, Nayana, Nina, Noia, Nola, Noleen, Noya, Nuala, Olathe, Qian, Ramani, Ramya, Raya, Remba, Rosabella, Rosalinda, Sang-Mi, Sarama, Shakeela, Shakilah, Shameena, Sheba, Sheina, Shiba, Shifra, Shifrah, Shoba, Shona, Shreya, Shrila, Shrini, Sigrid, Siri, Teagan, Tegan, Tifara, Tomomi, Uilani, Valenda, Valinda, Vashti, Venus, Viona, Wainani, Waseema, Wasima, Winifred, Winnie, Yafa, Yaffah, Yifat, Zahia, Zahiya, Zayna, Zeba, Zene

BIRD — FEMALE

Akilina, Aloma, Alondra, Aquilina, Arna, Ava, Avelina, Aveline, Avila, Bena, Branna, Branwen, Calandra, Calli, Callie, Chenoa, Chosovi, Colombe, Colombina, Doli, Dove, Dovey, Dovie, Dovina, Evelyn, Evlyn, Feige, Geiles, Halcyon, Jemima, Jonina, Kalandra, Kanit, Kenya, Lakenya, Lark, Larke, Linnet, Malina, Marilla, Mavis, Merla, Merle, Meryl, Muriel, Nika, Paloma, Penelope, Pennie, Penny, Petah, Raven, Ravenna, Robin, Robina, Robyn, Sparrow, Svenja, Teal, Teale, Tori, Tziporah, Wren, Yemima, Yona, Yonina

BIRD — MALE

Andor, Arden, Arnaldo, Arnaud, Arndt, Arne, Arnie, Arno, Arnold, Bertram, Bertrand, Bran, Brandan, Branden, Brandon, Callum, Calum, Chatan, Chayton, Colm, Corbin, Cormac, Drake, Falco, Falko, Gavin, Gawain, Gwayne, Hans, Hawk, Hawke, Hula, Iolani, Jonas, Kangee, Kangi, Kele, Makya, Malcolm, Merle, Merrill, Phoenix, Ramsay, Ramsey, Robin, Rook, Shea, Sven, Taven, Tavin, Wamblee, Yonah

BLESSING — FEMALE

Anneliese, Annelise, Ashera, Babette, Bakhita, Baraka, Bea, Beah, Beata, Beate, Beatrice, Beatrix, Beatriz, Belicia, Belita, Bella, Belle, Benedetta, Benedicta, Benedikta, Benicia, Benisha, Benita, Benoite, Bente, Bess, Bessie, Bessy, Beth, Bethan, Betsan, Betsie, Betsy, Betta, Bette, Bettie, Bettina, Betty, Bracha, Buffy, Chela, Eilis, Elisa, Elisabet, Elisabeth, Elisabetta, Elise, Elisha, Elisheva, Eliza, Elizabeta, Elizabeth, Elizaveta, Ellie, Elly, Elsa, Elsie, Elspeth, Elza, Helga, Helge, Ilsa, Ilse, Isabel, Isabela, Isabella, Isabelle, Isobel, Izabella, Izzie, Izzy, Jobeth, Kalyana, Keiko, Khaira, Khayra, Libbie, Libby, Liesa, Liesbeth, Liese, Liesl, Lisa, Lisbet, Lise, Lisette, Liz, Liza, Lizbet, Lizette, Lizzie, Lizzy, Macarena, Macaria, Masuda, Mazal, Olenka, Olga, Olya, Ponia, Sabela, Sabella, Sibeal, Talisa, Talisha, TaLisha, Talissa, Triana, Trixie, Ushara, Yelizaveta

BLESSING — MALE

Adom, Asher, Barack, Baruch, Ben, Benedetto, Benedict, Benedicto, Benedikt, Benito, Benôit, Bento, Chinua, Gadiel, Isad, Khair, Khayr, Macario, Makar, Makarios, Marzuq, Masud, Mubarak, Ngozi, Oleg, Shrini, Varada

BORN, REBORN, WELLBORN, HIGHBORN — FEMALE

Abeo, Abiola, Abiona, Ada, Adaline, Addie, Addy, Adela, Adelaide, Adele, Adelheid, Adelina, Adeline, Adelita, Adella, Adelle, Ailis, Ailish, Alette, Ali, Alice, Alicia, Alina, Alisha, Alison, Alissa, Alita, Aliz, Allie, Ally, Alyce, Alys, Alyson, Alyssa, Anastasia, Aseela, Asila, Asya, Benigna, Concepción, Concetta, Conchita, Della, Elke, Eugenia, Eugénie, Falala, Genesis, Heide, Heidi, Kenna, Kenner, Lani, Latasha, Lyssa, Masika, Medina, Menora, Menorah, Natalia, Natalie, Nataliya, Natalya, Natasha, NaTasha, Natasia, Natassa, Neema, Noella, Noelle, Oni, Owena, Pascuala, Renata, Renate, Rene, Renee, Renita, Stacey, Staci, Stacie, Stacy, TaLisa, Talisha, Talya, Taren, Taryn, Tasha, Tasia, Tyrona, Winona

BORN, REBORN, WELLBORN, HIGHBORN — MALE

Aldo, Anastasios, Benigno, Bowen, Eoghan, Eugen, Eugene, Eugenio, Ewan, Ewen, Gene, Gino, Hiram, Iraja, Jeno, Ken, Kenner, Kennet, Kenneth, Kenny, Kunto, Noel, Owain, Owen, Pascal, Pascual, Phoenix, Renato, René, Stacey, Stacy, Tasos, Tassos, Terrone, Ty, Tye, Tyrone

BOUNTIFUL, FRUITFUL, ABUNDANT, INCREASE — FEMALE

Darran, Efrata, Falala, Fifi, Ireland, Isadora, Isidora, Izzie, Izzy, Jalaina, Jalayna, Jo, Jobeth, Jodene, Jodi, Jodie, Jodine, Jody, Joette, Jojo, Joleen, Jolene, Joline, Josée, Josefa, Josefina, Josepha, Josephina, Josephine, Josette, Josie, Jozetta, Jozette, Khasiba, Lulla, Pepita, Spring, Talulla, Yosefa, Yosepha, Zuna

BOUNTIFUL, FRUITFUL, ABUNDANT, INCREASE — MALE

Che, Cuba, Daren, Darin, Daron, Darren, Effie, Efi, Efraim, Efrem, Ephraim, Faiz, Fayz, Giuseppe, Isidore, Isidoros, Izzie, Izzy, Jethro, Jody, Joe, Joey, Jojo, Jose, José, Josef, Joseph, Jozef, Khasib, Mazid, Pepe, Pepito, Quino, Sefi, Sepp, Yoo-Jin, Yosef, Yossi, Zavad, Zayd

BRAVE, COURAGEOUS, BOLD, VALOROUS — FEMALE

Aileen, Ailene, Andee, Andie, Andra, Andrea, Andreana, Andriana, Andrianna, Audra, Audrey, Audrie, Audrina, Audry, Bedelia, Bidelia, Birgit, Birgitta, Birgitte, Breana, Breanna, Breanne, Breda, Bree, Breena, Bria, Briana, Brianna, Brianne, Bridget, Brighid, Brigid, Brigida, Brigitte, Brina, Brita, Brites, Britt, Britta, Bryden, Chagina, Conlee, Dana, Devan, Devin, Dray, Drea, Drew, Drey, Ethel, Farrell, Farrol, Ferdinanda, Fernanda, Gitta, Gitte, Nora, Noreen, Norene, Ondrea, Petula, Reilly, Riley, Rylee, Ryley, Rylie, Veera

BRAVE, COURAGEOUS, BOLD, VALOROUS — MALE

Abhay, Akins, Arch, Archibald, Archie, Boden, Brian, Bryan, Bryant, Cade, Cadoc, Conley, Conrad, Corado, Dana, Danan, Devan, Devin, Devon, Eberhard, Eberhardt, Enapay, Erhard, Evert, Everett, Farrell, Fearghal, Ferdinand, Fergal, Fernand, Fernando, Gared, Garred, Garret, Garrett, Garrick, Gary, Gerard, Gerardo, Gerhard, Gerhardt, Gerry, Helmut, Hernando, Isamu, Jarret, Jarrett, Jaseer, Jasir, Jerald, Jerry, Jevin, Kade, Kekoa, Kennard, Kimbel, Koa, Konrad, Kort, Kuno, Kurt, Lalama, Leopold, Makoa, Nahoa, Nando, Ometz, Renard, Riley, Shange, Thibault, Tito, Titos, Titus, Uzi, Wyatt, Yong

BRIGHT, SHINING — FEMALE

Aarona, Aharona, Alberta, Albertina, Alohi, Amshula, Amsula, Anju, Ayah, Baheera, Bahira, Bahirah, Bahiya, Bahiyya, Berta, Bertha, Berthana, Berthe, Bertina, Bobbi, Bobbie, Candra, Chanda, Chandra, Deana, Deanna, Deanne, Dee, Dee Dee, Diana, Diandra, Diandre, Diane, Didi, Dyan, Electra, Elektra, Elettra, Febe, Gilberta, Halcyon, Kanta, Kashi, Kiana, Konane, Kyan, Lolia, Marilla, Meira, Meora, Merle, Meryl, Muneera, Munirah, Muriel, Nehara, Neve, Nia, Niamh, Orah, Phoebe,

Quiana, Roberta, Robin, Robina, Robyn, Roshana, Sania, Saniyya, Shirleen, Shirlene, Shirley, Shoba, Sorcha, Zahara

BRIGHT, SHINING — MALE

Aaron, Aharon, Akio, Akira, Al, Albert, Alberto, Albrecht, Altair, Anju, Areeb, Argos, Arib, Aron, Aubert, Baheer, Bahir, Barak, Bareeq, Barik, Bela, Bert, Berto, Bertram, Bertran, Bertrand, Bhanu, Bhasu, Bob, Bobbie, Bobby, Bobek, Chang-Ho, Dai, Del, Delbert, Dilbert, Egbert, Elbert, Feivel, Fivel, Gib, Gil, Gilbert, Gilberto, Haroun, Harun, Herb, Herbert, Herberto, Hob, Hubert, Hugo, Kent, Konani, Kwang-Ho, Lugh, Meir, Merrill, Ming, Muneer, Munir, Norbert, Oran, Pakala, Rob, Robert, Roberto, Robin, Rubert, Rupert, Sohrab, Sung-Wook, Uberto, Wilber, Wilbert, Wilbur, Yizhar, Zerach, Ziv

CHRISTIAN, CHRISTIAN-RELATED — FEMALE

Anunziata, Carol, Carole, Caryl, Caryll, Chris, Chrissie, Chrissy, Christa, Christelle, Christi, Christiana, Christiane, Christie, Christina, Christine, Christy, Corazón, Crista, Cristiana, Cristina, Cristine, Delora, Delores, Deloria, Dollie, Dolly, Dolores, Epifania, Ina, Keli, Kelley, Kellie, Kelly, Kerstin, Khristina, Kia, Kiersten, Kierstin, Kiley, Kirsten, Kirstie, Kirstin, Kirsty, Kris, Krista, Kristen, Kristie, Kristin, Kristina, Kristine, Kristy, Kyla, Kylie, LaTasha, Latasha, Lola, Lolita, Loris, Lou, Lourdes, Luz, Madonna, Malina, Natalia, Natalie, Nataliya, Natalya, Natasha, Natasia, Noella, Noelle, Nuria, Paisley, Santana, Talya, Tasha, Tiana, Tianna, Tina, Trinidad

CHRISTIAN, CHRISTIAN-RELATED — MALE

Baptiste, Battista, Bishop, Carsten, Chris, Christer, Christian, Christiano, Christopher, Christophoros, Cillian, Clark, Crisóforo, Cristián, Cristiano,

Cristo, Cristóbal, Cristoforo, Crosby, Gillean, Gillis, Karsten, Kelley, Kelly, Kester, Killian, Kirby, Kirk, Kris, Krister, Kristian, Kristofer, Kristoffer, Kristopher, Kyle, Lance, Malcolm, Monroe, Munro, Munroe, Noel, Paisley, Presley, Preston, Romeo, Santiago, Tiago, Topher, Trini, Trinidad, Tristian

COLOR — FEMALE

Adama, Adamina, Addison, Ahona, Ailbhe, Alba, Amber, Ambra, Amethyst, Anamosa, Aruna, Azura, Azure, Azzurra, Beryl, Bianca, Bianka, Blanca, Blanch, Blanche, Blanka, Bleu, Bronwen, Bronwyn, Burgundy, Candace, Candi, Candice, Candida, Candide, Candy, Carrie, Carry, Cayenne, Cerise, Cerule, Charice, Charise, Chenoa, Cherice, Cherise, Cherry, Chloe, Chloris, Ciara, Ciarra, Cloe, Cloris, Clover, Coral, Corelle, Cyan, Dan, Duana, Ebonie, Ebony, Eirwen, Esmeralda, Fenella, Fiala, Finola, Fionnuala, Flavia, Garnet, Garnette, Geiles, Griselda, Guinevere, Gwen, Gwendolen, Gwendoline, Gwendolyn, Gweneal, Gweneth, Gwyn, Gwyneth, Harita, Hazel, Ianthe, Indigo, Iola, Ivory, Jade, Jetta, Jette, Jolana, Jolanda, Juniper, Keira, Keri, Kerri, Kerry, Khloe, Kiera, Lainey, Laney, Lavender, Lesley, Leslie, Levana, Liaden, Lilac, Linnea, Loden, Melanie, Melany, Melina, Melony, Midori, Minda, Mindie, Mindy, Nea, Neela, Nila, Nola, Noleen, Nuala, Olive, Olwen, Olwyn, Phillis, Phyllis, Poppy, Qing, Qiong, Raven, Ravenna, Rhonwen, Rima, Rose, Rosie, Rosy, Rowena, Rowina, Rubí, Ruby, Saffron, Sapphira, Sapphire, Scarlet, Scarlett, Scarlette, Selda, Shani, Sharice, Sharise, Shasta, Siena, Sienna, Teal, Teale, Topaz, Viola, Violet, Violeta, Violette, Wendi, Wendy, Whitney, Winnie, Wynne, Yolanda, Yolande, Zelda, Zelde

COLOR — MALE

Adam, Adamo, Addison, Arjun, Arun, Bai, Blake, Bruno, Caesar, Carey, Cary, César, Cesare, Cezar, Ciar, Ciaran, Clancy, Cole, Coley, Daragh, Darrah,

Daven, Davin, Donn, Donovan, Doug, Dougan, Douglas, Duane, Dugan, Duncan, Dwayne, Dwight, Findlay, Findley, Finn, Fionn, Flann, Flavio, Floyd, Flynn, Gavin, Gawain, Gil, Gilroy, Gray, Grey, Griffith, Gwayne, Hinto, Irv, Irving, Jett, Keary, Keir, Kent, Kerry, Kieran, Kirwin, Les, Lesley, Leslie, Lloyd, Loden, Lootah, Monroe, Munro, Munroe, Neel, Nigel, Odhran, Odran, Oran, Oren, Orin, Phoenix, Radley, Red, Redd, Reed, Reid, Rogan, Rory, Rowan, Ruairi, Rufus, Rush, Russ, Russell, Rusty, Sapa, Satanta, Shappa, Slate, Taven, Tavin, Tito, Titos, Titus, Tucson, Whitley, Whitney, Wyn, Wynn

COUNSELOR, ADVISER — FEMALE

Alfreda, Avery, Avrielle, Conseja, Melva, Melvina, Monica, Monika, Monique, Musheera, Mushira, Rae, Raeleen, Ragna, Ralphina, Ramira, Ramona, Raylene, Rhetta, Rona, Ronette, Ronnell, Ronnette

COUNSELOR, ADVISER — MALE

Al, Alf, Alfred, Alfredo, Avery, Conrad, Corrado, Konrad, Kort, Kurt, LeeRon, Leron, Mel, Melvin, Mundo, Musheer, Mushir, Rafe, Rafer, Ragnar, Ragnvald, Raimundo, Rainer, Ralph, Ramiro, Ramón, Raoul, Raul, Ray, Raymond, Rayner, Raynor, Reggie, Regin, Reginald, Reginold, Reinaldo, Reine, Reiner, Renard, Renaud, Renny, Rhett, Rinaldo, Rolf

CROWN — FEMALE

Atara, Atira, Corona, Estefania, Kelila, Kitra, Livya, Stefana, Stefania, Stefanie, Stefany, Steffi, Steffie, Stephania, Stephanie, Stephany, Stevee, Stevie, Tiara

CROWN — MALE

Atir, Esteban, Etienne, Kalil, Stefan, Stefano, Stefanos, Stepan, Stephan, Stephanos, Stephen, Steve, Steven, Taj

DARK, NIGHT — FEMALE

Carrie, Carry, Ciara, Ciarra, Darcie, Darcy, Delaney, Duana, Jetta, Jette, Keira, Keri, Kerri, Kerry, Kiera, Laila, Laili, Lailie, Lainey, Laney, Layla, Leila, Leili, Lilith, Lillith, Lyla, Malinda, Maura, Melanie, Melantha, Melany, Melinda, Melony, Minda, Mindie, Mindy, Nisha, Rajani

DARK, NIGHT — MALE

Blake, Carey, Cary, Ciar, Ciaran, Daragh, Darcel, Darcy, Darrah, Daven, Davin, Delaney, Delany, Donovan, Doug, Dougan, Douglas, Doyle, Duane, Dugan, Dwayne, Jett, Keary, Keir, Kerry, Kieran, Kirwin, Maurice, Maury, Mo, Moe, Morrie, Morris, Morry, Odhran, Odran, Oran, Oren, Orin, Sapa, Sullivan, Sully, Taven, Tavin, Yiska

DELIGHTFUL, PLEASANT, CHARMING, SWEET — FEMALE

Abbie, Abby, Abi, Abigail, Adiva, Afric, Ananda, Aoife, Areta, Avigayil, Bevan, Bevin, Charisma, Charmaine, Charmian, Delice, Dulcia, Dulcie, Dulcinea, Eden, Ednah, Eula, Eulala, Eulalia, Eulalie, Euphemia, Gail, Gale, Gayle, Gioia, Lalia, Lalita, Lalitha, Manjika, Marini, Marley, Marlie, Marly, Min-Hee, Naamah, Namah, Nandini, Naomi, Noemi, Noshin, Olalla, Prita, Rakhima, Rama, Ramya, Ranjan, Shireen, Shirin, Tirza, Tirzah, Young-Hee

DETERMINED, STEADFAST, CONSTANT — FEMALE

Aamina, Ameena, Aminah, Asiya, Billie, Connie, Conny, Constance, Constancia, Constantina, Constanza, Etana, Haseema, Hasima, Hazima, Helma, Konstantina, Mina, Minna, Minnie, Minny, Rakina, Rakinah, Velma, Wilhelmina, Willa, Willetta, Wilma

DETERMINED, STEADFAST, CONSTANT — MALE

Aamin, Ameen, Amin, Bill, Billy, Constantine, Constantino, Dante, Duran, Eitan, Etan, Ethan, Eustace, Guglielmo, Guillaume, Guillermo, Haseem, Hasim, Hazeem, Hazim, Hector, Ittan, Katashi, Konstantin, Konstantinos, Kostas, Liam, Najih, Rakeen, Rakin, Søren, Uiliam, Viggo, Vilhelm, Vili, Wilbert, Wilbur, Wilhelm, Will, Willard, Willem, Willi, William, Wilmer, Zende

DIVINE — FEMALE

Ana, Asmani, Deana, Deanna, Deanne, Dee, Dee Dee, Devika, Diana, Diandra, Diandre, Diane, Diantha, Didi, Disa, Diviana, Divina, Dyan, Epifania, Hanita, Kiana, Lani, Mana, Quiana, Sangita, Surina

EARTH, EARTH KEEPER — FEMALE

Adama, Adamina, Addison, Aila, Avani, Demetria, Demi, Dimitra, Eartha, Gaea, Gaia, Georgene, Georgette, Georgia, Georgina, Georgine, Gigi, Gina, Ila, Ira, Jirina, Jorja, Moneka, Onatah, Siena, Sienna, Terra, Tierra, Tuwa

EARTH, EARTH KEEPER — MALE

Adam, Adamo, Adán, Addison, Bart, Bartholomew, Bartoli, Bartolomé, Bartolomeo, Clay, Clayton, Demetrio, Diji, Dima, Dimitri, Dimitrios, Dmitri, Dmitry, Garland, Georg, George, Georges, Georgi, Georgios, Georgy, Giorgio, Jiri, Jorg, Jorge, Jorgen, Jory, Jur, Jurek, Keb, Lance, Lanzo, Mahkah, Noma, Qeb, Terran, Tito, Titos, Titus, Yuri

ESTEEMED, EXALTED, HONORED, PRAISEWORTHY— FEMALE

Aarona, Adara, Agostina, Aharona, Aoloa, Augusta, Augustine, Fayola, Folami, Haamida,

Hadara, Hamida, Hamidah, Haseeba, Hasiba, Jaleela, Jalilah, Munifah, Omea, Saamia, Samia

ESTEEMED, EXALTED, HONORED, PRAISEWORTHY — MALE

Aaron, Abram, Adar, Agostino, Aharon, Ali, Aron, August, Augustine, Augustino, Augusto, Augustus, Austen, Austin, Avram, Ayinde, Chiram, Gus, Haroun, Harun, Hiram, Jahi, Jaja, Jalaal, Jalal, Jaleel, Jalil, Jaseem, Jasim, Mahib, Mahmoud, Mahmud, Mohammad, Muhammad, Munif, Shanley, Takashi, Timon, Tino, Tito

ETERNAL, EVERLASTING, IMMORTAL, INFINITE — FEMALE

Adel, Amara, Amaretta, Ambrosia, Amiti, Amrita, Anya, Erica, Erika, Khalida, Khalidah, Mauloa, Nili, Nitya, Perpetua, Sheridan

ETERNAL, EVERLASTING, IMMORTAL, INFINITE — MALE

Amaran, Ambrogio, Ambros, Amiad, Baki, Baqi, Cianan, Eilam, Eilif, Elad, Elam, Eric, Erich, Erick, Erik, Eryk, Javed, Khaleed, Khalid, Nityan, Phoenix, Sheridan, Soma, Thanos

FAMOUS, RENOWNED — FEMALE

Almira, Bobbi, Bobbie, Clotida, Elmira, Eloisa, Eloise, Gilberta, Loida, Loie, Loraina, Loraine, Lorena, Lorraina, Lorraine, Lou, Louisa, Louise, Luisa, Luise, Luiza, Lulu, Malou, Marilou, Marylou, Mira, Nola, Noleen, Ramira, Roberta, Robin, Robina, Robyn, Rolanda, Rosalinde, Rowena, Rowina, Winnie

FAMOUS, RENOWNED — MALE

Alois, Aloysius, Bob, Bobbie, Bobby, Bobek, Boris, Borys, Dodge, Elmer, Gib, Gil, Gilbert, Gilberto, Hob, Hodge, Ingmar, Ingvar, Kaulana, Lando, Lazlo, Lew, Lewis, Lothar, Lou, Louie, Louis, Ludwig, Luigi, Luis, Luther, Mongo, Nolan, Orlando, Radek, Ramiro, Roald, Rob, Robert, Roberto, Robin, Rod, Roddy, Roderick, Rodge, Rodney, Rodolfo, Rodrigo, Rodrigue, Roger, Rogério, Rolan, Roland, Rolando, Rolf, Rollo, Rowan, Rubert, Rudolf, Rudolph, Rudy, Rupert, Sem, Shem, Wilmer, Yash

FIRE, FLAME, CANDLE — FEMALE

Addison, Azar, Cande, Candelaria, Chandelle, Chondel, Edana, Edna, Eithne, Ena, Enya, Fina, Hayden, Ignacia, Kenna, Kenner, Lasair, Menora, Menorah, Nera, Pele, Serafina, Seraphina, Seraphine, Shandelle, Shondel, Topaz, Uriela, Uriella, Vesta

FIRE, FLAME, CANDLE — MALE

Addis, Addison, Aden, Agni, Aidan, Aiden, Aidis, Aodhan, Azar, Blaze, Brent, Brenton, Chandler, Egan, Fagan, Fagen, Hagan, Hagen, Hayden, Ignacio, Ignazio, Jaden, Jayden, Jomo, Keahi, Keegan, Ken, Kenner, Kennet, Kenneth, Kenny, Sandeep, Sandip, Serafim, Shaviv, Taden, Tayden, Ty, Tyce, Tye, Tyrus, Tyson, Uri, Uriah, Uriel

FLOWER — FEMALE

Adsila, Alissa, Alyssa, Amaryllis, Anarosa, Anemone, Azalea, Azalee, Azalia, Azalie, Azile, Bela, Bellarosa, Blossom, Calantha, Camellia, Chanda, Chanice, Chanelle, Chemeli, Chloris, Cloris, Dafna, Dafne, Dahlia, Daisy, Daphne, Delphina, Diantha, Fiala, Fiona, Fiorella, Fleur, Flora, Florence, Florens, Floretta, Florianne, Florissa, Gardenia, Giacinta, Gladdis, Gladys, Gulshan, Hadley, Hana, Heather, Honoka, Hua, Hyacinth, Hyacinthe, Hyun-Young, Ianthe, Ilima, Iona, Iris, Jacaranda, Jacinta, Jacinthe, Jasmine, Jasmyn, Jazmin, Jazmine, Jazz, Jessamine, Jessamyn, Ji-Young, Jolana, Jolanda, Jonquil, Kalei,

Kalia, Kamalika, Kamalini, Kiku, Kohana, Kundini, Lan, Lehua, Leilani, Leinani, Lian, Lil, Lila, Lilia, Lilian, Liliana, Lilike, Liliya, Lillian, Lillie, Lilly, Lily, Linnea, Lotem, Lotus, Magnolia, Malati, Malika, Malini, Malva, Melantha, Melba, Melia, Mio, Misaki, Nalini, Nasrim, Nazara, Nea, Nurit, Pansie, Pansy, Pema, Petal, Petula, Poppy, Raisa, Raizel, Rhoda, Romy, Rosa, Rosabella, Rosalia, Rosalie, Rosalinda, Rosana, Rosanna, Rose, Roseanne, Rosemary, Rosetta, Rosette, Roisin, Rosheen, Rosie, Rosina, Rosita, Rosy, Roza, Rozetta, Saki, Sakura, Sanna, Sausan, Senna, Shanna, Shoshanah, Shoshannah, Sihu, So-Young, Sue, Suellen, Suki, Sukie, Suma, Susan, Susana, Susanna, Susannah, Susanne, Susie, Suzan, Suzanna, Suzannah, Suzanne, Suzette, Suzie, Suzy, Tansy, Thalia, Viola, Violet, Violeta, Violette, Viona, Yamka, Yasmeen, Yasmin, Yolanda, Yolande, Young-Hee, Yuri, Zahra, Zalira, Zanna, Zinnia, Zusa, Zusanna

FORTUNATE, LUCKY — FEMALE

Ashera, Bakhita, Baraka, Fayola, Felice, Felicia, Felicidad, Felicie, Felicita, Félicité, Felicity, Felisha, Fortunata, Halona, Keiko, Khaira, Khayra, Masuda, Mazal, Oshra, Selda, Shreya, Shrila, Suh-Hyun, Ushara, Yoshi

FORTUNATE, LUCKY — MALE

Akhtar, Asher, Ben, Benj, Benjamin, Binyamin, Feliks, Felix, Fortunato, Gadiel, Isad, Khair, Khayr, Kichiro, Maddox, Madoc, Marzuq, Masud, Mubarak, Shrini, Venturo, Yoshiro

FRAGRANCE, PERFUME, MYRRH — FEMALE

Abeera, Abira, Aiveen, Atira, Cassia, Chameli, Fang, Fen, Gardenia, Jasmine, Jasmyn, Jazmin, Jazmine, Jazz, Jessamine, Jessamyn, Ketura, Kezia, Lakeisha, Lakisha, Keesha, Kesha, Keshia, Ketzia, Kezia, Kundini, Mae, Mai, Maire, Mairead, Mairona, Maja, Malati, Mamie, Manon, Mapuana,

Mari, Maria, Mariah, Mariam, Marian, Mariana, Marianna, Marie, Mariel, Mariella, Marielle, Marieta, Marika, Marion, Marionne, Marisa, Marise, Marissa, Marita, Mariya, Marja, Marla, Marlena, Marlene, Marlis, Marlissa, Marlo, Mary, Marya, Masha, Maura, Maureen, Maurene, May, Mea, Meah, Mia, Mimi, Miri, Miriam, Mirjam, Miryam, Mitzi, Moani, Moira, Moire, Mollie, Molly, Moreen, Moyra, Myra, Pollie, Polly, Randa, Rhoda, Ria, Rosalia, Rosalie, Rose, Rosemary, Rosette, Rosheen, Rosie, Rosy, Roza

FREE — FEMALE

Aditi, Amala, Ashima, Carla, Carlana, Carleen, Carleigh, Carlene, Carley, Carlie, Carline, Carlota, Carlotta, Carly, Carol, Carole, Carolina, Caroline, Carolyn, Carrie, Carry, Caryl, Caryll, Charlaine, Charlana, Charlayne, Charlee, Charleen, Charlena, Charlene, Charlie, Charline, Charlize, Charlotta, Charlotte, Cher, Cheryl, Clover, Fannie, Fanny, Franca, Francene, Frances, Francesca, Francette, Francine, Francisca, Françoise, Franka, Herut, Ina, Karla, Karlen, Karlie, Karlotte, Karly, Karola, Karolina, Karoline, Liberata, Liberty, Lina, Lotta, Lotte, Lysandra, Orma, Paquita, Sharla, Sharlaine, Sharlana, Sharlayne, Sharleen, Sharlena, Sharlene, Sheryl, Wilda

FREE — MALE

Burgess, Carey, Carl, Carlito, Carlo, Carlos, Carlton, Carolos, Carroll, Cary, Charles, Charley, Charlie, Charlton, Chaz, Chico, Chip, Chuck, Cisco, Darby, Dermot, Diarmaid, Dror, Francesco, Francis, Francisco, Franco, François, Frank, Franklin, Frans, Franz, Free, Hiram, Kanoa, Karl, Karol, Kermit, Liberato, Liberty, Libor, Lysander, Paco, Pancho, Quito, Shad

FRIEND — FEMALE

Aimée, Aleefa, Alifa, Alvena, Alvina, Ami, Amia, Amice, Amie, Amisha, Amishia, Amita, Amity, Amy, Aneesa, Anisa, Caragh, Dakota, Eddie,

Eddy, Edina, Edwena, Edwina, Elvina, Filomena, Huba, Khalila, Khalilah, Maitri, Melva, Melvina, Nadima, Nadimah, Najiah, Najiya, Nuan, Omatra, Philomena, Rafiki, Reut, Rowena, Rowina, Rue, Rut, Ruth, Selda, Sumitra, Tomomi, Wafeeqa, Wafiqa, Winnie, Zameela, Zamila

FRIEND — MALE

Akiki, Al, Alden, Aleef, Alif, Alvin, Alwyn, Amit, Amitai, Amitan, Auden, Audey, Audie, Boden, Dakota, Delwin, Ed, Eddie, Eddy, Edwin, Eldad, Elvin, Elvis, Erwin, Godwin, Irv, Irvin, Irwin, Itai, Jeb, Jebidiah, Jed, Jedidiah, Khaleel, Khalil, Lufti, Mel, Melvin, Nadim, Nikan, Nitis, Oman, Oscar, Oskar, Rafeeq, Rafi, Rafiq, Rowan, Tex, Tokota, Wafeeq, Wafiq, Winfred, Winfried, Winston, Yadid, Zameel, Zamil

FRUIT — FEMALE

Apple, Avalon, Beri, Berri, Betania, Beth, Bethanie, Bethany, Cerise, Charice, Charise, Cherice, Cherise, Cherry, Feige, Geneva, Liv, Livia, Livie, Livvy, Mei, Melina, Mio, Morela, Olive, Olivia, Prunella, Quince, Rimona, Sakura, Sharice, Sharise, Umeko

GARDEN, GARDENER — FEMALE

Carmel, Carmela, Carmelita, Carmen, Carmencita, Gana, Gania, Ganya, Georgeanne, Georgene, Georgette, Georgia, Georgina, Georgine, Gigi, Gina, Gulshan, Hortense, Hortensia, Janina, Janna, Jirina, Jorja, Lesley, Leslie, Mali, Melita, Riyaz

GARDEN, GARDENER — MALE

Bart, Bartholomew, Bartoli, Bartolomé, Bartolomeo, Carmelo, Carmine, Diji, Garth, Georg, George, Georges, Georgi, Georgy, Giorgio, Granger, Jiri, Jørgen, Jorge, Jörgen, Jur, Jurek, Les, Lesley, Leslie, Yuri

GENTLE, TENDER — FEMALE

Adina, Alima, Belinda, Bindi, Bindy, Brisa, Clemencia, Clementine, Dima, Gerlinde, Haleema, Halima, Halimah, Kehua, Klementina, Laka, Lalita, Lalitha, Lateefa, Latifah, Layaan, Linda, Lindie, Lindy, Lynda, Mayu, Mildred, Miliani, Miyu, Moani, Munisa, Nalini, Naseema, Nasima, Rosalind, Rosalinde, Rosalyn, Roslyn, Roz, Sanjana, Shu, Sieglinde, Teri, Terri, Terrie, Terry, Tirion, Yuko

GENTLE, TENDER — MALE

Cavan, Cavin, Clem, Clement, Clemente, Gareth, Gary, Gavin, Haleem, Halim, Ihsan, Keefe, Kevin, Kliment, Lateef, Latif, Munis, Naseem, Nasim, Shu, Taven, Tavin, Terence, Terrence, Terry, Torrie, Tory, Wen

GIFT — FEMALE

Adia, Aldora, Atiya, Atiyyah, Bogdana, Bohdana, Chanelle, Chanice, Chevonne, Dee, Dee Dee, Devan, Devin, Didi, Donatella, Dora, Doreen, Dorene, Doretta, Dori, Dorie, Dorinda, Dorine, Dorita, Dorona, Dorota, Dorotea, Dorothea, Dorothy, Ebun, Eudora, Genice, Genise, Gia, Gianna, Giovanna, Hadaya, Hanna, Hiba, Ioanna, Isadora, Isidora, Isoke, Ivana, Ivanka, Ivanna, Ivona, Izzie, Izzy, Jan, Jana, Janae, Jane, Janeka, Janelle, Janessa, Janet, Janey, Janice, Janie, Janika, Janine, Janiqua, Janique, Janis, Janita, Janna, Janne, Jannike, Jayne, Jaynie, Jean, Jeana, Jeanette, Jeanie, Jeanine, Jeanna, Jeanne, Jeannette, Jeannie, Jeannine, Jeannique, Jenessa, Jenique, Jenka, Jensen, Jensine, Jessa, Jessica, Jessie, Joan, Joana, Joani, Joanie, Johana, Johanna, Johna, Johnna, Jonell, Jonelle, Jonetta, Joni, Jonie, Jonna, Juana, Juanita, Lashonda, Lawhawna, Macey, Macie, Macy, Matana, Natana, Natanya, Noni, Rhonda, Seana, Seona, Shanda, Shanelle, Shanice, Shauna, Shawna, Sheena, Shilo, Shiloh, Shona, Shonda, Sian, Sine, Sinead, Siobhan, Sioned, Sunniva, Tabia, Teodora,

Thea, Theodosia, Theoroda, Vanja, Vanna, Vanya, Vonetta, Yochana, Zaneta, Zanita, Zhanna

GIFT — MALE

Bevan, Beven, Bogdan, Bohdan, Darshan, Darshawn, Darshon, Devan, Devin, Devon, Diosdado, Donat, Donatello, Donato, Dorian, Eion, Evan, Fyodor, Gianni, Giannis, Giovanni, Hanek, Hans, Iain, Ian, Ifan, Ioannis, Isidore, Isidoros, Ivan, Iwan, Izzie, Izzy, Jack, Jan, Janco, Janek, Janika, Jannik, Janos, Jashawn, Jathan, Jax, Jaxson, Jean, Jens, Jensen, Jess, Jesse, Jessie, Jevin, Jock, Johan, Johann, Johannes, John, Johnnie, Johnny, Jon, Jonathan, Jonny, Juan, Lashon, Macey, Macy, Matan, Mateo, Mathias, Mathieu, Mathis, Matt, Matteus, Matthew, Matthias, Matthieu, Matus, Nat, Natan, Nate, Nathan, Nathaniel, Netanel, Sean, Shai, Shane, Shawn, Shawnel, Shilo, Shiloh, Sion, Tad, Taddeo, Tadeo, Ted, Teddy, Teo, Teodor, Teodoro, Thad, Thaddeus, Theo, Theodor, Theodore, Theodoro, Theodoros, Theon, Van, Vanya, Yancey, Yancy, Yann, Yanni, Yannis, Yehonatan, Yianni, Yiannis, Yishai, Yonatan, Zane, Zavad, Zeb, Zebedee

GOD, ALLAH — FEMALE

Abeeda, Abida, Abiela, Abiella, Adel, Amania, Amanya, Amiela, Anneliese, Annelise, Anselma, Ariela, Ariella, Arielle, Aviela, Aviella, Avrielle, Azriela, Babette, Basha, Bashe, Batia, Batya, Belicia, Belita, Bella, Belle, Bess, Bessie, Bessy, Beth, Bethan, Betsan, Betsie, Betsy, Betta, Bette, Bettie, Bettina, Betty, Bogdana, Bohdana, Buffy, Chanda, Chanelle, Chanice, Chela, Chenia, Chenya, Chevonne, Daneisha, Danette, Dani, Dania, Danica, Daniela, Daniele, Daniella, Danielle, Danika, Danisha, Danni, Danya, Darsha, Datia, Datya, Dee, Dee Dee, Didi, Domenica, Dominga, Dominika, Dominique, Donata, Doreen, Dorene, Doretta, Dori, Dorie, Dorine, Dorita, Dorota, Dorotea, Dorothea, Dorothy, Eilis, Einya, Eliana, Elianna, Eliora, Elisa, Elisabet, Elisabeth, Elisabetta, Elise, Elisha, Elisheva, Eliya, Eliza, Elizabeta, Elizabeth, Elizaveta, Ellie, Elly, Elsa, Elsie, Elspeth, Elza, Emanuela, Emanuelle, Fifi, Foluke, Gabriela, Gabriele, Gabriella, Gabrielle, Gania, Ganya, Gavriel, Gavriela, Gavriella, Gavrielle, Gavrila, Genice, Genise, Gia, Gianna, Gilda, Giovanna, Gudrun, Hanna, Hazel, Henia, Henya, Ilsa, Ilse, Immanuela, Ioanna, Isabel, Isabela, Isabella, Isabelle, Isobel, Isoke, Ivana, Ivanka, Ivanna, Ivona, Izabella, Izzie, Izzy, Jalaina, Jalayna, Jan, Jana, Janae, Jane, Janeka, Janelle, Janessa, Janet, Janey, Janice, Janie, Janika, Janine, Janiqua, Janique, Janis, Janita, Janna, Janne, Jannike, Jayne, Jaynie, Jean, Jeana, Jeanette, Jeanie, Jeanine, Jeanna, Jeanne, Jeannette, Jeannie, Jeannine, Jeannique, Jenessa, Jenique, Jenka, Jensen, Jensine, Jeri, Jerri, Jerrie, Jessa, Jessica, Jessie, Jesúsa, Jo, Joan, Joana, Joani, Joanie, Joanna, Joanne, Joaquina, Jobeth, Jodene, Jodi, Jodie, Jodine, Jody, Joella, Joelle, Joette, Johana, Johanna, Johnna, Johna, Jojo, Joleen, Jolene, Joline, Jonell, Jonelle, Jonetta, Joni, Jonie, Jonna, Joquina, Josée, Josefa, Josefina, Josepha, Josephina, Josephine, Josette, Josie, Jozetta, Jozette, Juana, Juanita, Lashawna, Lashonda, Leandra, Leeya, Libbie, Libby, Libiya, Liesa, Liesbeth, Liese, Liesl, Lisa, Lisbet, Lise, Lisette, Liya, Liz, Liza, Lizbet, Lizette, Lizzie, Lizzy, Macey, Macie, Macy, Makaela, Makayla, Malina, Manuela, Maribel, Marybeth, Mashayla, Meisha, Michaela, Michalina, Michela, Michele, Micheline, Michelle, Micki, Miguela, Mika, Mikaela, Mikayla, Mikki, Mishaila, Mishcha, Mishka, Moriela, Neriah, Neriya, Noni, Obasi, Pepita, Rafaela, Rania, Raphaela, Raziela, Refaela, Sabela, Sabella, Sajida, Sajidah, Samanta, Samantha, Samuela, Seana, Selma, Seona, Shanda, Shanelle, Shanice, Shauna, Shawna, Sheena, Shelley, Shellie, Shelly, Shilo, Shiloh, Shirel, Shona, Shonda, Sian, Sibéal, Sine, Sinead, Siobhan, Sioned, Talisa, Talisha, TaLisha, Talissa, Tecla, Tekla, Teodora, Thea, Thekla, Theodora, Theodosia, Tiffanie, Tiffany, Timothea, Tobie, Toby, Uriela, Uriella, Vanja, Vanna, Vanya, Vonetta, Yelizaveta, Yisraela,

Yochana, Yoela, Yosefa, Yosepha, Zaneta, Zanita, Zhanna

GODDESS — FEMALE

Abril, Ambrosia, Amrita, Ana, Anonna, Aphrodite, April, Aranrhod, Asta, Astrid, Athena, Aura, Avril, Birgit, Birgitta, Birgitte, Breda, Bridget, Brighid, Brigid, Brigida, Brigitte, Brita, Brites, Britt, Britta, Chloris, Cleona, Cliona, Cloris, Dana, Denice, Denise, Diana, Diane, Dione, Dionisia, Dionne, Disa, Divina, Doris, Eira, Febe, Flora, Fortunata, Freja, Freya, Gill, Gillian, Gitta, Gitte, Giulia, Gudrun, Hareena, Hera, Inga, Inge, Ingrid, Iris, Isadora, Isidora, Jill, Jillian, Joceline, Jocelyn, Julia, Juliana, Julianna, Julie, Julienne, Juliet, Julieta, Juliette, Julita, Julitte, June, Juno, Keolani, Laka, LaNeece, Lanice, Lea, Lenice, Liane, Luna, Mae, Maia, Marcela, Marcelina, Marceline, Marcella, Marci, Marcia, Marcie, Marcille, Marcy, Maren, Marina, Marsha, Martina, Martine, Marty, May, Maya, Olimpia, Olympia, Pele, Phoebe, Pia, Reanna, Reanne, Rheanna, Rheanne, Rhian, Rhiana, Rhianna, Rhianne, Rhiannon, Riana, Rianna, Rianne, Rihanna, Selena, Selene, Selina, Surina, Thora, Tora, Venus, Vesta, Yuliva, Zalina, Zelena, Zina

GOD, ALLAH — MALE

Abdallah, Abdul, Abeed, Abid, Abidin, Achim, Adel, Adom, Adriel, Akim, Amadeus, Amal, Amiel, Ansel, Anselm, Anselmo, Anzelm, Arel, Ariel, Aviel, Aziel, Azrael, Azriel, Bevan, Beven, Bogdan, Bohdan, Chaniel, Che, Chimelu, Chinelo, Chinua, Corey, Cory, Dan, Dana, Danan, Daniel, Daniil, Danilo, Danny, Dano, Darshan, Darshawn, Darshon, Diosdado, Dom, Domenico, Domingo, Dominic, Dominick, Dominik, Dominique, Eilam, Elad, Elazar, Eldad, Eliam, Elias, Elijah, Elior, Eliot, Elisha, Elliot, Elliott, Ellis, Emanuel, Eoin, Evan, Ezekiel, Fyodor, Gabe, Gable, Gabriel, Gabrielo, Gadiel, Gamliel, Gavriel, Gavril, Geoff, Geoffrey, Geoffroi, Geoffry, Gianni, Giannis, Giole, Giovanni, Giuseppe, Godfrey, Godwin, Gottfried, Gustaf, Gustav, Gustavo, Hanek, Hans, Harel, Iain, Ian, Ifan, Imanuel, Immanuel, Ioannis, Isaiah, Ishmael, Ismail, Itai, Ivan, Iwan, Izzie, Izzy, Jack, Jan, Janco, Janek, Janika, Jannik, Janos, Jashawn, Jax, Jaxson, Jean, Jeb, Jebediah, Jed, Jedidiah, Jeff, Jefferson, Jeffrey, Jeffry, Jens, Jensen, Jerald, Jeremiah, Jeremy, Jerry, Jesús, Joab, Joachim, Joakim, Joaquin, Jock, Jody, Joe, Joel, Joey, Johan, Johann, Johannes, John, Johnnie, Johnny, Jojo, Jon, Jonathan, Jonnie, Jonny, Jools, José, Josef, Joseph, Josh, Joshua, Josiah, Jozef, Juan, Kaniel, Kim, Korey, Kory, Lashon, Laz, Lazar, Lazarus, Lazer, Lazzaro, Macey, Macy, Malcolm, Malkam, Manny, Manolo, Manuel, Mateo, Mathias, Mathieu, Mathis, Matt, Matteus, Matthew, Matthias, Matthieu, Matus, Micah, Micha, Michael, Michail, Michel, Michelangelo, Mick, Mickey, Mickie, Micky, Mico, Miguel, Mike, Mikhail, Mikkel, Misha, Mitch, Mitchel, Mitchell, Moriel, Nat, Nate, Nathaniel, Nechemya, Nehemiah, Netanel, Nic, Nili, Obadiah, Pepe, Pepito, Quino, Rafael, Rafer, Rafi, Raphael, Refael, Rephael, Sajeed, Sajid, Sam, Samuel, Samuelo, Sean, Sefi, Sepp, Shafat, Shane, Shaun, Shawn, Shawnel, Shay, Shaya, Shilo, Shiloh, Shmuel, Shua, Sion, Tad, Taddeo, Tadeo, Tawheed, Tawhid, Ted, Teddy, Teo, Teodor, Teodoro, Thad, Thaddeus, Theo, Theodor, Theodore, Theodoro, Theodoros, Theon, Tim, Timoteo, Timothee, Timotheos, Timothy, Tobiah, Tobias, Tobie, Tobin, Toby, Tuvia, Tuviah, Tuviya, Tuvya, Uriah, Uriel, Uziah, Van, Vanya, Yakim, Yancey, Yancy, Yann, Yanni, Yannis, Yehonatan, Yehoshua, Yeshaya, Yeshua, Yianni, Yiannis, Yirmeyahu, Yishmael, Yisrael, Yoav, Yochai, Yoel, Yonatan, Yosef, Yossi, Yusef, Zac, Zacarías, Zach, Zachariah, Zacharias, Zachary, Zacharya, Zack, Zak, Zane, Zeb, Zebedee, Zecharya, Zed, Zedekiah, Zeke

GODS — MALE

Aegis, Agni, Ambrogio, Ambros, Andor, Apollo, Chimelu, Chinelo, Chinua, Denis, Dennis, Denny, Deon, Deston, Dion, Dionisio, Dustin, Dusty,

Ganesh, Giles, Giuliano, Hanuman, Ingmar, Ingvar, Isidore, Isidoros, Issy, Izzy, Jools, Jules, Julian, Julien, Julio, Julius, Keb, Marc, Marcel, Marcello, Marcelo, Marco, Marcos, Marcus, Marek, Mario, Marius, Mark, Markos, Markus, Martin, Martino, Marty, Mordechai, Oscar, Óscar, Oskar, Qeb, Taran, Terrel, Terrell, Thorin, Tino, Tor, Tyrel, Tyrell, Yul, Yulian, Zeno, Zethus

GOOD — FEMALE

Agafya, Agata, Agatha, Agathe, Agathé, Alma, Anika, Aretha, Arizona, Benigna, Bona, Bonna, Bonnie, Bonny, Charita, Dara, Daria, Darice, Darya, Dobrila, Efimia, Eudora, Eunice, Eun-Sun, Gitel, Gittel, Glenda, Gwenda, Hasana, Hassana, Ide, Jia, Khaira, Khayra, Kisa, Kun-Sun, Lila, Mazal, Mema, Piala, Rhonda, Saguna, Shasa, Sheeva, Shifra, Shifrah, Siomha, Sumitra, Sushila, Taria, Tayiba, Tayibah, Tiva, Tobie, Toby, Tovah, Washta, Wema, Yoshi

GOOD — MALE

Akhtar, Arizona, Ben, Benigno, Benj, Benjamin, Benvenuto, Binyamin, Chang-Ho, Darian, Dario, Darius, Declan, Dobry, Evander, Hao, Hasan, Hasanat, Hassan, Huritt, Husayn, Hussein, Jia, Joon-Ho, Jung-Ho, Khair, Khayr, Kwang-Ho, Liang, Maddox, Madoc, Meged, Suman, Sung-Ho, Tayyib, Tiv, Tobiah, Tobias, Tobie, Tobin, Toby, Tov, Tovi, Tuvia, Tuviah, Tuviya, Tuvya, Winston

GRACE, GRACEFUL, GRACIOUS — FEMALE

Adiva, Altagracia, Altagrazia, Ana, Anabel, Anaïs, Anarosa, Anci, Aneesha, Aneta, Anezka, Anica, Anika, Anina, Anique, Anisha, Anita, Anja, Anke, Ann, Anna, Annabella, Annabeth, Annamaria, Anne, Anneliese, Annelise, Annette, Annie, Annika, Annisa, Annushka, Anouk, Anya, Carisa, Carissa, Chanah, Chanelle, Chani, Chanice, Channah, Chanya, Charice, Charis, Charissa,

Chelita, Chenia, Chenya, Cherise, Chevonne, Donanne, Genice, Genise, Georgeanne, Ghada, Ghadah, Gia, Gianna, Giovanna, Graca, Grace, Graciana, Gracie, Graciela, Graziella, Hanana, Hanita, Hanna, Hannah, Henia, Henya, Ioanna, Ivana, Ivanka, Ivanna, Ivona, Jan, Jana, Janae, Jane, Janeka, Janelle, Janessa, Janet, Janey, Janice, Janie, Janika, Janine, Janiqua, Janique, Janis, Janita, Janna, Janne, Jannike, Jayne, Jaynie, Jean, Jeana, Jeanette, Jeanie, Jeanine, Jeanna, Jeane, Jeannette, Jeannie, Jeannine, Jeannique, Jenessa, Jenique, Jenka, Jensen, Jensine, Jo, Joan, Joana, Joandra, Joani, Joanie, Joanna, Joanne, Johana, Johanna, Johna, Johnna, Jonell, Jonelle, Jonetta, Joni, Jonie, Jonna, Juana, Juanita, Juliana, Juliane, Julianna, Karis, Lashonda, Lateefa, Latifah, Lawshawna, Leann, Leanne, Liana, Lianna, Lianne, Luana, Luanna, Luanne, Ludmila, Mariah, Mariana, Marianna, Marianne, Maryanne, Naama, Naamah, Nan, Nancie, Nancy, Nannette, Neeta, Ninon, Nita, Pollyanna, Prasanna, Rosana, Rosanna, Roseanne, Santana, Seana, Seona, Shanda, Shanelle, Shanice, Shauna, Shawna, Sheena, Shona, Shonda, Sian, Sine, Sinead, Siobhan, Sioned, Suniti, Triana, Vanja, Vanna, Vanya, Vonetta, Yochana, Zaneta, Zanita, Zanna, Zareefa, Zarifah, Zayna

GRACIOUS — MALE

Ben, Bevan, Beven, Chaniel, Darshan, Darshawn, Darshon, Eoin, Evan, Fazl, Gianni, Giannis, Giovanni, Hanek, Hans, Iain, Ian, Ifan, Ioannis, Ivan, Iwan, Jack, Jan, Janco, Janet, Janika, Jannik, Janos, Jashawn, Jax, Jaxson, Jean, Jens, Jensen, Jock, Johan, Johann, Johannes, John, Johnnie, Johnny, Juan, Lashon, Lateef, Latif, Sean, Shane, Shaun, Shawn, Shawnel, Sion, Van, Vanya, Yancey, Yancy, Yann, Yanni, Yianni, Yiannis, Zane, Zareef, Zarif

GREAT, GLORIOUS, EXCELLENT — FEMALE

Adira, Agostina, Antoinette, Antonette, Antonia, Arya, Augusta, Augustine, Clio, Dagmar, Dylan,

Geona, Gloria, Gloriana, Glorianna, Indira, Jaleela, Jalilah, Kabeera, Kabira, Mahima, Maura, Maxene, Maxine, Meredith, Mira, Reanna, Reanne, Rheanna, Rheanne, Rhian, Rhiana, Rhianna, Rhianne, Rhiannon, Riana, Rianna, Rianne, Rihanna, Suniti, Sushila, Tecla, Tekla, Thekla, Tifara, Toinette, Toni, Tonia, Tonie

GREAT, GLORIOUS, EXCELLENT — MALE

Adir, Agostino, Antal, Anthony, Antoine, Anton, Antonello, Antonio, August, Augustine, Augustino, Augusto, Augustus, Austen, Austin, Bakari, Boris, Borys, Chiram, Cochise, Daiki, Daisuke, Dillon, Dima, Dylan, Gordan, Gordon, Grant, Gus, Hao, Hiroto, Hong, Jalaal, Jalal, Jaleel, Jalil, Jaseem, Jasim, Kabeer, Kabir, Kawa, Lazlo, Macsen, Macson, Magnus, Mahib, Maks, Manus, Massimo, Max, Maxim, Maximilian, Maximilien, Máximo, Maximus, Meged, Menewa, Meredith, Milos, Mirek, Miroslav, Radimir, Sujay, Tai, Tino, Tito, Tonio, Toño, Tony, Udara, Vlad, Vladimir, Wei, Yamato, Ziv

HANDSOME — MALE

Adonis, Al, Alain, Alan, Alano, Allan, Allen, Alun, Beau, Beaumont, Cadhla, Calix, Coinneach, Gavin, Hasan, Hassan, Husayn, Hussein, Jamaal, Jamal, Jun, Kavan, Kealan, Keelan, Ken, Kenner, Kennet, Kenneth, Kenny, Kenzie, Kevin, MacKenzie, Nohea, Polani, Quinlan, Shakeel, Shakil, Taven, Tavin, Waseem, Wasim, Wyn, Wynn, Zuri

HAPPY, JOYOUS, CHEERFUL, BLISSFUL, LAUGHTER — FEMALE

Abbie, Abby, Abeo, Abi, Abigail, Alair, Aleeza, Alegra, Alisa, Alissa, Alizah, Allegra, Ananda, Aoife, Ashera, Avigayil, Ayoka, Basima, Basimah, Basma, Bayo, Bea, Beah, Beata, Beate, Beatrice, Beatrix, Beatriz, Bliss, Blithe, Blythe, Chara, Charice, Charis, Charise, Charissa, Charmian,

Chedva, Cherice, Cherise, Damisi, Dayo, Delice, Duscha, Elza, Fana, Faraa, Farah, Farrah, Felice, Felicia, Felicidad, Felicie, Felicita, Félicité, Felicity, Felisha, Gae, Gail, Gaila, Gale, Gay, Gaye, Gayla, Gayle, Gayleen, Gilah, Gioia, Gwenyth, Gwyneth, Halona, Haniyya, Haniyyah, Hanna, Harsha, Hedva, Hilaria, Hilary, Hillary, Huan, Ilaria, Joi, Joisse, Joy, Joyce, Joye, Jubilee, Keiko, Lara, Larisa, Larissa, Latisha, LaTisha, Lecia, Leta, Leticia, Letitia, Letizia, Licia, Lisha, Luana, Makenna, Marnina, Merry, Mi-Kyoung, Nandini, Olina, Oshra, Prita, Renana, Rona, Rosie, Rosy, Sachiko, Sadiah, Sadiyah, Sameena, Samina, Sananda, Selda, Shankari, Sharmini, Shiran, Simcha, So-Young, Sunnie, Sunny, Tate, Tatum, Teshi, Tisha, Trixie, Ulani, Yamima, Yarona, Yi, Yu, Yukiko, Zelda, Zelde

HAPPY, JOYOUS, CHEERFUL, BLISSFUL, LAUGHTER — MALE

Alair, Asher, Ayo, Baseem, Basim, Basma, Caius, Elez, Ellery, Farih, Feliks, Felix, Gale, Gil, Gilon, Harshad, Hilario, Hilary, Huan, Ilar, Ilario, Isaac, Isaak, Isak, Ike, Ishaq, Kaius, Kalea, Mandu, Nandan, Nandi, Nirvan, Radimir, Ranjan, Ron, Sachi, Shankar, Sunara, Tait, Tate, Tatum, Teshi, Thabo, Winston, Yaron, Yitzchak, Yu

HEALTHY, HEAL — FEMALE

Afiya, Aiveen, Althea, Eira, Jian, Keolani, Mae, Mai, Maire, Mairead, Mairona, Maja, Mamie, Manon, Maretta, Mari, Maria, Mariam, Marian, Marie, Mariel, Mariella, Marielle, Marieta, Marika, Marion, Marionne, Marise, Marissa, Marita, Mariya, Marja, Marlis, Marlissa, Mary, Marya, Masha, Maura, Maureen, Maurene, May, Mea, Meah, Mia, Mimi, Miri, Miriam, Mirjam, Miryam, Mitzi, Moira, Moire, Mollie, Molly, Moreen, Moyra, Myra, Pollie, Polly, Rafaela, Raphaela, Refaela, Ria, Val, Valenda, Valentina, Valentine, Valeria, Valerie, Valeriya, Valery, Valinda

HEALTHY, HEAL — MALE

Asa, Asah, Balint, Daktari, Elazar, Galen, Galeno, Hale, Jace, Jason, Jazon, Jian, Kang, Ken, Kenta, Keola, Lazar, Lazarus, Lazer, Marion, Rafael, Rafer, Rafi, Raphael, Refael, Rephael, Val, Valentin, Valentine, Valentino

HELP, SERVE, SUPPORT — FEMALE

Alejandra, Aleka, Aleksandra, Alessa, Alessandra, Alessia, Alexa, Alexana, Alexandra, Alexandria, Alexia, Alexina, Alexis, Alondra, Andee, Andie, Azriela, Cindra, Cody, Dacey, Dacie, Dacy, Elazar, Eleazar, Gilda, Kody, Lexa, Lexi, Lexie, Lexy, Myla, Naseera, Nasira, Ofelia, Ophelia, Paget, Paige, Pilar, Pili, Rafeeda, Rafida, Sandi, Sandie, Sandra, Sandy, Sang-Mi, Sasha, Saundra, Shachee, Shandra, Sindra, Sondra, Tandra, Xandra, Zaheera, Zahirah, Zandra, Zanna, Zasha

HELP, SERVE, SUPPORT — MALE

Abdallah, Abdul, Alandro, Alasdair, Alastair, Alastar, Alec, Alejandro, Alejo, Alek, Aleksei, Aleksy, Alessandro, Alessio, Alester, Alex, Alexander, Alexandre, Alexandros, Alexei, Alexio, Alexios, Alexis, Ameed, Amid, Bharata, Birger, Cody, Daisuke, Elek, Elmo, Ezra, Gillean, Gilles, Gilroy, Hosea, Hoshea, Kaniel, Kody, Laz, Lazar, Lazarus, Lazer, Lazzaro, Lex, Miles, Milo, Myles, Naasir, Nasir, Obadiah, Page, Paget, Rafeed, Rafid, Sander, Sandros, Sandy, Sang-Ho, Sang-Min, Sasha, Sergei, Sergio, Sergios, Sven, Xander, Zaheer, Zahir, Zan, Zander

HOLY, SACRED — FEMALE

Agna, Agnes, Agnese, Agnessa, Anice, Annice, Annis, Ariadne, Ariane, Arianna, Arianne, Branwen, Bronwen, Bronwyn, Ceridwen, Ceridwyn, Chermona, Corazón, Dilwyn, Glenda, Glenis, Glennis, Glenys, Guinevere, Gwen Gwenda, Gwendolen, Gwendoline, Gwendolyn, Gwyn, Ines, Inés, Inessa, Inez, Jen, Jenn, Jenna, Jennie, Jennifer, Jenny, Jeri, Jerri, Jerrie, Kerani, Nessa, Nezza, Olenka, Olga, Olwen, Olwyn, Olya, Oni, Sanchia, Senga, Tegwen, Trinidad, Vesta, Vrinda, Wendi, Wendy, Winifred, Winnie, Wynne, Ynez

HOLY, SACRED — MALE

Agni, Devir, Dvir, Hieronymous, Jerome, Jeronimo, Jerry, Nevan, Nevin, Oleg, Panos, Sancho, Sinclair, Trinidad, Whakan, Wyn, Wynn

HONEST, TRUTHFUL, SINCERE, CANDID — FEMALE

Adeela, Adila, Amisha, Candace, Candi, Candice, Candida, Candide, Candy, Candyce, Cheng, Ernesta, Ernestine, Kalissa, Khalisa, Kupono, Leta, Letha, Sarala, Sati, Thea, Verusha, Yeshara, Yoo-Jin

HONEST, TRUTHFUL, SINCERE — MALE

Adeel, Adil, Cheng, Emmet, Ernest, Ernesto, Ernie, Ernst, Frank, Khalis, Makoto, Satyaki, Truman, Yasher, Yosher

HONOR, HONORABLE, NOBLE — FEMALE

Abiola, Ada, Adaline, Adara, Addie, Addy, Adela, Adelaide, Adele, Adelheid, Adelina, Adeline, Adelita, Adella, Adelle, Adina, Adira, Afric, Agostina, Ailani, Aileen, Ailene, Ailis, Ailish, Alberta, Albertina, Alette, Ali, Alice, Alicia, Alina, Alisha, Alison, Alissa, Alita, Aliz, Allie, Ally, Almira, Alyce, Alys, Alyson, Alyssa, Anju, Arya, Aseela, Asila, Audra, Audrey, Audrie, Audrina, Audry, Augusta, Augustine, Azeezah, Azizah, Bedelia, Berta, Bertina, Bidelia, Birgit, Birgitta, Birgitte, Breana, Breanna, Breanne, Breda, Bree, Breena, Bria, Briana, Brianna, Brianne, Bridget,

Brighid, Brigid, Brigida, Brigitte, Brina, Brita, Brites, Britt, Britta, Della, Dray, Drey, Earleen, Earlene, Earline, Elke, Elmira, Elvira, Elvire, Ethel, Eugenia, Eugenie, Fayola, Folami, Gitta, Gitte, Haamida, Hadara, Hamida, Hamidah, Haseeba, Hasiba, Heide, Heidi, Honora, Honoria, Honorine, Karima, Karimah, Kimiko, Lecia, Licia, Lisha, Lyssa, Mona, Nabeela, Nabilah, Nola, Noleen, Noreen, Norene, Obasi, Rafia, Rafiah, Sharifa, TaLisha, Talisha, Timothea

HONOR, HONORABLE, NOBLE — MALE

Adar, Adir, Adolf, Adolfo, Adolph, Adolphe, Agostino, Ahlf, Albert, Alberto, Albrecht, Aldo, Alfons, Alfonso, Ali, Alonso, Alonzo, Alphonse, Alphonso, Alphonzo, Aubert, August, Augustine, Augustino, Augusto, Augustus, Austen, Austin, Azeez, Aziz, Bela, Berto, Brian, Bryan, Bryant, Chiram, Daiki, Elbert, Eliot, Elliot, Elliott, Elmer, Erhard, Eugen, Eugene, Eugenio, Ewan, Ewen, Fons, Gene, Gino, Grady, Gus, Hasib, Hiram, Honoré, Jaja, Jeno, Kareem, Karim, Keefe, Lon, Lonnie, Lonny, Mahmoud, Mahmud, Mohammad, Muhammad, Nabeel, Nabil, Najeeb, Najib, Osei, Sharif, Tim, Timon, Timoteo, Timothee, Timotheos, Timothy, Tino, Tito, Titos, Titus, Varesh, Zevulun

HOUSE, HOME, DWELLING — FEMALE

America, Belen, Betania, Beth, Bethanie, Bethany, Dallas, Enrica, Enriqua, Harietta, Hariette, Harriet, Harrieta, Harrietta, Harriette, Henrietta, Henriette, Henrika, Henriqua, Hettie, Javiera, Jetta, Jette, Manara, Marta, Marte, Martha, Marthe, Martita, Meona, Xaviera

HOUSE, HOME, DWELLING — MALE

Amerigo, Beckett, Bo, Booth, Byron, Carey, Cary, Dallas, Emmerich, Enrico, Enrique, Graham, Hal, Hank, Harrison, Harry, Heinrich, Hendrik, Henri,

Henrik, Henrique, Henry, Imrich, Javier, Manar, Prescott, Quique, Rico, Royce, Tzion, Xavier, Zevulun, Zion

INTELLIGENT, KNOWLEDGEABLE, EDUCATED — FEMALE

Aaqila, Aarifa, Akeela, Akilah, Akili, Alima, Alimah, Anura, Aqila, Areefa, Arifa, Athena, Danesh, Faheema, Fahima, Gyanda, Ide, Ji-Min, Khabeera, Khabira, Ling, Min-Hee, Neora, Nevona, Quinn, Quinnie, Ru, Skyla, Skylar, Taleeba, Taleema, Talib, Talima, Zaheena, Zahina

INTELLIGENT, KNOWLEDGEABLE, EDUCATED — MALE

Aalim, Aaqil, Aarif, Akio, Aleem, Alim, Anura, Aqil, Areef, Arif, Baqir, Chanoch, Conall, Cong, Conn, Dhira, Enoch, Faheem, Fahim, Feivel, Frode, Gyan, Khabeer, Khabir, Min, Mwara, Naor, Navon, Pandita, Quinn, Ru, Rushdi, Sang-Min, Sekou, Skler, Skylar, Taleeb, Taleem, Talib, Talim, Zaheen, Zahin, Zhi

JEWEL, GOLD, SILVER — FEMALE

Adi, Amber, Ambra, Amethyst, Aranhod, Ariana, Arizona, Aurélie, Azura, Azure, Azzurra, Beri, Berri, Beryl, Bijou, Camber, Coral, Corelle, Cressida, Diamante, Esmeralda, Eun-Sun, Fidda, Garnet, Garnette, Gemma, Ghita, Giada, Golda, Goldie, Greta, Gretchen, Gretel, Griet, Ivory, Jada, Jade, Jaden, Jadyn, Jaiden, Jewel, Jewell, Jin, Jool, Jumana, Jumanah, Kim, Kimber, Kimberly, Kimbra, Madge, Mae, Maggie, Mai, Maisie, Maja, Mamie, Margalit, Margaret, Margarete, Margarita, Margaux, Marge, Margerie, Margery, Margherita, Margie, Margit, Margo, Margot, Marguerite, Marjaan, Marji, Marjie, Marjorie, Marjory, Marketa, May, Meagan, Meg, Megalyn, Megan, Meghan, Nasifa, Ofira, Opal, Oralee, Oralie, Oriana, Oriane, Orianne, Panna, Pearl, Pearle, Peg, Peggie, Peigi, Perla, Rita, Rubí, Ruby, Sapphira, Sapphire, Tiara, Topaz, Yu, Zlata

JOURNEYER, TRAVELER, STRANGER, FOREIGNER — FEMALE

Abiona, Alodia, Babette, Babs, Barb, Barbara, Barbee, Barbie, Barbora, Barbra, Barbro, Barby, Bea, Beah, Beata, Beate, Beatrice, Beatrix, Beatriz, Bobbi, Bobbie, Cheyenne, Dessa, Elodia, Elodie, Ferdinanda, Fernanda, Gershona, Hagar, Lawanda, Raida, Sojourner, Trixie, Varvara, Vonda, Wanda, Wendi, Wendy

JOURNEYER, TRAVELER, STRANGER, FOREIGNER — MALE

Doyle, Errol, Ferdinand, Fernand, Fernando, Geoff, Geoffrey, Geoffry, Geoffroi, Gershom, Gershon, Hernando, Jeff, Jefferson, Jeffery, Jeffry, Nando, Nocona, Ryder, Scout, Stian, Stig, Wendel, Wendell

JUDGE, JUSTICE, JUST — FEMALE

Adala, Dana, Daneisha, Danette, Dani, Dania, Danica, Daniela, Daniele, Danièle, Daniella, Danielle, Danika, Danisha, Danya, Dee, Dee Dee, Deena, Didi, Dina, Dinah, Hakeema, Hakima, Haseefa, Hasifa, Jestina, Justine, Justina, Piala, Tameeza, Tamiza, Tyra

JUDGE, JUSTICE, JUST — MALE

Adlai, Dan, Dana, Danan, Daniel, Daniil, Danilo, Danny, Dano, Haakim, Hakeem, Hakim, Hasif, Jung-Ho, Jung-Soo, Justice, Justin, Justino, Justus, Kapono, Kesi, Reinaldo, Ron, Ronald, Ronaldo, Shafat, Tameez, Tamiz, Terrel, Terrell, Tyr, Tyrel, Tyrell, Tyrrell, Zed, Zedekiah

KIND, COMPASSIONATE, MERCIFUL — FEMALE

Agafiya, Agata, Agatha, Agathe, Ahimsa, Alma, Anaïs, Anci, Aneesha, Aneta, Anezka, Anique, Anica, Anika, Anina, Anique, Anisha, Anita, Anja, Anke, Ann, Anna, Anne, Annette, Annie, Annika, Annisa, Annushka, Anouk, Anya, Ateefa, Atifa, Atsuko, Benigna, Bona, Bonna, Carissa, Caron, Chanah, Chani, Channah, Charice, Charis, Charise, Charissa, Cherice, Cherise, Clemencia, Clementine, Daya, Dobrila, Hanana, Hanna, Hannah, Hiro, Hui, Ihsan, Jo, Karis, Karuna, Kisa, Klementina, Laka, Lateefa, Latifa, Maitri, Mercedes, Mercee, Mercy, Mildred, Munisa, Myla, Naama, Naamah, Nan, Nancie, Nancy, Nanette, Ninon, Obioma, Piedad, Rahima, Rahimah, Sanjana, Santana, Shafeeqa, Shafiqa, Shu, Suh-Hyun, Tirion, Wema, Yuko

KIND, COMPASSIONATE, MERCIFUL — MALE

Ateef, Atif, Benigno, Clem, Clement, Clemente, Dobry, Fazl, Gareth, Gary, Gavin, Ihsan, Itai, Kevin, Kliment, Lateef, Latif, Lufti, Mahari, Miles, Milo, Munis, Myles, Noam, Raheem, Rahim, Shafeeq, Shafiq, Shu, Taven, Tavin

LIFE — FEMALE

Aisha, Aishah, Aoife, Asha, Asia, Ava, Bibiana, Bibiane, Chava, Chaya, Eshe, Eva, Eve, Evelina, Evita, Hava, Haya, Jivani, Laola, Lavita, Liv, Taneesha, Tanesha, Tanisha, Tivian, Viana, Vianna, Vita, Vivi, Vivian, Viviana, Vivianna, Vivie, Vivien, Vivienne, Viviette, Yeva, Zoe, Zoey, Zoya

LIFE — MALE

Abel, Ayush, Bion, Chai, Chaim, Chayim, Eldon, Haim, Hayyim, Jivana, Keola, Lif, Mo, Muamar, Muammar, Omar, Prana, Umar, Vian, Vidal, Vit, Vital, Vitale, Vitali, Vitaly, Vito, Yochai, Zissis, Ziven, Zoltan

LIGHT — FEMALE

Aileen, Ailene, Alcinda, Alonya, Aonani, Baheera, Bahira, Bahirah, Bahiya, Bahiyya, Behira, Cande, Candelaria, Chandelle, Chondel, Cinda, Eileen, Elaine, Elan, Elayne, Eleanor, Eleanora, Eleanore,

Elena, Eleni, Elenor, Eleonora, Eleanore, Elin, Elinor, Eliora, Ella, Ellen, Ellie, Ellinor, Elly, Evelyn, Evlyn, Fainne, Gayora, Giora, Halina, Helen, Helena, Helene, Hikari, Ilene, Ilona, Jalaina, Jalayna, Jyoti, Kalama, Kanta, Lainey, Laney, Lena, Lenci, Lene, Leni, Lenora, Leonor, Leonora, Leonore, Liora, Lora, Louella, Lucetta, Lucette, Lucia, Luciana, Lucienne, Lucila, Lucile, Lucille, Lucinda, Lucinde, Lucy, Luella, Luz, Malana, Manara, Meora, Ming, Nehara, Nelda, Nell, Nellie, Nelly, Nera, Neriah, Neriya, Noor, Nora, Nur, Nura, Nuriah, Nuriya, Onella, Orah, Raushana, Sania, Saniyya, Sorcha, Suellen, Svetlana, Tarani, Yeira, Yelena, Zahara, Ziva, Zivah, Ziya

LIGHT — MALE

Abner, Anwar, Avner, Avshalom, Baheer, Bahir, Bareeq, Barik, Deepak, Dillon, Dipak, Elior, Leeor, Leor, Luc, Luca, Lucas, Lucian, Lucien, Lucio, Lucius, Lugh, Luka, Lukas, Luke, Lux, Mandeep, Marici, Noor, Nur, Oran, Pradeep, Pradip, Shaviv, Sohrab, Unika, Uram, Uri, Uriah, Zerach, Ziv, Zohar

LOVE, BELOVED — FEMALE

Abebi, Abiba, Ahava, Ahavah, Ahuva, Ahuvah, Ai, Aiko, Aimée, Aimi, Aiveen, Amabel, Amada, Amanda, Ami, Amia, Amie, Amisha, Amishia, Amora, Amorette, Amy, Aneeqa, Aniqa, Annamaria, Aphrodite, Arzu, Asta, Avril, Azeezah, Azizah, Cairan, Cairenn, Cara, Cari, Caridad, Carina, Carine, Carisa, Carissa, Carita, Carol, Carole, Caron, Carrie, Carry, Caryl, Caryll, Carys, Cassidi, Cassidy, Charita, Charity, Cher, Cherie, Cherish, Cherry, Cheryl, Chiba, Darla, Darleen, Darlena, Darlene, Davette, Davida, Davina, Davita, Davona, Delphia, Desiree, Esmee, Felipa, Filipa, Filippa, Freja, Freya, Ghaliya, Ghaliyah, Grainne, Grania, Habiba, Habibah, Hiyam, Huba, Hulda, Ily, Kalia, Kari, Karita, Kassidy, Kendi, Kupenda, Kyna, Lalasa, Lalita, Lalitha, Libena, Lieba, Lolonyo, Lovee, Lovey, Luba, Lubya, Lyuba, Mabel, Mae, Mai, Maire, Mairead, Mairona,

Maja, Malou, Mamie, Mandie, Mandy, Manon, Maretta, Mari, Maria, Mariah, Mariam, Marian, Mariana, Marianna, Marianne, Maribel, Maricela, Marie, Mariel, Mariella, Marielle, Marieta, Marika, Marilee, Marilou, Marilyn, Marionne, Marisa, Marise, Marisol, Marissa, Maristela, Marita, Mariya, Marja, Marla, Marlena, Marlene, Marlis, Marlissa, Marlo, Mary, Marya, Maryanne, Marybeth, Marylou, Masha, Maura, Maureen, Maurene, May, Mea, Meah, Mia, Milada, Mimi, Miri, Miriam, Mirjam, Miryam, Mitzi, Moira, Moire, Mollie, Molly, Moreen, Moyra, Myra, Myrna, Nafisa, Omea, Philippa, Philomela, Pippa, Pippi, Pollie, Polly, Pollyanna, Prema, Ria, Romy, Rosemary, Sharice, Sharise, Sheri, Sherie, Sherrie, Sheryl, Suki, Thandi, Venus, Yakira

LOVE, BELOVED — MALE

Amadeus, Amado, Azeez, Aziz, Carey, Cary, Cassidy, Dafydd, Dai, Darold, Daud, Dave, Davey, David, Davy, Dawid, Dawud, Ehud, Eldad, Erasmus, Felipe, Felipo, Felippe, Filip, Filippo, Flip, Gannon, Habeeb, Habib, Jarel, Jeb, Jebediah, Jed, Jedidiah, Kama, Kassidy, Keefe, Lieb, Mano, Marion, Milos, Miloslav, Muheeb, Muhib, Oscar, Oskar, Phil, Philip, Phillip, Phillipe, Pip, Prem, Rasmus, Sajan, Tavi, Yadid, Yakir

MAN, MASCULINE — MALE

Akio, Anders, Andras, Andre, André, Andreas, Andrei, Andrés, Andrew, Andrey, Andy, Arsenio, Arsenios, Carey, Carl, Carlito, Carlo, Carlos, Carolos, Carroll, Cary, Charles, Charley, Charlie, Chaz, Chip, Chuck, Drew, Enosh, Evander, Kane, Karl, Karol, Nara, Ondro, Toshio, Truman, Xiong, Yasuo

MEADOW, PASTURE, FIELD, PLAIN — FEMALE

Ainslee, Ainsley, Ainslie, Ashleigh, Ashley, Ashlie, Bev, Beverley, Beverly, Caleigh, Hadley, Hailey,

Halle, Harleigh, Harley, Hayden, Hayley, Heather, Hialeah, Kaleigh, Kayley, Kim, Kimber, Kimberly, Kimbra, Lea, Leann, Leanne, Lee, Leigh, Lesley, Leslie, Liana, Lianna, Lianne, Marilee, Marley, Marlie, Marly, Meadow, Prairie, Reilly, Riley, Rylee, Ryley, Rylie, Savanna, Savannah, Shari, Sharice, Sharie, Sharise, Sharita, Sharon, Sharona, Sharrie, Sharry, Sherry, Shireen, Shirleen, Shirlene, Shirley, Whitley, Zavanna, Zavannah

MEADOW, PASTURE, FIELD, PLAIN — MALE

Ainsley, Arafat, Ashley, Berk, Brad, Bradley, Conway, Dudley, Farley, Gawain, Gwayne, Hadley, Haley, Harley, Hayden, Hayley, Heath, Huntley, Jaden, Jayden, Kemp, Lech, Lee, Leland, Les, Lesley, Leslie, Marley, Mead, Meade, Mort, Morton, Morty, Presley, Radley, Riley, Stan, Stanley, Taden, Taven, Tavin, Tayden, Wayland, Wes, Wesley, Whitley

MOON — FEMALE

Badra, Candra, Celina, Chanda, Chandra, Cinda, Cindy, Cinthia, Cinzia, Cynthia, Diana, Febe, Keiki, Kinda, Konane, Kynthia, Levana, Luna, Mahina, Masheed, Mashid, Mizuki, Parvani, Phoebe, Reanna, Reanne, Rheanna, Rheanne, Rhian, Rhiana, Rhianna, Rhianne, Rhiannon, Riana, Rianna, Rianne, Rihanna, Salena, Selena, Selene, Selina, Shashini, Taini, Zalena, Zalina

MOUNTAIN, HILL, CLIFF — FEMALE

Aarona, Aharona, Arlo, Brenda, Brenna, Bryden, Brynna, Chermona, Cinda, Cindy, Cinthia, Cinzia, Cynthia, Galila, Harlow, Hayden, Kendra, Kenya, Kinda, Kynthia, Lakenya, Marva, Mauna, Montana, Olimpia, Olympia, Paha, Pia, Sela, Shasta, Shelbie, Shelby, Shelley, Shelly, Shikah, Sierra, Tara, Taren, Tarina, Taryn, Torrance

MOUNTAIN, HILL, CLIFF — MALE

Aaron, Aharon, Arlo, Aron, Beaumont, Boden, Braden, Brandan, Branden, Brandon, Bryn, Cliff, Clifford, Clifton, Clint, Clinton, Clive, Craig, Galil, Gilad, Gilead, Giri, Givon, Harel, Harlow, Haroun, Harun, Hayden, Holt, Horst, Hub, Hubbell, Jaden, Jayden, Keanu, Kendrick, Kipp, Knox, Landan, Landon, Langdon, Linden, Lyndon, Marv, Marvin, Merlin, Merv, Mervin, Mervyn, Montana, Monte, Montgomery, Monty, Ross, Royle, Shelby, Shelley, Shelly, Taden, Tayden, Torrance, Torrie, Torry, Tucson, Tzion, Utah, Zion

MUSIC (SONG, SING, MELODIOUS, MUSICAL INSTRUMENT) — FEMALE

Aarona, Aharona, Aria, Bevan, Bevin, Carol, Carole, Caryl, Caryll, Chandelle, Chanice, Chantal, Chantay, Chanté, Chante, Chantel, Chantelle, Chantra, Chantrel, Chantrelle, Charmaine, Chondel, Cornelia, Harper, Jazz, Kanit, Kanti, Kerani, Keren, Kotone, Lark, Larke, Linnet, Lira, Lirit, Lirona, Lyra, Lyrica, Manjika, Mavis, Melodia, Melodie, Melody, Namale, Negina, Noella, Noelle, Odele, Philomela, Piper, Raneem, Rani, Rania, Ranim, Ranita, Renana, Riya, Robin, Robina, Robyn, Rona, Sangita, Shadia, Shadiya, Shandelle, Shanice, Shantel, Shantelle, Shantra, Shantrel, Shantrelle, Shirah, Shiran, Shiraz, Shirel, Shondel, Sonnet, Tehila, Tehilla, Wren, Yarona, Zemira, Zemirah

MUSIC (SONG, SING, MUSICAL INSTRUMENT) — MALE

Aaron, Aharon, Ahuli, Aron, Baird, Ballard, Chalil, Cornel, Cornelius, Cornell, Halil, Haroun, Harper, Harun, Jaran, Jaren, Jaron, Jubal, Kaleo, Karu, Leeron, Liron, Noel, Piper, Ran, Robin, Ron, Shofar, Tambe, Yaron, Yuval

NOBILITY, ROYALTY, PATRICIAN — FEMALE

Aubrey, Aubrie, Brenda, Brenna, Brisen, Brynna, Donia, Donna, Donya, Earleen, Earlene, Earline, Erica, Erika, Geena, Gina, Ginette, June, Juno, Kim, Kimber, Kimberly, Kimbra, Kimiko, Ladonna, Lani, Latrice, Lulla, Malina, Malka, Malkah, Midra, Pat, Patrice, Patricia, Patrina, Patrizia, Patsie, Patsy, Patti, Pattie, Patty, Payton, Peyton, Quanda, Quenby, Quenna, Reagan, Reanna, Regan, Regina, Reina, Reine, Rexene, Rheanna, Rheanne, Rhian, Rhiana, Rhianna, Rhianne, Rhiannon, Riana, Rianna, Rihanna, Riona, Ryan, Ryana, Ryann, Ryanne, Sadie, Sallie, Sally, Sara, Sarah, Sarana, Saranna, Sarina, Sarita, Shahana, Sheba, Shiba, Sura, Surah, Suri, Talulla, Tatiana, Tricia, Trish, Trisha, Zada, Zadie, Zara, Zarita

NOBILITY, ROYALTY, PATRICIAN — MALE

Aamir, Alberic, Ameer, Amir, Anolani, Auberon, Aubrey, Aubrie, Basil, Basile, Basilio, Baz, Brandan, Branden, Brandon, Breandan, Brendan, Brenden, Brendon, Caesar, César, Cesare, Cezar, Conner, Connor, Conor, Del, Delroy, Duke, Duna, Earl, Elroy, Eric, Erich, Erik, Errol, Eryk, Iolani, Ishah, Kahili, Kalei, Kennard, Kenton, Kimbel, Kingston, Leroy, Malcolm, Malkam, Moi, Naren, Negasi, Oba, Oberon, Paddy, Padraic, Padraig, Pat, Patricio, Patrick, Patrizio, Payton, Peyton, Prince, Quenten, Quintin, Quinton, Reagan, Rex, Riordan, Rordan, Rory, Roy, Ruairi, Ryan, Tor, Varesh, Vasily

OCCUPATION — FEMALE

Althea, Bailee, Bailey, Bailie, Chauncie, Chonsie, Deana, Deane, Deanna, Dee, Evette, Fabiana, Fabienne, Fabiola, Georgene, Georgette, Georgia, Georgina, Georgine, Gigi, Gina, Ivonne, Lavonne, Jirina, Jorja, Lavonne, Myla, Pastora, Penelope, Pennie, Penny, Tayler, Taylor, Tylar, Tyler, Tylor, Vonetta, Vonnie, Vonny, Yvette, Yvonne

OCCUPATION — MALE

Archer, Bailey, Baily, Bart, Bartholomew, Bartoli, Bartolomé, Bartolomeo, Baxter, Bishop, Bodie, Booker, Cade, Carter, Cash, Caspar, Casper, Chandler, Chauncey, Clark, Cooper, Cordell, Daktari, Dane, Dean, Deron, DeRon, Dex, Dexter, Diji, Fabian, Fabien, Fabio, Fabrice, Fabricio, Fabrizio, Fletcher, Forest, Forrest, Gaspar, Gaspard, Gaston, Georg, George, Georges, Georgi, Georgy, Giorgio, Granger, Howard, Igor, Ivar, Ives, Ivor, Jagger, Jasper, Jiji, Jorg, Jorge, Jorgen, Jory, Jur, Jurek, Kade, Kalei, Kaspar, Khayyam, Kyler, Lamont, Lamonte, Les, Lester, Macon, Marshal, Marshall, Mason, Miles, Milo, Myles, Nahele, Noma, Park, Parke, Parker, Porter, Ranger, Reeve, Rémy, Sawyer, Sheppard, Sherman, Skip, Spence, Spencer, Stew, Stewart, Stu, Stuart, Sven, Takumi, Tanner, Tannis, Tannon, Tavis, Taye, Tayler, Taylor, Thatcher, Travers, Travis, Trevis, Ty, Tye, Tylar, Tyler, Tylor, Walker, Wayne, Yuri, Yves

OCEAN, SEA — FEMALE

Adria, Adriana, Adrianna, Adrianne, Adrienne, Aphrodite, Coral, Doris, Dylan, Kailani, Kelsey, Kelsie, Lulu, Mae, Mai, Maire, Mairead, Mairona, Maja, Malou, Mamie, Manon, Maren, Mari, Maria, Mariam, Marian, Marie, Mariel, Mariella, Marielle, Marika, Marilla, Marilou, Marina, Marion, Marionne, Maris, Marisa, Marise, Marisol, Marissa, Marita, Mariya, Marja, Marlis, Marlissa, Marna, Marnie, Marva, Mary, Marylou, Masha, Maura, Maureen, Maurene, May, Mea, Meah, Meredith, Merle, Meryl, Mia, Mimi, Miri, Miriam, Mirjam, Miryam, Mitzi, Moana, Moira, Moire, Mollie, Molly, Moreen, Morgaine, Morgan, Morgana, Moyra, Muriel, Murphy, Myra, Nerida, Nerina, Nerissa, Oceana, Oceane, Oceania, Ondine, Pollie, Polly, Ria, Romy, Rosemary

OCEAN, SEA — MALE

Adrian, Adriano, Adrien, Dalen, Delmar, Dillon, Dylan, Holokai, Jamaar, Jamar, Kadhi, Kai, Kainui,

Kelcey, Kelsey, Lahar, Lamar, Malino, Marin, Marino, Marion, Marv, Marvin, Meredith, Merle, Merlin, Merrill, Merv, Mervin, Mervyn, Morgan, Mort, Mortimer, Murphy, Nalu, Nami, Ocean, Ross, Seymour, Skip, Urvil

PEACE, PEACEFUL, CALM, COMFORT, REST — FEMALE

Amity, An, Arina, Aryn, Eirini, Ena, Erin, Erina, Federica, Frederica, Fredonia, Fredrika, Frida, Frieda, Friede, Gala, Galina, Inga, Inge, Ingrid, Irena, Ireña, Irene, Irenka, Irina, Kimya, Lai, Lulu, Malina, Margea, Meona, Myla, Naima, Naimah, Nimah, Ning, Pacífica, Paz, Ping, Plácida, Raseena, Rasina, Razeena, Razina, Rena, Rochelle, Saleema, Salima, Salimah, Salome, Serena, Serene, Serenity, Shalva, Shalvah, Shanti, Sheeva, Shlomit, Shula, Siegfrida, Sigi, Siomha, Sushanti, Uma, Wilfreda, Winifred, Winnie, Yasu, Yasuko, Yrena, Yu, Zola

PEACE, PEACEFUL, CALM, COMFORT, REST — MALE

Absalom, Aksel, An, Avshalom, Axel, Bem, Cavan, Cavin, Corie, Corey, Dalen, Dima, Fedrico, Fred, Frederick, Frederico, Fredrick, Fredrik, Friedrich, Fritz, Galen, Galeno, Geoff, Geoffrey, Geoffroi, Geoffry, Godfrey, Gottfried, Humphrey, Humphry, Ingmar, Ingvar, Jalen, Jeff, Jefferson, Jeffrey, Jeffry, Kool, Korey, Kory, Luam, Mali, Malino, Malu, Manfred, Miles, Milo, Mirek, Miroslav, Mort, Mortimer, Myles, Naim, Nehemia, Ning, Nirvan, Noach, Noah, Pacífico, Pax, Paxton, Ping, Plácido, Radimir, Raseen, Rasin, Rico, Rocco, Roch, Rocky, Roque, Sal, Salaam, Salam, Salomon, Shama, Shefi, Shlomi, Shlomo, Siegfried, Sigfried, Sigi, Sol, Solomon, Vlad, Vladimir, Wilfred, Wilfrid, Winfred, Winfried, Yasu, Yasuo, Yu, Zalman, Zalmen, Zalmon

PLACE-NAME (TOWN, CITY, VILLAGE, STATE, COUNTRY) — FEMALE

Adria, Adriana, Adrianna, Adrianne, Adrienne, Africa, Africah, Alena, America, Arlene, Aryn, Ashanee, Ashani, Ashanti, Asia, Belen, Berlin, Bristol, Britney, Brittany, Caldonia, China, Cinda, Cindy, Cinthia, Cinzia, Cynthia, Dallas, Dana, Darcie, Darcy, Daryl, Delphina, Doris, Easton, Erin, Erina, Fannie, Fanny, Franca, Francene, Frances, Francesca, Francette, Francine, Francisca, Françoise, Franka, Gael, Inda, India, Iona, Ireland, Kelby, Kenya, Kinda, Kynthia, Lakenya, Lena, Lene, Lidia, Lindie, Lindsay, Lindsey, Lindy, Linni, Linnie, Linny, Linsay, Linsey, Linzi, Loraine, Lorna, Lorraine, Lourdes, Lyda, Lydia, Lydie, Mada, Madalena, Maddalena, Maddie, Maddy, Madeleine, Madeline, Madelyn, Madina, Magda, Magdalena, Magdalene, Malena, Malin, Marla, Marlena, Marlene, Marlo, Maya, Medina, Paisley, Paquita, Paris, Pariss, Payton, Peyton, Quenby, Romana, Sabina, Sabine, Selbie, Shelbie, Shelby, Tira, Tracey, Traci, Tracy, Venicia, Wallis

PLACE-NAME (TOWN, CITY, VILLAGE, STATE, COUNTRY) — MALE

Adrian, Adriano, Adrien, Ashton, Atticus, Bastien, Bret, Brett, Bruce, Burt, Burton, Cairo, Carlton, Charlton, Chico, Cisco, Clay, Clayton, Cliff, Clifton, Clint, Clinton, Colby, Crosby, Cuba, Dallas, Dana, Danan, Dane, Darby, Darcel, Darcy, Darold, Darrel, Darrell, Darryl, Dax, Des, Desmond, Dillon, Dorian, Easton, Francesco, Francis, Francisco, Franco, François, Frank, Franklin, Frans, Franz, Jarel, Keaton, Kelby, Kenton, Kipling, Kirby, Les, Lester, Lincoln, Lorne, Milt, Milton, Mort, Morton, Morty, Neville, Nili, Paco, Paisley, Pancho, Payton, Peyton, Orvil, Orville, Quenten, Quintin, Quinton, Quito, Reno, Roman, Romeo, Romano, Scott, Sebastian, Sebastien, Sebastiano, Shelby, Shelton, Tennessee, Tex, Tracey, Tracy, Trefor, Trev, Trevor, Tyrus, Tzion, Urban, Urbano, Wallace, Wally, Wes, Weston, Winston, Zion

PLANTS, HERB, SPICE — FEMALE

Abey, Anise, Anonna, Bela, Briony, Bryony, Carmel, Carmelita, Carmen, Carmencita, Cassia, Cayenne, Celyn, Chloe, Cinnamon, Cloe, Clover, Fabiana, Fabienne, Fabiola, Fern, Ferne, Fiona, Ginger, Grainne, Grania, Hailey, Haleigh, Hayden, Hayley, Hollie, Holly, Humita, Ivy, Katniss, Keesha, Keisha, Kesha, Ketzia, Kezia, Khloe, Lakeisha, Lakisha, Lesley, Leslie, Lotem, Malva, Marjolaine, Melita, Neta, Pepper, Phillis, Phyllis, Reilly, Riley, Romy, Rosemary, Rue, Rylee, Rylie, Ryley, Saffron, Sage, Senna, Taa, Takala, Vidonia, Viona

PLANTS, HERB, SPICE — MALE

Bruce, Carmelo, Carmine, Cillian, Dagan, Fabian, Fabien, Fabio, Farley, Gefen, Haley, Hayden, Hayley, Jaden, Jayden, Keaton, Killian, Les, Lesley, Leslie, Marlon, Mort, Morton, Morty, Nakos, Pezi, Ramsay, Ramsey, Riley, Royle, Rye, Rylan, Sage, Spike, Taden, Tayden

PROMISE, OATH — FEMALE

Anneliese, Annelise, Babette, Belicia, Belita, Bella, Belle, Bess, Bessie, Bessy, Beth, Bethan, Betsan, Betsie, Betsy, Betta, Bette, Bettina, Bettie, Betty, Buff, Chela, Eilis, Elisa, Elisabet, Elisabeth, Elisabetta, Elise, Elisha, Elisheva, Eliza, Elizabeta, Elizabeth, Elizaveta, Ellie, Elly, Elsa, Elsie, Elspeth, Elza, Ghislaine, Gilberta, Gisela, Gisella, Giselle, Gizella, Gizi, Ilsa, Ilse, Isabel, Isabela, Isabella, Isobel, Izabella, Izzie, Izzy, Jobeth, Libby, Liesa, Liesbeth, Liese, Liesl, Lisa, Lisbet, Lise, Lisette, Liz, Liza, Lizbet, Lizette, Lizzie, Lizzy, Sabela, Sabella, Sibeal, Talisa, Talisha, TaLisha, Talissa, Yelizaveta

PROTECT, GUARD — FEMALE

Aasimah, Alejandra, Aleka, Aleksandra, Alessa, Alessandra, Alessia, Alexa, Alexana, Alexandra, Alexandria, Alexia, Alexina, Alexis, Alondra, Andee, Andie, Anselma, Aseema, Asima, Billie, Brunhild, Brunhilde, Cindra, Edina, Eduarda, Edwena, Edwina, Elvira, Elvire, Foluke, Gerda, Haafiza, Hafiza, Hafizah, Hareena, Haseena, Hasina, Hasinah, Helma, Hera, Hilda, Hildegard, Lexa, Lexi, Lexie, Lexy, Magena, Melva, Melvina, Meredith, Mina, Minna, Minnie, Minny, Nedda, Nedra, Nedrah, Omatra, Rae, Raeleen, Ramona, Raylene, Sandi, Sandie, Sandra, Sandy, Sasha, Saundra, Selma, Shamira, Shandra, Sigi, Sindra, Sondra, Tandra, Tuesday, Velma, Wilhelmina, Willa, Willetta, Wilma, Xandra, Zandra, Zanna, Zasha, Zehira

PROTECT, GUARD — MALE

Aasim, Aegis, Alandro, Alasdair, Alastair, Alastir, Alec, Alejandro, Alejo, Alek, Aleksei, Aleksy, Alessandro, Alessio, Alex, Alexander, Alexandre, Alexandros, Alexei, Alexio, Alexios, Alexis, Alister, Ansel, Anselm, Anselmo, Anzelm, Aseem, Asim, Bill, Billy, Birger, Burk, Burke, Duarte, Eamon, Eamonn, Ed, Eddie, Eddy, Edmond, Edmondo, Edmund, Edmundo, Édouard, Eduard, Eduardo, Edvard, Edward, Edwin, Elek, Elmo, Folker, Foluke, Garan, Garen, Garren, Giles, Guglielmo, Guillaume, Guillermo, Haafiz, Hafeez, Halvard, Haseen, Hasin, Helmut, Howard, Ishah, Jaran, Jaren, Jaron, Kennard, Lalo, Lex, Liam, Magen, Malu, Mel, Melvin, Meredith, Mundo, Ned, Oman, Pala, Raimund, Raimundo, Ramon, Ray, Raymond, Sander, Sandros, Sandy, Sasha, Shomer, Siegmund, Sigi, Sigmund, Sigurd, Uilliam, Viggo, Vilhelm, Vili, Volker, Ward, Warren, Werner, Wilhelm, Will, Willard, Willem, Willi, William, Xander, Zander

PURE — FEMALE

Afeefa, Afifa, Agna, Agnes, Agnese, Agnessa, Agueda, Aikaterine, Aikaterini, Amala, Anice, Annice, Annis, Ariane, Arianna, Arianne, Cady, Cait, Caitin, Caitlin, Caitriona, Caleigh, Cami, Camila, Camilla, Camille, Cammie, Cammy,

Candace, Candi, Candice, Candida, Candide, Candy, Catalina, Catarina, Cate, Caterina, Catharina, Catharine, Catherine, Cathie, Cathleen, Cathryn, Cathy, Catina, Catrice, Catrin, Catrina, Catriona, Chastity, Dharmini, Ekaterina, Fateema, Fatima, Glenda, Glenis, Glennis, Glenys, Ines, Inés, Inessa, Inez, Jin-Sook, Jung-Ja, Kadi, Kady, Kaiti, Kaitlin, Kaitlyn, Kaleigh, Kalin, Kamilla, Karen, Kari, Karin, Karina, Karyn, Kasia, Katarina, Katarine, Katarzyna, Kate, Katelin, Katerina, Katharina, Katharine, Kathie, Kathleen, Kathryn, Kathy, Katie, Katina, Katinka, Katja, Katje, Katka, Katra, Katrin, Katrina, Katrine, Katriona, Katy, Katya, Kay, Kaya, Kaydi, Kaydy, Kayla, Kayleen, Kayleigh, Kayley, Kaylin, Kazia, Kittie, Kitty, Kiyoko, Kolina, Melia, Milla, Naqiya, Nessa, Nezza, Prasanna, Riju, Saafi, Safiya, Safiyya, Senga, Sharmeen, Sharmin, Shuchee, Taheera, Tahira, Trina, Triona, Vimala, Yekaterina, Ynez

RELATIVE — FEMALE (MOTHER, FATHER, DAUGHTER, SISTER, TWIN)

Abbie, Abby, Abi, Abiela, Abiella, Abigail, Abra, Abriana, Abrianna, Adanna, Ambala, Ana, Atiana, Aviela, Aviella, Avigayil, Avrielle, Ayda, Ayn, Basha, Bashe, Batia, Batya, Bechira, Cissy, Dana, Demetria, Demi, Dima, Dimitra, Gaea, Gaia, Gail, Gale, Gayle, Imogen, Imogene, Latanya, Latawnya, Madonna, Masika, Mina, Natane, Nina, Panik, Sissy, Tamsen, Tamsin, Tamsyn, Taneesha, Tanesha, Tania, Tanisha, Tanya, Tatiana, Tatienne, Tomasa, Tomasina, Winona

RELATIVE — MALE (FATHER, MOTHER, SON, BROTHER, TWIN)

Abe, Abner, Abraham, Abram, Abramo, Abrán, Absalom, Addison, Aksel, Aviel, Avner, Avraham, Avram, Avshalom, Axel, Barnabas, Barnaby, Barney, Barny, Bart, Bartholomew, Bartoli, Bartolomé, Bartolomeo, Ben, Benj, Benjamin, Binyamin, Bram, Broder, Brice, Bryce, Chibale,

Cormac, Demetrio, Dimitri, Dimitrios, Dmitri, Dmitry, Fitz, Garrison, Germain, Hagan, Hagen, Harrison, Ibrahim, Ichiro, Jackson, Jaxson, Joab, Junior, Kenzie, Kichiro, Luganda, Mac, Mack, MacKenzie, Madison, Maxwell, Namdi, Nelson, Prince, Pryce, Reuben, Reuven, Ronson, Ruben, Sonny, Tavis, Tavish, Thom, Thomas, Tip, Tipp, Tom, Tomas, Tomás, Tomasso, Vinson, Yoav, Yoshiro

ROCK, STONE — FEMALE

Alaina, Alana, Alanda, Alandah, Alani, Alanis, Alanna, Alanni, Alannis, Alayna, Alonda, Artia, Chandelle, Chanice, Chantal, Chantel, Chantelle, Chantra, Chantrel, Chantrelle, Chondel, Elandra, Harlow, Ilandra, Kim, Kimber, Kimberly, Kimbra, Lana, Loni, Lonie, Lorelei, Perrine, Peta, Petra, Petrah, Petrina, Petrine, Petrona, Sela, Shandelle, Shanice, Shantel, Shantelle, Shantra, Shantrel, Shantrelle, Shondel

ROCK, STONE — MALE

Al, Alain, Alano, Allan, Allen, Alun, Art, Arthur, Artur, Arturo, Carrick, Clive, Craig, Deston, Dustin, Dusty, Eban, Flint, Graham, Halle, Halsten, Halvard, Harlow, Kingston, Macon, Mason, Parnel, Parnell, Peader, Pedr, Pedro, Pete, Peter, Petros, Pierce, Piero, Pierre, Piers, Pietro, Pyotr, Rocky, Shamir, Slate, Stan, Stanley, Steinar, Sten, Stonewall, Torsten, Winston

RULER, LEADER, CHIEF, COMMANDER — FEMALE

Ailani, America, Arna, Cyrille, Donalda, Donanne, Donella, Donelle, Donette, Donia, Donna, Donya, Enrica, Enriqua, Erica, Erika, Federica, Frederica, Fredonia, Fredrika, Geraldine, Geri, Gerrie, Gladdis, Gladys, Hadia, Hadiya, Halle, Halley, Hallie, Hally, Haralda, Harietta, Harriet, Harrieta, Harrietta, Harriette, Henrietta, Henriette, Henrika, Henriqua, Hettie, Jeri, Jerri, Jerrie, Jetta, Jette, Keri, Kerri, Kerry, Meredith, Ricarda, Richelle,

Riki, Rikki, Rona, Ronnell, Ronette, Ronnette, Winema

RULER, LEADER, CHIEF, COMMANDER, LORD — MALE

Aamir, Adonis, Aksel, Ameer, Amerigo, Amir, Anolani, Arnaldo, Arnaud, Arnie, Arno, Arnold, Axel, Caesar, Cathal, César, Cesare, Cezar, Cirillo, Cirino, Cochise, Colin, Collin, Cy, Cyril, Cyrus, Dalil, Derek, Derick, Deron, DeRon, Dick, Didrik, Diedrich, Dieter, Dima, Dinesh, Dirk, Ditrik, Don, Donal, Donald, Donaldo, Donn, Donnie, Donny, Donovan, Duka, Duna, Earl, Emery, Emmerich, Enrico, Enrique, Eric, Erich, Erick, Eryk, Federico, Fred, Frederick, Frederico, Fredrick, Fredrik, Friedrich, Fritz, Ganesh, Garret, Garrett, Garrick, Gary, Gautier, Gerald, Geraldo, Geraud, Gerry, Giraldo, Griffith, Guido, Guy, Hadi, Hal, Halle, Hank, Harald, Harold, Harrison, Harry, Heinrich, Hendrik, Henri, Henrik, Henrique, Henry, Ihilani, Imrich, Ishah, Janesh, Jared, Jarel, Jarret, Jarrett, Jerald, Jerrad, Jerrod, Jerry, Jong-Soo, Jun, Keary, Kerry, Kim, Kimbel, Kiril, Kirill, Kona, Laird, Lazlo, LeeRon, Leolani, Leron, Mandara, Meredith, Minco, Moi, Naazim, Nagid, Nazeem, Netra, Nkosi, Olu, Prince, Quique, Radek, Ramiro, Reggie, Reginald, Reginold, Regis, Régis, Reinaldo, Renaud, Renny, Ricardo, Riccardo, Rich, Richard, Rick, Rickey, Ricky, Rico, Rikard, Rinaldo, Rod, Roddy, Roderick, Rodrigo, Rodrigue, Ron, Ronald, Ronaldo, Ronson, Rosh, Ryker, Sayyed, Sayyid, Shambe, Tiernan, Tierney, Torin, Tove, Tullie, Tully, Tyrus, Vadim, Varesh, Vlad, Vladimir, Waldo, Walt, Walter, Walther, Zethus

SEASONS — FEMALE

Abril, Akiko, April, Autumn, Aviva, Avivah, Avrielle, Avril, Chloris, Chun, Cloris, Genny, Ginette, Ginger, Ginnie, Ginny, Lavern, Laverne, Maia, Maya, Primavera, Qiu, Raabia, Rabia, Sommer, Spring, Summer, Teresa, Tereza, Teri, Terri, Terrie, Terry, Tess, Tessa, Theresa, Therese,

Thérèse, Traci, Tracie, Tracy, Treasa, Verena, Verna, Virginia, Vreni, Winter, Wynter

STAR — FEMALE

Aster, Astra, Danica, Danika, Estée, Estela, Estella, Estelle, Ester, Estera, Esther, Estrella, Halcyon, Hesper, Hester, Hokuala, Hoshi, Hoshiko, Lira, Lolia, Lyra, Maia, Maristela, Nahida, Nahidah, Namida, Seren, Sitara, Star, Starr, Starla, Starleen, Starlene, Starline, Stella, Stellina, Tara, Tarika, Trella, Vega, Venus, Zuhra

STRONG, MIGHTY, POWERFUL — FEMALE

Abira, Adira, Alima, Andee, Andie, Andra, Andrea, Andreana, Andriana, Andrianna, Apollonia, Apolonia, Arna, Aubrey, Aubrie, Audra, Audrey, Audrie, Audrina, Audry, Bedelia, Bernadetta, Bernadette, Bernadine, Bernarda, Bernardine, Berneen, Bidelia, Birgit, Birgitta, Birgitte, Breana, Breanna, Breanne, Breda, Bree, Breena, Bria, Briana, Brianna, Brianne, Bridget, Brighid, Brigid, Brigida, Brigitte, Brina, Brita, Brites, Britt, Britta, Bryden, Chela, Dray, Drea, Drew, Drusilla, Ebba, Ebbe, Ema, Emma, Emmie, Emmy, Erma, Ermin, Etana, Filomena, Gabriela, Gabriele, Gabriella, Gabrielle, Gavriel, Gavriela, Gavriella, Gavrielle, Gavrila, Geraldine, Geri, Gerrie, Gerta, Gertraud, Gertrud, Gertrude, Gibora, Giborah, Gitta, Gitte, Imelda, Imma, Irma, Jeri, Jerri, Jerrie, Jian, Kenda, Keri, Kerri, Kerry, Leeona, Leonor, Liona, Maddie, Maddy, Madison, Mana, Mathilda, Mathilde, Matilda, Matilde, Mattie, Matty, Matylda, Maud, Maude, Mildred, Milisent, Millicent, Millie, Milly, Nessa, Ondrea, Philomena, Ricarda, Richelle, Riki, Rikki, Rona, Ronette, Ronnell, Ronnette, Sela, Shachee, Thora, Tilda, Tilde, Tillie, Tilly, Tisha, Tora, Tressa, Truda, Trudie, Trudy, Ulla, Ursula, Val, Valencia, Valenda, Valentina, Valentine, Valeria, Valerie, Valeriya, Valery, Valinda, Veera, Virya

STRONG, MIGHTY, POWERFUL — MALE

Abir, Adir, Alberic, Amiram, Angus, Aonghas, Apollo, Arnaldo, Arnaud, Arnie, Arno, Arnold, Art, Arthur, Artur, Arturo, Auberon, Aubrey, Aubrie, Az, Azan, Azi, Aziel, Azrael, Azriel, Azud, Balin, Balint, Beño, Bernard, Bernardino, Bernardo, Bernhard, Bernt, Brian, Bryan, Bryant, Burk, Burke, Cairo, Conall, Dick, Dino, Dracos, Eberhard, Eberhardt, Eckart, Eckhart, Eitan, Ekon, Emmet, Emmett, Etan, Ethan, Everett, Evert, Eyal, Fearghas, Fergus, Ferris, Flint, Gabe, Gable, Gabriel, Gabrielo, Gale, Gared, Garred, Garrick, Gary, Gavriel, Geraldo, Gerard, Gerardo, Geraud, Gerhard, Gerhardt, Geri, Gerri, Gerry, Gibor, Gideon, Gidon, Giraldo, Griffith, Indra, Ittan, Jabbar, Jared, Jarel, Jarret, Jarrett, Jerald, Jerrad, Jerrod, Jerry, Jian, Kawa, Keary, Ken, Kenta, Kerry, Lee, Leeon, Len, Lennard, Lennart, Lenny, Leonard, Leonardo, Li, Lynard, Madison, Manfred, Maynard, Meinard, Meinhard, Narya, Oberon, Onam, Oswald, Oz, Ozzie, Plato, Qiang, Rayner, Raynor, Reggie, Reginald, Reginold, Regis, Régis, Renard, Renaud, Renny, Renz, Ricardo, Riccardo, Rich, Richard, Rick, Rickie, Ricky, Rico, Rikard, Rinaldo, Sabala, Shakra, Shamir, Socrates, Thorin, Tor, Uzi, Uziah, Uziya, Val, Valentin, Valentino, Valerio, Wei, Willard, Wyatt, Xiong, Zende, Zhuàng

SUCCESSFUL, VICTORIOUS — FEMALE

Ailsa, Berenice, Beri, Bernetta, Bernice, Berri, Cheng, Colette, Collette, Eunice, Faaiza, Faiza, Fayza, Helga, Helge, Jayna, Kaneko, Kelsey, Kelsie, LaToya, Latoya, Mansura, Niccola, Nicki, Nicola, Nicole, Nika, Nike, Nikki, Nikoleta, Ria, Roni, Ronnie, Siegfrida, Sieglinde, Sigi, Signe, Signy, Sigrid, Sigrun, Siri, Tori, Toria, Toriana, Torrie, Tory, Verona, Veronda, Veronica, Veronika, Véronique, Vickie, Vicky, Victoire, Victoria, Vika, Viki, Viktoria, Viktoriya, Vittoria, Zafira, Zafirah

SUCCESSFUL, VICTORIOUS — MALE

Bodie, Cheng, Claus, Cole, Coley, Colin, Collin, Enzo, Ghalib, Ghazi, Jayan, Jeta, Katsuro, Kelcey, Kelsey, Klaus, Mansur, Miklos, Nic, Niccolo, Nicholas, Nick, Nicky, Nico, Nicola, Nicolas, Niels, Nikita, Niklas, Nikolai, Nikolaos, Nikos, Nilolaus, Nils, Sanjay, Sheng, Shinda, Siegfried, Siegmund, Sigfried, Sigi, Sigmund, Sigurd, Sujay, Vic, Vicente, Vick, Vico, Victor, Víctor, Vijay, Vik, Viktor, Vince, Vincens, Vincent, Vincente, Vincenzo, Vinson, Vinzenz, Vittorio, Zafir

SUCCESSOR, CHANGE, TRANSFORM — FEMALE

Jackie, Jacklyn, Jacky, Jacoba, Jacque, Jacqueline, Jacquelyn, Jacquette, Jacqui, Jakova, Jamie, Yakova

SUCCESSOR, CHANGE, TRANSFORM — MALE

Akiva, Coby, Diego, Giacobbe, Giacomo, Hamish, Iago, Jack, Jacob, Jacobo, Jacques, Jaime, Jake, Jakob, Jakov, Jakub, Jalen, James, Jamie, Jax, Jaxson, Jay, Jim, Jimmy, Jock, Koby, Kuba, Santiago, Seamus, Shay, Tiago, Yakov, Yankel, Yancy, Yaqub

SUN, SUNRISE, SUNSET — FEMALE

Alba, Aliana, Anatolia, Aruna, Asia, Aurora, Aurore, Cyra, Dawn, Eliana, Éliane, Kira, Kyra, LaDawn, Marisol, Mihri, Roksana, Roshana, Roxana, Roxane, Roxanna, Roxanne, Roxie, Roxy, Sepideh, Solina, Solita, Sunnie, Sunniva, Sunny, Twila, Twyla, Vashati, Yoko, Zephira, Zora, Zorah, Zorina

SUN, SUNRISE, SUNSET — MALE

Asis, Bhanu, Bhasu, Cirino, Cy, Cyrus, Denzel, Dinesh, Koesh, Lahiki, Pakala, Pradosh, Samson, Shimson, Tawa

SUPERNATURAL — FEMALE (ELF, FAIRY, NYMPH)

Ailsa, Alfreda, Alvena, Alvera, Alvina, Aubrey, Aubrie, Avery, Avrielle, Elen, Elvina, Fay, Faye, Naida, Nerida, Nerina, Nerissa, Ondine, Reanna, Reanne, Rheanna, Rheanne, Rhian, Rhiana, Rhianna, Rhianne, Rhiannon, Riana, Rianna, Rianne, Rihanna, Shaelee, Shaleigh, Sheridan, Tatiana

SUPERNATURAL — MALE (ELF)

Al, Alberic, Alf, Alfred, Alfredo, Alvar, Alvaro, Alvin, Alwyn, Auberon, Aubrey, Aubrie, Avery, Elvin, Elvis, Oberon, Oliver, Olivier, Sheridan

SURNAME — FEMALE

Addison, Ashley, Bailey, Cameron, Carson, Casey, Cassidy, Channing, Dale, Dallas, Darcy, Delaney, Easton, Farrell, Greer, Hadley, Halle, Harley, Harlow, Harper, Hayden, Hayley, Hudson, Jensen, Kelby, Kelly, Kelsey, Kendal, Kenner, Kerry, Latham, Lesley, Lindsay, Lindsey, Logan, Loy, MacKenzie, Macy, Madison, Mallory, Marley, Marlow, Maxwell, Paget, Paige, Payton, Quenby, Reagan, Reese, Riley, Ryan, Selby, Shelby, Shelly, Sheridan, Sidney, Sydney, Tate, Torrance, Tracy, Tyler, Whitney

SURNAME — MALE

Adair, Addison, Archer, Arden, Ashford, Ashley, Bailey, Baird, Ballard, Baxter, Beaumont, Beck, Beckett, Berk, Bertram, Bertrand, Bishop, Boden, Booker, Bowen, Bradford, Bradley, Brady, Breck, Brenton, Brett, Brock, Brody, Bruce, Burgess, Burton, Cabot, Calder, Calvin, Camden, Cameron, Campbell, Carlin, Carrick, Carson, Carter, Casey, Cash, Cassidy, Chandler, Channing, Chauncey, Chester, Clancy, Clark, Clayton, Clifford, Clifton, Clinton, Clive, Colby, Conley, Conner, Connor, Conor, Conway, Cooper, Costello, Crosby, Curtis, Dack, Dale, Daley, Dallas, Daly, Darby, Darcy, Darryl, Dean, Delaney, Desmond, Dexter, Dillon, Donovan, Dougan, Douglas, Doyle, Drake, Dudley, Duran, Easton, Eldon, Eliot, Ellery, Elliot, Ellis, Emery, Emmet, Emmett, Ennis, Everett, Fagan, Farley, Ferris, Findlay, Findley, Fletcher, Ford, Franklin, Fraser, Gable, Galeno, Gannon, Garland, Garnet, Garnett, Garred, Garrison, Giles, Gillean, Gillis, Gilroy, Godwin, Gordan, Grady, Graham, Granger, Grant, Gray, Greer, Grey, Griffith, Guthrie, Hadley, Hale, Harley, Harlow, Harper, Harrison, Harvey, Hayden, Hayley, Hogan, Holt, Hubbell, Hudson, Humphrey, Hunter, Huntley, Innes, Innis, Irvin, Irving, Irwin, Jackson, Jagger, Jefferson, Jensen, Keary, Keaton, Keefe, Keegan, Keenan, Keir, Keith, Kelby, Kelly, Kelsey, Kemp, Kemper, Kendal, Kendall, Kendrick, Kennard, Kenner, Kent, Kenton, Kermit, Kerry, Kimbel, Kingston, Kipling, Kipp, Kirby, Kirk, Kirwin, Knight, Knox, Kyle, Laird, Lamong, Landan, Lane, Langdon, Larkin, Leith, Leland, Lennox, Lesley, Leslie, Lincoln, Linden, Logan, Lovell, Lyle, Lyndon, Macy, Macey, MacKenzie, Macon, Maddox, Madison, Madoc, Marley, Marlon, Marlow, Mason, Maxwell, Mead, Meade, Merrill, Milton, Mitchell, Monroe, Montgomery, Morton, Munro, Munroe, Murphy, Nelson, Nevin, Niles, Nolan, Norris, Novis, Oswald, Otix, Parker, Paxton, Payton, Peyton, Prescot, Prescott, Presley, Preston, Quinlan, Quinn, Radley, Rafferty, Ramsay, Ramsey, Randal, Randall, Reagan, Reed, Reese, Reeve, Reid, Ronson, Roscoe, Ross, Royce, Ryan, Sawyer, Scott, Seymour, Shane, Shanley, Shaw, Shelby, Sheldon, Shelley, Shelly, Sheppard, Sheridan, Sherlock, Sherman, Sidney, Sinclair, Slade, Slate, Sloan, Spencer, Stewart, Stuart, Sullivan, Sweeney, Sydney, Tanner, Tate, Tayler, Taylor, Terrell, Tierney, Torrance, Tracey, Tracy, Travers, Travis, Trent, Tully, Tyler, Tylor, Vinson, Wade, Walker, Ward, Warren, Wayne, Wesley, Weston, Whitley, Whitney, Willard, Woodrow

TREE, FOREST, WOODS — FEMALE

Acacia, Alameda, Alani, Alona, Ameera, Amira, Anina, Apple, Arizona, Ashley, Ashlie, Ashlyn,

Ashlynn, Asleigh, Aspen, Bryden, Cherry, Dafna, Dafne, Dalia, Dalya, Daphne, Dara, Darran, Dasi, Derryth, Ebonie, Ebony, Eila, Eilah, Eilona, Evette, Glenda, Glenna, Hadassah, Hazel, Ilana, Ilanit, Ivonne, Jacaranda, Jessenia, Juniper, Kai, Keitha, Kelley, Keli, Kellie, Kelly, Lara, Larenda, Larinda, Laura, Laure, Laurel, Lauren, Laurenda, Laurie, Lavern, Laverne, Lavonne, Lawanda, Liv, Livia, Livie, Livvy, Lora, Loreen, Loreena, Lorelle, Loren, Lorena, Lorenda, Loretta, Lori, Lorie, Lorin, Lorina, Lorinda, Lorine, Lowri, Lurella, Maple, Miki, Morela, Moriko, Myrtle, Olive, Olivia, Randa, Rowena, Rowina, Selby, Shakeda, Shelbie, Shelby, Silva, Silvia, Silvie, Silvy, Suzuki, Sylva, Sylvestra, Sylvia, Sylvie, Tamara, Tami, Tammie, Tammy, Taren, Taryn, Temira, Temirah, Tirza, Tirzah, Tyrona, Vanika, Verena, Verna, Vonetta, Vonnie, Vonny, Vreni, Wanda, Wendi, Wendy, Willow, Winnie, Yara, Yarah, Yesenia, Yvette, Yvonne

TREE, FOREST, WOODS — MALE

Adahy, Adair, Allon, Alon, Amir, Ankur, Arizona, Ash, Ashford, Ashley, Ashton, Berk, Braden, Branch, Calder, Cillian, Cochise, Collen, Daiki, Daragh, Daren, Darin, Daron, Darrah, Darren, Dekel, Derry, Eilon, Elon, Enzo, Eoghan, Ewan, Ewen, Fester, Forest, Forrest, Glen, Glenn, Grover, Holt, Horst, Ilan, Ives, Jaden, Jayden, Keith, Kelley, Kelly, Killian, Larkin, Larry, Lars, Laurence, Laurent, Lawrence, Laz, Lennox, Lenz, Lin, Linden, Loren, Lorencio, Lorens, Lorenz, Lorenzo, Loris, Lyndon, Lyront, Mander, Miti, Nahele, Nash, Oliver, Olivier, Park, Parke, Parker, Perry, Ranger, Renzo, Roscoe, Rowan, Shaked, Shaw, Silas, Silvano, Silvester, Silvino, Silvio, Sly, Song, Sylvester, Taden, Tayden, Terrone, Tomer, Ty, Tye, Tyrone, Vern, Verne, Vernon, Woodrow, Woody, Yves

TRUTH, TRUE, TRUSTWORTHY — FEMALE

Aamina, Aleta, Aletha, Alethea, Amana, Ameena, Aminah, Behira, Dilwyn, Dilys, Elvira, Elvire,

Haneefa, Hanifa, Imina, Jin-Sook, Kalissa, Khalisa, Leta, Letha, Mayu, Nika, Oleta, Oletha, Rafiki, Rita, Roni, Ronnie, Sati, Satya, Thea, Truth, Valda, Vera, Verena, Verita, Verna, Verona, Veronda, Veronica, Veronika, Veronique, Verusha, Vreni, Wafiya, Wafiyah, Yakini, Yoo-Jin, Zonta

TRUTH, TRUE, TRUSTWORTHY — MALE

Aamin, Aman, Ameen, Amin, Amitai, Amitan, Arch, Archibald, Archie, Emmet, Farouk, Faruq, Haneef, Hanif, Khalis, Makoto, Muni, Sadeed, Sadid, Satyaki, Shin, Truman, Zhong

UNITED, JOINED, TIED — FEMALE

Anneliese, Annelise, Babette, Becca, Becka, Becki, Beckie, Becky, Bekah, Belicia, Belita, Bella, Bellarosa, Belle, Belva, Bequita, Bess, Bessie, Bessy, Beth, Bethan, Betsan, Betsie, Betsy, Betta, Bette, Bettina, Beulah, Buffy, Chela, Eilis, Ekata, Elisa, Elisabet, Elisabeth, Elisabetta, Elise, Elisha, Elisheva, Eliza, Elizabeta, Elizabeth, Elizaveta, Ellie, Elly, Elsie, Elspeth, Elza, Hareena, Hera, Ilsa, Ilse, Isabel, Isabela, Isabella, Isabelle, Isobel, Izabella, Izzie, Izzy, Jobeth, Libbie, Libby, Liesa, Liesbeth, Liese, Liesl, Lisa, Lisbet, Lise, Lisette, Liz, Liza, Lizbet, Lizette, Lizzie, Lizzy, Malana, Maribel, Marybeth, Milan, Reba, Rebeca, Rebecca, Rebecka, Rebekah, Rebekka, Reva, Riki, Rikki, Rivka, Sabela, Sabella, Sibeal, Talisa, Talisha, TaLisha, Talissa, Tamsen, Tamsin, Tamsyn, Tomasa, Tomasina, Unity, Yelizaveta

VALLEY, GLEN, DALE — FEMALE

Ardela, Ardele, Ardella, Ardelle, Dale, Dallas, Deana, Deanna, Deanne, Dee, Della, Gayora, Giora, Glenda, Glenis, Glenna, Glennis, Glenys, Guadalupe, Hayden, Kenda, Kendal, Kendall, Keri, Kerri, Kerry, Loden, Lupe, Simi

VALLEY, GLEN, DALE — MALE

Ardel, Arden, Camden, Cavan, Cavin, Corey, Cory, Dale, Dallas, Dane, Dean, Del, Delbert, Delwin, Deron, DeRon, Dilbert, Gai, Glen, Glenn, Glyn, Hayden, Keary, Kendal, Kendall, Kerry, Korey, Kory, Logan, Perce, Percival, Percy, Sheldon, Slade

VIRTUOUS — FEMALE

Agueda, Aikaterine, Aikaterini, Aretha, Cady, Cait, Caitin, Caitlin, Caitriona, Catalina, Catarina, Cate, Catharina, Catharine, Catherine, Cathie, Cathleen, Cathrine, Cathryn, Cathy, Catina, Catrice, Catrin, Catrina, Chastity, Dharmini, Ekaterina, Fadeela, Fadila, Fang, Fateema, Fatima, Glenda, Kaiti, Kaitlin, Kaitlyn, Kalin, Karen, Kari, Karin, Karina, Karyn, Kasia, Katarina, Katarine, Katarzyna, Kate, Katelin, Katerina, Katharina, Katharine, Katherine, Kathie, Kathleen, Kathryn, Kathy, Katie, Katina, Katinka, Katja, Katje, Katka, Katra, Katrin, Katrina, Katrine, Katriona, Katy, Katya, Kay, Kaya, Kayla, Kayleen, Kaylin, Kazia, Keila, Kittie, Kitty, Kolina, Niqiya, Saguna, Sheela, Sook-Ja, Sushila, Taheera, Tahira, Trina, Triona, Wema, Yekaterina

WARRIOR, ARMY, WEAPON — FEMALE

Alvera, Arlo, Athena, Avrielle, Bari, Barri, Barrie, Bodil, Brenda, Brenna, Brunhilde, Brynna, Carol, Carole, Caryl, Caryll, Clotilda, Delaney, Earleen, Earlene, Earline, Edda, Edie, Edith, Eloisa, Eloise, Ermin, Fannie, Fanny, Franca, Francene, Frances, Francesca, Francette, Francine, Francisca, Françoise, Franka, Geraldine, Geri, Gerlinde, Gerrie, Gerta, Gertraud, Gertrud, Gertruda, Gertrude, Griselda, Gudrun, Halle, Halley, Hallie, Hally, Haralda, Harietta, Hariette, Harlow, Harriet, Harrietta, Harriette, Hedda, Hedvig, Hedwig, Heloise, Hettie, Hilda, Hildegard, Imelda, Jeri, Jerri, Jerrie, Joceline, Jocelyn, Keli, Kelley, Kellie, Kelly, Loída, Loie, Loraina, Loraine, Lorena, Lorraina, Lorraine, Lou, Louella, Louisa, Louise, Luana, Luanna, Luanne, Luella, Luisa, Luise, Luiza, Lulu, Maddie, Maddy, Madison, Malou, Marcela, Marcelina, Marceline, Marcella, Marci, Marcia, Marcie, Marcille, Marcy, Maren, Marilou, Marina, Marsha, Martina, Martine, Marty, Marylou, Mathilda, Mathilde, Matilda, Matilde, Mattie, Matty, Maud, Maude, Murphy, Myla, Paquita, Rhonda, Rhonwen, Tilda, Tilde, Tillie, Tilly, Tina, Truda, Trudie, Trudy, Tuesday, Tyra, Zelda, Zelde

WARRIOR, ARMY, WEAPON — MALE

Adair, Ahiga, Alois, Aloysius, Alvar, Álvaro, Alvaro, Arch, Archer, Arlo, Armand, Armando, Armin, Averil, Balin, Barrie, Barry, Bearach, Berach, Blade, Boris, Borys, Brant, Cade, Caden, Cadoc, Cai, Caiden, Carlin, Carroll, Cathal, Cathan, Chad, Chico, Cillian, Cisco, Clancy, Corin, Delaney, Delany, Dodge, Duncan, Earl, Eckart, Eckhart, Ed, Eddie, Eddy, Edgar, Edgard, Egil, Egon, Einar, Erwin, Evander, Findlay, Findley, Fletcher, Folker, Francesco, Francis, Francisco, Franco, François, Frank, Frans, Franz, Gared, Garnet, Garnett, Garred, Garret, Garrett, Garrick, Garrison, Garvan, Garvin, Gary, Gautier, Gavin, Gawain, Gerald, Geraldo, Gerard, Gerardo, Geraud, Gerhard, Gerhardt, Gerry, Gervaise, Gideon, Gidon, Giles, Giraldo, Guthrie, Gwayne, Hal, Halle, Hania, Harald, Harlow, Harold, Harrison, Harry, Harv, Harvey, Herb, Herbert, Herberto, Herman, Hodge, Humphrey, Humphry, Igor, Ivar, Ivor, Jared, Jarel, Jarret, Jarrett, Jarvis, Jerald, Jerrod, Jerry, Jomo, Kade, Kaden, Kai, Kane, Kekoa, Kelley, Kelly, Kemp, Kemper, Killian, Kim, Koa, Kondo, Lance, Lann, Lansa, Lew, Lewis, Lothar, Lou, Louie, Louis, Ludwig, Luigi, Luis, Luther, Madison, Makaha, Mando, Marc, Marcel, Marcello, Marcelo, Marco, Marcos, Marcus, Marek, Mario, Marius, Mark, Markos, Markus, Martin, Martino, Marty, Menewa, Miles, Milo, Mordechai, Murphy, Myles, Oliver, Olivier, Oscar, Óscar, Oskar, Paco, Pancho, Quito, Ragnar, Rainer,

Randal, Randall, Randolf, Randolph, Randy, Rayner, Raynor, Reiner, Rodge, Roger, Rogério, Shanley, Sloan, Steiner, Sven, Terrel, Terrell, Troy, Tyr, Tyrel, Tyrell, Tyrrell, Volker, Walt, Walter, Walther, Wayland, Werner, Wyatt

WATER (RIVER, STREAM, LAKE, SPRING, RAIN) — FEMALE

Arizona, Ashlyn, Ashlynn, Berlin, Bev, Beverley, Beverly, Brook, Brooke, Brooklyn, Channing, Chelsea, Chelsie, Clodagh, Delta, Dima, Eira, Eirwen, Fontana, Ghadir, Ginger, Inda, India, Jaleh, Jiang, Jordan, Katniss, Kehua, Kelby, Kelda, Keldah, Kenda, Kendal, Kendall, Lana, Lindie, Lindsay, Lindsey, Lindy, Linni, Linnie, Linny, Linsay, Linsey, Linzi, Lyn, Lynelle, Lynette, Lynn, Lynna, Lynnelle, Lynnette, Marilyn, Marlow, Maxwell, Maya, Mayana, Mayim, Megalyn, Mehli, Mistie, Misty, Mizuko, Naida, Nehara, Neva, Neve, Neves, Nieves, Noe, Rafeeda, Rafida, Rain, Raine, Rhea, Ria, Rilla, Sabrina, Sarita, Shannon, Shasa, Talia, Talya, Varana, Varsha, Wailani, Wainani, Yoki, Yukiko

WATER (RIVER, STREAM, LAKE, SPRING, RAIN) — MALE

Arizona, Arnon, Ashford, Beck, Bemidji, Brad, Bradford, Brook, Calder, Channing, Cliff, Clifford, Clive, Clyde, Detroit, Doug, Douglas, Ennis, Ford, Innes, Innis, Irv, Irving, Jafaar, Jafar, Jarek, Jordan, Jubal, Kelby, Kendal, Kendall, Lahar, Lech, Leith, Lincoln, Maks, Malek, Marlow, Max, Maxwell, Mo, Moe, Moise, Mort, Mortimer, Morton, Morty, Moses, Moshe, Musa, Nadish, Nehru, Nevada, Rain, Raine, Reno, River, Seymour, Shannon, Shui, Tennessee, Trent, Tucson, Wade, Van, Vance, Varil, Yuval

WEALTHY, RICH, PROSPEROUS — FEMALE

Abiola, Alodia, Ashira, Aud, Bhuti, Chaniya, Clover, Daria, Darice, Darya, Eddie, Eddy, Edie,

Edina, Edith, Eduarda, Edwena, Edwina, Elodia, Élodie, Ghania, Ghaniya, Helga, Helge, Hyun-Young, Khasiba, Kwasi, Lucretia, Lulla, Meera, Mira, Nagida, Nedda, Nedra, Nedrah, Neema, Oda, Odelia, Odette, Odila, Odile, Odilia, Shelley, Shellie, Shelly, Talulla, Taria, Ulla, Yaseera, Yasira, Yoo-Jin, Zuna

WEALTHY, RICH, PROSPEROUS — MALE

Adair, Ashir, Boo-Chun, Chang, Darian, Dario, Darius, Duarte, Eamon, Eamonn, Ed, Eddie, Eddy, Edgar, Edgard, Edmond, Edmondo, Edmund, Edmundo, Edoardo, Édouard, Eduard, Eduardo, Edvard, Edward, Edwin, Eniola, Ghani, Gitonga, Ingmar, Ingvar, Jethro, Khasib, Lalo, Mundo, Ned, Ola, Omar, Osher, Otis, Otto, Rafferty, Shelley, Shelly, Sung-Ho, Sung-Wook, Umar, Vasu, Yasir, Yassir, Yilma

WISE — FEMALE

Akili, Alfreda, Anina, Anura, Athena, Avery, Avrielle, Basira, Basirah, Busara, Danesh, Hakeema, Hakima, Hyun-Ja, Hyun-Ju, Hyun-Young, Ji-Min, Ji-Won, Ji-Young, Joceline, Jocelyn, Nadie, Nevona, Piala, Quinn, Quinnie, Ralphina, Sage, Shannon, Sofia, Sofía, Sofie, Sofiya, Sofronia, Sonia, Sonja, Sonje, Sonya, Sophia, Sophie, Zaheena, Zahina, Zofia

WISE — MALE

Al, Alf, Alfred, Alfredo, Avery, Basir, Bodhi, Conall, Conan, Conn, Conrad, Corrado, Dhira, Drew, Elvis, Frode, Ganesh, Gyan, Haakim, Hakeem, Hakim, Kavi, Konrad, Kort, Kurt, Navon, Ndidi, Prajna, Quinn, Rafe, Raimund, Ralph, Raoul, Rishi, Rushdi, Sage, Seanan, Shannon, Sionan, Sven, Toshio, Vidura, Wicasa, Zaheen, Zahin, Zhi

WOMAN, LADY, MISTRESS —
FEMALE

Almah, Beulah, Bevan, Bevin, Bhamini, Calandra, Calli, Callie, Cirilla, Cora, Corina, Corinna, Corrie, Cyra, Cyrilla, Cyrille, Donia, Donna, Donya, Doris, Farrell, Farrol, Geneva, Genevieve, Genny, Ginnie, Ginny, Hyun-Ja, Imogen, Imogene, Jung-Ja, Kalandra, Kira, Kora, Korinna, Kyra, Ladonna, LaDonna, Liadan, Lulla, Lysandra, Maida, Marta, Marte, Martha, Marthe, Martita, Nalin, Neva, Omana, Riva, Sheba, Shiba, Sook-Ja, Talulla, Winema

YOUNG, YOUTHFUL, CHILD —
FEMALE

Adamma, Addison, Aiko, Akiko, Alannah, Atsuko, Aviva, Avivah, Bala, Coleen, Colleen, Cora, Corina, Corinna, Corinne, Corrie, Gill, Gillian, Giulia, Hiroko, Honoka, Hoshiko, Jill, Jillian, Julia, Juliana, Juliane, Julianna, Julie, Julienne, Juliet, Julieta, Juliette, Julita, Julitte, Kabala, Kaneko, Kefira, Keiki, Keiko, Kelleen, Kenzie, Kimiko, Kiyoko, Kohana, Kora, Korinna, Liana, Liane, Lianna, MacKenzie, Maddie, Maddy, Madison, Maebh, Maeve, Maida, Maxwell, Mizuko, Moriko, Nalin, Navina, Ofra, Ophrah, Owena, Paget, Paige, Ramani, Reagan, Regan, Riva, Sachiko, Sarama, Sheridan, Tiponi, Umeko, Yasuko, Yoko, Yukiko, Yuko, Yuliya, Zita

YOUNG, YOUTHFUL, CHILD — MALE

Bowen, Cailean, Colin, Collin, Colt, Ewan, Ewen, Giuliano, Guri, Hogan, Jools, Jules, Julian, Julien, Julio, Julius, Junior, Kefir, Keifer, Kiefer, Kunto, Lovell, Ofer, Orson, Owain, Owen, Page, Paget, Ross, Sven, Tarun, Yul, Yulian

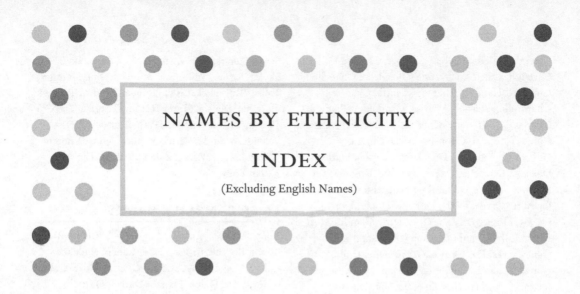

AFRICAN FEMALE NAMES

Abebi, Abeni, Abeo, Abiba, Abiola, Abiona, Adamma, Adanna, Adia, Afiya, Akili, Alima, Anika, Areta, Ashanti, Aster, Ayah, Ayda, Ayoka, Bayo, Becca, Binah, Busara, Chagina, Chaniya, Charlize, Dafina, Damisi, Dara, Dayo, Dina, Dziko, Ebun, Ekene, Eshe, Falala, Fana, Faraa, Fayola, Folami, Foluke, Hanna, Huba, Ijaba, Isoke, Janina, Jirani, Julisha, Kabala, Karungi, Kendi, Kimya, Kioni, Kisa, Koshi, Kupenda, Kwasi, Lewa, Lila, Lolia, Lolonyo, Makenna, Marini, Masika, Mchumba, Mema, Midra, Miyanda, Muna, Namale, Nayla, Neema, Nia, Niara, Nina, Noni, Obasi, Obioma, Oni, Orma, Rafiki, Remba, Safara, Sarama, Shani, Shasa, Sheba, Shiba, Sikia, Tabia, Teshi, Thandi, Tisha, Wema, Yakini, Zalira, Zene, Zola, Zuna

AFRICAN MALE NAMES

Abebe, Adio, Adisa, Adom, Akiki, Akins, Asis, Ayinde, Ayize, Ayo, Bakari, Bem, Chibale, Chimelu, Chinelo, Chinua, Daktari, Diji, Dini, Duka, Dumi, Duna, Ekon, Eniola, Foluke, Gitonga, Irungu, Jahi, Jaja, Jengo, Jomo, Jumbe, Kalei, Kazi, Keb, Kesi, Kobe, Kondo, Kunto, Kwanza, Lali, Lefa, Lencho, Lin, Luam, Luganda, Mahari, Malek, Mali, Mandara, Miti, Mo, Monde, Mongo, Mtima, Mugabi, Mwara, Namdi, Ndidi, Negasi, Ngare, Ngozi, Niko, Nkosi, Noma, Oba, Obama, Okal, Ola, Olu, Osei, Paki, Qeb, Sekou, Shambe, Shange, Shinda, Simba, Thabo, Themba, Tor, Unika, Yilma, Zaki, Zende, Zuri

AMERICAN FEMALE NAMES

Africa, Africah, Aila, Alani, Alanni, Alayna, Alcinda, Alexana, Aliana, Aloma, Alonda, Alyson, Amaretta, America, Amia, Amisha, Amishia, Aneesha, Anique, Anisha, Anissa, Apple, Arizona, Artia, Aryn, Ashanee, Ashani, Ashleigh, Asia, Aspen, Atiana, Avrielle, Azalee, Azalie, Azile, Balissa, Beah, Benisha, Berlin, Berthana, Bonna, Breana, Breanna, Breanne, Breena, Bria, Brianne, Brina, Britney, Brooklyn, Bryden, Cadence,

Caleigh, Calissa, Callisa, Camber, Carlana, Carleigh, Catrice, Cayenne, Chandelle, Chanelle, Chanice, Chantay, Chante, Chantra, Chantrel, Chantrelle, Charice, Charise, Charlaine, Charlana, Charlayne, Charlena, Cher, Chevonne, Cheyenne, China, Chondel, Chonsie, Cinda, Cindra, Cinnamon, Conless, Daneisha, Danisha, Darlena, Darnela, Darnella, Davette, Davita, Davona, Deena, Deloria, Delta, Desiree, Dessa, Diandra, Diandre, Dixee, Dixie, Donette, Donia, Donya, Dovey, Dovie, Dovina, Dray, Drey, Elandra, Elza, Erina, Eulala, Fantasia, Fauna, Felisha, Fredonia, Genesis, Genice, Genise, Georgeanne, Halle, Halycon, Ilandra, Ily, Inda, Ireland, Ivory, Jacque, Jacqui, Jaden, Jadyn, Jaiden, Jalaina, Jalayna, Jalinda, Jalissa, Janae, Janeka, Janessa, Janika, Janiqua, Janique, Jazmin, Jazmine, Jazz, Jelissa, Jenessa, Jenique, Jestina, Jonell, Jonelle, Jonetta, Jool, Jorja, Jubilee, Kadence, Kaitlin, Kaitlyn, Kaleigh, Kalin, Kalissa, Kameela, Kameelah, Karis, Kasey, Kassidy, Katelin, Katniss, Katra, Kaya, Kayleen, Kayleigh, Kayley, Kaylin, Keesha, Keila, Kelleen, Kenda, Kenner, Kenya, Kesha, Keshia, Kimber, Kinda, Kody, Krystal, Krystell, LaDawn, LaDonna, Ladonna, Lakeisha, Lakenya, Lakisha, LaNeese, Lanice, Lashawna, Lashonda, Latanya, Latasha, Latawnya, LaTasha, LaTisha, Latisha, LaToya, Latrice, Lavita, Lawanda, Lenice, Linzi, Lurella, Lurelle, Lynda, Lynelle, Lynnelle, Makaela, Makayla, Maretta, Marlissa, Marvela, Mashayla, Mea, Meah, Meisha, Megalyn, Mikayla, Mishaila, Mishcha, Mishka, Montana, Mystik, Mystique, NaTasha, Natasia, Neveah, Nezza, Nova, Novah, Oleta, Oletha, Oprah, Paris, Parris, Patrina, Pepper, Phillis, Piper, Quiana, Ravenna, Reanna, Reanne, Rheanna, Rheanne, Rhiana, Rhianna, Rhianne, Riana, Rianna, Rianne, Rihanna, Rilla, Ronnell, Rozetta, Rylee, Rylie, Sarana, Saranna, Senna, Serene, Serenity, Shanda, Shandelle, Shandra, Shanelle, Shanice, Shantra, Shantrel, Shantrelle, Sharice, Sharise, Sharita, Sharlaine, Sharlana, Sharlayne, Sharlena, Shonda, Shondel, Siena, Sienna, Sierra, Sindra, Sky, Skye, Skyla, Skylar, Skyler, Sojourner, Solina, Solita, Sommer, Talisa, Talisha, TaLisha, Talissa, Tandra, Taneesha, Tanesha, Tanisha, Taria, Tatum, Teagan, Tiara, Tivian, Tressa, Triana, Truth, Tuesday, Unity, Valenda, Valinda, Verita, Viana, Vianna, Vonetta, Willetta, Zada, Zadie, Zalena, Zalina, Zanita, Zasha, Zoey

AMERICAN MALE NAMES

Aden, Archer, Arizona, Asa, Barack, Blade, Blaze, Booth, Boothe, Brock, Cabe, Caden, Cadence, Caiden, Cage, Caige, Cairo, Caius, Calder, Calix, Coley, Colt, Dalen, Danan, Darcel, Darnell, Darold, Darshan, Darshawn, Darshon, Decimus, Deron, DeRon, Deston, Detroit, Dracos, Flip, Free, Gage, Gaige, Granger, Hawk, Hawke, Holt, Jace, Jaden, Jalen, Jamar, Jamarr, Jaran, Jarel, Jaren, Jaron, Jashawn, Jathan, Jax, Jaxson, Jayden, Jerrad, Jerrod, Jett, Jevin, Kade, Kaden, Kadence, Kaius, Kasey, Kassidy, Keaton, Keifer, Kenner, Kiefer, Koby, Kody, Kool, Kyler, Lashon, LeeRon, Leron, Lynard, Marvel, Marvell, Maverick, Merit, Montana, Neo, Nevada, Park, Parke, Piper, Rafer, River, Rook, Rush, Ryder, Ryker, Shawnel, Shim, Sky, Skylar, Skyler, Slade, Slate, Stonewall, Taden, Tayden, Tannis, Tannon, Tatum, Taven, Tavin, Tennessee, Terrone, Tex, Theon, Thorin, Trevis, Tristian, Tucson, Utah, Yancey, Yancy, Zephyrn, Zethus

AMERICAN INDIAN FEMALE NAMES

Abey, Adsila, Ahona, Anamosa, Anina, Anjeni, Ayita, Bena, Catori, Chenoa, Cheyenne, Chosovi, Dakota, Doli, Halona, Hialeah, Humita, Kai, Kanti, Kenda, Malila, Mina, Moneka, Nadie, Nalin, Namida, Natane, Nika, Niyol, Nova, Olathe, Onatah, Orenda, Paha, Panik, Petah, Shania, Shasta, Sihu, Simi, Taa, Taini, Takala, Tansy, Tiiva, Tiponi, Tuwa, Una, Urika, Washta, Winema, Winona, Yamka, Yoki, Zihna, Zonta

AMERICAN INDIAN MALE NAMES

Adahy, Ahiga, Ahuli, Bemidji, Chatan, Chayton, Cherokee, Cochise, Dakota, Enapay, Gomda, Hania, Hemene, Hinto, Honi, Hula, Huritt, Kangee, Kangi, Kavan, Kawa, Kele, Keokuk, Kuruk, Lansa, Lootah, Mahkah, Makya, Mato, Menewa, Minco, Nakos, Nantan, Nikan, Nitis, Nocona, Nodin, Ohanzee, Pezi, Quanah, Sapa, Satanta, Shappa, Tambe, Tapco, Tashunka, Tashunke, Tawa, Thonah, Tokota, Wamblee, Waneta, Whakan, Wicasa, Yiska

CHINESE FEMALE NAMES

An, Bao, Cheng, Cong, Chun, Dan, Fang, Fen, Hua, Huan, Hui, Jia, Jian, Jiang, Jiao, Jin, Lan, Lian, Liang, Ling, Mei, Ming, Ning, Nuan, Ping, Qian, Qing, Qiong, Qiu, Ru, Shu, Xian, Yi, Yu

CHINESE MALE NAMES

An, Bai, Bao, Chang, Cheng, Cong, Fa, Fang, Feng, Hao, Hong, Huan, Ji, Jian, Jie, Jin, Jing, Jun, Kang, Li, Liang, Lin, Long, Meng, Min, Ming, Ning, Ping, Qiang, Ru, Shen, Sheng, Shu, Shui, Shun, Song, Tai, Wei, Wen, Xiong, Xue, Yong, Yu, Zan, Zhi, Zong, Zhuang

DUTCH FEMALE NAMES

Anika, Anke, Annika, Anouk, Corrie, Elke, Emma, Gerda, Gilberta, Gisela, Helma, Jacoba, Janna, Jetta, Jette, Juliana, Karin, Katina, Katja, Katrina, Linda, Lotte, Magda, Marja, Mathilde, Mia, Mirjam, Rebekka, Stefana, Sybilla, Trudie, Trudy, Wilma, Xandra

DUTCH MALE NAMES

Abram, Alfons, Bart, Bram, Egbert, Elbert, Ernst, Erwin, Fons, Frans, Hans, Isaak, Jakob, Jozef, Justus, Kipp, Leopold, Lex, Manfred, Marius, Ruben, Rupert, Sander, Sem, Vincent, Wendel, Wendell, Wilbert, Willem, Xander

EASTERN EUROPEAN (CZECH, HUNGARIAN, POLISH) FEMALE NAMES

Aleksandra, Alina, Aliz, Anci, Aneta, Anezka, Angelika, Aniela, Apolonia, Barbora, Berta, Bianka, Blanka, Bogdana, Bohdana, Celina, Cili, Danica, Danika, Dobrila, Dominika, Dorota, Dusana, Estera, Febe, Fiala, Filipa, Florens, Gertruda, Gizella, Gizi, Halina, Hanna, Helena, Ilona, Irena, Irenka, Ivana, Ivanka, Ivona, Izabella, Jakova, Jana, Jenka, Jirina, Johana, Jolana, Julianna, Julita, Karin, Karina, Karola, Kasia, Katarzyna, Katinka, Katka, Kazia, Klara, Lenci, Libena, Lidia, Liliana, Lilike, Luba, Ludmila, Luiza, Mada, Magda, Marcelina, Marianna, Marika, Marketa, Marta, Matylda, Michalina, Milada, Mira, Morela, Olenka, Ondrea, Onella, Pavla, Petra, Phillis, Piroska, Regina, Romana, Sabina, Serafina, Teresa, Tereza, Truda, Zlata, Zofia, Zora, Zorah, Zorina, Zusa, Zuzanna

EASTERN EUROPEAN (CZECH, HUNGARIAN, POLISH) MALE NAMES

Aleksy, Alfons, Alois, Andel, Antal, Anzelm, Aron, Balint, Bela, Bobek, Bogdan, Bohdan, Borys, Cezar, Damian, Dano, Dawid, Ditrik, Dobry, Dominik, Dusan, Elek, Eryk, Feliks, Filip, Hanek, Havel, Imrich, Iwan, Jakob, Jakov, Jakub, Jan, Janco, Janek, Janika, Janos, Jarek, Jazon, Jeno, Jiji, Jozef, Jur, Jurek, Karol, Kuba, Lazlo, Lech, Libor, Lyront, Maks, Marek, Matus, Miklos, Milos, Miloslav, Mirek, Miron, Miroslav, Ondro, Radek, Radimir, Roman, Rubert, Teodor, Urban, Viggo, Vilhelm, Vili, Vit, Walter, Ziven, Zoltan

FRENCH FEMALE NAMES

Adeline, Adrienne, Agathe, Aimée, Alaina, Alair, Alette, Alexandra, Alexis, Alice, Alison, Aliz, Amélie, Amorette, Anaïs, Angèle, Angeline, Angélique, Anne, Annette, Anouk, Antoinette, Ariane, Arianne, Arielle, Augustine, Aurélie, Aurore, Avril, Babette, Barbara, Béatrice, Benoite,

Berenice, Bernadette, Bernardine, Berthe, Bibiane, Bijou, Blanche, Brigitte, Camille, Candide, Carine, Carole, Caroline, Catherine, Céleste, Célestine, Céline, Cerise, Chantal, Chanté, Charlene, Charice, Charline, Charlotte, Christelle, Christiane, Ciel, Claire, Clarisse, Claudette, Claudine, Clementine, Colette, Collette, Columbe, Constance, Corinne, Cosette, Cyrille, Danièle, Denise, Désirée, Diane, Dominique, Elaine, Eliane, Élodie, Élise, Éloise, Elvire, Emanuelle, Emeline, Esmée, Estée, Estelle, Eugénie, Eulalie, Eve, Fabienne, Félicité, Fifi, Fleur, Florianne, Francette, Francine, Françoise, Gabrielle, Geneviéve, Georgette, Georgine, Ghislaine, Gigi, Ginette, Giselle, Hannah, Hélène, Héloïse, Henriette, Honorine, Hortense, Hyacinthe, Isabelle, Jacinthe, Jacqueline, Jacquette, Jade, Jeanine, Jeanne, Jeannette, Jeannique, Joceline, Joëlle, Jolie, Jordane, Josée, Joséphine, Josette, Jozette, Judith, Julie, Julienne, Juliette, Julitte, Justine, Laure, Lise, Lisette, Louise, Lourdes, Lucette, Lucienne, Lucille, Lucinde, Lydie, Madeleine, Manon, Marceline, Marcille, Margaux, Margot, Marguerite, Marianne, Marie, Marielle, Marionne, Marise, Marjolaine, Marthe, Martine, Melisande, Michèle, Michilene, Mimi, Monique, Morgaine, Muriel, Nadia, Nadine, Nanette, Natalie, Nicole, Ninon, Noella, Nöelle, Noémi, Océane, Odette, Odile, Ondine, Oriane, Orianne, Patrice, Paulette, Paulina, Perrine, Philippa, Rachel, Reine, René, Reneé, Rochelle, Rosette, Roxanne, Sabine, Sarah, Séraphine, Simone, Sophie, Suzanne, Suzette, Sybille, Sylvie, Tatienne, Toinette, Valentine, Véronique, Victoire, Violette, Vivi, Vivienne, Yolande, Yvette, Yvonne

FRENCH MALE NAMES

Abel, Abraham, Adam, Adrien, Alain, Alair, Albert, Alexandre, Alexis, Alphonse, Anatole, André, Antoine, Armand, Arnaud, Arthur, Auberon, Aubert, Baptiste, Basile, Bastien, Benjamin, Benôit, Bernard, Blaise, Charles, Christian, Claude, Corin, Cyril, Damien, Daniel, David, Denis, Dimitri, Dion, Dominique, Donat, Edgard, Edmond,

Édouard, Émile, Étienne, Fabien, Fabrice, Fernand, Francis, François, Gabriel, Gaspard, Gaston, Gautier, Geoffroi, Georges, Geraud, Germain, Gervaise, Gilbert, Grégoire, Guillaume, Guy, Henri, Herbert, Honoré, Hubert, Hugo, Jacques, Jean, Joachim, Joseph, Jourdain, Jules, Julien, Justin, Laurent, Lionel, Louis, Luc, Lucien, Marc, Marcel, Marin, Marius, Martin, Mathieu, Matthieu, Maurice, Maximilien, Michel, Nicolas, Noël, Olivier, Pascal, Patrick, Paul, Philippe, Pierre, Raoul, Raphael, Raymond, Régis, Rémy, Renard, Renaud, René, Richard, Robert, Roch, Rodrigue, Roger, Roland, Salomon, Sébastien, Simon, Thibault, Thomas, Timothee, Tristan, Valentin, Victor, Vincent, Xavier, Yann, Yves

GERMAN FEMALE NAMES

Ada, Adele, Adelheid, Adria, Adriana, Agathe, Agnes, Alberta, Alena, Alexandra, Alfreda, Alina, Alodia, Amalia, Amalie, Amanda, Amelia, Andrea, Angela, Angelika, Anika, Anina, Anita, Anja, Anke, Anna, Anne, Anneliese, Annelise, Annette, Annika, Anselma, Antonia, Astrid, Augusta, Augustine, Aurora, Avelina, Barbara, Beata, Beate, Beatrix, Belinda, Bernardine, Berta, Bertha, Bertina, Bettina, Bianka, Birgit, Birgitte, Brigitte, Brunhilde, Cara, Carina, Carla, Cecilia, Charlotte, Christa, Christiana, Christina, Claudia, Clotilda, Corina, Corinna, Cornelia, Corona, Dagmar, Daniela, Debora, Dorothea, Ebba, Ebbe, Edith, Eleonor, Elisa, Elisabeth, Elise, Elke, Elsa, Emma, Erika, Erma, Ernesta, Ernestine, Esther, Eva, Felicie, Ferdinanda, Franka, Friede, Gabriele, Gerda, Gerlinde, Gerta, Gertraud, Gertrud, Gilberta, Gisela, Gitte, Greta, Gretchen, Gretel, Griet, Griselda, Gudrun, Halley, Hallie, Hally, Hanna, Hannah, Haralda, Hedwig, Heide, Heidi, Helena, Helene, Helga, Helma, Henriette, Hilda, Hildegard, Hulda, Ida, Ilona, Ilsa, Imma, Inga, Ingrid, Irene, Irma, Isabel, Isabella, Ivonne, Jana, Jette, Johanna, Jolanda, Josefa, Judith, Julia, Juliana, Juliane, Jutta, Kamilla, Karen, Karin, Karina, Karla, Karlotte, Karola, Karolina, Karoline, Katarina, Katerine,

Katharina, Katinka, Katja, Katrin, Katrina, Kerstin, Kirsten, Klara, Kris, Krista, Kristen, Kristin, Kristina, Kristine, Lara, Laura, Lena, Lene, Leni, Leona, Liane, Liesa, Liesbeth, Liesa, Liese, Liesl, Linda, Lisa, Lise, Lorelei, Lotte, Louisa, Luise, Lulu, Mada, Magda, Magdalena, Magdalene, Maja, Manuela, Margarete, Margit, Maria, Marianne, Marie, Marina, Marita, Marlene, Marlis, Martha, Marthe, Martina, Mathilde, Mia, Michaela, Milla, Mina, Minna, Minnie, Minny, Mirjam, Mitzi, Monika, Nadja, Natalie, Nicola, Nicole, Nina, Nora, Odelia, Odila, Odilia, Olga, Olivia, Patricia, Paula, Petra, Pia, Rakel, Raphaela, Rebekka, Regina, Renata, Renate, Rita, Rolanda, Romy, Rosalinde, Rosina, Rut, Ruth, Sabine, Sabrina, Sandra, Sara, Selda, Selma, Sibylla, Siegfrida, Sieglinde, Sigi, Silvia, Sofia, Sofie, Sonja, Sonje, Sophia, Sophie, Steffi, Steffie, Susanne, Svenja, Sybilla, Sybille, Sylvia, Tabea, Teresa, Thekla, Therese, Tilda, Tilde, Tina, Trudy, Ursula, Valda, Vanessa, Vera, Verena, Veronika, Viktoria, Vreni, Wanda, Wilhelmina, Wilma, Yvonne, Zenzi

GERMAN MALE NAMES

Achim, Adolf, Adrian, Ahlf, Alberic, Albert, Albrecht, Alex, Alexander, Alexis, Alfons, Alfred, Alois, Aloysius, Andreas, Anselm, Anton, Archibald, Armin, Arndt, Arne, Arno, Arnold, Arthur, Artur, August, Axel, Benjamin, Bernd, Bernhard, Bernt, Boris, Bruno, Burk, Christian, Claus, Daniel, David, Dennis, Derek, Derick, Dieter, Dietrich, Dirk, Eberhard, Eberhardt, Eckart, Eckhart, Eduard, Egon, Elias, Emil, Emmerich, Erhard, Erich, Erik, Ernst, Erwin, Eugen, Evert, Fabian, Falco, Falko, Ferdinand, Fester, Folker, Frank, Franz, Friedrich, Fritz, Gabriel, Garrick, Georg, Gerald, Gerhard, Gerhardt, Gilbert, Gottfried, Gregor, Gustaf, Gustav, Hagan, Hagen, Hans, Harald, Heinrich, Helmut, Hendrik, Horst, Hubert, Hugo, Isaak, Jakob, Jan, Joachim, Johan, Johann, Johannes, Jorg, Josef, Julian, Justus, Karl, Karsten, Kaspar, Kipp, Klaus, Konrad, Kris, Kristian, Kuno, Kurt, Lanzo,

Lennart, Lenz, Leo, Leon, Leopold, Lorenz, Lothar, Louis, Ludwig, Lukas, Luther, Magnus, Manfred, Marius, Markus, Martin, Mathias, Mathis, Max, Maximilian, Meinhard, Meinard, Michael, Nikolaus, Norbert, Oliver, Oskar, Otto, Patrick, Paul, Peter, Rafael, Raimund, Rainer, Ralph, Randolf, Raul, Reiner, Richard, Robert, Roderick, Roger, Roland, Rolf, Rudolf, Rupert, Sander, Sebastien, Sepp, Siegfried, Sigfried, Sigi, Sigmund, Silvester, Simon, Stefan, Stephan, Theodor, Thomas, Tobias, Torsten, Urban, Valentin, Viktor, Vincens, Vital, Vinzenz, Volker, Waldo, Walter, Walther, Wendel, Werner, Wilhelm, Willi, Winfried, Wolfgang

GREEK FEMALE NAMES

Acacia, Adona, Adonia, Agathe, Aikaterini, Aldora, Aleka, Alethea, Alexa, Alexia, Alexandra, Ambrosia, Anastasia, Anatolia, Andriana, Andrianna, Angeliki, Anna, Aphrodite, Apollonia, Aridne, Chara, Charis, Clio, Damaris, Danae, Daphne, Darice, Diantha, Dimitra, Dione, Dora, Dorcas, Dorkas, Dorothea, Echo, Efimia, Eirini, Elektra, Elena, Eleni, Eudora, Eugenia, Euphemia, Evangelia, Gaea, Gaia, Georgia, Grigoria, Helene, Hera, Ioanna, Iris, Isidora, Kaiti, Kalandra, Kalidas, Kalli, Kalliope, Kallisto, Kassandra, Katerina, Katina, Kolina, Konstantina, Kora, Korinna, Kynthia, Leandra, Lucia, Lydia, Magda, Marianna, Marina, Martha, Melantha, Melina, Melissa, Natalia, Natassa, Nike, Nikoleta, Odele, Olympia, Ophelia, Ourania, Penelope, Petra, Petrina, Philippa, Philomela, Philomena, Phoebe, Phyllis, Pia, Rena, Rhea, Sapphira, Selene, Sibyl, Sibylla, Sofronia, Sophia, Sotiria, Stefana, Stefania, Stella, Stellina, Sybilla, Tabitha, Tasia, Tessa, Thalia, Thekla, Theodora, Theodosia, Theresa, Timothea, Varvara, Xenia, Zoe

GREEK MALE NAMES

Adonis, Aegis, Alexandros, Alexios, Anatasios, Anatolius, Andreas, Angelo, Argos, Aristotle, Arsenios, Bion, Carolos, Christiano, Christophoros,

Dimitrios, Elias, Evangelos, Georgios, Giannis, Grigorios, Hieronymous, Ioannis, Isidoros, Konstantinos, Kosmas, Kostas, Leander, Lukas, Makarios, Markos, Matthias, Michail, Myron, Nikolaos, Nikos, Orion, Panos, Pavlos, Petros, Plato, Sandros, Sergios, Socrates, Sotirios, Spiro, Spyro, Stefanos, Stephanos, Tasos, Tassos, Thanos, Theo, Theodoros, Thomas, Timon, Timotheos, Titos, Titus, Yanni, Yannis, Yianni, Yiannis, Zacharias, Zeno, Zissis

HAWAIIAN FEMALE NAMES

Ahulani, Ailani, Alana, Alani, Alohi, Aniani, Anolani, Aoloa, Aonani, Hiilani, Hokuala, Honi, Ilima, Imina, Kailani, Kalama, Kalei, Kalia, Kanani, Kaui, Keala, Kehua, Keiki, Keolani, Kiana, Kolani, Konane, Kupono, Lai, Laka, Lana, Lani, Laola, Lea, Lehua, Leilani, Leinani, Luana, Lulu, Mahina, Malana, Malina, Mana, Mapuana, Mauloa, Mauna, Melia, Melika, Miliani, Moana, Moani, Naniloa, Noe, Olina, Omea, Pele, Ponia, Uilani, Ulani, Wailani, Wainani

HAWAIIAN MALE NAMES

Anolani, Holokai, Ihilani, Iolani, Kahanu, Kahili, Kai, Kainui, Kalea, Kaleo, Kane, Kanoa, Kapono, Kapuni, Kaulana, Keahi, Keanu, Keawe, Kekoa, Keola, Kilo, Koa, Kona, Konani, Lahiki, Lalama, Laniloa, Leolani, Makaha, Makani, Makoa, Malino, Malu, Mano, Moi, Nahele, Nahoa, Nalu, Nohea, Pakala, Polani

HINDU/INDIAN FEMALE NAMES

Aditi, Ahimsa, Amala, Ambala, Amisha, Amiti, Amrita, Amshula, Ananda, Anila, Anju, Anura, Anya, Aruna, Arya, Ashima, Ashni, Avani, Bala, Bela, Bhakti, Bhamini, Bhuti, Caitanya, Candra, Chameli, Chanda, Chandra, Charita, Charu, Darsha, Daya, Devika, Dharmini, Ekata, Eshana, Gyanda, Hanita, Harita, Harsha, Ila, Indira, Jayna, Jivani, Jyoti, Kalyana, Kamalika, Kamalini, Kanta, Karuna, Kashi, Kavala, Kerani, Kundini, Lalasa, Lalita, Lalitha, Lavanya, Leena, Lila, Mahima, Maitri, Malati, Mali, Malika, Malini, Manjika, Meera, Mira, Monika, Nalini, Nandini, Naseem, Navina, Nayana, Neela, Neeta, Nila, Nina, Nisha, Nita, Nitya, Omana, Omatra, Panna, Parvani, Pavana, Pema, Prasanna, Prema, Prita, Rajani, Ramani, Ramya, Riju, Rita, Riya, Roshana, Sabah, Sadhana, Saguna, Sakala, Sakalah, Salena, Samata, Sameena, Samina, Sananda, Sangita, Sanjana, Sarala, Sarani, Sarita, Sarvani, Sati, Satya, Sachee, Shameena, Shanti, Sharmini, Shashini, Sheela, Shikah, Shoba, Shreya, Shrila, Srila, Shuchee, Shushila, Sitara, Suma, Sumitra, Suniti, Surina, Sushanti, Tara, Tarani, Tarika, Uma, Vanika, Varana, Varsha, Vashati, Veera, Vimala, Vinata, Virya, Vrinda

HINDU/INDIAN MALE NAMES

Abhay, Aditya, Agni, Akama, Amaran, Anjay, Ankur, Aravinda, Arjun, Arun, Avikar, Ayush, Balin, Bandhu, Bhanu, Bharata, Bhasu, Bodhi, Darshan, Deepak, Dhira, Dinesh, Dipak, Gandhi, Ganesh, Giri, Gyan, Hans, Hanuman, Harshad, Indra, Iraja, Ishah, Janesh, Jayan, Jeta, Jivana, Kadhi, Kama, Karu, Kavi, Lahar, Mandar, Mandeep, Mandu, Marici, Milan, Muni, Nabha, Nadish, Nakin, Nandan, Nandi, Nara, Naren, Narya, Neel, Nehru, Netra, Nirvan, Nityan, Oman, Pala, Pandita, Parama, Pradeep, Pradip, Pradosh, Prajna, Prana, Prem, Puneet, Rama, Ranjan, Rasa, Rishi, Rohan, Sabala, Sajan, Sandeep, Sandip, Sanjay, Satyaki, Shakra, Shama, Shankar, Shasta, Shrini, Siddha, Soma, Sudama, Sujay, Suman, Sunara, Taj, Tarun, Udara, Urvil, Varada, Varen, Varil, Vasu, Vidura, Vijay, Vimal, Yash

IRISH FEMALE NAMES

Afric, Ailbhe, Aileen, Ailene, Ailis, Ailish, Aishling, Aiveen, Alannah, Alma, Ana, Aoife, Bedelia, Berneen, Bevan, Bevin, Bidelia, Breda, Bree, Briana, Brianna, Bridget, Brighid, Brigid,

Cairan, Cairenn, Cait, Caitin, Caitlin, Caragh, Carrie, Carry, Cassidi, Cassidy, Cathleen, Cathie, Cathy, Catrina, Catriona, Ciana, Cianna, Ciara, Ciarra, Clare, Cleona, Cliona, Clodagh, Codie, Cody, Coleen, Colleen, Dacey, Dacie, Dacy, Dana, Dara, Darcie, Darcy, Darran, Deirdra, Deirdre, Delaney, Devan, Devin, Duana, Edana, Edna, Eileen, Eilis, Eithne, Elan, Ena, Enya, Fainne, Farrell, Farrol, Finola, Fiona, Fionnuala, Gael, Geiles, Grania, Grainne, Honora, Ide, Imogen, Kady, Kaydi, Kaydy, Kate, Kathleen, Kay, Keela, Keeli, Keelin, Keely, Keeva, Kelley, Kelly, Keri, Kerri, Kerry, Kyna, Lana, Lasair, Liadan, Lulla, Maebh, Maeve, Maire, Mairead, Mairona, Maura, Maureen, Maurene, Moira, Moire, Mollie, Molly, Mona, Moreen, Moyra, Muriel, Murphy, Myrna, Neala, Nelda, Nessa, Niamh, Nola, Noleen, Nora, Noreen, Norene, Nuala, Oona, Oonagh, Payton, Peggie, Peggy, Peyton, Pollie, Polly, Quinn, Quinnie, Reagan, Regan, Reilly, Rhona, Riley, Riona, Roisin, Ryan, Ryann, Ryanne, Ryley, Seana, Senga, Shaelee, Shaeleigh, Shauna, Shawna, Sheridan, Sibeal, Sile, Sine, Sinead, Siobhan, Siomha, Sorcha, Talulla, Tara, Treasa, Triese, Tyrona, Ula

IRISH MALE NAMES

Addis, Aidis, Alan, Alastar, Alaster, Allan, Allen, Aodhan, Aonghas, Barrie, Barry, Bearach, Berach, Brady, Bran, Breandan, Brian, Brodie, Brody, Bryan, Cadhla, Cailean, Cane, Carey, Carlin, Carroll, Cary, Cassidy, Cathal, Cathan, Cavan, Cavin, Cian, Cianan, Ciar, Ciaran, Cillian, Clancy, Cody, Coinnech, Colin, Collin, Colm, Conall, Conan, Conn, Conner, Connor, Conor, Conway, Corey, Cory, Cormac, Coyt, Daley, Daly, Daragh, Darby, Darcy, Daren, Darin, Daron, Darrah, Darren, Declan, Delaney, Delany, Dermot, Derry, Desmond, Devan, Devin, Devon, Diarmaid, Dillon, Donal, Donn, Donovan, Dougan, Doyle, Drew, Duane, Dugan, Dwayne, Eamon, Eamonn, Egan, Ennis, Eoghan, Eoin, Fagan, Fagen, Fallon, Faolan, Farrell, Fearghal, Feargus, Fergal, Fergus,

Finbar, Finn, Fionn, Flann, Gannon, Garvan, Garvin, Grady, Hagan, Hogan, Ivor, Jarret, Jarrett, Kane, Kealan, Kean, Keane, Keary, Keefe, Keegan, Keelan, Keenan, Kelley, Kelly, Kermit, Kerry, Kevin, Kieran, Killian, Kirwin, Lann, Liam, Lorcan, Lugh, Manus, Murphy, Neal, Neil, Nevan, Niall, Nevin, Odhran, Odran, Oisin, Oran, Oren, Orin, Oscar, Paddy, Padraic, Padraig, Patrick, Peadar, Pierce, Piers, Quinlan, Quinn, Rafferty, Reagan, Renny, Reno, Riley, Riordan, Roc, Rogan, Ronan, Rory, Rowan, Ruairi, Ryan, Seamus, Sean, Seanan, Shane, Shanley, Shay, Shea, Sheridan, Sullivan, Sweeney, Tadhg, Taran, Teague, Teige, Tiarnan, Tiernan, Tomas, Torin, Tullie, Tully, Tyrone, Uilliam

ITALIAN FEMALE NAMES

Ada, Adele, Adelina, Adriana, Agata, Agnese, Agostina, Alba, Alberta, Alessa, Alessandra, Alessia, Alfreda, Alina, Allegra, Amanda, Amara, Ambra, Amelia, Andreana, Angela, Angelica, Angelina, Anna, Annabella, Annamaria, Annunziata, Anonna, Antonia, Arabella, Arianna, Ariela, Augusta, Aurora, Azzurra, Barbara, Beata, Beatrice, Bella, Bellina, Benedetta, Benicia, Benigna, Berenice, Bernadetta, Berta, Bertina, Betta, Bettina, Bianca, Bibiana, Bona, Brigida, Calida, Calista, Calliope, Callisto, Camilla, Capri, Cara, Carina, Carissa, Carla, Carlotta, Camilla, Carmela, Carmen, Carolina, Catarina, Cecilia, Celestina, Celia, Celina, Chiara, Cinzia, Clara, Clarissa, Claudia, Cloe, Colombina, Concetta, Constantina, Cornelia, Cosima, Cristiana, Cristina, Dafne, Damiana, Daniela, Daria, Debora, Demetria, Diamante, Diana, Dionisia, Diviana, Domenica, Donata, Donatella, Dora, Dorotea, Dulcia, Edda, Elena, Eleonora, Elettra, Eliana, Elisa, Elisabetta, Eloisa, Emanuela, Emilia, Emiliana, Emma, Enrica, Ernesta, Eugenia, Eulalia, Eva, Evangelia, Evangelina, Fabiana, Fabiola, Federica, Felice, Felicia, Felicita, Fernanda, Filippa, Fina, Fiorella, Flavia, Flora, Fortunata, Franca, Francesca, Gabriella, Gaia, Gemma, Ghita, Gia,

Giada, Giancinta, Gianna, Gina, Gioia, Giovanna, Gisella, Giulia, Graziella, Ilaria, Imelda, Isabella, Isidora, Lara, Laura, Leandra, Leonora, Letizia, Lia, Liberata, Lidia, Liliana, Lina, Lisa, Lorena, Loretta, Lucia, Luciana, Luisa, Maddelena, Manueala, Marcella, Marcia, Margherita, Maria, Marianna, Mariella, Marina, Marisa, Maristela, Marta, Martina, Matilde, Michela, Miranda, Mirella, Miriam, Monica, Nadia, Natalia, Niccola, Nora, Nunzia, Ofelia, Olimpia, Olivia, Oriana, Ottavia, Paola, Paolina, Patrizia, Perla, Pia, Placida, Primavera, Rachele, Rebecca, Regina, Renata, Rita, Roberta, Romana, Rosa, Rosabella, Rosalia, Rosetta, Rosina, Sabella, Sabina, Sabrina, Samanta, Samuela, Sandra, Sara, Serafina, Serena, Silvia, Simona, Sofia, Sonia, Sophia, Stefania, Susana, Susanna, Tabita, Tamara, Tecla, Teodora, Teresa, Tina, Valentina, Valeria, Vanessa, Vanna, Venicia, Vera, Veronica, Viola, Virginia, Vittoria, Viviana, Zoe

ITALIAN MALE NAMES

Abramo, Adamo, Adolfo, Adriano, Agostino, Alano, Alberto, Aldo, Alessandro, Alfonso, Alfredo, Allesio, Amadeus, Ambrogio, Amerigo, Angelo, Anselmo, Antonello, Antonio, Apollo, Armando, Arnaldo, Arsenio, Aturo, Augusto, Augustus, Bartolomeo, Basilio, Battista, Benedetto, Benigno, Benito, Benvenuto, Bernardino, Bernardo, Berto, Bruno, Carlo, Carmelo, Carmine, Cecilio, Celio, Cesare, Cirillo, Cirino, Claudio, Clemente, Constantino, Corrado, Cosimo, Cristiano, Cristoforo, Damiano, Danilo, Dante, Dario, Demetrio, Desi, Desiderio, Dezi, Dino, Dionisio, Domenico, Donato, Donotello, Edmondo, Edoardo, Efrem, Elmo, Emilio, Enrico, Enzo, Ernesto, Eugenio, Fabian, Fabio, Fabricio, Fabrizio, Federico, Fernando, Filippo, Flavio, Fortunato, Francesco, Franco, Galeno, Gerardo, Giacobbe, Giacomo, Gianni, Gilberto, Gino, Giole, Giorgio, Giovanni, Giraldo, Giuliano, Giuseppe, Gregorio, Guglielmo, Guido, Gustavo, Ignazio, Ilario, Jacobo, Lazzaro, Leandro, Leo, Leonardo, Liberato, Lorenzo, Loris,

Luca, Luciano, Lucio, Luigi, Macario, Manuel, Marcello, Marco, Marcus, Marino, Mario, Martino, Massimo, Maximus, Michelangelo, Milo, Niccolo, Nico, Nicola, Nunzio, Orlando, Ottavio, Paolo, Patrizio, Piero, Pietro, Placido, Primo, Raul, Renato, Renzo, Riccardo, Rinaldo, Roberto, Rocco, Rodolfo, Rodrigo, Rolando, Romano, Romeo, Salvatore, Sebastiano, Sergio, Silvano, Silvio, Stefano, Taddeo, Teo, Teodoro, Timoteo, Tito, Tommaso, Tonia, Uberto, Urbano, Valentino, Valerio, Venturo, Vico, Vincenzo, Vitale, Vito, Vittorio

JAPANESE FEMALE NAMES

Ai, Aiko, Aimi, Akiko, Asami, Atsuko, Chiyo, Cho, Hana, Hikari, Hiro, Hiroko, Hiromi, Honoka, Hoshi, Hoshiko, Kaneko, Keiko, Kiku, Kimiko, Kiyoko, Kohana, Kokoro, Kotone, Mari, Mayu, Midori, Miki, Mio, Misaki, Miyu, Mizuki, Mizuko, Moriko, Nami, Sachiko, Saki, Sakura, Suki, Suzuki, Takara, Tomomi, Umeko, Yasu, Yasuko, Yoko, Yoshi, Yukiko, Yuko, Yuri

JAPANESE MALE NAMES

Akio, Akira, Daiki, Daisuke, Hiroshi, Hiroto, Ichiro, Isamu, Katashi, Katsuro, Ken, Kenta, Kichiro, Makoto, Michi, Osamu, Ryuu, Sachi, Shin, Sho, Sora, Takashi, Takumi, Toshio, Yamato, Yasu, Yasuo, Yoshiro

JEWISH FEMALE NAMES

Abiela, Abiella, Abira, Adah, Adama, Adara, Addah, Adel, Adi, Adina, Adira, Adiva, Aharona, Ahava, Ahavah, Ahuva, Ahuvah, Aleeza, Aleta, Alima, Alisa, Alissa, Alita, Aliya, Aliyah, Alizah, Almah, Alona, Amalya, Amana, Amania, Amanya, Ameera, Amiela, Amira, Amita, Arela, Arella, Ariella, Arielle, Ashera, Ashira, Atara, Atira, Aviela, Aviella, Avigayil, Aviva, Avivah, Ayla, Azriela, Basha, Bashe, Batia, Batya, Bechira, Behira, Beulah, Bracha, Carmel, Chagit, Chaifa,

Chanah, Chani, Channah, Chanya, Chasida,
Chava, Chaya, Chedva, Cheifa, Chenia, Chenya,
Chermona, Chiba, Dafna, Dalia, Dalya, Dana,
Daniela, Daniella, Danielle, Danya, Dasi, Datia,
Datya, Davida, Delila, Delilah, Devora, Devorah,
Dinah, Dvora, Dvorah, Eden, Ednah, Efrata,
Eila, Eilah, Eilona, Einya, Eliana, Elianna, Eliora,
Elisheva, Eliya, Elza, Ester, Etana, Feige, Galila,
Gana, Gania, Ganya, Gavriel, Gavriela, Gavriella,
Gavrielle, Gavrila, Gayora, Geona, Gershona,
Gibora, Giborah, Gilah, Giora, Gitah, Gitel, Gittel,
Golda, Hadara, Hadassah, Hagar, Hagiya, Haifa,
Halil, Hanana, Hasida, Hava, Haya, Hedva, Henia,
Henya, Herut, Hillah, Ilana, Ilanit, Immanuela,
Kanit, Katania, Kataniya, Kefira, Kelila, Keren,
Keshet, Ketana, Ketura, Ketzia, Kitra, Laila, Lailie,
Leah, Leeat, Leebi, Leenoy, Leeona, Leeraz, Leeya,
Leili, Levana, Liat, Lieba, Libi, Libiya, Lilith,
Lillith, Linoy, Liora, Liraz, Lirit, Lirona, Livya,
Liya, Lotem, Magena, Mahira, Malka, Malkah,
Margalit, Margea, Marnina, Masada, Matana, Maya,
Mayana, Mayim, Mazal, Medina, Meira, Menora,
Menorah, Meona, Meora, Michaela, Mili, Miri,
Miryam, Mishala, Moria, Moriah, Moriela, Moriya,
Naama, Naamah, Nagida, Naomi, Nassana,
Natana, Natanya, Nava, Nechama, Nediva,
Negina, Nehara, Neora, Nera, Neriah, Neriya,
Neshama, Neta, Netiva, Nevona, Nili, Noia, Noya,
Nurit, Ofira, Ofra, Ophrah, Orah, Orpah, Oshra,
Rachel, Rachela, Rahel, Raisa, Raizel, Rani, Rania,
Ranita, Raz, Raziela, Rebekah, Refaela, Renana,
Reut, Reva, Rimona, Rishona, Riva, Rivka,
Rona, Salome, Sarah, Sela, Seraphina, Shakeda,
Shalva, Shalvah, Shamira, Shani, Sharon, Sharona,
Sheina, Shifra, Shifrah, Shilo, Shiloh, Shimona,
Shirah, Shiran, Shiraz, Shirel, Shlomit, Shoshanah,
Shoshannah, Shula, Simcha, Siona, Sura, Surah,
Talia, Talya, Tamah, Tehila, Tehilla, Temah,
Temira, Temirah, Teriah, Tifara, Tikvah, Timora,
Tira, Tirza, Tirzah, Tiva, Tivka, Tori, Tovah,
Tziporah, Uriela, Uriella, Ushara, Yaara, Yafa,
Yaffah, Yakira, Yakova, Yara, Yardena, Yarona,
Yashara, Yehudit, Yeira, Yemima, Yerusha, Yifat,

Yisraela, Yochana, Yoela, Yona, Yonina, Yosefa,
Yosepha, Zahara, Zara, Zehira, Zelda, Zelde,
Zemira, Zemirah, Zephira, Ziva, Zivah

JEWISH MALE NAMES

Abir, Adam, Adar, Adir, Adiv, Adriel, Aharon,
Akiva, Alon, Allon, Amal, Amiad, Amichai, Amiel,
Amir, Amiran, Amit, Amitai, Amitan, Amnon,
Amos, Ara, Arah, Arel, Ari, Ariel, Arnon, Arye,
Aryeh, Asaf, Asah, Asaph, Asher, Ashir, Atir,
Aviel, Avner, Avraham, Avram, Avshalom, Az,
Azan, Azi, Aziel, Azrael, Azriel, Barak, Baruch,
Ben, Binyamin, Chagai, Chai, Chaim, Chalil,
Chaniel, Chanoch, Chasid, Chiram, Chayim,
Dagan, Dan, Daniel, Datan, David, Dekel, Devir,
Dor, Dov, Dror, Dvir, Eban, Edan, Eden, Effie, Efi,
Efrayim, Ehud, Eilam, Eilon, Eitan, Elad, Elam,
Elazar, Eldad, Elez, Eli, Eliam, Elior, Elisha, Elon,
Emmet, Enosh, Etan, Eyal, Ezra, Feivel, Fivel,
Gadiel, Gai, Galil, Gamliel, Gavriel, Gavril, Gefen,
Gershom, Gershon, Gibor, Gidon, Gil, Gilad,
Gilon, Givon, Gomer, Guri, Hagai, Haim, Halil,
Harel, Hasid, Hayyim, Hersh, Hershel, Hevel,
Hillel, Hiram, Hirsh, Hirshel, Hosea, Hoshea,
Ilan, Imanuel, Immanuel, Ira, Itai, Ittan, Kaleb,
Kalev, Kalil, Kaniel, Kefir, Koresh, Lazar, Lazer,
Leeon, Leeor, Leeron, Leib, Leor, Lev, Levi, Liev,
Liron, Magen, Malachi, Malkam, Matan, Matar,
Meged, Meir, Menachem, Metav, Micha, Michael,
Mordechai, Moriel, Moshe, Nadav, Naftali, Nagid,
Naor, Naphtali, Natan, Nativ, Navon, Nechemya,
Netanel, Nisan, Nissan, Noach, Noam, Ofer, Ofir,
Ogen, Ometz, Onam, Oran, Osher, Pele, Peleh,
Rafi, Ram, Ran, Ravi, Refael, Rephael, Reuven,
Rom, Ron, Rosh, Seff, Sefi, Shafat, Shai, Shaked,
Shama, Shamah, Shamir, Shaul, Shavit, Shaviv,
Shay, Shaya, Shefi, Shem, Sheva, Shilo, Shiloh,
Shimon, Shimshon, Shlomi, Shlomo, Shmuel,
Shofar, Shomer, Shua, Sion, Tavi, Tiv, Tivon,
Tomer, Tor, Tov, Tovi, Tuvia, Tuviah, Tuviya,
Tuvya, Tziyon, Uram, Uri, Uriah, Uriel, Uzi,
Uziah, Uziya, Yadid, Yakim, Yakir, Yakov, Yankel,
Yarden, Yaron, Yashar, Yehonatan, Yehoshua,

Yehudah, Yeshaya, Yeshua, Yetzer, Yirmeyahu, Yishai, Yishmael, Yisrael, Yitzchak, Yitzhar, Yizhar, Yoav, Yochai, Yoel, Yonah, Yonatan, Yosef, Yosher, Yossi, Yuval, Zakai, Zalman, Zalmen, Zalmon, Zavad, Zebedee, Zecharya, Zerach, Zevulun, Zif, Ziff, Zion, Ziv, Zohar

KOREAN FEMALE NAMES

Eun-Sun, Huan-Ju, Hyun-Ja, Hyun-Young, Ji-Min, Jin-Sook, Ji-Won, Ji-Young, Jung-Ja, Kun-Sun, Mi-Kyoung, Min-Hee, Sang-Mi, Sook-Ja, So-Young, Suh-Hyun, Yoo-Jin, Young-Hee

KOREAN MALE NAMES

Boo-Chun, Chang-Ho, Jong-Soo, Joon-Ho, Jung-Ho, Jung-Soo, Kwang-Ho, Sang-Ho, Sang-Min, Sung-Ho, Sung-Wook

MUSLIM/PERSIAN FEMALE NAMES

Aamina, Aaqila, Aarifa, Aasima, Abeeda, Abeera, Abida, Abira, Adala, Adeeba, Adeela, Adiba, Adila, Afeefa, Afifa, Afroza, Aida, Aisha, Aishah, Akeela, Akifa, Akilah, Aleefa, Alifa, Alima, Alimah, Aliya, Amani, Ameena, Aminah, Aneeqa, Aneesa, Anisa, Aniqa, Aquila, Areefa, Arifa, Arzu, Aseela, Aseema, Asha, Asila, Asimah, Asira, Asirah, Asiya, Asmani, Ateefa, Atifa, Atira, Atiya, Atiyyah, Ayda, Azar, Azeezah, Azizah, Badra, Baheera, Bahira, Bahirah, Bahiya, Bahiyya, Bakhita, Baraka, Basheera, Bashira, Bashirah, Basima, Basimah, Basira, Basma, Danesh, Dil, Dima, Faaiza, Fadeela, Fadila, Faheema, Fahima, Faida, Faiza, Farah, Fareeda, Faridah, Farida, Farrah, Fateema, Fatima, Fayza, Fidda, Ghada, Ghadah, Ghadir, Ghaliya, Ghaliyah, Ghania, Ghaniya, Gulshan, Haafiza, Haamida, Habiba, Habibah, Hadaya, Hadia, Hadiya, Hafiza, Hafizah, Hakeema, Hakima, Haleema, Halima, Halimah, Hamida, Hamidah, Haneefa, Hanifa, Haniya, Haniyyah, Hasana, Haseeba, Haseefa, Haseema, Haseena, Hasiba, Hasifa, Hasima, Hasina, Hasinah, Hassana, Hazima, Hiba, Hiyam, Huda, Jaheeda, Jahida, Jaleela, Jaleh, Jalilah, Jameela, Jamilah, Janan, Janna, Jihan, Jinan, Jumana, Jumanah, Kabeera, Kabira, Kamila, Kamilah, Karima, Karimah, Khabeera, Khabira, Khalida, Khalidah, Khaira, Khalila, Khalilah, Khalisa, Khashia, Khasiba, Khatira, Khatirah, Khayra, Laila, Lateefa, Latifah, Layaan, Leila, Lila, Mahdia, Mahdiya, Maheera, Mahirah, Majeeda, Majida, Malak, Manara, Mansura, Maram, Marjaan, Masheed, Mashid, Masuda, Mihri, Mufeeda, Mufida, Muneera, Munifah, Munirah, Munia, Munisa, Munya, Musheera, Mushira, Nabeela, Nabilah, Nadeera, Nadima, Nadimah, Nadirah, Nafisa, Nahida, Nahidah, Naima, Naimah, Najiah, Najiya, Naqiya, Naseema, Naseera, Nashita, Nasima, Nasirah, Nasrin, Nazara, Nimah, Noor, Noshin, Nur, Nura, Nuriah, Nuriya, Raabia, Raazia, Rabiah, Rafeeda, Rafia, Rafiah, Rafida, Rahima, Rahimah, Raida, Rajia, Rajya, Rakhima, Rakina, Rakinah, Randa, Raneem, Ranim, Raniya, Raniyah, Raseena, Rashidah, Rasina, Raushana, Raya, Razeena, Razina, Raziyah, Rima, Riyaz, Roshana, Saafi, Saamia, Sabeera, Sabeeta, Sabira, Sabita, Sadiah, Sadiyah, Saffiyya, Safiya, Sahab, Sahla, Sajida, Sajidah, Saleema, Salima, Salimah, Samia, Samina, Saminah, Sania, Saniyya, Sausan, Sepideh, Shadia, Shadiya, Shafeeqa, Shafiqa, Shahana, Shaira, Shakeela, Shakilah, Shakira, Shakirah, Shareen, Sharifa, Sharmeen, Sharmin, Shirin, Taheera, Taheerah, Taleeba, Taleema, Taliba, Talima, Tameeza, Tameza, Tamiza, Taqia, Taqiya, Tayiba, Tayibah, Ulya, Vashti, Wafeeqa, Wafiqa, Wafiya, Wafiyah, Wajeeda, Wajida, Waseema, Wasima, Yamima, Yaseera, Yasira, Yasmeen, Yasmin, Zafira, Zafirah, Zaheeda, Zaheena, Zaheera, Zahia, Zahida, Zahina, Zahirah, Zahiya, Zahra, Zameela, Zameera, Zamila, Zamirah, Zareefa, Zarifah, Zayna, Zeba, Ziba, Ziya, Zuhra

MUSLIM/PERSIAN MALE NAMES

Aalim, Aamin, Aamir, Aaqil, Aarif, Aasim, Abaan, Aban, Abdallah, Abdul, Abeed, Abid, Abidin,

Adeeb, Adeel, Adib, Adil, Afeef, Afif, Ahmad, Ahmed, Akhtar, Akif, Aleef, Aleem, Ali, Alif, Alim, Amal, Aman, Ambar, Ameed, Ameen, Ameer, Amid, Amin, Amir, Anwar, Aqil, Arafat, Aram, Areeb, Areef, Arib, Arif, Arshad, Asad, Aseem, Aseer, Asim, Asir, Ateef, Atif, Azar, Azeez, Aziz, Azud, Baheer, Bahir, Baki, Baqi, Baqir, Bareeq, Barik, Baseem, Basheer, Bashir, Basim, Basir, Bizhan, Dabeer, Dabir, Dalil, Danesh, Daud, Dawud, Deen, Dil, Din, Fadeel, Fadil, Fahd, Faheem, Fahim, Faiz, Fareed, Farid, Farih, Farouk, Faruq, Fayz, Fazl, Fuad, Ghalib, Ghani, Ghazi, Haafiz, Haakim, Habeeb, Habib, Hadi, Hafi, Hafiz, Hakeem, Hakim, Haleem, Halim, Haneef, Hanif, Haroun, Harun, Hasan, Hasanat, Haseem, Haseen, Hasib, Hasif, Hasim, Hasin, Hassan, Hazeem, Hazim, Husayn, Hussein, Ibrahim, Ihsan, Isad, Ishaq, Ismail, Jaabir, Jabbar, Jabir, Jafaar, Jafar, Jahan, Jaheed, Jahid, Jalaal, Jalal, Jaleel, Jalil, Jamaal, Jamal, Jaseem, Jaseer, Jasim, Jasir, Javed, Kabeer, Kabir, Kamaal, Kamal, Kameel, Kamil, Kareem, Karim, Khabeer, Khabir, Khair, Khaleed, Khaleel, Khalid, Khalil, Khalis, Khasib, Khayr, Khayyam, Lateef, Latif, Lufti, Mahdi, Maheer, Mahib, Mahir, Mahmoud, Mahmud, Majeed, Majid, Manar, Mansur, Marzuz, Maseer, Masir, Masud, Mazid, Mohammad, Muamar, Muammar, Mubarak, Mufeed, Mufid, Mufiz, Muhammad, Muheeb, Muhib, Muneer, Munif, Munir, Munis, Musa, Musheer, Mushir, Mustafa, Naasir, Naazim, Nabeel, Nabil, Nadeer, Nadim, Nadir, Naim, Najeeb, Najib, Najih, Naqi, Naseem, Nasim, Nasir, Naveed, Navid, Nazeem, Nazif, Noor, Nur, Omar, Omid, Pir, Qaid, Qaim, Raaid, Raaji, Raashad, Raashid, Rafeed, Rafeeq, Rafi, Rafid, Raheem, Rahim, Rajih, Rakeen, Rakin, Raseen, Rashad, Rashid, Rasin, Razi, Ruhi, Rushdi, Sabeer, Sabir, Sadeed, Sadid, Safeer, Safir, Sajeed, Sajid, Salaam, Saladeen, Saladin, Salam, Samih, Sayyed, Sayyid, Shafeeq, Shafiq, Shakeel, Shakeer, Shakil, Shakir, Sharif, Sohrab, Taheer, Tahir, Taleeb, Taleem, Talib, Talim, Tameez, Tamiz, Taqi, Tareek, Tarik, Tariq, Taslim, Tawheed, Tawhid, Tayyib, Umar, Usamah, Wafeeq, Wafi, Wafiq, Waheeb, Wahib, Wajeed, Wajid, Waseem, Wasi, Wasim, Yaqub, Yaqut, Yasir, Yassir, Zafir, Zaheed, Zaheen, Zaheer, Zahid, Zahin, Zahir, Zameel, Zameer, Zamil, Zamir, Zareef, Zarif, Zayd

PORTUGUESE FEMALE NAMES

Agueda, Albertina, Benedicta, Bernarda, Brites, Caridad, Carlota, Constancia, Eduarda, Eliana, Elizabeta, Felipa, Fernanda, Fortunata, Francisca, Graca, Henriqua, Ines, Inez, Isabela, Joana, Joquina, Leonor, Madalena, Marta, Miguela, Neves, Priscila, Rosa, Rosita, Serafina, Vidonia

PORTUGUESE MALE NAMES

Alberto, Alexio, Alfonso, Alfredo, Angelo, Alvaro, Armando, Arnaldo, Augusto, Benedicto, Bento, Bernardo, Carlos, Cecilio, Clemente, Duarte, Edmundo, Eduardo, Felippe, Fernando, Fortunato, Francisco, Frederico, Gabrielo, Gilberto, Gregorio, Gustavo, Henrique, Herberto, Jacinto, Jaime, Jorge, Julio, Leonardo, Marcelo, Marcos, Mario, Matteus, Miguel, Modesto, Primo, Renato, Ricardo, Ronaldo, Santiago, Serafim, Silvino, Theodoro, Vicente, Vincente, Xavier

RUSSIAN FEMALE NAMES

Agafya, Agnessa, Akilina, Aleksandra, Alonya, Anastasia, Angela, Angelina, Anna, Annushka, Anya, Arina, Asya, Ayn, Darya, Diana, Dominika, Duscha, Ekaterina, Elena, Elizaveta, Elvira, Emma, Evelina, Gala, Galina, Georgina, Inessa, Irina, Ivanna, Izabella, Karina, Katerina, Katya, Khristina, Kira, Klara, Klementina, Kristina, Lara, Larisa, Lenora, Lieba, Liliya, Lubya, Ludmila, Luiza, Lyuba, Madina, Margarita, Marianna, Marina, Mariya, Marta, Marya, Masha, Misha, Nadya, Nataliya, Natalya, Natasha, Nika, Nina, Oksana, Olga, Olya, Polina, Rada, Raisa, Regina, Renata, Roksana, Roza, Sabina, Sasha, Sofiya, Sonya, Svetlana, Talya, Tamara, Tanya, Tasha, Tatiana, Tekla, Valentina, Valeriya, Vanya, Varvara, Vera, Veronika, Verusha, Vika, Viktoriya, Vita, Vonda, Yekaterina, Yelena, Yelizaveta, Yeva, Yuliya, Zaneta, Zhanna, Zina, Zlata, Zoya

RUSSIAN MALE NAMES

Abram, Adrian, Akim, Albert, Alek, Aleksei, Alexander, Alexei, Anatoly, Andrei, Anton, Arseni, Artur, Benedikt, Bogdan, Boris, Daniil, David, Denis, Dima, Dmitri, Dmitry, Dominik, Eduard, Efrem, Erik, Feliks, Fyodor, Georgi, Georgy, Grigori, Grigory, Igor, Isaak, Ivan, Kiril, Kirill, Kliment, Konstantin, Leo, Leonid, Lieb, Luka, Makar, Mark, Martin, Maxim, Mikhail, Miron, Misha, Moise, Nikita, Nikolai, Oleg, Pasha, Pavel, Pyotr, Radimir, Robert, Rolan, Sasha, Serafim, Sergei, Stepan, Vadim, Valentin, Vanya, Vasily, Viktor, Vitali, Vitaly, Vlad, Vladimir, Yakov, Yul, Yulian, Yuri

SCANDINAVIAN FEMALE NAMES

Ada, Adelina, Adriana, Agata, Agathe, Agna, Agnes, Alexandra, Alexis, Alicia, Alina, Amalia, Amanda, Amelia, Andrea, Anemone, Angela, Anika, Anina, Anita, Anja, Anke, Anna, Anne, Anneliese, Annelise, Annette, Annika, Anselma, Antonia, Arna, Asta, Astrid, Aud, Augusta, Augustine, Aurora, Barbara, Barbro, Beata, Benedikta, Bente, Bettie, Bettina, Betty, Birgit, Birgitta, Birgitte, Bodil, Brita, Britt, Britta, Camilla, Carina, Carita, Carol, Caroline, Catharina, Catherina, Cecilia, Celia, Charlotta, Christa, Christelle, Christina, Cilla, Cornelia, Crista, Cristine, Dagmar, Dagna, Dania, Daniela, Disa, Ebba, Ebbe, Edith, Eleonora, Elin, Elisabeth, Elise, Elke, Ella, Ellinor, Elsa, Emanuela, Emma, Erika, Ester, Eva, Evelina, Fredrika, Freja, Freya, Frida, Friede, Gerda, Gisela, Gitta, Gitte, Greta, Griet, Gudrun, Hanna, Hannah, Haralda, Hedda, Hedvig, Heide, Heidi, Helena, Helene, Helge, Henrika, Hilda, Hildegard, Hulda, Ilse, Inga, Inge, Ingrid, Irena, Irene, Irina, Irma, Ivonne, Janika, Janita, Janna, Janne, Jannike, Jensine, Johana, Johannna, Jonna, Josefa, Josefina, Judit, Judita, Judith, Julia, Juliana, Jutta, Kamilla, Kara, Karen, Kari, Karin, Karina, Karita, Karla, Karlotte, Karly, Karolina, Karoline, Katarina, Katarine, Katharina, Katja, Katje, Katrin, Katrina, Katrine, Kerstin, Kia, Kirsten, Klara, Kris, Krista, Kristen, Kristin, Kristina, Kristine, Laila, Lara, Laura, Lena, Lene, Liesa, Liese, Liesl, Linda, Linnea, Lisa, Lisbet, Lise, Liv, Lotta, Luise, Magda, Magdalena, Magdalene, Mai, Maja, Malena, Malin, Malou, Maren, Margaret, Margit, Maria, Marie, Marina, Marja, Marna, Marta, Marte, Martha, Marthe, Martina, Mathilde, Mia, Michaela, Mika, Mikaela, Milla, Monika, Nea, Nina, Nora, Oda, Ola, Olga, Olivia, Patricia, Paula, Petra, Petrine, Pia, Ragna, Rakel, Rebecka, Regina, Renate, Rita, Runa, Rut, Ruth, Sandra, Sanna, Sara, Selma, Sibylla, Signe, Signy, Sigrid, Sigrun, Siri, Sofia, Sofie, Sonja, Sunniva, Susanna, Susanne, Sylvia, Sylvie, Tea, Tekla, Teodora, Teresa, Therese, Thora, Tilda, Tilde, Tina, Tora, Tyra, Ulla, Ursula, Vanja, Vanna, Vega, Vera, Veronika, Viktoria, Vita, Vivi, Vivian, Wilhelmina, Yvonne

SCANDINAVIAN MALE NAMES

Adolf, Adrian, Aksel, Albert, Albrecht, Alex, Alexander, Alexis, Alf, Alfons, Alfred, Alvar, Anders, Andor, Andreas, Anton, Arne, Arno, Aron, Auden, August, Axel, Benedikt, Bente, Bernd, Bernhard, Bernt, Birger, Bjorn, Bo, Broder, Carl, Caspar, Chris, Christer, Christian, Claus, Dag, Daniel, David, Didrik, Dirk, Edvard, Egil, Eilif, Einar, Elias, Elof, Emanuel, Emil, Erik, Eugen, Filip, Frans, Fredrik, Frode, Gabriel, Garth, Georg, Gerard, Gerhard, Gerhardt, Gregor, Gustaf, Gustav, Hagen, Halle, Halsten, Halvard, Hans, Harald, Henrik, Igor, Ingmar, Ingvar, Isak, Ivar, Jakob, Jan, Jannik, Jens, Joakim, Johan, Johann, Johannes, Jorg, Jorgen, Josef, Karl, Kaspar, Kennet, Kim, Klaus, Knut, Konrad, Kort, Kris, Krister, Kristian, Kristofer, Kristoffer, Kristopher, Lars, Leif, Lennart, Leo, Lif, Lorens, Louis, Lukas, Magnus, Manfred, Marius, Mark, Markus, Martin, Mathias, Maximilian, Michael, Mikkel, Niels, Niklas, Nikolaus, Nils, Olaf, Olav, Oliver, Oskar, Otto, Paul, Peder, Ragnar, Ragnvald, Ralph,

Rasmus, Regin, Reine, Rikard, Roald, Robert, Roland, Rolf, Ruben, Rudolf, Salomon, Sander, Sigurd, Soren, Stefan, Steinar, Sten, Stephan, Stian, Stig, Sven, Tait, Teodor, Theodor, Thomas, Tobias, Tor, Torsten, Tove, Tyr, Ulf, Urban, Valentin, Victor, Viggo, Viktor, Vilhelm, Walter, Walther, Werner, Wilbert, Wilhelm

SCOTTISH FEMALE NAMES

Abi, Aileen, Ailene, Ailsa, Ainslee, Ainsley, Ainslie, Alexina, Alison, Bonnie, Bonny, Brenda, Cailin, Cait, Caldonia, Caitriona, Cameron, Carson, Catrina, Dallas, Davina, Donalda, Donella, Elspeth, Fenella, Finola, Fiona, Georgina, Gilda, Glenna, Greer, Iona, Isobel, Katriona, Keelin, Keitha, Kenna, Kiley, Kirstie, Kirstin, Kirsty, Kyla, Kylie, Lesley, Leslie, Lindsay, Lindsey, Logan, Lorna, MacKenzie, Mairead, Maisie, Malina, Malvina, Maura, Maxwell, Moira, Moyra, Nessa, Netta, Peigi, Rhona, Robina, Saundra, Seona, Shona, Sine, Sorcha, Triona

SCOTTISH MALE NAMES

Adair, Ainsley, Alan, Alasdair, Alastair, Alister, Angus, Aonghas, Archibald, Baird, Bruce, Caley, Callum, Calum, Cameron, Campbell, Carrick, Carson, Clyde, Coinneach, Craig, Dallas, Don, Donald, Donn, Doug, Douglas, Duncan, Evander, Ewan, Ewen, Fearghas, Fergus, Findlay, Findley, Fraser, Gavin, Gillean, Gillis, Gilroy, Glen, Glenn, Gordan, Gordon, Graham, Grant, Greer, Gregor, Guthrie, Hamish, Iain, Ian, Innes, Innis, Irvin, Irving, Ivor, Jamie, Jock, Keir, Keith, Kelvin, Ken, Kendrick, Kenneth, Kester, Knox, Kyle, Laird, Lamont, Leith, Lennox, Lesley, Leslie, Logan, Lorne, Mac, Mack, MacKenzie, Malcolm, Maxwell, Monroe, Montgomery, Munro, Munroe, Neal, Neil, Nevan, Nevin, Padraig, Peadar, Ramsay, Ramsey, Reed, Reid, Roderick, Ronald, Rory, Ross, Roy, Shaw, Sinclair, Stuart, Taven, Tavis, Tavish, Wallace

SPANISH FEMALE NAMES

Aarona, Abila, Abril, Ada, Adela, Adelina, Adelita, Adina, Adora, Adoracíon, Adriana, Ágata, Alameda, Alba, Alberta, Alegra, Alejandra, Aleta, Alicia, Alina, Alita, Alma, Almira, Alondra, Altagracia, Altagrazia, Alvera, Amada, Amalia, Amanda, Amelia, Amelina, Amora, Ana, Anabel, Anarosa, Angela, Angelina, Angelita, Anica, Anita, Antonia, Apolonia, Aquilina, Ariela, Aurora, Barbara, Beatriz, Belen, Belicia, Belita, Bella, Bellarosa, Benedicta, Benita, Bequita, Bernarda, Berta, Bertha, Betania, Bibiana, Blanca, Bona, Bonita, Brigida, Brisa, Calíope, Calista, Camila, Cande, Candelaria, Caparina, Caridad, Carina, Carisa, Carla, Carlota, Carmela, Carmelita, Carmen, Carmencita, Carolina, Catalina, Catarina, Catina, Cecilia, Celestina, Celia, Chela, Chelita, Clara, Clarisa, Claudia, Clemencia, Concepción, Conchita, Conseja, Constanza, Consuelo, Corazón, Cristal, Cristina, Damiana, Daniela, Davida, Débora, Destina, Diana, Dionisia, Dolores, Dominga, Dora, Dorita, Dorotea, Dulcinea, Elena, Eliana, Elisa, Elisabet, Elodia, Eloisa, Elvira, Ema, Emanuela, Emelina, Emilia, Emiliana, Enriqua, Epifania, Ernesta, Esmeralda, Esperanza, Estefanía, Estela, Ester, Estrella, Eugenia, Eulalia, Eva, Evangelina, Evita, Fabiola, Febe, Felicia, Felicidad, Felipa, Fernanda, Fidela, Filomena, Flavia, Flora, Fortunata, Francisca, Frida, Gabriela, Gilberta, Gisela, Graciana, Graciela, Guadalupe, Helena, Hermosa, Hilaria, Honoria, Hortensia, Ignacia, Imelda, Ina, Inés, Ireña, Iris, Irma, Isabela, Isidora, Jacaranda, Jacinta, Javiera, Jesenia, Jesúsa, Joaquina, Josefa, Josefina, Juana, Juanita, Judit, Julia, Julieta, Lara, Laura, Leandra, Leonor, Leticia, Lidia, Lilia, Liliana, Lina, Loída, Lola, Lolita, Lorena, Lourdes, Lucía, Luciana, Lucila, Lucinda, Luisa, Luna, Lupe, Luz, Macarena, Macaria, Madalena, Malena, Manuela, Maravilla, Marcela, Marcelina, Marcia, Margarita, María, Mariana, Maribel, Maricela, Marina, Marisa, Marisol, Maristela, Marita, Marta, Martina, Martita, Matilde, Maya, Melia, Melisa, Melita, Melodia,

Mercedes, Miguela, Milagros, Miranda, Modesta, Natalia, Nieves, Nita, Noemí, Nuria, Octavia, Ofelia, Olalla, Olimpia, Olivia, Pacífica, Paloma, Paola, Paquita, Pascuala, Pastora, Patricia, Paulina, Paz, Pepita, Perla, Perpetua, Petrona, Piedad, Pilar, Pili, Plácida, Primavera, Priscila, Quela, Rafaela, Ramira, Ramona, Raquel, Rebeca, Reina, Renata, Ricarda, Rita, Roberta, Rosa, Rosalia, Rosalinda, Rosana, Rosina, Rosita, Rubí, Rut, Sabela, Sabina, Sabrina, Samanta, Sanchia, Santana, Sara, Sarina, Sarita, Seferina, Selena, Sofía, Solana, Soledad, Sonia, Suelo, Susana, Tamara, Tea, Teodora, Teresa, Tierra, Tina, Tomasa, Trina, Trinidad, Valencia, Valentina, Valeria, Vega, Victoria, Violeta, Viona, Virginia, Viviana, Xaviera, Ximena, Yesenia, Ynez, Yolanda, Yrena, Zarita

SPANISH MALE NAMES

Abel, Abraham, Abrán, Adán, Adolfo, Alandro, Alano, Alberto, Aldo, Alejandro, Alejo, Alfonso, Alfredo, Alonso, Álvaro, Amado, Ambros, Andrés, Ángel, Angelo, Anselmo, Antonio, Aristo, Armando, Arnaldo, Arsenio, Arturo, Augustino, Augusto, Bartoli, Bartolomé, Basilio, Benedicto, Benito, Beño, Bernardino, Bernardo, Berto, Bruno, Carlito, Carlos, Carmelo, Cecilio, Celio, César, Che, Chico, Cirino, Cisco, Claudio, Clemente, Crisóforo, Cristián, Cristo, Cristóbal, Cuba, Damiano, Daniel, Danilo, Demetrio, Desi, Desiderio, Dezi, Diego, Dionisio, Diosdado, Domingo, Donaldo, Donato, Edmundo, Eduardo, Elias, Emanuel, Emilio, Enrique, Ernesto, Esteban, Eugenio, Fabio, Federico, Felipe, Felipo, Felix, Fernando, Fidel, Flavio, Fons, Fortunato, Francisco, Gabriel, Galeno, Gaspar, Geraldo, Gerardo, Gilberto, Goyo, Gregorio, Guillermo, Gustavo, Herberto, Hermán, Hernando, Hilario, Horacio, Hugo, Ignacio, Jacinto, Jacobo, Jaime, Javier, Jerónimo, Jesús, Joaquín, Jorge, José, Juan, Julio, Justino, Lalo, Lando, Leandro, Leo, Leonardo, Lobo, Lope, Lorencio, Lucas, Luis, Macario, Mando, Manny, Manolo, Manuel, Marcelo, Marcos, Martín, Martino, Mateo, Máximo, Mico, Miguel,

Milo, Modesto, Mundo, Nando, Nuncio, Octavio, Orlando, Óscar, Pablo, Pacífico, Paco, Pancho, Pascual, Patricio, Pedro, Pepe, Pepito, Plácido, Primo, Quino, Quique, Quito, Rafael, Raimundo, Ramiro, Ramón, Raúl, Reinaldo, Renato, Ricardo, Rico, Roberto, Rodolfo, Rodrigo, Rogelio, Rogério, Rolando, Roque, Sal, Salomon, Salvador, Samuelo, Sancho, Santiago, Seferino, Sergio, Silvano, Silvio, Tadeo, Teo, Teodoro, Tiago, Timoteo, Tino, Tito, Tomás, Toño, Trini, Trinidad, Valerio, Venturo, Vicente, Victor, Vidal, Vincente, Vito, Xavier, Ximenes, Zacarías

WELSH FEMALE NAMES

Aranrhod, Ariana, Bethan, Betsan, Branna, Branwen, Brisen, Bronwen, Bronwyn, Cari, Caron, Caryl, Caryll, Carys, Cate, Catrin, Celyn, Ceri, Ceridwen, Ceridwyn, Delwyn, Delyth, Derryth, Dilwyn, Dilys, Dylan, Eira, Eirwen, Elen, Elin, Eluned, Enid, Enida, Ermin, Glenda, Glenis, Glennis, Glynis, Guinevere, Gwen, Gwenda, Gwendolen, Gwendoline, Gwendolyn, Gweneal, Gweneth, Gwenyth, Gwyn, Isolde, Lewella, Llewella, Lowri, Luned, Marged, Mari, Meagan, Megan, Meghan, Meredith, Morgan, Morgana, Nia, Olwen, Olwyn, Owena, Piala, Rhian, Rhiannon, Rhonwen, Sabrina, Seren, Sian, Sioned, Tegan, Tegwen, Tirion, Winifred, Wynne

WELSH MALE NAMES

Alun, Alwyn, Andras, Arthur, Bevan, Beven, Bowen, Bran, Brice, Bryce, Bryn, Cadoc, Cai, Clyde, Collen, Dafydd, Dai, Drystan, Dylan, Evan, Gareth, Gawain, Geraint, Glyn, Griffith, Grigor, Gwayne, Huw, Iago, Ifan, Ilar, Ivor, Iwan, Kai, Kian, Lance, Llew, Llewelyn, Macsen, Macson, Maddox, Madoc, Merlin, Meredith, Mervin, Mervyn, Morgan, Owain, Pedr, Pryce, Rhys, Siôn, Tomas, Trefor, Trev, Trevor, Tristan, Vaughan, Vaughn, Wyn, Wynn

AFFIRMATION AUTHORS AND SOURCES

ABBEY, EDWARD (1929–89), American author

ABDU'L-BAHÁ (1844–1921), Persian theologian

ABIOLA, HAFSAT (b. 1974), Nigerian social reformer

ACKERMAN, DIANE (b. 1948), American author

ADAMS, GEORGE MATTHEW (1878–1962), American newspaper columnist

ADAMS, HENRY BROOKS (1838–1918), American journalist, historian, and author

ADAMS, JOHN (1735–1836), second US president

ADAMS, SCOTT (b. 1957), American cartoonist

ADAMS, THOMAS (1583–1653), English theologian

ADDISON, JOSEPH (1672–1719), English author and statesman

AELRED OF RIEVAULX (1110–67), English abbot and author

AESOP (c. 620–560 BCE), Greek moralist

AGUILAR, GRACE (1816–47), Jewish author

AITKEN, LARRY P. (dates unknown), Chippewa, founder of Leech Lake Tribal College (founded 1990)

AL-ADAWIYYA, RABIA (714–801), Sufi mystic and Muslim saint

AL-'ARABI, MUHYIDDIN IBN (1165–1240), Muslim mystic and author

ALBOM, MITCH (b. 1958), American author

ALCOTT, LOUISA MAY (1832–88), American author

ALDERMAN, EDWIN A. (1861–1931), American educator

ALEXANDER, CECIL FRANCES (1823–95), Irish poet and hymn writer

AL-GHAZALI (Abu amid Muammad ibn Muammad al-Ghazali, 1058–1111), Muslim theologian, jurist, philosopher, and mystic

AL-HALLAJ, MANSUR (Abi al-Mu i Husayn Manur al-Hallag, c. 858–922), Sufi mystic and author

ALI, MUHAMMAD (b. 1942), American boxer

ALIGHIERI, DANTE (1265–1321), Italian poet

ALLEN, JAMES (1864–1912), English author

AMBROSE, ST. (Aurelius Ambrosius, 340–397), bishop of Milan and saint

AMIEL, HENRI FRÉDÉRIC (1821–81), Swiss philosopher

ANAYA, RUDOLFO (b. 1946), Mexican-American author

ANDERSEN, HANS CHRISTIAN (1805–75), Danish author

ANDREWS, TED (1952–2009), American author

ANGELA OF FOLIGNO (1248–1309), Christian mystic

ANGELOU, MAYA (1928–2014), American author and activist

ANOUILH, JEAN (1910–87), French dramatist

APOLLINAIRE, GUILLAUME (1880–1918), French author

AQUINAS, THOMAS (1225–74), Christian theologian

ARCHIMEDES (c. 287–212 BCE), Greek mathematician

ARENDT, HANNAH (1906–75), German-born American philosopher and author

ARETINO, PIETRO (1492–1556), Italian author

ARISTOTLE (384–322 BCE), Greek philosopher

ARMSTRONG, NEIL (1930–2012), American astronaut

ARNE, THOMAS AUGUSTINE (1710–78), English composer

ARNIM, LUDWIG ACHIM VON (1781–1831), German author

ARNOLD, MATTHEW (1822–88), English author

ARNOLD, THOMAS (1795–1842), English educator and historian

ASCH, SHOLEM (1880–1957), American author

ASTELL, MARY (1666–1731), English author

ATHARVA VEDA (c. 1500–1000 BCE), Hindu sacred text

AUERBACH, BERTHOLD (1812–82), German-Jewish poet and author

AUGUSTINE OF HIPPO (Aurelius Augustinus Hipponensis, 354–430), Roman Catholic theologian and saint

AURELIUS, MARCUS (c. 570–475 BCE), Roman emperor

AUROBINDO, SRI (Ôrobindo Ghosh, 1872–1950), Indian activist, philosopher, yogi, guru, and poet

BAAL SHEM TOV (Yisroel ben Eliezer, 1698–1760), founder of Hasidic Judaism

BABA KUHI OF SHIRAZ (c. 980–1050), Sufi poet

BABYLONIAN TALMUD (c. 500), Hebrew religious text

BACALL, LAUREN (b. 1924), American actress

BACON, FRANCIS (1561–1626), English philosopher, statesman, scientist, jurist, and author

BAECK, LEO (1873–1956), Jewish rabbi

BAHU, SULTAN (Punjabi Bahoo, 1628–91), Muslim sufi and founder of the Sarwari Qadiri Sufi Order

BAILEY, PHILIP JAMES (1816–1902), English author

BAKER, KARLE WILSON (1878–1960), American poet

BALFOUR, ARTHUR (1848–1930), British prime minister

BALFOUR, CLARA (1808–78), English temperance leader

BALGUY, JOHN (1686–1748), English clergyman and philosopher

BALLOU, HOSEA (1771–1852), American Universalist theologian

BALTHASAR, HANS URS VON (1905–88), Christian theologian

BALZAC, HONORÉ DE (1799–1850), French author

BANCROFT, GEORGE (1800–91), American historian and statesman

BANGS, ED (dates unknown), wolf recovery coordinator (from 1988–2011), US Fish & Wildlife Service

BANKS, DENNIS (b. 1937), Objiwe activist and author

BARBOUR, JOHN (1320–95), Scottish poet

BARCA, PEDRO CALDERÓN DE LA (1600–81), Spanish dramatist and poet

BARRIE, JAMES M. (1860–1937), Scottish author and dramatist

BARTON, CLARA (1821–1912), American nurse

BARUCH, SHNEUR ZALMAN BEN (1747–1812), Jewish Orthodox rabbi

BASHŌ, MATSUO (1644–94), Japanese poet

BASIL OF CAESAREA, ST. (330–379), Eastern Orthodox bishop and saint

BAUDELAIRE, CHARLES (1821–67), French author

BEARD, CHARLES (1874–1948), American historian and economist

BEAUVOIR, SIMONE DE (1908–86), French existentialist, philosopher, feminist, and author

BECKETT, SAMUEL (1906–89), Irish dramatist

BEECHER, HENRY WARD (1813–87), social reformer and abolitionist

BEETHOVEN, LUDWIG VAN (1770–1827), German composer

BEGIN, MENACHEM (1913–92), prime minister of Israel

BENEDICT, POPE (Joseph Ratzinger, Sr. b. 1927), Roman Catholic pope

BEN-GURION, DAVID (1886–1973), Israeli statesman

BENJAMIN, PARK (1809–64), American poet, editor, and journalist

BERGSON, HENRI-LOUIS (1859–1941), French philosopher and Nobel Laureate

BERKELEY, GEORGE (1685–1753), English philosopher

BERNANOS, GEORGES (1888–1948), French author

BERNARD OF CLAIRVAUX (1090–1153), French Catholic abbot and saint

BERNSTEIN, LEONARD (1918–90), American composer

BERRA, YOGI (b. 1925), American baseball player

BERRY, THOMAS (1914–2009), Catholic priest

BESANT, ANNIE (1847–1933), English activist

BESTON, HENRY (1888–1968), American author and naturalist

BHAGAVAD GITA (c. 400 BCE), Hindu religious text

BISSET, JACQUELINE (b. 1944), English actress

BLACK ELK, WALLACE (1863–1950), Oglala Sioux holy man

BLAKE, WILLIAM (1757–1827), English poet, painter, and printmaker

BLASS, BILL (1922–2002), American fashion designer

BOILEAU-DESPRÉAUX, NICOLAS (1636–1711), French author

BOISTE, PIERRE-CLAUDE-VICTOR (1765–1824), French lexicographer

BOLTON, SARAH KNOWLES (1841–1916), American author

BORLAND, HAL (1900–78), American author

BOVEE, CHRISTIAN NESTELL (1820–1904), American author

BOYLE, HAL (1911–74), American columnist and Pulitzer Prize winner

BRADLEY, MARION ZIMMER (1930–99), American author

BRADLEY, OMAR (1893–1981), American general

BRADLEY, PRESTON (1888–1983), American clergyman

"BREASTPLATE OF ST. PATRICK" (c. 8th century), Irish hymn attributed to St. Patrick from the fifth century

BRIHADARANYAKA UPANISHAD (c. 1400–800 BCE), Hindu sacred text

BRONTË, EMILY (1818–48), English author and poet

BROOKS, PHILLIPS (1835–93), American clergyman

BROTHERS, JOYCE (1927–2013), American psychologist

BROWN, JOHN MASON (1900–69), American drama critic and author

BROWN, THOMAS EDWARD (1830–97), Scottish author

BROWNE, THOMAS (1605–82), English author and polymath

BROWNING, ELIZABETH BARRETT (1806–61), English poet

BROWNING, ROBERT (1812–89), English poet

BRUYÈRE, JEAN DE LA (1645–96), French author

BRYAN, WILLIAM JENNINGS (1860–1925), American statesman

BRYANT, WILLIAM CULLEN (1794–1878), American poet, journalist, and editor

BRYDGES, SAMUEL EGERTON (1762–1837), English author

BUBER, MARTIN (1878–1965), Jewish philosopher

BUCK, PEARL S. (1892–1973), American author and Nobel Laureate

BUDDHA (Siddhartha Guatama, c. 563–483 BCE), Indian prince, mystic, founder of Buddhism

BUECHNER, FREDERICK (b. 1926), American theologian

BULWER-LYTTON, EDWARD (1803–73), English author and playwright

BUNNER, HENRY CUYLER (1855–96), American poet

BUNZEL, RUTH (1898–1990), anthropologist and Zuni scholar

BURBANK, LUTHER (1849–1926), American botanist

BURKE, EDMUND (1729–97), English philosopher and statesman

BURNS, ROBERT (1759–96), Scottish poet

BURROUGHS, JEREMIAH (c. 1600–46), English clergyman

BURROUGHS, JOHN (1837–1921), American naturalist and essayist

BURTON, JIMALEE (b. 1920), Cherokee author

BURTON, ROBERT (1577–1640), English scholar

BUSCAGLIA, LEO (1924–98), American author

BUXTON, CHARLES ROBERT (1823–71), English philanthropist

BYRON, LORD (George Gordon Byron, 1788–1824), English poet

CADDY, EILEEN (1916–2006), Scottish spiritual leader

CAECUS, APPIUS CLAUDIUS (4th–3rd c. BCE), Roman statesman

CAEN, HERB (1916–97), American journalist

CALVIN, JOHN (1509–64), Christian theologian

CAMERON, JULIA (b. 1948), American author and artist

CAMPBELL, JOSEPH (1904–87), American mythologist and educator

CAMPBELL, THOMAS (1801–48), American painter

CAMUS, ALBERT (1913–60), French author, journalist, philosopher, and Nobel Laureate

CAPEK, KAREL (1890–1938), Czech author

CARLYLE, THOMAS (1795–1881), Scottish author

CARMICHAEL, ALEXANDER (1832–1912), Scottish folklorist

CARNEGIE, DALE (1888–1955), American author and lecturer

CARNEY, JULIA FLETCHER (1823–1908), American poet

CARROLL, LEWIS (Charles Lutwidge Dodgson, 1832–89), English author, logician, and photographer

CARSON, RACHEL (1907–64), American marine biologist and conservationist

CARVER, GEORGE WASHINGTON (1864–1943), American scientist, botanist, and inventor

CASALS, PABLO (1876–1973), Spanish cellist and conductor

CASTAÑEDA, CARLOS (1925–98), Peruvian-American author

CATHER, WILLA (1873–1947), American author

CATHERINE OF SIENA (1347–80), Catholic saint

CAUSSADE, JEAN PIERRE DE (1675–1751), French Jesuit priest and author

CERVANTES, MIGUEL DE (1547–1616), Spanish author, poet, and playwright

CHALMERS, THOMAS (1780–1847), Scottish clergyman

CHANDOGYA UPANISHAD (c. 1400–800 BCE), Hindu sacred text

CHANNING, WILLIAM ELLERY (1780–1842), American clergyman

CHAPIN, EDWIN HUBBELL (1814–80), American clergyman

CHAPMAN, ARTHUR (1837–1935), American poet

CHAPMAN, GEORGE (c. 1559–1634), English dramatist and poet

CHARDIN, PIERRE TEILHARD DE (1881–1955), French Jesuit priest, theologian, and paleontologist

CHATEAUBRIAND, FRANÇOIS-RENÉ DE (1768–1848), French author and statesman

CHEKHOV, ANTON (1860–1904), Russian author

CHESTERFIELD, LORD (Philip Stanhope, 1694–1773), English statesman

CHESTERTON, G.K. (Gilbert Keith, 1874–1936), English essayist and poet

CHILD, LYDIA MARIA (1802–80), American abolitionist and activist

CHOATE, RUFUS (1799–1859), American attorney

CHOPIN, KATE (1851–1904), American author

CHOPRA, DEEPAK (b. 1947), American author

CHRYSOSTOM, JOHN (347–407), archbishop of Constantinople

CHURCHILL, WINSTON (1874–1965), British prime minister

CICERO, MARCUS TULLIUS (106–43 BCE), Roman statesman

CLARKE, JAMES FREEMAN (1810–88), American clergyman

CLAUDIUS, MATTHIAS (1740–1815), German poet

CLAUSEWITZ, CARL VON (1780–1831), Prussian military theorist

CLAY, HENRY (1777–1852), American statesman

COCHISE (c. 1812–74), Chiricahua Apache chief

COELHO, PAULO (b. 1947), Brazilian author

COKE, EDWARD (1552–1634), English judge

COLERIDGE, HARTLEY (1796–1849), English author

COLERIDGE, SAMUEL TAYLOR (1772–1834), English poet and philosopher

COLLINS, MARVA (b. 1936), American Civil Rights activist

COLMAN, GEORGE, THE YOUNGER (1762–1836), English dramatist

COMMANDA, WILLIAM (Anishinàbe, 1913–2011), Algonguin spiritual leader

CONFUCIUS (551–479 BCE), Chinese philosopher

CONGREVE, WILLIAM (1670–1729), English playwright and poet

CONRAD, JOSEPH (Jozef Teodor Konrad Korzeniowski, 1857–1924), Polish-English author

CONSTABLE, HENRY (1562–1613), English poet

COOLIDGE, CALVIN (1872–1933), thirtieth US president

COOPER, SUSAN FENIMORE (1813–94), American author

CORNEILLE, PIERRE (1606–84), French dramatist

COSELL, HOWARD (1918–95), American sports journalist

COUSTEAU, JACQUES-YVES (1910–97), French undersea explorer and conservationist

COVEY, STEPHEN (b. 1932), American author

COWLEY, ABRAHAM (1618–67), English poet

COWPER, WILLIAM (1731–1800), English poet

CRAZY HORSE (Tashunkewitko, 1840–77), Lakota Sioux chief

CRISLER, LOIS (1940–73), American author

DAHL, ROALD (b. 1954), Welsh-born English author

DAISHONIN, NICHIREN (1222–82), Japanese Buddhist monk

DALAI LAMA, THE (Tenzin Gyatso, b. 1935), His Holiness the 14th Dalai Lama of Tibet

DAVIES, JOHN (baptized 1569–1626), English poet

DEMOCRITUS (c. 460–370 BCE), Greek philosopher

DICKENS, CHARLES (1819–70), English author

DICKINSON, EMILY (1830–86), American poet

DIDEROT, DENIS (1713–84), French philosopher

DISRAELI, BENJAMIN (1804–81), British prime minister

DIXON, RICHARD W. (1833–1900), English poet and theologian

DOBELL, SYDNEY (1818–89), English poet

DODSLEY, ROBERT (1704–64), English author

DOLE, ELIZABETH (b. 1936), American stateswoman

DONNE, JOHN (1572–1631), English poet and clergyman

DORRIS, MICHAEL (1945–97), American author

DOSTOEVSKY, FYODOR (1821–81), Russian author

DOUGLAS, WILLIAM O. (1898–1980), American Supreme Court justice

DOUGLASS, FREDERICK (1817–95), American social reformer, statesman, and author

DOV BAER OF MEZERITCH (c. 1704–72), Jewish Hasidic rabbi

DRUMMOND, HENRY (1851–97), Scottish clergyman and author

DUBOIS, W.E.B. (William Edward Burghardt, 1865–1963), American educator

DUFY, RAOUL (1877–1953), French painter

DUNBAR, WILLIAM (1465–1536), Scottish poet

DUNCAN, ISADORA (1877–1927), American dancer

DUNCOMBE, LEWIS (1711–30), English author

DURANT, WILLIAM JAMES (1885–1981), American historian, philosopher, and author

DUSE, ELEONORA (1884–1962), Italian actress

DYER, WAYNE (b. 1940), American author

DYKE, HENRY VAN (1852–1933), American author, educator, and clergyman

EARHART, AMELIA (1898–1937), American aviator

EARL OF SHAFTESBURY (Anthony Ashley-Cooper, 1671–1713), English statesman, philanthropist, and social reformer

EARLE, SYLVIA (b. 1935), American oceanographer

EBNER-ESCHENBACH, MARIE VON (1830–1916), Austrian author

ECKHART, MEISTER (1260–1328), Christian mystic

EDDY, MARY BAKER (1821–1910), founder of Christian Science

EDWARDS, AMELIA B. (1831–92), English author

EDWARDS, JONATHAN (1703–58), American theologian

EHRMANN, MAX (1872–1945), American author

EINSTEIN, ALBERT (1879–1955), German-American physicist and Nobel Laureate

ELIOT, CHARLES W. (1834–1926), American educator

ELIOT, GEORGE (Mary Ann Evans, 1819–80), English author

ELIOT, T.S. (Thomas Stearns Eliot, 1888–1965), English poet, playwright, and Nobel Laureate

ELIZABETH I (1558–1603), Queen of England

ELLISON, RALPH (1914–94), American novelist

ELOHAI NESHAMA (dates unknown), Jewish morning prayer

EMERSON, RALPH WALDO (1803–82), American author, poet, and philosopher

ENGELBREIT, MARY (b. 1952), American artist and editor

EPICTETUS (c. 55–135), Greek philosopher

ERASMUS (1466–1536), Dutch philosopher

ESTÉS, CLARISSA PINKOLA (b. 1945), American author and psychoanalyst

EURIPIDES (c. 480–406 BCE), Greek dramatist

EVELYN, JOHN (1620–1706), English author

EZRA, MOSES BEN IBN (c. 1055–1135), Jewish philosopher and poet

FAULKNER, WILLIAM (1897–1962), American author and Nobel Laureate

FEYNMAN, RICHARD (1918–88), Jewish-American physicist and Nobel Laureate

FLAUBERT, GUSTAVE (1812–80), French author

FLEMING, PAUL (1609–40), German poet and physician

FLETCHER, GILES (c. 1586–1623), English poet

FLETCHER, JOHN (1579–1625), English dramatist

FOCH, FERDINAND (1851–1929), French military theorist

FORBES, B.C. (Bertie Charles, 1880–1954), American founder of *Forbes Magazine*

FORSTER, E.M. (1879–1970), English author

FOSDICK, HARRY EMERSON (1878–1969), American clergyman

FOSS, SAM WALTER (1858–1911), American poet

FOX, EMMET (1886–1951), American theologian

FOX, MATTHEW (b. 1940), Christian theologian

FRANCIS, DIANA (1961–97), Princess of Wales

FRANCIS, POPE (Jorge Mario Bergoglio, b. 1936), Roman Catholic pope

FRANCIS OF ASSISI, ST. (Giovanni Francesco di Bernardone, 1182–1226), founder of the Catholic Franciscan Order and saint

FRANK, ANNE (1929–44), German diarist

FRANKL, VIKTOR (1905–97), Austrian psychiatrist and neurologist

FRANKLIN, BENJAMIN (1706–90), American statesman, scientist, and inventor

FREUD, ANNA (1895–1982), Austrian psychoanalyst

FROMM, ERICH (1900–80), German-born American psychologist and psychoanalyst

FROST, ROBERT (1874–1963), American poet

FRY, HAYDEN (b. 1929), American football coach

FULLER, THOMAS (1608–61), English clergyman and author

FUSELI, HENRY (1741–1825), English painter

GABIROL, SOLOMON IBN (c. 1021–58), Jewish philosopher

GAERTNER, JOHANNES (1912–96), German-Amercian poet and theologian

GALLIENNE, RICHARD LE (1866–1947), English author

GANDHI, INDIRA (1917–84), second prime minister of India

GANDHI, MAHATMA (Mohandas Karamchand, 1869–1948), first prime minister of India, spiritual leader, and activist

GARDINER, MARGUERITE (1789–1849), Irish author

GARFIELD, JAMES A. (1831–81), twentieth US president

GARRETT, GEORGE (1929–2008), American author

GATES, BILL (b. 1955), American businessman

GAULLE, CHARLES DE (1890–1970), French general and statesman

GAUTIER, THÉOPHILE (1811–72), French poet, dramatist, and novelist

GENEEN, HAROLD (1910–97), American businessman

GEORGE, DAN (1899–1981), Salish chief, author, poet, and actor

GERONIMO (Goyathlay, 1829–1909), Chircahua Apache chief

GESNER, KONRAD VON (1516–65), Swiss naturalist

GESSNER, SALOMON (1730–88), Swiss painter and poet

GHOSE, SRI CHINMOY (1931–2007), Hindu spiritual teacher

GIBRAN, KAHLIL (1893–1931), Lebanese-American author, artist, and poet

GILBERT, HUMPHREY (c. 1537–83), English navigator and statesman

GILPIN, LAURA (1891–1979), American photographer

GIOCONDO, FRA GIOVANNI (c. 1433–1515), Italian architect and scholar

GISSING, GEORGE (1857–1903), English author

GLADSTONE, WILLIAM EWART (1809–98), English prime minister

GOETHE, JOHANN WOLFGANG VON (1749–1832), German author, statesman, and philosopher

GOGH, VINCENT VAN (1853–90), Dutch painter

GOLDMAN, EMMA (1869–1940), American international activist

GOLDSMITH, OLIVER (1728–74), Anglo-Irish author, playwright, and poet

GOOD, JOHN MASON (1764–1827), English author

GORBACHEV, RAISA (1932–99), first lady of the USSR

GORDON, AARON DAVID (1856–1922), Jewish Zionist leader

GRACIAN, BALTASAR (1601–58), Spanish author

GRAHAM, MARTHA (1894–1991), American choreographer

GRAYSON, DAVID (Ray Stannard Baker, 1870–1946), American journalist

GREGORY THE GREAT (c. 540–604), Roman Catholic pope

GRISWOLD, ALFRED WHITNEY (1906–63), American historian and educator

GURNEY, DOROTHY (1858–1932), English poet and hymnwriter

HADITH OF THE PROPHET MUHAMMAD (c. 570–770), collected oral traditions

HAFIZ (Shams al-Din Muhammad Hafez-e Shirazi, c. 1320–89), Persian mystic and poet

HAHN-HAHN, COUNTESS IDA VON (1805–80), German author

HALE, EDWARD EVERETT (1822–1909), American clergyman

HAMMARSKJÖLD, DAG (1905–61), Swedish diplomat, economist, author, and Nobel Laureate

HAN SHAN (c. 730–850), Chinese poet

HAO, CH'ENG (1032–85), Chinese philosopher

HARGRAVE, FRANCIS (c. 1741–1821), English attorney

HART, JOSEPHINE (1942–2011), Irish author and theatrical producer

HART, MICKEY (b. 1943), American musician

HAUGHEY, CHARLES (1925–2006), Irish prime minister

HAWKING, STEPHEN (b. 1942), American physicist

HAWTHORNE, NATHANIEL (1804–64), American author

HAZLITT, WILLIAM (1778–1830), English essayist

HEINE, HEINRICH (1797–1856), German poet

HEMINGWAY, ERNEST (1898–1961), American author

HENLEY, WILLIAM ERNEST (1849–1903), English poet and editor

HENRI, ROBERT (1865–1929), American painter

HENRY, PATRICK (1736–99), American statesman

HERBERT, GEORGE (1593–1633), Anglican-Welsh poet and Anglican priest

HERODOTUS (c. 484–425 BCE), Greek philosopher

HERRICK, ROBERT (1591–1674), English poet

HERSCHEL, JOHN (1792–1871), English astronomer

HERZL, THEODOR (1860–1904), founder of modern Zionism

HESCHEL, ABRAHAM (1907–72), Jewish theologian

HESIOD (c. 750–650 BCE), Greek poet

HESSE, HERMANN (1877–1962), German-Swiss poet and author

HEVAJRA TANTRA (8th century), Buddhist text

HEYWOOD, JOHN (c. 1497–1580), English author

HILDEGARD OF BINGEN (1098–1179), Christian mystic

HILLMAN, JAMES (1926–2011), American psychologist

HOFFER, ERIC (1902–83), American philosopher

HOFFMANN, E. T. A. (Ernst Theodor Wilhelm, 1776–1822), German author and composer

HOFMANN, HANS (1880–1966), German-born American painter

HOLLOWAY, RICHARD (b. 1933), Scottish priest and author

HOLMES, ERNEST (1887–1960), American author

HOLMES, OLIVER WENDELL, JR. (1841–1935), US Supreme Court justice

HOLMES, OLIVER WENDELL, SR. (1809–94), American poet, physician, and author

HOMER (c. 800–700 BCE), Greek poet

HOOD, THOMAS (1799–1845), English poet

HOOVER, HERBERT (1874–1964), thirty-first US president

HOPKINS, GERARD MANLEY (1844–89), Jesuit priest and poet

HORACE (65–8 BCE), Roman poet

HOWITT, MARY (1799–1888), English poet

HUBBARD, ELBERT (1856–1915), American author and philosopher

HUGHES, LANGSTON (1902–67), American poet, activist, and playwright

HUGHES, THOMAS (1822–96), English author

HUGO, VICTOR (1802–85), French author

HUME, TOBIAS (c. 1569–1645), Scottish composer

HUMPHREY, HUBERT (1911–78), thirty-eighth US vice president

HUNT, LEIGH (1784–1859), English poet

HUXLEY, THOMAS HENRY (1825–95), English biologist and educator

IBSEN, HENRIK (1828–1906), Norwegian dramatist

I CHING: THE BOOK OF CHANGES (3rd and 2nd centuries BCE), Chinese classic text

IGNATIUS OF LOYOLA (1491–1556), Catholic theologian, founder of Jesuit Order, and saint

IKEDA, DAISAKU (b. 1928), president of Soka Gakkai International Buddism

INGE, WILLIAM RALPH (1860–1954), English theologian

INGERSOLL, ROBERT GREEN (1833–99), American statesman

IQBAL, MUHAMMAD (1877–1938), Muslim poet and philosopher

IRANAEUS (c. 130–201), Catholic Church father

IRVING, WASHINGTON (1783–1859), American author, historian, and statesman

ISAAC OF NINEVEH (d. c. 700), Eastern Orthodox bishop and theologian

ISA UPANISHAD (c. 1400–800 BCE), Hindu sacred text

ISSA (1763–1827), Japanese haiku poet

JACKSON, GLENDA (b. 1936), English politician and actress

JAMES, HENRY (1843–1916), American author

JAMES, WILLIAM (1842–1910), American psychologist and philosopher

JAMESON, ANNA (1794–1860), English author

JARMAN, DEREK (1942–94), English artist

JEFFERSON, THOMAS (1743–1826), third US president

JEKYLL, GERTRUDE (1843–1932), English horticulturist

JERROLD, DOUGLAS WILLIAM (1803–57), English dramatist

JOHN II, POPE (Karol Woljtyla, 1920–2005), Roman Catholic pope

JOHN OF THE CROSS, ST. (Juan de Yepes Alvarez, 1542–91), Catholic mystic and saint

JOHNSON, LADY BIRD (Claudia Alta Taylor, 1912–2007), American first lady

JOHNSON, SAMUEL (1709–84), English author, poet, editor, and lexicographer

JOHNSON, SONIA (b. 1936), American activist

JOLY, JOHN (1857–1933), Irish physicist

JONSON, BEN (1572–1637), English poet and dramatist

JOUBERT, JOSEPH (1754–1824), French essayist

JULIAN OF NORWICH (1342–1416), Christian mystic

JUMPING BULL (d. 1890), Hunkpapa Sioux war leader

JUNG, CARL (1875–1961), Swiss psychologist and psychiatrist

JUVENAL (c. 60–130), Roman satirist

KAFKA, FRANZ (1883–1924), Austrian author

KANT, IMMANUEL (1724–1804), German philosopher

KALIDASA (c. 5th century), Hindu Sanskrit poet and dramatist

KAPI'OLANI, QUEEN (1834–99), queen of Hawaii

KATHA UPANISHAD (c. 1400–800 BCE), Hindu religious text

KEATS, JOHN (1795–1821), English poet

KELLER, HELEN (1880–1968), American author and activist

KEMPIS, THOMAS À (c. 1380–1471), Christian monk and author

KEN, THOMAS (1637–1711), English bishop

KENA UPANISHAD (c. 1400–800 BCE), Hindu religious text

KENNEDY, JOHN F. (1919–63), thirty-fifth US president

KENNEDY, ROBERT F. (1925–68), US attorney general

KENYATTA, JOMO (1889–1978), first president of Kenya

KEOKUK (1767–1848), Sauk chief

KEROUAC, JACK (1922–69), American author

KETTERING, CHARLES F. (1876–1958), American inventor

KHAN, HAZRAT INAYAT (1882–1927), founder of the Universal Sufi Movement

KILMER, JOYCE (Alfred Joyce Kilmer, 1886–1918), American author and poet

KING, MARTIN LUTHER, JR. (1929–68), American clergyman, civil rights activist, and author

KINGSLEY, CHARLES (1819–75), English clergyman and author

KIPLING, RUDYARD (1865–1936), English author and poet

KISSINGER, HENRY (b. 1923), American statesman Nobel Laureate

KLEIN, ABRAHAM MOSES (1909–72), Jewish-Canadian poet

KNEBEL, KARL LUDWIG VON (1744–1834), German poet

KO-JI-KI (c. 500 CE), Hachiman Kasuga of the Shinto tradition

KOOK, ABRAHAM ISAAC (1864–1935), Jewish rabbi

KORDA, MICHAEL (b. 1933), English author

KORNFIELD, JACK (b. 1945), American Buddhist monk and author

KRISHNAMURTI, JIDDU (1896–1986), Indian philosopher and author

KROC, RAY (1902–84), American businessman

KRUGER, PAUL (1825–1904), South African statesman

KÜBLER-ROSS, ELISABETH (1926–2004), American psychiatrist

KUSHNER, HAROLD (b. 1935), American rabbi

LAMARTINE, ALPHONSE DE (1790–1869), French author

LAMB, CHARLES (1775–1834), English essayist

LAME DEER, JOHN (Fire, 1903–76), Lakota Sioux elder

LANDON, L. E. (Letitia Elizabeth Landon, 1802–38), English poet

LANDOR, WALTER SAVAGE (1775–1864), English author

LARCOM, LUCY (1826–93), American poet

LARSEN, JACK LENOR (b. 1927), American designer

LAW, WILLIAM (1686–1761), English theologian

LAWRENCE, D. H. (David Herbert, 1885–1930), English poet

LEC, STANISLAW (1909–66), Polish poet and aphorist

LEE, NATHANIEL (1655–92), English dramatist

LE GUIN, URSULA K. (b. 1929), American author

LEMARINE, ALPHONSE DE (1790–1869), French author

L'ENCLOS, NINON DE (1620–1705), French author

L'ENGLE, MADELEINE (1918–2007), American author

LESSING, GOTTHOLD EPHRAIM (1729–81), German philosopher and author

LETAKOTS-LESA (Eagle Chief, dates unknown), Pawnee chief

LEWIS, SINCLAIR (1885–1951), American author

LEYDEN, JOHN (1775–1811), Scottish poet

LINCOLN, ABRAHAM (1809–65), sixteenth US president

LINCOLN, VICTORIA (1904–81), American author

LINNÉ, CARL VON (1707–78), Swedish botanist

LLEWELLYN, RICHARD (1907–83), Welsh author

LOBEL, ARNOLD (1933–87), American author

LOMBARDI, VINCE (1913–70), American football coach

LONDON, JACK (John Griffith Chaney, 1875–1916), American author

LONERGAN, BERNARD (1904–84), Catholic priest, philosopher, and theologian

LONGFELLOW, HENRY WADSWORTH (1807–82), American poet

LOOKING HORSE, ARVOL (b. 1954), Hopi elder

LOPE DE VEGA (Félix Arturo Lope de Vega y Carpio, 1562–1635), Spanish playwright and poet

LOPEZ, BARRY (b. 1945), American author

LOREN, SOPHIA (b. 1934), Italian actress

LOVELACE, RICHARD (1618–57), English poet

LOWELL, JAMES RUSSELL (1819–91), American poet, editor, and diplomat

LUBBOCK, JOHN (1834–1913), English statesman and naturalist

LUCE, CLARE BOOTHE (1902–87), American playwright and diplomat

LUCRETIUS (Titus Lucretius Carus, c. 99–55 BCE), Roman poet and philosopher

LUTHER, MARTIN (1483–1546), Christian theologian

MA, SRI ANANDAMAYI (1896–1982), Hindu guru and saint

MAATHAI, WANGARI (1940–2011), Kenyan activist and Nobel Laureate

MABIE, HAMILTON (1845–1916), American author

MACARTHUR, DOUGLAS (1880–1964), American general

MACHETANZ, FRED (1908–2002), American painter

MACLEAN, NORMAN (1902–90), American author

MACLEOD, FIONA (William Sharp, 1855–1905), Scottish writer and poet

MAHABHARATA, THE (c. 8th and 9th centuries BCE), Hindu sacred text

MAHAPARINIBBANA SUTTA (c. 2nd century), Buddhist scripture

MAILER, NORMAN (1923–2007), American author and playwright

MAIMONIDES (Mosheh ben Maimon, 1135–1204), Jewish rabbi, philosopher, physician, and Torah scholar

MALRAUX, ANDRÉ (1901–76), French statesman and author

MANDELA, NELSON (1918–2013), South African activist and president

MANKUKYA UPANISHAD (c. 1400–800 BCE), Hindu sacred text

MANN, HORACE (1796–1859), American educator

MANN, THOMAS (1875–1955), German author and Nobel Laureate

MANSFIELD, LORD (William Murray, 1705–93), English judge

MANUEL, DON JUAN (1282–1348), Spanish author

MARDEN, ORISON SWETT (1850–1924), American author

MARE, WALTER DE LA (1873–1956), English poet and author

MARGOLIUS, HANS (1902–84), American philosopher and author

MARLOWE, CHRISTOPHER (1564–93), English dramatist and poet

MARTIN, AIMÉ (1781–1844), French author

MARVELL, ANDREW (1621–78), English poet

MASSINGER, PHILIP (1583–1640), English dramatist

MATISSE, HENRI (1869–1954), French artist

MAUGHAM, W. SOMERSET (1874–1965), English author

MAURIAC, FRANÇOIS (1885–1970), French author

MAXWELL, JOHN C. (b. 1947), Christian clergyman and author

McWHORTER, LUCULLUS VIRGIL (1860–1944), American frontiersman and scholar

MEAD, MARGARET (1901–78), American anthropologist

MELVILLE, HERMAN (1819–91), American author

MENCIUS (372–289 BCE), Chinese philosopher

MENDELSSOHN, MOSES (1729–86), Jewish philosopher

MENELIK II (1844–1913), emperor of Ethiopia

MERTON, THOMAS (1915–68), Roman Catholic mystic, monk, and author

METHOATASKE (1768–1813), Creek, mother of Techumseh

METTA SUTTA (c. 563–483 BCE), Buddhist text

MEYNELL, ALICE (1847–1922), English author and suffragist

MICHELANGELO (1475–1564), Renaissance sculptor and painter

MIDRASH (dates unknown), Homiletic teachings of the Hebrew Bible

MILLER, HENRY (1891–1980), American author and poet

MILLMAN, DAN (b. 1946), American author

MILLS, ENOS A. (1870–1922), founder of Rocky Mountain National Park

MILTON, JOHN (1608–74), English poet

MOMADAY, N. SCOTT (b. 1934), Kiowa-Cherokee author

MONTAIGNE, MICHEL DE (1533–92), French author

MONTESQUIEU, CHARLES DE (1689–1755), French political philosopher

MONTGOMERY, JAMES (1771–1854), English poet, editor, and hymn writer

MOORE, THOMAS (1779–1852), Irish poet

MORAN, LORD (Charles Wilson, 1882–1977), English physician

MORE, HANNAH (1745–1833), English author and philanthropist

MORLEY, CHRISTOPHER (1890–1967), American journalist and poet

MOTHER TERESA (1910–97), Albanian nun, missionary, and Nobel Laureate

MUIR, JOHN (1838–1914), Scottish-American naturalist and author

MUNDAKA UPANISHAD (c. 1400–800 BCE), Hindu sacred text

MURRAY, WILLIAM HUTCHISON (1913–96), Scottish mountaineer and author

MURROW, EDWARD R. (1908–65), American broadcast journalist

MUSTE, A. J. (Abraham Johannes, 1885–1967), American clergyman and activist

NACHMAN OF BRESLOV (1772–1810), Jewish rabbi and founder of Breslov Hasidism

NACHMANOVITCH, STEPHEN (b. 1950), American musician and author

NADER, RALPH (c. 1934), American political activist

NAGARJUNA (c. 150–250), Buddhist philosopher

NAISMITH, JAMES (1861–1939), Canadian-American sports coach and inventor of basketball

NAKASHIMA, GEORGE (1905–90), American woodworker and architect

NARADA DHARMA SUTRA (c. 6th century), Buddhist scripture

NEFERHOTEP (18th century), Egyptian king

NEVELSON, LOUISE (1900–88), Russian-born American sculptor

NEWTON, JOHN (1725–1807), British sailor and Anglican cleric

NEWMAN, JOHN HENRY (1801–90), Roman Catholic cardinal

NICEPHORUS THE SOLITARY (1198–1272), Greek Orthodox patriarch of Constantinople

NIEBUHR, REINHOLD (1892–1971), American theologian

NIETZSCHE, FRIEDRICH (1844–1900), German philosopher, poet, and author

NISARGADATTA MAHARAJ (1897–1981), Indian spiritual leader

NISHIDA, KITARO (1870–1945), Japanese founder of the Kyoto School of Philosophy

NKRUMAH, KWAME (1889–1979), first president of Ghana

NOBLE RED MAN (Mathew King, 1902–89), Lakota Sioux chief

OBAMA, BARACK (b. 1961), forty-fourth US president

O'DONOHUE, JOHN (1954–2008), Irish philosopher, author, and priest

OHIYESA (Dr. Charles E. Eastman, 1859–1939), Santee Sioux physician and author

OKAKURA, KAKUZ (1862–1913), Japanese scholar and poet

OLSON, SIGURD (1899–1982), American environmentalist and author

O'REILLY, JOHN BOYLE (1844–90), Irish poet, journalist, and author

O'SHAUGHNESSY, ARTHUR (1844–81), English poet

OVID (43 BCE–17 CE), Roman poet

PAGE, RUSSELL (1906–85), English landscape architect

PAINE, THOMAS (1737–1809), Anglo-American political theorist and author

PALEY, WILLIAM (1743–1805), English philosopher

PARK, BENJAMIN (1809–64), American poet

PARKER, CHARLIE (1920–55), American musician

PARKER, QUANAH (c. 1845–1911), Comanche chief

PARRY, JOSEPH (1841–1903), Welsh composer

PASCAL, BLAISE (1623–62), French mathematician, physicist, inventor, author, and philosopher

PATRICK, ST. (c. 387–493), Christian missionary

PEACE PILGRIM (Mildred Lisette Norman, 1908–81), American peace activist

PEALE, NORMAN VINCENT (1898–1993), American clergyman

PECK, M. SCOTT (1936–2005), American psychiatrist and author

PENN, WILLIAM (1644–1718), English philosopher and founder of the Province of Pennsylvania

PERÓN, EVITA (1919–52), first lady of Argentina

PETERS, TOM (b. 1942), American author

PETERSON, WILFERD (1900–95), American author

PETRARCH, FRANCESCO (1304–74), Italian poet

PICASSO, PABLO (1881–1973), Spanish painter

PIERCY, MARGE (b. 1936), American author

PINERO, ARTHUR (1855–1934), English actor and dramatist

PIRKEI AVOT (date unknown), Jewish religious text and compilation of ethical teachings

PLATO (427–347 BCE), Greek philosopher

PLAUTUS, TITUS MACCIUS (c. 254–184 BCE), Roman dramatist

PLOTINUS (205–270), Greek philosopher

PLUTARCH (c. 46–120), Roman historian

POE, EDGAR ALLAN (1809–49), American author

POKAGON, SIMON (1830–99), Potawatomi chief and author

PONTE, LORENZO DA (1749–1838), Austrian composer and poet

POPE, ALEXANDER (1688–1744), English poet

POSEY, ALEXANDER (1873–1908), Creek poet, humorist, journalist, and politician

POTOFSKY, JACOB (1892–1979), Ukrainian-born American trade unionist

POWELL, ADAM CLAYTON, JR. (1908–72), American clergyman and politician

POWELL, COLIN (b. 1937), American statesman and general

POWELL, ELEANOR (1912–82), American actress

POWHATAN (Wahunsenacawh, c. 1547–1618), Algonquin chief

PRAJNANPAD, SWAMI (1891–1974), Hindu spiritual leader

PRASNA UPANISHAD (c. 1400–800 BCE), Hindu sacred text

PRENTICE, GEORGE DENNISON (1802–70), American editor and poet

PRIOR, MATTHEW (1664–1721), English poet and diplomat

PRITCHETT, PRICE (b. 1941), American business adviser and author

PROCTER, BRYAN WALLER (1787–1874), English poet

PROUST, MARCEL (1871–1922), French author

PUSHMATAHA (c. 1765–1824), Choctaw chief

PYTHAGORAS (c. 570–495 BCE), Greek mathematician

QÖYAWAYMA, AL (b. 1938), Hopi potter

QÖYAWAYMA, POLINGAYSI (Elizabeth White, 1892–1990), Hopi author

QUEEN OF SHEBA (10th century BCE), ruler of ancient kingdom in Ethiopia

RAEL, JOSEPH (b. 1935), Ute-Pueblo author, shaman, artist, and founder of Sound Peace Chambers

RALEIGH, SIR WALTER (1552–1618), English poet and explorer

RAMDAS, SWAMI (1884–1963), Hindu philosopher and saint

RAND, AYN (1905–82), American author

RAY, JOHN (1627–1705), English naturalist

REAGAN, RONALD (1911–2004), fortieth US president

RED CLOUD (Makhpia-sha, 1822–1909), Oglala Sioux chief

RICHARDSON, SAMUEL (1689–1761), English author

RICHTER, JEAN PAUL (1763–1825), German author

RIG VEDA (c. 1500–1200 BCE), Hindu sacred text

RILKE, RAINER MARIA (1875–1926), German author and poet

RIMBAUD, ARTHUR (1854–91), French poet

RIVAROL, ANTOINE DE (1753–1801), French author

ROCHEFOUCAULD, FRANÇOIS DE LA (1613–80), French author and moralist

ROCKEFELLER, NELSON (1908–79), American philanthropist and vice president

ROETHKE, THEODORE (1908–63), American poet

ROGERS, WILL (1879–1935), Cherokee-American humorist

ROKEACH, ELEAZAR (c. 1176–1238), Jewish Kabbalist leader

ROOSEVELT, ELEANOR (1884–1962), American first lady and diplomat

ROOSEVELT, FRANKLIN D. (1882–1945), thirty-second US president

ROSE, WENDY (b. 1948), Hopi-Miwok author

ROSS, ALLEN C. (Ehanamani, b. 1940), Santee Sioux physician

ROSSETTI, CHRISTINA (1830–94), English poet

ROSTEN, LEO (1908–97), Russian-born American author, humorist, and educator

ROUSSEAU, JEAN-JACQUES (1712–78), French philosopher, author, and composer

ROWE, NICHOLAS (1674–1718), English author

ROYCE, JOSIAH (1855–1916), American philosopher

RUBENSTEIN, ARTHUR (1887–1982), Jewish pianist

RUFFINI, GIOVANNI (1807–81), Italian poet

RUIZ, DON MIGUEL (b. 1952), Mexican author

RUMI, JALALUDDIN (1207–73), Sufi mystic and poet

RUSH, BENJAMIN (1746–1813), American statesman

RUSKIN, JOHN (1819–1900), English artist and philosopher

RUTHERFORD, SAMUEL (1600–61), Scottish theologian

SAADI (Muslih-ud-Din Mushrif ibn-Abdullah Shirazi, c. 1184–1283), Persian poet

SAGAN, CARL (1934–96), American astronomer, astrophysicist, and author

SA'ID, ABU (Abu Sa'id Bahadur Khan, 967–1049), Sufi scholar and poet

SAINT-EXUPÉRY, ANTOINE DE (1900–44), French aviator, poet, and author

SALES, FRANCIS DE (1567–1622), Roman Catholic bishop and saint

SANAI, HAKIM (Hakim Abul-Majd Majdud ibn Adam Sana'i Ghaznavi, c. 1044–1150), Persian poet

SAND, GEORGE (Amatine Lucile Aurore Dupin, 1804–76), French author

SANDBURG, CARL (1878–1967), American author and poet

SANTAYANA, GEORGE (1863–1952), American poet and philosopher

SANT KA, TANEDA (1882–1940), Japanese poet

SAROYAN, WILLIAM (1908–81), American author

SARTON, MAY (Eleanore Marie, 1912–95), American poet and author

SATANTA (White Bear, 1830–78), Kiowa chief

SATHYA SAI BABA (1926–2011), Indian spiritual leader

SCHILLER, JOHANN FRIEDRICH VON (1759–1805), German poet, philosopher, historian, and dramatist

SCHOPENHAUER, ARTHUR (1788–1805), German philosopher

SCHUMACHER, E. F. (Ernst Friedrich, 1911–77), German-born British economist and author

SCHWEITZER, ALBERT (1873–1965), Franco-German missionary and theologian

SCOTT, WALTER (1771–1832), Scottish author, playwright, and poet

SENECA, LUCIUS ANNAEUS (5 BCE–65 CE), Roman statesman

SENESH, HANNAH (1921–44), Jewish resister and Israeli national heroine

SERTILLANGES, ANTONIN G. (1863–1948), French-Catholic philosopher

SHAKESPEARE, WILLIAM (1564–1616), English dramatist

SHAW, GEORGE BERNARD (1856–1950), Anglo-Irish playwright

SHELLEY, PERCY BYSSHE (1792–1822), English poet and dramatist

SHERIDAN, RICHARD BRINSLEY (1751–1816), Irish playwright and poet

SHINGIS (c. mid-1700s), Delaware chief

SHULA, DON (b. 1930), American football coach

SHVETASHVATARA UPANISHAD (c. 1400–800 BCE), Hindu sacred text

SIDNEY, PHILIP (1554–86), English author and statesman

SILESIUS, ANGELUS (1624–77), Christian mystic

SILLS, BEVERLY (1929–2007), American operatic soprano

SILVERSTEIN, SHEL (1930–99), American author

SINATRA, FRANK (1915–98), American singer and actor

SIVANANDA, SARASWATI (1887–1963), founder of yoga Vedanta Centers

SMILES, SAMUEL (1812–1904), Scottish author and reformer

SMITH, ALEXANDER (1830–67), Scottish poet

SMITH, ASHLEY (b. 1978), American author and speaker

SMITH, BETTY (1896–1972), American author

SMITH, LOGAN PEARSALL (1865–1946), American author

SMITH, SYDNEY (1771–1845), English theologian

SMOLLETT, TOBIAS (1721–71), Scottish poet and author

SNYDER, GARY (b. 1930), American author

SOCKMAN, RALPH W. (1889–1970), American theologian

SOCRATES (c. 470–399 BCE), Greek philosopher

SOPHOCLES (c. 496–406 BCE), Greek dramatist

SOUTH, ROBERT (1634–1716), English theologian

SOUTHEY, ROBERT (1774–1843), English poet

SPENSER, EDMUND (1553–99), English poet

SPINOZA, BARUCH (1632–77), Dutch philosopher

SRI GURU GRANTH SAHIB (1469–1708), Sikh sacred text

STEELE, RICHARD (1672–1729), Irish author and politician

STANDING BEAR, LUTHER (1903–39), Oglala Sioux chief

STANLEY, CHARLES (b. 1932), American clergyman

STANTON, ELIZABETH CADY (1815–1902), American social activist and abolitionist

STARK, FREYA (1893–1993), English explorer and author

STEINBECK, JOHN (1902–68), American author

STENDHAL (Marie-Henri Beyle, 1783–1824), French author

STERNE, LAURENCE (1713–68), Anglo-Irish author and clergyman

STEVENS, WALLACE (1879–1955), American poet

STEVENSON, ADLAI (1900–65), American statesman

STEVENSON, ROBERT LOUIS (1850–94), Scottish author and poet

STIRNER, MAX (Johann Kaspar Schmidt, 1806–56), German philosopher

STOPES, MARIE CARMICHAEL (1880–1958), Scottish author and social reformer

STOVER, MATTHEW (b. 1962), American author

STOWE, HARRIET BEECHER (1811–96), American author and abolitionist

SULTAN BAHU (1628–91), Muslim sufi and founder of the Sarwari Qadiri Sufi Order

SUTTA NIPATA (1st century), Buddhist sacred text

SVESTASVATARA UPANISHAD (c. 1400–800 BCE), sacred Hindu text

SWETCHINE, MADAME (Anne-Sophie Swetchine, 1782–1857), Russian mystic

SWIFT, JONATHAN (1667–1745), Irish satirist

SWINDOLL, CHARLES (b. 1934), Christian clergyman

SYMEON THE NEW THEOLOGIAN (949–1022), Orthodox Christian monk and saint

TABER, GLADYS (1899–1980), American author

TACITUS, PUBLIUS CORNELIUS (c. 56–117), Roman senator and historian

TAGORE, RABINDRANATH (1861–1941), Indian poet, essayist, dramatist, and Nobel Laureate

TAITTIRIYA UPANISHAD (c. 1400–800 BCE), Hindu sacred text

TAKATOMI, SENGE (1845–1918), founder of Izumo-Taishakyo Shinto

TALMUD (c. 500), first five books of Hebrew Bible

TAMMANY (c. 1628–98), Delaware chief

TAULER, JOHANNES (c. 1300–61), German theologian

TAYLOR, BARBARA BROWN (b. 1951), American clergyman and author

TAYLOR, BAYARD (1825–78), American poet

TAYLOR, JEREMY (1613–67), English theologian

TAYLOR, SUSAN L. (b. 1946), American editor

TEALE, EDWIN WAY (1899–1980), American naturalist, photographer, and Pulitzer Prize author

TECUMSEH (Shooting Star, 1768–1813), Shawnee chief

TEMPLE, WILLIAM (1881–1944), Archbishop of Canterbury

TEN BEARS (Paruasemana, c. 1790–1872), Yamparethka Comanche chief

TENNYSON, ALFRED (1809–92), Poet Laureate of the United Kingdom

TERESA OF AVILA (Teresa Sánchez de Cepeda y Ahumada, 1515–82), Carmelite nun and saint

THACKERAY, WILLIAM MAKEPEACE (1811–63), English author

THÉRÈSE OF LISIEUX (Marie-Françoise-Thérèse Martin, 1873–97), Roman Catholic mystic and saint

THOMAS, DYLAN (1914–53), Welsh poet and author

THOMAS, WILLIAM H. G. (1861–1924), English theologian

THOREAU, HENRY DAVID (1817–62), American author, poet, philosopher, abolitionist, and naturalist

THUCYDIDES (c. 455–400 BCE), Greek historian

TILLICH, PAUL (1888–1965), German theologian and philosopher

TOLLE, ECKHART (b. 1948), German-American author

TOLSTOY, LEO (Count Lev Nikolayevich, 1828–1910), Russian author and philosopher

TOURÉ, AHMED SÉKOU (Ahmed Seku Turah, 1922–84), first president of Guinea

TRAHERNE, THOMAS (c. 1636–74), English poet

TRIEBWASSER, TONIA (b. 1954), American poet

TRINE, RALPH WALDO (1866–1958), American author and philosopher

TRUTH, SOJOURNER (1797–1883), American abolitionist

TUBMAN, HARRIET (c. 1820–1913), American abolitionist and humanitarian

TUTU, DESMOND (b. 1931), social activist, South African Anglican archbishop, and Nobel Laureate

TWAIN, MARK (Samuel Langhorne Clemens, 1835–1910), American humorist and author

TZU, LAO (570–490 BCE), founder of Taoism

UESHIBA, MORIHEI (1883–1969), Japanese founder of Akido martial arts

ULLMAN, SAMUEL (1840–1924), American humanitarian and businessman

UPDIKE, JOHN (1932–2009), American poet and humanitarian

VALOIS, MARGUERITE DE (1553–1615), Queen of France

VAN DYKE, HENRY (1852–1933), American clergyman and educator

VERNE, JULES (1828–1905), French author

VICTORIO (1829–80), Chiricahua Apache chief

VINCI, LEONARDO DA (Leonardo di ser Piero da Vinci, 1452–1519), Italian painter, architect, mathematician, engineer, and inventor

VIRGIL (70–19 BCE), Roman poet

VIVEKANANDA, SWAMI (Narendranath Nath Dutta, 1863–1902), Hindu monk and founder of the Ramakrishna Order of Monks

VOLTAIRE (François-Marie Arouet, 1694–1778), French author, historian, and philosopher

WAITLEY, DENIS (b. 1933), American author

WALKER, ALICE (b. 1944), American author, poet, and activist

WASHINGTON, BOOKER T. (1856–1915), American educator and author

WATERS, FRANK (1902–95), Hopi author

WATSON, JOHN FORBES (1827–92), English physician and author

WEIL, SIMONE (1909–43), French philosopher, social activist, and Christian mystic

WEST, JESSAMYN (1902–84), American author

WEST, MAE (1892–1980), American actress

WHARTON, EDITH (1862–1937), American author

WHITEHEAD, ALFRED NORTH (1861–1947), English mathematician and philosopher

WHITEHEAD, WILLIAM (1715–85), English poet and playwright

WHITMAN, WALT (1819–70), American author

WHITTIER, JOHN GREENLEAF (1807–92), American poet and abolitionist

WIDMARK, JOY (b. 1970), American author

WIESEL, ELIE (b. 1928), Romanian-American author and Nobel Laureate

WILBERFORCE, SAMUEL (1805–73), Church of England bishop

WILCOX, ELLA WHEELER (1850–1919), American author and poet

WILDE, OSCAR (1854–1900), Irish author and poet

WILDER, THORNTON (1897–1975), American dramatist and author

WILLIAMS, WILLIAM CARLOS (1883–1963), American poet

WILLIAMSON, MARIANNE (b. 1952), American spiritual teacher and author

WILSON, JOHN (1788–1854), English poet

WILSON, WOODROW (1856–1924), twenty-eighth US president

WINCKELMANN, JOHANN JOACHIM (1717–68), German art historian and archaeologist

WINFREY, OPRAH (b. 1954), American television host, producer, media proprietor, and philanthropist

WINTER, WILLIAM (1836–1917), American drama critic and author

WOOLF, VIRGINIA (1882–1941), English author
WORDSWORTH, WILLIAM (1770–1850), English
    poet
WRIGHT, FRANK LLOYD (1867–1959), American
    architect
WULING, SHI (b. 1946), Buddhist nun

YAJUR VEDA (c. 1000–600 BCE), Hindu sacred text
YEATS, WILLIAM BUTLER (1865–1939), Irish poet
YOGANANDA, PARAMAHANSA (1893–1952), Hindu
    guru
YOGI, MAHARISHI MAHESH (1914–2008), Indian
    guru and founder of Transcendental Meditation
YOSHIDA, KENK (c. 1283–1350), Japanese author
    and Buddhist monk
YOUNG, EDWARD (1683–1765), English poet
YUEN, LOY CHING (1873–1960), Chinese Taoist
    poet
YUTANG, LIN (1895–1976), Chinese author and
    inventor

ZANGWELL, ISRAEL (1864–1926), Jewish author
    and humorist
ZHOU, ZHUANG (369–286 BCE), Taoist philosopher

ACKNOWLEDGMENTS
AND PERMISSIONS

My gratitude goes to my sister PJ for her editorial help and for believing in me. Great thanks to my agent and friend, Nancy Barton, for nursing me through the process with such grace and patience. Also, much gratitude to Jo Ann Deck and Fred Courtright for their invaluable guidance. Sincere appreciation to my editor, Georgia Hughes, for her encouragement and support, and a hearty thanks to Jeff Campbell and Kristen Cashman for their amazing eyes for detail.

Text is reprinted from the following sources by permission, with my special thanks!

Aitken, Larry P. *Two Cultures Meet: Pathways for American Indians to Medicine*. Copyright © 1990 by Garrett Park Press.

Armstrong, Virginia Irving, ed. *I Have Spoken: American History through the Voices of the Indians*. Copyright © 1971 by Swallow Press.

Baba, Sathya Sai. *Sathya Sai Baba Speaks*. Andhra Pradesh, India: Sri Sathya Sai Books & Publications Trust, vol. 1 (1959), vol. 6 (1996), vol. 10 (1960, 1970), vol. 12 (1973), vol. 13 (1975).

Barks, Coleman. *The Book of Love*. San Francisco: HarperOne, 2005. Copyright © 2005 by Coleman Barks.

———. *The Essential Rumi*. New York: HarperCollins, 1995. Copyright © 1995 by Coleman Barks.

———. *The Open Secret: Versions by Rumi*. Boston: Shambhala, 1999. Copyright © 1999 by Coleman Barks.

———. *Rumi: The Big Red Book*. San Francisco: HarperOne, 1999. Copyright © 1999 by Coleman Barks.

————. *Rumi: The Glance*. New York: Penguin, 1999. Copyright © 1999 by Coleman Barks.

Beck, Sanderson. *The Dhammapada*. Copyright © 1998. www.san.beck.org.

Buber, Martin. *Ten Rungs: Collected Hasidic Sayings*. Copyright © 1994 by Kensington Publishing Co.

Chittick, William C. *The Sufi Path of Love: The Spiritual Teachings of Rumi*. Copyright © 1983 by State University of New York. All rights reserved. Reprinted by permission.

Easwaran, Eknath (founder of the Blue Mountain Center of Meditation), trans. *The Bhagavad Gita*. Copyright © 1985, 2007. Reprinted by permission of Nilgiri Press, PO Box 256, Tomales, CA 94971. www.easwaran.org.

————. *The Dhammapada*. Copyright © 1985, 2007. Reprinted by permission of Nilgiri Press, PO Box 256, Tomales, CA 94971. www.easwaran.org.

————. *The Upanishads*. Copyright © 1985, 2007. Reprinted by permission of Nilgiri Press, PO Box 256, Tomales, CA 94971. www.easwaran.org.

Fox, Matthew. *Meditations with Meister Eckhart*. Copyright © 1983 by Inner Traditions / Bear & Co.

Hill, Norbert. *Words of Power*. Golden, CO: Fulcrum Publishing, 1999. Copyright © 1999.

Ladinsky, Daniel. *The Gift: Poems by Hafiz*. New York: Penguin Books, 1999. Copyright © 1999 by Daniel Ladinsky.

————. *The Purity of Desire: 100 Poems of Rumi*. New York: Penguin Books, 2012. Copyright © 2012 by Daniel Ladinsky.

————. *The Subject Tonight Is Love: 60 Wild and Sweet Poems by Hafiz*. New York: Penguin Books, 2003. Copyright © 1996 and 2003 by Daniel Ladinsky.

————. *A Year with Hafiz: Daily Contemplations*. New York: Penguin Books, 2011. Copyright © 2010 by Daniel Ladinsky.

Maitreya, Ven. Ananda, trans. *The Dhammapada* (1995). Revised by Rose Kramer. Reprinted with permission of Parallax Press, Berkeley, CA. www.parallax.org.

Neihardt, John G., ed. *Black Elk Speaks: Being the Life Story of a Holy Man of the Oglala Sioux, The Premiere Edition*. Copyright © 2008 by State University of New York. All rights reserved. Reprinted by permission.

Pilgrim, Peace. *Peace Pilgrim: Her Life and Work in Her Own Words*. Copyright © 1992 by Ocean Tree Books.

Prabhavananda, Swami. *The Upanishads: Breath of the Eternal*. Copyright © 1975 by Vedanta Press, Hollywood.

Owomoyel, Oyekan. *Yoruba Proverbs*. Copyright © 2005 by the Board of Regents of the University of Nebraska. Reprinted by permission of the University of Nebraska Press.

Shiva, Shahram, trans. *Rumi: Thief of Sleep*. Copyright © 2000 by Hohm Press.

Stewart, Julia, ed. *African Proverbs and Wisdom*. Copyright © 1997 by Kensington Publishing Corp.

Touchon, Cecil. *Gayani Meditations*. Copyright © 2007 by Cecil Library Publications.

Welker, Glenn. Hawaiian proverbs. Copyright © 1993–2014. www.indigenouspeople.net.

Wuling, Shi. *Path to Peace*. Copyright © 2006 by Amitabha Publications.

SCRIPTURE VERSIONS

Scriptures from the *21st Century King James Version* (KJ21), copyright © 1994 by Deuel Enterprises, Inc., Gary, SD 57237.

ABOUT THE AUTHOR

Neala Shane received her BA from Penn State University in religious studies. She began working on *Inspired Baby Names from Around the World* as a way to blend her passion for religions and names. She is fascinated by how people define and live their understanding of the Divine. During her research, Shane explored a variety of religious experiences, including studying Jewish Kabbalah as well as attending Sufi and Universal Peace dances and American Indian kiva chanting and sweat lodges.

Shane also volunteered as biography editor at the University of Colorado's Conference of World Affairs (2004–2007), which offers forums on international politics, diplomacy, science, technology, environment, spirituality, business, medicine, the arts, media, and human rights.

Shane currently volunteers as an ESL tutor for adults, and she recently tutored English in Nepal. She raised three children and is a delighted grandmother. She also recently celebrated her birthday by skydiving. Her passion continues to lie in discovering the places where universal truths intersect, as she believes that these are the sacred bridges we need in order to heal the world. She lives in Vancouver, Washington.